D1229402

How Was It Possible?

DISCARDED

DISCARDED

ReF
D
804.3
.H699
2015

How Was It Possible?

A Holocaust Reader

EDITED BY PETER HAYES

Foreword by Harvey Schulweis

Monroe College Library
New Rochelle, NY

University of Nebraska Press
Lincoln and London

© 2015 by the Jewish Foundation for the Righteous.
Acknowledgments for the use of copyrighted material
appear on pages 871–73, which constitute an extension
of the copyright page. All rights reserved.
Manufactured in the United States of America.

Library of Congress Cataloging-in-Publication Data
How was it possible?: a Holocaust reader / edited by
Peter Hayes; foreword by Harvey Schulweis.
pages   cm
Includes bibliographic references and index.
ISBN 978-0-8032-7469-3 (pbk.: alk. paper)
ISBN 978-0-8032-7489-1 (epub)
ISBN 978-0-8032-7490-7 (mobi)
ISBN 978-0-8032-7491-4 (pdf)
1. Holocaust, Jewish (1939–1945) 2. Holocaust,
Jewish (1939–45)—Causes. 3. Antisemitism—
Germany—History—20th century. 4. Jews—
Germany—History—twentieth century. 5.
Jews—Persecutions—Germany. 6. Germany—
History—1933–45. 7. Germany—Ethnic relations.
I. Hayes, Peter, September 7, 1946–, editor.
D804.3.H699 2015   940.53'18—dc23
2014039233

Set in Arno Pro by Renni Johnson.
Designed by A. Shahan.

CONTENTS

ILLUSTRATIONS

Photographs

Maps

Tables

Foreword

HARVEY SCHULWEIS

During the Holocaust thousands of non-Jews refused to be passive in the face of the evil they witnessed, rescuing Jews, often at risk to their own lives and the lives of their families. The Jewish Foundation for the Righteous (JFR) provides monthly financial support to such aged and needy non-Jews and educates future generations about their extraordinary acts of courage.

In 1986 Rabbi Harold M. Schulweis created the Foundation to fulfill the traditional Jewish commitment to *hakarat hatov*, the searching out and recognition of goodness. To this end, the JFR is committed to assisting those Righteous Gentiles who are in need. We must thank and support these extraordinary individuals who were the lone lights in the darkness. These unassuming and dignified people acted without expecting reward, then or now. Yet they express deep gratitude for the Foundation's support.

Rescuers serve as role models for us and for future generations. They teach us that, even in the midst of the worst evil in recorded history, each human being had the capacity to act humanely. Without their example, we are left only with the lessons of atrocity, hatred, and indifference to teach our children.

The JFR's national Holocaust teacher education program seeks to teach teachers the history of the Holocaust and, in this context, the significance of the Righteous as moral and ethical exemplars. As the Holocaust recedes in history, generations to come will never meet a Holocaust survivor or a Righteous Gentile, yet they must have an understanding of that terrible period. This Holocaust anthology, edited and introduced by Peter Hayes, provides such a resource.

The Jewish Foundation for the Righteous is pleased to partner with Professor Peter Hayes and the University of Nebraska Press in the publication of *How Was It Possible? A Holocaust Reader*.

TABLE 1. Estimate of Jews killed in the
Holocaust, by country of residence at
the time of deportation or death

Albania	591
Austria	65,459
Baltic states	272,000
Belgium	28,518
Bulgaria	11,393
Croatia	32,000
Czechoslovakia	143,000
Denmark	116
France	76,134
Germany	165,000
Greece	59,195
Hungary	502,000
Italy	6,513
Luxembourg	1,200
Netherlands	102,000
Norway	758
Poland	2,100,000
Romania	220,000
Serbia	10,700
USSR	2,100,000
Total	5,896,577

NOTES ON BORDERS

The figure for Albania refers to its dimensions *after* the annexation of Kosovo and western Macedonia in 1941. The figure for Bulgaria refers to its dimensions *after* the annexations of Thrace from Greece and Macedonia from Yugoslavia in 1941. The figure for Czechoslovakia refers to the Protectorate of Bohemia and Moravia and independent Slovakia minus the borderlands ceded to Hungary in 1939. The figure for Greece refers to its dimensions *after* the loss of Thrace in 1941. The figure for Hungary refers to its dimensions *after* the annexation of a border strip and Ruthenia from Slovakia in 1938–39, Northern Transylvania from Romania in 1940, and part of Vojvodina from Yugoslavia in 1941. The figure for Poland refers to the parts of the country annexed or occupied by Nazi Germany prior to 1941. The figure for Romania excludes Northern Transylvania but includes the provinces of Bessarabia and northern Bukovina ceded to the Soviet Union in June 1940 and regained in June 1941. The figure for the Soviet Union excludes Estonia, Latvia, and Lithuania but includes the territory annexed from Poland in 1939.

Sources: Wolfgang Benz ,ed., *Dimension des Völkermords* (1991), 15–16, 229–30, 238, 330, 351, 379; Jean Ancel, *The History of the Holocaust in Romania* (2011), 558; Yitzhak Arad, *The Holocaust in the Soviet Union* (2009), 521–25.

Introduction

PETER HAYES

The Holocaust, the Nazi attempt to eradicate the Jews of Europe, has come to be regarded as the emblematic event of the Twentieth Century, the epitome of the "era of ideologies" (Karl Dietrich Bracher) and the "age of extremes" (Eric Hobsbawm). One prominent scholar, Zygmunt Baumann, even has identified the Holocaust as the characteristic expression of the brutal, amoral rationality that he sees at the very heart of modern society. Such views crystallized relatively recently, largely since the 1970s, but they now signify a broad consensus about the major and ominous significance of the events that are the subject of this book.

Yet the Holocaust continues to resist comprehension. Despite thousands of books and the labors of countless historians and other scholars, novelists and memoirists, witnesses and judges, researchers and commissions, the topic often gives rise to a form of intellectual and emotional despair, a sense that the suffering unleashed was too great, too horrible, and too senseless to be accounted for by conventional explanatory processes, let alone grasped or understood. This feeling is, I believe, a reflex, an almost involuntary expression of revulsion at the barbarism of what happened. No matter how decent its origins, however, that reflex has harmful consequences. Above all, it stands in the way of learning from the Holocaust. The unfathomable can inspire awe, but not knowledge. Labeling something incomprehensible encourages and excuses turning attention elsewhere.

This book proceeds from the editor's twin convictions that the question the title asks—*How Was It Possible?*—is answerable and that the proof of this emerges from full and accurate descriptions of what the participants thought, said, and did. Yes, the assumptions, perspectives, and environments of those participants were often so different from ours as to be difficult to access. Yes, our ability to enter into their mental worlds is impeded by what stands between them and us: the distorting filter of knowledge about what came next. And, yes, making dreadful developments intelligible runs the risk of seeming to lend them a kind of intelligence or even justification; a French adage warns, "*tout comprendre, c'est tout pardonner,*" to understand all is to forgive all. But to shrink from these challenges is to abandon the subject of the Holocaust to demagogic exploitation in a host of contemporary arguments. Although historical knowledge generally does not lead to unanimity about why and how enormous cataclysms occurred, it often narrows down the range of defensible explanations. The result is not only enhanced understanding of the past, but also enriched capacity to counter misleading analogies to the present.

This book also reflects another of its editor's convictions: the Holocaust was National Socialist Germany's assault on the Jews of Europe. Nazism attacked many groups, but none for the same reason that it attacked the Jews, none with the same urgency, and none to the same extent. Hitler's ideology depicted the Jews as uniquely dangerous to Germany and therefore uniquely destined to disappear completely from the Reich and all territories subordinate to it. The threat posed by supposedly corrupting but generally powerless Sinti and Roma was far less, and therefore addressed inconsistently in the Nazi realm. Gay men were defined as a problem only if they were German or having sex with Germans and considered "curable" in most cases. Thus, the Nazi regime made no attempt to round up and kill the millions of homosexuals in Europe and eventually incarcerated only the small fraction of them deemed "incorrigible." Germany's murderous intent toward the handicapped inhabitants of European mental institutions and sanatoria was more comprehensive, since the Reich defined such people as drains on its resources everywhere within the German ambit, but here, too, implementation was uneven and life-saving exceptions permitted, especially in Western Europe. Not only were some Slavs— Slovaks, Croats, Bulgarians, some Ukrainians— allotted a favored place in Hitler's New Order, but the fate of most of the other Slavs the Nazis derided as sub-humans (*Untermenschen*) consisted of enslavement and gradual attrition, not the prompt massacre meted out to Jews after 1941. For all these reasons, this volume includes excerpts that relate Germany's erratic targeting of other populations to the Reich's relentless onslaught against the Jews in the years 1933–45, but keeps the primary focus on that onslaught.

The chapters of this book are designed to help readers answer a series of key questions: Why were Jews objects of hatred in Europe and why did that hatred vary by time and place? Why did Germans spearhead the assault in 1933–1945? Why were most European Jews unable to flee from their attackers? What sort of New Order did the Nazis envision and enact in Europe? Why and how did their policy toward Jews radicalize between 1939 and 1941 and did Jews respond? How did the Nazi regime kill so many people so rapidly? What role did collaborating non-Germans play in the persecution of the Jews and why? What sorts of people or institutions sought to protect Jews from the onslaught and why? What happened to survivors and the memory of their ordeal after 1945?

No single book on the Holocaust can capture every aspect of its origins, execution, and aftermath. I am acutely conscious of other questions worth asking, additional topics that merit inclusion, and many fine books and authors that have gone unrepresented in this compilation. My guiding purpose in selecting and editing the excerpts has been to provide readers with the most readable and reliable material available that will help them answer the individual questions listed above and the overarching question posed by the book's title. Of course, in the study of history, most answers are provisional, subject to alteration on the basis of new information and insights. But that prospect does not relieve us of the responsibility, here and now, to do the best we can with what we have.

EDITORIAL NOTE

Punctuation and spellings have been changed to conform to current American usage. Some paragraphing has been altered to save space within the volume. The format of the footnotes has not been standardized but generally follows the practice and form of the original texts (aside from the correction of spellings and punctuation). In a few instances, clear factual and statistical errors have been corrected.

Figure 2. Emile Zola's open letter *J'Accuse!* published on the front page of the Paris newspaper *L'Aurore*, Jan. 13, 1898. The letter passionately proclaimed Dreyfus' innocence and accused his denouncers of malicious libel. Jerusalem, J.N.U.L.

1. An open letter, *"J'Accuse . . . !"* (I accuse !), written by Emile Zola that was published on the front page of the Paris newspaper *L'Aurore*, January 13, 1898. The letter proclaims Alfred Dreyfus's innocence and accuses the French government of antisemitism. (Courtesy Yad Vashem.)

2. Marseilles, France . . . Summer 1942—Having studied in Germany during the 1930s, Abbé René de Naurois saw firsthand the threat that fascism posed within Germany and became an outspoken critic of Hitler and Nazism. When France fell to the Germans he realized that the threat now extended beyond the borders of the Reich. In 1941, he joined the resistance and was actively involved in smuggling Jews across the border into Spain. He provided false papers and refuge to those needing assistance. He hid Jews with families in the mountains and in Catholic institutions. Wanted by the Gestapo, the Abbé fled France in 1942. He joined the Free French and returned to his country with Gen. Charles de Gaulle during the Allied invasion at Normandy. Abbé de Naurois was decorated by General de Gaulle and received the *Croix de Guerre*. (Courtesy JFR Photo Archives.)

Introduction

PETER HAYES

Like all major events, the Holocaust had both long- and short-term causes. Many centuries of animosity toward Jews in Europe made an attempt to expel or eradicate them desirable to some people (i.e., provided motive), but only the conditions of a specific time period allowed the attempt to occur (i.e., provided opportunity). This chapter describes the changing and layered nature of the animosity and begins explaining why its eruption in the first half of the twentieth century surpassed all precedent.

For hundreds of years, the stigmatization of Jews in Europe stemmed from Christian religious teaching. Restrictions on what Jews could own or do or where they could live arose in order to: (1) demonstrate and defend the newer faith's claim to have superseded the older one in God's affection and (2) induce Jews to confirm this by converting. Misery and isolation were thus to be the lot of Jews, but not the extirpation meted out to every other form of religious dissent in Europe prior to the Reformation. They were to live in discomfort, both the Catholic and Orthodox churches taught, until such time that the Jews accepted the Gospel and thus heralded its triumph and the coming of the Kingdom of God.

This theological balancing act between punishment and preservation accounts for both the suffering and the survival of Jewry in Europe into the modern age. In the medieval and early modern eras, lay people periodically lost sight of why a group that had denied Christ's divinity should be treated differently from heretics and infidels and

lashed out at Jews, especially in times of adversity. Clergy and true believers increasingly portrayed rejecting Christ as allying with Satan and imagined all sorts of ways in which Jews did his work, from poisoning wells to kidnapping children for murderous rites. The consequences of this demonization sometimes took the lethal forms of massacres or mass expulsions. Yet, the treatment of Jews was never uniform in Christendom, and coexistence continued to alternate with persecution, even after Western or Catholic Christianity fragmented in the 16th century. Among Protestants, for example, Calvinists inclined to a respectful attitude toward Jewry, but followers of Martin Luther echoed the rage he expressed when the Jews proved no more willing to accept his Christianity than the one that it had reformed. After 1648, when the bloody and disastrous wars of religion ended in stalemate, the spread of the concept of religious toleration produced a decline in anti-Jewish violence in Western and Central Europe, but the same cannot be said about the Eastern part of the continent where Orthodoxy held sway.

The differences between Jews' experience in the two halves of the continent grew more marked during what historians call the "long nineteenth century," the years between the outbreak of the French Revolution in 1789 and the onset of World War I in 1914. In Western and most of Central Europe, the emancipation of the Jews from residential and professional restrictions in the wake of the French Revolution gradually became the accepted norm. Not so in the East, where the Russian Empire ruled over and enforced the Pale of Settlement that confined about half of Europe's Jewish population to relatively poor regions in today's Poland, Lithuania, Belarus, and Ukraine, and where the launching of pogroms and the forging of antisemitic propaganda, most notoriously *The Protocols of the Elders of Zion*, were favored tools of governance.

Even in the relatively enlightened parts of Europe, the situation of Jews remained ambiguous and contentious, and new forms of prejudice against them supplemented and in some circles replaced religious condemnation. For as their rights and opportunities expanded, Jews faced a backlash from two sorts of critics, those who argued that Jews had taken too little advantage of the new conditions and those who claimed they had taken too much. The first critique was the province of intellectuals and theologians for the most part, people who expressed disappointment that many Jews still observed their ancient traditions, beliefs, and rituals and thus failed to become indistinguishable from the population around them by embracing either its religion or its rationalism.

The second critique was more broadly based, recurrent, and vehement. Its proponents claimed that as the Jews had emerged from the ghettos and into the worlds of industry, trade, and the professions, they had become the principal beneficiaries of freedom of opportunity and competition. Invisible among college students, manufacturers, lawyers, and doctors in 1800, Jews seemed disproportionately present in all of these prized roles by the 1850s, even more so by the 1880s. Every social group that felt disadvantaged by economic and cultural change during the 19th century—from the nobility and the higher clergy to artisan producers and many farmers—spawned spokespeople dedicated to proving that its situation was not the result of market forces or technological change or new ways of thinking, but of a conspiracy on the part of the minority that was so obviously ascendant. Moreover, in an age of seeing and drawing profound distinctions among humans—spurred by scholarship in linguistics and science, by the burnishing of national identities, and by a new wave of colonial encounters with non-European peoples—numerous voices claimed to be able to demonstrate that the rise of the prospering group stemmed from innate and inbred traits that marked it off immutably from all others.

Yet neither critique succeeded in halting the pattern it attacked. Although the rise of Reform Jewry, primarily in German-speaking lands, narrowed the differences between Jewish and Christian religious observances, Western and Central European Jews mostly remained Jews and conscious of themselves as such. Despite the clamor of newspapers and political parties that sought to undo emancipation in almost every European country and the periodic occurrence of hate-laden incidents such as street riots, ritual murder trials, and the Dreyfus Affair, no roll back of Jews' civil rights took place. On the eve of World War I, Jews in Western and Central Europe were more secure, more integrated into their societies, and, on average, more prosperous than ever before. If they remained subject to discrimination in some quarters, the trend line of acceptance appeared to be in their favor.

The cataclysm of 1914–18 slowed or reversed that trend line in much of Europe. In the first place, Russia's sufferings and setbacks in World War I engendered a series of revolutions and a civil war from which the Bolsheviks emerged victorious. Communists rebelled in both Germany and Hungary, as well, though with less success. In all three uprisings, leaders of Jewish heritage (e.g., Leon Trotsky in Russia, Bela Kun in Hungary, Rosa Luxemburg and Kurt Eisner in Germany) played a prominent part, and opponents trumpeted this as proof of the alien menace Jews supposedly embodied. Especially but not only in Eastern Europe, a poisonous linkage of Jews with Bolshevism now reinforced their demonization by conservatives as instigators of destructive change.

In the second place, Germany's defeat toppled traditional institutions such as the monarchy, left behind intractable economic burdens, and set off an extended national debate over whom to blame. The German public divided deeply and almost evenly over whether responsibility lay with selfish elites that had misled the nation or sinister forces that had undermined it, chief among them the Marxists and the Jews. Germany's electorate also split sharply over the relative value of democratic decision-making or authoritarian rule. Still, one conviction united all political factions: the view that the victorious Allies had victimized Germany unfairly through the Versailles Treaty. Ultimately, a political deadlock between the competing sets of blamers allowed a clique of well-placed elitists and authoritarians to choose the winner. As a result, in January 1933 control over the most potentially powerful country in Europe, whose citizens felt aggrieved by the supposed injustices done to it, fell into the hands of Adolf Hitler, a man who soon became a dictator and who defined all Jews as his country's enemies.

The readings in this chapter lend detail to the main arguments of this introduction. Robert Wistrich's commentary on *antisemitism* traces its evolution from a religious to a pseudo-scientific formulation of the differences between Jews and others and highlights the prominence of these fateful ideas in late 19th century Austria, the land of Hitler's youth. Michael Burleigh and Wolfgang Wippermann's section on *racism* delineates the intellectual pedigree of the zoological poli-

tics later propagated by the Nazi Fuehrer. Amos Elon's account of *contradictions in Central Europe* reveals why that part of the world nonetheless offered Jews almost unparalleled, though not unlimited opportunities prior to World War I, and then began to turn on them during it. Even so, Klaus Fischer's summary of *Germany's turmoil* in the wake of the lost war makes clear that the depth of the nation's political polarization contributed more to Hitler's acquisition of power than the racist and expansionist ideology that was his guiding passion. Finally, Ezra Mendelsohn's survey of communal relations between the wars in *the interwar Jewish heartland* of East Central Europe, especially Poland, documents Jews' vulnerability to attack, even before the Nazis arrived.

The readings in this chapter alert readers to three key elements of the context in which Nazi Germany's assault on the Jews unfolded after 1933: the ideological inheritance that armed fomenters of hatred with a well-honed array of justifications for persecution; the political background that made the Nazi regime translate its racism into practice gradually and somewhat surreptitiously in the initial phase of Hitler's rule; and the geographical exposure of the largest concentration of European Jews, who lived where they were already at risk during the interwar years and where the Third Reich intended to obtain "living space." In addition, the excerpts will help readers begin assembling convincing answers to the most fundamental questions that historians must ask about the Holocaust: Why then (i.e., not earlier or later)? Why there (not elsewhere)?

Antisemitism

ROBERT S. WISTRICH

From *Antisemitism: The Longest Hatred*

"Antisemitism" is a problematic term, first invented in the 1870s by the German journalist Wilhelm Marr to describe the "non-confessional" hatred of Jews and Judaism that he and others like him advocated. The movement that began at that time in Germany and soon spread to neighboring Austria, Hungary, France and Russia was a self-conscious reaction to the emancipation of the Jews and their entry into non-Jewish society. In that sense it appeared to be a novel phenomenon, since, as the early antisemites were at pains to stress, they were not opposed to Jews on *religious* grounds but claimed to be motivated by social, economic, political or "racial" considerations.

Religious hostility in late nineteenth-century Europe was regarded by many intellectuals as something medieval, obscurantist and backward. There was clearly a need to establish a new paradigm for anti-Jewishness which sounded more neutral, objective, "scientific" and in keeping with the liberal, enlightened *Zeitgeist*. After all, Jews by virtue of their emancipation had become *equal* citizens before the law in European societies that, formally at least, had abandoned discrimination based on religious differences. Antisemitism that grounded itself in racial and ethnic feelings provided a way around this problem. By focusing attention on allegedly permanent, unchanging characteristics of the Jews as a social and national group (which depicted them as being fundamentally "alien" to their fellow citizens) the antisem-

ites hoped to delegitimize Jewish equality. They sought to restore the social boundaries that had begun to disappear in Europe, and they ultimately expected to return the Jews to their earlier pre-emancipated status.

"Antisemitism"—a term that came into general use as part of this politically motivated anti-Jewish campaign of the 1880s—was never directed against "Semites" as such. The term "Semitic" derived from the Biblical Shem, one of Noah's three sons, and designated a group of cognate languages including Hebrew, Arabic, Aramaic, Babylonian, Assyrian and Ethiopic, rather than an ethnic or racial group. Similarly, the contrasting term "Aryan" or "Indo-European," which became popular at this time, referred originally to the Indian branch of the Indo-European languages. Strictly speaking, "Aryans" were people speaking Sanskrit and related languages who had invaded India in prehistoric times and subjugated its indigenous inhabitants. Indians and Iranians were "Aryans" but Germans and North Europeans certainly were *not*, any more than European Jews, who no longer spoke Hebrew, could be meaningfully described as "Semites."

Nevertheless, in the late nineteenth century this pseudo-scientific nonsense became eminently respectable even among the European intellectual elites, so that the distinction between "Aryan" and "Semite" was easily grafted on to the much older distinction between Christian and Jew. As a result, for the last hundred years, the illogical term "antisemitism," which never really meant hatred of "Semites" (for example, Arabs) at all, but rather hatred of Jews, has come to be accepted in general usage as denoting *all* forms of hostility toward Jews and Judaism throughout history.

There is clearly a danger in using antisemitism in this overly generalized way, extending it to all times and places regardless of specific circumstances, differences between historical epochs and cultures, or other factors that might give the term more specificity and critical sharpness. Antisemitism is *not* a natural, meta-historical or a metaphysical phenomenon whose essence has remained unchanged throughout all its manifestations over the centuries. Nor is it an intrinsic part of the psychic structure of Gentiles, a kind of microbe or virus which invariably attacks non-Jews, provoking the "eternal hatred" for the "eternal people." Such a theory, which has some roots in the Jewish tradition ("Esau hates Jacob," the legacy of Amalek, etc.) and was adopted by early Zionists in Eastern Europe such as [Leo] Pinsker, [M.] Lilienblum and [Nachum] Sokolow, is quite unhistorical.

It ignores the fact that Jews have often been welcomed by the surrounding society; that their equality of status and integration was accepted as a binding legal and social principle in many countries during the modern period; and it crucially forgets that Jewish participation in cultural, scientific, economic and political life since the Western Enlightenment has in many respects been a remarkable success story. If antisemitism had really been a "hereditary disease of the Gentiles," or been based on an instinctive racial aversion to Jews (as antisemites sometimes claim), such a development would have been impossible. Admittedly, there has also been a backlash to Jewish integration, influence or success at some points in time—whether in first-century Alex-

andria and Rome, in medieval Muslim or Christian Spain, in fin-de-siècle Paris and Vienna or in Weimar Germany—but this pattern has definite historical causes and has nothing to do with any theory of innate Gentile antisemitism.

Any empirically valid discussion of antisemitism or hatred of Jews must, in my opinion, first of all come to terms with the problem of its historical continuity and development. This necessarily leads us back to the Hellenistic era, when a widespread Jewish Diaspora first emerged that was quite distinctive in the ancient world. Not only were the Jews the only monotheistic minority in this pagan world, bearers of a doctrine of election which claimed that Judaism was the sole truth, the supreme ethical teaching; not only did they persist in their historic existence as a separate social and religious group; not only did they refuse even to intermingle with the Gentiles because of their own dietary laws, Sabbath observance and prohibition on intermarriage; above all, this unique Diasporic nation which had set itself apart asserted spiritual supremacy over the polytheistic majority.

There is nothing surprising in the fact that such special characteristics and claims could provoke the hostility or resentment which one finds in Greek and Latin literature. To some extent this pre-Christian antisemitism looks like the normal, xenophobic prejudice that has prevailed between ethno-religious groups during virtually every period of history. But such a plausible conclusion ignores the *unique* character of the Jewish Diaspora, its unusual social cohesion, compactness and religiously sanctioned exclusiveness. This does not mean that the cause of antisemitism lay in the Jews themselves, but it can help us to understand how the peculiar brand of social hostility that we call by this name first arose as *one* possible response (there were of course others, ranging from admiration to indifference) to the reality of Jewish exclusiveness.

Pagan anti-Jewishness is important because it provided fertile soil for its Christian heirs, and it also reminds us that there was a significant form of hostility to Jews in Antiquity that *preceded* the birth of Christianity. Not a few early Christians had, for example, absorbed this Jew-hatred as a consequence of their pagan upbringing. Nevertheless, it is undeniable that Christianity would appear on the stage of history as a *negation* of Judaism in a much deeper sense than its pagan predecessors; that its theological polemics against Judaism were to be vital to its own identity far more than was the case for any other religion or culture. No other religion, indeed, makes the accusation that Christianity has made against the Jews, that they are literally the *murderers* of God. No other religion has so consistently attributed to them a universal, cosmic quality of evil, depicting them as children of the Devil, followers of Antichrist or as the "synagogue of Satan." The fantasies concerning Jews that were developed in medieval Christendom, about their plotting to destroy Christianity, poison wells, desecrate the host, massacre Christian children or establish their world dominion, represent a qualitative leap compared with anything put forward by their pagan precursors. Such charges, beginning with deicide, are peculiarly *Christian*, though in the twentieth century they have been taken up by Islam as well as by secular political religions such as Nazism or Bolshevism that have exploited the fiction of a Jewish world conspiracy.

Thus it is evident that Christian anti-Judaism and antisemitism did add a wholly new theological and metaphysical dimension to antisemitism that was absent in its pagan forerunners and quite distinct from the stigmatizing or persecution of other minority groups. The pervasive influence of Christianity (from the fourth century AD), on government, culture and society led to the marginalization of the Jews and their institutionalized oppression. The Christian theology which had usurped the Divine Promises to the Jews and proclaimed the Church as God's Chosen Elect, cast Israel in the role of God's forsaken, rejected and abandoned people—condemned to wandering and exile.

In the writings of the Church Fathers the negation of the Jews' religious and cultural values became a central motif. An overwhelmingly negative stereotype of the "deicide people" was transmitted through theological writings, the sermons of the clergy, the mystery and Passion plays, folklore, ballads and the plastic arts. This hostile collective stereotype of a Jewish people bearing the mark of Cain, a nation of Christ-killers and infidels in league with the Devil, became deeply embedded in the Western psyche following the massacres of Jews during the Crusades. During the next few centuries, new and even more irrational myths were added, that of the Jew as a ritual murderer, desecrator of the Host wafer, an agent of Antichrist, usurer, sorcerer and vampire. As Christianity spread among all the peoples of Europe, this devastating image crystalized until it was an integral part of European and Western culture, a fact that more than any other accounts for the pervasiveness of antisemitism to this day.

Jew-hatred no longer required any connection with real human relationships, indeed it no longer needed the presence of Jews at all. The stereotype had acquired a cultural dynamic of its own, as in medieval England after the expulsion of 1290, in Spain after the mass Jewish exodus of 1492, or in the "Judaizing" persecutions of Muscovite Russia. Even today, in post-Holocaust societies like Poland, Austria, or Romania where there are very few Jews left, one finds a similar phenomenon of "antisemitism without Jews." Nothing could make clearer the fallacy that antisemitism can be simplistically viewed as a "natural" or even a "pathological" response to a *concrete* Jewish presence, to Jewish activities, behavior or traditions.

The common denominator in all these societies is of course the impact of the Christian legacy and its translation over centuries into legalized discrimination, Jewish servitude, ghettoization and the narrow economic specialization of Jewry. Even where Jews converted in large numbers, as in late medieval Spain, the descendants of the converts were regarded with hostility and suspicion, leading to the Inquisition and "purity of blood" statutes that pointed the way to modern racial antisemitism. Not even the rise of humanism during the Renaissance and Reformation could successfully throw off the impact of the medieval image of the Jew. A reformer like Erasmus never dreamed of applying his humanist teachings on toleration to the Jews, who simply remained beyond the pale as far as he was concerned. Martin Luther, for his part, reiterated all the medieval myths about Jews, reinforcing rather than undermining them with an apocalyptic fury and vehemence all his own. Thus Luther's assault on the Papacy and the whole fabric of the Catholic Church, instead of liberating the Jews, made his Protestant followers more suspicious of them. Had they not refused to convert even after the great German Reformer had revealed to them the pure, unadulterated word of God? . . .

If the Reformation failed to bring any diminution of antisemitism, the eighteenth-century Enlightenment offered, at least on the face of things, a more promising prospect. There were Enlightenment writers who condemned the persecution of Jews as a way of attacking Christian intolerance. Their anticlericalism and concern for universal principles of human rights led them to a new conception of the status of the Jews, which found expression in the French Revolution of 1789. The Jews were not to be emancipated as a community but as *individual* human beings, the assumption being that, once oppression was removed, their distinctive group identity would disappear. There was no sympathy among the French revolutionaries for Judaism as such, which was generally viewed in Voltairean terms as a barbarous superstition.

The Enlightenment and the French Revolution demonstrated that anti-Judaism and antisemitism did not require a specifically Christian source of inspiration and could even be animated by anti-Christian sentiments. Enlightened Europeans and their radical successors in the nineteenth century, on the Left as well as the Right, were nevertheless still influenced by Christian stereotypes when they attacked Judaism or denounced the "Jewish" origins of Christianity. Even wholly secularized antisemites like Voltaire, Bruno Bauer, Richard Wagner and Eugen Dühring always assumed that Christianity was a superior religion to Judaism and did not hesitate to draw on Christian teachings to reinforce their own cultural or racist perspectives. They inherited the pervasiveness of the Christian antagonism to Jewry while no longer believing in its scheme of salvation, which had still retained an overriding commitment to the conversion of the Jews. This development opened up a dangerous situation whose demonic possibilities only became fully apparent with the rise of Nazism. For although Christianity had provided the seedbed on which Nazi racialist doctrines concerning the Jews could flourish, the Church still provided the Jews with an exit. If a Jew converted he was saved. There was no need for the extermination of the Jews because they had their place, even if it was a subordinate and degraded one, in the Christian world-order.

The Nazis took over all the negative anti-Jewish stereotypes in Christianity but they removed the escape clause. There was no longer any way in which even fully assimilated or baptized Jews could flee from the sentence of death which had been passed by the inexorable laws of race. In that sense, the "Final Solution," the purification of a world that was deemed corrupt and evil because of the very existence of the Jews, went beyond even the most radical Christian solution to the "Jewish Question." Hitler and Nazism grew out of a Christian European culture, but that does not mean that Auschwitz was preprogrammed in the logic of Christianity. Indeed, one could argue that the decline of religious belief by removing all moral restraints actually intensified the antisemitism that had been incubated for centuries under its protective shield. . . .

Antisemitism in Central Europe

The role that Jews played in the German-speaking culture of Central Europe from the middle of the nineteenth century until the rise of Hitler was unprecedented in its scale and quality. Indeed it is difficult to imagine the culture of modernity without the contributions of Marx, Freud, Einstein, Kafka, Mahler, Schoenberg, Wittgenstein and many others whose parents or grandparents had only recently been emancipated from life in the ghettos of Central Europe. Without the German-Jewish "symbiosis" there would have been no great cultural peaks like fin-de-siècle Vienna or Berlin during the Weimar Republic. Paradoxically, the Jews became victims of their very success in penetrating and remolding the agenda and the cultural axes of modernity in Central Europe. Identified by conservative and radical reactionary forces with the credo of liberalism or Marxism—with being standard-bearers of Western ideals of freedom, equality, and social

democracy—they were fated to be the first victims of the great counter-revolutionary backlash that culminated in National Socialism.

So deeply were Jews implicated in reshaping the culture, economy, and politics of societies like Germany and Austria, whose democratic traditions were weak and whose own national identity was insecure, that the antisemitism that developed in Central Europe assumed a uniquely racial and extremist quality. Racial antisemitism, grafted on to an older and still powerful Christian legacy of hate, served here to uproot at its very core the modern dream of assimilation, replacing it first with segregation, then expulsion, and finally mass extermination of the Jews.

Already in 1819, post-Napoleonic Germany, shaken by economic crisis and political upheaval, had experienced the anti-Jewish outbreaks known as the "Hep! Hep!" riots (a derogatory rallying cry against Jews). The goal of the agitation was to return the Jews to their previous ghetto status, following their entry into certain occupations, such as the civil service and the legal profession, which had been made possible by the Napoleonic conquest of Germany. Not only the mob but also the "educated" burgher classes, university professors like Friedrich Rühs and Jakob Fries, and student leaders, railed against acceptance of Jewish civic equality within a Christian state. A new kind of "Teutomania" came into being, rejecting the ideals of the French Revolution as alien to Germany, adopting a mystical cult of the German nation as an *Urvolk* ("natural folk"), deploring the commercialization of urban life, and attacking the Jews as despoilers of the German people (*Volksausplünderer*).[1] Throughout the nineteenth century German antisemitism would feed on this explosive ideological mix of romanticism, anticapitalism, *völkisch* nationalism, and hatred of Western liberal democracy.

Even radical intellectuals in Germany during the first half of the nineteenth century—like the Young Hegelians, Arnold Ruge, Bruno Bauer and Karl Marx—made, as we have seen, their own distinctive contribution to the subsequent emergence of a secular, anti-Christian antisemitism. They condemned the "fossilized," antihistorical character of Judaism, its religious separatism and its "exploitative" character, which, according to the radical Hegelians, had permeated bourgeois Christian society with a Judaic ethos. This depiction of Judaism as something alien and inferior that has nevertheless succeeded in "Judaizing" European society and culture finds its apogee in Richard Wagner's antisemitic tract, *Das Judentum in der Musik* (1850). Drawing on both the radical Hegelian and romantic nationalist traditions, Wagner identifies the "spirit of Judaism" with that of modernity, understood not as progress but as an expression of decadence and artistic decline.[2] As it was for the young Marx in the economic arena, so for Wagner, "liberation from Jewry" becomes the goal of redemption in the creative sphere.

But the great composer, one of the most influential antisemites of the modern age, goes much further than his contemporaries in his backlash against Jewry and the "abstract rationalism" that underpins emancipation. For Jewry's entry into modern society is perceived by Wagner as the infiltration of a wholly alien and antagonistic group whose success symbolizes the spiritual and creative crisis of German and European culture. The Jews represent the "evil conscience of our modern civilization" or, to quote another phrase much repeated by the Nazis, "the plastic demon of the decline of mankind." They embodied the corrupt, moneymaking principle of the new bourgeois world that Wagner held responsible for artistic decay.[3] The modern, educated, assimilated Jew is depicted by Wagner, already in 1850,

as "the most heartless of all human beings," alien and apathetic in the midst of a society he does not understand, whose history and evolution are indifferent to him. The Jew, wholly divorced from the *Volksgeist* (spirit of the folk), has no passion, no soul, no "inner capacity for life," no true music or poetry. He is a cold, loveless, purely cerebral being. Contemporary German-Jewish artists like the composers Felix Mendelssohn and [Giacomo] Meyerbeer, the poet Heinrich Heine or the radical writer Ludwig Boerne, are dismissed as arid, sarcastic and self-negating in their life and work.[4] The only redemption from this sterility lies in the "going under" of Jewry, its complete dissolution and disappearance.

Wagner's essentially racist vision of Jewry would have a profound influence on German and Austrian antisemites, including the English-born Houston S. Chamberlain, Lanz von Liebenfels, and above all on Adolf Hitler himself. Richard Wagner gave to German antisemitism a metaphysical pseudo-profundity, an aesthetic rationale rooted in the pagan world of classical Greece and a mythical quality that also finds expression in some of his operatic works as well as in his writings. The later Wagner, influenced by the racist philosophy of the French diplomat and historian Comte de Gobineau, is already a theorist of blood purity and the need to cleanse European civilization from the spiritual and physical pollution of the Jews. In 1881 he writes to Ludwig II of Bavaria: "I hold the Jewish race to be the born enemy of pure humanity and everything noble in it. It is certain that it is running us Germans to the ground, and I am perhaps the last German who knows how to hold himself upright in the face of Judaism, which already rules everything."[5]

It was in the late 1870s, in the decade immediately following formal Jewish emancipation in both Germany and Austria, that such ideas became commonplace and served as the basis for organized political antisemitism in Germany. It was the stock market collapse of 1873 in Vienna and then Berlin that provided the trigger by provoking an economic crisis which adversely affected the lower middle classes. It was against this background that radical German journalists like Otto Glagau and Wilhelm Marr wrote popular antisemitic tracts, and Prussian conservative publicists lashed out against the rule of the National Liberals ("Manchesterism" as it was often called), of Jewish financiers, and of the German Jewish-liberal press.[6] Both Glagau and Marr suggested that "the social question is nothing but the Jewish question," and the latter sought in 1879 to create an Antisemitic League, the first of its kind in Europe. His highly pessimistic book *The Victory of Judaism over Germanism* (1879), which put forward the thesis that "Germanism" was lost, since the Jews were already constructing their Jerusalem on the ruins of the new Germany, went through several editions and aroused extensive press comment.[7]

Far more effective than Marr, however, was the Lutheran court-preacher Adolf Stoecker, who in 1879 organized Berlin's first genuine antisemitic movement. Stoecker's bitter critique of Judaism and of modern German Jewry's "domination" of the press and the stock exchange combined traditional Lutheran theology with an anticapitalist appeal designed to win over the working-class to Throne and Altar. Although Stoecker's Christian Social Party failed in this objective, he remained one of the main propagators of a modern political antisemitism founded on Christian ideology in the Second German Reich.[8] His Catholic counterpart in Vienna, Karl von Vogelsang (an ex-Protestant German expatriate) who founded the conservative newspaper *Das Vaterland* in the 1870s, played a similar role in laying the ideological-political foundations of Austrian antisemitism. Here, too, the

assault on the Jews derived from a sharp critique of the Liberal hegemony and capitalistic exploitation of labor, combined with fear of secularizing trends in modern society and the resulting decline of Christian belief.

Racial antisemites like Eugen Dühring (a Berlin philosopher and economist), Theodor Fritsch, and the Hessian peasant leader Otto Boeckel took an even more intransigent, uncompromising view of the threat posed by emancipated Jewry to German society.[9] Moreover, they regarded Christianity as itself part of the problem since it was a "Semitic" religion that had imposed the "alien yoke" of the Old and New Testaments on the Germanic race, thereby inhibiting and distorting its natural instincts, its strength, virility, and heroic virtues. This racist trend of antisemitism had considerable appeal to university students in Germany and Austria, who in the early 1880s already began to exclude Jews from membership in their fraternities (*Burschenschaften*). In an age of formal equality when Jews had emerged as dangerous competitors in the liberal professions, especially journalism, medicine and law, racism had obvious attractions. It provided a way of reconstructing the social boundaries that had fallen with the ghetto walls—replacing them with new biological criteria based on blood and descent. In a secular, scientific and positivist age, "race" distinctions still had a certain objective, neutral quality to them and seemed more persuasive to many pseudo-intellectuals than outdated Christian theological concepts in which they no longer believed. Above all, the notion of race had a certain finality to it, suggesting that negative Jewish qualities were fixed and unchanging, hence not amenable to assimilation, conversion or any other attempts at social integration.

Anti-Jewish stereotypes, of course, had preceded racial thinking by centuries and existed quite independently of the emergence of this new ideology in the late nineteenth century. One could, like Paul de Lagarde, one of Germany's most prominent Orientalists and Bible scholars, radically negate Jewish existence without espousing racism.[10] De Lagarde, in calling for a Germanic Christianity that would completely eradicate its "Jewish" components, was one of the few nineteenth-century intellectuals to openly favor expulsion or imply approval for the physical destruction of German Jewry.

More influential at the time was the conservative nationalist historian, Heinrich von Treitschke, who had welcomed the Berlin antisemitic movement in 1879 with the famous slogan "The Jews are our misfortune" (*Die Juden sind unser Unglück*).[11] Von Treitschke gave academic legitimacy and respectability to what had hitherto seemed to be a rather disreputable, vulgar street movement. His demand for the total, unconditional surrender by German Jews of any distinctive Jewish identity did not openly employ racial arguments, but he did suggest that they remained an "alien" element in the German population who were largely to blame for the antisemitic response that their emancipation had aroused. Von Treitschke, like other Prussian conservatives, especially detested the "progressive" role that German Jews had played in promoting liberal ideas, radicalism and Social Democracy. Already in the Second Reich it had become fashionable to blame Jews for the policies of National Liberalism (Lasker, Bamberger), for stock-exchange capitalism (Rothschild, Bleichröder), and for revolutionary Marxism (Marx, Lassalle, Rosa Luxemburg). But what concerned the mandarin class in particular was the sense of Jews intruding into, subverting and ultimately controlling German intellectual and cultural life. This fear was rationalized as a desire to defend the semi-feudal, organic and "idealist" values of Germandom against the vulgar "materialism" with which Jews were supposedly corrupting the new capitalistic Germany. One finds such anxieties echoed across the political spectrum from radical economists like Werner Sombart to conservative monarchists like Houston S. Chamberlain.[12]

It was rare to find a German intellectual like Friedrich Nietzsche, who not only admired the Jews for their spiritual mastery and grandeur, while detesting "the stupidity, crudity and pettiness of German nationalism," but also vehemently dissociated himself from the "damnable German antisemitism, this poisonous boil of *névrose nationale*."[13] The German philosopher who took an axe to the Christian religion (he was also highly critical of the Jewish "slave rebellion in morals") deplored "these latest speculators in idealism, the antisemites, who today roll their eyes in a Christian-Aryan bourgeois manner and exhaust one's patience by trying to rouse up all the horned-beast elements in the people."[14] The problem was essentially a digestive one, for the German type, so Nietzsche believed, was "still weak and indefinite, so it could easily be blurred or extinguished by the stronger race." He had no doubt that the Jews were indeed "the strongest, toughest, and purest race now living in Europe," who could gain mastery over it if they so wished.[15] Yet, as Nietzsche stressed, they desired nothing but accommodation and absorption, to put an end to their centuries of wandering—to which purpose the German philosopher suggested that "it might be useful and fair to expel the antisemitic screamers from the country."[16]

The German antisemites in Nietzsche's day never constituted a major threat to the established social and political order. Their organizations were too divided among themselves, too limited in their electoral appeal and lacking in charismatic political leaders to obtain more than an ephemeral success at the polls. At the peak of their appeal during the Second Reich there were sixteen antisemitic deputies sitting in the Imperial Parliament-half of them from Hesse.[17] On the eve of the First World War party political antisemitism was clearly declining, but it would be very misleading to measure the impact of anti-Jewish feelings by such a narrow criterion. The influential Conservative Party adopted an openly anti-Jewish paragraph in its Tivoli Programme of 1892, and the ideologically affiliated Agrarian League (*Bund der Landwirte*) was a powerful ultra-conservative and antisemitic pressure group.[18]

If purely antisemitic rabble-rousers like Otto Boeckel, Hermann Ahlwardt, and Liebermann von Sonnenberg were ultimately unsuccessful, this was not so true of right-wing, imperialist lobbies like the Pan-Germanic League (*Alldeutscher Verband*), the *Deutschnationaler Handlungsgehilfenverband* (a white-collar trade union), the *Akademischer Turnerbund* (a gymnastics club) or the *Verein Deutscher Studenten* (an antisemitic students' movement). The impact of such lobbies and interest groups, imbued with an antiliberal, *völkisch*-national and antisemitic outlook, was considerably greater than that of ephemeral anti-Jewish political parties that rose and fell in accordance with the vagaries of the economy and the political system as a whole.[19] Moreover, as we have seen, organized antisemitism, which had first emerged in Germany after 1873, had a strong underpinning in cultural and religious stereotypes that remained entrenched in almost all sectors of the population. Once this potential was activated by the effects of defeat in the First World War, by inflation, massive economic depression, chronic political instability and the rise of a powerful mass movement of the Right, German antisemitism was rapidly transformed into a formidable political force.

Before 1914 it was, however, in German Austria and above all in Vienna that antisemitism first displayed its vote-catching efficacy. The Jews of Vienna, who formed about 8 per cent of the population, were heavily over-represented in the liberal professions, especially journalism, law and medicine; half of the students in the medical faculty in 1910 were Jewish. The Jews dominated the liberal educated class in fin-de-siècle Vienna and, even more than in Germany at that time, they seemed to be the creators, the critics, the impresarios and managers of German high culture. For Stefan Zweig they contributed nine-tenths of everything important in Viennese culture—an exaggeration, no doubt, but one containing enough truth to arouse the rage of the Austrian antisemites from Lueger to Hitler who denounced the "Judaization" of the press, art, literature and the theatre. The challenging innovations of Viennese Jews in psychoanalysis (Freud, Adler, Reich), in music (Mahler, Schoenberg), in literature, criticism and philosophy (Schnitzler, Salten, Beer-Hoffmann, Kraus) simply intensified the resentment of many Catholic Austrians.[20] Anti-Jewish theologians like August Rohling, author of the notorious *Der Talmudjude*, and Joseph Deckert railed against a "Semitic" conspiracy of powerful Jews who aimed at the subversion of the Catholic faith and even practiced, so they alleged, ritual murder as part of their hatred of Gentiles and insatiable drive for domination in Austria.[21] Antisemitic politicians like Schneider, Gregorig, Pattai, Lueger and Schoenerer disseminated these and other baseless slanders to a mass audience.

To some extent this fin-de-siècle Austrian antisemitism was a displaced reaction against the liberal capitalism that threatened those declining social strata, especially the Viennese artisans, with economic decline into the proletariat. Jewish industrialists and bankers as well as migrant peddlers from Galicia were seen as two sides of the same threat posed by capitalist modernization to the traditional way of life of the lower middle classes. While the multi-national Habsburg state valued the contribution made by Jewish enterprise to building up the railroads, financing the coalmines, pioneering sugar refining, establishing the beer industry, developing the iron and steel industry, the banking system and the metropolitan press, ordinary Austrians resented the dizzying ascent of the Jews in wealth and social status within one generation. It was all too easy and convenient to ascribe this success story to money-grabbing "materialism," dishonesty in business dealings or to a malevolent conspiracy to subjugate and oppress the Catholic majority.

The immensely popular resonance of anticapitalist antisemitism among the Viennese found its best expression in the spectacular career of Karl Lueger, the first democratic politician to triumph anywhere in Europe on an explicitly anti-Jewish platform.[22] Elected Mayor of Vienna in 1897, at the head of the Christian-Social Party, he retained power until his death in 1910 and was the first political role-model for the young Adolf Hitler, who admired him as "the greatest German *Bürgermeister* of all times." Lueger's attack on the Jews was a central part of his general assault on Liberal political hegemony in city politics and later of his defense of bourgeois class interests against the rising Social Democrats, most of whose intellectual leadership [in Austria] was Jewish, beginning with its founder Victor Adler. Lueger denounced Jewish influence in Hungary (coining the abusive term "Judeo-Magyars"), in Austrian banking, industry and commerce, in the Viennese Press, in medicine and the liberal professions. His Christian Social party called openly for segregation in the school system (though this was never imple-

mented), for banning the immigration of foreign Jews and for the restriction of Jewish influence in public life. Although officially Catholic in its discourse, the party had prominent agitators in its ranks, including Schneider, Gregorig. and priests like Father Deckert and Joseph Scheicher, whose populist antisemitism was as incendiary as that of any beer-swilling Pan-German racists. After his election to office in 1897 Lueger himself was more covert in his anti-Jewish rhetoric, limited as he was by Franz Joseph's imperial authority, which upheld the equality of all religious faiths and of all Austrian citizens before the law. Nevertheless, Lueger did not disown the more extremist Jew-baiters in his movement and did on occasion resort to racist remarks as well as carrying on surreptitious discrimination against Jewish employees of the municipality.[23]

Although the holder of an academic degree, Dr. Lueger did not hesitate to indulge in the crass anti-intellectualism so often directed by the more plebeian members of his party against Jews, free thinkers or socialists. Thus he frequently denigrated the universities and medical schools for being "Jew-infested" strongholds of atheism, free thinking, revolutionary subversion and the undermining of Christian morality. At the time of the 1905 Russian revolution, he threatened the Jewish community that if it supported the Social Democrats a pogrom could result. "I warn the Jews most expressly; for the same thing could perhaps happen as in Russia. We in Vienna are not antisemites [sic!], we are certainly not inclined to murder and violence. But if the Jews should threaten our fatherland, then we will show no mercy."[24]

The Christian Social Party, he declared on another occasion, was determined that the "Christian *Volk*" and not the alien Jews should be masters in their own house. His movement advocated "Christian solidarity," accompanied by an economic boycott of Jewish businesses to achieve this end, though such calls were rarely observed. It constantly campaigned against the *Verjudung* ("Judaization") of Austrian culture, though here too it met with little practical success. But it was more effective in implanting antisemitism in the hearts and minds of the younger generation, in making its discourse respectable and normal in public life, in linking it with a traditional, sentimental, religiously oriented Austrian Catholic patriotism.[25]

Lueger's conservative antisemitism was not incompatible with the toleration of baptized Jews or collaboration with wealthy, powerful Jewish capitalists whom the municipality needed to help fund its more ambitious projects for modernizing Vienna. This pragmatic, opportunistic approach had always been typical of Lueger's politics, and it did not change after he had embraced antisemitism as an integral part of his platform and ideology. He understood the value of antisemitism as a tactical weapon for attaining power but also recognized, unlike many of his rivals and his more extreme supporters, its limits once in office. His "war against the Jews" was carried out within the framework of a conciliatory, supranational Habsburg dynasty which deplored antisemitism as the politics of the street; mass violence within this *Rechtsstaat* (a state based on law) was rare, except in moments of crisis in Hungary, Galicia or Bohemia. There were no major economic crises such as characterized the post-1918 era in Austria. Nor were there any pogroms in Habsburg Vienna despite the hysterical diatribes of the more rabid Austrian antisemites. Viennese Jews were not stripped of their civil rights; there was no expropriation of Jewish wealth and, for all the anxiety and insecurity which antisemitism aroused, Jews continued to make a brilliant contribution to German-Austrian culture.

Nevertheless, Austrian antisemitism—that of Lueger and of his great rival, the Pan-German Georg von Schoenerer—provided the first model for Adolf Hitler's own war against the Jews, demonstrating to him its possibilities as a method of mobilizing the masses against a single, highly visible and vulnerable enemy. It was in prewar Vienna that the young Hitler would discover the "Jewish Question" and begin to link it inexorably with capitalism, Marxism, and the struggle for existence of the German nation. From Austrian Pan-Germanism Hitler took the biological, racist foundation of his world-view, and from Lueger he would learn how to use antisemitism as a political tool.[26]

NOTES

1. Eleanore Sterling, *Judenhaß: Die Anfänge der politischen Antisemitismus in Deutschland (1815–1850)*, (Frankfurt a.M, 1969).
2. O. D. Kulka, "Richard Wagner und die Anfänge des modernen Antisemitismus," *Bulletin des Leo Baeck Instituts*, 4, (1961), 281–300, on the connection between Wagner's political radicalism and racial antisemitism. See also Hartmut Zelinski, *Richard Wagner-ein deutsches Thema. Eine Dokumentation zur Wirkungsgeschichte Richard Wagners, 1876–1976* (Vienna/Berlin, 1983).
3. R. Wagner, *Das Judenthum in der Musik* (Leipzig, 1869), 10–12.
4. Ibid., 31–32.
5. Letter to Ludwig II, 22.XI. 1881. Quoted in J. Katz, *The Darker Side of Genius: Richard Wagner's Antisemitism* (London, 1986), 115. Katz's book is useful but unfortunately fails to grasp the passion and depth of Wagner's hostility to Jews. On this point, see Margaret Brearley, "Hitler and Wagner: the Leader, the Master and the Jews," *Patterns of Prejudice* 22, no. 2 (1988): 3–21.
6. Paul W. Massing, *Rehearsal for Destruction: A Study of Political Antisemitism in Imperial Ger-*

many (New York, 1949); P. G. J. Pulzer, *The Rise of Political Antisemitism in Germany and Austria* (London, 1988, revised ed.).

7. See the informative but otherwise disappointing biography by Moshe Zimmermann, *Wilhelm Marr: The Patriarch of Antisemitism* (New York, 1986).

8. Adolf Stoecker, *Christlich-Sozial: Reden und Aufsätze* (Berlin, 1890, 2nd ed.); Hans Engelmann, *Kirche am Abgrund: Adolf Stoecker und seine antijüdische Bewegung* (Berlin, 1984), 120–72.

9. U. Tal, *Christians and Jews in Germany: Religion, Politics and Ideology in the Second Reich, 1870–1914* (Ithaca/London 1975); Birgitta Magge, *Rhetorik des Hasses: Eugen Dühring und die Genese seines antisemitischen Wortschatzes* (Neuss, 1977).

10. Fritz Stern deals with de Lagarde in *The Politics of Cultural Despair: A Study of the Rise of German Ideology* (Berkeley, 1961).

11. For Treitschke's articles and the response which they drew, see W. Boehlich, ed., *Der Berliner Antisemitismusstreit* (Frankfurt a.M, 1965).

12. Werner Sombart, *Die Zukunft der Juden* (Leipzig, 1912), 52; Paul Mendes-Flohr, "Werner Sombart's *The Jews and Modern Capitalism*: An Analysis of Its Ideological Premises," *LBIYB* 21 (1976):87–107. Also Geoffrey C. Field, *Evangelist of Race: The Germanic Vision of Houston S. Chamberlain* (New York, 1981).

13. *Basic Writings of Nietzsche*. Translated and edited with commentaries by Walter Kaufmann (1968), appendix, 798.

14. Ibid., 594.

15. Ibid., 377.

16. Ibid. Nietzsche does, of course, also criticize the Jews, whose historic legacy he denounced as being responsible for "the slave-revolt in morals." This aspect of Nietzsche's approach to Judaism was as distorted as later efforts to turn him into a spiritual godfather of German Nazism.

17. Robert S. Wistrich, *Socialism and the Jews: The Dilemmas of Assimilation in Germany and Austria-Hungary* (London/Toronto, 1982), 275.

18. Hans Jürgen Pühle, *Agrarische Interessenpolitik und preussischer Konservatismus im wilhelminischen Reich* (Hanover, 1966).

19. Werner Jochmann, "Struktur und Funktion des deutschen Antisemitismus," in W. E. Mosse and A. Paucker, eds., *Juden im Wilhelminischen Deutschland, 1890–1914* (Tübingen, 1976), 389–477.

20. Robert Wistrich, *The Jews of Vienna in the Age of Franz Joseph* (London, 1989).

21. On the Rohling affair, I. A. Hellwing, *Der konfessionelle Antisemitismus im 19. Jahrhundert in Österreich* (Vienna, 1972).

22. Robert S. Wistrich, "Karl Lueger and the Ambiguities of Viennese Antisemitism," *Jewish Social Studies* 45 (1983): 251–62.

23. Richard S. Geehr, *Karl Lueger: Mayor of Fin de Siècle Vienna* (Detroit, 1990), 293.

24. Ibid., 200.

25. Wistrich, "Karl Lueger," 258–61.

26. Robert S. Wistrich, "Georg von Schoenerer and the Genesis of Modern Austrian Antisemitism," *The Wiener Library Bulletin* 29 (1976), new series, nos. 39/40, 21–29.

Racism

MICHAEL BURLEIGH AND WOLFGANG WIPPERMANN

From *The Racial State*

Racial ideologies and theories were not an exclusively German discovery. The word *Rasse* (race) is thought to derive from the Arabic *ras* (meaning "beginning, origin, head"). It entered the German language in the seventeenth century, as a loan word from English and French, and until the mid-nineteenth century was spelled with a "c" as Race.[1] However, in Germany racial ideologies enjoyed the widest currency and the greatest political salience: the Third Reich became the first state in world history whose dogma and practice was racism. Was this predictable? Was there a form of German *Sonderweg* [special path] in the development and diffusion of racial ideologies? If so, when did this begin? What does one mean by "race" and "racism"?[2]

Racial-Anthropological Theories

"Blacks and Whites are not distinct types of people, for they belong to one tribe, and yet to two different races."[3] With these words, written in 1775, Immanuel Kant both defined, and at the same time delimited, the concept of race. There were obviously different human races, however these belonged to a single "genus," because they "constantly produce fruitful children with one another, regardless of the great varieties which can otherwise be found in their form." It followed that the differences between the various human races were no guide to their "value." Most subsequent racial ideologues ignored this last crucial qualifi-

cation. They assumed that physical and psychological differences between individuals and races were an indication of their relative worth, and went on to construct racial hierarchies reflecting this assertion. In the late eighteenth century these claims were largely based upon external physical criteria. For example, the German theologian Johann Kaspar Lavater (1741–1801) attempted to deduce spiritual and psychological characteristics from physiognomy.[4] The Dutch anatomist Pieter Camper (1722–89) measured the "facial angles" of members of different races, in order to categorize them according to corporal stature and beauty.[5] The German physician Franz Joseph Gall (1758–1828) employed cranial measurement, in order, with the aid of this so-called phrenological method, to categorize the races in terms of intelligence, morality, and beauty.[6]

In a book published in 1798, entitled *Outline of the History of Humanity,* the Göttingen philosopher Christoph Meiners (1745–1810) categorized the peoples of the world according to their "beauty" or "ugliness."[7] The "fair" peoples were superior to all others, in terms of both beauty and intellectual achievements. By contrast, the "darker colored peoples" were "ugly" and "semi-civilized." A similar line of argument can be found in a book published in 1848 by the philosopher Carl Gustav Carus (1789–1869).[8] According to him, the universe was endowed with a soul that gradually took on material form: first, interstellar ether, then the solar system, and finally the planet Earth. In turn, the latter underwent a series of metamorphoses leading to the creation of Man. The complexions of the various human races reflected their degree of "inner illumination." The four great races were those of the dawn (yellow), day (white), sunset (red), and night (black). These races were also "related" to bodily organs; the Whites to the brain and the Blacks to the genitals. Following on from this, Carus attributed "the capacity for the highest spiritual development" to the "peoples of the day." The latter were therefore entitled to extend their "power over all inhabited parts of the world," and to hold sway over the uncivilized and ugly "peoples of the night." These few examples suffice to demonstrate that the transparent objective of these representatives of anthropological racism was to legitimize European colonialism. The claim that Blacks are less beautiful and less intelligent than Whites is still axiomatic to racist discourse in Europe and North America. In this respect Germany was hardly unique. However it is worth noting that German racial ideologists propounded the view that Africans and Asians were of "lesser racial value" at a time when the German states possessed no colonies, nor had any desire to do so.

Racial-anthropological theories also served to legitimize claims to hegemony among the European races themselves. This resulted in a very specific form of racist discourse, which developed in the late eighteenth and early nineteenth centuries. It had three distinct points of origin, which in the beginning were only loosely connected with one another. The first was a by-product of the value attached to ethno-cultural diversity by [Johann Gottfried] Herder, in his case as an attempt to redress the effects of French cultural and political hegemony.[9] Herder was anything but a racist. He explicitly rejected the concept of race, subscribed to a form of cultural relativism, detested everything that involved coercion and

conquest, and believed that the various peoples of the world would one day come together like the branches of a tree. However his claim that each "nation" disposed of a specific "national character" and "national spirit" gradually acquired exclusive overtones. Specifically, it became interlinked with a much older tradition of "Teutomania."[10] . . . Herder also celebrated the "tall, strong, and beautiful bodies" of the Germans, their "enormous blue eyes filled with the spirit of restraint and loyalty," and their "heroic cast of mind and great physical strength." Moreover, the Germans had laid the foundations of European freedom, civilization, and well-being, while defending it from the barbarians. It is important to bear in mind that these sentiments did not close his mind to the virtues of other peoples, most notably the Slavs, among whom his writings were highly esteemed. Put slightly differently, one could describe Herder's proto-nationalism as essentially cosmopolitan and emancipatory in character and intention.

Nonetheless, stereotypical representations of the ancient Germans multiplied in the form of vulgarized clichés like "Germanic loyalty" or "Germanic fortitude," which had unmistakably racist overtones. This Germanic cult fulfilled a twofold ideological function. Firstly, it represented a rejection of French claims to cultural and political hegemony. According to Arndt, Fichte, Jahn, and other national ideologists, the Germanic peoples were superior to the Latin French in corporal stature, beauty, bravery, and love of freedom. Secondly, the alleged cultural superiority of the Germans was also used to legitimize German rule over former West Slav and Polish territories. In this case, a number of ethnic stereotypes, some of which originated in the Middle Ages, were imbued with racist aspects. An example of this is the conceptual journey undergone by the slogan *"polnische Wirtschaft"* or "Polish mismanagement."

This was first used by the German Jacobin Johann Georg Forster (1754–94), as a means of encapsulating his distaste for the anarchic and oppressive character of the Polish noble Commonwealth.[11] However, his strictures upon a particular class soon slid into criticism of the Polish people as a whole. For in addition to his strictures upon the Polish *szlachta* [nobility], Forster condemned the "brutality" of the Poles in general, including the peasant victims of noble arbitrariness.

National stereotypes like these proliferated in the following period, chiefly as a means of legitimizing Prussian rule over part of partitioned Poland. For example, in 1801 the Prussian historian Johann Georg Friedrich Reitemeier claimed that the "uncleanliness" of the Slavs "was notorious from the earliest times."[12] Therefore the Slavs, and in particular the Poles, should consider themselves fortunate that the Germans had brought them "civilization and the comforts of luxury." Conquest by the Germans was "a revolution of the most beneficent sort." This cultural-political form of imperialism was given a historical-messianic quality through the claim that the Germans had a "mission" to resettle territories once inhabited by ancient Germanic tribes. Looked at in this way, the Slavs were history's squatters. Thus, in 1818, the historian Karl Adolf Menzel argued that the Germans had legitimate claims to those territories that "were already inhabited by the Germans in primeval times," by which he meant those territories once inhabited by eastern German tribes.[13]

The notion that the Germans were "bearers of civilization" to areas once settled by the "ancient Germans" became interconnected with Hegel's assertion that the Slavs, with the exception of the Russians, were "peoples without a history." The Germanization of former Slav territory was seen as an inevitable consequence of a presumptive "cultural gradient," declining from west to east, and of a "German drive to the east" that gradually assumed quasi-biological aspects. According to Moritz Wilhelm Heffter's *World Struggle of the Germans and Slavs* (1847), this last process was "the necessary consequence of the cultural-historical, intellectual and moral superiority which the cultivated always enjoy over the uncultivated."[14] . . . A putatively "timeless" German "drive" to the east was gradually imbued with the character of a gradual, but unstoppable process, akin to the regular migration of birds. An unreflective Social Darwinism also began to influence the terms of historical argument. This was clear in the case of Heinrich von Treitschke, who in an essay published in 1862 celebrated the "pitiless racial struggle" which the "Germans" had once waged against the heathen Prussians, Lithuanians, and Poles.[15] A form of "magic" emanated from "eastern German soil," for the latter had been "fertilized" by "the most noble German blood." Although Treitschke's object was to give historical legitimization to the process of "Germanizing" Prussia's Polish minority, rather than to license further imperialist conquests, his racialist celebration of a (mythical) genocide allegedly once practiced against the Prussians and Slavs would soon become a means of legitimizing claims to further territories in the east.

In addition to legitimizing, and in the Social Darwinian strain, "proving" the necessity of European imperialism and intra-European nationality conflicts, racial-anthropological theories also served to legitimize claims to hegemony by particular classes within societies. This was notably the case in France. In his *Essai sur la noblesse de France*, published in 1735, the Count Henri de Boulainvilliers argued that the French nobility was descended from Frankish-Germanic conquerors, while the townsmen and peasantry were the descendants of the ancient Gauls.[16] . . . Among those who subscribed to this "Frankish legend" was the Count Joseph Arthur de Gobineau (1816–82). Gobineau claimed that his own family was descended from this ancient Frankish aristocracy. Despite the fact that this claim was false, Gobineau clung to it with considerable tenacity, probably in order to divert attention from the present painful realities of the family. He had had an unsuccessful career as a middle-ranking diplomat, in the service of the parvenu Louis Bonaparte and, in his eyes, the equally detestable Third Republic. Gobineau regarded the latter as being symptomatic of a general decline. The question of why this decline had occurred was the main preoccupation of his *Essai sur l'inégalité des races humaines*, which was published between 1853 and 1855.[17]

In line with received racial-anthropological discourse, Gobineau claimed that the White, Yellow, and Black races were of "unequal" value. However, he then proceeded to argue that the rise and fall of civilizations was racially determined. All high cultures in world history were the work of "Aryans," and were based upon an aristocratic mode of rule. Cultures declined when this "Aryan" ruling caste interbred with members of the "racially less valuable" lower orders. This resulted, ineluctably, in rebellion by the "racially less valuable" against the "Aryan ruling race." Rebellions of this sort had occurred in ancient Egypt, Greece, and Rome. Likewise, the French Ancien Régime had been destroyed by a revolt of the Gallic plebs against a ruling elite descended from the Frankish nobility. A similar fate awaited every civilization in the world as a consequence of general racial interbreeding, although the effects of the latter, it should be stressed, were construed in socio-cultural rather than biological terms. A society that acknowledged no racial or social differences would make no progress in the field of culture. . . .

Racial-Hygienic Theories

Unlike Gobineau, whose work initially only appealed to a handful of reactionary aesthetes, Charles Darwin's *On the Origins of Species by Means of Natural Selection, or the Preservation of Favoured Races in the Struggle for Life* enjoyed massive success after its appearance in 1859.[18] Darwin was a reclusive Victorian gentleman scholar of a liberal, progressive cast of mind. He was opposed to slavery and strongly supported ideas of human equality by avoiding references to "lower" or "higher" races. He was concerned about poverty and established Friendly Societies in Kent. The Origins did not contain racial theories and was almost exclusively concerned with plants and animals. Nonetheless, Darwin, rather than Gobineau, was the involuntary progenitor of racist ideology, for he was responsible for the theory of natural selection as the mechanism of evolution. Selection was to become central to all subsequent racist discourse. It is important to emphasize here that Darwin himself was too intelligent and responsive to criticism to adhere to a fixed set of ideas, and that his theories themselves were composite and not intended for application to human society in a prescriptive sense. This was the "achievement" of Social Darwinians, who unlike Darwin himself used terms like "betterment" or "progress" in a morally loaded manner. Contrary to popular belief, Social Darwinism was not an exclusively right-wing concern. Social theorists who were politically antagonistic to each other could call themselves Darwinians simply by referring to different tendencies in Darwin's thought. This, and a generalized belief in science and progress, accounts for the existence of Social Darwinians who could be conservative, liberal, socialist, or Fascist.

According to Darwin, there was a constant struggle for existence in the plant and animal kingdoms. It would be won by those species that demonstrated that they were the most capable of adaption. These would be capable of reproduction. This process of natural selection would lead to the further development of the individual species. In order to counter criticism of the application of this theory to man, Darwin wrote *The Descent of Man*, in which he accounted for some human attributes by resorting to a theory of sexual selection. He also noted the counter-selective effects of modern civilization and suggested that breeding could make up for the diminishing impact of natural selection. This shift in his thought reflected the increasing influence upon him of his cousin Galton and the German zoologist Ernst Haeckel. . . .

Francis Galton (1822–1911) took the principle of selection further, in the interests of improving the biological health of the human race.[19] Healthy parents, by whom he meant members of the middle classes and the learned professions, should be encouraged to marry early and have as many children as possible. These should be issued with certificates of hereditary health. By contrast, those persons who failed this "Passed in Genetics" test were to be encouraged to emigrate to the land of "Cantsayanywhere." Man, in other words, was to take control of his evolutionary processes. Galton was the founder of hereditary health care, for which in 1883 he coined the term "eugenics," a program for improving the human race by genetic means. The prescriptive measures were not confined to the question of "judicious mating," but encompassed education, public health, and welfare. Darwin and Galton's ideas were gradually diffused throughout Europe and North America, where through the mediation of Herbert Spencer the notion of the "survival of the fittest" was used to legitimize laissez-faire capitalism.

Although the rampant individualist strain of Social Darwinism was not so successful in Germany, its collectivist and state interventionist variety was. The zoologist Ernst Haeckel (1834–1919) attempted to propagate Darwin's teachings, while converting them into a comprehensive quasi-humanist philosophy called "Monism."[20] This new philosophy was to be "based upon the real foundations of comparative zoology." Its "application to practical human affairs [would] open up a new path to moral perfection." Haeckel's Monism encountered considerable criticism from conservatives and enthusiasm from the Left that saw in him a champion of academic freedom, anti-clericalism, and collectivist solutions to social problems. However, neither his detractors nor supporters appeared concerned with Haeckel's racist presuppositions. These were much in evidence in his *History of Natural Creation*, a book that enjoyed considerable popularity within the German labor movement.[21] According to Haeckel's brand of anthropological racism, the "central races" were the "most highly developed and perfect . . . No other types of people can be compared either physically or intellectually with the central peoples. They alone have actually made history. They alone have been responsible for the cultural achievements which appear to raise the human race above the rest of nature."[22] Within the "central types of people," the "indogermanic" race was superior to the "hamosemitic" peoples. By virtue of their "more highly developed brains they would triumph over all other races and in the struggle for existence . . . [and] cast the net of their dominion over the entire world." However, in order to achieve this hegemony, selective breeding measures would be necessary. The model here was above all ancient Sparta, where the newly born were subjected to physical examination and selection.[23] . . .

This was not merely intended for metaphorical effect. Haeckel sincerely believed in the necessity for, and possibilities of, racial selective breeding. In a book, entitled *The Riddle of Life*, published in 1904, he explicitly advocated the killing of the sick:

> What profit does humanity derive from the thousands of cripples who are born each year, from the deaf and dumb, from cretins, from those with incurable hereditary defects etc. who are kept alive artificially and then raised to adulthood? ... What an immense aggregate of suffering and pain these depressing figures represent for the unfortunate sick people themselves, what a fathomless sum of worry and grief for their families, what a loss in terms of private resources and costs to the state for the healthy! How much of this loss and suffering could be obviated, if one finally decided to liberate the totally incurable from their indescribable suffering with a dose of morphia.[24]

Haeckel was not merely a harmless and uninfluential ideologist-cum-scientist. His eccentric philosophy was propagated through the Monist League, which he founded in 1906; and his ideas concerning racial selective breeding began to filter into rather more respectable scientific circles. The physician Wilhelm Schallmeyer (1857–1919) was particularly significant in this last respect.

In 1900 Schallmeyer had won first prize in a competition sponsored by the industrialist Friedrich Alfred Krupp, in response to the question "What can we learn from the principles of the theory of evolution for application to domestic political development and the laws of the State?"[25] Schallmeyer's response was published in 1903 as *Heredity and Selection in the Life of Nations: A Study in Political Science on the Basis of the New Biology*. According to Schallmeyer, the state had the duty to secure the biological capacity of its people. This would involve measures designed to increase the birthrate and the racial quality of its people. In this connection, Schallmeyer specified encouraging early marriage, the introduction of earnings-related child allowances, special payments to mothers, and licensed polygamy for especially racially "valuable" men. However, all of these measures were only to be available to those who had been examined by physicians expert in "socio-biological sciences." By contrast, those who failed the examination, and who were hence not to be issued with a certificate of fitness to marry, were to be prevented from reproducing. Schallmeyer thought that those of "lesser hereditary value" should be isolated and compulsorily sterilized. It should be noted, however, that Schallmeyer made no attempt to relate his "social biology" to racial-anthropological teachings. According to him, there were no pure races in Europe, and attempts to produce racial "thoroughbreds" were as meaningless as the preferential treatment of the "Nordic race."

This last matter preoccupied Alfred Ploetz (1860–1940). His central concern was reflected in a book entitled *The Efficiency of our Race and the Protection of the Weak*, which was published in 1895.[26] "Our" race was the "West Aryan" or "Germanic race," which was the "most outstanding civilized race," an assertion "about which there is nothing more to say." However, the "efficiency" of this Germanic race was threatened by "growing protection of the weak." Various measures would have to be taken to halt this last process. The conception of a child was "not to be left to accident, or to an over-excited moment, but rather regulated according to the principles which science has determined for the circumstances and times." If, despite these "principles," a deformed child should still be produced, then a "college of physicians, which decides concerning issues of citizenship, should prepare a gentle death, shall we say through a small dose of morphine." During wartime, only inferior persons should be sent to the front. Ploetz described these measures as "hygienic." Since they were ostensibly designed to improve the "qualities of our race," he coined the term "racial hygiene." Other scientists continued to use the term "eugenics."

Both tendencies ultimately reflected changing scientific conceptions of heredity. The hitherto dominant Lamarckian theory on the hereditability of environmentally acquired characteristics, which influenced Darwin's theory of evolution, was superseded by others that stressed genetic factors. The most extreme statement of the independence of heredity from the environment was August Weismann's theory of an autonomous, immutable "germ plasm."[27] Put simply, these discoveries ruled out the prospect of improving the mental or physical abilities of successive generations through education or sport, while emphasizing the predeterminedness of, for example, criminality or alcoholism. In this view of things, human beings became aggregates of "negative" or "positive" biological materials, their value as individuals being increasingly overshadowed by their contribution to the future of the collective, which could be construed as either the human race in general or one race in particular. Again, it is important to stress that there is no automatic correlation between these scientific ideas and types of political persuasion. Alfred Grotjahn (1869–1931), a theoretician of social hygiene with links with the right wing of the SPD [Social Democratic Party] (to which he owed his appointment as professor of social hygiene at Berlin University in 1920), advocated a combination of environmental improvement, isolation, and sterilization as a means of "amortizing" those elements who did not fit the socialist's profile of the "respectable" working classes. This included the insane, the "workshy," people with sexually transmitted diseases, alco-

holics, accident victims and so on. Where science led, socialism followed.[28] . . .

These scientific ideas did not unfold in a social void, and nor, as we shall see, were they the exclusive property of professional scientists. The scientists discussed above, and their adherents in applied health care, came from particular social classes, belonged to increasingly ramified professional structures, and lived within societies undergoing profound social and economic change. Specifically, these members of the educated bourgeoisie saw their urban "living space" threatened by hordes of fecund proletarians bearing the physical and psychological imprint of deplorable living and working conditions. Eugenics and racial hygiene were one response to the "social question."[29] While, socialist or otherwise, these responses also undoubtedly reflected genuine concern for suffering humanity, they also mirrored the frustrated modernizing arrogance of the educated bourgeoisie toward people apparently impervious to the verities of human betterment and progress, whether espoused by right-wingers or socialists. . . . Social Darwinists contributed the identification of low social position with "unfitness," or in other words, the idea that the poor must be unfit because they had failed in the "struggle of life." In some circles, concern about differential rates of fertility between the upper and lower social classes was related to the "counter-selective" impact of modern medicine and welfare, a notion which bore the imprint of Darwin as mediated by Galton. Put simply, welfare was obstructing the "natural" elimination of the "unfit."

Questions of quality also began to enter the orbit of questions of cost. Long before the health and welfare system faced a financial crisis, some pundits were applying cost-benefit calculations to the "asocial" and "handicapped." For example, in 1911 an essay competition solicited responses to the question: "What do inferior racial elements cost the state and society?" Although eugenicists differed about the comparable merits of "negative" and "positive" measures, the balance of opinion began to tilt toward the former. The North American example, specifically the introduction of a Sterilization Law in 1907 by the state of Indiana, appeared to lend this questionable practice an air of modern, democratic reasonableness. However, debates in Germany on these questions were overtaken by events. Specifically, the outbreak of the First World War resulted in a renewed emphasis upon population quantity rather than quality. The question of whether or not chronic alcoholics or habitual criminals should be sterilized was hardly the burning issue of 1914–18, when numbers counted.

The issue of quality resurfaced in the early 1920s. This was partly because of concern about the perceived "qualitative imbalance" resulting from the war's "mass annihilation of our genetically most valuable elements," partly a reflection of paranoia over the fecundity of neighboring races. . . . The onset of the Depression further reduced the gap between scientific and demographic advocates of "negative" eugenics and those engaged in the making of policy in an austere financial climate. Mass unemployment and a corresponding fall in tax receipts at all levels of government raised questions concerning the allocation of resources. Questions of cost served to lower the ethical threshold of politicians, who were also confronted by the weight of professional scientific opinion and the irrefutably gloomy prognostications of their own statisticians and demographic planners. By July 1932, the Prussian government had formulated a draft Reich Sterilization Law, which it forwarded to the Reich government that winter. By the time it arrived, the Reich government was in the hands of Adolf Hitler.

With Hitler very much in mind, it must be stressed that discussion of these questions was not confined to scientists, politicians, or government experts. Alongside, and often drawing from, the ideas we have been considering, were a host of scientifically illiterate pundits who subscribed to selective breeding in the interests of various types of Utopia. Bereft of objective scientific legitimization, the ideological and inhuman nature of their work is immediately transparent. This is clear in the case of the philosopher Friedrich Nietzsche. Prescriptively, in 1880, Nietzsche wrote that "the tendency must be toward the rendering extinct of the wretched, the deformed, the degenerate."[30] . . . Eight years later he outlined a series of measures for racial selective breeding.

Notwithstanding Nietzsche's interest in hyper-aristocratic quality, he accompanied the eugenicists along a dirigiste, technocratic, and inhuman route, albeit to a different destination. Beyond him and the scientists were a host of outright cranks, two of whom warrant some attention. Willibald Hentschel recommended the creation of "stud villages," in which men selected according to racial criteria should be encouraged to produce as many "highly valuable" little Germans as possible, through the good offices of up to ten women.[31] . . . Hentschel became the leading ideological light of the Artamanen League, whose members included, *inter alia*, Heinrich Himmler, Walther Darré, and Rudolf Höss, the later commandant of Auschwitz, all of whom were indebted to the racial Utopia propagated by their erstwhile mentor. Jorg Lanz, who preferred to style himself Lanz von Liebenfels, was somewhat further out in a paranoid, occultist darkness.[32] Lanz recommended the selective breeding of blonde, Aryan supermen. To this end, all suitable candidates were to be subjected to a stringent racial test. These fantasies were propagated through a journal called

"Ostara: Newspaper for Blond People." Although these ideas were abstruse and their advocates crazed, they nonetheless had a certain political effect. For example, many members of the Thule Society, who later supported the NSDAP, knew and respected Lanz's ideas. This may also have been the case with Adolf Hitler....

Racial Antisemitic Theories

By no means all of the racial hygienicists and eugenicists were either politically conservative or antisemites.[33] This last qualification applies to many of the scientists, pseudo-scientists, and for that matter Nietzsche too. Responsibility for fusing racial-hygienic and Social Darwinist ideas with antisemitism may be attributed to the (elective German) Englishman Houston Stewart Chamberlain (1855–1927).[34] According to Chamberlain, the Germanic peoples, but especially the Germans in the narrow sense, were superior to all other peoples in every respect. This superiority, which was based upon intellectual abilities rather than physical characteristics, was being threatened by another race, namely the Jews. For Chamberlain, the Jews were the Devil incarnate. They represented a demonic threat to the chosen German race. The reason for this was that, in contrast to the Jews, the Germans had no religion identical with their race. Christianity was essentially Jewish.

This rather unoriginal, racially motivated attack upon Christianity had consequences for both the Churches and the Jews. Instead of energetically refuting this nonsense, many Protestant and Roman Catholic theologians appeared to accept Chamberlain's views, for they themselves held the Jews responsible for liberalism, socialism, and Communism, not to speak of antisemitism itself. All of these evils were the product of secularization and modernization promoted by the Jews.

The latter were once again made the whipping boys for all adverse secular developments. This in itself was hardly new. However, the way in which racial antisemitism closed the only alternative option, namely that of conversion to Christianity, was an entirely novel development. Baptism no longer "liberated" the Jews from a racially rather than confessionally defined "Jewishness." The Jews were thus defined, and hence excluded, as the embodiments of general evils. Old legends and prejudices, notoriously that concerning ritual murder, were revived, and combined with more up-to-date conspiracy theories like the falsified *Protocols of the Elders of Zion*. As the embodiment of evil, the Jews were literally capable of anything and everything. This included responsibility for the alleged racial deterioration of the German people and the deliberate sabotaging of racial-hygienic solutions to the "social question" made available by modern science.

Racial antisemitic theories were not an exclusively German phenomenon. However in Germany they appear to have enjoyed especially wide currency and a high degree of political instrumentalization.[35] Although in contrast to Eastern Europe Germany's Jews were highly assimilated, their Emancipation, i.e., the achievement of formal legal equality, occurred relatively late, in 1869–71. Emancipation coincided with an equally belated, and comparatively rapid, industrialization of the German economy, and hence (partial) modernization of German society. The first great crisis of the German capitalist economy, the *Gründerkrise* of the early 1870s, coincided and was connected with the first wave of political antisemitism. The allegedly powerful and wealthy Jews were held responsible for the negative accompaniments of rapid industrialization and modernization. This convenient fiction found silent assent among Germany's ruling elites, for this modern strain of antisemitism had a negative, integrative utility in so far as fear of enemies, within and without, would bind the majority population more closely to the existing social order. This particularly affected the Jews after the First World War. Germany's Jews were held responsible for the "stab in the back" and the Revolution which had allegedly resulted in Germany's defeat, despite the fact that cemeteries were lined with the graves of young Jews who had fallen for their Fatherland. The Jews were also held responsible for the deployment by the French of colonial occupation troops on the Rhine, who then proceeded to seduce German women, thus undermining the "purity" of the "German race." German and foreign Jews were also allegedly involved in prostitution and the white slave trade, through which they hoped to encourage the spread of syphilis and other sexually transmitted diseases that would damage the "hereditary properties" of the "Aryan-Germanic race." Finally, "Berlin Jews" were even attempting to prevent the racial-hygienic improvement of the German people. The writer Artur Dinter plumbed further depths in racial conspiracy theory.[36] In a novel published in 1918, entitled *Sin Against the Blood*, he told the story of a "racially pure," blonde, blue-eyed German woman who was seduced by a Jew. Although she later managed to get away from him, and subsequently married an "Aryan," she and her husband nonetheless produced "typically Jewish-looking" children. Her "hereditary properties" had been permanently corrupted by a casual encounter with a Jew. This salacious and quasi-pornographic nonsense was sold in hundreds of thousands of copies. Writers like Dinter, Lanz, and scores of others found a sympathetic readership in Germany after the First World War. One of them was probably Adolf Hitler.

NOTES

1. Werner Conze, "Rasse," in Otto Brunner, Werner Conze, Reinhart Koselleck, eds., *Geschichtliche Grundbegriffe* (Stuttgart, 1984), 5: 135–78.

2. For the following, see the general surveys by George L. Mosse, *Towards the Final Solution: A History of European Racism* (New York, 1978), and *Nationalism and Sexuality: Respectability and Abnormal Sexuality in Modern Europe* (New York, 1985); Michael Banton, *The Idea of Race* (London, 1977); A. James Gregor, *The Ideology of Fascism: The Rationalism of Totalitarianism* (New York, 1969); Leon Poliakov, *The Aryan Myth: A History of Racist and Nationalist Ideas in Europe* (New York, 1974)

3. Immanuel Kant, *Von den verschiedenen Racen der Menschen* (Königsberg, 1775), 3.

4. Johann Kaspar Lavater, *Physiognomische Fragmente zur Beförderung der Menschenkenntnis und Menschenliebe*, Vols. 1–4, in *Johann Kaspar Lavaters ausgewählte Schriften*, ed. Johann Kaspar Orelli (Zurich, 1844).

5. Peter Camper, *Dissertation Physique* (Utrecht, 1791).

6. Franz Joseph Gall, *Vorlesungen über die Verrichtung des Gehirns* (Berlin, 1805).

7. Christoph Meiners, *Grundriss der Geschichte der Menschheit* (Lemgo, 1978; reprinted Königstein, 1981), 89.

8. Carl Gustav Cams, *Über die ungleiche Befähigung der verschiedenen Menschenstämme für höhere geistige Entwicklung* (Leipzig, 1848).

9. Johann Gottfried Herder, *Ideen zur Philosophie der Geschichte der Menschheit* (1785), *Herders Werke in 5 Bänden, ausgewählt und eingeleitet von Wilhehn Dobbeck* (Berlin, 1969), vol. 4.

10. For the following see George L. Mosse, *The Crisis of German Ideology: Intellectual Origins of the Third Reich* (London, 1964); Klaus von See, *Deutsche Germanen-Ideologie vom Humanismus bis zur Gegenwart* (Frankfurt am Main, 1970), *Die Ideen von 1789 und die Ideen von 1914. Völkisches Denken in Deutschland zwischen Französischer*

Revolution und Erstem Weltkrieg (Frankfurt am Main, 1975); Hans-Jurgen Lutzhöft, *Der nordische Gedanke in Deutschland 1920–1940* (Stuttgart, 1970); Wolfgang Emmerisch, *Zur Kritik der Volkstumsideologie* (Frankfurt am Main, 1971).

11. Johann Georg Forster in a letter to his wife dated 1785, *Georg Forsters Sämtliche Schriften*, ed. by his daughter (Leipzig, 1843), vol. 7, 489. On the following see also Wolfgang Wippermann, *Der "deutsche Drang nach Osten.' Ideologie und Wirklichkeit eines politischen Schlagwortes* (Darmstadt, 1981).

12. Johann Friedrich Reitemeier, *Geschichte der preussischen Staaten vor und nach ihrer Vereinigung in eine Monarchie* (Frankfurt an der Oder, 1801–5), 1: 33.

13. Karl Adolf Menzel, *Die Geschichte der Deutschen* (Breslau, 1818), 247.

14. Moritz Wilhelm Heffter, *Der Weltkampf der Deutschen und Slawen seit dem Ende des 4. Jahrhunderts nach christlicher Zeitrechnung, nach seinem Ursprunge, Verlaufe und nach seinen Folgen dargestellt* (Hamburg and Gotha, 1847).

15. Heinrich von Treitschke, "Das deutsche Ordensland Preussen," *Preussische Jahrbücher* 10 (1862): 95–151.

16. Comte Henri de Boulainvilliers, *Essais sur la noblesse de France* (Amsterdam, 1732).

17. Joseph Arthur de Gobineau, *Essai sur l'inégalité des races humaines* (Paris, 1853–5), 1–4; see also Michael Biddis, *Father of Racist Ideology: The Social and Political Thought of Count Gobineau* (London, 1970); E. J. Young, *Gobineau und der Rassimus. Eine Kritik der anthropologischen Geschichtstheorie* (Meisenheim, 1968).

18. Charles Darwin, *On the Origin of Species by Means of Natural Selection, or the Preservation of Favoured Races in the Struggle for Life* (London, 1959). For this and the following, see Hansjoachim W. Koch, *Der Sozialdarwinismus. Seine Genese und sein Einfluss auf das imperialistische Denken* (Munich, 1973); Gunther Mann, ed., *Biologismus im 19. Jahrhundert* (Stuttgart, 1973); Gisela Bock, *Zwangssterilisation im Nationalsozialismus. Studien zur Rassenpolitik und Frauenpolitik* (Opladen, 1986), Paul Weindling, *Darwinism and Social Darwinism in Imperial Germany* (Stuttgart, 1989), *Health, Race and German Politics between National Unification and Nazism 1870–1945* (Cambridge, 1989).

19. Francis Galton, *Hereditary Genius: Its Laws and Consequences* (London, 1863), *Inquiries into Human Faculty and its Development* (London, 1883), "Eugenics: Its Definition, Scope, and Aims," *Sociological Papers* 1 (1905): 45–50.

20. On Haeckel see Daniel Gasman, *The Scientific Origins of National Socialism: Social Darwinism in Ernst Haeckel and the German Monist League* (London, 1971).

21. Ernst Haeckel, *Natürliche Schöpfungsgeschichte. Gemeinverständliche wissenschaftliche Vorträge über die Entwicklungslehre* (Berlin, 1869); the 1911 edition is cited here.

22. Haeckel, *Natürliche Schöpfungsgeschichte*, 752.

23. Ibid., 154.

24. Ernst Haeckel, *Die Lebenswunder. Gemeinverständliche Studien über biologische Philosophie* (Leipzig, 1904).

25. Wilhelm Schallmeyer, *Vererbung und Auslese. Grundriss der Gesellschaftsbiologie und der Lehre vom Rassedienst* (Jena, 1903), and *Beiträge zu einer Nationalbiologie* (Jena, 1905).

26. Alfred Ploetz, *Die Tüchtigkeit unserer Rasse und der Schutz der Schwachen. Ein Versuch über Rassenhygiene und ihr Verhältnis zu den humanen Ideen, besonders zum Sozialismus* (Berlin, 1895).

27. August Weissmann, *Das Keimplasma. Eine Theorie der Vererbung* (Jena 1892).

28. Hans-Josef Steinberg, *Sozialismus und deutsche Sozialdemokratic. Zur Ideologie der Partei vor dem ersten Weltkrieg* (Berlin, 4th edition, 1976).

29. On the following themes see especially Paul Weindling, *Health, Race and German Politics between National Unification and Nazism 1870–1945* (Cambridge, 1989), 388ff. and Jeremy Noakes's seminal "Nazism and Eugenics: The Background to the Nazi Sterilization Law of 14 July 1933," in R. J. Bullen, H. Pogge von Strand-

mann, A. B. Polonsky, eds., *Ideas into Politics: Aspects of European History 1880–1950* (Beckenham, Kent, 1984), 75–94.

30. Friedrich Nietzsche, "Nachgelassene Fragmente Anfang 1880 bis Sommer 1882," in Giorgio Colli and Mazzino Montinare (eds.), *Nietzsches Sämtliche Werke* (Munich, 1980), 9: 250.

31. Willibald Hentschel, *Mittgart. Ein Weg zur Erneurung der germanischen Rasse* (Leipzig, 1904), *Varuna. Eine Welt-und Geschichts-Betrachtung vom Standpunkt des Ariers* (Leipzig, 1901). On Hentschel and the Artamanen, see Klaus Bergmann, *Agrarromantik and Grossstadtfeindschaft* (Mcisenheim, 1970); Bradley F. Smith, *Heinrich Himmler. A Nazi in the Making 1900–1926* (Stanford, 1971); Jost Hermand, *Der alte Traum vom neuen Reich. Völkische Utopien und Nationalsozialismus* (Frankfurt am Main, 1988), especially 140ff.

32. Jorg Lanz von Liebenfels, *Theozoologie* (Vienna, 1906). On Lanz see Wilfried Daim, *Der Mann, der Hitler die Ideen gab* (Munich, 1958).

33. From the vast literature on antisemitism see Hannah Arendt, *The Origins of Totalitarianism* (London, 1951); Peter G. Pulzer, *The Rise of Political Antisemitism in Germany and Austria 1867–1914* (New York, 1964); Reinhard Rürup, *Emanzipation und Antisemitismus, Studien zur "Judenfrage" der bürgerlichen Gesellschaft* (Göttingen, 1975); Norman Cohn, *Die Protokolle der Weisen von Zion. Der Mythos der jüdischen Weltverschwörung* (Cologne, 1969); Herbert A. Strauss, Norbert Kampe, eds., *Antisemitismus. Von der Judenfeindschaft zum Holocaust* (Frankfurt am Main, 1985). For the by no means uniform views of racial scientists and eugenicists concerning the "Jewish Question" see Weindling, *Health, Race and German Politics.*

34. Houston Stewart Chamberlain, *Die Grundlagen des neunzechnten Jahrhunderts* (Munich, 1899).

35. For antisemitism in Germany see, in addition to the works cited in note 37, Wanda Kampmann, *Deutsche und Juden. Die Geschichte der Juden in Deutschland vom Mittelalter bis zum Beginn des Ersten Weltkrieges* (Frankfurt am Main, 1979); Ismar Elbogen, Eleonore Sterling, *Die Geschichte der Juden in Deutschland* (Frankfurt am Main, 1966); Peter Gay, *Freud, Jews and other Germans: Masters and Victims in Modernist Culture* (New York, 1978); Werner E. Mosse, Arnold Paucker, eds., *Juden im Wilhelminischen Deutschland 1890–1914* (Tübingen, 1976), *Deutsches Judentum in Krieg und Revolution 1916–1923* (Tübingen, 1971), *Entscheidungsjahr 1932. Zur Judenfrage in der Endphase der Weitnarer Republik* (Tübingen, 1965); Monika Richarz, ed., *Jüdisches Leben in Deutschland. Selbstzeugnisse zur Sozialgeschichte im Kaiserreich 1871–1918* (Stuttgart, 1979), *Jüdisches Leben in Deutschland. Selbstzeugnisse zur Sozialgeschichte 1919–1945* (Stuttgart, 1982). More specialised areas are covered in Fritz Stern's masterly *Gold and Iron: Bismarck, Bleichröder and the Building of the German Empire* (London, 1977); Steven E. Aschheim, *Brothers and Strangers: The East European Jew in German and German Jewish Consciousness 1800–1923* (Madison, 1982); Jack Wertheimer, *Unwelcome Strangers: East European Jews in Imperial Germany* (Oxford, 1987).

36. Artur Dinter, *Die Sünde wider das Blut* (Leipzig, 1918).

Contradictions in Central Europe

AMOS ELON

From *The Pity of It All*

The two and a half decades before the Great War of 1914–18 are often obscured by the disasters that came afterward. As the historian Gordon A. Craig points out, these years are generally explored today "only for the clues they yield to the catastrophe that was to follow." This produces an "unfortunate distortion, for seen in its own right the period between 1888 and 1914 was characterized by . . . institutional stability, technological progress, and economic prosperity."[1] New developments belied old fears. Germany was economically and militarily the most powerful nation on the European continent, although war was increasingly considered unlikely, if only because of its exorbitant cost. Bourgeois life was firmly grounded in the rule of law. In *The World of Yesterday*, written after Hitler's rise to power, Stefan Zweig looked back at the "Golden Age of Security" half a century earlier, when he grew up as the son of well-to-do Viennese Jewish parents. Everything "seemed based on permanency, and the state itself was the chief guarantor of this stability." Whoever built a house looked upon it as a secure domicile for his children, grandchildren, and great-grandchildren. In his chronicle of a turn-of-the-century Berlin childhood, Walter Benjamin evoked a similar sense of bourgeois solidity in the prosperous lakeside suburb of Grunewald where his family lived. He grew up, he said, among a species that, no matter how compliantly it bowed to the minor whims of fashion, was

"wholly convinced of itself and its permanence." In his grandmother's "twelve- or-fourteen-room" home, with its upholstered window alcoves, walls lined with books, fine paintings, and precious objects, Benjamin noted "the almost immemorial feelings of bourgeois security that emanated from these rooms."[2]

The years of anxiety [in the 1870s] had not broken Jewish faith in German culture and its expected social and political ramifications; if anything, it had grown stronger. The process of acculturation continued. Three or four generations after *Bildung* [cultivation] struck roots among Jews, it was no longer "a recent acquisition" but a precious "heritage shared with other Germans."[3] What discrimination remained was deemed marginal and, in any case, unconstitutional—hence, a curable disease, bound to be short-lived.

Class privilege was still formidable and widely observed; indeed, it gave succor and protection to German Jews along with the rest of the bourgeoisie. "The well-dressed bourgeois, Jew or Christian, was a 'Herr' and had a right to be treated respectfully," the Zionist Richard Lichtheim remembered.[4] Lichtheim came from a family of Jewish doctors assimilated for five generations, descendants of the Königsberg radical democrat Johann Jacoby. Before 1914, Lichtheim claimed, he had never personally experienced antisemitism. Social exclusion was, if anything, partly self-imposed. Walter Benjamin recalled knowing no world other than the cloistered, privileged haven of his family, a "leased ghetto," a "gilded cage." Most middle-class Jews simply felt more comfortable in the company of other Jews.

They had to know their place, of course. Class-conscious, respectful conservatives like Zweig's father avoided dining at the Sacher, Vienna's most elegant hotel. He did so "not for reasons of economy—the difference in price from other hotels was insignificant—but because of a natural feeling of respect; it would have been distressing or unbecoming for him to sit at a table next to a Prince Schwarzenberg or Lobkowitz."[5] In the army, too, prejudice may have had less to do with religion than with social class. The regular officer corps was a fiefdom of the old landed aristocracy. In Prussia, there were relatively fewer non-aristocratic officers in the army in 1913 than in 1870. Jews were not given commissions, even in the Prussian reserves; in the Bavarian and Austrian reserves, however, they were. (The Bavarian army continued to exist after unification, though under the command of the kaiser.) The fact that prejudice was often applied inconsistently fueled hopes that it would soon be overcome.

Although not part of unified Germany, Vienna was nonetheless the most important center of German-language theater, literature, and music. According to Zweig, almost all the Viennese art and culture recognized and admired by the world was promoted, nourished, or created by Jews. Even after the election of the antisemitic rabble-rouser Karl Lueger as Vienna's burgomaster in 1895, Jews continued to live well there, Zweig maintained. Lueger's antisemitism was of a homespun, flexible variety—one might almost say *gemütlich*. Asked to explain the fact that many of his friends were Jews, Lueger famously replied, "I decide who is a Jew." Viennese Jews—at least Zweig's friends and acquaintances—were never personally affected. They were "free" from all "confinement and prejudice," Zweig insisted. "Neither in school nor in the university, nor in the world of literature" did Zweig experience the "slightest suppression or indignity as a Jew." Nowhere on the Continent was it easier to be a "European."[6]

The playwright Arthur Schnitzler was more circumspect. He testified to the existence of antisemitism, "an emotion rampant in numerous hearts," but insisted that it "did not play an important role politically or socially."[7] Schnitzler became the Viennese writer par excellence. One of his popular works of fiction, *The Road into the Open*, was so full of characters tormented by or for their Jewishness that it was later considered a proto-Zionist novel. In *My Youth in Vienna* (1912), Schnitzler commented that a Jew in public life "could not ignore the fact that he was a Jew; nobody else did, not the Gentiles and even less the Jews. You had the choice of being considered insensitive, obtrusive and fresh; or of being over-sensitive, shy and suffering from feelings of persecution."[8]

Schnitzler's pessimism in many ways better reflected fin-de-siécle Austria, which, under the aged Franz Joseph I, was a disintegrating empire of warring nationalities. While Stefan Zweig recollected an idyll, Robert Musil in his novel *The Man without Qualities* called Austria "Kakania," a word that spoke its own derision [the first two syllables have the same connotation in German as in English]. The satirist and playwright Karl Kraus said that Vienna was a "*Versuchsstation des Weltuntergangs*," a proving ground for the apocalypse.

In Germany, there was no such morbid twilight atmosphere. It was, by and large, a more hopeful, more orderly, and more law-abiding society, and though still only a semiliberal, semifeudal authoritarian society, it was also a remarkably stable and uncommonly creative environment, culturally and scientifically. Unlike Schnitzler, German

Jews saw only marginal evidence of the "Jewish problem." The leading quality newspapers—the *Berliner Tageblatt*, the *Vossische Zeitung*, and the *Frankfurter Zeitung*—rarely mentioned it. Fedor Mamroth, the Jewish literary editor of the *Frankfurter Zeitung*, stipulated in his will that his ashes be strewn in the sacred Rhine as a token of his abiding German fidelity and identity.

If the position of Germany's Jews was not perfect, it was certainly bearable—at least for the well-to-do—and even quite hopeful in the eyes of the intelligentsia. Intermarriage became common, increasing from 8.4 percent in 1901 to 29.86 percent in 1915.[9] Felix Theilhaber, a Zionist doctor in Munich, hysterically warned in 1911 that intermarriage and sinking birthrates—the result of modern women's uppityness, he lamented—would bring about the complete disappearance of German Jewry by 1950. According to Theilhaber, marriage among Jews had in the past been a "national-religious" institution, designed to "serve the preservation of the family and the nation"; now, however, it was increasingly "based purely on erotic attraction," as among Gentiles.[10] Theilhaber decried the recent decline of what he called "racial consciousness" among Jews. Philosophies could be abjured at will, he announced. "Blood" was more permanent.

Theilhaber traveled from one German Jewish community to another speaking out against "racial mixing" through intermarriage. [Franz] Kafka attended a speech in which Theilhaber warned of the biological damage caused by racial mixing: children of mixed marriages were likely to be decadent or morally depraved, and they often ended up as the worst antisemites. However preposterous, Theilhaber's stereotypes must be read in historical context. The vocabulary of sociobiology and "race" was then an integral part of civilized public discourse. More remarkable was the lack of response to Theilhaber's tirades. Intermarriage continued to flourish. In Breslau, a less "multicultural" city than Berlin, intermarriage rose from 11 percent in 1890 to 52 percent during the First World War, suggesting that integration was even more advanced in the provinces than was commonly thought.

Mixed love affairs were often still charged with atavistic fears. Kafka's infatuation with Milena Jesenska caused him nightmares. He consoled himself that since Milena was exactly thirteen years younger, fate had given her to him as a bar mitzvah present. The problems affected Gentile and Jew alike, of course. Theilhaber complained that they were, in too many cases, all too easily overcome. The Social Democratic lawyer Philipp Löwenfeld, shortly after his engagement to his Gentile girlfriend, was coldly received by her parents. Her father left him standing and asked curtly:

"What can I do for you?"

"I've come to inform you that your daughter and I intend to marry."

"That's out of the question."

"In that case, I'm free to leave. I only came for the sake of custom and propriety.... As you know, since we are both of age, we do not require your consent."

That broke the ice. Switching to the intimate "Du," the father said softly: "Please take a seat."[11]

Ritual differences between Jews and Christians continued to wane. As in countless other Jewish homes, Rabbi Wilhelm Klemperer's little boys said the following prayer as they were put to bed in the evening:

I trust in God and His embrace
In His mercy and good grace.

The evening prayer of Protestant children was only slightly different:

I trust in God and His embrace
In Christ's blood and His good grace.[12]

During the holiday season, Father Christmas and Father Hanukkah brought children their gifts. Reform Jews celebrated the Sabbath on Sunday. (By 1870, Reform, or Liberal, Judaism was dominant in virtually all urban centers.) Far from proving, as some claimed, that Reform Jews were indifferent to their faith, this shift demonstrated a continuing effort to retain it even as they amalgamated with the majority by sharing its day of rest. The theologian Hermann Cohen declared that Jews must be masters of the Sabbath, not its slaves.

Georg Tietz, a department store tycoon, remembered another manifestation of integration. As a schoolboy in turn-of-the-century Munich, every Saturday morning at nine he joined a "column of Jewish pupils" who were "marched from school to the nearby synagogue. . . . Most of the Catholic boys joined us there; in return, they invited us to a game of tag in the Frauenkirche on Sunday."[13] (Tietz's Latin teacher, however, was "loathsome." His name was Himmler; his son Heinrich later became chief of the Gestapo.)

The point of transition from traditional (that is, Orthodox) to Reform Judaism was noted by some as a moment of high drama. More than a half century after the fact, Victor Klemperer, a linguist and professor of Romance languages, still remembered it vividly. His father, Wilhelm, was the Orthodox rabbi of Landsberg an der Warthe, a small semirural community in West Prussia. The city register listed Dr. Klemperer as one of Landsberg's two "country preachers," the other being the Protestant pastor. Early in 1890, when Victor was nine years old, Dr. Klemperer applied for the position of "auxiliary preacher" at the new Reform temple in Berlin, where the congregants

no longer observed the dietary laws, the prayers were recited in German, and the Sabbath was celebrated on Sunday to the accompaniment of organ music. He was summoned to Berlin for an interview. Victor never forgot the afternoon his father's telegram arrived announcing, "Everything went well, thank God."[14] His appointment had been confirmed. That afternoon, Victor's mother gave him a dramatic foretaste of the new life awaiting him. She took him shopping. It was already getting dark. Not without "first carefully looking around," the mother entered a non-kosher butcher shop. In an excited but controlled voice she requested "mixed cold cuts, a little of every kind." Then she quickly and proudly hurried out. At home, immediately upon unwrapping the package, she sampled a slice herself and gave Victor one too. It hardly tasted different than their customary sausage. His mother chewed it with a radiant expression on her face. "This is what the others eat," she said. "Now we may eat it too."[15]

"Deep down, she certainly sensed something grander at the time," Klemperer said of his mother. The act of eating a pork sausage was "a form of communion."[16] It made her feel truly German. Half a century later in Nazi Dresden, fearing his imminent deportation, Klemperer proudly recalled his mother's gesture as a voluntary act of reform, not one imposed from above as in Russia, where Peter the Great had ordered all men to shave their beards, or in Turkey, where Kemal Ataturk had outlawed the fez.

Countless other memoirs testify to the growing estrangement of Jews from traditional ritual and custom. Fewer and fewer Jews, especially the educated and rich, were observant. Many were *konfessionslos*, creedless. Walter Benjamin's friend Kurt Hiller claimed that his parents were freethinkers. They had neither circumcised nor confirmed him. They would not even dream of having him baptized. "Theirs was a model point of view based on reason: Let the boy decide for himself when he's grown up. And that's exactly what I did when I chose to remain without a faith and cast my lot with the agnostics."[17] The writer Emil Ludwig (born Cohn) remembered that his parents practiced neither Judaism nor Christianity but rather the cult of *Bildung*. For the Cohns, the "practical" substitute for religion was moral education, while the "mystical" substitute was the worship of music.[18] Ludwig visited a synagogue for the first time, in Constantinople, only as an adult.

Walter Benjamin, who liked Easter eggs, felt only "mistrust" toward Jewish religious ceremonies. They "promised nothing but embarrassment."[19] The novelist Max Brod dismissed the religious instruction of his youth as "mere routine, boredom, something utterly exhausted and spent."[20] Franz Kafka "almost suffocated from the terrible boredom and pointlessness of the hours in the synagogue." They were, he said, "the rehearsals staged by hell for my later office life."[21] Kafka argued with his Jewishness throughout his life. The word Jew did not appear in any of his short stories or novels. The little religion he received at home he described as an "insignificant scrap" he was meant to cling to "for the sake of piety at least." But it was "a mere nothing, a joke—not even a joke." Four days a year his father went to synagogue, where he was, according to the son, "closer to the indifferent than to those who took it seriously."[22] . . .

Secularization was on the rise among adherents of all faiths. Religious observance declined among Protestants as among Jews. The philologist Fritz Mauthner hailed Jews for their more pronounced secularism. Their historical task once again was to lead the world, he said, this time as pioneers of modern "godlessness."[23]

Indifference to religion together with the hope of social improvement produced a new wave of conversion. The rate of baptisms among Jewish men jumped from 8.4 percent in 1901 to 21 percent in 1918. Converts came mostly from secularized families; as in previous waves of conversions, those who took the step were nominal Jews before and nominal Christians after. Most converted to Protestantism. In a caricature in the satirical magazine *Simplicissimus*, a Jew is asked why he insists on converting to Catholicism. "Well, you know," he answers, "there are far too many Jews among the Protestants." An antisemitic social register published in 1912, the *Semi-Gotha Almanach*, pretended to "expose" 1,540 converted Jewish families within the German nobility. . . .

Others were less conformist. Heinrich Braun, a socialist writer, was urged to convert to qualify for an academic post. He refused "despite the fact, or perhaps rather because, I have no deep connection to Judaism." Baptism, he quipped, "was much too Jewish."[24] Arthur Scholem, the father of Gershom Scholem, the scholar of Jewish mysticism, was a sober, assimilated, well-to-do Berliner and a confirmed German patriot. He felt that conversion was an "unprincipled, servile act" and avoided those of his relatives who had left the ancestral faith. Nonetheless, Scholem was a so-called Christmas Jew, celebrating both Jewish and Christian holidays. In his eyes, Christmas was a German *Volksfest*. The Scholems enjoyed their Christmas tree "as Germans, not as Jews," and their children enjoyed their presents.

The majority of assimilated Jews made similar accommodations, refusing baptism not so much out of any remaining religious sentiment as out of reluctance to face accusations of cowardice or treachery. Hermann Cohen decried baptism as "religious perjury."[25] The Zionist Lichtheim, like many other assimilated young men, briefly considered conversion—most of his uncles and cousins had already been baptized—but decided against it when his best friend, the scion of a noble Prussian family, warned him that taking that step would make him downright "despicable." The medievalist Harry Bresslau complained to his mentor, the great historian Leopold von Ranke, that religion was blocking his appointment as a professor. Ranke asked, "Why don't you convert? After all, you too are a 'historical' Christian." Bresslau refused to confirm his status as a historical Christian, whatever that meant. In the end he obtained a professorship anyway. Richard Willstätter, an organic chemist, was similarly stymied; he, too, refused. He eventually won a Nobel Prize. By contrast, Fritz Haber, another future Nobel laureate, became a Christian and forced his young bride to do likewise, only to wait another twelve years before achieving the rank of full professor. . . .

Assimilationists continued to put their trust in a better future, built not on such fragile elements as love and hope but on more sturdy political, cultural, and economic bases. They took heart from the failure of [Adolf] Stöcker's [Christian Social] party and from their accelerated acculturation within the German middle class. The increased political influence of Jews—because of their wealth and their role in the arts, sciences, and press—contributed to the growing confidence, as did the rise of the Social Democrats, who militated openly for human rights. There was a new willingness on the part of Jewish organizations to engage in direct political action. In March 1893, German Jews united to establish a national lobby, the *Centralverein* (Central Union of German Citizens of the Jewish Faith). It quickly became the largest representative Jewish body in the Reich. The name was carefully chosen to denote what the new *Verein* was and

was not. "We are not German Jews," the *Verein* said in one of its first statements. "We are German citizens of the Jewish faith." A time-honored taboo had nevertheless been broken: after a century of advancement through accommodation and manipulations behind the scenes, Jews finally dared to mobilize politically in defense of their civil rights. . . .

A few months before the birth of the new *Verein*, some of the more timid notables of the Berlin Jewish community had considered making another discreet and "humble" approach to the kaiser with earnest prayers and supplications for his "grace, protection, and support" against antisemitism. Nothing came of it. James Simon, the German Jewish "cotton king," advised them to desist. With the tired resignation of one who had tried and failed, Simon told his fellow notables: "Politically, there is no way to talk to him."

The new Verein ignored the conventional wisdom that stepchildren always be on their best behavior. It resolved to fight publicly, in the name of "pride," "manly courage," and "honor"—martial virtues highly regarded in the Germany of the kaisers. The mere launching of the new society unleashed the usual fears: it could amount to a public confession of the emancipation's failure. Jewish family magazines studiously ignored it at first. "One is almost tempted to say that initially the *Verein* met with more difficulties among coreligionists than among their enemies," according to its historian, Arnold Paucker.[26]

To counter these concerns, spokesmen for the *Verein* emphasized that it represented a religious rather than an ethnic minority. Since so many of its members were indifferent to religion, such insistence seemed somewhat beside the point. The truth was that the *Verein* represented a community not of faith but of fate. A widely shared family or clan culture continued to bind together believers and nonbelievers, linking the baptized with those who refused to convert.

The *Verein*'s initiatives were apparent in a number of areas. The association published a glossy magazine named, suggestively, *Im Deutschen Reich*—In the German Empire. As is often the case with such magazines, it was more widely distributed than actually read. Proclaiming that Jews had no more in common with their coreligionists in France or England than Catholics and Protestants with their coreligionists abroad, the magazine preached German patriotism as staunchly as it denounced baptism as dishonorable and called for more Jewish self-respect. The magazine warned its readers that if they would not fight for their rights no one would. In calling for Jewish self-assertion and condemning baptism—a practice forced on Jews by hypocrites to confirm their prejudices—the *Verein* helped, paradoxically, to promote [Martin] Buber's proto-Zionist "renaissance," a process of dissimilation among some of the most assimilated German Jews.

On the regional level, the new body advised and coordinated communities, student organizations, and other associated groups. Nationally, it acted as a parliamentary lobby, helped finance political campaigns, and joined non-Jewish efforts to promote tolerance and democracy. The *Verein* was a long-overdue act of political defiance. Its militancy was in contrast to the relative timidity of French Jews during the Dreyfus Affair. Had Germany truly been a constitutional monarchy, the *Verein* might have been more successful. In the circumstances, it was able to reach only the margins of power. Real power in Germany was centered not in the Reichstag but in the occult triangle of monarch, army, and bureaucracy.

Jewish university students were now often emboldened to challenge antisemites to duels, with occasionally fatal results. In fact, some grew so skilled at dueling that most elite student fraternities resolved that Jews no longer deserved chivalrous "satisfaction." . . .

The spectacle of intelligent young men fighting to become officers in the army reserves might seem ridiculous. In the context of the time and place it was a serious matter. Germany was a semi-militarized society. Martial imagery dominated the national fantasy; war monuments overlooked river valleys and public squares everywhere. Reserve officers enjoyed a special status. Schoolteachers, doctors, lawyers, professors, and businessmen listed their rank in the reserves on embossed calling cards. On Sedan Day, the anniversary of Bismarck's victory over France, Latin teachers appeared in their classrooms in full uniform with their medals and refought Caesar's battles on the blackboard in terms appropriated from Clausewitz and Moltke.[27] A commission in the army reserves was a sine qua non for senior careers in government. In May 1909, the *Frankfurter Zeitung* claimed that twenty-five to thirty thousand Jews, qualified by their educations to become officers, had served in the army since 1880. Not one had been promoted to officer, although some three hundred converts had.

The *Verein* spent a lot of time and money on this issue. At its instigation, Social Democratic deputies raised it annually in the Reichstag. But with no result. The ostensible official excuse was that candidates had to be accepted by the entire officer corps, a seemingly "democratic" feature. The alleged consensus among officers was that it was unthinkable for Jews to command Germans. The Reichstag had no say in the matter. The emperor shared the ingrained prejudice of the old officer class. Although he tried to secure a commission for the Jewish baron Albert Goldschmidt, he failed and did not press the matter. Goldschmidt had to be content with the post of attaché at the German embassy in London (the diplomatic corps was usually closed to Jews as well).

Owing mostly to declining birthrates, Jews were now a shrinking minority. Their representation in the population dropped by one-third, from 1.3 percent in 1880 to 0.9 percent thirty years later. To the majority of Germans they remained as visible as ever. They continued to believe in their ultimate integration. In retrospect, of course, they were wrong. At the time, though, as Peter Gay observes, they had good reason to believe they were right.[28]

What were the alternatives? In most other European countries, prejudice and discrimination seemed equally or more prevalent. With all its shortcomings, Germany stood out as a country where acculturation, social integration, and day-to-day tolerance seemed to have as good a chance as anywhere else in Western Europe. England in 1900 imposed strict limitations on Jewish immigration. In Italy, Jews were so few as to be almost invisible.

In Western Europe, antisemitism was generally thought to be most virulent in France. For nearly a century, French Jews had enjoyed the libertarian legacy of the 1789 revolution. In the mid-1890s, however, republican France was suddenly infected with the racial hatred generated by the trial of Captain Alfred Dreyfus, the only Jew on the general staff of the French army. Dreyfus, a wealthy Alsatian, was accused of spying on behalf of Germany and in 1894 was tried for treason. The eponymous affair institutionalized antisemitism in France in a manner thought unlikely in Germany. A cabal of soldiers, clericalists, aristocrats, politicians, frustrated monarchists, and pseudo-scientific savants—disciples of Joseph-Arthur de Gobineau, Edouard-Adolphe Drumont, Alphonse de Toussenel, and other racist theorists—agitated against Dreyfus and the community to which he belonged. Outside the courtroom where he was tried, the mob growled, "Death to the Jews." In the courtyard of the Ecole Militaire, where he was publicly stripped of his rank before being incarcerated on Devil's Island in French Guiana, he continued to proclaim his innocence. Most French Jews were cowed and passive. Alarmed German Jewish tourists in Paris hurried back to Frankfurt and Berlin. Hans Levy-Dorfmann, a young student of medicine at the Sorbonne, wrote his bride in Mainz that at the end of the academic year he would try to move back to a "decent German university."

The Dreyfus Affair convulsed France for more than a decade. The growing evidence that Dreyfus had been convicted of trumped-up charges seemed to poison the atmosphere even more: Jews were accused of being a pro-German fifth column, responsible for France's defeat in the war of 1870. In the *Allgemeine Zeitung des Judentums*, a correspondent wondered whether Jews could continue to live in France. The passionate anti-Dreyfus camp included not only socialites and *salonnières* but also the editors of *Le Figaro*, the poet Paul Valéry, the painter Edgar Degas, the politician and writer, Maurice Barrès, the ducs d'Uzès, de Brissac, de La Rochefoucauld, and de Luynes, and the comtesse de Martel (the model for Proust's Odette); and even the president of the republic. The Dreyfusards, who clamored for a retrial, were no less vocal socialists, republicans, anticlericalists, artists, and writers joined the cause, convinced that French democracy was at stake. Public disorder reached such a pitch that for a while it looked as if the army would rise up against the government to prevent a retrial and put an end to the republic. The violent upheaval reconfirmed German Jews in their patriotic fervor. They considered themselves lucky to live in an orderly country under a relatively benign regime.

Maximilian Harden (a convert, born Felix Ernst Witkowski), one of the most influential German political commentators prior to 1914, at first assumed that Dreyfus was guilty. As the affair grew in intensity and scope, Harden was shocked to see the alleged crime of one man ascribed to an entire community. He gave in to what for him was a rare show of pride in being a German—indeed gratitude for it—even under a government he hated and an emperor he despised. In Alsace-Lorraine, at the time of its annexation to Germany in 1871, thousands of Jews had chosen to leave for France "in order not to become Germans."[29] Many of those who had stayed now felt fortunate to be Germans.

In Eastern Europe, antisemitism was most savage in czarist Russia. At the turn of the century, five million Jews lived there as aliens among Russians, Byelorussions, Poles, Lithuanians, Letts, Estonians, Cossacks, Georgians, and Ukrainians, a multitude of diverse people, hostile to one another and especially to Jews. Most Russian Jews were confined by law to the so-called Pale of Settlement, a region permeated by poverty and hopelessness. The czar's chief adviser on Jewish affairs was Konstantin Pobedonostsev, a fanatical Slavophile. His formula for solving Russia's "Jewish problem" was simple: "one third must emigrate, one third convert, and one third must die."

Russia was the only European country that banned foreign Jews from entering it, at least in principle. Since it was also the only European country with a real border where foreigners were required to carry passports and were likely to be interrogated, German Jews were liable to be turned away at the frontier. Russia had also been notorious in recent years as the land of pogroms. The word *pogrom*—meaning "devastation" in Russian—was entering the international lexicon to describe violent outrages against a par-

ticular ethnic group. From the early 1880s, Russia's recurrent antisemitic pogroms were government-inspired diversions from the miseries of daily life. Nearly two million Jews fled Russia between 1880 and 1910; more than 100,000 crossed Germany every year on their way to North Sea ports and safer havens in North and South America. Relief funds for these emigrants and for those left behind were solicited among Jews all over Germany. The *Allgemeine Zeitung des Judentums* spoke of Russia as a land of hatred and iniquity, the great nineteenth-century Jewish "House of Bondage."

The novelist Arthur Landsberger (who committed suicide when the Nazis came to power) was convinced that even the United States was infested with "unparalleled antisemitism."[30] Eduard Lasker, on a visit to the United States shortly before his death, was shocked to discover a quota for Jews at Harvard University and a prohibition against Jewish guests at some of the best resort hotels. He concluded that though the United States might be more democratic than Germany in many ways, in terms of Jewish integration it lagged woefully behind. In 1891, Paul Dimidow cautioned in a pamphlet entitled *Where To? A Word of Warning to Western European Jews* that antisemitism had migrated to the United States together with the Russian Jews. And Ludwig Geiger, a Goethe scholar and quintessential *Bildungsbürger*, while protesting the lot of Eastern European Jews, noted that the situation elsewhere was worse. It was rare to find a Jewish professor in the United States and England. As late as 1911, the distinguished English historian Louis Namier was denied an Oxford fellowship by the warden and fellows of All Souls College because of his "Polish-Jewish origin."[31]

The status of Jews in Austria-Hungary was also more worrisome than in Germany. The Austrian Social Democrat Karl Kautsky wrote that Austrian antisemitism was more dangerous than the German variant because of its pseudodemocratic cast, which appealed to workers and oppressed nationalities. Visiting Austria in 1910, the scholar Victor Klemperer claimed that whereas he felt "abroad" in Italy or France, in Austrian-ruled Bohemia he sensed he was in "enemy territory."[32] Antisemitism, unequaled elsewhere in the West, was said to be rampant there.[33] Though Jews were prominent in Viennese cultural life and in the national economy, their condition throughout the multinational Habsburg empire was becoming ever more precarious. In Bohemia, Czechs hated them for being Germans and Germans despised them for being Jews. As the only minority truly loyal to the shaky Habsburg crown, they felt all the more politically isolated and exposed. Nowhere in Central Europe was their material plight as desperate as in the Austrian province of Galicia, where population growth combined with economic crisis to produce recurrent famines. Five thousand Galician Jews were said to starve to death annually....

The election system for the Prussian state parliament was based on rank and personal wealth, giving disproportional voting power to the nobility and the well-to-do middle class. Since most Jews were middle-class and more than half of them were self-employed in business or other entrepreneurial activities, the system enabled them to exert political influence beyond their numbers; most Jewish voters nevertheless continued to criticize this imbalance and to favor electoral and constitutional reform. By 1890, more than 60 percent of them supported the Social Democrats and similar opposition parties, voting against what Marxists would have called their class interests. By 1912, two years before the outbreak of war, 85 percent of the Jewish vote went to this largely pacifist left-of-center bloc.

Middle- and upper-middle-class Jewish voters were remarkably more liberal than other German middle-class voters. Wilhelm Liebknecht, the socialist leader and veteran of the 1848 revolution, found among them "a much greater sum of idealism than among non-Jews." August Bebel advised Engels in 1891 that "for decent company one must cultivate Jews." Engels was not sure this was a good thing but agreed that Jews had more brains than "others of the bourgeoisie."[34] As the National Liberal Party, for which most Jews had voted in the early 1870s, became increasingly conservative and chauvinist, middle-class Jews abandoned it and lent their support to the new left-of-center parties. By contrast, the non-Jewish German middle class had on the whole been liberal before 1871; in Bismarck's new Reich, however, much of its liberalism was eroded by relentless patriotic and martial propaganda. In his novel *Man of Straw*, Heinrich Mann portrayed with inspired bitterness the resultant servility, conformism, cowardice, and shallow religiosity of the post-1871 bourgeoisie. Henry Adams, who fondly remembered the unique cult of *Bildung* and civic virtue he had encountered on a visit to Germany half a century earlier, was sickened on a return visit to Nürnberg by the dominant bourgeois preferences in politics and in art. It conveyed to him a sense of hopeless failure and doom.

German Jews did not take the reactionary turn of the German middle class.[35] The assertion, occasionally still heard, that the Jewish bourgeoisie was as conservative as the rest of Germans is false. Arnold Paucker, an authority on the subject, concluded in 1976 that "nothing is more misleading."[36] The corollary claim, voiced in 1991 by the noted German historian Nicolaus Sombart, that "without Jews the liberal tradition in Germany might have vanished completely after the establishment of the Reich" is nevertheless overstated.[37] But there is no doubt that their abiding liberalism fueled the German democratic project.

The Social Democrats appreciated the growing support from Jewish voters; they were less pleased by the reputation it gave them in some circles as the "Jews' party." They did not, however, soften their stand on the obstacles Jews continued to face. On the contrary, in the Reichstag they kept up their protests against discrimination in the army, the bureaucracy, the diplomatic service, and the universities. Not only Jewish intellectuals and professionals but also businessmen and even department store tycoons supported them. It was the socialists' record on human rights and their unequivocal opposition to all forms of antisemitism that induced many Jewish capitalists to vote for them at a time when the party still advocated, at least in theory, the abolition of private property. Jewish middle-class support further increased after the party's rejection of doctrinaire Marxism. Ideologically, there seemed little difference between the Social Democratic leader Paul Singer, the kaiser's particular bête noire, and other prominent Berlin Jews, such as Oskar Tietz, Salman Schocken, and Walther Rathenau. Tietz and Rathenau shared Singer's mix of theoretical radicalism and sober, practical, liberal common sense. As a "class" in the Marxist sense of the word, the Jewish bourgeoisie remained an anomaly. They lived like bankers but voted like hard-pressed workers and leftist intellectuals.

The number of Social Democratic deputies in the Reichstag rose steadily after 1898. The party was the only one that, contrary to political wisdom, did not hesitate to present Jewish candidates. These candidates almost never converted; as a leading Jewish Social Democrat put it, one does not quit a persecuted minority. The Reichstag was not the only forum in which Jewish Social Democrats were quite visible. They were now also prominent among the advocates for disarmament, world peace, the abolition of royal prerog-

atives and of the death penalty, and other liberal reforms. Alfred Fried (winner of the 1911 Nobel Peace Prize) and Max Hirsch were among the founders of the German Peace Society. Its supporters included the Jewish publishing and advertising magnates Leopold Ullstein, Rudolf Mosse, and Leopold Sonnemann. Women's rights was yet another area of activity. . . .

At the turn of the century, middle-class German Jews prospered. A few grew rich. Of the two hundred wealthiest Prussian families, forty were said to be Jews. In Berlin they constituted 5 percent of the population but paid more than 30 percent of the city's taxes.[38] The richest man in Berlin was still the kaiser, for reasons perhaps of divine right, bribery, petty theft, legacy hunting, and treasonable treaties, as Karl Marx put it; the second-richest man was Fritz von Friedländer-Fuld, the converted son of a Silesian family of coal magnates.[39] An express bus commonly known as the "roaring Moses" ran every morning from Berlin's elegant suburb in the Grunewald forest, where bankers and brokers lived in large villas, to the new stock exchange building downtown. In Hamburg, where the Christian bourgeoisie was said to be far less prejudiced than that in Berlin, half the Jewish population lived in the two wealthiest quarters, Harvestehude and Rotherbaum. In Frankfurt, the average tax paid by Jews was four times higher than that of Protestants and eight times that of Catholics.

Grand synagogues rose in the main cities. Their gilded splendor—piety combined with swagger—was visible from afar and reflected the Jews' growing wealth and self-satisfaction. Neo-Romanesque or Gothic, some were hardly distinguishable from churches. The largest, most pompous synagogues were in garish pseudo-Moorish style, perhaps under the influence of Byron and the popular novels of Benjamin Disraeli, who had lent the proud Jews of medieval Spain an aura of marvelous nobility. The new synagogues recalled the golden age of tolerance in Moslem Spain and articulated the growing hope for a "symbiosis" similar to that between Jews and Moslems in thirteenth-century Cordoba and Seville. The Spanish decor also served to disassociate the rich Western Jews from their poor "primitive" coreligionists in Poland and Russia. Some families, including Theodor Herzl's, went so far as to invent a distant Sephardic genealogy. A few of the new synagogues were far too large for the needs of their increasingly secular middle- and upper-middle-class congregations, whose true house of worship was the opera house or the concert hall.

No other class in Germany (or the rest of Europe) carried love of art to as great lengths as did middle- and upper-middle-class Jews in turn-of-century Germany. The novelist Theodor Fontane (a self-confessed lover of the Prussian aristocracy) lauded German Jews for adorning their villas with music rooms rather than riding stables and for lining their walls with books instead of ancestral portraits. They were proud of their patronage of the arts. In 1881, a terrible fire swept through Vienna's Ringtheater, killing many in the audience. Reporting the disaster, the *Allgemeine Zeitung des Judentums* reveled in the "disproportionately" high number of Jews in theater audiences everywhere, compared with the very few who patronized beer halls.[40]

The hatemongers saw the phenomenon in a different light. Jewish art patrons were still inevitably ridiculed as parvenus. A contemporary caricature entitled "Friday Night," preserved at the Frankfurt Jewish Museum, shows ugly, hook-nosed, black-haired, corpulent men and bejeweled women—more like reptiles than human beings—occupying the first rows of a concert hall. Jewish nouveaux riches were the butt of countless jokes: A recently

converted stockbroker shows a visitor through his refurbished mansion. The living room is "genuine eighteenth century," he explains; the study, "sixteenth-century German Renaissance." Then the host marches his visitor quickly through a sparsely furnished room. "What's this?" the visitor asks. "Oh, nothing—just my late parents' old furniture." "I see," the visitor says. "It's the pre-Christian era!" . . .

Many Jews were now self-employed in commerce and related trades. Some were bankers. Almost half of all private banks were still said to be in Jewish hands but private banks were increasingly marginal, ceding ground to more powerful financial institutions. Much of the new national wealth was augmented by corporate and state institutions that provided the new industries with broader bases for expansion. The most important among those—the Reichsbank, the Deutsche Bank, the Dresdner and Darmstätter banks—had been founded, or were still run, by Jewish directors.

Apart from the banks, several of the new industries—medium- and large-sized chemical factories, metalworks, electrical, smelting, and printing plants, and mills—had been founded by enterprising Jews. They established the first German aircraft factory and department store chains and were among the first to introduce American production methods. Albert Ballin was perhaps the leading Jewish entrepreneur. From modest beginnings in a small family-owned travel agency in Hamburg, he rose to become one of the world's major shipping magnates, head of the Hamburg-America Line. Other prominent business leaders were the Hamburg banker Max Warburg (Ballin's close friend), the coal magnate Eduard Arnhold, the cotton magnate and art patron James Simon. Emil Rathenau and his son Walther were in a class by themselves. The elder Rathenau, known as the

"Bismarck of the German electric industry," introduced electric light and trams to most German cities.

The wealth, prominence, and intellectual acuity of these men brought them into personal contact with the kaiser. Some came to be known as the "kaiser's Jews" (*Kaiserjuden*)—a slightly derogatory term supposedly coined by the Zionist leader Chaim Weizmann. Unlike the court Jews of old, the *Kaiserjuden* did not administer the monarch's private investments; Gerson von Bleichröder had been the last of those. Ballin, Warburg, Arnhold, Rathenau, and the other *Kaiserjuden* were younger, more self-assured, better-educated, more fully assimilated and integrated into German life than Bleichröder and his ilk. The kaiser consulted them regularly on questions of financial and cultural policy, and they flattered him with large donations to his favorite charities. The kaiser was fascinated by self-made tycoons. Like his English cousin Edward VII, he actively sought the company of rich men, but unlike Edward he avoided becoming intimate with them. With few exceptions, the *Kaiserjuden* were not spared anxieties that came to embitter their assimilated coreligionists. They were envied for their influence and respected, but only up to a point. Warburg and Rathenau never felt that they "belonged" as, for example, the Krupps or Siemenses did, or as the Rothschilds, Sir Ernest Cassel, or Samuel Montagu (Baron Swaythling) did in England. The emperor treated the *Kaiserjuden* with exquisite civility, inviting them to private lunches and stag dinners in the palace or on his yacht. In theory, then, they were *hoffähig* (presentable at court); in practice they were not. Invitations to the palace were never extended to their wives. This rankled. . . .

In addition to its expanding economy and powerful army, Germany now also boasted an unrivaled educational system, excellent scientific and research facilities, and a rich cultural life. The combination of material strength with cultural wealth was unparalleled on the Continent.[41] It was apparent in every realm, in the sciences and in the arts. By 1913, more books were published in Germany annually—31,051 new titles—than in any other country in the world. In scientific research, German universities surpassed those of other European countries. The contribution of the Jews to this preeminence was enormous; in some fields, it was overwhelming. The reasons for such an outburst of creativity in so many different fields have long been a matter for speculation. They may have been social or psychological rather than religious since there was little if any religiously Jewish content in the works of Einstein, Freud, Mahler, Zweig, Werfel, Husserl, Hofmannsthal, Ehrlich, Willstätter, Mauthner, or even Kafka. Nor could the reasons have been "ethnic"—what is "Flemish" in Flemish art, what is "German" or "Jewish" in mathematics, physics, chemistry, music, or medicine? What, then, was behind this prodigious output? Was it self-conscious marginality? The stimulus of suffering and blows? The interplay between challenge and response? Tribal pressure? If "ease is inimical to civilization," as Arnold Toynbee has claimed, adversity was not without its rewards. Within a relatively short time, families once on the margins of established society, outside the general culture and language, produced a surprisingly high number of outstanding men and women in the arts and sciences. Some were the offspring of families comfortably well-to-do for generations; others were the sons and daughters of hardworking shopkeepers arid peddlers—Treitschke's pant-selling Jew boys—who had done well in business during the preceding decades. They had grown rich, producing talented scientists and literati to a decree far exceeding their numbers. In a familiar second- or third-generation phenomenon, the descendants of successful businessmen turned their backs on business and gravitated toward the arts and natural sciences, seeking full integration in the general culture and in many cases achieving it. Commenting on the proverbial industry of Jewish students, Einstein said that it was almost as though they had spent the last two thousand years preparing for university entrance exams. "Doctor" was said to be a Jewish first name. Some claimed that their parents had prodded them mercilessly to achieve better and better grades in school. "Good" was never good enough. They had to be excellent. By itself, this proved nothing, of course. Stern fathers pushing their children were a common feature of middle-class European life during the Wilhelminian and Victorian era.

A number of successful individuals came from the same family clusters. Walter Benjamin, Karl Marx, and Heinrich Heine were distant cousins. The intellectual genealogy of one remarkable North German Jewish family descended from a matriarch named Jente Hameln (1603–95). Nothing is known about Jente Hameln herself except that two centuries later her descendants included Felix Mendelssohn-Bartholdy, Heine, the jurist Eduard Gans, two Nobel Prize winners—the writer Paul Heyse and the chemist Adolf von Baeyer—the historian Johann Gustav Droysen, as well as the writers Johann Hermann Detmold, Theodor Lessing, Carl Sternheim, and Karl Wolfskehl.

The cumulative effect, however, transcended the contributions of any one family. It was as though a dam had given way to release a flood of talent. More Jews than ever entered journalism. Others became publishers, playwrights, novelists, poets, drama critics, gallery owners, theater directors, actors and actresses, concert pianists,

conductors, sculptors, and painters. By the early 1900s, some people came to believe that certain fields were actually "dominated" by Jews, so great was their presence. In 1912, Moritz Goldstein, a young Jewish journalist, delighted antisemites by publishing an article in the conservative magazine *Der Kunstwart* claiming that Jews now largely controlled German culture. As he saw it, "We are administrating the spiritual property of a nation that denies our right and our ability to do so."[42] A heated debate ensued in the pages of *Der Kunstwart* and elsewhere. Goldstein wanted Jews to stop pretending they were Germans. Germans, after all, only paid attention to "the Asiatic in us." The terms *control* and *administrate* were, of course, gross exaggerations. It was possible to contribute to a culture—even in a major way—without controlling or administrating it. While Jews played an important part in the arts and the press, nearly all the country's leading literary and artistic figures were non-Jews: Thomas Mann, Gerhart Hauptmann, Stefan George, Rainer Maria Rilke, and Hermann Hesse in literature; Richard Strauss and Wagner in music; Erich Heckel, Ludwig Kirchner, Karl Schmidt-Rottluff, and Franz Marc in painting. On the other, hand, Thomas Mann chose this moment to deny recurrent rumors that he was himself a Jew; his timing could not have been a mere accident. To prove his case, this scion of a North German patrician family (married to a woman of Jewish origin) asked: "What of *Buddenbrooks*, the book that made my name? What would it be if it had been written by a Jew? A snob's book!"[43]

One area in which Jews were especially prominent, though they were far from controlling it, was the sciences. The decades before the First World War saw tremendous progress in medicine, chemistry, electrochemistry, biology, mathematics, and physics, culminating in Einstein's general theory of relativity. A succession of remarkable break-throughs was facilitated partly by the German government and partly by privately endowed research institutes. In the natural sciences there was talk of a new German age of genius, second only to the era of Goethe, Schiller, Hegel, and Kant. A surprisingly large number of Jewish scientists—steeped also in humanistic culture to an extent that has since become quite rare—played a major role in this flowering. Students from all over the world flocked to their seminars and institutes. The historian Shulamit Volkov has identified thirty-nine leading German Jewish scientists born before 1880, ten of whom won Nobel Prizes.[44] Best known among the ten are Albert Einstein and Paul Ehrlich. Both came from well-to-do merchant families. Both suffered setbacks because of their origins. Einstein, the "new Newton, " radically changed our view of the universe; Ehrlich discovered chemotherapy, thus helping to save countless lives. Ehrlich's institute in Berlin rivaled Pasteur's in Paris and the Rockefeller Institute in New York. But for Ehrlich's early death, he would probably have won a second Nobel Prize for his contributions to immunology and for developing the first effective treatment for syphilis. The German pacifist Friedrich Foerster called Ehrlich the ideal German—"as God wanted Germans to be."[45]

Other Nobel laureates included Fritz Haber, the son of a prosperous dye merchant and alderman of the city of Breslau, who was honored for producing ammonia synthetically, a discovery immensely important in the production of artificial fertilizers. Einstein and Haber were close friends, though they were radically different in character and in their politics. Einstein was a cosmopolitan bohemian, Haber a stiff and disciplined German patriot. Einstein was a conscious Jew; Haber converted to Christianity. Even so, they formed a tight partnership, sustaining each other as scien-tists and as Jews. At home and abroad, they were celebrated as Germans, though Einstein always maintained that if their theories proved right Germans would hail them as heroes and Frenchmen would say they were Jews but that if their theories were disproved Germans would damn them as Jews and Frenchmen as filthy Germans.

Both worked at the new Kaiser Wilhelm Institute in Berlin, the major center of advanced research known as "the emperor's academic guard regiment" and particularly noteworthy for the significant role of Jews both academically and philanthropically. The institute's four main units were headed by Jews. Jewish philanthropists contributed more than a third of the donations to establish the institute and keep it running. The arms manufacturer Gustav Krupp was the largest donor (1.4 million Reichsmark), followed by the retired Jewish banker Leopold Koppel (1 million) and the *Kaiserjuden* James Simon and Eduard Arnhold.

Thorstein Veblen and Sigmund Freud maintained that the success of Jewish scientists resulted from their "creative skepticism," an outgrowth of their difficulties in gaining acceptance. Einstein evaded these difficulties by working for years in Switzerland, where he was granted citizenship; Haber had to convert. Volkov claims that, at least initially, many Jewish scientists who had been denied professorships and were forced to the margins of academic life were driven by these circumstances to pioneer and develop entirely new disciplines. They achieved breakthroughs that might not have been possible had they been tenured, overworked professors. The glory of German intellectual life, the unpaid *Privatgelehrte* or independent scholar, had to rely on an independent income; unable to get professorships, educated Jews often worked as independent scholars. Inherited income not only facilitated the adoption of liberal ideals but also enabled gifted young scientists to dedicate their lives to research and aspiring writers to be content with low or uncertain royalties. . . .

[In 1912,] the election results showed that most German voters disapproved of all racist politics. The antisemitic splinter parties effectively disappeared. The conservative right, which had campaigned against "Jew lovers," "Jewish money," and "Jewish-owned newspapers," suffered a serious setback. The Social Democrats, who had vigorously opposed antisemitic "Junkers and priests, knights and Christian saints," won an astounding 35 percent of the popular vote, doubling their strength and becoming the largest single party in the Reichstag. The number of Jewish deputies rose from eight to nineteen, of whom twelve were Social Democrats. The Social Democratic party was the envy of socialists throughout Europe. It had grown so fast it seemed almost irresistible and was widely expected to come into power soon, finally breaking, as it promised, the fetters of capitalism, militarism, feudalism, and antisemitic prejudice.

The brilliant young writer Kurt Tucholsky, eldest son of an affluent upper-middle-class Jewish family, rejoiced at the results. He had just published a highly successful novel, *Rheinsberg: A Picture Book for Lovers*, the story of an attractive young couple. The man, a student, is modeled on Tucholsky himself while his girlfriend is a witty, apparently non-Jewish Berliner. The lovers spend a blissful weekend in a remote country hotel in defiance of social and moral convention. The novel pictures a Utopian idyll, celebrating the symbiotic link between two appealing, openminded people. Many read it as a parable heralding the rise of a better world of political and erotic freedom.

Two years later, the First World War broke out. The liberal euphoria quickly proved to be mis-

placed. The 1912 elections notwithstanding, the ultrapatriotic voices in the Reichstag, in the military, in the popular press, and in the palace had their say. The Social Democrats agitated against the war, staging mass demonstrations in many cities. Their opposition collapsed at the last moment in the face of what seemed like overwhelming public support for war. The immediate cause of the war was the assassination of the Austrian crown prince in Sarajevo; the underlying cause was the rivalry of the great imperialist powers over the past two decades. In July 1914, it erupted in a continent-wide killing spree that embroiled Germany, France, England, Austria-Hungary, Serbia, Italy, and Russia. While decrying the orgy of "drunken" nationalism, Kurt Tucholsky immediately volunteered for war service. More than ten thousand other young German Jews did the same. One of them, Ludwig Frank, was a prominent Social Democratic Reichstag deputy. Only two days earlier, he, too, had attacked the cheap "coffeehouse enthusiasm" of the warmongers.[46] Like all other Social Democrats, by August 4 he had changed his mind and joined the majority in voting for the war budget demanded by the government. That same afternoon he enlisted. "I march in line with all the others, joyful and sure of our victory," he wrote.[47] Three weeks later he was killed in action. What had moved Frank and so many others? Abiding faith in Germany? Political opportunism? A lurking death wish, as was later speculated? Even Freud forgot himself for a moment. For the first time in his life he felt something like pride in being an Austrian national.

The Great War would prove, as George Kennan has written, the seminal catastrophe of the twentieth century. At the time, few if any suspected the extent of its horror. Max Reinhardt, the director who had revolutionized German theater and was recognized as "one of the first Austrian Jews to conquer Berlin," certainly did not.[48] He happened to be in Paris on the eve of the war attending the first premiere of a German work at the Paris Opera in nearly half a century: Richard Strauss and Nijinsky's biblical ballet *The Legend of Joseph*, staged by Diaghilev in Venetian costume.

As Harry Kessler, the librettist, noted, all of Paris was there, intellectuals as well as people in government and the Faubourg Saint-Germain set. "The premiere was the last, most spectacular parade of prewar Europe at its most brilliant, even as the catastrophe was already under way," Kessler later wrote. He had "unconsciously" woven the tragic horror of the moment into his libretto.[49]

Kessler remembered the festive supper party everyone attended at 2:00 a.m. to celebrate the event. Reinhardt, Diaghilev, and Marcel Proust were present, along with Hugo von Hoffmannsthal, Jean Cocteau, Richard Strauss, and the star of the show, Nijinsky of the Ballets Russes. Everyone expected a few days of war. In the early morning hours, Reinhardt and the other Germans and Austrians took the last available trains to reach the border before it closed. By the time he arrived back in Berlin, Reinhardt announced that the war was necessary in defense of German culture.

Albert Einstein was one of the few who did not share this view. He loathed German militarism. He had recently moved back from Switzerland to Berlin to take up an appointment at the Kaiser Wilhelm Institute, only "to discover for the first time that [he] was a Jew."[50] He was aghast at the headlong plunge toward war and the widespread readiness of leading intellectuals to welcome it. At times such as this, he noted, one realized "to what sad species of animal one belongs."[51] The scarcity of people around him who shared his anguish deepened his depression.

Einstein's dismay was further exacerbated by the pain of an agonizing divorce. Only "love of science" lifted him out of his "vale of tears."[52] His two boys were about to join his estranged wife in Switzerland. On July 29, Austria had just declared war on Serbia when Einstein saw them off at the Berlin railway station. Fritz Haber was at his side. Einstein spent the rest of the evening grieving over his loss and, presumably, quarreling with his friend. Haber did not share Einstein's despair over the coming war. On the contrary, he had already registered as a volunteer. Haber believed that in times of peace scientists belonged to the world but in times of war to their country. Like most other Germans, Haber expected a quick and easy victory. Nobody anticipated that the war would be long and awful and inaugurate a half century of mass killing, revolution, and chaos: the collapse of civilization in Germany, the rise of Nazi, Fascist, and Communist totalitarianism, and more than a hundred million dead. . . .

The first scene of Karl Kraus's monumental war drama, *The Last Days of Mankind*, takes place on the Ringstrasse, Vienna's elegant promenade. A Jewish couple is walking along.

> Newsboy: Extra! Extra! Heir to the throne assassinated! Killer arrested!
> Man (to his wife): Thank God he's not a Jew!
> His wife (pulls him away): Let's go home!

When war actually broke out, five weeks after the assassination, middle- and upper-middle-class urban Jews did not "go home." They joined up. By volunteering for war service long before being called up they hoped they would finally overcome the remaining informal impediments to full integration in German society. *Im Deutschen Reich*, the official organ of the *Centralverein*, the largest and most representative German-Jewish organization, announced that Germany was only defending its *Kultur*; the paper condemned "Russian malice," "French thirst for revenge," "English deviousness," and "Serbian lust for murder." The *Centralverein* itself solemnly called on its members "to serve the fatherland beyond the call of duty. Hasten to volunteer for service! All you men and women must dedicate yourselves to the fatherland through every kind of service." Eugen Fuchs, the chairman of the *Centralverein*, proclaimed himself German "down to my bones." He assailed "murderous Russia" and her allies, "insidious England" and "bloodthirsty France," for "maliciously" attacking Germany from the rear. He also allowed himself a bit of racism: in their greedy "struggle against German *Kultur*," the Allies had even enlisted "the help of Japan's yellow highway robbers."[53]

All traces of Jewish "cosmopolitanism" seemed to have vanished overnight. Jewish publications abounded in self-conscious tribal pride; a stream of stories appeared testifying to Jewish heroics and patriotic devotion. The *Allgemeine Zeitung des Judentums* insisted that the youngest German volunteer was a fourteen-year-old Jewish boy from Allenstein in East Prussia. The same paper also celebrated a Jewish soldier named Fischer said to have captured the first French flag of the war. When this turned out to be an error, the paper corrected itself with a poem:

First in battle and first to win
Was neither Jew nor Christian.
No liberal, Junker, or democrat:
The flag was caught by a German Soldat
    [soldier]!

The common experience of war was generally expected to cement firm new bonds among Germans of all faiths. The term used for that experience was *Erlebnis*, an emotionally charged word that refers more to a spiritual and even aesthetic phenomenon than to a physical and concrete one; a more accurate translation might be "rite of passage." A young Jewish volunteer, Julius

Holz, invoked his *Erlebnis* on December 7, 1914, his twentieth birthday, in a letter to his father from the front. He vowed to "fight like a man, as a good German of true Jewish faith and for the greater honor of my family." (Holz fell in battle in 1918. Twenty-four years later, on the eve of her deportation to an extermination camp, his eighty-one-year-old mother wrote the authorities asking to be spared in view of her son's death in action, as attested by attached documents. She received a one-line reply: "Your application to be released from 'labor service' is refused.")

Jews living in the more remote rural areas were probably more circumspect. The novelist Manes Sperber, who grew up in a small Galician town close to the Russian border, remembered his father telling a roomful of children and relatives, "For us the war is a terrible disaster."

"Why a disaster?" someone asked. "Our kaiser will be victorious and the czar will be defeated and will never oppress his subjects again."

"For us every war is a disaster," Sperber's father answered firmly. "No one in this room can be sure of his survival."[54]

In the main urban centers, liberal, leftist, and perhaps even some pacifist Jews were swayed by the prevailing emphasis on Russia. It was easier to endorse a war directed against the last despotic and openly antisemitic regime in Europe. At long last Russia would be punished for the pogroms of Kishinev, Homel, and Siberia, the philosopher Samuel Hugo Bergmann, a Zionist, noted in his diary.[55] He thanked the Lord that as an officer serving in the Austro-Hungarian army on the Russian front he would be able personally to avenge his people. A son of German-speaking Prague Jews, Bergmann saw himself as defending *Kultur* against the barbarians of the East. More than ever, he wrote, he felt part of German culture body and soul. "At least in war we are equal," another volunteer wrote home from the front line in France; shortly before he was killed.[56]

The hope for full integration was boosted considerably by the kaiser in a speech he gave from the throne on August 4 affirming his government's decision to go to war. The entire Reichstag and representatives of leading churches and synagogues were gathered in the White Hall of the imperial palace. The kaiser solemnly assured his audience by proclaiming that differences of religion, political affiliation, class, and ethnic origin no longer counted. He appealed to "all peoples and tribes of the German Reich . . . irrespective of party, kinship, and confession, to hold steadfastly with me through thick and thin, deprivation and death."[57] He added: "I no longer know any parties, I know only Germans," at which point the Reichstag broke into a "storm of bravos." No one, except perhaps Theodor Wolff of the *Berliner Tageblatt*, who witnessed the event, seems to have wondered whether the end of parties was actually a good thing in a democracy; over the next four years the country would, in fact, be governed by the military high command. Liberals commended the kaiser for his "noble" speech. Jews in particular were grateful. "The nation is like one family now," Paul Rieger of the *Centralverein* wrote. War had inaugurated a "divine peace" among all Germans; love of the fatherland had "torn down all dividing walls," he added happily.[58]

Several changes seemed at first to confirm the kaiser's promise. Some were cosmetic. Venom once directed at Jews was now diverted to "perfidious England," producing a solidarity that seemed to confirm Freud's dictum that it is easier to promote goodwill between two groups if there is a third they can both hate. The sociologist Werner Sombart, who only two years earlier had criticized Jews for their clannishness, now assaulted the English for their crass materialism, emphasizing the moral difference between German "heroes" and English "shopkeepers." Heine's bitter condemnation of England (Napoleon's "treacherous" jailers) brought him—six decades after his death—a brief spell of admiration even among antisemites. The leading "scientific" racist Houston Chamberlain lauded German Jews for doing their duty at the front and at home. Some such compliments were double-edged. On receiving his Iron Cross, the wounded Jewish poet Ernst Toller was told: "This should compensate for the stigma of your ancestry."[59]

Other changes were more significant. A few long-standing obstacles to the appointment of Jews to the higher ranks of the civil service and the judiciary were finally removed. Hundreds (later thousands) were given commissions in the army. Lieutenant Hugo Gutmann, a Jewish regimental adjutant, went to considerable lengths to secure Adolf Hitler an Iron Cross for bravery in the line of action. The divisional commander doubted that Hitler deserved it. Gutmann finally convinced him and personally affixed the medal to Hitler's chest.[60]

For several months after the outbreak of war, Jewish volunteers and conscripts felt little if any hostility in the ranks. In the name of the kaiser's "civic truce," the military authorities ordered the more radical antisemitic periodicals to refrain from anti-Jewish agitation. . . .

Disillusion was slow to sink in. Max Rothmann, a neurologist and professor in Berlin, had been one of the privileged few invited to attend the kaiser's August 4, 1914, speech in the White Hall of the imperial palace. He was there as a representative of the Berlin Reform synagogue community. Rothmann had been delighted to hear the kaiser say that all Germans were now equal in his eyes, irrespective of faith and ethnic origin. His family had long prided itself on its military tradition, and his elder son was already on his way to the

Western Front. Rothmann himself was a twice-decorated royal *Oberarzt*—chief doctor—in the Prussian army reserve. His father and grandfather had been decorated in the wars of 1815 and 1870, respectively.

Rothmann had another son, a fifteen-year-old. Soon after the kaiser's speech, Rothmann sought to enroll the boy in the Prussian cadet academy, believing like most other German Jews that the kaiser's words heralded a new era. A rude shock awaited him: his application was rejected. The excuse given was that the boy had taken Latin rather than English in the fourth grade. Rothmann supplied proof that other boys with similar records in his son's class had been accepted by the academy. He asked for an appointment with the principal. His request was refused without explanation.

Two months later, in October 1914, Rothmann's elder son fell in action. Rothmann turned to the army chief of staff, Helmuth von Moltke, informing him of his loss, and to the kaiser himself, renewing his request. The kaiser did not reply. The deputy war minister, Gustav von Wandel, wrote to Rothmann that cadet schools were Christian institutions: "Since your son adheres to the Jewish faith, the War Ministry regrets that it must reject your application." The chief of staff also wrote—to express "congratulations upon the heroic death" of his son, "who sealed his oath of loyalty to the fatherland with his heart's blood."[61]

Rothmann's bitter disappointment was not an isolated event. Far from uniting Germans and Jews, the war seemed only to deepen the gulf between them. As soon as the war turned sour, chauvinism turned inward. Rathenau saw it coming. "The more Jews die in this conflict," he wrote on August 4, 1916, "the more persistent will be their opponents' complaints that the Jews did nothing but sit behind the front lines profiteer-ing from the war. The hatred will double and triple."[62] Ferdinand Avenarius, the publisher of the high-brow *Kunstwart* magazine, warned a Jewish friend that Jews did not even begin to surmise the rage that was "boiling deep within the people." Such feelings were exacerbated by the sudden influx of impoverished Jews from occupied Poland and Russia, many brought against their will, to work in industry and agriculture. Living in abject conditions on the edges of the larger cities, they elicited revulsion.

The strategy of wearing down the enemy through sustained attrition proved self-defeating. It wore down the spirit of the army and demoralized the home front. A search for scapegoats ensued. The war was now said to drag on only because Jews like Rathenau and Ballin had not yet amassed enough money. The War Ministry was flooded with complaints about Jewish draft dodgers. Ludwig III, the king of Bavaria, held back his approval of Richard Willstätter . . . for a professorship at the University of Munich. On September 4, 1916, after repeated prodding by his minister of education, the king finally gave in, although not before warning the minister: "This is the last time I agree to the appointment of a Jew." It was indeed the last, Willstätter noted in his memoirs.[63]

In October 1916, when almost three thousand Jews had already died on the battlefield and more than seven thousand had been decorated, War Minister Wild von Hohenborn saw fit to sanction the growing prejudices. He ordered a "Jew census" in the army to determine the actual number of Jews on the front lines as opposed to those serving in the rear. Ignoring protests in the Reichstag and the press, he proceeded with his head count. The results were not made public, ostensibly to "spare Jewish feelings." The truth was that the census disproved the accusations: 80 percent served on the front lines.[64]

The Jew census had a devastating effect on German Jews, generating an unprecedented moral crisis among those on the front line. An artillery captain named Georg Meyer, in civilian life an accountant with Siemens in Berlin, felt as though he had been given a terrible slap in the face. "Now," he wrote,"I must endure it."[65] Two months later Meyer fell outside Verdun, one of twelve thousand Jews who gave their lives for Germany during the war.

Ernst Simon's reaction was even stronger. In 1914, Simon had fully shared the "intoxicating joy" of going to war. The Jew census turned this "de-Judaized aesthete," as he described himself, into a confirmed Zionist. The census was a "betrayal"; its popularity within the army horrified Simon. The dream of community was gone. In one horrendous blow, the census reopened the deep chasm that "could not be bridged by common language, work, civilization, and custom."[66]

Simon's reaction was particularly emphatic, and his conversion to Zionism was a relatively isolated event. Most Jewish soldiers, like Julius Marx, a young frontline volunteer, felt anger and frustration but did not sever their ties with their native country as Simon did after the war. In his diary, though, Marx recorded an infuriating exchange with his company commander:

> A while back I was summoned to see the company commander. A questionnaire was lying on the table.
>
> "Reporting!"
>
> "I have to take down your particulars," he said.
>
> "Might I ask, Lieutenant, what for?"
>
> 'Yes, well . . . the Ministry of War . . . someone suggested to the minister . . . they want to know how many Jews are serving on the front . . ."
>
> "And how many are behind the lines!? What kind of nonsense is this! What do they want

to do? Demote us to second-class soldiers and make us look ridiculous in the eyes of the entire army? They subject us to all kinds of harassment, refuse to promote us, and then wax indignant if they catch someone watching the war from the rear."
>
> 'You're absolutely right, but there's nothing I can do about it. So, what's your date of birth?"
>
> "Damn it to hell! So that's why we're risking our necks for this country?"[67]

The banker Max Warburg failed to convince the War Ministry to make the results of the census public. Instead, the ministry leaked some of its findings to a well-known antisemitic rabble-rouser, who then published two distorted papers on it. When, in the aftermath of the census, the Federation of Jews in France accused the German government of antisemitism, the government asked the kaiser's "friend" James Simon to counter the charge. Simon refused. He wrote Secretary of State Arthur Zimmermann that visible steps to end the prevailing discrimination would be more effective than denials.[68] The early warmonger Arnold Zweig decided after the census that he would rather be a prisoner of war than a German soldier. He published a macabre short story in *Die Schaubühne* called "Census at Verdun," in which the ghosts of the dead are summoned from their graves to complete the War Ministry's questionnaire.

NOTES

1. G. A. Craig, "The End of the Golden Age," *New York Review of Books*, November 4, 1999, 13.
2. W. Benjamin, *One-Way Street and Other Writings*, trans. E. Jephcott and K. Shorter (London, 1985), 328.
3. P. Gay, *Freud, Jews, and Other Germans* (Oxford, 1978), 78.

4. Unpublished ms. cited by H. Meier-Cronemeyer in *Germania-Judaica*; *Kölner Bibliothek zur Geschichte des deutschen Judentums* 8, nos. 1–2 (Cologne, 1969), 4.
5. S. Zweig, *The World of Yesterday* (London, 1945), 28.
6. Ibid., 30.
7. A. Schnitzler, *My Youth in Vienna*, trans. C. Hutter (New York, 1970), 63.
8. Ibid., 6.
9. *Zeitschrift für Demographie und Statistik der Juden*, January—February 1924, 25.
10. F. Theilhaber, *Der Untergang der deutschen Juden*, Munich, 1911.
11. Quoted in M. Richarz, *Bürger auf Widerruf: Lebenszeugnisse deutscher Juden, 1780–1945* (Munich, 1989), 310–11.
12. V. Klemperer, *Curriculum Vitae: Erinnerungen 1881–1918* (Berlin, 1996), 1: 96.
13. G. Tietz, *Hermann Ttetz: Geschichte einer Familie und ihrer Warenhäuser* (Stuttgart, 1965), 37, 53.
14. Klemperer, *Curriculum Vitae*, 1: 44.
15. Ibid.
16. Ibid., 44–45.
17. K. Hiller, *Leben gegen die Zeit* (Hamburg, 1969), 33.
18. E. Ludwig, *Geschenke des Lebens* (Berlin, 1932), 101.
19. W. Benjamin, *Berliner Kindheit um Neunzehnhundert* (Frankfurt, 1950), 47.
20. M. Brod, *Streitbares Leben* (Munich, 1969), 222.
21. F. Kafka, *Letters to Felice*, trans. J. Stern and E. Duckworth (New York, 1973), 502 (September 16, 1916).
22. F. Kafka, *Letter to His Father*, trans E. Kaiser and E. Wilkins (New York, 1966), 77.
23. W. Sombart, ed., *Judentaufen* (Munich, 1912), 77.
24. G. Kisch, *Judentaufen* (Berlin, 1933), 49.
25. Ibid., 17.
26. A. Paucker, "Zur Problematik einer jüdischen Abwehrstrategie in der deutschen Gesellschaft," *Juden im Wilhelminischen Deutschland*, ed. Mosse and Paucker, 487.
27. T. Lessing, *Einmal und nie wieder* (Gütersloh, 1967), 123.
28. P. Gay, Introduction to R. Gay, *The Jews of Germany: A Historical Portrait* (New Haven, 1992), xii.
29. E. Cahen, *Les héros de Wissembourg* (Paris, 1898), quoted in *Leo Baeck Institute Yearbook 28* (1983): 139.
30. A. Landsberger, *Judentaufen* (Munich, 1912), 4.
31. J. Namier, *Lewis Namier: A Biography* (Oxford, 1971), 101.
32. Klemperer, *Curricilum Vitae*, 1: 524.
33. *Leo Baeck Institute Yearbook 3* (1958): 81.
34. P. Pulzer, in Mosse and Paucker, *Juden im Wilhelminischen Deutschland*, 199.
35. E. Reichmann, *Flucht in den Hass* (Frankfurt, 1974), 172.
36. A. Paucker, in Mosse and Paucker, *Juden in Wilhelminischen Deutschland*, 492n.
37. N. Sombart, *Die Deutschen Männer und ihre Feinde* (Munich, 1991), 271.
38. S. Volkov, "Geschichte und Gesellschaft," *Zeitschrift für historische Sozialwissenschaft* 3 (1983): 338.
39. *Marx-Engels Werke* (Berlin, 1963), 12: 99.
40. *Allgemeine Zeitung des Judentums*, December 12, 1881, 862.
41. F. Stern, *Einstein's German World* (Princeton, 1999), 4.
42. *Der Kunstwart*, March 1, 1912.
43. R. Marwedel, *Theodor Lessing, 1872–1933: Eine Biographie* (Oldenburg, 1990), 138.
44. S. Volkov, *Jüdisches Leben und Antisemitismus im 19. und 20. Jahrhundert* (Munich, 1990), 146ff.
45. Quoted in F. Stern, *Verspielte Grösse* (Munich, 1998), 171.
46. L. Frank, *Aufsätze, Reden und Briefe* (Berlin, 1924), 348; R. Schay, *Juden in der deutschen Politik* (Berlin, 1923), 219ff.
47. J. Toury, *Die politischen Orientierungen der Juden in Deutschland* (Tübingen, 1966), 315.
48. Gay, *Freud, Jews, and Other Germans*, 158.
49. H. Kessler, *Künstler und Nationen* (Frankfurt, 1988), 279.
50. A. Einstein, *Ideas and Opinions*, trans. S. Bargmann (New York, 1964), 171.

51. Quoted in R. W. Clark, *Einstein: The Life and Times* (New York, 1971), 183.

52. Stern, *Einstein's German World*, 67.

53. E. Zechlin, *Die deutsche Politik und die Juden im Ersten Weltkrieg* (Göttingen, 1969), 88.

54. M. Sperber, *All das Vergangene* (Vienna, 1983), 121.

55. H. Bergmann, *Tagebücher* (Königstein, 1985), 59.

56. F. J. Strauss, ed., *Kriegsbriefe gefallener deutschen Juden* (Berlin, 1961), 22.

57. G. Kotowski et al., eds., *1914—1933: Historisches Lesebuch* (Frankfurt, 1968), 27.

58. P. Rieger, *Ein Vierteljahrhundert im Kampf um das Recht und die Zukunft der deutschen Juden* (Berlin, 1918), 61.

59. W. von Molo, *Erinnerungen und Begegnungen* (Stuttgart, 1957), 217.

60. A. Niekisch, *Gewagtes Leben* (Cologne, 1958), 283.

61. Facsimile in R. Vogel, *Ein Stück von Uns: Deutsche Juden in deutschen Armeen, 1813–1976,* (Mainz, 1977), 70.

62. Rathenau to W. Schwaner, quoted in V. Ullrich, *Die nervöse Grossmacht: Aufstieg und Untergang des deutschen Kaiserreichs, 1871–1918* (Frankfurt, 1997), 489.

63. Willstätter, *From My Life*, 235.

64. Vogel, *Ein Stück von Uns*, 149; *Leo Baeck Institute Yearbook* 19 (1974): 143.

65. Ullrich, *Die nervöse Grossmacht*, 485.

66. Simon, *Unser Kriegserlebnis*, 18.

67. J. Marx, *Kriegstagebuch eines Juden* (Frankfurt, 1964), 138.

68. *Leo Baeck Institute Yearbook* 10 (1965): 9.

Germany's Turmoil, 1918–1933

KLAUS P. FISCHER

From *Nazi Germany: A New History*

The defeat of a proud and arrogant nation, which up to the very last months of the war believed that final victory was within its grasp, is bound to cause a collective trauma with far-ranging consequences. . . . In the fall of 1918, . . . four ancient empires collapsed: the German, Austro-Hungarian, Russian, and Ottoman. With the collapse of these ancient monarchies disappeared old symbols of authority that were not so easily replaced. The trauma of defeat and the collapse of ancient authorities opened the floodgates to years of violence, revolution, and extremism. It is against this postwar chaos, which extended into the 1920s and was later rekindled by the Great Depression, that the growth of political pathology must be seen. In Germany, as elsewhere in Europe, a generation of political extremists roamed the political landscape in search of a messianic leader who could redeem them from meaningless sacrifices on the battlefield and restore a collective sense of purpose that had disappeared with the old authorities.

When Germany faced inevitable defeat, those who had been most responsible for the disaster—the leaders of the military establishment—deftly stepped aside and let new democratic leaders take the blame. As early as September 29, 1918, the day the Hindenburg line cracked, the German high command finally awoke to the reality of defeat. The Second Reich was drawing to a close. The emperor was by now a virtual nonentity, as he had

been during most of the war; and when the military high command asked Chancellor Hertling to open negotiations for an armistice, it became painfully obvious even to die-hard supporters of the monarchy that President Woodrow Wilson and the Western allies did not want to negotiate with the kaiser and his military autocrats. The old order had become a diplomatic liability because Woodrow Wilson, enamored by lofty democratic sentiments, insisted that he would not bargain with the emperor or the military but only with the true representatives of the German people. This amounted in some way to an incitement to revolt or, at the very least, to a strong expectation, backed up by menacing threats, that the German people replace the monarchy with a more acceptable democratic government.[1]

The Allied powers, of course, were not the only catalysts of sweeping changes in Germany. By the middle of 1918, the Allied blockade was exacting a grim toll in the form of widespread starvation, food riots, political strikes, and plain lawlessness, made all the more serious by a worldwide influenza epidemic that killed twenty million people. . . . In Berlin, banks were failing, food rations were reduced even further, people died of the influenza virus, and the kaiser's credibility had reached rock bottom. Although the emperor dismissed Chancellor Hertling, who was widely regarded as a stooge of the military, the appointment of Max von Baden, his liberal cousin, did not improve his popularity. . . . Baden now sent his final note to Wilson, informing him that the

German military was now fully subject to civilian control. The American president replied on November 5, stating that peace could be made in accordance with his Fourteen Points although he made one important reservation: Germany, he insisted, would be held liable for all damage done to Allied property. This was an ominous indication of what was in store for Germany: the imposition of "war guilt," reparations payments, and territorial losses.

On November 8, 1918, the German armistice commission, led by Matthias Erzberger, a leading Catholic Center politician and a catalyst of the peace resolutions in the Reichstag, arrived in the French village of Rethondes in the forest of Compiègne to parley with Marshal Ferdinand Foch, the supreme generalissimo of the Allied armies on the western front. Negotiating in a railroad car, later used by Hitler to dictate peace to the French in 1940, Foch presented several tough conditions to the German side before fighting would cease. The Germans were given two days, November 9 and 10, to respond to the Allied proposals. This presented a real problem to the German delegation because during the course of these two days the German emperor resigned, a republic was proclaimed, and Max von Baden handed over all of his authority to an interim president, Friedrich Ebert. In view of these events, the French wondered whether they were really dealing with the legal representatives of Germany. However, on November 10, Ebert sent a message agreeing to the armistice terms. The next day, November 11, the armistice was signed.

The terms of the armistice were anything but lenient. Germany was given two weeks to withdraw from Alsace-Lorraine and from all other invaded territory. All German territory west of the Rhine was to be occupied by Allied troops. The Germans were to evacuate East Africa. Germany also forfeited an enormous amount of cannons, machine guns, planes, and trucks. All submarines were to be surrendered, and the whole German fleet was to be put into Allied hands. The treaties of Brest Litovsk and Bucharest, made with Russia and Romania respectively, were declared null and void. Finally, Germany was to free Allied prisoners even though the Allies were not required to free German prisoners. The armistice was clearly designed to convince the Germans that they had lost the war. All was now quiet on the western front.

Inside Germany, however, all was not quiet on any front. While the German delegation agonized over the terms of the armistice in their railroad car in the forest of Compiègne, total confusion broke out in Germany. On November 9, Kaiser William abdicated his throne and a republic was proclaimed by the Social Democrat Phillip Scheidemann. The kaiser's hasty departure for exile in Holland left a political vacuum that several factions, including the Communists, attempted to fill. The Russian defeat in war had brought the Bolsheviks to power, and there were good reasons to suspect that similar developments might occur in Germany. This is certainly how Lenin perceived the situation from his vantage point in Moscow in November 1918. The Bolshevik autocrat spoke of Russia and Germany as twins and looked to the more industrialized Germany as his advanced outpost in the coming struggle with capitalism. Directly and indirectly, the Russian Communists gave enthusiastic support to their German comrades in hopes that a communized Germany would be the catalyst for a communized Europe....

In the first two weeks of November, a reenactment of the Russian Revolution seemed to be taking place in Germany. This is certainly how a temporarily blinded young corporal by the name of Adolf Hitler, who was recovering from a poison gas attack at Pasewalk in Pomerania, perceived the political situation. In reality, the fear of a Communist revolution was much exaggerated because the German situation did not resemble the Russian. In Russia, the urban working class was proportionally much smaller than the German working force; it was also less disciplined along formal union lines and lacked the tradition of skilled craftsmanship that predisposed the German worker toward a more conservative political outlook. Both the Russian peasants and workers hated the tsarist regime and longed for its violent overthrow. Under the impact of a disastrous war, an elite cadre of revolutionaries skillfully mobilized these seething resentments and, taking advantage of the blunders of the first or moderate revolution of March 1917, staged a second revolution that put an end to the traditional order in Russia. The Bolsheviks imposed a one-party dictatorship on Russia and gradually assembled the instruments of mass control that such a rule inevitably necessitates: a revolutionary army (the Red Army), a secret police (Cheka), forced labor camps for political opponents, and a pliant cadre of government officials executing the will of the reigning autocracy.

By contrast, in Germany there was only one revolution, and that one left the traditional social structure essentially undisturbed.[2] The decisive political shift of power in Germany had taken place during the last month of the war when the ruling elites, composed of the aristocracy, the upper middle class, and the High Command of the Armed Forces, were politically displaced for the moment by the forces of social democracy, especially by the parties in the Reichstag that commanded the loyalties of the workers and portions of the middle classes.

The largest of these left-wing parties was the Social Democratic Party. Founded in 1875, the party had gone through a hectic period of external persecution and internal dissension. In 1914 the party had reluctantly voted to support the war effort; but in doing so, it had spread further dissent into the rank and file, precipitating a walkout by the dissidents who formed a new party in 1917 called the Independent Socialist Party. The aim of this new radical party was to establish genuine socialism in Germany and bring an immediate halt to the despised war. The Independent Socialists were supported by the more radical Communists who had been organized into the Spartacist League by two remarkable revolutionaries—Rosa Luxemburg and Karl Liebknecht. Supported by many disenchanted workers, these Spartacists, named after the ill-fated Roman slave leader Spartacus, called for a Communist regime modeled on Bolshevik rule in Russia; they favored immediate revolution, expropriation of industry and landed estates, and the establishment of "soviets" or workers' councils. Their leader, Karl Liebknecht, was the son of Wilhelm Liebknecht, friend of Karl Marx and one of the founding fathers of the Social Democratic Party. Karl Liebknecht broke with the party in 1914 because he could not go along with its support of the war. Liebknecht was a short, slender man who wore a pince-nez, sported a military moustache, and gave the overall impression of a minor clerk in the civil service rather than a dangerous subversive. Yet Liebknecht was a man of unshakeable determination and revolutionary zeal. . . .

With a sizeable part of the German left rallying around Liebknecht and his second-in-command, the gifted ideologue Rosa Luxemburg—a stout, crippled, but combative agitator in her middle forties—the Majority Socialists (Social Democrats) struggled to maintain their control over the German workers. Ostensibly Marxist in their orientation, the Majority Socialists showed little interest in ideology and even less in subverting the social order for Communism.... They wanted to raise the general standard of living for the working people in the context of a modern democratic society. Their leader, Friedrich Ebert, typified these relatively moderate expectations. Born in 1871, the son of a humble Catholic tailor, Ebert was apprenticed as a journeyman saddle-maker and, by dint of hard work, gradually rose to the chairmanship of the saddlers' union in Bremen. His good sense, jovial character, and pragmatic outlook made him popular among the rank and file and led to his election to the Bremen city council before he was thirty.... In 1912 Ebert became a deputy of his party to the Reichstag; in 1913 he succeeded August Bebel as head of the German Social Democratic Party (SPD).

The Majority Socialists admired Ebert's tact and diplomatic aplomb; they liked his flexibility on ideological issues. In fact, Ebert was not doctrinaire on ideological questions; he ... strongly believed in parliamentary democracy, preferably in republican but under certain conditions also in monarchical form. His bête noire was lack of organization and lack of good order. He believed that everything should be done according to some acceptable protocol and that decisions should never be forced on constituted authorities by the irrational actions of crowds and rabble-rousers.[3] This is why Ebert threw his authority behind the government of Prince Max von Baden in October 1918, because he genuinely feared a social revolution that would lead, as in Russia, to a Bolshevik coup. The prospect of a Bolshevik revolution filled Ebert and his colleagues, including his right-hand man, Philipp Scheidemann (1863–1939), with horror.

The center of political gravity was thus shifting in the fall of 1918 from the imperial elites to the Majority Socialists. The crucial day was November 9, 1918. In order to prevent the Independent Socialists and the radical Spartacists from gaining control over the working population of Berlin, the Majority Socialists demanded the abdication of Kaiser William, who had moved to army headquarters at Spa for his own protection....

When the Majority Socialists, after repeated inquiries to the chancellery, did not receive definitive news of the emperor's abdication—for William was still toying with the idea of reasserting his control—they made good on their earlier threat of withdrawing their representatives from Max's cabinet. The man who now forced everybody's hands and decided the fate of postwar German politics was Max von Baden. On his own authority, he announced the kaiser's abdication and called for elections to a constituent assembly and the establishment of a regency. Max von Baden then resigned in favor of Friedrich Ebert. The emperor, who was still at Spa [in occupied Belgium] with his high-ranking military leaders, referred to this decision by his cousin as "bare-faced, outrageous treason," but his support among the German people had eroded to such an extent that ... William boarded a special train that carried him into exile in Holland. He never saw Germany again.

Germany in Revolutionary Turmoil

At noon on November 9, 1918, while Philipp Scheidemann was eating a bowl of potato soup in the Reichstag dining hall, a crowd of soldiers rushed into the hall and accosted him with the ominous news that Liebknecht was already speaking from the balcony of the imperial palace and was ready to proclaim the Soviet Republic of Germany. Recalling his horrified reaction, Scheidemann later wrote, "Now I clearly saw what was afoot. I knew his [Liebknecht's] slogan—supreme authority for the workers' councils. Germany to be therefore a Russian province, a branch of the

Soviet. No, no, a thousand times no!"[4] Scheidemann then rushed to one of the large windows of the Reichstag and addressed a throng of cheering Berliners with the startling news that "the accursed war is at an end . . . The emperor has abdicated . . . Long live the new! Long live the German Republic!"[5] When Scheidemann made this startling announcement, the news of the emperor's abdication had not been released, and even Liebknecht had not fully marshaled his forces. Thus, when Friedrich Ebert heard that his second-in-command had proclaimed a republic, "His face turned livid with wrath," as Scheidemann later recalled. Ebert banged his fist on a table and yelled at the embarrassed culprit: "You have no right to proclaim a Republic!"[6] Germany had received a republic by accident; and the fact that it was proclaimed by a Socialist would stigmatize it from the moment of its birth.

Later that day, Liebknecht's troops managed to occupy the deserted imperial palace, and it was from there that Liebknecht proclaimed a free Socialist republic, promising "to build a new order of the proletariat." By nightfall no one knew who was really in power in Berlin because two republics had been proclaimed successively. The issue, however, was actually decided on that very evening. As Friedrich Ebert tried to work out the implications of the day's events in his mind in the chancellor's private office, one of the office phones, which turned out to be a secret line to military headquarters at Spa, began to ring. Unaware of this secret line, Ebert was startled to hear General Groener on the other end of the line. The general briefly recapitulated the day's events at Spa: he informed Ebert that the emperor had abdicated and was on his way to Holland and that an orderly withdrawal of Germany's front-line armies would commence immediately. In response to Ebert's question as to where the army stood in the present crisis, the general replied that the army would support Ebert's government if, in turn, the new government would support the officers' corps, maintain strict discipline in the army, and oppose Communism. Much reassured, Ebert agreed to these friendly overtures; by doing so, he concluded that much criticized marriage of convenience between the fledgling democratic republic and the traditional military-industrial complex. . . . By agreeing not to tamper with the traditional structure of the German army, Ebert and his Majority Socialists unwittingly helped to perpetuate a military establishment that despised the democratic process. Throughout the Weimar Republic the military became a frequent rallying point for right-wing extremists who wanted to destroy the democratic republic.

Yet without the support of the army Ebert's government would probably not have survived the attacks launched against it by the extreme revolutionary left. By Christmas of 1918, Ebert was skating on very thin ice indeed; his cooperation with the military had exposed him to charges of counterrevolutionary activities. Playing for time, he invited three Independent Socialists to join his newly formed cabinet and temporarily endorsed the radicals' claim that all sovereignty resided in the council of soldiers and workers. Privately, he made it clear that he abhorred government by councils of workers and soldiers. The present situation, as he saw it, called for a sound constitutional method by which power would be transferred to a publicly elected constituent assembly that would then proceed to frame a constitution acceptable to the nation.

Ebert's hopes of a peaceful and orderly transition to parliamentary government required the restoration of law and order, and the most effective means of bringing this about still resided in Germany's armed forces. Unfortunately, many army units were melting away quickly in the wake of the general withdrawal from enemy territories and the impending plans to demobilize most of the units. Even in defeat, however, the army managed to preserve its dignity. General Groener succeeded so brilliantly in marching almost two million troops home to Germany that it created the illusion, especially in Berlin, that the German army had not really been defeated at all. On November 11, the day the armistice was signed in France, the vanguard of eleven army divisions staged a spectacular parade by marching up Unter den Linden to the sounds of cheers and hurrahs, with the band striking up "Deutschland, Deutschland, über Alles." Ebert himself reviewed the troops from a specially erected platform, declaring, "I salute you who return unvanquished from the field of battle."[7] The aura of militarism was still so powerful that not even a Socialist could admit publicly that the German army had been defeated.

In the general confusion following the tenuous transfer of power from the old ruling elites to the makeshift cabinet assembled by Friedrich Ebert, the ingrained German sense of order had prevented not only a complete political breakdown but a possible Communist seizure of power as well. Moreover, in order to avoid the collapse of German industry, representatives of employers sat down with trade unionist leaders and worked out mutually beneficial agreements that recognized the existence of independent trade unions and their right to collective bargaining. Finally, to safeguard the integrity of the civil service system, Ebert called upon all state officials to remain at their posts, a measure for which he was much criticized because the managerial elite of the old civil service was bound to be hostile to democracy. Yet only a small minority of Socialists, consisting largely of radicalized shop stewards and Spartacists, resisted these stabilizing policies set forth by Ebert and his Majority Socialists. Even within the councils of workers and soldiers there was determined opposition to following the Russian example of violent or "root-and-branch" revolution. . . .

Weimar and Versailles

Between 1919 and 1933, Germany was subject to two major documents: the Treaty of Versailles, which determined how Germans responded to foreign powers, and the Weimar Constitution, which regulated the political life of Germans until Adolf Hitler decided to tear up both documents. Although the Weimar Constitution was one of the most democratic constitutions in the world in 1919, Richard Watt's clever judgment that the constitution began and ended as a document in search of a people remains a sad and tragic fact.[8] By the same token, one could argue that the Treaty of Versailles was also a document that began and ended in search of a single people willing to accept all of its provisions. Neither of these documents proved to be acceptable to the German people, and the fourteen-year history of the Weimar Republic (1919–33) witnessed persistent attempts, especially by the parties of the extreme ends of the political spectrum, to repudiate both.

On January 19, 1919, the German people went to the polls to elect 421 deputies to the National Constituent Assembly. . . . The results harbored several positive signs: the German people clearly decided in favor of moderation and appeared to be willing to experiment with social democracy, though few Germans understood what democracy entailed in practice. In addition, the parties on the extreme ends of the political spectrum suffered a noticeable setback. . . . Despite these positive indications, one could also detect certain long-range problems. The elections had revealed that the voters did not show overwhelming support or enthusiasm for any party. This meant that no single party was able to claim a clear mandate for governing and that the only way in which the democratic process could be made to work was to form coalition cabinets. Such makeshift arrangements, however, threatened to produce internally divided governments, since the policy makers represented different ideological views and reported to different constituencies. Indeed, throughout the life of the Weimar Republic, stable democratic government was constantly undermined by unpopular minority cabinets and internally weak grand coalitions.[9] . . .

The framers of the constitution, in their eagerness to preserve a sense of historical continuity, retained the word *Reich* in referring to the new republic. It was not clear just how the idea of empire, with all the imperial symbols it evoked, and the idea of a democratic republic could be harmonized. The truth was that the contradictions inherent in such efforts caused psychic dissonances that were made all the more acute by the pressures of economic hardship and national humiliation. Throughout the life of the republic, the average German was treated to frequent public spectacles in which the feudal classes, dressed in their resplendent uniforms, medals, and ribbons, strutted up and down the streets of German cities taunting the democratic establishment. Funerals and patriotic meetings invariably prompted gaudy displays of aristocratic splendor and created the impression, first, that nothing had changed since the fall of the monarchy, and, second, that the traditional classes somehow had a monopoly on patriotism.

The framers of the constitution were sensitive to the fact that strong executive leadership was required in order to unify the divided nation. It was for this reason that the president of the republic was endowed with more power than was customary under other parliamentary systems. The office of the Presidency was a compromise between a constitutional monarch and a parliamentary president. He was to be elected by the German people for a period of seven years (Article 41). The constitution specified that the president had to be elected by a majority of the voters, and that runoff elections, during which different candidates could be appointed, had to be arranged if no candidate achieved a clear majority. The president's powers were extensive: he appointed the chancellor; served as commander in chief; appointed and removed all military officers; possessed the right to dissolve the Reichstag; and in times of national emergency, he was empowered to suspend civil liberties and intervene with the help of the armed forces to restore public safety and order. This innocuous article (Article 48) gave little concern in 1919 because the constitution also specified that the Reichstag could repeal a president's emergency decree. In addition, the constitution also provided for countervailing powers by insisting that every order or decree issued by the president had to be countersigned by the chancellor.

The chancellor and his ministers formed the government of the Reich. The chancellor himself was appointed and could be dismissed by the president, and the ministers he chose also had to be approved by the president. The chancellor's government had to have the confidence of the Reichstag; and if the Reichstag chose to withdraw its confidence in the chancellor or any of his ministers, the particular individual had to resign. Furthermore, should any member of the government violate the constitution, the culprit could be brought before the Supreme Court (*Staatsgerichthof*) for trial.

Legislative power was vested in a bicameral house composed of the Reichstag and Reichsrat.

Members of the Reichstag or lower house were elected for four years by universal suffrage (female and male citizens of twenty years and over) and in accordance with a new principle of representation called "proportional representation."[10] This meant that voters cast their votes for a party and not for individual candidates. Each party drew up lists of names and waited for the election results to see how many candidates on the list were eligible for the Reichstag. For each sixty thousand votes a party was guaranteed one seat in the Reichstag. Although this system of proportional representation seemed to represent the popular will more closely than any other, it also fragmented the political process into a host of different and mutually antagonistic parties. Since most parties stood a good chance of garnering sixty thousand votes, even the smallest parties could gain a handful of seats in the Reichstag.... Such proliferation of parties created a very unfortunate impression of the democratic process in the minds of most Germans who saw the resulting confusion as a validation of their authoritarian prejudices, namely, that democracy spells chaos and corruption....

On January 18, 1919, one day before the German people went to the polls to elect members to the National Constituent Assembly, the peace conference assembled in Paris to make the world safe for democracy, a phrase that had been coined by H. G. Wells in August 1914 to explain the meaning of the Allied cause. Unfortunately, after months of bitter wrangling, the conference succeeded in the opposite: it made the world safe from democracy.[11] The peace treaty, supposed to create a just and lasting world, was not made among coequal powers, but was summarily imposed upon the vanquished with menacing threats that left no doubt that war would be resumed if they failed to sign....

The public reaction in Germany can only be described as a profusion of public fury. Germans had not experienced such a sense of unity since the opening of the war; they felt betrayed and humiliated. The new democratic government, which had to bear the onus of the treaty, even contemplated armed resistance. Chancellor Scheidemann went on record by telling the nation that the intent of the proposed treaty was to make Germans "slaves and helots . . . doing forced labor behind barbed wire and prison bars" and that it was dishonorable to accept the treaty.[12] Despite the German reaction, the Allied powers refused to budge, giving the Germans one week to sign the treaty. This, in turn, caused a government crisis in Germany, with Scheidemann and his entire cabinet resigning in protest. The new government, headed by Gustav Bauer, another Social Democrat, realized that resistance was fruitless and urged the National Assembly to sign the document. On June 22, following bitter and acrimonious debates, the National Assembly finally yielded. The formal signing took place on June 28 in the same Hall of Mirrors in the Versailles Palace where Bismarck had proclaimed the German Empire in 1871.

The provisions of the Versailles Treaty can be seen as treating three basic themes: territorial losses, reparations, and punitive actions aimed at reducing Germany to the level of a minor power. Concerning outright territorial losses, Alsace-Lorraine, as expected, reverted to France, and all German overseas possessions were parceled out among the victors. Acrimonious discussions occurred over the fate of the Rhineland, with the French demanding that the left bank of the Rhine be detached from the rest of Germany and set up as an independent state. Although this extreme proposal was rejected, the peacemakers did agree to detach the left bank of the Rhine along with fifty kilometers of territory on the right bank of the river. Such territory was designated a neutral zone; within that zone Germany was prohibited from establishing any military presence. Moreover, this "demilitarized zone" was to be occupied by Allied troops for a period of fifteen years. The Saar Valley, with its rich coal deposits, was to be placed in French hands for the same period of time; its citizens would then be given a choice whether they wanted to join Germany or France.

To the east, the Allied powers wanted to set up strong buffer states against Bolshevism. As a result, . . . large numbers of Germans would now find themselves living in Poland and Czechoslovakia. In the case of Poland, the peacemakers decided to give the new state access to the Baltic Sea, but by cutting a "corridor" to that sea, they cut off East Prussia from the rest of Germany. The city of Danzig, located at the end of the corridor, became a "free city," politically independent but economically available to Poland. The problem of Danzig and the corridor, involving disputed territory and ethnic conflicts, would poison the relationship between Germany and Poland in the inter-war period, ultimately providing Hitler with a pretext for triggering World War II.

The fate of other territories, east or west, was to be decided by democratic plebiscites. Upper Silesia, a rich mining area, was annexed by Poland after a disputed plebiscite, while the rest of Silesia went to Germany. Although plebiscites were regarded by the Allies as an expression of national self-determination, they were not always honored when the decision was likely to run counter to the expected outcome of the victors. Thus, when the Austrians wanted to join Germany, the peacemakers set aside self-determination in favor of national self-interest, prohibiting the *Anschluss* on the grounds that this would add too much territory and too many people to Germany. The same

argument was made in respect to the Sudetenland and the Tyrol. Over three million Germans lived in the mountainous provinces of Bohemia and Moravia—two regions that the peacemakers had given to the new state of Czechoslovakia, ostensibly to provide the Czechs with more defensible frontiers. The Germans who lived in these regions were called Sudeten Germans after the mountain belt separating Bohemia and Silesia. Strictly speaking, these Germans had formerly belonged to the Habsburg Empire, but now found themselves as a minority within the new Czechoslovakian state. The same was true of those Germans living in the South Tyrol, for when the Brenner Pass was given to the Italians for strategic military reasons, the Germans in the South Tyrol now suddenly found themselves living in Italy.

The clauses of the Versailles Treaty dealing with reparations were the most punitive because they were based on the self-serving belief that Germany was solely responsible for having caused the war. The peacemakers' claim that Germany was responsible for the war was summed up in Article 231 of the treaty, subsequently referred to by the Germans as the "war guilt" clause: "The Allied and Associated Governments affirm and Germany accepts the responsibility of Germany and her allies for causing all the loss and damage to which the Allied and Associated Governments and their nationals have been subjected as a consequence of the war imposed upon them by the aggression of Germany and her Allies."[13]

In practice, this statement declaring Germany guilty of having caused all the damage and suffering of World War I was intended to be a moral justification for reparations. The peacemakers were determined to hold Germany liable for all the material damage caused by four years of devastating warfare; but since they could not translate this claim into a measurable or sensible amount of money, the treaty remained silent on the full amount of payments the Germans were expected to dole out to the victors. In the meantime, the treaty forced Germany to pay two billion dollars in gold before May 1, 1921, and to relinquish extensive deliveries of coal, chemicals, river barges, and most of the German merchant marine fleet. The German delegation at Versailles was further informed that a special Inter-Allied Reparations Commission would be convened to settle Germany's final obligations. The German counterargument that this amounted to a blank check, obligating Germany in advance to pay any amount the victors wanted to impose, was categorically rejected by the Allies without explanation.

No other provisions of the Versailles Treaty poisoned the postwar period as much as the articles that concerned reparations; and when the Inter-Allied Reparations Committee finally announced the total bill in 1921, a staggering sum of thirty-five billion dollars in gold, even Allied statesmen doubted that Germany could afford such exorbitant obligations. No Hitlerian demagogue was required to point out that such vindictive measures would cripple Germany's economy. Similar arguments were already being made on the Allied side, notably by John Maynard Keynes, then a young Cambridge economist and a member of the British delegation to the Paris Peace Conference. In a dispassionate work of analytical reasoning entitled *The Economic Consequences of the Peace* (1921), Keynes persuasively argued that reparations really aimed at the destruction of economic life in Germany and that by doing so, they would ironically also threaten the health and prosperity of the Allies themselves.[14]

Keynes denounced the peacemakers as hypocrites and political opportunists whose pious promises of a just and lasting peace had led only to "the weaving of that web of sophistries and Jesu-

itical exegesis that was finally to clothe with insincerity the language and substance of the whole treaty."[15] He recommended the reconstruction of the German economy as a precondition to a general European recovery. Helping the Germans back on their feet, however, would require a scaling down of reparations, cancellation of war debts, reduction of inflation, and massive reinvigoration of German industry through international loans. Keynes even proposed an extensive free common market under the aegis of the League of Nations. His immensely stimulating and controversial ideas were roundly condemned by the defenders of the Versailles Treaty because they amounted, in essence, to a repudiation of the treaty at the moment of its birth.

Equally shattering as the economic provisions of the Versailles Treaty were the terms relating to the future of the Germany military. The German army was to be reduced in size to a volunteer force of one hundred thousand men. Of these, no more than four thousand could be officers, and their term of service was limited to twenty-five years, while that of the enlisted personnel was limited to twelve years. The strength of this small volunteer force was to be further impaired by depriving it of tanks, aircraft, and other "offensive" weapons. Similarly, the German navy was to be dismantled except for a token surface-vessel force not exceeding ten thousand tons. The German battle fleet was to be delivered into Allied hands, but when the German officers who had taken the fleet to the naval harbor of Scapa Flow in the Orkney Islands learned of the fate that was in store for their ships, they cheated the Allies of their prize by scuttling fifty of the sixty-eight ships.[16] Finally, with an eye toward the heart of the German military establishment, the treaty called for the abolition of the general staff, the war college, and all cadet schools. Adding insult to injury, the peacemakers also demanded that Germany hand over the kaiser and other war leaders for trial on charges of violating the laws of war.

The End of Money

[In the early 1920s] Germany's economic position was deteriorating daily as a result of runaway inflation. These inflationary difficulties stemmed primarily from a series of imprudent government fiscal policies that originated in World War I.[17] The German government did not try to finance the war by taxation but rather by floating internal bonds. In addition, the government also removed restrictions on the circulation of notes not covered by gold reserves. . . . As war costs increased, the government resorted more and more to the printing presses, driving up the amount of currency in circulation and devaluing the mark. By 1918 the mark stood at half the gold parity of 1914. The war hid the problem of inflation, but the pressures of defeat, coupled with the economic burdens imposed on Germany by the Versailles Treaty, brought the problem to the surface in dramatic terms. The whole German economy was now cracking under the impact of years of deficit spending and burdensome obligations imposed by the Allies.

The immediate cause of the collapse of the German economy was the invasion of the Ruhr by the French on January 11, 1923. The French Prime Minister, Raymond Poincaré, was a Germanophobe who strongly believed that the Germans were willfully deceiving the Allies that they could not faithfully meet their financial obligations. The French had already spent billions of francs in restoring their war torn areas, expecting the Germans to pay for every penny of it. Poincaré adamantly rejected [German Chancellor Wilhelm] Cuno's request for a moratorium on reparations payments and then tried to galvanize other Allied powers into supporting military intervention. Neither the British nor the Americans, however, believed that an Allied invasion of the Ruhr was justified. Poincaré pressed on regardless, merely waiting for a legal pretext. This came when the Reparations Commission declared Germany in default on the delivery of 140,000 telegraph poles.

On January 11, 1923, a French-Belgian force invaded the Ruhr, seized its industries and mines, and stirred up separatist feelings aimed at further weakening the unity of the Reich.[18] French occupying troops acted harshly and brutally. Bloody clashes were the order of the day. The German government responded to the French invasion with a policy of "passive resistance," which meant that all economic activity came to a standstill in the Ruhr. The German economy now became unglued because the government, in an effort to subsidize the Ruhr workers who had gone on strike, resorted to printing more and more paper money. Inflation reached fantastic heights; unemployment soared. Even with the best intentions, the German government simply could not meet all of its social obligations; it was already chafing under the weight of its obligations to the Allies, to its war veterans, to the unemployed, to the aged.

Germans were caught in a vortex from which there seemed no escape. The world was upside-down: a simple penny postage stamp cost 5 million marks, an egg 80 million, a pound of meat 3.2 billion, a pound of butter 6 billion, a pound of potatoes 50 million, a glass of beer 150 million. Prices changed from day to day, prompting people to rush to the stores armed with satchels of worthless money to buy simple necessities.

To many Germans this period seemed like an economic apocalypse. Konrad Heiden has referred to it as the "end of money,"[19] the end of roseate visions of material affluence, and the end of all secular faiths in progress. We might add that it also seemed like the end of faith in government, its good word, and its assurance that the savings of ordinary citizens would be protected. For nine years, Germans had sacrificed their lives and their savings to the government. In return, the government had squandered a third of the national wealth in a futile war as a result of which war loans, savings, and investments were now worthless. The savings of thrifty middle-class Germans were wiped out. It was not uncommon for German savers to receive polite letters from bank managers informing them that "the bank deeply regrets that it can no longer administer your deposit of sixty-eight thousand marks, since the costs are all out of proportion to the capital. We are therefore taking the liberty of returning your capital. Since we have no banknotes of small enough denominations at our disposal, we have rounded out the sum to one million marks. Enclosure: one 1,000,000 mark bill."[20] To add insult to injury, the envelope was adorned by a canceled five million mark postage stamp.

While the majority of middle-class Germans were ruined by the collapse of 1923, never fully regaining their trust in the government, a few clever financial manipulators grew fabulously wealthy by securing massive bank credits, promptly investing in "physical values" (real estate, businesses), and repaying the debts with devalued money. It was in this manner that Hugo Stinnes, already a wealthy man before 1923, bought up at random large numbers of businesses, including banks, hotels, newspapers, paper mills, and so on. Stinnes affected the frugal mentality of the clerk and coal miner he had once been, but there were hundreds like him who spent garishly and contributed much to the growing atmosphere of moral decadence and cynicism, an atmosphere that has been so vividly captured in the music, art, and popular entertainment of the 1920s. While a few grew rich, the country

as a whole steadily deteriorated. Unemployment increased, farmers hoarded their produce, manufacturing dropped, and millions of thrifty savers lost all of their savings.

On August 12, 1923, Ebert appointed Gustav Stresemann, leader of the German People's Party, as chancellor of the new government. The new chancellor, destined to become one of the most important statesmen of the Weimar Republic, faced staggering problems: the Ruhr was occupied by the French; Communist-Socialist regimes had taken power in Thuringia and Saxony; Communist insurrections plagued Hamburg; Bavaria had fallen into the hands of right-wing reactionaries who threatened to secede from the Reich; Germany's eastern borders were threatened by the Poles; and the mark stood at 4.6 trillion [U.S.] to the dollar. It was in this volatile atmosphere that an obscure corporal of World War I, leader of a growing right-wing party, determined to overthrow the Weimar Republic. His name was Adolf Hitler.

Mein Kampf

Hitler's worldview was not based on formal academic traditions, but was primarily rooted in pseudo-history and mythology. It was a pervasive mood based on atavistic forces rather than on formal systems or logically articulated concepts. Its dynamic force, in other words, resided in myths and tribal prejudices. This is why all attempts to construct a formal lineage of intellectual precursors to Nazism—Fichte, Hegel, Treitschke, Wagner, Nietzsche—have been simplistic and reductionist. Hitler and other spokesmen of Nazi ideology were anti-intellectuals who were motivated largely by propagandistic purposes. Their affinity was closer to those minds that dwelled in the demimonde of popular prejudices and cranky opinions (racists, occultists, health faddists, and so on). It was from *völkisch* racial tracts that Hitler derived much of his information about the world. Although *Mein Kampf* [the book Hitler wrote in the mid-1920s] makes reference to a few famous German authors, these references are invariably misleading and distorted. The ideas he derived from them are generally altered to fit the Procrustean bed of his own hate-filled mentality.

In sum, Hitler's *Weltanschauung* was a system of prejudices rather than a philosophy based on well-warranted premises, objective truth-testing, and logically derived conclusions. Hitler was well aware of this. In politics, he believed, there is greater cognitive value in myths and feelings than in science or reason. Approaching *Mein Kampf* from this perspective, we can readily identify four major prejudices: a racist interpretation of history, a social Darwinist view of life and nature, a preference for the militaristic style of life, and a belief in transforming Germany into a world power.

The bedrock of Hitler's worldview, what he called his "granite foundation," was the belief in the biological and cultural superiority of the Aryan race. This belief formed the basis of his philosophy of history and his political ideology. Hitler was a crude naturalist who explained human nature on the analogy of nature. His concept of nature, however, was not the benign view of the eighteenth-century Enlightenment but the cruel Darwinian view that nature is red in tooth and claw and always favors the strongest or fittest. Moreover, he assumed a law of nature that promotes what he termed "higher breeding." In order to promote human progress, nature encourages the stronger specimen to mate with the stronger, while discouraging the propagation of the weak. By interfering in this process, we sin against the natural order of things.

Hitler actually believed that nature was endowed with an intelligible design; he was con-

vinced, for example, that "nature thinks aristocratically," makes "certain corrective decisions about the racial purity of mortal beings," does not like bastards, and "inexorably revenges the transgressions of her laws"[21] [subsequent references to page numbers for quotations from *Mein* Kampf appear in the text in parentheses]. Hitler seems to have based these sweeping generalizations on little more than uninformed prejudices about higher forces. In fact, throughout *Mein Kampf* he is preoccupied with abstract forces such as nature, fate (*Schicksal*), providence (*Vorsehung*), the Goddess of Misery, the Goddess of History, and so on. It goes without saying that these forces support the truth of his convictions.

He assumes that the strength and weakness of man rest solely in the blood (469). There is superior blood and inferior blood; unless we artificially interfere in nature's aristocratic design, the superior blood will inevitably overcome the inferior blood. In Hitler's view the best blood is obtained when animals mate solely with representatives of their own species—titmouse seeking titmouse . . . (389). Any crossing between beings of not quite the same type produces inherently weaker or infertile types. Strength, resilience, and intelligence are the result of racial purity, struggle, and the mating of superior types with each other.

Since human nature is part of nature, the same biological laws of racial purity are applicable. Here, too, nature encourages sharp separations between the racial groups, while also promoting uniform characteristics within each group. Thus the white, black, or yellow person seeks his or her own kind. Since human racial groups are qualitatively different, it follows that crossbreeding undermines racial purity and produces inferior offspring. The worst blood defiling occurs when the Jew mates with the Aryan. Hitler seems to feel that this almost amounts to mating across species, a biological absurdity because no human group has speciated.

Hitler divided the human race into three distinct and qualitatively different groups: Aryan culture-founders, culture-bearers, and culture-destroyers (389). This taxonomy rested on two essential criteria—self-serving ethnocentrism and the racist belief that skin pigmentation is a primary determinant of cultural achievement. Only the Aryan creates culture; he is the Prometheus of mankind "out of whose bright forehead springs the divine spark of genius at all times" (389). Asiatic people, Hitler conceded, possess high culture, but only because the Aryan has provided the creative impetus for it. In the absence of Aryan influences, the Japanese, for example, would fall back into the sleep from which the Aryans aroused them in the nineteenth century. Other racial groups are equally uncreative, and Africans are incapable of even being culture-bearers. In an obviously irritated mood, Hitler denounced all well-meaning efforts to raise primitive blacks to the level of culture-bearers, arguing that this would have to be at the expense of retarding the progress of able Aryans, an effort that would be as self-defeating as it would be unnatural (640).

As to the Jew, he is without genuine culture because he is not capable of creating one. The Jew merely exploits what others have created; he is a pure parasite feeding on the body of healthy cultures, "a sponger who, like a harmful bacillus, spreads out more and more if only a favorable medium invites him to do so" (419–20). The Jew has always lived a furtive existence in other people's communities, where he secretly built up his own state under the guise of a religious community. His great lie, Hitler insisted, is that he is only religiously different, while in other respects being as German as a German or as English as an Englishman. On the contrary, Hitler was convinced that the Jews are "always a people with definite racial qualities and never a religion" (421).

Moreover, Hitler also believed in the existence of a Jewish world conspiracy, as foretold in *The Protocols of the Elders of Zion*. In his lengthy survey of the secret machinations of the Jews over the ages, Hitler revealed that he passionately believed in a conspiratorial view of history according to which the Jews are the real causal forces behind events. In other words, the great changes in European society are not directly the result of great economic transformations, revolutions, or wars—the sort of events covered by ordinary historians—but the result of secret connivings by malicious Jews behind the scenes. Thus, every destructive event is unmasked by Hitler's paranoid mind as being plotted by a scheming Jew, whether it is the rapacious money-lending Jew, the Jew as court Svengali, the Jew as bleeding-heart liberal, the Jew as parliamentary democrat, the Jew as pacifist, or the Jew as Bolshevik. The end result is the same: the Jew incites social divisiveness, hollows out a healthy community from within, and thus prepares the way for the final takeover of the world.

The irrational logic of this argument led Hitler to conclude that the Jew must be the personification of the devil, the spirit who always subverts (447). As a consequence of his delusional system of ideas, Hitler could literally envision "bow-legged Jew bastards" lurking behind the corners of dark alleys in order to rape and therefore defile young Aryan girls (448). This and other passages in *Mein Kampf*, especially the long section in chapter 10 of book 1 dealing with syphilis, clearly point to a potentially malignant pathology. The whole book reverberates with dark ruminations about blood defiling and blood poisoning by demonic Jews. The author rants and raves about nature-abhorring bastards and appeals to our sacred obligation to keep the blood pure. Here are only a few samples (with corresponding page numbers) of Hitler's prejudiced epithets, describing the Jews as: Personifications of the devil (447), dealers of Aryan blood (448, 826–27), ferment of decomposition (666, 952), blood-suckers and vampires (426–27, 451), purveyors of prostitution and syphilis (78), rapists of Aryan women (448, 826), harmful bacillus (420), maggots (75), poisoners (76, 312), pestilence (76), bow-legged bastards (619), foul-smelling creatures (75), fungi (160), regents of the stock exchange (930), great masters of lying (313, 412), members of a different race (74), wire-pullers (772, 911).

Hitler was passionately convinced that a people's historical greatness depended upon the purity of its blood. Whenever a people permits itself to become bastardized, it *"sins against the will of eternal Providence"* (452; emphasis added). Elsewhere, he called race pollution the original sin (928). Although the Jew has seriously undermined the German blood and spirit, the German people can recover its racial purity by ruthlessly weeding out inferior types from within and by preventing alien races from poisoning the group from without.

The *völkisch* state, therefore, has a clear-cut mission: to breed the most racially pure, fertile, and healthy specimens, so that, at length, the entire national group participates in the blessing of a "high-bred racial treasure" (609). From these strictures it is only a short step to Himmler's racial stud farms, the ss elite, and the extermination of inferior breeds (Gypsies, Asiatic inferiors, cripples, the mentally retarded, and Jews). The antidote to what Hitler perceived to be a clear and present danger of race pollution was to keep the blood pure and to eliminate the Jew before the Jew destroyed the German. To Hitler, this was an "all or nothing" proposition because the Jew is the "great agitator for the complete destruction of

Germany. Wherever in the world we read about attacks on Germany, Jews are their fabricators" (906). Germany must therefore devise a state policy in order to eliminate the Jew. . . .

In sketching the future Nazi state, Hitler made it clear at the outset that the *völkisch* state must be based on the principle of personality rather than the decisions of majorities. In other words, the state must be organized like a military chain of command culminating in one man who decides for the whole (669–70). Effective organizations, whether political, economic, or educational, are governed best when governed by strong leaders. Men of genius are never born out of general elections; they are bred. The Western democratic process, he argued, encouraged mediocrity, lack of responsibility, and habitual obstructionism. He rejected the idea that every individual had a constitutional right to participate in shared governance; only the select few have or ever will exercise meaningful power in any system, even in those systems that are ostensibly based on majority rule. The masses must not be deluded into believing that they can actually exercise power. This must be done for them by gifted leaders who rise from their midst and express their longings while also expressing the good of the nation. The interest of the people is not always synonymous with the good of the nation; in fact, the masses often crave selfishly, so that by giving them rights without corresponding responsibilities, they will tend to take from the state rather than give to it.

In opposition to what he termed decadent Western democracy, Hitler proposed to establish a "German type of democracy" by which a leader is freely chosen by the people and then given full responsibilities to do what he has to do (116). There would be no obstructionist parties, state institutions, or special-interest groups to thwart the mandate that has been given to the leader by the *Volk*—in short, there would be no cumbersome countervailing powers to executive leadership at all. That such unlimited executive power has historically resulted in tyranny is conveniently ignored. The fact is that Hitler had no conception of the state at all, other than in the form of the personal dictatorship he craved for himself. In his racially pure state, power would be exercised by a charismatically gifted leader who ruled through a one-party system and delegated dictatorial power to his subordinates. It would be a vertical system of dictatorial empowerment, starting with the führer at the top of the pyramid and extending downward by way of intermediate führers right down to the father führer in each German family. . . .

In his remarks on foreign policy, Hitler took a strident pan-German position, arguing that the future of Germany resided in the conquest of living space. He differed with many prewar imperialists, however, in rejecting the acquisition of overseas colonies on the grounds that Germany was not a traditional sea power and should not become entangled again in a major conflict with the British Empire. Imperial Germany had been right in pursuing an expansionist policy, but wrong in pursuing it overseas. No sacrifice should have been too great to gain England's favor because England is a great Germanic nation with as equal a claim to territorial expansion as Germany. Hitler believed that England and Germany were natural allies, provided they left each other alone to pursue their territorial ambitions in different parts of the world. It is not entirely clear how or why Hitler expected the English to support German dominance on the Continent, especially since he was well aware of the traditional British policy of favoring a balance of power on the Continent. His views of England consisted of a combination of wishful thinking and misinformation. He assumed

that the English regarded the French as a greater threat than they did the Germans because the war had made [the French] the strongest power on the Continent and also because the French, like the English, were a colonial power, and thus a serious overseas competitor to English imperial interests. He realized that the English did not want to see any continental state rise to the position of a world power, but he also believed that the English would probably support a German world power whose economic and territorial interests did not infringe upon England's overseas empire.

As to the French, they are "the German people's irreconcilable mortal enemy" (902). The English might not want Germany to be a world power, but the French desire that Germany have no power at all. The French, he thought, posed a mortal danger because Jewish financial interests there were working hand in glove with rabid chauvinists to destroy Germany as a nation. He also saw the French people becoming more and more "negrofied," thereby also posing a profound racial threat to Germany (907–8). He strongly believed that French policy toward Germany had not changed since Louis XIV, namely to encourage the balkanization of Germany into small states and to build up a solid hegemony over the Continent. In order to thwart France's grand design, Germany must search for powerful allies, regain its military greatness, and find new soil and territory in order to support its population. In *Mein Kampf*, he was quite explicit about all three: Germany, he argued, should align itself with England and Italy against France, break the shackles of Versailles, and search for *Lebensraum* (living space) in that part of the world where its ancestors had traditionally pursued their imperial ambitions— eastern Europe.[22]

Germany's natural sphere of interest, Hitler believed, was in eastern Europe and the vast spaces of Russia (179, 892). A growing race requires space in order to achieve national greatness and attain the status of a world power. If Germany confined itself to the limited space allotted to it by the Versailles Treaty, it would cease to be a great power in the world. Hitler was a believer in the conventional Eurocentric mythology that European powers could rule the world provided that they pursued a ruthless policy of territorial expansion and economic growth. In fact, he assumed a direct causal connection between territorial expansion by force of arms and economic growth, rejecting the liberal democratic view that nations could also be great by pursuing a peaceful policy of free enterprise, as was subsequently proved by postwar Germany and Japan.

Hitler rationalized these blatantly imperialistic views in purely Machiavellian and frequently crude social Darwinian terms, holding that "might alone makes right" (949), that "one makes alliances only for fighting" (959), that nature does not know political borders, and that conquering the vast spaces of Russia is racially and geopolitically right because the area is populated only by the "scum of humanity"—Jews, Asiatic inferiors, and Communists (959–60). In fighting Russia, Hitler believed, one would be able to reduce two of the deadliest poisons in one full swoop—Jews and Communists.

Hitler's aims, then, were crystal-clear: domestically, he proposed to breed a higher race, weeding out "impurities of the blood" and "un-German" attitudes (liberal, democratic, pacifistic, Communistic, and so on), while internationally promising to elevate Germany to the ranks of a world power. In fact, in the chapter on future alliances after the war, Hitler delivered both a prophecy and a deadly threat to Germans and to the world by saying that "Germany will be either a world power or will not be at all" (950).

Hitler was also quite explicit on the means by which these grand visions were to be attained—that is, how he would mold a relatively small nation, limited in resources and manpower, and transform it into the strongest power in the world. He would nationalize and fanaticize the masses through unrelenting propaganda until, at last, shaped into a superbly organized fighting force, the German masses would carry out their sacred racial mission. The chief strategy in Hitler's arsenal of gaining, maintaining, and expanding power was propaganda. Without propaganda, it is impossible to reach the heart of the people and imbue them with a sense of purpose or mission. Effective propaganda, Hitler believed, did not rest on logic or reason but rather on faith and emotions. The masses are not comfortable with ambiguities or skeptical habits of mind; they crave certainty. In order to reach their hearts, where the deeper convictions are always rooted, it is necessary to teach them a fanatically one-sided doctrine; for once the masses have found a political faith, it is very difficult to undermine it. Knowledge is more easily undermined than faith. History teaches us, Hitler insisted, that the "driving force of the most important changes in this world has been found less in a scientific knowledge animating the masses, but rather in a fanaticism dominating them and in a hysteria which drove them forward" (968).

The success of a movement, Hitler felt, did not depend on enlightening the voters but rather on the manipulation of mass affections or disaffections. Hitler, therefore, made no distinction between education and propaganda; the two were virtually synonymous in his mind. However, propaganda is simply a means to an end rather than an end in itself. The end of politics, of course, is power—the alpha and omega of life itself. Propaganda can be effective only if it promotes a firm set of ideological positions. Any technique, no matter how reprehensible, is justified in promoting such ideological convictions. Since politics in the modern age has become largely quantitative by appealing to the largest number of voters, the propagandist must always address the capacities inherent in the group mind or mentality, which is just another way of saying that the masses are inherently limited in their mental capacities and can understand only simple ideas: "All propaganda has to be popular and has to adapt its spiritual level to the perception of the least intelligent of those toward whom it intends to direct itself. Therefore its spiritual level has to be screwed the lower, the greater the mass of people which one wants to attract. . . . The more . . . it exclusively considers the feelings of the masses, the more striking will be its success" (232–33).

It is another function of propaganda to hammer home, by endless repetition if necessary, a few clearly articulated notions, preferably in vivid pictorial images. Moreover, since propaganda aims at persuasion rather than instruction, it is far more effective to appeal to the emotions than to the rational capacities of crowds. This can always be done more effectively through the spoken word and in settings where masses of people can be reached. The heart assents more easily than the mind, especially when a demon speechmaker unleashes the seductive powers of emotionality. Hitler believed that crowds are more impressionable and gullible than individuals; they are apt to believe the unbelievable. In tact, they swallow the big lie more easily than the small lie, which would suggest that the biggest promises or claims are more persuasive than the humbler truths. Hitler also held that "people, in an overwhelming majority, are so feminine in their nature and attitude that their activities and thoughts are motivated less by sober consideration than by feeling and sentiment" (237). . . .

In the end, people are persuaded effectively only when the last vestiges of doubt have been removed from their minds. This cannot be accomplished by objective presentation of all sides of an issue, but rather by the insistence that only one side is the absolute truth. The task of propaganda, Hitler insisted, is to stress exclusively the doctrine one is advocating and to contrast it sharply with its false alternative. In political discourse there are no shades of grey but only the positive or the negative, love or hate, right or wrong, truth or the lie (236–37).

Critical or analytical habits of mind, at any rate, were dismissed by Hitler as Jewish or intellectual and thus unwanted in the *völkisch* state. In several appallingly anti-intellectual passages, Hitler let it be known that he would change the whole direction of German education by getting rid of intellectuals and by emphasizing the education of the will rather than the brain. Intellectuals are a source of grave danger to group cohesion because they lack the will to believe by instinct. They are overeducated apes "stuffed with knowledge and intellect, but bare of any sound instinct and devoid of all energy and courage" (642–43). Their theoretical knowledge estranges them from the healthy folk below, so that what is required in the *völkisch* state is a periodic infusion of healthy blood from the masses into the ranks of enervated intellectuals. . . .

Such attitudes were undoubtedly based on Hitler's own failures in the Austrian school system, but they also expressed widespread resentments with an elitist and authoritarian school system in general. Although Hitler's rhetoric against the German-Austrian school system contained an undertone of crude egalitarianism, it was in actual fact elitist to the core, except with a different emphasis: instead of promoting a caste of intellectual mandarins recruited from the upper classes, Hitler proposed to groom a classless elite from the ranks of the racially pure and politically correct candidates. Among themselves, the chosen elite would practice a kind of democratic camaraderie, the sort of fraternal experience that Hitler associated with the trenches in World War I. In fact, the education of the trenches should serve as a model for the education of the new army-state.

It does not require hindsight to understand the implications of Hitler's ideas. Anyone who bothered to study *Mein Kampf* with an open mind before Hitler's seizure of power could not have had any doubts as to what would be in store for Germany if this man were entrusted with absolute power. . . .

The Breakdown of Parliamentary Democracy

In December 1929 the German government was in a tailspin of financial calamities, facing a shortfall of 1.5 billion marks in anticipated revenues while at the same time trying to finance an unemployment insurance program whose annual cost, calculated in 1928 on the basis of 800,000 unemployed, had now more than tripled under the impact of 2.8 million idle workers. The financial crisis, in turn, triggered a political crisis that went far beyond the issue of unemployment insurance to the very breakdown of parliamentary democracy itself. The controversy over unemployment insurance, which split the great coalition government of Hermann Müller, was just the opening round in a lengthy and divisive battle of political self-destruction. When the government ran out of money by the end of 1929, the Reich finance minister, Rudolf Hilferding, proposed a tax on tobacco and an increase in insurance premiums from 3 to 3.5 percent.[23] Although a Social Democrat, Hilferding resorted to strict conservative fiscal policies of raising taxes and slashing spending, measures that caused an immediate howl of protest from

diverse interest groups and led to a humiliating defeat of his program in the Reichstag.

However, the republic was not threatened, as a current joke had it, by a half-percentage increase in insurance rates; rather, the threat came from the renewed outbreak of political extremism on both the left and the right. If the German people had possessed confidence in the republic and its leaders, the flood of economic bad news that now began to inundate them might have been more bearable; but the sad fact was that even before the Great Depression, the German people displayed little trust in their democratic institutions. The initial assault on democracy, however, was not orchestrated by Adolf Hitler, who certainly benefited from it, but by political intriguers in the German military.[24] A few powerful military schemers, notably General [Kurt von] Schleicher, undermined the Müller government in two ways: first, by persuading Hindenburg not to empower the chancellor to pass his fiscal program by emergency decree, thus almost certainly assuring his downfall, and, second, by actively promoting Heinrich Brüning as Müller's successor. . . .

The new chancellor was a bald, bespectacled, and ascetic-looking patrician who projected the persona of an austere Jesuit priest, which may explain why the crafty Schleicher referred to him as "Ignaz." Born in Münster, the son of a Catholic vinegar merchant, Brüning had studied law, philosophy, and political economy at various German universities, graduating with a doctoral degree in political economy from the University of Bonn in 1914. He spent his formative years not only in the academy but also in the trenches, serving his country during the war as a commander of a small machine-gun unit on the western front. The experience of witnessing the deaths of many men under his command instilled in him a Spartan sense of duty and a strong conviction that the greatest virtue resided in holding out in the face of even insurmountable obstacles. . . . Although Brüning was an honorable man, he was not an inspiring leader. A confirmed bachelor, the new chancellor was by temperament a taciturn and suspicious man who avoided the glare of publicity and shied away from intimate human contacts. Brüning was, at best, a competent midlevel civil servant, comfortable in the world of party caucuses and small political circles. As Heinz Höhne has pointed out, his natural impulse was to solve problems in bureaucratic-authoritarian terms by relying on personal contacts and special connections, plotting his strategy in the backroom like a chess master but knowing nothing about the feelings, prejudices, phobias, and hatreds of ordinary people.[25]

The new chancellor was also politically out of touch with many ordinary Germans. Brüning was actually a romantic conservative with a fondness for lost causes such as restoring the Hohenzollern monarchy. Idolizing the aged Field Marshal von Hindenburg, perhaps more the legend than the man, he envisioned the old man as a stalking horse to a restored monarchy. He believed that this could be accomplished by extending the president's term of office for life and having him serve as a sort of interim crowned head, a *Reichsverweser* [Regent], until the day when the monarchy would be reestablished. Brüning's fantasy bore little resemblance to reality, except that Hindenburg was in fact his political raison d'être; for without the field marshal's support, his government would have quickly collapsed, as time would prove later, because it was not based on broad parliamentary support.

In terms of economics, the new chancellor was essentially a laissez-faire liberal who, like Herbert Hoover in the United States, believed that the economic crisis was merely one of those cyclical downturns that would eventually bottom out and reverse itself without active government interference. Deploring the bloated welfare state as detrimental to economic growth, Brüning favored deflationary policies aimed at reducing taxes and government spending.[26] Although this initially endeared him to big business, his actual fiscal policies, greatly modified under the pressure of competing interest groups, alienated sizable elements within both business and labor. . . .

With the help of Hindenburg and his conservative retainers, Brüning effectively destroyed the democratic process. By resorting to the extraconstitutional device of Article 48 as a primary means of governance, Brüning tacitly accepted unconstitutionality as a preferred alternative to parliamentary democracy. At the very time of worsening economic crisis, he dissolved the Reichstag, passed his program by presidential decree, and recklessly called for new elections, to be held in September 1930. With the benefit of hindsight, we can see that Brüning had committed several fatal errors: first, he had relegated parliament and parties to the political periphery and thus reduced the chances of collective decision making; second, by sanctioning governance by emergency decree, he tied himself dangerously close to the mercurial whims of the aging field marshal; and third, by calling elections at a time of heightened radicalism and widespread alienation, he was inviting the further growth of political extremism, as was born out by the fateful election of September 14, 1930.

The Nazi Upsurge and the End of Brüning

Hitler knew that his hour had struck with the coming of the Great Depression. Relying on his uncanny political intuition, he tirelessly built up a close psychological rapport with those who had been hurt by the depression. He did this by presenting himself as an ordinary and caring man who empathized with the suffering of the German people and promised them radical change. His appeal was not to a particular class or ideology but to the German people as a whole. He soothed middle-class fears of lawlessness by promising to restore law and order, gratified conservatives with promises of a national resurgence, pleased the military by evoking visions of a splendid new army, and confidently reassured the workers that no one would ever face poverty and unemployment under National Socialism. Above all, he reminded all of his audiences that they were not to blame for the crisis because they were victims of the system. He knew the agents of their suffering, could identify the culprits, and with the aid of the German people would wage a war of liberation, ridding the German people of their tormentors and leading them to a glorious future.

With all the remarkable energy he could muster, Hitler began to woo the German people in speech after speech, traveling the length and breadth of Germany; and behind him was the ubiquitous Nazi Party, a veritable perpetual motion machine that was drowning out all other parties in the intensity of its propaganda, the commitment of its rank and file members, and the organizational talents of its leaders.

Young people were particularly attracted by the movement's visionary zeal; they identified with its radical approaches and admired its innovative tactics of building mass support. They joined in droves. Membership in the SA increased by leaps and bounds, and it attracted Germans from all walks of life—the unemployed, students, former veterans, workers, and farmers. Its reputation began to acquire a certain magical quality because those who joined believed that the SA would groom the future saviors of Germany. By 1930, thanks to the mythmaking genius of Dr.

Goebbels, the SA was also beginning to produce martyrs who could serve as shining examples to future storm troopers.

In February 1930 a young Berlin SA leader, Horst Wessel, was killed by a Communist. Wessel was the son of a prominent Protestant minister, then deceased, who had defied his mother by joining the SA, abandoning his legal studies at the University of Berlin, and consorting with a prostitute with whom he had fallen in love.[27] On January 14, 1930, the prostitute's former pimp, accompanied by several Red Front comrades, broke into Wessel's apartment and shot him in the mouth during a scuffle. Mortally wounded, Wessel lingered on for several days in a hospital. Joseph Goebbels, among others, made a daily pilgrimage to his hospital bed. It turned out that Wessel had published a stirring poem in Goebbels's newspaper, *Angriff*; the poem, entitled "*Die Fahne hoch*" (Raise high the flag), would become the battle hymn not only of the SA but of the Nazi movement as a whole. When Wessel finally succumbed to his injuries, Goebbels staged an elaborate funeral for the dead SA man and transfigured him into a national martyr. The carefully arranged solemnity of the funeral, replete with a roll call for the dead, lugubrious rhetoric, and sentimental pathos, turned into a bloody brawl as Communists threw stones over the cemetery wall and sent the mourners ducking for cover behind the tombstones. Yet all this was grist for Goebbels's propaganda mill. Now he could really "beat the living shit out of the murderers," as he had previously written, and excoriate the red mob: "As the coffin came to rest in the cool ground there went up outside the gates the depraved cry of the subhuman. . . . The departed, still with us, raised his weary hand and beckoned into the shimmering distance: Forward over the graves! At the end of the road lies Germany."[28] Such sentimental schmaltz for the dead would later became standard fare by which the Nazis tried to pull at the heartstrings of gullible Germans. . . .

The election of September 14, 1930, represented a turning point in the fortunes of the Nazi Party. When the votes were in, the Nazis had scored a major breakthrough, receiving 6.4 million votes (18 percent of the total vote) and seating 107 out of 577 deputies in the Reichstag. This made the Nazi Party the second largest party in the Reichstag. The Social Democrats were still the largest party, but their representation in the Reichstag since the last election in 1928 had dropped from 153 to 143 seats. The third largest party was the Communist Party, which also increased its representation by polling 4.6 million votes and receiving 77 seats in the Reichstag. The liberal parties of the middle, except for the Center Party, were all seriously crippled by the election. . . . The smaller parties on the right, on whom Brüning had been counting, lost heavily also. . . .

The election clearly mirrored the extreme polarization of German politics and also indicated that the enemies of the republic were gaining the upper hand over its defenders. Simple arithmetic ruled out the construction of some form of prorepublican government coalition.[29] With the growth of extremism on both the left and the right it was impossible for Brüning to command a majority in the Reichstag.

The Nazi upsurge can be attributed primarily to the depression that had ruined many German businesses and led to a tragic increase in unemployment. The depression, in turn, stirred up a pervasive fear of impending political chaos leading to an acute crisis in confidence in the democratic system. Many Germans blamed the system for the crisis, laying the depression squarely at the feet of what they perceived to be a failing democracy. As a result, the German middle class, already

alienated from the republic by the crisis of 1923, stigmatized the "system" as criminal and incompetent. All sorts of antidemocratic ideas, articulated in bold and urgent terms by conservative pundits, came thundering down on perplexed Germans from all sorts of newspapers, books, and journals. These spokesmen of the conservative right argued that the coming of the masses in politics signaled what Edgar J. Jung called the "*Herrschaft der Minderwertigen*" (rule by the inferior) and the institutionalization of mediocrity and vulgarity.[30] They indicted the whole range of democratic forms—constitutions, parties, elections—as unsuited to Germany's traditions. They scorned democratic principles as empty shibboleths fabricated by parties or demagogues to disguise their self-interest or their lust for power. Democracy, according to these spokesmen, was inherently contradictory because an amorphous mass of people could not actually define goals, set policies, or literally govern itself. Elitism, they insisted, was a fact of life that could not be covered up by rhetorical fig leaves pleasing to the masses. Societies have been and always will be governed by elites, by the stronger, more powerful, and more gifted sort of people. Even in democracies we find that the wealthy few usually pull the real levers of power. It follows, as Oswald Spengler put it, that "the fundamental right of the mass to choose its own representatives remains pure theory, for in actuality every developed organization recruits itself."[31] For replacements for this corrupt Western-type of democracy, these antidemocratic spokesmen looked variously to a restoration of the monarchy, a dictatorial presidential government, a military junta, an authoritarian model based on Spengler's notion of "Prussian socialism," or a "German-type" of plebiscitarian democracy in which the mass entrusts its fate to a charismatic dictator.

The Nazis were undoubtedly beneficiaries of popular antidemocratic theories that they themselves did not create. The election of September 14, 1930, had shown the existence on both the right and the left of a longing for charismatic leadership, a wish to dismantle the egalitarian welfare state, a desire for an autocratic state run by civil-servant experts, a craving for dictatorship, and a longing for a harmonious folk community (*Volksgemeinschaft*) based on racial Utopias. Hitler exploited these fears and longings; he did not create them.

Nor did Hitler alone create the preconditions that led to the collapse of democracy. As previously seen, the use of extraparliamentary dictatorship was initiated by Brüning and Hindenburg and subsequently enlarged by Papen and Schleicher. In other words, Germany had been well prepared for dictatorial rule before Hitler became chancellor.

The September election produced an immediate bandwagon effect on the Nazi movement. As Joachim Fest observed, it even became chic to join the party, particularly after one of the kaiser's sons, Prince August Wilhelm ("Auwi"), became a member.[32] . . .

On January 8, 1932, Joseph Goebbels noted in his dairy that "the chess game for power has begun,"[33] a judgment that was certainly vindicated by subsequent events. The year 1932 was densely packed with momentous events, but the real chess moves—the ones that would propel Hitler into power—took place behind the scenes in government offices or private drawing rooms. Hitler turned out to be a superb chess player on both the public and the private level; and when the year was over, his goal of checkmating his opponents was within his grasp. . . .

The year 1932 would test Hitler's political skills on many occasions, especially in the public limelight. There were no less than five grueling elections in 1932—four national elections and one

important state election in Prussia—exerting further strains on the democratic process at a time when most German voters were more concerned with the cancerous growth of unemployment than the electoral process. By the end of the year German voters were thoroughly tired of the machinations of parties, the dissimulations of politicians, and the whole democratic process itself. They longed for an end to the political squabbles; and sadly, many Germans now looked to the Nazis to liberate them from further political involvement. As one perceptive observer put it: "National Socialism was a revulsion by my friends against parliamentary politics, parliamentary debate, parliamentary government—against all the higgling and the haggling of the parties, their coalitions, their confusions, and their connivings. It was the final fruit of the common man's repudiation of the rascals. Its motif was, Throw them all out."[34]

President Hindenburg's term of office was scheduled to expire on May 5, 1932. It took considerable pressure by his immediate entourage to persuade the eighty-four-year-old president, now in failing health and showing disturbing signs of senility, to run again for public office for the good of the fatherland. The old man at first demurred, citing old age and failing vigor, but eventually saw merit in the argument that he was probably the last bulwark against political anarchy. However, his hope to be spared another election was dashed when Brüning failed to gain the support of the Reichstag for his plan to extend the president's term of office without new elections. Accordingly, Germans geared up for a major presidential election, to be held on March 13, 1932. The Communists fielded their leader Ernst Thälmann, a former transportation worker and dedicated Moscow operative for Joseph Stalin, while the nationalists chose Theodor Duesterberg, second-in-command of the paramilitary *Stahlhelm*. It was not until three weeks before the elections were scheduled that a fourth candidate stepped forward—Adolf Hitler. Hitler had been a "stateless" person since 1925 and was therefore ineligible for public office unless he obtained German citizenship. He did this by first finding a law that stated that Reich citizenship was automatically conferred on all those who held a state citizenship. Next, on February 26, Hitler finagled an appointment for himself as a councilor (*Regierungsrat*) in the Nazi-controlled State of Brunswick; because the appointment automatically carried with it citizenship in that state, Hitler was now also a full-fledged citizen of the Reich.

The campaign was bitter and divisive. Hitler toured Germany by car from one end to the other, promising to wage a campaign "such as the world has never seen before." His stamina was remarkable. In fact, during 1932 he gave a total of 209 public speeches, something no candidate has ever done before or since.[35] Fifty thousand phonograph records of Hitler's speeches were made and distributed; propaganda movies were quickly unloaded on theater owners throughout Germany. Joseph Goebbels, who had been the driving force behind Hitler's effort to run for the presidency, brought out a special illustrated magazine highlighting the campaign issues. Needless to say, columns of the SA marched up and down the streets of Germany singing, chanting, brawling, and drowning the country in a sea of posters and banners.

Despite such unparalleled agitation, which dwarfed anything the opposition was able to muster, Hindenburg won an impressive victory over Hitler on March 13, 1932. The aging president received 18,651,497 votes (49.7 percent), while Hitler garnered 11,339,446 votes (30.2 percent). Thälmann, the Communist candidate, received 4,983,341 (13.3 percent) and Duesterberg 2,547,729 (6.8 percent). Since Hindenburg had not received the necessary majority, the constitution called for a runoff election that would decide the issue by a simple plurality. . . . In view of the violent intensity of the last campaign, the government limited actual campaigning to only one week (April 3–10), making it difficult for Hitler to marshal the full force of his movement. However, Hitler managed to use the short time available to him in a very effective and clever manner: he chartered a plane and . . . began his famous "flights over Germany," visiting twenty-one cities in just one week.[36]

These grandstanding gestures brought much publicity, but they did not bring electoral victory. Hindenburg won 19,359,983 votes (53 percent), while Hitler came in a strong second with 13,418,547 (36.8 percent) votes. Hindenburg had gained more than one-half of the votes and was reelected for another seven years, although few expected him to live out the full tenure of his office. Hitler had received more than a third of the votes—an impressive achievement—but it now appeared that his popularity had reached its peak. Gregor Strasser, among others, warned Hitler that the party had reached its apex and that Hitler should therefore abandon his "all or nothing" tactics in favor of a more conciliatory approach, perhaps involving cooperation with other parties. . . .

Hitler's hope of conquering the Reich government by capturing control over the individual state governments turned out to be as misplaced as his earlier plan to seize control of the top through the office of the presidency. The outcome of the state elections was quite similar to that of the second presidential election. The Nazis gained a leading position in all states except Bavaria, but they were unable to capture sole control of any major German state. . . . In the State of Prussia, where three-fifths of the German people resided, the ruling SPD government of Otto Braun was badly mauled by spectacular Nazi gains and could maintain itself in power only as a caretaker government until a majority could be obtained in a runoff election.[37] As in many other state governments, the Nazis on the right and the Communists on the left controlled a majority of mandates, effectively paralyzing the democratic process by preventing the formation of a viable republican coalition. In other words, the "Nazicommunists" were holding the nation at ransom.[38]

The "Hunger Chancellor," i.e., Heinrich Brüning, was still stubbornly pursuing his conservative retrenchment policies; but far from improving Germany's dire economic situation, the measures he chose to mend the economy were self-defeating and contradictory. By raising taxes, cutting wages, and slashing government spending, he discouraged investments, undermined the creation of new jobs, lowered consumer spending, and further fueled unemployment and public suffering. The impact of these policies continued to be devastating, especially on the unemployed. At the time of the Nazi upsurge in September 1930, there were roughly 3 million unemployed; one year later, that figure had risen to 4.35 million; and in 1932, it stood at 5.1 million.[39] Brüning blamed the depression on reparations and hoped that his government would be able to convince the Western powers to abolish them. Much of his efforts were therefore directed toward foreign policy, but these efforts did not come to fruition until reparations were abolished in July 1932—too late to benefit the Brüning government. At any rate, reparations were only part of Germany's economic problems. Brüning accomplished nothing in dealing with these problems; on the contrary, he exacerbated them by a dogged pursuit of self-defeating remedies without a mandate from anyone other than a mercurial and senile president who was about to cave in to Brüning's enemies.

Again General Schleicher sang loudest in this chorus of Brüning detractors. Schleicher warned Hindenburg that Brüning was a weak leader because he had failed miserably in containing the radicals (on both the right and the left). . . . The old man had never really liked Brüning because of his aloof manners and his Catholicism. He also blamed his chancellor somewhat irrationally for failing to extend his presidential term of office, thus forcing him twice into a humiliating popularity contest with a Communist (Thälmann) and a Bohemian corporal (Hitler). Although he had won this contest, Hindenburg knew that a large number of Germans had voted against him, including the citizens of Tannenberg and the Masurian Lake district, where he had won his legendary victories in World War I. By the end of May, Brüning tendered his resignation. As Golo Mann put it, "He was dismissed because he felt himself dismissed; the ex-lieutenant felt that he could not remain in command if the Field-Marshal did not wish him to remain."[40]

The Papen and Schleicher Periods

In picking a successor to Brüning, President von Hindenburg relied again on the dubious advice of Schleicher, who had persuaded him that Franz von Papen was the best man for the post. Most Germans had trouble placing the new chancellor's name. . . . Intellectually, the new chancellor was bereft of any realistic plans for solving Germany's staggering socioeconomic problems, other than proposing to form a solid block of upper-middle-class interests against the forces of the left. Since Papen was a clever socialite whose network of acquaintances gave him access to a host of different interests—higher clergy, military leaders, industrialists, landed aristocracy, intellectuals—Schleicher concluded that the new chancellor might be able to neutralize the left and perhaps even co-opt the better elements of the Nazi movement. In addition, Papen was a witty and amusing raconteur—qualities that endeared him to Hindenburg, who affectionately took to calling him by the diminutive "Fränzchen."

Many thoughtful Germans, however, were shocked by the appointment of Papen; they could not help but wonder about a system that had given them a series of undistinguished and unrepresentative leaders. The chancellors of the 1920s, with the exception of Stresemann, had been grey, colorless, flat, and eminently forgettable. Brüning had been a bony ascetic with little parliamentary standing. Papen was worse: he was fatuous, pretentious, intellectually empty, and enjoyed no parliamentary support whatsoever. The French ambassador, Andre François-Ponçet, famous for his astute and pithy maxims about various political characters, informed his government shortly after Papen's appointment that the new chancellor "enjoyed the peculiarity of being taken seriously by neither his friends nor his enemies. He gave the impression of an incorrigible levity of which he was never able to rid himself. . . . He was reputed to be superficial, blundering, untrue, ambitious, vain, crafty and an intriguer."[41] These negative qualities, well known to most insiders, did not seem to have worried the wire-puller behind the scenes, General Schleicher, who brushed off the objection by a close friend that Papen did not have a strong head by saying: "He doesn't have to have. He's a hat!"[42]

The dashing Papen immediately went to work and assembled a cabinet of aristocratic top hats so unrepresentative that it was dubbed the "cabinet of barons," for five of its members were aristocrats and two were industrialists. Schleicher, who had jobbed Papen into power, took over the Ministry of Defense. Papen had as little backing and even less popular support than Brüning. . . .

On June 4, 1932, Papen dissolved the Reichstag and scheduled new elections for July 31. . . . The Nazis pulled off a stunning victory, polling 13.7 million popular votes and receiving 230 seats in the Reichstag, thus replacing the Social Democrats as the largest party in Germany. The two other major antirepublican parties, the Communists and the Nationalists, also gained heavily, making it impossible to form a workable coalition government. The three major antidemocratic parties now controlled 356 seats or more than one-half of the total 608 seats in the German Reichstag.

Since the Nazis were now the largest party in the Reichstag, it became clear to both their friends and enemies that they could not be excluded from some share in governing Germany. For the next six months the conservative clique around the president tried to negotiate some kind of accommodation with Hitler that would stop just short of giving him the chancellorship or to fob him off with a few cabinet posts; but true to his ideological convictions, Hitler rejected all of these offers. He wanted everything or nothing. Sooner or later, he believed, the sheer gravitational pull of his movement would overwhelm all of his opponents. He knew that after the July elections the Papen government, or any similar government, not only lacked popular standing, but could not even count upon firm support from the conservative right. Its only support, in fact, continued to be the approval of the president; but, as Brüning had discovered to his great disappointment, that support was precarious. Alan Bullock put Germany's dilemma in sharp relief when he said that "with a voting strength of 13,700,000 electors, a party membership of over a million and a private army of 400,000 S.A. and S.S., Hitler was the most powerful political leader in Germany, knocking on the doors of the Chancellery at the head of the most powerful political party Germany had ever seen."[43] . . .

On September 12, 1932, the Reichstag reconvened for a few turbulent hours. Even before it opened, Papen had already secured Hindenburg's approval for its dissolution, setting November 6 as the date for new elections. . . . The NSDAP lost two million votes and thirty-four Reichstag seats; its national standing declined from 37.4 percent to 33.1; percent and its representation in the Reichstag dropped from 230 to 196. However, the November 6 elections had not resolved anything because the Nazis and the Communists were still controlling half of the Reichstag seats. Moreover, Papen's minority government was still despised and had virtually no support. After being stalemated by the refusal of the major parties to support his government, Papen resigned from his office on November 17, though he accepted Hindenburg's request to carry on for another two weeks until a new government could be formed.

On November 19 and 21 Hitler and Göring conducted confidential discussions with president Hindenburg about the possibility of a Hitler chancellorship. The old gentleman appears to have been willing to entertain the idea of appointing Hitler as chancellor, provided that he could form a workable majority in the Reichstag. Knowing that this would be difficult, if not impossible, Hitler countered with a proposal of governing the country as a presidential rather than a parliamentary chancellor, backed up by the same emergency powers as Papen. Through [Otto] Meissner, Hindenburg later replied in writing that he could not accept Hitler's plan because "a presidential cabinet led by you would necessarily evolve into a one party dictatorship."[44] . . .

On December 2, 1932, Schleicher became chancellor, while at the same time retaining his post as minister of defense and automatically inherit-

ing Papen's position as Reich commissioner for Prussia. Few German military leaders had ever enjoyed so much power, but in this case it had been acquired at great cost and at the expense of a long line of victims. . . . He soon discovered that his influence did not reach very far beyond his offices in the *Bendlerstrasse* [the address of the Defense Ministry]. . . . By the middle of January, Schleicher's position was steadily deteriorating. What happened next was a series of private meetings between Hitler and the conservative clique surrounding the president. In retrospect, these meetings appear Byzantine and lurid, with many of them taking place in the house of Joachim von Ribbentrop, an empty and pretentious social climber who was trying to graft himself onto the Nazi bandwagon through his wealthy social connections. Papen met Hitler at Ribbentrop's house in Dahlem on January 10, 18, and 22.[45] The third meeting was the most decisive because Papen now decided to enmesh Hindenburg's son, who was widely regarded as an incompetent and insensitive pretender, along with the spineless but obedient bureaucrat Meissner in his machinations to form a Hitler-Papen government. . . .

The next morning, January 23, the well-informed Schleicher called State Secretary Meissner and asked him what the president's son had discussed the previous evening. Presumably not receiving a satisfactory answer, he then marched into President Hindenburg's office, admitted that he had failed to gain broad support for his government, and requested presidential support for four emergency measures—dissolution of the Reichstag, postponement of elections for three months, declaration of a state of emergency, and prohibition of the Nazi and Communist parties. Hindenburg objected that these measures were likely to provoke civil war and reminded the general that he himself had opposed a similar plan by Papen in December. Schleicher responded by saying that the situation had greatly deteriorated since that time and that only a concerted attack on the Nazis and the Communists could stave off a political catastrophe.[46] After discussing Schleicher's proposals with Meissner, Hindenburg made up his mind to reject the proposals; he was determined that he would not even give Schleicher authorization to dissolve the Reichstag, a request he had granted without compunction to the previous two chancellors. It was clear that Schleicher was finished, but the old gentleman still vacillated for another seven days about the choice of a successor.

For the next seven days intensive negotiations took place aimed at bringing Hitler into the government with certain restrictions. . . . Hindenburg was now a torn man, but he gradually succumbed to the arguments of the men he thought he could trust—his son Oskar, Papen, and Meissner. Yet as late as January 27, he could still tell several high-ranking generals who came to see him: "Surely gentlemen, you would not credit me with appointing this Austrian corporal Chancellor."[47] What troubled the old man more than anything else was the danger that Hitler could gain control over the Reichswehr. If he could be assured that a Hitler appointment was checked and balanced by trusted conservatives, especially in the Defense Ministry, he might be willing to support a Hitler government after all. It so happened that he had already decided upon a candidate who was to succeed Schleicher in the Defense Ministry—Werner von Blomberg, an enemy of Schleicher who was currently a delegate to the disarmament conference in Geneva. Blomberg had been commander of the army district for East Prussia, and so was well known to Hindenburg; but what the old man did not know was that Blomberg was a strong Nazi sympathizer.

On January 28, Schleicher met his cabinet, and a unanimous decision was made to resign if the president refused to dissolve the Reichstag. Schleicher then went to the president and repeated his previous proposals. The old man flatly turned him down. . . . The stage was set for the arrival of Hitler, Hugenberg, Papen, and the other members of the new government. . . . On the morning of January 30, Oskar von Hindenburg was dispatched to the Anhalter railroad station to pick up Blomberg and to rush him to the presidential palace for his swearing in as new defense minister . . . . By 12:40 the word of Hitler's appointment was out. Watching the presidential palace from the Kaiserhof Hotel, Hitler's entourage could see the beaming Hermann Göring proclaim the news to a cheering crowd. Hitler's car emerged from the driveway shortly afterward. Joining his entourage at the Kaiserhof, tears in his eyes, Hitler celebrated his remarkable triumph—a triumph, however, that would not have been possible without the intrigues of Schleicher and Papen, the political myopia of German voters and parties, the narrow self-interest of the military-industrial leaders, and the senility of the "Wooden Titan," Paul von Hindenburg.

Conclusion: Who Supported Hitler?

If economic stability had been restored and maintained during the Weimar Republic, the Nazi movement would have never amounted to anything more than a small, xenophobic group of unregenerate misfits, but with the economic collapse, first of 1923 and then of 1929, it began to amalgamate misguided sympathizers who joined out of economic self-interest because they had been frightened into believing that the only alternative was the destruction of the middle class and the triumph of Communism. In order of precedent, the following groups were amalgamated step-by-step into the Nazi movement—the lower middle classes, who were afraid of being deprived of their social status; substantial elements of the more prosperous *Mittelstand* who fell victim to scare tactics that their businesses or possessions were subject to immanent expropriation by Communism; and disenchanted workers whose loyalty to nation exceeded their loyalty to class.

In the end, however, it was Hitler's organizational and charismatic genius that made it possible for the Nazi Party to attract a broad segment of the German population. Party membership lists and electoral data reveal that the Nazi Party was able to appeal beyond its hardcore followers and attract apparently incompatible social groups.[48] Hitler seems to have known intuitively that voting patterns are shaped not only by class affiliation but by group prejudices. Hitler reasoned that if he could successfully nationalize the masses, indoctrinating them with ethnic prejudices, he could effectively diffuse economic divisions and reintegrate heterogeneous elements into one national community (*Volksgemeinschaft*). He was right. Between 1923 and 1933 he created the basis for such a mass party (*Sammelpartei*), a concept so novel that it eluded the comprehension of most observers at the time: "The idea that a fanatical petty bourgeois could, by claiming to be socialist, labour, and nationalist all in one, direct a mass movement and that he might be victorious, was sociologically too novel and politically too unwanted to be readily comprehended."[49] . . .

Who, then, voted for Hitler? A broad but not a majority segment of the German electorate. The highest vote that Hitler received in a free election (July 31, 1932) was 37.3 percent—that is, only three out of every eight votes. But given the polarization of German politics, that margin was higher than that of any other party, making the Nazi Party "the long-sought party of the middle-class concentra-

tion."[50] The Nazi victory of July 1932 generated enough momentum for the Nazis to be able to exploit the weaknesses of their opponents and capitalize on their own organizational strengths. What came to Hitler's aid was the mediocre leadership of opposition parties, the defects of the Weimar Constitution, the universal hatred of the Versailles Treaty, a growing mood of totalitarianism, and the gradual defection of key members of the ruling elite. Capitalizing on the tactical and managerial superiority of the Nazi Party and his own manipulative talents, Hitler simply outwitted the only group that could still block him in 1932—the conservative clique around President Hindenburg.

The Weimar Republic failed because there were not enough strongly committed republicans to save it. In normal times, the republic might have been able to muddle through, as illustrated by its modest resurgence in the middle years (1924–29); but in times of turbulent and chaotic changes, its weaknesses became fatal liabilities. Amid a climate of mutual fear and paranoia, many Germans regressed to a "quick-fix," authoritarian solution; and given the predominance of right wing, nationalistic attitudes, such a solution was bound to originate from the political right.

NOTES

1. Erich Eyck, *A History of the Weimar Republic*, trans. Harlan P. Hanson and Robert G. L. Waite, 2 vols. (Cambridge MA: Harvard Univ. Press, 1962), 1: 37–39.
2. A good summary of scholarly views on the German revolution of 1918–19 is contained in Reinhard Rürup, "Problems of the German Revolution of 1918–19," *Journal of Contemporary History* 3 (1968): 109–35. The most acute analysis of the survival of prewar institutions (armed forces, civil service, education) into the postwar

period is [Karl] Dietrich Bracher, *Die Auflösung der Weimarer Republik: Eine Studie zum Problem des Machtverfalls in der Demokratie* (Villingen, Schwarzwald: Ring-Verlag, 1960).

3. Golo Mann, *The History of Germany since 1789*, trans. Marian Jackson (New York: Praeger, 1968), 332.

4. Philipp Scheidemann, *The Making of New Germany: The Memoirs of Philipp Scheidemann,* trans. J. E. Mitchell (New York: Appleton, 1929), 2: 262.

5. Ibid., 2: 264.

6. Ibid.

7. Friedrich Ebert, *Schriften, Aufzeichnungen und Reden* (Dresden: C. Reissner, 1926), 2: 127–30.

8. Richard M. Watt, *The Kings Depart* (New York: Simon & Schuster, 1968), 314.

9. [Karl] Dietrich Bracher, *The German Dictatorship*, trans. Jean Steinberg (New York: Praeger, 1970), 75.

10. On the practice and shortcomings of proportional representation, see Eyck, *History of the Weimar Republic*, 1: 70–71.

11. On the range of historical judgments of the Versailles Treaty, see Ivo J. Lederer, ed., *The Versailles Settlement: Was It Foredoomed to Failure?* (Boston: D. C. Heath, 1960).

12. Scheidemann quoted by Gordon Craig, *Germany, 1866–1945*, 425.

13. U.S. Senate, *Treaty of Peace with Germany*, 66th Cong., 1st sess., 1919, Senate Doc. 49.

14. John Maynard Keynes, *The Economic Consequences of the Peace* (New York: Harcourt, Brace & Howe, 1920), 15–16.

15. Ibid., 51.

16. For the fate of the German navy, see Langhorne Gibson and Paul Schubert, *Death of a Fleet* (New York: Coweard-McCan, 1932).

17. On the complexities of the German economic collapse of 1923 there is an excellent summary of views in Fritz Ringer's documentary collection entitled *The German Inflation of 1923* (New York: Oxford Univ. Press, 1969).

18. On the Ruhr question, see Paul Wentzcke, *Ruhrkampf: Einbruch und Abwehr im Rheinisch-westfälischen Industriegebiet* (Berlin: R. Hobbing, 1930).

19. Konrad Heiden, *Der Fuehrer: Hitler's Rise to Power* (Boston: Houghton Mifflin, 1944), cha7.

20. Ibid., 127.

21. Adolf Hitler, *Mein Kampf* (New York: Reynal & Hitchcock, 1941), 84, 580, and 603.

22. The term *Lebensraum*, popular among pan-German writers before World War I, was rarely used by Hitler in *Mein Kampf*. Hitler used such terms as "soil and territory," "space," or "roots" (*Scholle*), terms that would later evoke a whole Nazi ideology of "blood and soil." The most popular work on this theme of *Lebensraum*, published in the same year as Hitler's second volume of *Mein Kampf* (1926), was Hans Grimm's best-seller *Volk ohne Raum* (People without space).

23. Höhne, *Machtergreifung*, 63–65.

24. The following studies provide an excellent guide to the role of the Reichswehr in undermining parliamentary government: Craig, *Politics of the Prussian Army*; Walter Goerlitz, *History of the German General Staff, 1657–1945*, trans. Brian Battershaw (New York: Praeger, 1957); and Thilo Vogelsang, *Reichswehr, Staat und NSDAP* (Stuttgart: Deutsche Verlags-Anstalt, 1962).

25. Höhne, *Machtergreifung*, 96–97.

26. Turner, *German Big Business and the Rise of Hitler*, 160.

27. For a detailed reconstruction of Wessel's case, including the trial of his murderers, see Imre Lazar, *Der Fall Horst Wessel* (Munich: Wilhelm Heyne Verlag, 1980).

28. Quoted by Heiber, *Goebbels*, 70.

29. Peukert, *Weimar Republic*, 209.

30. Edgar J. Jung, *Herrschaft der Minderwertigen* (Berlin: Deutsche Rundschau, 1927).

31. Oswald Spengler, *Politische Schriften* (Munich: Beck, 1932), 189.

32. Fest, *Hitler*, 289.

33. Joseph Goebbels, *Vom Kaiserhof zur Reichskanzlei: Eine historische Darstellung in Tagebuchblättern* (Munich: Eher, 1934), 20.

34. Milton Mayer, *They Thought They Were Free* (Chicago: Univ. of Chicago Press, 1955), 101.

35. Consult the excellent chronicle of Hitler's activities in Milan Hauner, *Hitler: A Chronicle of His Life and Time* (New York: St. Martin's Press, 1983).

36. Fest, *Hitler*, 320.

37. See Braun, *Von Weimar zu Hitler* (Hamburg: Hammonia Norddeutsche Verlagsanstalt, 1949], 218–42.

38. Bracher, *Auflösung*, 503–4.

39. Bracher, *German Dictatorship*, 169.

40. Mann, *History of Germany*, 403.

41. Quoted by Wheeler-Bennett, *Nemesis of Power*, 246.

42. Gottfried Reinhold Treviranus, *Das Ende von Weimar: Heinrich Brüning und seine Zeit* (Düsseldorf: Econ Verlag, 1968), 334.

43. Bullock, *Hitler*, 218.

44. Quoted by Bracher, *Auflösung*, 666.

45. In order to dispel the charges of being a shabby intriguer, Papen denied having seen Hitler from January 4 to 22 (*Memoirs*, 236). But this is contradicted by Ribbentrop's later recollections (*Zwischen London und Moskau: Erinnerungen und letzte Aufzeichnungen*, 38–39). See also Höhne, *Machtergreifung*, 247–48, 250–51; and John Weitz, *Hitler's Diplomat: The Life and Times of Joachim von Ribbentrop* (New York: Ticknor & Fields, 1992), 53–55.

46. Meissner, *Die Machtergreifung*, 166–67.

47. *Auflösung*, 714.

48. Childers, *The Nazi Voter*, 13–14.

49. Pierre Aycoberry, *The Nazi Question: Essay on the Interpretations of National Socialism, 1922–1975* (New York: Pantheon, 1981), 15.

50. Childers, *The Nazi Voter*, 262.

The Interwar Jewish Heartland

EZRA MENDELSOHN

From *The Jews of East Central Europe Between the World Wars*

The interwar years in East Central Europe, a short but well-defined period no longer than a single generation, witnessed the dramatic and unexpected triumph of the national principle and the formation of such new states as Poland, Czechoslovakia, Latvia, and Lithuania. During these years previously subjugated nationalities struggled to overcome staggering difficulties and to establish viable states which, so it was hoped, would never again be brought under foreign domination. . . . For the student of modern Jewish history, East Central Europe during the interwar years is of particularly dramatic interest. For one thing, these years may be justly regarded as a period of grim rehearsal for the tragedy of East European Jewry during World War II. In most of the new states, relations between Jews and gentiles were bad from the very beginning, and in all of them these relations deteriorated sharply during the 1930s. In Hungary Jewish emancipation was actually revoked, while in Poland and Romania the emancipation won in 1918–1919 proved to be no guarantee of equality. Almost everywhere the "Jewish question" became a matter of paramount concern, and antisemitism a major political force. . . .

A second major consideration is internal developments within the Jewish communities. During the 1920s and 1930s modern Jewish political movements, largely the creation of tsarist Russia, flourished in Eastern Europe as they never had

before and as they never would again. In some countries, most notably Poland, secular Jewish nationalism and Jewish socialism were transformed almost overnight into mass movements that were able to wrest control of the Jewish community from its more traditional leaders. The Jewries of Poland, Galicia, Lithuania, Bessarabia, and Bukovina underwent what might be termed a process of politicization and nationalization not unlike that which was affecting their gentile neighbors. Even the Orthodox population, traditionally strong in Eastern Europe, organized itself into modern political parties which adopted many of their secular adversaries' characteristics. Along with the striking politicization of East European Jewry went efforts to implement the tenets of the now triumphant ideologies. In fact, East Central Europe between the wars was the major testing ground for modern Jewish politics: thus the remarkable, though ultimately unsuccessful, efforts to establish extraterritorial national autonomy for the Jews, one of the chief aims of most Jewish nationalist parties; thus Zionist efforts to promote mass emigration (*aliyah* in Hebrew) to Palestine, which for the first time became a practical option for large numbers of Jews fleeing Eastern Europe. And then there was the attempt made by the Jewish left both to promote a proletarian Jewish culture and to forge alliances with the non-Jewish left in order to topple the "bourgeois" states of the region and to replace them with socialist or Communist regimes. Finally, the antinationalist Orthodox Jewish parties sought to perpetuate the old Jewish way of life by establishing new institutions and by instituting working relationships with the various regimes. . . .

The demographic decline of East European Jewry and the more important process of economic decline resulted by the 1930s in the impoverishment of hundreds of thousands of Jews in Poland, Romania, and the Baltic States. An additional theme emphasized here has to do with the different though related processes of acculturation (by which is meant the Jews' adoption of the external characteristics of the majority culture, above all its language) and assimilation (by which is meant the Jews' efforts to adopt the national identity of the majority, to become Poles, Hungarians, Romanians "of the Mosaic faith," or even to abandon their Jewish identity altogether). Were the Jews in these lands growing closer to their neighbors, or further apart? And did the Jews' willingness or lack of willingness to acculturate and assimilate have any impact on attitudes toward them? These are among the most vital questions the historian of post-emancipation Jewry can ask, along with the no less important question as to the efficacy of the various Jewish political proposals for solving the Jewish question.

. . . In Poland, Hungary, Czechoslovakia, Romania, Lithuania, Latvia, and Estonia resided the major Ashkenazi (i.e., of German origin) Jewries, almost all of which, except for pre–World War I Romanian Jewry, had previously resided either in tsarist Russia or in Habsburg Austria-Hungary. . . . Even within this rather limited area there was enormous diversity, both in general and among the various Jewish communities. . . . Despite this evident diversity, certain shared characteristics imparted to East Central Europe a large measure of unity. Most obvious was the fact that, with the exception of the Czech lands, this was an economically and socially backward region that did not

make great economic progress during the interwar years. The majority of the inhabitants were peasants, the percentage of city dwellers was low, and cities were often regarded as foreign enclaves by a hostile peasantry and by the gentry-derived intelligentsia. There was little industrialization, and the commercial class was often "non-native." The old elites—landowners, the clergy—retained considerable power, although they had to share it with the emerging intelligentsia and bourgeoisie, and sometimes even with the rapidly organizing peasantry. To the problems of how to overcome backwardness and poverty was added another shared by most East Central European lands— political inexperience.

The new states faced the extraordinarily difficult task of nation-building after centuries of dependence, a task made all the more difficult by the degree of external hostility to their still fragile independence. . . . All these states were anti-Communist and antirevolutionary, and most perceived the Soviet Union as their most dangerous antagonist. Most began their lives as democracies, at least on paper, and all, with the familiar Czechoslovak exception, moved to the right during the interwar years. This was only to be expected, given their anti-Soviet orientation, the control exerted by the traditional elites, and the weak if not nonexistent traditions of democracy and liberalism. In most of these lands the principal political struggle was not between left and right (the left tended to be quite weak), but rather between right and extreme right. The principal internal threat to the stability of such countries as Poland, Hungary, and Romania in the 1930s emanated from the so-called native fascist movements, such as the Iron Guard in Romania and the Arrow Cross in Hungary. This struggle, in which the Jewish question played a great role, had fateful consequences for the local Jewish communities.

Another major problem which plagued all the lands of East Central Europe was that of the minority nationalities. Despite the triumph of the national principle after World War I, the political boundaries in East Central Europe were not, and indeed could not, be drawn according to strictly ethnic criteria. Most of the countries discussed here regarded themselves as nation-states, but in fact they were not. One-third of the population of Poland, for example, was non-Polish. The minorities were often regarded as threats to the status quo and as disloyal elements interested in redrawing the frontiers in order to accommodate their own national interests. . . . The determined efforts of such countries as Poland and Romania to establish centralized states and to promote the interests of the dominant nationality inevitably clashed with the grievances, real or imagined, of the national minorities. This led to the flourishing of extreme nationalism, which may be regarded as the ruling ideology of East Central Europe between the wars. In this region nation was exalted over class, and unbridled nationalism was rarely tempered by social idealism. . . .

From the Jewish perspective, the East Central European environment as it has been described here offered little grounds for optimism. Generally Jews have flourished in lands of cultural and religious tolerance, political liberalism, stability, and economic growth. In interwar East Central Europe they were confronted, rather, with chauvinism and intolerance, instability, economic stagnation, and extreme right-wing politics. Moreover, the traditional safety valve of emigration had been blocked by the new restrictions inaugurated by the United States and other Western nations. Many observers were quick to point out, even at the beginning of this period, that the old multinational Habsburg empire was a much more favorable environment from the Jewish point of view

than were the successor states, and some went so far as to insist that even the tsarist empire was preferable. It can be argued, too, that the neighboring Soviet Union was a much more friendly place for the Jews than were most of the new East European states. In the Soviet Union the dominant ideology was based on class rather than nation, the old conservative (and antisemitic) elites had been destroyed, and economic dynamism was beginning to transform a typically backward East European state into a modern, industrialized colossus. In comparing the fate of the Jews in the Soviet Union with that in East Central Europe during the interwar period, one might conclude that in the latter the environment was bad for the Jews while not necessarily being bad for Judaism—that is, collective Jewish religious, cultural, and even political expression—whereas in the former Jews as individuals were able to prosper while Judaism as a religion, and indeed all forms of specifically Jewish creativity, withered away. In certain countries of East Central Europe, most notably Poland, the hostile environment was no impediment to the flourishing of Jewish culture of either the secular or the religious variety.

If East Central Europe was far from being a unified region, despite certain characteristics common to most of its countries, the same was true of the Jewries of East Central Europe. Not only was there no such thing as "East Central European Jewry," but also it made little sense to speak of "Czechoslovak Jewry," "Romanian Jewry," or even "Polish Jewry." There was a world of difference between the basically middle-class, acculturated Jewish communities of Bohemia and Moravia in western Czechoslovakia and the poverty-stricken, Yiddish-speaking, Orthodox Jewry of Subcarpathian Rus in eastern Czechoslovakia. And there was little to unite the Jewish community of Wallachia, in old, pre—World War I Romania, with the Jewish community of Bessarabia, annexed to Romania after the war. The same can be said of the Jews of central (or Congress) Poland and of Polish Galicia, or of the Jews in northern and southern Latvia. . . . Viewed broadly, two basic "types" of Jewish communities in East Central Europe emerge—a "West European type" and an "East European type." The East European type was characterized by the relative weakness of acculturation and assimilation, the preservation of Yiddish speech and religious Orthodoxy (sometimes of the extremely conservative Hasidic variety), and a lower middle-class and proletarian socioeconomic structure. A typical East European Jewish community had a high birth rate and a low rate of intermarriage, and, while it was largely urban in nature, many of its members still lived in the old-style *shtetl* (small Jewish town). In such a community a certain degree of acculturation and secularization had occurred, but such acculturation and secularization, which took place gradually in the context of socioeconomic backwardness and general anti-Jewish hostility, most typically led not to assimilation, but to modern Jewish nationalism of one form or another. There existed in this type of community two legitimate forms of Jewish identity—religious (meaning almost always Orthodox, since Reform Judaism was virtually unknown) and national (usually secular national). Finally, East European Jewish communities usually constituted a rather large percentage within the general population, especially within the urban sector, and played a highly conspicuous role in local economic life, particularly in commerce. In lieu of a "native" middle class, these communities were often correctly identified as the local equivalent of a bourgeois class.

The West European type was characterized by a high degree of acculturation, aspirations toward assimilation, and a general tendency to abandon both Yiddish and Orthodoxy, accompanied by a readiness to embrace some form of Reform, or liberal, Judaism. From a socioeconomic point of view, such Jewish communities tended to be middle class; from a demographic point of view, they were highly urbanized, though they rarely constituted a remarkably high percentage within the general urban population. The typical West European Jewry possessed a low birth rate and often a high rate of intermarriage; its sense of Jewish identification was usually religious, not national secular.

The West European type of Jewish community obviously closely corresponds to the Jewries of such Central and West European countries as Germany, France, and England. In East Central Europe it was found in Bohemia and Moravia (the so-called Czech lands), in Hungary, in certain parts of Latvia, and in Romanian Wallachia. The East European type was found in Galicia, central (Congress) Poland, Polish Lithuania, independent Lithuania, Subcarpathian Rus, Bukovina, Bessarabia, and southern Latvia. . . . There is an obvious correlation between the degree of economic development, and the type of Jewry. Usually, though not invariably, the more developed the region, the more Western the type of Jewry; the less developed, the more Eastern. . . .

The implications of this typology for the internal development of the various Jewish communities of East Central Europe were very important. In the East European communities, autonomous Jewish culture flourished during the interwar years, as did the new Jewish politics. In these communities Zionism, Jewish socialism, and modern Hebrew and Yiddish schools and literature thrived, along with a new Jewish leadership based on mass support from within the community. Here, too, were voiced demands for Jewish national autonomy. In the West European-type communities, on the other hand, autonomous Jewish politics and culture were much less in evidence. Jews participated much more in the cultural life of the majority nationality and were much less attracted to the various forms of modern Jewish nationalism. Their leaders were quite different, as were the policies they followed. It is extremely doubtful, however, if the type of community had much to do with Jewish-gentile relations.

In modern Jewish history in the Western world, the classical pattern has been progression from non-acculturation and non-assimilation to acculturation and efforts to assimilate, from the physical and spiritual ghetto to integration, of one sort or another, into the broader society. In interwar East Europe this pattern is not in evidence. The East European-type communities, despite a certain, and sometimes even an impressive, degree of acculturation during the 1920s and 1930s, remained basically Yiddish-speaking, lower middle class and proletarian, and strongly influenced both by religious Orthodoxy and by modern separatist Jewish nationalism. Once again we may contrast this situation with that of Soviet Jewry, a typical East European community at the outset of the interwar period, but well on its way to becoming a West European-type community by the end of the 1930s. This dramatic change was a function of the ruling ideology and of the economic dynamism of the Soviet state. In East Central Europe the combination of intolerant, antisemitic nationalism, right-wing politics, and economic stagnation made such a change impossible. . . .

Poland

. . . During the nineteenth century the lands which had once constituted the Polish state belonged to the Prussian (later German), Russian, and Austro-Hungarian states. . . . The sudden and unexpected collapse of the three partitioning powers in 1917–

1918 made the rebirth of a Polish state inevitable. The borders of the new state, however, were the subject of lengthy diplomatic and military maneuvers, and were not permanently settled until 1923. The new borders did not satisfy those Polish maximalists who hoped for a return to the vast territories of the prepartition Polish state, but they were large enough to satisfy most nationalists. In the east the Poles made good their claims to Vilna (Wilno), and while they failed to annex Kiev, once a Polish city, they did annex the province of Volynia, previously part of the Russian Ukraine. These and other eastern areas were generally known during the interwar period as the *kresy* (borderlands). All of formerly Habsburg Galicia, including its heavily Ukrainian eastern half (whose capital was Lwów), was incorporated into the new state, as was nearly all of [formerly Russian] Congress Poland. In the west, Poland obtained part of Upper Silesia (after a plebiscite in 1921), part of Austrian Silesia (shared with the new state of Czechoslovakia), Poznán, and part of Pomorze [Pomerania]. (Danzig, also claimed by Poland, was made a free city.) The national appetite for borders which contained such Polish ethnic islands in non-Polish seas as Vilna and Lwow, as well as extensive territories in mixed Polish-German regions, rendered the new Poland not a nation-state but, rather, a state of nationalities. . . .

According to the census of 1921, the population of Poland was 27,176,717; approximately one-third of this number were non-Poles. The largest non-Polish nationality was the Ukrainian group, followed by Jews, Belorussians, and Germans.[1] The Slavic minorities—Ukrainians and Belorussians—possessed a territorial base in the kresy and in eastern Galicia as well as aspirations for political independence. Indeed, the Galician Ukrainians, whose national consciousness was particularly strong, had proclaimed the independent West Ukrainian Republic in 1918, and, although this state was crushed by Polish arms, the hope of establishing a great Ukrainian state lived on. Ukrainian and Belorussian nationalism was particularly dangerous for the Poles, since both these nationalities might well be tempted to look eastward, to the Ukrainian and Belorussian Soviet republics, for inspiration and assistance. Thus the problem of the Slavic national minorities was inextricably connected with the threat of Soviet irredentism and the spread of Communism within Poland. By the same token, the German population of the western regions was naturally suspected of hoping and working for the return of German rule. It was less logical to accuse the Jews of plotting either to establish their own state within Polish borders or to destroy the Polish state through the intervention of its allies abroad, but such accusations were the stock in trade of numerous Polish antisemites. In short, for many Poles the national-minorities problem constituted a serious challenge to the integrity of the state, and the question of how to deal with it became a major issue in interwar Polish politics. . . .

The Jews of Poland

During the interwar period the Polish state conducted two censuses, the first in 1921 and the second ten years later. According to the first census there were 2,855,318 Jews (by religion) in Poland, or 10.5 percent of the population. By 1931 the number had grown to 3,113,933, but the percentage had dropped to 9.8. This was by far the largest Jewish community in non-Communist Europe, and also the community that made up the highest percentage within the general population. Only in British Palestine was there a higher proportion of Jews.[2] Even more impressive was the extremely high percentage of Jews in Polish cities. In 1921 the Jews constituted nearly one-third of the entire urban

population of the country, and in the eastern provinces of Volynia and Polesie over one-half. Such numbers were interpreted by Polish antisemites as proof that Polish cities were dominated by "foreigners," against whom a holy war must be waged by the native middle class.

Despite their strong urban bias, the result of rapid urbanization during the nineteenth century, many Polish Jews remained in the countryside. In 1931, 23.6 percent of all Jews resided in villages; in the *kresy* and in Galicia the percentage was higher than in the more urbanized region of former Congress Poland. The situation in the *kresy*, where the Jews constituted the urban class par excellence, but where a very large number of all Jews resided in villages, is typical of the demographic situation in the most backward areas of Eastern Europe. In such regions Jews truly dominated the cities, but the cities were relatively small and relatively few in number, and thus unable to absorb large numbers of Jews who remained in the little towns (*shtetlekh*).

No dramatic changes occurred in the Jewish demographic structure during the interwar period. The tremendous growth that characterized Jewish demography in Eastern Europe during the nineteenth century slowed, although we should emphasize that in Poland the Jewish population continued to grow in absolute terms. Nonetheless, in Poland as everywhere else in East Central Europe, the Jewish percentage within the population declined. In Warsaw, for example, the 310,332 Jews counted in the 1921 census constituted 33.1 percent of the general population, whereas by 1931 the 352,659 Jews constituted 30.1 percent. The Jewish rate of natural increase, though significant, was lower than that of the Poles, the Ukrainians, and the Belorussians (though higher than that of the Germans), and during this period Poles were urbanizing at a faster rate than were Jews. Also, proportionately more Jews than non-Jews emigrated, and, although emigration in general did not have a major impact on Jewish demography, it was fairly substantial during the early 1920s.[3] There was, on the other hand, very little intermarriage or conversion, in contrast with rates of intermarriage and conversion in Hungary and Bohemia-Moravia. In Poland, as elsewhere in East Central Europe, there was no parallel to the demographic revolution that changed the foundations of Jewish life in the Soviet Union—the result of the abolition of the old Pale of Settlement and the dramatic Jewish internal migration to the great cities of the interior.[4]

The economic structure of the Jewish population naturally reflected the urban character of the community. If most Poles were employed in agriculture, the overwhelming majority of Jews were employed in commerce, industry, and the professions. Moreover, if most Poles in the non-agrarian sector tended to be engaged in industry, most Jews, at least in 1921, were employed in commerce. This meant that Jews were relatively more dominant in the latter category than in the former. This was the typical pattern in Eastern Europe....

Between 1921 and 1931 one important change took place. That by the latter date more Jews derived their income from "industry" (42.2 percent) than from "commerce" (36.6 percent) was a most unusual situation so far as the Jews were concerned and unparalleled in any other country in East Central Europe. Some observers called this a process of "proletarization," while others, more realistically, termed it a process of pauperization.

As for the influence of Jews within the general Polish economy, it was most pronounced in commerce and in the professions. The data . . . illustrate the general rule that the more backward the region in Eastern Europe, the more predominant the role of Jewish commerce. Thus in Gali-

cia, and most especially in the *kresy*, the Jews were *the* commercial class, while in the more developed central region their role was less conspicuous. The role of Jews in industry was considerably less pronounced; in 1931 a grand total of 2,537,669 people were employed in industry, of whom only 506,690, or 19.97 percent, were Jews. Nearly one-half of all those engaged in the clothing industry were Jews....

In general, the Jewish population in interwar Poland may be termed lower middle class and proletarian, with a numerically small but important intelligentsia and wealthy bourgeoisie. A leading Polish historian and student of the period has estimated that the Jewish bourgeoisie numbered 100,000 (including dependents); the petty bourgeoisie, 2,000,000, the working class, 700,000; the professionals and intelligentsia, 300,000.[5] The Jewish proletariat was not a proletariat of the great factories and mines, it was, rather, a proletariat consisting almost entirely of craftsmen employed in light industry. The typical Jewish worker was a shoemaker, baker, or tailor who worked in a small shop, possibly with a few other journeymen, but often alone....

Various factors were at work in producing this anomalous situation. It was often asserted, with some degree of accuracy, that Jews preferred to be self-employed and resisted being absorbed into the factory proletariat. More important was the fact that Jews were rarely employed in non-Jewish firms, and relatively few Jews owned large factories. The problem of Saturday work was also of importance in this regard, since Jews usually refused to work on the Sabbath, and any factory that employed both Jews and non-Jews would therefore have to close down two days a week. Finally, that non-Jewish workers often regarded factory jobs as their monopoly and resisted Jewish incursions was a natural phenomenon in light of the existence of chronic unemployment.[6] In the 1930s there were some signs in Poland that the situation was changing, as more and more Jews, driven by economic necessity, sought work in factories. But until the very end the Jewish working class, though large and politically as well as socially important, remained a most un-Marxian unit, in the sense that it was far from being a working class of the great industrial establishments.

If the typical Jewish worker was a tailor, the typical Jewish "merchant" was a small shopkeeper or owner of a stall in the local market, working alone or with the help of his family. Of all Jews active in commerce in 1931, 78.6 percent were self-employed and did not employ workers (among non-Jews the percentage was significantly lower, 42.5).[7] There were, of course, wealthy Jewish merchants, just as there were wealthy Jewish industrialists, and in general the Jewish bourgeoisie played an important role in the Polish urban economy.[8] But great Jewish industrialists, merchants, and bankers were much more prominent in the economic life of nineteenth-century Russian Poland than they were in the interwar period, when the state came to play a dominant role in economic life and did its best to exclude Jews from positions of influence. . . .

The Jewish economic condition in Poland at the outset of the interwar period, as in other economically backward regions of Eastern Europe, was undeniably gloomy. On the one hand, it could be asserted, and often was, that Jews "dominated" the economy; on the other, the community itself was poor, existing to a dangerous extent on foreign relief funds and cursed with an unhealthy economic structure. One of the great questions which faced the Jewries of independent Poland was whether the economic performance of the new state, and its economic and social policy, would permit the kind of economic breakthrough

into the ranks of the middle class which had been experienced by the Jews of Central and Western Europe and which would be experienced by the Jewish communities of North America and the Soviet Union during the interwar period. The future of Polish Jewry depended to a great extent on the answer to this fateful question.

The two Polish censuses of 1921 and 1931, along with their demographic and economic data, also supply very interesting and revealing material on the national character of the Polish Jewries. The number of Jews in Poland cited above refers to "Jews by religion," but Polish citizens were also asked to state their national affiliation (in 1921) and their mother tongue (in 1931). Obviously the largest number of Jews is yielded by the question "What is your religion?" but a very large number of "Jews by religion" also declared themselves to be "Jews by nationality." In the 1921 census, 2,044,637 Jews declared themselves to be Jews by nationality, or 73.76 percent of the total number of Jews by religion. . . . The data from the 1931 census on language affiliation are no less interesting, and perhaps even more revealing. All in all, 79.9 percent of Polish Jewry declared Yiddish to be its mother tongue, and 7.8 percent obeyed the command of the Zionist movement and declared (falsely) its mother tongue to be Hebrew. Those who described themselves as Polish-speaking from childhood obviously belonged to the acculturated segment of the Polish Jewish community. . . .

The data presented above portray a Jewish community that, despite its evident heterogeneity, was basically lower middle class and proletarian, and both unassimilated and unacculturated—although, as we shall see, by the 1930s acculturation was making rapid strides forward. It was not only largely Jewish in speech and in national feeling, but also, of course, deeply rooted in traditional religious Judaism, whether of the Hasidic or anti-Hasidic (misnagdic) variety. The cultural and political activities of the interwar Polish Jewry were determined both by its essentially Eastern-type characteristics, inherited from the past centuries, and by its confrontation with the nationalistic, antisemitic, backward, but nonetheless modernizing Polish state.

The Jewish Question in the New Poland

... One of the hallmarks of the new Jewish politics in Eastern Europe, which developed chiefly in the late-nineteenth-century Russian empire ... was the principle that the Jews were a nation like all other nations. The fact that they had no territory of their own was not regarded as an indication that they were no less a legitimate national entity than the Ukrainians or the Poles. Whether or not the Jews ought to aspire to a territory and state of their own was a bone of contention among the competing Jewish political parties, but most Jewish nationalists, whether Zionist or anti-Zionist, believed that so long as Jews lived in the East European diaspora they should enjoy both civil and national rights. ...

Jewish national autonomy meant different things to different people. Its most fundamental meaning was that the Jews, like other minority nationalities, whether territorial or extraterritorial, should be granted the right to develop their national life with the help of public funds. In practical terms this meant above all the right to establish state-supported Jewish schools conducted in Jewish languages (either Yiddish or Hebrew). More far-reaching plans called for state support for a wide range of Jewish cultural, social, and economic institutions and, on the political level, for a state-recognized official Jewish democratic body whose elected leaders would represent the Jews in parliament and in the government. Some Jewish nationalists even demanded that the Jew-ish national representation in parliament be guaranteed in accordance with the Jewish proportion of the general population. ...

It is important to emphasize that not all East European Jews were interested in the various schemes for Jewish national autonomy. This was obviously true of the assimilationist sector, and it was true of many acculturating Jews as well. It was also true of most Orthodox Jews. The last were naturally hostile to all secular ideologies, and the fact is that almost all the adherents to Jewish national autonomy had in mind secular national autonomy—secular Jewish national schools, for example. That the religious leadership of the Polish Jewish communities could no more support the secular ideology of national autonomy than they could support the Marxist ideology of the Jewish socialist Bund was a fact known, and exploited, by the Polish government.

Jewish demands for national autonomy in Poland were set forth by Jewish leaders at the Paris peace conference of 1919, at which time these leaders attempted to persuade both the great powers and the Polish politicians that the granting of such demands would serve both the Jewish and the Polish interests. ... In the end, Poland signed (in June 1919) a Minorities' Treaty with the victorious powers, of which two articles specifically mentioned the Jews. The first called upon the Polish government to allow for the existence of Jewish schools, controlled by Jewish authorities and funded by the state. The second forbade the government to compel the Jews to violate their Sabbath. ...

The Poles bitterly resented having been coerced into signing the Minorities' Treaty. They regarded it as an intolerable act of interference on the part of the great powers and blamed the Jews for having engineered its acceptance. The treaty was ratified by the *Sejm* [Polish parliament] only after all shades of opinion had denounced it, and its text was first published by the Polish government in its official organ as late as December, 1920. The secular national Jewish leadership, on the other hand, regarded its passage as a great victory. It was, so thought the optimistic Zionists, a "magna carta" in that it specifically referred to the Jews as a minority with national, not only religious, rights. It signified, so they thought, the beginning of a new era in Polish-Jewish relations and a foundation upon which the glorious edifice of Jewish national autonomy in Poland would be erected.[9] From our vantage point, however, such optimism is difficult to understand. . . . The traditional antisemitism of the Polish political elite was reinforced by the experience of World War I and by the events in Poland, particularly in the ethnically mixed border regions, during the immediate postwar period. Far from being regarded as potential allies, as they were in Lithuania and in Bohemia, the Jews were generally regarded as enemies of the Polish cause. Their effort to force Jewish national autonomy down the Poles' throats with the aid of foreign powers was seen as yet another example of their basically hostile attitude toward the Polish state. . . .

Attitudes toward the Jews were part and parcel of attitudes toward the nationalities question as a whole. If the Jews represented, as always, a special and particularly troublesome case, they could not be isolated from the more general difficulty posed by one-third of the Polish population's being ethnically non-Polish. The basic issue that confronted Polish politicians was whether Poland was a multinational state by definition or a Polish nation-state despite the undeniable existence of numerous non-Poles. Adoption of the first position implied granting extensive national rights to the "territorial minorities" in the east, the Ukrainians and the Belorussians, as well as

giving special status to the German minority in the west. It also implied a greater willingness, at least, to consider the Jews' demands for national autonomy. If, on the other hand, Poland was to be regarded as a nation-state, the implications were quite different. In this case the nationalities would not receive special rights, efforts would be made to polonize the country, and the interests of the Polish element within the population would be promoted at the expense of the non-Poles. It was this latter position that was adopted by the great majority of Polish political parties and was, in fact, implemented. The Ukrainians and the Belorussians were often regarded as an "ethnic mass" which, with the right treatment, eventually could be merged with the Polish nation. Ukrainian demands for autonomy in eastern Galicia were turned down, as were their requests to establish a Ukrainian university in Lwów. Ukrainian- and Belorussian-language elementary schools were permitted to exist but were under strong pressure to polonize; their numbers declined over the years. Members of these Slavic nationalities did not have an easy time in pursuing careers in the Polish civil service, and they encountered discrimination in all walks of life. The Germans, too, faced similar discrimination and received little satisfaction so far as their nationalist demands were concerned. True, negotiations were occasionally held between the Poles and the various nationalities (including the Jews), but the "agreements," if reached, failed to endure. The fact is that most Polish leaders adhered to the slogan "Poland for the Poles." The non-Poles would have to conform, suffer in silence, and in the end either emigrate or undergo polonization.[10] The Polish nation, it was felt, had not shed its blood and sacrificed its sons in order to establish a state in which vast territories and important financial resources would be controlled by non-Poles.

The Jewish question, of course, was quite different from the Ukrainian, Belorussian, or German question. On the surface it appeared to be a less dangerous and difficult one. The Jews, after all, possessed no territorial ambitions in Poland and had no armed allies on Poland's borders. They were traditionally a politically loyal, if culturally and religiously nonconformist, population, and there was no reason why they should not prove to be loyal citizens of the Polish state. It cannot be denied, however, that they constituted a problem for the rulers of the state. The vast majority of Jews were clearly very different from the Polish majority—in religion, speech, culture, customs, and economic behavior. Should the state attempt to polonize them or not? Should they be allowed to continue to predominate in Polish cities and in Polish commerce? Polish politicians brought to the Jewish question a set of attitudes much more complex than those they brought to the Ukrainian or even the German question. The Jews, after all, were not Christians, and the Catholic church, one of the most influential of all Polish institutions, had long waged a campaign against them. Antisemitism was not at all the same as anti-Ukrainian reeling—it had much deeper and more emotional roots. Moreover, the Jews were to be found everywhere in Poland and were highly visible. If the Ukrainians and the Belorussians were concentrated in the far-off villages of Galicia and the kresy, the Jews were to be found in great numbers in the very centers of Polish political and cultural life—in Warsaw, Cracow, Lwów, and Vilna. What was to be done with them? . . .

The decline in the number of antisemitic excesses from 1921 on brought relief to the Jewish community, but it did not lead to a new era of peace and understanding between Poles and Jews. It soon became clear that the Polish state, though committed by its constitution to treat all of its citizens as equals, was no less committed to the National Democratic mission to weaken the Jewish population. One way in which this is done was to see it that virtually no Jews were hired in those sections of the economy controlled by the state. For example, the Polish bureaucracy was to all intents and purposes *Judenrein* [Jew-free]. In Galicia, where Jews had been employed in the civil service before the war, they were pensioned off. In municipal bureaucracies the same situation prevailed.[11] Of 72,721 elementary school teachers in Poland in 1931, only 2.2 percent were Jews; and 4,429 high school teachers, only 2.8 percent.[12] Jewish doctors were not hired in state hospitals, and Jewish lawyers were not employed by state institutions. Jewish professors in Polish universities were virtually unknown; even the great historian Szymon Askenazy, one of Poland most distinguished scholars, could not obtain a chair in Warsaw. There were hardly any Jewish officers (aside from doctors) in the Polish army. The number of Jewish students in Polish universities, which were here as elsewhere in Eastern Europe hotbeds of antisemitism, declined dramatically during the interwar years-from 24.6 percent in 1921–1922 to 8.2 percent in 1938–1939.[13] True, an effort in 1923 to institute a legal *numerus clausus* (Jewish quota) in the universities was thwarted by Jewish protests in Poland and by opposition abroad, but the universities as autonomous institutions were able to see it that fewer and fewer Jews were admitted.

Aside from not hiring Jews in the civil service, other ways were found to strike at the Jewish economic interest. Jewish businessmen found it difficult to get state loans, and Jewish artisans found it no less difficult to obtain work licenses. The government passed a law forbidding work on Sunday, which was hailed by some as a progressive piece of legislation, and which had in fact been a long-standing demand of the Polish labor movement, but which was interpreted by the Jews quite differently, since it meant that many Jews were unable to open their businesses two days out of the week.[14] The effect of this law on the Jewish economy, and the impact of the other measures described, led one Jewish leader to accuse the Poles of carrying out a policy of economic "extermination" against the Jewish population and of creating an environment even more hostile to the Jews than that of tsarist Russia.[15] This assessment was influenced by other anti-Jewish acts inspired by the government, such as the effort to expel from Poland Jews accused of not having Polish citizenship and the electoral law which made it especially difficult for Jews and other scattered minorities to elect representatives to the *Sejm*.

"Extermination" was certainly far too strong a word to use, at least in the 1920s, but even in this first decade of Polish independence, which later appeared to many Jews as a kind of golden age of Polish democracy and tolerance, it was clear that the Jewish condition was tragic. The triumph of Polish nationalism meant the unleashing of latent antisemitism that struck at all Jews, assimilated and unassimilated, Orthodox, and secular. This triumph, along with the generally bad economic situation, made much worse by the Depression of the 1930s, meant the end to any reasonable hopes that the Jews might improve their already desperate economic situation and make a breakthrough into the middle class. On the contrary, the poverty of the land and the policy of its government led toward the ever-increasing impoverishment of large sections of the Jewish community, whose miserable plight was one aspect of the general impoverishment of the Polish population in the 1930s.

Jewish Politics in Poland in the 1920s

When viewed as a whole, Jewish politics in Poland possessed certain special characteristics. For one thing, the degree of divisiveness and factionalism was surprisingly great, all the more so in view of the relatively homogeneous nature of the Jewish social structure. The Jews, unlike the other national groups of the region, possessed neither a peasantry nor a landed aristocracy and thus were spared political parties based on these two groups. Nonetheless, the number of Jewish political organizations in independent Poland was remarkable. To be sure, political divisiveness in Eastern Europe was not a Jewish monopoly, but there were certain specific reasons for its prevalence among the Jews. The question of where the Jewish problem was to be solved, "here" or "there," did not confront any other national group in the region, and neither, except in a few marginal cases, did the question of linguistic orientations. Moreover, the question of which identity to assume, secular national or religious, was more acute among the Jews than among the other nationalities. Finally, since the Jews enjoyed no political power, there was little incentive to prevent political factionalism. The absence of real rewards for sticking together meant that ideological differences led almost inevitably to organizational splits. On the other hand, traditional notions of Jewish unity and the fact that the antisemites often made no distinctions among Jews usually failed to lead to Jewish political unity.

Along with divisiveness went a remarkably high degree of political mobilization within the Jewish community. Not all Jewish parties were mass organizations; some, in fact, were the creations of one man and a typewriter. But on the whole the historian of interwar Polish Jewry cannot fail to be struck by the fact that Polish Jewry, especially Polish Jewish youth, was highly politicized. An important collection of hundreds of autobiographies of Jewish teenagers, available in the archives of the Jewish Scientific Institute (Yivo) in New York, demonstrates that for young Polish Jews, particularly in the 1930s, joining a political youth movement or party was the norm, the expected thing to do. Why was this the case? One obvious reason was the very acuteness of the Jewish question itself, which obliged many Jews, young people particularly, to seek solutions in the political arena. If political activism is a function of extreme situations, we should not be surprised that so many Jews turned to politics. The Jewish dilemma in Poland, in both its economic and its political aspects, also had the effect of lessening the traditional authority of the parents and of religion in the Jewish household. Economic collapse and violent antisemitism, along with the secular, democratic, and modernizing character of the new Polish state, meant that Jewish children were less likely to look to their parents or to their rabbis for guidance and more likely to place their hopes in one or another of the new political organizations, both Jewish and non-Jewish. They were, in other words, more likely to "run away" to the Pioneer, to the Bund, or to the Polish Communist Party. Parental opposition, once formidable, weakened during this period and was usually not strong enough to dissuade them. The generational war between parents and children often took the form of a war over the political orientation of the youth, whose rejection of parental attitudes and whose growing indifference to religious authority resulted in the swelling of the ranks of the Jewish parties.

Another characteristic of Jewish politics in Eastern Europe was that the party or the youth movement took on the attributes of a state within a state, dispensing a wide range of services not always connected with its ideological position. Such services, from running elementary and high schools to administering summer camps, helped give party members the feeling that they resided in a "new world," as opposed to the "old world" of the home and the synagogue. It is clear that the party served as a kind of substitute both for the family and for the secular state, which notably failed to treat its Jewish citizens equally and was not interested in granting them the kind of services they needed. To be a Bundist or a member of *Poale Zion* was to belong to a separate world with its own cultural, social, and economic institutions. The parties, therefore, were important in aiding Polish Jews in compensating for their alienation from the antisemitic, Catholic, Polish nationalist state.

All the major Jewish parties in Poland, with the important exception of *Agudes yisroel*, were committed to what they termed the "new Jewish politics." This signified that they had broken once and for all with the old Jewish political traditions of seeking a modus vivendi, at all costs, with the authorities. They denounced such traditional behavior as demeaning. The "new Jew," they reasoned, possessed national pride and would proudly demand his rights as a Jew and as a free man. Adherents to the new Jewish politics would therefore not be afraid to anger the gentiles. It was this point of view that lay behind Jewish political activity at the Paris peace conference, where Jewish national rights were demanded even though such demands obviously angered the Poles. And the fact that *Agudes yisroel* rejected this stance in favor of time-honored Jewish political practices made this religious party the object of disgust and scorn in Zionist, Folkist, and Bundist circles. The new Jewish politics flourished in interwar Poland as nowhere else in the diaspora....

Aspects of Jewish Cultural Life

Just as interwar Poland became the center of autonomous Jewish politics in the Jewish diaspora, so it also became the center of autonomous Jewish culture, whether secular or religious, whether in Hebrew or in Yiddish. The yeshivas for which Poland had been so famous in the Jewish world continued to flourish, and new institutions of traditional Jewish learning were founded by the two new religious parties, Agudes yisroel and the Mizrachi.[16] Along with the preservation of traditional Jewish culture went the remarkable experiment to create in Poland a secular Jewish national culture based on Yiddish which was designed to serve as one of the cornerstones of Jewish national autonomy. Never before in modern Jewish history, and for that matter never again, would this version of autonomous Jewish culture make such deep inroads into Jewish life. If in the Soviet Union the regime clamped down on Yiddish culture in the 1930s, and if in America acculturation and assimilation sentenced Yiddish to a gradual but inevitable decline, Poland remained the ideal setting in which the "folk language" and the "folk culture," in its new, modern form, could thrive. Moreover, the unification of Congress Poland with Galicia and the eastern borderlands, while causing serious problems for Jewish politics, was a blessing for Jewish culture. Indeed, the role of Litvaks in Yiddish cultural life in the capital was so great as to cause some grumbling in Polish Jewish circles with regard to the "foreign invasion" from the Lithuanian-Belorussian lands.[17]

One dramatic example of the success of Yiddish culture in Poland was the Yiddish press, with its two mass-circulation dailies in Warsaw (*Haynt* and *Moment*) and hundreds of other daily and weekly newspapers in the provinces. Jewish newspapers also appeared in Hebrew and in Polish, but neither of these languages, especially not the former, could compete with Yiddish.[18] Another example was the flourishing of the Yiddish theater.[19] Interwar Poland also became a great center of Yiddish literature . . . and produced such talented authors as Y. Y. Trunk (1887–1961), Oizer

Varshavsky (1898–1944) and I. J. Singer (1893–1944). It was also the milieu in which the most famous of modern Yiddish writers, Isaac Bashevis Singer (b. 1904, known simply as Bashevis in Yiddish) made his literary debut.[20] Along with literature went the development of Yiddish literary criticism and new efforts to promote an understanding of Jewish history and culture. In 1925 the Jewish Scientific Institute (Yivo) was founded in Vilna. The Yivo quickly became the main scholarly institution of the secular Yiddish cultural movement, and its various publications helped lay the foundation for modern academic work on Yiddish language and literature. . . .

If modern Yiddish culture in the interwar period found a center in Poland, modern Hebrew culture fared less well. The Hebrew press, supported by the Zionist movement, was not nearly so successful as its Yiddish rival, and the new Hebrew theater and literature were now concentrated in Tel Aviv and Jerusalem rather than in Warsaw and Vilna. Hebrew, of course, was not a spoken language of Polish Jewry, and in an age of mass-circulation newspapers and novels, the small, cultural elite that had traditionally supported Hebrew culture could not compete with popular tastes and habits. . . .

In their choice of a Jewish school, Polish Jewish parents revealed a markedly conservative character, preferring the traditional religious schools to the Bundist or Zionist alternatives. The majority of all Jews of school age attended Polish state schools rather than Jewish private ones. According to [Chaim] Kazdan, about sixty percent of all Jewish pupils studied in state schools, although it should be emphasized that this figure includes Jewish pupils in those state schools which catered exclusively to Jews (the so-called *Szabasowki* that exempted Jews from writing on Saturday) and that many Jewish pupils studied both in Jewish and in state schools.[21] On the high school level the majority of Jewish pupils attended Jewish schools, since Polish high schools, unlike Polish elementary schools, discriminated against Jews.

The reasons for the preference of state over Jewish education among Polish Jews are obvious. Polish state schools, after all, were free. And even if they were sometimes antisemitic, they dispensed a Polish education. . . . The new Jewish generation was at least to some extent becoming culturally polonized, whatever the findings of the 1931 census, and in this sense the old Polish Jewish assimilationist dream of a Polish-speaking Jewry was realized during the interwar period. . . .

The ever-growing encroachment of Polish on Jewish life did not mean that the Jews were assimilating into Polish society. It did, however, indicate the severe obstacles confronted by the adherents to Jewish national cultural autonomy everywhere in Poland, with the exception of the still not polonized *kresy* . . . . It is safe to assume that, had independent Poland survived for another twenty years, modern Yiddish and Hebrew culture and schools would have inevitably declined, to be replaced by Jewish cultural creativity in the Polish language.

Before the war some Jews had played a major role in Polish cultural life, and this trend continued into the interwar period. Indeed, only in Hungary, and of course in interwar Soviet Russia, did Jews penetrate so deeply into the cultural life of the majority nationality in Eastern Europe. The presence of a small but important Polish Jewish cultural elite demonstrates the heterogeneous character of Polish Jewry.

The 1930s: The Reemergence of Violent Antisemitism and the Jewish Reaction

During the 1930s, and particularly in the last four years of Poland's existence as an independent state, violent antisemitism made a dramatic reappearance. It was accompanied by redoubled efforts to strike at the Jews' economic interests and to remove the Jews, as many as possible, from Polish economic and intellectual life. A complex combination of factors, having to do with the transition from democracy to right-wing authoritarianism, economic depression, and events outside Poland's borders, was responsible for these ominous developments. In Poland, as in most other states of East Central Europe, the last decade of the interwar period witnessed a struggle for power between moderate and extreme right-wing nationalists in the context of an economic crisis and the rising influence of Nazi Germany. The Jewish question, in Poland as elsewhere, proved to be an integral part of a political struggle the outcome of which was to determine who would rule the country.

The first great blow to Poland's democratic form of government—Pilsudski's coup d'état of 1926—was regarded by most Polish Jews as a positive event. This was not because they opposed democracy, but rather because they regarded Pilsudski as a moderate nationalist, a federalist and therefore possibly sympathetic to the concept of national autonomy, a bitter enemy of the National Democrats, and a former socialist opposed to antisemitism as a political or economic weapon. He was also seen as a strong man who would put a stop to the endless political and social strife that some Jews believed was the main cause of Polish antisemitism. To a certain degree Pilsudski's ten years in office as the supreme arbiter of Poland's fate justified these expectations. He was successful in holding the extreme antisemites in check and welcomed the participation of Jews in his government lists during elections to the *Sejm*. His prime minister in the years immediately following the coup, Kazimierz Bartel, was generally regarded as friendly to the Jews and made a few statements opposing economic antisemitism. However, Pilsudski and his camp, popularly known as the *Sanacja* (cleansing), took no steps to alter the state's basic attitude toward the Jews, just as they did little to win the affection of the Ukrainians and Belorussians. The Jews continued to receive virtually no state funds for their cultural institutions, and they remained the victims of wide-ranging economic discrimination. The Great Depression, which struck Poland with a vengeance in 1929, rendered the impact of this economic antisemitism all the greater. In short, despite Pilsudski's refusal to embrace antisemitic slogans, the Jewish crisis intensified. If the Jews sincerely mourned Pilsudski after his death in May, 1935, they mourned him as the lesser evil, as a man much to be preferred to his National Democratic and fascist-leaning opponents. . . .

The roots of the unprecedented wave of antisemitism that characterized the post-Pilsudski period are certainly to be found in pre-1935 Poland. One is the already mentioned economic crisis, which heightened social tensions and inevitably worsened Polish-Jewish relations. Another important factor was the rise of Nazism in Germany. Polish nationalists had much to fear from a resurgent Germany, but they were greatly impressed by Hitler and the prominent role of antisemitism in the Nazi ideology. Of particular significance was the influence of Nazism on the younger National Democrats. In 1934 some right-wing radical youth split off from Dmowski's party and formed the National Radical Camp (ONR), clearly based on the Nazi model; its members were described by Moshe Kleinbaum, a leading Zionist, as "Polish Hitlerites."[22] And the National Democratic movement itself, called since 1928 the National Party, veered ever more sharply to the right, its antisemitism "greatly encouraged by the impunity with which Hitler was able to deprive of political rights the wealthiest and most powerful Jewish

community in Europe."[23] As was the case elsewhere in East Central Europe, the universities became centers of anti-Jewish agitation and riots, much of it in emulation of the Nazis. Dmowski himself, despite his longstanding anti-German views and his devotion to Catholicism, did nothing to stem the growing tide of pro-Nazi feeling within his party.[24]

While the right-wing opposition took comfort from Hitler's triumph, the Polish government took steps to come to terms with the new regime on its western border. In 1934 Poland and Germany signed a nonaggression pact, thus signaling the Polish government's apparent belief that it had nothing to fear from Hitler. This in turn naturally increased Nazi influence within Poland. In July of the same year, Goebbels visited Poland and lectured at the University of Warsaw. Many Polish dignitaries, including the prime minister, attended his lecture, which dealt, among other things, with the National Socialist attitude toward the Jewish question.[25] . . .

After the death of Pilsudski, Poland was ruled by a small circle of Pilsudski loyalists who lacked their revered leader's charisma and who enjoyed little popular support. The new regime's legitimacy was based on an antidemocratic constitution, initiated by Pilsudski himself, which supplanted the liberal constitution of 1921. In 1936 a new ruling political organization called the Camp of National Unity (OZON) was established, the electoral success of which was guaranteed by the new constitution. It should be stressed, however, that even now Poland did not become a totalitarian state. The most serious threat to the rule of the "colonels," as Pilsudski's followers were called, came from the right—from the National Party and its fascist offshoot, the ONR. In the struggle that took place in the context of growing social unrest and an increasingly dangerous international situation, the Jewish question became a major issue, as each side, seeking popular support among the impoverished Polish masses, attempted to outdo the other in its devotion to the anti-Jewish campaign.[26]

During the post-Pilsudski years the government's attitude toward the Jewish question was fairly clear. In the short run, the Jews' role in the Polish economy and in all other walks of life was to be drastically reduced. In the long run, emigration was the only solution. In a declaration of 1937 the government, which refused to allow Jews to join the ruling party, defined its Jewish policy as follows:

> We have too high an idea of our civilization and we respect too strongly the order and peace that every state needs to approve brutal antisemitic acts which harm the dignity and prestige of a great country. At the same time, it is understandable that the country should possess the instinct compelling it to defend its culture, and it is natural that Polish society should seek economic self-sufficiency.[27]

This last reference to "self-sufficiency" meant that the government lent its official sanction to unbridled economic antisemitism. This policy was given its most famous formulation by Prime Minister Slawoj-Skladkowski, who said in 1936, "Economic struggle [against the Jews] by all means [*owszem*]—but without force."[28] But the main thrust of official policy toward the Jews was to promote the cause of Jewish emigration. The problem was, of course, that it was not clear where the Jews could go. The Polish government did its best to soften British opposition to emigration to Palestine, and, if Zionism meant Jewish emigration to that country, no one was more Zionist than Poland's leaders in the late 1930s. Poland also linked the issue of Jewish emigration to its demands for colonies overseas. Thus in 1936 Madagascar was put forward as a suitable Polish colony and as a promising region for Polish Jewish settlement.[29] . . .

Both economic antisemitism and "pro-Zionist" leanings were very much present in pre-1935 Poland, and neither can be regarded as a new departure. What was new was the government's open and vocal espousal of these principles, the immediate causes of which were its weakness, its fear of the extreme right, and its antidemocratic tendencies. In its Jewish policy it received the full support of the Polish Catholic church, long a bastion of antisemitism and, of course, an institution of great influence and authority. The church was a veteran supporter of the National Democrats, and some priests were among the most active propagators of antisemitism in the country. In 1936 Cardinal August Hlond, head of the Polish hierarchy, published a special pastoral letter on the Jewish question in which he opposed Nazi racist doctrines but condemned the Jews as atheists and revolutionaries. He also lent the authority of the church to economic antisemitism.[30]

The main difference between the attitude of the extreme right-wing opposition and that of the government and the church to the Jewish question had to do with means, not ends. While the political and religious establishments deplored violence, the right embraced it. And if the church, at least, resisted Nazi racism, thereby seeking to protect Jewish converts to Catholicism, the right had no such scruples. Both establishment and opposition, the *Sanacja* and the *Endeks*, agreed that "Jewish influence" in Poland must be done away with. What this meant was clear, although how it was to be achieved was not. The centrist Peasant Party, an amalgam of the various peasant factions of the 1920s, also lent its voice to the anti-Jewish chorus. In 1935 this party declared that:

all citizens in Poland irrespective of creed and nationality must enjoy equal rights. The Jews, however, as has been proved, cannot be assimilated and are a consciously alien nation within Poland. As a middle class they occupy a far more important position in Poland than in other countries, so that the Poles have no middle class of their own. It is, therefore, most vital for the Polish state that these middle-class functions shall more and more pass into the hands of the Poles. We must realize this objective not through fruitless acts of violence, which only brutalize the nation, but above all through the development of the cooperative movement in the country. While we profess the principle of equal rights for the Jews in Poland, we shall nevertheless aim to solve the Jewish problem through the emigration of Jews to Palestine and other places.[31]

This left the Polish Socialist Party as the only important political organization clearly opposed to antisemitism, and even within its ranks there was no unanimity on the Jewish question. Thus in 1936 one of its spokesmen published a pamphlet advocating Jewish emigration, a position denounced by the Jewish ally of the PPS, the Bund.[32] Nonetheless, in Poland, as was not the case in Hungary, a political organization of considerable and even growing strength set its face clearly against the government-inspired antisemitic campaign. Gentile opposition to antisemitism, therefore, was not restricted, as it was in other countries, to a courageous but lonely and isolated group of intellectuals and priests who viewed with alarm the emergence of virulent racism on the Nazi model. From the Jewish point of view, and particularly from the point of view of the Jewish left, this was a fact of some importance. But it is also true that the PPS was too weak to blunt

the antisemitic campaign. Its stand, therefore, was of greater moral than practical significance.

The war against the Jews during 1935–1939 took many forms, ranging from legislative efforts to brutal attacks. In 1936, for example, legislative action was initiated in the *Sejm* to outlaw *shkhite* (ritual slaughter). This attack on one of the most fundamental aspects of Jewish religious practice caused a tremendous storm in the Jewish world, where it was interpreted as a first step toward revoking Jewish emancipation. A law forbidding *shkhite*, closely modeled on Nazi German legal precedents, was actually passed by the *Sejm* in 1936, but was eventually amended by the government to allow a certain amount of ritually slaughtered meat for Jews in areas where they made up more than three percent of the population.[33]

Another dominant theme in the antisemitic movement was the effort to establish "ghetto benches" in Polish universities. In some of these institutions the Jewish students, whose number was rapidly dwindling, were required to attend lectures in segregated areas of the classroom; this system was inaugurated at the Lwów Polytechnicum in 1935, and later at the University of Vilna. From 1937 on, physical attacks against Jewish students became ever more common, and several Jewish students were actually murdered. The ghettoizing of Jewish students was the first skirmish in the campaign to segregate (and eventually oust altogether) Jews in the white-collar professions. In 1937 various associations of doctors and journalists adopted the "Aryan paragraph," thereby making Jewish membership impossible.[34]

Most serious, however, was the economic boycott of Jewish businesses, an age-old tactic which now resurfaced with explicit government support. Bands of antisemitic enthusiasts invaded the marketplaces of Polish towns and villages and warned Christian Poles not to do business with Jewish merchants. Behind them stood a well-organized movement, spearheaded by National Democrats but supported by the various Polish economic organizations of merchants and artisans. Christian businessmen were supplied with special signs attesting to their "Aryan" nature, which were displayed for all to see. Pressure (not all of it gentle) was brought to bear on Christian Poles not to do business with Jewish firms, not to deal with Jewish agents, and not to rent apartments to Jews. The right-wing press often published the names of Christians who failed to obey the boycott. Thus in 1937 the *Warszawski Dziennik Narodowy* informed its readers that a certain von Richwald had purchased a radio from a Jewish store in Poznań Province and that a civil servant from Radom had taken a ride in a Jewish cab.[35]

The enforcers of the boycott had frequent recourse to violence. Jewish stalls in marketplaces and at fairs were destroyed; Jewish storekeepers and artisans in little towns were terrorized and forced to abandon their shops. In such an atmosphere it did not require much for attacks on Jewish shopkeepers to degenerate into pogroms directed against the entire local Jewish population. From 1936 on, such pogroms were a common occurrence, once again reviving a phenomenon familiar in Poland during the prewar period. According to a list prepared by Yankev Leshchinski, during 1935–1936, 1,289 Jews were wounded in antisemitic attacks in over 150 towns and villages in Poland, a number based on reports in the Polish press and probably much too low. "Hundreds of Jews were killed."[36]

The impact of all this on the Jewish population, both from the economic and psychological point of view, was enormous. During the 1930s, the period of the Great Depression when the entire population of Poland underwent a process of pauperization, it began to appear as though not only

the Polish Jewish youth had "no future" in the country, but that the entire Jewish community was in dire peril. The most telling aspect of the economic crisis was the decline in the number of Jewish-owned stores. During the years 1932–1937 the Jewish economist Menakhem Linder carried out a study of the Jewish-owned shops in eleven towns in the Bialystok region. In 1932 there were 663 Jewish-owned shops in these towns, which constituted 92.0 percent of the total number of shops; by 1937 there were 563 Jewish-owned shops, which constituted 64.5 percent of the total number. The figures show that the crucial year in this decline was 1936–1937, the reason being the renewed boycott. The decline was nationwide, although it was particularly evident in the eastern borderlands, where Jewish domination of commerce was so pronounced. By 1938, according to one authority, the share of Jewish-owned enterprises in Polish commerce had sunk below 50 percent, and no end to the precipitous decline was in sight.[37]

That the economic boycott was less effective in the industrial sector (which, as we know, meant chiefly craft production) is one reason for the Jewish tendency toward "proletarianization" in the 1930s. But more important than proletarianization was pauperization. The Great Depression, the antisemitic campaign, and the competition of a "native" bourgeoisie and of peasant cooperatives combined to push more and more Jews below the poverty line. As early as 1934 the percentage of Jews who appealed for some form of relief during the Passover holiday was alarmingly high—in Galicia nearly one-third of the Jewish population, in fifty-eight selected urban localities needed such aid. And the worst was yet to come. The vigorous, even heroic efforts of foreign Jewish relief organizations to halt the economic decline saved many Jews from starvation, but were unable to reverse the trend.[38] By the eve of World War II, Polish Jewry was an impoverished community with no hope of reversing its rapid economic decline. . . .

In this new state, beset with seemingly intractable internal and external problems, only nationalism and the Catholic Church served as unifying factors. Both Polish nationalism and Polish Catholicism were by their very nature exclusive, antipluralistic, and antisemitic. And, since there was little in the way of a tolerant, pluralistic, liberal political tradition in modern, as opposed perhaps to medieval, Poland, nothing stood in the way of the triumph of extreme national-religious intolerance from which all the minorities in the state suffered and which, because of the special nature of the anti-Jewish tradition and the economic vulnerability of the Jews, was particularly threatening to the Jewish minority.

It is true that the Polish state, unlike Hungary and Romania, refrained from enacting anti-Jewish legislation in the late 1930s. It is also true that in Poland, unlike in most other East European countries, there was considerable opposition to the extreme antisemitism of the late 1930s. But, in the development of Jewish-gentile relations, there was little essential difference between Poland and the other major states of the region, with the important exception of Czechoslovakia. The combination of traditional hatred of Jews, the triumph of nationalism, internal weakness, and the role of the Jewish question in the struggle for power between the moderate right and the extreme right typified the situation not only in Poland, but in other East European states as well. In this respect, as with regard to internal Jewish developments—acculturation, economic decline, political divisiveness, the failure of national autonomy and Zionism to solve the Jewish question—Poland may serve as a paradigm of the Jewish experience in interwar East Central Europe. . . .

NOTES

1. For data and a discussion of the difficulties of ethnic statistics, see Rothschild, *East Central Europe*, 34–36.
2. On Jewish demography in Poland, see Mahler, *Yehude polin ben shte milhamot ha-olam* (Tel Aviv, 1968), 18–36; Szyja Bronsztejn, *Ludnośćżydowska w Polsce w okresie mi ędzywojennym* (Warsaw, 1963). See also Bronsztejn, "The Jewish Population of Poland in 1931," *Jewish Journal of Sociology* 6, no. 1 (July 1964): 3–29. The 1921 census did not include parts of the provinces of Vilna and Silesia.
3. For figures on Jewish emigration 1921–1931, see Bronsztejn, *Ludnośćżydowska*, 97. During this period 292,832 Jews emigrated; of these, 184,500 left during 1921–1925. See also Aryeh Tartakower, "Jewish Emigration from Poland in the Post-War Years," *Jewish Social Service Quarterly* 16, no. 3 (March 1940): 273–79.
4. On the remarkable changes in Soviet Jewish demography, see Mordecai Altshuler, *Ha-kibuts ha-yehudi be-vrit ha-moatsot bi-yamenu* (Jerusalem, 1980), 11–20.
5. Janusz Żarnowski, *Spoleńczestwo drugiej rzeczy-pospolitej* (Warsaw, 1973), 391.
6. For a discussion of this question, see Mendelsohn, *Class Struggle in the Pale* (Cambridge, Eng., 1970), 19–23.
7. Mahler, *Yehude polin*, 133.
8. See Zarnowski, *Spoleczeństwo*, 263–78.
9. For the quotation see Mendelsohn, *Zionism in Poland*, 107. See also Netser, *Maavak yehude polin*, 162.
10. See the following Polish studies: Andrzej Chojnowski, *Koncepcje polityki narodowościowej rzgdów polskich w latach 1921–1939* (Wroclaw, etc., 1979); Jerzy Tomaszewski, "Konsekwencja wielonarodowościowej struktury ludnosci Polski 1918–1939 dla procesów integracyjnych spoleczeństwa," in *Drogi integracji spoleczeństwa w Polsce XlX–XXw.*, ed. Henryk Zielinski (Wroclaw, etc., 1976), 109–38. See also Alexander

Groth, "Dmowski, Pilsudski, and Ethnic Conflict in Pre-1939 Poland," *Canadian Slavic Studies* 3 (1969):69–91; Joel Cang, "The Opposition Parties in Poland and Their Attitude towards the Jews and the Jewish Question," *Jewish Social Studies* 1, no. 2 (1939): 241–56.

11. Mahler, *Yehude polin*, 159–60.

12. Ibid., 170.

13. Ibid., 172.

14. On economic antisemitism, see the survey by Yeshaye Trunk, "Der ekonomisher antisemitizm in poyln tsvishn di tsvey velt-milkhomes," in *Studies,* ed. Fishman, 3–98.

15. This term was used by Yitshak Grünbaum at a Zionist conference in 1925; see Mendelsohn, "Polish Zionism between Two Wars," *Dispersion and Unity* 17–18 (1973): 82, quoting from *Haynt* 55 (March 5, 1925).

16. Sh. Z. Kahana, "Ha-moreshet ha-masoratit shel yehude polin*," Sefer ha-shanalyorbukh* 2 (1967): 34–70; Yitshak Levin, "Yeshivat hokhme lublin," ibid., 381–88; Shmuel Mirski, ed., *Mosdot tora be-iropa be-vinyanam u-ve-horbanam* (New York, 1956), 1–413, 561–603.

17. See Nakhmen Mayzel, *Gevn amol a lebn* (Buenos Aires, 1953), 17–18.

18. For bibliographies of the Yiddish press, see Yisroel Shayn, *Bibliografie fun oysgabes aroysgegebn durkh di arbeter parteyen in poyln in di yorn 1918–1939* (Warsaw, 1963); idem, "Bibliografie fun yidishe periodike in poyln," in *Studies,* ed. Fishman, 422–83. For studies of the Jewish press, see *Fun noentn over*, vol. 2 (New York, 1956), which deals with the Jewish press in Warsaw; Khaim Finkelshtein, *Haynt, a tsaytung bay yidn, 1908–1939* (Tel Aviv, 1978). See also David Flinker et al., eds., *Itonut yehudit she-hayta* (Tel Aviv, 1973), and Marian Fuks, *Prasa żydowska w Warszawie 1823–1939* (Warsaw, 1979).

19. See Mikhol Vaykhert, *Zikhroynes, Varshe*, vol. 2 (Tel Aviv, 1961), for a memoir on the Yiddish theater in Poland. See also Yitskhok Turkov-Grudberg, "Dos yidishe teater in poyln tsvishn

beyde velt-milkhomes," *Sefer ha-shanal yorbukh* 2 (1967): 325–58.

20. Dov Sadan, *Sifrut yidish be-folin ben shte milhamot ha-olam* (Jerusalem, 1964); Y. Y. Trunk, *Di yidishe proze in poyln in der tkufe tsvishn beyde velt-milkhomes* (Buenos Aires, 1949); Mayzel, *Gevn amol a lebn.*

21. Kazdan, *Di geshikhte fun yidishn shulvezn*, 550–51.

22. Meltser, *Yahadut polin*, 13. See also Roman Wapihski, *Narodowa Demokracja 1893–1939* (Wroclaw, etc., 1980), 299–329.

23. Polonsky, *Politics*, 370.

24. Micewski, *Z geografii politycznej ii rzeczypospolitej. Szkice* (Warsaw, 1964), 21.

25. Yosef Teeni, *Aliyat Hitler la-shilton ve-hashpaata shel ha-antishemiyut al matsavam shelyehudepolin ba-shanim 1933–1939* (Ph.D. diss., Hebrew University, 1980), 61. See also Meltser, "Yahse polin-germaniya ba-shanim 1935–1938 ve-hashpaatam al baayat ha-yehudim be-folin," *Yad va-shem, kovets mehkarim* 12 (1977): 145–70.

26. For a good analysis of the situation, see Wynot, "'A Necessary Cruelty': The Emergence of Official Antisemitism in Poland," *American Historical Review* 76, no. 4 (October 1971): 1035–58. See also Korzec, *Juifs en Pologne*, 239–74.

27. As quoted in Polonsky, *Politics*, 424.

28. As quoted in Trunk, "Der ekonomisher antisemitizm," 65. See also Meltser, *Yahadut polin*, 45–46.

29. Meltser, *Yahadut polin*, 127–54; Leni Yahil, "Madagascar: Phantom of a Solution for the Jewish Question," in *Jews and Non-Jews in East Central Europe*, ed. Vago and Mosse, 315–34; Meltser, "Ha-diplomatiya ha-polanit u-vaayat ha-hagira ha-yehudit ba-shanim 1935–1939," *Gal-ed* 1 (1973): 211–49.

30. Teeni, *Aliyat Hitler*, 11–12.

31. As quoted in Joel Cang, "The Opposition Parties in Poland," 249.

32. Meltser, *Yahadut polin*, 12.

33. Ibid., 85–98.

34. Ibid., 99–105; Korzec, "Antisemitism in Poland," 94–98.

35. Trunk, "Der ekonomisher antisemitizm," 52. On the boycott, see ibid., 48–60; Meltser, *Yahadut polin*, 42–50, 190–205.

36. Trunk, "Der ekonomisher antisemitizm," 54; Yankev Leshchinski, "Ha-praot be-folin," *Dapim le-hekerha-shoa ve-ha-mered* 2 (February 1952): 37–92; Leshchinski, *Erev khurbm* (Buenos Aires, 1951).

37. Meltser, *Yahadut polin*, 204.

38. On the work of the Joint Distribution Committee in Poland in the 1930s, see Yehuda Bauer, *My Brother's Keeper: A History of the American Jewish Joint Distribution Committee 1929–1939* (Philadelphia, 1974), 190–209.

2 Nazism in Power

Reichspräsident von Hindenburg und Reichskanzler
Adolf Hitler begrüßen sich am 21. 3. 33 in Potsdam.

3. Chancellor Adolf Hitler greets German President Paul
von Hindenburg at the opening ceremonies for the new
Reichstag in Potsdam on March 21, 1933. (United States
Holocaust Memorial Museum, courtesy of B. I. Sanders.)

4. Berlin, Germany . . . September 1942—In 1938 Erna Puterman was working as a seamstress in Berlin where she met Frieda Adam (*left*), a coworker. The two teenage girls became friends. Even when Erna was forced to change jobs because she was Jewish, Frieda continued her friendship with Erna. Frieda refused to be intimidated by the anti-Jewish laws and climate. Life became increasingly difficult and exceedingly harsh for the Jews of Germany. In September 1942 Erna's mother was arrested and later sent on one of the early transports to Auschwitz. Erna was left to care for her brother, who was deaf. Not knowing what to do, Erna went to Frieda for help and advice. Frieda's response to Erna was immediate: "As long as there is food for us, there will be food for you, too." Thus in September 1942, Erna and her brother went into hiding, which lasted for more than two years. Frieda had three small children, ages six, four, and two, and a husband in the German army. Frieda said of her husband, "He was an evil man. Everyone was evil back then." When Frieda's husband discovered that she was hiding two Jews he began to blackmail her. Late in 1944 Frieda was forced to find Erna and her brother another place to hide. They all survived the war. (Courtesy JFR Photo Archives.)

Introduction

PETER HAYES

Adolf Hitler came to office determined to reverse the emancipation of Germany's Jews by stripping them of citizenship and the right to hold office; excluding them from the civil service, journalism, education, and the arts; and banning intermarriage with non-Jews. He expected these measures to reduce not only the influence of Jews over the rest of the nation, but also their very numbers in Germany, and he intended to accelerate that process by barring Jewish immigration and expelling all Jews who had entered the country since the outbreak of World War I. As of 1933, however, neither his nor his Party's planning appears to have gone beyond a program of degrading, segregating, and diminishing German Jewry and the stated eventual goal of its "removal" (in German: *Entfernung*) from the Reich. Cruel and harsh as this was, it was not yet a plan to massacre. Although Nazi rhetoric toward the Jews always was implicitly murderous—calling them vermin, parasites, bacilli, and cancers likened them to things to eradicate—Hitler initially was content, for the most part, with metaphorical menace.

In the early years of the Third Reich, the Nazi leadership could not be sure of what it could get away with in dealing with German Jews. After all, over half of the German population had never voted for Hitler, Nazis had only 3 of 12 seats in the Cabinet appointed on January 30, 1933, and President Hindenburg for a while retained the decisive political position. Hitler and his associates knew that they needed time to win most Germans over to his conviction that persecuting Jews was a necessary defensive act, indispensable to national survival. Moreover, the new regime needed stability and an appearance of moderation in order to generate an economic revival that would secure Hitler's hold on power and to lull Britain and France into tolerating the rearmament program that would propel his quest for "living space." Hitler the ideologue was obsessed with Jews, but Hitler the politician and expansionist dared not let his obsession show too much.

The readings in this chapter examine how the Nazi regime used a combination of carrot and stick from 1933 to 1939 to make the ostracism and impoverishment of German Jewry into the increasingly vicious collective project of an increasingly Nazified society. The excerpt by Eckert Conze and his colleagues on the International Historians Commission on the German Foreign Office and Nazism presents that institution as representative of the fateful readiness of *elite* portions of German society to offer *cooperation* with the Third Reich, to place themselves swiftly at its service, and to overlook its brutalities in order to achieve common goals. The eyewitness report by Sebastian Haffner, the pen name of Raimund Pretzel, a non-Jew whose disgust with Nazism led him to emigrate from Germany in 1938 and to record these recollections the following year, depicts the atmosphere of *street-level coercion* by which Nazis intimidated both opportunists and opponents into conformity during 1933. Thomas Kühne's analysis of the multiple ways in which Germans learned to accept *the claims of commu-*

nity and to recognize moral obligations only to "Us," not "Them," lays bare the process by which Nazism eroded ordinary Germans' decency thereafter.

Avraham Barkai's meticulous summary of *Aryanization*, the process by which the jobs and possessions of German Jews were transferred to other Germans from 1933 to 1939, captures the diabolical combination of stop-and-go persecution at the national level—characterized by flurries of discriminatory actions in 1933, 1935, and 1938 and lulls in between—with steady pressure on the livelihoods of Jews from Nazi activists and officeholders at the local level, below the radar of most foreign observers. As a result, by late 1937, almost five years after Hitler took power, nearly one-third of the German Jews had fled the country, some 60% of their businesses and 40–50% of their wealth had become the property of someone else or the German state, and the Jews who remained had been pushed into an impoverished economic ghetto, where most of them worked for themselves or each other. Yet this was not enough for Hitler, who by now saw war coming faster than Jews were leaving and dreaded a repetition of their supposed undermining of Germany during World War I. The result was the avalanche of persecutory measures that descended on the Jews in 1938 and culminated in the pogrom of November 9–10.

As the indoctrination of Germans and the infliction of "social death" on Jews gathered force, only ineffectual opposition arose either at home or abroad. Those few Germans who succored Jewish friends did so quietly and privately; everyone else simply turned away or cheered on the Nazi hooligans. Although more vocal criticism erupted overseas and gave rise to retaliatory boycotts of German goods, these actions did little to dampen either the urge in Britain and France to avoid war by appeasing Hitler or the resurgence of the German economy that raised his popularity. The pogrom had, at least for a time, an adverse effect on Germany's image abroad and, for a brief period, a positive effect on the chances of Jews finding refuge elsewhere.

But, beneath the surface and little noticed at the time, the pogrom had a far more ominous outcome for the Jews of Germany and Europe. The burst of violence set free a new vocabulary about their future. The unprecedented word choice reflected the mounting mathematical frustration among Nazi policy-makers, who after the addition of the Jewish populations of Austria and the Sudetenland during 1938 now saw even less chance than Hitler had discerned in late 1937 of ever driving all the Jews out of the Reich, let alone doing so before war began. The final reading selection—consisting of a reported remark by Vice Minister (*Staatssekretär*) Ernst von Weizsäcker of the German Foreign Office in November 1938, an article in the ss journal *Das Schwarze Korps* during the same month, and a speech by Adolf Hitler to the Reichstag two months later—documents the appearance of *talk of annihilation* (*Vernichtung*). As yet, it was mentioned only as something that would happen under certain conditions. Nonetheless, in contrast to the preceding years in which the direction of Nazi policy consistently had been referred to as "removal" or "exclusion" of the Jews, the thought of murder was now out in the open.

Elite Cooperation

ECKART CONZE, NORBERT FREI, PETER HAYES,
AND MOSHE ZIMMERMANN

From *Das Amt und die Vergangenheit*;
translated by Peter Hayes

At the head of the German Foreign Office [in January 1933] was Constantin *Freiherr* [Baron] von Neurath, a career diplomat who had gained the trust and support of [President Paul von] Hindenburg. A pronounced anti-intellectualism and a political attitude that assigned primacy to military strength provided a common bond between the two men. Their friendship also rested on a shared passion for hunting. From 1922 to 1930 Neurath was the German Ambassador in Rome, and in June 1930 he took over at Hindenburg's behest the same position in London, the Foreign Office's most important ambassadorship. Having ascended in the late 1920s, thanks to Hindenburg's patronage, to the first among equals of leading diplomats, Neurath was Hindenburg's preferred candidate to succeed Stresemann as Foreign Minister in 1929, but not yet politically acceptable. In June 1932, Hindenburg had to persuade him to join the Papen Cabinet because Neurath did not want to exchange his London posting for a Ministry in a government that he did not expect to last long. A little over half a year later, the new Chancellor was Adolf Hitler.

With Neurath a man reached the top of the Foreign Office whose biography guaranteed a continuation of the high-pressure negotiating stance of [Chancellor Heinrich] Brüning's presidential cabinet. As Ambassador in Rome he had observed at close range how Mussolini had brought a war-shaken Italy into the "stability" of a dictatorship. Ever since, fascist Italy was his model for the Reich. One day, he said in 1923, the first great year of crisis for the Weimar Republic, "a Mussolini also [must] come to us," and ten years later, he was prepared to do everything he could in order to make Hitler into a second Mussolini.[1] Neurath, who saw in National Socialism only a German variation on Fascism, trusted like others in the Cabinet of "national concentration" in the strength of the "Framing Concept" [the conservatives' illusion that they had Hitler surrounded in the Cabinet] and hoped that the union of the national right would bring about an authoritarian reform of the state that would smooth the way to a revisionist foreign policy largely independent of parliament and backed by a strong army. For these reasons, he applied himself to stabilizing the new government and legitimizing it internationally.

Many of the leading diplomats shared this point of view, especially Ulrich von Hassell, Neurath's successor as Ambassador in Rome. He owed his entrance to the Foreign Service in April 1909 to Neurath, his fraternity brother. Badly wounded in September 1914, Hassell worked for a time as private secretary to his father-in-law, Grand Admiral Tirpitz. In the Foreign Office, he counted as one of the most articulate advocates of an economic and trade policy whose overt goal was German dominance in southeastern Europe. He argued that Germany's return to great power status should be accompanied by a rapprochement with fascist Italy. The two states had to work together because both could achieve their territorial goals only by proceeding against France, which clung to the political status quo like no other country. Like Neurath, Hassell saw in the Nazi takeover the hope for "stability not only for our domestic, but also for our foreign policy." Driven by powerful ambition, he wanted to play a leading role under the government or, as he wrote to his wife, "to be an active fighter, that means to influence." His career ended in 1944 in front of the People's Court, where he was indicted for participating in the attempt on Hitler's life of July 20, 1944. Facing certain death, he declared he had "not agreed with the Weimar system and therefore welcomed National Socialism in 1933."[2]

Friedrich von Prittwitz und Gaffron was the very opposite of Neurath and Hassell and the only leading diplomat who resigned in early 1933. Before he became the Ambassador in Washington, he had served six years in Rome as Neurath's second-in-command. Their different political standpoints emerged repeatedly even in this period. Whereas Prittwitz pledged himself to the "consistent search for international understanding," Neurath favored confrontation.[3] It was highly symbolic that Prittwitz submitted his resignation in March 1933 to Neurath of all people, saying that he had never made a secret of his political attitudes, which were rooted in a liberal conception of the state and in republican principles. Because leading members of the new national government condemn these principles, he could "for reasons of both personal decency and professional duty" not continue to serve without "betraying himself." . . .

The resolute action of the 49-year-old Prittwitz, who ended his steep career rise overnight, found no imitators, contrary to his expectations. Characteristic of the predominant attitude among leading diplomats was the example of Bernhard von

Bülow, the State Secretary since 1930. A nephew of the former Reich Chancellor of the same name and godchild of [Kaiser] Wilhelm II, Bülow unmistakably rejected National Socialism. Paradoxically, the successful revisions of the Treaty of Versailles achieved at the end of the Weimar Republic made him oppose Nazism for fear that Hitler's policies would endanger the gains. On the other hand, he was sure that the Foreign Office would "survive even a Nazi government without major direct damage to foreign policy," as he wrote to his close friend Prittwitz a year before the Nazis came to power.[4] This formulation hinted at what distinguished Bülow's behavior after January 30 [1933]: the certainty that this was merely a transitional period and that Hitler would fall. The Nazis' failed experiment would cause them to lose their central political position and the power relations would be rearranged; then one could gather together social support for a reconstruction of the state according to conservative and authoritarian ideals. Wish and reality could hardly have diverged more clearly. Shortly before his death in 1936, Bülow provided an explanation for why he remained in office, despite his reservations about Nazism, that a majority of diplomats surely shared and that after the war resurfaced in nearly all attempts at self-justification: "One does not leave his country in the lurch because it has a bad government."[5]

The ruling structure of the Nazi regime did not permit such a distinction between state and government. This must have been apparent to Bülow, who was steeped in an "almost religious feeling for the fatherland," in the judgment of the French Ambassador to Berlin.[6] In any case, in May 1933 he drafted a hand-written resignation letter that he then did not submit. The draft implies that Bülow wanted to get a series of leading diplomats to submit similar letters in order to win back their lost influence. In one passage, later crossed out, Bülow wrote that he was submitting his resignation also in the names of the Ambassadors in Paris, London, and Moscow.[7]

With Roland Köster in Paris, Leopold von Hoesch in London, and Herbert von Dirksen in Moscow, Bülow hoped for a collective withdrawal. The three ambassadors personified the leading diplomats of the Weimar Republic. Nearly the same age and tied together in friendship, they had entered the Foreign Service of the German Empire and ascended to high positions after the Revolution of 1918–19. They came from privileged and wealthy families and were Protestants, doctors of law, and former reserve officers who kept a critical distance from the proletarian Nazi mass movement. But, unlike the resolute Prittwitz, the hesitant Bülow, and the hyperactive Hassell, with whom they shared not only many political convictions, but also the belief that they could influence political developments, these ambassadors were not in the least prepared to put a stick through the spokes of history.

Apparently Köster was the quickest to draw conclusions from the events that followed January 30. At the same time as Bülow was drafting his resignation, Köster traveled twice for conversations with Hoesch in London, with the knowledge and perhaps on the instructions of the State Secretary. Whatever they discussed, they ultimately found no basis for a collective threat to resign. In the end, all four men remained in the service of a regime that they rejected and thus helped to bridge the transition from the nationalist great power politics that they represented to the ideologically racist foreign policy of the Third Reich. The increasing isolation of Germany after 1933 reduced their room for maneuver, but provided a welcome justification for remaining in office. Their rejection of Weimar democracy made them receptive to the promises of an authoritarian state that

pushed opposition to the Versailles Treaty. They regarded the violent excesses of Hitler's takeover as "events that go with revolutions" that over time will "gradually fade away."[8]

Bülow's draft of his resignation noted that the reordering of Germany had "brought appearances and events to light that are incompatible with the dignity and security of the Reich and with the continuation of a healthy foreign policy."[9] . . . [Yet] had antisemitism been the only distinguishing characteristic of the new regime, it would have encountered little challenge from the diplomats. They were worried solely about Germany's reputation. "Foreigners have trouble understanding the anti-Jewish actions because they have not personally experienced the inundation with Jews," noted the rising Envoy Ernst von Weizsäcker with regard to the boycott. "The fact remains that our position in the world has suffered and that the political and other consequences will soon be apparent." Weizsäcker belonged to the group of officials who worried about the future because they feared things could get out of control if the radical elements in the Nazi Party got the upper hand. Therefore, he believed that he had to give the regime "all forms of support and experience . . . and help see to it that the now commencing second phase of the current revolution becomes genuinely constructive."[10]

With his view that "the specialist cannot simply quit the field," Weizsäcker "was in good company," he later wrote.[11] Like Weizsäcker, most German career diplomats, the majority of whom had entered the diplomatic service during the German Empire, continued their work without interruption under the new regime. Through every previous change of government in the sixty-three-year history of the Office, it had gone about its business. Without doubt the government of January 30, 1933, was appointed in constitutional fashion, but it had legitimated terror from the outset. As its violent character became ever more apparent, the members of the old guard at the Foreign Office by no means abandoned their posts, and many of them stayed on into the war years. The same elite that had served the Kaiser and, in their eyes, survived the Weimar Republic would become the supporters of the Nazi policies of conquest and annihilation. . . .

The First Attacks on Jews

As the assaults on the rights of Jewish citizens began to mount after the Reichstag elections of March 6, 1933, the Foreign Office felt compelled to react to the disorder. So the diplomats worked on a justification. Even after World War II, Ernst von Weizsäcker expressed the view that Germany in the early 1920s had "opened the borders too widely in the East. The inflation drew in too many Jews," who had made themselves "into a great power."[12] State Secretary Bülow took the same position in March 1933, saying that he had referred repeatedly in conversations with diplomats to the "strong influx of Eastern Jews" who had been granted citizenship in large numbers by the Social Democratic government of Prussia. The municipal administration in Berlin and the public hospitals had become completely "jewified," and one could not overlook the "advance of Jews in the judiciary, the universities, and the schools and many other places since 1918." Regarding all of this, Bülow surmised that, "numbers must be available" that the representations abroad "could use," and he wondered whether Nazi Party offices or Interior Ministry officials could "privately" provide facts and figures. "With a number of concrete examples" diplomats could make a better case in dealing with the accredited foreign representatives in Berlin, most of whom were "absolutely not pro-Jewish."[13]

The assignment to gather material that could be used to explain to foreigners the basis of the antisemitic movement in Germany went to the State Secretary's nephew Vicco von Bülow-Schwante, who had just been appointed to the Foreign Office and placed at the head of the revived German Section. The offspring of a widely ramified family of diplomats and soldiers, Bülow-Schwante, who was born in 1891, had pursued a military career until a riding accident made him unsuitable for field service during World War I, and he was seconded to various foreign missions. He withdrew from the military and diplomatic services after the war out of antirepublican conviction and turned to managing his estates. A member of the right-wing German National People's Party (DNVP) since 1928, he also led the Foreign Section of the paramilitary *Stahlhelm* [Steel Helmet] formations. In that capacity he strengthened the organization's partnership with the Italian fascist paramilitary forces and sought to intensify ties to Mussolini. He also strove relatively early to achieve partial cooperation with the Nazi Party and as early as the end of 1929 won Hitler over to the idea of a joint propaganda campaign with the DNVP and the *Stahlhelm*. Bülow-Schwante's appointment to the Foreign Service as head of the German Section reflected the "Unification of the National Right" that President von Hindenburg desired.[14]

The reestablishment of the German Section in the Foreign Office indicated that a new era had begun. As matters stood, a section whose responsibility included the "observation of domestic political events of importance to foreign policy" as well as the "observation of the effects of foreign countries on domestic political conditions" could be understood only as an intrusion on the autonomy of the Foreign Office.[15] That the handling of the "Jewish question" fell within the purview of the German section was also ominous.[16]

Of course, there had been a German Section, responsible for the interaction between domestic and foreign policy, from 1919 to 1931. In that respect, the section was not a "foreign body," and its leaders had been recruited from the diplomatic service. The new element now was the lateral entrant Bülow-Schwante. His chief assistant until 1936 was Hans Röhrecke, a career diplomat specializing in domestic questions, and then Walter Hinrichs, a trained lawyer who had served in World War I as an officer and joined the Foreign Service in 1919. Emil Schumburg, to whom the handling of the "Jewish Question" was assigned, looked back on a similar career.[17] Born in 1898 the son of a general in the army medical service, he completed secondary school at the age of eighteen and volunteered for the military, which he left in 1919. After a law degree and several foreign trips, he entered training for the diplomatic service on January 1, 1926. . . .

Bülow's directive of March 13, 1933, to have statistics collected concerning the disproportionate "advance of Jews" in German public life marked, in effect, the first stop on the way to the "final solution of the Jewish question." Bülow-Schwante acted on the State Secretary's assignment immediately. At the Reichstag session of March 24 that approved the Enabling Act, he took Propaganda Minister Goebbels aside and asked for his help. In rapidly developing contacts between the German Section and the Propaganda and Interior ministries details were talked over and statistics and pamphlets assembled. The personnel of the German section had to show a good deal of initiative because they found the available material "very thin and only partially useable for the purposes of propaganda abroad."[18] Finally, the process yielded the "journeyman's qualifying piece" of the German Section, approved by Bülow and Neurath, which was sent to all Germany's overseas missions exactly three months after Hitler's accession.

The document opened by declaring that foreigners regarded "the Jewish question in Germany almost without comprehension" because of "a lack of knowledge of the relevant conditions." It was nonetheless a fact that after 1918 "political life, governing power, and the intellectual life of the nation [had been] subjected to extraordinarily strong Jewish influence." "The current events" constitute nothing but "a reaction against the trend since 1918." In particular, the "high number of Jewish parliamentary deputies and political functionaries in the Social Democratic and Communist parties" had given "Jewry in general an influence in public life, government, the judiciary, and the bureaucracy inappropriate to its proportion of the population." Deploying statistics, the document sought to prove that Jews were not only over represented in certain professions, but also statistically significant presences among "criminals" and "the mentally ill in need of hospitalization."[19]

The German Section followed up with another circular letter almost a year later, claiming that "foreign Jews" as well as "German Jewish emigrants" had unleashed against Nazi Germany "an incitement with lies and atrocity stories of the sort not seen since the war propaganda of the Allies." "This agitation led ultimately to a boycott of German goods," against which Germany defended itself on April 1, 1933. In the process, the National Socialist government demonstrated its full authority by succeeding in "directing the spontaneous public rage against Jewry during the days of revolution into orderly channels." Since then, "the Jewish question in Germany" had assumed "a peaceful and steady development" that approached in stages the political goal: exclusion of Jewry from public offices and services but fundamental preservation of its economic and social freedom of action." Despite "Jewish agitation propaganda," the "dejewification of public life" in Germany would continue along established lines.[20]

Such circular letters, intended to provide foreign missions with talking points, usually went through extensive preparations involving multiple stages between drafting in the Section and endorsement by the State Secretary or the Minister. In the process, little masterpieces of dialectics came into being. Thus, two months after the April boycott, one could read in a press release that even "German Jews of calm judgment" would "recognize the boycott day and the ensuing measures against Jewish domination as proof of great statesmanship." Because the "completely disciplined execution" had "opened a vent for pent up antisemitic tendencies, . . . the pressure of constant fear that these . . . might someday explode had been removed from German Jewry."[21]

The antisemitic propaganda that the Foreign Office spread abroad to justify unjust practices was not inspired by the Propaganda Ministry or any Party office, as there was no need for either to act. In this instance, the Foreign Office proceeded with the professionalism of an established agency not satisfied with mere implementation, but seeking to participate in and advise on policy as well. Thus, Bülow-Schwante recommended that the Propaganda Ministry under all circumstances should hold fast to a rigorous line on the Jewish question for foreign policy reasons. There should be no contact with Jewish organizations. Even if boycotts of German exports had adverse economic effects, the damage to foreign policy would be much greater, if "the slightest readiness" of Germany "even to confer with" Jewish organizations became apparent, as that "will be interpreted as a sign of weakness." German diplomatic and consular offices were directed "under no circumstances" to respond to overtures of this sort.[22]

This policy was followed. In September 1934, the Embassy in London reported on an approach by a prominent Jewish columnist. He sought initially an official German statement that "some German citizens of the Jewish faith had been unjustly pulled into suffering for the misdeeds of their coreligionists who caused the measures that the government directed at Jewry." In addition, he wanted a declaration "that in the future those German citizens of the Jewish faith who conduct themselves as good Germans can live unrestricted and free in Germany."[23] If the German government indicated that it was prepared to make such a statement, a delegation of British Jews could travel immediately to Berlin for further conversations.

The answer was unequivocal. Drafted by Bülow-Schwante, edited by Neurath, and signed by Bülow, it established that "a negotiation or conclusion of an agreement concerning the Jewish question with any Jewish organization or representative Jewish group, whether in Germany or abroad" was out of the question. "If one day the Jewish question is to be taken up, that must solely be as an expression of strength, not weakness . . . Relenting on the Jewish question under economic or political pressure would not calm the domestic or foreign policy situation or satisfy the Jewish opponents, but would undermine the fundamental ideological position of National Socialist Germany. The worse the economic situation becomes, the less one should consider compromise on the Jewish question." Those were the final words of the text that was sent immediately to all German foreign postings.[24] A copy went to the Party and state agencies with which the Foreign Office was in constant contact on this matter, including the Racial Policy Office of the NSDAP, whose leader Walter Gross had discussed thoroughly the "adverse effects of German racial policy abroad" with "Jewish officer" Schumburg only a few days earlier.[25] . . .

The Foreign Office was continuously in the picture and part of the search for a "solution to the Jewish question." Its primary task consisted throughout in justifying the persecution of the German Jews to foreigners. To that end, the Office employed Hitler's constant conflation of Jewry and Bolshevism, appealed to the European bourgeoisie's fears of the "Bolshevik menace," and praised the Reich as a "bulwark" against it. "To have deflected the danger of new misery in Europe is the greatest service of Adolf Hitler," went the message announced by German diplomats to the entire world.[26]

NOTES

1. HSTAS [Main State Archive, Stuttgart] Q 3/11, Bu 385, Neurath an Mathilde von Neurath, November 25, 1923.

2. ADAP [Documents on German Foreign Policy] C I, Nr. 64, Hassell an Neurath, March 8, 1933; ADAP, E VIII, Nr. 228, Aufzeichnung Sonnenhol, Verhandlungen vor dem Volksgerichtshof am 7.9.1944 .

3. PAAA [Political Archive of the Foreign Office] R 28268, Prittwiz an AA, October 20, 1926.

4. PAAA, R 29517, Bülow an Prittwitz, January 25, 1932.

5. Peter Krüger and Erich J.C. Hahn, "Der Loyalitätskonflikt des Staatssekretärs Bernhard Wilhelm von Bülow im Frühjahr 1933," *Vierteljahreshefte für Zeitgeschichte* 20, 410.

6. Andre François-Poncet, *Botschafter in Berlin 1931–1938* (Berlin: 1962), 276.

7. Krüger and Hahn, *Vierteljahreshefte für Zeitgeschichte* 20, 398.

8. IMT [International Military Tribunal] v. 16, Aufzeichnung, June 22, 1946, 657.

9. Krüger and Hahn, *Vierteljahreshefte für Zeitgeschichte* 20, 397.

10. Leonidas Hill, ed., *Die Weizsäcker-Papiere*, vol. 2: 1933–1950, 70–71.

11. BA [Federal German archive] Nachlass Ernst von Weizsäcker, N 1273, v. 82, hand written memorandum, no date [1950].

12. BA, Nachlass Weizsäcker, N 1273, v. 50: Lebenserinnerungen, Vatikan, September 1945.

13. ADAP, C I, Nr. 79, Memorandum by Bülow for Bülow-Schwante, March 13, 1933.

14. AdR [Akten der Reichskanzlei], *Kabinett Schleicher*, v. 1, Nr. 79, *Tagebuchaufzeichnung Lutz Graf Schwerin von Krosigk*, February 5, 1933; IfZ [Institut für Zeitgeschichte] zs 1021, Aufzeichnung Jacobsen über Gespräch mit Bülow-Schwante am 9.11.1965, November 10, 1965; Hermann Graml, *Zwischen Stresemann und Hitler. Die Aussenpolitik der Präsidialkabinette Brüning, Papen und Schleicher* (Munich, 2001), 113–69.

15. PAAA, R 98651, Hauszirkular Bülows, March 20, 1933.

16. ADAP, C III, Anhang II, Geschäftsverteilungsplan, Juni 1934–März 1935.

17. Ibid.

18. PAAA, r98468, Aufzeichnung Bülow-Schwante, April 20, 1933.

19. Ibid., Runderlass Bülow-Schwante an alle Missiionen, April 30, 1933.

20. PAAA, R 99292, Runderlass Bülow-Schwante an alle Missionen, February 28, 1934.

21. PAAA, R 984980, Runderlass Bülow-Schwante an alle Missionen, June 6, 1933.

22. PAAA, R 99530, Bülow-Schwante an Propagandaministerium, January 31, 1934.

23. PAAA, R 99574, Bismarck an das AA, September 27, 1934.

24. PAAA, R 99531, Neurath an alle Missionen sowie an Rudolf Hess, das Reichsinnenministerium und das Propagandaministerium, October 30, 1934; Aufzeichnung Bülow-Schwante, October 16, 1934.

25. PAAA, R 99346, Aufzeichnung Schumburg, October 24, 1934.

26. PAAA, R 984980, Runderlass Bülow-Schwante an alle Missionen, June 6, 1933.

Street-Level Coercion

SEBASTIAN HAFFNER

From *Defying Hitler*

At first the revolution only gave the impression of being a "historical event" like any other: a matter for the press that might just possibly have some effect on the public mood.

The Nazis celebrate January 30 as their day of revolution. They are wrong. There was no revolution on January 30, 1933, just a change of government. Hitler became Chancellor, by no means the Führer of a Nazi regime (the cabinet contained only two Nazis apart from him). He swore an oath of allegiance to the Weimar constitution. The general opinion was that it was not the Nazis who had won, but the bourgeois parties of the right, who had "captured" the Nazis and held all the key positions in the government. In constitutional terms, events had taken a much more conventional, unrevolutionary course than most of what had happened during the previous six months. Outwardly also, the day had no revolutionary aspects, unless one considers a Nazi torchlight procession through Wilhelmstrasse or a minor gunfight in the suburbs that night as signs of a revolution. . . .

For most of us outsiders, the experience of January 30 was that of reading the papers—and the emotions we felt while we were doing so.

At about five o'clock the evening papers arrived: "Cabinet of National Unity Formed—Hitler Reich Chancellor."

I do not know what the general reaction was. For about a minute, mine was completely correct:

icy horror. Certainly this had been a possibility for a long time. You had to reckon with it. Nevertheless it was so bizarre, so incredible, to read it now in black on white. Hitler Reich Chancellor . . . for a moment I physically sensed the man's odor of blood and filth, the nauseating approach of a man-eating animal—its foul, sharp claws in my face.

Then I shook the sensation off, tried to smile, started to consider, and found many reasons for reassurance. That evening I discussed the prospects of the new government with my father. We agreed that it had a good chance of doing a lot of damage, but not much chance of surviving very long: a deeply reactionary government, with Hitler as its mouthpiece. Apart from this, it did not really differ much from the two governments that had succeeded Brüning's. Even with the Nazis it would not have a majority in the Reichstag. Of course that could always be dissolved, but the government had a clear majority of the population against it, in particular the working class, which would probably go Communist, now that the Social Democrats had completely discredited themselves. One could prohibit the Communists, but that would only make them more dangerous. In the meantime the government would be likely to implement reactionary social and cultural measures, with some antisemitic additions to please Hitler. That would not attract any of its opponents to its side. Foreign policy would probably be a matter of banging the table. There might be an attempt to rearm. That would automatically add the outside world to the 60 percent of the home population who were against the government. Besides, who were the people who had suddenly started voting Nazi in the last three years? Misguided ignoramuses for the most part, victims of propaganda, a fluctuating mass that would fall apart at the first disappointment. No, all things considered, this government was not a cause for alarm. The only question was what would come after it. It was possible that they would drive the country to civil war. The Communists were capable of going on the attack before a prohibition against them came into force.

The next day this turned out to be the general opinion of the intelligent press. It is curious how plausible an argument it is, even today, when we know what came next. How could things turn out so completely different? Perhaps it was just because we were all so certain that they could not do so—and relied on that with far too much confidence. So we neglected to consider that it might, if worse came to worst, be necessary to *prevent* the disaster from happening. . . .

You did not see or hear anything that was any different from what had gone on before. There were brown SA uniforms on the streets, demonstrations, shouts of "*Heil*" but otherwise it was "business as usual." In the Kammergericht, the highest court in Prussia, where I worked as *Referendar* [report writer and candidate for the higher civil service] at that time, the process of the law was not changed at all by the fact that the interior minister enacted ridiculous edicts. The newspapers might report that the constitution was in ruins. Here every paragraph of the Civil Code was still valid and was mulled over and analyzed as carefully as ever. Which was the true reality? The chancellor could daily utter the vilest abuse against the Jews; there was nonetheless still a Jewish *Kammergerichtsrat* (Berlin Supreme Court judge) and member of our senate who contin-

ued to give his astute and careful judgments, and these judgments had the full weight of the law and could set the entire apparatus of the state in motion for their enforcement—even if the highest officeholder of that state daily called their author a "parasite," a "subhuman," or a "plague." Who cut the worse figure? Who was the butt of the irony of the situation?

I must admit that I was inclined to view the undisturbed functioning of the law, and indeed the continued normal course of daily life, as a triumph over the Nazis. They could behave as raucously and wildly as they wished. They could still only stir up the political surface. The depths of the ocean of life remained unaffected. . . .

It was only the next morning that I read about the Reichstag fire, and not until midday that I read about the arrests. Around the same time a decree of Hindenburg's was promulgated. It abolished freedom of speech and confidentiality of the mail and telephone for all private individuals, while giving the police unrestricted rights of search and access, confiscation and arrest. That afternoon men with ladders went around, honest workmen, covering campaign posters with plain white paper. All parties of the left had been prohibited from any further election publicity. Those newspapers that still appeared reported all this in a fawning, fervently patriotic, jubilant tone. We had been saved! What good luck! Germany was free! Next Saturday all Germans would come together in a festival of national exaltation, their hearts swelling with gratitude! Get the torches and flags out!

Thus the press. The streets were exactly the same as always. The cinemas were open. The law courts sat and heard cases. No sign of a revolution. At home people were a little confused, a little anxious, and tried to understand what was happening. That was difficult, very difficult, in such a short time.

So the Communists had burned down the Reichstag. Well, well. That could well be so, it was even to be expected. Funny, though, why they should choose the Reichstag, an empty building, where no one would profit from a fire. Well, perhaps it really had been intended as the "signal" for the uprising, which had been prevented by the "decisive measures" taken by the government. That was what the papers said, and it sounded plausible. Funny also that the Nazis got so worked up about the Reichstag. Up till then they had contemptuously called it a "hot air factory." Now it was suddenly the holy of holies that had been burned down. Well, what suits their book, don't you agree, my friend, that's politics, isn't it? Thank God we don't understand it. The main thing is: the danger of a Communist uprising has been averted and we can sleep easy. Good night.

More seriously: perhaps the most interesting thing about the Reichstag fire is that the claim that it was the work of the Communists was so widely believed. Even the skeptics did not regard it as entirely incredible. That was the Communists' own fault. They had become a strong party in recent years, and had again and again trumpeted their "readiness." Nobody believed they would allow themselves to be "prohibited" and slaughtered without putting up a fight. During the whole of February we had been permanently at "eyes left," waiting for the Communist counterstrike. The Communists were determined people, with fierce expressions. They raised their fists in salute, and had weapons—at least, they used guns often enough in the everyday pub brawls. They boasted continually about the strength of their organization, and they had probably learned how to do "these things" in Russia. The Nazis, had left no one in doubt that they wanted to destroy them. It was natural, indeed obvious, that the Communists would retaliate. It was only sur-

prising that there had been nothing of the kind so far.

It took a long time for the Germans to realize that the Communists had been sheep in wolves' clothing. The Nazi myth of the Communist putsch that had been averted fell on fertile ground that had been prepared by the Communists themselves. Who would have believed that there was nothing behind the facade of raised fists?

What is a revolution? Constitutional lawyers define it as a change of constitution by means not foreseen therein. By this definition the Nazi revolution of March 1933 was not a revolution. Everything went strictly "by the book," using means that were permitted by the constitution. At first there were "emergency decrees" by the president of the Reich, and later a bill was passed by a two-thirds majority of the Reichstag giving the government unlimited legislative powers, perfectly in accordance with the rules for changing the constitution.

Now, that is obviously shadow boxing, but even if we look at things as they really were, there is still room for doubt whether what happened that March really deserves the name of a revolution. From a simple, commonsense point of view, one would say that the essential characteristic of a revolution is that people violently attack the established order and its representatives, police, army, etc., and overcome them. It need not always be thrilling and glorious. It can be accompanied by atrocities, brutality, plunder, murder, and arson. At all events, we expect revolutionaries to be on the attack, to show courage, risk their lives. Barricades may be out of date, but some form of spontaneity, uprising, commitment, and insurrection seem to be an essential part of a genuine revolution.

None of that was to be found in March 1933. The events were a combination of the most disparate ingredients. What was completely absent was any act of courage or spirit by any of the participants. The month of March demonstrated that the Nazis had achieved an unassailable position of power: through terror, celebration and rhetoric, treachery, and finally a collective breakdown—a million individuals simultaneously suffered a nervous collapse. More bloodshed has accompanied the birth of many European states, but none came into being in a more loathsome way.

European history knows two forms of terror. The first is the uncontrollable explosion of bloodlust in a victorious mass uprising. The other is cold, calculated cruelty committed by a victorious state as a demonstration of power and intimidation. The two forms of terror normally correspond to revolution and repression. The first is revolutionary. It justifies itself by the rage and fever of the moment, a temporary madness. The second is repressive. It justifies itself by the preceding revolutionary atrocities.

It was left to the Nazis to combine both forms of terror in a manner that invalidates both justifications. In 1933 the terror was practiced by a real bloodthirsty mass (namely the SA—the SS did not play a part until later), but this mass acted as "auxiliary police," without any emotion or spontaneity, and without any risk to themselves. Rather, they acted from a position of complete security, under orders and with strict discipline. The external picture was one of revolutionary terror: a wild, unkempt mob breaking into homes at night and dragging defenseless victims to the torture chambers. The internal process was repressive terror: cold, calculated, official orders, directed by the state and carried out under the full protection of the police and the armed forces. It did not take place in the excitement following a victorious battle or danger successfully overcome—nothing of the kind had happened. Nor was it an act of revenge for atrocities committed by the other side—there had been none. What happened was a nightmarish reversal of normal circumstances: robbers and murderers acting as the police force, enjoying the full panoply of state power, their victims treated as criminals, proscribed and condemned to death in advance.

An example that became public knowledge because of its scale occurred some months later in the Cöpenik area of Berlin, where a Social Democratic trade unionist defended himself, with the help of his sons, against an SA patrol that broke into his home at night to "arrest" him. In obvious self-defense he shot two SA men. As a result, he and his sons were overcome by a larger troop of SA men and hanged in a shed in the yard that same night. The next day, the SA patrols appeared in Cöpenik, in disciplined order, entered the homes of every known Social Democrat, and killed them on the spot. The exact number of deaths was never made public.

This form of terror had the advantage that, according to the circumstances; one could either shrug one's shoulders and speak of "the unavoidable, if regrettable, side effects of any revolution"—using the justification for revolutionary terror—or point to the strict discipline and explain that public law and order were being maintained and that these actions were required to prevent revolutionary disorder overwhelming Germany: the justification for repressive terror. Both excuses were used in turn, depending on the audience being addressed. . . .

The Nazis never showed anything but the sly, pale, cowardly face of a murderer denying his crime. While they were systematically torturing and murdering their defenseless victims, they daily declared in fine, noble words that not a single hair of anyone's head would be harmed, and that never before had a revolution shed less blood or been conducted more humanely. Indeed, only a few weeks after the atrocities began, a law was passed that forbade anyone, under pain of severe penalties, to claim, even in the privacy of his own home, that atrocities were taking place.

Of course, it was not the intention to keep the atrocities secret. In that case they would not have served their purpose, which was to induce general fear, alarm, and submission. On the contrary, the purpose was to intensify the terror by cloaking it in secrecy and making even talking about it dangerous. An open declaration of what was happening in SA cellars and concentration camps—in a public speech or in the press—might still have led to desperate resistance, even in Germany. The secret whispered rumors, "Be careful, my friend! Do you know what happened to X?" were much more effective in breaking people's backbones.

The effect was intensified by the way one was permanently occupied and distracted by an unending sequence of celebrations, ceremonies, and national festivities. It started with a huge victory celebration before the elections on March 4—*"Tag der nationalen Erhebung"* (Day of National Rising). There were mass parades, fireworks, drums, bands, and flags all over Germany, Hitler's voice over thousands of loudspeakers, oaths and vows—and all before it was even certain that the elections might not be a setback for the Nazis, which indeed they were. These elections, the last that were ever held in prewar Germany, brought the Nazis only 44 percent of the votes (in the previous elections they had achieved 37 percent). The majority was still against the Nazis.

If you consider that terror was in full swing, that the parties of the left had been prohibited from all public activity in the decisive final week before the elections, you have to admit that the German people as a whole had behaved quite decently. However, it made no difference at all. The defeat was celebrated like a victory, the terror intensi-fied, the celebrations multiplied. Flags never left the windows for a whole fortnight.

A week later Hindenburg abolished the Weimar national flag, which was replaced by the swastika banner and a black, white, and red "temporary national flag." There were daily parades, mass meetings, declarations of gratitude for the liber-ation of the nation, military music from dawn to dusk, awards ceremonies for heroes, the dedica-tion of flags, and, as a final climax, the tasteless display of the "Day of Potsdam"—with the trai-tor Hindenburg visiting the grave of Frederick the Great, Hitler swearing loyalty to something or other for the nth time, bells tolling, a solemn pro-cession to church by the members of the Reich-stag, a military parade, swords lowered in salute, children waving flags, and a torchlight parade.

The colossal emptiness and lack of meaning of these never-ending events was by no means unin-tentional. The population should become used to cheering and jubilation, even when there was no visible reason for it. It was reason enough that people who distanced themselves too obviously—sshh!—were daily and nightly tortured to death with steel whips and electric drills. Better to cel-ebrate, howl with the wolves, *"Heil, Heil!"* Besides, people began to enjoy doing so. The weather in March 1933 was glorious. Was it not wonderful to celebrate in the spring sunshine, in squares decked with flags? To merge with the festive crowds and listen to high-sounding patriotic speeches, about freedom and fatherland, exaltation and holy vows? (It was certainly better than having one's belly pumped up with a water hose in some hidden SA cellar.)

People began to join in—at first mostly from fear. After they had participated, they no lon-ger wanted to do so just from fear. That would have been mean and contemptible. So the nec-essary ideology was also supplied. That was the spiritual basis of the victory of the National Socialist revolution.

At the end of March the Nazis felt strong enough to initiate the first act of their real revolution, a revolution not against some constitution or other, but against the basis of human society on earth, a revolution that, if nothing is done, will stop at nothing. The first diffident move was the boycott of the Jews on April 1, 1933.

It had been thought up by Hitler and Goebbels over tea and biscuits at Obersalzberg in Bavaria the Sunday before. On Monday the papers carried the peculiarly ironic headline "Mass Demonstrations Announced." From Saturday, April 1, they said, all Jewish shops would be boycotted. SA troops would stand guard in front of them and prevent anyone from going in. All Jewish doctors and lawyers were also to be boycotted. SA patrols would check their consulting rooms to ensure that the ruling was obeyed.

One could see the advances that the Nazis had made in just one month by considering the justification for the boycott. The myth of a Communist coup that had been used to override the constitution and remove civil liberties had been carefully and plausibly constructed. They had even felt the need to supply some direct evidence in the form of the Reichstag fire. The justification for this new affront was a barefaced insult and mockery of those who were expected to act as though they believed it. The boycott was to be carried out as a defense and reaction against the totally unfounded horror stories about the new Germany that the German Jews were alleged to have cleverly spread abroad. Yes, just so.

Further measures were added, in the next few days (some of them later temporarily rescinded). All "Aryan" shops had to sack their Jewish employees. Then all Jewish shops had to do so too. Jewish shops had to pay their "Aryan" employees in full during the period they were closed by the boycott. Jewish owners had to withdraw from their businesses and install "Aryan" managers. And so on.

At the same time a great "education campaign" against the Jews was set in motion. The Germans were informed through pamphlets, posters, and meetings that it had been a mistake to consider the Jews as human beings. In reality they were a kind of "subhuman" animal, but with the characteristics of a devil. The consequences that would be drawn from this were not spelled out for the moment. Still, the campaign slogan was given out as "*Juda verrecke*" (Perish Judah). A man who had hitherto been unknown to most Germans was appointed as leader of the boycott: Julius Streicher.

All this aroused in the German people something one might not have expected after the previous four weeks: widespread alarm. A murmur of dissent, suppressed but audible, spread through the land. The Nazis sensed that they had gone too far for the moment, and withdrew some of their measures after April 1. Not, however, without first allowing these to unleash the full force of their terror. By now everyone knows to what extent the Nazis have changed their true intentions.

Apart from the terror, the unsettling and depressing aspect of this first murderous declaration of intent was that it triggered a flood of arguments and discussions all over Germany, not about antisemitism but about the "Jewish question." This is a trick the Nazis have since successfully repeated many times on other "questions" and in international affairs. By publicly threatening a person, an ethnic group, a nation, or a region with death and destruction, they provoke a general discussion not about their own existence, but about the right of their victims to exist. In this way that right is put in question.

Suddenly everyone felt justified, and indeed required, to have an opinion about the Jews, and to state it publicly. Distinctions were made between "decent" Jews and the others. If some pointed to the achievements of Jewish scientists, artists, and doctors to justify the Jews (justify? what for? against what?), others would counter that they were a detrimental "foreign influence" in these spheres. Indeed, it soon became customary to count it against the Jews if they had a respectable or intellectually valuable profession. This was treated as a crime or, at the very least, a lack of tact. The defenders of the Jews were frowningly told that it was reprehensible of the Jews to have such-and-such a percentage of doctors, lawyers, journalists, etc. Indeed, percentage calculations were a popular ingredient of the "Jewish question." People discussed whether the percentage of Jews among the members of the Communist Party was not too high, and among the casualties of the Great War perhaps too low. (This is the literal truth. I heard this argument in the mouth of an educated man with a Ph.D., who reckoned himself a member of the cultured class. He argued quite seriously that the twelve thousand Jewish dead in the Great War was too small a proportion of the Jewish population in comparison with the corresponding number of "Aryans" killed, and derived from this a certain justification for Nazi antisemitism.)

Today it is quite clear that Nazi antisemitism had nothing to do with the virtues or vices of the Jews. The interesting thing about the Nazis' intention to train the Germans to be persecutors of the Jews throughout the world, and if possible exterminate them, an intention they made no secret of, is not the justification they gave. That is such utter nonsense that it is demeaning even to take it seriously enough to argue against it. It is the intention itself that is significant. It is something new

in the history of the world: an attempt to deny humans the solidarity of every species that enables it to survive; to turn human predatory instincts, that are normally directed against other animals, against members of their own species, and to make a whole nation into a pack of hunting hounds. . . .

Friday, March 31. Tomorrow things would get serious. I still could not quite believe it. I scanned the papers, looking for signs of any mitigation, perhaps some movement toward a more reasonable, acceptable position. There was nothing. Just the intensification of some measure or other and pedantic instructions about the details of the action and the manner in which it was to be executed.

Otherwise it was business as usual. Looking at the steady bustle and traffic on the streets, one had no sense that anything special was about to take place. Jewish shops were still open and trading as usual. Today one was still permitted to shop there. It would not be prohibited until tomorrow, at 8 a.m. precisely.

I went to the *Kammergericht*. It stood there, cool and gray as always, set back from the street in a distinguished setting of lawns and trees. Its halls were filled with the hushed fluttering of attorneys in their batlike, black silk gowns, carrying briefcases under their arms, with concentrated, serious expressions on their faces. Jewish attorneys were pleading in court as though this were a day like any other.

Not being due in court, I went to the library (as though this were a day like any other), settled down at one of the long worktables, and started reading a document about which I had to give an opinion. Some complicated affair with intricate points of law. I carried the heavy legal tomes to my place and surrounded myself with them. I looked up decisions of the high courts of the Reich and made notes. As always, the high-ceilinged, spacious room was filled with the inaudible electricity of many minds hard at work. In making pencil marks on paper, I was setting the instruments of the law to work on the details of my case, summarizing, comparing, weighing the importance of this or that word in a contract, investigating what bearing this or that clause would have on the matter, according to the precedents. When I scribbled a few words something happened, like the first cut in a surgical operation: a question was clarified, a component of a judicial decision put in place. Not the final decision, naturally: "It is thus irrelevant whether the plaintiff . . . so it remains to investigate whether . . ." Careful, precise, silent work. Everybody in the room was similarly immersed in their own cases. Even the ushers, somewhere between beadles and policemen, moved more quietly here in the library, and seemed to try and make themselves invisible. The room was full of extreme silence, a silence filled with the high tension of deeply concentrated work. It was like a silent concert. I loved this atmosphere. At home I would have been unable to work today, here it was perfectly easy. Your thoughts just could not stray. It was like being in a fortress, or better, a test tube. No breath came in from the outside world; here there was no revolution.

What was the first noticeable noise? A door banging? A distant sound like an order being given? Suddenly everybody raised their heads and strained to hear what it was. The room was still utterly quiet: but the quality of the silence had changed. It was no longer the silence of concentrated work. It was filled with alarm and agitation. There was a clatter of footsteps outside in the corridor, the sound of rough boots on the stairs, then a distant indistinct din, shouts, doors banging. A few people got up and went to the door, looked out, and came back. One or two approached the ushers and spoke quietly with them—in here no one ever raised their voice. The noise from outside grew stronger. Somebody spoke into the silence: "SA." Then, not particularly loudly, somebody else said, "They're throwing out the Jews," and a few others laughed. At that moment this laughter alarmed me more than what was actually happening. With a start I realized that there were Nazis working in this room. How strange.

Gradually the disturbance took shape—at first it had been intangible. Readers got up, tried to say something to one another, paced about slowly to no great purpose. One man, obviously a Jew, closed his books, packed his documents, and left. Shortly afterward somebody, perhaps a superintendent, appeared in the doorway and announced clearly but calmly, "The SA is in the building. The Jewish gentlemen would do well to leave." Almost at once we heard shouts from outside: "Out with the Jews!" A voice answered, "They've already gone," and again I heard two or three merry giggles, just as before. I could see them now. They were *Referendars* just like me. . . .

The scouts later explained what had happened in the main part of the building. No atrocities, why, certainly not! Everything went extremely smoothly. The courts had, for the most part, adjourned. The judges had removed their robes and left the building quietly and civilly, going down the staircase lined with SA men. The only place where there had been trouble was the attorneys' room. A Jewish attorney had "caused a fuss" and been beaten up. Later I heard who it was. He had been wounded five times in the last war, had lost an eye, and even been promoted to captain. It had probably been his misfortune that he still remembered the tone to use with mutineers.

In the meantime, the intruders had arrived at the library. The door was thrust open and a flood of brown uniforms surged in. In a booming voice, one of them, clearly the leader, shouted, "Non-Aryans must leave the premises immediately." It struck me that he used the careful expression "non-Aryans," but also a rather colloquial expression for "premises." Someone, probably the same person as before, answered, "They've already left." Our ushers stood there as though they were about to salute. My heart beat heavily. What should I do, how keep my poise? Just ignore them, do not let them disturb me. I put my head down over my work. I read a few sentences mechanically: "The defendant's claim that . . . is untrue, but irrelevant . . ." Just take no notice!

Meanwhile a brown shirt approached me and took up position in front of my worktable. "Are you Aryan?" Before I had a chance to think, I said, "Yes." He took a close look at my nose—and retired. The blood shot to my face. A moment too late I felt the shame, the defeat. I had said "Yes"! Well, in God's name, I was indeed an "Aryan." I had not lied, I had allowed something much worse to happen. What a humiliation, to have answered the unjustified question as to whether I was "Aryan" so easily, even if the fact was of no importance to me! What a disgrace to buy, with a reply, the right to stay with my documents in peace! I had been caught unawares, even now. I had failed my very first test. I could have slapped myself.

As I left the Kammergericht it stood there, gray, cool, and calm as ever, set back from the street in its distinguished setting. There was nothing to show that, as an institution, it had just collapsed. There was also nothing about my appearance to show that I had just suffered a terrible reverse, a defeat that would be almost impossible to make good. A well-dressed young man walked down Potsdamer Strasse. There was nothing untoward about the scene. Business as usual, but in the air the approaching thunder of events to come. . . .

April 1, 1933, had been the first climax of the Nazi revolution. In the following weeks, events showed a tendency to revert to being merely matters for the press. Certainly the terror continued, as did the celebrations and parades, but no longer in the *tempo furioso* of March. Concentration camps had become an institution. One was advised to get used to that fact and mind one's tongue. The *Gleichschaltung*—placing Nazis in controlling positions of all ministries, local agencies, boards of large companies, committees of associations—continued, but it now took a pedantic, orderly form with laws and regulations. It no longer had the wild, unpredictable character of the "individual actions" of the previous months. The revolution became official. It became a fact, something that a German is used to accommodating and putting up with.

It was again permissible to visit Jewish shops. One was still told not to do so, and permanent posters described one as a "traitor to the race" if one did, but it was permitted. There were no SA guards at the doors. Jewish civil servants, doctors, lawyers, and journalists were still dismissed, but now it happened legally and in an orderly fashion, by paragraph such-and-such of the Civil Code, and there were exceptions for veterans and people who had been employed before the war. Could one ask for more? The courts, which had been suspended for a week, were allowed to resume their sessions and pass their verdicts. However, judges could now be removed, quite legally and according to law. The judges, who could be ousted at a moment's notice, were told that their powers had been immeasurably increased. They had become "people's judges," "sovereign judges." They need no longer anxiously follow the letter of the law. Indeed, it was better if they did not. Understood? . . .

One day—I do not remember what heresy I had just uttered—one of my co-*Referendars* took me aside, looked closely into my eyes, and said, "A word of warning, colleague. I have your best interests at heart." Another close look. "You're a republican, aren't you?" He put a placatory hand on my arm. "Shh. Don't worry. I am one too at heart. But you must be more careful. Don't underestimate the fascists." (He used the word "fascists.") "Skeptical comments are no use nowadays. You're only digging your own grave. Don't fancy that there's anything to be done against the fascists now! Certainly not by open opposition, believe me! I think I know the fascists better than you. We republicans must howl with the wolves."

That was the voice of the republicans. . . .

The world I had lived in dissolved and disappeared. Every day another piece vanished quietly, without ado. Every day one looked around and something else had gone and left no trace. I have never since had such a strange experience. It was as if the ground on which one stood was continually trickling away from under one's feet, or rather as if the air one breathed was steadily, inexorably being sucked away.

What was happening openly and clearly in public was almost the least of it. Yes, political parties disappeared or were dissolved; first those of the left, then also those of the right; I had not been a member of any of them. The men who had been the focus of attention, whose books one had read, whose speeches we had discussed, disappeared into exile or the concentration camps; occasionally one heard that one or another had "committed suicide while being arrested" or been "shot while attempting to escape." At some point in the summer the newspapers carried a list of thirty or forty names of famous scientists or writers; they had been proscribed, declared to be traitors to the people and deprived of their citizenship.

More unnerving was the disappearance of a number of quite harmless people, who had in one way or another been part of daily life. The radio announcer whose voice one had heard every day, who had almost become an old acquaintance, had been sent to a concentration camp, and woe betide you if you mentioned his name. The familiar actors and actresses who had been a feature of our lives disappeared from one day to the next. Charming Miss Carola Neher was suddenly a traitor to the people; brilliant young Hans Otto, who had been the rising star of the previous season, lay crumpled in the yard of an ss barracks—yes, Hans Otto, whose name had been on everyone's lips, who had been talked about at every soiree, had been hailed as the "new Matkowski" that the German stage had so long been waiting for. He had "thrown himself out of a fourth-floor window in a moment when the guards had been distracted," they said. A famous cartoonist, whose harmless drawings had brought laughter to the whole of Berlin every week, committed suicide, as did the master of ceremonies of a well-known cabaret. Others just vanished. One did not know whether they were dead, incarcerated, or had gone abroad—they were just missing.

The symbolic burning of the books in May had been an affair of the press, but the disappearance of books from the bookshops and libraries was uncanny. Contemporary German literature, whatever its merits, had simply been erased. Books of the last season that one had not bought by April became unobtainable. A few authors, tolerated for some unknown reason, remained like individual ninepins in the wreckage. Otherwise you could get only the classics—and a dreadful, embarrassingly bad literature of blood and soil, which suddenly sprang up. Readers—always a minority in Germany, and as they were daily told, an unimportant one at that—were deprived of their world overnight. Further, since they had quickly learned that those who were robbed might also be punished, they felt intimidated and pushed their copies of Heinrich Mann and Feuchtwanger into the back rows of their bookshelves; and if they dared to talk about the newest Joseph Roth or Jakob Wassermann they put their heads together and whispered like conspirators.

Many journals and newspapers disappeared from the kiosks—but what happened to those that continued in circulation was much more disturbing. You could not quite recognize them anymore. In a way a newspaper is like an old acquaintance: you instinctively know how it will react to certain events, what it will say about them and how it will express its views. If it suddenly says the opposite of what it said yesterday, denies its own past, distorting its features, you cannot avoid feeling that you are in a madhouse. That happened. Old-established democratic broadsheets such as the *Berliner Tageblatt* or the *Vossische Zeitung* changed into Nazi organs from one day to the next. In their customary, measured, educated style they said exactly the same things that were spewed out by the *Angriff* or the *Volkischer Beobachter*, newspapers that had always supported the Nazis. Later, one became accustomed to this and picked up occasional hints by reading between the lines of the articles on the arts pages. The political pages always kept strictly to the party line.

To some extent, the editorial staff had been replaced; but frequently this straightforward explanation was not accurate. For instance, there was an intellectual journal called *Die Tat* (Action), whose content lived up to its name. In the final years before 1933 it had been widely read. It was edited by a group of intelligent, radical young people. With a certain elegance they indulged in the long historical view of the changing times. It was, of course, far too distinguished, cultured, and profound to support any particular political party—least of all the Nazis. As late as February its editorials brushed them off as an obviously ephemeral phenomenon. Its editor in chief had gone too far. He lost his job and only just managed to save his neck (today he is allowed to write light novels). The rest of the editorial staff remained in post, but as a matter of course became Nazis without the least detriment to their elegant style and historical perspective—they had always been Nazis, naturally; indeed better, more genuinely and more profoundly so than the Nazis themselves. It was wonderful to behold: the paper had the same typography, the same name—but without batting an eyelid it had become a thoroughgoing, smart Nazi organ. Was it a sudden conversion or just cynicism? Or had Messrs. Fried, Eschmann, Wirsing, etc. always been Nazis at heart? Probably they did not know themselves. Anyway, I soon abandoned the question. I was nauseated and wearied, and contented myself with taking leave of one more newspaper.

The Claims of Community

THOMAS KÜHNE

From *Belonging and Genocide*

In early 1939, trying to adjust to his London exile, Sebastian Haffner was disgusted when he thought of Germany. He had recently left his home country with his Jewish fiancée. As an Aryan whose closest friends in Germany had been Jews, he was appalled by the Nazis' brutal harassment of and violence against the Jews. Even more frightening to him was how rapidly the Nazis had awakened the "readiness to kill" among his compatriots. According to his assessment, the "whole nation, Germany," was infected "with a germ that causes its people to treat their victims" as if they were "wolves." The Germans were not "subjugated" (to Hitler and the Gestapo), they were "something else, something worse," Haffner wrote, "they are 'comraded,' a dreadfully dangerous condition.... They are terribly happy, but terribly demeaned; so self-satisfied, but so boundlessly loathsome; so proud and yet so despicable and inhuman." "Widely praised, harmless male comradeship," Haffner said, "completely destroys the sense of responsibility for oneself."[1] And as such, he believed, comradeship had become "demonic" as well as pandemic in Germany.

"The Life of an Individual Must Not Be Set at Too High a Price"

No Nazi would have agreed with Haffner's devastating evaluation, but all of them would have proudly confirmed that the Third Reich had elevated comradeship to a state virtue. In truth, the Nazis glorified precisely what Haffner condemned. What Haffner took as a horrible pathology was the moral foundation of the Third Reich. The National Socialist movement understood itself as born in the trenches, with the goal of transferring the frontline comradeship to the entire German Volk. In 1933, that vision seemed to become reality. The veterans' movement welcomed the apotheosis of comradeship as "the basis of the new Reich." "Our yearnings are fulfilled," exclaimed the *Kyffhäuser*; "finally, the bridge from frontline experience to state building is complete."[2] Even Catholics, though opposing the Nazi movement, were swept along by the "feeling of national and German emotion" that "has seized our people," as the Catholic Teachers Organization exulted. "We have succeeded in breaking through the un-German spirit that prevailed in the revolution of 1918."[3]

The term *comradeship* was ubiquitous in the Third Reich. All Hitler Youth and Labor Service units were called "comradeships" (*Kameradschaften*). College students would meet in comradeships instead of in fraternities. Apprentices for all kinds of occupations were to be trained in comradeships. Even artists would come together no longer in art colonies but rather in comradeships. Nazi Germany presented itself as a great "national comradeship," with a broad range of institutions and aids to overcome party struggle, class divisions, the lacunae of an unfinished nation, and any appearance of "egoism" and loneliness.[4]

But despite the euphoria of 1933, Nazi leaders, thinkers, and propagandists understood that the

Volksgemeinschaft—the national comradeship—was far from complete. The Nazis may have called their "seizure of power" and the nazification of state institutions in 1933 a revolution, but they knew that a "transitory period" would be needed to "reeducate" their countrymen, as Heinrich Himmler once admitted. "National Socialism is not at the end of its days but only at the beginning," Hitler said in 1938, explaining why the Nazi state forced its youth into various organizations. Ridding them of "class consciousness or pride in status" and educating them "to think as Germans and act as Germans" would require thorough training.[5]

In fact, Hitler's "social revolution" was to lead to "something completely new and totally revolutionary," as the historian Yehuda Bauer has stated. Rooted in social Darwinist obsessions that saw history as a constant struggle between peoples for dominance and in the conviction that Germans were superior to any other nation, the Nazi revolution was planned and carried out as a racial rather than as an economic revolution. In other words: it aimed at a new class structure which went beyond any Marxist category. Despite its ongoing propaganda against class divisions, the Nazi state did not seriously touch the gap between middle and working classes. But millions of people seen as racially inferior were to be annihilated or enslaved—a revolution that would have changed class hierarchies far more profoundly. Nazi racial politics intended to distribute the properties and homelands of these people among Aryans. Those "subhumans" that would be spared from annihilation were to be installed as a new underclass beneath the real Aryan society. Hitler's Germany would thus become a welfare state based on the expropriation and exploitation of "inferiors." Millions of slaves from all across Eastern Europe would provide "the menial labor that would allow Aryans to pursue higher pleasures."[6]

Before World War II, the brutal basis of glory was not subject to public announcement; the people's comrades, or *Volksgenossen*, received a foretaste of the glorious future of the *Volksgemeinschaft* in seemingly harmless ways. Nazi Germany discarded the burdens of the Versailles Treaty, regained its national pride, and reclaimed its military power. With the economy recovering, full employment, mass consumerism, and a comprehensive welfare program came within reach. The state tourist and leisure agency, *Kraft durch Freude* (literally Strength Through Joy), announced the production of an inexpensive car for the masses, the *Volkswagen*, which promised happiness for every citizen in the near future. Until then, relatively inexpensive radios and tourist trips anticipated what would come. Everyone, or more precisely, every *Volksgenosse*, would live better than before.[7]

But in the Nazi utopia, the promise of the Promised Land was not milk and honey. Rather it was liberation from the selfish dynamic that burdened modern societies with endless conflicts. Material well-being and private happiness were promoted in the Third Reich only so long as they oiled the engines of national harmony. No pleasure without indoctrination was the law that governed mass consumerism and leisure activities. Radios transmitted the speeches of Hitler and Goebbels, Nazi spies sniffed out the ideological conformity of Germans relaxing on tourist trips, and the Volkswagen driver, traveling through the country, was to internalize the grandeur of the German fatherland. All these activities served the same goal as the huge national rallies that the Nazi Party held in Nuremberg: to reinforce the unity and harmony of the *Volksgemeinschaft*.

Understood as a national regeneration, the Nazi revolution aimed at the ethics, minds, and hearts of the Aryans to overcome their ideological divisions rather than their economic ones. Whereas Karl Marx had argued that being impacts consciousness, the Nazis based their revolution on the reverse assumption: consciousness was to determine being.[8] Winter Aid, or *Winterhilfswerk*, was established in 1933 to solicit donations for the needy and to replace the welfare organizations of the Weimar Republic, the trade unions, and the Christian churches. Hundreds of thousands of Germans committed themselves to helping. "With the aid of this tremendous society," Hitler said in 1937, "countless people are . . . regaining the firm belief that they are not completely lost and alone in this world, but sheltered in their *Volksgemeinschaft*—that they, too, are being cared for." As Hitler explained, this statewide charity would give Christian and socialist traditions "practical life." Such charity would not drop from heaven. "People are not born socialists, but must first be taught how to become them." Winter Aid served as not only a shelter for those in need, but also an "insurance against lack of common sense," Hitler announced. It was a program to turn the *Volksgenossen* into "practical" socialists.[9]

Donating to Winter Aid was mandatory. "*You too must sacrifice*," propaganda posters reminded Germans continuously. Pressure and control were omnipresent. Landlords issued forms to make householders report what they had donated, and teachers encouraged students to collect contributions from their parents, so as not to be listed on a classroom display board as a black sheep. Whoever did not contribute ran the risk of public denunciation and ostracism. In Flensburg, businessman Otto Schrader failed to contribute to Winter Aid and was immediately taken into "protective custody," as the local newspaper reported. Thus publicly outlawed, he promised to integrate himself "fully and wholly into the *Volksgemeinschaft*" through significant contributions to Winter

Aid. "Finally the training program was effective," the paper stated smugly.[10]

Rather than putting Christian and socialist ideals into practice, Nazi welfare in fact abandoned them. Neither voluntary as a matter of individual empathy nor universally addressed to all persons in need, charity in the Third Reich reeked of compulsion—and exclusion. No non-Aryan benefited, and whoever did not contribute was considered an enemy of the fatherland. Becoming a "practical" socialist, that is, a National Socialist, meant to absorb the rigid dichotomies of racist distinctions between Them and Us. Whether applying for a marriage loan from the state or for a vacation trip with Strength Through Joy, virtually every activity was meant to reveal, and to make one think about, one's racial origins. The Nazi welfare program aimed simultaneously at the ideological elevation and the racial purification of the German nation. In the schools, students now learned about the nation as a "community of blood," a "community of mind," "a community of fate and struggle," and a "community of work."[11] The envisioned *Volksgemeinschaft* would be rid of Jews and other supposedly racially inferior groups, and at the same time insiders would be converted, reformed, and made uniform—not just outwardly but inwardly, in their thinking and habits.

Winter Aid and other welfare programs in Nazi Germany promised charity to achieve conformity. They demanded self-sacrifice and attempted to erase "egotism" and selfishness, the mental conditions that were blamed for the divisions of Weimar society and for Germany's surrender in 1918. As one pedagogue said, "What an individual is worth is to be measured by the yardstick of the people, i.e., he will be measured by his achievements for the totality."[12] The virtues of individual life had no place in the Nazi Utopia. Addressing his military entourage in late 1941 and considering the massive losses of German soldiers in the aborted drive to reach Moscow, Hitler explained: "The life of an individual must not be set at too high a price. If the individual were important in the eye of nature, nature would take care to preserve it. Amongst millions of eggs a fly lays, very few are hatched out—and yet the race of flies thrives." So the end goal was a state in which every citizen knew he lived and died solely for his species—the Aryan *Volksgemeinschaft*.[13]

Hitler's martial rhetoric was directed to his military audience and its bloody environment. Military power relied on unity and self-sacrifice; egotism and selfishness, synonyms for individuality and private group interests, were seen as the most decisive detriments to it. The war on Europe, the expansion of *Lebensraum* in the East, and the subjugation of millions of people were inconceivable without domestic homogeneity, attainable only by ideological regimentation. And vice versa: war forged unity and strengthened community. In 1927 Hitler had outlined the basics by conjuring a mythical past "where there was no class division. This was in the platoons at the front line. There must be a chance to establish such unity at home as well. Why did it work at the front line? Because opposite was the enemy, and you were aware of the threat he constituted." Hitler's conclusion was: "If you want to amalgamate our people into a unity, the first thing you have to do is to create a new front line with a mutual enemy, so that everybody knows: We have to be united, because the enemy is the enemy of all of us."[14]

"The Aim Is Always the Same, Namely to Declare an Enemy"

No community and no unit exists without the "other": those who do not belong, who really or supposedly threaten the community either physically or just by looking different, by pursuing different ways of life, by harboring different experiences and visions—thus by challenging the identity of those who belong. If there is no enemy, one has to be invented. The larger and the more complex the in-group (as in industrial societies), the more difficult it is to obtain uniformity.

In 1932 Carl Schmitt, later a major political philosopher of the Nazis, outlined what a state had to do to reach "internal peace." It had to decide "upon the domestic enemy"—the enemy within. "Whether the form is sharper or milder," he explained, "explicit or implicit, whether ostracism, expulsion, proscription, or outlawry are provided for in special laws or in explicit or general descriptions, the aim is always the same, namely to declare an enemy." The inner enemy was to be considered "the other, the stranger . . . he is, in an especially intense way, existentially something different and alien."[15] Thus, the cohesion of the people's community was based not just on threatening clichés about imperialist England or subhuman Slavs, but even more on tracking down, identifying, persecuting, and terrorizing "domestic enemies."

Combining established antisemitic traditions, popular eugenic discourse, and anticommunist resentment, the Nazis chose "the Jew" as the racial paradigm of a "domestic enemy" and painted a frightening picture of a conspiracy being planned and executed inside and outside Germany. Endless propaganda, decisive legislation, constant harassment, and brutal terror transformed assimilated Jews into a German menace. "The Jew" served to unite the Aryan *Volksgemeinschaft*. In Osnabrück, the Nazi Party county leader (*Kreisleiter*) Münzer spoke in August 1935 to a crowd of twenty-five thousand people about the "Jewish question." It was not just about "antisemitism in a traditional sense," he said. It was "not just a fight against Jews as such, but a fight for the German soul . . . The Führer wants each German to be really aware of the Jewish menace and to recollect his own German identity in order to understand that any softness toward the Jew damages the German people."[16]

Many Germans agreed; they fabricated a widespread sense of national belonging by excluding the Jews. In 1937, the Jewish Victor Klemperer saw a picture in the *Stürmer*, the radical antisemitic Nazi newspaper, which showed "two girls at a seaside resort. Above it: "Prohibited for Jews," underneath it: "How nice that it's just us now!" Klemperer, who strongly identified himself as a German and had long taken pride in being a World War I veteran, understood the "horrible significance" of these words. To Germans, being "just us now" meant to live without Jews. "I have not only outwardly lost my Fatherland. . . . My inner sense of belonging is gone," noted Klemperer in his diary.[17] Ousting Jewish citizens strengthened the Aryans' sense of belonging. Clients boycotted their Jewish shopkeepers, patients boycotted their physicians, and students ostracized their Jewish classmates and professors. The Nazi government and party agencies dissolved Jewish associations and escalated into destroying houses and synagogues, Aryanizing businesses, and, long before the Holocaust started, forcing Jews to emigrate after stripping them of most or all their possessions.

To be sure, not all Germans acted alike. Relatively few used violence, and not all ostracized their former Jewish colleagues, neighbors, and friends. Many Germans felt uneasy about openly attacking them, and some continued to shop in Jewish stores, much to the displeasure of the Nazi leaders. Consequently the Osnabrück *Kreisleiter*, in his 1935 speech, agitated not only against Jews but also against those Germans who still kept in touch with Jews. Such Germans were branded as *Volksverräter*, traitors of the German people. In covering its local issues, the *Stürmer* publicly denounced the names and addresses of those *Volksgenossen* who still shopped with Jews. Very few non-Jewish Germans were able to resist such pressure. Most of them conformed one way or another, not always hating Jews yet modifying their behavior in ways that propelled the vision of a *Volksgemeinschaft* "cleansed" of the Jews. Beginning in 1933, the German Jews lived in a state of constant fear.

One of these Jews was Lilli Jahn, who did not emigrate and was murdered in Auschwitz. Raised in a Jewish family in Cologne, well educated in the arts, theater, and music, she studied medicine and fell in love with a non-Jewish fellow medical student, Ernst Jahn. In 1926, they married and moved to Immenhausen in Hesse to set up a medical practice. They missed urban life but enjoyed "some refined company . . . the local clergyman, their colleagues . . . and the local landowner, a highly cultivated man," observed Lilli's closest friend, Lotte Paepcke, also a Jewish woman married to a gentile. The Jahns were welcome—so they thought. Until 1933 "Just imagine," wrote Lilli to friends on April 2, the day after the infamous nationwide boycott of Jewish shops, lawyers, and physicians, "they also boycotted my Amadé [her husband] because he has a Jewish wife!" All of a sudden, the Jahns were ostracized by their neighbors and even their friends. One day the local landowner appeared with a minor cut and asked the doctor to take care of it. "Purely in passing," he also wanted to "make it clear that he and his wife would, alas, be temporarily compelled to sever relations with the doctor and his family." The doctor shouldn't take it personally, his patient added. So did a colleague, excusing himself for no longer socializing with Ernst. "'Nothing could ever detract me from my respect for you and your lady wife, but circumstances.' . . . Six months later the clergyman came to say that he had now received his third warning from Party headquarters and that their pleasant chats at the doctor's home must unfortunately cease." And another half year later, Lilli wrote in a letter to friends: "Our ostracism here in Immenhausen is now more complete than anyone could have dreamt. SA [the Nazi paramilitary group] headquarters has forbidden Bonsmann to cross our threshold!! The fact that he had obeyed this prohibition requires no comment." Bonsmann had been Ernst's friend and colleague. Now he was an SA man.[18]

Again, not all Germans followed Nazi boycott appeals. Shortly before November 1938, when Nazi thugs destroyed synagogues all over Germany, murdered scores of Jews, and sent thirty thousand to concentration camps, Lotte Paepcke's father, Max Mayer, stated that some Aryans readily accepted the "relentless expulsion" of the Jews from the body politic and "mindlessly" recited the slogans supplied by the propagandists. To a large extent, however, Max Mayer said, "people reject this persecution, aware of the falsity and injustice of such slogans, but unable to assist their victims." Mayer's diagnosis was quite right. The Security Service of the SS, the *Sicherheitsdienst* (SD), came to the same conclusion by "x-raying" ordinary Germans' opinions. Many of them inconspicuously or even demonstratively ignored the Nazi appeals to boycott Jewish shops, doctors, and lawyers. And when anti-Jewish violence escalated into the Kristallnacht pogrom in 1938, many Germans were shocked. To be sure, the motives of such discontent were disparate. Embarrassment of the educated middle class about the disgrace of German civilization was paralleled by concerns of workers "calculating the number of extra hours they will need to work to repair the damage done to German national property."[19]

The Germans' attitude toward the Jews during the Nazi era cannot easily be reduced to a common denominator, as historians have often attempted. Lilli Jahn's fate is a particularly tragic example. Her husband Ernst did what so many Germans did—yield to the antisemitic pressure. In 1942, he divorced his wife and left her unprotected; in fact, he handed her on a plate to the death machinery. It was not so much the hatred of Jews but indifference toward them—a silent or passive complicity—that established mass support of Nazi racial politics in the 1930s. Most Germans accepted the pseudo-legal measures that led to the exclusion of Jews from social life and to their expropriation. At the same time, many Germans despised the violent acts perpetrated by radical Nazis. Such ambivalence rarely alleviated the terror experienced by the Jews. But it troubled the regime. While symbolic gestures and concerns of Aryans about the fate of the Jews grew fainter, the Nazi leaders knew that the *Volksgemeinschaft* was not as united and ideologically synchronized as they wanted it to be. And the Germans' attitude toward the Jews was not the only thing that did not satisfy the regime's desire for totalitarian control. Throughout the 1930s Gestapo and Nazi block wardens, charged with supervising their neighbors, reported from all over Germany on the many former Social Democrats and Communists who continued to spread discontent with the regime by word of mouth. Discontent could not be tolerated. While propaganda wrapped the utopia of a grand community in the tinsel of consumerism and charity, a different notion of *Volksgemeinschaft* took on ever sharper shape, one that was welded together by violent terror outwardly, but also by psychic terror inwardly.[20]

Learning community in the way Hitler envisioned it meant becoming sensitive to anything and anybody who did not conform or who did not fit the standards of a racially and ideologically homogeneous society. The *Volksgemeinschaft* was threatened not only by racially alien elements such as Jews or Sinti and Roma, but also by biologically and hereditary defectives, and by a broad range of "asocials" or "community aliens" (*Gemeinschaftsfremde*) like homosexuals, whores, alcoholics, tramps, beggars, who, though not clearly criminal, were considered unable to adapt themselves to the community. These were to be eliminated, sterilized, or taken into "preventive detention."[21] The hunt for the enemy within was so insidious because it spread uncertainty. What exactly was "asocial" behavior? Some categories were established, but only to open a vast gray area. "Whoever challenges our unity, will end up at the stake," announced Baldur von Schirach, the national leader of the Hitler Youth, in 1934. What precisely challenged the unity of Hitler Youth? The very boy who, instead of enjoying the pleasure of comradeship in the Hitler Youth, wasted his time with a stamp collection at home or with spontaneous adventure trips with his friends was suspected of being a social outcast. Nazi propagandists, jurists, doctors, and pedagogues worked ambitiously to categorize all kinds of "community pests" in order to make the *Volksgenossen* detect the slightest deviance. Among these categories were the "coward," the "shirker," the "grind," the "troublemaker," the "griper," the "peacock," the "uncontrolled," the "schemer," and the "loner." Although the lone wolf was not necessarily a criminal, as a military psychologist noted uneasily, his behavior could be considered a "preliminary stage of desertion." Desertion, though, from any unit was the epitome of treason, the ultimate betrayal of one's comrades and community. And whoever did not conform or obey but just tried to be himself was considered a possible deserter—a traitor of the *Volksgemeinschaft*.[22]

"Their Comrades Are Their Conscience"

Not all carriers of social pathogens were automatically deemed hopeless. Unlike the persecution of the Jews, the treatment of Aryan outsiders was flexible. Preparing for total war, the *Wehrgemeinschaft*, or martial community, needed to mobilize as much manpower as possible.[23] Thus, the rhetoric of extermination that threatened "community aliens" or "community pests" left the door open for converting the troublemakers into useful *Volksgenossen*, or at least into cannon fodder. In a 1935 lecture on how to build comradeship the physician Horst Buchholz drew on an extreme case of "egotism" to show what the right social setting could achieve. Three years earlier he had treated a man who suffered from a severe case of asthma as well as extreme myopia. Solely concerned with himself, the patient had sought refuge in Indian mysticism and Schopenhauer's solipsist philosophy. Overall, he had "completely disowned the real world and any real people." A hopeless case of egotism, Buchholz's audience might have concluded at this point. The specialist, though, knew of a therapy that would work a miracle. Instead of wasting time with medicine or sanatoria, Buchholz, a psychiatrist and specialist in internal medicine, sent his patient into a "strong school of community—the SA." There, his patient found what he needed: "duties and engagement on the one hand, comradely support for his many little disabilities on the other hand." Proudly, Buchholz added: "The patient has been healthy for three years." Buchholz left no doubt about the point of it all. Egotism was not to be treated for the individual's ailments but to remove the obstacles on the road to "our grand mutual goal, the German *Volksgemeinschaft*."[24]

To cleanse Germans of "egotism," to construct a new people and a grand community, the Nazi state forced young boys and also, less insistently, girls, into a sophisticated, life-long training program. As Hitler explained in a speech in December 1938, "Boys join our organization at the age of ten." Four years later, "they move from the *Jungvolk* to the Hitler Youth. . . . And then we are even less prepared to give them back into the hands of those who create class and status barriers, rather we take them immediately into the Party, . . . into the SA or into the SS," after which they "are polished for six or seven months" in the Labor Service. And if there "are still remnants of class consciousness or pride in status, then the *Wehrmacht* will take over the further treatment for two years" and after that, "to prevent them from slipping back into old habits once again, we take them immediately into the SA, SS, etc., and they will not be free again for the rest of their lives."[25]

German boys from the age of ten to eighteen joined the Hitler Youth. In 1933 one of three did so, from 1939 on almost everyone joined. As part of their training, usually a couple of weeks per year, they spent some time in a camp. Adults also were asked to join a training camp for a certain period. From 1933 through 1939, about 70 percent of German teachers participated in at least one training camp. From 1935 on, the compulsory camps of the National Labor Service—*Reichsarbeitsdienst*, or RAD—enforced a six-month work schedule on all males between the ages of eighteen and twenty-five. And from 1935 until 1945, the *Wehrmacht* drafted about seventeen million men for military service, which began with a training period in the barracks—a special kind of camp. The *Waffen*-SS added another million.[26]

Unlike the pre-Nazi youth movement, which had allowed any boy or girl to leave camp whenever he or she liked, the Nazis organized camps militarily. Youths were subjected to a hierarchical structure and to a strict and uniform daily sched-

ule of education, training, and service. Housed in tents or barracks, they were separated for weeks, months, or even years from what had been their normal life; jobs, possessions, friends, and relatives were no longer of importance. Initially strangers, once isolated from the rest of the society in a "community of fate," these young people had to get along, whether they liked it or not. Whereas in modern society an individual lives, works, plays, and sleeps in different places with different people, Nazi camps were organized as "total institutions." This is the label the sociologist Erving Goffman coined for prisons, hospitals, monasteries, and military barracks where all of these activities occur in the same place, with the same people answering to a single authority.[27] And so it was in Nazi youth camps. All camp members wore uniforms as the symbol of their equality, all were required to work, sleep, and play together, and all were subjected to a tight daily schedule that included exercises, classes, meals, sleeping, but very little leisure time.

What did young Germans learn in these camps? Total institutions can serve different goals. Whereas prisons or concentration camps are purported to save the "good" society from "bad" people, military-like barracks or training camps were supposed to "improve" people's ideological dispositions, mental conditions, or social skills. Separation from relatives and friends also "condensed" social interaction in the camp, providing the optimal prerequisites for brainwashing or "assimilation," as a leading Nazi pedagogue, Ernst Krieck, wrote. The camp brought together youths so that they would "all adopt the same type [of personality] and a similar lifestyle."[28]

Sebastian Haffner took his own experience as a paradigmatic example of how such "assimilation" worked in National Socialist Germany. In early 1933 he had just finished law school and was preparing to establish his professional life. After the Nazis came into power, though, he learned that civil service candidates like him had to join a training camp for some weeks before being permitted to take their legal exams. After receiving his call-up papers, he traveled to Jüterboog, a village on the plains of Brandenburg, quite a distance from Berlin, where he had grown up. The camp was located outside of Jüterboog. Not knowing how to get there from the train station, he and some prospective comrades deliberated about whether to order limousines. Some SA men, who looked forward more eagerly to the camp than Haffner, ultimately decided for them. They knew that entering a training camp in comfortable cars was not an appropriate option. Instead, they ordered the crowd to "form up in threes" and to march. And out of the deep uncertainty that would never leave him in the weeks to come, Haffner remembers, "we obeyed."

Surprisingly to Haffner, ideological indoctrination did not play a major role in the Jüterboog camp. There were no lessons on antisemitism, Nazi eugenics, the "Lebensraum" ideology, the leadership principle, or on the heroic past of the NSDAP. Slowly Haffner learned that the lessons were much more subtle than mere indoctrination. Camp life fostered togetherness, military order, and, most important, the practice of comradeship, which was to replace the security of family and friends Haffner had been used to in civilian life. If one's feet smelled, one was obliged to wash them "every morning and every evening. That is a rule of comradeship." And it was not just about personal hygiene. More important were fitness exercises and paramilitary drills, bellowing "Heil Hitler," marching around the camp, and singing military songs.

And beyond obeying orders, even without supervision, the comrades practiced comradeship on their own. "Civilian courtesy" was scorned with the abundant use of crudities and profanity. The "ritual reciting of lewd songs and jokes" served to vilify bourgeois love. Comradeship "actively decomposed" both "individuality and civilization" and elevated men above "civilized tenderness." A highlight of such decomposition was the boyish prank "of attacking a neighboring dormitory at night with 'water bombs,' drinking mugs filled with water to be poured over the beds of the defenders. . . . A battle would ensue, with merry 'Ho's and 'Ha's and screaming and cheering. You were a bad comrade if you did not take part. . . . It was taken for granted that comradeship prevented those who had been attacked from telling tales."

The group did not need a superior authority to run its internal affairs but restored order on its own. Individuals were powerless, but comradeship offered empowerment. The night after a dormitory raid "we had to be prepared for a revenge attack." Revenge restored order just as ostracism did. "If someone committed a sin against comradeship" by acting superior or showing off or exhibiting "more individuality than was permissible, a nighttime court in the barracks would judge and condemn him to corporal punishment. Being dragged under the water pump was the punishment for minor misdemeanors." Someone who "favored himself in distributing butter rations," however, suffered a "terrible fate." He was "dragged from his bed and spread-eagled on a table. 'Every man will whack Meier once, no one is excused,' the judge thundered." And the victim was well advised to accept what the group did to him. "By the dark laws of comradeship that governed us, independently of our individual wills, a complaint would have put him in danger of his life."

In his memoir Haffner drew ambivalent conclusions about what all this meant. Comradeship, he wrote, "can become a means for the most terrible dehumanization" as it "relieves men of responsibility for their own actions, before themselves, before God, before their conscience. They do what all their comrades do. . . . Their comrades are their conscience and give absolution for everything." This analysis reveals the rage of an individualist who had been compelled to betray his personal identity and illustrates what Siegfried Kracauer had described fifteen years earlier. Comradeship "de-personalizes the individual mind." In the camp, Haffner had no privacy. Friends and relatives were cut off. With the young men isolated from these securities, uncertainty ruled the camp and could be overcome only by merging into the community of comrades. In the training camp, young men replaced their previous individual identities with a new group identity, one that pertained exclusively to a male society. On the other hand, Haffner also wrote that in the camp, he began to partake of the "happiness of comradeship. . . . It was a pleasure to go for a cross-country run together in the morning, and then to go naked into the communal hot showers together, to share the parcels that one or another received from home, to share also responsibility for misdemeanors that one of your comrades had committed, to help and support one another in a thousand little ways."[29]

"A Feeling of Absolute Superiority"

From time immemorial the cultural codes for men have been drastically different than those for women. In preindustrial societies, boys participated in initiation rites that separated them from women and initiated them into becoming men—to think, feel, and behave like other men, to adopt and internalize manly social qualities. Boys were sent to the men's hut to learn male conformity and male solidarity. How that happened varied from one culture to another. Sometimes

homosexual practices were included, sometimes not. Usually, these rites were dramatically framed, torture and humiliation playing a major role. Only these activities seemed to guarantee the desired result.[30] . . .

Similar patterns of male initiation were still at work in modern societies, and so also in Nazi Germany. Crucial is how they relate to their political context. Nazi Germany inflated these traditions and deployed them to fabricate a *Volksgemeinschaft* of its own.

To become a real man, a "momma's boy" needed to erase any infantile, egocentric identities that were rooted in the female world of his family. To knock out his private identity and to give him a new, truly male identity, he was sent to "schools of manliness"—the military, the Labor Service, or the Hitler Youth. Educators in interwar Germany justified and organized such training as a "period to break up the wrong consciousness," to reshape completely the entire personality of a youth. Max Momsen, a college director in Cottbus, explained in 1935 how camp training worked. "When camp service seizes the body and compels it to a certain concise performance, it also forces the body into certain mental and emotional habits, which consist first of all in relinquishing all that is individual and selfish. . . . The private self, the individual, will be broken. This might be a hard and painful procedure. It is inevitable, though, for the sake of a higher and larger community."[31]

The boy who was to become a full member of this larger community had to start from scratch. Accepting status as lowest on the pecking order was the first step.[32] The new recruit was made to do "things he would have decisively refused to do as a pampered mother's boy"—cleaning, mending, darning, making beds, peeling potatoes, folding the wash, all the things that "mama" had done for him and that were "not at all a man's job."[33]

Thus, ironically, for a boy to become a real man, he had to become a woman first. For the moment, he lost any gender identity. The dramatic humiliation rite followed the "principle of the lower service."[34] Only there, at the lowest step of the ladder in the hierarchical structure of male bonding, could a new identity be ascribed to him. Mother's boy had "to go through an entire system of tortures" executed by his comrades or his superiors in order "to be acknowledged as a real man and no longer be considered just a young whippersnapper."[35]

Although the camp or barrack was devoid of women, its "anti-structure" was not without the symbolic power provided by the dichotomies and hierarchies of a gendered system. Although cleaning, darning, and cooking were not ordinarily valued as men's work, "female jobs" still had to be done in an exclusively male institution. "A man has to do things by himself. So does the soldier. When in the battlefield, he also is on his own."[36] Embedded in this popular appeal is the kernel of a powerful idea: in an all-male society, the male bond is independent of the rest of the world, in particular from women. It is sovereign. It creates the world from scratch. Humiliation, thus, was designed as the starting point of a period of suffering, which would eventually lead to redemption.

It was all about community—the sovereignty of the community but also its collective responsibility. If one comrade failed in some task or merely stepped out of line, the entire group was blamed and penalized. To handle collective responsibility, the group sought inner conformity. "Comradeship entails strong discipline and oppresses the malicious, unreliable and uncomradely elements," as military pedagogue Erich Weniger stated. The outsider represented the "other"—the needed enemy for those who wanted to belong, just as cohesion of the good society "needs" its criminals, as George Herbert Mead wrote in 1918. "The

attitude of hostility toward the lawbreaker has the unique advantage of uniting all members of the community in *the emotional solidarity of aggression*." Observing that "nothing unites the members of a group like a common enemy," the sociologist Albert Cohen has concluded that external and internal enemies are, in a way, exchangeable. Either of them "arouses the sentiments of community and revives a waning solidarity." This, again, is the reason why communities need the deviant. He may "function as a 'built-in' out-group, and contribute to the integration of the group in much the same way as do witches, devils, and hostile foreign powers."[37] . . .

Anybody who failed to adapt to the mood of his group and resisted demands to sacrifice himself on the altar of the "Us" was almost sure to find himself in the outsider role. In the military, your superior was at hand not only as the teacher of comradeship but also as its catalyst. He tortured the recruits with mud baths, locker room and dormitory roll calls, masquerades, and confinement to barracks. But shared hatred of the tormentor ensured a certain harmony within the group, even collective joy and collective power. "We have imperceptibly grown together into firm comradeship" through the harassment they suffered in the first weeks of serving together, wrote a Wehrmacht recruit to his friend in the Hitler Youth. Now they felt like "nobody can get to us."[38] Another recruit, Kurt Kreissler, was enthusiastic about "an iron comradeship" that had grown out of his and his roommates' hatred of their superiors. "Almost nothing can shake us anymore, not even when our first lieutenant bawls us out," he noted in his diary.[39] Former Wehrmacht soldier Harms Karl Vorster recalled the nasty trick he and his comrades played on a malicious superior. After their sergeant got drunk and fell fast asleep one night, his soldiers secured a padlock around his testicles and kept the key. The next day was awful for him, as he had to carry out his duties with his hand in his trouser pocket to try and minimize his discomfort. His recruits, though, were delighted, and they stuck together when the sergeant demanded that the culprit reveal himself. Together they got through the inevitable punishment with conspiratorial indifference.[40]

Amid uncertainty, loneliness, and powerlessness, comradeship provided security, togetherness, and strength. It often took the form of little "conspiracies," even as it protected the culprit trapped in the workings of the military or paramilitary obedience and subjugation machine. While Hans Lorenz and his comrades were at a pub—their first such excursion after three weeks in the military—his belt and his gun were stolen. Three days of detention awaited him; a soldier was responsible for his gear, and there were no excuses. His comrades, however, held "a council of war" and decided that one of them would report sick every day so that Hans could borrow the "sick" soldier's gun and a belt. They continued this scheme until they were permitted another pub visit, at which time Hans managed to procure a gun and a belt in the same way he had lost his own.[41]

Those who achieved a sense of security through comradeship amid the insecurity of a totalitarian state and the reins of a "total institution" shared an exceptional feeling—the "feeling of absolute superiority," as Klaus Ewald, a former student in one of the *Napolas*, the paramilitary Nazi elite schools, put it. There, war games fostered an even stronger sense of togetherness than did the hunt for outsiders or little conspiracies against superiors elsewhere. "Over there is the enemy," students were told as they were introduced to field exercises. "We are going to attack. First we have to get through that hollow, then approach the hill over there: we'll fan out and move forward to face the enemy and provide each other with fire protection. I'll be shooting, you'll jump; together we keep the enemy down, then another one will take over protective fire, he moves forward, and so on—that is total working together."[42]

A new social order was emerging. Who was in and who was out, who was above and who was below, what was to be done and what was to be left out—all this was to be redefined. Middle-class ethics and customs no longer counted. "We really had to swelter and freeze, we had to get soaked in our tents. We might curse about it, and it might bring out our nastier side, but we always came back to the communal group," said Wilfried Glatten. This atmosphere lent itself to a "conspiratorial community," which Nazi propaganda loved to conjure. It radiated an aura of revolt, upheaval, and protest, not against the political regime but against a supposedly outdated social climate— the musty smell of bourgeois privacy, security— and boredom.[43] . . .

NOTES

1. Sebastian Haffner, *Defying Hitler* (New York, 2002), 143f, 199, 290f.
2. *Kyffhäuser*, September 3, 1933, 614f; *Stahlhelm*, January 27, 1935; ibid., January 29, 1933 (!), "We are creating the nation!"
3. Quoted in Deborah Dwork and Robert Jan van Pelt, *Holocaust. A History* (New York, 2002), 68f.
4. Cornelia Schmitz-Beming, *Vokabular des Nationalsozialismus* (Berlin, 1998), 343–45.
5. Hitler speech, December 4, 1938, in Jeremy Noakes and Geoffrey Pridham, eds., *Nazism, 1919–1945. A History in Documents and Eyewitness Accounts*, 2 vols. (New York, 1983–84), 1: 417; Felix Kersten, *Totenkopf und Treue, Heinrich Himmler ohne Uniform* (Hamburg, 1952), 184.
6. Yehuda Bauer, "Overall Explanations, German Society and the Jews, or: Some Thoughts About

Context," in *Probing the Depths of German Anti-semitism. German Society and the Persecution of the Jews, 1933–1941*, ed. David Bankier (Jerusalem, 2000), 16; Ian Kershaw, *The Nazi Dictatorship: Problems and Perspectives of Interpretation*, 4th ed. (London, 2000), 161–82 (social classes); Eric D. Weitz, *A Century of Genocide. Utopias of Race and Nation* (Princeton, 2003), 110 (slaves).

7. Shelley Baranowski, *Strength Through Joy. Consumerism and Mass Tourism in the Third Reich* (Cambridge, 2007).

8. David Schoenbaum, *Hitler's Social Revolution. Class and Status in Nazi Germany 1933–1945* (London, 1967), 76; Claudia Koonz, *The Nazi Conscience* (Cambridge MA, 2004), 59f, 73f, 133f, 145; Peter Fritzsche, *Life and Death in the Third Reich* (Cambridge MA, 2008).

9. Max Domarus, *Hitler. Speeches and Proclamations 1932–1945. The Chronicle of a Dictatorship* (Wauconda, 1992), 2: 955.

10. Poster of the 1934–35 campaign, http://www.dhm.de/lcmo/objckte/pict/plio3466/index.html, accessed January 28, 2009. See Lore Walb, *Ich, die Alte—ich, die Junge. Konfrontation mit meinen Tagebüchern 1933–1945* (Berlin, 1997), 72f; *Deutschland-Berichte der Sopade*, vol. 2, 1935 (Frankfurt, 1980), 200f. (February 2, 1935).

11. Noakes and Pridham, *Nazism, 1919–1945*, 1: 437.

12. Leutloff, "Deutsche Volksbildungsarbeit," *Bericht. Weltkongreß für Freizeit und Erholung Hamburg vom 23.-30. 7. 1936* (Berlin, 1937), 586, quoted in Franz Janka, *Die braune Gesellschaft. Ein Volk wird formatiert* (Stuttgart, 1997), 253.

13. H. R. Trevor-Roper, ed., *Hitler's Table Talk, 1941–1944. His Private Conversations* (New York, 2000), 142. Contrary to what Hannah Arendt suggests (*The Origins of Totalitarianism* [New York, 2004, originally 1951], 565), these statements did not refer to the inmates of concentration camps but to the Aryan *Volksgemeinschaft*. Hitler's public elaborations were less cynical; Joachim C. Fest, *Hitler* (New York, 1974), 433–36.

14. *Adolf Hitler in Franken. Reden aus der Kampfzeit* (Nuremberg, 1938), 83.

15. Carl Schmitt, *The Concept of the Political* (New Brunswick, 1976), 46f and 27.

16. Otto Dov Kulka and Eberhard Jäckel, eds., *Die Juden in den geheimen NS-Stimmungsberichten 1933–1945* (Düsseldorf, 2004), Document no. 1109 (DVD). More generally, see Omer Bartov, "Defining Enemies, Making Victims: Germans, Jews, and the Holocaust," *American Historical Review* 103 (1998): 258–71.

17. Victor Klemperer, *I Will Bear Witness. A Diary of the Nazi Years, 1933–1941* (New York, 1998), 233f, August 17, 1937.

18. Martin Doerry, ed., *My Wounded Heart. The Life of Lilli Jahn, 1900–1944* (New York, 2004), 50f, 57, 61, 64f; Michael Wildt, *Volksgemeinschaft als Selbstermächtigung. Gewalt gegen Juden in der deutschen Provinz, 1919–1939* (Hamburg, 2007), 191–93, 202f (*Stürmer*); generally, see Saul Friedländer, *Nazi Germany and the Jews. The Years of Persecution, 1933–1939* (New York, 1997), and Marion Kaplan, *Between Dignity and Despair. Jewish Life in Nazi Germany* (New York, 1998); Bankier, *Probing the Depths of German Antisemitism.*

19. Doerry, *My Wounded Heart*, 77f; David Bankier, *The Germans and the Final Solution. Public Opinion Under Nazism* (Oxford, 1992), 86f; Frank Bajohr and Dieter Pohl, *Der Holocaust als offenes Geheimnis. Die Deutschen, die NS-Führung und die Alliierten* (Munich, 2006), 39–43.

20. Richard Evans, *The Third Reich in Power, 1933–1939* (New York, 2005); Ian Kershaw, *Popular Opinion and Political Dissent in the Third Reich. Bavaria 1933–1945* (Oxford, 1983); Sheila Fitzpatrick and Alf Lüdtke, "Energizing the Everyday," in *Beyond Totalitarianism. Stalinism and Nazism Compared*, ed. Michael Geyer and Sheila Fitzpatrick (Cambridge, 2009), 266–301. On "indifference" as a category to describe Germans' attitude toward anti-Jewish politics, see Carolyn J. Dean, *The Fragility of Empathy After the Holocaust* (Ithaca, 2004), 76–105.

21. Michael Burleigh and Wolfgang Wippermann, *The Racial State: Germany 1933–1945* (Cambridge, 1991), 75–197; Robert Gellately and Nathan

Stoltzfus, eds., *Social Outsiders in Nazi Germany* (Princeton, 2001).

22. Hermann Göring, *Reden und Aufsätze* (Munich, 1938), 226–44; Karl Mierke, "Gefährdete Kameradschaft," *Soldatentum* 6 (1939), 138–41, 188–95; Hermann Foertsch, *Der Offizier der deutschen Wehrmacht*, 5th ed. (Berlin, 1941), 56, 67; Schulz, "Loslösung und Einfügung im Soldatenleben," *Soldatentum* 4 (1937): 2–10; Kurt Kreipe, "Versager im soldatischen Friedensdienst," *Soldatentum* 2 (1935): 79–82; Gerathewohl, "Eigenart und Behandlung des Einzelgängers," *Soldatentum* 5 (1938): 163–68; Baldur von Schirach, *Die Hitler-Jugend. Idee and Gestalt* (Berlin, 1934), 85 (stake).

23. [Erich] Ludendorff, *The Nation at War* (London, c. 1936, originally German [1935]).

24. [Horst] Buchholz, "Aufbau der Gesinnung und des Kameradschaftsgeistes," *Kongreßbericht der deutschen allgemeinen ärztlichen Gesellschaft für Psychotherapie iiber die Tagung in Breslau vom 3.-6. Okt. 1935* (Heidelberg, 1935), 72–77.

25. Noakes and Pridham, *Nazism, 1919-1945*, 1: 417.

26. Michael Kater, *Hitler Youth* (Cambridge MA: 2004); Jürgen Schiedeck and Martin Stahlman, "Die Inszenierung 'totalen Erlebens.' Lagererziehung im Nationalsozialismus," in *Politische Formierung und soziale Erziehung im Nationalsozialismus*, ed. Hans-Uwe Otto and Heinz Sünker (Frankfurt, 1991), 167–202; Gerhard Kock, "*Der Führer sorgt für unsere Kinder . . .*" Die Kinderlandverschickung im Zweiten Weltkrieg (Paderborn, 1997), 144–49; Kiran Klaus Patel, *Soldiers of Labor. Labor Service in Nazi Germany and New Deal America, 1933-1945* (New York, 2005), 190ff. On the figures see also Koonz, *The Nazi Conscience*, 157; newspaper report on teacher camps from 1937 in Noakes and Pridham, *Nazism, 1919–1945*, 1: 432–35.

27. Erving Goffman, *Asylums. Essays in the Social Situation of Mental Patients and Other Inmates* (Garden City, 1961).

28. Ernst Krieck, *Nationalsozialistische Erziehung*, 4th ed. (Osterwieck, 1937), 9–13.

29. Haffner, *Defying Hitler*, 257–91.

30. Arnold van Gennep, *The Rites of Passage* (Chicago, 1960); David Gilmore, *Manhood in the Making. Cultural Concepts of Masculinity* (New Haven, 1990), chap. 7; Frank W. Young, *Initiation Ceremonies. A Cross-Cultural Study of Status Dramatization* (Indianapolis, 1965), 24–41, 63–104.

31. John Remy, "Patriarchy and Fratriarchy as Forms of Androcracy," in *Men, Masculinities and Social Theory*, ed. Jeff Hearn and David Morgan (London, 1990), 43–54; for "momma's boy" see *Das junge Deutschland* (1944), 85–90, and for pre-Nazi Germany see *Arbeiterjugend* (1926), 108, *Das junge Deutschland* (1928), 159–68; for "school of manliness" see Ute Frevert, *A Nation in Barracks. Modem Germany, Military Conscription and Civil Society* (Oxford, 2004), 162, and Patel, *Soldiers of Labor*, 216; for "wrong consciousness" see Helmut Stellrecht, *Neue Erziehung* (Berlin, 1942), 61; Max Momsen, *Leibeserziehung mit Einschluß des Geländesports* (Osterwieck, 1935), 19f.

32. Guido Knopp, *Hitler's Children* (Phoenix Mill, 2004), 139–43.

33. *Wir Mädel*, 1940–41, 812; Jesco von Puttkamer, *Deutschlands Arbeitsdienst* (Oldenburg, 1938), 24, 41.

34. Stellrecht, *Neue Erziehung*, 61.

35. F. Lehmann, *Wir von der Infanterie*, 3d ed. (Munich, 1934), 18.

36. *Wir Mädel* 1940–41, 812, 814.

37. Erich Weniger, *Wehrmachtserziehung und Kriegserfahrung* (Berlin, 1938), 118; cf. Hans von Seeckt, *Gedanken eines Soldaten* (Leipzig, 1935), 9f; for recent sociological research, see Michael S. Kimmel, "Masculinity as Homophobia. Fear, Shame, and Silence in the Construction of Gender Identity," in *Theorizing Masculinities*, ed. Harry Brod and Michael Kaufmann (Thousand Oaks, 1994), 119–41; George Herbert Mead, "The Psychology of Punitive Justice," *American Journal of Sociology* 23 (1918): 590f; Albert K. Cohen, *Deviance and Control* (Englewood Cliffs, 1966), 8f.

38. Hermann Melcher, *Die Gefolgschaft* (Berg, 1990), mf.

39. Memoirs of Kurt Kreissler (pseudonym), 1: 5 (author's copy); Friedrich Grupe, *Jahrgang 1916*.

Die Fahne war mehr als der Tod (Munich, 1989), 66–68.

40. Author's interview with Harms Karl Vorster (pseudonym), 1994. Cf. Erhard Steininger, *Abgesang 1945. Ein Erlebnisbericht* (Leer, 1981), 95f; Max Bauer, *Kopfsteinpflaster. Erinnerungen* (Frankfurt, 1981), 100–102.

41. Hans Lorenz, *Graubrot mit Rübenkraut. Ein zeitgeschichtliches Schicksal* (Moers, 1993), 108f, 117. Cf. Weniger, *Wehrmachtserziehung und Kriegserfahrung*, 122; Wilhelm Reibert, *Der Dienstunterricht im Reichsheer. Ein Handbuch für den deutschen Soldaten*, 6th ed. (Berlin, 1934), 96; Friedrich Altrichter, *Das Wesen der soldatischen Erziehung* (Oldenburg, 1942), 129–34; Joseph Goebbels, "Soldat im Kampf der Geister," *Das Reich*, October 12, 1941, front page.

42. Author's interview with Klaus Ewald, 1995; Knopp, *Hitler's Children*, 18f, 132f; Bernd Hainmüller, *Erst die Fehde—dann der Krieg. Jugend unterm Hakenkreuz—Freiburgs Hitlerjugend* (Freiburg, 1998).

43. "Verschworene Gemeinschaft," *Völkischer Beobachter*, January 24, 1939; Omer Bartov, "The Conduct of War: Soldiers and the Barbarization of Warfare," in *Resistance Against the Third Reich, 1933–1990*, ed. Michael Geyer and John W. Boyer (Chicago, 1994), 48f.

Aryanization

AVRAHAM BARKAI

From *From Boycott to Annihilation*

Even before January 30, 1933, violent acts against Jewish individuals had not been uncommon. In Jewish neighborhoods in the large metropolitan centers, such acts and incidents were as much a part of the everyday "street scene" as the brawls between members of the SA and the Communists. Yet the police had tried to maintain public law and order. Now the SA was itself part of the police force—sporting arm bands labeled Auxiliary Police and armed with carbine rifles, its men patrolled the streets. Terror against political opponents and against Jews had been legalized. In the "better" sections of town, such as along the fashionable Kurfürstendamm in Berlin, that terror remained low-key as long as there was a desire in the party leadership to avoid antagonizing the still-hesitant, solid middle-class burghers and foreign visitors to the city. In the poorer neighborhoods and in outlying regions, the SA was able, unencumbered, to give free rein to its passions.

The first victims of this violence were the *Ostjuden*, the Jews from Eastern Europe. The great majority of these Jews had only recently come to Germany in the period around World War I, and they adhered faithfully to their religious customs and traditions. Easily recognizable by their beards and forelocks, their distinct dress and headwear, they personified the image of "Jewry as a foreign race." It proved easy to mobilize the xenophobic animosity of broad sections of the population against such an "alien" group of Jews. For the most part, they were poor people of modest means: small merchants trading in low-price goods, workers who made inexpensive articles of clothing in tiny shops or, for example, cut and pasted rubber raincoats. Those Eastern Jews who were even poorer traveled as itinerant peddlers through the rural countryside, their case of samples in hand, earning the enmity of the local storeowners.[1]

There are numerous eyewitness accounts of the brutal terror to which Jewish tradesmen were exposed even before the organized boycott of April 1, 1933. Two will be cited here as representative examples. Along with Berlin, Munich, and several cities in Saxony, the Eastern Jewish population was concentrated in the industrial cities in western Germany. It was there that an especially rabid antisemitism festered and spread. On March 20, 1933, in Dortmund,

> members of the SA and SS dragged the butcher Julius Rosenfeld and his son from the Dortmund stockyards through the streets of the city to a brickyard at the Voss pit. Rosenfeld and his son were lined up against the wall several times and threatened with pistols. They were forced to sing the "Horst Wessel Song," and were greeted by a rain of blows when they arrived at the brickyard. The young Rosenfeld was forced to set fire to his father's beard with a burning newspaper. After this, father and son were compelled to jump into a clay-pit. After five hours, the elder Rosenfeld was released

and sent home under the condition that within two hours he bring a slaughtered ox to his tormenters as a ransom for the release of his son.[2]

The second report comes from Duisburg:

> On March 24, a civilian accompanied by an armed member of the SS gained forced entry into the furniture store of the Polish Jew AAC, who apparently had antagonized his competitors by underselling them. The SS man accosted the Jew with his fists and left him covered with blood. AAC proceeded in this condition to the precinct station, where he was told that the police were powerless to act in such cases. On April 1, he was taken into protective custody, since there were fears of further acts of violence.[3]

The businesses owned by Eastern European Jews were not the only ones affected by reprisals. Especially during the month of March 1933, larger firms as well—mainly Jewish department stores and other retail shops—were singled out as targets for more or less violent demonstrations. Several newly installed mayors distinguished themselves in particular in this connection. Apparently, the National Socialist "revolution" was proceeding at too slow a pace for their taste; they felt it should be speeded up by so-called *Einzelaktionen*, "individual actions" against Jewish stores and businesses. The *Kampfbund für den gewerblichen Mittelstand* (League of Struggle for the Commercial Middle Class) appointed "commissars" everywhere to close stores or even to try to have them expropriated. This development took on such independent momentum that the government in Berlin found it necessary to intervene in order to maintain "peace and quiet in the economy" during those critical months marked by the consolidation of Nazi power and continuing massive unemployment. For this purpose, Hugenberg, the economy

minister, appointed an experienced and proven National Socialist "expert on the economy"— Otto Wagener, former director of the Section on Economic Policy of the NSDAP—as special commissioner for economic affairs. Moreover, Hitler and his "deputy," Rudolf Hess, also issued urgent warnings against these autocratic and arbitrary *Einzelaktionen*.[4]

There were also excesses directed against Jewish doctors and lawyers. At its convention on March 14, 1933, the League of National Socialist Lawyers called for a purge of all courts as well as new elections to the bar associations in order to make sure these were "free of all Jews and Marxists." Earlier, there had been reports from various areas of the Reich of courthouses that had been occupied and scenes of "angry crowds" pushing their way into courtrooms. Subsequent to this and even before the official boycott and their "legal" barring from the profession by the Civil Service Law (*Berufsbeamtengesetz*) of April 7, 1933, Jewish judges and district attorneys had "been requested to take a short vacation."[5] The League of National Socialist German Physicians, which even before the takeover of power had engaged in an aggressive boycott directed against Jewish doctors, also distinguished itself now by a series of further measures. These were aimed in particular at doctors who had been members of the Association of Socialist Physicians. Many of them were arrested and manhandled. An accelerated boycott and a campaign of denunciations and repression was initiated against other doctors; these cost a number of lives.[6]

It was no accident that these first spontaneous antisemitic boycott actions were initiated specifically by the two professional groups. Even before 1933, the ranks of these professions had been marked by the presence of an especially virulent antisemitism.

In small trade ... the fear of superior competitors led to a particularly intensive animosity toward Jews. A similar situation prevailed among university graduates. ... Antisemitism, which had become socially acceptable already in the late 19th century, especially through the influence of Heinrich von Treitschke, found more fervent adherents in the educated middle classes after 1918 than in any other social stratum. ... A material cause suggests itself as an explanation for the antisemitic involvement of doctors and lawyers: they had dealings with an especially large number of Jewish colleagues, and figured that without that competition they would be better off.[7]

The intention to exclude Jewish competitors is certainly not the only explanation for the receptivity to antisemitic notions among these strata. An additional causal factor was a general aversion in such circles toward modern industrial society and the "system" of the Weimar Republic, which they saw embodied in the Jews. However, even if one attributes the antisemitic impulses of the Nazis primarily to their ideological "image of the enemy," one must consider the fact that "in the rank and file of the party, economically motivated antisemitism was virulent," and that "at the lower levels of local district leadership," the noisy rowdy antisemitism of the SA hordes was motivated by a desire for unobtrusive personal enrichment at the cost of Jewish retail trade.[8] The situation was probably not much different among antisemitic university students and graduates.

Although the struggles against the department stores, "against trusts and corporations," and against "Jewish high finance" were high on the list of priorities in the program and propaganda of the NSDAP as prime goals of economic antisemitism, it was the medium-size and small Jewish shops that were initially hardest hit by the measures after the Nazi takeover of power. The Jewish banks and large concerns and even the hated department stores were to remain largely unaffected for several years. It is true that in the early weeks following the Nazis' attaining power, as well as on the Boycott Day of April 1, the customary SA patrols were posted in front of several department stores. These SA troopers acted to prevent customers from entering the premises of stores; however, the proprietors and managers were generally able to find ways to utilize personal connections—as well as the concern of the new rulers regarding the continuing unemployment situation—to their advantage. In many instances, the employees of such large firms, for the most part non-Jewish, appealed to the government and to party officials not to endanger their jobs by boycott actions.[9] The example of the department store firm Hermann Tietz shows that such intervention by employees resulted in a certain success. As late as the middle of 1933, Tietz had obtained a large consolidation loan from the state treasury with Hitler's express consent, since the Tietz firm did, after all, employ fourteen thousand workers, mainly non-Jews. Consequently, the large Jewish concerns were able to profit temporarily from the general economic upswing and the rise in consumer demand that were already in evidence in 1933.[10]

Boycott Day, April 1, 1933

The organized boycott on April 1, 1933, ordered by the NSDAP party leadership on March 28, was the temporary high point of those "spontaneous" excesses, though by no means their end. The "Action Committees ... for practical planned implementation of the boycott of Jewish businesses, Jewish products, Jewish doctors and Jewish lawyers," which were immediately formed everywhere, were to be "extended out to reach into the smallest farming village in order to strike a blow at Jewish tradesmen, especially in rural areas."[11] . . .

The April 1 boycott was successful in its fundamental and, in the view of this author, consciously planned function. It set the stage for tightening the screw of economic discrimination and the ousting of the Jews from the economy. Efforts were made to push on with this process—cautiously, in a veiled manner, yet nonetheless consistently. . . . There could no longer be any doubts within the population about the political objectives after this boycott, which had been organized by the top echelons of party leadership and at least condoned by all government offices. Efforts to oust Jews from active economic life were given their official stamp of legitimating approval by the boycott, even if the temporary postponement of their final realization was explained by an openly admitted "exigency of the moment." Helmut Krausnik has given a precise picture of the interacting factors:

> In this phase when the National Socialist regime was still attempting to consolidate its power, the *pseudolegality* of the entire procedure was both an essential feature of totalitarian rule and an aspect in keeping with the unavoidable consideration given to the foreign policy situation and the attitude of the majority of the population. Because even in broad circles of the German burgher classes, there was probably an emotional aversion to violent actions and the unrestrained character of the anti-Jewish agitation of the NSDAP, especially in its effects on the "individual" Jews. . . . The focus of official Jewish policy up until 1938 lay, on the one hand, in the so-called *legal exclusion* of the Jews; on the other . . . in a step-wise but systematic, relatively *unobtrusive*—yet for this very reason all

> the more effective—*police-administrative practice* of suppression and terrorizing. The total atmosphere was, moreover, essentially determined and shaped by an unceasing, officially tolerated *moral defamation and discrimination* of Jews by the Party.[12] (emphasis in original)

In this respect, the limitation of the boycott to only one day, which Goebbels had already announced the evening of March 31 and which was finally proclaimed formally by the government on April 4, is of little import.[13] Its function, namely, to legitimize anti-Jewish measures in the economic field, had been fulfilled after the first day. The creeping boycott that commenced at that point demonstrates that this signal was understood by interested individuals and offices. In any event, the somewhat surprising retreat from the public stage indicates that the new rulers were still uncertain about reactions abroad and the potential political and economic consequences. In a discussion in the Reich Chancellery at noon on March 31, consideration was given to a proposal to call off the boycott set for the next day if the governments of the three Western major powers would issue a declaration denouncing the "atrocity propaganda" by midnight.[14] . . .

The Civil Service Law and the Liberal Professions

One week after Boycott Day, the Law for the Reestablishment of the Professional Civil Service (*Gesetz zur Wiederherstellung des Berufsbeamtentums*, or *Berufsbeamtengesetz*; hereafter Civil Service Law) was enacted. This can be regarded as the first comprehensive law involving economic discrimination against the Jews, though Jews are not specifically mentioned in the title of the law.[15] Its proclamation was preceded by protracted discussions in various ministries. These discussions had little to do with Jews or Jewish policy but were closely connected with the worries, by no means unfounded, of the civil bureaucracy in regard to its constitutional privileges. Once these had been tampered with, even if only as far as Jews and "politically untrustworthy individuals" were concerned, then further interference in the civil service could not be ruled out.[16]

The law issued on April 7 stipulated that civil servants of "non-Aryan" origin were to be retired immediately. The first implementation ordinance on the legislation defined as "non-Aryans" all those persons who had even one "non-Aryan" grandparent. It obligated all civil servants to which the law was applicable to prove their "Aryan" descent. This definition and the exceptions spelled out in the Civil Service Law served as an example and basis for the legal exclusion of the workers and clerical employees in government service who did not have professional civil servant (*Beamte*) status, along with lawyers and physicians. Corresponding regulations and decrees were issued in the course of the ensuing weeks—in express reference to the Civil Service Law and using the same criteria and exceptions—for Jewish attorneys and notaries public; Jewish doctors in state-supported health insurance clinics; medical students, postgraduate assistants, and lecturers at universities; and even members of professional associations such as the German Pharmacists' Association.[17]

Only after long argument and debate did it prove possible to arrive at the exact definition of "non-Aryan" descent contained in the Civil Service Law. Various ministries had, up until April 1, voiced reservations, and Jewish organizations had attempted to utilize established connections with higher government offices to achieve some toning down of its regulations. Symptomatic of the still prevailing feeling of insecurity among the new rulers at this time is the fact that such efforts were

actually successful in some cases. The Association of Jewish War Veterans (RjF) was able, with the help of the aging Field Marshal von Mackensen, to induce Reich President von Hindenburg to intervene directly with Hitler to limit the scope of the law. Soldiers who had fought at the front, fathers or sons of those who had fallen in battle, and all veteran government workers who had been given civil-servant status before August 1, 1914, were exempted. The files attest to this decision by Hitler, expressly termed a "gesture of concession" toward the Reich president.

It would certainly have been more difficult to induce Hitler to make such concessions on this matter if he had had even an approximative idea of just how large the group of these "exceptions" would turn out to be. Apparently, he and those around him were totally convinced by their own propaganda (according to which the Jews in World War I had, for the most part, supposedly been "shirkers" and soldiers who had wangled desk jobs to avoid front-line duty) and believed that the regulations of exclusion would be applicable to only a small number of Jewish "combat veterans." However, after issuance of the law and its various derivative prohibitions on professional employment, it turned out that a quite sizable number of Jews were able to continue working in their professions for several years as a result of the regulations governing exceptions.

The Civil Service Law affected only a relatively small segment of Jewish professionals directly.... At the beginning of 1933, the number of Jews with permanent civil service jobs at all levels of the bureaucracy did not exceed five thousand for the entire Reich. After the Civil Service Law was enacted, the June 1933 census figures indicated that there were still twenty-five hundred Jewish officials in the civil service; of these, some two hundred held senior positions. Despite various forms of harassment and unobtrusive measures to oust them from their jobs, a number of them were able to remain at their desks until the enactment of the Nuremberg Laws in September 1935. Among other things, the 1935 laws were designed to "amend the oversight" of 1933. In any event, those who had been categorized as "exceptions" under the 1933 legislation had the advantage of being able to collect their pensions for a few more years. In this case too, it was probably a concern among "Aryan" *Beamten* about the inviolability of guaranteed privileges as civil servants that was the underlying, decisive motive, rather than any solicitude regarding the fate of their dismissed Jewish colleagues. The Jewish civil servants who had been summarily dismissed were cheated out of at least a portion of their entitled retirement pensions by unobtrusive procedural measures, such as a shrewdly devious way of calculating their official age of retirement. This was before such pension payments were completely abolished by subsequent "legal" measures in the following years.[18]

Compared with its immediate impact, the indirect effect of this law was of far greater importance. Since the regulations contained in the Civil Service Law were taken as a model for numerous professions, at least until the enactment of the Nuremberg Laws, the group of those affected was far larger than just those few thousand remaining Jewish civil servants. Jewish doctors and lawyers were among the first to feel its immediate effects. Long before the enactment of the 1933 legislation, there had been a campaign in the courthouses against Jewish judges, district attorneys, and lawyers. Hans Kerrl, Reich commissioner for legal affairs in Prussia, in a radio announcement on the eve of the April 1 boycott, had issued an order enjoining Jewish attorneys from entering court buildings.[19] This led to violent scenes in a large number of courthouses. Kerrl issued a further

directive on April 3 banning the appointment of Jewish law graduates as court interns. One day later, he issued a general prohibition barring all Jewish attorneys from entering court premises.[20]

The zeal exhibited by Kerrl, a former minor court secretary, reflects the particular level of aggression against Jewish members of the legal profession. According to estimates at the time, approximately thirty-five hundred such jurists, categorized as "Jewish by religion"—the overwhelming majority of whom were attorneys with their own private practice or employed in private law firms—were affected by the legislation. Only some three hundred Jews held posts as judges or district attorneys.[21] Thus, the Civil Service Law had a direct effect initially on only about 40 percent of Jews in the legal profession. Most of these came under the provisos of the regulations on exceptions as former war veterans or as senior attorneys with long government service records. In addition to the group directly affected, there were, however, another almost two thousand "non-Aryan" legal interns and recent law graduates who now had no prospect whatsoever of finishing their formal professional training and being licensed to practice in Germany.[22]

The League of National Socialist German Lawyers, surprised by the large number of Jewish attorneys covered by the clauses on exceptions, stepped up its efforts for further limitations on Jews in the profession. The Third Ordinance on Implementation of the Civil Service Law, issued May 6, 1933, restricted the scope of the combat-veteran category.[23] Judges who insisted on returning to their court positions after the vacation ordered on April 11 were "encouraged" by means of arbitrary transfers and various forms of harassment to retire "voluntarily." The situation was made so difficult for those Jewish attorneys still in practice that in Berlin, for example, they worked out a system for which days of the week they would appear at court, in order to prevent "seething rage among the populace" from boiling over as a result of an excessive number of Jewish lawyers at court on any given day.[24] The now totally nazified professional association prohibited its members from operating joint practices with Jews or even sharing joint premises with "non-Aryan" attorneys. In addition, all public offices were enjoined from engaging the services of Jewish attorneys.

The boycott propaganda against Jewish lawyers that continued to be spewed out by the newspapers was hardly necessary any longer. After all, what rational "Aryan" plaintiff—or even Jewish, for that matter—would, under the existing circumstances, have let himself be represented by a Jewish counsel? Thus, after a short time, even the Jewish attorneys still licensed to practice found themselves engaged in preparing documents and papers for their mainly Jewish clientele outside the walls of the courtroom. Other lawyers were able to find temporary employment with Jewish organizations or the local Jewish *Gemeinden* [communities]. . . .

The approximately eight thousand Jewish physicians practicing in Germany at the beginning of 1933 fared little better than their coreligionists in the legal profession. They were concentrated particularly in the large metropolitan centers; in Berlin, for example, they constituted, according to unofficial estimates, between one-third to one-half of all practicing doctors.[25] A number of them had been instrumental in establishing the system of public medical care and occupied senior positions there. In contrast, there were only a few Jewish doctors on the staffs of government hospitals in the provinces. The majority of Jewish doctors was in private practice and operated clinics that generally enjoyed an excellent reputation among the population. Until the advent of the Third Reich,

the economic situation of Jewish physicians was correspondingly favorable. They were often those listed with the highest incomes in the tax rolls of the local Jewish *Gemeinden*.

The professional envy of non-Jewish doctors in the Weimar Republic was probably only one of the reasons the League of National Socialist German Physicians developed into the breeding ground for a particularly virulent strain of antisemitism. It would appear that the combination of "racist-genetic" medicine and research together with antisemitism was principally ideological in nature. This thesis is also supported by the fact that a number of high-ranking doctors in the ss, some quite notorious, participated directly in the mass murder of Jews in World War II.[26] Even before the Nazis came to power, the League of National Socialist German Physicians had embarked on an especially vicious propaganda campaign to boycott Jewish doctors. This campaign now reached its high point in a veritable barrage of slander and violence. Many Jewish doctors were shipped off to concentration camps, where they were maltreated and did not return alive.[27]

The first national legislative measure against Jewish doctors was at the initiative of Labor Minister Franz Seldte. On April 22, 1933, he issued an order barring all "non-Aryan" doctors from work at state-supported health-insurance clinics and hospitals, with the exception of those "exempted categories" included in the Civil Service Law.[28] At the local level, several towns and states had anticipated this measure by instituting exclusion decrees on their own initiative. In Bavaria, all Jewish school doctors were dismissed from service effective immediately. In Berlin and many other cities, the welfare offices were issued a directive instructing them not to refer patients to Jewish doctors for treatment. The Physicians' Association in Duisburg, at the instruction of the county chief of the NSDAP, stamped referral slips for appointments with specialists with the words: "Not valid for Jewish doctors." After the Jewish doctors still in practice had made a formal complaint, referring to their seniority and status as war veterans, the party county chief informed the Physicians' Association confidentially that it was apparently compelled to reinstate these doctors. He added, however, that they should take their good time in so doing: in any case, the rubber stamps should be stored safely away for future use. Even though the sources are somewhat unclear on this matter, it appears improbable that the Jewish doctors in Duisburg were ever again able to practice in unrestricted fashion.[29] Similar situations prevailed in numerous other cities.

Along with such open and "legal" measures, the quiet boycott against Jewish doctors and the campaign of intimidation among patients were perhaps even more effective. More than half of all Jewish doctors were forced to abandon the profession by the middle of 1933 as a result of this coordinated process of repression and harassment. In the beginning, they did not yield without putting up a fight. At a time when even the official Jewish leadership still believed it could rely on traditional legal norms of the constitutional state to guarantee the economic basis for continued survival of Jews in Germany, Jewish doctors also made frequent confident appeals on their own behalf to government agencies and the courts. However, they were soon forced to recognize the hopelessness of any prospect for intervention by the authorities and to accept the restriction of their practices to Jewish patients only. Or they could explore another option: namely, emigration. In that respect, Jewish doctors were doubtless far better off than their Jewish compatriots in the legal profession, since their professional skills and reputation allowed them a swifter and

smoother transition to building a new existence in their country of emigration.[30]

Along with Jewish lawyers and doctors, there were also some five thousand Jewish university graduates and persons active in other "free professions" in Germany in 1933. In view of the discrimination practiced at German universities well into the Weimar period, the figure of eight hundred university faculty members was indeed a significant number. Jewish writers and journalists constituted a group almost equal in size and included some of the most important names in German literature and journalism at the time. Musicians were especially prominent among the approximately three thousand Jewish professional artists. Like the small number of Jewish "leaders in economic life," this was a numerically modest yet highly conspicuous elite, with substantial influence on the educated urban middle classes and the young intelligentsia.

The German Jews in the Weimar Republic were proud of the achievements of these elite groups; they basked in their fame and repeatedly cited them as living proof of the "German-Jewish symbiosis." . . . In the eyes of the Nazis who had taken power, they were, however, the embodiment of a racially alien "Jewish spirit" that was supposedly "polluting" the German folk soul. The party program had called for the immediate removal of Jews from cultural life, and Joseph Goebbels, the new Minister of Popular Enlightenment and Propaganda, began its implementation soon after the party took power.

University teachers had been directly affected by the Civil Service Law. Two hundred of these, who enjoyed an international reputation in their fields far beyond the borders of Germany received appointments at universities abroad during the course of 1933. However, after April 1933, nearly 350 Jewish faculty members were left without jobs.[31]

The ousting of the other Jews active in various areas of cultural life was implemented by introducing special legislation. Although the Reich Chamber of Culture Law enacted on September 22, 1933, did not contain any express "paragraph on Aryans," it made any professional activity in literature, the press, the theater, music, and the plastic arts dependent on membership in a corresponding "chamber"—and such membership was denied to Jews.[32] In addition, a special law regulating editorship of publications was enacted on October 4, 1933, barring Jewish or "partly Jewish" newspaper editors.[33]

The Civil Service Law and other legislation enacted in the early months of 1933 affected an estimated 12,000 to 13,000 Jews—that is, approximately 5 percent of the 240,487 gainfully employed Jews listed in the census of June 16, 1933. . . .

The Independent Middle Classes

After the boycott had been called off and decrees by the government and party denouncing "individual actions" had been published in an attempt "to calm the economy," the repressive measures against Jewish retail trade were continued by other means—less conspicuous but no less effective.

Despite all official admonishments and warnings from Berlin, however, the open and violent attacks against Jewish businesses went on unabated, especially in the smaller towns. Uniformed men posted before shops prevented customers from entering, and the photographs of those who shopped at Jewish stores continued to appear in the local press or in the *Stürmer* display case, accompanied by captions such as "traitor to the people" and "lackey of the Jews." The *Gauleiter* in the Palatinate, Josef Bürckel, formulated very clearly the difference between public declarations and practical continuing boycott terror in his reply to "repeated inquiries . . . regarding the question of department stores and the treatment of Jewish businesses":

> Various decrees are cited that could lead to misunderstandings in this matter. The following remarks should be of use to all concerned:
> 1. Before the takeover of power, the department store for us was the junk-shop which had brought ruin upon the small businessman. This judgment will stand for all time to come. The same holds when it comes to the treatment of the Jewish question.
> 2. We old Nazis do not care at all about the decrees issued by some boastful Nazi upstart or other. For us, there is nothing but the fulfillment of the program in accordance with the wishes of the Führer.[34]

The local party leaders, many of whom had become town mayors and or had advanced to other high positions in administration, had various means and ways at their disposal to discriminate against Jewish businesses and tighten the screw of economic pressure. Despite a guideline of the Reich Cabinet of July 14, 1933, expressly stipulating that public contracts were to be awarded only by the agencies officially authorized—without any interference by other organizations, especially the *Kampfbund für den gewerblichcn Mittelstand*,[35]—Jewish firms had few prospects of being considered for such government contracts. This guideline remained in force until August 1938 but left local agencies sufficient latitude so that they could give preference to the "Aryan" firms in every local posting of a public tender. The available sources make it clear that in only a few cases were Jewish firms able to win public contracts after 1933. Such successful firms were, for all practical purposes, without any serious competitors in a specific area because of their scale and their many years of experience.[36]

Another means of boycotting Jewish retail tradesmen "administratively" was the prohibition by welfare offices and other local agencies against using welfare vouchers to purchase goods in Jewish stores. Such vouchers were issues to recipients of welfare or young married couples. When this practice led in 1933 to complaints to the government by Jewish organizations, it was prohibited by various official agencies, yet was generally continued at local level by other means. In Duisburg, for example, the corresponding rubber stamps were collected from the welfare offices (and dutifully stored away for future use!); at the same time, the welfare recipients were told they had to make their purchases at specific shops—"Aryan," of course. Posters appeared in the welfare offices warning welfare recipients against spending money "from public sources" for purchases in Jewish shops.[37]

A prohibition on shopping in department stores or Jewish shops was also introduced for municipal employees. In a number of cities, there initially were disputes with the old municipal bureaucracy about this measure, which referred to a decision by Hitler in October 1933.[38] However, all evidence suggests that regional and local party offices, as well as government agencies, disregarded such instructions from Berlin after a short time, extending the prohibition generally in effect for all Nazi Party members to all municipal employees in a number of towns. When complaints from Jewish organizations and intervention by the central government in Berlin increased in Westphalia, the district governor (Regierungspräsident) in Arnsberg informed the Reich Ministry that the regulations regarding the protection of Jewish economic enterprises from unlawful "individual actions" could not be implemented "without serious disruption of public peace and order." He therefore requested not to be bothered any longer by such matters; they

should be dealt with by direct contact with the NSDAP, the SA, and the SS, which were themselves exercising an "open boycott."[39]

In actual fact, the open and violent boycott actions continued unabated throughout the entire year 1933, especially in the small towns but also in the large metropolitan centers. In June, uniformed SA and SS men in Dortmund blocked entry to all Jewish shops for two full weeks, manhandling customers wishing to get by them.[40] The large number of similar incidents, attested to by the available sources, proves very clearly that the actual situation of Jewish retail trade cannot be evaluated solely on the basis of the legal measures in effect or their temporary absence.... Even after the announced end of the boycott, the small retail tradesmen continued to be the principal target of measures of economic harassment. Such measures were practiced by party organizations, generally with the tacit toleration of local government and municipal authorities and with the active involvement of interests deriving a direct financial benefit from the boycott.

On the other hand, as long as the problem of mass unemployment remained unresolved, the large department stores and commercial firms were protected from encroachments for a short time simply by dint of their economic importance and the size of their work forces. If they understood how to adapt to the new circumstances, Jewish industrial concerns were also able to profit from the general upturn in the economy. Boards of directors were reshuffled, and in many cases the name of the firm was "Germanized" even before sizable blocks of stock had changed owners—a common practice in subsequent years in the wake of the intensified "Aryanization" process. In these early years of National Socialist rule, Jewish economic activity at various levels persisted, and the fate of the small bourgeois upper class, even at this time, was by no means identical with that of the Jewish population as a whole.[41]

Beginnings of a "Jewish Economic Sector"

Increasingly, Jewish blue-collar and white-collar workers could hope to find jobs only with Jewish employers. As long as the number of independent Jewish firms and businesses was still relatively large, it was possible to facilitate procurement of many jobs and apprenticeship positions in this way. This then represented the beginning of the development of an independent—though by no means autarkic—Jewish economic sector previously nonexistent in Germany. The more the vocational and job prospects of Jews were restricted as a result of legislation, "spontaneous" boycott, or administrative measures and chicanery, the closer the Jewish community joined together, closing ranks in economic respects as well. And the more hopeless the legal battle to maintain existing positions in the economy proved to be, the clearer was the recognition by ever increasing numbers of Jews that in their struggle for economic survival they could rely only on themselves and perhaps on the support of their coreligionists abroad. Jewish economic life thus began to undergo a restructuring: more and more, Jews were now working for and employing Jews, assuring themselves a livelihood by means of economic intercourse among themselves.

As in other areas, Jewish young people here too showed themselves to be more inventive and farsighted than many adults or than a number of the Jewish organizations. As early as May 1933, an appeal was circulated by the National Committee of Jewish Youth Leagues, signed by Ludwig Tietz and Georg Lubinski. It called on the local branches of all Jewish youth organizations to take an active part in efforts to procure jobs for the Jewish unemployed. Each member was obligated to locate at least one vacant job or apprenticeship by making inquiries among friends and relatives. An effort was to be made to find places for individual agricultural training ("individual *hachshara*") among local farmers—if necessary only in exchange for food and lodging and even with the supplementary payment of a small sum of money to the farmer. In the course of a few weeks, several hundred positions, mainly agricultural apprenticeships, were located and arranged in this manner.[42]

Beginning during the Weimar Republic, appreciable numbers of Jewish blue-collar workers and even more white-collar personnel had found employment in Jewish-owned firms. This was one by-product of the antisemitic boycott that had already intensified at the time of the Depression; it was also a consequence of intentional efforts undertaken by the Jewish job placement offices. A large proportion of these workers were dismissed during the course of the April boycott under pressure from NSBO (Nazi Factory Cell Organization) officials and other Nazi functionaries. Attempts by large Jewish concerns to reemploy them after Boycott Day were unsuccessful. The Jewish placement bureaus thus concentrated their efforts principally on small and medium-size Jewish plants, in which as a rule there were no NSBO factory cells and the supervision by the DAF [German Labor Front] was less effective. In a number of cases, the employment of new Jewish workers was combined with the awarding of contracts by Jewish institutions to the employment firms. In this way, both the new Jewish employee and his or her Jewish employer came to benefit economically from the arrangement.[43]

The Jewish newspapers were also mobilized in the search for jobs. The success of recurring appeals in the press appears to have been only negligible in the early period, when circulation figures for the Jewish press had just started to climb at a slow pace. But it was at this juncture that the importance of Jewish newspapers for the subsequent development of the Jewish economic sector began to emerge and make itself felt. Clearly articulated in the columns of these papers were the urgency of the need to procure gainful employment for Jewish workers and an appeal to the feeling of Jewish solidarity: as, for example, in an article published in September 1933 with the characteristic title "We accuse!" The article criticized Jewish master craftsmen, cooks, barbers, tailors, and other artisans because they were prepared to take on Jewish apprentices only in exchange for the payment of an apprentice fee. This was denounced as an attempt to try to profit from the distressful hard times. Where should these people, who sometimes did not even have enough for a warm meal, get the necessary money to pay such fees?[44]

Along with press releases, the *Wirtschaftshilfe* issued a mimeographed bulletin entitled "*Vermittlungsdienst*" (Exchange Service). Its first issue in the spring of 1933 reflected the desperate situation faced by the jobless and impoverished. Doctors and lawyers appealed to their colleagues in particular, requesting to be kept in mind when they were buying tea, coffee, or soap. Their wives advertised assistance with various types of written work and knitting. Dismissed judges and state attorneys offered their gowns for sale or their legal libraries "at bargain prices." The mimeographed pages also carried requests for and offers of capital investment, ranging from RM 3,000 to RM 40,000, although there were more requests than offers. Frequently, factories or shops were offered for sale at what appeared to be completely ridiculous prices: for example, a "shipping firm in Mannheim" for the incredible sum of RM 1,000; or a doctor's practice, completely equipped and

with a family home, in an office whose rent was prepaid until April 1935—RM 5,000 to RM 6,000![45] The sources do not indicate whether buyers were found for the properties. Yet how desperate must the situation have been for those who had placed the ads.

And so it was that the Jewish economic sector came into being—unplanned and by no means conceived as the long-term solution to the crisis situation of German Jewry—in the early months of the Nazi regime at the initiative of individuals and groups who suddenly found themselves jobless and without any income. Many may have taken the assurances of the new rulers at face value—namely, that Jews had nothing to fear in the field of the vocational trades—and thus ventured in such trades to build a new basis for their continued economic existence in Germany. Others sold off their legal or medical practices in order to emigrate to a new homeland. It seemed reasonable to everyone in need of help to turn first to their own community....

The Illusion of a "Grace Period"

After the regime had established itself, open violence against Jews was confined to sporadic incidents. Legislation likewise dealt only rarely with Jewish economic activity. Even the announced and anticipated new economic restrictions in the wake of the Nuremberg Laws of September 1935 failed to materialize. Among many contemporaries at the time, there thus arose the illusion of the advent of an economic "grace period"—a view that even today is widespread in the historical literature. In actual fact, however, the process of ousting Jews from the economy in Germany and expropriating their assets pressed ahead with inexorable consistency.

Initially, the brunt of this process was felt more in the smaller towns and rural areas of the provinces than in the large metropolitan centers, and it generally was carried out in quiet and relatively unobtrusive ways. The Nazis had understood that Jewish owners of small and medium-size shops and firms could be motivated to sell their businesses for a mere fraction of their real worth—without the introduction of legislation that created a stir or public proclamations but rather by resorting to threats, intimidation, and small-scale violence wherever deemed necessary. In the early period, nonetheless, many Jewish firms improved their economic situation. They too were able to profit from the general economic upturn, insofar as it was possible for them to continue to operate their businesses. Yet the process of displacement was the dominant feature in these years, and by 1937 the Jews were already a crushed and significantly weakened group, both demographically and economically....

Until September 1935, very little new legislation was introduced aimed at restricting Jewish economic activity. Such new laws basically confirmed the existing status quo. In March 1934, by decree of the Finance Minister, the exclusion of Jewish firms from the program for redemption of welfare vouchers became official policy.[46] Similarly, the banning of Jewish doctors or doctors related by marriage to Jews (*versippt*) from the various government-supported health insurance schemes, even if they had been World War I veterans, became official with the issuance of an order by the Reich minister of labor on May 17, 1934.[47] A corresponding exclusion order barring dentists was issued in February 1935.[48] ...

The Nuremberg legislation, in particular the Reich Citizenship Law (Reichsbürgergesetz) of September 15, 1935,[49] provided a basis for further economic measures. Such measures, however, were not introduced until a much later date. Those who felt the pinch initially were the remaining Jewish civil servants and members of certain selected professions, such as pharmacy, in which only a few Jews still remained active.[50] ... It was not until 1936, when the German economy had reached full employment, that the Nazis began to plan and, beginning in 1937, to implement the complete and total removal of Jews from the German economy, the envisioned *Entjudung der deutschen Wirtschaft*. That marked the actual turning point. ...

At party level, the *Gauwirtschaftsberater* (district economic advisers; hereafter DEAs) in particular were officially responsible in all matters relating to the ousting of Jews from the economy. This position of adviser had been created within the framework of the Economic Policy Section in the Munich national headquarters of the NSDAP even before the 1933 takeover in order to advise *Gauleiter* about economic questions in accordance with guidelines issued by Munich. After 1933, the DEAs were under the control of the Commission for Economic Policy directed by Bernhard Köhler until his death in 1939 and subordinate to the dynastic power of the respective *Gauleiter*. There is no doubt about the decisive function that the DEAs and their bureaucratic staffs had in implementing economic policy toward the Jews.[51] Extensive files were assembled in their offices covering every single Jewish business in their area of authority, and the development of these businesses was carefully monitored. Sources included reports filed by "inside planted informers" and information from competitors, as well as data supplied by tax offices and the local chambers of commerce and industry. ...

The anti-Jewish boycott was not a one-time or sporadic phenomenon but rather a process that spread and deepened at a slow, steady pace. It was promoted systematically by its adherents. The trade associations and the DAF attempted to prevent the forging of business ties with Jewish suppliers by perusal of the account books of non-Jewish firms. Specialist associations, such as that of the egg and poultry importers, many of whom were Eastern European Jews, excluded Jews by means of an arbitrary "Aryan Paragraph" in their statutes.[52] Although there was no "legal" basis for such regulations, a prohibition on purchasing at Jewish stores was put into effect for civil service workers, and labor courts accepted its violation as grounds for dismissal.[53] Middle-class credit institutions denied loans to Jewish businessmen, and outstanding loans and mortgages were canceled for the most minor reason. This method was also recommended in the press as an effective way of plunging Jewish business owners into liquidity problems and then forcing them to sell their businesses "at bargain prices" to "Aryans." . . .

The last university teachers and government officials who were still in their posts were dismissed on the basis of the Nuremberg Laws. By a series of technical administration manipulations, they were then often cheated out of their pension rights, either completely or in part.[54] Jewish teachers were soon teaching only at Jewish schools; because of the high level of antisemitic incitement among schoolchildren, such schools had had an increased number of pupils even before the official exclusion of Jewish children from the public schools. More than two thousand Jewish artists found employment in Jewish cultural life, even though such jobs were insufficient to live on. The Reich Chamber of Culture was busy devising ever new methods to cut off all possibilities of gainful employment for Jews "creative in cultural life"— from artists to newspaper vendors. In the autumn of 1935, the press reported with satisfaction that all stages of film production and distribution, previously an area in which Jews were heavily represented, were finally "free of Jews" (*judenrein*) and

that the remaining 140 Jewish motion-picture theater owners would soon be dealt with as well.[55]

The worst off were the blue-collar and white-collar workers. At the end of 1937, thirty to forty thousand of them were out of work, even though there was already a lack of workers in certain sectors of the economy. Among their ranks were many who had previously been self-employed and who were now dependent on the labor market after having given up their businesses.[56] Only those employed by small and medium-size Jewish enterprises were able to profit from the general economic upswing. In the large firms, even those owned by Jews, more and more Jews were dismissed under the pretext that it was too much to ask of "Aryans" to work together in the same firm with Jews. This was accepted by the labor courts as grounds for dismissal. In the civil service, a similar reason for dismissal was the argument used against the few remaining Jewish government workers that they could not be expected to swear the legally required oath of allegiance to the Führer and identify with him and his philosophy.[57]

Foreign workers, or those who had been made stateless by the July 1933 law rescinding naturalizations of the foreign-born, were in particularly dire straits.[58] Even before the Nazi takeover, foreigners had had to renew their work permit on an annual basis, but those who had lived in Germany for more than ten years were generally released from this regulation. Beginning in 1934, such certificates of release were no longer issued. The Eastern European Jews, who were in any case among the most impoverished groups within German Jewry, were thus deprived of any possibility for legal gainful employment and became increasingly dependent on public and Jewish welfare. In addition, the threat of deportation hung over them, although such deportations were rare before 1937 out of consideration for bilateral agreements with countries with a large number of resident German citizens.[59]

The opinion is still widespread in the historical literature that Jewish businesses were not transferred to non-Jewish ownership until relatively late (i.e., during the final years prior to the outbreak of the war) and that this transfer was generally carried out by administrative means. In actual fact, "Aryanization" had already begun in 1933 in the form of "voluntary" sales. In the course of the accelerating process of displacement of Jews from economic life, the number of these "transfers," at prices that were more and more unfavorable for the Jewish sellers, increased from year to year. Old Guard party stalwarts and middle-class party functionaries were the principal gainers. In reality, the supposed "grace period" was in fact "open season" for Nazi owners of small businesses who were out to make a "killing" in the property market.

The approximately one hundred thousand independent Jewish firms in 1932 were distributed roughly as follows:[60]

Area of business: Number of firms
Retail trade: 55,000
Wholesale and export: 8,000
Artisan crafts: 9,000
Industry: 8,000
Free professions: 12,000
Other: 10,000

This estimate may not be exact, but it presents a fairly reliable picture of the actual relative figures. The borders between categories are also a bit fuzzy in these statistics. . . . In addition, these figures include only Jews classified as "Jewish by religion," so-called *Glaubensjuden.* Persons "Jewish by race," so-called *Rassejuden* (i.e., those of only partial Jewish descent and/or Jews not professing the Jewish religion) were not listed in the 1933 census as Jews.

In the autumn of 1935, the periodical *Deutsche Zukunft* estimated the number of still-existing Jewish firms and businesses at seventy-five to eighty thousand and assumed an approximately equal number of firms owned by "Jews by race and Jews from mixed families (*Mischlinge*)."[61] The second figure is doubtful and impossible to verify, but the first can be regarded as relatively reliable. Thus, according to these two estimates, a total of some 20 to 25 percent of all Jewish businesses had either been liquidated or transferred to "Aryan" hands by the middle of 1935. Apparently, these were businesses located largely in villages or small towns, where Jews were much more at the mercy of the boycott campaign and had less capacity to resist in economic terms than Jews in the metropolitan centers. One consequence of this was the mass migration of population to the cities, which is also confirmed by demographic statistics.

The Expanded "Jewish Economic Sector"

Only a smaller number of the large Jewish department stores and businesses were able to retain their Jewish directors and a clientele not directly exposed to the pressures of the party. With this one exception, the Jewish community must now live in its own framework, and is increasingly taking on the character of a new type of ghetto. A ghetto which is admittedly not surrounded by walls, yet which is cut off from economic as well as social and intellectual contact with the surrounding world. The typical German Jew today is a middle-aged man, whose children have emigrated and who ekes out a meager existence as a small businessman in one of the larger cities.[62]

This description, taken from the 1937 annual report of the major British assistance organization for German Jewry, the Council for German

Jewry, paints an accurate picture. The developments described had been forced on the German Jews by external circumstances, and the "Jewish economic sector" had evolved over the course of the years against their will. At the end of 1936, voices still could be heard among the Jewish public decrying a Jewish "economic ghetto" and rejecting any abandonment of positions still in Jewish hands.[63] Yet the pressure of circumstances proved to be stronger.

Naturally, it is impossible to speak about any sort of autarky of the Jewish sector for the simple reason that Jews were dependent on goods and services that they were unable to manufacture or supply themselves. However, as producers and employees, they were increasingly dependent on the internal "Jewish market," which was becoming ever smaller. Those who had left active economic life lived first off the proceeds from liquidation and lifelong savings and then off their very bone and substance. Or they were dependent on Jewish welfare, financed by funds from Jews still able to contribute, or, to a lesser extent, by assistance from coreligionists abroad.

The administrative bureaucracies of the Jewish *Gemeinden* and organizations had not only been enlarged to help cope with the growing tasks, they represented a kind of "scheme for creation of jobs" from the funds of the Jewish public sector. These monies derived largely from tax revenues paid by the German Jews themselves. Jewish doctors found work in an impressive publicly supported health system, equipped with hospitals and clinics, children's homes, homes for the aged, and rural convalescent homes. Former lawyers were able to make use of their knowledge and experience in Jewish administration. Teachers were placed in the significantly expanded Jewish educational system and in adult education, often as language teachers in courses preparing for emigration. Writ-

ers and journalists worked for the Jewish press and in Jewish publishing houses, which flourished on a scale hitherto unknown.[64]

This development was also reflected in the ad sections of Jewish newspapers, which published the addresses of still practicing Jewish doctors and dentists and of attorneys whose licenses were still valid. Even without any special appeal, most Jews frequented Jewish physicians and specialists. Jewish boardinghouses in spas announced the availability of kosher cuisine. They were preferred by non-orthodox clientele as well, even before signs proclaiming "Jews not wanted" made their appearance in most hotels. The advertisement sections of the papers became more and more voluminous and reflected all facets of the "Jewish economic sector": ads from job seekers and, far less frequently, want ads for vacancies, announcements concerning stores and artisan shops and businesses of all kinds, apartments and rooms to rent—a diversified picture of everyday occupations and needs, which necessarily brought together again individuals who had long been estranged from the Jewish community. The process of economic liquidation was also manifested in the pages of these papers: businesses and properties, furniture, and concert pianos were offered for sale at bargain prices "due to emigration."[65]

The bureaus of the *Wirtschaftshilfe* increasingly became offices for the provision and coordination of services in the "Jewish sector." The bulletin *Vermittlungsdienst* stopped publication in 1936 because no corresponding responses were forthcoming from the numerous ads offering something for sale or requesting capital. Jews who had capital as a result of liquidation of businesses or other sources generally were wary of investing it in Jewish enterprises. They increasingly preferred various forms of liquid accounts, which were then available to them whenever needed for emigration or purposes of everyday living. On the other hand, the *Wirtschaftshilfe* bureaus and the Jewish *Gemeinden* and organizations now had at their disposal a large number of newly established direct contacts as well as persuasive "means of advertising" in order to stimulate mutual Jewish economic intercourse. Loans could be granted in the form of shipments of goods from Jewish commercial firms and manufacturers. The extensive orders placed by Jewish institutions were also given, wherever possible, to Jewish suppliers. Jewish sales representatives and agents were furnished with recommendations to Jewish firms. The agricultural teaching farms and artisan crafts training centers bought their supplies from Jewish firms; in turn, they passed on their own produce and products wherever possible to those same concerns for distribution and sale. This is also true in the case of hospitals, schools, and welfare organizations—in short, the entire Jewish "public" sector. That sector, taken as a whole, represented a quite sizable market in its own right.[66]

Jewish workers, both blue- and white-collar, were even more dependent on the Jewish sector than the self-employed. Even after full employment was reached in the German economy, it was almost impossible for them to be hired by non-Jewish employers because the prerequisite for such employment was formal membership in the DAF Jewish employers, especially smaller firms, figured out various ways to circumvent these regulations. Even larger enterprises sometimes devised ways to retain at least a portion of their Jewish work force and, in some instances, to treat these workers in exemplary fashion. . . .

Early in 1935, the regulation of the compulsory employment booklet was introduced. It affected foreign and stateless Jews in particular. Even Jewish employers were prohibited from offering such people legal employment unless they had an employment booklet, and they were usually denied such a document. The closing down of the Jewish employment bureaus on January 1, 1937, had even more dire consequences for all Jewish jobless. From then on, the Jewish unemployed were dependent on the public employment offices. They had little prospect of being included in the lists there and were often subject to discrimination and abuse. The semi-legal, internal system of job referral and procurement, largely without any written documents, was continued, with steadily decreasing success. In view of the rapidly multiplying tasks it had to grapple with, the Jewish economic sector and the internal Jewish labor market were able to offer less and less assistance.[67]

Jewish Welfare and Relief Work

With accelerating displacement from active economic life, the number of Jews directly in need of financial aid rose from year to year. The steadily mounting expenditures on welfare are vivid testimony to the gradual pauperization of German Jewry, though they also testify to its willingness to sacrifice and its sense of solidarity.

According to law, needy Jews were supported until November 1938, and to a limited degree thereafter, by public welfare. Jewish welfare services were actually supposed to provide only additional subsidiary assistance, principally within an institutional framework. In actuality, however, the welfare sections of the Jewish *Gemeinden* had been obliged, beginning in late 1935, to report to the German authorities about the direct support payments they were providing. The public welfare offices then initiated a policy of deducting these amounts from the public welfare payments based on standard schedules.[68] Especially "zealous" offices devised on their own initiative additional ways to harass the Jewish community. Once again, it was the "capital of the movement" [Munich] that led the way: Mayor Fiehler endorsed the view of the municipal welfare office that welfare for Jews was to be "interpreted according to the basic principles of the National Socialist world-view," even when specific regulations were lacking. According to a communication of the German *Gemeindetag* (National Association of Municipalities) at the end of 1936, even if needy Jewish applicants "should be supported in accordance with the as yet unrestricted laws," this did not mean that "a non-Aryan necessarily had to be given equal rights with an Aryan member of the community in all areas of welfare." Accordingly, Jewish welfare recipients were excluded from many benefits. An official who had approved a stay in a convalescent home for a Jewish applicant was transferred as a form of punishment.[69]

Since Fiehler was also chairman of the *Gemeindetag*, his devices were soon imitated elsewhere. Standard payment amounts were arbitrarily lowered for Jews, and various occupational groups (e.g., teachers) remained without any support whatsoever. Jews had already been excluded from the special assistance benefits for recently married couples or families with many children.[70]

As a result of this discriminatory treatment and the mounting number of needy Jews, applicants turned more and more to the Jewish *Gemeinden* and the *Reichsvertretung* [National Representation of German Jews] for assistance. At the same time, the revenues of the *Gemeinden* were declining due to the fact that often it was precisely the more affluent members of the Jewish community who emigrated. More and more rural *Gemeinden* had to be designated as "*Gemeinden* in distress" because they were no longer able to balance the budget by their own means and had to obtain subsidies from the Reichsvertretung. As early as 1935, almost a third of all German Jews required continuous

or temporary financial assistance in some way, such as supplementary relief aid during the winter months, for example. At this time, more than a third of the public funds of the Jewish *Gemeinden* were already being directly or indirectly expended on welfare support. In 1935, such expenditures accounted for 35 percent of the total budget of the Berlin *Gemeinde*; in Aachen, that figure reached a level of 40 percent.[71] The overwhelming proportion of these funds was supplied by German Jews themselves, with only negligible help forthcoming from Jewish communities abroad....

Beginning with the winter of 1935–1936, German Jews also bore the expenses for the program of *Jüdische Winterhilfe* (Jewish Winter Relief Aid; hereafter JWH), along with the standard *Gemeinde* taxes. In addition, the so-called blue card was introduced to raise funds for welfare assistance; stamps were supposed to be pasted in on a monthly basis.[72] Everyone was expected to participate in this solidarity campaign for donations, and for that reason there were stamps ranging in value from 25 pfennigs to 5 marks. The blue card brought in on average no more than a half million marks annually. Nonetheless, this solidarity action must also be regarded as an impressive accomplishment in material terms, considering the economic situation the German Jews found themselves in....

Along with this, the *Geimeinden* maintained soup kitchens and supplied the needy with cheap or free groceries, which were generally provided to them in a discreet manner. The soup kitchens distributed 66,350 warm meals in Berlin in 1934 and sent 11,200 food packets. By 1937, the corresponding numbers had risen to 78,700 meals and 26,400 packets. In relation to the entire Jewish population of Berlin, these figures do not appear very high. But if one considers that the Jewish population was on the decline and that this type of support was meant only for the poorest individuals, the statistics testify to the deepening pauperization of this lowest underclass.[73]

The Demographic and Economic Situation

At the beginning of 1938, there were still between 350,000 and 365,000 Jews living in the *Altreich*— that is, within the borders of 1937.[74] The Jewish population had thus declined by between 160,000 and 175,000 since January 1933. Most of that number had emigrated, and the difference in vital statistics between births and deaths is estimated to have been thirty to thirty-five thousand. The Jewish population was still dispersed in some 1,400 *Gemeinden*; however, 612 of these had been classified as "communities in distress," and a further 120 small *Gemeinden* were facing imminent dissolution. Nearly 65 percent of all Jews were concentrated in seven large communities; 140,000, amounting to some 40 percent of all Jews left in Germany, lived in Berlin.

At this point, Jews still holding jobs were, almost without exception, working for Jewish employers. Consequently, the employment situation was largely dependent on the number of still extant Jewish firms and businesses. Some 60 to 70 percent of enterprises owned by Jews in January 1933 were no longer in Jewish hands. This estimate is confirmed by figures given by the *Judenreferent* (Adviser on Jewish Affairs) in the Economy Ministry, Alf Krüger. Krüger listed the number of Jewish firms as of April 1, 1938, at exactly 39,552.[75] Jewish retail trade had been particularly hard hit by this process of liquidation: In July 1938, of the formerly more than fifty thousand Jewish retail shops, there were, according to official statistics, only about nine thousand left in the *Altreich*, including the sales outlets of Jewish craft enterprises. A total of 3,637 of these were located in Berlin.[76] Even these shops were facing a bitter struggle for survival, especially in the smaller provincial towns and villages.

The reporting of all Jewish assets and property was ordered by decree in April 1938.[77] The registration took several months and, as preserved documents indicate, no form of property and assets was excluded. The results are summarized in a confidential circular of the Economy Ministry dated November 28, 1938.[78] It stated that the value of reported Jewish assets and property in the entire area of the Reich, including Austria, was approximately RM 8.531 billion gross RM 7.123 billion net after deduction of debts and other obligations. Of this RM 112 million were in agricultural properties, and RM 2.343 billion in urban real estate. Active business capital constituted only RM 1.195 billion, approximately 14 percent of reported total wealth. Since the total amount included some RM 2 billion listed as assets of Jews in Austria—where "Aryanization" was only in its early stages at the time, April 1938—the proportion of capital still invested in business firms in the *Altreich* proper was probably even lower. The sum of RM 4.481 billion, equivalent to about 60 percent of the total amount, was listed in the category "other types of assets," and was emphasized as being "vulnerable assets . . . readily seizable." These consisted of various forms of disposable assets, invested in bank notes, securities, and the like, for the most part apparently the proceeds from the sale of businesses already liquidated.

Jewish property and assets in the Altreich have been estimated at RM 10 to 12 billion for the year 1933. This had declined to half of that amount by April 1938, whereas only about a third of all German Jews had emigrated within that same period. . . .

The Process of Legal Exclusion Is Stepped Up

All preparations for the final exclusion of Jews from the economy had been completed by the spring of 1938; one could now press ahead with their realization. Every Jew, or non-Jewish partner of a Jewish spouse was obligated to declare all assets in the country or abroad exceeding the value of RM 5,000. In blunt language, Section 8 formulated the purpose of this *Verordnung*: the Plenipotentiary for the Four-Year Plan "was authorized to take steps to ensure the utilization of assessable assets in the interests of the German economy." A directive issued at the same time subjected "any sale or leasing of an industrial, agricultural or forestry enterprise and the order of usufructuary rights" to firms under Jewish ownership to official confirmation by the "higher administrative authorities."[79] . . .

The groundwork was being laid here for the subsequent total despoliation of the German Jews—here still euphemistically termed "utilization of assets," or, more bluntly, as "seizure" (*Erfassung*). The "*Sühneleistung*" (Atonement Penalty) levied on the Jews after the November pogrom and later special taxes were assessed on the basis of the declaration of assets of April 1938, although it was conceded in the already quoted November 28 circular of the economy minister that since that survey "substantial assets, impossible even to estimate in monetary terms, had been sold below their true value to non-Jewish businessmen."[80]

The official form for registration of assets was a many-paged questionnaire in which it was necessary to list every type of possession, down to the last detail: securities, properties, insurance policies, outstanding unpaid debts, valuable paintings, luxury articles—nothing could be left out.[81] In addition, by means of various semiofficial hints and ambiguous reports in the press, Jews were encouraged not to declare their assets below their true value. Thus, for example, Undersecretary Brinkmann stated in a press conference, attended by foreign journalists, that Jews

had been allowed to determine the value of their assets themselves, so that in the event of a takeover, the owner might be compensated by the government in interest-bearing securities.[82] Ernst Herzfeld also reported that the "suspicion, possibly launched by the Nazis, was widespread that there was an intention to 'purchase' Jewish assets in return for complete or partial compensation. Naturally, nothing more than the declared value would be indemnified. . . . These considerations caused a fair number of individuals to declare the value of their real estate and other assets to be higher than the actual taxable worth."[83]

The Third Ordinance of the Reich Citizenship Law[84] was published on June 14, 1938. It defined exactly what sort of industrial concern and what form of business—such as a private trading company or limited liability company—"should be considered as Jewish in the sense of the Reich Citizenship Law." In respect to companies, it was sufficient if one Jew was in senior management or on the board of directors or if one-quarter of its capital was in Jewish hands. In addition, an "industrial firm dominated in actual fact by Jewish influence"—however that was to be interpreted—was classified as being "Jewish." One month later, in a circular by the interior minister dated July 14, 1938, the listing of all still existing Jewish enterprises was ordered.[85] By means of detailed individual regulations, the authorities hoped to make sure that not a single Jewish business would be overlooked. The lists were also supposed to include businesses formerly owned by Jews, whose owners had, "for all external appearances," left the firm, "if there is a likely suspicion that they still control the concern's management." In this case as well, the competent authorities were instructed to look carefully into the "dominant influence" in firms belonging to "persons with Jewish relatives" or "of mixed descent" (*Mischlinge*). . . .

The Law on Changes in Trade Regulations of July 6, 1938, excluded Jews from various occupations that they were still permitted, at least formally, to pursue.[86] Of decisive and serious impact . . . was the prohibition on the vocation of peddler (itinerant tradesman) and on the "practice of a trade outside one's official town of residence" by the owner of a firm or traveling sales representatives. Many former independent businessmen and unemployed workers had flocked to these occupations as an alternative that held out the prospect of a modest income. . . .

The Fourth Ordinance of the Reich Citizenship Law of July 25, 1938,[87] rescinded the licenses of all Jewish doctors still in practice, effective September 30, 1938. However, the interior minister was given the authority to permit an exception: certain Jewish doctors who had lost their positions could treat Jews, using the professional title of *Krankenbehandler*, "practitioner for the sick." All others were prohibited from the practice of medicine, effective immediately. Since January 1, 1938, Jewish doctors had no longer been allowed to treat patients covered by health insurance schemes for white-collar workers. Since May, they had been barred from accepting welfare patients for treatment.[88] At this juncture, the prohibition mainly affected Jewish patients from the health insurance schemes and on welfare; non-Jewish patients were rarely given referrals to Jewish doctors. In many welfare offices, bills and certificates signed by Jewish doctors were no longer recognized as valid. Of the 3,152 Jewish doctors still in practice at that time in the *Altreich*, only 709 received permission to treat Jewish patients as a *Krankenbehandler*; the figures for Berlin were 426 out of a total of 1,623 practicing physicians.[89]

The Fifth Ordinance of the Reich Citizenship Law of September 27, 1938,[90] excluded all still practicing attorneys. Analogous to the special regula-

tion of the Fourth Ordinance, the judiciary was authorized to grant permission to so-called *Konsulenten*, "counsels for legal advising and representation of Jews." At that time in the *Altreich*, there were still 1,753 Jewish lawyers; even before this ordinance, they had had an almost exclusively Jewish clientele. Now, a total of only 172 (40 of them in Berlin) were licensed as *Konsulenten*. Like the doctors, these *Konsulenten* were prohibited from using their earlier professional designation in any form whatsoever on signs or letterheads. The decree also regulated the fee schedule of such *Konsulenten*: a portion of their income from services had to be paid to a Reich Office for Compensation. . . .

The Pogrom: Prelude to Expropriation and Expulsion

On October 28–29, 1938, some eighteen thousand Jews holding Polish citizenship were deported across the Polish border. This first mass deportation to the East was an anticipation of later "deportations" (*Aussiedlungen*) during the war, in its manner of implementation and in the indifferent reaction among the populace and by foreign governments. Jews were arrested at night in their homes, herded together for a short time in jails and at other collection points, loaded onto railway cars, and taken to the border. Because the Polish government, after a brief hesitation, had closed the crossing point into Poland, more than eight thousand Jews were forced back over the German border. They had to stay out under the open sky in a no-man's land between Neu-Bentschen and Zabaszyn in Posen, exposed to the rain and cold, until Jewish relief organizations managed to arrange emergency housing and food for them.[91]

Among the Jews expelled to Zabaszyn was the family of Sendel Grynszpan (Grünspan) from Hannover. Their son Herschel, who had already emigrated from Germany, fired the shots on November 7 that killed the German legation secretary, vom Rath, in Paris. According to Herschel's own testimony, this was to avenge the injustice suffered by his parents. That assassination served as the direct pretext for the pogrom of November 9–10, 1938, euphemistically and bizarrely termed *Reichskristallnacht.*

The night of November 9–10, most of the still existing synagogues in Germany and Austria went up in flames. The police and fire department had received instructions only to protect adjacent buildings from a possible spreading of the fire; otherwise, they were advised to let "popular anger" take its course. According to Heydrich's instructions, "Jewish stores and homes [should] only be destroyed, not plundered." "Special care should be taken in business streets to make sure that non-Jewish shops were definitely protected from possible damage." In addition, the Gestapo ordered "the arrest in all districts of as many Jews—especially prosperous ones—as could be accommodated in the jails" and to "establish immediate contact with the relevant concentration camps regarding the quickest possible internment of Jews in these camps."[92]

These instructions, except for that pertaining to plundering, were adhered to in exemplary fashion. Almost one hundred Jews were murdered that night, and thirty thousand largely affluent Jews were placed in concentration camps. It is not known how many of them perished there. Seventy-five hundred Jewish businesses were demolished during the pogrom, and there cannot have been many more than this figure still in existence at the time.

There are various, in part contradictory descriptions of the details of the pogrom, its underlying causes, the question of who gave the direct order, and the reactions of the population. It is certain that Goebbels played a central role in organizing the "spontaneous" excesses after having obtained Hitler's consent at the annual meeting of the party Old Guard in Munich. There is clear evidence for both the participation of the SA and SS and the passive complicity of the police. In contrast, Göring claimed that the reports had taken him totally by surprise. Yet what angered him was only the destruction of property and the expected financial burden for the insurance companies as a result. In his own words, he would have much preferred that, instead of this destruction, two hundred Jews had been murdered instead.[93]

There are quite differing reports as to the behavior of the population. For example, the writer Jochen Klepper entered in his diary on November 10: "All the store windows of Jewish businesses were smashed today, and fires set in synagogues, though without any danger [to life]. A short walk through Jewish neighborhoods is enough to show one that once again, the population does not condone what has happened. I was able to see that with my own eyes." One day later, he noted that "what Hanni [his Jewish wife] has to report today about the reactions she heard from … the wife of the naval officer, women at the bakery, men down at the newspaper stand, and even the next-door neighbor of the demolished Jewish shop (probably the last) is sufficient proof: now as before, there is no need to despair when it comes to the true intentions of the German people."[94] The British consul general in Cologne reported on November 14, 1938, that "there is nervousness amongst middle-class Germans, who in general disapprove. They dare not, however, voice their disapproval. . . . The industrialists say that they have no influence with the party, who have made such a point of racial purity that the Führer must carry his theories to their logical conclusion. . . . Yet I am inclined to think that the Führer knows his Germans. Amongst the masses of Germans who have nothing at stake, there is observable a certain amount of 'Schadenfreude' ('joy in mischief')."[95]

Undoubtedly, these and all other conflicting reports, based on the personal experiences of their authors, possess a certain kernel of truth. However, the timing of the pogrom was by no means accidental, and the shots fired in Paris served only as a convenient pretext. Beginning in the autumn of 1937, the radicalization of public antisemitism functioned to promote the propagandistic preparations for a series of measures and laws directed against Jews. The effect on various groups in the population may well have differed. The declared goal of Jewish policy was the final prohibition of any kind of economic activity by Jews—in order to pressure them into emigrating more quickly. However, there was a desire to retain Jewish assets and "utilize" them for war preparations. The temporary conclusion of this process was the prospective immediate expropriation of a portion of Jewish assets and the freezing of the remainder. Detailed plans had been drawn up for this. The following quotation from a newspaper proves that these plans were being prepared with public knowledge, and that their implications were also correctly understood by contemporaries:

> For a long time now, National Socialism has been making preparations to take decisive economic measures in the wake of the political conclusion it has arrived at in dealing with Jews. . . . The regulation on inventory-taking introduced this year by the government [indicates] the coming efforts to enhance economic performance and the necessary exclusion of Jewish influence in the economy. In one or another form, therefore, the special utilization of Jewish capital would have come about any-

how, sooner or later. The shots fired in Paris . . . however, have triggered an early start.[96]

The author of this article was mistaken only in the last sentence. The Nazis had not been able to foresee the shots in Paris, but those shots did not come too early. Rather, all indications are that not only did the assassination provide the pretext for the pogrom, but that it occurred at a quite suitable time. Three weeks prior to the pogrom, and fourteen days after conclusion of the Munich Agreement, Göring had declared in a closed meeting that "Jews now must be driven from the economy." Their assets would have to be transferred in orderly manner to the Reich and not be squandered as a "welfare system for incompetent party members."[97] The German Federation of Banks and Savings Associations had informed its members on October 28 that the Foreign Currency Control Office, headed by Heydrich since July 1938, was preparing "security orders" for Jewish assets, "by which the control of the owners over their various assets is to be restricted." On August 19, the Economy Ministry had ordered those offices dealing with registration of Jewish assets to finish the work by September 30, if necessary by engaging additional personnel, "in order to make preparations for a possible seizure of part of Jewish assets for the purposes of the German economy."[98] In the tax offices and at the Gestapo and police offices, bolstered by assistance from the respective chambers of commerce and DEAs, lists of affluent Jews were drawn up. Fifteen hundred Jews arrested in July and already in concentration camps were required to build additional barracks.[99] In view of all of these preparations, the shots in Paris would appear to have been a bit too delayed in coming.

Immediately after the pogrom, the measures that had been prepared were set in motion. Hitler's notion of a "Guaranty Association for Jews"

(*Judengarantieverband*) could finally now be made a reality: the "special taxation" approved by him two years earlier was now levied as a "*Sühneleistung*," in the form of the one-time penalty of RM one billion. In addition, Jews were required to "restore the appearance of the streets" without being paid the insurance claims they were entitled to; those insurance monies had been pocketed by the state on the basis of a special decree. . . . In the meeting held on November 12, 1938, in the Aviation Ministry, there was an exchange with the representative of the insurance firms; they were then allowed to retain a portion [i.e., most] of this money, thus also profiting from the transaction.[100]

That same day saw the issuance of the First Ordinance on the Exclusion of Jews from German Economic Life.[101] This ordinance prohibited almost all still extant options for gainful employment and ordered the dismissal of employees without any right on their part to claim pensions or compensation. On November 21, an implementation order by the economy minister[102] stipulated that the *Sühneleistung* penalty was to be in the form of a tax amounting to 20 percent of the assets reported in April, quite independent of whether the respective Jew was still actually in possession of such declared assets. Any changes that had occurred since were subject to affirmation only by the higher administrative office. In October 1939, the tax was hiked to 25 percent of reported assets, since the total of RM 1 billion had supposedly not been reached.[103]

In actual fact, however RM 1.127 billion was collected. If one adds to this the Flight Tax payments levied on emigrants from November 1938 until the outbreak of the war, the resultant total is a figure of an estimated RM 2 billion in Jewish assets that flowed "legally" and directly into the coffers of the Reich in this brief period. If this amount is compared with the figures based on the registra-

tion of declared assets in April 1938, and allowing for accelerated plundering in the meantime, this RM 2 billion probably constituted half or more of the total assets still in Jewish hands. This does not include "profit from Aryanizations" pocketed by individuals or Jewish "contributions" to party organizations.[104] How these "contributions" were "encouraged" is reported by the Reich treasurer of the NSDAP to Reichsleiter Bormann in a letter of December 2, 1938:[105]

A few members of the Party from the district headquarters appeared at the homes of the Jews in question. First of all, they proceeded to cut the telephone wires. Then they presented the Jew with "contribution certificates" which had been prepared by a notary. The Jew was told that he had an opportunity to make a contribution. If he dared to resist, they responded by threatening to shoot. The assets taken from the Jews . . . included houses, automobiles and radios.

It is not clear from the letter whether or to what extent Jewish assets were retained, but the Reich treasurer must have had a similar suspicion:

In some districts, there are organizations implementing the liquidation of Jewish assets; in other districts, this is basically dependent on the DEA . . . . The great danger exists that the Gauleiter may in some cases take advantage of the situation to set up "black" slush funds which they control independently, without my approval.

The Ordinance on Utilization of Jewish Assets of December 3, 1938, marked the temporary conclusion of this phase.[106] It stipulated the "forced Aryanization" of all Jewish firms that were still in existence but had been prohibited from operating since the pogrom. At the same time, an order was issued requiring the deposit of cash, securities, jewelry, and other valuables in blocked accounts, and control over these assets was made subject to a formal permit. Trustees appointed by the authorities directed the "Aryanization" of Jewish businesses that were still deemed useful. "Unjustified profits due to *Entjudung*" were not seized by the Reich until February 1939.[107] Since the ordinance was not retroactive, it was tantamount to locking the stable door after most of the horses had already escaped—or in this instance, had been stolen.

The tactics of the German rulers aimed at driving Jews out of the country by means of increased economic and physical pressure had the desired effect. In the years 1938–1939, approximately 120,000 Jews left Germany, almost as many as in the entire preceding five years.[108] Most of them had been a short while before still relatively affluent individuals who had hesitated to part from their possessions; now they fled the country penniless. They had been literally fleeced, stripped of their possessions by "legal" means. What remained to them after the "treatment" they were accorded by the tax offices had to be left in blocked accounts, which were almost completely inaccessible. Such accounts were then confiscated by the Reich at a later date by means of new "legislation." The henchmen of the SA and SS also got their spoils: Despite the fact that they had valid emigration papers, many thousands in KZ-camps were able to get out only after they had left sizable sums of money, cars, and other property to local party groups or even individual Nazis as "voluntary contributions."

NOTES

1. See S. Adler-Rudel, *Ostjuden in Deutschland 1880–1940* (Tübingen, 1959). For the Nazi period, see especially Maurer, 190ff., which emphasizes the difference between the "legal" considerations regarding the foreign status of the Eastern Jews and everyday bureaucratic practice.

2. Affidavit, Julius Rosenfeld, in Knipping, 25f.

3. Buchloh, 131. See similar descriptions from other localities in Drobisch, 78f.; Krausnick, 31 if.; Düwell, 83f.

4. See Barkai, *Wirtschaftssystem*, 87ff.

5. Adam, 47f.

6. Ball-Kaduri, 49f.

7. H. A. Winkler, in Martin-Schulin, 283.

8. B. Martin, in Martin-Schulin, 299.

9. HStaA Düsseldorf, Reg. Aachen, 211/23883.

10. Uhlig, 52f., ii5ff.

11. Order of the Party direction of the NSDAP, dated March 28, 1933; in Scheffler, 69f.

12. Krausnick, 315f.

13. Genschel, 51, 54.

14. BAK, R 43 II, no. 600, 63f.

15. Walk, I/38. Laws and ordinances are generally cited according to the collection edited by Josef Walk et al. The interested reader will find details there on the original and complete publication of the various individual laws, etc.

16. See Adam, 51ff.

17. The individual laws and ordinances in Walk; lawyers and patent attorneys: 1/66; doctors in state-supported health insurance programs: I/71; pharmacists: I/72; government employees lacking civil-service status: I/74, 86, 98; university teachers, schoolteachers, notaries public: I/90.

18. Conrad Kaiser YV, 01/25; Ball-Kaduri, 97f.

19. Walk, I/20.

20. Ibid., I/35, 1/37.

21. ALBI/Jm, no. lib, *Statistischer Bericht des Zentralausschusses für Hilfe und Aufbau*, no. 516, May 12, 1933. The Central Committee was formed even before the establishment of the *Reichsvertretung der deutschen Juden* (after 1935: *Reichsvertretung der Juden in Deutschland*, cited hereafter as *Reichsvertretung*). After it was established, the Central Committee became, for all practical purposes, a section within the *Reichsvertretung*. Nevertheless, annual reports and other publications in the

first few years continued to appear in part under its letterhead. These will generally be quoted as publications of the *Reichsvertretung*.

22. *RV/Arb.* 1933, 32f.; *C. V. Zeitung*, August 10, 1933.

23. Walk, I/90.

24. Blau, "Vierzehn Jahre," 23f. (on the biography of Bruno Blau, see Richarz, vol. 3, 459); Herzfeld, 5f.

25. ALBI/Jm, B 11, 11 a, Statist. Abteilung der Reichsvertretung. According to the census of June 16, 1933, there were still 5,557 Jewish doctors in Germany, amounting to just under 11 percent of all doctors in the area of the Reich. See Bennathan, 111.

26. See Z. Zofka, "Der KZ-Arzt Josef Mengele: Zur Typologie eines NS-Verbrechers," *VfZ* 34 (1986), especially 250ff.; M. Kater, "Doctor Leonardo Conti and His Nemesis," *Central European History* 18 (1985): 299–325.

27. S. Ostrowski, YVA, 01/16; Ball-Kaduri, 45ff.

28. Walk, I/71.

29. Ibid., I/20, I/24; Adam, 49, 67ff; StA Duisburg, Best. 500, no. 307.

30. *RV/Arb.* 1933, 34f.; Adler-Rudel, 139.

31. Adler-Rudel, 137; *RV/Arb.* 1933, 35f.

32. Walk, I/248.

33. Ibid., I/264.

34. Quoted in Genschel, 82.

35. Walk, I/173; GStaA Dahlem, Re151, no. 3576.

36. Thus, for example, in the case of a firm in Essen that was "Aryanized" in 1937 with the aid of the Gestapo.

37. StA Duisburg, Best. 500, no. 136. In detail in H. Zimmermann, "Untersuchungen zur Geschichte der Duisburger Judengemeinde 1933–1945," unpublished graduate thesis (Staatsexamen), 1969, 16ff. (copy in StA Duisburg).

38. Buchloh, 108; Genschel, 8if.

39. StaA Münster, Reg. Arnsberg IG/572.

40. Knipping, 33f.; similarly in Munich: Hanke, 100ff.

41. Herbert Strauss regards these differences as so pronounced that he speaks about "the existence of 'two Jewish economies'" and "the 'two economies' characteristic of the Jews of the period"; see Strauss 1980, 345.

42. Schaeffer, file no. 26.

43. Ibid.; Szanto, *Erinnerungen*, 150ff.

44. *C.V. Zeitung*, September 15, 1933.

45. Wirtschaftshilfe der jüdischen Gemeinde Berlin, Wiener Library, Tel Aviv, PC3/4, no. 4. The official exchange rate of the reichsmark was pegged early during the Nazi period at an overvalued RM 2.5 to the U.S. dollar (instead of the long-standing rate of 4.2 to the dollar) but was manipulated in an extremely complex manner, resulting in multiple rates, depending on type of transaction. Cf. Howard S. Ellis, *Exchange Control in Central Europe* (Cambridge, Mass., 1941), especially 233–42. Also Gustav Stolper et al., *The Germany Economy: 1870 to the Present* (New York, 1967), especially 329 (chart).

46. Walk, I/354.

47. Ibid., I/391.

48. Ibid., I/517. See also World Jewish Congress 1937, 37; Genschel, 90, n6ff.

49. Walk, I/636.

50. Ibid., II/46; 140.

51. Barkai, *Wirtschaftssystem*, 39f. Especially useful data on the role of the district economic advisors in ousting Jews from the economy and Aryanizations can be found in the extensive files in the State Archives of North-Rhine Westphalia, Munster.

52. *Westfälische Landeszeitung*, May 3, 1936; *Frankfurter Zeitung*, April 17, 1936.

53. Muellerheim, 14.

54. *RV*, annual reports, 1934–1936; Adler-Rudel, 137; YVA, 01/25.

55. Adam, 132; *Frankfurter Zeitung*, September 25, 1935.

56. World Jewish Congress 1937, 31; Adler-Rudel, 132.

57. Representative of many press reports: *Israelitisches Familienblatt*, March 26, 1936; *Frankfurter Zeitung*, September 17, 1936, October 20, 1936; *Germania*, October 18, 1936; *Der Gemeindetag*, January 5, 1937; *JWSP*, 1933/34, 219ff.

58. Walk I/172, 198.

59. Maurer, I95ff.

60. My estimate is based on the census and occupational survey of June 1933, data in Bennathan,

Marcus, *Krise* (1931), and the figures calculated in the Statistics Office of the Reichsvertretung; and in particular the studies cited by Herbert Kahn on retail trade (1934) and Jewish crafts (1936).

61. Quoted in Genschel, 125; see also *Jüdische Rundschau*, November 1, 1935.

62. Council, 1937, 7.

63. Margalioth, "Tendencies," 348f.

64. *RV/Arb.* 1934–37; see Poppel, *Salman Schocken and the Schocken Verlag, YLBI* 17 (1972): 93ff.; M. T. Edelheim-Muhsam, "The Jewish Press in Germany," *YLBI* 1(1956): 163ff.; E. Simon, "Jewish Adult Education in Germany as Spiritual Resistance," *YLBI* 1(1956): 68ff.

65. "Die jüdische Presse als Wirtschaftsspiegel," *Israelitisches Familienblatt*, April 2, 1937.

66. *RV/Arb.* 1934, 59f.; 1936, 102f.; Adler-Rudel, 133ff.; Szanto, *Erinnerungen*, I37f.; *idem*, "Economic Aid," 221f.

67. *JWSP*, 1937, 1ff.

68. An order in this connection was not issued until after the November 1938 pogrom (Walk HI/20). On the previously customary procedures, see *RV/Arb.* 1935, 45; Hanke, 263f.; Adler-Rudel, 159f.

69. Hanke, 263f.

70. Adam, 133, 191f.

71. Strauss 1980, 342; Adler-Rudel, 161f; Bauer, 125; *RV/Arb.* 1935, 49.

72. Adler-Rudel, 166f.

73. Adler-Rudel, 168.

74. The annual report of the *Reichsvertretung* for 1937 gives a figure of approximately 350,000. I believe the estimate by Strauss of 365,000 is more accurate. See Strauss 1980, 326.

75. A. Krüger, *Die Lösung der Judenfrage in der Wirtschaft: Kommentar zur Judengesetzgebung* (Berlin, 1940), 44. Genschel lists this source, but nonetheless estimates that only 25 percent of the businesses and a much smaller percentage of manufacturing enterprises had been "Aryanized" by the autumn of 1937 (136). It is possible that the liquidated Jewish firms have not been included.

76. *Textil-Zeitung*, December 3, 1938; *Berliner Morgenpost*, November 25, 1938.

77. Walk II/457; 458.

78. GStaA Dahlem, Rep. 151 no. 1658a, RWM, Ill/Jd. 8910/38, November 28, 1938.

79. Walk II/458.

80. GStaA Dahlem.

81. An original copy of the questionnaire can be found in the Wiener Library, Tel Aviv, under PC 3/51.

82. *Foreign Relations of the United States; Diplomatic Papers 1938*, 2: 366.

83. Herzfeld, 43.

84. Walk II/487.

85. Walk II/503.

86. Walk II/500.

87. Walk II/510.

88. Adam, 188.

89. Leibfried, 11.

90. Walk II/547.

91. S. Milton, "The Expulsion of Polish Jews from Germany: October 1938 to July 1939—Documentation," *YLBI* 29 (1984): 169–99.

92. Telegram, signed Heydrich, November 10, 1938, *IMT*, vol. 27, 491; see also Scheffler, 73flf.

93. *IMT*, vol. 37, PS-1816; Kochan, 107, 131f.

94. Jochen Klepper, *Unter den Schatten Deiner Flügel. Aus den Tagebüchem der Jahre 1932–1942* (Stuttgart, 1956), 675f.

95. General Consul Bell, November 14, 1938, in *Papers concerning the Treatment of German Nationals in Germany 1938–39* (London, HMSO, 1939), 17.

96. *Berliner Börsen-Zeitung*, November 19, 1938.

97. *IMT*, vol. 37, PS-1301, session of October 14, 1938.

98. HStaA Düsseldorf, OFD Düsseldorf, Br. 1026/276, RWM, express letter, August 19, 1938.

99. YVA, 01/249; Scheffler, 28f.; Kochan, 34.

100. Walk III/7, 13; Drobisch, 602; *IMT*, vol. 37, PS-1301, session of October 14, 1938.

101. "Erste Verordnung zur Ausschaltung der Juden aus dem deutschen Wirtschaftsleben." Cf. Walk III/8.

102. Walk III/21; full text in GStaA Dahlem, Rep. 151, no. 2193.

103. Walk IV/23; GStaA Dahlem, ibid.

104. Hilberg, 92.

105. BAK, NSi, Vorl. 430, published in Patzold, *Verfolgung*, 193ff.

106. "Verordnung über den Einsatz des jüdischen Vermögens." Cf. Walk III/46.

107. Walk III/132; full text in GStaA Dahlem, Rep. 151, no. 1658a, RWM, III Jd./1/2082/39.

108. Strauss 1980, 326; Rosenstock, 377.

109. E. Kogon, *Der SS-Staat. Das System der deutschen Konzentrationslager* (Frankfurt am Main, 1965), 193f.

Talk of "Annihilation"

ERNST VON WEIZSÄCKER'S REMARKS TO A SWISS DIPLOMAT,
NOVEMBER 15, 1938, FROM *DOCUMENTS DIPLOMATIQUES SUISSES*

The Swiss Minister in Paris, W. Stucki, to the Chief of the Political Department [of the Swiss Foreign Ministry], G. Motta, November 15, 1938

> Yesterday. . . . Mister [Vice-Minister Ernst] von Weizsäcker, who had stayed in Paris [after the memorial service for Ernst vom Rath], telephoned me. . . . I invited him to lunch today with my family. He has just left after we thoroughly discussed assorted important questions in open and friendly manner. . . . I turned the conversation to the currently acute Jewish question. Mr. von W. did not make the least effort to defend what has been undertaken, both legally and illegally, in Germany against the Jews. Without compromising his reputation, he expressed to me his great regret that once again a very bad attitude toward Germany was created throughout the entire world. In his opinion, the National Socialist Party is so deeply engaged in conflict with Jewry that it cannot turn back, cannot even stand still. The remaining circa 500,000 Jews in Germany should immediately be deported somewhere because they cannot stay in Germany. If, however, as has been the case to date, no country will take them in, they surely are going sooner or later toward their complete annihilation.

"JEWS, WHAT NOW?" FROM *DAS SCHWARZE KORPS*, NOVEMBER 24, 1938

The Jews must be driven from our residential districts and segregated where they will be among themselves, having as little contact with Germans as possible. . . . Confined to themselves, these parasites will be . . . reduced to poverty. . . . Let no one fancy, however, that we shall then stand idly by, merely watching the process. The German people are not in the least inclined to tolerate in their country hundreds of thousands of criminals, who not only secure their existence through crime, but also want to exact revenge. . . . These hundreds of thousands of impoverished Jews [would create] a breeding ground for Bolshevism and a collection of the politically criminal subhuman elements. . . . In such a situation we would be faced with the hard necessity of exterminating the Jewish underworld in the same way as, under our government of law and order, we are accustomed to exterminating any other criminals—that is, by fire and sword. The result would be the actual and final end of Jewry in Germany, its absolute annihilation.

HITLER'S REICHSTAG SPEECH, JANUARY 30, 1939, FROM *NAZISM 1939–1945*

Europe cannot find peace until the Jewish question has been solved. . . . On this day I should like to say one thing that may be memorable for others as well as for us Germans. In the course of my life I have very often been a prophet and have usually been ridiculed for it. During the time of my struggle for power it was in the first instance only the Jewish race that received my prophecies with laughter when I said that I would one day take over the leadership of the state, and with it that of the whole nation, and that I would then among other things settle the Jewish problem. Their laughter was uproarious, but I think that for some time now they have been laughing on the other side of their face. Today I will once more be a prophet: if the international Jewish financiers in and outside Europe should succeed in plunging the nations once more into a world war, then the result will not be the Bolshevizing of the earth, and thus the victory of Jewry, but the annihilation of the Jewish race in Europe!

3 Impediments to Escape

5. Passengers aboard the *St. Louis*, granted a temporary haven in Belgium, prepare to disembark at the port of Antwerp. The photograph is taken from the page of an illustrated feature article on the *St. Louis* refugee ship published in the weekly newsmagazine *Paris Match*, June 17, 1939. On May 13, 1939, over nine hundred Jewish passengers sailed from Hamburg, Germany, aboard the *St. Louis* in search of safe heaven. Turned away by Cuba and the United States, the ship was forced to return to Europe. Four European countries (Great Britain, France, Belgium, and the Netherlands) accepted the passengers, but within a few months war broke out in Europe and the refugees in three of these countries found themselves once again under German rule. Many of them were killed during the Holocaust. (U.S. Holocaust Memorial Museum, courtesy of Clark Blatteis.)

6. Pau Basse Pyrenees, France . . . September 1942—"My family was on the *St. Louis*, that doomed ship that no country seemed to want. We made our way to southern France, like so many refugees from Germany. We were from Berlin. In May 1939, my mother and father rented a small apartment in the home of Eliette Carapezzi Enard. In August 1942, my parents and I were arrested and taken to Gurs camp. The *Oeuvre de Secours aux Enfants* (OSE), the main Jewish organization working to safeguard children in France, was operating in Gurs. The OSE would take children out of the camp and place them in convents and homes throughout the region, passing them off as Christians. I was taken out of Gurs and placed with the Enards. I was so sick and malnourished. My French mother, Eliette, nursed my wounds and brought me back to health. I lived in a very loving atmosphere for four years as a member of their family. My parents died in Auschwitz in 1942. In 1946, Eliette took me to Paris where she gave me to the OSE, which arranged to send me to the United States to live with my aunt and uncle in New York City." This was the testimony given by Judith Koeppel Steel, the little girl saved by Eliette. (Courtesy JFR Photo Archives.)

Introduction

PETER HAYES

In view of the barriers that Jews had to overcome in order to escape from Nazi persecution during the 1930s, the wonder is that so many managed to find refuge. By the time Hitler invaded Poland on September 1, 1939, some 60% of the Germans defined as Jews by the Nazi regime in 1933 had managed to flee the Third Reich. So had about 67% of the Jews of Austria, which Germany had annexed in March 1938. Less fortunate were the Jews of the Sudetenland and the Czech provinces of Bohemia and Moravia, who fell into Hitler's hands in October 1938 and March 1939; only about one-quarter of them got away before World War II began. Moreover, the relatively high emigration rates for Germany and Austria mask how difficult flight was, how precarious the prospects and how narrow the margin of success. Fully half of those who got out did so only in the nick of time in 1938–39, when the escalation of Nazi cruelty momentarily shamed the wider world into taking more of them in.

Why was escape so difficult? By the post-World War I era, the massive human mobility of the preceding century had become a thing of the past. No longer could a person or group turn its back on oppression for the price of a railroad and/or steamship ticket. Virtually all relatively developed nations had introduced schemes of immigration control and supervision, everything from quota systems on how many people could enter from each other country per year (e.g., the United States) to landing requirements and visas that restricted who could disembark and how long

she or he could stay (e.g., Great Britain). With the exception of countries such as France that had been literally bled white by the Great War, most nations went from welcoming immigrants to mistrusting them and encouraging them to move on. The shift reflected the rampant cultivation of national identities and ethnic hierarchies in the last quarter of the nineteenth century, along with mounting concerns for national security in the face of violent radical movements such as anarchism and Bolshevism in the early decades of the twentieth.

By the time the Nazis came to power, the Great Depression had furnished a new justification for these restrictions. Keeping out foreigners now meant fending off competitors for scarce employment. Even had racists, drawing on the full available arsenal of calumnies, not agitated loudly in many countries against admitting supposedly "undesirable" or "unassimilable" Jewish refugees, the self-centered assertion that "the boat is full" might have sufficed to keep the doors nearly barred. In any case, during the 1930s national public opinions opposed, usually by overwhelming margins, admitting significant numbers of refugees from Nazi persecution. What the populace resisted, especially in democratic states but even in most Latin American dictatorships, politicians also did.

Economic and political constraints operated powerfully even in Palestine, where the local populace had no official voice in making immigration policy. Seen by Zionists as the future site of a Jewish state, this former territory of the Ottoman Empire had passed to the League of Nations in 1918, which designated Great Britain as the governing or mandatory power. It had gone on record in the Balfour Declaration of 1917 as favoring "a national home for the Jewish people" in Palestine, but then backtracked during the 1930s because of rising resistance on the part of the indigenous Arab population. Faced with growing prospects of war in both Europe and East Asia, the leaders in London sought to pacify the Middle East and thus to secure Egypt and the Suez Canal, "the jugular vein of the Empire" (Bernard Wasserstein), by holding down the flow of Jewish immigrants into Palestine. A series of increasingly restrictive definitions of Palestine's capacity to absorb new laborers culminated in the White Paper of May 1939 that capped future Jewish immigration at 15,000 people in each of the following five years.

The Nazi regime played adroitly on these conditions. As it stripped its Jews of all they had, it fostered fear abroad that they would become a burden on receiving states, thus strengthening resistance to providing refuge. Such resistance, the Reich's spokespeople pointed out, indicated that no one else wanted the Jews either, which supposedly vindicated Nazi antisemitism. Conversely, every sign of sympathy for German Jews by foreign governments attested, the Nazis claimed, to the power of international Jewry and once more vindicated Nazi antisemitism. Above all, German policy makers and propagandists knew that foreign governments worried that accepting large numbers of German Jews would set a precedent that invited the increasingly antisemitic governments of Poland and Lithuania to provoke a far larger exodus. This bogeyman played a decisive part in the spectacular failure of the Evian Conference in July 1938, at which the representatives of thirty-two countries mouthed sympathy for the plight of Jews in Germany, but offered almost no practical relief.

For all of these reasons, Jews trying to leave Nazi Germany faced enormous internal and external obstacles. At home, the increasing depredations of the German financial authorities complicated the task of deciding when to leave and created a gauntlet of preconditions that were difficult to fulfill. On the foreign side, satisfying the intricate prerequisites for visas, completing the extensive paperwork, obtaining the necessary funds, including sometimes for bribery, and coping with the arbitrariness of the responsible consular officials took a heavy toll.

The readings in this chapter detail both the governmental and the psychological or emotional impediments to escape that confronted German Jews. Richard Breitman's and Alan Kraut's account of *United States refugee policy* reveals how bureaucratic inertia and public opinion overrode empathy except in the aftermath of the pogrom of 1938 and restricted Franklin Roosevelt's capacity and willingness to act. The results included admitting some 79,000 fewer Jews to the U.S. in 1933–39 than the already restrictive quota system allowed. Even so, the U.S. offered more German Jews asylum than any other country. Eugen Weber's portrait of changing attitudes in *France* during the 1930s outlines the degree to which refugee policy became a political football there and rising domestic tensions translated into mounting animosity to foreigners. Louise London's close examination of immigration policy in the *British Empire* stresses the constraints built into the country's self-image as a "transit" nation, especially at a time when the Dominions would not accept large numbers of refugees and Arab resistance in British-occupied Palestine limited its utility in this respect. The report of the Independent Commission of Experts on the measures *Switzerland* took to discourage refugees from entering the country shows how difficult flight to that nearby potential haven was and how few people accomplished it. Rebecca Boehling's and Uta Larkey's portrait of a group of Jewish relatives who made it to *Palestine* provides insight into the difficulties not only of getting out of Germany, but also of making the transition to the new, unfamiliar surroundings. Finally, Marion Kaplan traces the dilemma of *going and staying* as German Jews experienced it during the 1930s and illuminates the influence on both choices of age, class, and gender.

In many respects, the story of the *St. Louis*, a refugee ship that left Hamburg with 937 Jews aboard on May 13, 1939, and was permitted to land only 28 of its passengers in Cuba and none of them in the United States, parallels the larger tale of Jews' struggle to escape from Nazi persecution during the 1930s. The passengers barely got out of Germany before World War II began and found refuge only with great difficulty. At the last minute, four nations (Holland, Belgium, France, and Great Britain) flinched at the thought of making the ship return to Germany and granted asylum to the passengers. Like the majority of Jews in Nazi hands prior to 1939, they reached safety by a hair's breadth. Moreover, when the Nazis overran Western Europe in 1940, 532 of the Jews from the *St. Louis* were trapped anew, like approximately 100,000 other Jewish refugees from Germany, Austria, and the Czech provinces. They thus rejoined at least 350,000 Jews who had been unable to escape the Greater German Reich by then, along with approximately two million Jews in the parts of Poland annexed or subordinated to Germany. All were henceforth at the mercy of the Nazi New Order.

The United States and Refugees, 1933–1940

RICHARD BREITMAN AND ALAN M. KRAUT

From *American Refugee Policy and European Jewry, 1933–1945*

The United States had a tradition of serving as a refuge for European emigrants. Unlike any other country in the world, the United States was not only populated by immigrants; it was also a society that touted itself as a sanctuary for the world's "homeless, tempest-tost." It also possessed land, resources, and civic ideals embracing religious and political freedom. More than 2.5 million Jews had found a haven in the U.S. during the late nineteenth and early twentieth centuries.

The legend of the open or "golden" door was in some ways misleading, however. For a long time American sympathy for the victims of persecution and poverty abroad was expressed not through a positive immigration policy but through one of benign neglect. The vast expanse of the continent and the expanding industrial economy generally made immigrants seem an asset rather than a problem requiring legislative action. Even before the massive immigration from southern and eastern Europe peaked after the turn of the century, however, there were problems. As John Higham and other scholars have observed,[1] nativism was deeply rooted in the loam of American culture. The price of an open society democratically governed has been the recurrent fear of subversion by new arrivals unfamiliar with—and, therefore, possibly unappreciative of—republican ideals. Moreover, part of the white Anglo-Saxon Protestant majority that cast the mold for American values

looked with suspicion upon racial and religious minorities already in the United States—blacks, Orientals, Roman Catholics, as well as Jews.

Government began to impose immigration restrictions upon nationalities: first, against the Chinese and Japanese but, later, after World War I, against Europeans as well. The era of mass immigration came to an abrupt halt. The visa system instituted at the end of the war and the new immigration laws of 1921 and 1924 established maximum annual levels of immigration from each European country (quotas) as well as various qualifications for immigrants. The overall yearly ceiling of quota immigrants was 153,774 in 1929, when the new quota system became fully operable. Western hemisphere countries were exempted from the quota system as were certain professionals whose skills were in short supply.

The Great Depression amplified demands for additional requirements and reductions. President Hoover and the State Department took a key step in 1930 without congressional authorization. The State Department was already using a provision of the 1917 Immigration Act to limit immigration from Mexico: any Mexican considered "likely to become a public charge," i.e., unable to support himself, was denied a visa. The public charge clause, first included in an 1882 law, was originally aimed at persons who lacked physical or mental skills required for constructive employment. But there was another way to interpret "likely to become a public charge"—anyone unlikely to obtain a job under current market conditions. In a September 1930 press release, President Hoover announced a new policy of rigorous enforcement of this LPC clause with regard to potential immigrants from Europe.[2] This Hoover barricade in front of the "golden door" was still in place when thousands of Jews began to seek escape from Nazi Germany in 1933.

The LPC clause was among the most potent of the devices that allowed the State Department, acting through American consuls and vice consuls abroad who issued visas to potential immigrants, to regulate the level of immigration administratively. Beginning in 1933 and continuing throughout the 1930s, government agencies and officials debated whether the Roosevelt administration should reverse Hoover's sharp cutback in immigration and whether it should offer special consideration to victims of Nazi persecution.

Congress might have acted on its own or turned back the administration's initiatives. . . . But there were always divergent voices in Congress on immigration policy. . . . Although the advocates of immigration restriction usually outnumbered the supporters of liberalization, Congress never actually intervened to pass new immigration laws. The numerous restrictionist voices on Capitol Hill, however, were audible at the White House.

Inertia was on the side of the restrictionists. But there were influential advocates of a positive refugee policy. In April 1933 Supreme Court Justice Louis Brandeis wrote to his friend and political confidant Felix Frankfurter, then a professor at Harvard Law School: "F.D. [Franklin Delano Roosevelt] has shown amply that he has no antisemitism. . . . But this action, or rather determination that there shall be none [i.e., no change in the Hoover immigration policy] is a disgrace to America and to F.D.'s administration."[3] Frankfurter himself, already an informal advisor to the president, professed to be slightly more optimistic about American assistance to those persecuted in

Germany. He wrote to Secretary of Labor Frances Perkins on the same day: "My thanks for the memorandum concerning the treatment of political refugees. . . . I shall continue to refuse to believe that, alone of all Western Governments, this Administration will remain without public action or utterance in the face of such [Nazi] assault on the decencies of civilization."[4] Partly through the efforts of Frankfurter, Perkins, and similarly minded people, the number of Jewish refugees admitted to the United States gradually increased through the 1930s. But a new tightening of immigration rules and regulations in 1939–41, the result of wartime fears, reduced the flow of refugees to a trickle, precisely at the time when the Nazis began to practice mass murder against the Jews. The American cutback was in part a reaction to conscious German efforts to stimulate antisemitism abroad.

The tightly restrictionist phase of American policy did not change until late in the war. A good part of the reason has to do with bureaucracy. Even those who championed the cause of European Jews found themselves confined to the channels and bound by the procedures of the bureaucratic system. Bureaucracy, as Max Weber observed in a famous essay, was the *sine qua non* of the modern democratic state.[5] Bureaucracies follow precedents and usually restrict themselves to their assigned tasks. The two overriding concerns of the American government in the Roosevelt era were economic recovery and protection of the United States against a hostile fascist coalition. Lacking presidential or congressional backing for a positive refugee policy, few bureaucrats were willing to consider the rescue of persecuted foreigners as compatible with the defense of the national interest.

Our research makes clear that such figures as Assistant Secretaries of State Wilbur Carr, George Messersmith, Breckinridge Long, Commissioner of Immigration Daniel MacCormack, and many other officials at lower levels of authority devised and carried out adjustments to immigration regulations that had a major effect upon the level of immigration to the United States. Although some of these individuals may have been biased against Jews, we find that bureaucratic indifference to moral or humanitarian concerns was a more important obstacle to an active refugee policy.

President Roosevelt's most frequent role was in deciding not to alter the outcome of the bureaucratic process, although he had the power to do so. When he did intervene, he sometimes liberalized immigration policy (1938) but sometimes tightened it as well, particularly as war approached. . . . In all, just over 120,000 Germans and Austrians were admitted into the U.S. as immigrants between 1933 and 1944, the overwhelming majority (roughly 90 percent) of them Jews. When one takes into account Jewish immigration from other European countries as well as nonquota immigration and visitors, one arrives at a maximum figure of approximately 250,000 refugees from Nazism who entered the United States during those years.[6] The comparable figure for Great Britain, a far smaller country, is about 70,000; that for spacious Canada, however, is less than 5,000.[7] The American record was not the worst. But the United States failed to do even what its own immigration laws allowed. The overall annual quota (153,774) was never filled during this period; immigration never exceeded 54 percent of the quota. Even the quota of 25,957 for Germany was rarely filled. This was not because of lack of demand for immigration visas. . . . Conscious decisions to apply regulations in a manner to reduce immigration held the flow well below what the quota laws allowed. . . .

Our findings suggest that . . . humanitarian considerations are not easily translated into govern-ment policy. Official indifference to suffering in faraway lands and unwillingness to take responsibility for persons whose care might require tax dollars is still with us . . .

Roosevelt's refugee policy, not unlike some of his economic policies, can best be understood as two policies: compliance with the restrictionist legislation in place since the 1920s and a symbolic humanitarianism extended to a suffering minority.[8] During his first two administrations, the most consistent quality of Roosevelt's policy toward European Jewry was his noninterference with the national quota system that Congress had passed in 1924. Roosevelt never failed to listen sympathetically to individual Jews and to Jewish organizations who petitioned the White House for relief of their coreligionists. But, even when FDR privately assured Jewish leaders that he would act to ease the suffering of their European brothers, he dissociated himself from public statements and other policies that singled out Jewish refugees for special assistance because they were targets of special abuse in Germany.

The president's dual course, largely charted by the political winds, was uneven. Often Roosevelt sought to deflect Jewish pressure from the White House. Between 1933 and 1936, FDR relied on the federal bureaucracy as a trapdoor through which to drop the nettlesome issue of refugees. The New Deal coalition had little to gain and much to lose by taking a stand on an issue that so aroused voters' moral, economic, and social sensibilities. The leniency in administrative procedures that visa applicants experienced after FDR's reelection bears the earmarks of a discreet White House initiative, designed to have a salutary but limited impact upon the flow of refugees. Even after his landslide victory, the president preferred such modest concessions to directly confronting the conflicting demands of refugee advocates and restrictionists. Rather, Roosevelt sought to defuse the issue with a call for an international forum on refugees in 1938. The other nations of the world were as little prepared for gestures of humanitarianism as the United States was, and little was accomplished. But the escalation of German persecution of the Jews, culminating in *Kristallnacht* on November 9, 1938, would not permit the White House to remain silent. With more symbol than substance, FDR denounced the persecution. By the eve of his bid for a third term in 1940, Roosevelt was confronting a war in Europe. The president was not alone in his fears that Nazi or Soviet agents might be infiltrating the United States camouflaged as refugees. This suspicion effectively put an end to any hopes that Roosevelt would finally throw open America's doors to a substantial number of European Jews . . .

Roosevelt was no stranger to the Jews. In the New York State gubernatorial election of 1928, FDR received more votes from the Jewish community than did his Republican opponent, Albert Ottinger, a Jew, who spent much of the campaign defending himself against charges of insufficient piety lodged by Jews more observant than he. In 1932, Roosevelt got strong Jewish support, collecting at least three Jewish votes to every one of Hoover's. In 1936, Roosevelt got 96 percent of the votes in the nation's most Jewish ward in Chicago's Cook County . . . [9]

By 1935, the government was peppered with young, talented Jews such as Isador Lubin and Charles Wyzanski Jr. (Labor), Robert Nathan (Treasury), Nathan Margold, Abe Fortas, Saul K. Padover, and Felix Cohen (Interior), Jerome Frank (Agriculture), David Lilienthal (TVA), and David K. Niles (WPA). While Roosevelt occasionally turned for advice to Justice Louis Brandeis, the elder statesman of progressivism, the presi-

dent was much closer to Harvard Law professor Felix Frankfurter, to political confidant Benjamin Cohen, who drafted much of the New Deal's critical legislation, and to speechwriter Samuel Rosenman. The latter had joined Roosevelt while FDR was still governor of New York and was responsible, along with Raymond Moley, for the phrase "New Deal." In his cabinet Roosevelt included Henry Morgenthau, Jr., highly respected on Wall Street, as head of the Treasury Department. [10]

Roosevelt did not capitulate to demands stoked by hatemongers, such as Father Charles Coughlin, William Dudley Pelley, and the leadership of the Ku Klux Klan, that he curb the number of Jews in his administration. Haters who referred to his administration as the "Rosenberg Administration" found FDR unruffled. Still, the master politician who had honed his instincts in the same New York Democratic party that included Tammany Hall never permitted his admiration for Jewish talent to cloud his instincts. FDR's Jewish appointments rarely exceeded the realities of the Democratic party's ethnic demography. Of 192 judicial appointments, Roosevelt gave 7 to Jews and 52 to Catholics. Only Morgenthau ever reached a cabinet-level position, and only Abe Fortas, at the Interior Department, reached the rank of an undersecretary. As historian Leonard Dinnerstein has observed, "one's fingers and toes" would be sufficient to count the number of Jews in policy-making positions in the Departments of State, War, Navy, and Commerce, the Federal Reserve Board, the Federal Trade Commission, the U.S. Tariff Commission, and the Board of Tax Appeals. [11]

Moreover, American Jewry could not convert these appointments, nor even their electoral support of Roosevelt, into sufficient pressure to persuade FDR to aid German Jewish refugees during the 1930s. Within weeks of his inauguration, Roosevelt was hearing from prominent Jewish friends and political cronies on the subject. While conversations with Irving and Herbert Lehman, and his personal favorite Felix Frankfurter, succeeded in getting FDR's attention, the results were less than dramatic. Roosevelt shunted the matter into the bureaucracy's hopper. When the refugee question became the subject of a tug-of-war between the State and Labor departments, Roosevelt treated Jewish pleas for a humanitarian gesture as he did all problems for which he had no comfortable solution—with distance. . . .

In April 1933, FDR pursued the same restrictionist immigration policy as his Republican predecessor. He remained aloof as State Department officials such as Undersecretary William Phillips and Assistant Secretary Wilbur Carr tangled with Secretary of Labor Frances Perkins over the refugee issue in 1933. Though both sides sent documents and memoranda to the White House, there is no evidence that the president acted.

Instead, Roosevelt stood to the side and let the pugnacious bureaucrats nip at each others' heels until the attorney general could render an opinion on the legal issues involved, especially the controversial proposal to allow relatives and friends of a refugee to post bonds guaranteeing that the refugee would not become a public charge. In the end, FDR did not respond to New Dealer Perkins's call for a humane, generous refugee policy. He accepted State's strict enforcement of the LPC clause. State's policy enjoyed broad public support and the backing of increasingly important factions in the young New Deal's coalition such as the AFL. The fate of Roosevelt's economic programs and the political viability of the New Deal clearly took precedence over assisting foreign nationals in distress.

Between 1933 and 1936, FDR approached the refugee issue circumspectly. He offered a symbolic

humanitarianism, continuing to meet with Jewish spokesmen but largely in an effort to mollify the American Jewish community without making any promises. Jewish leaders, such as Rabbi Stephen Wise, recognized that stiff congressional opposition to refugee policy reform made Roosevelt wary of the issue. But without the assent of "General Headquarters," as Wise termed the White House, non-Jewish congressional advocates of reform, such as Senators Joseph T. Robinson (D-Arkansas) and Elbert Thomas (D-Utah), were hesitant to raise the politically divisive issue. In the early summer of 1933, the American Jewish Committee and the American Jewish Congress were in rare agreement that a debate on the House floor "could lead to an explosion against us."[12] Wise, both popular and controversial because of his commitment to public protest on behalf of Jewish refugees, had long desired a private audience with Roosevelt. Not until January 1936, however, did the summons to Hyde Park finally come. The president greeted Wise warmly. Known for his monumental ego and pride in being a Washington insider, Wise was charmed by FDR. The rabbi's critics, especially those in the Yiddish press, argued that Wise was duped, co-opted by the wily Roosevelt. One prominent Yiddish journalist suggested that all FDR had to do was place his arm around Wise's shoulder and warmly intone his first name—"Steve, Steve"—and the rabbi was disarmed.[13] . . .

Though Wise may have been even less immune than most to the Roosevelt charm, he did not fail to let Roosevelt know that the State Department's continued lack of cooperation was angering the American Jewish electorate. Using Felix Frankfurter as his pipeline to the Oval Office, Wise warned FDR that failure to act decisively on behalf of Jewish refugees might cause Jewish voters to switch to the Republicans in 1936. Others, such as

Frankfurter and Herbert Lehman, continued to urge Roosevelt to speak out before November.[14]

When Roosevelt finally took public action, it was not to order modification of U.S. immigration policies or procedures. In August 1936, the president spoke out on the need to rebuild Palestine, the Jews' ancient homeland. The following month, he discussed with his cabinet the British intention of curbing the number of Jewish refugees admitted to Palestine. He urged the British not to close the Middle East safety valve. Still, despite the flurry of presidential inactivity regarding the quota system, by late 1936 the word probably reached officials at State that Roosevelt would appreciate some leniency on visa policy administration. By December 1936 refugees were experiencing an unusual easing of consular requirements, especially on matters of documentation and proof of support.

Roosevelt's ringing victory in the 1936 election—60.8 percent of the vote—was a mandate to continue the projects and policies of the first administration. There is no evidence that FDR perceived his reelection as an opportunity to do more and send the Congress a comprehensive immigration reform bill. Public sentiment toward the Jews suggested that such an initiative would be politically risky. A 1937 poll conducted by the American Institute for Public Opinion indicated that 38 percent of those polled thought that antisemitism in the United States was increasing. Another poll conducted almost a year later revealed that, though 81 percent of the sample did not think there would be a "widespread campaign against the Jews in the U.S.," 48 percent did think that the persecution of the Jews in Europe was "partly" their own fault.[15] Even more important, though, by 1937 Roosevelt's own political capital was declining. His hold on Congress was tenuous at best. That summer a group of conservative Democratic senators broke with Roosevelt

to join Republicans in an anti–New Deal bloc. Alienated by FDR's failure to balance the budget and to continue business's recovery, the coalition, which included Vice President John Nance Gardner, sought to frustrate Roosevelt's reform legislation and eventually carry the party away from the New Dealers.[16] Such political circumstances made it even more unlikely that FDR would take the political risk necessary to support liberalization of immigration restrictionism. But Germany's invasion of Austria in March 1938 raised issues that Roosevelt could not avoid. Austrian Jews almost immediately felt the sting of Nazi anti-Jewish policies. Jewish property was seized; some Jews were expelled from the country; still others were dragged off to concentration camps. Lines lengthened at American consulates.

At a cabinet meeting on March 18, 1938, Roosevelt asked his advisors whether the United States could aid Austrian political refugees; he did not single out the Jews for special mention though much of the Nazi abuse was directed at them. Recalling that the United States had been a haven for Germans during the last century, Roosevelt seemed to believe that the United States should again put out the welcome mat. He ordered the combination of German and Austrian quotas to give an increased number of Austrians a chance for an American visa from the unused portion of the German quota, which was considerably larger than Austria's. Roosevelt then asked the cabinet whether a bill he would initiate to increase the quota was likely to pass. Warned that it would not, FDR quickly abandoned the idea.[17] A battle in Congress always involved calling in favors and using up valuable patronage and personal credit. Experienced in legislative duels, the president chose not to fight when he could not win. And there is ample evidence that many congressmen would have been pressured to vote against the president. An Opinion Research Corporation Poll taken in March, the same month as the Anschluss, revealed that 75 percent of the respondents opposed the admission of "a larger number of Jewish exiles from Germany (17 percent were agreeable and 8 percent had no opinion).[18] Instead, FDR announced his intention of coaxing other countries to take from one hundred to one thousand Austrian families each. Any assistance to the Austrian families in need would lighten whatever burden the United States would eventually undertake.

Even those Jewish leaders pressing FDR hardest for action were acutely aware that there were political constraints on Roosevelt. Stephen Wise and others looked on with "amazement and horror" when Congressman Emanuel Celler introduced a bill into Congress that would suspend the quota provisions of the 1924 immigration law for refugee visa applicants. Referring to the bill as "almost . . . the work of an agent provocateur," Wise feared that an anti-immigration backlash would make impossible Roosevelt's intended liberal policies toward the Austrian Jews. The rabbi even quoted his "elevator lad," who said, "'It is all right to take care of the Austrian Jews, but I cannot afford to give up my job for them.'"[19]

Several days after the cabinet meeting on March 18, the president responded to the entreaties of Morgenthau and ordered Sumner Welles to expedite the liberalization of immigration procedures. Welles was also instructed to appeal to Latin America to take some refugees.[20] Roosevelt wanted to go still further in internationalizing the refugee issue. He announced an invitation to other countries to join with the United States in establishing a special international committee to promote and support emigration from Germany and Austria. Roosevelt also suggested that, domestically, the government assist in mobilizing private

organizations that could fund the emigration process. He signed a public appeal to the American people, reminding them of the American tradition of offering asylum to refugees. Roosevelt's only change in the draft Morgenthau prepared was to strike the words "religious" and "racial refugees" and to substitute "political refugees."[21] Even though he wanted to rescue the oppressed, Roosevelt reverted to his symbolic policy, an approach that would cost the United States government little and make few drains on his own political budget. If Hitler found it valuable to publicize the Jewish identity of his victims, Roosevelt found it equally expedient to obscure the religious identity of those he would see rescued. . . .

As usual, Roosevelt's political instincts were on target. Measures of public opinion suggest that even the limited hope his efforts offered refugees was more generous than that which the majority of Americans might have extended. A Fortune poll published the same month that the [Evian] international conference convened reported that two-thirds of the respondents (67.4 percent) agreed that "with conditions as they are we should try to keep them [the refugees] out." Only 18.2 percent took Roosevelt's more moderate attitude that "we should allow them to come but not raise our immigration quotas." Far fewer, 4.9 percent of the sample, wanted to "encourage them to come even if we have to raise our immigration quotas." The other 9.5 percent were apathetic and did not know where they stood on the controversy.[22]

The shattering of glass in the cities and towns of Germany in November 1938, *Kristallnacht*, was heard in even the most apathetic American towns. Press coverage thrust the story before the American public and its reluctant president.[23] FDR was forced to respond. Still, the increasing unpopularity of a remilitarized Germany made Roosevelt's task easier. He could recall Ambassador Hugh Wilson "for consultation" and issue a strongly worded communiqué without apprehensions of a political backlash. Indeed, over 70 percent of those Americans polled on the recall of Wilson favored the move.[24] On November 15, FDR told reporters that he "could scarcely believe that such a thing could occur in twentieth century civilization."[25] Though he still did not modify the quota system, a generous Roosevelt did order the Labor Department to extend the visitors' visas of over 12,000 German Jewish refugees in the United States for another six months. So often had Roosevelt spoken the words and phrases that speechwriter Samuel Rosenman had written for him that the situation almost seemed reversed when Rosenman wrote, "I do not believe it either desirable or practicable to recommend any change in the quota provision of our immigration law."[26] Roosevelt could afford an act of generosity; more would be an extravagance he would not chance. . . .

By late November, Roosevelt had become quite interested in finding alternative plans of refuge for the Jews. He saw colonization as an alternative to Palestine, which the British were jealously guarding. FDR hoped to raise private funds to purchase a sanctuary to accommodate over five million people and become the foundation of a permanent Jewish homeland.[27] Not unlike Lincoln who sought to remedy America's race problems by colonizing slaves and black freedmen abroad, FDR was hoping to relocate an unwanted population. Over the next two years, he considered locations in Africa, Asia, and even Alaska for his colonization plan. Any plan was open to consideration that avoided the public antagonism and congressional opposition that quota revision would likely entail.

After the elections of 1938, FDR could afford even less to antagonize Congress. Worsening economic recession and the anti-New Deal coalition of conservative Democrats and Republi-

cans forged in 1937 had taken their toll at the polls. During the spring of 1938, Roosevelt launched an assault against New Deal opponents in party primaries. In a fireside chat he denounced these "Copperheads," a term borrowed from the Civil War era when it was used by Republicans to describe antiwar, ergo disloyal, Democrats.[28] He then barnstormed the country, speaking in behalf of Democrats loyal to the New Deal and attacking their opponents. But, except for the victories of Alben Barkley and Elmer Thomas in Kentucky and Oklahoma respectively, the trip was a failure. Candidates he supported lost in Georgia, South Carolina, and Maryland. In some states, such as Nevada and Colorado, the president actually avoided open fights with candidates he felt he could not beat. In the November elections, Republicans picked up eighty-one seats in the House, won eight seats in the Senate, and netted thirteen governorships. Despite their gains, the Republicans lost twenty-four of the thirty-two Senate elections. The New Deal was not moribund, but the Republican party was rising from the ashes of 1936. Controversial legislation on immigration was the last thing that most New Dealers in Congress wanted, and there is no evidence that FDR was prepared to take the attendant risks of supporting bills to expand quotas for the refugees.

While the president was thinking of which far-off land would prove both hospitable to the refugees and politically affordable to their benefactors, especially himself, the problem was brought to American shores. In May 1939, the president was presented with a crisis that could not be solved through his favorite technique of management and conflict: 933 passengers of the *St. Louis*, the majority of them Jewish refugees, were seeking a temporary home in Havana, Cuba. Over 700 of them had already applied for American visas, even securing affidavits of support. They wished to await their turn in Havana. When the Cubans denied permission for the ship to dock, the passengers telegrammed FDR for help, informing him that 67 passengers held American quota registration numbers. While diplomats stumbled over technicalities, the president left the telegram unanswered. The *St. Louis* returned to Europe, where only the extraordinary efforts of the Jewish Joint Distribution Committee prevented the passengers from returning to Germany and the likelihood of concentration camps. Roosevelt could have clipped the red tape with an executive order, but by so doing he would have created an extraordinary exception. The passengers adrift did not fit into any standard category—tourist, visitor, or visa-holding immigrant—and exceptions set precedents. The president would not take the risk of alienating the Cubans, perhaps his own State Department, and, most of all, the American public.

Similarly Roosevelt distanced himself from the humanitarian efforts of Senator Robert F. Wagner and Representative Edith Nourse Rogers to legislate refugee rescue. Their bill called for the transfer of 20,000 German children to the United States over a two-year period, in excess of the quota limit. Roosevelt's well-known response to an appeal for presidential endorsement was to scribble "File No Action" on the memorandum.[29] Once again the president accurately assessed the mood in Congress and, beyond that, among the public generally. The bill, emasculated by amendments, died in committee in the summer of 1939. Six months earlier George Gallup's pollsters had determined that 66 percent of the American people opposed the admission of 10,000 refugee children from Germany that year.[30] With another presidential election on the horizon and little amelioration of the hostility to immigrants, Roosevelt must have calculated the costs and benefits of his sup-

port. With the bill likely to lose, he could gain few supporters but lose many votes the following November by endorsing this compassionate but ill-fated and perhaps naive bill, votes that 20,000 youngsters arriving over a two-year period could not repay for many elections to come.

By the fall of 1939, FDR was preoccupied with the war in Europe and the politics of the homefront. The two converged in the threat of fifth column subversives. Throughout 1939 and 1940, the president and millions of other Americans feared that foreign subversives might be planted among the refugees by the warring powers, especially Germany and the Soviet Union. Now national security fears seemed an additional justification for restrictionism. While the president did not wish to alarm Americans unnecessarily, neither did he wish to lull them into a false security.

During the last months of 1939, in the light of national security fears, Roosevelt spoke with fresh enthusiasm about colonization as the only viable solution to the refugee problem. Colonization remained a solution that, when discussed in the abstract, provoked little public opposition, definitely an advantage with another presidential election coming. When Brandeis visited FDR in October 1939, Roosevelt raised the possibility of creating a new agency, a favorite New Deal tactic. This resettlement agency would be headed by Bernard Baruch. Brandeis, less than enthusiastic, commented that "Baruch would be more likely to consider colonization of Jews on some undiscovered planet than Palestine."[31] Roosevelt abandoned the agency idea but maintained an interest in large-scale resettlement schemes.

A month after Brandeis's visit, Roosevelt held extensive talks with Interior Secretary Harold Ickes on the use of Alaska as a refugee sanctuary.[32] Roosevelt was considering settling 10,000 individuals in Alaska, annually, for the next five years. Anticipating the criticism that such an endeavor might create a national enclave of Jews that might resist Americanization, the president had even considered limiting the proportion of Jews to 10 percent of the settlers. Early in 1940, an Alaska colonization act, the King-Havenner bill, was debated in Congress. Under the proposed legislation, refugees between 16 and 45 years of age who qualified for the new jobs that would be created in agriculture, forestry, fishing, mining, and fur farming could come to Alaska outside the immigration quota limits. Wives and children of the refugees would also be allowed to enter. In spite of the many economic benefits that the bill contained for the development of Alaska, the bill died in subcommittee for much the same reasons that the Wagner-Rogers bill failed to reach the floor. Public opposition was vocal, especially in Alaska. Immigration opponents in the forty-eight states saw it as a backdoor to America for refugees. Though Roosevelt was enthusiastic about the Alaska plan, once the bill was introduced the president backed away from it. Undersecretary of State Sumner Welles cautioned the president that the bill's passage would require new laws restricting immigration into the United States from the territory of Alaska. Again Roosevelt would have found himself locked in confrontation with congressional restrictionists. FDR withdrew to the sidelines, still intrigued by the idea of resettlement—especially in Africa. . . .

The plight of Jewish refugees was never a matter demonstrably critical to the national interest. It was a humanitarian issue of limited concern to most Americans, as public opinion polls and congressional opposition to the Wagner-Rogers legislation amply demonstrate. Roosevelt wisely established a dual policy, one restrictionist and the other symbolically humanitarian. He eschewed confrontations that placed him in opposition to

overwhelmingly public sentiment. Restrictionism, on the other hand, seemed very much in the public interest, especially in an era of economic depression. The result was that the issue of visas for Jewish refugees between 1933 and 1940 became bogged down in the bureaucratic machinery.

NOTES

1. John Higham, *Strangers in the Land: Patterns of American Nativism, 1860–1925* (New Brunswick NJ: 1955). See also Higham's essays in *Send These To Me: Jews and Other Immigrants in Urban America* (New York, 1975).

2. Robert A. Divine, *American Immigration Policy, 1924–1952* (New Haven, 1957), 62–63; White House Press Release, September 8, 1930; A. Dana Hodgdon to Undersecretary of State Joseph P. Cotton, September 11, 1930; Cotton to Hodgdon, September 12, 1930; Secretary of State Henry L. Stimson to Secretary of Labor James J. Davis, November 21, 1930; and Assistant Secretary of State Wilbur J. Carr to J. P. Cotton, November 15, 1930, NA RG 59, 150.062 Public Charge (hereafter PC) 8, 9, 44, 45 respectively. These documents also indicate that the State Department was concerned about possible criticism of the new interpretation of the public charge clause.

3. Louis D. Brandeis to Felix Frankfurter, April 29, 1933, Felix Frankfurter Papers, Box 29, Library of Congress (hereafter LC).

4. Frankfurter to Frances Perkins, April 27, 1933, Frances Perkins Papers, Columbia University.

5. "Bureaucracy," in H. H. Gerth and C. Wright Mills, *From Max Weber: Essays in Sociology* (New York, 1971), 224.

6. Herbert A. Strauss, "Jewish Emigration from Germany: Nazi Policies and Jewish Responses (II)," *Leo Baeck Institute Yearbook 26* (1981): 359. David S. Wyman's modification of tabulations by Maurice R. Davie, *Refugees in America* (New York, 1947), 23–24, 27, in Wyman, *Paper*

Walls, 218–19. This is roughly consistent with the National Refugee Service's estimate that almost 210,000 "Hebrew" immigrants and nonimmigrants entered the United States between 1933 and June 30, 1943. If we allow for another 2,000 Jews entering the U.S. between July 1, 1943, and the end of 1944, that would mean that there were roughly 38,000 non-Jewish refugees.

7. Abella and Troper, *None Is Too Many*, vi.

8. The importance of symbolic politics is best described by Murray Edelman, *The Symbolic Uses of Politics* (Urbana, 1964). Recent scholarship suggests that FDR's tax policies, for example, were really two: "one a revenue workhorse, the other a symbolic showpiece." See Mark H. Leff, *The Limits of Symbolic Reform: The New Deal and Taxation, 1933–1939* (Cambridge, 1984), 2–3.

9. Burns, *Roosevelt: The Lion and the Fox*, 104; Lawrence Fuchs, "American Jews and the Presidential Vote," *American Political Science Review* 49 (1955): 385–401; and Dinnerstein, "Jews and the New Deal," 474.

10. Dinnerstein, "Jews and the New Deal"; and Feingold, "'Courage First and Intelligence Second,'" 443–44.

11. Dinnerstein, "Jews and the New Deal," 475.

12. Wise to Frankfurter, June 6, 1933, Wise papers, Box 109, Correspondence—Zionism, AJHS.

13. Simon Weber, interview with Alan M. Kraut, August 17, 1983.

14. Report of a Visit of Dr. Stephen S. Wise to President Roosevelt at Hyde Park, Mon. October 5, 1936 [verbatim transcript, according to Wise's cover letter to Frankfurter, October 6, 1936], Wise Papers, Box 68, Federal Government—Presidential File, AJHS.

15. Hadley Cantril, ed., *Public Opinion, 1935–1946* (Princeton, 1951), 381–82.

16. James T. Patterson, *Congressional Conservatism and the New Deal: The Growth of the Conservative Coalition in Congress, 1933–1939* (Lexington, 1967), 160–63.

17. Morgenthau Diaries, March 22, 1938, vol. 116, FDRL; and Ickes, *Secret Diary*, vol. 2, 342–43. See also Stewart, "United States Policy," 273.

18. This poll was conducted by the Research Opinion Corporation in March 1938. It is cited in Charles Herbert Stember et al., *Jews in the Mind of America* (New York, 1966), 148. A later Opinion Research Corporation poll, commissioned by the American Jewish Committee in May 1938 revealed that 82 percent of the polling sample opposed increased immigration of Jewish refugees. See Chronological File, September-December 1938, American Jewish Committee Archives.

19. Wise to Frankfurter, March 30, 1938, Wise Papers, Box 109, Correspondence-Zionism, AJHS.

20. Moffat Diary, March 21, 22, 1938, Moffat Papers, Houghton Library, Harvard; and Welles to Morgenthau, March 23, 1938, Morgenthau Diaries, vol. 116, FDRL.

21. Morgenthau Diaries, March 18, 1938, vol. 116, FDRL.

22. Stember, *Jews in the Mind of America*, 145.

23. Lipstadt, *Beyond Belief*, 98–109.

24. Cantril, *Public Opinion*, 382.

25. Statement by President, November 15, 1938, reprinted in *Franklin D. Roosevelt and Foreign Affairs* (Clearwater, 1981), 2d ser., vol. 12, 83.

26. Rosenman to FDR, December 12, 1938, President's Personal File, FDRL.

27. FDR Memorandum for the Undersecretary of State, November 26, 1938, OF 20, FDRL; Morgenthau to FDR; and Bowman to FDR, November 21, 25, 29, 1938, President's Secretary's File, Box 177, FDRL.

28. Burns, *Roosevelt: The Lion and the Fox*, 360–61.

29. Morse, *While Six Million Died*, 268; and Stewart, "United States Policy," 527.

30. Stember, *Jews in the Mind of America*, 149.

31. Brandeis discussion with FDR quoted in Alpheur Thomas Mason, *Brandeis: A Free Man's Life* (New York, 1946) and cited in Shafir, "Impact of the Jewish Crisis on American German Relations, 1933–39," vol. 2, 970.

32. Harold L. Ickes, *The Secret Diary of Harold L. Ickes*, vol. 3, *The Lowering Clouds, 1939–1941* (New York, 1954), 56–57. See also Wyman, *Paper Walls*, 102.

France: From Hospitality to Hostility

EUGEN WEBER

From *The Hollow Years*

The more the twentieth century advanced, the more France was to attract foreigners, benefit from them, resent them, reject them. When the century opened, the large, under populated country—only thirty-eight million—counted over a million aliens. Then came the war, the dark swaths it cut, the opportunities it created. Immigration boomed. In 1921 foreigners made up less than 4 percent of the country's population. Ten years later they counted almost double that number. France had become the world's leading host of immigrants, ahead of the United States. In Paris, where in 1921 foreign residents represented 5.3 percent of the capital's population, ten years later they stood at 9.2 percent and accounted for a quarter of all persons arrested by police.[1]

Inevitably, critical voices arose to denounce the dregs of the world flowing into the hexagon, too numerous to assimilate, too barbarous to keep the peace, weighing on the country's jails, on its medical resources, poisoning the race, or using [foreign] gold to buy and parcel out the unspoiled countryside.[2] When in 1928 the perfume millionaire François Coty set out to challenge the established press by bringing out a daily that sold for ten cents instead of twenty-five, his populist *Ami du Peuple* specialized in chauvinism, and the editorial articles that Coty signed were mostly written by a professional antisemite, Urbain Gohier.[3] By 1930 *L'Ami du Peuple* printed a million copies and claimed three million readers. So xenophobia always found a public.

One regular contributor to Coty's papers *L'Ami* and *Le Figaro* was a wild art critic, Camille Mauclair—symbolist, anarchist, and early Dreyfusard reconverted to the antisemitism of his Alsatian parents by hatred of art merchants and of speculators. Mauclair had his work cut out hounding the false esthetics of so-called modern painting, the pictorial Soviet of the Ecole de Paris, the metics [the generic pejorative term for aliens in France] busy spoiling French taste, the importers of hideous Expressionist works, the Jews (Kisling, Chagall, Pascin, Soutine, Lipchitz), half Jews (Picasso!), Masons, Communists (Signac), and other Bolshevik agents. "One really does not have to be xenophobic," he explained in *Les Métèques contre l'art français* (1930), "to feel concern at the growing number of metics who, brandishing a naturalization certificate whose ink is scarcely dry, install themselves in France to judge our artists without an intimate sense of our race....[4]

Reducing the foreign workforce was a mainstream proposal. One of Blum's trusted aides, Georges Monnet, Socialist deputy of the Aisne and future minister of agriculture under the Popular Front, joined Edouard Herriot and many others in calling for quotas, which parliament voted by 1932. Right- and left-wing governments had encouraged immigration. Now they encouraged outmigration. Some 43,000 foreigners left France in 1930; they would be 93,000 in 1931, 108,000 in 1932. In the five years after 1931 half a million foreigners left the country; the number of foreign residents in Paris shrank by over a third.[5]

Some of the shrinkage was due to the rising level of naturalizations, which provoked as much revulsion as did the alleged burden of aliens themselves. In 1927 a newly passed law had simplified the Byzantine process of naturalization. Many took advantage of the new facilities: ten times as many in the eight years beginning 1927 as in the eight years before that. By 1936, 70 percent of naturalized French citizens had got their papers in the decade since 1927. How really French were they? How French were they perceived to be? When in 1935 the newly elected Miss France turned out to be a recently naturalized young German, Mlle. Pitz, "hostile reactions" persuaded the winner to resign. Her title went to the runner-up, Mlle. Giselle Préville. "*Miss France sera française!*"[6]

All along the line the professional classes rebelled against foreign competition. Students flowed into France, many from Eastern Europe, graduated from law or medical faculties, then stayed on in the country to undercut good French lawyers, or more especially doctors, and steal their practices. In 1934 access to the French bar was regulated; naturalized foreigners were prevented from practicing law for ten years after becoming French. In 1939 the Paris Faculty of Letters counted 28 percent foreign students, the Faculty of Medicine 34 percent. One medical student in three came from abroad; too many planned to stay. With one doctor for every 1,650 inhabitants France was seventeenth in the world of medical rankings, way behind the United States with one doctor per 753 inhabitants or the UK with one per 822 inhabitants. But the profession clamored for protection against foreign invasion of a field it described as overcrowded, and the Right, always strong in medicine, pressed the case. In winter 1935 the *Action Française* called for a strike in medi-

cal faculties, to exclude foreigners from competition for internships or externships, prohibit them from temporarily replacing interns, [and] prohibit doctors naturalized for less than ten years from practicing at all. *Je Suis Partout* (February 9, 1935) denounced "*Les métèques médecins*"; the Latin Quarter erupted in its high-spirited fashion ("*A bas les métèques! La France aux Français!*"). In summer 1935 the exercise of medicine—already hedged in 1933—was further limited, medical and dental practice restricted to naturalized foreigners who had performed their military service in the French Army.[7] . . . These restrictive laws were among the few measures that the general public was able to extract from its elected representatives, and "it was only in suspicion and hostility" that a relative national unanimity was realized.[8] . . .

The Jewish population of France, less than ninety thousand at the turn of the century, had more than doubled by 1930 and stood around three hundred thousand in 1939.[9] Yet even at its highest the proportion of Jews in a French population forty-one million strong remained unimpressive: about 0.7 percent. Most of the French never saw a Jew or wouldn't know one if they saw him, but few, if challenged in 1930, would lack a view of Jews. Churchgoing Catholics knew them as the people who killed the Son of God—a faux pas of which Easter Week provided annual reminders. The urban populace, especially in Paris, connected them with capitalism and capitalist exploitation or else with low-paid competition that cut even closer to the bone. But there was too—above all— the diffuse prejudice that a well-informed Jesuit described as "antisemitism of principle—latent and quite general."[10] One did not have to hate Jews to think ill of them, to prefer to avoid them, and, of course, not to want one's offspring to marry one. Emmanuel Berl remembered the father of a girl he courted who would not want her to marry him because he was Jewish, "but he would not have wanted him if his father had been a dentist or a bailiff . . . antisemitism had a certain innocence."[11]

Many well-known intellectuals quite innocently reflected their negative image of Jews on one level or another: André Gide, François Mauriac, Romain Rolland, Georges Duhamel. . . . Some probably had honed their prejudice abroad, like Paul Morand, who married a Romanian, Princess Soutzo; some, like Paul Léautaud and Marcel Jouhandeau, spilled bile on Jews among many others; some fitted native stereotypes into their writings, like Georges Simenon, many of whose minor unpleasant characters are Jewish; some, like Jacques Feyder or Robert Brasillach, resented Jewish success greater than their own; some—Brasillach again—let homosexuality drive them into the arms of Rexists and of Nazis; some, like Marcel Arland, found antisemitic criticism good in parts, just like the curate's egg; some, like Edmond Jaloux, didn't much blame the Germans, explaining "that the Jews had taken all the money in Germany and kept the Germans from living."[12]

Reasons or rationalizations there were many. Yet it all came down to one thing. For Jean Giraudoux, as for so many others, the Jews were not as other French; they were not French whatever passport they might carry; they were simply "other." They also—whatever the exceptions—did not belong at certain levels of society or of administration, which may be why in 1930, when Jean Filippi passed the competitive examination to the Financial Inspectorate, of nineteen "admissible" candidates, one who had been well placed in preparation was simply excluded for his Jewishness.[13] That was our Jesuit Father Joseph Bonsirven's "antisémitisme de principe," latent and mostly dormant when not challenged. But it took little to stir the embers.

The Right, of course, had been actively associated with antisemitism since the 1880s. In 1930 the main antisemitic rag of those far-off days, *La Libre Parole*, was revived: a straw in the wind. In 1931 Georges Bernanos, Catholic dropout of the *Action Française*, reburnished the memory of Edouard Drumont, France's antisemitic pope. But where the Right led, the Left was not slow to follow. Antisemitism offered licit opportunities for xenophobia and patriotic ire that did only modest violence to internationalism. Jews had long been the resident aliens par excellence. In France they were associated with the German enemy. War had exacerbated chauvinism, and Jews were its first and most obvious focus. In 1920, for example, the afflux of Jews fleeing East European upheavals coincided with a plague epidemic that made fifteen victims in the poorer parts of Paris. Socialist and royalist legislators agreed in blaming Jewish refugees for turning the capital into a nest of microbes; the Communist *Humanité*, the radical *OEuvre*, joined the carping chorus.[14]

When, in 1923, Emile Delavenay left his native Savoy for the Lycée Louis-le-Grand in Paris to prepare for the competitive entrance examination of the *Ecole Normale Supérieure*, he was struck by the aggressive antisemitism that some of his fellow students showed. Attending the Lycée Montaigne a few years later, the future Cardinal Lustiger, son of poor Polish immigrants who always spoke French badly, had to face fights and insults because he was "a dirty Jew." Yet at a girls' lycée a student from Martinique "with skin the color of coffee with very little milk" was tormented and ostracized worse than any Jewess. Being Jewish simply made tricky situations worse.[15]

Jews were not especially prominent among the foreigners that flowed to Paris in the 1920s. Good Frenchmen could focus their prejudices as easily on Ruritanians or on Yankees. Bécassine, at Clocher-les-Bécasses, was shocked by the parakeet accent of a South American *Rastat-quéros*; a slightly more sophisticated observer, Paul Morand, objected to the flood tide of Cubans and Brazilians. . . . And when the more or less financial, more or less conservative *Petit Bleu* denounced the strange foreign faces filling the terraces of Montparnasse cafés, its description, explicit enough, nevertheless avoided specifying to whom "the circumflex noses, overdark hair, coppery skin," belonged.[16]

Then, early in 1933, Germany went over to Nazism, and by the end of the year over twenty thousand Germans had sought refuge in France. Between 1933 and 1939 some fifty-five thousand Germans passed through the country—not many compared with the more numerous representatives of other nationalities, but a bone of contention in those contentious times. Many of the exiles had an international reputation: Heinrich Mann, Lion Feuchtwanger, Alfred Döblin, Bertolt Brecht. Others, like Walter Benjamin, Arthur Koestler, Hannah Arendt, and Giselle Freund, whose camera was her only fortune, were going to acquire one. Numbers remained small: twenty-five thousand or so year in year out, about one third of them in Paris; and Jews represented less than one third of that until 1938.[17]

Their output was prodigious. Concerts, ballets, public lectures sprinkle the contemporary press but cannot hold a candle to the printed word. Between 1933 and 1939 about three hundred books by exiled German authors were to be translated into French, besides a mass of articles in French newspapers and periodicals. Albrecht Betz, who studied their activities, has counted a remarkable yearly average of forty books and two hundred articles in France during these years. More relevantly, most of these were oriented to the Left, whether Socialist or Communist, which meant

that the politics of German emigration melded with the internal politics of France. Even Lion Feuchtwanger, better known for his historical novels, published *Moscou 1937*, the story of his trip to Russia that detailed the comforts and joys he and his wife had discovered in the land of the future. For the intellectuals whom German nationalism had rejected, the modern world and modern civilization began with the French Revolution, with the rights of man the Revolution had proclaimed, with the democracy to which its heirs aspired. . . . No wonder that conservatives of all stripes, however disgusted by Hitler's treatment of dissenters and Jews, did not want to see the ill treated taking refuge in their country. No wonder that the governments of a Third Republic already riven by dissension did not want it aggravated by more sources of mischief. By fall of 1933 the first sympathy had waned; the refugees' welcome had cooled to more restrictive policies. Official statistics show that 616 political refugees were expelled or refused admission in 1933 alone.[18]

As the years passed, Jewish and refugee became synonymous: "[F]irst one, then ten, then a hundred, then fifty thousand . . . Paris absorbs them all." Paris was turning into a New Zion, insinuated Paul Morand, into Canaan-on-the-Seine, suggested *Candide*, while *Candide's* more vociferous sidekick, *Je Suis Partout*, spread alarm about "Foreigners in France," "The Exodus of Israel," and "France Invaded." France, Paul Morand made one of his Jewish characters rejoice, had become "God's own concentration camp" for Jews who, no sooner sheltered, knew only to cause trouble for their hosts.[19]

"Invasion" was a favorite image, and though most German Jews only used France as a staging area before moving on, their German associations served them ill. For Emile Buré, Clemenceau's old associate of *L'Aurore*, now master of his own republican and nationalist publication, *L'Ordre*, the immigrants were "the Uhlans of German revenge." And why not? As François Coty pointed out in his *Figaro*, if French Jews claimed to be French, German Jews could hardly claim they were not German. Curiously this seemed to be borne out by the way some Jews behaved. In her contribution to the multiauthored *La France et l'Allemagne 1932–1936*, Rita Thälman mentions one German Jew—Alfred Rosenthal—distributing Nazi films like *Horst Wessel*, another—Samuel, better known as Lucien Leuman—who used his position as publicity director of a film company to aid Nazi propaganda in France, and a third, the American Walter Ruthmann, whom she describes as an agent of Goebbels.[20]

Of course, reactions to the refugees varied widely. When, in 1933, Albert Einstein decided not to return to Berlin, the French government at the behest of the minister of education, Anatole de Monzie, created for him a chair of mathematical physics at the Collège de France. We know that Einstein went to Princeton instead, but the offer of a chair at France's premier institution of higher learning had evoked almost unanimous approval. The only false note came from the likes of Coty, who denounced him as an agent of the international Jewish-Bolshevik conspiracy, like his patron Monzie, "the most active agent of the Soviets in France." Coty was thinking of Einstein's reluctant involvement in 1932 with Henri Barbusse's world antiwar congress, which the physicist criticized as a waste of time and from which he dissociated himself when he learned it was Communist-dominated. But Einstein was indeed for peace, as he was against fascism. His pacifism, his antifascism, his Jewishness would have got him into hot water had he not sensibly opted to leave Europe for the United States.[21]

Not all Jewish refugees were Einsteins; not all French observers were Cotys. Some traditional-ists objected to wealth or vulgarity far more than they did to Jewishness. Some sympathized with Jewish victims of German barbarism because their oppressors were German. Some good Catholics like the Comte Jean de Pange, hoped Hitler was less awful than he seemed while they also tried to defend his prey. But most attempts to evoke sympathy for Jews abutted on stubborn prejudice: Anti-antisemitism simply did not sell.[22] Paul Morand's *France la doulce*, first published in the leftish weekly *Marianne* in 1933, then as a book by Gallimard in 1934, turns about a French film industry colonized by interlopers. The film producers are all foreign—Jews, Greeks, Romanians, Armenians—and ignorant of French or Western culture. But they know their business. The German Jew, to take one example, rejects the idea of a film friendly to Jews because it would not sell in Germany and would prefer an antisemitic script with more public appeal.

If antisemitism sold better, and increasingly well with time, that was less because Jewish numbers grew in some frightening fashion (we have seen they did not) than because Jews became associated in the public mind first with disturbances of the peace, then with directly threatening the cause of peace itself.

Stephen Schuker has pointed out how "recent Jewish immigrants . . . belonged to Communist-affiliated groups that appeared to be sapping the State from within." Many of them had come not from Germany—whose Jews dressed and behaved in "respectable" fashion—but from farther east, where both Jewishness and antisemitism were more obtrusive and crass. Many of the poorer, less Orthodox immigrants from Poland picked up their political training in rough left-wing schools. They suspected the "Jewish fascism" of middle-class French Jews and preferred to emphasize the worldwide war against working-class oppression rather than "the insignificant struggle between Germans and Jews." Eastern Jews spoke Yiddish and joined Communist cells. The Yiddish Workers' Theater put on "revolutionary" plays; Yiddish schools and choirs sang songs like "We are workers' children . . . our father is on strike: the police fires on workers in the streets . . . when I grow up I'll be a hero, a soldier, a Communist." The *Croix Angévine* did not have to tell the truth in order to sound plausible when it claimed that metics predominated among the Communists demonstrating in February 1934. But Jews represented a further menace still. Militant Jews, more aggressive than their native fellows because more desperate, "actively campaigned for a boycott against goods from Nazi Germany and proselytized in favor of various forms of intervention to aid their persecuted brethren abroad."[23] Scarcely a way to endear themselves to French pacifists, and a perfect excuse for xenophobes to argue that foreigners whose own legal position in France was in doubt were trying to embroil the country in their private quarrels.

Symbol of this dangerous drift was Leon Blum, head of the Socialist party and, after the elections of 1936, of the French government, too. Some Blumophobes, of whom there were many and of many kinds, attacked the Socialist leader as a warmonger. In fact, he had spent most of his early career arguing for moral disarmament and leading his party in voting against defense budgets. That did not prevent his enemies from denouncing his antifascism as aggressive and his politics as likely to lead to war. It stood to reason: Blum was Jewish; Jews wanted war. *Candide* called on the French to oppose the war Blum wished to wish on them; *Je Suis Partout* illustrated the grave of Private Durand, killed in the coming war: "Died for ~~France~~ Israel."[24] Such views were not limited to the Right. Raymond Abellio, then active on the Left, makes clear that the anti-Nazism and the

"bellicism" of Blum and of his—often Jewish—friends were attributed by more steadfastly pacifist comrades to Semitic prejudice. Semitism and bellicism appeared to coincide; so, increasingly, would antibellicism and antisemitism. Like the pacifist wing of the Socialist party ranged behind Paul Faure, a growing portion of the Left came to associate its search for peace with opposition to Jewish warmongering.[25]

By 1936 Alain himself, the peaceful rationalist, assumed that all German refugees "preached Holy War. If it breaks out under Blum, antisemitism will rule in France. . . . Beyond this double fanaticism, I see no possibility of war. . . ." For Alain, the Jewish fanatic and the anti-Jewish fanatic were as one. For many others, anti-Jewish fanatics presented no particular problem; Jewish ones were a present threat. As *L'Echo de la Nièvre* complained, it was just the foreigners who fled their own country like cowards who were most obstinate in pressing their foolish hosts to battle. "They, of course, would stay behind, providing company for French women. . . ." "Don't defend Benda, don't defend Blum," wrote André Suarès to Jean Paulhan. "When war breaks out, civil or foreign, you will see an explosion of antisemitism and they will be largely responsible for it."[26]

By 1938, when Suares traced his lines, antisemitism was exploding—precisely because old prejudices were stirred up by new fears. The more disturbing the apprehensions of war, the livelier the gossip about Jews working to stir fear and hatred. During the Munich crisis rumors of Jews secretly working for war were particularly rife. There were demonstrations against the Jews in Paris and in provincial centers like Lyons, Dijon, and Epinal; Jewish shop windows were smashed; foreign-looking individuals were attacked in the streets. Near the Gare de l'Est two Jews speaking Yiddish were surrounded by a hostile crowd accusing them of defending Hitler; in working-class Belleville two immigrants alleged to have cried, "Long live Hitler! Long live Germany!" got away by the skin of their teeth; other Jews were charged with inciting young people to avoid mobilization. The hostile crowds—and apparently police, too—were using Jews as mirror images of their own discontent.[27]

Emmanuel Bed remembered Céline's explaining his father's business failure, which led the old man to blame Jesuits and Jews: "*Crois-tu qu'il était con!*" Then, in 1937, came *Bagatelles pour un massacre*, and in 1938 *L'Ecole des cadavres*—paroxysms of fear and loathing for those who, in Céline's eyes, were leading France back into carnage. The democracies wanted war, they would have it, and the Jews had drugged and dragged them into it. "War for the bourgeoisie was shitty enough; but now war for the Jews."[28] Desperate, exasperated, outrageous, torrential, frenzied, raging, Céline was as ferocious as he was frantic—snarling, ranting, roaring, sneering, spitting his fury, his spite, his bile, too malignant to be funny, too excessive to be taken seriously, untranslatable, untranslated, and yet reviewed with the sort of respect a professional deserved when unbalanced, with the sort of detachment that suggests that, by then, almost nothing shocked. In the *Nouvelle Revue française*, Marcel Arland regretted the excessive tone of *Bagatelles*: A little more equity and nuance and the book's indictment (of a society hopelessly tainted by black and Jewish blood) would have been more effective.[29]

Col. François de La Rocque, who opposed the anti-Jewish tendencies of some *Croix de Feu*, was savaged for it by the *Action Française* and by some of his more militant adherents. Pope Pius XI, who, in September 1938, declared antisemitism "inadmissible," was ignored by many faithful, including the Assumptionist Fathers of *La Croix*. Who could blame them when the grim prayer *Pro perfidis Judaeis* [for the perfidious Jews] continued to impress the faithful on Good Fridays?[30] It would be only in April 1939 that a decree-law prohibited incitements to hatred for reasons of religion or race.[31] Six months before that, almost coincident with Hitler's *Kristallnacht*, the activities of resident aliens had been restricted, the hunt for the arrest and expulsion of illegal aliens had become more urgent. One has the impression that by late 1938 and early 1939 antisemitism had become endemic.

NOTES

1. Ralph Schor, *L'Opinion française et les étrangers, 1919–1935* (1985), 34–35; André Kaspi and Antoine Marès, *Le Paris des étrangers* (1989), 14–15, 30.
2. See Jean-José Frappa, *A Paris sous l'oeil des métèques* (1926), 206 and passim; *Le Matin*, January 1926, for series on "Paris, l'hospice du monde"; *Paris-Soir*, January 9, 10, 1930.
3. See Urbain Gohier, *Paroles d'un Français* (1930), 279–87: "La France aux barbares." Schor, *L'Opinion*, 179, calls *L'Ami du Peuple's* contents an anthology of xenophobia.
4. Camille Mauclair, *L'Ami du Peuple*, August 15, 1929; Mauclair, *Les Métèques*, 10, 111, 141, 146; also his *Crise de l'art modern* (1944). Novelist, poet, journalist, and critic, Mauclair (1872–1945), who had been a friend of Mallarmé's and one of the first supporters of Dreyfus, turned racist and antisemitic in the late 1920s and collaborated under the Occupation.
5. Georges Mauco, *Les Etrangers en France* (1932), 543; Kaspi, Marès, *Paris*, 18; Schor, *L'Opinion*, 366, 603; Henri Noguères, *La Vie quotidienne au temps du Front populaire* (1977), 78. Pierre Hamp, *Braves Gens de France* (1939), 189, 192, comments harshly on foreigners (like Dr. Roubinoff, an exploitative crook) who come to practice in France with insufficient training. More convinc-

ingly, Erich Maria Remarque's *Arch of Triumph* (New York, 1945) turns about the Paris life of a highly qualified German surgeon exploited by his French colleagues. Ravic, Remarque's hero, has no papers and no license to practice in France, but Paris doctors are only too glad to have him do their work for a pittance and leave to them the credit and the gain.

6. Schor, *L'Opinion*, 562, 584.

7. Ponty, *Polonais*, 317; *Etudes démographiques: Les Naturalisations en France* (1942), 45; *Echo de Clamecy*, June 1, 1935.

8. Schor, *L'Opinion*, 611, 724.

9. Schor, *L'Opinion*, 613.

10. Quoted in ibid., 182. Late-nineteenth-century antisemitism had capitalized on dormant prejudice; the Dreyfus Affair had publicized and spread it; the comradeship of the war had stilled it; economic crisis brought all the old stereotypes out again.

11. Berl, *Interrogatoire par Patrick Modiano* (1976), 17.

12. Paul Morand, *Bucarest* (1935), 160–61; Paul Léautaud, *Journal littéraire 12* (1962): 50, 57, 116, 213; Marcel Jouhandeau, *Comment je suis devenu antisémite* (1936–39); Pierre Assouline, *Simenon* (1992), 277, 285; Simenon, *Les Caves du Majestic* (1939); for Brasillach, Dominique Arban, *Je me retournerai souvent* (1990), 68–69, and Geraldi Leroy, in *Intellectuels des années 30* (1989), 256; for Arland, see Louis-Albert Revah, *Julien Benda* (1991), 234, and *Nouvelle Revue française*. February 1, 1938, 303–10; for Jaloux, *Journal de l'abbé Mugnier* (1985), 573.

13. Jacques Body, *Giraudoux et l'Allemagne* (1975), 329–30; AO, Jean Filippi, 1, 1.

14. Schor, *L'Opinion*, 79.

15. Emile Delavenay, *Témoignage* (Aix-en-Provence, 1992), 73; Jean-Marie Cardinal Lustiger, *Dare to Believe* (New York, 1986), 39; Susan Zuccotti, *The Holocaust, the French and the Jews* (New York, 1993), 23.

16. *Semaine de Suzette*, December 20, 1934; Paul Morand, *France la Doulce* (1934), 51; *Petit Bleu*, May 9, 1932.

17. Michael Marrus and Robert Paxton, *Vichy France and the Jews* (New York, 1981), 36; Albrecht Betz, *Exil et engagement* (1991), 89–92.

18. Betz, op. cit., 109; *Emigrés français en Allemagne: Emigrés allemands en France 1685–1945* (1983), 129. Reading Arthur Koestler's memoirs of those years, one realizes how many of the more visible and audible exiles were Communists or Communist sympathizers and how many anti-Fascist associations functioned as Communist fronts. *The Invisible Writing* (London, 1954), 198, 231, and passim.

19. Morand, *France*, 48, 129; *Candide*, January 25, 1934; *Je Suis Partout*, April 22 and 29, 1933, October 13, 1934, February 9, 1935.

20. Buré in *L'Ordre*. March 8, 1933; Coty in *Figaro*. April 2, 1933; Thälmann in *La France et L'Allemagne 1932–1936* (1980), 169. The Jewish "invasion" was also featured in a series of articles by Raymond Millet, published by the authoritative *Le Temps* in spring 1938 and reprinted by the author under the title *Trois millions d'etrangers en France* (1938).

21. Harry Paul, ms., "Science on the Right," 16; *Figaro*. May 18, 1933, "Le Communisme au Collège de France"; and press comment in *OEuvre*. April 10 and 13, 1933; *Echo de Paris*. April 19, 1933; *Echo de la Nièvre*. April 22, 1933. As Thomas Glick and his contributors have shown in *The Comparative Reception of Relativity* (Boston, 1987), 113, 137, and passim, Einstein's theories did not receive a warm welcome among the French scientific community.

22. Jean de Pange, *Journal* (1965) II, 261, April 1, 1933, and 268, April 15, 1933: "Hitler? Lui faire crédit."

23. Stephen Schuker, *Jews in Modem France* (Hanover NH 1985), 145, 170; Weinberg, *Les Juifs* 52, 157; *Croix Angévine*. February 11 and 18, 1934.

24. *Candide*. October 10, 1935; *Action française*. August 22, 1936; *Je Suis Partout*. July 17, 1939. Thus *L'Ami du Peuple*, November 20, 1933: "The metics of the Judeo-Masonic Revolutionary International who live at our expense and abuse our hospitality . . . may lead us straight to the most

awful war where France would fight on behalf of Israel."

25. Raymond Abellio, *Ma dernière mémoire* 3 (1980): 48–49; *Je Suis Partout*, August 7, 1938. Not just the Left either. In *François de Wendel en République* (1976), 549, Jean-Noël Jeanneney shows the great industrialist inclined to discount warnings of Nazi menace and rising German power when these came from Jews. If his friend and political ally Georges Mandel supports the British alliance, Wendel asks himself in the mid-1930s, is he not being carried away "by his Jewish hatred against Germany"?

26. Alain, *Correspondance avec Elie et Florence Halévy* (1958), 311, August 6, 1936; *Echo de la Nièvre,* September 24, 1937; *Correspondance Jean Paulhan et André Suarès, 1925–1940* (1987), 208–9, November 19, 1938; Thus in May 1938 Emile Roche, the influential director of the Radical *République*, wrote his friend and patron Joseph Caillaux that the "Franco-Russian" supporters of Czechoslovakia were simply out to sink Hitler, who was "guilty only of having put German Jews in concentration camps, for the motor of all this campaign, if it is Russian, is also Jewish." Emile Roche, *Avec Joseph Caillaux* (1980), 187. Uncompromising humanist and rationalist, Julien Benda (1867–1956) was a prominent and prolific figure perhaps best known for his *Trahison des clercs* (1927), which denounces the mobilization of passions as political forces and the descent of intellectuals into the political arena, where they abandon higher principles that it is their mission to defend for short-term intoxications.

27. Marrus and Paxton, *Vichy France*, 40; Weinberg, *Les Juifs*, 212–23. Hostility to Jews also grew because Jewish entries from Poland and other nearby countries where antisemitism grew steadily worse were becoming more numerous, and illegal entries may have outnumbered legal ones. Ponti, *Polonais.* 319, estimates eighty to ninety thousand by 1939. Poles in general did not have a good press in the fall of 1938, when Polish miners in the Nord were credibly reported to have paraded with shouts of "Heil Hitler!" Gillet and Hilaire, *De Blum*, 202. Ponty, 346, refers to similar reports and rumors in many parts of France.

28. Berl and Modiano, *Interrogatoire*, 126; Céline, *Bagatelles*, 86; *L'Ecole*, 25.

29. Arland, *Nouvelles Rome française*, February 1, 1938, 303–10; Jacqueline Morand, *Les Idées politiques de Louis-Ferdinand Céline* (1972), 47, plausibly links Céline's paranoiac pacifism and his equally paranoiac antisemitism.

30. Maurice Pujo, *Comment La Rocque a trahi* (1938) and the anonymous, undated *La Rocque et les juifs*; Pierre Pierrard, *Juifs et Catholiques Français* (1970), 273, for the Pope's explicit words, which probably explained Céline's dubbing Achille Ratti "Isaac Ratisch."

31. It was under the provisions of this so-called Marchandeau decree, named after the minister of justice who signed it, that some of the more antisemitic portions of Drieu La Rochelle's *Gilles* were censored in October 1939 and only restored under Vichy. The integral edition of the work would be published in 1942.

The Unreceptive British Empire

LOUISE LONDON

From *Whitehall and the Jews, 1933–1948*

The year 1905 saw Britain take the first step in creating its modern system of immigration control. Prior to this time, immigration itself was not subject to legal controls, although records were kept of immigrant landings.[1] The Aliens Act 1905 was designed to stem the influx of Jews from eastern Europe. It introduced port controls, operated by immigration officers who inspected aliens on arrival. The new controls were highly selective. The vast majority of alien passengers were not subject to inspection. The act's inspection provisions applied only to aliens travelling steerage class, used by the poorest passengers, and then only on a ship carrying more than a specified number, in practice twenty, of alien passengers in that class. So small groups of steerage class passengers escaped inspection. No cabin class passengers were inspected. Aliens subject to inspection had to pass a poverty test. Failure made them liable to be refused entry as "undesirable immigrants."[2] The mad, the diseased, and the criminal were also to be excluded. Aliens refused leave to land had a right of appeal to Immigration Boards.

Concern to preserve the United Kingdom's tradition of granting refuge led to the inclusion in the 1905 act of a limited concession for asylum seekers. It took the form of an exemption from refusal on grounds of poverty. The exemption was confined to refugees seeking entry solely to avoid prosecution or punishment on religious or political grounds or for an offence of a political character, or persecution, involving danger of imprisonment or danger to life or limb, on account of religious belief.[3] No mention was made of racial persecution or religious persecution that fell short of endangering liberty, life or limb. . . .

In 1919 both the right of appeal to Immigration Boards against refusal of leave to land and the provision exempting refugees from the poverty test were abolished. No trace of legal protection for refugees remained on the statute book. . . . Home Office discretion, then, was the only hope left to refugees. The British tradition of asylum still counted for something, despite having no legal basis. It was invoked repeatedly during the years of Nazi persecution. The government would assert that British policy remained in accordance with tradition as far as possible. Its critics would counter that the humanitarian claims of refugees were not satisfied by treating them no worse than other foreigners. Aliens were, after all, now subject to the most stringent controls.[4]

In truth, the basis of policy had changed beyond recognition since prewar days. Britain was no longer a country of immigration. Strict controls on aliens were now the rule. Entry leading to permanent settlement was restricted to two categories of foreigners only: those whose presence offered some benefit to the country or people with strong personal or compassionate grounds. . . .

All passengers required passports or other papers establishing nationality and identity from the time of the First World War onward. The War Office's Military Intelligence Department ran an elaborate system of surveillance of alien passports by means of visas. After the war, the government decided to continue the visa system for security purposes as well as for immigration control. A visa is a form of entry clearance. This means that, where a visa is a prerequisite of entry, anyone arriving at a port without one is normally refused admission. In the interwar years, aliens from designated foreign countries, whatever the purpose of their journey, needed to obtain visas at a British post abroad before setting out. A visa was issued, on payment of a prescribed fee, provided the alien's plans complied with the Aliens Order and there were no personal objections. Normally, visa decisions were made on the spot by passport control officers (PCOs), who were responsible to the Passport Control Department (PCD) of the Foreign Office but received their instructions, in effect, from the home secretary.[5] . . .

From 1933 onward the immigration of Jewish refugees from Germany to Britain was controlled by a partnership between the Home Office and voluntary committees. The most significant of these organizations were the Jewish Refugees Committee (JRC) and its associated funding bodies, set up by Anglo-Jewish leaders in response to the first wave of refugees in the spring of 1933. The Jewish organization undertook the management of the refugee influx and underwrote its costs. Having shouldered these risks and responsibilities, Jewish leaders also expected to have a say on refugee admissions. Indeed, they made several important interventions which led the Home Office to adjust its approach to the Jewish refugees" cases. But the crucial aspect of the relationship was the advantage it offered the government. Over these years, the government came to rely on the Jewish insurance against any risk to public funds when considering applications from Jews from Germany. This arrangement required no for-

mal changes in the established system of control. Nor did the government commit itself to a policy of granting asylum. Indeed, it believed that keeping refugee policy to a minimum was a way of avoiding unwelcome obligations to refugees. Practice and policy both evolved, but in a piecemeal way, the product of the pressures of the moment and decisions on particular cases. . . .

Refugees from Germany, most of them Jews, started to arrive at British ports at the end of January 1933. The immigration authorities reported that up to 400 Germans, most of whom were thought to be Jews, had been admitted as visitors by March 30. A handful had been denied entry; refusals stood at fewer than ten. Then, in early April, a further 150 or so entered in just three days.[6] These figures were unsettling for the Home Office, not only because of the dramatic increase, but also because of the financial implications.

British policy toward the refugees revolved around the issue of finance. On April 5, 1933, Home Secretary Sir John Gilmour raised refugee matters in the Cabinet for the first time . . . He explained that, although most of the Jews entering under the Aliens Act were "persons of the professional classes on temporary visits," some were "Jews who were completely destitute."[7] The Home Office wished to give a speedy response to an initiative from Jewish leaders that appeared to remove the risks entailed in admitting destitute Jews. The Jewish leaders were offering a guarantee that the Jewish community would undertake responsibility for refugees. Gilmour said that representatives of the Jewish community had visited the Home Office "with a scheme to provide money and work for destitute Jews."[8] They were also asking whether controls could be relaxed to ease the entry of refugees.[9] Ministers agreed to set up a new Cabinet committee chaired by the home secretary to examine the Jewish proposals. . . .

The Jewish proposals were set out in a document signed by Neville Laski KC, president of the London Committee of Deputies of British Jews, better known as the Board of Deputies, Lionel L. Cohen KC, chairman of the Board's Law, Parliamentary and General Purposes Committee, Leonard G. Montefiore, president of the Anglo-Jewish Association, and Otto Setoff. The most important element in its seven short paragraphs was the guarantee that no refugee would become a burden on public funds: "all expense, whether temporary or permanent accommodation or maintenance, will be borne by the Jewish community without ultimate charge to the state."[10] The guarantee was open-ended. No limit was set on the numbers to whom it would apply, but it was not designed to lead to long-lasting commitments.

Jewish leaders intended the refugees' stay to be temporary. Re-emigration played a crucial part in their proposals. They stated that negotiations were in progress "with a view to the ultimate transmigration of the refugees to countries other than England." The community would look after refugees, from the moment they landed until their eventual departure. Representatives of the Jews' Temporary Shelter (JTS) would meet all continental trains. The authorities were asked to telephone with advance details of Jewish refugee arrivals. Emergency accommodation had been secured for up to 500 at the JTS and other hostels. More permanent homes would be found among the Jewish community. An organizing committee chaired by Schiff would supervise the new arrangements. The illiberal proposal that it be made a condition of entry that newly arrived refugees register at the JTS was not taken up by the government.[11] The package of proposals bore the hallmark of the Anglo-Jewish tradition, in which charitable aid to poor Jewish migrants went hand in hand with minimizing the embarrassment they caused.

However, the grand commitment of the guarantee was without precedent.

In return, Jewish leaders wished the government to throw open its doors. First, as the Home Office reported, they asked, "that all German Jewish refugees from Germany should be admitted without distinction." Secondly, "those already admitted for the purpose of visits or who may be admitted in the future should be allowed during the present emergency to prolong their stay indefinitely."[12]

These requests bristled with difficulties. The government was being asked to bestow a new right of asylum on all German Jewish refugees. Moreover, the Jewish guarantee, while open-ended, was aimed at emergency admissions on a temporary basis. The Jewish request that the government allow open-ended admissions in return confused the matter of temporary versus indefinite stays. The Home Office warned that further admissions could lead to the presence of a considerable number of German Jews who wished to remain indefinitely. In theory, the Home Office could refuse extensions of stay. In practice, it might prove difficult to insist that refugees return to Germany unless conditions there changed. Eventually, the question of maintenance or work was bound to arise. The possible transfer of the center of the fur trade from Leipzig to London would create room for some Jewish fur traders. But, for the rest, if the numbers in Britain grew, how feasible were the plans of the Jewish community to send refugees to other parts of the empire? The Home Office was confident that the Jewish community could afford to implement its guarantee of temporary maintenance. The main long-term issue for the Cabinet committee was, therefore, the possibility that admissions might ultimately result in "a considerable addition to the permanent population of this country."[13]

However, an immediate decision was needed on the current issue of control. Should immigration restrictions be relaxed as the Jewish proposals envisaged? Alternatively, should controls be tightened? Neither course appealed to the Home Office. It preferred to leave the controls more or less as they were. The meeting agreed. The committee confirmed that the imposition of strict landing conditions should continue. It also accepted a new proposal put forward by Sir Ernest Holderness of the Home Office, that refugees be required to register with the police immediately on arrival, rather than after the usual three months.[14]

For the government, the great attraction of the Jewish initiative was the offer of finance. So, while the committee rejected the Jewish suggestion of granting a right of asylum and recommended telling Jewish leaders that there could be no question of relaxing entry restrictions for German Jews, it wished to make use of the Jewish guarantee. It therefore suggested that the reply should also say that, in the cases of refugees already admitted temporarily, applications for further extensions would be considered "provided that the Jewish Community were prepared to guarantee, so far as might be necessary, adequate means of maintenance for the refugees concerned." This form of words literally made consideration of all future extensions dependent on the guarantee.[15] . . .

The immediate problem posed by the refugees was solved. Their fate in the long run was not. The interim arrangements agreed in April 1933 governed refugee admissions for nearly five years, during which the Cabinet did not discuss the subject again. Meanwhile, the demand for settlement grew steadily, but it was granted only in selected cases. . . .

For most refugee Jews, coming to the United Kingdom was an emergency measure, a temporary substitute for permanent refuge overseas. In 1933

the British government shared the Jewish view that Palestine could make a more substantial contribution than the United Kingdom to solving the Jewish refugee problem. It took care not to inflame Arab hostility to Jewish immigration by allowing in large numbers of German refugees. Nevertheless, to facilitate the entry of German Jews, it announced adjustments to Palestine's immigration procedures, covering both immigrants in the laboring category and persons possessing defined amounts of capital.[16] Later, the Colonial Office estimated that, in 1933–36 alone, 32,754 German Jews had been admitted to Palestine.[17] In the five years from 1933 to 1937, Palestine provided permanent homes for perhaps four times as many Jews from Germany as the estimated 10,000 who were temporarily in Britain by the end of that period.[18] Understandably, therefore, a senior Foreign Office official in 1935 described Palestine as "our contribution to the refugee problem."[19]

The empire also seemed to offer possibilities. In the inter-war years Britain cooperated with dominion governments to support migration to Canada, Australia and New Zealand. Immigrants of British stock were preferred and certain emigrants could obtain assisted passages, but by 1933 such arrangements were at a low ebb.[20] Jewish organizations and the British government, largely motivated by the wish to reduce refugee numbers in the United Kingdom, decided to explore the possibility of resettling German Jews in the dominions and colonies.[21] In the summer of 1933, Humbert Wolfe, principal assistant secretary responsible for the Ministry of Labor's Employment and Training Department, approached the Canadian government about settling Jewish doctors in remote areas of Canada. When this failed, he explored possibilities with the other dominions, but was met there too by the reaffirmation of strict immigration regulations. . . .

The precise reasons dominion governments gave for their lack of enthusiasm varied, but all were worried about Jewish immigration. Lord Bledisloe, governor-general of New Zealand, expressed sympathy, especially for "German scientists of Semitic origin," but stated that, even if there were openings, his government would be reluctant to take any step . . . from humanitarian motives which might leave the impression that German Jews of any description were being welcomed to this Dominion during a period of acute economic depression to the possible detriment of New Zealanders." He feared "that immigrants from Germany might be at heart, if not openly, Communists, and spread revolutionary propaganda to the social unsettlement of the local community."[22] Cooper informed dominion governments of steps the Home Office had taken to prevent "Communists and other undesirable aliens from Germany" entering "in the guise of refugees.[23]

Dominion governments were disinclined to surrender any part of their controls. They kept a grip on refugee arrivals by handling cases on their individual merits and refusing to commit themselves to admitting certain classes or specified numbers. The Australian Department of the Interior opposed group immigration schemes for Jews, claiming that Jews as a class were not desirable immigrants because they did not assimilate and generally preserved their identity as Jews. Australian Jewish organizations also preferred to restrict the size of groups entering the country. But discreet small-scale emigration to Australia of selected refugees was arranged, with Anglo-Jewish leaders providing much of the impetus. Michael Blakeney's research has shown that Australia reduced requirements for landing money in the cases of individuals, especially those nominated by persons or organizations guaran-

teeing that they would not be a charge on the state. . . .

British officials and Jewish leaders concluded in March 1937 that, "any attempt to force the pace, or to do anything spectacular, would only result in increased restrictions, as had been the case in South Africa."[24] In 1933–35 South Africa had admitted over 1,000 Jewish refugees. But when refugee immigration increased in 1936, agitators alleged that the country was being flooded by "unassimilable" Jewish immigrants. Severe restrictions ensued. The cash deposits now demanded from intending immigrants were beyond the means of Jews from Germany, [who were] prohibited from taking out more than a twentieth of the required sum. Jewish organizations in Germany, with financial help from the CGJ and other Jewish relief organizations abroad, chartered a boat, the *Stuttgart*, which succeeded in landing 537 refugees in Cape Town, just ahead of the deadline for the new deposits. The boat's arrival led to further antirefugee agitation and a hastily passed Aliens Act introduced an Immigrants Selection Board, with absolute power to grant or deny permits. Among other requirements, aliens had to show that they would become "readily assimilable" with the country's white inhabitants and not pursue an overcrowded occupation. The numbers of German Jewish immigrants fell off dramatically, although restrictions eased slightly after *Kristallnacht*. In all, South Africa admitted between 6,000 and 7,000 refugees in the 1930s.[25]

Immediately after *Kristallnacht*, Britain approached dominion governments again. Canada was unmoved. The high commissioner stated that "unfortunately the Jews were not generally good settlers on the land, they hastened into towns and cities." In places like Toronto with large numbers of Jews "any increase would start an antisemitic movement."[26] Canada took non-Jewish refugees from Czechoslovakia in 1938–39, but could only accommodate negligible numbers of European Jews: under 5,000 between 1933 and 1945.[27] Australia offered to take 15,000 over three years (the high commissioner, S. M. Bruce, had urged his government to agree to 30,000), but less than half arrived.[28] In all, Australia took some 10,000 refugees from Nazism, not counting those included in war-time deportations of internees from Britain.[29] The dominions held to their position throughout and even after the war. . . .

German and Austrian passport holders coming to the United Kingdom had not required visas since 1927. . . . In early March 1938, as an exodus from Austria seemed imminent, the idea of bringing back visas for Germans resurfaced within the Home Office. C. B. McAlpine, a principal in the Aliens Department, put the case in favor. Refugee numbers in Britain were growing. Germans admitted as visitors were applying to remain as refugees. Austrian Jews were investigating refuge and an influx was to be expected. Getting rid of refugees would become increasingly hard. The numbers of stateless ex-Germans would grow as a result of a new German decree removing citizenship from exiles who failed to register at a consulate within three months. If Austrian Jews fled after a German takeover they might also become stateless either because of the new decree or because they would not be accepted as German citizens. Once stateless, people became undeportable. Refugees who still held a nationality were technically deportable, but an outcry could be expected if it became known that the government was deporting refugees to Germany. The Home Office did not want the extra work of large numbers of port refusals. Nor did it relish the inevitable criticism from a public that regarded forcible return to Nazi persecution as inhuman. Thus, it was difficult to enforce either expulsion

or exclusion. The prospect of voluntary departures was also fading, since stateless and impoverished Jews found it increasingly difficult to gain admission abroad, even on a temporary basis. In early 1938 an estimated 10,000 Jewish refugees were present in the United Kingdom. McAlpine suggested that the benefits refugees had brought were outweighed by the danger of a spread of anti-Jewish feeling. The proper course, he concluded, "if the restriction of Jewish immigration was deemed to be a national necessity," was to use a visa requirement "to prevent potential refugees from getting here at all." It would then be possible to select immigrants "at leisure and in advance."[30] Other officials claimed that visas would not help and it was preferable to strengthen control at the ports.[31]

These leisurely deliberations were interrupted on March 11, 1938, by the news that Germany had annexed Austria. Immediately, arrivals of Jews with Austrian passports increased. A number were refused entry. More refugees were expected once Austria's borders reopened. Within hours of the German occupation, the Home Office learned with dismay that the Jewish guarantee no longer held good for new admissions.[32] Schiff may have been the bearer of this devastating news. He was the signatory of a follow-up letter two days later stating regretfully that, in response to developments in Germany and recently in Austria, the CGJ had decided it must limit its liability under the guarantee given in 1933. His committee's expenditure on refugees from Germany, he pointed out, had amounted to over £60,000 the previous year and would reach the same figure in the current year. The CGJ would honor its commitments to refugees who had already entered. But it had decided that the guarantee would not extend to new admissions. The only exceptions would be for cases where the Jewish organization had given its prior approval. Schiff added, "we shall, of course, do our best to look after the welfare of all refugees who find themselves stranded here."[33]

Any remaining hesitation about visas within the Home Office now evaporated. To adjust government policy took less than a week. Home Secretary Sir Samuel Hoare, raising the issue in Cabinet on March 16, reported that "many persons were expected to seek refuge from Austria." Referring to visas, he said he "felt great reluctance in putting another obstacle in the way of these unfortunate people." He also mentioned a "curious" MI5 [British Intelligence] report "suggesting that the Germans were anxious to inundate this country with Jews, with a view to creating a Jewish problem in the United Kingdom." The Cabinet assigned a small group of ministers to deal with the question. They were to adopt "as humane an attitude as possible" and to avoid "creating a Jewish problem in this country."[34]

The Home Office's object was to prevent the unplanned accumulation of many more Jewish refugees in the United Kingdom. Total exclusion was not the intention. Rather, so the Home Office argued, a change in procedure was required to meet the new need to preselect refugees abroad. Questions of quantity and quality had not posed a problem so far, but it had become necessary to address them.[35] Investigations by the passport control officer would have a better chance of picking out potential refugees than would controls at the ports, where the opportunities for making enquiries were too limited.[36]

On April 1 a Jewish deputation was given advance notice of the imminent changeover to visas. The home secretary explained his approach to the future selection of refugee entrants: "It would be necessary for the Home Office to discriminate very carefully as to the type of refugee who could be admitted to this country. If a flood of the wrong type of immigrants were allowed in there might be serious danger of antisemitic feeling being aroused . . . The last thing which we wanted here was the creation of a Jewish problem." The deputation reportedly said they "entirely agreed with this point of view." Indeed, Schiff endorsed the need for visas, for Austrians in particular: "It was very difficult to get rid of a refugee . . . once he had entered and spent a few months in this country. The imposition of a visa was especially necessary in the case of Austrians who were largely of the shopkeeper and small trader class and would therefore prove much more difficult to emigrate than the average German who had come to the United Kingdom."[37] When MPs subsequently raised questions about the barrier the visa requirement presented to refugees, ministers were able to cite the refugee organizations' support for reviving visas.[38]

The Home Office proceeded to implement its new policy of preselection. Instructions to PCOs on investigating applicants left no doubt that the purpose of the new visa procedure was to regulate the flow of refugees. The regulations assumed that applicants "who appear to be of Jewish or partly Jewish origin, or have non-Aryan affiliations" and claiming to be travelling to Britain for some temporary purpose were likely to be potential refugees, "whose real object is to apply, after arrival, to be allowed to remain indefinitely." The PCO's task was to distinguish such persons from *bona fide* applicants for visitors' visas. If a suspected emigrant persisted in claiming to be a visitor, he should be warned that he would be expected to leave at the termination of his visit and required to sign an undertaking to do so. He should also be warned that, if he overstayed, steps would be taken to compel his return, "notwithstanding any plea to the contrary." Once the PCO decided he was dealing with a refugee case, the applicant was usually ineligible for a visa unless he or she fell into the exclusive category of desirable immigrants set out in the new regulations. This elite consisted of people with international reputations in science, medicine, research or art, or successful industrialists wishing to make preliminary visits in connection with transferring their businesses to Britain, together with other persons of standing in these fields. Their applications were either to be granted on the spot or not refused without sanction from London. At the opposite end of the scale stood the mass of potential applicants—the rank and file in commerce and the professions—who were not eligible for entry at all. However, exceptions might still be made for political cases and for people who had offers of hospitality, or other means of temporary support in the United Kingdom. The scope for exceptions maintained a degree of flexibility, especially where safeguards were available against refugees becoming a public charge.[39] . . .

The reintroduction of visas solved one problem for the Home Office even as it created another. The physical mass of refugees had been contained on the continent and difficulties at the ports largely avoided. Immigration officers were spared the distasteful duties of conducting endless quayside investigations, refusing Jews leave to land, and forcing them to go back to the continent. The burden of initial face-to-face contact with applicants had been shifted abroad to passport control and consular officials, who came under the Foreign Office. In Germany and Austria, consular posts were overwhelmed with applications and people seeking advice. The Home Office was soon snowed under by an avalanche of paper— applications, certificates, photographs, affidavits and frantic, heart-rending letters. Officials, barely coping with the files of refugees in Britain, were now also burdened with applications referred back from Vienna, Berlin, and elsewhere. Every day brought queries from friends and relatives of persons still abroad. Congestion in the Home Office interview room became a serious problem.[40] . . .

The Aliens Department enlisted the aid of the Coordinating Committee, an umbrella organization recently set up, with Home Office encouragement, by the main refugee organizations. The voluntary organizations helped by dealing with incoming correspondence and investigating visa applications. If persons wrote to the Foreign Office appealing for assistance or advice on entry to Britain, they were generally referred to the German Jewish Aid Committee (GJAC), as the JRC was now known; in other cases the correspondence itself was forwarded to the GJAC.[41] One consequence of having the voluntary organizations deal with letters was that the government itself never kept a systematic record of individuals who approached it for help. Departments were thus partly insulated from the desperate plight of Jews seeking escape from Nazism.

Figures from Austria in the summer of 1938 give an idea of the scale of the demand for refuge. The director of passport control said in early July that a "very large number of unclassified persons" had applied since the *Anschluss* for advice and taken away forms, but not so far put in applications. In addition, visas granted in the first half of 1938 alone to Austrian subjects totaled 2,740, refusals approximately 420, and 545 cases, including some already disposed of, had been referred for decision in London. The number of staff dealing with visas in Vienna had been increased from four to fifteen.[42] Locally engaged staff were employed as reception clerks to manage the crowd. By September, staff were dealing with 200 enquiries a day about emigration to various parts of the British Empire and accepting over 100 visa applications daily. From May to September 1938 the Consulate had also given out 16,000 forms in connection with possible emigration to Australia.[43]

As the situation of Jews on the continent deteriorated, the Home Office came under increasing pressure to reexamine admissions. Activists at home pressed the government for a more generous policy. It was also necessary to provide a British contribution to international discussions on the admission policies of countries of refuge and settlement at the forthcoming Evian conference, fixed for early July. In the preceding month the Home Office produced what was in essence a restatement of existing policy. Nevertheless, it contained hints of movement toward a more positive approach. The statement said that numbers "depended largely on the opportunities and rate of absorption, and, as regards artisans, on the attitude of the Trade Unions." However, the Home Office was prepared to admit several classes of refugee: those prepared to start businesses; young people for training or education; professional persons; those with academic qualifications; and between 2,000 and 3,000 artisans per year.[44] . . .

In reality, no move had been made to liberalize the substance of admissions policy, but the pressure to appear more liberal was being felt. The submission opened with the sonorous claim that Britain was now prepared "on the ground of humanity to adopt an even more liberal policy in the matter of admission and employment," but confined within the narrow limits occasioned by domestic, demographic, and economic problems and the fact that it was "not a country of immigration."[45] The object was largely exhortatory. The exaggerated, yet studiedly imprecise picture of Britain's contribution was designed to stimulate other nations to greater generosity. At the conference, Lord Winterton urged other countries of refuge to follow the United Kingdom in being ready to absorb a certain proportion of refugees.[46] . . .

The pressure for absorption of refugees already in the country was growing, prospects for re-emigration were shrinking, and pressure for more generous admissions mounting. The Home Office responded by insisting that the cases of persons who might seek permission to remain permanently—and this category now encompassed virtually all Jews—must be scrutinized with the utmost care before permission to set foot in Britain could be granted. Thus, preselection was explicitly linked to absorption. The result was a system riven with contradictions. Refugees were granted admission on a temporary basis, yet people were required to have qualifications for permanent settlement in order to obtain merely temporary refuge. Many people who could only qualify for temporary refuge were refused admission, in case they stayed on. . . .

The Czech crisis of September 1938 created further pressure for admissions. People from Czechoslovakia started to arrive at the ports and some were refused entry. It was not possible to reintroduce visas for holders of Czechoslovak passports quickly, since revocation of the visa abolition agreement required three months' notice that had to be given on a quarter-day. On the first possible date the Czechs were notified that visas would be required as from April 1, 1939. Meanwhile, Holderness warned that Czech nationals faced close interrogation at the ports and the likelihood of refusal.[47] Admitting large numbers of refugees from Czechoslovakia was regarded as out of the question.[48]

By October 1938, the policy of restriction could be said to be working only in the sense that it was keeping out most refugees who wished to enter. The demand for refuge was running at an unprecedentedly high level. Neither the Home Office nor the refugee organizations could cope with the ever-growing pressure of work, despite efforts to spread the burden by involving other departments. The system inevitably delayed all cases that passed through it. Representatives of the refugee organizations told the Home Office that the system was at breaking point. Although voluntary organizations were acquiring a greater measure of control over admissions, they lacked the administrative capacity to cope. The government would not provide the extra funds they needed.[49] The Coordinating Committee stated that there was "a complete breakdown on the official side, of the policy of selected immigration through the approved voluntary organizations."[50] It sent a deputation that complained that the government was admitting persons not previously authorized by the voluntary committees. Winterton found himself in the odd position of defending the Home Office's right to admit aliens not approved by the refugee bodies.[51] On October 28, Schiff and Davidson told Cooper that the government had admitted too many refugees from Austria who should not have been admitted at all because they seemed to have no prospects of suitable employment or of emigration. Schiff suggested calling a halt to admissions, at least temporarily, until those already admitted had been assimilated or re-emigrated. This could be done without announcing any change of policy.[52]

The government's waning ability to deal with the workload was clear from the arrears in the processing of naturalization applications. The Home Office was already badly behind when the applications of refugees who completed the statutory five years" residence were added to its pile of work. By May 1938 the arrears figure was over 2,000. . . .

The refugee crisis assumed new diplomatic significance in late March 1938 when Roosevelt called for an international meeting on the refugee problem to launch a new committee of government representatives "for the purpose of facilitating the emigration from Austria, and presumably from Germany, of political refugees."[53] Nations where refugees had found or hoped to find a haven agreed to gather at Evian in France in early July to discuss collective action on the refugee problem.[54]

As the danger of a European war came closer, the Foreign Office was alert for signs that the isolationism of the Americans might be giving way to a readiness to become involved in European problems. Thus when Roosevelt suggested the conference, the attractive possibility of boosting Anglo-American cooperation led to agreement within Whitehall that "on political grounds alone" it was desirable to accept the American proposals in principle.[55] As Makins recalled, he and his colleague "grabbed" the opportunity.[56] But British policy-makers were suspicious of the proposal for the new agency. The proposed Intergovernmental Committee on Refugees (IGC) was bound to create potential problems and unwelcome pressures. The British at first tried to prevent the new agency from coming into existence, but, once they realized that it would be difficult to stop, they acquiesced in its formation at the Evian conference.

In previous years the Foreign Office and the Treasury had agreed that to spend money or establish machinery for dealing with the refugees would risk perpetuating the problem, so such activities should be left to the private organizations.[57] . . . Whitehall officials also feared that helping people in the Reich would provoke additional problems for Jews in Poland, Romania, and elsewhere, including Hungary. At the May 1938 session of the Council of the League [of Nations], Poland and Romania had already mentioned their desire for aid to help reduce their Jewish populations. Before the Evian conference, Sir John Hope Simpson, director of the Royal Institute of International Affairs' Refugee Survey, argued that, if the proposed IGC failed to act to relieve the acute position of the Jewish populations in these countries, persecution was sure to follow. He regarded this problem as more serious than the problem faced by German and Austrian refugees.[58] Foreign Office officials shared Simpson's concerns, but came to the opposite conclusion, namely that any action by the IGC to relieve the position of Jews in these countries would be a cue for further persecution. At Evian they therefore tried to convince Polish and Romanian observers that their governments should not look to the IGC for assistance.[59] The government, reluctantly, was being drawn into establishing new international machinery on the refugee problem. . . .

There was a logic behind the apparently contradictory postures which British policy-makers adopted toward the IGC. The logic becomes apparent once it is understood that the government did not assign vital importance to the IGC's success; as mentioned, the government's overriding objective was rather to ensure that the IGC did not interfere with British sovereignty over refugee policy. The Foreign Office also wished to discourage the growth of the refugee problem on the continent and to limit its impact on the United Kingdom. It was therefore determined to show the German government and other interested spectators, Poland and Romania in particular, that the United Kingdom could not be blackmailed into taking destitute Jews off other nations' hands. The priority, therefore, was not to help refugees. It was to force Germany and other governments wishing to unload their Jewish populations to play according to internationally agreed rules. British ministers and officials were determined that no aspect of the government's refugee policy would be dictated by any external force-be it a foreign state, an international organization, or even the sheer pressure of the refugee exodus. In this context, the Evian conference could be viewed as a success for British policy. The demands of Poland and Romania for help in getting rid of their Jews had been

consigned to the sidelines. The question of Palestine had been kept off the conference agenda. The United Kingdom had not been forced into any new commitments. . . .

National concerns shaped British policy on every aspect of aid to refugees. As regards immigration, the government doggedly upheld its sovereign right to choose how many refugees it would admit and to decide cases on their individual merits. Spokesmen further claimed that only a very limited number of refugees could be absorbed, because the United Kingdom was "not an immigration country"—a place of first refuge and transit, yes, but not of permanent settlement.

The government never envisaged mass settlement within the empire. The dominions' continuing reluctance to admit Jewish refugees was scarcely challenged.[60] In late 1938 and 1939 certain colonies, especially British Guiana, Kenya, and Northern Rhodesia, were put forward publicly by ministers as possible places of settlement. Makins wished that these offers were genuine; he personally viewed Northern Rhodesia as the best possibility. But he acknowledged that talk of such prospects was largely bluff: "In all fairness it has to be admitted that the offer of British Guiana and Tanganyika is largely an illusory one, and this must inevitably become apparent in due course."[61] Palestine had been allowed to take in a relatively large number of Jewish refugees on a permanent basis until, in response to Arab opposition, Britain imposed increasing restrictions in the controversial White Paper of May 1939 and finally established a quota for Jewish immigration. When the notion was floated that the IGC could require a commitment to absorbing specific numbers in any part of the empire, Britain rejected that too. British policy-makers' failure to act to provide settlement prospects for refugees from Nazism reflected fears that to do so might stimulate Poland and Romania to force out their Jewish populations in a state of destitution. The main use to which government put the IGC was thus negative: it would support nothing except action by the IGC; the IGC achieved nothing, so nothing was done. Thus it turned out that, for British purposes, a key function of the IGC was to contain both the size of the refugee problem and the demand for refuge and to do so merely by existing, rather than by acting. . . .

As far as finance was concerned, British policy maintained that relief, emigration, and settlement should be paid for by refugees themselves or by private organizations and not by governmental contributions. Any departure from this policy was believed to risk increasing and perpetuating the refugee problem, by encouraging the emigration and expulsion of destitute Jews. As the crisis deepened, Treasury officials questioned strict adherence to a zero-cost policy, but for the moment the policy remained intact.

On the afternoon of November 21 [1938] the prime minister made a Commons statement. It was largely devoted to an enumeration of the steps the government was taking to survey the possibilities of settlement in the colonial empire, especially plans to lease large areas of British Guiana. On further admissions to the United Kingdom, Chamberlain merely reiterated that numbers were "limited by the capacity of the voluntary organizations dealing with the refugee problem to undertake the responsibility for selecting, receiving and maintaining" refugees. He stated that since 1933 the government had permitted about 11,000 refugees to land, in addition to some 4,000 to 5,000 who had since re-emigrated. He dismissed as "premature" the suggestion by Eleanor Rathbone MP of a loan for refugee maintenance. Other questioners were told to await the home secretary's speech that evening.[62] Chamberlain's statement

was widely reported in the North American press. Hoare's speech aroused much less interest abroad since it concerned domestic policy only.

Hoare set out the government's new approach later the same day during a Commons debate on refugee policy.[63] The need for careful selection was his starting point. He warned that mass immigration was likely to encourage the growth of fascism, although he did not use the word. He also stressed the importance of preventing "an influx of the undesirable behind the cloak of refugee immigration." The government therefore needed to check in detail the individual circumstances of adult refugees, a process bound to involve "a measure of delay." Individual cases would be investigated by voluntary organizations represented on the Coordinating Committee, whose recommendations the Home Office accepted. The main issue was whether refugees could support themselves. The 11,000 German refugees who had come to live in Britain in the years 1933 to 1938 had set up industries that provided jobs for 15,000 British workmen; they had thus improved rather than damaged British employment prospects. These benefits, Hoare claimed, were due to "very careful selection." In reality the creation of most of these jobs dated from the period prior to the revival of mandatory preselection.

Hoare admitted that the admissions system had been strained "to breaking point" in the preceding ten days, but with thousands of applications per day, strain was inevitable. The machinery was now being greatly expanded, he announced. Moreover, while the Home Office would stick to individual selection for persons who might stay permanently, selection procedures would be modified for people coming for temporary refuge, for whom a less detailed scrutiny was permissible. Those expected to re-emigrate were "a class of case which we can deal with en masse," he said, and could be admitted on an unprecedented scale and more speedily. Transmigrants would be provided with a temporary home, on the understanding that, "at some time in the future, they will go elsewhere for their permanent home." The government would also look kindly on proposals for training for eventual resettlement in the colonial empire, such as an existing scheme to train "Jewish boys for agriculture and Jewish girls for domestic service." Large numbers of "non-Aryan children" could be admitted without the individual checks used for older refugees, provided they could find responsible sponsors. All children whose maintenance could be guaranteed could come. Jewish parents would accept separation from their children to save them from danger in Germany. Hoare commended to his fellow countrymen this "chance of taking the young generation of a great people." He asserted the government's anxiety to help, promised "the utmost support" for the voluntary organizations' work and vowed to show "that we will be in the forefront among the nations of the world in giving relief to these suffering people." ...

In early November, when refuge was sought for German refugees being turned out of Yugoslavia, Holderness had said, "We are not prepared to be made the dumping ground of Europe."[64] Cooper considered that the November pogrom had been designed to rouse sympathy abroad so that the doors of receiving countries would be opened to admit larger numbers than they had previously been prepared to accept, and that this hope had been largely fulfilled.[65] But the Home Office remained totally opposed to the mass immigration of refugees and totally committed to preselection. Home Office ministers steadfastly resisted the idea of setting up a facility similar to Ellis Island in the USA, where persons whose entry had not been approved could remain while their cases were being investigated.

Hoare told the Commons that it was undesirable to allow a "stagnant pool" of refugees to develop in the United Kingdom.[66] The Home Office continued to require admissions to be linked to jobs or re-emigration.[67]

The Home Office had accepted the principle of letting in large numbers of children. Samuel had returned from the Jewish leaders' November 15 meeting with Chamberlain in a hopeful frame of mind. He reported to the CGJ's Executive Committee that he felt the prime minister appreciated the difficulties of the situation and wished to help and that, where the entry of children was concerned, Chamberlain would support any suggestion approved by the Home Office. Mrs. Rebecca Sieff, having spoken to Cooper, was convinced that the home secretary would be prepared to waive formalities. In preparation for expanded immigration, a new appeal, chaired by Lord Rothschild, was being launched in the Jewish press. Plans were outlined to bring 5,000 children from Germany. Schiff also suggested approaching trades unions, adding that, if refugees could not work, they might come for training for re-emigration.[68] Jewish leaders' assessment of Chamberlain's position, several days prior to Samuel's meeting with Hoare, is consistent with Cabinet records showing Chamberlain's key role in widening refugee admissions. The crucial Jewish promise was the collective guarantee of financial responsibility for children given to Chamberlain on November 15. On November 21, the date of the refugee debate, Hoare reached agreement with Samuel and several Jewish and other religious workers on streamlining children's admission; Samuel recorded in his memoirs that Hoare agreed that children could enter "without the slow procedure of passports and visas" and that Jewish leaders gave a guarantee "that they should be emigrated as soon as they were old enough and conditions allowed."[69]

British consular officials in Germany exerted themselves to speed up departures for the United Kingdom. The PCO in Berlin, Captain Frank Foley, acting without instructions, arranged with the American consul to grant visas to persons stopping in Britain in transit to the USA, but was asked to await new procedures developed by the Home Office.[70] British officials based in Germany knew that evidence that a British visa had been authorized could secure a man's release from a concentration camp. Thus it was important to grant visas quickly and to minimize the time lag between visa authorization and release. The consul in Frankfurt, R. T. Smallbones, had an agreement with the local secret police that they would release prisoners on being told that a visa had been granted. Even though Hoare was enthusiastic, Makins failed to interest Home Office officials in developing more systematic procedures for notifying the German authorities of visas granted to detainees. Cooper argued that it was up to the prisoner's friends and family to do this.[71]

The voluntary committees could now select a wide range of refugees for entry. The representatives they sent to the continent worked in conjunction with German Jewish organizations, notably the *Reichsvertretung*, identifying suitable candidates. Lists of approved names were then submitted to the Home Office. These lists, or "nominal rolls," largely replaced the elaborate process of individual visa applications, notably in children's cases, and made possible the use of group visas. Other refugees still came under the standard visa system, but recommendations from the voluntary organizations were often accepted in lieu of investigation by the authorities. The Home Office also arranged with the GJAC that people aged thirty-five to fifty selected to enter on the basis of guarantees would be required to prove only suitability for emigration or in special cases

absorption in the United Kingdom, rather than the existence of firm and valid arrangements to re-emigrate within two years.[72]

In a special effort to save men from German concentration camps, the CGJ set up a refugee transit camp at Richborough in Kent on the site of an abandoned army camp. The American Jewish Joint Distribution Committee agreed to subsidize some 20 percent of upkeep costs. A Jewish worker in Berlin recalled that the lucky ones who went to Richborough were chosen from over 10,000 applicants. Julian Layton, an Anglo-Jewish representative who helped with selection in Germany, felt a strong personal commitment to assisting men who did not have means but who would be suitable for re-emigration. Layton and his companions successfully proposed a policy of releasing CGJ funds to help such men and in early January the project obtained approval from the Home Office. Men aged eighteen to forty-five going to the camp were accepted as transmigrants. The endorsement on their passports described them as admitted "pending re-emigration." However, the reality of these re-emigration prospects was often questionable and in some cases fictitious. For example, Werner Rosenstock, who worked for the *Reichsvertretung* in 1939, and arrived in the United Kingdom just before the war, recalled that statements by refugees that they planned to re-emigrate to Shanghai were often based on nothing more than the fact that Shanghai did not require visas. The camp filled rapidly. It had been intended to accommodate 5,000 refugees, but a lower limit of 3,500 was agreed. Some 3,350 men and 220 women and children were temporarily lodged at Richborough when war broke out. Only 100 had re-emigrated by November 1939.[73]

There was no quota for children. However, a subcommittee set up by the CGJ to promote large scale children's emigration considered the admission of about 10,000 as an upper limit. The numbers climbed from 1,544 in January 1939 to 9,354 by the end of August.[74] The vast majority (7,482) were classified as Jews, the rest as Christians (1,123) and "undenominational" (749). The large number of arrivals in late 1938 led to the utilization of summer camps as short-term accommodation. The camps were impossible to heat properly, but the children had warm clothes, so few needed the additional clothing donated by Marks and Spencer.[75]

Admission saved the children's lives. Exclusion sealed the fate of many of their parents. Three-quarters of the unaccompanied children in England by July 1939 had parents left behind in Greater Germany, in most cases with no means of support. . . .

In the last months before the war, the British authorities realized that the influx of refugees was getting out of control while hardly any were leaving. Samuel intimated to the CGJ in late 1938 that the Home Office felt unease about the establishment of transit camps, "as . . . a pool of refugees might be formed in England."[76] The Home Office had given permission for Richborough Camp, but, by January 1939, Hoare already regarded the accumulation of transmigrants as a problem. A new Cabinet Committee on the Refugee Problem, set up under his chairmanship, held six meetings before the outbreak of war. Hoare used the committee to promote the reduction of refugee numbers in the United Kingdom. At its first meeting he complained about the "very embarrassing" delay in arriving at a detailed scheme for the permanent settlement of refugees allowed in on a temporary basis. Making specific reference to the training camp at Richborough, he expressed concern that a "stagnant pool of refugees" remained in the country; in fact the camp was not yet ready to accept inmates.[77] A few weeks later Hoare sug-

gested earmarking some of the men training at Richborough for settlement in British Guiana. He sought Foreign Office action to curtail irregular immigration to British colonies or Palestine by parties of Jewish refugees without visas. Such immigration, he said, was causing difficulties in his own department; presumably he meant that it was using up opportunities for re-emigration from the United Kingdom. Randall told him the Foreign Office had concluded that it was a waste of time to try to influence the German government to stop stimulating the exodus of Jews without visas.[78]

The committee's interim report to the Cabinet in July 1939 stated that the refugee organizations were in no position to finance colonial settlement schemes such as the British Guiana project. Indeed, there was a danger that their funds would be inadequate to meet existing commitments. Of some 40,000 refugees in the country, the majority were transmigrants, admitted on the strength of guarantees that the cost of their maintenance would not fall on public funds. The funds of the refugee organizations that had undertaken responsibility for these guarantees had been strained to the utmost, principally by delays in re-emigration. Unless a large number emigrated soon, refugees were likely to fall on public assistance, an outcome the Home Office was most anxious to avoid. The report concluded that in these circumstances the government should no longer refuse to offer financial support for refugee settlement and re-emigration. It advised agreeing in principle to make funds available on a basis proportional to amounts subscribed privately, provided other governments would also contribute, although the only country whose cooperation should be regarded as essential was the USA. The United Kingdom should take a lead on these issues at the forthcoming meeting of the IGC "in view of the gravity of the situation in this country."[79]

Hoare's committee advocated this major reversal of previous policy because it considered that the United Kingdom now had a refugee problem, which should be solved urgently through the provision of settlement opportunities abroad. It should be done at government expense because no other source was available.

The new position, while it represented an important turnaround regarding public funds, was also aimed at saving future expenditure on public assistance. It was consistent with the policy of keeping the United Kingdom as a country of transit. The proposed injection of British finance was aimed at increasing opportunities to emigrate from the United Kingdom, not at expanding the chances of escape from Nazi territory. In mid-July the Cabinet agreed [to] these proposals in principle.[80] The government communicated its offer of funds first to the Americans, then to the IGC, reiterating the concern that without such action countries of refuge would "be left with large numbers of refugees who cannot be absorbed."[81] But it was too late. In September, war broke out, rendering British contributions for settlement projects inconceivable in the foreseeable future.

NOTES

1. Vaughan Bevan, *The Development of British Immigration Law* (London, 1986), 63–65.
2. Aliens Act 1905, s. 1 (3).
3. Ibid.
4. Sir John Gilmour, *Hansard*, House of Commons, vol. 276, cols. 2557–8, April 12, 1933; Sir Samuel Hoare, ibid., vol. 333, cols. 991–4, March 22, 1938; Makins, minute, February 16, 1935; Sir John Hope Simpson, *The Refugee Problem: Report of a Survey* (London, 1939), 345.
5. "Control of Passengers," March 29, 1923, PRO CAB 15/10, 21–24; H. R. Foyle to W. Wilson, May 5, 1939, PRO T162/847/E20500/3.
6. Holderness, "Copy of note given to S of S for use at the meeting of the Cabinet on April 5, 1933," April 4, 1933, PRO HO 213/1630; Conclusions, Committee on Aliens Restrictions AR (33) 1st Cons., April 6, 1933, PRO CAB 27/549. This file contains the committee's records: its composition and terms of reference; Gilmour, memorandum, "The Present Position in regard to the Admission of Jewish Refugees from Germany to this Country," April 6, 1933; the record of its sole meeting, Conclusions, Committee on Aliens Restrictions AR (33) 1st Cons., April 6, 1933; its report CP 96 (33), April 7, 1933; and other documents.
7. Cab. 23 (33) 5, April 5, 1933, PRO CAB 23/75.
8. Ibid. This evidence is further discussed in London, "British Immigration Control Procedures and Jewish Refugees, 1933–1942," Ph.D. thesis, University of London (1992), 78–80.
9. Neither this last request nor any mention of "work" appears in the written proposals from the Jewish leaders. It is possible that they raised them when they called at the Home Office.
10. "Proposals of the Jewish Community as regards Jewish Refugees from Germany," n.d., Appendix I to Gilmour, "The Present Position," n. 6 above (original in PRO HO 213/1627).
11. Ibid.
12. Gilmour, "The Present Position," n. 6 above.
13. Ibid.
14. CP 96 (33) AR (33) 1st Cons., n. 6 above; Aliens Restriction Act 1914, s. 1 (1) (f), and Aliens Order 1920, art. 6.
15. CP 96 (33) AR (33) 1st Cons., n. 6 above.
16. Conclusions AR (33)1, n. 1\6 above; Simon, *Hansard*, House of Commons, vol. 276, cols. 8210–12, April 13, 1933.
17. Sir J. E. Shuckburgh to Makins, June 30, 1938, PRO FO 371/22538, W8786/104/98, f. 6.
18. Strauss, "Jewish Immigration" (I), table 1, 346; Strauss, "Jewish Immigration" (II), table 10, 354–55.
19. M. D. Peterson, February 18, 1935, PRO FO 371/19676, W1370/356/98, f. 113.

20. Empire Settlement Act 1922; Civil Estimates, Class II, 7, "Oversea Settlement," PRO DO 175/14508/4, 1–10.

21. Fuller details are in London, "British Immigration," 103–13.

22. Bledisloe to Thomas, December 22, 1933, PRO DO 57/175/14414/11.

23. References to destroyed DO files of September 18 and October 17, 1933, PRO DO 5/10.

24. Sir John Loader Maffery, permanent under secretary CO, minute, March 24, 1937; G. F. Plant, memorandum of meeting with Felix Warburg, March 31, 1937, PRO DO 57/175/ 14414A/3.

25. Frieda H. Sichel, *From Refugee to Citizen: A Sociological Study of the Immigrants from Hitler-Europe Who Settled in Southern Africa* (Cape Town, 1966), x, 13–25.

26. MacDonald, memorandum of meeting with Vincent Massey, November 29, 1938, PRO DO 121/2.

27. Abella and Troper, *None Is Too Many*, xxii, 131.

28. MacDonald, memorandum, December 1, 1938, PRO DO 121/2.

29. F. Straton to official secretary, Office of High Commissioner for the UK, March 28, 1945, PRO DO 57/1331/Ml 164/5; see also Blakeney, *Australia*.

30. C. B. McAlpine, memorandum, March 1, 1938, PRO HO 213/94.

31. H. Jones, minute, March 15, 1938, PRO FO 372/3282, T3398/3272/378, f. 8.

32. William Strang, memorandum of telephone conversation with Holderness, March 12, 1938, M. J. Creswell, Sir A. N. Noble, R. M. Makins, memoranda, March 14, 1938, PRO FO 372/3282, T3272/3272/378, f. 1; Sherman, *Island Refuge*, 86–93.

33. Schiff to under secretary (HO), March 14, 1938, PRO T 161/997/S45629; C. D. C. Robinson to Sir Nevile Bland, March 14, 1938, PRO FO 372/3282, T3398/3272/378, f. 8.

34. Cab. 14 (38) 6, March 16, 1938, PRO CAB 23/93.

35. Memorandum regarding Austrian refugees, probably by Holderness, n.d., March 1938, PRO HO 213/3.

36. Robinson to Bland, March 14, 1938, PRO FO 372/3282, T3398/3272/378, f. 8.

37. HO minutes of meeting with deputation, April 1, 1938, PRO HO 213/42.

38. R. A. Butler, *Hansard*, House of Commons, vol. 335, cols. 843–4, May 4, 1938; Hoare, ibid., vol. 338, cols. 2300–1, July 21, 1938.

39. PCD, circular, "Visas for Holders of German and Austrian Passports entering the United Kingdom," April 27, 1938, PRO FO 372/3283, T6705/3272/378, f. 326, esp. paragraphs 1, 2, 3, 6–9.

40. Holderness, minute, June 22, 1938, PRO HO 45/24773/435958/60.

41. Minutes, April 1, 1938, PRO HO 213/42, 3; PRO HO 213/268; Simpson, *The Refugee Problem*, 338–39; Sherman, *Island Refuge*, 99–100.

42. Jeffes, minute, July 9, 1938, A. W. Urquhart, minute, n.d., mid-July 1938, PRO FO 372/3284, T9255/9423/3272/378, f. 167.

43. P. Stanley Sykes to E. H. Ranee, October 5, 1938, attaching memorandum by G. W. Berry, Assistant PCO Vienna to inspector general of passport control, London, September 26, 1938, PRO FO 366/1036, X9278/84/50, f. 52.

44. Record of interdepartmental meeting, "Intergovernmental meeting at Evian," June 8, 1938, PRO FO 371/22527, W8127/104/98, f. 150; Cooper to Makins, July 2, 1938, PRO FO 371/22528, W8853/104/98, f. 60.

45. "Contribution," July 11, 1938, PRO FO 919/9.

46. Lord Winterton, speech, July 6, 1938, "Intergovernmental Committee, Evian––July 1938, Verbatim Report of the First Meeting CI/E/CRI," PRO FO 919/8.

47. Holderness to W. I. Mallet, November 2, 1938, PRO FO 371/21586, CI3325/11896/12, f. 253.

48. Makins, minute, October 27, 1938, PRO FO 371/21585, C12940/11896/12, f. 47.

49. *Jewish Chronicle*, December 9, 1938, 7, 21; Bentwich, *They Found Refuge*, 54–5.

50. Ormerod to Winterton, October 18, 1938, PRO HO 213/1636.

51. Correspondence, 20– October 8, 1939, ibid.

52. Cooper, memorandum, October 29, 1938, ibid., Sherman, *Island Refuge*, 155–8.

53. US Embassy, memorandum, March 24, 1938, Noble to E. A. Shillito, March 28, 1938, PRO T 160/842/F13577/01/1.

54. Sherman, *Island Refuge*, 95–97, 100–23.

55. Minutes of interdepartmental meeting, March 28, 1938, PRO T 160/842/F13577/01/1.

56. Lord Sherfield (Roger Makins), interview with the author, December 13, 1990.

57. See, e.g., Herbert Brittain (Treasury) to Strang, July 31, 1935, PRO FO 371/19677, W7002/356/98, f. 172.

58. Makins, minute, "Consideration of the Refugee Question at the 101st Session of the Council," May 14, 1938, Simpson to Makins, June 8, 1938, PRO FO 371/22527, W6714/7399/104/98, f. 47.

59. Skrine Stevenson, minute, July 6, 1938, PRO FO 371/22528, W8851/104/98, f. 31; Makins, minute, ibid., quoted in Sherman, *Island Refuge*, 116.

60. DO, "Memorandum as to the attitudes of the Dominions toward the proposals to be discussed at the International Conference at Evian," June 1938, R. A. Wiseman to Makins, June 20, 1938, PRO FO 371/22527, W8012/104/98, f. 136.

61. Shuckburgh to Makins, June 30, 1938, Makins, minute, December 1, 1938, PRO FO 371/ 22538, W8786/15621/104/98, f. 6.

62. Chamberlain, House of Commons, vol. 341, cols. 1313–17, November 21, 1938.

63. Hoare, ibid., cols. 1427–83, November 21, 1938.

64. Holderness to Makins, November 4, 1938, PRO FO 371/22536, \V 14633/104/98, f. 93.

65. Cooper, memorandum, December 16, 1938, PRO HO 213/1639.

66. Hoare, *Hansard*, House of Commons, vol. 342. col. 3082, December 22, 1938; ibid., vol. 345, cols. 2455–7, April 3, 1939.

67. Record of interdepartmental meeting, November 16, 1938.

68. Minutes, Executive Committee meeting, November 17, 1938, CBF, reel 1, file 20.

69. Samuel, *Memoirs*, 255.

70. Correspondence, 24–November 8, 1938, PRO HO 213/100.

71. Correspondence, November 8–December 28, December 29, 1938–January 12, 1939, PRO FO 371/21753, C14141/14718/16070/2311/18, f. 165; correspondence, November 9–December 23, 1938, PRO FO 371/21757, C13766/15535/2412/18, f. 349; for Home Office views, see correspondence, PRO HO 213/101.

72. Coordinating Committee minutes, January 13, 1939, AJ 43/14/114.

73. Julian Layton, interview with the author, April 20, 1988; correspondence etc., January—November 1939, CGJ, "Report by Mr Layton, Mr Gentilli and Mr Baron on the selection of refugees for the Richborough Camp" (n.d., covering visit February 19–March 3, 1939), AJDC 592; Hubert Pollack, "Was nicht in den Archiven steht," n.d., 497/55 01/17, Yad Vashem Archive, Jerusalem; Dr. Werner Rosenstock, interviews with the author, April 19, 1988, May 6, 1989.

74. *Movement for the Care of Children from Germany: First Annual Report, 1938–1939*, PRO HO 213/302.

75. Correspondence, December 1938–January 12, 1939, PRO MH 55/689.

76. Minutes, CGJ Executive meeting, December 29, 1938, CBF reel 1, file 2.

77. CRP (39) 1st meeting, January 24, 1939, PRO CAB 98/1.

78. CRP (39)3rd meeting, March 1, 1939, 4th meeting, May 9, 1939, ibid.; Randall, minute, March 1, 1939, PRO FO 371/24080, W3734/520/48, f. 89.

79. Hoare, Interim Report, Cabinet Committee on the Refugee Problem CP 151 (39), July 7, 1939, PRO CAB 98/1.

80. Cab 37 (39), July 11, 12, 1939, PRO CAB 23/100; Sherman, *Island Refuge*, 242–50.

81. Text of statement by UK representative to IGC on July 19, 1939, LIC 32, AJ 43/37/48.

Switzerland

INDEPENDENT COMMISSION OF EXPERTS SWITZERLAND — SECOND WORLD WAR

From *Switzerland, National Socialism, and the Second World War*

Civilian Refugees between 1933 and 1937

A large number of people left Germany immediately after the National Socialists took power in January 1933. The two largest groups were, on the one hand, politically persecuted communists and social democrats; and on the other, Jews who were under threat of antisemitic violence, boycotts and legalized discrimination. In spring 1933, the Swiss Federal authorities passed a law, which was to remain in force until 1944, distinguishing between political and other refugees. Political refugees were those who were under personal threat owing to their political activities. The Federal authorities were extremely reticent to recognize political refugees; communists in particular were not welcome. According to an instruction issued by the Federal Department of Justice and Police (*Eigdenössisches Justiz-und Polizeidepartement*, EJPD) only "high state officials, leaders of left-wing parties and well-known authors" should be accepted as political refugees. On the basis of this restrictive interpretation of the term "refugee," Switzerland granted political asylum to only 644 people between 1933 and 1945, of these, 252 cases were admitted during the war. The Federal Council had the final decision on granting political asylum; political refugees were the responsibility of the Federal Prosecutor's Office (*Bundesanwaltschaft*), which was part of the EJPD.[1]

All other refugees were considered simply as foreigners from a legal point of view and were subject to the stipulations of the Federal Law on Residence and Settlement of Foreigners of March 26, 1931, which came into force in 1934. From an administrative point of view, they were the responsibility of the cantonal police, which issued so-called tolerance permits (valid for a few months only), residence permits, and settlement permits. The Police Division of the EJPD coordinated cantonal policy regarding foreigners; as the highest authority, the Police Division had to approve the issuing of work permits and longer-term residence permits in particular. In addition, the Division could lodge an objection to cantonal decisions. Between 1933 and 1938, however, the cantons still enjoyed a good deal of freedom in the way they implemented their policy with regard to refugees. Some cantons adopted a very restrictive policy while others freely issued tolerance permits. The latter were granted on the condition that the recipient did not engage in gainful employment and left Switzerland as soon as possible.[2] Switzerland saw itself as a transit state, a halfway station for refugees where they would organize their emigration to other countries such as France, the Netherlands or the USA. In view of the restrictive policy adopted by Switzerland after the end of the First World War, it was hardly worth considering as a place of permanent residence. In his manual for emigrants published in 1935, the Jewish sociologist Mark Wischnitzer wrote, "The ban on employing foreigners is implemented to the letter in Switzerland." He also mentioned the authorities' fight against "over-foreignization" (*"Überfremdung"*), which had negative repercussions in particular for Jewish emigrants.[3] Accordingly, at the end of 1937 there were only around 5,000 refugees in Switzerland.[4]

Increased Persecution of Jews and Introduction of the "J"-Stamp for Passports in 1938

With the intensification of anti-Jewish measures in Germany after 1937, the annexation of Austria in March 1938, the pogroms in November 1938, and the subsequent complete exclusion of Jews from the German economy, the situation became considerably more tense. Between the annexation and the outbreak of the war in September 1939, over 100,000 Jews emigrated from Austria alone, of whom an estimated 5,500 to 6,500 came to Switzerland for a longer or shorter period. The total number of refugees in Switzerland thus rose to between 10,000 and 12,000 in 1938/39.[5] The attempt made by the international community to agree on a common policy on the question of refugees at the Evian Conference in July 1938 failed.[6] On the contrary, numerous countries imposed further restrictions on admission. The Swiss Federal Council strengthened border protection and adopted a series of administrative measures: on March 28, 1938, it made it compulsory for all holders of Austrian passports to have a visa; on August 18, 1938, it decided to refuse entry to all refugees without a visa; and from October 4, 1938, German "non-Aryans" were also obliged to obtain a visa.

As early as April 1938, Switzerland held discussions with Germany in order to set up measures that would enable the border authorities to distinguish between Jewish and non-Jewish German citizens. When the Federal Council was weighing the idea of making it compulsory for all German citizens to obtain a visa, the German authorities feared that this would signal detrimental consequences for foreign affairs and that other countries would introduce similar measures. For this reason, they agreed to identify the passports of German Jews with a "J." Contrary to the Federal Council and the Swiss Embassy in Berlin, Heinrich Rothmund, the Head of the Police Division at the EJPD, ultimately came out in favor of making visas compulsory for all Germans in order to be able to exert more efficient control over all German emigrants. Furthermore, he recognized the discriminatory and legally dubious character of the Germano-Swiss agreement. It was quite possible that such discrimination would be extended to Swiss Jews, since the bilateral agreement gave the Third Reich the right to demand that Swiss passports be similarly marked. With regard to Rothmund's doubts, Federal Councilor Giuseppe Motta said, "The Federal Council unanimously approved the agreement with Germany. It also approved (unanimously too) the press release. Mr. Rothmund can therefore put aside the little scruples that are bothering him."[7]

The measures agreed in August 1938 to turn back unwanted immigrants were implemented ruthlessly; despite their awareness of the risk refugees ran, the authorities often turned them over directly to the German police. It even happened that border guards struck refugees with the butts of their rifles to bar them from crossing the border.[8] Nevertheless, several thousand Austrian Jews found refuge in Switzerland, in many cases owing to the efforts of Paul Grüninger, a police captain of St. Gallen, who until the beginning of 1939 allowed hundreds of people to enter the country illegally. He was dismissed in spring 1939, and at the end of 1940 was found guilty by the St. Gallen district court of violating his official powers and falsifying documents. It was not until 1993, long after his death, that he was politically rehabilitated after the cantonal government had refused several applications from the 1960s on; two years later he was also legally rehabilitated by the St. Gallen district court.[9] There were also Swiss consular officials in Italy and Austria who generously issued entry visas to Austrian refugees, for which they were reprimanded by the government.[10] Ernst Prodolliet, for example, a consular employee in Bregenz, was told during his disciplinary hearing that "Our consulate's job is not to ensure the well-being of Jews."[11]

Outbreak of the War: Returning Emigrants, Emigrants, Military Refugees

The outbreak of the Second World War in September 1939 changed the political context fundamentally. Firstly, the war made it difficult for refugees present in Switzerland at the time to emigrate to a third country. Secondly, apart from those persecuted under the German dictatorship, the subsequent years brought tens of thousands of refugees as a consequence of the war to Switzerland. The first wave of arrivals in September 1939 was made up of over 15,000 Swiss people from abroad who came back to their home country and needed work and accommodation; between then and May 1945, another 41,000 Swiss joined them in returning home.[12]

The outbreak of the war drastically restricted the possibility of moving on for refugees who were already in Switzerland. Nevertheless, during the first two years of the war a few hundred people managed to emigrate to a third country; but between 1942 and 1944 it was practically impossible to leave Switzerland. The Federal Council reacted to the outbreak of the war and the obvious failure of the concept of Switzerland as a transit country with a decree passed on

October 17, 1939, that defined the legal status of emigrants: emigrants were obliged to leave the country as quickly as possible; they were forbidden to engage in political activities, in activities that breached Switzerland's neutral status, and in gainful employment—under threat of deportation. Furthermore, this decree, which was backed up by the authority of the Federal Council, created a legal basis for the practice, introduced in 1940, of interning emigrants in civilian work camps and demanding a financial contribution from the wealthier ones in favor of refugee relief organisations.[13] In principle, both the setting up of the work camps and the levying of financial contributions from emigrants were welcomed by the aid organizations, although they did not always approve of the way in which this policy was implemented. These contributions represented financial relief for the organizations that had been supporting the refugees since 1933 and had reached the limits of their financial capacity by the end of 1938. The aim of the work camps was to occupy the immigrants, who were forbidden to take up gainful employment, for the benefit of the country; at the same time, internment was a means of control and discipline. At the outbreak of the war there were between 7,000 and 8,000 immigrants in Switzerland, including around 5,000 Jews; during the war the country hosted a total of 9,909 immigrants, i.e., between September 1939 and May 1945 an estimated 2,000 refugees were allowed to enter the country and issued a tolerance permit.[14] In addition, between the outbreak of the war and the end of 1941, over 200 refugees who had entered Switzerland illegally and whom the authorities considered it untimely to deport, were interned on the basis of the law on foreigners.[15] Thus in contrast to 1938 and the period after 1942, the first two years of the war saw relatively few civilian refugees entering Switzerland. At the same time there is documentary evidence that during the same period over 1,200 people were refused entry, of whom 900 tried to get into Switzerland in June 1940, mainly along the border with France.[16]

NOTES

1. Koller, *Entscheidungen*, 1996, 22–24.

2. Ludwig, *Flüchtlingspolitik*, 1957, 24–27. Koller, *Entscheidungen*, 1996, 24f.

3. Wischnitzer, *Juden*, 1935, 177.

4. UEK, *Flüchtlinge*, 2001 (Publications of the ICE), section 3.1.

5. Hoerschelmann, *Exilland*, 1997, 12. UEK, *Flüchtlinge*, 2001 (Publications of the ICE), section 3.1.

6. Weingarten, *Hilfeleistung*, 1981, Adler-Rudel, *Evian Conference*, 1966, 214–41, and 1968, 235–73. Citrinbaum, *Participation*, 1977. See also section 3.7.

7. FA, E 2001 (E) 1970/217, vol. 206, Rothmund to Feldmann, May 24, 1954, and other documents on the question as to whether Ludwig should mention this note (original French) in his report. In accordance with a suggestion from Rothmund himself and a request from the EPD, Ludwig agreed not to publish the note for the sake of Motta's reputation.

8. Koller, *Entscheidungen*, 1996, 65f. UEK, *Flüchtlinge*, 2001 (Publications of the ICE), section 4.3–3.

9. Keller, *Grüninger*, 1993. UEK, *Flüchtlinge*, 2001 (Publications of the ICE), appendix 2: Biographische Angaben zu Paul Grüninger (1892–1972).

10. UEK, *Flüchtlinge*, 2001 (Publications of the ICE), chapter 4.1.2. See also Rothmund to Bonna, November 23, 1938, in: DDS, vol. 12, no. 454, 1045–47 (original German).

11. FA, E 2500 (-) 1990/6, vol. 141, record of E. Prodolliet's hearing, February 20, 1939. With regard to Prodolliet cf. Keller, *Grüninger*, 1993, 77–82.

12. Stadelmann, *Umgang*, 1998, 64.

13. Ludwig, *Flüchtlingspolitik*, 1957, 170f.

14. Ludwig, *Flüchtlingspolitik*, 1957, 164 and 318.

15. Koller, *Entscheidungen*, 1996, 87. Koller states that 212 civilian refugees were interned between September 1, 1939, and December 31, 1941. Robert Jezler's report dated July 30, 1942, records a total of 308 foreigners interned by the Police Division on January 1, 1942; see DDS vol. 14, no. 222, 721 (original German).

16. Koller, *Entscheidungen*, 1996, 94.

Palestine

REBECCA BOEHLING AND UTA LARKEY

From *Life and Loss in the Shadow of the Holocaust*

A few months after their March 1935 wedding, Lotti (née Steinberg) had emigrated to Palestine with her husband Hans, one of the two sons of Flora and Julius Kaiser-Blüth. Julius and his half-brother Karl owned Mannsbach & Lebach Company on the Lindenstrasse in Cologne, a textile factory that manufactured occupational clothing until it was "Aryanized" in December 1938.[1] Hans had been an active member of the Zionist youth organization, Blue and White (*Blau-Weiss*).[2] Studying in Munich and Berlin, he was trained as a mechanical and electrical engineer.[3] Although he had gotten an apprenticeship with the prestigious Deutz Company in Cologne, he could not find work in his profession once the Nazis came to power. Hans did manage to get hired as a commission-only sales representative for Palestine by the MAN (Machine Factory Augsburg-Nuremberg) Company in March 1935, but only after it was clear that he would be emigrating to Palestine.[4] Lotti met Hans Kaiser-Blüth in a Hebrew class organized by the Zionist movement in Cologne.[5] Hans, unable to find work in Germany and a committed Zionist, . . . had already made immigration plans when he first met Lotti. Within a matter of months Lotti and Hans married and planned their move to Palestine. . . .

Lotti's decision to emigrate to Palestine was definitely influenced by feeling excluded and trapped in Germany without a professional future, yet she clearly retained a strong sense of German identity.

We know of only a few instances in which Lotti felt she needed to stand up for herself as a Jew in Nazi Germany. One such incident highlights the ludicrous claims of antisemitic propaganda and the stereotypical assumptions about Jews, as well as Lotti's self-confidence. It occurred on a trip she took after her grand wedding, when she visited her "very dear relatives," the Bachrachs in Plettenberg, to say good-bye before leaving for Palestine. A man wearing Nazi Party insignia entered her train compartment, sat across from her and proceeded to flirt with her. When she pointed out to him that she was both married and Jewish, he expressed his disbelief, remarking on her "lack of racial characteristics." She told him off, stressing to him that he was giving a Jew this "compliment."[6] Examples of such "mistaken identity" were fairly widespread. Once the Nazi propaganda effectively portrayed Jews as "the other," ordinary Germans often had no compunction about pointing out who "looked Jewish."

Lotti's marriage into the wealthy Kaiser-Blüth family presented her with a more promising personal and professional future, as well as access to a new homeland. In addition to providing the necessary funds for them to emigrate to Palestine, Lotti's in-laws also purchased state-of-the-art Siemens equipment for her new dental practice. In 1922 the British mandate government of Palestine established immigration applicant categories according to the personal assets, profession or age of the applicant or his or her familial relationship to a resident of Palestine. The Kaiser-

Blüths provided the necessary funds so that Lotti and Hans were eligible for a Capitalist Certificate, also known as category A1, which was limited to prospective immigrants with significant personal assets. Immigrants applying under this category had to prove that they had liquid assets of at least LP (Palestine pounds) 1,000, equal to 1,000 British pounds, with 50 percent or more in cash.[7] At the time of Lotti and Hans's immigration LP 1,000 were worth about 15,000 RM.[8] This was more than the annual income of a lawyer or doctor.[9] A couple, or parents and one or two children under the age of 18, were allowed to immigrate on one certificate.

Immigration to Palestine had become financially more attractive to German Jews after the summer of 1933 due to the *Ha'avarah* [Transfer] Agreement.[10] In short, this controversial agreement between Zionist leaders and the Nazi government was geared to stimulate German-Jewish immigration to Palestine by means of favorable financial conditions and selling German goods to Palestine.[11] It also helped the dire foreign currency situation in Nazi Germany, as reflected in the reasoning behind the Reich Flight Tax. In the first years of the Nazi regime the exchange of Reichsmarks for other currencies was strictly limited, but then in 1936 it was forbidden altogether.[12]

Under the *Ha'avarah* Agreement, however, prospective immigrants from Germany to Palestine could bypass these currency exchange restrictions by depositing their Reichsmark funds into blocked accounts in one or other of those banks approved by the Palestine Trust Society for Advice to German Jews Inc. (known as the *Paltreu*).[13] They would then receive a *Ha'avarah* certificate, which entitled them to the equivalent of their blocked funds in Palestine pounds in the form of imported German goods or property in Palestine.[14] Importers of German goods in Pales-

tine deposited the funds for the purchase of these goods with the Anglo-Palestine Bank. This was where Lotti and Hans, and, after their arrival in Palestine, Kurt and Hanna, did all their banking.[15]

The *Ha'avarah* Agreement drew international criticism from many corners and was hotly debated when it was made public. Some opponents pointed out that this agreement only facilitated the immigration of wealthy Jews into Palestine, while the poorer majority would remain in Germany. Jewish opposition came mostly from groups outside Germany that advocated an economic boycott and rejected any deals with the Nazi regime. However, the *Ha'avarah* Agreement enabled a major resettlement of German Jews to Palestine. Most of the 60,000 German Jews who emigrated to Palestine between 1933 and the outbreak of World War II were direct or indirect beneficiaries of the *Ha'avarah*.[16] During this same period some 100 million RM were transferred to Palestine.[17]

The chances for Jewish engineers to work in their profession in Palestine were significantly lower than in many other countries of immigration.[18] Even though engineers who came as active Zionists received some support in finding jobs, they were often unemployed for a long time and had to work in unrelated fields. Palestine, which in the 1930s was only at the beginning of its industrialization, had a limited need for engineers or for many other professionals. Hans Kaiser-Blüth's connection to the German Zionist Federation (ZVfD) and his contract with the MAN Company as one of their sales representatives for Palestine allowed him to make some business deals through the *Ha'avarah* Agreement. Hans's son Michael later recalled that it was his father's representation of the MAN Company that helped get him a work permit in Palestine.[19] For Hans and many others in his situation the *Ha'avarah* Agreement provided a financial foundation on which to build, but, as it turned out, not a solid or lasting one.[20]

One of the reasons for Hans's fluctuating business success was the precarious political and economic nature of the *Ha'avarah* Agreement. By the end of 1935 he had managed to complete his first successful business deal.[21] This coincided with increased Jewish emigration from Germany after the Nuremberg Laws of September 1935.[22] In order to facilitate the flight of Jews from Germany to Palestine, but perhaps also to encourage it under the *Ha'avarah* Agreement, German imports to Palestine had to be competitively priced. The Ha'avarah therefore introduced measures in 1935 that effectively lowered the price of imported German goods and made them more competitive on the Palestinian market.[23] Hans's brief success in concluding a business deal at that time might have occurred owing to this 1935 economic stimulus.

More Jews immigrated to Palestine in 1935 than in any other year (61,900). The same year, however, saw the lowest annual share of German Jewish immigrants to Palestine (14 percent of total Jewish immigration) than in any other year from 1933 to 1941.[24] The total of German-Jewish immigration during these eight or more years amounted to 24 percent of all Jewish immigration to Palestine. Of all German Jews, only about 10 percent (about 60,000) immigrated to Palestine during the Nazi regime.[25] Of these 60,000 German Jews, 80 percent settled in cities,[26] almost half of them in Tel Aviv.[27] In other words, Hans and Lotti belonged to that minority of German Jews who immigrated to Palestine but once there, were part of an overall Jewish immigrant majority who decided on urban living.[28] Lotti and Hans settled in Tel Aviv, which was founded by Jews in 1909, not far from the ancient Arab harbor town of Jaffa. By 1936 the Jewish population in Palestine

was about 28 percent of the total, the Arab population constituting almost 72 percent.[29]

Although there are few extant descriptions of Lotti and Hans's first months in Palestine, it is quite certain that, like most German-Jewish immigrants in the mid 1930s, they experienced a difficult period of adjustment. Arriving in the extreme summer heat, they had to get used to an entirely foreign environment, climate, and lifestyle. They were lucky to have landed at the modern harbor of Haifa rather than Jaffa, where many immigrants had to jump from their ship into little boats, in which Arab workers rowed them to the beach.[30] Even though life was not easy for Lotti in those first months, and many amenities and the infrastructure that she had taken for granted in Germany were no longer part of everyday life, she reminisced fondly even decades later about the pioneer spirit, "the sense of belonging together, the mutual help" in Palestine.[31]

Lotti recalled their wonderful reception in Palestine from some of Hans's Zionist connections: "From the very beginning we had a very nice circle of people around us. We felt very welcome."[32] In Palestine the Association of German Immigrants (HOG),[33] part of the Jewish Agency for Palestine,[34] was very active in providing initial help, although with limited resources. It often distributed information fliers and organized Hebrew-language courses for new immigrants from Germany.[35] . . .

When describing their lifestyle in Palestine to her family, Lotti made sure to sound very upbeat and to emphasize what they would be used to, especially the availability of familiar food items, and the desirable, such as frequent visits to the beach, which was walking distance from their apartment. In the hot October days of 1935, Lotti bragged about serving her husband a three-course meal for lunch-"soup, potatoes, cucumber salad and steak on one day; bouillon, chicken thighs with cream sauce, beans, and pudding for dessert on the next."[36] Like many German-Jewish immigrants in Palestine, Lotti maintained the cooking style she had learned in Germany. Many German Jews disliked unfamiliar food like hummus and techina,[37] but often enjoyed the abundance of local vegetables.[38] Even though Lotti claimed optimistically that the climate would be manageable for everybody, she admitted a few days later in the same letter to her sister that Hans had initially suffered terribly owing to the unfamiliar heat. He had been lethargic, irritable, and unable to work.[39]

Lotti and Hans, similar to other bourgeois Jews from Germany, furnished and decorated their apartment with European flair. In a family photo from 1936 Lotti and Hans sit around their tastefully set table for *Kaffee und Kuchen*, complete with white table linen, a bouquet of flowers and delicate china cups and saucers. The elegant old-world glass cabinet, displaying valuable china and glass items, the comfortable sofa, and the print of Vermeer's *Girl with a Pearl Earring* further contributed to this picture of bourgeois taste and comfort. The traditional dark and heavy interior design favored by this *Bildungsbürger* [cultivated middle class] couple from Germany, including bookcases with classical literature, seems to clash with the intensely bright outdoors. A 1936 photograph from Lotti and Hans's balcony reveals newly built rows of three- and four-storied white houses in the Bauhaus or International style. The street looks bare, with very little vegetation and only the occasional young tree.[40]

Lotti hoped to set up her dental practice immediately upon arrival in Palestine. But the dental instruments and equipment that her in-laws shipped were held up for a year in the port of Jaffa because of unrest in Palestine.[41] After arriving, she did manage to begin treating patients, using space at the office of other dentists she knew. One such office, she bragged, "was located in one of the most modern buildings that one of the best architects had built for himself."[42] Once she was able to set up her own office, she managed to establish a successful and well-regarded dental practice. Lotti treated a younger family friend in Tel Aviv, who was originally from Plettenberg. He recalled sixty-five years later: "Lotti was one of the best dental surgeons, and also certainly one of the most attractive ones." With very few of Hans's business deals actually coming to fruition and his parents unable to continue their initial financial support due to unfavorable German regulations, the majority of the family income was generated through Lotti's dental practice.[43]

After Hans and Lotti got themselves settled in Palestine, Hans's parents and Lotti's mother, Selma, visited them there, albeit on separate occasions. Yet neither considered staying or immigrating at the time. The Kaiser-Blüths visited Lotti and Hans in the summer of 1936 for about three or four weeks. This timing is remarkable, since tensions in Palestine had worsened just before. Presumably the trip was planned long in advance, and the passage had already been paid. In April 1936 the Arab Higher Committee (AHC), led by the controversial Grand Mufti of Jerusalem, Haj Amin El-Husseini, demanded an end to all Jewish immigration to Palestine and the prohibition of land transfer to Jews.[44] The AHC declared a general strike, which was followed by riots protesting the surge of Jewish immigration to Palestine.[45] One major center of the strike and riots was Jaffa, the ancient harbor not far from Tel Aviv where Lotti's dental equipment was held up. Between April and June 1936 almost every issue of the weekly *Jüdische Rundschau*, a publication of the German Zionist Federation in Berlin, featured front-page articles on the violent unrest in Palestine. Articles entitled "Bloody Riots in Jaffa"[46] and "Continued Arab

Terror"[47] reported on the outbreak of violence at several locales. Nevertheless, the elder Kaiser-Blüths followed through with their planned visit to Palestine. . . .

Julius, not at all tempted to move himself or his assets to Palestine, still believed that the Nazi regime would pass quickly and that he and his profitable business in Cologne would ride out the hard times.[48] Even as late as the end of 1938, following the November Pogrom, Julius would still not waver from his determination to stay in Germany. . . .

Selma visited Lotti and Hans in the spring and summer of 1937. . . . Selma had to stay much longer in Palestine than she had intended owing to an emergency operation (an appendectomy) and the subsequent recuperation. Lotti accompanied her mother back home to Essen in September 1937, with a stopover in Italy.[49] In retrospect Lotti very much regretted not having tried to convince her mother to stay with them in Palestine.[50] But both during and for months after her visit in Palestine, Selma did not even consider emigration/immigration.

In the interim, the AHC increasingly contested further Jewish immigration to Palestine. The British government sought a territorial solution to the ethnic conflicts in Palestine and proposed two states, a Jewish one and an Arab one. When the plan was made public in July 1937, a new spate of violence erupted in Palestine. The leadership of both Jewish and Arab constituencies rejected the idea of this Partition Plan.[51] Still trying to honor the 1917 promise of the Balfour Declaration to establish a "national home" for the Jews, the British government did not achieve a workable solution for all involved.[52]

In July 1938, when world leaders were meeting at the Evian Conference to discuss the refugee crisis of German Jews, the situation in Palestine remained tense. The front-page news in the Zionist *Jüdische Rundschau* in Germany caused great worries among Lotti's friends and relatives: "In recent days a large number of terror acts, attacks and battles were reported from Palestine. The total number of Jewish deaths was seventeen. In Tel Aviv and Haifa several bombings cost the lives of many victims."[53] The newspaper even commented on "conditions that resemble a civil war."[54] Lotti's friends Lucie and Chaim, who had visited Tel Aviv at about the same time Selma did, recalled to Lotti: "We now only have our memories [of our visit last year], because the situation has so drastically changed. I have followed the present horrible events with interest and compassion. Unfortunately, the outcome is still unclear . . . Do you have any plans for the future or are you holding out and waiting for better times?"[55] Lotti's 81-year-old *Tante* Johanna, her father's sister, was also very worried about Lotti: "We all wish and hope that the government [in Palestine] will succeed in reestablishing law and order for everybody in the country so that the economy will flourish again."[56]

Interestingly, in her letters Lotti expressed much concern about the unsettling events in Germany but did not comment on the violence in Palestine.[57] In turn, Lotti's friends and relatives in Germany voiced their fears about Palestine but did not reflect on their own situation in letters. Of course, they were always conscious of censors and might not have wanted to risk having their letters intercepted or being punished for writing about the dangers for Jews in Germany. Both sides perceived the other to be in greater danger than the situation in which they found themselves. Lotti might have wanted to spare her friends and relatives such bad news, but . . . such events did not directly affect her daily life. At that time Lotti also had many private concerns: In addition to being overworked, suffering from migraines, feeling ill for several weeks herself, and running her busy practice, she also had taken care of a sick friend.[58] Furthermore, she was still hoping that her loved ones would leave Germany for Palestine and likely wanted to avoid giving them any unfavorable impression. Lotti remained positive that Palestine would become the future home for her siblings and her older family members.[59]

Lotti's dental practice was flourishing by early 1938,[60] as evident in descriptions about her "good clientele"[61] and the fact that she "could afford shopping sprees."[62] The fact that Lotti was able to open her own successful dental practice after a relatively short time in Palestine was mainly possible due to the high-end dental equipment that her in-laws had purchased for her. Many other professionals often had to accept menial work and a severe drop in social status.[63]

While Lotti had become a successful dentist, Hans's business was suffering terribly. The details of the development of the *Ha'avarah* Agreeement show that by 1938 the funds had been reduced by more than half compared with the previous year.[64] Hans was unaware in 1938 of the conflicts in Germany between the Reich Economics Ministry, the Foreign Office and the Interior Ministry regarding continuing support of the *Ha'avarah* Agreement and their economic impact on his business chances.[65] Moreover, when the 1936 Nazi rearmament program, the Four Year Plan, swallowed up more and more foreign currency, the Reich Economics Ministry drastically reduced the volume of German goods allowed for exports under the *Ha'avarah* Agreement. The Ministry created a list of German products that could or could not be exported to Palestine.[66] The MAN machinery that Hans was trying to bring into Palestine might well no longer have been allowed for import. This would offer one further explanation for his declining business deals. Despite the political controversies, the reduced number of German goods cleared under the *Ha'avarah* Agreement, rising transfer costs and the drastically declining exchange value of the money needed for a "capitalist certificate," the volume of goods involved in the *Ha'avarah* Agreement peaked in 1937.[67] However, just one year later the amount of goods transferred had sunk drastically to an all-time low.[68] A very disappointed Hans reported to Marianne that his business had suffered because of the political situation in Palestine and Europe in the summer of 1938. He received another blow when the transfer of certain machinery was discontinued in the fall. Nevertheless, he was already pursuing the sale of alternative products and was hoping for other, larger projects.[69]

Although Hans's income fluctuated and remained below his own and Lotti's expectations, their standard of living was rather high compared with that of many other *olim*, the Hebrew term for legal immigrants. While many memories of immigrants who settled in Palestine in the 1930s stressed the unifying pioneer spirit and the sense of community and belonging in *Eretz Israel*, the realities at the time were often more complicated. The frictions within the *Yishuv* (Jewish community), primarily between Eastern European and Western European Jewish immigrants and refugees, many of whom had fled Nazi Germany, often arose from different cultural practices and customs, as well as from the perceived social class differences related to Jewish identity and religiosity. The "language battle" of the 1930s between Yiddish and Hebrew was decided in favor of the latter.[70] Lotti and Hans, however . . . like many other immigrants from Germany, continued to speak German at home and in their social circles. As was the case with most immigrants, however, they used more and more Hebrew words in their correspondence. Many of these words, such as *ima* (mother) and *osereth* (household helper), *assutah* (maternity ward), *b'rith milah* (circumcision celebration), indicate the intersection of this German-speaking family with the Hebrew-speaking "outside world."

The Jewish immigrants from Germany, dubbed *yekkes* (*Jeckes*), often recalled their difficulties in learning Hebrew.[71] Even though the Association of German Immigrants (HOG) offered language courses, the combination of obsolete teaching methods, the perceived lack of encouragement to practice everyday Hebrew, and German Jews' deep attachment to German language and culture often hindered a speedy acculturation process.[72] While no statistics on Hebrew-language acquisition by German-Jewish immigrants to Palestine are available, anecdotal evidence suggests that many more men than women enrolled in intensive language courses so that they could improve their chances of finding work.[73] Of course there was a stronger presumption that men rather than women would need to join the workforce. In the case of Lotti and Hans, however, it was Lotti who, as a service professional in a field in demand, had to learn Hebrew in order to communicate with her patients, and as a result she spoke Hebrew better than Hans. Their son recalled: "She was more involved in the East European milieu where Hebrew was much more common. She had a mixed group of patients."[74] . . .

Even more pressing than getting their older family members out of Germany was the urgent need to help Kurt [Steinberg; Lotti's brother]. His arrest and incarceration in the aftermath of the November Pogrom set into motion his sisters' intense rescue attempts in the United States and in Palestine. . . . Lotti and Hans deposited LP 200 with the British consulate in Frankfurt for what Kurt described as an "interim stay" in Palestine.[75] Lotti and Hans also submitted the

necessary paperwork to the consulate to secure a tourist visa for Kurt. Lotti had offered to obtain for Kurt a certificate or residence permit for him until he could emigrate to the United States.[76] She wanted to be sure that he would agree and waited to get word from him once he was released from the concentration camp. Kurt's telegram reached a very worried Lotti in Palestine on December 2: "I am back. Send deposit slip and notarized invitation immediately."[77] Thanks to what Lotti called her "connections," she managed to send Kurt the required papers the same morning, including a notarized invitation and a receipt for funds wired to Germany.[78] Yet for some reason these efforts to get him to Palestine were unsuccessful. Fortunately, however, a few weeks later the sympathetic British consul in Cologne, J. E. Bell, granted a desperate Kurt and his soon-to-be wife Hanna one of the last tourist visas to Palestine. . . .

Kurt and Hanna were welcomed upon their arrival by Kurt's thrilled sister Lotti and her husband Hans. The reunion must have been so moving that Kurt, barely finding words to express his utter delight and joy, left it up to the recipient of his letter to imagine his emotions. He commented in an understated manner: "Well, and then . . . What shall I say? We talked and we all were happy." Kurt expressed how very much he was looking forward to the next night when the two couples were planning to celebrate his and Hanna's wedding with a festive meal, a roast goose.[79]

The euphoria surrounding Kurt and Hanna's arrival, however, soon gave way to everyday concerns about employment, housing and setting up lives in a completely alien culture. Not choice, but dire circumstances and luck led Kurt and Hanna to Palestine. For the first few months they shared a crowded household together with Lotti and Hans, who were expecting their first child in June. This was a taxing time for all. A shortage of apartments in Tel Aviv made it very difficult for new refugees to find a place to rent. Luckily, Lotti discovered that the family of one of her patients was about to move out of their one-room apartment. She arranged for Kurt and Hanna to get this apartment, even at a reasonable rent. To live in their own one-room apartment greatly helped Kurt and Hanna's process of adjustment. Kurt raved about their new place. Even though their furniture had not arrived, they were very happy with their modest but independent living conditions.[80] As newly-weds Kurt and Hanna had not yet lived together anywhere on their own and were now quite happy to do so.

Almost immediately after Kurt and Hanna moved out, however, Hans's brother Ernst, who had just immigrated from Germany, moved in with Lotti and Hans.[81] Again, the initial joy of having another family member join them in Palestine soon collided head-on with the challenges of everyday life. This was a particular burden for the pregnant Lotti. It would be more than seven months before she and Hans would have their small apartment to themselves again. Similar to Kurt, Hans's brother Ernst Kaiser-Blüth considered Palestine only a stepping-stone on his way to the United States. But, unlike the initial reaction of Kurt, who was thrilled to be out of Germany, where he suffered internment and maltreatment at KZ Buchenwald, Ernst's first observations and critical attitude toward Palestine did not bode well for even a short stay there. Ernst was among the lucky few young or middle-aged Jewish men who had not been interned in a concentration camp following the November Pogrom. He presumably felt less concerned about survival than about finding an acceptable new homeland, and wrote: "You are lucky that you went directly to America. There is nothing to gain here. The smart ones here are the ones who live off their savings. That way they lose less than if they worked."[82] Ernst expected to stay in Palestine for only a few months, as his relatively low registration number for the U.S. quota seemed to guarantee his immigration to the States by the end of 1939.[83]

At the beginning of their new lives in Palestine, Kurt worked for several weeks on a *moshav*, or cooperative farm, that raised chickens in Ramoth Hashavim and where Günter, one of his university friends, also worked.[84] Kurt and Hanna's son, Gideon, explained:

> Well, there are *kibbutzim* and *moshavim*. The *kibbutzim* had no private property, and everything was according to communist principles. Everything belonged to everybody: To each according to his needs, from each according to his abilities. *Moshavim* were something different. They also exist today. Everybody has a piece of land: one grows bananas; the other has chickens, and so on. But they have a communal system of distribution . . . my father, the state's attorney (*Oberlandesgerichtsrat*), worked in a chicken coop.[85]

Lotti recalled in a 1988 interview that in Palestine "Kurt and Hanna had a very, very difficult time at the beginning."[86] Trained in Germany as a lawyer in Roman rather than Anglo-American common law, Kurt could not work in his profession. Yet he was eagerly looking for jobs and needed to make a living quickly.[87] Kurt lived on the *moshav* for a few weeks but then left because he made hardly any money there. Back in Tel Aviv, Kurt decided to enroll in a Hebrew-language course and take private lessons in English conversation.[88] He was still intent on emigration to the United States and in the meantime hoped to increase his job opportunities with British employers. Hanna, without any special education or training in Germany or Palestine, did find a job as a waitress but lost it after a short time, presumably because she could not speak Hebrew.[89]

Another worry for Kurt was Hanna's and his temporary legal status. As a German lawyer and bureaucrat Kurt was still psychologically tied to following the rules and felt the urgent need to have all their papers in order. Given his plans to stay in Palestine only temporarily, he hesitated to take any steps to set up even semi-permanent residency in Palestine and agonized over the decision to apply for a renewal of their tourist visas. He had heard a rumor that it would be better not to alert the immigration officials to the upcoming deadline. But not having the correct legal papers would have, as Kurt put it, "gone against my convictions."[90] To Kurt's great relief, Marianne and Arthur Stern's affidavits for his immigration to the United States had arrived at the U.S. consulate in Stuttgart.[91] Kurt and Hanna's tourist visas were renewed for another three months at the beginning of May 1939, apparently because Kurt was able to produce the proof of sufficient funds. Whether the affidavits for immigration to the United States helped them to get their tourist visas for Palestine renewed is not clear. However, Kurt seemed to think it did and was glad to have them. With regard to how the British officials in Palestine treated immigrants, especially tentative ones, Kurt wrote: "They are very petty toward all groups of immigrants here right now."[92] Kurt did not know at the time that the British Parliament was developing drastic changes in immigration policies, which were published two weeks later in a White Paper. The White Paper effectively and drastically limited Jewish immigration to Palestine to a total of 75,000 people over a five-year period, beginning in 1939.[93]

Lotti, who had adjusted rather quickly and quite well to life in Palestine, became a little impatient with what she perceived as Kurt's reluctance to pursue new opportunities and what she considered his "passivity" in looking for jobs. Lotti saw Kurt as a "typical German academic," who lacked pragmatism and made mountains out of molehills instead of vigorously embracing new challenges.[94] Yet Lotti might have underestimated the effects of Kurt's traumatic experiences and the stress of his last months in Nazi Germany, as well as his initial culture shock. Kurt and Hanna did adjust to their new realities, but that, of course, took some time.

Kurt's search for work eventually met with some success. He waited for weeks to receive approval by the British for a job with a "very important [British] distributor of books, newspapers and journals" at the end of May.[95] He was first hired as a salesman on a probationary basis, with minimal income. After two months he and Hanna were supposed to be able to open a combination newspaper stand/bookstore in the main British military camp on the outskirts of Sarafand, where a new shopping center was planned.[96] Kurt was very much looking forward to receiving the British authorities' final approval and prepared himself for his new job by reading a lot of British and American publications. Kurt's delight at being able to recommend English-language journals and books to Marianne was offset by the difficulties he experienced a few weeks later:[97]

This matter takes its normal course, which means here a particularly slow one. I like the job and think that we will have a decent income. However, the construction in Sarafand has not even started. This is not my company's fault, which is very interested in a faster pace. The military government is to blame for the slow progress. And before the opening I cannot demand any income. But I have to admit that I am not being exploited, but trained. If it should take much longer, I will get another advance.

But no matter how long it will take, I consider it better to just follow this lead, which seems to be a solid company, instead of looking for some kind of inferior job. This would always limit me, and even this I would need to find first.[98]

Kurt and Hanna's financial situation was now very serious. All that Hanna earned was LP 4 a month as a part-time waitress.[99] At that time Hans calculated that the monthly subsistence income needed for a couple was LP 10.[100] This was indeed subsistence level, considering that in the mid 1930s the General Federation of Laborers in *Eretz Israel* (*Histadrut*) calculated that a bachelor needed to earn a minimum of LP 8 plus LP 3 for any additional person per household.[101] Kurt and Hanna's difficult material situation was exacerbated by the fact that their entire container with furniture, clothing and household items had been held up in the harbor of Antwerp already for eight months when war broke out.[102] As it turned out, Kurt and Hanna never saw their belongings again. . . .

In the spring of 1939 news from Palestine was not good. In an effort to curb Arab revolts and discontent over the growing number of Jewish immigrants, the British government released its White Paper. After that, further Jewish immigration would be contingent on the agreement of the Palestinian Arabs. The White Paper also severely restricted Jewish land acquisition and aimed at a bi-national state with a Jewish minority of about one-third of the total population.[103] After the White Paper was publicized enormous Jewish demonstrations erupted in Tel Aviv. Kurt and Hans were among those protesting. Kurt, for one, deeply resented:

this recent British policy, if one could call it that. The way the British now treat the promises they once made [the Balfour Declaration] and their "solution" to the future of Palestine is

unbelievable . . . You might have heard or read about the demonstrations here in the news. Hans and I were among the 50,000 protesters, a quarter of the population of 200,000. We all marched in wonderful order and discipline— and unlike Nazi Germany without any pressure—to the stadium, where we listened to speeches in Hebrew and sang the Hatikvah.[104]

The White Paper represented a significant setback for the Jewish population in Palestine and those remaining in Europe who had hoped to immigrate. Just as the number of European Jews seeking refuge in Palestine rose dramatically, the British government all but closed its doors to Jewish immigration.

NOTES

1. Julius to Lotti and Hans, December 9, 1938, Cologne KC. Cf. Becker-Jákli, *Das jüdische Krankenhaus*, 243, 252, 464. Karl Kaiser-Blüth had been a member of the board of the Cologne Jewish community since 1931 and a member of the board of trustees of the Jewish hospital in Cologne, the Israelitsches Asyl.

2. Michael Keynan (Hans and Lotti's son) to Rebecca Boehling, April 24, 2005, e-mail. This organization, founded in 1912, prepared young German-Jewish people for life in Palestine, including Hebrew lessons, classes on Jewish history and tradition, and life on a *kibbutz*. Cf. Walter Laqueur, *Generation Exodus: The Fate of Young Jewish Refugees from Nazi Germany* (Hanover NH: Brandeis University Press, 2001), 5.

3. Michael Keynan to Uta Larkey, March 10, 2009, email. Hans earned his *Diplom Ingenieur* degree in Germany (Dipl. Ing.).

4. The contract was signed by MAN representatives and Hans Kaiser-Blüth on March 4, 1935, in Nuremberg. Copy of MAN contract provided by Gabriele Mierzwa, Museum und Historisches

Archiv (VMM), manroland, Augsburg, April 21, 2009.

5. Interview with Michael Keynan, June 29, 2006, Tel Aviv, conducted by Uta Larkey. A family picture shows Lotti and Hans together in November 1934.

6. Interview with Lotti, November 2, 1988, IN 291, recorded at the Alte Synagoge Archives, Essen.

7. PHILO-Atlas, *Handbuch*, 142.

8. Due to several regulations, the exchange rate had increasingly worsened: In 1933, LP 1,000 equaled about 12,500 RM, in 1937, 20,000 RM, and from late 1938 until September 1939, 40,000 RM. See Barkai, *From Boycott to Annihilation*, 101.

9. In 1936 the annual income in Germany of a lawyer was about 10,800 RM, and that of a doctor about 12,564 RM. See Kater, *Doctors Under Hitler*, 33.

10. This agreement originated in a private initiative between Sam Cohen, the director of Hanotea Ltd. (an investment company for citrus orchards and equipment) in Palestine and the Reich Economics Ministry. For more information see Edwin Black, *The Transfer Agreement* (New York: Carroll & Graf, 2001).

11. On August 7, 1933, representatives of the Jewish Agency for Palestine, the German Zionist Federation (ZVfD) and the Reich Economics Ministry signed the *Ha'avarah* Agreement. See Barkai, *Hoffnung und Untergang*, 167.

12. Juliane Wetzel, "Auswanderung aus Deutschland," in Benz, ed., *Die Juden in Deutschland*, 464.

13. The Jewish-owned banks, Warburg in Hamburg and Wasserman in Berlin, acted on behalf of the *Paltreu*. Corresponding to the *Paltreu* was the Ha'avarah Trust and Transfer Office Ltd. in Tel Aviv. Cf. Black, *Transfer Agreement*, 249.

14. Francis Nicosia, *The Third Reich and the Palestine Question* (Austin: University of Texas Press, 1985), 47.

15. Lotti to Marianne, June 17, 1938, Tel Aviv OC.

16. Wetzel, "Auswanderung aus Deutschland," 467.

17. Friedländer, *Nazi Germany and the Jews*, 63.

18. Yoav Gelber and Walter Goldstern, *Vertreibung und Emigration deutschsprachiger Ingenieure nach Palästina 1933–1945* (Düsseldorf: VDI Verlag, 1988), 76.

19. Interview with Michael Keynan, June 29, 2006, Tel Aviv, conducted by Uta Larkey.

20. Gelber and Goldstern, *Vertreibung und Emigration*, 76.

21. Marianne's Notebook, December 31, 1935, Bern OC.

22. Werner Feilchenfeld, Dolf Michaelis and Ludwig Pinner, *Haavara-Transfer nach Palästina und Einwanderung deutscher Juden 1933–1939* (Tübingen: J.C.B. Mohr, 1972), 44.

23. Ibid., 51. Ha'avarah Ltd. granted a "bonification" to the importing companies in Palestine, a certain sum that was deducted from the asking price for imported goods. This lowered the price of German goods, which then could be offered at a competitive price in Palestine. After their arrival, the importing companies paid the net difference to Ha'avarah Ltd.

24. Ibid., 90. In 1939, however, the German-Jewish immigration rate climbed to 52 percent, an all-time high.

25. Friedländer, *Nazi Germany and the Jews*, 63. One-third of Jews from Germany emigrated to Palestine on a Capitalist Certificate. See Richarz, ed., *Jewish Life in Germany*, 341.

26. Samih K. Farsoun and Christina Zacharia, *Palestine and the Palestinians* (Boulder CO: Westview Press, 1997), 76.

27. Joachin Schlör, *Endlich im gelobten Land? Deutsche Juden unterwegs in eine neue Heimat* (Berlin: Aufbau Verlag, 2003), 121.

28. Ibid., 76. About 85 percent of Jews lived in the three major urban centers: Tel Aviv–Jaffa, Jerusalem and Haifa.

29. Farsoun and Zacharia, *Palestine and the Palestinians*, 78. For a critical analysis of the foundation of Tel Aviv see Mark LeVine, *Overthrowing Geography: Jaffa, Tel Aviv and the Struggle for Palestine 1880–1948* (Berkeley: University of California Press, 2005), 6off.

30. Gideon Greif, Colin McPherson and Laurence Weinbaum (eds.), *Die Jeckes: Deutsche Juden aus Israel erzählen* (Cologne: Bohlau, 2000), 30.

31. Interview with Lotti, November 2, 1988, IN 291, recorded at the Alte Synagoge Archives, Essen.

32. Ibid.

33. *Hitachdut Olej Germania* (Association of German Immigrants) was founded in 1932 in Palestine as an immigrants' aid organization.

34. The Jewish Agency for Palestine was founded by Jewish leaders in Palestine, among them Chaim Weizman, as a representational body for Jews in Palestine. It was formally recognized in 1929 under Article 4 of the British mandate for Palestine. It was to be a "public body for the purpose of advising and cooperating with the Administration of Palestine in such economic, social and other matters as may affect the establishment of the Jewish national home and the interests of the Jewish population in Palestine." See http://avalon.law.yale.edu/20th_century/palmanda.asp#art4 (accessed November 27, 2009). The Jewish Agency also administered the Palestine Immigration Office (*Palästina Amt*) in different German cities.

35. Gerda Luft, *Heimkehr ins Unbekannte: Eine Darstellung der Einwanderung von Juden aus Deutschland nach Palästina 1933–39* (Wuppertal: Peter Hammer Verlag, 1977), 120. Luft emigrated to Palestine in 1924 and was the Palestinian correspondent for the *Jüdische Rundschau*. She was the first wife of Chaim Arlosoroff, one of the initiators of the *Ha'avarah* Agreement.

36. Lotti to Marianne, October 1, 1935, Tel Aviv OC.

37. Techina, similar to tahini, is a flavored sesame paste essential for many Middle Eastern dishes.

38. Greif, McPherson and Weinbaum (eds.), *Jeckes*, 32.H.

39. Lotti to Marianne, October 1, 1935, Tel Aviv OC.

40. Zamenhoff Street, where Hans and Lotti lived, is today a leafy residential street in the center of busy Tel Aviv, off Dizengoff Square. Tel Aviv, also called the "White City," became in 2003 a UNESCO World Heritage Site for its 1930s Bauhaus or International architectural style.

41. Schreiber, "Die Familie Steinberg-Kaufmann," 7.

42. Interview with Lotti, November 2, 1988, IN 291, recorded at the Alte Synagoge Archives, Essen.

43. Zeew (Wolfgang) Neufeld to Uta Larkey, July 10, 2008, Tel Aviv, email. He died a few months later, at age 85, in December 2008.

44. The Arab Higher Committee (AHC) replaced the Palestine Arab Congress in 1936. The AHC was the central political organ and representative of Palestinian Arabs. Cf. Farsoun and Zacharia, *Palestine and the Palestinians*, 106.

45. Abraham Edelheit, *The Yishuv in the Shadow of the Holocaust: Zionist Politics and Rescue Aliya, 1933–1939* (Boulder CO: Westview Press, 1996), 131.

46. "Blutige Unruhen in Jaffa," *Jüdische Rundschau*, 41/32 (April 21, 1936).

47. "Weiterer Araberterror," *Jüdische Rundschau*, 41/46 (June 9, 1936).

48. Interview with Lotti, November 2, 1988, IN 291, recorded at the Alte Synagoge Archives, Essen.

49. Lotti did not mention this visit in her 1988 interview, but Michael, her son, found postcards sent to Selma in Palestine from her loved ones in Germany at this time. Michael Keynan to Rebecca Boehling, April 24, 2005, email.

50. Alicia Frohmann stressed the pain and regret her mother Lotti experienced over this "lost opportunity" to have saved her mother Selma. Interview with Alicia Frohmann, April 27, 2005, Miami, Florida, conducted by Rebecca Boehling. Michael Keynan mentioned in his 2006 interview that as a child he often asked his parents why they had not locked up his grandparents, "all three of them," in a bathroom during their respective visits in Palestine. Interview with Michael Keynan, June 29, 2006, Tel Aviv, conducted by Uta Larkey.

51. The Zionist Congress supported the partition idea but disagreed with the proposed border. The AHC rejected the partition idea altogether. See Nicosia, *The Third Reich and the Palestine Question*, 111.

52. The question of Palestine as "a land twice promised" is still debated by historians. The answers depend on their interpretation of the McMahon-Hussein correspondence (1915) and the Balfour

Declaration (1917). Whether or not Palestine was indeed twice promised, the British government clearly sent mixed messages and, arguably, in the midst of fighting a world war and trying to win over diverse allies, made pragmatic and contradictory commitments.

53. *Jüdische Rundschau*, 43/59 (July 26, 1938).

54. "Die Gefahr versämter Gelegenheiten," *Jüdische Rundschau*, 43/60 (July 29, 1938).

55. Chaim and Lucie to Lotti, August 10, 1938, Stettin FC.

56. Johanna Steinberg Moses to Lotti, June 17, 1938, Hanover FC.

57. One exception is the mention of her canceled vacation trip to Cyprus "due to the extremely critical political situation. . . . Taking trips here in the country is no pleasure right now." Lotti to Marianne, September 30, 1938, Tel Aviv OC.

58. See letters from Lotti to Marianne, April 6, 1938, July 1, 1938, and August 16, 1938, Tel Aviv OC.

59. Lotti to Marianne, July 1, 1938, Tel Aviv OC.

60. Johanna Steinberg Moses to Lotti, June 17, 1938, Hanover FC. Johanna wrote: "I was very pleased to hear that your practice is doing so well. You are a hard-working, courageous woman."

61. Interview with Michael Keynan, June 29, 2006, Tel Aviv, conducted by Uta Larkey.

62. Lotti to Marianne, April 6, 1938, Tel Aviv OC.

63. Luft, *Heimkehr ins Unbekannte*, 47. Luft noted that among her more than a hundred German-Jewish interview partners, only two wealthy immigrants were able to maintain their standard of living.

64. Feilchenfeld, Michaelis and Pinner (eds.), *Haavara-Transfer*, 45.

65. The Interior Ministry was committed to increased Jewish emigration from Germany to Palestine. While the Reich Economics Ministry was very much in favor of the continuation of the terms of the initial agreement, the Foreign Office cautioned against further collaboration with Zionist leaders after the 1936 Arab revolts. The Arab Chamber of Commerce had requested a revision of the *Ha'avarah* Agreement in a note to the German Consulate. For more information on the specifics of this conflict, see Nicosia, *The Third Reich and the Palestine Question*, 126–40 and Appendix 9.

66. Feilchenfeld, Michaelis and Pinner (eds.), *Haavara-Transfer*, 51.

67. Ibid., 69f.

68. Ibid., 45. Presumably it took a while for these changed conditions to have an impact on the actual transfer.

69. Hans to Marianne, October 1, 1938, Tel Aviv OC.

70. Luft, *Heimkehr ins Unbekannte*, 118. Cf. Gelber und Goldstern, *Vertreibung und Emigration*, 116. The Organization for Enforcing the Hebrew Language, supported by several Hebrew-language papers and other publications, actively encouraged the use of Hebrew, sometimes to a fault. The immigrants from Germany deeply resented the boycott of the German language in parts of the *Yishuv* and assured their opponents that they spoke the language of Goethe, not Hitler.

71. The etymology of this originally derogatory, teasing term coined in the 1930s to describe German immigrants is still debated. Some relate it to the German custom of always wearing a jacket, or *Jacke*, no matter what the climate or circumstances. See Gabriele Koppel, *Heimisch werden–Lebenswege deutscher Juden in Palästina* (Hamburg: Europäische Verlagsanstalt, 2000), 8. Others attribute the term to a derivation of a word for "joker," a Geek or a *Jeck*. See Shlomo Erel, ed., *Jeckes erzählen: Aus den Leben deutschsprachiger Einwanderer in Israel* (Vienna: LIT Verlag, 2004), 410. Tom Segev and Gideon Greif explain that the term is actually a Hebrew acronym meaning "block-headed Jew" (Jehudi Kshe Havana). See Tom Segev, *The Seventh Million: The Israelis and the Holocaust* (New York: Henry Holt, 2000). Cf. Greif, McPherson and Weinbaum (eds.), *Jeckes*. German Jews were often perceived as naïve, unwilling or unable to adapt to a Middle Eastern lifestyle, always proper and hard working. See Martina Kliner-

Fruck, *"Es ging ja ums Uberleben": Jüdische Frauen zwischen Nazi-Deutschland, Emigration nach Palästina und ihrer Rückkehr* (Frankfurt am Main: Campus Verlag, 1995), 132.

72. Luft, *Heimkehr ins Unbekannte*, 120f.

73. Kliner-Fruck, *"Es ging ja ums Uberleben,"* 153.

74. Interview with Michael Keynan, June 29, 2006, Tel Aviv, conducted by Uta Larkey.

75. Kurt to Marianne, February 9, 1939, Tel Aviv OC.

76. Selma to Marianne, November 22, 1938, Essen and Lotti to Marianne, December 5, 1938, Tel Aviv OC.

77. As quoted by Lotti in letter to Marianne, December 5, 1938, Tel Aviv OC.

78. Ibid.

79. Kurt to several family members in the United States and Germany, February 9, 1939, Tel Aviv OC.

80. Kurt and Hanna to Marianne, May 3, 1939, Tel Aviv OC.

81. Kurt to Marianne, May 3, 1939, Tel Aviv OC.

82. Kurt, Lotti and Ernst to Marianne, May 22, 1939, Tel Aviv OC.

83. Ernst's registration number was 10327. Kurt to Marianne, May 3, 1939, Tel Aviv OC.

84. Letter from Marianne to Arnold, March 22, 1939. She mentioned that Kurt worked as a *poël*, which she translated as *Landarbeiter* (farmworker).

85. Interview with Gideon Sella, June 28, 2006, Tel Aviv, conducted by Uta Larkey. *Kibbutzim* and *moshavim* are the plural forms.

86. Interview with Lotti, November 2, 1988, IN 291, recorded at the Alte Synagoge Archives, Essen.

87. Kurt to Marianne, May 3, 1939, Tel Aviv OC.

88. Ibid.

89. Lotti to Marianne, April 30, 1939, Tel Aviv OC.

90. Kurt to Marianne, February 9, 1939, Tel Aviv OC.

91. Kurt to Marianne, February 19, 1939, Tel Aviv OC.

92. Kurt to Marianne, May 3, 1939, Tel Aviv OC.

93. For the text of the 1939 White Paper, see http://avalon.law.yale.edu/20th_century/ brwhi939.asp (accessed January 2, 2010).

94. Lotti to Marianne, April 30, 1939, Tel Aviv OC.

95. Kurt to Selma and Henny, June 3, 1939, Tel Aviv OC.

96. Lotti to Marianne, May 28, 1939, Tel Aviv. Sarafand was the name of an Arab village about 2 miles from Rishon le-Zion where Kurt and Flanna moved.

97. Kurt to Marianne, June 14, 1939, Tel Aviv OC.

98. Kurt to Marianne, July 10, 1939, Tel Aviv OC.

99. Lotti to Marianne, May 28, 1939, Tel Aviv OC.

100. Hans to Marianne, April 30, 1939, Tel Aviv OC.

101. Luft, *Heimkehr ins Unbekannte*, 48.

102. Even though Selma urged Kurt in almost every letter from October 1939 to March 1940 to arrange for the transport of the container with his furniture and other belongings from Antwerp to Tel Aviv, at times of war this was very unlikely.

103. Hershel and Abraham Edelheit (eds.), *History of Zionism: A Handbook and Dictionary* (Boulder CO: Westview Press 2000), 525. For the text of the British White Paper of 1939, see http://avalon.law.yale.edu/20th_century/brwhi939.asp (accessed November 21, 2009).

104. Kurt to Marianne, May 22, 1939, Tel Aviv OC. The *Hatikvah* (Hope), written in the 1880s, expresses the ancient hope of the Jewish people to be a free people in the Land of Israel. The *Hatikvah* became the unofficial anthem of the Zionist movement in the late 1880s and the national anthem of the State of Israel after 1948.

Going and Staying

MARION KAPLAN

From *Between Dignity and Despair*

Jews fled the personal hostility of villages and smaller towns by seeking the anonymity, and hence relative safety, of large cities. A teenager noted that by 1935 Jews in his small town could no longer go to cafes, the pool, or parks, not to mention the "Hitlerplatz," which no Jew could enter because of its name. After moving to Berlin in 1935, he enjoyed the freedom of not being recognized among the larger population. Ann Lewis also remarked that she was glad to be a Berliner, grateful—like many of her elders—for her relative freedom. Economic strangulation, occurring most quickly in small towns, also provoked migration. By 1935–36, in some small towns over 80 percent of the Jewish population was destitute. As people migrated in search of work, local Jewish communities dwindled in number and in resources. By 1937, 200 of the 1,600 communities had dissolved and over 600 of those remaining required outside subsidies. A large proportion of the migrants were women. Many sought jobs as domestics and would later become the sole support of families left behind.[1]

For those left behind, the loneliness was of "such a degree and so sudden . . . as had never before been experienced even in Jewish history." Family and friendship circles shrank. In 1936, one woman described the feeling of leaving a woman friend as "dying a little."

Female friendships—There is something sisterly. . . . Parting from a friend! Last hour together. Suitcases . . . are packed, the furniture stored, the apartment . . . stands empty and . . . appears almost hostile. . . . Will we elderly people ever see each other again? . . . Will friendship last . . . ? . . . A personal story from an individual fate but also a community fate for us Jews; for who does not feel . . . this tear, this shock . . . during separation, emigration, departure! *Partir c'est mourir un peu!*

By 1938, Jewish newspapers had concluded: "We must learn to endure loneliness."[2]

In the families that migrated, women had to adjust their household to a new urban environment: crowded apartments, unskilled jobs, and public constraints, not to mention deteriorating political circumstances. Women who stayed in big cities participated as never before in social welfare work within Jewish communities and Jewish women's organizations to integrate the steady stream of newcomers. Jewish communities and organizations worked to provide the new arrivals with shelters, soup kitchens, and used clothing and furniture centers. They also expanded orphanages, old-age homes, and meal and transportation subsidies. Often women volunteered in such endeavors while prodding their own families to emigrate.

As emigration became more and more crucial, women usually saw the danger signals first and urged their husbands to flee Germany. Among rural Jews, "the role of women in the decision to emigrate was decisive. . . . The women were the prescient ones . . . the ones ready to make the decision, the ones who urged their husbands to emigrate." Urban Jewish women had similar reactions. Marta Appel described a discussion among friends in Dortmund about a doctor who had just fled in the spring of 1935. The men in the room, including her husband, a rabbi, condemned him.

The women . . . found that it took more courage to go than to stay. . . . "Why should we stay here and wait for our eventual ruin? Isn't it better to go and to build up a new existence somewhere else, before our strength is exhausted by the constant physical and psychic pressure? Isn't the future of our children more important than a completely senseless holding out . . . ?" All the women shared this opinion . . . while the men, more or less passionately, spoke against it. I discussed this with my husband on the way home. Like all other men, he . . . couldn't imagine leaving one's beloved homeland and the duties that fill a man's life. "Could you really leave all this behind you to enter nothingness?" . . . "I could," I said, without a moment's hesitation.

The different attitudes of men and women described here suggest that gender significantly determined the decision between flight and fight.[3]

Women were more inclined to emigrate because they were not as integrated into the public world. For example, they rarely saw themselves as indispensable to the Jewish public. One man declared in his memoirs that he could not leave Germany because he thought of himself as a "good democrat" whose emigration would "leave others in the lurch" and would be a "betrayal of the entire Jewish community."[4] Rabbi Leo Baeck, the official leader of German Jewry, evinced similar feelings. Offered safe permanent passage by two Britons in 1939, he responded: "I will go, when I am the last Jew alive in Germany."[5]

Women were also less involved than men in the economy, even though some had been in the job market their entire adult lives. This had several effects. First, Jewish men had a great deal more to lose. Only when they could no longer make a living were some men willing to leave. To emigrate before they had lost their positions or before their businesses or professional practices had collapsed would have required men to tear themselves away from their life work, their clients, and colleagues. There were other considerations as well. The daughter of a wealthy businessman commented: "When the Nazis appeared on the scene, he was too reluctant to consolidate everything and leave Germany. He may have been a bit too attached to his status, as well as his possessions." But even businesswomen appeared less reluctant than their spouses to emigrate. One wealthy female manufacturer, whose husband managed her inherited business, wanted to flee in 1933. He refused. She insisted that at least they both learn a trade (which later served them well in Shanghai).[6] In short, the family could be moved more easily than a business or profession. In light of men's close identification with their occupations, they often felt trapped into staying. Women, whose identity was more family-oriented than men's, struggled to preserve what was central to them by fleeing with those they loved.

Women's subordinate status in the economy probably eased their decision to flee, since they were familiar with the kinds of work, generally domestic, they would have to perform in places of refuge. Lore Segal described how her mother, formerly a housewife and pianist, cheerfully and successfully took on the role of maid in England, whereas her father, formerly a chief accountant in a bank, experienced his loss of status as a butler and gardener with great bitterness.[7] Even when both sexes fulfilled their refugee roles well, women seemed less status-conscious than men. Perhaps women did not experience the descent from employing a servant to becoming one as intensely as men, since their status had always been determined by that of their father or husband anyway.

Finally, women's lesser involvement in the economy allowed them more time for greater contact with a variety of non-Jews, from neighbors to schoolteachers. Jewish men worked mostly with other Jews in traditional Jewish occupations (in specific branches of retail trades, in the cattle trade, or in independent practices as physicians and attorneys). They may have been more isolated than women from non-Jewish peers (though not from non-Jewish customers). This spared them direct interactions with hostile peers but also prevented the awareness of deteriorating circumstances garnered from such associations. Many Jewish men were isolated further as the boycotts of Jewish concerns grew, for the clientele of Jewish businesses that survived turned predominantly Jewish. And discriminatory hiring meant that Jewish blue- and white-collar workers found opportunities only within the Jewish economic sector. In 1936, some Jews decried a "Jewish economic ghetto," and in 1937 the Council for German Jewry in London reported that the German-Jewish community lived in a "new type of ghetto . . . cut off from economic as well as social and intellectual contact with the surrounding world."[8] In contrast, Jewish women (even those who worked in the same "Jewish ghetto") picked up other warning signals from their neighborhoods and children.

Men and women led relatively distinct lives, and they often interpreted daily events differently. Although women were less involved than men in the work world, they were more integrated into their immediate community. Raised to be sensitive to interpersonal behavior and social situa-

tions, women had social antennae that not only were more finely tuned than their husbands' but also were directed toward more unconventional— what men might have considered more trivial— sources of information. For example, an American Jewish couple who resided in Hamburg during the 1930s were alerted to danger by household help. The wife wrote: "Any woman knows . . . her best source of information are the servants. . . . I received more information from Harold . . . than I could have received at the best . . . intelligence office."[9] Women registered the increasing hostility of their immediate surroundings unmitigated by a promising business prospect, a loyal employee or patient, or a kind customer. Their constant contacts with their own and other people's children probably provided them with further warning signals—and they took those signals seriously.

Men, on the other hand, felt more at home with culture and politics. Generally more educated than their wives, they cherished what they regarded as German culture—the culture of the German Enlightenment. This love for their German liberal intellectual heritage gave men something to hold on to even as it "blunted their sense of impending danger." When Else Gerstel argued with her husband about emigrating, he, a former judge, insisted that "the German people, the German judges, would not stand for much more of this madness."[10]

One could argue that men were more "German" than women not only with regard to their education but also with regard to their sense of patriotism. Even in a situation gone awry, there were war veterans who refused to take their wives' warnings seriously. These men had received reprieves in 1933 because of President Hindenburg's intervention after the exclusionary April laws (although the reprieves proved to be temporary). Their wives typically could not convince them that they, too, were in danger. One woman, who pressed her husband to leave Germany, noted that he "constantly fell back on the argument that he had been at the front in World War I."[11] Most men expressed their arguments in terms of having served their country and, hence, having certain rights. Nevertheless, the "front" argument had a deep emotional core, for the war experience had aroused strong feelings of patriotism.

A widespread assumption that women lacked political acumen—stemming from their primary role in the domestic sphere—gave women's warnings less credibility. One woman's prophecies of doom met with her husband's amusement: "He laughed at me and argued that such an insane dictatorship could not last long." Even after their seven-year-old son was beaten up at school, he was still optimistic. Many men also pulled rank on their wives, insisting that they were more attuned to political realities: "You're a child," said one husband. "You mustn't take everything so seriously. Hitler used the Jews . . . as propaganda to gain power—now . . . you'll hear nothing more about the Jews."[12] Often the anxious partner heard the old German adage: "Nothing is ever eaten as hot as it's cooked."

Men, therefore, attempted to see the "broader" picture, to maintain an "objective" stance, to scrutinize and analyze the confusing legal and economic decrees and the often contradictory public utterances of the Nazis. Men mediated their experiences through newspapers and broadcasts. Politics remained more abstract to them, whereas women's "narrower" picture—the minutiae (and significance) of everyday contacts—brought politics home. Summing up, Peter Wyden recalled the debates within his own family and those of other Berlin Jews:

It was not a bit unusual in these go-or-no-go family dilemmas for the women to display more energy and enterprise than the men. . . .

Almost no women had a business, a law office, or a medical practice to lose. They were less status-conscious, less money-oriented than the men. They seemed to be less rigid, less cautious, more confident of their ability to flourish on new turf.

The Berlin artist Charlotte Salomon, who painted a stunning exploration of her life while awaiting her fate in southern France in 1941–42, depicted this dilemma. She portrayed her short grandmother looking up to her tall grandfather, whose head is above the frame of the painting. The caption reads: "Grossmama in 1933: 'Not a minute longer will I stay here. I'm telling you let's leave this country as fast as we can; my judgment says so.' Her husband almost loses his head."[13]

Even given the gender differences in picking up warning signals and yearning to leave, it is crucial to recognize that these signals occurred in stages. Alice Nauen and her friends "saw it was getting worse. But until 1939 nobody in our circles believed it would lead to an end" for German Jewry. Interspersed with personal, daily observations, women's assessments were often more on target than men's, but obviously women could also be confused by Nazi policies and events. When Hanna Bernheim's sister, who had emigrated to France, returned for a visit in the mid-1930s, the sister wanted to know why the Bernheims remained in their south German town. Hanna Bernheim replied:

First of all it is so awfully hard for our old, sick father to be left by all his four children. Second there are so many dissatisfied people in all classes, professions and trades. Third there was the Roehm Purge and an army shake up. And that makes me believe that people are right who told us "Wait for one year longer and the Nazi government will be blown up!"

Moreover, these signals were often profoundly mixed. As we have seen, random kindnesses, the most obvious "mixed signals," gave some Jews cause for hope. One woman wrote that every Jewish person "knew a decent German" and recalled that many Jews thought "the radical Nazi laws would never be carried out because they did not match the moderate character of the German people."[14] Ultimately, confusing signals, often interpreted differently by women and men, as well as attempts by the government to rob Jews of all their assets, impeded many Jews from making timely decisions to leave Germany.

Women and men often *assessed* danger differently, reflecting their different contacts and frames of reference. But *decisions* regarding emigration seem to have been made by husbands. Despite important role reversals, both men and women generally held fast to traditional gender roles in responding to the political situation—unless they were overwhelmed by events.

The common prejudice that women were "hysterical" in the face of danger worked to everyone's disadvantage. Charlotte Stein-Pick begged her father to flee in March 1933. Her husband brought her father to the train station only moments before the ss arrived to arrest the older man. Not knowing about the ss visit, her husband said upon returning home: "Actually, it was entirely unnecessary that your parents left, but I supported you because you were worrying yourself so much." Stein-Pick also overheard a private conversation in a train on November 6, 1938, two days before the November Pogrom, in which the participants discussed what was about to happen to Jewish men. "When I arrived home I implored my husband and a friend who lived with us to leave . . . immediately. . . . But my counsel was in vain. They believed my nerves had given way: how should these people have known anything and one could not have built

camps big enough." Another husband believed his wife to be completely overwrought when she suggested—in 1932—that he deposit money in a Swiss bank. While cabaret artists were already joking about people taking trips to visit their money in Switzerland, her husband refused. In this case, the belief that women should keep out of business matters made it even less likely that her suggestions would be heeded. If women's appraisals were considered too emotional in general, pregnancy discredited them completely, since men considered pregnant women especially high-strung. A month before the Germans annexed Austria, a Viennese Catholic wife told her Jewish husband that Hitler meant trouble for him and packed all of his things. But she could not persuade him to depart; he attributed her worries to her pregnancy.[15]

Men's role and status as breadwinners made them hesitant to emigrate and gave them the authority to say no. Else Gerstel fought "desperately" with her husband of twenty-three years to emigrate. A judge, he refused to leave, insisting: "There is as much demand for Roman law over there as the Eskimos have for freezers." Describing their dispute as a great strain on their marriage, she wrote, "I was in constant fury." Another wife recalled her attempt to convince her husband to flee: "A woman sometimes has a sixth feeling. . . . I said to my husband, '. . . we will have to leave.' He said, 'No, you won't have a six-room apartment and two servants if we do that.' . . . I said, 'Okay, then I'll have a one-room flat . . . but I want to be safe.'" Despite his reluctance, she studied English and learned practical trades. His arrest forced their emigration to Australia, where she supported the family.[16]

In the rare cases in which husbands followed their wives' assessment and emigrated, the wives either recruited other male friends to help convince the husbands or were themselves professionals whose acumen in the public world was difficult to deny. Marie Bloch had read Hitler's *Mein Kampf* in 1929 and insisted on sending her children out of the country in 1933. Her husband refused to leave his factory and could not "give up the thought that the Germans would see in time what kind of a man Hitler was." After the Nuremberg Laws she knelt in front of his bed, begging him to leave. Distraught, she asked him whose opinion he would respect and invited that friend to their home. The friend told them to flee to the United States where he, himself, was heading. Only then did her husband agree to go. A woman lawyer had an easier time convincing her spouse, since she had been politically aware and active. It was her decision to flee: "My husband saw that I was consumed with anxiety. Despite his good job, he decided to leave Germany with me." They fled only as far as France, where he was later caught by the Nazis and murdered in Auschwitz, while she managed to join the Resistance. In retrospect, she wished she had thanked him—which she never did—"for his selfless decision . . . for this most ardent proof of his love that he had ever given me."[17]

In the late 1930s, events often jolted families into leaving, with women sometimes taking the lead. In early 1938, one daughter reported that her mother "applied to the American authorities for a quota number without my father's knowledge; the hopeless number of 33,243 was allocated. It was a last desperate act and Papa did not even choke with anger anymore " Her parents and young brother were deported and murdered. After narrowly escaping battering by a Nazi mob in her small hometown, another woman convinced her husband to "pack their things throughout the night and leave this hell just the next day." After the November Pogrom, some wives broke all family conventions by taking over the decision making

when it became clear that their husbands' reluctance to flee would result in even worse horrors. Else Gerstel's husband had been arrested but not imprisoned, and he still "had no intention of leaving Germany, but I sent a telegram to my brother Hans in New York . . . 'Please send affidavit.'"[18]

Sometimes the "Aryan" wives of Jewish men took the lead. Verena Hellwig, for example, feared for her two "mixed" (*Mischling*) children even as her husband, also of "mixed blood," insisted on remaining in Germany until his approaching retirement. When her teenage son could not find an apprenticeship, she spoke to a Nazi official. He told her that people of "mixed blood" were "our greatest danger. They should either return to Judaism . . . and suffer the fate of the Jews or they should be prevented from procreating, like retarded people." She had reached her turning point: "Her homeland was lost"; "Germany was dead" for her. She soon emigrated to England with her son, followed by her daughter. This meant a temporary separation from "her husband, [her] best friend," but she had to find a future for her children.[19] . . .

Obstacles to Emigration

. . . . After November 1938, "essentially everyone tried to find a possibility of emigrating."[20] Still, immigration restrictions in foreign countries and Nazi bureaucratic and financial roadblocks stymied Jews. Countries of potential refuge thwarted Jewish entry. Elisabeth Freund described her and her husband's many attempts to leave Germany:

It is really enough to drive one to despair. . . . We have filed applications for entry permits to Switzerland, Denmark, and Sweden . . . in vain, though in all these countries we had good connections. In the spring of 1939 . . . we obtained an entry permit for Mexico for 3,000 marks. But we never received the visa, because the Mexican consulate asked us to present passports that would entitle us to return to Germany, and the German authorities did not issue such passports to Jews. Then, in August 1939 we did actually get the permit for England. But it came . . . only ten days before the outbreak of war, and in this short time we were not able to take care of all the formalities. . . . In the spring of 1940 we received the entry permit for Portugal. We immediately got everything ready and applied for our passports. Then came the invasion of Holland, Belgium, and France. . . . A stream of refugees poured into Portugal, and the Portuguese government recalled . . . all of the issued permits. It was also good that in December 1940 we had not . . . paid for our Panamanian visas, for we noticed that the visas offered us did not . . . entitle us to land in Panama.

Freund was frustrated with friends who urged them to leave Germany: "As if that were not our most fervent wish." She agonized: "There are no more visas for the U.S.A. My husband has made one last attempt and asked our relatives in America by wire for the entry visas for Cuba. . . . No other country gives an entry permit to German Jews any longer, or is still reachable in any way."[21]

Once they received permission to *enter* a foreign country, Jews still had to acquire the papers to *exit* Germany. "Getting out . . . is at least as difficult as getting into another country and you have absolutely no notion of the desperation here," wrote sixty-six-year-old Gertrud Grossmann to her uncomprehending son abroad. Getting the required papers took months of running a bureaucratic gauntlet, which many women faced alone, meeting officials who could arbitrarily add to the red tape at whim: "There was no rule and every official felt like a god."[22]

Bella Fromm summarized the plight of all German Jews: "So far I have gathered a collection of twenty-three of the necessary documents. I have made a thorough study of the employees and furniture in fifteen official bureaus . . . during the hours I have waited." Bewildered, she reported that she did not yet have all the papers she needed—and this was a few months before the November Pogrom. Afterward, Mally Dienemann, whose sixty-three-year-old husband languished in Buchenwald, raced to the Gestapo to prove they were ready to emigrate. Next she rushed to the passport office to retrieve their passports.

> After I had been sent from one office to another . . . I had to go to . . . the Emigration Office in Frankfurt, the Gestapo, the police, the Finance Office, [send] a petition to Buchenwald, a petition to the Gestapo in Darmstadt, and still it took until Tuesday of the third week, before my husband returned. . . . Next came running around for the many papers that one needed for emigration. And while the Gestapo was in a rush, the Finance Office had so much time and so many requests, and without certification from the Finance and Tax offices . . . one did not get a passport, and without a passport a tariff official could not inspect the baggage.[23]

Finally arriving in Palestine in March 1939, Rabbi Dienemann died from his ordeal.

By 1939, new arbitrary laws slowed emigration even more. Even with a U.S. affidavit in hand, Else Gerstel could not simply leave "immediately," as her brother abroad urged. "It was impossible even to buy the ship tickets before we had the official permits. And that meant to pay taxes that were much higher than everything we owned. There were several months of red tape, desperate struggle." The elderly were physically ill equipped to endure the strains of this paper chase. Gertrud

Grossmann confided by letter: "I dread going to the consulate and possibly standing around there for hours, which is physically impossible for me." The situation deteriorated so much that by 1940 she wrote her son: "Your emigration [in 1938] was child's play compared to today's practically insurmountable difficulties."[24]

As the government harassed the desperate Jews, individual Germans sought to enrich themselves at Jewish expense and Jews, often women, since the men were in camps, regularly encountered corruption. Charlotte Stein-Pick, anxious to get her husband out of a camp and expecting to receive visas from the American consulate imminently, was shocked to learn that there were Germans at the embassy who expected bribes in order to forward her papers. She went to a lawyer, who informed her that it would take 3,000 marks to pay off the swindlers: "I ran around bewildered. . . . In spite of everything, we German Jews still continued to resist believing the terrible corruption which National Socialism brought with it." In a respectable shipping company's elegant office on Berlin's exclusive boulevard, *Unter den Linden*, another desperate woman had to hand over a 100-mark payoff for a place on a ship's waiting list. Moreover, she had to participate in the expensive farce of paying for round-trip tickets because, even though the Germans would have blocked their reentry, her family's visas to Cuba had to be tourist visas. Since this family had hidden money before the government blocked it, she was able to pay for the trip.[25] A situation like this was frustrating and nerve-racking before the war; it could cost Jewish lives thereafter.

Even before the pogrom, the government had no intention of letting Jews escape with their money or property. Afterward it blocked bank accounts more stringently and robbed potential emigrants more thoroughly. In Berlin, the Gestapo set up a special "one-stop" emigration bureau where: "the emigrating Jew was fleeced, totally and completely, in the manner of an assembly line." When they entered they were "still . . . the owner[s] of an apartment, perhaps a business, a bank account and some savings." As they were pushed from section to section "one possession after the next was taken." By the time they left, they had been "reduced to . . . stateless beggar[s]," grasping one precious possession, an exit visa.[26]

Nazi avarice is illustrated by the experience of the Bernheim family. They left in July 1939, falling prey to the Nazi decree of February 1939 that expropriated all valuable stones and metals from Jews. Thus, before emigrating, Hanna Bernheim packed a suitcase and headed for a Nazi "purchasing post" to give up her valuables:

There were many people who had three, five suitcases, full of marvelous things: old [bridal] jewelry, Sabbath candles and goblets . . . beautiful old and modern plates. . . . The young officials were in high spirits. . . . These treasures, often collected by generations, were thrown together. . . . They were small-minded enough to take jewelry not at all precious as to the . . . value, but precious to us as souvenirs of beloved persons.

Shortly thereafter, at the airport, agents examined Bernheim's hatbox and confiscated a brass clock, toiletries, and underwear. The guard even insisted on a body search. She recalled: "The propellers started . . . and I could only beg the woman to do the examination immediately. She was nice and correct, helped me with dressing, and the French pilot waited. And so I flew out of . . . hell."[27] Nazi insatiability was so great that a dentist warned one woman to see him before departing "and have him cover a gold crown and filling I had with a white coating. A patient of his had missed her ship while the gold in her mouth was removed by a Nazi dentist."[28]

Despite chaos and barriers, the largest number of Jews to leave in one year emigrated directly after the November Pogrom, reaching 78,000 in 1939. The United States, Palestine, and Great Britain took the most German Jews, but Jews left no escape route untried, as the 8,000 who fled to Japanese-occupied Shanghai show. By September 1939, about 185,000 (racially defined) Jews still remained in Germany; their numbers sank to 164,000 by October 1941, when Jewish emigration was banned. Another 8,500 managed to escape between 1942 and 1945. Exact figures of those who left Germany as a result of racial persecution cannot be established, but a good estimate is between 270,000 and 300,000 Jews. That is, close to three-fifths of German Jews managed to flee Germany. Yet approximately 30,000 of those who got out were later caught by the Nazis in other European countries. Ultimately, about half of those Jews who had lived in Germany in 1933 could save themselves through emigration to safe countries. Their friends and relatives who remained behind were murdered.[29]

Packing for Good

When Jews finally reached the stage of packing, they believed their departure would be permanent. Women took charge. As Berta Kamm put it: "Only a woman knows how much there is to deliberate and resolve in such a rushed departure." Packing was so clearly considered "women's work" that some women stayed behind to do it, sending men and children ahead. Packing quickly became an art as Nazi rulings and red tape skyrocketed. To emigrate with one's belongings, one had to receive a permit from the Finance Department. This permit was obtainable only after preparing lists of all the items one wished to take.

Lisa Brauer spent an entire week writing "endless lists, in five copies each . . . every item entered, every list neatly typed, and in the end I could only speak and breathe and think in shoes, towels, scissors, soap and scarves." Another woman recalled how "a science of emigration advisement came into being [and these advisers] prepared the lists. For example, one was not allowed to say 'one bag of sewing supplies,' but had to detail every thimble, every skein of wool, every snap." Also one could not take just anything: "Only those things were allowed which had been purchased before 1933." Other items could be taken only in limited amounts and only "if the complete purchase price was paid to the Gold-Discount-Bank once again."[30]

After completing the lists, and often with ship or plane tickets in hand, Jews had to await the authorization of the Finance Department. Despite official policy encouraging emigration, the Nazi bureaucracy dawdled and delayed Jewish emigration. Again, connections and bribes seemed to speed up the process and, again, women had to master the world of officialdom and the art of bribery. To obtain the necessary papers before her boat departed, Lisa Brauer begged for assistance from a former student whom she knew was married to someone in the Finance Department. She arrived at the student's door early one morning, when it was still dark, "to avoid being seen and recognized by curious neighbors." Shortly thereafter, a clerk from the Finance Department appeared at her home. Brauer offered him any books in her library. "Three days later I got my appointment at the Finance Department."[31]

With the arduous packing accomplished and papers in hand, some families sent the freight containers, known as "lifts," to interim stations, frequently ports in Holland. They remained there until the family knew its final destination. Some families lost their possessions when access to their containers was cut off by the German invasion of Holland. But others could not even consider packing most of their possessions, since the giant containers and the surcharge demanded by the Nazis for every item cost too much. One man recalled "that these giant containers . . . stood in front of many houses in my neighborhood, with the designation . . . New York or Buenos Aires or Haifa. However, most emigrants could not afford such costly things and traveled to foreign lands with only a few suitcases."

Many emigrants, mourning their loss, sold their homes and furnishings for a pittance. Lisa Brauer, trying to create what she viewed as a dignified moment amid her misfortune, set the table with coffee and cake and invited neighbors to purchase items: "Only a few . . . took advantage and tried to grab as much as they could carry." Dismantling her home after the November Pogrom, Alice Baerwald wrote: "It was so terribly difficult to destroy . . . what one had created with so much love." She had cultivated every plant around the house: "Flowers, nothing but flowers, that was my joy. . . . My children had played and laughed here and romped in the grass with the dogs. And now suddenly to sell to total strangers." The city of Danzig decided the price of her house and chose the buyer. She then sold the contents of her home to "Aryan" purchasers, many of whom complained of their plight. Since Nazi ideology asserted that Germans suffered because of Jews, many Germans could simultaneously ignore Jewish suffering, exploit Jews, and lament their own lot. A pastor's wife proclaimed, "We're suffering just as much as you," but Baerwald retorted, "only with the difference that you're buying and I'm selling."[32]

It was clear to the emigrants that their German neighbors were benefiting greatly from their misery and doubtlessly clear to these Germans as well. Placing an ad in the paper, Lotte Popper tried to sell her "bedroom, living room, kitchen furniture." The ad was simply one among many other ads by Jews. She commented: "Yes, the Aryans had it good. They could now beautify their homes cheaply with the well-cared-for furniture of emigrating Jews." Only "the stupid among the populace were persuaded not to buy anything which had been used by Jews. The others, however, crowded the auction rooms, for the belongings [of Jews] were to be had for a song."[33]

Packing gave some women the chance to smuggle valuables out of the country. What their ingenuity managed to salvage was paltry compared with what the Nazis stole from them. Still, it helped some families subsist for a short time when they arrived penniless at their destination and saved precious mementos. While most women packed feverishly under the scrutiny of one or two officials,[34] some women managed to bribe these officials. One woman, who smuggled gold, silver, and jewelry into her bags, commented on the officials who demanded huge payoffs to make this possible: "This corruption of the Germans, which grew into the monstrous, rescued the lives and a modest existence for many people, particularly Jews." A few women bribed officials without consulting their husbands. They knew full well that their plans would have been vetoed, but they hoped to save some valuables for their immediate needs abroad. Else Gerstel, the wife of a judge, hid silverware with "Aryan" friends until the night before she packed. She then paid off packers to hide the silver while "seven Gestapo men were watching." She also smuggled other valuables in a secret compartment of her desk, built especially for this purpose: "I had risked of course the concentration camp and my life, probably all our lives. Alfred had no idea of what I had done. The night before we arrived in Cuba I whispered the whole story in his ear."[35]

Other women smuggled jewelry or money abroad for their relatives. Visiting her grandchild in Switzerland, one grandmother smuggled jewelry on each trip. Alice Baerwald, a resident of Danzig, agreed to smuggle her sister-in-law's jewelry from Berlin to Danzig in order to mail it to her when she emigrated. It was not yet forbidden to send one's own jewelry from Danzig, a "free city" according to the Treaty of Versailles, and she could claim it belonged to her. Then other elderly family members begged her to take their jewelry to Danzig too. None of them wanted to become dependent upon their adult children once they arrived abroad. Even more fearfully, she agreed, noting that "if someone caught me, I'd be finished." A few years later, she reflected: "One lived . . . in such danger that one . . . forgot completely that there could still be a normal life elsewhere. . . . Naturally one did many forbidden things, but because, in fact, everything was forbidden to us Jews, one had absolutely no choice."[36]

Women committed "illegal" acts not only to support their families but also to help the community at large. Beate Berger, for example, smuggled money from Berlin to Palestine in order to buy land for a children's home. Faithful friends, too, helped Jews take valuables abroad. The patient of one Jewish doctor, who was driven to commit suicide because of Nazi persecution, helped the doctor's widow smuggle jewelry and fur coats to Switzerland. She even accompanied the family to the border to assure their safety.[37]

While for many, "packing reduced a lifetime of possessions into three suitcases," for others, the clothing, shoes, and linens they packed had been donated by the Jewish Winter Relief Agency. Having sold the little they had to pay for their voyage, they had nothing left to take with them. The Jew-

ish organization proclaimed: "They should not be uprooted and arrive in a foreign country with the mark of poverty stamped upon them."[38]

Final Farewells

In fear for their lives, some people fled immediately after the pogrom. Alice Oppenheimer, with exit papers in hand and a husband in Buchenwald, packed bags for her five children and looked up the next train to Switzerland. It would leave on a Saturday. Because she was religiously observant, she phoned a rabbi for his advice regarding travel on the Sabbath. He told her to disregard the prohibition against travel since her life was in danger. She left with only some jewelry to sell in Italy in order to tide the family over until its departure for Palestine: "I could sell only a few articles, and those I practically gave away. I had to have some money in hand. How else could I proceed with five children? [In Italy] I bought a loaf of bread for them and said: 'I cannot give you any more to eat, or I won't have enough money.'" Several days later they embarked for Palestine, where they met up with the sixth child. Her husband also joined them, freed after sixteen days in a concentration camp because of his Palestine certificate. Oppenheimer remarked that the camp had "transformed a still youthful man into an old man whom I failed to recognize when he finally landed by boat at Tel Aviv."[39]

For those lucky enough to leave Germany, most faced painful farewells with friends and relatives. "More and more, one learned to say farewell," wrote one woman, as she listed friends who had scattered over the entire world. Moreover, all worried that those left behind would face increasing torment, and neither side knew whether they would ever see each other again. Fleeing shortly after the pogrom, Toni Lessler said her farewells in the only public place left for Jews, the railroad station café. There, no one noticed a few Jewish people visiting with each other. Referring to the Zoo station in Berlin, Lessler wrote:

> As we looked around . . . we saw similar groups to ours . . . friends and relatives who were taking leave from one another, none of whom could find any other meeting place than this dismal train station . . . in the midst of renovation and which offered the most inhospitable sojourn imaginable. I am unable to say how many tears were shed that evening.

When Elisabeth Freund finally escaped, shortly after Germany invaded the Soviet Union, her good-byes were excruciating. In the midst of real terror, having experienced bombings, forced labor, and the removal of Jews to tighter quarters, she tried not to break down: "Just no tears. One must not start that, otherwise one cannot stop. Who knows what will become of these people. In a situation like this, one can no longer say farewell in a conventional way."[40]

Individuals took leave in their own personal ways of what had been their *Heimat*—an almost untranslatable, nostalgic word for a romanticized homeland. In 1962, Ann Lewis and her parents described their feelings as they embarked for England. Ann, ten years old at the time, recalled the farewell at the train station:

> Relatives and friends—perhaps twelve or fifteen people—had gathered to see us off. . . . Everyone had brought presents . . . flowers, chocolate, sweets, magazines, books. I have never forgotten this picture of the little knot of our friends and relations, standing close together as if to give each other mutual comfort, waving to us as the train carried us away. Sometimes I am surprised how often it comes into my thoughts. Although this leave-taking occurred when I was still so young, it marked

the most important turning point of my life . . . the fundamental break with my roots.

Her mother wrote:

> We are waiting at *Bahnhof* Zoo. . . . Many relatives and friends are there with flowers and presents. The train comes into the station, we get in, the children are excited and are looking forward to opening their presents—the train begins to move, we wave. Everything vanishes, we sit down—try not to think—dull apathy—mind a complete blank, vacant, oppressed, not a single tear. Courage—we *must* win through.

Her father wrote:

> It is comfortable in the compartment . . . the luggage-racks are crammed with suitcases. . . . The four . . . are silent . . . the two adults, their faces looking serious and tired, are gazing with unseeing eyes through the windows, deep in thought. . . . Barely a quarter of an hour from now . . . Germany will lie behind them—Germany, the country which had been their home, where they had experienced happiness and suffering, the land whose language they had spoken—Germany, the country whose landscape was so dear to them . . . the Germany of poets, of thinkers, and of the great composers.[41]

Strikingly, even as both parents experienced relief, their farewell thoughts echoed the general orientation of women and men when contemplating emigration: most women covered their pain and maintained a courageous front, while many men looked back, mourning for the country and culture they had once loved and had now lost. Adding to these differences . . . were more immediate concerns: women looked forward to a safer environment for their families, while men agonized about how to support them.

It was terribly distressing for Jews to leave their homeland, family, and friends, especially when they saw the present suffering and feared for the future of those left behind. They also worried about how they would fare abroad. Their anguish notwithstanding, these émigrés were the lucky ones, and not only in hindsight. When Toni Lessler confided to a friend that "emigrating is terribly hard," he responded tearfully, "Remaining here is much harder!"[42]

Who Stayed Behind?

A gender analysis of the desire to emigrate . . . highlights women's and men's unique expectations, priorities, and perceptions. Women wanted to leave well before their men. Paradoxically, it does not follow that more women than men actually left. To the contrary, fewer women than men left Germany. Why?

Although life was becoming increasingly difficult in the 1930s, there were still compelling reasons to stay. First, women could still find employment in Jewish businesses and homes. They could also work as teachers in Jewish schools, as social workers, nurses, and administrators in Jewish social service institutions, and as clerical workers for the Jewish community. And older, educated women found jobs in cultural and social service fields within the Jewish community. Hedwig Burgheim, for example, found challenging and important work. In 1933, she was forced to resign as director of a teacher training institute in Giessen. Thereafter she directed the Leipzig Jewish Community's School for Kindergarten Teachers and Domestic Services, which trained young people for vocations useful in lands of emigration. After the November Pogrom, her own attempts at emigration having failed, she taught at the Jewish school and, by 1942, headed the old-age home in Leipzig.

Along with its residents, she was deported in early 1943 and died in Auschwitz. Martha Wertheimer, a journalist before 1933, also found her skills in demand thereafter. She plunged into Jewish welfare work, while also writing books and plays, contributing to the Jewish press, and tutoring English to earn extra money. She escorted many children's transports to England; worked twelve-hour days without pausing for meals in order to advise Jews on emigration and welfare procedures; took great joy in leading High Holiday services at the League of Jewish Women's Home for Wayward Girls; and organized education courses for Jewish youth who had been drafted into forced labor. Ultimately, she wrote a friend in New York that, despite efforts to emigrate, she was no longer waiting to escape: "A great dark calm has entered me, as the saying of our fathers goes 'Gam zu le'tovah' ('this, too, is for the best')." She continued: "It is also worthwhile to be an officer on the sinking ship of Jewish life in Germany, to hold out courageously and to fill the life boats, to the extent that we have some."[43]

While the employment situation of Jewish women helped keep them in Germany, that of men helped get them out. Some men had business connections abroad, facilitating their immediate flight, and others emigrated alone in order to establish themselves before sending for their families. Among Eastern European Jews who returned east between 1934 and 1937, for example, the majority were male, even though almost half of them were married. A handful of men, some with wives, received visas to leave Europe from groups hoping to save eminent intellectuals and artists. Women's organizations agreed that, if there was no choice, wives should not "hinder" husbands from emigrating alone, but they argued that it was often no cheaper for men to emigrate without their wives.[44]

Before the war, moreover, men faced immediate physical danger. Men who had been detained by the Nazis and then freed, as well as boys who had been beaten up by neighborhood ruffians, fled Germany early. After the November Pogrom, in a strange twist of fortune, the men interred in concentration camps were released only upon showing proof of their ability to leave Germany immediately. Families—mostly wives and mothers—strained every resource to provide the documentation to free these men and send them on their way while some of the women remained behind. Alice Nauen recalled how difficult these emigration decisions were for Jewish leaders:

> Should we send the men out first? This had been the dilemma all along. . . . If you have two tickets, do you take one man out of the concentration camp and his wife who is at this moment safe? Or do you take your two men out of the concentration camp? They took two men out . . . because they said we cannot play God, but these are in immediate danger.

Even as women feared for their men, they believed that they themselves would be spared serious harm by the Nazis. In retrospect, Ruth Klüger reflected on this kind of thinking and the resulting preponderance of women caught in the trap: "One seemed to ignore what was most obvious, namely how imperiled precisely the weaker and the socially disadvantaged are. That the Nazis should stop at women contradicted their racist ideology. Had we, as the result of an absurd, patriarchal short circuit, perhaps counted on their chivalry?"[45]

Despite trepidations, parents sent sons into the unknown more readily than daughters. Bourgeois parents worried about a daughter traveling alone, believing boys would be safer. Families also assumed that sons needed to establish economic

futures for themselves, whereas daughters would marry. In 1935, one family sent its son to Palestine because "it was proper for a young man to try to leave and find a job elsewhere." His parents were reluctant to send their daughter abroad. Like other young women, socialized to accept their parents' judgment, she consented to remain behind and even made it "possible for him to go abroad by supporting him financially." As more and more sons left, daughters remained as the sole caretakers of elderly parents. One female commentator noted the presence of many women "who can't think of emigration because they don't know who might care for their elderly mothers . . . before they could start sending them money. In the same families, the sons went their way." Leaving one's aging parent—as statistics indicate, usually the mother—was the most painful act imaginable. Ruth Glaser described her own mother's agony at leaving her mother to join her husband, who had been forbidden reentry into Germany: she "could not sleep at night thinking of leaving her [mother] behind." Men, too, felt such grief, but more left nonetheless. Charlotte Stein-Pick wrote of her husband's anguish: "This abandonment of his old parents depressed him deeply. . . . He never got over this farewell. . . . To be sure, he saw that we could never have helped them, only shared their fate. I almost believe he would have preferred it."[46]

As early as 1936, the League of Jewish Women noted that far fewer women than men were leaving and feared that Jewish men of marriageable age would intermarry abroad, leaving Jewish women behind in Germany with no chance of marrying. Still, the League was not enthusiastic about emigration to certain areas because of anxiety about the possibility of forced prostitution. The League of Jewish Women also turned toward parents, reminding them of their "responsibility to free their daughters" even though daughters felt "stronger psychological ties to their families than sons do, [which] probably lies in the female psyche." As late as January 1938, one of the main emigration organizations, the Aid Society, announced that "up to now, Jewish emigration . . . indicates a severe surplus of men." It blamed this on the "nature" of women to feel closer to family and home and on that of men toward greater adventurousness. It also suggested that couples marry before emigrating, encouraged women to prepare themselves as household helpers, and promised that women's emigration would become a priority. Yet only two months later the Society announced it would expedite the emigration of only those young women who could prove their household skills and were willing to work as domestics abroad.[47] Jewish organizations also provided less support to emigrating women than to men.[48]

That some women and men took the advice to marry before going abroad, or came upon the idea on their own, can be seen from marriage ads in Jewish newspapers. These ads frequently included the requirement that the future spouse be amenable to emigration. For example, in 1936, one woman sought a "marriage partner . . . with the possibility of emigration," while another woman gave the value of her dowry in Swiss francs. A businessman offered a "pretty, healthy, and young woman" the opportunity of emigrating to Palestine together. By 1938, almost every ad announced the desire or ability to emigrate, occasionally boasting "affidavit in hand." Some may have entered into phony marriages before emigrating to Palestine. Since a couple, that is, two people, could enter on one certificate, a quick marriage of convenience, to be continued or broken upon arrival, saved an extra life.[49]

Families were often reluctant to consider Palestine, and the *kibbutz*, as an alternative for daughters. One survey of graduating classes from several Jewish schools in late 1935 showed that 47 percent of the boys but only 30 percent of the girls aimed for Palestine. Statistics for the first half of 1937 indicate that of those taking advantage of Zionist retraining programs, only 32 percent were female. Overall, fewer single females than males emigrated to Palestine: between 1933 and 1942, 8,209 "bachelors," compared with 5,080 "single" females, entered from German-speaking lands.[50]

Those young women who actually wound up in Palestine preferred the cities. The majority of German-Jewish girls and young women did not take available positions on *kibbutzim* or in agricultural training centers but rather took jobs as cooks or milliners. Better jobs, such as social workers, kindergarten teachers, and nurses, were much harder to find. While emigration consultants encouraged young women to take up the adventures of *kibbutz* life, articles appearing on Palestine, often written by committed Zionists, must have given pause. In one such article, the male author described a situation in which eight young women cared for fifty-five young men. They cooked, washed "mountains" of laundry, darned hundreds of socks, and sewed ripped clothing, working long days and into the night. But even more was expected of them. They were to do the emotional housework as well:

> A friendly word at the right time will bring a young man to his senses who once had a dozen shirts . . . and now noticed that his last carefully maintained shirt was taken by another. . . . Whether the kibbutz thrives is up to the girls! They have to mother one, be a comrade to the other . . . and have the endlessly difficult task of always remaining in a good mood [and] smiling.

Such reports, plus the numerous news items regarding Arab-Jewish discord, left most young women looking elsewhere for refuge.[51]

The growing disproportion of Jewish women in the German-Jewish population also came about because, to begin with, there were more Jewish women than men in Germany. In 1933, 52.3 percent of Jews were women, owing to male casualties during World War I, greater marrying out and conversion among Jewish men, and greater longevity among women. In order to stay even, a greater absolute number of women would have had to emigrate. The slower rate of female than male emigration, however, meant that the female proportion of the Jewish population rose from 52.3 percent in 1933 to 57.5 percent by 1939. After the war, one woman wrote:

> Mostly we were women who had been left to ourselves. In part, our husbands had died from shock, partly they had been processed from life to death in a concentration camp and partly some wives who, aware of the greater danger to their husbands, had prevailed upon them to leave at once and alone.... Quite a few of my friends and acquaintances thus became martyrs of Hitler.[52]

A large proportion of these remaining women were elderly. Age, even more than being female, worked against timely flight; together they were lethal. Between June 1933 and September 1939, the number of young Jews in Germany under age thirty-nine decreased by about 80 percent. In contrast, the number of Jews over sixty decreased by only 27 percent. As early as 1936, a Jewish woman released from prison for her work in the communist resistance recuperated in a sanatorium. She remarked upon its "dismal milieu": "The guests [were] nearly all old people who had remained behind by themselves. Their children were either in prison camps or in Palestine, the U.S.A., and still farther away.... [They] longed for death." By 1939, the proportion of people over sixty had

increased to 32 percent of the Jewish population; by 1941, two-thirds of the Jewish population was past middle age. In Berlin alone, the number of old-age homes grew from three in 1933 to thirteen in 1939 and to twenty-one in 1942. Already in 1933, the elderly had consisted of a large number of widows, the ratio being 140 Jewish women over the age of sixty-five to 100 men. By 1937–38, 59 percent of the recipients of Jewish Winter Relief aged forty-five and over were female. In 1939, 6,674 widowed men and 28,347 widowed women remained in the expanded Reich.[53]

In short, in slightly less than eight years and drastically increasing after the November Pogrom, two-thirds of German Jews emigrated (many to European countries where they were later caught up in the Nazi net), leaving a disproportionate number of old people and women. Jewish newspapers featured articles about old women whose children had emigrated, whose living quarters were small, whose help had disappeared, whose finances were meager. Thrown together, sometimes in old-age homes, sometimes as paying guests in the homes of other Jews, these women passed their days reliving memories of better times. Financial worries plagued them, but they were even more tormented by not knowing their children's exact whereabouts or circumstances. They constituted a "community of old people, who supported . . . and consoled each other." When Elisabeth Freund, one of the last Jews to leave Germany legally in October 1941, went to the Gestapo for her final papers, she observed: "All old people, old women" waiting in line.[54]

NOTES

1. Teenager (from Lippehne near the Eichwald) in Limberg, *Durften*, 213–15; Lewis, LBI, 251–52; destitution in Kramer, "Welfare," 183. In the first

three months of 1937, for example, over 55 percent of migrants were women. Quack, *Zuflucht*, 60–61.

2. *IF*, June 25, 1936; *CV*, March 10, 1938, 3.

3. Rural Jews in Baumann, "Land" (Baden-Württemberg), 40; Appel in Richarz, *Leben*, III, 237. This gender-specific reaction in dangerous situations has been noted by sociologists and psychologists: men tend to "stand their ground," whereas women avoid conflict, preferring flight as a strategy. See also: Kliner-Fruck, "*Über-leben*" 79. Although there were also women who were afraid to leave, they were in the minuscule minority. Gay, "Epilogue," 364.

4. Gompertz, LBI, 7.

5. Leonard Baker, *Days of Sorrow and Pain: Leo Baeck and the Berlin Jews* (New York, 1978), 238.

6. "His status" in Berel, LBI, 16; Shanghai couple described by their daughter, Evelyn Rubin, at Queens College, December 1988, and in the *Long Island Jewish Week*, November 19, 1978.

7. Lore Segal, *Other People's Houses* (New York, 1958). See also: Quack, *Sorrow* and *Zuflucht*, chaps. 4 and 6.

8. Women in the economy in Claudia Koonz, "Courage," 285, and *Mothers*, chap. 10; Jewish sector in Barkai, *Boycott*, 2–3, 6–7, quotes on 80–83.

9. Axelrath, Harvard, 37.

10. "Impending danger" in Koonz, "Courage," 287; "judges" in Gerstel, LBI, 71.

11. Segal, LBI, 45–46, 61. See also: Drexler, Harvard, Hamburger, LBI, 40–41; Spiegel, *Retter*, 15; Hilda Branch in Rothchild, *Voices*; Eisner, *Allein*, 8; Morris, "Lives," 93.

12. "He laughed" in Segal, LBI, 45–47, 61; "so seriously" in Allport, "Personality," 3.

13. Wyden, *Stella*, 47; Salomon in Felstiner, *Paint*, 74. Carol Gilligan's theories may apply here: men tend to view and express their situation in terms of abstract rights, women in terms of actual affiliations and relationships. *In a Different Voice: Psychological Theory and Women's Development* (Cambridge MA, 1982).

14. Nauen, *Research Foundation*, 8; Bernheim, Harvard, 53; "decent German" in Hamburger, LBI, 41, 46.

15. Stein-Pick, LBI, 2, 38; Swiss bank in Bamberger, LBI, 5; pregnancy in Deutsch, Harvard.

16. Gerstel, LBI, 71; "sixth feeling" in Foster, *Community*, 28–30.

17. Bloch, Research Foundation, 6, 8; the lawyer was Braun-Melchior, LBI, 32.

18. "Quota" in Strauss, LBI, chap. 8, 44; "hell" in Bernheim, Harvard, 45; Gerstel, LBI, 76.

19. Hellwig, Harvard, 25–26. See also Edel, *Leben*, 149–50; Bab, LBI, 180.

20. Psychologists in Allport, "Personality," 4; "everyone" in Lange, *Davidstern*, 27.

21. Freund in Richarz, *Life*, 413–15.

22. Letter from Gertrud Grossmann, January 17, 1939; "god" in Bernheim, Harvard, 51.

23. Fromm, *Blood*, 238 (July 20, 1938); Dienemann, Harvard, 35.

24. Post-1939 laws in Bernheim, Harvard, 63–64; Gerstel, LBI, 76. See also: Nathorff, LBI, 127–33; letters from Gertrud Grossmann, January 3, 1939; February 22, 1940.

25. Stein-Pick, LBI, 37; also bribes to have husbands released from camps in Moses, Harvard, 44; pay-off in Brauer, LBI, 51.

26. Alexander Szanlo in Barkai, *Boycott*, 152.

27. Bernheim, Harvard, 55–56, 66; see also Lessler, LBI, 33.

28. Gerstel, LBI, 76, 80, 86.

29. Strauss, "Emigration," I, 317–18, 326–27.

30. Kamm, Harvard, 27, 31; "women's work" in Freyhan, LBI, 7; Brauer, LBI, 56; "before 1933" in Freund, LBI, 144–45. See also: Bab, LBI, 198; Limberg, *Durften*, 203.

31. Brauer, LBI, 57.

32. Containers in Lange, *Davidstern*, 30; Brauer, LBI, 55; Baerwald, Harvard, 65–67.

33. Popper, Harvard, 75; "stupid" in Honnet-Sichel, Harvard, 80.

34. Brauer, LBI, 54, writes of a bailiff (*Gerichtsvollzieher*) and Freund, LBI, 178, of a custom's official (*Zollbeamter*) coming to the home. See also: Glaser, LBI, 71.

35. "Corruption" in Moses, Harvard, 44–45; Gerstel, LBI, 77–79.

36. Grandmother in Glaser, LBI, 38; Baerwald, Harvard, 73, 75. Blocked accounts and prohibitions re money in Walk, *Sonderrecht* (April and December 1936); Barkai, *Boycott*, 100, 138.

37. Berger in Scheer, *Ahawah*, 265; patient in Lixl-Purcell, *Women*, 53.

38. "Packing" in Vogel, *Forget!*, 202; "uprooted" in Schwarz, "Tschaikowsky," 119.

39. Lixl-Purcell, *Women*, 78.

40. "Farewell" in Bab, LBI, 193; Lessler, LBI, 34; Freund in Richarz, *Life*, 423.

41. Lewis, LBI, 275–77.

42. Lessler, LBI, 33.

43. *JWS*, 1937, 7–13; 27, 78–81; Barkai, "Existenz-kampf," 163; Burgheim, archives, LBI; Hanno Loewy, ed., *In mich ist die grosse dunkle Ruhe gekommen, Martha Wertheimer Briefe an Siegfried Guggenheim* (1939–1941), Frankfurter Lern-und Dokumentationszentrum des Holocaust (Frankfurt am Main, 1993), 6, 9, 13, 15, 22, 37.

44. Returning east in Maurer, "Ausländische," 204; "hinder" in BJFB, December 1936, 5.

45. Men beaten in Eisner, *Allein*, 8; Nauen (whose father was secretary of the *Hilfsverein* in Hamburg), Research Foundation, 15; Klüger, *leben*, 83.

46. "Proper" in Morris, "Lives," 43; "the sons" in BJFB, April 1937, 5; Glaser, LBI, 26, 71; Stein-Pick, LBI, 46. Another daughter who remained with her parents in Erika Guetermann, LBI.

47. BJFB, December 1936, 1. Bundesarchiv, Coswig: 75C Jüd. Frauenbund, Verband Berlin, folder 37. Protokoll der Arbeitskreistagung vom November 2, 1936; Aid Society (Hilfsverein) in CV, January 20, 1938, 5; March 3, 1938, 6.

48. For example, in 1937, of the 7,313 émigrés supported by the emigration section of the Central Organization of Jews in Germany, there were approximately 4,161 men and 3,041 women. The *Hilfsverein* supported 3,250 men and 2,512 women. The Palestine Bureau supported 911 men and 529 women. *Informationsblätter*, January/February 1938, 6–7. Overall immigration into the U.S. showed a higher proportion of men, evening out only in 1938–39. See: *AJYB 5699* (1938–39) (1938), 552–54; *5701 (1940–41)* (1940), 608–9; *5702 (1941–42)* (1941), 674–75; Quack, "Gender," 391.

49. Businessman in IF, March 5, 1936; "affidavit" in IF, October 13, 1938, 16; see also Klemperer, *Zeugnis*, 1, 462 (February 1939). Phony marriages in Wetzel, "Auswanderung," 453; Kliner-Fruck, "*Überleben*" 140; Backhaus-Lautenschläger, *standen*, 62.

50. Surveys in JWS, 1935, 188. *Informationsblätter*, August/October 1937, 60. Palestine statistics in "Jewish Immigration from Germany during 1933–1942 (includes Austria . . . Czechoslovakia and Danzig . . .)," reprint from "The Jewish Immigration and Population" issued by the Dept. of Statistics of the Jewish Agency.

51. *JWS*, 1933–34; "friendly word" in IF, January 16, 1936, 15; June 25, 1936, 9.

52. "Mostly" in Lixl-Purcell, *Women*, 92. Women were also a majority of the Jewish populations of German-dominated Europe: Hilberg, *Perpetrators*, 127; IF, February 27, 1936; Blau, "Population," 165.

53. On age, see Strauss, "Emigration," I, 318–19, and Blau, "Population," 165; "dismal" in Rothschild, LBI, 125–26; old age homes in Gruner, "Reichshauptstadt," 242, 251; Winter Relief in Vollnhals, "Selbsthilfe" 405, and BJFB, October 1938, 4.

54. Disproportionate number of elderly women in Richarz, *Leben*, 61; *JWS*, 1937, 96–97, 161–63, 200–201; Klemperer, *Zeugnis*, 1, 475; IF, January 16, 1936; Freund, LBI, 146.

4 The New Order in Europe

7. Adolf Hitler and his entourage in front of the Eiffel Tower shortly after the fall of France. With Hitler are Albert Speer, Wilhelm Keitel, Martin Bormann, and other Nazi officials. June 28, 1940. (Courtesy of Bildarchiv Preussischer Kulturbesitz, Heinrich Hoffmann.)

8. Minsk, Belarus . . . August 1941— After the Germans occupied Minsk in 1941, Tamara Osipova, a student, joined a partisan group made up of mostly students and teachers. From August 1941 to September 1942 these partisans fought against the Germans and worked to rescue Jews from the Minsk ghetto. Tamara and her mother, Maria, went to the ghetto and smuggled out dozens of Jewish women and children. Risking their lives, the mother and daughter often had to bribe local officials to save these Jews. Maria was then responsible for obtaining forged identity papers while Tamara worked to find safe places for the women and children to hide. Elena Krechetovich was one of the many women they smuggled out of the ghetto. After obtaining forged identity papers for Elena, Tamara and Maria were able to get her a job at the local hospital. Along with many others rescued by Tamara and Maria, Elena sought shelter in their home and survived the war. (Courtesy JFR Photo Archives.)

Introduction

PETER HAYES

The Third Reich conquered most of Europe in four great offensives within just twenty-seven months: first, in September 1939, Germany swept over Poland; second, between April and June 1940, Hitler's troops subdued Denmark, Norway, the Netherlands, Belgium, Luxemburg, and France; third, in April 1941, Nazi forces occupied Yugoslavia and Greece, thus building upon Germany's alliances with Hungary, Romania, and Bulgaria to obtain complete control of the Balkans; and fourth, between June and December 1941, the *Wehrmacht*, along with Finnish, Hungarian, Italian, and Romanian army units, invaded the Soviet Union and advanced to the gates of Moscow. By the time "the hinge of fate" (Winston Churchill) turned and Germany's adversaries began to push it back in North Africa and at Stalingrad in November 1942, the Nazis had imposed their so-called New Order on all of continental Europe with the partial exceptions of four officially neutral countries: Sweden, Switzerland, Spain, and Portugal.

Driven by two central principles—racism and economic exploitation—this New Order inflicted enormous violence and suffering on the subject populations, including even some Germans. Massive, racially motivated violence characterized the New Order's very inception, as the first two readings in this chapter make clear. Robert Proctor shows how the outbreak of the fighting provided Hitler with an excuse for *culling the German Volk* of tens of thousands of allegedly "useless eaters," disabled inhabitants of sanatoria and asylums within the Reich, eventually by means that forecast the

operations of the death camps. Götz Aly and Susanne Heim outline the massive *rearranging of populations* in the parts of Poland annexed to Germany, as Heinrich Himmler took responsibility for transferring to the region half a million ethnic Germans from the Soviet Union and Southeastern Europe, expelling enough Poles to make room for the arrivals, and meanwhile "Germanizing" select groups of the residents and slaughtering the Polish intelligentsia. The resettlement program disrupted the Nazi regime's efforts to maximize agricultural production, and this was not the only way in which Himmler's project proved ill conceived. Long delays in finding homes for the repatriated Germans meant that many of them spent years in "internment barracks," in some cases mental institutions that only recently had become available through the murder of their previous residents.

Yet, such confusion and mismanagement not only failed to deter Himmler and his aides from planning demographic engineering on an even larger scale in the occupied Soviet Union, but also made them think in more sweepingly murderous terms. Timothy Snyder's description of *racial war in the German East* details the Hunger Plan drawn up by German officials prior to the invasion, which foresaw the starvation of some 30 million people in order to allow the German Army to live off the conquered land, and the General Plan for the East (*Generalplan Ost*), a document drafted and periodically revised by Himmler's staff, which envisioned gradual German colonization of the Baltic region, the Crimea and parts of Ukraine, and the vicinity of Leningrad, along with the enslavement and decimation over time of the indigenous people. Although both plans proved unrealizable, the toll taken by German policy and military operations in the Soviet Union was staggering: at least 16 million people killed, almost half of them civilians.

With the exception of Serbia, the rest of Nazi-occupied Europe was spared this sort of carnage, but not the other costs of defeat and subjugation. Greater Germany lived off the food, goods, labor, and money of the occupied states, and it was the only country in continental Europe to post an increase in national income during World War II. The positions of other nationalities on the Nazi racial hierarchy became their ranks on the food chain, as Germans had access to the largest quantities and best quality food, followed in descending order by Nordics, Latins, most Slavs, Sinti and Roma, and Jews. Götz Aly's analysis of the forms of *individual and governmental plunder* decreed by German policy makers paints a vivid picture of not only the Reich's exactions, but also of the inflationary pressures that they caused nearly everywhere. Germany confiscated massive stockpiles of industrial raw materials and military materiel each time a country fell, and then allowed its troops to pick local markets clean while the Reich imposed huge occupation charges. As a result, by 1943, one-third of the national incomes of France and Norway were flowing to Germany; by March 1944, the Reich estimated that France had provided cash and kind worth more than 35 billion Reichsmarks, Holland 12 billion, and Belgium more than 9 billion. Shortages and rationing became almost universal (the great exception was Denmark) and highly discriminatory along racial lines.

Just as important in sustaining the German war effort and the country's living standards was the massive flow of *forced labor* that Ulrich Her-bert documents. By August 1944, 7.6 million foreigners were working in Germany, and they made up more than a quarter of the total workforce, including almost half of all people employed in agriculture. Among them were some 1.8 million Belgian, French, Italian, Polish, and Soviet prisoners of war. Poland and the Soviet Union provided almost two-thirds of the civilians, some 3.8 million people, most of them lured with false promises of comfortable working conditions or simply rounded up by German forces and shipped to the Reich. Once there, these Eastern laborers (*Ostarbeiter*) were subjected to discriminatory wage and tax rates and calorie allocations and to strict regulations designed to prevent contact with the surrounding German population. Also treated particularly harshly were the almost 600,000 Italians working in Germany, more than two-thirds of them soldiers interned by the Reich after the Italian capitulation to the Allies in September 1943.

In retrospect, the most striking feature of the Nazi New Order is its counterproductive and myopic nature. It offered almost nothing positive or promising to anyone other than Germans and their Balkan affiliates, e.g., Slovakia, Croatia, Bulgaria, Romania, and Hungary. It imposed heavy economic burdens that undermined initial enthusiasm for the arrival of the Germans in some places, e.g., Ukraine, and initial willingness to collaborate with them in others, e.g., France, and then stoked resistance to occupation. It was profligate with lives and resources, simultaneously ruthless, corrupt, and wasteful.

Nazi aggression brought unprecedented destruction and upheaval to Europe between 1939 and 1945. Thirty-six and one-half million Europeans died from war-related causes, over half of them civilians. At least fifty million persons became homeless. By 1943, thirty million inhabitants had been uprooted and transplanted, and

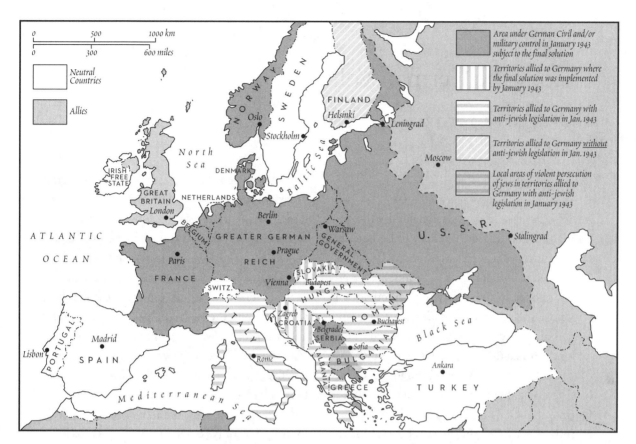

Map 1. Europe, January 1, 1943. Based on map by Jacques Chazaud. From *Voices and Views: A History of the Holocaust,* edited, with introductions, by Debórah Dwork (The Jewish Foundation for the Righteous, 2002).

that was before the Red Army's advance toward Berlin set millions more in motion. As the war came to an end, transportation collapsed almost everywhere under hails of bombs and shells, food supplies slumped, currencies became worthless, workplaces went dark, infections spread, and a return to prosperity appeared inconceivable. Amidst the seemingly endless devastation and suffering, many people could not recognize the distinctness and extremity of what Hitler and his henchmen had done to Europe's Jews.

Culling the German Volk

ROBERT N. PROCTOR

From *Racial Hygiene*

In early October of 1939, designated by the government as the year of "the duty to be healthy," Hitler authored a secret memo certifying that "Reichsleiter Bouhler and Dr. Brandt are hereby commissioned to allow certain specified doctors to grant a mercy death [*Gnadentod*] to patients judged incurably sick by critical medical examination."[1] By August 24, 1941, when the first phase of this "adult operation" was brought to an end, over 70,000 patients from more than a hundred German hospitals had been killed, in an operation that provided the stage rehearsal for the subsequent destruction of Jews, homosexuals, communists, Gypsies, Slavs, and prisoners of war.[2] ...

Wonderful Parks and Gardens

According to the postwar testimony of Hitler's personal physician Karl Brandt, Hitler decided even before 1933 that he would one day try to eliminate the mentally ill. In fact, shortly after the rise of the Nazis, several NSDAP *Gauleiter* were authorized to perform secret euthanasia operations in certain insane asylums.[3] It was not until 1935, however, at the Nazi Party Congress in Nuremberg (the *Parteitag der Freiheit*), that concrete plans for the destruction of all of Germany's "lives not worth living" were discussed. The logic for the destruction was presented by Gerhard Wagner, Führer of the National Socialist Physicians' League, in a speech before the congress.

In his speech Wagner assailed liberalism and Marxism for having denied "the inherently different value" of the lives of different individuals. According to Wagner, the doctrine of equality (*Gleichheitslehre*) was even worse in its effects ("biologically speaking") than the Russian revolution, insofar as it led one "to value the sick, the dying, and the unfit on a par with the healthy and the strong." Wagner argued that the average family size of "inferiors" was nearly twice that of healthy families; as a result, the number of mentally ill had grown by 450 percent in the last seventy years, while the population as a whole had increased by only 50 percent. Inferiors thus lived on at the expense of the healthy: "more than one billion Reichsmarks is spent on the genetically disabled; contrast this with the 766 million spent on the police, or the 713 million spent on local administration, and one sees what a burden and unexcelled injustice this places on the normal, healthy members of the population." Wagner noted that steps were being taken to reverse this trend, and that, indeed, while much of the world still clung to what he called the insane idea of equality (*Wahn der Gleichheit*), Germany as a nation had begun to recognize, once again, "the natural and God-given inequality of men."[4]

Not included in published records of the time, however, was Wagner's solution to the problem. According to Brandt's postwar testimony, Hitler told Wagner at this time that if a war should break out, then he (Hitler) would authorize a nationwide program of euthanasia; Brandt also recalled that "the Führer was of the opinion that such a program could be put into effect more smoothly and rapidly in time of war, and that in the general upheaval of war, the open resistance anticipated from the church would not play the part that it might in other circumstances."[5]

The association of euthanasia and war was not fortuitous. If the healthy could sacrifice their lives in time of war, then why should the sick not do the same? This was Hoche and Binding's argument, and it became a fashionable one among the Nazis. One American writer recognized this thinking as early as 1941, when he pointed out that the handicapped and mentally ill "were not killed for mercy. They were killed because they could no longer manufacture guns in return for the food they consumed; because beds in the German hospitals were needed for wounded soldiers; because their death was the ultimate logic of the national socialist doctrine of promoting racial superiority and the survival of the physically fit."[6] The Nazis made this link explicit. On August 10, 1939, when Nazi leaders met to plan the euthanasia operation, Philipp Bouhler, head of the Party Chancellery, declared that the purpose of the operation was not only to continue the "struggle against genetic disease" but also to free up hospital beds and personnel for the coming war.[7] The underlying philosophy was simple: patients were to be either cured or killed. Accordingly, Leonardo Conti, Wagner's successor as Reich Health Führer, allowed individuals capable of productive work to be excluded from the operation. . . .

The destruction of life not worth living was glorified in Nazi literature and art. In 1936 the ophthalmologist Helmut Unger published his widely read novel *Sendung und Gewissen* (Mission and conscience), which told the story of a young woman who, suffering from multiple sclerosis, decides that her life is no longer worth living and asks to be relieved of her misery. Her husband, a doctor, recognizes her plight and agrees to give her poison. In a grand act of humanity, the husband gives his wife a fatal injection of morphine, while a friend of his (also a doctor) accompanies the act with soothing and romantic music at the piano. The doctor, Terstegen, is accused of murder and brought to trial, where he refuses to let his colleagues invent an alibi for him, because he is convinced he has done no wrong. "Would you," asks Terstegen, "if you were a cripple, want to vegetate forever?" He is finally acquitted on grounds that his act constituted an act of mercy; in a critical scene, the words of the Renaissance physician Paracelsus are recalled: "medicine is love."[8] Unger's novel was important in helping to prepare the ground for the euthanasia program. In the fall of 1935, Gerhard Wagner ordered the book made into a movie designed to dramatize the plight of the incurably ill. The film (*Ich klage an!* ["I Accuse"]) was released in Berlin in the early war years, where it was a great success.[9]

Humanistic propaganda notwithstanding, the argument for the destruction of life not worth living was at root an economic one. In 1934, for example, the journal *Deutsche Freiheit* in Saarbrücken published a small pamphlet by Dr. Heilig, a representative of the Nazi Physicians' League for Altena and Lüdenscheid. In his pamphlet, Heilig argued:

> It must be made clear to anyone suffering from an incurable disease that the useless dissipation of costly medications drawn from the public store cannot be justified. Parents who have seen the difficult life of a crippled or feeble-minded child must be convinced that, though they may have a moral obligation to care for the unfortunate creature, the broader public should not be obligated . . . to assume the enormous costs that long-term institutionalization might entail.[10]

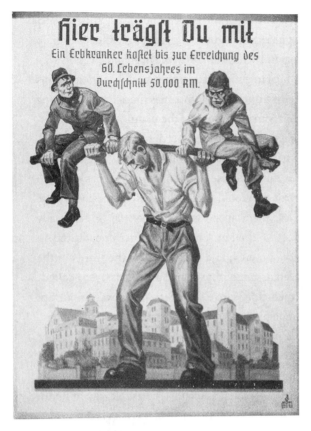

 hier trägst Du mit

Ein Erbkranker kostet bis zur Erreichung des
60. Lebensjahres im
Durchschnitt 50.000 RM.

9. "You Are Sharing the Load! A Genetically Ill Individual Costs Approximately 50,000 Reichsmarks by the Age of Sixty." This poster, from an exhibit on racial hygiene produced by the Reichsnährstand, illustrates the burden the mentally ill place on the healthy German population. (Image from Walter Gross, "Drei Jahre rassenpolitische Aufklärungsarbeit," *Volk und Rasse* 10 [1935]: 335, courtesy USHMM.)

Heilig also stated that it made no sense for persons "on the threshold of old age" to receive services such as orthopedic therapy or dental bridgework; such services were to be reserved for healthier elements of the population.

Heilig's comments are typical within the Nazi medical profession. Popular medical and racial hygiene journals carried charts depicting the costs of maintaining the sick at the expense of the healthy; schoolbooks asked students to calculate the costs of maintaining the frail and invalid.

Adolf Dorner's 1935–36 high school mathematics textbook, for example, included the following problems:

Problem 94

In one region of the German Reich there are 4,400 mentally ill in state institutions, 4,500 receiving state support, 1,600 in local hospitals, 200 in homes for the epileptic, and 1,500 in welfare homes. The state pays a minimum of 10 million RM/year for these institutions.

I. What is the average cost to the state per inhabitant per year? II. Using the result calculated from I, how much does it cost the state if:

A. 868 patients stay longer than 10 years?
B. 260 patients stay longer than 20 years?
C. 112 patients stay longer than 25 years?

Problem 95

The construction of an insane asylum requires 6 million RM. How many housing units @ 15,000 RM could be built for the amount spent on insane asylums?[11]

Such problems did not remain in the realm of theory. After the war, documents presenting detailed calculations of the "savings" achieved through the euthanasia operation were found in a safe in the castle at Hartheim (one of six euthanasia institutions equipped with gas chambers). Euthanasia officials calculated that the "disinfection" (murder) of 70,273 individuals in the course of the operation . . . saved the German economy an average of 245,955.50 RM per day (88,543,980.00 RM per year); if one assumed an average institutional life expectancy of ten years, the Reich had been saved expenses in excess of 880 million RM. Officials also noted that by the end of 1941, 93,521 hospital beds had been freed up by the operation.[12]

Even before the euthanasia operation, other aspects of Nazi social policy reflect this same philosophy. In 1933, the first year of Nazi government, expenditures for the handicapped and invalid were drastically cut. German medical insurance companies paid 41.5 million RM for invalids—10 million less than in 1932, in the depths of the recession.[13] Many homes for the elderly or infirm closed in the early years of the Nazi regime; the total number of nurses caring for the ill dropped from 111,700 in 1933 to 88,900 in 1934. According to the *Statistisches Reichsamt*, the number of hospitals and other medical care institutions fell from 3,987 in 1931 to 3,219 in 1935; the number of beds per 1,000 population fell in the same period from 5.7 to 4.5.[14]

These policies were supported by Germany's most prominent racial hygienists. Otmar von Verschuer, for example, attacked Germany's entire system of socialized medicine on the grounds that it interfered with the natural tendency for individuals to sort themselves out according to "inner genetic potential." Verschuer argued that socialized medicine could seriously impair the racial hygiene of a people, and that the German state had been far too eager to support "the weak, the laggard, and the inferior."[15] Fritz Bartels, Gerhard Wagner's right-hand man in the Nazi Physicians' League, phrased this in even stronger terms. He accused Marxists in the "14-year humiliation" (*14 Jahre Schmach*—Nazi language for the Weimar Republic) of having built "palaces for the mentally ill," "wonderful parks and gardens" for those inferior beings that inhabit Germany's mental institutions. Bartels noted that this would soon have to stop. This, after all, was the lesson of history: "From time immemorial, the nation has always eliminated the weak to make way for the healthy. A hard, but healthy and effective law to which we must once again give credence. The primary task of the physician is to discover for whom health

care at government expense will be worth the cost."[16] For the Nazi medical philosopher, support for the mentally ill was simply not worth the cost. In the course of the thirties, funds allotted to care for the mentally ill gradually fell, reaching 40, 39, or even 38 pfennig per person per day.[17] It was not such a large step from here to remove all care entirely.

The Child-Murder Operation

The program to destroy lives not worth living began in a relatively innocuous fashion. In the fall of 1938, a father by the name of Knauer wrote to Hitler asking that his child, born blind, retarded, and without an arm and a leg, be granted a "mercy death," or euthanasia. Hitler instructed his personal physician Karl Brandt to determine in consultation with the child's physicians whether or not the facts were as stated in the father's letter. Brandt was instructed that if the report proved to be accurate, then he was empowered to allow the physicians to grant the child euthanasia. Werner Catel, the physician in charge of the child, agreed to allow the child to die a "merciful death."

The case of Knauer provided a model on which other euthanasia actions would be carried out. In May 1939, only a few months later, Brandt notified Hans Hefelmann that Hitler had asked him (Brandt) to appoint an advisory committee to prepare for the killing of deformed and retarded children. Hitler's Chancellery was to be directly responsible for the operation; but to maintain secrecy, the project was organized under the cover name Committee for the Scientific Treatment of Severe, Genetically Determined Illness (*Reichsausschuss zur wissenschaftlichen Erfassung von erb- und anlagebedingten schweren Leiden*). Members of the committee included Karl Brandt, Helmut Unger, the pediatrician Ernst Wentzler, the psychiatrist Hans Heinze, and the pediatrician Werner Catel. The entire process of euthanasia was to be conducted under the strictest secrecy (*Geheime Reichssache*); Hefelmann, in testimony after the war, noted that only those physicians from whom a "positive attitude" could be expected were asked to participate in the operation.[18]

On August 18, 1939, just fourteen days before the invasion of Poland, the Committee for the Scientific Treatment of Severe, Genetically Determined Illnesses produced a secret report, delivered to all state governments, asking that midwives or doctors delivering any child born with congenital deformities such as "idiocy or Mongolism (especially if associated with blindness or deafness); microcephaly or hydrocephaly of a severe or progressive nature; deformities of any kind, especially missing limbs, malformation of the head, or spina bifida; or crippling deformities such as spastics [*Littleschen Erkrankung*]" register that child with local health authorities. The ostensible reason given for this registration was "to clarify certain scientific questions in areas of congenital deformity and mental retardation."[19] The order also required that doctors with any child in their care up to the age of three and suffering from any of these infirmities report this child to local health offices; doctors throughout the Reich were sent elaborate questionnaires for this purpose. Registration orders were published in many medical journals; the ailments listed in the orders were simply added to the list of other things requiring medical notification—such as venereal disease, births and deaths, childbed fever, certain contagious diseases, and genetic illnesses falling under the Sterilization Law.[20] Midwives were paid 2 RM for every registration.

Questionnaires returned by physicians or midwives were assembled in Berlin at the desk of Hans Hefelmann, business director of the operation. Hefelmann sent the questionnaires to Profes-

sors Catel, Heinze, and Wentzler to be sorted for "selection" (extermination). Children slated to die were marked with a plus sign; children allowed to live were marked with a minus sign. Decisions were made entirely on the basis of these questionnaires; those doing the selection never examined the children in person or consulted the families or guardians. Children marked with a plus sign were ordered into one of twenty-eight institutions rapidly equipped with extermination facilities, including some of Germany's oldest and most highly respected hospitals (Eglfing-Haar; Brandenburg-Görden; Hamburg Rothenburg and Uchtspringe; Meseritz-Obrawalde, among others). Parents were told that the transport was necessary to improve treatment for their child.[21]

Methods of killing included injections of morphine, tablets, and gassing with cyanide or chemical warfare agents. Children at Idstein, Kantenhof, Görden, and Eichberg were not gassed but were killed by injection; poisons were commonly administered slowly, over several days or even weeks, so that the cause of death could be disguised as pneumonia, bronchitis, or some other complication induced by the injections. Hermann Pfannmuller of the hospital at Eglfing-Haar slowly starved the children entrusted to his care until they died of "natural causes." This method, he boasted, was least likely to incur criticism from the foreign press or from "the gentlemen in Switzerland" (the Red Cross).[22] Others simply left their institutions without heat, and patients died of exposure. Nazi medical men could thus argue that their actions were not technically murder, for they were simply withholding care and "letting nature take its course."[23] Parents were informed with a standardized letter, used at all institutions, that their daughter or son had died suddenly and unexpectedly of brain edema, appendicitis, or other fabricated cause; parents were also informed that, owing to the danger of an epidemic, the body had to be cremated immediately.

This first part of the children's euthanasia was originally restricted to children up to three years old. In December 1940, however, Hefelmann, in conference with hospital doctors administering the program, agreed that the three-year-old boundary might "occasionally be overstepped."[24] On July 12, 1941, *Reichsstatthalter* Mehlhorn ordered all doctors, nurses, and medical personnel to register not just infants but all minors known to have crippling handicaps; teachers who noticed such handicaps among their pupils were required to register those children with health authorities. Anyone failing to register such individuals could be fined up to 150 RM or face imprisonment up to four weeks.[25] By the autumn of 1941, the children's euthanasia program had been expanded to include children up to eight, twelve, and even sixteen and seventeen years old, partly to make up for the slowdown of the adult program discussed later in this chapter.[26]

Jewish children were originally excluded from this operation, on the grounds that they did not deserve the "merciful act" (*Wohltat*) of euthanasia. In 1943, however, the program was broadened to include healthy children of unwanted races: in May 1943 the psychiatric hospital at Hadamar began exterminating Jewish children. Altogether, more than 5,000 children were killed in this first phase of the German euthanasia program.[27]

Adult Euthanasia

The child murders were only one part of a much larger program designed to rid Germany of its weak, handicapped, and "inferior." Here again, the program was planned and administered by medical professionals.

On July 18, 1939, Hans Hefelmann reported to Viktor Brack that Hitler had authorized Leon-ardo Conti to begin a process of adult euthanasia (*Erwachseneneuthanasie*). The message had been given to Hefelmann, in utmost secrecy, by the ophthalmologist Helmut Unger; Unger, in turn, had been informed of the authorization earlier in the year by Reich Physicians' Führer Gerhard Wagner. By the summer of 1939, Conti (Wagner's successor), Philipp Bouhler (Party Chancellery leader), and Herbert Linden (coauthor of the Blood Protection Law) had worked out a plan for the extermination of all of Germany's mental patients. Three ostensibly scientific/medical organizations were created to administer the destruction of mental patients and handicapped children. The Working Committee for Hospital Care provided letterhead for operations correspondence; the Charitable Foundation for Institutional Care was responsible for arranging financial details; and the Nonprofit Patient Transport Corporation was responsible for transporting patients to extermination institutions.[28] Each organization was subordinated to the Committee for the Scientific Treatment of Severe, Genetically Determined Illness, the body established in the summer of 1939 to administer all euthanasia operations. The operation was given the code name T-4, derived from the address of the Nonprofit Patient Transport Corporation, located at Tiergartenstrasse 4 in Berlin.

In October 1939 the first euthanasia applications were sent to psychiatric institutions, where they were evaluated by forty-eight medical doctors—including most notably Werner Heyde, Friedrich Mauz, Paul Nitsche, Friedrich Panse, Kurt Pohlisch, Carl Schneider, and W. Villinger. For their services, the physicians received five pfennig per survey if they evaluated more than 3,500 applications per month, and ten pfennig if they evaluated fewer than 500 per month. From a total of 283,000 applications evaluated, roughly 75,000 patients were marked to die.[29]

The first executions of adult mental patients were carried out during the military campaign against Poland. On January 9, 1940, Dr. Hildebrandt, the future head of the Office of Race and Settlement, reported to Himmler the "elimination [*Beseitigung*] of approximately 4,400 incurable mentally ill from Polish insane asylums," and further, "the elimination of approximately 200 incurable mentally ill from the asylum at Konradstein." Most of these were simply shot, as part of the cleanup work of *Einsatzgruppen* deployed by the Security Service (SD) close behind advancing German armies. Patients were also killed in certain parts of Germany near the front—especially in Pomerania (near Danzig)—and in West Prussia.[30] At about the same time, physicians began to develop techniques that could be used to destroy the entirety of Germany's mental patient population. In early January 1940, Brack, Brandt, Conti, and Bouhler met in the psychiatric hospital at Brandenburg, near Berlin, to conduct the first large-scale test of adult euthanasia. August Becker, a chemist employed by the Reich Criminal Police Office, described this first "experiment" as follows:

> I was ordered by Brack to participate in the first euthanasia trial run in the Hospital at Brandenburg, near Berlin. It was in the first part of January 1940 that I traveled to the hospital. Special apparatus had been constructed for this purpose at the hospital. A room, similar to a shower with tile floors, had been set up, approximately three by five meters and three meters high. There were benches around the edge of the room, and on the floor, about ten centimeters above the ground, there was a water pipe approximately one centimeter in diameter. In this tube there were small holes, from which the carbon monoxide gas flowed.

> The gas containers were outside the room and were already attached to one end of the pipe. . . . In the hospital there were already two crematoria ovens ready to go, for burning the bodies. At the entrance to the room, constructed similar to that of an air-raid shelter, there was a square peep hole through which the behavior of the subjects [*Delinquenten*] could be observed. The first gassing was administered personally by Dr. Widmann. He operated the controls and regulated the flow of gas. He also instructed the hospital physicians Dr. Eberl and Dr. Baumhardt, who later took over the exterminations in Grafeneck and Hadamar. . . . At this first gassing, approximately 18–20 people were led into the "showers" by the nursing staff. These people were required to undress in another room until they were completely naked. The doors were closed behind them. They entered the room quietly and showed no signs of anxiety. Dr. Widmann operated the gassing apparatus; I could observe through the peep hole that, after a minute, the people either fell down or lay on the benches. There was no great disturbance or commotion. After another five minutes, the room was cleared of gas. SS men specially designated for this purpose placed the dead on stretchers and brought them to the ovens. . . . At the end of the experiment Viktor Brack, who was of course also present (and whom I'd previously forgotten), addressed those in attendance. He appeared satisfied by the results of the experiment, and repeated once again that this operation should be carried out only by physicians, according to the motto: "The needle belongs in the hand of the doctor." Karl Brandt spoke after Brack, and stressed again that gassings should only be done by physicians. That is how things began in Brandenburg.[31]

TABLE 2. Killing stations

KILLING STATION	PERIOD OF OPERATION	NUMBER KILLED
Grafeneck	January 1940–December 1940	9,839
Brandenburg	February 1940–September 1940	9,772
Bernburg	January 1941–September 1941	8,601
Hadamar	January 1941–August 1941	10,072
Hartheim	May 1940–May 1941	18,269
Sonnenstein	June 1940–August 1941	13,720

The carbon monoxide used in this and subsequent operations (or "disinfections," as they were commonly known) was recommended for use by toxicologists at the Reich Criminal Police Office's Institute for Criminal Technology.[32] After taking the gold out of the teeth, the bodies were sent to be burned in newly installed crematoria.

The Brandenburg experiment served as a model for subsequent executions. Hospitals at Grafeneck, Bernburg, Sonnenstein, Hadamar, Brandenburg, and the castle at Hartheim near Linz were all specially outfitted with gas chambers disguised as showers and crematoria to burn the bodies.[33] Young, inexperienced doctors were chosen to run the facilities.

The original intent of those who planned the euthanasia operation was to scale it according to the formula 1,000:10:5:1—that is, for every 1,000 Germans, 10 needed some form of psychiatric care; 5 of these required continuous care; and among these, 1 should be destroyed.[34] Given a German population of 65–70 million, this meant that 65,000–70,000 individuals should have been included within the operation. And in fact the program kept closely to this schedule. By the end of August 1941, when the gassing phase of the operation was stopped, 70,273 individuals had been killed. The committee responsible for overseeing the operation kept meticulous records, and today we have an accurate account of how many were killed, and where.[35]

It is important to recognize the banality of the operation. In 1941 the psychiatric institution at Hadamar celebrated the cremation of its ten-thousandth patient in a special ceremony, where everyone in attendance—secretaries, nurses, and psychiatrists—received a bottle of beer for the occasion.[36]

Operations on such a scale are not easy to keep quiet. Rumors had begun to spread in 1940 that children were being killed. Some people began to notice identical form-letter death announcements appearing in newspapers; others complained when they were notified that their child had died of "appendicitis," even though the child's appendix had been removed years before. Suspicions also began to grow (especially around the hospital at Hadamar) that homes for the elderly were going to be emptied; some elderly began to refuse commitment to rest or retirement homes. In the spring of 1940, after a number of parents complained that their children had been killed, state prosecutors filed charges of murder against the directors of two institutions. Charges were quickly dropped, however, when the courts were informed that Hitler himself had guaranteed the immunity of all persons involved. Subsequently procedures were developed to prevent such difficulties. Martin Bormann ordered that letters notifying parents of their child's death be varied in both form and content. Himmler suggested showing films on heredity and mental disease in order to quell the "ugly public opinion" that had grown in the mountainous area surrounding the extermination hospital at Grafeneck;[37] such films had been used since early in the regime as part of an effort to harden public attitudes against "weaker" elements in the population.[38] The regime also took more forceful steps. Parents who resisted turning over their children to the hospitals were declared incompetent and deprived of custody. In other cases, reluctant parents were sent to forced labor camps, and their children were placed in the custody of the state. By the summer of 1941, protests (especially from the Catholic church) had become sufficiently frequent to cause a certain amount of concern among those administering the operation; on August 24, 1941, Hitler ordered Brandt to stop gassing patients in psychiatric institutions. By this time, however, the original goal of eliminating 65,000–70,000 patients had already been achieved.

The killings continued, however, throughout the war and even for some time after. After the fall of 1941, the character of the euthanasia operation changed dramatically. Until August 1941, the program had been centrally administered through Hitler's Party Chancellery. Beginning in 1942, responsibility for administering euthanasia was shifted away from the Chancellery and back to individual hospitals. The methods of killing also changed. Whereas earlier killings had been primarily by means of gas chambers, killings after the fall of 1941 were achieved through a combination of injections, poisonings, and starvation. Euthanasia took on less the character of a single,

Reichwide "operation" and more the character of normal hospital routine.[39] . . .

Doctors were never *ordered* to murder psychiatric patients and handicapped children. They were *empowered* to do so, and fulfilled their task without protest, often on their own initiative. Hitler's original memo of October 1939 was not an order (*Befehl*), but an empowerment (*Vollmacht*), granting physicians permission to act. In the abortive euthanasia trial at Limburg in 1964, Hefelmann testified that "no doctor was ever ordered to participate in the euthanasia program; they came of their own volition." Himmler himself noted that the operations undertaken in psychiatric hospitals were administered solely by medical personnel.[40]

Two further dimensions to this situation have emerged from recent research. First, most of those physicians who did object complained primarily that the operation was not, strictly speaking, legal. In the early years of the program, some of those administering the operation (Brack and Lammers, for example) were sufficiently concerned about this complaint that they drew up plans for a euthanasia law with the help of several of Germany's racial hygienists . . . and yet the law was never passed. The decision was made instead to keep the question of euthanasia a "private matter"— between doctors and their patients. The killings were performed contrary to German law, though authorized by government officials; Hitler assured those responsible for administering the program that he would bear full responsibility for all that was done.[41]

The West German historian Götz Aly has shown that in many cases, parents of handicapped or retarded offspring were eager to rid themselves of the stigma of having "defective children." Many parents wrote to hospitals to ask if their child could be relieved of his or her misery and be granted euthanasia. The euthanasia operation was not an entirely unpopular program; in fact, it appears to have received a broad level of public support throughout the country.[42] ...

Similarly, the elimination of the adult mentally ill was not an entirely unpopular program. By the end of the thirties, propaganda bodies had whipped up such fear and hatred for the mentally ill—one Bielefeld physician compared the genetic defective to a "grenade" waiting to explode[43]—that the elimination of these people seemed a logical or even humane measure. Support for the euthanasia of the mentally ill was apparently one reason that steps were taken, in the spring and summer of 1939, to coordinate a single, nationwide euthanasia program: as Aly has shown, Nazi authorities formulated standardized procedures for killing mental patients partly out of fear that, in war conditions, individual *Gauleiter* might begin destroying patients on their own.[44]

NOTES

1. *Der Prozess gegen die Hauptkriegsverbrecher vor dem internationalen Militärgerichtshof*, vol. 26 (Nuremberg, 1947), 169. The language of the command (*"Gnadentod unter Verantwortung"*) was taken in part from Helmut Unger's 1936 kitsch novel, *Sendung und Gewissen*.

2. For background on the killings, see the comprehensive study by Ernst Klee, *"Euthanasie" im NS-Staat* (Frankfurt, 1983).

3. Klee, *"Euthanasie,"* 46–47. Paul Wulf, himself a victim of the Nazi sterilization program, recalls that in 1936 a number of patients in psychiatric institutions were killed by injections. See his *"Zwangssterilisiert,"* in *Erfassung zur Vernichtung*, ed. Roth, 7.

4. *"Unser Reichsärzteführer spricht,"* *Ziel und Weg*, 5 (1935): 431–37.

5. Mitscherlich and Mielke, *Medizin ohne Menschlichkeit*, 184.

6. Michael Straight, "Germany Executes Her 'Unfit,'" *New Republic*, May 5, 1941, 627–28. See also W. L. Shirer, "Mercy Deaths in Germany," *Reader's Digest*, July 1941, 55–58.

7. Friedrich Kaul, *Nazimordaktion T-4* (Berlin [East], 1973), 58; see also Mitscherlich and Mielke, *Medizin ohne Menschlichkeit*, 191–92.

8. Helmut Unger, *Sendung und Gewissen* (Berlin, 1936).

9. See the commentary on the film *Ich klage an!* in ARW, 2(1941): 237.

10. Reported in IAB, October/November 1934, 159–60.

11. Adolf Dorner, *Mathematik im Dienste der nationalpolitischen Erziehung* (Frankfurt, 1935).

12. Klee, *"Euthanasie,"* 340–41.

13. W. Goeze, "Gesundheitsfürsorge in der Invalidenversicherung 1933," *Reichs-Gesundheitsblatt*, 10(1935): 183.

14. IAB, June/July 1936, 82–83.

15. Verschuer, *Erbpathologie*, 38–39.

16. IAB, November/December 1935, 124–25.

17. Klee, *"Euthanasie,"* 46.

18. Ibid., 79.

19. *Informationsdienst des Hauptamtes für Volksgesundheit der NSDAP*, November 1942, 75. Kurt Blome issued the 1942 version of these orders. See also DA, 70(1940): 142. Klee in his *"Euthanasie"* includes a reproduction of this secret *Runderlass* of the Reich Ministry of the Interior (80–81).

20. Eugen Stähle, "Die Hebammen von Heute," *Wiener Klinische Wochenschrift*, 55(1942): 561–66.

21. Kaul, *Nazimordaktion T-4*, 36.

22. Mitscherlich and Mielke, *Medizin ohne Menschlichkeit*, 193.

23. Kaul, *Nazimordaktion T-4*, 33.

24. Ibid., 50.

25. "Der öffentliche Krüppelfürsorge im Reichsgau Wartheland," ARW, 2(1941): 231.

26. Mitscherlich and Mielke, *Medizin ohne Menschlichkeit*, 211–12.

27. Ibid., 191, 212.

28. These three organizations were the *Reichsarbeitsgemeinschaft Heil-und Pflegeanstalten*; the

Gemeinnützige Stiftung für Anstaltspflege; and the
Gemeinnützige Kranken-Transport-G.m.b.H.

29. Müller-Hill, *Tödliche Wissenschaft*, 17.

30. Klee, "*Euthanasie*," 95–98.

31. Cited in Kaul, *Nazimordaktion* T-4, 77–78.

32. Müller-Hill, *Tödliche Wissenschaft*, 17.

33. Ibid., 17–19.

34. Kaul, *Nazimordaktion* T-4, 64.

35. Aly, "Medizin gegen Unbrauchbare," in Aly et al., *Aussonderung und Tod* (Berlin [West], 1985), 23. Records for these figures can be found in roll 18, T-1021, National Archives, Washington DC.

36. Wertham, *A Sign for Cain*, 157.

37. Kaul, *Nazimordkation* T-4, 106–12.

38. Klee, "*Euthanasie*," 53.

39. Aly, "Medizin gegen Unbrauchbare," 19—31.

40. Wertham, *A Sign for Cain*, 167.

41. Mitscherlich and Mielke, *Medizin ohne Menschlichkeit*, 186–88.

42. Götz Aly, paper delivered to the Free University's Institut für Geschichte der Medizin in Berlin, July 1985.

43. Klee, *Euthanisie*," 48.

44. Aly, "Medizin gegen Unbrauchbare," 14–19.

Rearranging Populations

GÖTZ ALY AND SUZANNE HEIM

From *Architects of Annihilation*

The Break-Up of the Old Order

Since the start of the war and with the victory of our arms, the old order in Europe is breaking up. . . . The principles of a healthy ethnic and geographical order, which have remained mere theory in the absence of the freedom to plan and organize, are now close to being put into practice.

—KONRAD MEYER, "Grossraumprobleme der Agrarpolitik und Betriebslehre"[1]

Five weeks after the outbreak of war, on October 6, 1939, Hitler proclaimed his intention of "creating a new ethnographic order" in Europe . . . through "a resettlement of nationalities." . . . At the same time, Hitler announced "efforts to clarify and settle the Jewish problem."[2] The very next day, Hitler made Himmler responsible for organizing the logistical side of this violent expulsion of whole peoples. Himmler promptly styled himself Reich Commissioner for the Strengthening of German Nationhood (*Reichskommissar für die Festigung deutschen Volkstums*, or RKF) and set up an office of the same name that was to prepare and carry out the task of population redistribution. . . . Within a few months Himmler's small office had grown into a powerful, wide-ranging institution that set the tone of policy, underpinned by a whole network of banks, limited companies, planning groups, an "industry start-up and advi-

sory agency," and regional planning staffs. All these bodies were armed with the authority to issue instructions to existing institutions. Between them they employed many thousands of people: SS men, social workers and community liaison staff, architects, auditors, administrators, agronomists, bookkeepers. . . .

All these different skills and activities were harnessed to a single purpose: to organize resettlement policy in the annexed regions of western Poland—or the "reincorporated eastern territories," as they were viewed from a German perspective. People were dispossessed and driven from their homes, others were drafted in to replace them. The RKF wound up many businesses, amalgamated others, handed them over to new owners. It made credit available, planned new roads, communications and energy supply systems, reorganized entire villages and towns, and set itself the task of "completely changing the face of the countryside."[3] The first prerequisite for this was that the Reich Commissioner for the Strengthening of German Nationhood should "transplant entire ethnic contingents," as Himmler put it.[4] . . .

The western regions of Poland annexed in the wake of the German invasion, covering an area as large as Bavaria and Schleswig-Holstein put together and with a population of 9.5 million, were to be Germanized as quickly as possible and their economic systems adapted to the needs of the German Reich. To that end, the planners at the RKF proposed to expel the Jewish population and a portion of the native Polish population to the

Map 2. German Partition of Poland, 1941–1944. Based on map by Jacques Chazaud. From *Voices and Views: A History of the Holocaust,* edited, with introductions, by Debórah Dwork (The Jewish Foundation for the Righteous, 2002).

central provinces of the former Polish Republic, the so-called Government General. The houses, farms, shops and workshops of the deportees were either closed down, demolished or allocated to ethnic Germans "repatriated" from the Baltic states, Soviet-occupied eastern Poland, and later Romania.

The Reich Commissioner for the Strengthening of German Nationhood was thus creating not just a new "ethnographic order," but also a new economic and social order. While its activities were mainly concentrated in the annexed eastern territories, it was not long before the local representatives of the RKF were at work in all German-occupied or annexed territories, where people were sorted into categories—"persons of German origin," "persons suitable for Germanization," or "members of a dependent minority race—and the various ethnic and minority groups were displaced and resettled.[5] In being thus categorized, people were either confirmed in their civil and social rights or summarily stripped of them. Those judged "suitable for Germanization" received adequate supplies of food, and the men were quickly conscripted into the *Wehrmacht*. Those who were classed as "belonging to a dependent minority race," on the other hand, not only forfeited immediately all claims to a pension, but henceforth belonged to a population group without human rights that could be shunted around at will.

On October 30, 1939, Himmler issued an order for the following resettlement operations to be carried out in the period between November 1939 and February 1940: "(1) From the former Polish, now German provinces and territories: all Jews. (2) From the province of Danzig-West Prussia: all Congress Poles. (3) From the provinces of Posen [later known as the *Warthegau*], South and East Prussia, and Upper Silesia: a yet to be determined number of particularly hostile Polish nationals."[6]

A so-called immediate-action plan called for the deportation "by the beginning of the census on 17.12.39" of "a sufficient number of Poles and Jews to make room for the incoming Baltic Germans." This plan applied only to the *Warthegau*. Looking further ahead, a long-term plan set forth future resettlement operations for the whole of the "eastern provinces." The idea was not simply to replace the Jewish and a portion of the non-Jewish population in the annexed eastern territories with ethnic Germans, but at the same time

to reduce the population density. The planners judged that this would allow them to amalgamate groups of farms and so create more profitable economic units. In order to achieve this the RKF decreed that for every ethnic German moving into the area at least two Poles or Jews must be expelled; in many regions the figure was much higher. The whole process relied on meticulous forward planning. In December 1939 a report by senior SS and police commander Warthe stated: "The critical factors determining the number of evacuees from each district are the ethnic composition of the local population, its political complexion, and its socioeconomic structure. [. . .] It should be borne in mind that we are not dealing here with some indiscriminate mass deportation, but with a very specific group of persons who first have to be identified and documented and then taken away." For every person who was to be deported the German authorities filled out an evacuation card. This card then went the rounds of the "ethnic German index, the deferral index, the Ukrainian and Russian index and the transport index," where it was carefully checked against the records held by each. In addition a special commission examined the deportation application and made a final decision.[7]

According to a report on the "resettlement of Poles from the new Reich territories," prepared by Eduard Könekamp as an observer at the German Foreign Institute in December 1939, a routine had quickly been established:

As ethnic Germans from the Baltic states, Volhynia, and Galicia come pouring into the new Reich territories, particularly the *Warthegau*, an equivalent number of Poles from matching occupations are being evacuated at the same rate. Depending on the number of German farmers, traders, skilled tradesmen, etc., who are registered with the immigration offices, a corresponding number of jobs, houses, and farms previously held or occupied by Poles must be made available for them. If, for example, an incoming batch of immigrants from the Baltic states contains twenty German master bakers, then twenty Polish bakeries in Posen and the rest of the Warthegau must be evacuated.[8] The German immigrants then move into these premises [. . .] Initially the evacuation of residents from the towns was not carried out selectively, but simply block by block. This often meant that railway workers and other persons working in vital industries were evacuated, causing economic disruption. Today evacuations are carried out on the basis of specially prepared lists. Polish intellectuals are evacuated as a matter of priority. Polish agricultural workers, domestic staff and factory workers are allowed to remain.[9]

On January 30, 1940, a conference convened by Himmler and chaired by Heydrich reviewed the first phase of the resettlement program and discussed how all the agencies involved might best coordinate their efforts. These agencies included the RKF itself, the commander (and the inspectors) of the security police and the SD [Security Service], the senior SS and police commanders in the annexed eastern territories and the Government General, the Ethnic German Agency (*Volksdeutsche Mittelstelle* or VoMi), and the Central Trust Agency for the East. The Central Office for the Security of the Reich had no less than nine representatives around the table. Adolf Eichmann was present, as was the economics specialist and head of the SD in Germany, Otto Ohlendorf. Heydrich told the assembled delegates that apart from the 87,000 Poles and Jews who had been deported in order to make room for ethnic Germans from

the Baltic states, an "uncontrolled" and so-called illegal emigration had taken place. By this he meant the mass exodus of people trying to escape the German terror. Heydrich also reported on the especial zeal displayed by his officials, who had ensured "that in the evacuations carried out to date the original quotas have not only been met, but have been exceeded." He gave notice of further deportations in the "very near future": "40,000 Jews and Poles to facilitate the relocation of Germans from the Baltic States" and "120,000 Poles to facilitate the relocation of Germans from Volhynia." He also announced the deportation of the entire Jewish population from the "new eastern districts" (*Ostgaue*), some 450,000 people, and of the 30,000 or so gypsies from the German Reich.[10] But the limited transport capacity of the German railway system, the *Reichsbahn*, and food shortages in the Government General were thought likely to cause problems in this regard.

Section IV in the Central Office for the Security of the Reich was responsible for all resettlement operations, and not just for the "Jewish transports." On December 21, 1939, Heydrich had issued the following instructions regarding the "clearance of the eastern provinces": "It is necessary for practical reasons to have all security-related matters handled by a central agency while the program of clearances in the eastern territories is being implemented. As my special adviser in charge of Section IV at the Central Office for the Security of the Reich I have appointed SS *Hauptsturmführer* Eichmann, with SS *Hauptsturmführer* Günther as his deputy. The offices of this special department are located in Berlin W 62 at Kurfürstenstrasse 115/116."[11] By January 8, 1940, Eichmann was already chairing his first meeting with representatives of various ministries on the subject of the "evacuation of the Jews and Poles in the very near future."[12]

Germanization

As the term itself suggests, Germanization was not about "repatriating" families who had thought of themselves as Germans for generations past, but about dividing the subjugated peoples into "useful" and "useless" groups. It was also about offering the option of collaboration to individuals who were willing to conform and to those who were particularly needed. It was about pursuing a brutal and calculated policy of divide and rule and destroying ethnic cultures and identities. Quite simply, Germanization meant "creaming off human resources" for the social and economic "rebuilding of the Reich" and the conduct of the war. The threat of starvation, dispossession, and possible deportation was used to "soften up" the subject populations and make them "more receptive" to Germanization. Persons who were deemed unsuitable for Germanization were thereby cleared for deportation.

The "guidelines for the Germanization of Polish families" issued in March 1942 state: "The Germanization of families of other nationalities is not primarily intended to swell the ranks of the German nation by incorporating persons of predominantly Nordic-Dinaric blood, but rather to sap the quality of the leadership caste in the foreign ethnic stock." Experience has shown, the author continues, "that particularly among the leaders of the Polish insurgents and resistance movement there is a high preponderance of Nordic blood, which predisposes them to play a more active part in events than the more fatalistic Slavic elements. . . . For this reason in particular the more racially valuable strains should be creamed off from the Polish nation." Only the Reich Commissioner for the Strengthening of German Nationhood, the NSDAP, and the SD were able to recommend the Germanization of persons belonging to "depen-

dent minority races." The eligibility criteria were as follows: "The family must stand out from the rest of the Polish population *and* [the writer's emphasis] the ethnic German population by virtue of its general demeanor, diligence, cleanliness, and healthiness, even if it is living in impoverished circumstances." Furthermore, families deemed suitable for Germanization must not only stand out from the average of the indigenous population, but must also "be above the average for the equivalent social class in the Reich." Factors rated highly by the RKF included the desire to better oneself and the willingness to conform, rather than any characteristics relating to national origins. On this point the guidelines are quite specific: "A poor knowledge of German or a political past is no impediment."[13]

The mentally ill, social misfits, active Communists, persons living in so-called mixed marriages, and other maladjusted types could not become Germans. To qualify for this "privilege," candidates must be given a clean bill of health medically, genetically, and politically. Without this, such persons were classed as "racially undesirable" even if they were ethnic Germans.[14] Moreover the general policy was not to Germanize persons over the age of forty-five. The reason given was as follows: "The German nation would burden itself with such persons, not simply in demographic terms, but also in purely social terms. The persons concerned are capable of fully productive work only in very few instances, and since they are unlikely to produce further offspring they constitute an unnecessary burden on the body of the nation."[15]

The social utopia envisaged by the RKF was not dictated primarily by a sentimental German nationalism. Its supreme goal was to establish a German-speaking master race on the one hand, and on the other hand to eradicate, or at least enslave, large groups of so-called inferior peoples.

Through the "creaming off" of so-called superior elements, the social fabric of these peoples was to be destroyed. At the same time, the demographers at the RKF had it in mind to replace their own "inferior" population inside the German Reich with these newly acquired "human resources": after all, plans were already being made to eliminate more than a million "antisocial elements," "misfits," and "idlers" from the Reich.[16]

Himmler regarded the policy of Germanization as part of that strategy he had summarized in a memorandum of May 1940. In contrast to his early decrees he now embraced Germanization as an effective instrument of social restructuring. For in the meantime it had dawned on the National Socialist leadership too that the manpower needed for the far-reaching imperialistic plans of the German Reich could not be supplied from their own population alone. Under the title "Some thoughts on the treatment of the dependent minority races in the East," Himmler's memorandum called for the population in the East to be "broken up into countless small fragments and particles,"[17] a policy expressly endorsed by Hitler. In future Polish children should only have four years of primary schooling, learning "simple arithmetic allowing them to count to a maximum of 500." Their "highest precept," Himmler avers in his memorandum, must be "to obey the Germans and to be honest, hard-working and well-behaved." However, these much-quoted remarks did not apply to all Polish children. Himmler planned to use this process to sift out those Polish families who wanted a better education for their children, exploiting their aspirations as a criterion and lever for Germanization:

Parents who wish from the outset to give their children a better education, both at primary school level and later on at a secondary school, must submit an application to the senior ss and police commander. The application will be decided primarily on the basis of whether the child is racially pure and matches up to our requirements. If we acknowledge the child as being of our blood, it will be explained to the parents that the child will be sent to a school in Germany, where he or she will remain for the duration. . . . The parents of these children of good blood will then be given a choice: either they must give up their child . . . or the parents must undertake to move to Germany and become loyal citizens of the Reich. Their love of their child gives us a powerful hold over them, in that the child's future and education depend on the loyalty of the parents.

When these children, with or without their parents, had arrived in Germany, Himmler insisted that they were "not to be treated like lepers," but "accepted and integrated into German life after changing their names." If these measures were "systematically implemented," after ten years or so there would only be an "inferior population" living in Poland, a "leaderless nation of workers," destined to collaborate, under strict supervision, in the "eternal civilizing deeds" of the German nation.[18] A few weeks after drafting this memorandum Himmler estimated that approximately one-eighth of the total Polish population could be Germanized in this manner.[19]

The concept was extended with the onward march of German military aggression: "There are still a few Goths left in the Caucasus and the Crimea," observed Himmler in 1942, and he intended to "bring them out and make them into true Germans." "After the war," he continued, he would "despatch ss commanders to every country to bring out the good blood from the indigenous population via the children. The ss commander would turn up in plain clothes and present himself as a helpful, caring man, showing kindness to the children, telling them about free school places, and then bringing them back to Germany with him."[20]

The fact that Himmler's plans for Germanization applied primarily to children in the first instance had to do with his belief that young persons should be nurtured and encouraged solely on their merits, without regard to their social origins and the old social hierarchies and class structures. They would then, so Himmler presumed, be especially loyal to Nazi ideas and thinking. Naturally the desire not to create a society top-heavy with elderly people also played its part here: through the relocation of children and juveniles from "dependent minority races" to the German Reich the population structure would shift in favor of young persons with a healthy capacity for work, and a more favorable ratio between productive labor and welfare costs.

On September 12, 1940, Himmler issued a decree regulating the "future composition of the population" in the annexed eastern territories.[21] According to this, the people living there were to be divided into the following four categories: A = German nationals, i.e., "true" or "fully-fledged" Germans; B = "persons of German origin who must be taught to become fully-fledged Germans again, who therefore possess German nationality but not, initially, the rights and status of full Reich citizenship." Persons in this category were generally to be deported to the prewar Reich for "re-Germanization." This course of action was mandatory, however, for category C persons, defined as "valuable members of the dependent minority races and German renegades who possess German nationality subject to revocation." By far the largest category was D, into which the Reich Commissioner for the Strengthening of German Nationhood placed all those "foreign nationals who do not possess German nationality." Of these eight million or so Polish men and women, the authorities were to "sift out" those "who constitute a valuable addition to the population of the German nation"; their number was fixed in advance by the decree at "a maximum of one million persons."

In the same decree, and on the basis of these categories, Himmler ordered the introduction of a further system for classifying the population, the so-called *Deutsche Volksliste* [DVL-German National List]. This divided the Germans and those deemed "worthy of Germanization"— essentially the persons assigned to categories A, B and C—into four classes and conferred upon them differing sets of civil and social rights. . . . Members of the first two classes were to be "deployed for the work of reconstruction in the East," while those placed in classes 3 and 4 would be "brought up as fully-fledged Germans—or re-Germanized, as the case may be—through an intensive program of education in Germany over a period of time." (This normally meant deporting the persons concerned for forced labor on German farms.) Those assigned to class 4 of the German National List, together with "racially valuable members of dependent minority races (Ukrainians, Great Russians, White Russians, Czechs and Lithuanians)" were to be given German nationality subject to revocation.[22] They were kept under close surveillance by the security police. As a reward for conformity and good behavior they might hope to receive German citizenship after a few years. "Those who decline to be re-Germanized," it was tersely noted, "will be subject to action by the security police." In other words, they would be placed in a concentration camp or murdered. As Himmler noted in a jotting: "All Germanic blood to us or be wiped out."[23]

For the annexed eastern territories, a total of 977,000 people were registered in classes 1 and 2 of the German National List, while those registered in classes 3 and 4 numbered 1,928,000; together they amounted to approximately one-third of the population. Two-thirds of those registered were placed in class 3 of the List. All the remaining members of the "dependent minority races"—i.e., the majority that did not qualify for the List—were classed as "client subjects of the German Reich, with limited native citizens' rights."[24] They were effectively without rights in the face of harassment by the authorities, and they could be deported at any time. But if they displayed evidence of good behavior they might be rewarded with promotion to the lower ranks of the Germanization hierarchy. These arrangements did not apply to Jews or gypsies.

The numbers of those selected for Germanization varied considerably from one region to the next. This did not reflect the arbitrary whims of individual *Gauleiter*, but the agrarian and industrial policy aims of the RKF for each region. And when the shortage of manpower became acute in the last two years of the war, the RKF dramatically increased the quotas for Germanization.[25] In the technical jargon of the population planners this process was also known as *Umvolkung* (ethnic conversion).

Resettlement in Annexed Western Poland

To confiscate and then administer agricultural land in the annexed eastern territories the RKF set up a central land office. This agency was supported by regional land offices, which . . . were now used to push through a "land reform" designed to serve German interests by supplementing the terror tactics of expulsion with a systematic reordering of the conditions governing land tenure. Special maps were drawn up in the land offices. They were used to locate and identify agricultural property earmarked for confiscation. On these maps, land and soil quality were correlated with ethnic grouping, so that one could tell by looking at the map "which types of land were occupied by German farmers and which by Poles."[26] The purpose was to ensure that any better-quality land still owned by Poles was now handed over to Germans. But the Polish farmers were to be evicted even from the poorer-quality land, as these areas were designated for forestation or "landscaping."[27]

As soon as the land had been confiscated and arrangements were in place for deportation and resettlement, the RKF's resettlement units went into action. The staff of these units was responsible for installing the incoming ethnic Germans in "new" farms and houses. The transit camps in which they had been temporarily housed up until then were often former mental or nursing homes that had been cleared by murdering the inmates under the "euthanasia" program. Now the ethnic Germans were given apartments and houses from which Polish and Jewish families had been evicted. The realities of resettlement are described in many surviving reports; a small selection is cited below.

A certain Mr. Schick, employed in the Katowice Trust Agency, describes a resettlement operation that he was invited to observe by the SS:

On Sunday 17 May 1942 the SS resettlement unit, together with the local police battalion, carried out the eviction of some 700 persons in Todygowicz and installed new settlers in their place. [. . .] The evicted Poles were given just half an hour to vacate their properties, and consequently took just the bare essentials with them such as clothing and linen, while the furniture, carpets, household articles, sewing machines and pianos stayed behind. The incoming settlers were supplied with new furniture by the NSV and will sell the furniture left behind by the Poles.[28]

Walter Quiring, a colleague of the Dr. Könekamp of the German Foreign Institute in Stuttgart, supplies a number of important additional details in his own account: "The evacuated Poles are taken first of all to transit camps in Litzmannstadt [Lódz]. Here they are processed and classified according to racial group. Approximately 8 per cent of the total—those belonging to racial groups I and II—are taken back to Germany to be assimilated. A further 15–20 per cent are also sent to Germany for labor service, while the rest are sent east into the Government General."[29]

In 1946 Franciszka Jankowska, a Pole, gave the following account of her expulsion:

On 23 April 1940, it was a Tuesday, at 4.00 a.m., when we were all still asleep, two uniformed Germans entered the room. They ordered us to get dressed at once and leave the house. We were terrified, and suspected that we were being deported. Suddenly I noticed smoke in the room. I grabbed my two youngest children and got them out of the house. The children were only dressed in their night shirts, I had taken them straight from their beds. The fire spread rapidly. The Germans began to fire on the burning house, shooting into the flames, I'm sure they were trying to kill my husband. I learned from our neighbor, Jacub Pszczolkowski, that my husband didn't get away, but was killed. I and my four children were taken along with other evacuees to a camp in a factory in Lodz. When we left the camp they gave us 20 zlotys each. I had no way of supporting myself and my children, and so was dependent on charity aid from the local population.[30]

Eduard Könekamp describes an evacuation operation of this kind from a German perspective:

In the camp on the very outskirts of the town about 20 buses came in one after the other, bringing a total of 700 evacuees. They came piling out of the vehicles, laden with suitcases, rucksacks, bundles tied up in sheets, prams and children's toys, eating utensils, coats and blankets. It rained incessantly. We were standing around in a sea of mud. A few lamps cast their dim light over the scene. Children, rudely awoken from sleep and distraught, were crying. We saw old women in their eighties and nineties. A man wearing the ribbon of the Iron Cross (second class)—a German secondary-school teacher who had chosen to work in Poland—and we saw our countess, ladies in half-veils and fine furs. An implacable but just fate was here being visited upon individual Poles, and upon the ruling class in particular.[31]

In the wake of these brutal evacuations, incoming ethnic Germans were installed as soon as possible. The process is described by Walter Quiring:

I was particularly impressed by the way the resettlement in Janowice (in the Lentschütz district) was organized. The resettlement unit sent a car for me at 4.30 a.m. [...] Our first destination was the transit camp in Zgierz. Parked outside the gate was a line of brown buses normally used to take German workers on vacation trips. The luggage was just then being put on board. The new colonists were sitting in a school hall eating their breakfast. The head of every family had a piece of white paper hung around his neck with the number of his farm written on it (and already the numbering ran from 1441 upwards). I talked to the new colonists. One of them, Selent, had taken part in the Manchurian campaign in 1904–1905. His family had been sent to Siberia in 1915, while he served at the front with the Russian army. After the war he went to America for a few years, to make enough money to build up his farm in Volhynia again. [...] We leave with the second group. The people are put on the buses in the order of their farm numbers. [...] At a farm halfway there we meet up with the police unit of 50 or so men who have been working there during the night. Janowice comes into view up ahead. [...] Then the first carts arrive. No. 1441. A pale, elderly farmer in a poor state of health. "This here is your farm," the ss man tells him. It's a small, blue-painted Polish cottage. It seems to me that the farmer turns a shade paler. He slowly approaches the high wooden gate. His wife stays on the cart, as if rooted to the spot. "And the second farm over there, the neighboring one, that's yours as well..." continues the ss man. "Now that's more like it," he seems to be thinking. I accompany the people as they tour the house. They wander slowly from room to room, examining everything closely. Nobody says a word. Now and then the farmer points to an object and says to his wife, "Look!" We wish the people good luck and go over to the next house.[32]

The practical implementation of the resettlement policy involved both the Party and the Central Office for the Security of the Reich. The NSDAP was represented on the ground by the Ethnic German Agency (VoMi), which had been set up in 1936 with the object of integrating ethnic Germans living abroad more effectively into German political life.[33] The VoMi was headed by ss Obergruppenführer Werner Lorenz. As soon as the "repatriations" of Germans living abroad began, the establishment of the VoMi was steadily

expanded. By June 1941 it had been promoted to the status of an ss *Hauptamt* or central office.

The Central Office for the Security of the Reich (*Reichssicherheitshauptamt* or RSHA) exercised control over resettlement policy through two institutions: the *Einwandererzentrale* (EWZ or Immigration Bureau), responsible for the repatriation of ethnic Germans from abroad, and the *Umwandererzentrale* (UWZ or roughly Resettlement Bureau), responsible for the expulsion of the indigenous population. The EWZ was headed by ss *Standartenführer* Dr Martin Sandberger,[34] who was also deputy *Gruppenleiter* in the RSHA and later gave the order for mass shootings of civilians in the Soviet Union. The head of the UWZ, in charge of deportations, was Adolf Eichmann.

In October 1939 the RKF had founded the German Resettlement Trust Company [German acronym: DUT] for the purpose of "administering and safeguarding the property rights" of ethnic Germans who were resettled in conquered territories. Its activities were "many and various," but according to its charter the Company was primarily concerned with "the orderly transfer of settlers' assets from the country of origin to the new settlement area." By the end of 1940, half a million Germans living abroad were "on their way home," and as such were under the care of the DUT. The Company's last annual report (for 1943) ends with a balance-sheet total of half a billion Reichsmarks. By December 31, 1942, its 1,700 employees had provided for the needs of exactly 806,106 settlers, handing over to them "confiscated Jewish properties and assets" or leaving them furniture and household goods "previously owned by Poles and Jews."[35] Any additional household goods required were commandeered by the RKF from other sources—the Lodz ghetto, for example, where the RKF also continued to have new furniture made until 1944.[36]

The whole system worked as follows. The Foreign Office concluded bilateral agreements with the Baltic republics, the Soviet Union, and Romania governing the resettlement of ethnic Germans. The RKF then resettled these German families—whose forebears had emigrated to eastern and southeast Europe in previous centuries—in the annexed territory of western Poland. The property they had left behind in their old homeland was valued by the DUT, and the government of that country had to make a lump-sum payment of equal value to the German Reich, usually in the form of deliveries of raw materials or food. In theory the German government should then have reimbursed the resettled families for the assets they had left behind. In practice the government pocketed the revenues from the resettlement trade and compensated the resettled families with the stolen property of the displaced Jewish and Polish population. So the German state and the Four-Year Plan Authority, which was responsible for imports of raw materials and food, made a tidy profit from this triangular transaction, which was based on expulsion and deportation. The negotiations over a resettlement agreement with Romania may serve as an example. In this instance the Foreign Office valued the assets left behind by the settlers in Romania at approximately 50 million Reichsmarks, for which the Romanian government was expected to make payment-in-kind by supplying oil to an equivalent value. At the end of 1942 the RKF reported to Hitler: "To date the work carried out by the Reich Commissioner has cost approximately 770 million Reichsmarks of public money. An additional 225 million Reichsmarks has been spent through the German Resettlement Bank on renovating and equipping the farms taken over by the settlers in the annexed Eastern territories. By and large the costs of resettlement have been met by utilizing the property and assets formerly belonging to the ousted dependent minorities, without payment of compensation and without recourse, therefore, to public money."[37] . . . At the same time the DUT functioned as a bank dealing specifically with the financial aspects of resettlement.[38] It gave loans to the incoming colonists to help them get started and made sure that the new property allocated to them was broadly equivalent to what they had left behind.

The DUT and RKF collaborated closely with the Central Trust Agency for the East (*Haupttreuhandstelle Ost* or HTO). While the RKF was responsible for confiscating and reallocating agricultural holdings and forestry land, the Central Trust Agency for the East performed the same function vis-à-vis commercial and industrial assets. The latter body was set up by the Four-Year Plan Authority and remained a permanent fixture as a self-contained "business unit" within the parent institution.[39] The Central Trust Agency for the East administered the businesses it confiscated on a temporary basis and made them over to new owners; but only, of course, if its auditors rated them as "a paying proposition" when measured against German criteria of productivity. To administer urban real estate the Agency set up a separate limited company, the GHTO. So by extending its reach through the Central Trust Agency for the East the Four-Year Plan Authority was able to bring industry and commerce and urban real estate under its control and in this way became directly involved in countless deportation operations and expulsions of Jews. The RKF selected the new owners for confiscated businesses and properties, was sometimes involved in hiring new workers for the expropriated firms, and supplied new tenants and landlords. The Central Trust Agency and the RKF also undertook joint public relations initiatives.[40] But above all else the Central Trust Agency for the East combined hard-headed economic interests with practical resettlement policy. Its "entire work" was "placed in the service of strengthening the war economy of the German Reich" and implementing the "principles of the Four-Year Plan."[41]

NOTES

1. Konrad Meyer, "Grossraumprobleme der Agrarpolitik und Betriebslehre," *Arbeitstagung des Forschungsdienstes. Dresden, Oktober 1942* (*Agrarpolitik-Betriebslehre*, Sonderheft 18), Neudamm 1943, 5–15.

2. Reprinted in: *Der grossdeutsche Freiheitskampf*, Berlin 1942, 67–100.

3. Himmler on questions of resettlement, on the occasion of a visit to Madrid on October 22, 1940; Federal Archive, R 49/20; as quoted in: Karl Heinz Roth, "Erster 'Generalplan Ost' (April/Mai 1940) von Konrad Meyer," *Mitteilungen der Dokumentationsstelle zur NS-Sozialpolitik* I (1985), No.4, document 4.

4. Ibid.

5. As of August 1, 1942, there were RKF representatives for the following regions: Warthegau, Danzig-West Prussia, Upper Silesia, East Prussia, the Government General, Steiermark, Kärnten, Lorraine, Luxembourg, Alsace, Tirol-Vorarlberg, Salzburg, the Sudetenland, Norway, the Netherlands, the Reich Commissariat for the Ostland [the occupied Baltic states], Southern Russia (Kiev) and France (Buchheim, 249 f.). On the work of the Reich Commissioner for the Strengthening of German Nationhood in Slovenia, see the excellent regional study by Tone Ferenc: *Quellen zur nationalsozialistischen Entnationalisierungspolitik in Slowenien 1942–1945*, Maribor 1980.

6. *Biuletyn Glownej Komisji Badania Zbrodni Hitlerowskich w Polsce* (hereinafter cited as *Biuletyn*), Warsaw 1960, vol. 12, document 9F.

7. Report submitted by senior SS and police commander Warthe, December 18, 1939; ibid., document 23F.

8. Könekamp's information about the ratio of numbers was probably wrong even then. But if not, then it was not long before the number of those who were deported to make way for the incoming ethnic Germans was increased (see, 95).

9. Bericht von Dr Könekamp–Polenfahrt vom 29.11. bis 9.12.39; Federal Archive, R 57 neu/31.

10. *Biuletyn*, document 71F.

11. Letter from Heydrich to the commander of the security police and SD in Cracow and to the inspectors of the security police and SD in Breslau, Posen, Danzig, and Königsberg, dated December 21, 1939; *Biuletyn*, document 32F.

12. Memorandum of January 8, 1940, by SS Obersturmführer Franz Abromeit; ibid., documents 37–39F.

13. Richtlinien für die Eindeutschung polnischer Familien des SS-Führers im Rasse-und Siedlungswesen beim Höheren SS-und Polizeiführer/Südost; Federal Archive/BDC, Günther Stier.

14. Old and sick persons, who would otherwise have been suitable for Germanization, were expressly rejected as an "undesirable addition to the blood stock" (Federal Archive/BDC, SS-HO/4992). To qualify as an ethnic German, one had to speak German and have no more than "one grandparent of foreign ethnic origin." Such persons were "to be naturalized as a matter of principle unless there were objections on genetic, political or security-related grounds" (Zum Entwurf einer Dienstanweisung für die EWZ (undated), Federal Archive/BDC, SS-HO/3180–3254).

15. Die "Deutsche Volksliste" in Posen. Bericht über ihre Entstehung und die Entwicklung des Verfahrens, a report prepared by Herbert Strickner in the winter of 1942–43 and reprinted in: Karol Marian Pospieszalski, *Niemiecka Lista Narodowa w "Kraju Warty"* (*Documenta Occupationis Teutonicae*, vol. IV), Poznan 1949, 117; on the dating of the report, see ibid., 326.

16. Aly/Roth, 105–8.

17. Memorandum of Himmler's of May 28, 1940, reprinted in: *VfZG* 5 (1957), 194–98.

18. Ibid.

19. Himmler's notes on plans for future colonization by German farmers, June 24, 1940; Federal Archive NS 19/184; as quoted in: Ackermann, *Himmler*, 300 ff.

20. Record of the remarks made by the SS Reichsführer on August 14, 1942, following his visit to Kiev; Federal Archive NS 19 neu/1446; as quoted in: ibid., 273.

21. Erlass für die Überprüfung und Aussonderung der Bevölkerung in den eingegliederten Ostgebieten; State Archive of Katowice, Bodenamt/1a, 53 ff. Cf. *Documenta Occupations Teutonicae*, vol. IV.

22. People in classes 1 and 2 of the German National List were granted German nationality and Reich citizenship, while those in class 3 received only German nationality, without Reich citizen status.

23. Notes for a speech that Himmler gave at a conference of SS and police commanders in Hegewald on September 16, 1942; Federal Archive NS 19/4009.

24. Later the Jewish and gypsy populations were formally excluded from the category of "client subjects;" see for example order No.779/42 of June 8, 1942, circulated by the president of the regional labor office and Reich trustee for labor in Upper Silesia; State Archive of Katowice, Gauarbeitsamt OS/577, 56.

25. In Slovenia the RKF granted German nationality subject to revocation to 500,000 out of a total of 800,000 residents, while in Lorraine the proportion was even higher, 500,000 out of 600,000 (cf. Czesiaw Madajczyk, *Die Okkupationspolitik Nazideutschlands in Polen 1939–1945*, Berlin 1987, 469).

26. Memorandum of May 7, 1940, Ref.: planning maps; State Archive of Katowice, Bodenamt/ld, l.

27. Notes for a speech by Himmler before a gathering of senior Party officials and *Gauleiter* in Berlin on December 10, 1940; Federal Archive NS 19/4007.

28. Note for the file made by Mr. Schick, employed in the Saybusch branch office of the Katowice Trust Agency, on May 20, 1942; State Archive of Katowice, HTO/9797, 88.

29. German Foreign Institute Commission, report by Dr. Quiring, No.9 ('Secret'), Litzmannstadt, April 19, 1940; Federal Archive, R 57 neu/15.

30. As quoted in: Wladyslaw Bartoszewski, "SS-Obersturmbannführer Karl Adolf Eichmann. Ein Beitrag zur Liste seiner Verbrechen," *Zachodnia Agencja Prasowa* (Warsaw) 4 (April 1961): 13.

31. See note 10.

32. See note 30.

33. Hans Buchheim, "Rechtsstellung und Organisation des Reichskommissars für die Festigung deutschen Volkstums," *Gutachten des Instituts für Zeitgeschichte*, vol. I, Munich 1958, 259.

34. Robert L. Koehl, RKFDV: *German Resettlement and Population Policy 1939–1945*, Cambridge 1957, 64.

35. See also the annual reports of the German Resettlement Trust Company (DUT) for the years 1940–43; they are kept in the library of the World Economic Institute in Kiel.

36. See also the documents recording the activities of Leo Reichert, head of the central department of economics at the RKF; Federal Archive/BDC, personal file of Leo Reichert.

37. Political Archive of the Foreign Office, reference files Luther/Schriftverkehr L-Sch/1940/vol. 4; film 3890, frame 2443784. On December 10, 1940, Himmler calculated that the stolen assets used to fund the work of the RKF in Poland already totaled 3.3 billion Reichsmarks.

38. The composition of the supervisory board is an indication of the disparate interests that were brought together in the DUT. Those with a seat and a vote on the board were: ministerial section head Dr. Hugo Fritz Berger, representing the Reich Ministry of Finance; Hans Kehrl, representing both the Four-Year Plan Authority and the Reich Ministry of Economic Affairs; chairman of the supervisory board was Wilhelm Keppler, undersecretary in the Foreign Office assigned to special duties, who for a long time had been Hitler's personal adviser on economic matters and the principal intermediary between the NSDAP and the business community, and

who had cofounded the "Heinrich Himmler Circle of Friends" (cf. Emil Helfferich, *1932–1946. Tatsachen. Ein Beitrag zur Wahrheitsfindung*, Jever 1969). Also represented of course were the NSDAP, the Reichsbank, manufacturing industry and the private banking sector, and-by three members-the SS.

39. This took effect with the issue of a decree by Göring on October 19, 1939; see Ministerprasident Generalfeldmarschall [Hermann] Göring, ed., *Haupttreuhandstelle Ost. Materialsammlung zum inneren Dienstgebrauch* (Berlin 1940).

40. See for example the series of publications *Die wirtschaftlichen Entwicklungsmöglichkeiten in den eingegliederten Ostgebieten des deutschen Reiches*, of which more than ten issues appeared.

41. Hugo Ratzmann, *Wesen und Aufgabe der Treuhandstelle Posen. Vortrag, gehalten am 28. Januar 1940 anläßlich der ersten grossen nationalsozialistischen Führertagung des Warthegaus in der Gauhauptstadt Posen*, Posen 1940, 9.

Racial War in the East

TIMOTHY SNYDER

From *Bloodlands*

Whether as enemies or as allies, and despite their different ideologies, the Soviet and Nazi leaderships faced the same basic question. How could a large land empire thrive and dominate in the modern world without reliable access to world markets and without much recourse to naval power? Stalin and Hitler had arrived at the same basic answer. The state must be large in territory and self-sufficient in economics, with a balance between industry and agriculture that supported a hardily conformist and ideologically motivated citizenry capable of fulfilling historical prophecies—either Stalinist internal industrialization or Nazi colonial agrarianism. Both Hitler and Stalin aimed at imperial autarky, within a large land empire well supplied in food, raw materials, and mineral resources. Both understood the flashy appeal of modern materials: Stalin had named himself after steel, and Hitler paid special attention to its production. Yet both Stalin and Hitler understood agriculture as a key element in the completion of their revolutions. Both believed that their systems would prove their superiority to decadent capitalism, and guarantee independence from the rest of the world, by the production of food.[1]

As of late 1940 and early 1941, war factored into this grand economic planning very differently for the Soviets than it did for the Nazis. By then Stalin had an economic revolution to defend, whereas Hitler needed a war for his economic transformation. Whereas Stalin had his "social-ism in one country," Hitler had in mind something like National Socialism in several countries: a vast German empire arranged to assure the prosperity of Germans at the expense of others. Stalin presented collectivization itself both as an internal class war and as a preparation for the foreign wars to come. Hitler's economic vision could be realized only after actual military conflict—indeed, after a total military victory over the Soviet Union. The secret of collectivization (as Stalin had noted long before) was that it was an alternative to expansive colonization, which is to say a form of internal colonization. Unlike Stalin, Hitler believed that colonies could still be seized abroad; and the colonies he had in mind were the agrarian lands of the western Soviet Union, as well as the oil reserves in the Soviet Caucasus. Hitler wanted Germany, as he put it, to be "the most autarkic state in the world." Defeating Britain was not necessary for this. Defeating the Soviet Union was. In January 1941 Hitler told the military command that the "immense riches" of the Soviet Union would make Germany "unassailable."[2]

The willingness of the British to fight on alone after the fall of France in June 1940 brought these contradictions to the fore. Between June 1940 and June 1941, Britain was Germany's lone enemy, but stronger than it appeared. The United States had not joined the war, but President Franklin D. Roosevelt had made his commitments clear. In September 1940 the Americans traded fifty destroyers to the British for basing rights in the Caribbean;

as of March 1941 the president had the authority (under the "Lend-Lease" act) to send war materiel. British troops had been driven from the European continent when France had fallen, but Britain had evacuated many of them at Dunkirk. In summer 1940 the *Luftwaffe* engaged the Royal Air Force, but could not defeat it; it could bomb British cities, but not intimidate the British people. Germany could not establish air superiority, a major problem for a power planning an invasion. Though an amphibious assault upon the British Isles would have involved a major crossing of the English Channel with men and materiel, Germany lacked the ships necessary to control the waters and effect the transport. In summer 1940 the *Kriegsmarine* had three cruisers and four destroyers: no more. On July 31, 1940, even as the Battle of Britain was just beginning, Hitler had already decided to invade his ally, the Soviet Union. On December 18 he ordered operational plans for the invasion to "crush Soviet Russia in a rapid campaign."[3]

Hitler intended to use the Soviet Union to solve his British problem, not in its present capacity as an ally but in its future capacity as a colony. During this crucial year, between June 1940 and June 1941, German economic planners were working hard to devise the ways in which a conquered Soviet Union would make Germany the kind of superpower that Hitler wanted it to become. The key planners worked under the watchful eye of Heinrich Himmler, and under the direct command of Reinhard Heydrich. Under the general heading of *Generalplan Ost* ss *Standartenführer* Professor Konrad Meyer drafted a series of plans for a vast eastern colony. A first version was completed in January 1940, a second in July 1941, a third in late 1941, and a fourth in May 1942. The general design was consistent throughout: Germans would deport, kill, assimilate, or enslave the native populations, and bring order and prosperity to a humbled frontier. Depending upon the demographic estimates, between thirty-one and forty-five million people, mostly Slavs, were to disappear. In one redaction, eighty to eighty-five percent of the Poles, sixty-five percent of the west Ukrainians, seventy-five percent of the Belarusians, and fifty percent of the Czechs were to be eliminated.[4]

After the corrupt Soviet cities were razed, German farmers would establish, in Himmler's words, "pearls of settlement," utopian farming communities that would produce a bounty of food for Europe. German settlements of fifteen to twenty thousand people each would be surrounded by German villages within a radius of ten kilometers. The German settlers would defend Europe itself at the Ural Mountains against the Asiatic barbarism that would be forced back to the east. Strife at civilization's edge would test the manhood of coming generations of German settlers. Colonization would make of Germany a continental empire fit to rival the United States, another hardy frontier state based upon exterminatory colonialism and slave labor. The East was the Nazi Manifest Destiny. In Hitler's view, "in the East a similar process will repeat itself for a second time as in the conquest of America." As Hitler imagined the future, Germany would deal with the Slavs much as the North Americans had dealt with the Indians. The Volga River in Russia, he once proclaimed, will be Germany's Mississippi.[5] ...

The Soviet Union was the only realistic source of calories for Germany and its west European empire, which together and separately were net importers of food. As Hitler knew, in late 1940 and early 1941 ninety percent of the food shipments from the Soviet Union came from Soviet Ukraine. Like Stalin, Hitler tended to see Ukraine itself as a geopolitical asset, and its people as instruments who tilled the soil, tools that could be exchanged with others or discarded. For Stalin, mastery of Ukraine was the precondition and proof of the triumph of his version of socialism. Purged, starved, collectivized, and terrorized, it fed and defended Soviet Russia and the rest of the Soviet Union. Hitler dreamed of the endlessly fertile Ukrainian soil, assuming that Germans would extract more from the terrain than the Soviets.[6]

Food from Ukraine was as important to the Nazi vision of an eastern empire as it was to Stalin's defense of the integrity of the Soviet Union. Stalin's Ukrainian "fortress" was Hitler's Ukrainian "breadbasket." The German army general staff concluded in an August 1940 study that Ukraine was "agriculturally and industrially the most valuable part of the Soviet Union." Herbert Backe, the responsible civilian planner, told Hitler in January 1941 that "the occupation of Ukraine would liberate us from every economic worry." Hitler wanted Ukraine "so that no one is able to starve us again, like in the last war." The conquest of Ukraine would first insulate Germans from the British blockade, and then the colonization of Ukraine would allow Germany to become a global power on the model of the United States.[7]

In the long run, the Nazis' *Generalplan Ost* involved seizing farmland, destroying those who farmed it, and settling it with Germans. But in the meantime, during the war and immediately after its (anticipated) rapid conclusion, Hitler needed the locals to harvest food for German soldiers and civilians. In late 1940 and early 1941 German planners decided that victorious German forces in the conquered Soviet Union should use the tool that Stalin had invented for the control of food supply, the collective farm. Some German political planners wished to abolish the collective farm during the invasion, believing that this would win Germany the support of the Ukrainian popula-

tion. Economic planners, however, believed that Germany had to maintain the collective farm in order to feed the army and German civilians. They won the argument. Backe, Göring's food expert in the Four-Year-Plan Authority, reputedly said that the "Germans would have had to introduce the collective farm if the Soviets had not already arranged it."[8]

As German planners saw matters, the collective farm should be used again to starve millions of people: in fact, this time, the intention was to kill tens of millions. Collectivization had brought starvation to Soviet Ukraine, first as an unintended result of inefficiencies and unrealistic grain targets, and then as an intended consequence of the vengeful extractions of late 1932 and early 1933. Hitler, on the other hand, planned in advance to starve unwanted Soviet populations to death. German planners were contemplating the parts of Europe already under German domination, requiring imports to feed about twenty-five million people. They also regarded a Soviet Union whose urban population had grown by about twenty-five million since the First World War. They saw an apparently simple solution: the latter would die, so that the former could live. By their calculations, the collective farms produced just the right amount of food to sustain Germans, but not enough to sustain the peoples of the East. So in that sense they were the ideal tool for political control and economic balance.[9]

This was the Hunger Plan, as formulated by May 23, 1941: during and after the war on the USSR, the Germans intended to feed German soldiers and German (and west European) civilians by starving the Soviet citizens they would conquer, especially those in the big cities. Food from Ukraine would now be sent not north to feed Russia and the rest of the Soviet Union but rather west to nourish Germany and the rest of Europe. In the German understanding, Ukraine (along with parts of southern Russia) was a "surplus region," which produced more food than it needed, while Russia and Belarus were "deficit regions." Inhabitants of Ukrainian cities, and almost everyone in Belarus and in northwestern Russia, would have to starve or flee. The cities would be destroyed, the terrain would be returned to natural forest, and about thirty million people would starve to death in the winter of 1941–42. The Hunger Plan involved the "extinction of industry as well as a great part of the population in the deficit regions." These guidelines of May 23, 1941, included some of the most explicit Nazi language about intentions to kill large numbers of people. "Many tens of millions of people in this territory will become superfluous and will die or must emigrate to Siberia. Attempts to rescue the population there from death through starvation by obtaining surpluses from the black earth zone can only come at the expense of the provisioning of Europe. They prevent the possibility of Germany holding out until the end of the war, they prevent Germany and Europe from resisting the blockade. With regard to this, absolute clarity must reign."[10]

Hermann Göring, at this time Hitler's most important associate, held overall responsibility for economic planning. His Four-Year-Plan Authority had been charged with preparing the German economy for war between 1936 and 1940. Now his Four-Year-Plan Authority, entrusted with the Hunger Plan, was to meet and reverse Stalin's Five-Year Plan. The Stalinist Five-Year Plan would be imitated in its ambition (to complete a revolution), exploited in its attainment (the collective farm), but reversed in its goals (the defense and industrialization of the Soviet Union). The Hunger Plan foresaw the restoration of a preindustrial Soviet Union, with far fewer people, little industry, and no large cities. The forward motion of

the *Wehrmacht* would be a journey backward in time. National Socialism was to dam the advance of Stalinism, and then reverse the course of its great historical river.

Starvation and colonization were German policy: discussed, agreed, formulated, distributed, and understood. The framework of the Hunger Plan was established by March 1941. An appropriate set of "Economic Policy Guidelines" was issued in May. A somewhat sanitized version, known as the "Green Folder," was circulated in one thousand copies to German officials that June. Just before the invasion, both Himmler and Göring were overseeing important aspects of the postwar planning: Himmler the long-term racial colony of *Generalplan Ost*, Göring the short-term starvation and destruction of the Hunger Plan. German intentions were to fight a war of destruction that would transform eastern Europe into an exterminatory agrarian colony. Hitler meant to undo all the work of Stalin. Socialism in one country would be supplanted by socialism for the German race. Such were the plans.[11] . . .

Chiune Sugihara, the Soviet specialist among Japanese spies, spent that spring [of 1941] in Königsberg, the German city in East Prussia on the Baltic Sea, trying to guess the date of the German invasion of the Soviet Union. Accompanied by Polish assistants, he made journeys through eastern Germany, including the lands that Germany had seized from Poland. His estimation, based upon observations of German troop movements, was mid-June 1941. His reports to Tokyo were just one of thousands of indications, sent by intelligence staffs in Europe and around the world, that the Germans would break the Molotov-Ribbentrop Pact and invade their ally in late spring or early summer.

Stalin himself received more than a hundred such indications, but chose to ignore them. His own strategy was always to encourage the Germans to fight wars in the west, in the hope that the capitalist powers would thus exhaust themselves, leaving the Soviets to collect the fallen fruit of a prone Europe. Hitler had won his battles in western Europe (against Norway, Denmark, Belgium, Luxembourg, the Netherlands, and France) too quickly and too easily for Stalin's taste. Yet he seemed unable to believe that Hitler would abandon the offensive against Great Britain, the enemy of both Nazi and Soviet ambitions, the one world power on the planet. He expected war with Germany, but not in 1941. He told himself and others that the warnings of an imminent German attack were British propaganda, designed to divide Berlin and Moscow despite their manifest common interests. Apart from anything else, Stalin could not believe that the Germans would attack without winter gear, which none of the espionage reports seemed to mention.[12]

That was the greatest miscalculation of Stalin's career. The German surprise attack on the Soviet Union of June 22, 1941, looked at first like a striking success. Three million German troops, in three Army Groups, crossed over the Molotov-Ribbentrop line and moved into the Baltics, Belarus, and Ukraine, aiming to take Leningrad, Moscow, and the Caucasus. The Germans were joined in the invasion by their allies Finland, Romania, Hungary, Italy, and Slovakia, and by a division of Spanish and a regiment of Croatian volunteers. This was the largest offensive in the history of warfare; nevertheless, unlike the invasion of Poland, it came only from one side and would lead to war on one (very long) front.

German officers had every confidence that they could defeat the Red Army quickly. Success in Poland, and above all in France, had made many of them believers in Hitler's military genius. The invasion of the Soviet Union, led by armor, was to

bring a "lightning victory" within nine to twelve weeks. With the military triumph would come the collapse of the Soviet political order and access to Soviet foodstuffs and oil. German commanders spoke of the Soviet Union as a "house of cards" or as a "giant with feet of clay." Hitler expected that the campaign would last no more than three months, probably less. It would be "child's play." That was the greatest miscalculation of Hitler's career.[13]

Ruthlessness is not the same thing as efficiency, and German planning was too bloodthirsty to be really practical. The Wehrmacht could not implement the Hunger Plan. The problem was not one of ethics or law. The troops had been relieved by Hitler from any duty to obey the laws of war toward civilians, and German soldiers did not hesitate to kill unarmed people. They behaved in the first days of the attack much as they had in Poland. By the second day of the invasion, German troops were using civilians as human shields. As in Poland, German soldiers often treated Soviet soldiers as partisans to be shot upon capture and killed Soviet soldiers who were trying to surrender. Women in uniform, no rarity in the Red Army, were initially killed just because they were female. The problem for the Germans was rather that the systematic starvation of a large civilian population is an inherently difficult undertaking. It is much easier to conquer territory than to redistribute calories.[14] . . .

The German occupiers never had the ability to starve when and where they chose. For the Hunger Plan to be implemented, German forces would have had to secure every collective farm, observe the harvest everywhere, and make sure that no food was hidden or went unrecorded. The *Wehrmacht* was able to maintain and control the collective farms, as were the ss and local assistants, but never so effectively as the Soviets had done. Germans did not know the local people, the local harvest, or the local hiding places. They could apply terror, but less systematically than the Soviets had done; they lacked the party and the fear and faith that it could arouse. They lacked the personnel to seal off cities from the countryside. And as the war continued longer than planned, German officers worried that organized starvation would create a resistance movement behind the lines.[15]

Operation Barbarossa was supposed to be quick and decisive, bringing a "lightning victory" within three months at the latest. Yet while the Red Army fell back, it did not collapse. Two weeks into the fighting, the Germans had taken all of what had been Lithuania, Latvia, and eastern Poland, as well as most of Soviet Belarus and some of Soviet Ukraine. Franz Haider, chief of staff of the German army, confided to his diary on July 3, 1941, that he believed that the war had been won. By the end of August, the Germans had added Estonia, a bit more of Soviet Ukraine, and the rest of Soviet Belarus. Yet the pace was all wrong, and the fundamental objectives were not achieved. The Soviet leadership remained in Moscow. As one German corps commander noted pithily on September 5, 1941: "no victorious Blitzkrieg, no destruction of the Russian army, no disintegration of the Soviet Union."[16]

Germany starved Soviet citizens anyway, less from political dominion than political desperation. Though the Hunger Plan was based upon false political assumptions, it still provided the moral premises for the war in the East. In autumn 1941, the Germans starved not to remake a conquered Soviet Union but to continue their war without imposing any costs on their own civilian population. In September Göring had to take stock of the new situation, so disastrously different from Nazi expectations. Dreams of a

shattered Soviet Union yielding its riches to triumphant Germans had to be abandoned. The classic dilemma of political economy, guns or butter, was supposed to have been resolved in a miraculous way: guns would make butter. But now, three months into the war, the men carrying the guns very much needed the butter. As the war continued beyond the planned twelve weeks, German soldiers were competing with German civilians for limited food supplies. The invasion itself had halted the supply of grain from the Soviet Union. Now three million German soldiers simply had to be fed, without reducing food rations within Germany itself.[17]

The Germans lacked contingency plans for failure. The troops had a sense that something was wrong; after all, no one had given them any winter coats, and their night watches were getting cold. But how could the German population be told that the invasion had failed, when the Wehrmacht still seemed to be pushing forward and Hitler still had moments of euphoria? But if the Nazi leadership could not admit that the war was going badly, then German civilians would have to be spared any negative consequences of the invasion. Grumbling of stomachs might lead to the grumbling of citizens. Germans could not be allowed to make a sacrifice for the troops on the front, at least not too much, and not too soon. A change in domestic food policy might allow them to see the truth: that the war, at least as their leaders had conceived of it, was already lost. Backe, Göring's food specialist, was sure about what had to be done: the Soviets would have to be deprived of food so that Germans could eat their fill.[18]

It was Göring's task to spare the German economy while supplying the German war machine. His original scheme to starve the Soviet Union after a clear victory now gave way to an improvisation: German soldiers should take whatever food they needed as they continued to fight a war that was already supposed to be over. On September 16, 1941, just as the timeline for the original "lightning victory" was exceeded, Göring ordered German troops to live "off the land." A local commanding general was more specific: Germans must feed themselves "as in the colonial wars." Food from the Soviet Union was to be allocated first to German soldiers, then to Germans in Germany, then to Soviet citizens, and then to Soviet prisoners of war. As the *Wehrmacht* fought on, in the shorter days and longer nights, as solid roads gave way to the mud and muck of autumn rains, its soldiers had to fend for themselves. Göring's order allowed their misconceived war to continue, at the price of the starvation of millions of Soviet citizens, and of course the deaths of millions of German and Soviet and other soldiers.[19] . . .

During the summer of 1941, some German soldiers had shared their rations with hungry Soviet civilians. A few German officers had tried to ensure that Soviet prisoners of war were fed. In autumn this would have to cease. If German soldiers wanted to eat, they were told, they would have to starve the surrounding population. They should imagine that any food that entered the mouth of a Soviet citizen was taken from the mouth of a German child.[20] German commanders would have to continue the war, which meant feeding soldiers, which meant starving others. This was the political logic, and the moral trap. For the soldiers and the lower-level officers, there was no escape but insubordination or surrender to the enemy, prospects as unthinkable for German troops in 1941 as they had been for Ukrainian communists in 1932.[21]

In September 1941, the three *Wehrmacht* Army Groups, North, Center, and South, greeted the new food policy from rather different positions. Army Group North, tasked to conquer the Baltic States and northwestern Russia, had laid siege to Leningrad in September. Army Group Center raced through Belarus in August. After a long pause, in which some of its forces assisted Army Group South in the battle for Kiev, it advanced again toward Moscow in early October. Army Group South meanwhile made its way through Ukraine toward the Caucasus, much more slowly than anticipated. Platoons of German soldiers resembled the communist brigades of a decade before, taking as much food as they could as quickly as possible.

Army Group South starved Kharkiv and Kiev, the two cities that had served as capitals of Soviet Ukraine. Kiev was taken on September 19, 1941, much later than planned, and after much debate about what to do with the city. Consistent with *Generalplan Ost*, Hitler wanted the city to be demolished. The commanders on site, however, needed the bridge over the river Dnipro to continue their advance east. So in the end German soldiers stormed the city. On September 30 the occupiers banned the supply of food to Kiev. The logic was that the food in the countryside was to remain there, to be collected by the army and then later by a German civilian occupation authority. Yet the peasants around Kiev found their way into the city and even ran markets. The Germans were unable to seal the city as the Soviets had done in 1933.[22]

The *Wehrmacht* was not implementing the original Hunger Plan but rather starving where it seemed useful to do so. The *Wehrmacht* never intended to starve the entire population of Kiev, only to ensure that its own needs were met. Yet this was nevertheless a policy of indifference to human life as such, and it killed perhaps as many as fifty thousand people. As one Kievan recorded in December 1941, the Germans were celebrating Christmas, but the locals "all move like shadows, there is total famine." In Kharkiv a similar policy killed perhaps twenty thousand people. Among them were 273 children in the city orphanage in 1942.[23]

Hitler's plans for Leningrad, the old capital of imperial Russia, exceeded even Stalin's darkest fears. Leningrad lay on the Baltic Sea, closer to the Finnish capital Helsinki and the Estonian capital Tallinn than to Moscow. During the Great Terror, Stalin had made sure that Finns were targeted for one of the deadliest of the national actions, believing that Finland might one day lay claim to Leningrad. In November 1939 Stalin had ensured for himself the enmity of the Finns by attacking Finland, which was within his area of influence according to the terms of the Molotov-Ribbentrop Pact. In this Winter War, the Finns inflicted heavy losses and damaged the reputation of the Red Army. They finally had to concede about a tenth of their territory in March 1940, giving Stalin a buffer zone around Leningrad. So in June 1941 Hitler had a Finnish ally, since the Finns naturally wanted to retake land and take revenge in what they would call the "Continuation War." But Hitler did not want to take Leningrad and give it to the Finns. He wanted to remove it from the face of the earth. Hitler wanted the population of Leningrad exterminated, the city razed to the ground, and then its territory handed over to the Finns.[24]

In September 1941, the Finnish Army cut off Leningrad from the north, as the Army Group North began a campaign of siege and bombardment of the city from the south. Though German commanders had not all known about Hitler's most radical plans for Soviet cities, they agreed that Leningrad had to be starved. Eduard Wagner, the quartermaster general of the German army, wrote to his wife that the inhabitants of Leningrad, all 3.5 million of them, would have to be left to their fate. They were simply too much for the

army's "provision packet," and "sentimentality would be out of place." Mines were laid around the city to prevent escapes. The surrender of the city was not forthcoming, but had it come it would not have been accepted. The German goal was to starve Leningrad out of existence. At the very beginning of the siege of Leningrad, on September 8, 1941, German shells destroyed the city's food warehouses and oil tanks. In October 1941 perhaps 2,500 people died of starvation and associated diseases. In November the number reached 5,500, in December, 50,000. By the end of the siege in 1944, about one million people had lost their lives.[25] . . .

The greater the control the *Wehrmacht* exercised over a population, the more likely that population was to starve. The one place where the *Wehrmacht* controlled the population completely, the prisoner-of-war camps, was the site of death on an unprecedented scale. It was in these camps where something very much like the original Hunger Plan was implemented.

Never in modern warfare had so many prisoners been taken so quickly. In one engagement, the *Wehrmacht* Army Group Center took 348,000 prisoners near Smolensk; in another, Army Group South took 665,000 near Kiev. In those two September victories alone, more than a million men (and some women) were taken prisoner. By the end of 1941, the Germans had taken about three million Soviet soldiers prisoner. This was no surprise to the Germans. The three German Army Groups were expected to move even faster than they did, and thus even more prisoners could have been expected. Simulations had predicted what would happen. Yet the Germans did not prepare for prisoners of war, at least not in the conventional sense. In the customary law of war, prisoners of war are given food, shelter, and medical attention, if only to ensure that the enemy does the same.[26]

Hitler wished to reverse the traditional logic. By treating Soviet soldiers horribly, he wished to ensure that German soldiers would fear the same from the Soviets, and so fight desperately to prevent themselves from falling into the hands of the enemy. It seems that he could not bear the idea of soldiers of the master race surrendering to the subhumans of the Red Army. Stalin took much the same view: that Red Army soldiers should not allow themselves to be taken alive. He could not counsel the possibility that Soviet soldiers would retreat and surrender. They were supposed to advance and kill and die. Stalin announced in August 1941 that Soviet prisoners of war would be treated as deserters, and their families arrested. When Stalin's son was taken prisoner by the Germans, he had his own daughter-in-law arrested. This tyranny of the offensive in Soviet planning caused Soviet soldiers to be captured. Soviet commanders were fearful of ordering withdrawals, lest they be personally blamed (purged, and executed). Thus their soldiers held positions for too long and were encircled and taken prisoner. The policies of Hitler and Stalin conspired to turn Soviet soldiers into prisoners of war and then prisoners of war into non-people.[27]

Once they had surrendered, Soviet prisoners were shocked by the savagery of their German captors. Captured Red Army soldiers were marched in long columns, beaten horribly along the way, from the field of battle to the camps. The soldiers captured at Kiev, for example, marched over four hundred kilometers in the open air. As one of them remembered, if an exhausted prisoner sat down by the side of the road, a German escort "would approach on his horse and lash with his whip. The person would continue to sit, with his head down. Then the escort would take a carbine from the saddle or a pistol from the holster." Prisoners who were wounded, sick, or tired were shot on the spot, their bodies left for Soviet citizens to find and clean and bury.[28]

When the *Wehrmacht* transported Soviet prisoners by train, it used open freight cars, with no protection from the weather. When the trains reached their destinations, hundreds or sometimes even thousands of frozen corpses would tumble from the opened doors. Death rates during transport were as high as seventy percent. Perhaps two hundred thousand prisoners died in these death marches and these death transports. All of the prisoners who arrived in the eighty or so prisoner-of-war camps established in the occupied Soviet Union were tired and hungry, and many were wounded or ill.[29]

Ordinarily, a prisoner-of-war camp is a simple facility, built by soldiers for other soldiers, but meant to preserve life. Such camps arise in difficult conditions and in unfamiliar places; but they are constructed by people who know that their own comrades are being held as prisoners by the opposing army. German prisoner-of-war camps in the Soviet Union, however, were something far out of the ordinary. They were designed to end life. In principle, they were divided into three types: the *Dulag* (transit camp), the *Stalag* (base camp for enlisted men and noncommissioned officers), and the smaller *Oflags* (for officers). In practice, all three types of camps were often nothing more than an open field surrounded by barbed wire. Prisoners were not registered by name, though they were counted. This was an astonishing break with law and custom. Even at the German concentration camps names were taken. There was only one other type of German facility where names were not taken, and it had not yet been invented. No advance provision was made for food, shelter, or medical care. There were no clinics and very often no toilets. Usually there was no shelter from the elements. The official calorie quotients for the prisoners were far below survival levels and were often not met. In practice, only the stronger prisoners, and those who had been selected as guards, could be sure of getting any food at all.[30]

Soviet prisoners were at first confused by this treatment by the *Wehrmacht*. One of them guessed that "the Germans are teaching us to behave like comrades." Unable to imagine that hunger was a policy, he guessed that the Germans wanted the Soviet prisoners to show solidarity with one another by sharing whatever food they had among themselves. Perhaps this soldier simply could not believe that, like the Soviet Union, Nazi Germany was a state that starved by policy. Ironically, the entire essence of German policy toward the prisoners was that they were not actually equal human beings, and thus certainly not fellow soldiers, and under no circumstances comrades. The guidelines of May 1941 had instructed German soldiers to remember the supposedly "inhuman brutality" of Russians in battle. German camp guards were informed in September that they would be punished if they used their weapons too little.[31]

In autumn 1941, the prisoners of war in all of the Dulags and Stalags went hungry. Though even Göring recognized that the Hunger Plan as such was impossible, the priorities of German occupation ensured that Soviet prisoners would starve. Imitating and radicalizing the policies of the Soviet Gulag, German authorities gave less food to those who could not work than to those who could, thereby hastening the deaths of the weaker. On October 21, 1941, those who could not work saw their official rations cut by twenty-seven percent. This was for many prisoners a purely theoretical reduction, since in many prisoner-of-war camps no one was fed on a regular basis, and in most the weaker had no regular access to food anyway. A remark of the quartermaster general

of the army, Eduard Wagner, made explicit the policy of selection: those prisoners who could not work, he said on November 13, "are to be starved." Across the camps, prisoners ate whatever they could find: grass, bark, pine needles. They had no meat unless a dog was shot. A few prisoners got horsemeat on a few occasions. Prisoners fought to lick utensils, while their German guards laughed at their behavior. When the cannibalism began, the Germans presented it as the result of the low level of Soviet civilization.[32] . . .

In the starving Soviet Union in autumn 1941, the *Wehrmacht* was in a moral trap, from which National Socialism seemed to offer the only escape. Any remnants of traditional soldierly ideals had to be abandoned in favor of a destructive ethic that made sense of the army's predicament. To be sure, German soldiers had to be fed; but they were eating to gain strength to fight a war that had already been lost. To be sure, calories had to be extracted from the countryside to feed them; but this brought about essentially pointless starvation. As the army high command and the officers in the field implemented illegal and murderous policies, they found no justification except for the sort that Hitler provided: that human beings were containers of calories that should be emptied, and that Slavs, Jews, and Asians, the peoples of the Soviet Union, were less than human and thus more than expendable. Like Ukrainian communists in 1933, German officers in 1941 implemented a policy of starvation. In both cases, many individuals had objections or reservations at first, but the groups in the end implicated themselves in the crimes of the regime, and thus subordinated themselves to the moral claims of their leaders. They became the system as the system became catastrophe. It was the *Wehrmacht* that established and ran the first network of camps, in Hitler's Europe, where people died in the thousands, the tens of thousands, the hundreds of thousands, and finally the millions.

Some of the most infamous prisoner-of-war camps were in occupied Soviet Belarus, where by late November 1941 death rates had reached two percent *per day*. At *Stalag* 352 near Minsk, which one survivor remembered as "pure hell," prisoners were packed together so tightly by barbed wire that they could scarcely move. They had to urinate and defecate where they stood. Some 109,500 people died there. At *Dulag* 185, *Dulag* 127, and *Stalag* 341, in the east Belarusian city Mahileu, witnesses saw mountains of unburied corpses outside the barbed wire. Some thirty to forty thousand prisoners died in these camps. At *Dulag* 131 at Bobruisk, the camp headquarters caught fire. Thousands of prisoners burned to death, and another 1,700 were gunned down as they tried to escape. All in all at least thirty thousand people died at Bobruisk. At Dulags 220 and 121 in Homel, as many as half of the prisoners had shelter in abandoned stables. The others had no shelter at all. In December 1941 death rates at these camps climbed from two hundred to four hundred to seven hundred a day. At *Dulag* 342 at Molodechno, conditions were so awful that prisoners submitted written petitions asking to be shot.[33]

The camps in occupied Soviet Ukraine were similar. At *Stalag* 306 at Kirovohrad, German guards reported that prisoners ate the bodies of comrades who had been shot, sometimes before the victims were dead. Rosalia Volkovskaia, a survivor of the women's camp at Volodymyr Volynskyi, had a view of what the men faced at the local *Stalag* 365: "we women could see from above that many of the prisoners ate the corpses." At *Stalag* 346 in Kremenchuk, where inmates got at most two hundred grams of bread per day, bodies were thrown into a pit every morning. As in Ukraine in 1933, sometimes the living were buried along

with the dead. At least twenty thousand people died in that camp. At *Dulag* 162 in Stalino (today Donetsk), at least ten thousand prisoners at a time were crushed behind barbed wire in a small camp in the center of the city. People could only stand. Only the dying would lie down, because anyone who did would be trampled. Some twenty-five thousand perished, making room for more. *Dulag* 160 at Khorol, southwest of Kiev, was one of the larger camps. Although the site was an abandoned brick factory, prisoners were forbidden to take shelter in its buildings. If they tried to escape there from the rain or snow, they were shot. The commandant of this camp liked to observe the spectacle of prisoners struggling for food. He would ride in on his horse amidst the crowds and crush people to death. In this and other camps near Kiev, perhaps thirty thousand prisoners died.[34]

Soviet prisoners of war were also held at dozens of facilities in occupied Poland, in the General Government (which had been extended to the southeast after the invasion of the Soviet Union). Here astonished members of the Polish resistance filed reports about the massive death of Soviet prisoners in the winter of 1941–1942. Some 45,690 people died in the camps in the General Government in ten days, between October 21 and 30, 1941. At *Stalag* 307 at Deblin, some eighty thousand Soviet prisoners died over the course of the war. At *Stalag* 319 at Chelm some sixty thousand people perished; at *Stalag* 366 in Siedlce, fifty-five thousand; at *Stalag* 325 at Zamosc, twenty-eight thousand; at *Stalag* 316 at Siedlce, twenty-three thousand. About half a million Soviet prisoners of war starved to death in the General Government. As of the end of 1941, the largest group of mortal victims of German rule in occupied Poland was neither the native Poles nor the native Jews, but Soviet prisoners of war who had been brought west to occupied Poland and left to freeze and starve. Despite the recent Soviet invasion of Poland, Polish peasants often tried to feed the starving Soviet prisoners they saw. In retaliation, the Germans shot the Polish women carrying the milk jugs, and destroyed whole Polish villages.[35]

Even had the Soviet prisoners all been healthy and well fed, death rates in winter 1941–42 would have been high. Despite what many Germans thought, Slavs had no inborn resistance to cold. Unlike the Germans, Soviet soldiers had sometimes been equipped with winter gear; this the Germans stole. The prisoners of war were usually left without shelter and without warm clothing, enduring temperatures far below freezing. As the camps were often in fields, no trees or hills broke the ruthless winter winds. Prisoners would build for themselves, by hand in the hard earth, simple dugouts where they would sleep. At Homel three Soviet soldiers, comrades, tried to keep one another warm by sleeping in a tight group. Each would have a turn sleeping in the middle, in the best spot, taking the warmth of his friends. At least one of the three lived to tell the tale.[36] . . .

The organization of the camps in the east revealed a contempt for life, the life of Slavs and Asians and Jews anyway, that made such mass starvation thinkable. In German prisoner-of-war camps for Red Army soldiers, the death rate over the course of the war was 57.5 percent. In the first eight months after Operation Barbarossa, it must have been far higher. In German prisoner-of-war camps for soldiers of the western Allies, the death rate was less than five percent. As many Soviet prisoners of war died on a single given day in autumn 1941 as did British and American prisoners of war over the course of the entire Second World War.[37]

Just as the Soviet population could not be starved at will, the Soviet state could not be destroyed in one blow. But the Germans certainly tried. Part of the idea of the "lightning victory" was that the Wehrmacht would cover terrain so quickly that the soldiers, and the trailing *Einsatzgruppen*, would be able to kill Soviet political elites and Red Army political officers. The official "Guidelines for the Behavior of the Troops in Russia," issued on May 19, 1941, demanded a "crackdown" on four groups: agitators, partisans, saboteurs, and Jews. The "Guidelines for the Treatment of Political Commissars" of June 6, 1941, specified that captured political officers were to be killed.[38]

In fact, local Soviet elites fled to the east; and the more elite such people were, the more likely they were to have been evacuated or to have had the resources to arrange their own escape. The country was vast, and Hitler had no ally invading on another vector who might be able to capture such people. German policies of mass murder could affect the Soviet leadership only in the lands that were actually conquered: Ukraine, Belarus, the Baltic States, and a very thin wedge of Russia. This was not very much of the Soviet Union, and the people in question were not of critical importance to the Soviet system. People were shot, but with only minimal consequences for the Soviet state. Most Wehrmacht units seemed to have little difficulty in obeying the "commissar order"; eighty percent of them reported having executed commissars. The military archives preserve the records of 2,252 shootings of such people by the army; the actual number was probably greater.[39]

Shooting civilians was mainly the task of the *Einsatzgruppen*, one that they had already performed in Poland in 1939. As in Poland, the *Einsatzgruppen* were assigned to murder certain political groups so that the state would collapse. Four *Einsatzgruppen* followed the Wehrmacht into the Soviet Union: A following Army Group North into the Baltics toward Leningrad, B following Army Group Center through Belarus toward

Moscow, C following Army Group South into Ukraine, and D following the 11th Army in the extreme south of Ukraine. As Heydrich clarified in a telegram of July 2, 1941, after having issued the relevant orders orally, the *Einsatzgruppen* were to kill communist functionaries, Jews in party and state positions, and other "dangerous elements." As with the Hunger Plan, so with the elimination of people defined as political threats: those in confinement were most vulnerable. By mid-July the orders had come through to carry out mass murder by shooting in the Stalags and Dulags. On September 8, 1941, *Einsatzkommandos* were ordered to make "selections" of the prisoners of war, executing state and party functionaries, political commissars, intellectuals, and Jews. In October the army high command gave the *Einsatzkommandos* and the Security Police unrestricted access to the camps.[40]

The *Einsatzkommandos* could not screen the Soviet prisoners of war very carefully. They would interrogate Soviet prisoners of war in their holding pens, immediately after they were taken. They would ask commissars, communists, and Jews to step forward. Then they would take them away, shoot them, and throw them into pits. They had few interpreters, and these tended to remember the selections as being somewhat random. The Germans had imprecise notions of the ranks and insignia of the Red Army, and initially mistook buglers for political officers. They knew that officers were allowed to wear their hair longer than enlisted men, but this was an uncertain indicator. It had been some time since most of these men had seen a barber. The only group that could easily be identified at this point were male Jews; German guards examined penises for circumcision. Very occasionally Jews survived by claiming to be circumcised Muslims; more often circumcised Muslims were shot as Jews. German doctors seem to have collaborated willingly in this procedure; medicine was a highly nazified profession. As a doctor at the camp at Khorol recalled: "For every officer and soldier it was, in those times, the most natural thing that every Jew was shot to death." At least fifty thousand Soviet Jews were shot after selection and about fifty thousand non-Jews as well.[41]

The German prisoner-of-war camps in the East were far deadlier than the German concentration camps. Indeed, the existing concentration camps changed their character upon contact with prisoners of war. Dachau, Buchenwald, Sachsenhausen, Mauthausen, and Auschwitz became, as the SS used them to execute Soviet prisoners of war, killing facilities. Some eight thousand Soviet prisoners were executed at Auschwitz, ten thousand at Mauthausen, eighteen thousand at Sachsenhausen. At Buchenwald in November 1941, the SS arranged a method of mass murder of Soviet prisoners that strikingly resembled Soviet methods in the Great Terror, though exhibiting greater duplicity and sophistication. Prisoners were led into a room in the middle of a stable, where the surroundings were rather loud. They found themselves in what seemed to be a clinical examination room, surrounded by men in white coats—SS-men, pretending to be doctors. They would have the prisoner stand against the wall at a certain place, supposedly to measure his height. Running through the wall was a vertical slit, which the prisoner's neck would cover. In an adjoining room was another SS-man with a pistol. When he saw the neck through the slit, he would fire. The corpse would then be thrown into a third room, the "examination room," be quickly cleaned, and the next prisoner invited inside. Batches of thirty-five to forty corpses would be taken by truck to a crematorium: a technical advance over Soviet practices.[42]

The Germans shot, on a conservative estimate, half a million Soviet prisoners of war. By way of starvation or mistreatment during transit, they killed about 2.6 million more. All in all, perhaps 3.1 million Soviet prisoners of war were killed. The brutality did not bring down the Soviet order; if anything, it strengthened Soviet morale. The screening of political officers, communists, and Jews was pointless. Killing such people, already in captivity, did not much weaken the Soviet state. In fact, the policies of starvation and screening stiffened the resistance of the Red Army. If soldiers knew that they would starve in agony as German captives, they were certainly more likely to fight. If communists and Jews and political officers knew that they would be shot, they too had little reason to give in. As knowledge of German policies spread, Soviet citizens began to think that Soviet power was perhaps the preferable alternative.[43]

As the war continued into November 1941, and more and more German soldiers died at the front and had to be replaced by conscripts from Germany, Hitler and Göring realized that some prisoners of war would be needed as labor inside the Reich. On November 7 Göring gave the order for positive selections (for labor). By the end of the war more than a million Soviet prisoners of war were working in Germany. Mistreatment and hunger were not easily overcome. As a sympathetic German observer noted: "Of the millions of prisoners only a few thousand are capable of work. Unbelievably many of them have died, many have typhus, and the rest are so weak and wretched that they are in no condition to work." Some four hundred thousand prisoners sent to Germany died.[44]

By the terms of the German plans, the invasion of the Soviet Union was an utter fiasco. Operation Barbarossa was supposed to bring a "lightning victory"; in late autumn 1941, no victory was in sight.

The invasion of the Soviet Union was supposed to resolve all economic problems, which it did not. In the end, occupied Belgium (for example) was of greater economic value to Nazi Germany. The Soviet population was supposed to be cleared; in the event, the most important economic input from the Soviet Union was labor. The conquered Soviet Union was also supposed to provide the space for a "Final Solution" to what the Nazis regarded as the Jewish problem. Jews were supposed to be worked to death in the Soviet Union, or sent across the Ural Mountains, or exiled to the Gulag. The Soviet Union's self-defense in summer 1941 had made yet another iteration of the Final Solution impossible.[45] . . .

The fate of some of the Soviet prisoners who were released from camps in the east suggested what was to come for the Jews. At Auschwitz in early September 1941, hundreds of Soviet prisoners were gassed with hydrogen cyanide, a pesticide (trade name Zyklon B) that had been used previously to fumigate the barracks of the Polish prisoners in the camp. At about the same time, other Soviet prisoners of war were used to test a gas van at Sachsenhausen. It pumped its own exhaust into its hold, thereby asphyxiating by carbon monoxide the people locked inside.

NOTES

1. See Streit, *Keine Kameraden*, 26–27. Oil was necessary: industry and agriculture. Here, too, Germany was dependent upon imports, and true autarky seemed to require the conquest of the Soviet Caucasus and its oil fields.

2. Consult Tooze, *Wages of Destruction*, 409, 424, 429, 452. For the "most autarkic state in the world," see Kennedy, *Aufstieg*, 341. On the oil reserves, see Eichholtz, *Krieg um Öl*, 8, 15, *passim*. Compare Hildebrand, *Weltreich*, 657–58. The German was convinced that Soviet resources

were needed to fight the war; see Kay, *Exploitation*, 27, 37, 40 and "immense riches" at 212.

3. On Germany's naval capacity, see Weinberg, *World at Arms*, 118; also *Wages of Destruction*, 397–99; and Evans, *Third Reich at War*, 143–46. Quotation: Mazower, *Hitler's Empire*, 133. Alan Milward long ago drew attention to the cause of the assumption of a rapid victory; see *German Economy*, 40–41.

4. On *Generalplan Ost*, see Madajczyk, "Generalplan," 12–13, also 64–66; Aly, *Architects*, 258; Kay, *Exploitation*, 100–101, 216; Wasser, *Himmlers Raumplannung* 51–52; Tooze, *Wages of Destruction*, 466–67; Rutherford, *Prelude*, 217; Mazower, *Hitler's Empire*, 206, 210; and Longerich, *Himmler*, 597–99.

5. On Himmler, see Longerich, *Himmler*, 599. On Hitler, see Kershaw, *Hitler*, 651. See also Tooze, *Wages of Destruction*, 469.

6. *Deutschösterreichische Tageszeitung*, March 3, 1933; Kershaw, *Fateful Choices*, 267. On the percentage cited, see Kay, *Exploitation*, 56,143.

7. Quotations: Kay, *Exploitation*, 211, 50, 40. See also Tooze, *Wages of Destruction*, 469; and Kershaw, *Hitler*, 650.

8. Quotation: Gerlach, *Kalkulierte Morde*, 342. The institutional apparati are clarified in Kay, *Exploitation*, 17–18, 148.

9. Kay, *Exploitation*, 138, 162–63.

10. On the "extinction of . . . a great part of the population," see *Verbrechen der Wehrmacht*, 65. The long quotation is in Kay, *Exploitation*, 133; see also Gerlach, *Kalkulierte Morde*, 52–56. Given the settlement patterns of Soviet Jews, these "superfluous people" included not only Russians, Belarusians, Ukrainians, and Balts but at least three quarters of the Soviet Jewish population as well.

11. Kay, *Exploitation*, 164. In June, Hitler confirmed Göring's overall responsibility for economic planning.

12. Burleigh, *Third Reich*, 484, 487.

13. Quotations: Römer, *Kommissarbefehl*, 204. Regarding Hitler's quotation, see Kershaw, *Hit-*

ler, 566. See also Pohl, *Herrschaft*, 64; and Bartov, *Hitler's Army*, 16.

14. On the use of civilians as human shields, see the order of May 13, 1941, text in *Verbrechen der Wehrmacht*, 46. See also Bartov, *Hitler's Army*, 71; Pohl, *Herrschaft*, 71, and discussion of women in uniform at 205; Römer, *Kommissarbefehl*, 228, also 551; and Gerlach, *Kalkulierte Morde*, 774.

15. *Verbrechen der Wehrmacht*, 344; Pohl, *Herrschaft*, 185; Gerlach, *Kalkulierte Morde*, 266.

16. Quotation: Arnold, "Eroberung," 46.

17. Compare Edele, "States," 171. The problem of feeding German soldiers without reducing food rations is examined in Tooze, *Wages of Destruction*.

18. Gerlach, *Kalkulierte Morde*, 798. As Tooze has pointed out, Germans were indeed willing to make economic sacrifices for the war effort; see *Wages of Destruction*.

19. Streit, *Keine Kameraden*, 143, 153. On Walther von Reichenau (September 28), see Arnold, "Eroberung," 35.

20. Streit, *Keine Kameraden*, 143, 153. Compare Kay, *Exploitation*, 2.

21. See Keegan, *Face of Battle*, 73; Gerlach, *Kalkulierte Morde*, 51; Forster, "German Army," 22; and *Verbrechen der Wehrmacht*, 288.

22. Arnold, "Eroberung," 27–33.

23. On Kiev, see Berkhoff, *Harvest*, 170–86, maximum death total (56,400) at 184; also Arnold, "Eroberung," 34. On Kharkiv, see Pohl, *Herrschaft*, 192; *Verbrechen der Wehrmacht*, at 328, gives a minimum of 11,918.

24. Kay, *Exploitation*, 181, 186.

25. Wagner was in 1944 one of the plotters against Hitler. See *Verbrechen der Wehrmacht*, at 193 and 311, for quotations. One million is the estimate usually given in the Western literature; see, for example, Kirschenbaum, *Siege*; and Salisbury, *900 Days*. The Soviet estimate is 632,000; see *Verbrechen der Wehrmacht*, 308. On food and fuel, see Simmons, *Leningrad*, 23.

26. On the numbers cited, see *Verbrechen der Wehrmacht*, 209. On the projected number of prisoners, see Gerlach, *Kalkulierte Morde*, 783.

27. Bartov, *Hitler's Army*, 87; Polian, "Violence," 123; Overmans, "Kriegsgefangenpolitik," 800–801. See also Merridale, *Ivan's War*, 28; and Braithwaite, *Moscow*, 165.

28. Berkhoff, *Harvest*, 94–96; Gerlach, *Kalkulierte Morde*, 845–57. For a general perspective on the treatment of prisoners of war, see the superb Keegan, *Face of Battle*, 49–51.

29. Polian, "Violence," 121. Datner estimates 200,000–250,000; see *Zbrodnie*, 379.

30. Overmans, "Kriegsgefangenpolitik," 805; Gerlach, *Krieg*, 24.

31. On "comrades," see Dugas, *Vycherknutye*, 30.

32. On the chain of authority, see Streim, *Behandlung*, 7. Quotation: Pohl, *Herrschaft*, 219; also Gerlach, *Kalkulierte Morde*, 801. See also Overmans, "Kriegsgefangenpolitik," 808. On cannibalism, see Shumejko, "Atanasyan," 174; and Hartmann, "Massenvernichtung," 124.

33. On ration cuts, see Megargee, *Annihilation*, 119. For "pure hell," see *Ich werde es nie vergessen*, 178. On Minsk, see *Verbrechen der Wehrmacht*, 227–29; Gerlach, *Kalkulierte Morde*, 768, 856; Gerlach, *Krieg*, 51; Polian, "Violence," 121; Overmans, "Kriegsgefangenpolitik," 807; and Beluga, *Prestupleniya*, 199. On Bobruisk, see Pohl, Herrschaft, 224. On Homel, see Pohl, *Herrschaft*, 224; and Dugas, *Sovetskie Voennoplennye*, 125. On Mahileu, see Pohl, *Herrschaft*, 224–25. On Molodechno, see Gerlach, *Krieg*, 34; and Megargee, *Annihilation*, 90; also Bartov, *Hitler's Army*, 79.

34. On Kirovohrad, see *Verbrechen der Wehrmacht*, 239–44. On Khorol, see Pohl, *Herrschaft*, 226. On Stalino, see Pohl, *Herrschaft*, 227; and Datner, *Zbrodnie*, 404.

35. Motyka, "Tragedia jencow," 2–6; Kopowka, *Stalag 366*, 47. On the 45,690 people who died in the General Government camps, see Dugas, *Sovetskie Voennoplennye*, 131. Compare Mlynarczyk, *Judenmord*, 245 (250,000–570,000).

36. On the lack of warm clothing, see Bartov, *Eastern Front*, 112. On the three Soviet soldiers, see Dugas, *Sovetskie Voennoplennye*, 125.

37. Compare *Verbrechen der Wehrmacht*, 188.

38. On the intention to kill Soviet elites, see Kay, *Exploitation*, 104. On Hitler in March 1941, Streim, *Behandlung*, 36. For the text of the guidelines, see *Verbrechen der Wehrmacht*, 53–55.

39. On the 2,252 shootings, see Römer, *Kommissarbefehl*, 581.

40. On July 2, 1941, see *Verbrechen der Wehrmacht*, 63; Kay, *Exploitation*, 105; and Kershaw, *Fateful Choices*, 453. On the instructions given to the *Einsatzgruppen* and their fulfillment, see Datner, *Zbrodnie*, 153; Streim, *Behandlung*, 69, 99; and Berkhoff, *Harvest*, 94. On October 1941, see Streit, "German Army," 7.

41. Pohl, *Herrschaft*, 204 (and 153 and 235 for the estimates of fifty and one hundred thousand). Overmans estimates one hundred thousand shootings in "Kriegsgefangenpolitik," 815. Arad estimates eighty thousand total Jewish POW deaths; see Soviet Union, 281. Quotation (doctor): Datner, *Zbrodnie*, 234. On medicine as a nazified profession, see Hilberg, *Perpetrators*, 66.

42. Streim, *Behandlung*, 102–6.

43. For an estimate at the low end, see Streim, *Behandlung*, 244: minimum 2.4 million. For estimates of 3–3.3 million, see Pohl, *Herrschaft*, 210; Overmans, "Kriegsgefangenpolitik," 811, 825; Dugas, *Sovetskie Voennoplennye*, 185; and Hartmann, "Massenvernichtung," 97. For an estimate at the high end, see Sokolov, "How to Calculate," 452: 3.9 million. On morale, see *Verbrechen der Wehrmacht*, 204.

44. On November 7, 1941, see Gerlach, *Kalkulierte Morde*, 817. Compare Gerlach and Werth, "State Violence," 164. See also Streim, *Behandlung*, 99–102, 234. On the four hundred thousand total deaths among those released, see Pohl, *Herrschaft*, 215. Quotation (Johannes Gutschmidt): Hartmann, "Massenvernichtung," 158; a similar estimation by Rosenberg is in Klee, "Gott mit uns," 142.

45. Belgium: Kay, *Exploitation*, 121.

Plunder, Individual and Governmental

GÖTZ ALY

From *Hitler's Beneficiaries*

Hitler's Satisfied Thieves

On September 3, 1939, Heinrich Böll—then a soldier in the *Wehrmacht*—wrote his family in Cologne that he couldn't imagine what he was going to do with his "fantastic wage of 25 marks." Sometime later, Böll reported that he was able to purchase a half pound of coffee, back then a luxury item, in Rotterdam for "all of fifty pfennigs." He sent the coffee home, expressing his regret that as a common soldier he was "allowed only one 500-gram package per week." "I'm not very optimistic about Mother's hopes for more coffee," he went on to write from the northern French coast. "But please send me whatever money you have. Perhaps I'll be able to step up my efforts on the coffee front. It can be German money. I'll just exchange it in the canteen."[1]

At that point in the war, German soldiers were allowed to receive up to 50 marks per month—their families transferred the money via army postal service, and it was paid out in the native currency of the countries where soldiers were stationed. Soon the allowance was raised to 100, and before Christmas 1939 it went up to 200 marks, "so that soldiers at least have the opportunity to buy the customary presents."[2] The increase drew a word of caution from the *Wehrmacht* intendant in charge of Belgium: "I cannot help but mention that, thanks to this measure, the country's shelves are in danger of being stripped completely bare."[3] Soldiers in the Netherlands were allowed to

receive the massive monthly sum of 1,000 marks (around $12,000 today) for shopping purposes. The German bank commissioner complained that "the largest sums" of German money were flowing into Holland from relatives of *Wehrmacht* soldiers and that the influx would necessarily lead to "damaging effects in currency matters." German economists overseeing Belgium's finances were astonished to find that, in the first year of occupation, relatives of *Wehrmacht* soldiers had transferred some 34 million marks—and that figure did not include the members of the Fifteenth and Sixteenth Armies—via the army postal service. They warned of "untenable consequences" if they were to have to pay out those transfers from their budget for occupying Belgium. The Finance Ministry, however, turned a deaf ear to their complaints.[4]

And despite the official regulations, soldiers were allowed to take as much money with them as they wanted when entering or leaving Germany during their frequent leaves. In the fall of 1940, the Reichsbank board of directors expressed concern about the situation at the currency exchange office in the Herzogenrath train station near Germany's western border. The office was "under extraordinary pressure from *Wehrmacht* soldiers in transit," noted one board member, yet employees in Herzogenrath had been "instructed to exchange any and all sums."[5] Starting in January 1941, German customs officials gave up the sporadic "checks for currency" they had been performing on soldiers. Such checks, it was concluded, only caused delays at the border and "irritated" the soldiers.[6]

In 1941, the amount of money soldiers entering Belgium could legally exchange was raised to 300 Reichsmarks—considerably more than the average monthly wage of a German worker. Occupation authorities pleaded for the exchange limit to be capped at 50 marks per person, arguing that they needed "to protect the [Belgian] currency" and "curb the inflationary increase in hard currency."[7] The quartermaster general objected, "pointing out that troops from the Eastern Front" on leave in Belgium "were especially in need of relief."[8] The *Wehrmacht* High Command refused the request "on general grounds of troop support."[9] The army field postmaster general reported regularly about the "huge numbers of packages in his territory being sent back from the field to Germany."[10]

German soldiers literally emptied the shelves of Europe. They sent millions of packages back home from the front. The recipients were mainly women. When one asks the now elderly witnesses about this period in history, their eyes still gleam at the memory of the shoes from North Africa, the velvet, silk, liqueurs, and coffee from France, the tobacco from Greece, the honey and bacon from Russia, and the tons of herring from Norway—not to mention the various gifts that poured in from Germany's allies Romania, Hungary, and Italy.[11]

An open letter, published in 2003, from this author to older readers of the weekly newspaper *Die Zeit* asked them to share their recollections. Many respondents reported that what they received depended on whether they were lucky enough to have generous relatives. "I remember a number of nice things," one woman wrote, "that friends and relatives would proudly unpack from parcels received from 'abroad.' ... People had more respect for the sender and compared him favorably with those who hadn't sent anything back."

People who received such luxuries "boasted and bragged to others who had gotten only letters."[12] Interestingly, while female respondents offered accurate descriptions of the period, the men, without exception, denied ever having sent a single package home.

On October 1, 1940, the customs border between Germany and the Protectorate of Bohemia and Moravia was abolished, prompting the Reich protector, the Nazi leader in those territories, to complain about the uninhibited "purchasing frenzy" among German soldiers. "The luggage nets of the express trains," wrote another German official, "are packed to the roof with heavy suitcases, bulky packages, and stuffed bags." Even officers and high-ranking bureaucrats, he continued, were cramming their luggage with "the most extraordinary consumer goods—furs, watches, medicines, shoes—in nearly unimaginable quantities."[13]

Wolf Goette, a young actor at the German theater in Prague who would later have a successful career in East Germany, wrote back home: "Please write and tell me if there's anything I can bring back. I'll do my very best." He added: "Yesterday we bought a wonderful desk. We're always being accosted by a colleague named Wiesner. He's become a true antiques dealer. Yesterday he purchased a marvelous Empire-era etching. Today it was a Gothic Madonna from Spain. It's not the worst idea in the world to invest your money in such tangible assets." In another letter to his family, he wrote: "I've noted your various requests. Yesterday I purchased four kilos of cocoa for you (7 per kilo)." For a relative or acquaintance nicknamed Rolli, Goette procured "a supply of perfume and eau de cologne as well as some light-colored leather gloves for Donna." For a certain Jürgen Müller, who had sent him money, Goette obtained "a portable electric cooking stove together with a pot and a pan." He continued to take orders for goods from his family: "How many sheets of Japanese paper should I get hold of? A sheet costs fifty reichspfennig. Has the package with the seeds arrived yet? Today I sent off the fifth package of books you requested. I'll send the rest later with the final transport."[14]

In an open letter written for but then censored by the daily newspaper in Worms, Fritz Boas, a junior officer stationed in France, reported the following: "The first thing one does is to 'storm' the shops. . . . Everyone has something to buy for his nearest and dearest back home. Today a letter from 'Mama' arrived requesting some material, if possible thin-striped brown, to make a formal dress, some chamois, and—if manageable—a couple of bars of fine soap and some whole-bean coffee. That's all for now, darling, she says. I'll write soon to tell you what else I'd like. Wait, I almost forgot. Do you still have almonds and white elastic bands?"[15]

"I'm going to pack the butter and the soap (four big bars)," wrote Heinrich Böll, "so that I can send them with the noon mail." He then issued his regular, although officially forbidden, request to his family for more money ("best concealed in a cake") for purchases. A few days later, Böll was again keeping accounts: "I sent another pound of butter yesterday. That makes four in all that are currently en route, as well as a package with a giant 400-gram bar of soap for Mother in honor of her name day. I'm 40 marks in debt, but I'm waiting for your package full of surprises." He didn't have to wait long. A short time later, he reported back home: "I've received the book 'Barbara Naderer' with what was inserted in it. That makes 60 marks (10 from you and 50 from my parents). . . . If you can ensure that things continue this way, I won't have to pass on all the splendid things on the 'black market.' . . . I'd be genuinely happy if I could send you something."[16]

On one occasion it was "a nice engraving from Paris." On others it was cosmetics, three pounds of onions for his mother, a pair of ladies' shoes, and nail scissors. At one point, Böll announced he was undertaking "an exhausting shopping spree" the following day, hoping "to stumble across something" for himself and his wife, Annemarie.[17] A few weeks later, he reported to his mother: "After mess, I returned to my quarters and sweated over the task of packing. No fewer than 11 packages in all: 2 for a comrade, one for the staff sergeant, and 8 for me: 2 for you, one with butter and one with writing paper, 2 for [his brother] Alois's family, and 4 for my family. I'll put the eggs in a package this week because I didn't have enough to send two. You'll be able to get some at home." No sooner had these orders been filled than the young soldier was back in shopper's heaven: "In Paris, I should be able to find some nice things, definitely some shoes for you and some material."[18]

The French nicknamed the tens of thousands of German soldiers like Boas and Böll "potato beetles" (doryphores). Of them, historian Henri Michel has written: "Loaded down with heavy packages, German soldiers departed from the Gare de l'Est for home leave. Their luggage was crammed with lingerie, specialties from Paris, and luxury goods of every description. They had been acquired in countless petty transactions, but they did significant damage to the French national economy, playing a significant role in the development of the black market and inflation. They were the reason it was increasingly difficult for everyday French people to procure the basic necessities."[19]

Liselotte S., whose father worked as a medical orderly in France, recalled in 2003:

I know that my mother sent my father money every month. He used it to buy things we lacked at home: coffee, cocoa, cheese, chocolate in various forms, shoes for my mother, for me, and our apprentices, fur-lined and plain leather gloves, once even a pair of motorcycle gloves. . . . Every day packages from France arrived in the mail. My mother also sent money to my father's buddies whose wives didn't have access to the maximum amounts allowed. One time two fur coats arrived—I was only twelve and had to grow into mine. My father used to get around the limits on the amounts he could send by taking packages to other *Wehrmacht* units stationed nearby. As a driver for the chief medical officer, he had plenty of opportunities, and once the mail delivered ten packages tied together. Whatever we couldn't use in our two-person household, we would swap for other good and services. Workmen who repaired the house and kept up the garden profited from them.[20]

The story was much the same in all the other countries Germany occupied, although the desired goods were often more difficult to come by than in France. A German customs investigation, for instance, cited the following passages from a letter written home to his wife by a soldier stationed in Poland: "The packages for you, my father, and Frieda went out the day before yesterday. Be on the lookout for them when they arrive. . . . The shoes are on their way. . . . I got some material for a couple of pairs of pants for Otto." Anticipating his home leave, he announced: "Ilse won't have to worry about a lack of Easter surprises. I'm well supplied, and I'll be bringing everything home for Easter. Nice things that you probably can't get anymore in Germany. I try to think of everything and get everything I can for you, and you show your gratitude by not writing. Do you think that's fair? You don't need to save the coffee I sent—I'll bring more at Easter.

You can give Ida some of the cocoa you've got at home. I've got enough of that as well for you."[21]

In the Baltic States, Reich Commissioner Hinrich Lohse determined that substantial amounts of money were being imported from Germany and exchanged. He reported that soldiers were buying up whatever was available and "then shipping the purchased wares out of the territory."[22] These purchases for export were made possible by extremely high exchange rates, which quadrupled the value of the mark against the ruble. The rate had been set to the advantage of German soldiers with the aim of facilitating plunder. Unlike in the conquered nations of Western Europe, cash could be imported into, then exchanged and spent in, the occupied parts of the Soviet Union with a minimum of "bureaucratic nonsense." Soldiers were allowed to take 1,100 marks worth of RKK [Reich Credit Bank] certificates, rubles, and German currency with them, as well as 600 zlotys (around 300 Reichsmarks) for travel expenses through the General Government of Poland. The only objection raised at the Economics Ministry meeting during which those limits were set came from senior government counsel Hoffmann of the Eastern Economics Staff, who pointed out that they would cause "what amounts to a total clearance sale in the East."[23] The introduction of German currency was only restricted much later—after an urgent request by occupation authorities.[24]

In a letter published in 1954, Otto Bräutigam, a former department head at the Nazi ministry in charge of occupied territories in the East, recalled: "Because of the low prices, the Baltic States were a true El Dorado for German soldiers and the civilians who followed them. There was a gigantic shopping spree." Bräutigam knew whereof he spoke. On August 6, 1941, the first day after his arrival in Riga, he wrote of "buying some things in the '*Wehrmacht* department store.'" "There wasn't a lot available," he complained, but then added: "My driver has gotten hold of 25 kilos of butter, which we split in the spirit of fairness."[25]

A soldier's daughter who was born in 1934 reported: "Among the bright spots were the packages my father sent us from the East: tin cans with excellent butter and delicious black tea from his company's stopover in Riga. I can particularly remember the clunky and at first far too large blue shoes and boots, which served me well and kept my feet dry until after the war. I was proud of the satchel of Russian leather I used as a school knapsack. My father 'organized,' as people used to say back then, various leather articles for me. A thick green woolen blanket always accompanied us whenever we children were evacuated to the countryside, as well as a dark-blue knitted sweater with a blue-and-white collar."[26]

In October 1943, when Heinrich Böll was transferred from France to the Crimea, he made one last shipment of butter home, "as a tribute from 'douce France.'" In the heavy fighting of early December, he suffered a minor head wound that probably saved his life. He landed in a military hospital in Odessa, where he wrote: "You can buy anything you want at the bazaar here." He was then sent to convalesce in Stanislawow, Poland, in what is now Ukraine, where he immediately sent one package of chocolate and one bar of soap back home. Shortly before returning to Germany on leave, he wrote: "I'm constantly asking myself if there's anything nice here I can bring you. I've given up on my dream of getting you a pair of these lovely, warm Polish booties. The price is simply too high."[27]

Even in the depths of winter in 1943, while the *Wehrmacht* was suffering catastrophic defeats on the battlefield, the soldiers of the Eighteenth Army near Leningrad managed, according to statistics from the military post office, to send more than

3 million packages home. They were filled with items that had been plundered, bought at bargain prices, or left over from food rations. To the disappointment of the soldiers, probably because of state restrictions the packages traveling in the other direction were markedly fewer. By then the government was seeking to conceal the extent to which Germans were enriching themselves at the cost of others. According to accounts by the military postmaster general, Karl Ziegler, his department was required "to burn all records of total statistics compiled for the military postal service."[28]

In Norway, occupying German soldiers also did their level best to empty the country's shelves, even though the Norwegians depended on imported food for their survival. While the number of packages shipped from Norway was restricted, occupation authority staff members were allowed to send 2.5 kilos of goods home per month.[29] The packages mainly contained fish, and there was a lively trade in fox fur.[30] For Christmas 1942, the *Wehrmacht* High Command relaxed the restrictions and even set up a "herring transfer station" to transport "barrels of herring privately purchased by vacationers" via sealed express freight trains to the northern German city of Gustrow. From there, the herring was distributed throughout the Reich.[31]

Only in 1944, when military defeat seemed probable and dissatisfaction among the Norwegian population had reached a critical level, did Reich Commissioner Josef Terboven try to limit the plundering of Norwegian herring to between 7 and 8 kilos annually per soldier. In April 1944, the chief intendant reported that he was doing his best to get the limit raised to between 10 and 12 kilos, although he added that his efforts had "regrettably not yet yielded a final result."[32]

Considering that normal weekly meat and fish rations in Germany at this point were 350 grams (less than a pound), the herring imports represented a nutritional increase of around 50 percent for German housewives. Moreover, that figure includes only officially permitted imports—it doesn't take into account vacationers' prohibited but tolerated practice of bringing fish back with them on passenger trains. In summer 1944, officers finally began disciplining a handful of German soldiers for "illegal herring exports."[33] A few months earlier, in December 1943, the *Wehrmacht* chief intendant in Norway had noted dryly, "Request rejected," after learning of the Reich commissioner's plans to stop the illegal smuggling.[34] Meanwhile authorities in charge of the German occupation troops had noted as early as summer 1942 that Norwegians were "considerably undernourished."[35]

Even in areas where the military situation was hopeless, officers responsible for troop welfare continued to pander to what had quickly become the habitual greed of German soldiers. In April 1943, encircled army divisions in the Kuban region along the Black Sea ordered one million small-package stamps with the inscription "one small package/front-homeland."[36] In the winter of 1944–45, the commander of 6,000 soldiers trapped by British troops on the island of Rhodes distributed some 25,000 such stamps.[37] In October 1944, the *Wehrmacht* High Command approved a measure allowing Germans entering occupied Italy to exchange 100 Reichsmarks in RKK certificates for lire and to spend the money there. The Finance Ministry protested that the practice would further destabilize the currency and endanger the supply of basic necessities in Italy, and the decision was reversed six weeks later.[38]

Private purchases in the month of August 1943 in occupied France totaled 125 million Reichsmarks. Even allowing for the devaluation of the franc, the equivalent would be hundreds of millions of dollars today.[39] Private purchases drove up inflation, disrupted occupation authorities' attempts to control the market, and undermined all forms of economic stability. Stability, however, was precisely what was required to ensure the long-term exploitation of the resources of an occupied country. The functionaries responsible for running occupied economies repeatedly tried to restrict the number of packages sent through the military postal service and to subject German soldiers to customs and currency checks. But customs officials described such checks as "truly precarious" situations that often led to "unfortunate confrontations" and "rebellion and insults."[40] The few occasions when customs officials actually did confiscate goods or currency inevitably "called forth a general mood of bitterness among the troops."[41]

As early as October 1940, to maintain troop morale, Göring had completely abolished the already liberal limits on what soldiers could purchase, dismissing "worries raised from various quarters that stores in the occupied territories would soon be stripped bare" as "negligible."[42] In the same breath he condemned "the measures instituted to enforce restrictions on purchases and shipments" as "psychologically intolerable." Instead he ordered that German soldiers in hostile countries be allowed to buy everything they could afford, with no greater restrictions than applied to native citizens. Existing "prohibitions on the purchases of furs, jewelry, carpets, silks, and luxury items" were to be "immediately" lifted. Also to be abolished were restrictions on the numbers of packages soldiers were allowed to send back home through the military postal service. (Limits on packages in the other direction were retained.)

Göring used the occasion to formulate what became known as the "Schlep Decree" (*Schlepperlass*): "The basic restrictions on the transport of purchased items by soldiers on leave, etc., are to be lifted. Soldiers should be allowed to take with them whatever they can carry so long as it is intended for their own personal use or that of their dependents."[43] Göring also ordered the free shipment through the military postal service of packages weighing up to 1,000 grams (with 200-gram leeway) "in unlimited numbers." On July 14, 1942, customs officials quietly lifted the regulations governing packages whose weight exceeded that limit.[44]

Taking the same view as most of his soldiers, Hitler praised the *Wehrmacht* as "the most natural middleman available to a soldier who wants to send something to his wife or children." In the summer of 1942, he admonished Admiral Erich Raeder: "When soldiers bring something home from the Eastern Front," it is "a bonus that benefits the homeland."[45] On occasions in which individual officers and customs officials tried to put a stop to uninhibited plundering, the Führer vented his rage on behalf of the troops: "To put it bluntly: What can I take with me from the East? Treasures of art? They don't exist. All that's left is food to stuff your mouth. Nothing better can happen to it than that it be given to a soldier's family here at home."[46] Around the same time, Hitler remarked that a soldier on home leave "should be considered the ideal and simplest means of transport and should be given as much food as he can physically carry."[47]

The chief of the *Wehrmacht* High Command, Field Marshal Wilhelm Keitel, quickly translated these statements into a personal decree of the Führer's. The edict read: "Food, intoxicants, and tobacco brought back from occupied territories to the Reich by members of the *Wehrmacht* on home leave or official business, insofar as they are carried by hand, are to be made immediately exempt from all forms of control and confiscation."[48] In early August 1942, at a high-level meeting devoted to the topic of food supplies, Göring returned to the issue. According to the minutes of the meeting, Göring interjected: "Is the finance minister in attendance?" The deputy minister replied: "Yes, sir! Reinhardt here!" Göring then continued: "Mr. Reinhardt, desist with your customs checks. I'm no longer interested in them. . . . I'd rather have unlimited amounts of goods smuggled in than have custom duties paid on nothing at all."

At the same meeting, Göring issued even more drastic statements. Angered by occupation authorities who were trying to stabilize France's currency to facilitate its long-term exploitation, Göring thundered: "It has been said that we need to restrict soldiers' access to their pay or it will cause inflation in France. But inflation is what I want to see more than anything else. . . . The franc should be worth nothing more than a sheet of a certain type of paper used for a specific purpose. That will hit France exactly the way we want to hit France."[49]

In her autobiography, a librarian who worked in Hamburg during the Third Reich described the consequences of this attitude: "We didn't suffer any privations. . . . Our food, clothing, and shoe vouchers were honored. Our men were still bringing back meat, wine, textiles, and tobacco from the occupied territories." When the same eyewitness traveled to Cologne in the summer of 1943, after her parents' home was hit by an Allied bomb, she found the train station crammed with soldiers on leave from the Eastern Front whose homes had also been destroyed: "There they stood, having traveled day and night, laden down with knapsacks and packages." Even as late as Christmas 1944, the author's brother, who had been given last-minute leave, was able to produce "a whole goose, half a suckling pig, and a large slab of bacon from his luggage." He also brought home, apparently from his *Wehrmacht* rations, "coffee, tea, schnapps, and cigarettes."[50]

The effects of Hitler's order, as transmitted by Keitel, to suspend all customs checks are described in an urgent communication from customs officials in the city of Kiel, near the German-Danish border: "There is no doubt that the majority of goods imported by members of the *Wehrmacht* into German territory under the guise of "comrades' 'luggage' are to be sold at dramatically inflated prices. It is equally beyond doubt that members of the *Wehrmacht*, especially of the navy and the *Luftwaffe*, are engaged to a considerable extent in such black market activities—for the purpose of personal profit."[51] Deputy Finance Minister Reinhardt intervened to end the quarrels and complaints on Germany's northern and eastern borders by invoking Hitler's decree: "It is the Führer's will that as many foodstuffs as possible be brought back home from the occupied eastern territories and that customs authorities take a hands-off approach."[52]

By sweeping aside restrictions maintained by *Wehrmacht* intendants, Hitler and Göring encouraged Germans in their spirited, organized, and extremely popular drive to loot the shelves of occupied Europe. At the beginning of the war, the *Wehrmacht* had decreed that products scarce in Germany could be imported duty-free into the Reich in "amounts of up to 5 kilos in weight"—a relatively modest allotment.[53] The limit was initially maintained despite constant reports from various authorities that it was being exceeded. But by summer 1940, political pressure had forced the *Wehrmacht* High Command to double the amount.[54]

Göring's Schlep Decree, which legalized the near-unlimited transport of goods from occupied Europe to Germany, was politically motivated. Measured against figures from September 1940,

the number of packages sent via military post from France to Germany immediately quintupled and settled at an average of 3.1 million a month.[55] On November 1, 1940, soldiers' pay was increased by 50 percent in Poland, Norway, and Holland, by 20 percent in France and Denmark, and by 25 percent in Belgium. The pay raises were intended to "enable members of the *Wehrmacht* to satisfy their consumer needs to a greater extent."[56] On behalf of the *Wehrmacht* leadership, Quartermaster General Eduard Wagner, Field Marshal Walther von Brauchitsch, and Lieutenant General Hermann Reinecke endorsed the decree. . . .

Heavily Burdened in France

The armistice treaty required France to pay a daily tribute of 20 million Reichsmarks—an unprecedented sum—to its occupier. Nonetheless, the Reich Finance Ministry complained that the sum was too modest and lobbied to have it increased. High-ranking ministry officials justified their demands with innocuous-sounding arguments: care, they said, should be taken to avoid "unnecessarily burdening" a later peace treaty "with obligations pertaining to financial matters and money-transfer policies."[57] By January and February 1943, the daily demands of the *Wehrmacht*, not including the purchasing sprees ordered by Göring and Speer, had reached 29 million Reichsmarks. As the administrative council of the Reich Credit Bank ascertained, the total expenditures created "a need for French currency of approximately 35 million Reichsmarks a day, or around one billion marks per month."[58]

The rampant greed of the occupiers meant a drastic increase in the amount of money in circulation in France. State expenditures for civilian needs in all of France totaled some 130 billion francs per year between 1941 and 1943. Initially, occupation costs amounted to roughly the same, essentially doubling the state's budget. But in the final two years of the occupation, those costs shot up rapidly. The huge jump in 1943 was a direct result of German military defeats in Eastern Europe and increases in arms production. A similar phenomenon can be observed in all the countries occupied by Germany. At a meeting of Nazi leaders in Berchtesgaden on April 28, 1943, Göring complained that "the financial contributions from France are insufficient." There was a need, he said, for "a serviceable taxation apparatus to take in direct taxes." Changing the system, Göring suggested, should be a major priority.[59]

In addition to daily payments toward occupation costs, France was soon forced to provide hefty clearing advances to finance the export of goods to Germany. Between 1941 and 1943 advances were increased from 20 to 45 billion francs, and budgetary estimates for 1944 reached nearly 90 billion. France was also required to pay for the quartering of German occupiers as well as Italian troops in the southeast of the country. The *Wehrmacht* raised money by imposing collective fines on individual cities. Nantes, for example, was required to pay an extra 10 million francs in the first nine months of the occupation. In Cherbourg and Bordeaux, the figures were 6 million and 2 million francs, respectively.[60] These sums do not include the value of property requisitioned by the *Wehrmacht* during its surprisingly swift march through the country.

In response to German pressure, French tax revenues increased significantly between 1941 and 1943—from 68.2 to 101 billion francs. But the budget deficit grew just as fast, increasing from 160 to 220 billion francs. The shortfall for 1944 was projected to be 317 billion. As a result of German greed, state expenditures were more than triple normal state revenues.[61]

How much did France end up handing over to Germany in the course of the occupation? Esti-

mates vary but a fairly accurate picture can be gleaned from the figures provided by several different agencies. According to an official Reichsbank report in the spring of 1944, total occupation costs paid to the Reich by France amounted to 680 billion francs. In addition, 120 billion francs in goods and services were exported to Germany—about half of which had been financed on credit.[62] Since the occupation continued for another four months, another 10 percent can be added to this total. After the liberation of France, new finance minister Aimé Lepercq would claim that Germany had bled the country for the equivalent of 900 billion francs.[63] The French national debt had risen during the occupation by more than a trillion francs.[64] The Bank for International Settlements calculated the occupation costs demanded from France in 1944 to have been 35.25 billion Reichsmarks or 705 billion francs, not including clearing debts. These sums do not include contributions paid by Alsace-Lorraine, which was more or less treated as a part of Germany or by southeastern France, where the money went to Italy.

Taken together, these estimates support the conclusion that direct German revenues from France exceeded 800 billion francs or 40 billion Reichsmarks. In the unsentimental estimation of Reichsbank director Hartlieb, the plundering provided "effective relief for the Reich budget and ultimately spared Germany from having to take out credit from the national bank, while also greatly burdening France's budget and currency."[65] In 1959, Pierre Arnoult, a historian of the occupation, summarized the German technique of maintaining the appearance of fairness by paying for needed goods and services in the local currency. "They didn't take anything away from us by force," he wrote. "They purchased everything correctly—but with money they took from us."[66]

The French finance minister was required to transfer payments for ongoing occupation costs to the account of the Reich Credit Bank in Paris. Just as individual Germans essentially stole French goods by purchasing them with worthless RKK certificates, the Reich continually raided this occupation fund for expenses that had nothing to do with France. For example, of the 6.5 billion Reichsmarks (21.3 million per day) of contributions France paid between January and October 1942, the Reich used 720 million marks to procure "horses, food, and amenities for the eastern troops"—that is, German armies fighting in the Soviet Union. A further 840 million marks were officially allocated for "black market purchases, stocks and bonds, and works of art."[67]

The fiduciary basis was laid in the first few weeks after Germany's invasion. A bank account designated "Occupation Costs France B" was set up to receive funds for the ongoing, considerably inflated expenditures of the *Wehrmacht* and its soldiers. A parallel account, "Occupation Costs France A" was established for money that was then "loaned" to finance German attempts at self-enrichment. In the first six months of the occupation, a number of large sums of money were, to use the official lingo, "diverted." They included 536 million Reichsmarks for the families of "French workers deployed in Germany"; 250 million for the Economics Ministry "for raw materials and the acquisition of partial stock holdings"; 9 million for the Food Ministry "for the purchase of livestock"; and 5 million for the Transport Ministry for the acquisition of a large portfolio, deposited in France, of stocks in the International Sleeper Carriage Company of Brussels.[68] The policy division of the Finance Ministry deposited revenues earned in France into Account A for the explicit "use of the Finance Ministry."[69]

The Reich used various means to conceal its campaign of plunder and theft. For example, the exchange rate between the franc and the mark, which had been set to benefit German buyers, was selectively manipulated: the official rate was one Reichsmark to 20 francs, which represented a 25 percent devaluation of the prewar French currency, but for outstanding German accounts receivable, the prewar exchange rate was used. To take another example, the Finance Ministry pocketed around 5 million Reichsmarks in savings left behind by French people expelled from Alsace and Lorraine. And if all else failed, funds could simply be transferred from Account B when Account A ran out of money: on March 3 and October 9, 1941, transfers of 600 and 900 million francs, respectively, were made at the behest of the Finance Ministry.[70]

"Private" companies and purchases were also used to conceal monies that were in fact going to the Reich. In the short interval between May 16 and October 14, 1942, a Nazi-owned company called Roges, ostensibly founded to trade in raw materials, received transfers of 700 million francs for acquisitions in France. The funds came not via Account A but directly from Account B, which was supposed to be devoted exclusively to costs arising from the occupation.[71] Meanwhile, private citizens and officials alike redeemed a total of 2.5 billion Reichsmarks in RKK certificates (1.3 billion of them in 1943), which were never recorded from Account A.[72] RKK certificates were not handed out for free. They first had to be paid for in Reichsmarks, creating revenues for the German treasury.

In September 1943, Nazi armaments minister Albert Speer began to buy French machinery for German factories through a newly founded company called Primetex, for which 300 million francs in start-up money had been secretly siphoned off from the occupation costs budget.[73] Primetex operated alongside Roges.[74] Its CEO was ministerial director Wilhelm Bender of the Finance Ministry. Its stated mission was "the acquisition and commercial exploitation of confiscated goods in all occupied areas as well as the purchase, storage, and resale of raw materials essential to the war effort."[75]

The balance sheets for the Occupation Costs France A account are today held at the French National Archive in Paris. A glance at the accounts for the period 1940 to 1943 reveals a common thread. In all recorded transactions, government offices, companies, and private individuals from Germany paid Reichsmark equivalents for major purchases they had made in francs. The Finance Ministry was at pains to conceal that it simply kept these sums of Reichsmarks, while paying for French goods with francs siphoned from the occupation costs budget. . . . Likewise, German investors, firms, and banks that bought French stocks paid the going rate in Reichsmarks, which ended up in the German treasury, while French vendors were paid in francs from the budget set aside for occupation costs.[76] The Reich also forced the French government to pay out francs for purchases made by private German companies in France, while Berlin retained the Reichsmark equivalents the companies had paid into a state institution called the German Settlement Bank. . . .

Like private companies, German government agencies wasted no time tapping into the funds extorted from the French state. On December 5, 1940, the Army High Command drew 20 million Reichsmarks from Occupation Costs Account A to purchase general necessities. Shortly before Christmas that year, senior officials in the Propaganda Ministry went on a shopping spree for the equivalent of 750,000 marks, and a Berlin-based association of German goldsmiths helped itself to 500,000 marks.[77] On December 17, 1940, the mayors of the cities of Düsseldorf, Essen, and

Wuppertal began to make purchases in France. They were followed by the mayor of Frankfurt and the president of the Rhine region on January 20 and 21, respectively. On February 21, 1941, the mayor of Berlin sent an acquisition team, outfitted with 701,000 marks, to France.[78] The gourmet food wholesaler Riensch & Held and another food company, Emil Koster AG, bought up delicacies to take the sting out of the privations of wartime. On October 17, 1940, Karl Haberstock, Hitler's personal art buyer, received 1.5 million francs from Account A. Shortly before that, the Economics Ministry had transferred a sum equivalent to 75,000 marks to the Reich treasury via the bogus General Retailing Corporation.[79] . . .

The economic consequences for France were severe. As the delegate to the Armistice Commission who was responsible for French finances remarked: "To the extent that products were imported to Germany from France and the purchasing price flowed back into the German Settlement Bank and thereby into the Reichsbank, the French Finance Ministry was forced to take out the equivalent amount in francs in state loans to pay off French creditors. The positive effects this had on the value of the Reichsmark were mirrored in the negative effects it had on the value of the French franc."[80]

The German Settlement Bank had the same address and telephone number as the Reichsbank, and the two institutions used identical forms, strongly suggesting that the former was a division of the latter. And in fact, the Handbook for Civil Servants, published by the Reichsbank in 1941, explicitly stated as much.

NOTES

1. Böll, *Briefe*, 14–15, 90, 102, 111. The quotations that follow are taken from the more than three hundred single-spaced pages of Böll's letters.

Böll's wife, Annemarie, edited out numerous passages, many of which seem to have been about gifts that her husband sent or brought back home from the front.

2. Feldpostamt 405, BA-MA RH24/5/181; progress report no. 1 of intendant, MBB/NF (Fritsch), July 1–December 31, 1940, BA-MA RW36/118, 88.

3. German Commissioner of the Central Bank of the Netherlands (Wohlthat), Material für den Januarbericht an Hitler [Material for the January Report to Hitler], February 10, 1941, BA R2/30701.

4. RFM (Breyhan) to MBB/NF (Wetter), August 9, 1941, BA R2/274, 142–43.

5. Reichsbank board of directors to RFM, November 21, 1940, BA R2/56061, 469.

6. Reichsbank office, Rostock, to Reichsbank board of directors, May 16, 1941, BA R2/56058, 48.

7. MBB/NF to OKH, December 1, 1941, BA R29/3, 36–62.

8. RKK administrative council, July 21, 1942, BA R29/4, 59–60.

9. Managing intendant, MBB/NF, progress report no. 6, July 1–December 31, 1942, BA-MA RW36/127, 16; final report of MVB/NF, Währung und Finanzen [Currency and Finances], winter 1944–45, 13–14, 18, BA-MA RW36/225.

10. July 6, 1942, BA-MA RW36/95.

11. The information was gathered as part of a survey carried out by the author among elderly women in his circle of relatives and acquaintances.

12. Adelheid B. to G. Aly, May 20, 2003.

13. Dennler, Passion, 31 (October 1940); Chmela Report, NID-14615.

14. Wolf Goette (1909–1995) to his family and to A., July 6, December 20, 1940; June 13, October 5, October 31, November 17, 1941; April 28, 1942, Stiftung Archiv der Akademie der Künste, Berlin, Wolf-Goette-Archiv, Prague, 1939–42, Goettes Briefe/I, 157; Goettes Briefe/II, 192, 210, 316; Goettes Briefe/III, 23, j51, 65; 2./Familienbriefe Prag, vol. 4, 213ff.

15. Umbreit, "Kontinentalherrschaft," 236; Latzel, Soldaten, 135–38.

16. Böll, Briefe, 845, 874, 902–3.

17. Ibid., 619, 663, 694, 765, 833.

18. Ibid., 738, 798.

19. Michel, Paris, 298–99.

20. Liselotte S. to G. Aly, May 25, 2003.

21. Confiscated letters of the soldier Schwabe (December 2, 1939–June 16, 1940) BA R2/56100, 54–61. On mass theft by German soldiers in Poland, see Böhler, Auftakt.

22. RKK administrative council, December 16, 1941, BA R 29/3, 18–23.

23. RWM, Conference on Currency Regulations for the Occupied Soviet Territories, September 8, 1941, BA R2/56060, 18–30. The regulation was issued on September 16, 1941, ibid., 102.

24. Reichsbank board of directors to RFM, August 17, 1942, ibid., 118, 143ff.

25. Bräutigam, Uberblick, 53–54; Oertel, "Reichsbank," 159; Heilmann, "Kriegstagebuch," 140.

26. Marlene F. to G. Aly, November 14, 2003; on the comparable situation in Belarus, see Gerlach, Morde, 260–65.

27. Böll, Briefe, 924, 975, 986ff., 999–1000.

28. Schmitt and Gericke, "Feldpost," 62; Ziegler, "Erinnerungen," 48. On the positive supply situation of German troops in the second and third winters of the war, see Rass, "Menschenmaterial," 246.

29. Customs Regulations for Members of the Wehrmacht BA R 2/58094.

30. Wehrmacht commander, Norway, Shipping and Personal Carrying of Wares, July 14, 1941, BA R2/58094, 155–56.

31. The reason for the measure was the intervention of Swedish customs, since the leave transports passed through Swedish territory, Wehrmacht Chiefs of Staff, January 9, 1943, BA R2/58094, 260.

32. Progress report of chief intendant, Norway (January 1–March 31, 1944), BA-MA RW7/1711b, 87.

33. Ibid. (April 1–June 30, 1944), 243.

34. Ibid. (October 1–December 31, 1943), 6.

35. RKK administrative council, July 1, 1942, BA R29/3, 223–24; SS Main Office (Klumm) to

Reichsführer Brandt, November 9, 1944, in Petrik, *Okkupationspolitik*, 215–16.

36. Schmitt and Gericke, "Feldpost," 3–4.

37. Oberleitner, *Feldpost*, 190–91.

38. RFM (Schwerin von Krosigk) to chief of the OKW, October 24, 1944, BA R2/14554, 2; R 2/323. At the start of Germany's occupation of northern Italy, Field Marshal Rommel had issued restrictions on "the bringing of goods back to Germany," September. 21, 1943, BA R2/30601.

39. Lt. Int., MBiR to OKH, July 27, 1943, BA R 2/14553, 46–53.

40. RFM to OFP, Würzburg, June 12, 1940, BA R 2/56059, 33.

41. Customs authority, RFM (Siegert), Kontrolle der Wehrmachtangehörigen (durch die Hand des Herrn Staatssekretärs dem Herrn Minister) [Monitoring of Wehrmacht Members (hand-delivered by the state secretary to the minister)], June 13, 1942, BA R2/56061, 28.

42. Feldpostamt 406, July 1940, BA-MA RH24/6/319; Gericke, *Feldpost*, 61–62.

43. OKW, October 10, 1940; conference chaired by Göring on the economic exploitation of occupied territories, October 7, 1940, LArch, Berlin, A Rep. 92/105, 106–8.

44. OKW (Reinecke), Über den Versand und die Beschlagnahme von Feldpostpäckchen [On the Shipment and Confiscation of Military Mail Packages], July 14, 1942, LArch, Berlin, A Rep. 92/105, 115.

45. Hitler, *Monologe*, 363–64 (August 25 and 26, 1942).

46. Ibid., 346 (August 16, 1942).

47. *Hitlers Tischgespräche*, 182 (July 17, 1942).

48. Keitel, August 16, 1942, LArch, Berlin, A Rep. 92/105, 116. On September 17, 1942, the Finance Ministry declared that Hitler's decree also applied to those entering from wartime allied and friendly states.

49. Göring to StS RK, and Mbfh., August 6, 1942, IMG, vol. 39, 388, 391.

50. Seydelmann, *Balance*, 105, 130, 182.

51. ZFS, Kiel, progress report, August 1, 1942–January 31, 1943, BA R2/56104, 53.

52. Reinhardt to the OFP responsible for eastern borders, January 28, 1942. The decree was later extended for the Reich's northern, western, and southern borders, October 7, 1942, BA R2/31099.

53. Foreign Office, Berlin (Wiehl), to RFM, Hamsterkäufe in Dänemark [Hoarding in Denmark], April 27, 1940, BA R2/56058, 13.

54. RKK main administration to Reichsbank board of directors, October 5, 1940, BA R2/56045, 14.

55. MBIF, army field postmaster, diary (July 1–December 31, 1940, and January 1–June 30, 1941), BA-MA RW35/1390, 26; 1391, 18.

56. H.V.Bl., November 4, 1940; Frank to Keitel, November 25, 1940, BA-MA RW7/1710a, 85–86; RKK administrative council, February 16, 1942, BA R29/2, 234.

57. RFM (Berger) to Foreign Office, Berlin, September 9, 1940, NA RG 338/case 11/F44, microfilm 884–85.

58. RKK administrative council, February 27, 1943, BA R2/13502, 110.

59. Göring conference at Berchtesgaden, April 28, 1943, NA RG238/case Xl/microfiche 28 (NG-3392). Michel was among the participants.

60. French note on German-French relations [April 1941] PAAA (BA) 61136; German embassy, Paris (Gerstner), to Foreign Office trade division, July 3, 1941, AN AJ 40/1021, 49–50.

61. Schachtschnabel, "Finanzwirtschaft; Der französische Staatshaushalt," *Bank-Archiv* (1943), 76; RWM, monthly status report for France, February 10, 1944, NA T 71/59, 750–52. In 1942, according to German reports, 157.5 billion francs were siphoned off from the French budget for occupation costs and clearing advances. This amount was more than the total "expenditures for French purposes" (153.9 billion francs). In 1943, these expenditures fell to 143.4 billion, while occupation costs and clearing advances rose to 281.6 billion francs—that is, 200 percent of French state expenditures. Progress report (Schaefer), April 5, 1944, PAAA R106959, 2–3; aide-memoire (Hartlieb and Hemmen), Französische Finanzlage und Vorschläge zur Deckung der Ausgaben

[The French Economy and Suggestions for Covering Expenditures], May 7, 1943, Archive de la Banque de France 1397199501/12.

62. Archive de la Banque de France 1397199501/12, 1; progress report (Hartlieb), February 1945, HAdDB B 330/4600, 7, 15.

63. Französiche Finanzlage [The French Financial Situation] (Germany embassy, Madrid), January 21, 1945, PAAA R 106959.

64. Progress report (Hartlieb), February 1945, HAdDB B330/4600, 65, 76ff.

65. Ibid., 5; Evolution de la trésorerie et des dépenses publiques 1938–1945, SAEF B0060911/1.

66. Arnoult, "Finances," 39.

67. Foreign office trade division (Reinel), November 7, 1942, BA R2/14552, 68; OKW (Kersten) to Foreign Office, Berlin, November 6, 1942, PS-1741.

68. RFM (Berger) to Four-Year Plan (Gramsch), January 15, 1941, BA R29/1, 25–26. On the actual uses of the money, see RKK main administration to RFM, February 21, 1941, ibid., 89; Umbuchungen [transfers] 1941 BA R29/2, 82, 163ff.; RFM (Bayrhoffer) to RVM, December 10, 1940, AN AJ 40/1124 (Besatzungskosten A IV [Occupation Costs Account A IV]); Feindvermögen [Enemy Assets] AN AJ 40/589, 42.

69. RFM (Mayer), Result of Calculations 1941, August 6, 1942, R2/24250.

70. Account A VI of the RKK, Paris, 1941 AN AJ 40/1124; WaKo, May 24, 1941, NG-3630.

71. RFM, October 14, 1942, Reich secret BA R2/14552, 15; MBiF, intendant director to OKW, January 18, 1943, 114ff.

72. Progress report (Hartlieb), February 1945, HAdDB B330/4600, 6, 11.

73. RFM, Primetex, November 30, 1942, BA R2/14553, 35–36.

74. Papiers Monange, Postwar Investigations, SAEF B57045.

75. Aufbau, Aufgaben und bisherige Tatigkeit der Roges [Expansion, Mandate, and Current Activity of Roges] [February 1942] BA R2/30536, 3–4.

76. RFM (Bussmann) to RHK, October 24, 1940, AN AJ 40/1124. (There are hundreds of examples of these practices in this unpaginated file.) Heinz Schmid-Lossberg, Rüstungskontor GmbH, etc., June 8, 1945, SAEF R57045, 12.

77. RFM to RHK, December 6 and 9, 1940, AN AJ 40/1124.

76. Besatzungskosten-Kto. Frankreich A I [Occupation Costs Account France A I], Finance ministry announcements (October 15, 1940–April 5, 1943) AN AJ 40/1124.

79. RFM to RHK, October 17, 1940, NA AJ 40/1124.

80. Progress report (Hartlieb), February 1945, HAdDB B 330/4600, 17.

Forced Labor

ULRICH HERBERT

From *Hitler's Foreign Workers*

Forced Recruitment in the East

Forced conscription for labor was nothing new in the occupied territories of the Soviet Union. The military administration had, quite early on, conscripted Soviet citizens as laborers for the German occupation forces.[1] The transition to recruitment for work in the Reich was thus fluid. However, the methods employed by the various military authorities were not uniform, and ranged from conscription orders (accompanied by the taking of hostages) to voluntary recruitment. In the spring of 1942, when the labor authorities began to recruit Soviet civilian workers for work in Germany, the Supreme Command of the Second Army summarized the experience gathered to date by the military authorities: "Voluntary recruitment will not be successful. Forced conscription without comprehensive preparations, especially in terms of propaganda, leads to injustices; it requires a large bureaucracy for the registration and guarding of workers, creates bad blood, and undoubtedly strengthens partisan activity. . . . As a remedy, the army recommends the introduction of obligatory labor service."[2] Initially, the civilian authorities had given no thought whatsoever to recruiting workers on a voluntary basis. Experience with coercive recruitment in Poland immediately suggested the extensive application of force, although first thoughts about the employment of Soviet civilian workers in the Reich had been conditioned by reports that some people in the East were markedly pro-German.

The basis of coercive recruitment was an ordinance issued on December 19, 1941, by the Eastern Ministry: "all inhabitants of the occupied Eastern territories are under a public obligation to work according to their capacity."[3] However, right from the beginning the German authorities preferred to use force. This was not only because they assumed that the recruitment of voluntary workers in the Soviet Union would prove a failure: the idea that Soviet workers might refuse to go to Germany was viewed as an outright affront, and a recruitment campaign in which the German Reich had to *request* the Soviet population to come to Germany was regarded as degrading to the Germans and undeserved by the Russians. In a conversation with [Plenipotentiary for Labor Deployment Werner] Mansfeld on January 23, Göring remarked "that over the longer term, Germany could not request the workers of the occupied territories to work in Germany, with only limited success, and then offer them the incentive of ever higher wages. If the previous recruitment campaign had proved unsuccessful, it would be necessary to consider the introduction of compulsory labor service in Germany." With this in mind, Mansfeld then issued his guidelines to the offices in the occupied territories.[4] He told them that the aim was still voluntary recruitment, but in order to achieve a satisfactory result, the German authorities would "have to be able to order, with all requisite vigor, those measures necessary to bolster voluntary recruitment of workers for deployment in Germany."...

The figures for the number of workers needed were high. On February 24, 1942, Mansfeld requested 380,000 agricultural and 247,000 industrial workers; in collaboration with the Eastern Ministry, they were apportioned among the various regions in the form of "obligatory work gangs." There were to be 290,000 agricultural workers from the Ukraine alone, 50,000 industrial workers from Stalino, 30,000 from Kiev.[5]

The extensive recruitment drive by the German authorities in the occupied Eastern territories was launched by the beginning of the year. . . . The approach was two-pronged. While press advertisements and posters wooed applicants with the splendid prospects that awaited them if they chose to work in Germany, the German authorities simultaneously forced the local administration to conscript large numbers of workers within a short time by issuing call-up orders. In February 1942, the mayor of Kiev wrote to the heads of the district administrations: "The Municipal Commissariat has ordered the municipality to organize the voluntary departure of Kiev residents between the ages of 16 and 55 who are fit and able to work (at least 20,000 persons) for work in Germany. . . . You are hereby ordered to ensure that from April 7, a daily quota of at least 50 persons from each district report to Lvovskava St. for duty. . . . Anyone who willfully evades his obligation to work should be brought before the police."[6]

In order to fulfill the quotas for these weekly transports, the village elders and rural mayors (*starosti*) appointed by the military government were required to provide a fixed number of workers by a specified date. Consequently, the immediate conscriptions were often carried out by local forces, who bore the brunt of popular indignation. The director of the assembly camp for skilled workers in Kharkov described in October 1942 how such "conscription operations" looked in practice:

> The frequently corruptible *starosti* and village elders often have their chosen skilled workers taken from their beds in the middle of the night, and then locked up in cellars until they are sent off in transports. Since the workers are often not allowed any time to pack, etc., many of them arrive . . . in the assembly camp with completely inadequate gear. It is quite common for these village militiamen to threaten and beat skilled workers, and this has been reported from most communities. In a number of cases, women were beaten so badly they were unable to walk.[7]

In order to give the conscription operations added emphasis, the German authorities finally resorted to terror in individual instances, so as to intimidate the workers and make any refusal appear pointless. Such cases became more frequent as more and more Soviet people opposed recruitment. In the autumn of 1942, the foreign mail censorship office in Berlin reported from the occupied Eastern territories on the basis of letters it had evaluated:

> So as to make sure that the transports of workers reach the specified target, men and women, including teenagers aged 15 and above, are reportedly being picked up on the street, at markets and during village celebrations, and then speeded away. For that reason, the inhabitants are frightened, hide, and avoid going out in public. According to the letters examined, flogging as a punishment has been supplemented since the beginning of October by burning down farmsteads or entire villages as a reprisal for the failure of townships to produce the

labor required. This latter measure has been reported from a whole series of localities.

Such an action was described in a letter by a village resident from Bielosirka in Ukraine:

The order came to provide 25 workers, but no one reported, all had fled. Then the German gendarmerie arrived and started to set fire to the houses of those who had run off. . . . The people who rushed over were not allowed to put out the fires, they were beaten and arrested, so that six farms burned down. In the meantime, the gendarmes had set other houses ablaze. The people fell to their knees, kissing the hands of the gendarmes, but they started beating them with rubber truncheons and threatened to burn down the entire village. . . . During the fire, the [Ukrainian] militia went through the nearby villages, arresting and imprisoning the workers. Wherever they failed to find a worker, they locked up the parents until their children showed up. They raged like this all night long in Bielosirka. . . . Nowadays people catch people the way knackers used to snatch stray dogs.[8]

This combined system of promises, social pressure, and brutal terror was organized on a pattern first field-tested in Poland. It was introduced by Mansfeld and the Economic Staff East, and was then massively implemented by [Mansfeld's successor, Fritz] Sauckel. The recruitment commissions now assigned by the GBA [Plenipotentiary for Labor Deployment] consisted of civil servants from the Eastern Ministry and representatives of the various state labor offices responsible for the individual districts in the East. The latter had simultaneously been appointed as "special adjunct officers" (*Sonderführer des Heeres*) in order to facilitate smooth cooperation with the military authorities.[9]

This construction, coupled with Sauckel's constant and vociferous emphasis on his "authority from the Führer," proved highly effective, and the numbers of recruited civilian workers skyrocketed. In 1942, according to Sauckel's figures, 1,480,000 civilian workers were brought from the Soviet Union to Germany—1,416,000 just in the period beginning April 1, amounting to some 40,000 weekly—along with 456,000 prisoners of war.[10]

However, Sauckel's reports, written in the grandiloquent party style with a heavy propagandistic element, are embellished. The figures used are based on the reports of the recruitment commissions, which included in their statistics all laborers scheduled to be sent to Germany, no matter whether they ran away before being put on a transport, died on the journey, were "weeded out" by the SD [Security Service of the SS] or sent back from Germany due to infectious disease, old age and infirmity, pregnancy, etc. Instead of the almost 1.5 million Soviet workers recruited according to the data of the recruitment commissions, the statistics of the labor offices indicated that at the end of November 1942, there were 1,125,000 Eastern workers in Germany. Even if December is included, there is still a difference of almost 700,000 between the two totals.[11] Nonetheless, these are incredibly high figures. In a relatively short period, some 1.5 million civilian workers and prisoners of war from the Soviet Union had been placed at the disposal of the German economy. At the end of November 1942, the ratio of Soviet to non-Soviet foreign workers, civilian and POW, was 53:100, while the ratio of Soviet to German workers had risen to 8 for every 100.

For a long time, the labor deployment authorities were convinced that recruitment quotas could still be substantially increased. Sauckel visited Ukraine at the end of May and noted after

TABLE 3. Employed foreign workers in Germany, 1941–1942 (including POWs)

NATIONALITY	AS OF SEPTEMBER 25, 1941	AS OF NOVEMBER 20, 1942	DIFFERENCE
Belgians	121,000	130,000	+9,000
French POWs	952,000	931,000	−21,000
French civilians	49,000	134,000	+85,000
Italians	271,000	198,000	−73,000
Yugoslavs	108,000	117,000	+9,000
Dutch	92,000	155,000	+63,000
Poles	1,025,000	1,315,000	+290,000
Soviet civilians/POWs	257,000	1,612,000	+1,355,000
Czechs	158,000	193,000	+35,000
Other	343,000	118,000	−225,000
Total	3,506,000	4,665,000	+1,159,000

Note: Figures based on *Der Arbeitseinsatz im (Groß-) Deutschen Reich*, 1941–42.

his return: "As far as labor is concerned, a first glance around the villages and cities is sufficient to show that there are enough people to guarantee the required number of workers for Germany. Indeed, if you limit the German perspective to the necessities of war, there is even a surplus."[12]

Forced Recruitment in the West

The enormous efforts of the regime in 1942 to bring as many foreign workers as possible to Germany had rapid and major success. In his final report at the end of 1942, Sauckel proudly announced that since the beginning of the year, "more than 3 million foreign workers, including POWs, had been made available" to the German war economy. Of these, some 570,000 were from France, Belgium and the Netherlands.[13] ... However, the figures from his own office, based on the reports of the labor offices, which counted only workers actually deployed (and with an upward margin of error, since transferred replacements were also registered as new arrivals), yielded a somewhat different picture:

The effective increase in workers from Holland, Belgium, and France together during this phase was below 10,000 per month, while it was 20,000 in the case of Poles and 100,000 for Soviet workers. Between April and December, the figure for the Soviet Union swelled to nearly 200,000 per month. This conspicuous difference between the published figures and the actual deployment of Western workers can be explained by the fact that Sauckel was doctoring the figures, inflating them so as to appear to have kept his promises and avoid losing political influence. "Recruitment" here is often tantamount to "registration" or "legal obligation to serve as a worker." In Belgium, for example, 77,414 persons had been registered for labor duty in Germany in the period from October 1942 to March 6, 1943. Of these 67,775 had actually reported, 19,024 of whom were subsequently released as "unfit for duty." 48,751 were conscripted or volunteered, of whom 4,947 refused to work in Germany. Thus, of the 77,414 originally registered, only 43,804, some 56 percent, were actually deployed.[14]

The second reason [for the statistical discrepancies] was that the Western workers in Germany had limited work contracts, generally for six months or one year. After this, the employers and authorities discovered to their surprise and chagrin that workers frequently were not prepared to extend their contracts, and returned home. This development reached such proportions that the Economic Group Aviation Industry reported: "We also took the opportunity at the weekly 'personnel exchange' in the Aviation Ministry to underscore the alarming difficulties that must arise for our member firms if foreigner contracts are not extended as quickly as possible."[15]

Speer and Milch relayed industry's complaints to Hitler and successfully called for rapid changes. Hitler stipulated "that there must be an end to six-month contracts for foreign workers. . . . Instead, contracts should be concluded which provide for the payment of some sort of one-off compensation for longer-term deployment (more than half a year)."[16]

In fact, many firms began to keep Western workers even against their will, after consulting with the labor offices and using legislation valid for German workers. In June 1942, for example, the personnel director of the Krupp cast steel plant (Gußstahlfabrik, GSF) in Essen told the company's subsidiaries that foreigners whose contract had expired and who were unwilling to continue working should be conscripted by the labor office. Nonetheless, the numbers returning home remained high until the Law on Conscription for Service of September 4, 1942 (for the

French; October 6, 1942, for the Belgians) stipulated that open-ended service contracts should become the rule.[17]

Moreover, the German recruitment offices in the occupied Western territories wooed workers with a veritable pack of lies about conditions in Germany. The recruiters were paid on a commission basis and thus had a vested interest in pushing up the number of recruits in any way they could. The SD reported numerous cases in which French or Belgian workers had been lured to Germany with promises they could live in a private apartment, would be paid above standard wage scales, could be employed in the same firm as their wives, would be given vacation when they wanted, etc. When confronted with the realities of life in the Reich, they returned home after a few weeks.[18] Such fluctuations account for at least part of the difference between recruitment and deployment figures. Returnees also caused problems for the regime in that they served as a conduit for accurate information: they quickly spread the latest news about the true situation of foreign workers in Germany. That rendered recruiting even more difficult, because despite the relatively high wages, most workers from the occupied Western countries still saw working in Germany as a decidedly unattractive proposition. Not only were the hours long, but Nazi repression was severe, heavy-handed, and keenly felt by the Western workers. Moreover, since the beginning of 1942 if not before, it had become clear that workers who went to Germany might well not be allowed to go home. This was a dilemma for the regime that characterized its entire policy: If the authorities abandoned compulsory conscription in order to lure more workers from the West, they could expect that those already working in the Reich would run from Germany in droves. If they were kept in Germany by coercion, it was unlikely there would be any further voluntary enlistments.[19]

Along with compulsory conscription, other significant factors in this connection were the regulations for treatment of civilian workers and the situation of the just under one million French POWs, whose fate and living conditions in Germany were carefully watched. Since the end of 1941 numerous civilian and military offices in Germany had attempted to improve the circumstances of these prisoners by moderating the regulations on their treatment and surveillance, so that reports about their poor situation in the Reich would no longer hamper intensified recruitment in the West. Thus, by October 1941 rules for French and Belgian POWs had already been relaxed: individuals could leave the camp as a reward for good behavior, take "walks" in closed groups (they were "mainly intended to show the POWs something of German culture"), attend religious services, and receive visits from their womenfolk. Since Western prisoners were often employed as skilled workers or in building-repair groups as roofers or glaziers, many were able to move around town quite freely.[20]

Improved rules for treatment were also issued for industrial workers from the Western territories. According to the altered regulations summarized in an information leaflet issued by the GBA in May 1942, the Western workers had the same rights as German workers when it came to wages, working conditions, separation compensation, working hours, overtime supplements and taxes. They were assured good dormitories and food as well as vacation and home leave. Only when it came to the "duration of the employer-employee relationship and its dissolution" were things spelled out in plain German: the labor contract was considered to be binding for an indefinite period. Permission from the labor office was needed in order to quit, and "refusal to take up work without reason, unwarranted absenteeism, and insubordinate shirking" were considered to be "breach of work contract."[21] ...

There was no doubt that if recruitment from the occupied Western territories was to be increased, certain relaxations in the rules on treating civilian workers and prisoners of war from the West were crucial. And the German arms industry was urgently in need of skilled workers, especially from France.[22] In his April 1942 "Program," Sauckel had commented that he wished to meet "one quarter of the entire demand for foreign workers" by manpower from the West. In particular, some 150,000 French skilled workers were to be brought to Germany.[23] Initially, this was to be effected through a step-up in voluntary enlistments. Consequently, the recruitment campaign was extended to the non-occupied area of France, and a large bureaucracy was set up, employing more than 700 Germans by the beginning of August.[24] Yet it soon became clear that, as a German administrative director put it, "the goal that has been set cannot be achieved if we follow the path of voluntary recruitment."[25] Sauckel's "Order No. 10" of August 22, 1942, instructed the German authorities in France, Belgium, and the Netherlands to issue legal ordinances for coercive measures ("duty to report, restrictions on job changing, compulsory labor service, compulsory training") immediately.[26]

Additionally and as a kind of compensation, the German authorities simultaneously accepted the proposal of the head of the Vichy government, Pierre Laval, that one prisoner of war should be released for every civilian worker recruited in France, though they did not accept the ratio proposed by Laval. On June 6, Hitler agreed to the release of 50,000 French POWs from agriculture in exchange for the deployment of 150,000 French

TABLE 4. Polish workers in Germany, September 1941–May 1944, in thousands

	POLES FROM THE GG			UKRAINIANS FROM FORMER POLISH TERRITORY			TOTALS		
	M	F	TOTAL	M	F	TOTAL	M	F	TOTAL
Sept. 25, 1941	744	262	1,006	—	—	—	744	262	1,006
May 20, 1942	719	278	997	83	35	118	802	313	1,115
Oct. 10, 1942	792	328	1,120	129	64	193	921	392	1,313
Nov. 20, 1942	786	330	1,116	131	66	197	917	392	1,313
Sept. 30, 1943	—	—	—	—	—	—	1,092	526	1,618
May 15, 1944	—	—	—	—	—	—	1,083	540	1,623

M = male; F = female

Note: Calculations based on *Der Arbeitseinsatz im (Groß-) Deutschen Reich*, 1941–43. The difference in figures, in comparison with table 22 there, is due to the differential counting of "Ukrainians," depending on whether only those Ukrainians resident in the expanded *Generalgouvernement* are included or all Polish Ukrainians.

civilian workers in Germany—the beginning of the so-called *relève*.[27]

The transition to recruitment based solely on conscription in the West, especially in France, was a logical consequence of National Socialist labor policies. Voluntary recruitment, operating exclusively through social pressure, would have presupposed further improvements in the living conditions of the Western workers in Germany, up to and including a set of regulations similar to those for German workers. Yet even that would not have guaranteed increased recruitment, because the political repression affecting the German work force was not likely to be particularly attractive to foreigners from Western Europe. There was no ideological strategy for integrating Western workers into the political "Fortress Europe," which would bind the population of the occupied Western territories to the political goals of Nazi Germany, urging them to put up with poor living conditions temporarily in light of the prospect of a distant, worthwhile political and economic goal. Moreover, such a strategy contradicted the German victory mentality of 1942. . . .

If the existing conditions were retained, recruitment quotas could be achieved only by coercion. But if workers were recruited by force, would they perform? This approach would also lead necessarily to intensified anti-German sentiment in the countries involved. Once the Germans had decided, in the late summer of 1942, to push ahead with compulsory conscription, the reactions were not long in coming. The German secret service in France reported in early November that "as a consequence of the Law on Conscription for Service, more formerly indifferent people [are shifting over] to the opposite camp. . . . In numerous circles today, one can encounter an atmosphere of embittered rejection of everything that is German. . . . Even if that is not as yet manifested openly, there is nonetheless an unmistakable danger that a substantial proportion of the population may have become even more receptive than before to enemy agitation."[28] This in turn pinned down additional German security forces in the occupied territories, and within Germany itself-a vicious circle that was becoming ever more constricted, or, as Homze put it: "The Germans were on a treadmill; the faster they ran, the faster they had to run."[29]

Propaganda and Terror in the *Generalgouvernement*

German occupation policy in Poland could operate free from political constraints, in particular any considerations about the attitude of the population toward Germany. Nevertheless, there had been a marked drop in the influx of Polish labor to Germany since the beginning of 1942. Effective new recruitment from the *Generalgouvernement* (GG) thus amounted to some 110,000 between September 1941 and the end of November 1942 or approximately 7,800 a month. Since the former Poland now served as a back-up area for the German Eastern front, the need for manpower there had skyrocketed, especially since Polish industry had been harnessed for German arms manufacture, although not on the same scale as in the Western occupied areas.[30] Since the autumn of 1941, it was only in the areas of Poland formerly occupied by the Soviet Union that large contingents of Polish workers had been conscripted.

In Poland as in France, the conflict between a policy of increased mobilization of local industry to serve the needs of German war production on the one hand, and the pressing demands from Reich labor authorities and employers for more foreign labor on the other, was never really resolved: it remained a juxtaposition of conflicting interests, often unregulated. It was a struggle to achieve everything at once: increased Polish production, more voluntary enlistment of Polish

workers for deployment in the Reich, and more forced conscriptions.

[Hans] Frank's administration in the GG had ceased to base its recruiting propaganda on a prospective improvement of conditions for Poles in Germany. The authorities involved were well aware that such propaganda was unlikely to score much success. The minutes of the RSHA *Arbeitskreis* meeting held on May 28, 1942, commented tersely: "In light of the increase in coercive conscription instead of recruitment, B. [Baatz] considers propagandistic intentions to be illusory."[31] Nonetheless, an attempt was made in early November 1941 to grant several weeks' home leave to "Polish civilian workers who had proved their worth."[32] The *Generalgouvernement* authorities planned to showcase this decision, with appropriate propaganda hype.

In Cracow, for example, those back on home leave were to be given a reception by representatives of the labor offices, and then taken to the camp for agricultural workers. "At the camp, they will be served a meal and given some drink and tobacco, and perhaps sweets for the ladies." Reports on the event should be carried by the Polish illustrated paper, the weekly newsreel *Deutsche Wochenschau*, and the radio. Finally, the plan was to make two large banners inscribed with the words: "Greetings, agricultural workers, on your vacation trip back home!" and "Polish agricultural workers from the Reich, welcome back home!"[33]

The entire affair was a total fiasco. Of the 1,338 vacationers in the Warsaw district, for example, only 547 showed up for the trip back to Germany. In his report, the Warsaw district chief commented that "a large proportion of those on leave were unwilling to return to their jobs in the Reich," and he was forced to conclude that "the principle of unconditional voluntary service must be abolished. The foreign-policy considerations that were decisive in regard to the strict implementation of this principle are no longer valid, since it was never really believed abroad that these workers had been voluntarily recruited."[34]

The operation also ran up against criticism in Germany. The SD reported that "there was a strong sense of indignation amongst the rural population," and individual comments had an uncommonly severe tone: "'Home leave is nothing but a way for these guys, who'd at last gotten used to doing a bit of work thanks to good handling, to disappear.' . . . 'Our soldiers in the World War spent four to five years in captivity and weren't allowed home during the war, and this Polish riffraff, these criminals, are being shown such consideration.'"

The SD also noted Germans were complaining that the Poles were even being allowed to ride on express trains. And people were grousing that it was downright "tactless" to have to read reports in the media like: "A banner proclaims to the heroes from the Reich: 'Vacationers, welcome back home!'" People were outraged, and the SD pointed out that it was therefore very questionable whether the "advantages achieved by granting the Polish civilian workers vacation time (easier recruitment in the GG, better job performance, less sexual intercourse with Germans) outweigh the drawbacks (vacationers not returning, extra burden on public transport, etc.)."[35]

The granting of leave and permission to return to Poland were therefore halted: "Polish agric. workers can, in individual cases, be told that the reason for the ban on vacation and home leave is the spread of typhus in the GG. However, we should avoid disseminating this explanation in public, especially in the press."[36]

But this did not reduce demands from authorities in the Reich for manpower from the GG. When Sauckel assumed office, he launched his first "action" or recruitment drive, the "Agricul-

tural Workers Recruitment Drive 1942," with the aim of bringing further contingents of Polish workers to Germany. The basis for the operation was to be the coercive recruitment that had already been authorized and effectively utilized down to the beginning of 1941: conscription by age-group (year of birth), compulsory registration, withdrawal of support payments, etc. Polish youths were likewise to be included, "among whom there may also be weaker young boys aged 13 to 15."[37]

Nonetheless, results were poor, so that the ordinance of compulsory service was reinforced in May, making it possible in principle to conscript all Polish workers for deployment in Germany. Implementation of this ordinance was, once again, largely left to the Polish mayors and village councils. They were required to register all persons in their community and to conscript individuals for compulsory service according to the quotas assigned.[38]

The administration in Cracow was well aware of the possible political repercussions of these drives. In May 1942, state secretary Bühler reported the following:

A survey of 27,000 defense plant workers showed that only 42 of them had reported voluntarily. But if police coercion is to be used, the upshot will be that many workers will no longer show up for work, because of their fears of being hauled off to the Reich. A further suggestion from the Reich is to launch a sweep operation against people in the streets of larger cities. The hope is that such an operation could yield 52,000 workers. All such notions are totally erroneous, and if people really wish to try methods like these, they will, without any doubt whatsoever, endanger reinforcements for the front.[39]

Bühler's suspicions were certainly logical. Nonetheless, the large swoops in villages and towns were initiated in the spring of 1942 in order to meet the conscription quotas by any means necessary.[40]

At the end of 1942, a Polish self-administration office in Warsaw commented on these forced round-ups:

> On November 23 in Gorlice (Jaslo District), the state commercial school was surrounded by the police while morning classes were in session. All contact between the young people and their parents was cut off. In the evening, the young men and women were indiscriminately loaded onto freight cars and transported without warm clothing or food to the mass camp in Cracow.... The forced recruitment operation on November 24 at the commercial school in Jaslo proceeded in a similar fashion. The last two grades with youngsters below the age of 17 ... were transported to the mass camp at Cracow. There, the young people who were weak and completely unfit for heavy labor were not, despite their youth, thoroughly screened and then sent back, but were designated for further transport somewhere else.[41]

Reports about such incidents spread like wildfire in the *Generalgouvernement*, causing fear and anxiety in the population. That was in fact the aim of such methods: to induce Polish workers to report voluntarily for fear of being picked up during a swoop and bundled off to Germany.

The Frank administration was well informed about the use of such methods, but preferred to blame them on "over-enthusiastic subordinates" or shift responsibility to the authorities in Berlin. When Sauckel came to Cracow in August, Frank obsequiously promised him more than 140,000 more workers, "because we will use the police to get hold of them." Yet at the same time, he criti-

cized what he termed those "firebrands in Berlin." Whereupon Sauckel, in his customary style, assured Frank that he would prevent labor deployment from "ever becoming a mark of disgrace, a blemish stigmatizing the German nation in the eyes of the world." He would make sure that the Poles were treated fairly in the Reich, because "foreigners are terribly persnickety about justice."[42]

As in the occupied Soviet territories, so in Poland: reports on the real situation of agrarian workers deployed in Germany loomed as the greatest single obstacle to further recruitment. Frank frequently underscored this point, since the stories filtering back about the poor treatment of Poles in the Reich were also a convenient excuse for the comparatively low success rate in recruiting new workers from the GG. At a government meeting at the beginning of December, he commented with pride that when it came to recruitment, the *Generalgouvernement* "topped the list of all the countries in Europe, both absolutely and comparatively." However, "we would have been able to send at least 50 percent more voluntary workers to the Reich if the Poles were treated better there." It was high time "to put an end to the scandal of the continued ill-treatment of Poles in the Reich." All in all, the Poles deployed there had proved their worth. "Naturally, we have to admit that they are not high-quality material," but "as I see it, the difference between Czechs and Polacks is not all that great."[43] ...

The basic regulations on all important questions in connection with Polish workers in the Reich had been spelled out in a number of decrees issued in the first two years of the war, and these remained in effect even after the increase in foreigner deployment which began in early 1942. One change was that after inclusion of the Soviet workers, the Poles had advanced one rung up the racial ladder: the regulations on treatment for the

Ostarbeiter were clearly more stringent than those for Poles. The Poles were often given supervisory functions at jobs where they had been employed for a long period and were now being supplemented by Soviet workers. The practice went so far that the RSHA *Arbeitskreis* had to stipulate that this supervisory function by Polish workers was applicable solely to other foreign workers, not to German workers. We can therefore assume that there had been a number of instances of Poles supervising Germans.[44]

However, this trend toward "upgrading" the Poles after the advent of Soviet workers was offset by a new bid to further regiment the daily life of the Poles: a whole series of regulations and orders was enacted over the course of the year, often involving the strangest trifles. Frequently these measures were pure harassment and denigration, and sometimes seem quite ridiculous if one considers the administrative effort expended on them by the German authorities. For example, the Justice Ministry instructed that Poles in detention awaiting trial should no longer be addressed as "Mr." (Herr), since a Pole was not a Herr. The RSHA forbade Poles to wear any medals or decorations, which should be taken from them and put in safekeeping. Poles were not to be served by German barbers—well, in some cases this was permissible, but only if special separate equipment was used. Poles were not allowed radios, were completely banned from fast and express trains, and could use public transport only with a special permit.[45] They were prohibited from attending public church services; only once a month were they allowed to participate in a special church service. "The singing of songs and hearing of confession in Polish is prohibited."[46]

There was no change in labor law for Poles, but new regulations were issued for Polish children: "There are no particular objections to Polish chil-

dren being employed beyond the limits set down in the Youth Protection Act."[47]

If we scrutinize the regime's policy on foreign workers from the beginning of the "Eastern campaign" to the turning point after Stalingrad in terms of its results, this phase marks the abandonment of a policy of temporary deployment as an "emergency stopgap measure." With the importation of millions of Soviet workers, if not before, foreigners had become the cornerstone of the edifice of German labor deployment and the German war economy. . . .

Scope and Structure of the Employment of Foreigners

After the continuing massive recruitment of new foreign workers in 1943 and 1944, the proportion of foreigners in the total work force of the Greater German Reich stabilized at roughly 25 percent. In some industries critical to armaments production, and in agriculture, it was substantially higher, while only few foreigners were employed in the consumer goods industries and office jobs (see table 5). Thus, in August 1944, almost half of all those employed in agriculture were foreign nationals. In mining, construction, and metals, foreigners accounted for about one in every three workers. In the summer of 1944, the total number of foreign workers was divided roughly equally between three sectors: agriculture, heavy industry, and other industrial branches. Until the beginning of 1942, foreigner deployment had been concentrated in agriculture; now that was no longer the case. Two-thirds of the Poles and French POWs were employed in agriculture; yet the majority of workers added since 1941 had been deployed in industry. This trend is especially manifest in the case of the last group of foreigners to be conscripted, the Italian military internees: only seven percent were employed in agriculture; 42 percent

TABLE 5. German and foreign workers in selected occupational categories, August 1944

CATEGORY	TOTAL EMPLOYED	FOREIGNERS	CIVILIAN WORKERS	POWS	PERCENTAGE OF FOREIGNERS
Agriculture	5,919,761	2,747,238	2,061,066	686,172	46.4
Mining	1,289,834	433,790	196,782	237,008	33.7
Metals	5,630,538	1,691,329	1,397,920	293,409	30.0
Chemicals	886,843	252,068	206,741	45,327	28.4
Construction	1,440,769	478,057	349,079	128,978	32.3
Transport	1,452,646	378,027	277,579	100,448	26.0
Printing	235,616	9,668	8,788	880	4.1
Textiles and clothing	1,625,312	183,328	165,014	18,314	11.1
Commerce and banking	1,923,585	114,570	92,763	21,807	6.0
Administration	1,488,176	49,085	39,286	9,799	3.3
Total economy*	28,853,794	7,651,970	5,721,883	1,930,087	26.5

* Includes workers in some minor industries not detailed above.

Note: Calculations based on *Der Arbeitseinsatz im Großdeutschen Reich*, No. 10, October 31, 1944.

were sent to work in the metal industry, compared with a 22 percent average for all groups of foreigners. Among Soviet POWs, the disproportionate percentage deployed in mining (some 25 percent) is conspicuous. Russians, Italians and Poles accounted for more than 80 percent of all foreigners employed in mining. Almost half of all French civilian workers were in the metals sector, a consequence of the high proportion of skilled workers recruited from France. Of the 5.7 million foreign civilian workers registered in August 1944, 1,924,912 were women, exactly one third. The foreign female laborers were predominantly from the East (87 percent), contrasted with 62 percent of the men. The lower a given group was in the Nazi political and racial pecking order, the higher the percentage of women, ranging from three percent among the Hungarians (allied with Germany) to

51.1 percent of the civilian workers from the Soviet Union. To stress the magnitude of female Eastern labor: in the summer of 1944, there were more female Eastern workers in Germany than civilian male and female workers from Belgium, France and Holland combined!

It is difficult to provide an accurate picture of the distribution of skills among foreign workers in the Reich as a whole. However, it is instructive to note that of the approximately 1.8 million foreign civilian workers deployed in metals and construction at the end of March 1944, about half were unskilled, and the other half semi-skilled or skilled. Evidently efforts by employers and the authorities to deploy foreigners at skilled jobs in line with their qualifications had already had some success.[48]

As for regional distribution, the proportion of foreigners was highest in those areas heavily dominated by agriculture. If we include the figures for POWs, then just under half of all employees in these farming areas were foreigners.[49] Since the percentage of female German workers in the countryside was especially high, there were many areas in the East of the Reich where twice as many foreigners were employed as German males.[50] In the Ruhr, the proportion of foreigners among civilian workers hovered around 18 percent, slightly below the average for the Reich. However, the number of POWs deployed in coal-mining was particularly high. If they are added to the total, the proportion of foreign workers at the beginning of 1944 in the Essen Labor District was 23.4 percent.[51]

This short overview of the statistics on foreigner employment in the last year of the war indicates that a quarter of all those working in the German economy were foreign nationals; in industries crucial to defense, they amounted to a third of the work force, and in agriculture, nearly half. The foreign workers made their mark on everyday life in both agricultural areas and the cities. In Berlin, for example, there were almost 400,000 foreign laborers; Hamburg had 63,000, Königsberg 70,000, Munich 65,000, while Magdeburg, Leipzig, Nuremberg and Linz each had some 60,000.[52]

NOTES

1. See, for example, the order from the 20th Motorized Infantry Div. of September 17, 1941, to the residents of Schlüsselburg: "All inhabitants between the ages of 15 and 55 must report before headquarters by 1 p.m. on September 17. They will be taken for labor service and will be fed and treated well. . . . Any male inhabitants who ignore this command and are found in Schlüsselburg or within a 10 km radius of the town or on the eastern bank of the Neva will be shot." Doc. NOKW 2986.

2. AOK 2 to Army Group B, n. d. (spring 1942); Doc. NOKW 2772, partially reproduced in Norbert Müller, ed., *Deutsche Besatzungspolitik*, 293–4.

3. Eastern Ministry, "Verordnung über die Einführung der Arbeitspflicht in den besetzten Ostgebieten," December 19, 1941, Doc. 1975 PS, IMT, vol. 29, 186. The third implementation ordinance of November 16, 1942, states that the obligation to work may "also extend to the performance of services outside the area of territorial validity of this ordinance"; ibid.

4. Memo of Foreign Ministry, January 23, 1942, on discussion between Göring and Mansfeld; Doc. NG 3752. Economic Staff East, Main Group Labor, Rachner, to Offices in the East, January 26, 1942, Doc. USSR 381, IMT, vol. 39, 491.

5. Decree, Business Group Labor Deployment of the Four-Year Plan Office, February 24, 1942; mentioned in a letter from the Eastern Ministry to the Reich Commissioners, March 6, 1942, Doc. 580 PS, IMT, vol. 26, 161.

6. Report, Armaments Commando Dessau, February 13, 1942, Institut fur Zeitgeschichte (hereafter IfZ) MA 41.

7. Report, Director of the Assembly Camp for Skilled Workers in Kharkov, October 5, 1942, Doc. 054 PS, IMT, vol. 25, 103–4.

8. Excerpts from the confidential report on the popular mood, ABPS Berlin, on letters from the occupied Eastern territories examined in the period from September 11 to November 10, 1942, Doc. 018 PS, IMT, vol. 25, 77–8; similar reports are frequent and there is a steep rise in their numbers, especially from the autumn of 1942 onward.

9. Letter from GBA to the Directors of the Commissions of the Former Business Group Labor Deployment in the Occupied Eastern Territories, March 31, 1942, Doc. 382 USSR, IMT, vol. 39, 496; GBA to Economic Staff East, Rachner, March 31, 1942, ibid., 494.

10. Report by GBA on labor deployment in 1942; Doc. 1739 PS, IMT, vol. 27, 578ff.

11. Figures based on *Der Arbeitseinsatz im (Groß-) Deutschen Reich*, 1942–43, and the report by the

Business Group Labor Deployment (Beisiegel), March 23, 1942, BA R 41/281. The number of Soviet prisoners deployed in the Reich at the end of 1942 was roughly 500,000; however, at the end of February that year there were already some 180,000 POWs working in the Reich, so that here too Sauckel's figures are exaggerated by over 100,000.

12. Report by Sauckel on his trip to the Ukraine, May 26–31, 1942, BA R43 II/652, 183ff.

13. "Bericht des GBA über den Arbeitseinsatz im Jahre 1942" (Report by GBA on Labor Deployment 1942), Doc. 1739 PS, IMT, vol. 27, 578ff.

14. Report of recruitment offices, March 1943 BA R41/276, fols. 17–18.

15. Letter, Economic Group Aviation Industry, n.d. (early 1942), quoted in Seeber, "Zur Rolle der Monopole," 16.

16. Discussion between Speer and Hitler, February 19, 1942; Boelcke, *Deutschlands Rüstung*, 66.

17. Ihn to individual Krupp plants, June 1942, Doc. NIK 6705; cf. Pfahlmann, 33–4.

18. *MadR*, February 12, 1942, BA R58/169, fol. 146.

19. On the French workers in Germany, see the studies by Durand, Evrard, Frankenstein and Fridenson, and Milward, "French Labor." For Holland, Sijes, and Hirschfeld, *Fremdherrschaft*, 117–54; idem, "Arbeitseinsatz."

20. Decrees, OKW/Sec. POWs, October 3, 1941, December 8, 1941, December 31, 1941, January 8, 1942; AES, Part 2, A IIIe, 8ff.; OKW/General Wehrmacht Office/POWs, Order, March 20, 1942, "betr. Auflockerung der Bewachung von französischen und belgischen Kriegsgefangenen" (Re: Easing of Regulations on the Guarding of French and Belgian POWs), AES, Part 2, A IIIe, 25ff.; Merkblatt "Verhalten gegenüber Kriegsgefangenen" (Leaflet "Behavior Toward POWs"), OKW/Sec. POWs, May 21, 1942, AES, Part 2, A IIIe, 40ff.

21. "Merkblatt für ausländische gewerbliche Arbeitskräfte" (Leaflet for Foreign Industrial Employees), May 1942; issued by Labor Ministry/GBA, Circular 529/42, May 4, 1942, BA RD89/15, 1942, 295.

22. Cf. Janssen, *Das Ministerium Speer*, 82–3; however, he personalizes the connection so strongly that the contradictions between political aims and the material constraints of the war economy turn into a duel between Sauckel and Speer, in which Sauckel plays the villain and Speer the hero.

23. "Das Programm des GBA," April 20, 1942, in *Handbuch des GBA*, 27ff. When Sauckel was in Paris in May, he even demanded 250,000 skilled workers; cf. Jäckel, Frankreich, 224.

24. Ibid.

25. Michel, Head of Administrative Staff, Office of German Military Commander in France, to State Secretary Barnaud, August 26, 1942; Doc. F-530, IMT, vol. 5, 543–44.

26. "Anordnung des GBA Nr. 10 betr. den Einsatz von Arbeitskräften der besetzten Gebiete," August 22, 1942, and "Durchführungsbestimmungen," October 29, 1942, in *Handbuch des GBA*, 97ff. The administrative regulations were issued in France on September 4, in Belgium on October 6; cf. Evrard, 53ff. After the war, a Belgian worker described how such forced recruitments might look: "Before the war, I had a job with the Belgian railways. At 9 a.m. on the morning of May 15, 1943, I visited a bicycle dealer in Proven and noticed a German car in the market place. There were German military police there who had picked up some men and were loading them into the car. When I got home, I told my wife what had happened. I didn't suspect anything, and wanted to go see who had been taken away. But my wife advised me not to, so I stayed at home. I was standing at the front door of the house, when I suddenly caught sight of that same German car turning around in front of my door and heading back the way it had come. But it stopped in front of my place, three German military police officers jumped out, one armed with a rifle and two with revolvers. They surrounded me and ordered me, without any further explanation, to accompany them. I didn't know why I was being picked up. Later on in Germany, how-

ever, I learned there had been a mistake. I had been registered as unemployed, born 1920 and unmarried; in fact, I worked for the Belgian railways, was born in 1902 and was married." Affidavit, L. Alleweireldt, September 25, 1947, Doc. NIK 12955; Durand, *La captivité*; idem, "Vichy."

27. The transformation of all French POWs into conscripted civilian workers, on analogy with the Poles, had been rejected by Hitler; Situation Report, WRA, June 1, 1942, BA/MA RW 4/v. 308, fol. 260; report, WRA (IV a), January 1943 BA/MA RW 19 WI/IF 5/3690, 27.

28. "Stimmungsbericht des Militärverwaltungschefs in Frankreich über die Anwerbung vom 10.10 bis 9.11.1942" (Situation Report on Recruitment by Military Administrative Head in France, October 10–November 9, 1942) BA R 41/267, fol. 240.

29. Homze, 137.

30. See Madajczyk, *Okkupationspolitik*, 564ff., 577ff.; Broszat, *Polenpolitik*, 106ff; Dlugoborski and Madajczyk, 404ff.

31. Meeting, RSHA *Arbeitskreis*, May 28, 1942, minutes BA R16/162.

32. *MadR*, February 26, 1942, makes reference to these regulations of January 1, 1941, BA R58/168, fol. 202ff. With an order on March 31, 1941, the right to vacation time and home leave was nullified in the case of Poles, *RABl* 1941, 195.

33. Discussion notes, Main Dept. of Propaganda GG, November 26, 1941, *Doc. occ.* X, Doc. IV.28.

34. Report, Governor of Warsaw District to Frank, February 10, 1942, *Doc. occ.* X, Doc. IV.33.

35. *MadR*, February 26, 1942, BA R58/169, fol. 302ff.

36. *Reichsbauernführer* to Rural Farmer Associations, February 25, 1942, *Doc. occ.* IX, Doc. No. 111.

37. Government of GG, Labor Dept., to subordinate authorities, March 23, 1942, *Doc. occ.* X, Doc. IV.34. Cf. also letter from Sauckel to Greiser, Governor in Warthegau, April 15, 1942, *Doc. occ.* IX, Doc. No. 116.

38. VO zur Sicherstellung des Kräftebedarfs für Aufgaben von besonderer staatspolitischer Bedeutung (Dienstpflichtverordnung)" (Order on Procurement of Personnel for Tasks of Special National Importance [Order on Obligatory Service]), May 13, 1942, *Doc. occ.* X, Doc. IV.39; see, for example, the letter from the District Chief in Lublin (rural) to the Council Head in Lubartov, November 13, 1942, *Doc. occ.* X, Doc. IV.44.

39. *Diensttagebuch*, May 11, 1942, 495.

40. Diary entry by Bühler on discussion of main department heads, December 8, 1942, quoted in *Deutschland im zweiten Weltkrieg*, vol. 3, 372.

41. Memo, n.d. (end of 1942), on registering schoolchildren for labor, *Doc. occ.* IX, Doc. No. 136.

42. *Diensttagebuch*, entry of August 18, 1942, 544–5.

43. Speech by Frank to the GG government in session, December 9, 1942, *Diensttagebuch* 585ff.

44. Meeting, RSHA *Arbeitskreis*, May 28, 1942, and November 17, 1942, minutes BA R16/162.

45. In the order of regulations enumerated: letter of Justice Ministry, December 1, 1941, BA R22/3373, fol. 41; Decree, Reichsführer-SS and Chief of the German Police (S IV D (for. workers), December 10, 1941, *Doc. occ.* X, Doc. I.20; Trade Corporation Schneidemühl to Regierungspräsident Schneidemühl, January 20, 1942, *Doc. occ.* IX Doc. No. 108; Decree, Chief of Security Police, June 16, 1942, *Doc. occ.* IX, Doc. No. 119; Head office, Reichsbahn, Posen to Governor of Warthegau, July 2, 1942, *Doc. occ.* IX, Doc. No. 121; Order, Transport Minister, October 1942, *Doc. occ.* IX, Doc. No. 135.

46. Cf. Decree, Reichsführer-SS and Chief of the German Police, July 26, 1942, GStAB 1 Js 4/64, Doc. A 52.

47. Decree, Labor Ministry, June 12, 1942, in Küppers and Bannier, *Einsatzbedingungen*, 111.

48. Ibid., Nos. 6, 7 and 8, August 21, 1944.

49. The Gau District Labor Offices with the highest percentage of foreigners (civilian workers only) in 1944 were: East Prussia (33.9%), East Hanover (32.5%), Lower Saxony (32.3%), Kurhesse (31.2%), Pomerania (30.7%). The lowest proportions of foreigners at this time were reported from Baden (12.6%), Hamburg (13.6%), Upper Silesia (13.4%) and Danzig (13.3%). In September 1944, the Reich average was 27%. Based on

Der Arbeitseinsatz im Großdeutschen Reich, No. 11/12, December 30, 1944, 4.

50. In the summer of 1944, there were approximately 140,000 POWs and 235,000 foreign civilian laborers working in East Prussia, a total of roughly 375,000 foreigners, compared with some 200,000 male German workers.

51. Report, Director, District Labor Office Essen, January 1944, StAM OP 5141.

52. Expert Opinion, Audit Office, GSF, November 20, 1942, Doc. NIK 4021.

5 Jews in the Nazi Grip

10. Helen Verblunsky, a young girl in the Kovno ghetto (Lithuania), as she delivers milk to one of her mother's customers. Her mother, Tova, smuggled milk into the ghetto, which she obtained from Lithuanians in exchange for articles of clothing. Helen looked after her younger brother, Avramaleh, while her parents worked on forced labor brigades. During the Children's *Aktion* on March 27, 1944, seven-year-old Avramaleh was forcibly taken from Helen. He never returned. Helen and her parents were deported to Stuthoff in July, 1944. Upon arrival, her father, along with all the other men, was shipped to Dachau. Helen and her mother never saw him again. Mother and daughter succeeded in staying together until liberation, 1941–1943. (U.S. Holocaust Memorial Museum, courtesy George Kadish / Zvi Kadushin.)

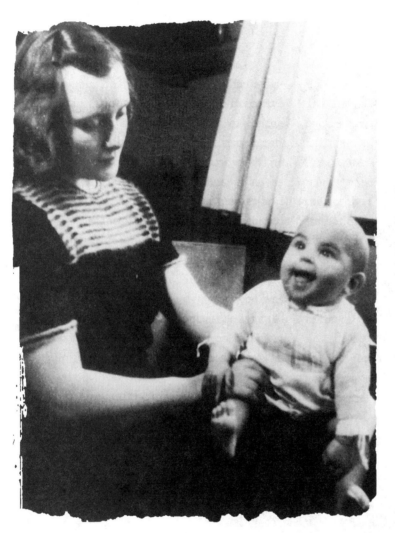

11. Amsterdam, the Netherlands . . 1942—Marion Pritchard with Erica Polak. Marion Pritchard was studying to become a social worker when Germany invaded the Netherlands in May 1940. One day she witnessed Germans throwing young Jewish children onto a truck for deportation. It was a shocking sight, and Marion was overwhelmed with rage. The twenty-two-year-old student decided then that she would do whatever she could to rescue Jewish children. In 1942 she was asked by her friend "Miek," who was also a member of the Dutch resistance, to find a hiding place for a Jewish friend and his three small children. When Marion could not find a place, Miek persuaded his mother-in-law to let Marion, Fred Polak, and his children, Lex, Tom, and Erica, move into the servants' quarters of her house in the country. Miek had built a hiding place under the floor in case the Germans came looking for Jews. All four of them could fit in the space. One night three Germans and a Dutch Nazi came to search the house. Marion had put the Polaks under the floor but had not had time to give Erica, the baby, her sleeping powder. The search party left after failing to find any Jews. The baby started to cry, so Marion let the children climb out of the hiding place. The Dutch Nazi returned half an hour later; he saw the children sleeping and the hiding place uncovered. Marion knew she needed to act quickly. She reached for a gun that Miek had given her and killed the Dutchman. The Polaks stayed with Marion until the end of the war. During the German occupation of the Netherlands, she helped save approximately 150 Jewish children. (Courtesy JFR Photo Archives.)

Introduction

PETER HAYES

During the initial phase of their subjugation of Europe, the Nazi leaders still acted as though their objective with regard to the Jews remained "removing" them from German territory. But once the fighting began, that goal became more elusive. The conflict disrupted most transportation for refugees and reduced the already low receptiveness to them abroad. In the meantime, the growth of the German Empire meant the multiplication of the number of Jews within it. Clearly, a continued policy of terrifying Jews into leaving was unlikely to produce the Jew-free (*judenrein*) Reich that Hitler desired.

As a result, even before Warsaw surrendered, the Nazi regime began laying the basis for a policy of compulsory deportation. On September 21, 1939, Chief of the German Security Police Reinhard Heydrich directed his subordinate offices in occupied Poland to enforce "the concentration of the Jews from the countryside into the larger cities . . . which either are railroad junctions or at least lie on railroad lines." So far as possible, responsibility for the implementation of not only this policy, but also all subsequent German orders regarding the new areas of residence was to be imposed upon Jewish Councils of Elders (*Judenräte der Ältesten*) composed of current community leaders. Six days later, Heinrich Himmler, the head of the Nazi SS (*Schutzstaffel*) and of the German police, created a new Main Office for the Security of the Reich (RSHA) under Heydrich and entrusted him with overall responsibility for "the Jewish Question." Within this organization, Adolf Eichmann,

an SS officer who had supervised the fleecing and expatriation of thousands of Austrian Jews during 1939, assumed control of the "Jewish Department" that was to handle the logistics of the incipient ghettoization and the ultimate deportation. In short, less than one month after invading Poland and adding approximately two million Jews to its realm, the Nazi regime had devised a system of segregating these people from the surrounding population, positioning them for swift round up later, stripping them of all their immovable and most of their movable property in the process, and turning the leaders of their communities into the executors of German policy.

Although the Germans conceived of this program rapidly, they translated it into practice in Poland unevenly and haltingly. Events moved fastest in the regions annexed to the Reich, namely Eastern Upper Silesia, West Prussia, and the so-called *Warthegau*. The last named was the location of the city of Lodz, which became on May 1, 1940, the first large-scale ghetto to be sealed off from the outer world. Initially with 153,177 residents crammed into 1.6 square miles of a slum district that lacked indoor plumbing, the Lodz ghetto became under Hans Biebow, its German administrator, and Chaim Rumkowski, its Eldest of the Jews, the most self-sustaining and the longest lasting of the Jewish population centers, even though it was now officially within Germany. In contrast, Warsaw's ghetto in the German-occupied rump of Poland, the General Government, was not closed off until November 1940, and its staggering congestion—at the outset, more than 400,000 Jews were confined to 1.3 square miles—made it less manageable and more lethal. Further to the east, in Lublin, the gates did not shut on some 40,000 Jews until April 1941, and the permeability of the ghetto boundaries, as with many of the smaller sites, remained much greater.

The variability of ghettoization had a number of causes. The chaotic and contradictory nature of German population policy in Poland slowed implementation, as did shortages of personnel and transportation. German administrators squabbled about whether and how ghetto inmates were to be kept alive and thus about how much trade they could do with their environs and with the occupying regime. Above all, no one seemed to know how long the ghettos were to last and where the denizens someday were to be sent. German planners spoke consistently of eventually consigning the Jews to a "reservation," but kept changing its location. Early in the occupation of Poland, an eastern region around the village of Nisko was the destination of choice. Following the defeat of France in June 1940, attention shifted to the island of Madagascar, a French colony off the east coast of Africa that interwar antisemites often had mentioned as a possible destination for European Jews. Later that year, after the German failure in the aerial Battle of Britain quashed the prospect of transporting Jews by sea and turned Hitler's thoughts toward the invasion of the Soviet Union, its Arctic regions and Siberia were discussed as possibilities. With each change of venue came a deferral of deportation and thus among the German occupiers a declining sense of urgency about completing the ghetto system, as well as declining patience with its existence.

Despite variations among the ghettos in everything from the date of their establishment to the quality of their leadership, they all operated to constrict and sooner or later to suffocate Jewish life. Subjected to ever mounting scarcity, Jews were pitted against each other in the struggle for food, clothing, shelter, and sheer survival, and their ability to sustain one another both materially and morally eroded steadily. The readings in this chapter trace this excruciating process in occupied Poland and contrast it with the less conspicuous mechanisms of grinding Jews down that the Nazis applied in Western Europe prior to the onset of deportations from there in 1942.

Isaiah Trunk cautions against facile retrospective judgments in his depiction of the intractable dilemmas that the Nazi system of *indirect rule* imposed on the Jewish Councils and the atmosphere of arbitrary terror in which they worked. Passages from the diary of Chaim Kaplan, who died at Treblinka but whose writings were found hidden in a kerosene can at a farm outside of Warsaw in 1963, trace the increasingly debilitating *isolation and impoverishment* of that city's Jews from the fall of 1939 until the eve of massive deportations in the summer of 1942. Gordon Horwitz narrates the ultimate example of the *"choiceless choices"* (Lawrence Langer) that ghetto leaders faced, the moment in September 1942 when Chaim Rumkowski beseeched the remaining Jewish laborers to prolong their own lives by sacrificing their children and aged relatives to fulfill the latest round of German deportation quotas. Samuel Kassow describes the dedication to *leaving a record* of what the Germans had done and the Jews had suffered that propelled the "Oyneg Shabes" clandestine archive in Warsaw, even as its contributors lost confidence in their own survival. Yisrael Gutman shows that the classic instance of Jewish armed resistance, the Warsaw Ghetto Uprising of 1943, like the later camp uprisings at Treblinka and Sobibór, occurred—indeed, could only occur—when the remaining Jews realized that they were about to be wiped out and thus had *nothing to lose* by fighting back. Felicja Karay tells the story of some of the few Jews left alive in Poland in 1943–44, the *women slave laborers* who toiled under atrocious conditions at a German munitions factory. Finally, Martin Dean details the process of *robbery in the Netherlands* that stripped Dutch Jews of their rights and property as a prelude to their deportation, yet largely stopped short of ghettoization.

Taken altogether, these readings remind us of how collectively powerless Jews were, especially while Germany was ascendant, to affect their fates. Young, fit, and unencumbered individuals could take flight or seek hideouts, but whole communities could not. Totally outgunned by hateful enemies, lacking escape routes, surrounded by largely hostile populations, usually inhabiting terrain that offered little cover, unsure until at least 1942 of the Nazis' intentions, and steadily drained of their strength, most Jews in the Nazi grip seemed to have only two alternatives: to die defiantly or to play for time.

Indirect Rule

ISAIAH TRUNK

From *Judenrat*

The Organizational Structure of the Jewish Councils

The Councils were conceived by the Nazis not as an instrument for organizing life in the ghettos or for strengthening the structure of the ghetto, but the opposite; as an instrument which, in their hands, would help them to realize their plans concerning the Jewish population in the occupied territories and, in particular, their extermination plan. The Councils were permitted, at most, to take care of distributing the meager supplies and maintaining a certain standard (only too low) of sanitation (for the continuous epidemics would also threaten the Nazis themselves); they were permitted to preserve "peace and order" as understood by the authorities.

The ramified Jewish organization was originally created to carry out, precisely and efficiently, all the regulations and directives of the occupation authorities. This was the definition of its role in the very first document about the Council of Elders (the "urgent letter" of Heydrich of September 21, 1939), in the regulation concerning the establishment of the Jewish Councils of November 28 of the same year, issued by Hans Frank, and in official Nazi declarations dealing with Jewish self-rule in the occupied territories. The Councils had to serve only one purpose—to execute Nazi orders regarding the Jewish population.

Other activities undertaken by the Councils, with the consent of the authorities, in the sphere of internal ghetto life (social welfare, economic and cultural work) were performed, in fact, outside their prescribed tasks. Such other activities, which dealt with the internal requirements of the Jewish population, were sometimes accorded a certain degree of tolerance, and even of encouragement; they served the Nazi-propagated illusion that the continued existence of the ghettos was guaranteed and concealed the Final Solution (*Endziel*) from the Jews for as long as necessary.

The tasks of the Councils can be divided into three classes:

1. Tasks imposed by the authorities, such as conduct of the census of the Jewish population, the supply of forced labor, registration of candidates for the work camps, for deportation, etc.

2. Routine tasks in social welfare, medical care, and in the economic and cultural fields— tasks which were, in the main, a continuation of prewar communal activities.

3. New tasks made essential by the complete elimination of the Jewish population in the ghetto from governmental and municipal services, such as food supplies, the management of the ghetto dwellings, industry, health, police and judicial services, etc.

These varied duties of the Councils necessitated the growth of a ramified, administrative apparatus. The organizational structure of this apparatus expanded as the isolation of the Jewish population from the general, governmental, and municipal framework was completed. . . . The Nazi-created Jewish ghetto necessarily became a Jewish city *sui generis*, linked to the main city only by slender links that had to be maintained for purely technical reasons, e.g., lighting, water-supply, sewage, and limited telephone connection (up to a certain period). Generally the ghettos were cut off from the normal postal services and, in some ghettos, special post offices were opened. Suitable administrative machinery had, therefore, to be created in the ghettos to serve the needs of the Jewish population in those matters normally dealt with by the government and the municipality. It was also necessary to set up special departments to carry out the orders and directives of the authorities with regard to forced labor, collection of taxes, delivery of various materials and merchandise, of forced-labor workers, transfers, evacuations, and the like.

From the start of the occupation, the Germans excluded Jews from the benefits of social services such as pensions for war invalids, sick benefits, etc.[1] Jewish bank accounts were withheld and Jewish property confiscated;[2] forced labor duty for the Jews was ordered.[3] In many places the Jews were also excluded from the general system of food supply. As a result of all these measures, even before the ghettos had been established, Jews were faced with most urgent tasks: to provide in short order some social and medical services, if only on a minimal scale; to take care of food supply and distribution; and to search for new sources of income for countless people eliminated from the national economies and from state and community frameworks.

A particularly urgent field of activities demanding immediate attention was the necessity to provide shelter for the overflow of homeless people who had lost all their possessions as a result of the war operations. Masses of desolated, penniless

refugees surged from their ruined dwelling places into the larger communities, where some sort of lodgings had to be found for them. The ranks of these unfortunates were soon augmented by the thousands of Jews the Germans threw out of their homes. The Germans complemented this deluge of aimlessly wandering people without any tangible means of existence by systematic spoliation of Jewish property and by relentless, random arrests for forced labor. By such measures these people's economic existence was entirely broken down.

New departments had to be established, and old ones revitalized or reorganized by the Councils, to cope with this ever increasing responsibility and with the overriding necessity to deal with the hostile authorities on a daily basis. The departments of welfare and medical care, food supply, and forced-labor duty were the earliest ones established. Later came the crucial moment when the Jews were enclosed in the ghettos, where, according to the plans of the Nazis, the "ghetto autonomy" was to be complete and self-sustaining in all sectors of community life. It then became particularly important to extend the existing administrative apparatus . . . to include policing of the ghetto area, management of real estate to organize the food distribution, etc. . . .

The departments of registration and vital statistics came into being quite early, in accordance with Heydrich's circular letter of September 21, 1939, which ordered the Councils to carry out a census of the Jewish population according to age. At the end of October 1939 a statistical bureau was established in Warsaw following the order to take a census of Jews residing in the Polish capital. The census took place on October 28.[4] In Lublin the registration department was established on February 22, 1940, and its first duty was to carry out the census there.[5] In Lodz a department for this purpose was established on May 9, 1940, soon after the Jews were closed up in the ghetto.[6] Prior orders during October 1939 had directed the forced labor department to carry out the registration of males eighteen to sixty years old and females twenty-two to fifty-five years old.

To take care of the deliveries of merchandise ordered by various authorities, there were established in some of the ghettos special offices, such as the acquisition office (*Beschaffungsamt*) at Lwów, the material deliveries office (*Sachleitungskomission*) at Zólkiew, etc.[7]

The "resettlement" of the Jews into the overcrowded ghettos—for the most part located in desolate, squalid, slum-ridden sections of the towns—suddenly forced upon the community leaders extremely heavy responsibilities: to move the worldly goods of thousands of dislodged families; to find the living space necessary to shelter them, to try to distribute this insufficient room among the people rendered homeless on short notice, to move dislodged institutions of public service into some new quarters, to speed up repairs of ruined buildings to create additional living space. These agonizing tasks all demanded simultaneous solution. Among the new departments that mushroomed in the ghettos, those that dealt with providing homes were necessarily among the first and most important to come into being. Initially called resettlement departments or commissions, they were renamed tenants' departments as time passed.

It was also necessary to serve in other fields. Isolated in the ghettos, robbed of personal property, forced to give up their businesses and positions of employment, and, as a rule, even compelled to surrender their homes, native Jews and refugees alike, businessmen and salaried workers, had been deprived of their livelihood and customary means of sustenance. All required immediate attention and assistance in their search

for some means of support for themselves and their families. People had to start all over from scratch. Trade had to be organized, new sources of income created. Simultaneously, it was necessary to plan and bring to life a network for distribution of allotted food rations, to open schools, to make arrangements for distribution of mail (as a rule the Jews were excluded from general postal service), to establish management of real estate, and, in places like Lodz, to take over servicing gas and electricity for the ghetto on behalf of the municipality. Last, but not least, when Passover approached, some of the ghettos created *ad hoc* commissions to take care of seasonal necessities, such as providing matzoth.

The administrative structure of the Councils grew in stages, accretions depending on the realities of life in the ghetto, the necessity to take care of ever growing tasks for the ghetto inmates, and the heavy duties imposed by the occupation authorities. The structure of the Councils also depended on the type of the ghetto: whether life was totally regimented by a forceful bureaucratic apparatus or some opportunities for free enterprise were left to the inmates. Added to everything else, the enormous paper work demanded by the supervisory authorities necessitated the establishment of new offices, if only to diminish the heavy workload of existing departments....

A Council seldom remained unaltered from beginning to end of its existence. Usually the opposite took place. Council members escaped, took cover, resigned, were arrested, were killed on the spot, or were deported; and others were nominated to take their places.

The reasons for this fluctuation among the Council members were twofold: an internal reason stemming from the Jews themselves, and an external one stemming from the Germans. In the majority of known cases, Jewish communal or civic leaders were unwilling to join the Councils. Elected or nominated members were moved to accept and, once accepting, to continue in their difficult positions only out of a fear of reprisals by the Gestapo or a sense of responsibility toward defenseless coreligionists, under the illusion that as Council members they might be in a position to ease the lot of the Jews. However, Council members perceived or imagined what they could expect. Naturally there were exceptions. Some ambitious individuals tried to get nominated as Council members for egoistic reasons, believing in the power ostensibly vested in them by the Germans. These included some who tried to play the role of intermediaries between the Germans and the Jews even before the Councils had been established.

The terror inflicted on the Jews and the Councils by the Germans from the very start of the occupation strongly influenced many Council members to relinquish the dangerous office, apprehensive of tasks the Germans might have in store for them.

There were various perilous means of avoiding membership in the Councils. Escape with or without one's family, was one of them, particularly at the early stages of occupation before the ghettos came into being. For example, we read concerning the first members of the Tarnow *Judenrat* that they

> have quickly gotten the right idea about the Germans' intentions. Dr. Josef Apner, the pride of the judicial profession in Galicia, whom the Germans forced to take over the leadership of the Council, soon relinquished his position, for he understood what the Germans would be asking of him. His substitute Lenkowicz, and the Council member Waksman, escaped to Lwów right after all the prayer houses and synagogues went up in flames one day.[8]

In Szczebrzeszyn "the members of the first Council quickly relinquished their office and, for the most part, escaped to the Russian-occupied area. Another Council was then elected."[9] An eyewitness account of events in Kalisz relates that "the Jewish Council disintegrated before the expulsion in the fall of 1939. The majority of the Council members escaped."[10] The first chairmen of the original Councils in Kolo, Plock, Przemysl, Boryslaw, Kutno, and many other places, also ran away.[11] In Warsaw six Council members were allowed to leave Poland in the winter of 1939–1940. A seventh member escaped abroad.[12] Later, when free travel for Jews was strictly curtailed, it became very difficult to escape.

Another form of expressing unwillingness to serve on the Jewish Councils was to resign. This, however, was highly dangerous. It required a lot of courage and determination to take such a step. In the *Gazeta Zydowska* (No. 16, February 25, 1941) an answer was printed to two inquiries addressed to the "Legal Corner." The inquirers were advised that changes of Council chairmen or changes in the composition of the Councils could take place only by a decision of the *Stadt-* or *Distrikthauptmann* or by voluntary resignation. The editor cautioned, however, that this was his own personal opinion based on an interpretation of the order establishing the Jewish Councils; he did not know whether the pertinent authorities would accept this view, since the order did not specifically mention the length of tenure of members or the procedure for changing the composition of the Councils. In the prevailing atmosphere of constant terror "voluntary resignations" were as unrealistic an idea as were the accounts themselves in the *Gazeta Zydowska*.

There were other cases of repression directed at Council members trying to resign. In Nowy Sącz a member resigned at the end of 1941 "because he was of the opinion that the Council ought to refuse to deliver Jews for the labor camps and let the Gestapo itself take whomever they wanted." Apparently at the demand of the German authorities, the ghetto police delivered him to the Gestapo. He was not seen any more.[13] A member of the Jewish Council at Kozienice (Radom district) resigned during the first weeks of the occupation and found refuge on the "Aryan" side. There were subsequent rumors that the Pole who had given him shelter killed him and buried him in a cellar. When his body was exhumed after the war, it was found that his head had been severed from his body.[14] "At first, respectable civic leaders in Krzemieniec participated in the Council. . . . After a short while, however, when they had realized its true character and tasks, they resigned."[15] A member of the Plock Jewish Council hid himself to avoid serving.[16] The first chairman of the Council at Bursztyn resigned. He had been appointed by the Ukrainian mayor, "but chose rather to work at hard labor together with all other Jews."[17] Another member gave the same mayor a suit as a gift to be released from serving on the Council.[18] In Ozierany, Council members tried to be released from membership on the local Council (although others paid large amounts for the privilege of becoming Council members").[19] The first chairmen of the Councils at Czyzów, Nowy Dwór, Staszow, and others also resigned.[20]

As a rule, however, nominated Council members, fearing Gestapo reprisals, did not resign or ask to be released from service. Those who gathered enough courage to try to get permission to resign were given "friendly advice" not to do so. Adam Czerniakow notes in his Diary under the date January 26, 1940: "In view of these events [cash extortions from the Council], I have asked the SS to relieve me of the chairmanship, because I am in no position to lead the community in such abnormal times. I was advised not to do so [for his own good]."

The makeup of Councils or the hierarchy of their membership was liable to changes because of internal controversies. The attitude prevailing in a given Council was also a very important factor. Changes in Council memberships, dismissal of old members, and nomination of new ones were, to a certain degree, the result of struggles and divergent opinions about tactics that should be used vis-à-vis the German authorities. Sometimes the struggles degenerated into wrangles about authority, in which the Germans became involved. Thus the first chairman of the Chmielnik Jewish Council had to resign under the pressure of opposition against him within the Council and the relief committee.[21] The sources do not always supply information as to the reasons for changes in the composition of the Councils, limiting their information to the mere fact that change took place. What actually happened in many cases can only be surmised by drawing analogies to known causes of change in other places.

Changes in the personnel of the Councils in Upper Eastern Silesia were made by Moshe Merin, chief of the Union of Jewish Communities in that part of the occupied territory. He made changes in order to pack the Councils with his own people.

In Czestochowa the presidium dismissed 10 Council members for "sabotaging the Council's activities" in 1940.[22] A former member of the Bursztyn Jewish Council relates that three members, including the chairman, were removed. They were replaced by three others who had previously been sent to the *Kreisamt* in Rohatyn to deliver a cash contribution ordered by the authorities. Whether this change was initiated by the Germans or by the Jews themselves is not indicated in the pertinent account. It is possible that the success of their mission to Rohatyn (under the protection of the Ukrainian police commandant) won the approval of the *Kreischef*, who may have forced upon the Bursztyn Council the decision to co-opt them to the Council in place of three members who had been fired.[23]

For the most part the German authorities instigated changes in the personnel of the Councils. The Germans bullied the Councils in every respect; they fired, arrested, and killed chairmen and members who happened to fall into the bad graces of the authorities, refusing to become obedient tools in the execution of German atrocities or violating the arbitrary rules in other ways. No legal norms were applied in the treatment of the Councils by the Germans. The principle of "local leadership" reigned supreme and without mercy. Whenever they considered it suitable to their own interests, the Germans would reduce or augment the number of Council members, disregarding their own orders concerning the number of the Council members (such as, for instance, Frank's order of November 28, 1939). In place of persons removed from the Councils, the Germans brought in people in whom they apparently had more confidence. Numerous chairmen and Council members were removed because they displeased the Germans by their independent attitudes or because their German masters simply did not like them. It often happened that the memberships of entire Councils were replaced by hand-picked people chosen from a list of names prepared in advance. Some of the Germans' protégés were placed in top positions. In cases where they could not find people suitable for their aims within the functioning Councils, they nominated new members from outside the Councils. . . .

Changes in the composition of the Councils or in the hierarchy of their members occurred especially often before or during "resettlement actions," when the authorities needed the full cooperation of the Councils and the ghetto police. As a rule, when Council members and policemen were themselves caught up in the deportations, they were replaced by new, though greatly reduced, Councils and police forces.

Sources illustrating the fluctuation caused by German interference, including arrests and murders of dismissed members, are so abundant that we must limit ourselves to only a small number of illustrations pertaining to the various occupied areas. The first Vilna Jewish Council of Ghetto No. 1 (the short-lived Ghetto No. 2 existed till the end of October 1941 and had its own Council) was established on July 4, 1941, with a membership of 10 (one resigned). On July 24 the Council received an order to increase the number of its members to 24, but at the beginning of August (the exact date is unknown), the *Gebietskommissar* ordered the Council to reduce its membership to the previous number.[24] On September 2, Schweinenberg, a Gestapo officer, came to the Jewish Council, arrested 5 Council members and 11 other persons (mainly Council functionaries who happened to be present on the premises at the time), and sent them all to the Lukishki jail for not delivering 10 carts on time as ordered (the order had been received the previous day, but because all carts belonging to Jews had long since been confiscated, the Council had hired five carts from gentiles and sent them to the headquarters of the *Ypatinga* [Lithuanian special police], which, however, had sent them back). None of these 16 persons returned from jail. Only six persons, of whom one was a Council member, were allowed to remain in the Council building after their documents had been checked. The Council actually stopped its activities.[25] When the ghetto was established, the Gestapo nominated one of the remaining Council members as head of the third

Council. The new chairman co-opted three members of the second Council and one more member from outside the Council. Thus this Council was limited to only five members.[26]

In Lódz, 20 or so of the 31 members of the first *Beirat* (the advisory council established during the first 10 days of October 1939), were summoned to the Gestapo office on November 7, 1939. All were arrested and deported to a penal camp not far from Lódz. . . . Some of the *Beirat.* members were shot to death or tortured, others were sent to concentration camps in Germany and perished there, and five members were sent to Cracow during the partial expulsion of Lodz Jews to certain parts of the Government General.[27] In the beginning of February, Rumkowski asked the police authorities to issue passes to members of his second Council.[28]

The first chairman of the Jewish Council at Lwów was Dr. Josef Parnas, a man in his seventies. He was a strong-willed person with a great deal of pride, descended from a noble, prosperous family, who had served as an officer in the Imperial Austrian Army. Dr. Parnas was arrested in October or November 1941, allegedly because he had refused to deliver Jewish forced laborers, and was shot in jail. The second chairman, Dr. Adolf Rotfeld, a prewar member of the executive of the Zionist organization in Eastern Galicia, died of "natural causes" in February 1942, according to pertinent sources—after only a few months in office. The third chairman, Dr. Henryk Landsberg, a well-known lawyer and prewar civic leader, was publicly hanged together with 11 Jewish policemen on the balconies of the Council building in September 1942. This was in reprisal for a Jewish butcher's resisting arrest by an ss-man, who happened to drop dead during the squabble. On the same day, 175 Council functionaries were shot. Dr. Eberson was then nominated Council chair-

man, saying, according to a witness, "I have gladly accepted the nomination. Maybe they will shoot me soon." His gloomy prediction came true. During the "action" that took place from January 5 to 7, 1943, Dr. Eberson was shot, together with a number of other Council members, after reporting for "selection" as ordered. Other Council members hid themselves. However, according to the witness who heard him say why he accepted the nomination to head the Council, Dr. Eberson committed suicide. Some of the Council members were sent to the camp at Janowska Street.[29]

In Horodenka (*Distrikt Galizien*) a Jewish Council of three members was established on orders from *Kreishauptmann* Winkler. After a while a "deceitful and money-greedy ss-man" was appointed *Kreishauptmann*. He dismissed the Council and appointed a larger one. Only the chairman of the former Council was included in the new Council.[30]

The story of the Council of Elders in Belchatów (*Wartheland*) is characteristic for the unceremonial, despotic manner in which the Germans governed the Councils. At first, the Council there consisted of 12 members, but in March 1940, apparently on orders from the *Kommandant* of the local gendarmes, the Council was reduced to three members. It seems that after the intervention by the local German mayor on April 2, 1940, the Council was enlarged to five members. But the new Council was not of long duration. It was dismissed on October 18, 1940, and a new one was appointed. The new chairman lasted for only a few days. He was arrested on October 23 and another chairman was nominated. He functioned until July 2, 1941. The composition of the entire Council was changed on that day and a new chairman, two members of the so-called *Beirat*, and new chiefs of welfare, food, forced labor, and other departments were appointed. This Council, the sixth one, functioned only until September 24, 1941, when the German mayor again ordered a change in its composition. The chairman of the fourth, formerly dismissed, Council was appointed to head the new one. Only two *Beirat* members remained. The chiefs of the departments were also changed. It is not known how long this, the seventh, Council was allowed to function.[31] Some reasons for these repeated changes in the composition of the Belchatow Jewish Council can be derived from the mayor's letter of October 20, 1940 (i.e., two days after the dismissal of the third Council), apparently addressed to the Council chairman, in which he and other dismissed members were accused of grumbling and agitating against the authorities. They all were warned of severe punishment if they tried to interfere with the authority of the new Council.[32] The extreme fluctuation of the Belchatów Jewish Council may have come also as a result of personal intrigues by some of its members who were trying to win the mayor's support for their personal aspirations.

In Konskie (Radom district) at the beginning of 1940 the Jews were ordered to elect a new Council in place of the first one.[33] The same happened in Mir, Mlawa, Kielce, and in many other places.[34] In Jaworów (*Distrikt Galizien*), the chairman was changed four times,[35] in Krzemieniec three times. The first chairman in Krzemieniec, Dr. Ben-Zion Katz, was condemned to death for not delivering a second list of Jews ostensibly for labor duty (he told the Germans that he would submit a second list after the men on his first list returned). A second chairman, the lawyer Jonas Grynberg, suffered a nervous breakdown, and only the third one lived till the tragic end of the ghetto.[36]

Some of the members of the Lancut Council (*Distrikt Galizien*) were arrested at the end of March 1942 during a conference called by the Gestapo at Jaroslaw. The majority of the Council members, expecting nothing good from the "conference," simply did not show up. According to another version, the German mayor warned one Council member, Dr. Pohorile, not to go. Eight members were therefore saved. Those who went to the "conference" were ordered to deliver 10 hostages. They refused and were arrested. Together with six other Jews seized randomly in the street, they were sent to Jaroslaw. All were shot in mid-July 1942. The authorities nominated a new Council, with the lawyer Rubin Nadel as its chairman.[37]

We have already indicated that before or during "resettlement actions" the authorities changed or reduced the Councils. In the Lublin Ghetto, during an extraordinary meeting on March 31, 1942 (an "action" had started there on the 17th), four ss-men came to the Council and told them, among other things, that the 24-man Council then in operation was to be reduced to 12 members. Six of the old Council, in addition to the vice chairman, one of the office functionaries, and five outsiders, were to be included in the new Council. The remaining 18 Council members were to be "resettled" in the next transport. The Council members destined for "resettlement" and who had their residence outside the ghetto (this was a rare privilege) were given a chance to go home, guarded by the Security Police, to fetch any personal belongings they might need. After that, their apartments would be sealed. The ss-men gave cynical assurances that the chairman and one member of the old Council would take over leading positions on the Council and in the jss [Jewish Social Welfare] in their new domicile because they had the necessary experience. The ss-men then nominated the vice chairman to be chairman of the new Council and nominated and assigned the duties of a three-member Council presidium.[38]

After the "action" in Horodenka, the *Kreishauptmann* called in Jewish representatives and, expressing his condolences for what had happened, accused the Ukrainians of requesting that the Germans decrease the number of Jews in town. He ordered the establishment of a new Council headed by Moryc Filfel, one of the "useful" Jews who had been released from among some Jews assembled in a prayer house for "resettlement."[39] In August 1942 the authorities nominated a new chairman of the Krasnobród Council (Lublin district), one month before the "resettlement action." He functioned until the ghetto was liquidated in February 1943.[40]

In Stanislawów (*Distrikt Galizien*) the authorities nominated new Councils after almost every "action." The first Council was nominated on July 26, 1941, immediately after the Germans had occupied the town. It was dismissed after the first slaughter, on October 12, 1941. The tenure of the second Council lasted till July 1942. All its members were then arrested and were not seen any more. Neither did the third Council last for long. In August 1942 all its members were arrested and publicly hanged. The fourth Council lasted until the liquidation of the ghetto in February 1943. Its members were shot on the 23rd of that month.[41]

Of the 24 members of the Jewish Council in Radom only 3 remained after the first "resettlement action" in mid-August 1942. The survivors were Dr. L. Fastman (who became Council chairman), Dr. N. Szenderowicz, and Dr. Zabner. Dr. Zabner and his wife committed suicide after they were arrested in the building of the criminal police. They had been accused of sending their two children over to the "Aryan" side in the course of the "resettlement." A certain Leon Yames replaced Dr. Zabner. Dr. Fastman was arrested on January 10, 1943, and sent to Auschwitz for not reporting that Dr. Dimant had come back to the ghetto from Szydlowiec (a nearby town). Ten days later, on January 20, Dr. Szenderowicz was

nominated Council chairman. On May 1, 1943, the Gestapo summoned all members and functionaries of the Council, carried them away to Wolanów (near Radom), where most of them were shot. The chairman and the members who survived were sent to Auschwitz.

The Attitude of the Councils toward Physical Resistance

Before analyzing Council attitudes toward physical resistance against the Germans, three aspects of the problem should be taken into account: (*a*) the objective chances for resistance, (*b*) resistance in relation to other prospects for rescue, and (*c*) the ethical positions of diverse segments of the Jewish population on the very idea of physical resistance. These matters are complicated, and we shall limit ourselves here to discussing only a few of them:

1. The situation of the Jews in the tightly sealed ghettos was such that the objective conditions for physically resisting the Nazi extermination machine with some hope of success simply did not exist.

2. The number of able-bodied males capable of fighting was continually reduced as a result of demographic changes among the ghetto inmates.

3. Because of complete isolation, it was next to impossible to get arms from the outside world, even if they had been offered.

4. There was a complete lack of arms (for instance, the Organization of Jewish Fighters in the Warsaw Ghetto was able to accumulate no more than 10 old pistols up to January 18, 1943, the day of the first attempt at armed resistance).

5. Gentile neighbors were hostile to the Jews except for certain democratic and socialist circles, parts of the liberal intelligentsia, and some of the clergy.

6. An endless mass of often conflicting German orders frustrated any plans for counteraction. The Jews in the ghettos were rendered physically and mentally weak by constant hunger, disease, and relentless terror. These conditions brought about widespread apathy and a fatalistic attitude, rendering long-range planning impossible, as is demonstrated by events in Vilna, Bialystok, and Czestochowa.[42] In addition, the perfidy of the Germans, sudden raids, roundups, and the graduated scale of extermination actions all contributed to the emergence of the illusion that the Jews who remained after each action would survive.

7. The Jewish underground movement could not rely on direct aid from any institution abroad, while the non-Jewish resistance groups systematically received arms, manpower, training, and money from their respective governments-in-exile in London. Without this support they could not exist, grow, or effectively perform.

Of the two basic forms of physical resistance, in the ghettos and in partisan units, the latter offered better prospects for rescue. Considering the chronology of the Holocaust, however, even these prospects were not too bright. It is important to bear in mind that the partisan movement in Eastern Europe, which perhaps provided a chance of rescue for small groups of escapees from the ghettos (because of the generally hostile attitude of the non-Jewish environment, purely Jewish resistance groups had very little chance of holding out), became a serious factor as late as the second half of 1942, at a time when the vast majority of Jews in the *Ostland* and the Ukraine had already been murdered, and when extermination in the areas of the Government General and the incorporated territories was already in full swing. Incidentally the partisan movement could have meaning only

for those ghettos in Eastern Europe situated close to Soviet partisan units, the only ones that were not openly hostile to escapees from the ghettos. The other ethnic partisan groups in that area—Polish, Latvian, Lithuanian, and Ukrainian (except the very small Communist groups)—not only did not admit Jews, but fiercely combatted ghetto refugees who tried to find shelter in the woods.

These and other tragic circumstances thwarted efforts to create meaningful Jewish resistance in the ghettos. To bring the problem into historical perspective it is sufficient to compare the objective fighting possibilities of Jews enclosed in ghettos to those of the resistance movements of non-Jewish segments of the populations in the occupied territories. It is clear that the prospects for armed Jewish resistance leading to rescue were quite minimal. Only young people in good health had a chance to free themselves from the condemned ghettos and reach the partisans, after hazardous peregrinations. The large majority of ghetto inmates—mothers with children, old, sick, emaciated people—were not able to go the long, dangerous way. Not many of those who joined the so-called family camps—groups connected with purely Jewish partisan groups (of the Belsky brothers, for instance)—survived.

There also were unfavorable subjective circumstances for physical struggle. Even during these most difficult times the Jews were confident that the world was not lawless. It was unthinkable that a government in the very heart of civilized Europe, even a Nazi one, should openly hold as its main political goal the physical elimination of an entire people, and it was unthinkable that the world would let it happen. This was one of the reasons why people did not believe in the terrible truth until the very end, when it was too late to plan or undertake anything. When the hideous truth revealed itself in its full horror on the thresholds of gas chambers or on the brinks of mass graves, the victims may have pondered whether it was worthwhile to fight for life after all in a world of limitless bestiality and passive silence.[43] It should also be borne in mind that the Orthodox population of non-Soviet Eastern Europe (constituting perhaps half the inmates of the ghettos) grew up amid the age-old Jewish tradition of spiritual heroism and martyrdom in times of oppression and was therefore historically and mentally unprepared and mostly opposed to the concept of physical resistance. These people were armed with quite different weapons: prayers and faith that the Almighty would have mercy on His oppressed people—that a miracle would happen in the end.

Another factor crippling the will to armed resistance was the nightmare of collective responsibility mercilessly imposed on the occupied areas by the Nazis—the fear that innocent people would suffer because of the resistance of small groups, that for each endeavor to resist or escape from the ghetto into the woods the Nazis would inflict collective reprisals on particular families and even on the entire ghetto. This anxiety sometimes rendered helpless even the most courageous young people in the underground organizations. As long as they remained in the ghettos with their parents and siblings, their feeling of responsibility for their families was a restraining factor against joining the resistance. Only on the eve or during the course of the last liquidation actions, when the end was obviously inescapable, did groups of young people or entire families escape from ghettos in Eastern Poland and *Ostland*, where there was a better chance to join partisans in the adjacent woods. They often paid a high price for their courageous endeavors.

One more factor hampering organized resistance by the Jews was the deep-seated conviction prevalent among some of the ghetto inmates—particularly the workers, artisans, and experts working for the benefit of the German war machine—that they had a good chance to survive because of their work but that this chance would be destroyed by attempts at resistance. This was the fundamental tenet of the entire rescue conception of the Jewish Councils, a tenet that adversely influenced the ghetto inmates by weakening their will to resist.

The majority of ghetto inmates maintained that resistance was not a real alternative to their desperate situation. They feared that it might even speed the liquidation process by giving the Germans an excuse to implement bloody repressions.[44] . . .

Believers in the idea of resistance could be found only among the politically conscious inmates—mostly party-affiliated young people. But even these men quarreled among themselves because of fear for the fate of helpless ghetto inmates and of their loved ones, and also because of their inability to agree on where the armed struggle with the enemy should be undertaken. Some believed that the Jewish resistance movement bore a historical responsibility to protect the lives and honor of the oppressed Jewish masses within the ghetto walls; others maintained that, in view of extremely adverse conditions for fighting within the ghetto, the best thing to do was to leave and join the partisans. Heated and prolonged discussions went on in the Vilna, Bialystok, and Warsaw Ghettos.[45]

Councils also grappled with this problem and sources testify to their dramatic, passionate discussions. One report describes the soul-searching debate of the Siauliai Jewish Council: on February 5, 1943, the Council of Elders called a meeting of the coworkers of the ghetto administration, the ghetto court, and members of the *Hechalutz* [Zionist pioneer] organization to discuss the burning problem: whether to start immediately to resist or to wait a little longer; whether to escape to the woods or join the Lithuanian resistance movement with which some contact had been established prior to the meeting. An evasive answer had been received from the Lithuanian underground: there were not enough arms, it would be hard for escapees to hide, etc. It became clear in the course of the discussion that only well-organized and armed young people had any chance of escaping from the ghetto into the marshlands of northeastern Lithuania, where Soviet partisans operated. Women, elderly or weak people, and children had no chance. As most of those attending the meeting were in these categories, the proposal to escape from the ghetto was rejected. The chairman, Mendel Leibowicz, suggested that the inmates be given arms to prepare for resistance within the ghetto and that the ghetto be set in flames on all sides at the critical moment, so that inmates would have a chance to escape. E. Yerushalmi, to whom we are indebted for this report, notes that apart from arms and a detailed plan, a strong will and readiness to sacrifice women and children were also needed. Those present at the meeting lacked both. This was the main reason why no underground organization was created in Siauliai.[46] . . .

We may therefore conclude that, as with other problems, there was no uniform opinion among the Jewish Councils on the problem of resistance. There were Councils with an extremely negative attitude both to resistance within the ghetto and to escape from the ghetto to join the partisans in the woods. On the other hand, there were Councils that sympathized with the resistance groups and supported them morally and materially. Still others were ambivalent, wavering in their attitude. There were also Councils that actively participated in resistance during the last period of the ghettos' existence.

NOTES

1. VBIGG, No. 13 (December 21, 1939), Par. 5; VBIGG 1, no. 18 (March 13, 1940), Par. 8.
2. VBIGG, Part 2 (1940): 23.
3. VBIGG, No. 1, 6–7; No. 13 (December 21, 1939); No. 14 (December 23, 1939).
4. *Bericht Warschau*, 7.
5. *Sprawozdanie*, 56.
6. ZC, Doc. 110.
7. Zaderecki, 445; testimony by Rabbi David Kahane, 15–16 (YIA); Gerszon Tafet, *Zalada Zydów zoliewskich* (Lódz, 1946), 25–26.
8. Turne. *Kiyum un khurbn fun a yidisher shtot* (Tel Aviv, 1954), 810, 811.
9. *Yilon leinformatsye veyediyot*, No. 4 (1952), 113.
10. Testimony No. G-28/328, 11–12 (YaVA).
11. Questionnaire No. 179; Questionnaires Nos. 281, 285, 286, 288, 289; in the first months of the occupation five members left for Warsaw; Questionnaire No. 355; Questionnaire No. 849.; RA, 2, No. 1155.
12. Questionnaires Nos. 49, 50, 52, 54, 65, 68.
13. Questionnaire No. 191.
14. Questionnaire No. 213.
15. *Pinkos Kremenets*, 252.
16. Questionnaire No. 284.
17. Questionnaire No. 244.
18. Testimony by Abraham Kalisher (YIA).
19. *Sefer Ozheran vehasviva, Encyclopaedia* (1959), col. 487.
20. *Yizkor-bukh Chizheve*, 926–27; testimonies Nos. G-53/679, B-48/681, in YaVA; *Sefer Stashev*, 418.
21. *Pinkos Khmielnik*, 731.
22. Brener, *op. cit.*, 15: from a source emanating from the Council (Rocznik 2, 11), which listed two different slates of Council members, it is evident that 10 persons left the Council and were replaced by others.
23. *Sefer Burshtyn, Encyclopaedia* (1960); testimony by Abraham Kalisher, 10.
24. Kruk, *op. cit.*, 25–28.
25. Ibid., 46–48.
26. Ibid., 69, 71; Dvorzhetsky, *op. cit.*, 44.

27. *Lodzher geto*, 30.

28. Eisenbach, *Getto Łódzkie*, 21–22.

29. Friedman, *Encyclopaedia*, 674–75; Diary of Zvi Radletsky (File E/37-2-2 in YaVA); testimony by Rabbi David Kahane.

30. *Sefer Horodenko*, 287.

31. AJHI, "Mss. about Cities," File No. 151, 29, 31, 105, 127.

32. Ibid., 30, 36. A denunciation against the Council chairman was placed before the Gestapo by the mayor on November 16, 1941, in which the chairman was accused of having contacts with smugglers (on whose behalf he interceded before the authorities) and with persons arrested by the Gestapo for political reasons. One can easily imagine the fate in store for a person so accused.

33. G.Z., No. 11 (August 28, 1940).

34. Testimony by Haim Wierzba in the YIA; *Pinkos Mlave*, 405–6; *Sefer Kelts*, 13; Dr. Peltz was allegedly deported to Auschwitz for refusing to perform lethal injections on sick people in the Jewish hospital.

35. Druk, *op. cit.*, 12–16.

36. *Pinkos Kremenets*, 268.

37. *Sefer Lantsut*, 363–64; English section of the book, xxxvi–xxxvii.

38. Minutes of the Council, No. 16/140, of the same date.

39. *Sefer Horodenko*, 290.

40. *Krasnobród, sefer zikaron* (Tel Aviv, 1956), 345, 352.

41. Ami Weitz, *Al Khorvotekha Stanislavuv* (Tel Aviv, 1947), 28, 44, 76–78, 95.

42. *Dapim min hadleyka*, 93–94; Brener, *op. cit.*, 64–65.

43. I. Trunk, "Yidisher vidershtand in der nazi-tkufe," *Shtudies in yidisher geshikhte in poyl*n (Buenos Aires, 1963), 302–3.

44. Reports on the "Witenberg day" in the Vilna Ghetto by Nusia Dlugi, Breine As, Shimon Palewski, Zhenie Berkman, and Mark Dvorzhetsky, *YIVO-Bleter* 30, no. 2: 188–213.

45. R. Korczak, *op. cit.*, 167–68; *Dapim min hadleyka*, 97–107 (minutes of the meeting of the members of the kibbutz Dror, in Bialystok February 27, 1943); address by Yitzhak Cukierman (Antek) at a meeting held in kibbutz Yagur, published in *Nasze Slowo* (Warsaw, April 1948); *Sefer hapartizanim hayehudim*, vol. 1 (Merkhavia, 1958), 570.

46. Yerushalmi, *op. cit.*, 315.

Isolation and Impoverishment

CHAIM KAPLAN

From *Scroll of Agony*

October 16, 1939

Life moves along by itself. There is no transportation, no water, no electricity. Everything creeps, and this has given foundation to flourishing rumors that the conquerors won't remain here. But there is one thing the conquerors do not ignore, that they return to incessantly, as though from the very outset they had come here for that purpose alone. A certain psychosis of hatred and loathing toward "the *Jude*" has infected them, and if they do anything with care and forethought, it is in the Jewish area.

Here are a few pearls in the course of one day: First, Mayor Starzynski, in the name of the local commissar appointed by the German military command, announced with special pleasure that the German-appointed courtyard commandants are required to furnish a list of the residents of each courtyard who require public assistance, and on the basis of this, everyone will receive a legal document entitling him to receive, free of charge, bread, meals, clothing, and linen which the city will furnish at its own expense—except for the Jews.

Second, in a conversation which lasted two minutes, and which assumed the character of an order through the addition of a threat that "otherwise, they alone are responsible for their lives," the Jewish Council was ordered to furnish a list of the Jewish residents of Warsaw from sixteen to sixty years of age. For what purpose? Nobody knows. But it is certain that it's not for the benefit of the Jews. Our hearts tell us that a catastrophe for the Jewry of Poland is hidden in this demand.

Third, Rosensztat, a Jewish pharmacist from Grzybowska Street, came to the conquerors with a request for "spirits," without which no drugstore can function. They asked him if he was a Jew. When he said yes, they informed him that he wouldn't receive any until he fired his Jewish employees, and that the manager, who until now had been Rosensztat himself, must also be an Aryan. Henceforward it is forbidden for the Jewish owner to cross the threshold of his own pharmacy. The Aryan manager will send the monthly accounts to him at home.

Fourth, the price of merchandise has gone down unnaturally—because everyone is afraid of confiscation. Jews plead with their Christian acquaintances to accept certain sums for safekeeping, so that they won't have to deposit anything in excess of 2,000 zloty in the bank under the supervision of the conqueror. But the Christian "friends" refuse, because their merchants' association has forbidden its members to give assistance to Jews in any form whatsoever.

Fifth, today Moshe Indelman, an editor of the newspaper *Hajnt*, was arrested. They told his wife that if her husband didn't return, she could find out about his fate at Third of May Street. M.I. is my friend and comrade. . . .

October 18, 1939

Our lives grow gloomier from day to day. Racial laws have not yet been formally decreed, but actually our defeat is inevitable. The conqueror says bluntly that there is no hope for Jewish survival. There is room for the assumption that a beginning is being made now.

So far there has been free trade in the streets. This is a trade of pennies, whose practitioners are boys and girls, young men and women driven to this sort of business by poverty. It is destined to be forbidden. It too will be taken out of the hands of the Jews. Every public place shows hatred and loathing toward the Jews. Isolated incidents of blows and violence against Jews have grown too numerous to count. Eyewitnesses tell horrifying stories, and they are not exaggerations.

The future of the schools for Jewish children is not yet known. In general the conquerors have no dealings with Jewish representatives. We are like grains of sand. There is no prior consultation regarding our own lives. They make decrees by themselves and there is no changing them. Reasons are not required. There is only one reason—to destroy, to kill, to eradicate.

Let anyone who wishes to consider the depths of the tragedy of Polish Jewry come to the Joint [American Joint Distribution Committee] building (13 Leszno Street) and see the vale of tears. But even the Joint has no legal authority, and the conqueror knows nothing of its existence. It is our good fortune that the Joint's funds are in the hands of the American consulate and the enemy has no access to them. Otherwise he would confiscate them to the last cent. But the Joint's relief money is like a drop in the ocean. Great God! Are you making an end to Polish Jewry? "The populace" cannot understand: Why is the world silent?

October 19, 1939

There are no schools, elementary or high, Jewish or Polish. Many school buildings were burned, and a school that has been burned will never rise again, with so many people homeless. Even the schools that remain are in ruins. There isn't a building in Warsaw whose windows haven't been broken, particularly on the side facing the street—and when any glass is available, they raise the prices exorbitantly. . . .

October 21, 1939

Some time ago I stated that our future is beclouded. I was wrong. Our future is becoming increasingly clear. Today the legal destruction began, with an order barring Jews from the two branches of the economy in which 50 per cent of the Jewish community supported itself. It makes one's blood freeze, and a man is ready to commit suicide out of desperation. This isn't just a small economic deprivation that makes things difficult but will not endanger our survival. It is a savage slash that has no equal in the history of the oppression of the Jewish people. The cruel decree is short and decisive, comprising only seven paragraphs, but it suffices to topple our entire economic structure. The decree says: It is strictly forbidden for Jews to trade in textile goods (manufactures) and processed hides (leather) and any sort of manufacturing that involves these materials. With terrible savagery the ax has struck at the most active artery of the Jewish economy. All violators of this order will be severely punished, even by capital punishment. After this it will be proper to say "blessed be the righteous judge" [the prayer said at funerals] for Jewish business in Poland. Besides the traders in hides and fabrics, thousands of Jews who were indirectly supported from this will be deprived of all livelihood. . . .

May 2, 1940

In a spiritual state like the one in which I find myself at this time, it is difficult to hold a pen, to concentrate one's thoughts. But a strange idea has stuck in my head since the war broke out—that it is a duty I must perform. This idea is like a flame imprisoned in my bones, burning within me, screaming: Record! Perhaps I am the only one engaged in this work, and that strengthens and encourages me.

When the conqueror runs rampant, he makes no distinction between Jews and Poles, even though he knows the Jew has no thoughts of revolt. The Pole is beaten for whatever sin he commits; the Jew is beaten day and night at every opportunity, whether he has sinned or not. When the day of reckoning comes the tyrant lumps them both together, and there is no escaping his wrath,

The prison on Dzielna Street is filled with prisoners, and therefore the entire area around it has become a place ripe for depredations. Gendarmes visit the area frequently, and every one of their visits leaves an impression on the bodies of Jews. The Nazis pass like a storm through the Jewish streets, whose inhabitants know from experience that many of them will come out of it toothless and eyeless. It is an attack of beasts of prey, devoid of any human feeling, upon innocent people walking unaware through the street. And not only upon men—women too are included. Even a mother standing by her baby's cradle is not secure against sudden attack. Sometimes the Germans beat people about the shoulders with long whips while sitting in a car driven along close to the curb; sometimes they pour down their blows while they stand outside the car. Then you see before you animals on two legs: murderous faces, a terrible fury of wild men in destructive rage. Whoever falls into their hands is reduced to a heap of bones. As I say, the Nazis make no distinction between men and women or, in the case of women, between a young girl and a mother beside a cradle. Today I saw with my own eyes how a Jewish baby's cradle

was turned upside down after they had beaten the miserable mother until she fell under the weight of her suffering. Her hysterical screams echoed through the entire street, but the Nazi gendarme carefully finished his "job" before he returned to his car.

Jewish passersby are aware of every appearance of a car whose occupants are the servants of the Führer. When they first notice it from a distance, a flight begins, an escape into the doorways of the houses. In a single instant the street takes on the appearance of a graveyard. In every place they go there is silence, and you won't find a single living soul on the street. Thousands flee, but many are caught. Fear reigns in every corner.

This is the custom every day of the year, so that occurrences of this sort are a fleeting thing, an act of the moment. Whatever happens, happens—and then the danger passes. Everyone returns to his work and his occupation. Life makes its own demands.

October 8, 1940

Jewish Joke I: The Germans are beating the Jews because England doesn't want to make peace; the Poles are beating them because the same England did not prepare herself properly for battle and is being defeated.

Jewish Joke II: The Führer asks Frank, "What evils and misfortunes have you brought upon the Jews of Poland?"

"I took away their livelihood; I robbed them of their rights; I established labor camps and we are making them work at hard labor there; I have stolen all their wealth and property." But the Führer is not satisfied with all these acts. So Frank adds: "Besides that, I have established *Judenraten* [*sic*] and Jewish Self-Aid Societies."

The Führer is satisfied, and smiles at Frank. "You hit the target with the *Judenraten*, and Self-

Aid will ruin them. They will disappear from the earth!" . . .

Frank came to Warsaw to inaugurate the aid project for next winter. Notices written in German in huge letters joyfully announced his arrival. *Volksgenossen* [Germans] were ordered to hang out flags in honor of the guest. German Warsaw was jubilant. And do not be surprised when I say "German Warsaw," even though its German population is only a negligible minority. Here quantity is not important, quality is the determinant. One German outweighs a thousand Poles and tens of thousands of Jews.

The Germans have the power now, and they are the real lords of the city. The war broke out for their benefit, and they were a main political cause of the conquest of Poland and its loss of sovereignty. The whole world was created just for them. Poland is no longer Polish even ethnographically. Don't ask where twenty million Poles disappeared to! German science which serves Nazism has caused them to disappear—and not more than ten million Poles can be found. And those who remain are obviously not worthy to rule. As for the Jews, they don't count at all. They are cattle. When the conquerors' newspapers wrote about Lodz and its industrial development they didn't mention the Jews even obliquely. It was as if they had never existed.

Frank's coming made no special impression on the city. They didn't turn out to see him and his companions; in fact the population pretended not to notice him. Everyone ignored this tyrant whose wickedness and cruelty are even greater than that of the Führer. This is good. It is a sign that the Poles have a political sense. Even though great military and political changes bode ill for their future, they remain stubborn. You will not find one single public-spirited citizen among them who is willing to be the conquerors' representative, to talk to his people and make them realize that they cannot change reality and must accept the yoke of German rule—like Hacha in Czechoslovakia and Quisling in Norway.

October 10, 1940

Clouds are covering our skies. Racial segregation is becoming more apparent each day. Yesterday an order was published that the Jews must make way before every German, both soldiers and civil servants in uniform. Making way means that the Jews must step aside until the Germans leave the sidewalk. You must always keep your eyes open and guard yourself against daydreaming and conversation lest you fail to do the proper honor to a Nazi you encounter. Today we have already had our first victims, who were beaten because of the order. You go out trembling, full of panic lest you meet a Nazi.

All people whose ancestors did not stand before Mount Sinai are allowed to walk in the streets until eleven at night. For Jews outside the walls, the curfew is seven; inside the walls, nine. In the morning, no Jew who lives outside the walls can be on the street before eight.

The Jewish trolley is a mockery of the poor. Trolley cars with white trim (for Aryans only) with two cars pass by empty, while dozens of passengers wait at the stop; no one dares to enter the empty cars because it is not a Jewish trolley. In the Jewish tram, the crowding and pushing make it almost impossible to breathe. No one standing can sit down, and no one sitting can get up. The passengers neither sit nor stand, but rather hang—it is like the plague of darkness in the land of Egypt. There is no filthier place, capable of spreading contagious diseases, than a Jewish trolley on a single ride, where everything is infected, when sick people sweat and slobber on you.

Yet with all this the Jews are "content with their lot" and say decisively that the maximal evil has not yet come, that there is some sort of psycho-logical barrier preventing the conquerors from pouring their full wrath upon us. Here the Jews surmise: What will happen to us when a new war breaks out between the conqueror and Russia-America? Then we will simply be eradicated. The Bolshevik land will again be called a Jewish state and the United States all the more so.

October 12, 1940, End of Yom Kippur, 5701

On the New Year we prayed illegally. The ban on communal worship was still in effect. In secret, in side rooms near the dark, closed synagogues we prayed to the God of Israel like Marranos in the fifteenth century.

But one day before the eve of the Day of Atone-ment the *Zyd* newspaper reached us from Cracow, bringing us permission for communal worship. This permission was not unconditional, however. It is still forbidden to pray publicly in the syn-agogues, and they remain locked. The law was relaxed only to permit communal worship in small groups in private homes, on condition that they don't make noise and that there is no crowding.

The Jewish community of Warsaw left noth-ing out in its prayers, but poured its supplications before its Father in Heaven in accordance with the ancient custom of Israel. To our great sorrow, as the day drew to a close, at a time when the gates of tears were still open, we learned that a new edict had been issued for us, a barbaric edict which by its weight and results is greater than all the other edicts made against us up to now, to which we had become accustomed.

At last the ghetto edict has gone into effect. For the time being it will be an open ghetto, but there is no doubt that in short order it will be closed. In Lodz the ghetto edict was not carried out all at once, but rather step by step, and many signs indicate that it will be the same in Warsaw. After

the ghetto plan was postponed two weeks ago, we were almost tranquil. But the enemy of Israel neither sleeps nor slumbers.

Before the thirty-first of October the Jews who live in the streets outside the walls must move lock, stock, and barrel to the streets within the walls; and all the Aryans (read Poles) living in the streets within the walls must move to the Aryan quarter. To a certain extent the edict has hurt the Poles more than the Jews, for the Poles are ordered to move not only from the ghetto, but from the German quarter as well. Nazism wants to separate everyone—the lords by themselves, the under-lings by themselves, the slaves by themselves. The blessed and the accursed must not mingle.

A hundred and twenty thousand people will be driven out of their homes and will have to find sanctuary and shelter within the walls. Where will we put this great mass of people? Most of them are wealthy, accustomed to beautiful apartments and lives of comfort, and they will be totally impov-erished from now on. Their businesses and live-lihoods were directly connected with the areas where they lived. In leaving their homes they are also leaving their incomes.

The Gentiles too are in mourning. Not one tradesman or storekeeper wants to move to a strange section, even to an Aryan section. It is hard for any man, whether Jewish or Aryan, to start making his life over. And so the panic in cap-tured Warsaw, occupied by harsh masters, is great. As I have said, for the time being we are in an open ghetto; but we will end by being in a real ghetto, within closed walls.

Hundreds of Germans are coming in, refugees from the English bombs, half-mad women with their children. They complain angrily to their fat, comfortable relatives who are enjoying the spoils of a strange land out of all danger. An eyewitness reports that a German soldier dared to write these words on the wall of one of the trolley cars: *"Wir fahren hin und her. Wir haben kein Heimat mehr*! [We ride back and forth. We have no more homeland!].

Maybe this is the beginning of the removal of the yoke that Churchill is trying so hard to accomplish . . .

November 10, 1940

The conquerors' radio emphasized and reemphasized that this is not a ghetto, but rather a Jewish quarter, like the Polish quarter or the German quarter. In whispers, the constant rumor was that Roosevelt had a hand in these concessions. The oppressed Jewish masses enjoy rumors of this sort. It is good in our terrible troubles to believe that some mighty hand is guiding us, that our sufferings are seen and our sighs are heard. But we woke up, and our souls were empty.

In our favor there were flourishing, unfounded rumors; against us there were unalterable, hard facts. All the concessions were blown away like smoke. A time extension was given only once, and that was for the benefit of the Poles. We had hopes for Praga, that the edict would be softened in its favor, but it was a dream. By the fifteenth of November not a Jew will be left there. A city of fifty thousand Jews is going into exile.

Most significantly, in all the thoroughfares leading to the Aryan quarters high walls are being erected blocking the paths to the Aryan world before us. At present only the streets united with the Jewish ghetto by car tracks are still open. Wherever you turn the murderers have blocked the way. Moreover, the walls being erected now are higher and sturdier than the ones that were put up earlier. Before our eyes a dungeon is being built in which half a million men, women, and children will be imprisoned, no one knows for how long. The *Judenrat* is building this great mass grave with

its own funds. All of this is a clear proof, because if the conquerors wished to leave the ghetto open they would not need to build high, fortified walls to block the path of life before us.

The *Judenrat* is burdened with much other work in preparing to organize life within a closed ghetto. Under its supervision a Jewish police force is being recruited which will have authority over the buried-alive Jews of the ghetto. Nine thousand young men have already registered as candidates for this force. By the way, each applicant included a five-zloty registration fee, which even the abject poor paid in the hope of being accepted for the ghetto police, although there will be salary for these policemen. Among the other preparations are negotiations with the Aryan owners of pharmacies in the Jewish quarter. In the area set aside for the ghetto there were formerly twenty-one pharmacies, seven of them Jewish, the rest Aryan. As soon as the conquerors came the Jewish druggists were pushed out of their businesses. Now, with the creation of the ghetto, the conquerors intend to leave in the area only eleven pharmacies, which will be under the supervision of the *Judenrat* and will once again have Jewish personnel. The same applies to the management of Jewish-owned apartment houses. From now on there will be no room for Aryan managers. The houses will be turned over to the control of the *Judenrat*, which will employ the agents removed from them by force and deprived of their livelihoods. All of these are bad signs.

The day is not distant when we will be penned in like cattle, forcibly removed from the outside world like a camp of unclean lepers. . . .

November 19, 1940

If it were said that the sun has darkened for us at noon it would not be merely a metaphor. We will molder and rot within the narrow streets and the crooked lanes in which tens of thousands of people wander idle and full of despair.

The matter of food supplies, in particular, has contributed to confusion. Since communication between us and the villages is cut off, our food will be given to us by the conquerors. This will amount to ninety-percent starvation. What good will ten decagrams of coarse bread a week do?

Anger at black marketeering has become tremendous. The wealthy and even the ordinary well-to-do had hoarded food. Only the poor are left with nothing, because they couldn't afford to stock up. It is they who are the victims of the black marketers and it is hard to see them in their distress. There is nowhere to earn a penny. Toil and poverty were their lot even in ordinary times, and now a ton of coal costs 800 zloty; a loaf of coarse bread, three zloty; a litre of milk, two zloty; a kilo of butter, 30 zloty. And so on. . . .

December 2, 1940

Life in the ghetto is becoming "normal." The chaos lasted no more than a week. When half a million people are locked in a small cage, faced with hunger, privation, epidemics, atrocities, naturally it causes a stir. Even the conquerors were confused. This is a unique political experiment. The intention was to starve and impoverish us in body and in spirit, to segregate us from the outside world; to undermine our very existence. A great project of this sort demands extraordinary exertions and cannot be brought into effect by words alone. But to our sorrow, it must be admitted that the tyrants succeeded.

Entry and exit permits are given only to Aryan officials who hold posts in one of the government institutions within the ghetto. Certain Jews too get permits of this sort, and these include the Jewish Gestapo agents, the destroyers from our midst, as well as an insignificant number of indi-

viduals who fill some important position of service for the government in an institution outside the ghetto boundaries. Aside from these, there are also Jewish boys under the age of ten, who, not being marked by the "badge of shame," sometimes manage to sneak across the border because the border guards do not recognize that they are the children of the inferior race. These children are clever, and they are sent by their parents to buy food cheaply. Usually they are successful in their mission and bring home bargains. This week I got a bargain of this sort myself: a quarter-kilo of butter for six zloty, which our relative Emek brought in from the other side of the wall. God bless him!

While the rich were hoarding food the poor were going around mourning and desolate, their eyes expressing anger at those complacent people upon whom the famine had not yet made an impression. This jealousy, which was like a fire contained within their bones, prompted such talk as: "Let them hoard to their hearts' content. When we're starving we will take it by force. Justice does not require allowing the bourgeoisie to enjoy all good things at a time when the people are dying of starvation." . . .

April 3, 1941

Like the Egyptian Passover, the Passover of Germany will be celebrated for generations. The chaotic oppression of every day throughout this year of suffering will be reflected in the days of the coming holiday. Last year the Joint's project was functioning full force. It was not conducted properly and many people criticized it, but in the last analysis it fed the hungry and brought the holiday into every Jewish home. We lacked for nothing then.

This year everything is changed for the worse, and we are all faced with a Passover of hunger and poverty, without even the bread of poverty. First of all, the Joint has divested itself of all activity in connection with the holiday. In effect it has disappeared from the communal stage, and its voice is no longer heard. Self-Aid support is also a matter of leaning on a shattered reed, and the new taxes did not help to ease its burdens. We thought they would quiet our fears about the support of the soup kitchens, but we were wrong. We Jews are not afraid of a Jewish government. Many evade payment of the tax, and no threat of punishment does any good with the misers. If the Jews of Warsaw who are able to pay had obeyed Czerniakow's decree and turned over the tax of two zloty apiece each month willingly, the problem of feeding the hungry would not be so serious. The courtyard committees who were charged with the assessments had to fight the miserable creatures for every penny. A strong, healthy father of a family of five, who spends 30 zloty a day for the needs of his household and whose home is filled with good things, was ready to put out the eyes of the chairman of the courtyard committee because he would not give him a reduction on his assessment of two zloty per person. "A poor man like me pay ten zloty a month? God in heaven!"

And so there were arguments and quarrels in every courtyard. The members of the courtyard committees are the scapegoats.

The end result is that the collection of the tax goes on with the greatest difficulty. In theory the recalcitrants should be punished, and there is even a special office for this purpose. But this punishment-machine does not function at the necessary tempo. The courtyard committees overlook much, out of their unwillingness to make enemies, and the punishment office overlooks much for personal reasons. The result of all this is that the tax has not improved the situation and the soup kitchens are closed almost every other day.

As the holiday drew near, the Self-Aid made the customary Passover appeal for money for the poor. But this project was born in an unlucky hour and its results will be nil. At present—one week before the holiday—the project's treasury is empty.

What, then, will we eat during the eight days of the coming holiday? I am afraid we will turn our holiday into a weekday. For prayer there are no synagogues or houses of study. Their doors are closed and darkness reigns in the dwelling places of Israel. For eating and drinking there is neither matzoth nor wine. . . .

January 4, 1942

The words of the poet have come true in all their dreadful meaning: "'Tis not a nation nor a sect but a herd." Gone is the spirit of Jewish brotherhood. The words "compassionate, modest, charitable" no longer apply to us. The ghetto beggars who stretch out their hands to us with the plea, "Jewish hearts, have pity," realized that the once tender hearts have become like rocks. Our tragedy is the senselessness of it all. Our suffering is inflicted on us because we are Jews, while the real meaning of Jewishness has disappeared from our lives.

Our oppressors herded us into the ghetto, hoping to subdue us into obedient animals. Instead, however, we are splitting and crumbling into hostile, quarrelsome groups. It is painful to admit that ever since we were driven into the ghetto our collective moral standard has declined sharply. Instead of uniting and bringing us closer, our suffering has led to strife and contention between brothers. The Nazis, possibly with malice aforethought, put us in the hands of the *Judenrat* so that we might be disgraced in the sight of all. It is as if they were saying, "Look at them! Do you call them a people? Is this your social morality? Are these your leaders?"

It is not at all uncommon on a cold winter morning to see the bodies of those who have died on the sidewalks of cold and starvation during the night. Many God-fearing, pious souls, who, if the day happens to be the Sabbath, are carrying the *tallith* [prayer shawl] under their arms, walk by the corpses and no one seems to be moved by the sight. Everyone hastens on his way praying silently that his will not be a similar fate. In the gutters, amidst the refuse, once can see almost naked and barefoot little children wailing pitifully. These are children who were orphaned when both parents died either in their wanderings or in the typhus epidemic. Yet there is no institution that will take them in and care for them and bring them up as human beings. Every morning you will see their little bodies frozen to death in the ghetto streets. It has become a customary sight. Self-preservation has hardened our hearts and made us indifferent to the suffering of others. Our moral standards are thoroughly corrupted. Disgraceful as it may sound, we must admit the bitter truth: Everyone steals! Petty thievery, such as picking pockets or stealing a hat or an umbrella, is common. Because kosher meat is terribly expensive, people have relaxed their observance of the laws regarding the eating of kosher food. Not only atheists and derelicts are guilty of this, but synagogue sextons and pious men as well.

Nazism has forced Polish Jewry to degrade itself thus. Nazism has maimed the soul even more than the body! . . .

Choiceless Choices

GORDON J. HORWITZ

From *Ghettostadt: Łódź and the Making of a Nazi City*

Soon enough the unsettling anxieties of that dreadful summer [1942] were to culminate in the terrible realization that the sick, the elderly, and above all the children of the Łódź ghetto were indeed targeted for removal. What had occurred in the Jewish communities in the outlying provinces was to happen here as well. In spite of the growing sense of threat, the blow, when it came, was experienced as a shock of unimagined magnitude, leaving those who survived it forever scarred. All that [Chaim] Rumkowski [the head of the Jewish Council] had staked in attempting to secure his people's survival by diligently serving the Germans, accommodating their perceived economic goals, and obediently executing even the most unwelcome of their demands, was to be tested as never before.

At seven o'clock on the morning of Tuesday, September 1, three years to the day since the invasion of Poland and a day similarly beautiful and bright, pedestrians walking past the ghetto hospitals on Łagiewnicka, Drewnowska, and Wesoła streets noticed what struck them as the curious if at first unalarming appearance of what were described as military trucks just then driving up to the buildings.[1] Of late, rumors had circulated to the effect that in order to clear space for the creation of additional workshops, the hospitals were soon to be closed, their patients and medical facilities transferred to barracks currently under construction on Krawiecka and Tokarzewski streets.[2] But this work was nowhere near completion, and even more unsettling, it would have been highly unusual for the Germans to send military transports to the ghetto to accomplish the task. Apprehension mounted as observers took note of the unusually heavy presence of Jewish policemen in the vicinity of the hospitals, keeping the growing crowds, increasingly drawn by the strange goings-on, from approaching. That same apprehension quickly turned to panic when they saw the Germans roughly forcing patients out of the buildings, even pushing some children from the windows, and piling them onto the vehicles. Stunned, bystanders soon realized that they were witnessing not just the closure of the hospitals but the beginning of the wholesale deportation of the patients.[3]

[Hans] Biebow [the head of the German ghetto administration] was on the scene, a fact he would acknowledge at his postwar trial in 1947 even while denying in the face of eyewitness testimony that he had approved or participated in such acts of brutality.[4] One of those Jewish eyewitnesses, hiding in a linen closet of the Łagiewnicka Street hospital to avoid being seen, first spied Biebow passing along the corridor in the company of two unidentified "high-ranking" men in uniform. Biebow was speaking of the need to speed the operation. Shortly thereafter, patients at the nearby medical facility on Mickiewicza Street, by now alerted to the threat, began climbing from the windows and taking flight. Biebow rushed to the scene. Rounding the corner at Łagiewnicka

Street, quickly assessing the fast-moving events unfolding before his eyes, he reportedly struck a woman and, seizing a man by the hair, dragged him back to the building before hustling down to the corner and shouting for uniformed assistance.[5] Szyja Teitelbaum, who had been passing through the vicinity, remembered noticing Biebow shouting at three young people; he ordered them into a garden and made them turn to face a tree. When Gestapo officers Fuchs and Stromberg arrived, the men "all drew their revolvers and fired. Biebow was standing in the middle. I got a good look," Teitelbaum insisted, "because I was standing at a distance of 6–7 meters from the incident."[6] Hersz Janowski, a ghetto cart driver, also spotted Biebow in the company of these same agents participating in the murder of three youths, aged in his estimation around sixteen to seventeen years old. "Each of the three Germans shot one of the boys from behind," he said, and Biebow was heard crudely joking about it.[7]

Meanwhile, Rumkowski, "in the hospital on Drewnowska Street since early morning," appears to have been attempting, with unspecified success, to intervene, presumably in order to exempt certain individuals from the *Aktion*, as did the director of the Order Service's Special Department, Dawid Gertler, who, taking up position in the main hospital on Łagiewnicka Street, was "surrounded by petitioners of every sort."[8] The Germans were not in the least inclined to let any escapees off the hook. The Jewish Order Service was consequently charged with hunting them down and delivering them for removal with the rest. The Germans demanded a quota of two hundred persons, instructing that should some of the fugitive patients prove unrecoverable, their relatives were to be seized in their stead; also declared eligible for seizure was anyone "who had applied for admittance to the hospital," regard-

less of whether he or she had been a patient on the morning of September 1. The Order Service complied as instructed.[9]

The following Friday, September 4, was intensely sunny and hot. At two in the afternoon posters went up announcing an assembly set for 3:30 in the fire department square, where at last Rumkowski and other leaders were going to address the ghetto. In advance of the assembly rumors had it that perhaps the children were to be spared after all, or that the *Aktion* was to be put off for another three months. But these were only conjectures. In tears, mothers were already nervously crowding around officials to appeal on behalf of their children. On the main pedestrian bridge over Zgierska Street there was unusually heavy traffic. Rumkowski's carriage had been seen passing at high speed. The atmosphere was feverish. It looked, said one observer, as if "all hell has broken loose." On top of everything else, with the shops and workplaces now to be closed the following day, people were worried about the shortfall in the day's rations. Amid the restlessness of the moment, however, there were pockets of apparent calm. . . . But the general mood of the ghetto was tense, if not desperate. Another rumor had it that Polish workers, operating under German supervision, were digging graves on Wolborska Street. Everyone anxiously awaited the promised words of the chairman.[10]

Even in advance of definite news, parents were half crazed over the prospect of losing their children. "Mothers race about in the streets, one shoe on and the other off, half of their hair combed and the rest unkempt," wrote Josef Zelkowicz, "kerchiefs half draped over their shoulders and half dragging on the ground." As yet, however, the worst had not happened. "They still have their children. They can still clutch them fiercely to their shriveled bosoms. They can still kiss their clear eyes. But what will happen afterwards, in another hour, tomorrow? Rumor has it that the children will be removed from their parents today and sent away on Monday. Sent away—where?"[11] But at least "for now, for the moment, every child is still with his mother." In consequence, mothers would lavish small luxuries upon their children: their "last loaf of bread" and, if available at all, some margarine to go with it, even a bit of sugar.[12] "Today, the ghetto has cast aside all thoughts of the future. It is living for the moment, and for the moment every mother is clutching her child." Attended with such unexpected solicitousness, the children could not help but wonder: "Am I ill?" Yet logic led them to ask: "If I am ill, why am I walking about the streets? Why don't they make me stay in bed? Why don't they take me to a doctor?" Zelkowicz knew the truth: "But they are very ill, these wretched Jewish children. They are like baby birds, and like sick birds they are doomed to die."[13] Facing imminent deportation, an elderly person of sixty-five or older might in the end give up, resigned to an unalterable fate, reasoning that "one can't live forever anyway, and what does it matter anymore—to die a few days, a few weeks, even a few years earlier than otherwise?" Again likening the endangered ghetto youngsters to little birds, Zelkowicz could not countenance the same resignation with respect to "the children, who have just poked through their eggshells, whose first glimpse of God's world was through the prism of the ghetto, for whom a cow or a chicken are creatures from the land of fantasy, who have never sensed the fragrance of a flower, the shape of an orange, or the flavor of an apple or pear—is their fate sealed? Must they experience the terror of death at this early juncture[?]"[14]

Time's relentless passage never seemed more acute. No one cheated time. Whether old or young, with each passing day, everyone was one

day closer to death. But the inhabitants of the ghetto also knew that for every man, woman, and child there existed in the accounts of the ghetto population registry a second, representational self in which, for administrative purposes, his or her official age was listed. Although time could not be fooled, records were alterable: if only on paper, an elderly person might miraculously be made to appear suddenly more youthful, a little boy or girl instantly more mature. A clean erasure, perhaps, or a precise mark, and at a stroke what was a 3 could be reborn a 13. But the Department of Population Records, under the pressure of the hour, was made off limits. On the night of September 3–4, its bureau was "sealed" to public access.[15]

Meanwhile, at 4 Koscielny Street the Evacuation Committee (the Resettlement Commission referred to in the *Chronicle* [the daily record of developments and events compiled by Jewish officials in the ghetto]) had set up headquarters on a separate floor of the same building as the population registry, where employees were busily compiling lists of candidates for removal from the ghetto.[16] Yet, given the widespread uncertainty over the precise age categories involved, the evacuation bureau was quickly thrown into a state of "chaos, commotion and confusion." Apparently at the start even the chief members of the committee, "Mr. Jakobson, Mr. Blemer, Mr. Rosenblatt, Mr. Neftalin, and Mr. Greenberg," were in the dark with regard to where they were to draw the lines defining the targeted population, and this uncertainty resulted in contending interpretations of the edict. If, as the decree asserted, "the stipulated age was from one to ten," did that not mean that infants under twelve months were excluded and to be left untouched? Or was the measure actually to be "applied to children from the age of one minute up to nine years and three hundred and sixty-five days"? So too there were "similar disagreements about the elderly: did it include those aged sixty-five, or did it begin only after the completion of one's sixty-fifth year?"[17] Nor was it at all clear whether possession of papers might serve to exempt an individual from eligibility for removal.[18]

Ghetto inhabitants were only too aware that, however the regulation was interpreted, even those who were healthy, employed, and neither too young nor too old were hardly out of the woods. And should they be spared, they still had to worry about the fate of their children and elderly parents. For word got out, and this time it was true, that together the young children and the elderly, even when all had been seized, would constitute only about thirteen thousand persons, while the demanded quota amounted to some twenty thousand. If so, this meant that others outside the targeted categories would be taken as well. And given the reports that exemptions were to be made for the families of ghetto police and firemen, and workshop managers and other officials as well—a rumor that would also turn out to be true—it was clear that the circle of potential victims would have to widen even further to make up "the difference." As always, those who lacked rank and connections would be the most exposed. Such awareness only spurred the desperation and panic in the streets.[19] Scenes at the remaining food centers still open that day were especially tense. "The shoving and congestion were so terrible that even people who pushed their way through to the distribution yard received their potatoes helter-skelter amid an orgy of fury and madness. Most of the mob, however, after a full day of queuing, went away just as they had come—with empty sacks."[20]

On the afternoon of the fourth, in anticipation of Rumkowski's arrival a crowd estimated at 1,500, among them a large number of concerned parents with children at their side, and many elderly men and women, gathered outside the firehouse at 13 Lutomierska Street to await further news of their fate. In spite of the bright sun and the intense heat of the lengthening afternoon, a cluster of spectators, shunning the patch of shade off to the side, claimed positions close to the speaker's platform. Determined to keep the public at a more comfortable remove so as to control the crowd, the ghetto fire chief, Henryk Kaufman, officiously directed those in front to step aside. Given the evident anxiety gripping those present, Kaufman's brusque demeanor seemed strikingly inconsiderate, and was likely, Zelkowicz thought, a reflection of a lack of concern born of the knowledge that whatever the scope of the impending tragedy, he and his own family would remain unaffected.[21]

Belatedly, at 4:45 Rumkowski appeared, making his way to the podium accompanied by two advisers, Dawid Warszawski, "senior manager of the needleworkers' workshop," and Stanislaw-Szaja Jakobson, head judge of the ghetto court and experienced co-coordinator of the year's prior deportations.[22] It was clear at a glance that Rumkowski himself was weak, unsteady; his movements were slow and painful, and he seemed to shuffle forward like "a frail old man who can barely put one foot in front of the other." Rumkowski's crown of "white hair" now appeared noticeably unattended, displaying "unkempt tufts" atop a head that was no longer held erect but was uncharacteristically "stooped, as if he [could] hardly hold it atop his shoulders." As for his mouth, "the tsk-tsk motions of his lips" left no doubt that from them would issue "not even one word of consolation."[23]

Reticent, holding back, Rumkowski came forward only to announce that Warszawski would be the first to address the assembly. Warszawski immediately laid out the details of the decree, forthrightly acknowledging its terrible dimensions while arguing that the ghetto must bow to its demands in full and at all costs. To be sure, he offered a word on Rumkowski s behalf, noting the irony that of all people, this man whose life had been dedicated to the education of children should now be compelled to take upon himself the anguish of directing the forcible removal of young children from the ghetto. Sad as this surely was, Warszawski insisted that for the community there was "no choice" but to submit. "The sentence has been handed down. It is irrevocable. They are demanding sacrifices and sacrifices must be made." By way of justification he invoked the specter of events known to be occurring in Warsaw, where that very summer, in operations still under way, the ghetto was being ruthlessly cleared of nearly its entire population: "There was a decree such as this in Warsaw, too. We all know—it is no secret—how it was carried out." Although his name was not mentioned, in what may have been a veiled allusion to the passive defiance of Adam Czerniaków, head of the Warsaw Jewish Council, who, faced in July with an order to assist in assembling children and others for deportation, had taken his own life, Warszawski, speaking for the Jewish leadership in Łódź, declared that failure to cooperate with the decree would only compel the Germans to use their own forces to do the job. "But we have decided to do it ourselves," he explained, "because we do not want and are unable to transform it into a horrific, terrible disaster." In order to avoid a repetition in their streets of what was happening in Warsaw, there could be no other choice but to cooperate and carry out the evacuation by their own hands, and in this way alone at least ameliorate the effect. "Can I give you any solace? Any comfort?" he said to the crowd. "I can tell you only one thing. It may calm and console you a little: It seems, according to all indications, that we will be able to stay on here uneventfully after the decree."[24] He would be right

about that point, but it is doubtful that any who heard it could have followed the weak logic of a final, supposedly consoling thought: Warszawski asked them to consider that, in the conceivable event that Litzmannstadt [the German name for Lodz] might be subject to air assault, and inhabitants of the ghetto forced quickly to seek shelter, it would be better if adults were not encumbered by the elderly and the very young. Coming at the end of an otherwise forthright presentation, the idea, to say the least, sounded unconvincing.[25]

Judge Jakobson, next to mount the dais, could only underscore Warszawski's sad revelations, though adding that, of the figure of twenty thousand which his predecessor had noted would constitute the ultimate number of deportees the Germans were demanding, the projected daily quota would be three thousand.[26] More significantly, Jakobson revealed that "to prevent disasters" during the course of the operation the entire ghetto would be subject to a curfew.[27] It was clear, however, in whose interests it was to confine the population to their residences for the duration of the roundup. "Everyone knows that the Evacuation Committee wanted it this way to make its work easier," wrote Zelkowicz. "How simple it is to make everyone wait at home and be ready to be hauled away, obviating the need for a search."[28] All the same, both Warszawski and Jakobson had at least been forthcoming in regard to "the truth about the number of deportees, the types of people to be sent away, and the curfew," an improvement, Zelkowicz thought, over proffering "half-truths, rumors and random conjectures." But the assembled had yet to hear from Rumkowski. It was now his turn to speak.[29]

This time there would be none of his typical bombast, none of his famed self-puffery; today there would be no haughty declarations, no scolding, no admonitions, no threats. The man was obviously troubled, his vaunted ego visibly injured. "The President cries like a little boy," Zelkowicz recorded. "One can see how the agony of the masses has buffeted him, how grievously the decree has hurt him though it applies to him neither directly nor indirectly. These are not crocodile tears. They are Jewish tears, emanating from a Jewish heart."[30] Rumkowski would not dwell on the matter, but in what may have been an effort to evoke from listeners at least a small measure of empathy, even if it was only an expression of self-pity rising to the surface of his awareness, he spoke sorrowfully of his own childlessness, compensated by the many years he had dedicated to the care of children. It was for him a matter of personal anguish to have to bend to a demand that he surrender the young. "I lived and breathed together with the children," he told the crowd. "I never imagined that my own hand would have to bring the sacrifice to the altar."[31] Yet he was careful to concede the greater suffering of parents whose impending loss was immeasurable and crushing. "I understand you, mothers. I see your tears. I also sense the throbbing of your hearts, fathers, who will have to go to work the day after they have taken away your children, when only yesterday you amused yourselves with your beloved offspring. I know and feel all of this."[32] He would not be so presumptuous as to think he could lessen their hardship. "I bear no tidings of consolation today. Neither have I come to calm you today, but rather to expose all of your pain and sorrow. I have come like a thief to deprive you of that which is dearest to your hearts."[33]

Yet he was not going to abandon hope of winning understanding for his position. So unexpected had been the emptying of the hospitals that even he had been unable to prevent harm to his own in-laws. Of course, for some time he had been doing his best to reduce the exposure of young people in the ghetto to new threats. He had endeavored to put more and more of them to work. Touching on the decisive order of the moment affecting the elderly and the young, he indicated that he had not received it until the afternoon of the previous day. He had succeeded, he claimed, in reducing the initial demand from 24,000 victims to 20,000. Though his fervent appeal to exclude nine-year-old children from the general order of deportation had categorically been denied, those aged ten and older had in the end been granted an exemption. Inadequate as this was, he asked the ghetto to take some solace in this small concession. In any case, he wished it known that he had done all that he possibly could; he had even dropped down on his "knees and begged" the Germans to reconsider, "but it was useless."[34] Be that as it may, like his lieutenants, Rumkowski saw no choice but to submit to the edict in exchange for permission to conduct the removal of the young, the elderly, and the ill with the community's own forces. In this way alone might the ghetto avoid the brutality and violence sure to follow should the Germans send in their own troops to carry out the order.[35]

From the start, Rumkowski told his audience, confronted by the edict, he and his trusted associates had been "guided not by the thought 'How many will perish' but 'How many can be saved.'"[36] He reminded them of the fate of the population of the provincial communities, with which they were familiar. "Hardly a thousand Jews reached the ghetto from small towns where seven to eight thousand Jews used to live." The choice facing the Jews of Lodz was as stark as this. "So what's better? What do you want? To leave eighty to ninety thousand people [alive] or to destroy them all, Heaven forfend?" With that, his listeners might have sensed the man finding toward the end of his oration a measure of his familiar dominant bearing. In any event, knowing that in carrying out the order he was a criminal in their eyes, he embraced once more the comparison he knew suited him at this moment only too well. "It takes the heart of a thief to demand what I am demanding of you. But put yourselves in my place, think logically, and draw the conclusion yourselves. I cannot behave otherwise, since those who may be saved far outnumber those whom we are ordered to hand over."[37]

The logic of the argument, cruel as it surely was, was compelling. But given the exhaustion of a last desperate appeal to the Germans to modify their demand, was there truly no alternative to submission and compliance? It is worth noting that Rumkowski remained, as ever, publicly silent about the fate of the deportees. He offered no hope that they were merely being shifted to a new location. His reference to the altar and to sacrifice left little room for conjecture that even the children would survive the journey, though as Zelkowicz and the *Chronicle* attest, speculation to that effect still circulated. But the likelihood of their death—by what means still remained beyond confirmation and beyond imagining—left parents in tears. The members of Rumkowski's audience that afternoon of September 4 were not entirely passive in their grief. At the very moment when he relayed to them the Germans' promise that "if you hand over the sacrifices by yourself, it will be quiet"—that is, compliance would "prevent further sacrifices" and the community would be left in peace—people were heard to shout: "'We'll all go'; 'Mr. President, don't take only children; take one child from families that have other children!'" Rumkowski responded that he would not accept such "hollow clichés," adding, "I haven't the strength to argue with you."[38]

Apart from the question of substituting youngsters from larger families for those who were their parents' only children—yet another grievous choice implied by the already insane terms of the edict—what if Rumkowski had accepted the logic of those who shouted "We'll all go" and on that Friday afternoon had announced that, at the potential cost of the dissolution of the ghetto, he would not lend his own hand to the destruction of the elderly, the sick, and most especially the young? It would have been a courageous act, and Rumkowski and the ghetto he administered would have been honored for it on that day and on all days of remembrance thereafter. Nevertheless, as Rumkowski knew, it took little imagination to comprehend that such defiance would constitute a direct challenge to a German security establishment whose cruelties both the leaders and the inhabitants of the ghetto had long endured. In all likelihood such an act would have brought the Lodz ghetto to a swift and bloody end. Well before reaching this terrible juncture, Rumkowski knew what to expect from any overt act of defiance. Any Jewish leader who resisted such a decree would have to reckon not just with death but with torture as well. Rumkowski would not have forgotten the fate of the first *Beirat* and the treatment that preceded their deaths in autumn 1939. And they had done nothing to provoke their torment. But what of a symbolic refusal, one that cheated the Gestapo of the satisfaction of vengeance against a defiant Jewish underling? In his speech Rumkowski had alluded briefly to his own death, if only in the context of wondering if he would live long even after compliantly executing the impending decree. He would have known about Czerniaków's suicide, undertaken in the face of similar pressures, only weeks before in late July. But if the idea of following a similar course crossed his mind now, he dismissed it, whether out of understandable reluctance to take his own life or because Czerniaków's gesture, honorable as it was, had done nothing to prevent the mass deportation that followed. In Warsaw, others had been found to carry out the order.[39] The world would not read of Rumkowski's suicide or of a courageous ghetto whose people chose, by his word or by his example, to be led away to their deaths rather than offer up with their own hands their aged, their sick, and above all their defenseless young; nor would we hear of those who might have rushed the wooden fence posts and the wires, to die there under fire or, if successful in fleeing the precincts of the ghetto, hunted down and shot in the countryside beyond or, more likely, in the streets of the nearby city.[40]

The words of Warszawski and Jakobson indicate that in advance of addressing the public, internal discussion of how to respond had been going on among a small circle of leaders close to Rumkowski. Others were consulted as well, or at least informed in advance. Speaking of this moment long afterward Arnold Mostowicz would recall:

When Rumkowski learned that the Germans had decided to remove all the sick, the elderly, and the children, he called a meeting of doctors. . . . I took part in that meeting. In the course of it ninety percent of the doctors agreed that it had to be done, that the decision must be observed. At the same time they were fully aware that to those deported it meant death. Naturally you can ask me—and it would be a fair question—how did I react? Well, I reacted in the most cowardly way imaginable: I said nothing. I cannot tell you what made me act that way, except one thing which I am sure of now. . . . Personally, I was under no threat; that was one of the reasons for my silence, but it would be too easy to say that it was the only reason. I guess I kept quiet because I was ashamed to say that we should do as the Germans told

us, since there was no escape from their decision, but at the same time to admit that it was an utter disgrace.[41]

The speeches ended and evening approached, marking the conclusion of a crushing day. "The sun dips to the west. Dusk has come. As the sun sets, everyone feels the encroachment of impending events," Zelkowicz wrote, groping to express the unrelieved terror of that moment. "No one believes in miracles anymore. All three speakers made it clear that the decree is irreversible— twenty thousand Jews must be deported from the ghetto. Sent away for good. Never to be seen again." Surely "there has never been a sunset like today's." On other days, sunset had brought to the residents of the ghetto the promise of rest. It was the time

when you returned to your wife after a day at work. After a whole day apart, parents and children gathered for a pitiable dinner. In the courtyard they met with neighbors who declaimed their woes and they breathed musty air into their lungs—musty but, nevertheless, better than the air inside the cramped apartments. Every day, people yearned for sunset. Today, however—how many years of people's lives would they forfeit to keep the sun from setting, to make this day last interminably, to avert the bleak, grotesque morrow forever?[42]

"Once night falls, everyone trembles at the sight of his lengthening shadow." The courtyards are abandoned as people return to their homes to wait out the darkness, or to wait out time's passing:

So the ghetto residents sit in their apartments. Many of them do not even turn on a light. Why bother? For what purpose should people see their own agony and tears in other faces? In other rooms, however, the lights are on. Mostly, these are rooms inhabited by children to whom the hideous decree applies. The best beds have been prepared for these children. Mothers and fathers stand at these beds, not to safeguard the children's slumber or to drive away the ghetto flies, but to contemplate them in their last remaining hours. They can still be together; the parents can still engrave their children's faces into their memory.[43]

A sentence of death hovered over the elderly, too. Who, Zelkowicz asked, will watch over them on this night? For them hope is all but extinguished. The old are so obviously useless to the Germans. While death likely also awaited the young, there was at least the sliver of a chance that, under parental protection, children might yet be spared the worst.[44] But as for the elderly, though once their lives had been filled with family, many now were all alone. Zelkowicz thought of them; surely they must "amble along the walls of their rooms, like shadows of stray dogs on a moonlit night in some Godforsaken place." Their fate was grim, their future all but annulled. If any could be sure that this ghetto night was their last on earth, it was they. Their smallest sensory perceptions, momentarily experienced in the vanishing here and now, would be among their last." So the elderly totter along the walls of the narrow rooms that they now love and cherish so. Even the spider webs and the stains of fleas on the walls have become dear to their hearts." Among them, "who knows what the morrow, and the day after, will look like? Will they have a room at all, or will they share a pit with two hundred, with a thousand people, men, women, children all together—those who have been 'discarded'?" For the last time they enjoyed the comfort of a mattress, a pillow, some sheets, a coverlet: this "bug-infested bedding," uncomfortable as it was, had "suddenly become

agreeable" and, in a sense, "their live-in doctor. It allows them to refresh themselves and to relax for a few hours. In their dreams, it reflects the faces of their dear children and grandchildren. How dear this bedding is to an old man in his final hours!" Thus drawn "to that place, to that side of life, to the land of dreams," for one final time an old man might find himself in the company of those who had given a declining life its meaning.[45]

From the outset the ghetto had endured an unsettled relationship with time; ultimately the Jews of Łódź staked all hope on waiting out the Germans until their fortunes failed and the war came to an end. There was always the possibility that through perseverance, through merely holding out, the great remnant might be saved and, once freed, reenter the world. The ghetto would not endure forever. Just as, with all certainty, they knew that at this very moment there existed a world beyond the ghetto, they knew as well that there would be a time to come after it. Whether they might live to experience that future was another matter. Possibly they would. In this hope they could only wish that the intervening time would pass as quickly as possible, that the day of liberation might be near. It was only when a sentence of death drew nearer still that they wanted nothing so much as for time to slow, for the present to be never-ending. But time for them did pass, as time does. Who but a Joshua [the Israelite leader for whom, the Bible says, God made the sun and moon stand still] had the power to delay it?[46] And so the sun set on this day, as on all days before and after, just as surely as it would rise up again and again with each new dawn.

Worry undermined slumber. "Here and there a broken heart issues a groan that emanates from an open window like the sound of an overused violin string, a bleat from a strangled throat like the sound of a slaughtered calf. A child occasionally screams in his restless sleep like the last flickering of a dying candle." But the people knew that nearby existed a kind of peace, the enjoyment of which fed off the misery of the ghetto. It pierced the night with sounds from farther afield. "From that side of life, from the other side of the barbed-wire fence, the ghetto sometimes hears the clatter of a passing streetcar or the screech of a hoarse phonograph record, like the mocking of a drunk nomad who has been placed in charge of the pointless lives of a hundred thousand leprous dogs, that tomorrow or the next day will get their just deserts. 'Cling-clang—one in five to be torn away. Clank-clank—one Jew in five.'"[47]

Night vanished. A new day began. By seven o'clock on the morning of Saturday, September 5, the streets were filled. In anticipation of the curfew, people headed out in the hope of stocking up on any available foodstuffs. "It is utterly impossible to stay at home. Everyone runs out. They literally run—rushing, hustling, as if propelled by someone wielding a whip."[48] For all the commotion there was also an uncharacteristic atmosphere of quiet: "No one converses, it's as if people have left or forgotten their tongues at home. Acquaintances do not offer greetings, as if ashamed of each other. They freeze as they walk. They freeze as they stand in lengthy queues at the distribution points and the vegetable yards. An eerie silence has overtaken the ghetto."[49] Such anxious motion brought to mind a picture of "sinners' souls circulating in the netherworld. This is exactly how they would look: lips buttoned in stubborn silence, eyes filled with a great terror." For Zelkowicz, hellish visions evoked further images of a grotesque metamorphosis: "The three bridges in the ghetto swarm with hundred-headed snakes, an encampment of snakes that moves continually back and forth, hither and yon. The creatures racing about, scurrying in the thick air, are people."[50]

The Jewish police made ready to comply with the tasks ahead, prepared, as on prior occasions, to see to it that orders were carried out. This time they would be assisted by ghetto firefighters, whose cooperation had also been sealed by the promise of safety for their own children and relations and extra servings of bread and sausage to fill their bellies and provide needed energy for the work. Ghetto porters and teamsters, among them men of considerable strength, making up what came to be known unofficially as the White Guard (taking their name from the powdering of "flour, sugar, and rice" that stuck to their garments), were needed as well. These strong men were said to have undertaken preparations to defend their young by mounting guard at the thresholds of their residences "with axes in [their] hands." The display of force proved unnecessary; their cooperation was purchased like that of the police. Their children protected, the transport workers went to work assisting in the operation.[51] Their young children and those of the Jewish police, firemen, and workplace managers—recipients of passes exempting them from resettlement—were brought to a shelter on Łagiewnicka Street, protected for the duration of the Aktion. Removing their small sons and daughters to the shelter when it opened on Sunday, even many of these privileged fathers were anxious, unsure at first that the pledge they had been given would hold.[52]

Even in advance of the curfew, set to begin at 5 p.m., the Jewish police started collecting the first of those marked for capture. They began by emptying the old age homes, a relatively effortless undertaking, for the victims were physically weak, isolated from others, certain to be on the premises and there for the taking. In such a place the police could be sure of getting off to a successful start; there they could practice their technique, developing a feel for the Aktion while encountering as little difficulty as possible. "There, as they say, the table's been set. Everything can be taken as is," wrote Zelkowicz. "No need to be selective. Everything is old and fit to be 'thrown on the garbage heap.'"[53] So too "in the old-age homes, the policemen can work in a calm and businesslike way. No one disturbs or annoys them; there are no mistakes. . . . They load the old men and women onto the wagons like pieces of scrap metal."[54]

That would prove the standard procedure, soon to be extended to the ghetto as a whole: those to be removed would climb up onto horse-drawn wagons, guarded by Jewish police and driven by ghetto teamsters to designated assembly points or holding areas established inside the newly cleared hospitals and on the grounds of the ghetto's Czarnieckiego Street prison. From there, in successive transports, they would be loaded onto German trucks that exited the ghetto bound for Chelmno. On that initial weekend morning as well, the first of the carts filled with children were spotted being loaded on Rybna Street. Zelkowicz would record that in stark contrast to grieving parents and other adults nearby, the youngest of the children, apparently oblivious to their fate, were beside themselves with excitement, if also a bit confused. "These children see no reason to cry," he wrote:

> They are quite content: they have been placed on a wagon and they are going for a ride! Since when have children in the ghetto had such an opportunity? If it were not for all those wailing people, if their mothers and fathers had not screamed so as they placed them in the cart, they would have danced to the cart. After all, they are going for a wagon ride. But all that shouting, noise and crying upset them and disrupted their joy. They jostle in the elongated wagon bed with its high barriers, as if lost, and their bulging eyes ask: What's going on? What

do these people want from us? Why don't they let us take a little ride?[55]

Oskar Singer, however, noted that there were also older children, more experienced in ghetto life and its misfortunes, who appeared soberly resigned in the face of what was happening to them.[56] Afterward—apparently on the evening of September 5—the men of the Jewish Order Service saw to the roundup of the children in the Marysin [a neighborhood of the ghetto] homes. While some of the estimated 850 youngsters who had been staying there had left in advance of the *Aktion*, Rumkowski, arriving to oversee the removal, made sure that none evaded capture or were left behind.[57]

Confined to their residences, people confronted the knowledge that their own parents, husbands, wives, daughters, sons, sisters, and brothers were potentially targeted for removal, if not already taken, perhaps never to be seen again. The tension and grief, difficult enough to endure by day, became immeasurably worse with the onset of darkness. From the perspective of the following day, Zelkowicz reviewed the distinctive mood prevailing during the nighttime hours of the fifth, wondering: "Who could sleep tonight? Mothers whose children had been taken from them? Men whose wives, their helpmeets, had been taken? People whose ailing loved ones were removed from their beds? . . . The ghetto tosses on its bed and knows no sleep. The aching, enfeebled bones cannot lie still. The ghetto's brain is incurably feverish. All those screams and roars, sighs and groans that split the silence of the night through the open windows and doors have landed on its heart." Sounds of anguish traversed the darkness. For the bereaved, night brought not the least diminution of their suffering: "Hours have passed since these woes, these agonies, were inflicted on those wretched people, but the situation has not calmed down one bit. Mothers have not yet tired of shrieking, fathers' wellsprings of tears have not yet been sealed, and the silence of the night amplifies the reverberations of the screaming and sobbing."[58]

NOTES

1. Josef Zelkowicz, *In Those Terrible Days: Notes from the Lodz Ghetto*, trans. Naftali Greenwood (Jerusalem: Yad Vashem, 2002), 251. *Chronicle*, entry for September 1, 1942, 248, credited to Zelkowicz.

2. *Chronicle*, 249. Zelkowicz, *In Those Terrible Days*, entry for September 1, 1942, 251.

3. Zelkowicz, *In Those Terrible Days*, 251–54. *Chronicle*, entry for September 1, 1942, 248–49. On the pushing of children from windows, see testimony of Dr. Donat Szmulewicz-Stanisz, in Jerzy Lewinski, *Proces Hansa Biebowa* (Warsaw: PRS, 1999), 107, and of Bronyka Szyldwach, in *Preserved Evidence: Ghetto Łódź*, ed. Anna Eilenberg-Eibeshitz, vol. 1 (Haifa: H. Eibeshitz Institute for Holocaust Studies, 1998), 256–57.

4. Note the exchange in Lewinski, *Proces Hansa Biebowa*, 67.

5. Testimony of Aleksander Klugman, ibid., 139–40.

6. Testimony of Szyja Teitelbaum, ibid., 112.

7. Testimony of Hersz Janowski, ibid., 111.

8. *Chronicle*, entry for September 1, 1942, 249.

9. *Chronicle*, entry for September 2, 1942, 249.

10. Rosenfeld, *In the Beginning*, Notebook E, entry for 4 [September 1942], 121. Oskar Rosenfeld, *Wozu noch Welt: Aufzeichnungen aus dem Getto Łódź*, ed. Hanno Loewy (Frankfurt am Main: Verlag Neue Kritik, 1994), entry for 4 [September 1942], 148.

11. Zelkowicz, *In Those Terrible Days*, 264.

12. Ibid., 264–65.

13. Ibid., 265.

14. Ibid., 266.

15. Ibid., 267–68.

16. Ibid., 268. *Chronicle*, 250–51.

17. Zelkowicz, *In Those Terrible Days*, 268–69.

18. Ibid., 269.

19. Ibid., 270–71.

20. Ibid., 273.

21. Ibid., 274–75.

22. Ibid., 276. The account in the *Chronicle* refers to Rumkowski's address as having taken place at 4:00 p.m., entry for September 14, 1942, 250.

23. Zelkowicz, *In Those Terrible Days*, 276.

24. Ibid., 277.

25. Ibid., 277–78.

26. Ibid., 278.

27. Ibid.

28. Ibid., 279.

29. Ibid.

30. Ibid., 280.

31. Ibid.

32. Ibid., 282.

33. Ibid., 281.

34. Ibid., 280–83.

35. Ibid., 280–82.

36. Ibid., 281.

37. Ibid., 283.

38. Ibid., 282–83.

39. In addition, elsewhere the Nazis proved equally capable of carrying out evacuations without the direct cooperation of the councils. See Yehuda Bauer, *Rethinking the Holocaust* (New Haven: Yale University Press, 2001), 77–78.

40. In other ghettos, however, such attempts were made, though with very limited success. See Dov Levin, "The Fighting Leadership of the *Judenräte* in the Small Communities of Poland," in *Patterns of Jewish Leadership in Nazi Europe, 1933–1945: Proceedings of the Third Yad Vashem International Historical Conference*, ed. Yisrael Gutman and Cynthia Haft (Jerusalem: Yad Vashem, 1979), 134, 136–42. Leni Yahil, *The Holocaust: The Fate of European Jewry*, trans. Haya Galai (New York: Oxford University Press), 471–72.

41. Quoted in *Fotoamator* (1998), dir. Dariusz Jablonski, Apple Film Productions, English version trans. Alina Skibihska and Wolfgang Jöhling.

42. Zelkowicz, *In Those Terrible Days*, 286.

43. Ibid., 287.

44. Ibid., 288.

45. Ibid., 288–89.

46. Ibid., 286. On the theme of wishful halting of time, see also Bernard-Henry Lévy, *War, Evil, and the End of History* (Hoboken NJ: Melville House, 2004), 224–25.

47. Zelkowicz, *In Those Terrible Days*, 289.

48. Ibid., 300.

49. Ibid., 301.

50. Ibid.

51. Testimony of Matithiahu Jakubowicz, cited in Eilenberg-Eibeshitz, *Preserved Evidence*, 261.

52. Ibid. Zelkowicz, *In Those Terrible Days*, 349–51.

53. Zelkowicz, *In Those Terrible Days*, 302.

54. Ibid., 303.

55. Ibid., 307.

56. Oskar Singer, *Im Eilschritt durch den Gettotag . . . ,* ed. Sascha Feuchert, Erwin Leibfried, Jörg Recke *et al.* (Berlin: Philo, 2002), 137. Zelkowicz, *In Those Terrible Days*, 307–8.

57. Isaiah Trunk, *Lodz Ghetto: A History*, ed. and trans. Robert Moses Shapiro (Bloomington: Indiana University Press, 2006), 244–45. Yakov Nirenberg, "Di geshikte fun lodsher geto," in *In di yorn fun yidishn khurbn* (New York: Farlag Unser Tsait, 1948), 270. Rosenfeld, *In the Beginning*, Notebook H, entry for July 12 [1943], 196.

58. Zelkowicz, *In Those Terrible Days*, 343–44.

Leaving a Record

SAMUEL D. KASSOW

From *Who Will Write Our History?*

The Oyneg Shabes [Joy of the Sabbath] was not just a clandestine archive; it was also a tightly knit collective, a secret but vital component of the larger alternate community that had developed out of the house committees and the *Aleynhilf* [the Jewish Self-Help Organization]. Using the *Aleynhilf* as a base, [Emanuel] Ringelblum slowly and methodically assembled a group of collaborators that ranged from the most prominent leaders of prewar Polish Jewry to impoverished refugees. Of all the Jewish historians in prewar Poland, Ringelblum most regarded history as a collective enterprise. Now, in the middle of a national disaster, it was this collective effort that shaped the archive and imbued it with a sense of purpose. As Ringelblum wrote, probably in late 1942:

> The members of the Oyneg Shabes constituted, and continue to constitute, a united body, imbued with a common spirit. The Oyneg Shabes is not a group of researchers who compete with one another but a united group, a brotherhood where all help one another . . . Each member of the Oyneg Shabes knew that his effort and pain, his hard work and toil, his taking constant risks with the dangerous work of moving material from one place to another—-that this was done in the name of a high ideal. . . . The Oyneg Shabes was a brotherhood, an order of brothers who wrote on their flag: readiness to sacrifice, mutual loyalty, and service to [Jewish society].[1]

Over time, the Oyneg Shabes brought together men and women from a wide spectrum of prewar Polish Jewry: wealthy businessmen and poor artisans, rabbis and Communists, Yiddishists and Polish-speaking intellectuals, teachers and journalists, economists and leaders of youth groups. Some were part of a small executive committee, an inner circle that raised money, made policy, and decided what to study and what to collect. A larger group contributed essays and reports commissioned by the archive. This group ranged from frequent contributors to those who only submitted one or two essays or testimonies. Some members only copied, typing or writing out duplicate and triplicate copies of incoming material; isolated from everyone else except Ringelblum and his closest secretaries, were Israel Lichtenstein and his two teenaged helpers, David Graber and Nahum Grzywacz. They concealed the documents in the Borochov School on Nowolipki 68 and waited for the order to bury them under the school basement. Although exact numbers are difficult to establish, approximately fifty to sixty people (including copiers and transcribers) were involved in some way with the archive, from its beginning in 1940 until the ghetto uprising in 1943.

The Oyneg Shabes had more luck in saving documents than in saving people. Although thousands of pages survived in the tin boxes and in the milk cans (a significant part of the archive was most certainly lost), little more than random traces remain of the men and women who wrote the documents, gathered them, copied them, and hid them. As most of the Oyneg Shabes collaborators died with their entire families, few survivors could provide more than the barest biographical details of those who perished. The fate of the Oyneg Shabes collective reflected the fate of interwar Polish Jewry: the destruction was so complete and so calamitous that all too often only disconnected scraps of information remained. The few biographies of those who contributed to the archive, published largely in Yiddish books and journals, are short and sketchy, some little more than a paragraph, and often they are little more than hagiographies.

Some members of the Oyneg Shabes did not even have the luck to find some small memorial in an article or biographical dictionary. Those who wrote in Polish fell between the cracks: they did not merit entries in the standard Yiddish literary lexicons, nor were they famous enough for inclusion in the biographical dictionaries of Polish literature. There are scant details on the young student Salomea Ostrowska, a productive worker in the archive. Stanislaw Rozycki . . . has left no traces beyond his penetrating essays on the ghetto streets and on his experiences in Soviet-occupied Lwów. Many members of the archive left little more than a name. Hardly any had a grave. Only three survived: Hersh Wasser, his wife Bluma, and Rachel Auerbach.

Only a small inner circle—the so-called executive committee—knew the entire scope of the archive's agendas and membership. Most Oyneg Shabes work proceeded on a need-to-know basis. Once contributors received an assignment, they were not supposed to discuss it with anyone, even if they suspected that their interlocutor was also working for the archive. They did know, however,

that a secret organization with a national mission had asked them for help.

The Oyneg Shabes, although a diverse group, had particular characteristics. Although several contributors, such as Daniel Fligelman, were totally unknown figures before the war and were "discovered" by the Oyneg Shabes through the *Aleynhilf* or the refugee committees in the Warsaw Ghetto, Ringelblum had managed to assemble an executive committee of stature and achievement. It included prominent prewar communal leaders and well-to-do businessmen. Virtually all members of the executive committee of the Oyneg Shabes had been active in prewar Jewish cultural life. In the ghetto, the entire executive committee also served in the leadership of the *Aleynhilf*. Apart from the executive committee, most Oyneg Shabes collaborators were teachers, economists, and journalists, all recruited from the Jewish intelligentsia.

If any one prewar institution shaped the ethos of the Oyneg Shabes it was clearly the YIVO [Yiddish Scientific] Institute, for prior to the war several members had worked in some way for the YIVO in its Warsaw branch, in Lodz, or in Vilna. These included Ringelblum, Hersh Wasser, Eliyahu Gutkowski, Yitzhak Giterman, Abraham Lewin, Shie Rabinowitz, Shmuel Winter, Aaron Koninski, Shimon Huberband, Menakhem Linder, Rachel Auerbach, Cecylia Slapakowa, Jerzy Winkler, Yitzhak Bernstein, Yehezkiel Wilczynski, and others. Many were scholars in their own right who had already published work on history, literature, folklore, or economics. In the YIVO they had seen that political differences need not preclude collaboration to advance Yiddish culture. The Oyneg Shabes merely extended a path that they had already chosen.

But Ringelblum understood that the archive could work only by reaching out and recruiting new members. Hersh Wasser, one of the two secretaries of the Oyneg Shabes, recalled that Ringelblum had told him that the archive had to become "the property of the entire Jewish people [*der kinyn fun gantsn yidishn folk*]." There could be no room for ideological and political quarrels. Anyone whom the staff considered a valuable worker and able to keep secrets was eligible for membership. According to Wasser, Ringelblum never wanted the archive to be known as a Left *Poalei Tsiyon* [LPZ=Marxist Zionist] archive or even an archive with any ideological slant or bias.[2] If YIVO activists were over-represented in the leadership of the Oyneg Shabes, they still made room for fervent champions of Hebrew (Eliezer Lipe Bloch) and for Jewish poets and writers who wrote in Polish (Henryka Lazowert, Gustawa Jarecka).

Wasser recalled that the executive committee, as part of this effort to make the Oyneg Shabes as inclusive as possible, reached out to the strongest and best-organized political party in the ghetto—the Bund. The Bund refused the Oyneg Shabes request to work together and set up its own archive.[3] As usual the Bund preferred to work alone, especially when the potential partners were Zionists or, worse, members of the LPZ, with whom the Bund had long had chilly relations.[4] But even though the Bund as a party decided to go its own way, several Bundists worked in the Oyneg Shabes Archive on their own, such as Shie Rabinowitz, who was on the executive committee; David Cholodenko, who was a judge in literary contests; Leyb Goldin, who contributed a valuable fictionalized essay on hunger; and Yehezkiel Wilczynski, who conducted interviews, transcribed documents, and left many of his own studies on the history of Polish Jewry. Furthermore, it is entirely probable . . . that, when news first reached the ghetto of the Nazis' extermination program, the Bund and the Oyneg Shabes

worked together to inform Jews abroad and the Polish Government-in-Exile in London.[5]

Communists also joined the Oyneg Shabes. One of the most important editors of the underground Communist press in the ghetto, Yehuda Feld (whose real name was Yehuda Feldworm) played a significant role in the archive. Feld worked in the CENTOS [Central Organization for the Care of Orphans], had extensive contact with children and refugees, and filed important and informative reports on them for the Oyneg Shabes. He also compiled a collection of short stories of ghetto life, *In di tsaytn fun Homen dem tsveytn* (In the days of Haman the Second).[6]

Ringelbum had been preparing for the archive as soon as the war began. Shortly before the Germans invaded Poland, he began a diary. This diary revealed very little about his personal emotions and practically nothing about his family. Especially in the first year of the war, it resembled the random notes and jottings of a historian who was planning a major book after the war. By day Ringelblum heard countless stories from the hundreds of people who passed through the offices of the *Aleynhilf*; at night he recorded them in his diary.[7]

German soldiers, in the year prior to the ghetto's establishment, frequently raided Jewish apartments to requisition them or in search of valuables. In those circumstances, Ringelblum believed, most Jews were too scared to write. Instead of keeping diaries and journals, prominent journalists and writers burned incriminating papers and books.[8] Therefore Ringelblum began keeping records in his diary fully aware that he bore a special responsibility to document events that would otherwise be forgotten.

He quickly realized, however, that these fears were exaggerated. Although the Germans did all they could in the first months of the occupation to destroy the Polish political underground, they cared little about what the Jews wrote or said. When they raided Jewish homes, they were interested in valuables, not manuscripts.[9]

That being the case, Ringelblum believed that it was feasible to organize an underground archive to study Jewish life under the Nazi occupation and to collect documentation. He knew from the beginning that it had to be a collective enterprise. No one individual could even begin to think about interviewing sources, gathering documents, and ensuring that the material would remain hidden and secure. On November 22, 1940, he convened a meeting that formally organized the archive.[10]

Over time Ringelblum and his associates built this "band of comrades" by a process of trial and error. Several people disappointed him and were quietly dropped. Others, totally unknown before the war, became indispensable. Today it is clear that the Oyneg Shabes succeeded in part because alongside an executive committee that provided direction and focus, many of the members of the archive wrote on topics they chose themselves. This interplay of central direction, focused research, and individual initiative produced an enormous variety of material. Thanks to the Oyneg Shabes, a large number of very different people, with diverse points of view and interests, ensured breadth of coverage and a variety of opinions and approaches. In the middle of a war, Ringelblum believed, it was best to cast as wide a net as possible. How could one know, after all, what information future historians would find "important"? In the archive Ringelblum came closest to realizing his prewar dream of a history "of the people and by the people." . . .

A generation earlier, in the middle of the First World War, the Yiddish writer Y. L. Peretz had urged his fellow Jews to document their wartime experiences. A nation that had pride and self-

respect did not leave the writing of its history to enemies. Jews, Peretz warned, had to ensure that future historians would work with Jewish sources and not depend on hostile documents and testimony.[11] Until early 1942 the Oyneg Shabes, like Peretz in the First World War, had believed that the end of the war would see a revitalized Jewish community in Poland with the archive a buttress to national self-awareness and a means to create a "usable past" for the future. But by the spring of 1942 the workers of the Oyneg Shabes began to realize that, instead, they might be writing the last chapter of the eight-hundred-year history of Polish Jewry. Nonetheless their work had a purpose. Even if they did not survive, they could still determine what that last chapter would say and who would write it. Their work and sacrifice would create a record that would bring the killers to justice. They might still leave a legacy for future generations.

In the summer of 1943, in the Majdanek concentration camp, Isaac Schiper told a fellow inmate that,

Everything depends on who transmits our testament to future generations, on who writes the history of this period. History is usually written by the victor. What we know about murdered peoples is only what their murderers vaingloriously cared to say about them. Should our murderers be victorious, should they write the history of this war, our destruction will be presented as one of the most beautiful pages of world history, and future generations will pay tribute to them as dauntless crusaders. Their every word will be taken as gospel. Or they may wipe out our memory altogether, as if we had never existed, as if there had never been a Polish Jewry, a ghetto in Warsaw, a Maidanek. Not even a dog will howl for us.

But if *we* write the history of this period of blood and tears—and I firmly believe we will—who will believe us? Nobody will *want* to believe us, because our disaster is the disaster of the entire civilized world. . . . We'll have the thankless job of proving to a reluctant world that we are Abel, the murdered brother.[12]

Ringelblum, more optimistic than Schiper, had no doubt that the world would believe what had happened—if confronted with the proper evidence. He intended to amass a record whose thoroughness, objectivity, and sheer scope would force "future generations" to look the truth in the face.

The Uniqueness of the Oyneg Shabes

The Oyneg Shabes Archive was the largest secret archive in Nazi-occupied Poland, but it was not the only one. In the Vilna Ghetto, Jewish librarians and writers—for example, Herman Kruk, Avrom Sutzkever, and Shmerke Kaczerginski—gathered and buried books and documents.[13] In the Bialystok Ghetto, a young resistance leader, Mordecai Tenenbaum, who had almost certainly learned about the Oyneg Shabes during his brief stay in the Warsaw Ghetto, set up a ghetto archive and incorporated it into the Jewish underground organization.[14] In the Lodz Ghetto, Ghetto Elder Chaim Rumkowski established an archive as a separate department of the ghetto administration—and seemed to turn a blind eye as it became a major center of testimony and documentation.[15] There was also a secret archive in the Kovno Ghetto, working closely with the *Judenrat*.

After the war much of the material gathered by these archives survived. Most of the Lodz Ghetto Archive was unearthed from a dry well and from a secret burial place under the former ghetto fire department. (The Germans discovered a third cache and destroyed it.) In 1944, Avrom Sutz-kever and Shmerke Kaczerginski returned to Vilna and dug up many of the documents they had buried—as well as Kruk's important diary. In Bialystok Mordecai Tenenbaum had entrusted the archive to a sympathetic Pole. The Pole disappeared but, miraculously, many of the archive's documents surfaced after the war.

Countless individuals worked on their own to record what they saw. In hundreds of ghettos, hiding places, jails, and death camps, lonely and terrified Jews left diaries, letters, and testimony of what they endured. For every scrap of documentation that surfaced after the war, probably many more manuscripts vanished forever.

But the secret archives could accomplish much more than solitary individuals. They drew their strength from the collective energy of dedicated workers who could pool their talents and establish a hierarchy of priorities and objectives. The more diverse the archival staff and the greater the range of their prewar political and cultural backgrounds, the more likely it was that the archive would develop fruitful contacts and sources of information. Archives, although not entirely free of politics, generated a sense of common purpose that helped allay political rivalry. A collective could mobilize financial resources and gain the protection of important people in the Jewish Councils or social welfare organizations more easily than individuals. In some ghettos the official Jewish leadership and the archival staffs came together in a complex relationship fraught with mutual suspicion and mutual need. Ghetto leaders might feed the archive important documents—even as they concealed others.

In some important respects the Oyneg Shabes Archive resembled the archives in other ghettos. All collected documentation and testimony, and all worked in varying degrees of secrecy. Many leaders had earned respect before the war and claimed some authority in the ghetto community. In Lodz, for instance, Henryk Neftalin had been a prominent and esteemed attorney. Herman Kruk had headed one of the largest Yiddish libraries in Poland, the Bund's Grosser Library in Warsaw; in the Vilna Ghetto he not only organized the library but turned it into a major institution of the ghetto's cultural life and used it as the base for his documentation project.[16] Avrom Sutzkever and Shmerke Kaczerginski had already made their mark in prewar Vilna as promising young poets in the literary group *Yung Vilne*, and if few people outside his youth movement, *Dror*, had heard of Mordecai Tenenbaum before the war, in the Bialystok Ghetto he headed the Jewish resistance, acquiring authority and status that gave the archive legitimacy.[17]

But there were also important differences between these other archives and the Oyneg Shabes. In Lodz, Vilna, and Bialystok the archives enjoyed varying degrees of official "cover" and encouragement, and received financial help—some more than others—from the official ghetto leaders, who in turn used the archives to convey information and tell their side of the story. The Oyneg Shabes, on the other hand, had only minimal contacts with the *Judenrat*. Indeed, it saw itself as an integral part of the ghetto's alternative community.

In the Lodz Ghetto, the archive functioned simultaneously as an official department and as a semi-clandestine organization. But it was obvious that the archive staff did not feel free to criticize Rumkowski or gather any material it wished.[18] In the Vilna and the Bialystok ghettos, the archives were not under *Judenrat* control. However, both Jacob Gens, the commandant of the Vilna Ghetto, and Ephraim Barash, the head of the Bialystok *Judenrat*, maintained contact with the archives. Barash gave Mordecai Tenenbaum financial

help and a place to work and handed over valuable *Judenrat* records even as he withheld other particularly sensitive documents.[19] In Vilna relations between ghetto commandant Jacob Gens and Herman Kruk were quite cool. But Gens knew about Kruk's diary and archive, and he occasionally sought him out in order to tell his side of the story.[20]

The Oyneg Shabes, on the other hand, gave the *Judenrat* a wide berth. (Shmuel Winter was an "exception that proved the rule.") Ringelblum noted that more than once the Oyneg Shabes had passed over potential recruits just because they had connections to the *Judenrat*. Ringelblum and *Judenrat* president Adam Czerniakow had little in common. Ringelblum knew that Czerniakow was keeping a diary, and Ringelblum's name was in Czerniakow's address book, but there is no evidence that they shared any confidences or that Czerniakow called Ringelblum in for the kind of secret meetings that took place in Vilna or Bialystok with Gens and Barash. The Oyneg Shabes did interview the *Judenrat* officials Israel Milejkowski and Henryk Rozen as part of its survey of Jewish leaders and intellectuals, but here, too, no evidence suggests that either Milejkowski or Rozen knew that this was an Oyneg Shabes project.

Changing Priorities: The Evolution of the Oyneg Shabes

Ringelblum's sweeping and ambitious agenda for the Oyneg Shabes outstripped in scope and ambition those of other archives. Over time this agenda came to embrace the collection of artifacts and documents, the study of Jewish society, the gathering of individual testimony, the documentation of German crimes, and the alerting of the outside world to the German mass murder. These goals often overlapped and were pursued simultaneously by the archive.

The Oyneg Shabes Archive collected both texts and artifacts: the underground press, documents, drawings, candy wrappers, tram tickets, ration cards, theater posters, invitations to concerts and lectures. It took copies of the convoluted doorbell codes for apartments housing dozens of tenants. There were restaurant menus advertising roast goose and fine wines, and a terse account of a starving mother who had eaten her dead child. Carefully filed away were hundreds of postcards from Jews in the provinces about to be deported to an "unknown destination." The Oyneg Shabes preserved the poetry of Wladyslaw Szlengel, Yitzhak Katzenelson, Kalman Lis, and Joseph Kirman. It preserved the entire script of a popular ghetto comedy, "Love Looks for an Apartment," and long essays on the ghetto theaters and cafes. The first cache of the archive also contained many photographs, some seventy-six of which survived.[21]

The Oyneg Shabes retained hectographed readers used in the ghetto schools and reports that nurses wrote in the ghetto orphanages. After July 22, 1942, the archive collected the German posters announcing the Great Deportation, among them one promising that anyone who voluntarily reports for deportation will be given three kilograms of bread and a kilogram of marmalade. Crammed into the milk cans of the second cache were penciled notes whose shaky handwriting betrayed the desperation of their authors. These scraps of paper—smuggled out of the *Umschlagplatz* [literally: the reloading place, i.e., the collection point for Jews being deported from Warsaw]—were frantic appeals for a last-minute rescue. Among the last documents buried in the second cache were posters calling for armed resistance.

The Oyneg Shabes commitment to comprehensive documentation went hand in hand with another important commitment, namely, post-

war justice. Its model in this regard was Eliyahu Cherikover, who had established the remarkable archive that documented the Ukrainian pogroms of 1919–21. The evidence amassed by Cherikover had helped acquit Shalom Schwarzbard, who in 1926 had assassinated Ukrainian leader Semyon Petlura and was subsequently tried for murder in a French court. This quest to gather evidence explained why the archive collected enormous amounts of material from as many localities as possible. At first glance much of this material was repetitious. But it did confirm, town by town and village by village, exactly what the Germans did, when they did it, who gave the orders, and who helped them do it. If the Oyneg Shabes did not keep these testaments, then who would?

In time the Oyneg Shabes, unlike most of the other archives, also acquired a new role as a center of "civil resistance."[22] Eventually the Oyneg Shabes turned into an information center of the Jewish underground, disseminating news about the extermination of Polish Jewry via the Polish underground abroad, issuing bulletins, and warning surviving Jews to drop their illusions about German intentions.

Priorities of the Oyneg Shabes constantly shifted to reflect changing circumstances. Broadly speaking, the Oyneg Shabes went through different periods. From the outbreak of the war until the establishment of the ghetto, Ringelblum kept his notes, gathered information, and scouted out potential collaborators. When the ghetto was established in the fall of 1940 the work of the archive, paradoxically, became easier. Fear of German searches lessened; the Nazis, intensely following the activities of the Polish underground, seemed to have little interest in what Jews said or wrote. Thus, in addition to the "social space" created by the house committees and the *Aleynhilf*, a new kind of "cultural space" emerged in the ghetto that made it easier for Ringelblum to develop the archive.

One manifestation of this "cultural space" was the expansion of a large and varied underground press published by the political parties and youth groups.[23] The archive made the collection of these newspapers a major priority; indeed, without the Oyneg Shabes, very few newspapers and pamphlets would have survived. Like the archive, they provide priceless information about life in the ghetto, political debates, Polish-Jewish relations, and how Jews followed the military situation. The underground press and the archive covered many of the same themes: daily life in the ghetto, complaints about *Judenrat* and police corruption, escalating mortality from hunger and disease, problems in the labor camps, events in the provinces, the plight of children and refugees, street humor, and ghetto folklore. Ultimately a complementary relationship developed between this underground press and the Oyneg Shabes. The press put out edited versions of reports for the archive. Several members of the executive committee of the Oyneg Shabes—including Hersh Wasser, Eliyahu Gutkowski, and Shmuel Breslav—also edited underground newspapers. In October 1941, the underground press began to publish the first accounts of mass executions. By the spring of 1942 the Oyneg Shabes would publish an underground bulletin of its own, full of information about the oncoming "Final Solution."

While the archive itself had to remain secret, it indirectly benefited from the ability of the underground press to disseminate information, remind readers of prewar values and moral codes, and foster a community. The flow of information disseminated by the underground newspapers helped create an awareness of the need to record what was happening, and their moral and political exhortations bolstered a determination to use this

testimony to bring to justice not only Nazi perpetrators but also Jews who had failed the moral tests of national solidarity and honesty. The underground press, through its articles on the military situation, became the major source of information in the ghetto about the war. Even when things looked bleakest, such as after the fall of France in June 1940, the underground press furnished commentaries that kept hope alive.

By the fall of 1941 a new period began when the Oyneg Shabes decided to institute a major study of Jewish life under the Nazi occupation—the "Two and a Half Years" project. No sooner had the Oyneg Shabes begun this project than news began to arrive about Nazi massacres, first in the eastern territories, then in Chelmno, and then in the provinces surrounding Warsaw. Racing against time to complete the "Two and a Half Years" project, Ringelblum and the staff now faced a new challenge—to gather and disseminate information about the Nazi killings.

The Oyneg Shabes Archive was uncovered in two separate caches: the first in September 1946 and the second in December 1950. The first cache covered the period from the beginning of the war until August 3, 1942, the day Lichtenstein, Grzywacz, and Graber buried the documents.[24] A third cache . . . was buried under Swietojerska 34 and would have documented the critical months of March and early April 1943, when the ghetto was preparing for armed resistance. Despite dogged searches, it was never found.[25]

Unfortunately the physical condition of the first and second parts of the archive differed considerably. The first part had been packed into boxes of tin or sheet zinc. Lichtenstein did not have the time to weld them shut, and water seeped into all the boxes.[26] Many documents that had been written in ink were illegible, and many photographs were destroyed. Paper clips corroded, further damaging the materials. Much of the first part of the archive was covered with a thin fungus. The whole collection required years of painstaking restoration work, which remains incomplete. Indeed, only in the late 1980s, thanks to a grant from the United States Holocaust Memorial Museum, were major resources available for physical restoration.[27]

The second part of the archive, discovered in December 1950, had been packed in aluminum milk cans that protected the contents from water seepage. Therefore the condition of these documents was much better. The materials of the second cache reflected the vastly different conditions that the Oyneg Shabes faced after the onset of the Great Deportation. The archive was no longer in a position to conduct the careful studies of ghetto life begun in 1941. The children were gone, along with the schools, orphanages, and house committees. On the other hand, compared to the first cache, the second contained a much higher proportion of official records: *Judenrat* documents, German correspondence and orders, and records of the *Aleynhilf*. Before the onset of the Final Solution, Ringelblum did not assign priority to the collection of German documents or even *Judenrat* materials. The Germans, he figured, would preserve these records in their own files. But after the Great Deportation began, the Oyneg Shabes tried to collect as many official records and *Judenrat* materials as possible. Ringelblum also asked Yitzhak Zuckerman to procure archival materials from Michal Weichert's Jewish Self-Help Society, whose central offices were in Krakow.[28] The second cache contained as much material as the archive was able to gather about Treblinka, the Great Deportation itself, and the reactions of the surviving Jews. It documented psychological transformations that marked the ghetto inhabitants after the conclusion of the first stage of the extermination process in September 1942: anger at the Jewish police and the *Judenrat*, shame at the lack of resistance, determination that "the next time" the Jews would fight back. The Oyneg Shabes painstakingly documented the world of the "shops" that had replaced the ghetto after the Great Deportation. The second cache also contained important materials about the first armed confrontation between the ZOB [Jewish Fighting Organization] and the Germans in January 1943. And as the last members of the Oyneg Shabes faced death, they put their own personal documents in the second cache: university diplomas, personal writings, and so on. Ringelblum left the entire manuscript of his unpublished "History of Warsaw Jewry," and Opoczynski left many of his prewar writings.

Neither Wasser nor Auerbach believed that the ten boxes of the first cache contained all the material that the Oyneg Shabes had collected by August 1942. Even taking into account documents that had been damaged by water, they still believed that Lichtenstein and his young helpers must have buried other boxes.[29] Indeed, certain essays that Ringelblum cited in his essay on the Oyneg Shabes did not turn up.[30] In his letter to the YIVO written on March 1, 1944, Ringelblum mentioned "more than twenty [*tsvey tsendlik*]" boxes. We will probably never know the answer.

Working In Secret

The Oyneg Shabes staff was small enough to ensure efficiency and secrecy but large enough to fan out all over the ghetto in search of material. Ghetto teachers brought in children's essays in neat copybooks, and postal workers submitted the last postcards sent by provincial relatives before their deportation to an "unknown destination." In the pestilential refugee centers Oyneg Shabes interviewers risked their health to collect firsthand accounts of brutal expulsions and of the desperate efforts to hang on to life in overcrowded former synagogues and schools that often housed hundreds of starving people. The staff of the Oyneg Shabes interviewed Jewish intellectuals about the future of the Jewish people, and children about their dreams for "after the war." When refugees arrived in the Warsaw Ghetto from the Soviet-occupied zone, the Oyneg Shabes spared no effort to obtain their testimony.

The Oyneg Shabes quickly established a distinct organizational framework. The executive committee supervised the everyday work of the archive. Grouped around the executive committee were a few dozen writers and copiers. One list of Oyneg Shabes workers in Hersh Wasser's handwriting includes thirty-seven names and addresses.[31] Many of those listed had no recorded writings in the archive and were probably copiers. The list was far from complete; missing were such names as Kon, Winter, Giterman, Landau, Auerbach, and Slapakowa. Judging by who was included and who was absent, a plausible assumption might be that those on the list were receiving regular payments from Wasser but not those with sufficient means or stable employment.

Ringelblum and the executive committee, at their customary Saturday meetings to discuss the activities and plans of the archive, formulated questionnaires that were used to guide the "Two and a Half Years" project, and presumably they discussed the recruitment of new members. The committee probably reviewed the inventories of archival materials that were compiled by Hersh Wasser and Menakhem Kon's account book of income and expenditures.[32] By 1942, the executive committee as a whole, rather than individual Oyneg Shabes members, often met with refugees and survivors and heard firsthand accounts of the escalating mass murder.[33] The executive committee must have approved the decision to issue an Oyneg Shabes underground publication in the spring of 1942 that publicized the German killings. At the height of the Great Deportation in August 1942 the executive committee met to decide the eventual destination of the archive, the YIVO in New York City.[34]

Secrecy was paramount. The staff constantly worried that the slightest mistake, the smallest misjudgment could destroy the entire project. Prospective recruits were carefully scrutinized.[35] The archive rejected some potentially valuable contributors because of their links to the *Judenrat*, to the Jewish police, or to the "Thirteen."[36] Perhaps this explains the absence of the great historian Isaac Schiper as a member or contributor to the archive: Ringelblum noted with some consternation in his diary that Schiper had accepted invitations for dinner with Abraham Gancwajch, the leader of the "Thirteen."

The few diaries left by members of the Oyneg Shabes clearly revealed the importance of secrecy. In the hundreds of pages of the Ringelblum diaries, the Oyneg Shabes is barely mentioned—and then only in the most roundabout way. In the diary Hersh Wasser kept in the Warsaw Ghetto, he refers to "interesting OS meetings" and nothing more. Abraham Lewin in his diary also avoided any discussion of the inner workings of the archive. Rachel Auerbach had known the writer Peretz Opoczynski before the war and would see him from time to time in the Warsaw Ghetto. She learned only after the war that Opoczynski was, like herself, one of the major contributors to the Oyneg Shabes.

After the onset of mass extermination, when personal survival appeared more doubtful than ever, Ringelblum decided to write about the archive in an essay contained in the cache of documents discovered in 1950. That essay, along with terse memoirs by Hersh Wasser and postwar essays by Rachel Auerbach, constitute the only sources on the archive written by insiders. Considering that only three members survived the war, such a paucity of sources is not surprising.

Underpinning the activities of the Oyneg Shabes was a group of copiers and transcribers.[37] Sometimes authors would hand over compositions to the Oyneg Shabes, which would then be copied. Another category of materials consisted of interviews that were conducted by an Oyneg Shabes member. Depending on the interviewer and the circumstances, these ranged from almost verbatim transcripts to loose paraphrasing.[38] The archive tried to make multiple copies of each document to safeguard the information, whether the document was an original composition or the transcript of an interview. Copies were sometimes typed and sometimes handwritten. Of course photographs, posters, or original artifacts could not be copied. Coded letters in various alphabets or symbols appear on the front of documents, as well as abbreviations that refer to various members of the Oyneg Shabes. Certain symbols, for instance, designate "transports" of documents that Hersh Wasser classified, organized, and transferred to a hiding place.[39]

After the war, when the archive was unearthed, it became very difficult to distinguish between originals and copies. In the first cache many copies survived but the originals did not. Documents often had names or initials, but in many cases it was impossible to know whether these names referred to the original author or to the name of the person who made the copy or who transcribed the interview. Thus, after the war, certain essays thought to have been written by Rabbi Huberband were actually his transcriptions of what he heard from a second party. After the war Hersh Wasser identified authorship of certain

documents, but these notations were not always correct.[40]

To ensure secrecy, Ringelblum and the staff decided to build a "firewall" between the inner circle of the Oyneg Shabes and Lichtenstein's group, the three men who would receive physical custody of the materials, and, at a signal, bury them. As the materials from Wasser slowly piled up in the hideout in the school, Lichtenstein and his teenaged helpers would read the documents and discuss what they meant. Just before he helped bury the first cache on August 2–3, 1942, David Graber, nineteen years old at the time, recalled,

> My own work was rudimentary—I would pack and hide the material. But nevertheless it was so interesting. There was so much variety, so much that one could learn. Until late into the night we would sit with Comrade Lichtenstein, look through the documents and talk.... First were the photographs of Jews being beaten ... there were many photographs. Then came the reports of the lives of Jews in the provinces, in Lodz. This was hard to read.... How horrible was the report about the gassings in Chelmno, told by Grojanowski. We were so shaken ... that we could not work the whole next day.[41]

It is now clear that when they buried the first cache of the archive on the night of August 2–3, 1942, they worked in great haste. Staring death in the face, they had no time to classify the materials or to sort out copies from originals, which should have gone in different boxes to increase the chances of survival. In fact, when the boxes were opened, many documents were jumbled together, copies along with originals.[42]

From the very beginnings of the archive, the entire staff of the Oyneg Shabes knew they had to risk their lives to collect information. As noted earlier, it was especially perilous to go into the disease-ridden, squalid, and overcrowded refugee centers, and many members of the Oyneg Shabes indeed came down with typhus. Some, such as Rabbi Huberband and Peretz Opoczynski, recovered, but others, like Bernard Kampelmacher, died. Still, despite the dangers, the Oyneg Shabes was a godsend for many of Ringelblum's recruits. It provided a moral lifeline, an occupation, and a reason to go on living. Members felt needed and part of a community.

The staff of the Oyneg Shabes had to find a way to gather material without compromising security. The far-flung activities of the *Aleynhilf* provided excellent cover, since practically the entire Oyneg Shabes—and especially the inner circle—worked in this organization. The *Aleynhilf's* activities allowed members to gather descriptions of practically every forced labor camp in the General Government and helped to camouflage one of the archive's most important projects, the collection of information on events in cities and towns outside Warsaw and in the Soviet-occupied zone. Under the guise of ascertaining the needs of the refugee population, Hersh Wasser and others arranged hundreds of interviews, investigating each interviewee's background and, Ringelblum noted, often waiting until the interview ended to make notes.[43]

The soup kitchens were another major resource from which the Oyneg Shabes gathered material. Rachel Auerbach would identify "clients" who could provide important information, and Ringelblum would send useful individuals to the kitchens for extra food.

Public writing contests proved another excellent source of material and provided a welcome degree of subterfuge. In January 1942 the "Jury and Executive" of a writing contest (which actually consisted of key members of the Oyneg Shabes staff) announced a public competition on a number of themes: a monograph on Jewish life in a city, Polish-Jewish relations, Jewish converts to Catholicism in the ghetto, schools, children, bribery and corruption, smuggling, any particular aspect of the ghetto economy, house committees, entertainment and dissolute behavior in the ghetto, the refugee shelters, the September 1939 campaign, and the Jewish police. There were other themes as well, but much of the document is illegible. The "jury" also announced that it would consider themes that were not on the list.[44] The prizes, ranging from one thousand zlotys for first place to one hundred for sixth place were a significant incentive at a time when a common wage was four to six zlotys a day. The jury reserved the right to divide prizes. Still another competition invited young people to write about their life in the ghetto: essays, diaries, edited correspondence, or even fiction from working youth, middle-class youth, members of the intelligentsia, and students.[45]

The executive committee, and especially Menakhem Kon, collected the money that the Oyneg Shabes needed to function. Expenses included paper and supplies, honoraria for essays, and money to buy food and medicine for key members of the project. There were also many extraordinary expenses that could not be anticipated. For example, when "Szlamek" escaped from the death camp in Chelmno in January 1942, it was Hersh Wasser who took him in hand, found him a place to stay in the Warsaw Ghetto, and then sent him to the provinces [to Zamosc, where he was caught in a round up in April and sent to his death at Belzec]. Kon recorded that the Oyneg Shabes gave Szlamek payments totaling about one thousand zlotys in February and March 1942. Further, in 1942 and 1943 the Oyneg Shabes published information bulletins in Yiddish and in Polish—presumably at its own expense.

One account ledger for the Oyneg Shabes, in Menakhem Kon's handwriting, lists disbursements of at least 55,298 zlotys between November 1940 and July 1942.[46] Other account books probably existed, as the archive continued to work after July 1942. This one extant account book establishes that the archive was spending at least 2,500 zlotys a month and probably much more. Most of the disbursements seem to have been small regular payments to the members of the archive plus periodic purchases of paper and ink and other incidentals. On August 28, 1941, the book recorded an outlay of 390 zlotys to procure tin boxes—no doubt for storing the documents.

There is no question that many—perhaps most—of the archive's expenses were also tucked into the much larger budget of the *Aleynhilf*, as most of the Oyneg Shabes worked there. Although their salaries were meager, these were monies the archive did not have to account for. The same held true of food. As we have already seen, Ringelblum, Gutkowski, or Wasser would send up to sixty people a day to Rachel Auerbach's soup kitchen. It is likely that the kitchen on Leszno 40 was not the only one the Oyneg Shabes used.

Where did the Oyneg Shabes get its funds? Although Yitzhak Giterman was on the executive board, Hersh Wasser insisted in his postwar account that the Oyneg Shabes received no direct help from the Joint Distribution Committee. Wassers's memory must have failed him, since Kon's account ledger shows several payments of 750 zlotys from the Joint as well as regular income from the "SPS" (perhaps the *Aleynhilf*?). Kon's ledger also showed regular and sizable donations from three individuals in particular: Shmuel Winter, Shie Rabinowitz, and Alexander Landau.

Ringelblum kept reminding the men and women of the Oyneg Shabes that they "had to work badly." In other words, the collaborators had

to remember that "the best was the enemy of the good." Given the conditions in the ghetto, it was pointless to pretend that writing, research, and interviews could meet the prewar standards of a university or a scholarly journal. And security came first. If getting a particular piece of information proved too risky, then it was better to forgo the opportunity.

As time went on Ringelblum worried that too many Jews were becoming complacent about alleged German lack of interest in their political activities and in the underground press. Ringelblum was present at a noisy meeting of the *Hashomer Hatzair* [Socialist Zionist Youth Movement] held a short distance from German gendarmes. The cheers and singing could easily be heard outside the building, and the whole scene reminded Ringelblum of a raucous prewar rally. He began to fear that the Germans might indeed care about this clandestine activity, especially if they suspected a possible connection between the Jewish and the Polish secret press.[47] At any rate, the Germans shattered the widespread sense of false security on the night of April 17–18, 1942, when they suddenly descended on the ghetto in the late hours of a Friday evening with lists of names. The lists seemed random, although later many Jews believed that many of the victims had been connected in some way to the underground press. Small groups of Gestapo agents knocked on apartment doors, politely asked certain individuals to come with them, and then shot them in the street. The bodies were left lying in pools of blood. One of the most prominent victims, as we have seen, was Ringelblum's longtime comrade from the YIVO and the IKOR [Yiddish Cultural Organization], the Oyneg Shabes activist Menakhem Linder. Yitzhak Zuckerman, a future leader of the Jewish Fighting Organization, narrowly escaped the same fate. That evening Ringelblum had been planning a lecture in

Rachel Auerbach's soup kitchen on the subject of martyrdom (*Kiddush Hashem*) in Jewish history. Forewarned that something was afoot, he abruptly cancelled the lecture.[48]

What would the Germans do next? If they were onto the underground press, surely they would be doubly anxious to track down the secret archive. At least one member of the Oyneg Shabes executive committee, Menakhem Kon, urged Ringelblum to leave the Warsaw Ghetto as soon as possible.[49] Ringelblum ignored these pleas, but the archive decided to lay a false trail to deceive the Germans. Shortly after the April massacre, the Oyneg Shabes put out the word that it had stopped its activities. Then, in absolute secrecy, Ringelblum and the executive committee invited a much smaller cadre to continue working.

The onset of the Great Deportation in July 1942 threw the Oyneg Shabes into temporary disarray, but Ringelblum and his staff soon regained their bearings. Although the Germans deported many important members, much of the core group survived the first phase of the deportation, which halted on September 12, 1942. Even during that terrible summer the Oyneg Shabes held meetings and charted its future course of action. It now began to pay special attention to documenting the deportation process. When the first escapees from Treblinka appeared in the Warsaw Ghetto, the Oyneg Shabes sat them down to give detailed accounts. When the temporary lull began in September 1942 the Oyneg Shabes resumed its work, composing more questionnaires and learning as much as possible about the state of mind of the remaining Jews. The archive paid special attention to the "shops." It also began to issue an informational bulletin in Polish, *Wiadomosci*. Sometime in February 1943 Ringelblum ordered the burial of a second cache—the milk cans that were found in 1950.[50]

NOTES

1. Ringelblum, *Ksovim fun geto*, 2:101–2. Of course, the "brotherhood" included several women: Rachel Auerbach, Cecylia Slapakowa, Henryka Lazowert, Gustawa Jarecka, and Bluma Wasser.

2. Hersh Wasser, "Vi iz es geven?" *Unzer veg* (March 1954).

3. Ibid.

4. For an excellent study of the Bund in wartime Poland, see Daniel Blatman, *Levna'an heruteinu v'herutkhem: ha-Bund b'Polin 1939–1949* (Jerusalem, 1996).

5. On this possibility, see Ruta Sakowska, "Biuro Informacji i Propagandy KG Armii Krajowej a Archiwum Ringelbluma," BZIH, nos. 162–63 (1992): 19–34.

6. AR 1, no. 457. Reprinted in Yehuda Feld, *In di tsaytn fun Homen dem Tsveytn*, ed. Ber Mark (Warsaw, 1954). For biographical details on Feld, see Samuel Niger and Jacob Shatzky, eds., *Leksikon fun der nayer Yidisher literatur*, 8 vols. (New York, 1956–81), 7:413–14.

7. Hersh Wasser recalled that Ringelblum was always writing something down. As he rushed from meeting to meeting in the *Aleynhilf* or the IKOR, Ringelblum was always jotting down impressions on any handy scrap of paper. See Wasser, "A vort vegn Ringelblum Arkhiv."

8. Ringelblum, *Ksovim fun geto*, 2:77.

9. Ibid.

10. Ibid. This took place in his apartment on 18 Leszno Street.

11. Quoted in Roskies, *The Literature of Destruction*, 209–10.

12. Alexander Donat, *The Holocaust Kingdom* (New York: Holt Rinehart and Winston, 1965), 211; quoted in Alvin Rosenfeld, *A Double Dying* (Bloomington and London: Indiana University Press, 1980), 37–38.

13. On archives in the Vilna Ghetto Archive, see Kruk, *The Last Days of the Jerusalem of Lithuania*; Avrom Sutzkever, *Vilner geto* (Buenos Aires, 1947), 112–17; Yitzhak Arad, "Ha-arkhiyon ha-mehtarti

shel geto Vilna," in *Mi'gniza*, ed. Israel Gutman (Jerusalem, 1997), 151–61; and David Fishman, *Embers Plucked from the Fire: The Rescue of Jewish Cultural Treasures in Vilna* (New York, 1996).

14. The best short treatment of the secret archive in the Bialystok Ghetto is Sarah Bender, "Arkhiyon hamahteret bi'Bialystok," in Gutman, *Mi'gniza*, 121–33. Sec also Bronka Klebanski, "Al Mordecai v'al arkhiyono," in Mordecai Tenenbaum-Tamaroff, *Dapim min ha'dleka: pirkei yoman, mikhtavim, maamarim* (Jerusalem, 1984), 205–15. On Tenenbaum's elliptical reference to the Oyneg Shabes, see his "Mikhtav rhaverim," in *Dapim min ha'dleka*, 99.

15. The best overview of the Lodz Ghetto Archive can be found in Dobroszycki, *The Chronicle of the Lodz Ghetto*, ix–lxviii.

16. On Kruk, see *idem*, *The Last Days of the Jerusalem of Lithuania*; see also Samuel David Kassow, "Vilna and Warsaw, Two Ghetto Diaries: Herman Kruk and Emanuel Ringelblum," in Shapiro, *Holocaust Chronicles*, 171–217.

17. Klebanski, "Al Mordecai v'al arkhiyono," 205–15.

18. See Dobroszycki, *The Chronicle of the Lodz Ghetto*, xxvi–xxviii.

19. Sarah Bender, "Arkhiyon hamahteret bi'Bialystok," in Gutman, *Mi'gniza*, 122–23. Barash [also] passed on to Tenenbaum crucial information about Treblinka, including documents and photographs found in articles of clothing that had been sent from Treblinka to the Bialystok ghetto.

20. [See] . . . Kruk, *The Last Days of the Jerusalem of Lithuania*, 406.

21. See AR 1, no. 1222. They included street scenes of the ghetto, starving children, the Jewish police, the building of walls, smugglers throwing sacks of flour across the ghetto walls, people listening to loudspeakers on the street, and so on.

22. Discussed by Ruta Sakowska in her "Opór cywilny getta warszawskiego," *BZIH*, nos. 86–87 (1973): 79–81.

23. See Kermish, *Itonut ha-Mahteret ha-Yehudit b'Varsha*, xxvii–lxxxi; Daniel Blatman, "Itonut

mahtcret v'hevra," in *idem*, ed., *Geto varsha, sipur itonai* (Jerusalem, 2002), 7–87; Gutman, *The Jews of Warsaw*, 146–54.

24. According to Tadeusz Epsztein, who has prepared the most comprehensive catalogue of the archive, the first cache contained 25,540 pages of material and the second held 9,829 pages. The latter covered August 1942 until February 1943. Epsztein, "Introduction to the Catalog of the Warsaw Ghetto's Underground Archive," 3–4.

25. Rachel Auerbach wrote that a special cellar had been prepared for that part of the archive. See Yad Vashem Archives, Rachel Auerbach Collection, P-16–82, 15.

26. Epsztein, "Introduction to the Catalog of the Warsaw Ghetto's Underground Archive," 4.

27. Ibid., 5.

28. Zuckerman, *A Surplus of Memory*, 112.

29. Yad Vashem Archives, Rachel Auerbach Collection, P-16–82, 15.

30. Examples are essays by Henryka Lazowert on a Jewish family, and by Shie Perle on Lwow.

31. AR 1, no. 1152.

32. Copies of these lists can be found in AR 1, nos. 1147 and 1176.

33. See Lewin, *A Cup of Tears*, 107.

34. Ibid., 141. The archive remained in Warsaw, however, at the Jewish Historical Institute.

35. Wasser, "A vort vegn Ringelblum Arkhiv."

36. Named after its headquarters on Leszno 13, the "Thirteen" . . . furnished information to the Gestapo. This organization emerged as a rival to the *Judenrat* and the Jewish police. See Gutman, *The Jews of Warsaw*, 90–94.

37. The major activity of some members was copying and transcribing, whereas others performed several functions at once, for example, writing diaries, interviewing, copying, and transcribing.

38. See Epsztein, "Introduction to the Catalog of the Warsaw Ghetto's Underground Archive," 13.

39. On the complex difficulties of sorting out copies from originals, see ibid., 7–15.

40. Ibid.

41. AR 1, no. 432.

42. Epsztein, "Introduction to the Catalog of the Warsaw Ghetto's Underground Archive," 13. When the first cache was discovered in 1946, the staff of the Jewish Historical Institute numbered the tin boxes and noted the contents of each.

43. Ringelblum, *Ksovim fun geto*, 2:87.

44. AR 1, no. 134. Reprinted in Kermish, *To Live with Honor*, 27–28.

45. Ibid.

46. AR 2, 210.

47. Ringelbium, *Ksovim fun geto*, 1:353; diary entry of May 12, 1942.

48. Auerbach, *Varshever tsvoes*, 185.

49. Ringelblum, *Ksovim fun geto*, 2:102.

50. According to Epsztein, the latest date found on material in the second cache was February 1, 1943.

Nothing to Lose

YISRAEL GUTMAN

From *The Jews of Warsaw, 1939–1943*

The First Day of the Uprising

On the eve of Passover, the festival of freedom, 1943, the Germans opened the final stage of their campaign to annihilate all trace of the Jewish community of Warsaw. This time, however, the penetration of German troops into the ghetto did not come as a surprise, for throughout the month of April persistent rumors had brought "the last stirring of life in the ghetto" to a halt. "Every day," Tuvia Borzykowski wrote, "and even a number of times each day, all the Jews would stop whatever they were doing and dash for shelter."[1] The least suspicion of heightened activity among the enemy's forces was sufficient to alarm the entire population and engender a state of alert. Nonetheless, the Jews could not ignore the approach of the Passover holiday. With a determination that had characterized the Jews for centuries and a resourcefulness that had reached unprecedented proportions during the occupation, the surviving remnant of the Warsaw ghetto prepared to celebrate the Passover, taking care to acquire the ritual Passover foods (matzos and wine) and cleansing their eating and cooking utensils as prescribed by religious law.

On April 18, 1943, the ghetto received reports—including authoritative information from the "Aryan" side—that the massing of troops had been noted in Warsaw and the Germans were evidently about to initiate the decisive *Aktion* against the ghetto. The lookout posts that had been set up in buildings throughout the ghetto were now reinforced, and the night of April 18 was spent watching and waiting. At 1:00 or 2:00 a.m. came the first reports on the deployment of enemy forces along the ghetto wall—units of the German gendarmerie and the Polish Police, who surrounded the ghetto with a cordon of guards 25 meters apart. Z.O.B. [Jewish Fighting Organization] runners dashed from house to house alerting the population that an *Aktion* was expected the next morning. In many cases their warning was superfluous, since the tenants had already received word from the regular lookouts on the rooftops. Many residents of the ghetto abandoned their festive tables and gathered together in large groups. "No Jew slept that night. Belongings, underwear, bedding, [and] provisions were packed and taken into the bunkers."

The Z.O.B. was put in a state of high alert. "At one in the morning," Borzykowski wrote, "the command received the latest reports, on the basis of which all the groups were mobilized immediately."[2] [Marek] Edelman noted that the news arrived at 2:00 a.m.: "All the combat groups were alerted immediately, and at 2:15—that is, in about fifteen minutes—they had taken up their combat positions."[3] As the forces were mustered, each fighter received a steel combat helmet and a knapsack filled with "underwear, provisions, [and] first-aid materials. In addition to the standard weapons at his disposal, every fighter was now given bombs, Molotov cocktails, etc."[4] Chaim

Frimmer described the preparations for battle at the Z.O.B.'s principal position in the Central Ghetto:

> In the evening a state of alert was proclaimed and the passwords were changed. Now we knew that the Germans were readying themselves for an *Aktion* in the ghetto. A single password was established for the fighters in all the groups—"Jan—Warsaw"—[and] we began fortifying the positions. The approach to the gate of the courtyard was blocked by a wagon that we turned wheels-up. We removed closets and the rest of the heavy furniture from the apartments and stacked them in the gateway. The windows were fortified with sandbags. People were assigned to their various positions. . . . I received an order from Berl Braudo to check the weapons and pass out ammunition to the men. We filled baskets with Molotov cocktails and passed them on to the positions. . . . Mordecai Anielewicz arrived and went into Yisrael [Kanai's] room. After consultation they came out and walked through the rooms and apartments, selecting appropriate spots for positions. People from other groups came to receive provisions, battle rations—rusks, sugar, groats. "Cjank" [doses of cyanide] was passed out to certain people, especially those whose tasks required them to be mobile and heightened their chances of being caught by the Germans and tortured during interrogation.[5]

In his summarizing report on the fighting in the ghetto, General Stroop mentioned the factors that moved the Germans to initiate the final *Aktion* on April 19:

> In January 1943, following his visit to Warsaw, the *Reichsführer*-S.S. [Himmler] ordered the S.S.-*und Polizeiführer* of the Warsaw District [von Sammern] to transfer the equipment and armament plants located in the ghetto, *including their workers and machinery*, to Lublin. The execution of this order became hopelessly bogged down, because both the management of the factories and the Jews resisted the transfer by every means imaginable. As a result, the S.S.-*und Polizeiführer* decided to carry out the transfer of the factories by force in a large operation that was scheduled to last for three days.[6]

In January 1946, Franz Konrad, the ss officer in charge of the *Werterfassung* [registering valuables] in von Sammern's headquarters, gave testimony that related to the first day of the April *Aktion*:

> A week before Easter 1943—it was a Sunday morning—S.S. *und Polizeiführer* von Sammern convened a meeting of the heads of the Security Police, *Obersturmbannfüher*-S.S. Hahn, the commanders of the S.S. units in Warsaw, [the commanders] of the cavalry and infantry reserve units, the commanders of the "Sipo" [Security Police] and the "Orpo" [Regular Police], and the officers in his headquarters (myself among them). At this meeting we were notified that on Monday he intended to transfer out the Jews who still remained in the Warsaw ghetto. During the discussion about the appropriate time for sending the various S.S. and police units into action, *Brigadeführer* Jürgen (Josef) Stroop entered and announced that he had been appointed to the post of S.S.-*und Polizeiführer* by order of the *Reichsführer*-S.S.[7]

That same day, April 18, the Polish Police was put under alert (Polish policemen were slated to take part in the encirclement of the ghetto). The declaration of a state of alert was evidently passed on to circles in the Polish underground, who in turn warned the ghetto underground that an *Aktion* might commence the next day.

The question remains whether the Germans were aware of the activities and preparations going on in the ghetto—i.e., that an armed Jewish force was deploying for resistance. It is absolutely certain that the commanders of the SS and the police knew that a resistance force was being organized in the ghetto and that they could expect armed opposition to any forthcoming *Aktion*. After all, the Germans had already experienced combat skirmishes in January. Even though they had experimented with the strategy of a relatively long waiting period and attempted to dismantle the ghetto by means of persuasion—as if disregarding the fact that an underground force was preparing itself to give battle whenever the *Aktion* began— the way in which von Sammern approached the forthcoming *Aktion*—namely his mobilization of an impressive military force and convening of the heads of the commands in Warsaw—indicates that he knew the April *Aktion* would not resemble the previous "resettlement operations" because this time the Jews could resist. All the same, it appears that von Sammern did not appreciate the extent of the resistance or know of the widespread network of bunkers in the ghetto. We may assume that he expected the forthcoming resistance to resemble the street fighting during the January deportation, meaning that the insurgents would try to attack the German troops head on. Von Sammern therefore decided to send in a large force on the first day of the operation in order to break the resistance with a single mighty blow. He likewise accepted as fact the claims of [Walter] Tobbens [a German manufacturer in the ghetto] that the Z.O.B. had foiled the peaceful evacuation of the population by pressure and terror tactics and that once the hard core of insurgents had been eliminated, the deportation would go smoothly, since the remainder of the Jews did not support the fighting underground.

The unfolding of events in the ghetto after the mass deportation in the summer of 1942 had undermined von Sammern's credit with Himmler, who decided to place the final task of liquidating the ghetto in the hands of a man who was new to Warsaw but had a reputation as an experienced police commander. Before being posted to Warsaw, Jürgen Stroop had served in the SS and Police Command in eastern Galicia and was regarded as a vigorous man who had proven his abilities and determination in operations against the partisans. Stroop reached Warsaw before the initiation of the *Aktion*, on the evening of April 17. The next day he appeared at the meeting called by von Sammern but did not immediately assume command of the operation, evidently preferring to remain in the position of a supervisor who would be ready to enter into action whenever intervention proved necessary or when the time appeared ripe to assume command. In reply to questions addressed to him after the war, Stroop reported, *inter alia*:

> The German command, and particularly my predecessor as *S.S.-und Polizeiführer*, von Sammern, did not take even the mildest resistance into account. A number of trouble-free deportations had preceded the final *Aktion*, so that Dr. von Sammern assumed that the final deportation would also be executed smoothly. Only on the eve of the *Aktion* did he receive a report that armed resistance could be expected. Of course, he didn't believe it, but for the sake of discipline he passed on the full assessment to [Friedrich] Krieger [commander of police in occupied Poland], so that the latter could act accordingly.[8]

It is unreasonable to believe that von Sammern assumed the forthcoming evacuation would resemble the *Aktionen* of the past or that he was surprised to receive a report pointing out the possibility of resistance and personally did not believe it. It is entirely possible, however, that von Sammern did not wish to admit his concern to Stroop or even to brief his successor on the true situation. Confessing to the truth of the matter would not improve his position or personal situation. At the same time, it is imperative to emphasize that the Germans never even imagined the potency of the resistance. General Rowecki, the commander of the A.K. [*Armia Krajowa* (Home Army), the underground military resistance organization of the Polish government-in-exile], noted in his report on the uprising to the London-based government that "the resistance of groups of Jewish fighters was far beyond all expectations and took the Germans by surprise," and a survey of the Polish underground appraising the situation from May 8 to 14 stated: "The Germans regarded the prolongation of resistance in the ghetto as a stain on their reputation. The oversight that allowed such a line of resistance to come into being cost the commander of the ss and the police in the Warsaw District, von Sammern, his post. Police general Stroop was appointed in his place."9

While imprisoned in Poland, Stroop wrote:

The residents of the ghetto knew about all the moves of the German authorities. They were ready for anything and took appropriate counter-measures. Thus the building of shelters in cellars, which was done in accordance with orders, was exploited for the construction of bunkers to defend the ghetto, and this was kept from the German authorities. Col. von Sammern told me that despite the secrecy, as early as April 17th [the Jews] were informed by telephone of the hour when the operation would begin! In my opinion, this was the crucial reason for the failure of the operational units under

[von Sammern's] command to penetrate [the ghetto] during the morning hours of April 19, 1943! [The Jews] were prepared and were not intimidated by the use of armor and half-tracks (they had incendiary bottles, powerful home-made bombs, revolvers, low-caliber rifles, and even German uniforms). But they underestimated the fighting power of the police stationed in Warsaw.10

The irony at this stage was that the isolated and doomed Jews were preparing for the German attack and were forewarned of its imminence, while the omnipotent German regime, backed by secret police and a network of informers of all kinds and nationalities, knew essentially nothing of what was going on in the ghetto. This important achievement must be credited to the success of the fighting organizations in the ghetto, particularly the Z.O.B., in purging the ghetto of destructive elements and preparing it for the impending trial.

According to Stroop's report for April 20, the "Grand *Aktion*" commanded by von Sammern began at 3:00 a.m. on April 19 with an encirclement of the ghetto by reinforced troops. (As we have noted, the Jewish sources report that the lookouts spotted these forces at 1:00 or 2:00 a.m.) At 6:00 a.m., Stroop's report continues, came "the deployment of Waffen-S.S. to the extent of 850/16" (i.e., 850 soldiers and 16 officers). Simha Ratajzer, a Z.O.B. fighter, subsequently described how the German forces entering the ghetto appeared from a lookout post in the Brushmakers' Area:

At 4:00 in the morning we saw a column of Hitlerites at the Nalewki passage moving toward the Central Ghetto. [The column] marched and marched without end, a few thousand strong. Behind it came a few tanks, armored cars, light cannon, and a few hundred ss troops on motorcycles. "They're marching like they're off to war," I commented to Zippora, my partner in the position, and suddenly I sensed how weak we were. What are we and our force against an armed and equipped army, against tanks and armored cars, while we have only revolvers and, at best, grenades in our hands. . . .[11]

The German force penetrated the ghetto in two columns. One marched along Nalewki Street while the second (which had entered the gate at the corner of Gesia and Zamenhofa streets) intended to spread out along the other main artery in the Central Ghetto, Zamenhofa-Mila. The Jewish forces in the Central Ghetto were deployed at three points: (1) a force composed of three Z.O.B. combat squads took up position on the upper floors of the buildings at the corner of Gesia and Nalewki streets; (2) four Z.O.B. squads, together with the area headquarters and the general headquarters of the organization, were located in positions at the intersection of Zamenhofa and Gesia streets; (3) the Z.Z.W. [Jewish Military Union] force in the Central Ghetto, which comprised the union's principal contingent, fortified itself in the sector of Muranowska Square. For months the fighters had been preparing escape routes over the rooftops, so that it would be possible to get from house to house without going out into the streets.

The first armed clash occurred on Nalewki Street, at the corner of Gesia, where two Z.O.B. combat squads (under the command of Zecharia Artstein and Lolek Rotblat) came into contact with the Germans. A German column moving up the center of the road while singing boisterously was attacked at the corner by forces positioned in the building at 33 Nalewki Street. The surprise was total and the power of the fire—especially the bombs and hand grenades—inflicted injuries to the enemy and sowed havoc in its ranks, so much so that the Germans retreated and dispersed, leaving their casualties lying on the street. Then the German troops tried to organize a counterattack. This time they no longer exposed themselves in the center of the street but hugged the walls of the buildings and sought shelter in the entrances. The heavy German fire met with only sporadic response from the Jewish side, but the Jews enjoyed a clear advantage: the Germans could not operate without exposing themselves. As one fighter explained in his memoirs, "while we were concealed in our positions," the Germans were easy targets. This second battle likewise ended in a German retreat. There were no casualties to the Jewish side.

While this clash was taking place on the corner of Nalewki and Gesia, the main battle of April 19 raged at the corner of Zamenhofa and Mila streets. Four squads of Z.O.B. fighters (under the command of Berl Braudo, Aaron Bryskin, Mordecai Growas, and Leib Gruzalc) positioned themselves around the square that dominated the intersection. Nearby, the Germans had chosen a place to establish an improvised headquarters. The arrival of their equipment—including tables, benches, and communications instruments—was followed by the end of the main German column. Jewish policemen were forced to march at the head of this column to serve as a human wall and protect the German units by absorbing any burst of fire from the Jewish insurgents.

Chaim Frimmer, a fighter in Braudo's squad who viewed the German deployment and subsequent battle from one of the lookout posts, described the events as follows:

At five in the morning a loud rumble was heard. Suddenly I saw from my lookout on the balcony that cars had come through the ghetto gate. They reached the square, stopped, and soldiers got out and stood to the side. Then a truck arrived carrying tables and benches. . . . Wires were laid, and telephones were placed on them. Other cars came with soldiers bearing machine guns. Then motorcycle riders arrived [and] some ambulances and light tanks could be seen stopping by the entrance. . . . At six a column of infantry entered. One section of the column turned into Wolynska Street and the other remained in place, as if awaiting orders. Before long the Jewish Police came through the gate. They were lined up on both sides of the street and, as ordered, began to advance toward us. I would report everything to a fighter lying down not far from me [who in turn passed word on] to the command room, where Mordecai [Anielewicz], Yisrael [Kanal], and others were seated. When the column of Jewish Police reached our building, I asked how to proceed: Attack or not? The reply was to wait; Germans would surely follow, and the privilege of taking our fire belongs to them. And that's exactly what happened: After the Jewish Police crossed the street, an armed, mobile German column began to move. [I was ordered to wait] until the middle of the column had reached the balcony and then throw a grenade at it, which would serve as a signal to start the action. . . . Immediately thereafter grenades were thrown at the Germans from all sides, from all the positions on both sides of the street. Above the tumult of explosions and firing, we could hear the sputter of the German *Schmeisser* [a submachine gun used by the German army] operated by one of our men in the neighboring squad. I myself remained on the balcony and spewed forth fire from my Mauser onto the shocked and confused Germans. . . . The battle lasted for about half an hour. The Germans retreated leaving many dead and wounded in the street. . . . Again my eyes were peeled on the street, and

then two tanks came in, followed by an infantry column. When the tank came up to our building, some Molotov cocktails and bombs put together from thick lead pipes were thrown at it. The big tank began to burn and, engulfed in flames, made its way toward the *Umschlagplatz*. The second tank remained in place as fire consumed it from every side.[12]

The first of Stroop's daily reports described the progress of the fighting during the early morning hours of April 19 from the German viewpoint:

As soon as the units deployed, a premeditated attack by the Jews and the bandits; Molotov cocktails were thrown on the tank and on two armored cars. The tank was burning fiercely. At first, this attack caused [our] forces to retreat. Our losses in the first action were 12 men (6 ss men, 6 Trawniki men [Eastern European auxiliaries]). At close to eight o'clock, the second attack under the command of the undersigned.

It was only after the war, during his trial in Poland, that Stroop added details on what had happened from the moment that the forces under von Sammern's command were repulsed until Stroop assumed command of the operation:

At 6:00 a.m. on April 19, Col. von Sammern initiated the *Aktion*, and he remained in command of it—by mutual agreement—since he had made all the preparations and was familiar with the place. I consented to come to the ghetto, which I had never seen before, at about 9:00 a.m. on April 19. At around 7:30, von Sammern turned up at my lodgings and announced that all was lost, that the forces he had sent into the ghetto had retreated and there were already dead and wounded. I can't remember how many. Von Sammern said that he would call Cracow and request that "Stuka" planes bomb the ghetto to quash the rebellion that had broken out. I told him not to because I wanted to review the situation on the spot. . . . I asked for a map of the ghetto and entered through the gate, while bullets showered down on me incessantly. . . . I handled the forces according to the rules of street fighting, lining storm troopers along both sides of the main street so that they would not go charging forward blindly, as had evidently happened before. I issued the appropriate orders to the commanders of the units. My intention was to gain control of at least the buildings on the main street.

According to [Tuvia] Borzykowski, the battle resumed on Nalewki Street about three hours after the German retreat. The enemy troops removed mattresses from the *Werterfassung* warehouse near the Z.O.B. positions and constructed a protective barricade as they continued to fire. They operated in groups and were careful not to expose themselves to the snipers firing from the positions. When the barricade was set on fire by Molotov cocktails, the Germans threw their own incendiary bottles into the building at 33 Nalewki Street, where the Z.O.B. position was located, setting it aflame. The fighters, who were forced to abandon their position and seek cover, evaded the Germans waiting for them in the street by escaping over the rooftops. The positions on Zamenhofa also came under heavy fire, and the order to withdraw was given as a hail of bullets pierced the ceilings of the rooms where the fighters were stationed. Those fighters took shelter in the bunker that housed their headquarters on Zamenhofa Street.

Stroop also reported that at about 7:30 his forces came up against "very strong resistance from a block of buildings, accompanied by machine-gun fire."[13] This is a reference to the battle that broke out in Muranowska Square, where the main con-

tingent of the Z.Z.W. was located. In the course of the fighting, the Z.Z.W. unfurled a blue-and-white flag and the national flag of Poland. One of its members reported that on the day of the first battle, a machine gun had reached the unit through the tunnel that extended to the "Aryan" side.[14] It was stationed in a position that dominated the entire square and effectively blocked the German advance. Each of the German attacks met with stiff resistance. Edelman noted that during the battle a tank was hit and set aflame, "the second one that day."[15] According to Stroop, "a special combat unit silenced the enemy, penetrated the buildings, [but] did not catch the enemy itself. The Jews and the criminals were fighting everywhere, position by position, and at the last moment they escaped and fled over the rooftops or through underground passages."[16]

On the first day of battle, then, the Jewish fighters attacked from three focal points. In each case, it was the insurgents who opened fire and surprised the enemy. The Germans were forced to withdraw from the ghetto after the first clash, and von Sammern lost his lead when he realized the strength of the Jewish resistance. When Stroop assumed command of the operation, he proceeded cautiously, adopting the tactics of house-to-house fighting. Yet he too was forced into a difficult and drawn-out battle in Muranowska Square. The losses to the Jewish side that day were relatively light. One member of the Z.O.B. fell (Yechiel from Growas's squad, who fired the submachine gun), while the Z.Z.W. probably lost a larger number of people.[17] The casualties on the German side (according to Stroop's reports) were one dead and twenty-four wounded, including fourteen ss men, two German gendarmes, six men from the Trawniki unit, and two Polish policemen.[18]

As early as the first day of the uprising, the Germans also met with opposition from a totally unexpected source—i.e., the resistance of the ghetto's population at large, which the Germans dubbed "the battle of the bunkers." Stroop described the nature and significance of this line of resistance in his comprehensive survey: "The number of Jews trapped in and removed from the buildings was very small. It turned out that Jews were hiding in sewers and specially equipped bunkers. During the first few days, only a few bunkers were believed to exist; but as the major operation continued, it became clear that the entire ghetto was systematically equipped with cellars, bunkers, and passages." Stroop's report on the first day of the fighting concludes: "During the search only 200 Jews were caught. Afterward storm troops were sent into action against the bunkers known to us with orders to bring out their inhabitants and demolish the bunkers themselves. About 380 Jews were caught in this operation. The presence of Jews in the sewers was discovered."[19]

Thus we learn from Stroop's report that as a result of a day of stubborn fighting, which cost the Germans heavy losses, 580 Jews were trapped—about 1 percent of the ghetto's population at the time. According to Stroop, this "accomplishment" was achieved because the Germans knew the location of some of the "shops," and most of the victims of April 19 were trapped in them. On the first day of the operation, then, in addition to the organized and determined armed resistance of the fighting organizations, the Germans came up against the phenomenon of tens of thousands of people fortified below ground . . .

The Turning Point in the Uprising

As we have seen, after the initial days of battle, the German command reached the conclusion that the way to overcome the insurgents was to burn down or demolish the ghetto's buildings, thereby forcing the Jews to come out into the open. On

April 26 Stroop reported that "during today's operation many housing blocks were set aflame. This is the only and ultimate way to defeat the rabble and scum of the earth and bring them above ground." His April 22 report illustrated this form of warfare and its results:

> The fire that raged all night drove the Jews who—despite all the search operations—were still hiding under roofs, in cellars, and in other hiding places out of the housing blocks in order to escape the flames in one way or another. Scores of burning Jews—whole families— jumped from windows or tried to slide down sheets that had been tied together, etc. We took pains to ensure that those Jews, as well as others, were wiped out immediately.

Initially the Germans allocated three days for the liquidation of the ghetto. Stroop was naturally interested in accelerating the pace of the operation and evidently thought that the fire and demolition would achieve his aim quickly. On the fifth day of the *Aktion*, April 23, he believed that the revolt had come to an end. He therefore divided the ghetto into twenty-four sectors and ordered his troops, likewise divided into units according to sector, to comb the area in a final search. In his report for April 23, Stroop noted that "the troops were notified that the *Aktion* will end today," but it soon became evident that his announcement was premature, for "the Jews and the hooligans are [still] to be found in a number of blocks."[20]

The principal difficulty confronting Stroop at this stage of the uprising was the "battle of the bunkers," which continued for close to a month and evidently did not end even on May 16, 1943— the day on which he officially pronounced the close of the "Grand *Aktion*" in the ghetto. After the war, during his interrogation, Stroop repeatedly stressed that "We did not find out about all the bunkers and strongholds set up and equipped for the uprising until after the start of the battle!" In each of his daily reports, he spoke of dozens of bunkers being discovered, cleaned out, and blown up. On May 24, 1943, when he replied in writing to questions addressed to him by Krieger, Stroop testified that 631 bunkers were destroyed during the "Grand *Aktion*."

The Germans needed special facilities for their campaign against the bunkers, such as police dogs, special listening devices to detect sounds underground, and poisonous gas for the bunkers whose inhabitants refused to come out. A gas of the chlorine variety was also used to annihilate the inhabitants of the bunkers, since the Germans would not dare to infiltrate the labyrinth of hiding places. Stroop does not mention the use of gas in his reports and would not confess to it even after the war. In both cases, he insisted that only smoke bombs were used to clear out the bunkers, but the truth is that many were killed by the poisonous gases used against these hideouts. In fact, it was the gas, more than anything else, that forced the victims to come out. There were also many cases of delayed complications and respiratory diseases, and people so affected later died in "*Revir*," the special section for the sick in the Majdanek concentration camp.[21]

All of these measures did little to bring about the swift defeat of the bunkers. On the contrary, the "battle of the bunkers" turned into a drawn-out operation in which the Germans made slow progress. The condition of the bunkers' inhabitants—meaning the entire population of the Central Ghetto, including the fighters—steadily deteriorated until it turned into a state of unrelieved suffering and torture. At the beginning of the uprising, the Germans set fire to individual buildings or housing blocks, but in the course of time the fire spread until it engulfed the entire ghetto.

Many bunkers collapsed as a result of the blaze and the consequent buckling of building walls. When only the skeletons of buildings remained, the cellars grew so hot that it was impossible to breathe in them. But the Germans did not content themselves with the results of the fire and went on to blow up what remained of the gutted structures. Bunkers became uninhabitable and were abandoned. Yet even under these circumstances, the population of the bunkers did not give up the struggle, and they began to wander from bunker to bunker or seek cover among the ruins. One memoir described the scene in a central bunker at 30 Franciszkanska Street, where a number of injured Z.O.B. members found shelter:

> I can't think of anything but breathing air. The heat in the bunker is unbearable. [But] it's not only the heat. The steaming walls give off an odor as if the mildew absorbed during decades had suddenly been released by the catalyst of heat. And there's no air. I sit here open-mouthed, as do all those around me, deluding ourselves that we can gulp down some air. There is no talk in the bunker [because] it is more difficult to breathe when you talk. But from time to time shouting [and] scuffles break out; nerves are taut, and for the most part the shouts are over nothing. We haven't eaten for twenty-four hours. Only dry bread is left and the water is more or less fit for drinking. All the food has spoiled. The heat and the odor have tainted it, so that the ample reserves are inedible.[22]

In another memoir, a man who wandered from one hiding place to another described the situation in one of these shelters: "The new hideout was not the most pleasant of places. It was crowded; cold crept through your bones; we had to stand in water above our hips; and the water pipe—which was in contact with the electricity cable—was electrified . . ."[23] Despite it all, however, the inhabitants of the bunkers refused to surrender. They continued to struggle under great stress and intolerable physical conditions, and every instance of successfully evading the Germans was regarded as deliverance.

In addition to the sophisticated devices for exposing the bunkers, the Germans also employed informers, who were promised their lives in return for revealing the whereabouts of the bunkers' entrances. The Germans hauled these informers along with them, and when the entrance to a bunker was breached, they were ordered to call out in Yiddish for everyone to come out, since the bunker had been exposed and only those who would come out willingly had a chance of saving themselves. The Germans also forced the informers to stand directly in front of the entrance, since the initial response to their call was often a round of gunfire.

The "battle of the bunkers" proved to the Germans that the Jews were determined not to surrender themselves. On April 24, Stroop reported: "From time to time it became clear that despite the terror of the raging fire, the Jews and the hooligans preferred to turn back into the flames rather than fall into our hands." And on May 4 he confessed in his daily battle report: "Uncovering the bunkers becomes more difficult. Often it would be impossible to find [them] were it not for the treachery of other Jews. The command to leave the bunkers voluntarily is almost never obeyed; only the use of smoke bombs forces the Jews to respond to it."

Many bunkers were the strongholds of recalcitrants who not only preferred death by fire or gassing to capture but even fought back. Often they were members of the fighting organizations who had found their way into the bunkers and

resisted when the Germans arrived, though it must be added that the armed struggle of individuals and unaffiliated groups focused primarily on the defense of the bunkers. On April 26 Stroop detailed a number of incidents of this nature:

> The entire former Jewish residential quarter was again combed today by the same storm troopers going over the same sectors. That way I hoped that the commanders would approach as far as the open lines of the housing blocks and courtyards familiar to them so that they could advance further and infiltrate the labyrinth of bunkers and underground passages. Almost all the storm troopers reported some resistance, but it was broken by firing back or blowing up the bunkers.[24]

The fortified labyrinth of subterranean bunkers and tunnels made the ghetto into a unique partisan fighting ground. Since a substantial portion of the bunkers were not uncovered by the police dogs, listening devices, or informers, the network of shelters that protected the remains of Warsaw's Jewish community posed a serious challenge to the Germans. A clear-cut order demanded that every Jew be trapped and liquidated or sent to a camp. Yet in the heart of a large metropolis, clandestine Jewish life continued to go on below ground, and even after weeks of employing the most radical and brutal tactics, the Germans had difficulty snuffing it out. The "battle of the bunkers" held down German troops and, above all, took time. And that time—the days and weeks—was precisely what discomfited the Germans most. The *Aktion*, conceived as a three-day final purge of the Warsaw ghetto, had turned into a drawn-out and far from routine battle in which German military and police forces were pitted against Jewish civilians holed up in bunkers. In full view of the Polish public, under the curious and mocking gaze of the population of a city that was the focus of constant security problems, the "battle of the bunkers" was regarded as a blot on the Germans' prestige and a serious security risk.

The full-scale battle fought by the members of the combat organizations lasted primarily for the first three days of the uprising. From then on the Germans generally succeeded in overcoming the pockets of resistance, driving the fighters out of their positions and forcing them to retreat into the bunkers, which thereafter served as bases for the combat forces. Although the network of sub-terranean shelters had originally been regarded as refuges for the noncombatant population, it now assimilated the fighters as well, allowing them to continue their struggle. It was from these bunkers that bands of fighters went out on raids and attacked the enemy. If the hundreds of fighters had been forced to operate in an unpopulated ghetto or were opposed by a hostile population, the Germans would probably have suppressed the rebellion during the first days of open com-bat. While it is true that not all of the bunkers willingly accepted the fighters, for their presence was regarded as an additional risk and provoca-tion of the Germans, most of them welcomed the combatants with open arms and agreed to place the defense of the bunker in their hands. As a rule, therefore, the network of bunkers played an important role in the Warsaw ghetto uprising by considerably extending the life of the revolt. In point of fact, it took the Germans longer to quell the Warsaw ghetto uprising than it had taken them to defeat entire countries. Moreover, the stand of the population in the bunkers accorded the uprising the character of a popular revolt in which thousands of civilians took part. Thus it was to the credit of the bunkers that the outburst of the com-bat squads developed into a partisan struggle that went on for an extended period of time.

On April 23, Mordecai Anielewicz wrote to his comrade Yitzhak Zuckerman, who was stationed on the "Aryan" side of the city:

> I can't begin to describe the conditions under which the Jews are living. Only an elect few will hold out under them. All the others will perish, sooner or later. Our fate is sealed. In the bunkers where our comrades are hiding, it is not even possible to light a candle at night for lack of air. . . . During the day they sit in the hideouts. Starting in the evening we go over to the partisan method of action. At night six of our companies go out with two tasks before them: armed reconnaissance and the acquisi-tion of arms.[25]

Marek Edelman wrote in *A Fighting Ghetto*:

> Because conditions had changed so much, the Z.O.B. revised its tactics [and] attempted to defend larger concentrations of people hid-ing from the Germans in bunkers. Thus, for example, two Z.O.B-squads (Hochberg's and Berek's) moved a few hundred people from a shelter that had been blocked on 37 Mila Street to 7 Mila Street in broad daylight. This [lat-ter] position, which contained a few thousand people, was held for over a week. In the mean-time, the burning of the ghetto was drawing to a close. Places of shelter are sorely lacking and—even worse—there is a shortage of water. The fighters are going down into the shelters together with the civilian population. There they will continue to fight as best they can. The battles and clashes take place mostly at night now. During the day the ghetto is like a city of the dead. Only on the totally darkened streets do Z.O.B. squads meet up with German units. Whoever fires first has the advantage. Our units circulate through the entire ghetto, [and] every

night many from both sides are killed. The Germans and Ukrainians go out only in large units and more often than not set up ambushes.[26]

Thus even after all hopes of remaining underground for a prolonged period—perhaps even until the end of the war—were dashed, the alliance between the fighters and the many civilians living in the bunkers held fast. Even the bunker housing the Z.O.B. headquarters at 18 Mila Street, in which the organization's command and principal force found refuge, was not a Z.O.B. bunker per se but had been set up by a group of hardened smugglers. The fighters, for their part, combined the continuation of the armed struggle with the defense of the bunkers. Yet both the fighters and civilians in the ghetto realized that the situation generated by the resistance could only be temporary.

Stroop's reports reveal that the armed clashes continued, and the troops charged with wiping out the bunkers were forced to operate under combat conditions. On April 23 he reported that "the Jews and the thugs restrained themselves until the last moment in order to pour intense fire on the units." On April 24 he commented that "from time to time the Jews continued to shoot, almost until the end of the operation. . . ." The next day Stroop noted that "today, as well, there was occasional armed resistance, and three revolvers and explosives were captured in one of the bunkers." Three days later he made note of the fact that "the external appearance of the Jews being caught now implies that the turn of the . . . leaders of the rebellion has come. Swearing against Germany and the Führer and cursing the German soldiers, they hurled themselves out of windows and off balconies." His report for April 28 stated that "today, as well, armed resistance was exhibited and broken in a number of places." On May 2 Stroop recorded that "the ss patrols operat-

ing at night sometimes met up with armed resistance from the Jews." The next day he elaborated that "in most cases, the Jews fought with weapons before abandoning the bunkers," and "last night shots were aimed at some of the patrols operating in the ghetto." On May 4: "In order to catch the Jews totally off guard, the troops on patrol wrapped their shoes in rags and other materials at night. Thirty Jews were shot to death in clashes with the patrol units." On May 5: "Today, as well, Jews fought in a number of places before being captured." As late as May 13 he wrote:

While mopping up one of the bunkers, a real battle took place in which Jews not only opened fire with .08-caliber revolvers and Polish Wiss pistols, but even tossed oval-shaped, Polish-manufactured hand grenades at the ss men. After a few of the bunker's [fighters] were brought out and stood waiting to be searched, one of the women slipped her hand under her dress in a flash and—as has often happened—pulled a hand grenade out of her underwear, released the cap, and hurled it at the men who were searching her, while she herself jumped back quickly and took cover.[27]

Descriptions of battles in the bunkers were also available from Jewish sources. Marek Edelman described one such battle in a bunker at 30 Franciszkanska Street, a building with a number of courtyards and sophisticated bunkers . . . :

. . . The shelter on 30 Franciszkanska Street, which housed an operative base of fighters who had broken through from the Brushmakers' Area, was uncovered on May 3. The men fought one of the most outstanding battles from the technical point of view. It lasted for two days, and 50 percent of our men fell. Berek was killed by a grenade. . . . It is difficult to speak of victory when people are fighting for their lives and so many are lost, but one thing can be said of this battle: We did not allow the Germans to execute their plans.[28] . . .

Starting in the first week of May, Stroop repeatedly noted in his reports that the struggle with the hard core of insurgents had begun and that he was engaged in annihilating the focal points of the revolt. On May 15 he reported:

Last night patrol units in the ghetto reported that they did not come up against Jews, except on rare occasions. . . . In the exchange of fire that took place during the afternoon hours—when the thugs again fought with Molotov cocktails, revolvers, and homemade hand grenades—after the gang was destroyed, one of the policemen (Orpo) was wounded by a bullet in his right thigh. The last block that remains intact . . . was searched a second time and then destroyed by a special commando unit. Toward evening the synagogue in the Jewish cemetery, the mortuary room, and all the surrounding buildings were blown up or set to the torch.

It was the destruction of the largest Jewish synagogue in Warsaw—a building of special architectural design located outside the boundaries of the ghetto—that symbolized the "victory" over Warsaw's Jewish community and the end of the fighting in the ghetto. On May 16 Stroop wrote: "One hundred and eighty Jews, thugs, and the scum of humanity were killed. The 'Grand Aktion' ended at 20:15 [8:15 p.m.] with the demolition of the Warsaw synagogue."

Yet it was clear to Stroop that concluding the operation was not equivalent to wiping out all the bunkers and Jews who had fortified themselves in the ghetto. Despite his firm resolve, Stroop did not succeed in completing the liquidation of the

ghetto. On May 13 he reported that he intended to conclude the "Grand Aktion" on May 16 "and turn over the task of the forthcoming operations . . . to a police battalion. . . ." Indeed, on May 16 he noted that he would charge said police battalion with "continuing or concluding the actions that have yet to be carried out."[29]

Proof of the fact that the Jewish resistance was not suppressed during the four weeks of the "Grand Aktion" under Stroop's command can be found in the daily reports of the Polish "Blue Police" that describe the situation after May 16. The report for May 18 states: "Jewish units emerge from underground and attack the Germans by surprise. At night the SS men withdraw to the borders of the ghetto; there is not a single German in the ghetto. SS men claim that thousands of Jews are hiding out among the ruins and in the underground niches." On May 20 the "Blue Police" review noted: ". . . Shots in the ghetto night and day. Sometimes they are accompanied by loud blasts of explosives—the demolition of certain buildings and the tossing of grenades by both sides." On May 21 there was again mention of "shooting in the ghetto from light weapons and both sides throwing grenades." On May 22 and 23:

. . . Gunfire from light and automatic weapons and the sound of explosions. According to an unconfirmed report, Himmler's visit has made it certain that the area of the ghetto will be attacked and the wall surrounding it will be raised higher because the German police and SS men involved in security work in the ghetto are suffering heavy losses and the number of German functionaries who have fallen is excessive.

The report of May 27–31 states:

On the 27th, 28th, 29th, and 30th of this month, exchanges of fire day and night, especially during the night of May 30; and during the day of May 31, heavy fighting [raged] on Prze-jazd and Leszno streets. . . . Jews attempted to break through to the "Aryan" side. On the other hand, during the day the Germans continue to pull Jews out of the bunkers and from under burned-out buildings and shoot them on the spot.

Finally, the last report we have from this source, covering June 1–2, states:

The situation in the ghetto appears to be deteriorating. . . . Today the borders of the ghetto were surrounded by strong ss units and armored cars penetrated [the area]. We can expect the Germans to take far-reaching steps against the Jews in hiding. According to information from the "G" [probably the Gestapo], the German casualties who have fallen in the course of liquidating the Jews have been very heavy.[30]

Information from reliable Jewish sources also testifies to the presence of people in the ghetto after May 16, the date proclaimed by Stroop as the conclusion of the "Grand *Aktion*." In his book *The Last Ones*, Arie Najberg described the situation in the ghetto between May 19 and May 26:

The strategy of the operation constantly changed. Up to then they had used armed force aided by technical support—fire, dynamite, listening devices—and sometimes by dogs. But as the *Aktion* progressed, it became more difficult to uncover the remaining bunkers and more difficult still to capture people alive. They therefore turned to ruses. When they entered an area, the German companies would bring along Poles and a Jewish informer. The informer would walk around in the courtyards and call out various names or shout in Yiddish: "Jews come out! The war is over!" The

Poles served as "bait": They were supposedly sent from the "Aryan" side to bring help to the Jews. But we who were hiding in the gutted buildings could hear the orders exactly as they were given, and we were not fooled. We also warned all the [other] Jews in our area.

From our point of view, it is interesting to note that Najberg writes of the weeks before and after May 16 as one continuous period. He was totally unaware that Stroop had proclaimed the conclusion of the "'Grand *Aktion*" and many other Jews like him—ignorant of how the situation appeared to the Germans or what forces were being used to suppress the uprising and expose the people in hiding—continued to hide and fight. Najberg wrote of meeting hundreds of Jews at night, of battles and skirmishes with Germans and Poles in the area of the ghetto, of the building at 4 Walowa Street, which contained 150 people on June 3, 1943 (the day on which it was destroyed), and was referred to by its inhabitants as a "hotel." He described the residents of the bunkers in June 1943: "Those living in the shelters became harrowingly thin and looked like skeletons. After six weeks in these graves, they looked like ghosts frightened of the living."

Despite everything, groups of the "last survivors" holding out among the ruins or in the bunkers succeeded in making contact with individual Poles who helped them get out of the ghetto and infiltrate the Polish side of the city. Of Najberg's group, which numbered forty-five people living among the ruins, four remained alive on September 26, 1943—more than five months after the outbreak of the revolt—when, still armed, they stole across the border to the "Aryan" side.

According to a Polish source, small mutually isolated groups of totally exhausted Jews remained in the ghetto until October. Individual survivors of these groups, like Najberg's band, succeeded in crossing over to the Polish sector of the city in September and October 1943 via the sewers and other passages.[31] We also know of one bunker that remained populated until January 1944.[32] In September, the Germans sent a battalion of Polish laborers into the ghetto and ordered them to demolish the infrastructures and walls that were still standing in the area. Those who still remained in hiding evidently met their deaths during these demolition activities, although a few individuals continued to live in dugouts, totally cut off from nature, light, and human company.

The ghetto was destroyed. Hitler's Third Reich had accomplished its mission. No Jews or Jewish dwellings remained in the Warsaw ghetto.

NOTES

1. Borzykowski, *Bein Kirot Noflim*, 26.
2. Ibid., 29.
3. Edelman, *Getto walczy*, 52–53.
4. Borzykowski, *Bein Kirot Noflim*, 29.
5. Aharon Carmi and Chaim Frimmer, *Min ha-Deleka ha-Hi* (*From that Conflagration*) (Tel Aviv, 1961), 215 (the memoirs of Chaim Frimmer).
6. See Kermish, *Mered Getto Varsha*, 128.
7. See Konrad's statement in Blumental and Kermish, *Ha-Meri ve-ha-Mered*, 370.
8. Kermish, *Mered Getto Varsha*, 189–90.
9. See Mark, *Powstanie w getcie warszawskim*, Document No. 102, 335, 337.
10. Kermish, *Mered Getto Varsba*, 206.
11. See Blumental and Kermish, *Ha-Meri ve-ha-Mered*, 249.
12. Carmi and Frimmer, *Min ha-Deleka ha-Hi*, 216–17.
13. Kermish, *Mered Getto Varsha*, 138–39, 211.
14. See the selection from the memoirs of Dr. Walewski in Lazar, *Mezada shel Varsha*, 245–46.
15. Edelman, *Getto walczy*, 55.
16. Kermish, *Mered Getto Varsha*, 139.
17. According to Halperin, eight members of *Betar* [Revisionist Zionists] fell that day, including a member of the command, Eliyahu Halberstein. See *Ha-Emet al ha-Mered be-Getto Varsha*, 21.
18. A full list of the wounded and their names appears in Wulf, *Das Dritte Reich*, 65–66.
19. Kermish, *Mered Getto Varsha*, 139.
20. Kermish, *Mered Getto Varsha*, 149.
21. See Yisrael Gutman, *Anashim va-Efer: Sefer Auschwitz-Birkenau* (*People and Ashes: The book of Auschwitz-Birkenau*) (Tel Aviv, 1957), 196–97.
22. Gutman, *Mered ha-Nezurim*, 362.
23. B. Goldman, "75 Yom be-Getto Varsha ha-Ole be-Lehavot" ("75 Days in the Burning Warsaw Ghetto") in Blumental and Kermish, *Ha-Meri ve-ha-Mered*, 281.
24. Kermish, *Mered Gretto Varsha*, 151–52, 156, 171.
25. See Zuckerman and Basok, *Sefer Milhamot*, 158.
26. Edelman, *Getto walczy*, 61.
27. Kermish, *Mered Getto Varsha*, 149, 152, 154, 159, 161, 170, 172–73, 186. In each case of a reference to Stroop's reports, I refer the reader to the Hebrew translation in Kermish. At the same time, I have checked each translation against the original German and sometimes believe it necessary to render certain corrections; hence the differences between Kermish's version and the English translations given here.
28. Edelman, *Getto walczy* 62.
29. Ibid., 187, 192.
30. See Blumental and Kermish, *Ha-Meri ve-ha-Mered*, 345.
31. Arie Najberg, *Ha-Ahronim: Be-kez ha-Mered shel Getto Varsha* (*The Last Ones: At the End of the Warsaw Ghetto Uprising*) (Tel Aviv, 1958), no-11, 133–34, 189–91.
32. Yad Vashem Archive, 0-3/714 (testimony of Stefania Fiedelzeid, who lived in a bunker within the area of the ghetto until January 1944).

Women Slave Laborers

FELICJA KARAY

From *Women in the Holocaust*

The Nazis established fourteen factory-labor camps for Jews in the Radom district of Poland. The Skarzysko-Kamienna labor camp, which was in operation from April 1942 until August 1944, was the largest, oldest, and most important of these factory camps. I shall use it as my model in describing the fate of women in the labor camps.[1] . . .

The Organization of the Camp

The state ammunition plants in the city of Skarzysko-Kamienna were built in 1927. With the German occupation, they were placed under the stewardship of the German munitions concern Hasag (Hugo Schneider *Aktiengesellschaft*, Hasag-Leipzig). To help meet wartime production needs, a Jewish camp was established on the plant premises. On October 15, 1942, the camp had 4,361 inmates, including 1,771 women.[2] There was a practical reason for the relatively high proportion of women (which was unusual in armament factories): Hasag paid the ss in Radom five zlotys per day for each male laborer but only four zlotys for each woman.[3]

All the Hasag factories in Skarzysko were divided into three *Werke* (sections), and the camp also had three divisions corresponding to the *Werke*. Each camp was a separate unit governed by three authorities: the German commander; the factory guard (*Werkschutz*), consisting of Ukrainians who were responsible for security, routine administration, and executions; and the Jewish internal administration (*Lagerverwaltung*), composed of the camp elder (*Lagerälteste*), the police force, and miscellaneous officials.

In each camp a three-echelon social structure corresponded to the three large transports that reached the camp. First, Jews from the ghettos of Radom were mobilized, starting in the summer of 1942. By late June 1943, this "Radom echelon" numbered 6,408 people, of whom about half were women.[4] That summer, approximately 2,000 men and women from the Majdanek concentration camp were added to the workforce. Because the letters KL were printed on their clothing, they were called *kaelnik* or *kaelanka*. Another 2,500 inmates arrived from the Plaszów camp in November 1943, forming the "Plaszów echelon." In all, roughly 25,000 Jews passed through the Skarzysko camp, and at least 20,000 of them are believed to have perished.[5]

A class hierarchy also emerged, headed by the "prominents," the leaders of the internal administration and their assistants. Below them were the "bourgeoisie," a handful of inmates who managed in various ways to smuggle valuables and money into the camp and to trade in them. Most inmates belonged to the "proletariat," who struggled to survive and to avoid descending to the bottom of the hierarchy, the *Musselmänner*—those who lost their will to live and looked like corpses.

For both male and female inmates, the chances of survival depended on such personal factors as age, health, and occupation. Level of education, cultural background, and social origin had little, if any, effect. The inmates' fates were, however, directly linked to their jobs and the statuses they had managed to acquire in the camp's class structure.

The three *Werke* differed in size, type of production, and the supervisors' attitude toward the Jewish prisoners. The Polish laborers who toiled with the Jews were residents of Skarzysko and surrounding towns and returned home at the end of the day. The Jews were marched from the camps to the factories and back again each day, escorted by the Jewish police and their assistants. Many Poles were appointed junior managers; thus they, together with *Volksdeutsche* (ethnic Germans who lived in Eastern Europe) and the few Germans, supervised the inmates' work. The Jewish police were in charge of doling out the soup at the noon recess, an extremely important function in view of the starvation in the camp.

Like the men, the women worked in two shifts, day and night, without adequate sanitary conditions and without work clothes. At first, they found it harder to adjust to the work than the men, many of whom had been skilled or unskilled laborers. It was difficult for a woman who had been a housewife, a seamstress, or a high school student to become, in a matter of days, a skilled worker who could operate a complicated machine. Several women eventually became experts; their testimonies provide an amazingly detailed description of their work.

Women were posted to various departments, including the most difficult, the *Granatenabteilung* (shell department). Here, a shell cleaner, for example, carried eighteen hundred shells, weighing nine pounds each, to the polishing machines in a ten-hour shift. When the women from the Plaszów transport arrived, the Polish workers warned them that they would not last more than

a few months. To their good fortune, relates Zona Horowicz, some decent people among the Poles promised to help.[6] In *Werk* A, the largest, most women manufactured light ammunition for the infantry. The output expected of them was constantly being raised, and the assembly line work demanded intense concentration. Many women were employed in the departments that finished and inspected ammunition parts. Although this work was not arduous, anyone who earned the displeasure of the German women managers faced a bitter fate. Marianne Tietge was notorious for her blows and kicks to the genitals of men and women alike, and Dora Pawlowska was no better.[7] *Werk* B turned out anti-aircraft ammunition. Here, two German overseers, Georg Hering and Wilhelm Leidig, were famous for their cruelty. When a large quantity of *Schmelz* (defective pieces) built up, they sentenced the workers, men and women, to forty or sixty lashes on their naked torsos.

Women who, through bribery or "pull," obtained work in the kitchen, the flake mill, the vegetable patch, or the mess hall of the *Werkschutz* were much better off than the production workers, for their jobs enriched their diet and gave them an opportunity to pilfer food to sell in the camp. The women used various strategies to obtain these prized jobs. One woman torched the machine at which she worked and bribed her Polish supervisor with a bottle of vodka; to her joy, she was transferred to the flake mill, where a *Volksdeutsche* named Laskowski protected his workers.[8]

Werk C was the most infamous site in the entire Radom district. In the notorious "death department" (*Menschenmordende Abteilung*), underwater mines were packed with yellow picric acid powder, a substance that turned the workers into green-haired monsters with black hands. Next to the "*Pikryna*" was a production floor for land-based mines; its key chemical, TNT, gave the prisoners reddish-pink skin. Women in both departments were employed to weigh the powder and sort and pack the mines. And because mortality among the men was so high, women were also put to work at the presses.[9] In the department where the shell cases were filled, it was the women's task to stir the boiling TNT, with two seconds per stir, 1,800 stirs per hour, and 21,600 in a twelve-hour shift, all without sitting.[10]

A world away from these torture chambers was the most coveted workplace, the detonator department. This was easy labor, although detonators were known to explode. The director, Hermann Schmitz, treated the inmates very decently . . .[11] His kindness notwithstanding, Schmitz personally surrounded himself with the most beautiful women.

All ethnic groups in the factory labor force—Germans, Ukrainians, Poles, *Volksdeutsche*—displayed rampant antisemitism and a wish to exploit the inmates to maximum advantage, as laborers and as individuals. In day-to-day life, however, treatment of Jews varied enormously. The Jews' most extensive daily contact was with the Poles who worked in the factory. The Polish foremen in Section 58 of *Werk* C were notorious throughout the camp for their bestial cruelty.[12] Generally speaking, almost all the male former prisoners complain of beatings and extortion by the Poles, whereas the women express few grievances.

The factory, with all its complex problems, was only one arena in the struggle for survival. Living conditions in the camp, determined above all by Hasag's wish to save on production costs, affected the prisoners' fate no less. Conditions at the camps in *Werke* A and B were better than in *Werk* C, but only marginally. Officially the inmates in all three camps received, twice a day, three-quarters of a liter of watery soup with dried potato flakes, two hundred grams of bread baked partly with the same potato flakes, ersatz coffee, and occasionally a dollop of jam. Twice a week, a spoonful of sugar was added to the soup. On entering the camp, prisoners were stripped of personal valuables, including extra clothing and shoes. When their only set of clothing wore out, it was "replaced" with paper sacks; instead of shoes, the prisoners received wooden clogs. They were not given utensils, soap, or towels.

The first contingents of prisoners at Skarzysko, male and female, were housed on an abandoned production floor at *Werk* A known as *Ekonomia*, which had four-tier bunks but no mattresses or blankets. The barracks built subsequently were extremely overcrowded and infested with lice, fleas, and bedbugs. Nevertheless, they were more comfortable than *Ekonomia*, which as late as December 1942 still accommodated 1,316 women and 933 men.[13] The latrines and shower huts were also inadequate, and hot water was unheard of. Once a month, the prisoners were taken to a public bath in *Werk* A for a hot shower and disinfection of clothing.

Disease spread rapidly under such conditions. The lack of underwear made women especially susceptible to urinary-tract infections. Dysentery and foot sores were also common. Seasonal outbreaks of typhus claimed hundreds of lives. Although each *Werk* had its "clinic" (*Revier*) and medic, no medication was available, and the first doctors appeared only in 1943. Until the spring of 1943, selections were carried out twice a week in each camp, and all the ill and infirm were sent to *Werk* C, where they were murdered by the *Werkschutz* at the "shooting range" (*Schießstand*).

Sexual Harassment and Assault

The testimonies of prisoners contain several allusions to sexual harassment by overseers even though Germans were prohibited from *Rassen-*

schande (racial shame—that is, behavior beneath the dignity of one's race). The Germans, most of them young bachelors, attempted to quench their libido by exploiting the Polish women in the factory, although this was explicitly prohibited. Much more dangerous were approaches to Jewish women that might be construed as *Rassenschande*. In all three *Werke*, however, there were rumors of "forbidden sexual liaisons" and the exploitation of Jewish women. The inmates in Fritz Schwinger's department at *Werk* A knew the identity of his lover but turned a blind eye because Schwinger was a decent person who helped his workers. At *Werk* B, factory manager Walter Glaue occasionally picked out a young woman in addition to his steady lover. When Bella Sperling was executed on charges of sabotage, rumor had it that Glaue had impregnated her and therefore wished to get rid of her.[14]

More conventional courtships also took place: the young German Porzig, for example, asked the beautiful Rena Cypres whether she would welcome him if he visited her after the war. The women could not tell whether Hermann Schmitz, the popular department head at *Werk* C, had a Jewish lover, but they forgave him his eccentricities. When a factory manager decided to distribute underwear to the female prisoners, Schmitz ordered "his girls" to lift their skirts in order to show what was lacking.[15]

The most famous tryst in the factory took place in the *Werkzeugbau* department (for instrument production). Everyone noticed that the foreman, Hugo Ruebesamen, tended to loiter excessively in the vicinity of the most beautiful Jewish woman in the department. The supervisor was informed, and he flayed the woman until she bled in an attempt to force her to admit that she had had sexual relations with Ruebesamen. When she would not, she was sent to the ss headquarters in Radom, from which she disappeared without a trace. Although

Ruebesamen also refused to confess, he was sentenced to three months' imprisonment.[16]

Sex between Poles and Jews was forbidden, but several Poles "started up" with attractive young Jewish women. The testimonies do not indicate whether these seductions ended in intercourse, which would have been difficult to conceal under factory conditions, or in mere groping in dark corners. Gafczynski, supervisor of the garden at *Werk* B, would invite women to "work" with him in the greenhouses on cold winter days, and several of these women became pregnant. When he tried to seduce a married woman, her husband made sure that officials in high places became aware of it, and the amorous gardener was dismissed.[17]

Nevertheless, German commanders were reluctant to deprive themselves of any of life's pleasures, and in all three *Werke*, there were known cases of individual and collective rapes of Jewish women. Dozens of testimonies mention the *Werkschutz* commander Fritz Bartenschlager, who would sometimes attend selections in order to choose "escort girls." In October 1942, for example, five of these women were taken to a feast at his apartment, where they were ordered to serve the guests in the nude and were ultimately raped by the revelers. In January 1943, when Bartenschlager's visitors included ss district commander Herbert Boettcher and Franz Shippers, the ss commander of Radom, three women, including nineteen-year-old Gucia Milchman, who was renowned throughout the camp for her extraordinary beauty, were brutally raped and then murdered.[18]

Other commanders chose the most beautiful young women of each newly arrived transport as personal "housemaids." (Almost all these women were later killed.) When Paul Kiessling, camp commander at *Werk* C in 1942, tired of his "maid," he sent her to Hans Schneider, *Werkschutz* commander at *Werk* A. Schneider discovered that the woman was pregnant and dispatched her to the "shooting range."[19] Rank-and-file Ukrainian guards are not known to have taken part in this behavior, evidently because they were barred from the camp when off duty."[20]

Markowiczowa of *Werk* C

At the Skarzysko camp, in accordance with German policy, all internal administration officials were men. The sole exception was Fela Markowiczowa, camp commander at *Werk* C, who had attained her position on her own merit. She succeeded in developing relations with the factory management and the camp authorities and knew how to bribe Germans and Ukrainians to allow her free rein in administering the camp. The Hasag management was satisfied with this arrangement because Markowiczowa's heavy-handed regimen met their needs.

At *Werk* C, the "yellow kingdom," where dozens of people starved to death each day and scores were slaughtered in the nearby forest, the proud, intelligent, vigorous, and uninhibited Markowiczowa ruled with an iron fist. Indeed, her subjects called her "the queen" or "Katherine II."[21] Markowiczowa placed members of her family in key positions in the administration, organized a "royal court" in a family barrack known by the prisoners as the White House, and distributed all jobs in the camp for payment or by whim. She included several members of the intelligentsia in her "royal council" and was not averse to offering help to the camp writer, Mordchai Strigler. Her "royal guard" was composed of strapping young policemen, from whom the queen derived double benefit: the large sums of money that she charged for the positions and a supply of lovers. On the positive side, however, she not only allowed the prisoners to engage in cultural activities, but actually supported them.

Markowiczowa hated women and appointed none to any position of importance. All of her police, their commanders, and those in charge of the bread storeroom, the clothing storeroom, and the prisoner registration office were men. The women had to make do with positions as overseers of a barrack or a room (*Blockälteste*, *Stubenälteste*) or as nurses at the infirmary; a few became supervisors of labor details.

Trade and Commerce

In order to live, prisoners were obliged to seek ways to become part of the economic life of the camp through labor, trade, and services. This activity went on in all Nazi camps. In Skarzysko, the "Radom women" were the first to take up crafts. Although most of them were destitute, they had smuggled in all manner of small items that turned out be lifesavers—sewing needles and thread, knitting needles, scissors, mirrors, bowls, Primus stoves, clothing, even bedding. They obtained their raw material as the men did, by "organization"—that is, pilfering from the factory—thus risking the death penalty for "sabotage." Yarn and fabric were also brought in by Poles who ordered the finished products from the prisoners. To get the materials past control at the factory gates, it was necessary to bribe the *Werkschutz* men, who quickly learned that this was a good source of additional income.

Many men in the camp were skilled cobblers, tinsmiths, carpenters, and so on. Although the women had a narrower range of skills, they knew how to exploit their abilities. Seamstresses and knitters rarely lacked customers; a female prisoner would knit a sweater for a Polish boss or sew a shirt for a supervisor in exchange for bread. Some women made children's clothes or underwear from the rags handed out at the factory for use in cleaning the machines; others produced dolls that they sold to Polish workers at the factory.[22]

The women in the ammunition quality-inspection department unraveled the gloves they were given and used the yarn to knit lacy scarves and muffs, for which there were always buyers. There was also a "cosmetics" market; chalk (used to mark shelves) and machine oil were made into a special "cream" that served as both blush and lipstick. On several occasions the makeup saved exhausted women from death during selections.[23] Embroiderers also found work: when a German supervisor named Mierschowa discovered that Ala Neuhaus was a superb embroiderer, she released Neuhaus from her job at the machine so that she could spend most of her time embroidering for her.[24]

Even in the camps, women could not get by without a handbag in which to conceal a morsel of bread, a rag that served as a towel, a sliver of soap, a comb, a soup plate, a spoon. Ala Erder and her mother manufactured bags out of the jute-cloth aprons that were handed out at the factory. The aprons were hard to smuggle into the camp, but the risk was worth taking, for the bags, embroidered with colored threads extracted from rags, were easily sold to both Jews and Poles.[25]

Some women peddled their products at the factory and in the camps. Others, who had no special skills, sold small slices of bread, a handful of cigarettes, sugar cubes, or garlic cubes. Some women bought miscellaneous foodstuffs from the Poles and sold them to "cooks," who mixed them into the local broth, heated the result in cans over a bonfire, and sold it to all customers. Some obtained apple peels from the Poles, dried it, and made it into a "tea" that added flavor to a cup of boiling water.[26] Women who lacked the small amount of money needed to start a "business" would turn to the "services": washing and cooking for prominents, mending clothes, and cleaning the barracks.

Underground Activities

The subject of Jews' labor in ammunition factories leads into their role in sabotaging production. Such sabotage could be performed in three possible ways: reducing output, introducing defects, and stealing the product for the Polish partisans in the nearby forests. Women from the Plaszow transport, for example, damaged the anti-aircraft shells that they filled by imprecision in threading. They were frequently beaten for this deliberate carelessness.[27]

It was possible to pilfer ammunition for the partisans only with the collaboration of the Poles. Ziuta Hartman and her Polish supervisor, together with several other inmates, organized the systematic transfer of "scrap"—crates of ammunition—to a cache in a forest.[28] At the Pikryna, the Polish foreman, Kopecki, persuaded Towa Kozak and a friend to steal cubes of TNT for the partisans. He threatened to "wring [the girls'] necks if they dared chirp."[29] Many such escapades failed. Lola Mendelewicz, working for the infantry at *Werk* A, stole rounds of ammunition and gave them to her boyfriend, Edek, who passed them on to the partisans. When they decided to escape, they were both tracked down and executed.[30]

Women also played a significant role in organizing underground assistance from outside—the transfer and distribution of money donated by Jewish and Polish relief organizations in Warsaw. Starting in late 1943, these funds began to reach the camp in various clandestine ways. "Distribution committees" were set up at all three *Werke*.

Mutual Assistance

. . . . In extreme cases, the last hope for survival was mutual assistance. Women expressed contrasting opinions on the availability of such aid. Roza Bauminger, a forty-year-old teacher, claimed that human interaction in the camps descended to the level of utter bestiality, survival of the fittest, and the abuse of the weaker by the stronger. But Frania Siegman, a genial young woman, described friendships and willingness to help.[31]

At Skarzysko, as in all Nazi camps, the desperate battle for life and death led to violence among all the prisoners, women included. The men were at least united by the traditional education they had received as children and their general command of Yiddish. This was not the case with the women. The Radom women were steeped in conservative tradition and Jewish folklore, and they spoke only Yiddish. The *kaelniks* were a more heterogeneous group, which included assimilated women, several nightclub stars from the big city, and Bund members who adhered to secular Yiddish culture. Most of the Plaszow contingent had secondary or higher education, spoke only Polish, and were totally assimilated. The veterans sarcastically termed them *Krakower inteligenz* (Krakow intelligentsia).

Relations between prominents and rank-and-file inmates were marked by undisguised hatred. Many testimonies recount violence by Jewish policemen against both classes. Most women supervisors of the barracks maintained tolerable relations with women prisoners and were not accused of brutality. At *Werke* A and C, however, several Jewish "nurses" were infamous not only for pilfering their patients' food rations and remaining belongings, but also for euthanasia.[32]

Alongside these manifestations of hostility were many manifestations of mutual aid in the Skarzysko camp. It was usually confined to one echelon and administered by small cells. The basic mutual-aid cell was composed of survivors from the same family—a married couple, a mother and daughter, sisters and brothers. Single men and women first looked for *landsmannschaft* survivors—Jews from the same city—who sometimes helped one another. Although the authorities insisted that residential arrangements coincide with workplaces, former neighbors tried to share the same barracks. Thus, a Skarzysker barrack, a Szydlowcer barrack, and other locality-specific barracks emerged.[33]

Women inmates developed close relationships and devised new ways to help each other: either pairing by age, with the older looking after the younger, or forming "camp families" composed of four to five women who shared a shack, their labor, and their possessions. In some groups the oldest woman took several younger women under her wing.[34] In *Werk* C, youth groups coalesced along ideological or political lines—for instance, members of the Zionist youth movement *Akiva* supported each other, as did Bund members from Warsaw, who joined up with resident Bundists from small towns in the Radom district.[35]

Mutual assistance was especially important at times of illness. Any patient who survived the deadly typhus epidemic of the winter of 1943–1944, which claimed the lives of almost all the women of the Haszow echelon, did so with others' assistance. The angels of mercy included Mrs. Carmel, who looked after her young comrades, and Drs. Wasserstein and Rotbalsam, who provided medical assistance. There were also nurses worthy of the name, male and female, such as Zosia and Szaweslajn, who on several occasions removed patients from the infirmary at the last moment, carrying them on their backs, and thus saved them from selection.[36]

Bunk Romances among Jewish Inmates

Romantic liaisons among the Jewish inmates were inevitable. Such couplings of "*kuzyns*" (cousins) became widespread in all three *Werke*. The *Krakower inteligenz* women at first rejected the advice of the experienced *kaelniks* that they find *kuzyns* if they did not wish to meet a quick death. These educated and assimilated young women regarded even the local prominents as "trash that rose to the surface in the tempest of the war and that would sink after the storm passed;"[37] they could not imagine having an affair with some miserable cobbler from the shtetl who did not even speak Polish. Their resistance, however, eroded with the ravages of time, disease, hard labor, and, above all, fear of famine. The best solution was to find a *kuzyn* from among the Plaszów men, especially those assigned to the local police.

In the spring of 1944, the prisoners' living conditions improved slightly, as Hasag came to realize that the prospects of obtaining new transports of Jews were nil and the survivors in the camp were too depleted to meet the requisite pace of output. Better nutrition and living conditions also revived social life. Now it was not only the prominents who sought a *kuzynka*, but also rank-and-file men. There were also reverse cases of women who had managed to obtain good positions or small amounts of money and could now choose their own lovers. Even some women who worked at Pikryna found *kuzyns*, despite their off-putting appearance. . . .

Why did this phenomenon become an integral part of the camp experience? Many of the inmates were young, single, and in search of a soul mate or of the possibility of commingling: others sought material assistance: but most believed that life would be easier with a partner. The institution of *kuzyns* was an important manifestation of the will to survive. Several of these relationships turned into true love, leading to marriage after the war. . . .

The "bunk romances" had their dangerous aspects. Although many women stopped menstruating under the afflictions of hard labor and malnutrition, impregnation was frequent. Pregnant women were singled out for death in every selection. Abortion was out of the question; although the camp had doctors, instruments and medications were unavailable. Some women managed to conceal their condition until the last minute by various ruses (for example, by wearing girdles or loose clothing). In one shocking case described by Towa Kozak, an unknown Jewish woman at the factory delivered her baby in the toilet; as soon as they were discovered, mother and child were murdered.

If women were in the camp when they went into labor, they were helped by their friends or the local doctor. Their babies, however, were taken from them immediately and, in most cases, abandoned in a distant shack until they died. The writer Mordchai Strigler, a prisoner who performed janitorial work in the camp, attests to having found corpses of babies under bunks and in garbage heaps. Dr. Wasserstein's testimony tells the tragic account of a baby who had been hurled into a container of corpses and could not be saved.[38]

Babies had no right to exist in the Skarzysko camp, but several children circulated in the three *Werke*. Boys and girls between the ages of twelve and fourteen were considered fit for work. In most cases, both the Poles and the Germans protected them. . . . In other cases, however, children were beaten for failing to meet work quotas or for suspected sabotage. . . .

Evacuation

The day of reckoning came in late July 1944. The advancing Soviet forces halted at the Vistula, giving the Skarzysko management time to evacuate the factories and camps. A rumor spread of preparations for a selection. "Queen" Markowiczowa and her family fled from *Werk* C one night, and at least 250 inmates escaped through openings cut in the camp fence. The escapees included nearly all the Bund members, Hedzia and Henoch Ross, and most of the policemen. The openings, however, turned out to have been a German trap; nearly all the fugitives were murdered in the nearby forests by Germans, *Werkschutz*, and Poles.[39]

Before the evacuation, a selection took place in all three *Werke*. All inmates who were physically spent, most pikrynists, and all those who were ill were sent to their deaths, as were young men who had displeased the Germans for various reasons. Some women faced death with exceptional courage. At *Werk* A, where all the ill inmates were evacuated, young Dr. Greenberg refused to abandon her ailing mother and accompanied her to her death.[40] At *Werk* B, Linka Goldberg beseeched the German commander Haas to spare her mother's life, and he finally consented.[41] When Giza Leinkram saw her mother being taken to the trucks with the other victims, she chased her, and her mother barely managed to push her away at the last moment. At *Werk* C, the two Fortgang sisters and Dr. Mina Krenzler—young women whom the Germans had selected to join the transport of the living—chose to die with their mothers. When Dora Rozenblat was separated from her mother, she refused to abandon her and assaulted a policeman. The *Werkschutz* men, unable to separate them, shot both as the entire camp looked on.[42] Some of the 6,500 men and women inmates who remained alive were transferred to the Hasag factories in Czestochowa, Leipzig, and Buchenwald.

NOTES

1. Felicja Karay, *Death Comes in Yellow: Skarzysko-Kamienna Slave Labor Camp* (Amsterdam: Harwood Academic Publishers, 1996).

2. Juden, Stärkemeldung am 15.10.1942, Hasag-Werke Skarzysko-Kamienna (hereafter: Stärke meldung), Adam Rutkowski Collection YV, 0–6/37–3.

3. Raul Hilberg, *The Destruction of the European Jews* (Chicago: Quadrangle, 1961), 336.

4. Hasag Werke Skarzysko-Kamienna, Betriebskarte, Bundesarchiv Koblenz (hereafter: BA), R 3/2040.

5. Skarzysko-Kamienna, forced-labor camp, *Encyclopedia of the Holocaust*, ed. Israel Gutman (New York: Macmillan, 1990), 1360.

6. Zona Horowicz, testimony YV, 0–16/1156.

7. Marianne Tietge, Urteil in Kamienna Prozess YV, TR-10/7, 12; Hana Zajdenwerg, testimony YV, 0–33/1820.

8. Luna Lipszyc, testimony YV, 0–33/1844.

9. Maria Szechter, "Pikryna dziala, Prasy." Dokumenty zbrodni i meczenstwa, Polish (Kraków: Zydowska Komisja Historyczna, 1945), 45–48. Maria Szechter-Lewinger delivered a horrific account of her work at the press as part of a four-inmate team that had to manufacture 1,650 cubes of TNT in each shift.

10. Zahawa Sztok, testimony YV, 0–33/1843.

11. Eda Jewin, testimony YV, 0–33/1838.

12. Sala Fass, testimony YV, 0–16/1352.

13. Stärkemeldungen, December 1942.

14. Henryk Greipner, testimony YV, 0–33/1815; Rywka Lewin-Abramowicz, 0–33/1810.

15. Rina Cypres, testimony YV, 0–33/1857.

16. Anklageschrift, Kamienna Prozess YV, TR-10/7, 28.

17. Giza Leinkram-Szmulewicz, testimony YV, 0–33/1841.

18. Hayim Milchman, testimony YV, M-1/E/1972/1973; Srul Najman, Akta w sprawie Franz Schippers YV JM/3786.

19. Lola Arlajtman-Rozenfeld, testimony YV, 0–33/1806.

20. Luna Lipszyc, testimony.

21. Szraga Knobler, testimony YV, 0–33/3674; Roza Bauminger, testimony YV, 0–16/828.

22. Hana Zajdenwerg, testimony.

23. Ester Hendelsman-Kerzner, testimony YV, 0–33/1826.

24. Ala Neuhaus, testimony YV, 0–33/1833.

25. Ala Erder, testimony YV, 0–33/1817.

26. Paulina Buchholz-Schneider, testimony YV, 0–33/E/l 42–2–1.

27. Felicja Bannet, testimony YV, 0–16/828; Malka Finkler-Granatstein, 0–3/3323.

28. Zivta Hartman, testimony YV, 0–33/1851.

29. Towa Kozak, testimony YV, 0–33/1828.

30. Fryde Mape-Zonszajn, *Pinkas Chmielnik* (Tel-Aviv, 1960), 847.

31. Roza Bauminger, *Przy pikrynie i trotylu: Obóz pracy przymusowej w Skarzysku-Kamiennej*, Polish (Kraków: Centralna Zydowska Komisja Historyczna, 1946), 43; Frania Siegman, testimony YV, 0–3/2979.

32. Regina Finger, testimony YV, 0–16/161; Anna Warmund, 0–33/1849.

33. Fela Blum, testimony YV, 0–33/1839; Zahawa Kampinski, 0–33/1849.

34. Malka Cukerbrot-Hottner, testimony YV, 0–33/1655.

35. Moshe Kligsberg, "Henoch Ross," in *Doyres Bundisten*, ed. J. S. Hertz, Yiddish (New York: Unser Zeit, 1956), 3: 412–15.

36. Henryk Greipner, testimony; Helena Zorska YV, 0–33/1797.

37. Rina Taubenblat-Fradkin, testimony YV, 0–16/249.

38. Mordchai Strigler, *In di fabrikn fun toit*, Yiddish (Buenos Aires: Union Central Israelita Polaca en la Argentina, 1948); Adam Wasserstein, testimony YV, 0–16/1043.

39. Strigler, *Goiroilos*, 268–84.

40. Menasze Hollender, testimony YV, 0–3/1012.

41. Irena Bronner, testimony YV, 0–33/1851.

42. Roza Bauminger, *Przy pikrynie*, 59–60.

Robbery in the Netherlands

MARTIN DEAN

From *Robbing the Jews*

The spoliation of Jewish property in the Netherlands proceeded in accordance with streamlined practices developed previously inside the Reich. *Reichskommissar* Dr. Arthur Seyss-Inquart and his *Generalkommissar für Finanzen und Wirtschaft* (Minister for Financial and Economic Affairs, GkFW) Hans Fischböck—both of them from Austria—were careful to apply lessons learned previously to ensure firm state control over the process.[1] The Dutch historian, Gerard Aalders, characterizes the Nazi looting of the Jews in the Netherlands as an orderly confiscation decreed by the state—"robbery by decree."[2] The main complications resulted from the need to conceal the ultimate aim of the German measures, including through the use of camouflaged institutions, to enable the goal of complete confiscation to be achieved. Despite considerable cooperation by some Dutch financial institutions, there were no indigenous plans for any form of spoliation, and so the entire policy had to be imported and directed by the Germans.

As part of the concealment strategy, the German civil administration sought to bring all forms of Jewish property under its control in a series of carefully prepared stages. A report prepared by the Security Police in the Netherlands at the end of 1942 explained that the first step had been to restrict the ability of Jews to freely dispose of their own property, followed by compulsory registration measures and finally the obligation to surrender property. The aim of these measures was to prevent Jewish property escaping in an uncontrolled fashion, so that it could be prepared for important tasks of the Reich, especially covering the costs incurred by the removal of the Jews.[3] ...

The major innovation in the Netherlands was the rapid concentration of nearly all Jewish movable wealth at the Bank of Lippmann, Rosenthal & Co., Sarphistraat (LiRo) under the provisions of two decrees issued in August 1941 and May 1942. In practice, this was a refined version of the measures taken in the Reich to register Jewish property and control it in blocked accounts overseen by the Currency Offices. Nominally, the property remained in the possession of Dutch Jews in blocked accounts at LiRo, at least until the beginning of 1943 when it was transferred into a single collective account. By this time, the deportation of Jews from the Netherlands was already in full swing. The concentration of all Jewish property in one financial institution considerably simplified both the collection of property and its ultimate confiscation.

Seizure of Property of Persons Who Fled and of "Enemies"

After its establishment on May 29, 1940, initially the new civil administration under *Reichskommissar* Seyss-Inquart was concerned to avoid civil disturbances and therefore did not move immediately against Jewish property. As in Luxembourg, the first measures were directed instead against "enemy property," which of course affected the property of Jews and others who had fled the country during the invasion.[4] Under a decree of June 14, 1940,[5] "enemy property" had to be registered with the *Deutsche Revisions-und Treuhand* AG (DRT), a German accountancy firm. The DRT, acting together with Fischböck's Ministry for Financial and Economic Affairs (GkFW), directed the appointment of administrators and their subsequent supervision. In total, the "Enemy Property" section of the GkFW managed capital with a value of about 1.2 billion florins (or RM 900,000).

As in the Reich, the Germans administered non-Jewish enemy property in the Netherlands in trust until the end of the war, but it was not confiscated for fear of possible reprisals against their own investments that had been frozen abroad.[6] The property of several hundred Dutch Jews who had fled was initially also placed in trust in accordance with the "Enemy Property" regulations. Subsequently, however, it was unlawfully sold in 1942 and 1943, together with other Jewish property, and the proceeds paid into an account of the DRT at the LiRo bank.[7]

The "Enemy Property" regulations did, however, serve as a potential model for the treatment of Jewish property, perhaps allaying the fears of some Jews when the civil administration ordered Jewish property registration in the summer of 1941. Significantly, Fischböck subsequently charged the "Enemy Property" section of the GkFW with the supervision of the administration of Jewish property by the LiRo Bank, revealing the close connections between these two policies.[8]

Communal Organizations

Reichskommissar Seyss-Inquart ordered the registration and reformation of non-commercial organizations and foundations in two decrees issued on September 20, 1940, and February 28, 1941.[9] ... The second decree resulted in the liquidation of Jewish organizations, with the funds being paid into accounts at the *Vermögensverwaltungs-und Rentenanstalt* (Property Administration and Pension Institute, VVRA) under the direction of the Commissioner for Non-Commercial Organizations and Foundations, Hans Werner Müller-Lehning. The liquidation of about one thousand Jewish organizations is estimated to have brought in 10 million fl.[10]

Aryanization of Jewish Businesses

With regard to Aryanization, *Reichskommissar* Seyss-Inquart and *Generalkommissar* Fischböck were eager to avoid the excesses that had occurred in Austria during the initial "wild Aryanizations" in March 1938. Therefore, they were careful to establish several new institutions to maintain close state control over the process. Their aim was to ensure that a realistic price was paid in the Netherlands and that applicants had suitable business experience and adequate capital.[11]

The first stage in the process of Aryanization was the registration of Jewish businesses, according to the terms of Decree 189/1940 of October 22, 1940.[12] The decree included a definition of who was a Jew and made the sale of Jewish businesses subject to official permission. All "Jewish businesses" (those with one Jewish partner or director, or in which Jews owned more than 25 percent of the capital) had to register their assets and liabilities with the *Wirtschaftsprüfstelle* (Office of Economic Investigation, WPS) by November 30, 1940. By the end of November, 19,000 businesses had complied, and ultimately about 21,000 "Jewish" firms were registered. A Security Police report from this period notes that Dutch Jews were reluctant to sell their companies voluntarily, partly because of the difficulties involved in emigrating and also the inability to convert Dutch guilders into hard currency that would be of use abroad. There was also a fear on the German side that the best objects might fall into the wrong hands, and so the Nazis began to prepare at the local level for a compulsory Aryanization program similar to that implemented in Germany during 1938.[13]

At the end of 1940, Seyss-Inquart obtained the Führer's approval in principle to proceed with compulsory Aryanization. Following the disturbances that culminated in the Amsterdam dockworkers strike in February 1941, fear of public opinion no longer remained a reason for delay.[14] Therefore, in March a further "Aryanization decree"[15] was introduced to provide the legal basis for the forced sale and liquidation of Jewish enterprises and their placement under the control of trustees. The WPS, which had been built up around the economic staff that had served in the German General Consulate in Amsterdam, then proceeded to appoint trustees and supervise their work. The Jewish enterprises bore the costs of administration.[16] A few Jewish businesses had already been placed in trusteeship under the "Enemy Property" laws, which had prepared the way for their Aryanization prior to the March 1941 decree.

As elsewhere, implementation of Aryanization still took considerable time, as difficult decisions had to be made in thousands of cases about the appointment of trustees, whether to Aryanize or liquidate, and how to find suitable buyers. According to a report by Reichskommissar Seyss-Inquart to the head of the Party Chancellery, Martin Bormann, dated January 27, 1942, of the approximately one thousand businesses dealt with to that date, some four hundred had been taken over by Dutch businessmen (valued at 60.5 million fl.) and 340 by Germans (valued at 103 million fl.); the remaining 260 were reserved for veterans of the ongoing war (*Kriegsteilnehmer*). The German authorities exploited their control over Aryanization to sup-

port German businesses and entrepreneurs trying to gain a foothold in the Netherlands while allowing some Dutch entrepreneurs to pick up many of the smaller businesses. In particular, the Dresdner Bank established its own subsidiary in the Netherlands, the Handelstrust West, which became very active in support of German Aryanization bids.[17] Other individuals in Germany made applications for Aryanization opportunities in the Netherlands via the Regional Economic Advisers (*Gauwirtschaftsberater*) of the Party.[18]

Ultimately, about two thousand firms were Aryanized and about ten thousand liquidated, although the WPS had still not decided on the fate of one thousand cases by the end of the occupation. Roughly 8,000 of the 21,000 firms originally identified as Jewish-owned or under Jewish influence managed to escape this definition by reducing the level of Jewish ownership and paying a fine (1 percent of capital).[19] . . .

The proceeds from Aryanization sales were paid into accounts at the VVRA, which in turn was supposedly to make one hundred quarterly payments over twenty-five years into blocked accounts opened for the former Jewish owners at LiRo (with no interest paid).[20] . . . The money paid to the Property Administration and Pension Institute was mostly converted into both Reich and Dutch government bonds, placing this large financial resource directly at the government's disposal.[21]

After the beginning of large-scale deportations from the Netherlands in July 1942, the WRA ceased further payments into individual Jewish accounts at LiRo, and on instructions from Fischböck the existing accounts were consolidated into a single collective account in 1943.[22] Thus, ultimately the proceeds from Aryanization flowed conveniently to the state. It is very hard to assess the precise amount raised from Aryanization in the

Netherlands, as most prices paid were still well below market value.[23] In general, Aryanization was conducted more quickly and with greater central direction in the Netherlands than in Germany or other parts of Western Europe; its implementation was linked closely in time to plans for the deportation of Dutch Jews from the summer of 1941 onward. Thus, the Nazi civil administration was able to direct Aryanization centrally in a very comprehensive manner, making it an instrumental part of the confiscation process.[24] . . .

The Registration of Jewish Property— The First LiRo Decree

After the May meeting, the comprehensive confiscation of private property from the Dutch Jews was implemented in a "pseudo-legal" and concealed manner. The first stage was the concentration of Jewish liquid property at LiRo, in accordance with the so-called First LiRo Decree issued on August 8, 1941.[25] The new centralized LiRo Bank, created in summer 1941, involved a deliberate deception: in an attempt to allay Jewish fears, the new bank used the same name as a well-established Jewish bank that had already been Aryanized.[26]

All Dutch financial institutions were obliged to transfer Jewish bank accounts and share certificates to LiRo. When they complained that they would lose about 5 percent of their current business as a result, they received assurances that they would receive commissions in connection with the conversion of Jewish wealth into fixed interest securities.[27] Top-secret guidelines on the treatment of the Jewish bank accounts and securities holdings (depots) established at LiRo made clear that these were intended to be blocked accounts, from which only a fixed amount could be withdrawn each month by the Jewish owners to meet their ordinary living expenses. The regulations permitted only a few exceptions to these limits, for extraordinary payments such as taxes or doctor's bills, in response to written applications to the Inspection Department at LiRo.[28]

. . . The complex requirements of the decree were an onerous burden for the Jews and the banks, which had to cope with a morass of new regulations.[29] A Jewish man who was arrested in Amsterdam for the illegal possession of share certificates in November 1941 protested that he thought it was the responsibility of the bank to transfer the shares automatically and that therefore he had not known anything about it himself.[30] Officials at LiRo complained repeatedly about "passive resistance" to the measure by Dutch banks that had failed to transfer their Jewish accounts. In particular, they feared that wealthier individuals were escaping the net. For example, a number of prominent Jewish former stockbrokers had not registered any property with LiRo by November.[31] Despite the careful registration in August 1941 of 140,522 "full-blooded" Jews in the Netherlands by the German authorities, it remained a difficult task for the Dutch banks and insurance companies to identify their Jewish customers.[32] . . .

The Conversion of Shares into Government Bonds

A considerable portion of Jewish assets in the Netherlands was invested in shares and government securities. According to the internal accounts of LiRo, by 1945 it had received about 300 million fl. in securities, nearly three-quarters of all incoming Jewish property. By comparison, cash and bank deposits came to only 55 million fl.[33] Therefore, the treatment of Jewish share capital is of considerable significance for understanding the confiscation process.

On November 17, 1941, *Reichskommissar* Seyss-Inquart instructed the LiRo Bank to begin converting Jewish assets into German and Dutch government bonds, as soon as the process of concentration had "been largely completed."[34] This conversion was postponed initially, due to concerns at LiRo that compliance with the First Decree had been slow and incomplete. However, in the first months of 1942, LiRo started the conversion process with a massive sale of Jewish shares. The timing could hardly have been worse though, as it coincided with a fall in the stock market caused by Japanese advances in the Far East. The financial press was well informed about the action, as LiRo did little to conceal the origins of these sudden large sales.[35]

The conversion of Jewish property in this way was a revival of Göring's 1938 plans to convert Jewish assets into low-interest government bonds and help finance rapidly mounting state debt. At the same time, it represented an important further step toward confiscation, as the nominal owners of the shares were (of course) not consulted. The Jews of Amsterdam were quite shocked when it was revealed in March 1942 that many of their shares had already been converted into government bonds. The Jewish Council protested that there was no legal basis for these sales and expressed the fear that they would inevitably accelerate the impoverishment of the Dutch Jews.[36]

The large-scale sale of Jewish shares in the Netherlands was facilitated by the cooperation of many Dutch stockbrokers. With regard to the sale of most shares, it is difficult to reconstruct precisely who was involved. However, throughout the war, trade continued in so-called American certificates issued by Dutch financial institutions based on U.S. shares. Their value rose steadily, as the Dutch currency fell against the dollar with the increasing expectation of an Allied victory. From the available records, Gerard Aalders concludes

that 136 of the 375 members of the Amsterdam stock exchange dealt in formerly Jewish-owned shares of this type and that most must have been aware of the fact that they were stolen.[37]

The massive sale of Jewish shares in the Netherlands was exploited by the Nazis to repatriate some foreign shares to boost their foreign currency reserves. In addition, German companies took an interest in purchasing shares of some Dutch companies in order to penetrate the local market. For example, the German insurance company Allianz purchased 300,000 fl. in shares of the Dutch insurance company, Ass. Mij. de Nederlanden van 1945, from Jewish or "Enemy Property" sources in April 1942.[38] The main purchasers of Jewish-owned shares were in fact Dutch stockbrokers, though some may have been acting as intermediaries for German buyers.

The Second LiRo Decree

In May 1942, the Second LiRo Decree secured the funds already registered and demanded the surrender to LiRo of almost all remaining Jewish valuables. In addition, it reduced the limit for monthly withdrawals by Dutch Jews to 250 fl.[39] This decree completed the official transfer of Jewish private wealth to the LiRo Bank initiated in August 1941, although it did not openly specify actual confiscation. Hitler preferred to defer acknowledgment of the confiscation policy until the Jews had been physically removed, partly out of concern for public opinion.[40] . . .

The cessation of further payments to Jews from LiRo ordered in November 1942 and the ensuing liquidation of individual accounts marked the final steps in the confiscation process. As one subsequent German report put it, with the transfer to a collective account, "the individual property of the respective payees [individual Jewish account owners] is submerged and the delivered values are to be viewed as confiscated by the *Reichskommissar*."[41] Beginning in January 1943, account holders no longer received statements from LiRo, and the remaining Jews in need of support had to make applications to the Jewish Council, which paid them from funds made available by LiRo.[42] This reflected another element of prewar German schemes: using the Jewish communal organization to ensure that Jews did not become a burden on the state.[43] The conversion from individual blocked accounts to one single combined account also destroyed the record of the money's original provenance, considerably complicating the process of postwar restitution to surviving Jews and the heirs of those murdered in the Nazi concentration and death camps.

Diamonds, Precious Metals, Jewelry, and Other Cultural Property

The value of precious metals, diamonds, jewelry, and cultural property (just over 5.1 million fl. according to internal records) surrendered to the LiRo Bank was relatively small compared with the financial assets collected.[44] However, LiRo had to compete with other agencies . . . for many items,[45] and some jewelry and precious metals were extracted by the confiscation and blackmailing efforts of the Security Police. LiRo processed its share of these items fairly quickly, completing the resale of most by the end of 1943. Valuations were performed by a variety of auction houses and brokers who received commissions of 1 or 1.5 percent. Many artworks and other cultural items were sold at less than their value or were simply surrendered to other German agencies, such as the *Dienststelle Mühlmann*, which acquired artworks in the Netherlands under the authority of Seyss-Inquart.[46]

The total value of the silver processed by LiRo was almost twice that of the gold, but the prices paid were well below the international market value, as LiRo also paid for the smelting costs of silver bullion and gold was sold at official prices kept artificially low. In agreement with the *Reichsstelle für Edelmetall* (Reich Office for Precious Metals), the most valuable silver was to be sent to Berlin and the remainder smelted locally or sent to Degussa.[47] Jewelry was sold mainly to German firms or government agencies. The main purchaser was General Commissar Schmidt, who put a stop to the sale of diamonds in January 1943 and then purchased more than 1 million fl. in jewelry and precious stones from LiRo between March and May 1943. The distorted priorities of the Nazi regime are reflected in the fact that these diamonds were intended primarily as ornaments to be worked into the casings of Germany's highest military decorations.[48]

The Amsterdam diamond industry itself was treated initially with some caution due to the fragile nature of the trade, which relied heavily on the skills and business connections of the many Jewish craftsmen and brokers who owned some 80 percent of it. In this industry, Aryanization was largely deferred until 1944, as maintaining the supply of diamonds—especially industrial—was vital to the German war effort. Dutch diamond workers and their families were protected at first from the deportations, although by June 1943 most had been rounded up and carried off to the transit camp at Westerbork, from where some were subsequently deported to the East.[49]

As the German authorities were particularly concerned to recover any hidden stocks of diamonds and to prevent them being smuggled out of the country, the offer of protection from deportation was also used to extract remaining diamonds via blackmail, although in many cases German officials subsequently reneged on their promises of protection. After their arrests in May and June of 1943, some diamond company owners were released, as the Four-Year Plan had commissioned the company of Bozenhardt brothers to buy up remaining diamond stocks for sale on the world market in exchange for foreign currency. The official fixed price was actually paid during this action to facilitate resale on the world markets with acceptable paperwork.[50]

By the end of 1944, only part of the extorted diamonds had been sold, as their sale in neutral countries was encountering growing difficulties. Nevertheless, diamond workers had better chances of survival than most Dutch Jews, not only because they were arrested later but also thanks to Himmler's plans (never realized) to continue exploiting their special skills at the Bergen-Belsen concentration camp.[51] ...

Life Insurance and Pensions

Life insurance policies had to be registered with LiRo both by the Jewish owners and the companies themselves following the Second LiRo Decree; LiRo then proceeded to recall the capitalized values of [i.e., to cash out or redeem] the registered policies in accordance with the deadline of April 1, 1943, set for the completion of all of LiRo's work.[52] However, officials at LiRo confronted a number of practical difficulties and were not satisfied with the level of cooperation by Dutch insurance companies. For example, in July 1942, the Inspection Department of LiRo complained about new policies being issued after the First LiRo Decree in which the payee was a Dutch company, but the beneficiary was a Jew. In December 1942, it reported that a major life insurance company was refusing to make further pension payments for deported Jews unless it received a declaration from the commandant of Westerbork Camp that the beneficiary was still alive.[53] In response to such tactics, a more explicit decree

covering the termination of insurance policies and pensions was issued in June 1943 (VO 54/1943), intended to overcome such legal obstruction. LiRo's own research revealed that not all Jewish policies were being declared by the companies, and ultimately it seems that barely 80 percent of Jewish polices were ultimately surrendered. In total, some 22,368 policies were surrendered, with a combined value of about 25 million fl.[54]

Real Estate

Jewish real estate in the Netherlands was dealt with under a separate decree of August 11, 1941, which called for its registration with a new institution, the *Niederländische Grundstücksverwaltnng* (Dutch Real Estate Administration, NGV) that was founded five days later.[55] Subsequently, the NGV was responsible for the administration and sale of registered Jewish real estate and mortgages, with the assistance of trustees. As with industrial property, the proceeds were initially to be paid into blocked accounts for the former owners at LiRo via the VVRA, in installments over twenty-five years. In total, 20,000 properties and 5,600 mortgages were registered, with an estimated value of 150 million and 22 million florins, respectively.[56]

In practice, the prices paid were frequently well below the market value. This was partly a result of the reluctance to buy former Jewish property, especially in the countryside, reinforced by the wariness of Dutch mortgage institutions to lend money for this purpose. Germany's declining military fortunes after the battle of Stalingrad in February 1943 certainly made investment in former Jewish property an increasingly risky proposition. However, it is not clear whether the reluctance of Dutch institutions and individuals to participate in sales of Jewish-owned real estate was motivated primarily by political or economic calculations.[57]

Clearing Jewish Apartments
after the Deportations

The processing of Jewish household effects actually began in the Netherlands before the deportations, as the ERR [Operations Staff Rosenberg] confiscated and exploited the property of Jews who had managed to flee during the Nazi invasion. The process of concentrating Jews before the deportations, which began in early 1942, also involved the registration of their household property by the *Hausraterfassungsstelle*, a special section affiliated with the Central Office for Jewish Emigration; it had both Jewish and Dutch staff. The ERR then cleared the houses.[58] This division of labor was maintained after the mass deportations began in July 1942. Ultimately, the Germans deported more than 75 percent of the Jewish population in the Netherlands (107,000 out of 140,000).[59]

By the end of June 1944, the contents of more than 29,000 dwellings had been cleared, with most of the property being sent to Germany in the course of the so-called Furniture Action (*Möbel-Aktion*) for the benefit of German victims of Allied bombing. Furniture remaining in the Netherlands was either given to the *Wehrmacht* for its own use, or the low-quality pieces were sold to Dutch wholesalers. The sort of benefits obtained by some Dutch collaborators can be seen from the May 1943 example of the Dutch ss-*Standartenführer* Feldmeijer, who requested an apartment equipped with items "suitable for entertaining prominent guests." His request was duly met with articles removed from a former Jewish residence.[60] . . .

As Presser observes, the process of clearing Jewish apartments took place in full view: "Everyone in the vicinity, even those who had not seen the victims dragged away under cover of darkness,
could not but observe the furniture vans being loaded up in broad daylight."[61]

Beneficiaries and Corruption

A large bureaucracy requiring numerous forms in multiple copies was necessary to organize the plundering of the Dutch Jews. According to Presser, "some of the laborers in this vineyard were not beyond collecting a few windfalls. But . . . most did their work meticulously and honestly." Today, the extensive records they created mean that, despite the loss of some important documents, the process of confiscation can still be reconstructed. The documents do reveal several notable cases of corruption within LiRo itself, mainly because there was no effective way to control the activities of the staff and most of the "clients" had been deported.[62]

The various opportunities for enrichment certainly facilitated the progressive removal of the Jews, despite the lack of widespread support for German anti-Jewish policies among the Dutch population as a whole. According to one German report, the Dutch police were especially interested in stealing coffee, tea, tobacco, and cash while arresting Jews. They frequently forbade Jews to take any luggage with them on the grounds that the Germans would take it anyway.[63]

The role of the "bounty hunters" in the Netherlands, who collected rewards for exposing Jews in hiding, has recently become a topic of more intensive research. Despite denials during their postwar trials, it appears that financial rewards were the prime motives for the Dutch civilian staff of the "*Recherchegruppe Henneicke*" under the control of the Central Office for Jewish Emigration, who helped arrest for deportation as many as eight or nine thousand Jews.[64] Funds to reward these people were advanced from confiscated Jewish property.[65] The DSKs also set up a similar system of local informants to track down concealed Jewish property. In March 1942, the DSK proposed offering rewards to attract informants, to be paid as a percentage of the amount recovered on a sliding scale.[66] It is still not clear how widespread participation in these activities was.

As elsewhere, there were also local initiatives to mop up Jewish property overlooked by the house-clearing squads. A fifty-one-year-old housewife wrote in her diary on July 3, 1943, "I and Truus went over some Jewish homes, but there was little to get—all the essentials had gone, including underclothes and linen. The next-door neighbors had got there first; all I could find was a few trifles and Truus got a pedal car and some other toys. But the whole business is highly dangerous, for if they catch you they send you to the Vught concentration camp."[67] Support for Jews in hiding was often rendered in return for financial rewards.[68] Therefore, the effectiveness of the asset-stripping campaign, begun comprehensively before the start of the deportations, also reduced the chances of Jews surviving to the liberation. To salvage something of their property, some Jews turned to Dutch friends and neighbors, the so-called *Bewahrier*, to "look after" their property until their return. However, even for those few Jews who did return, it was not always easy to reclaim their possessions.

Assessment of Confiscations in the Netherlands

The most striking aspects of the confiscation process in the Netherlands were (1) the careful preparation of the action in coordination with planning for the deportations and (2) its rapid and comprehensive implementation. In the key months from August 1941 to May 1942, the legislative framework of confiscation in the Netherlands was assembled, accompanying the key transition in German policy from forced emi-gration to deportation and physical destruction.[69] By the fall of 1941, detailed planning for the removal (*Aussiedlung*) of the Jews from the Netherlands was already underway, with Hitler's explicit approval.[70] The actual implementation still took time to prepare, but in the meantime the two LiRo Decrees effectively concentrated and secured almost all Jewish assets at the LiRo Bank. As one internal LiRo report maintained, "it was important to secure Jewish property as far as possible before the deportations, as otherwise considerable amounts would inevitably go astray"[71] Thus, there was even a parallel between the concentration of Dutch Jews for deportation and the concentration of their assets.

What happened to confiscated Jewish property in the Netherlands? In practice, only a small part was actually used for financing the Final Solution. Of the total income from Jewish property, almost certainly in excess of one billion fl.,[72] only about 25 million fl. were made available to the Gestapo for the establishment of two Jewish camps and other administrative costs in the Netherlands. The bulk of the money remained in the accounts of LiRo and the VVRA. According to Seyss-Inquart, in talks with Reich Finance Minister Graf Lutz Schwerin von Krosigk, it had been agreed that the major part would be retained for purposes inside the Netherlands.[73] However, the rapid processing of Jewish property provided an almost immediate boost to Germany's shaky war finances, as much of it was quickly converted into Dutch and German government bonds, starting even before the deportations. The haul also brought in some vital foreign currency, though only part of the diamonds and foreign securities collected were actually sold in the neutral countries due to increasing difficulties encountered in these markets by 1944.

Most striking is the effectiveness of the confis-cation policy, securing according to the rough calculations of Helen Junz as much as 94 percent of Jewish property on Dutch soil.[74] Even some overseas assets were repatriated through the blackmail schemes and extensive registration of property. Significantly, a very large part of the proceeds went directly into the hands of the state. . . . The German authorities also exploited the policy of Aryanization to pursue other German aims, including German penetration of the Dutch economy and its "rationalization" through the liquidation of many smaller and inefficient firms. The looting was also used to reward some Dutch collaborators, although the role of the Dutch as beneficiaries remained limited, as the appetite for Jewish property was restrained and much of the furniture was shipped to Germany.

What was the role of Dutch institutions and Dutch society in this massive and highly effective plunder campaign against Jewish property? It is important to stress that very few initiatives came from the Dutch population or the Dutch administration. Although many Dutch citizens were prepared to take a risk and invest in former Jewish property, the reservations they expressed here were much greater than in Austria or Germany. The warnings against purchasing Jewish property—warnings issued by the Dutch government in exile—were widely known and to some extent heeded, especially as faith in an Allied victory always remained alive and grew steadily from 1943.[75]

The legalistic approach taken by the German authorities to the confiscation of Jewish property in the Netherlands was successful, as Dutch civil servants and private institutions were generally law-abiding and obeyed German instructions. . . . In many respects, the system of bureaucratic "confiscation by decree" in the Netherlands proved very successful for the Germans, even by comparison with other Western European countries. The

clear priorities of the Nazi-run civil administration planning for the eventual incorporation of the Netherlands into the Reich also played a role.[76] In the Netherlands, the comprehensive confiscation of Jewish property was carefully coordinated with the development of the Final Solution, transferring the bulk of Jewish wealth directly into the hands of the state by methods first conceived in Austria and the Reich.

NOTES

1. See Götz Aly and Susanne Heim, *Vordenker der Vernichtung: Auschwitz und die deutschen Pläne für eine europäischer Neuordnung* (Hamburg: Hofmann und Campe, 1991), 44–45; and A. J. van der Leeuw, "Reichskommissariat und Judenvermögen in den Niederlanden," in A. H. Paape, ed., *Studies over Nederland in oorlogstijd* ('s-Gravenhage: Martinus Nijhoff, 1972), 237–49, here 237–38.

2. Gerard Aalders, "Die Arisierung der niederländischen Wirtschaft: Raub per Verordnung," in Alfons Kenkmann and Bernd-A. Rusinek (eds.), *Verfolgung und Verwaltung: Die wirtschaftliche Ausplünderung der Juden und die westfälischen Finanzbehörden* (Münster: Oberfinanzdirektion Münster, 1999), 122–37.

3. Eichmann Trial, document T-536, Gestapo Report on the development of the Jewish Question in Holland, December 31, 1942.

4. G. Aalders, "Niederlande: Wirtschaftliche Verfolgung," in W. Seibel, ed., *Holocaust und "Polykratie" in Westeuropa, 1940–1944: Nationale Berichte* (December, 2001), 129.

5. VO 26/1940 über die Behandlung des feindlichen Vermögens.

6. See Stephan H. Lindner, *Das Reichskommissariat für die Behandlung feindlichen Vermögens im Zweiten Weltkrieg* (Stuttgart: Franz Steinert, 1991).

7. G. Aalders, "Niederlande: Wirtschaftliche Verfolgung," 136–37.

8. BAL, R 177/203, Dr. Schröder. GKFW an Herrn von Karger, LiRo, March 4, 1942.

9. VO 145/1940; VO 41/1941.

10. G. Aalders, *Geraubt!*, 192–95.

11. G. Aalders, "Niederlande: Wirtschaftliche Verfolgung," 130.

12. VO 189/1940 über die Anmeldung von Unternehmen.

13. USHMM, RG-41, ACC.1997.A.1007, Netherlands Institute for War Documentation (NIOD), reel 301, Meldungen aus den Niederlanden (BdS reports), November 29, 1940.

14. NARA, RG-242, T-120, reel 3271, E554244–45, Aufzeichnung betr. Arisierung in Holland, March 1, 1941.

15. VO 48/1941, über die Behandlung anmeldepflichtiger Unternehmen, March 12, 1941.

16. G. Aalders, "Niederlande: Wirtschaftliche Verfolgung," 139–40.

17. R. Hilberg, *Die Vernichtung*, vol. 2, 599–601.

18. Jacob Presser, *The Destruction of the Dutch Jews* (New York: E. P. Dutton, 1969), 367–68.

19. G. Aalders, *Geraubt!*, 202; R. Hilberg, *Die Vernichtung*, vol. 2, 602–3.

20. G. Aalders, *Geraubt!*, 200–201; see also Jean-Marc Dreyfus, "L'aryanisation economique aux Pays-Bas (et sa comparison avec le cas français), 1940–1945" (unpublished paper presented at the United States Holocaust Memorial Museum in summer 2001), 8.

21. A. J. van der Leeuw, "Reichskommissariat und Judenvermögen in den Niederlanden," in A. H. Paape, ed., *Studies over Nederland in oorlogstijd*, 237–49, here 242.

22. Ibid., 244–47; see also, for example, BAL, R 177/214, GkFW an DSK Niederlande. February 26, 1943.

23. Gerard Aalders, *Nazi Looting: The Plunder of Dutch Jewry during the Second World War* (Oxford: Berg, 2004), 281, gives an estimate of 150 to 200 million fl.

24. For this comparative insight, I am indebted to J. M. Dreyfus, "L'aryanisation economique," 23–26.

25. VO 148/1941, über die Behandlung des jüdischen Vermogens.

26. For details of this process, see G. Aalders, *Gelraubt!*, 221—326.

27. USHMM, RG-41, Ace. 1997.A.1007 (NIOD), reel 391, Nbg. Doc. NID-13754, LiRo internal memo, August 19, 1941.

28. BAL, R 177/203, undated guidelines on LiRo accounts created under VO 148/1941.

29. J. Presser, *The Destruction of the Dutch Jews*, 72–73.

30. USHMM, RG-14.001M (Gestapo Düsseldorf), reel 5, statement of J. S., November 19, 1941.

31. BAL, R 177/203, LiRo Inspectie an GkFW, November 24 and November 26, 1941; see also similar correspondence on March 18, 1942.

32. See G. Aalders, "Niederlande: Wirtschaftliche Verfolgung," 133: of these, 22,252 were foreign nationals (14,652 from the Reich). The Dutch banks did not have records telling them which customers were Jewish and which were not.

33. G. Aalders, *Geraubt!*, 388: the total income received by LiRo was just over 425 million fl.

34. USHMM, RG-41, Acc.1997–A.0117 (NIOD), reel 131 (Collection 97, Alfred Flesche, 1940–1945) RK to LiRo, November 17, 1941; see also G. Aalders, *Geraubt!*, 273.

35. G. Aalders, *Geraubt!*, 273–78.

36. See BAL, R 177/203, Joodsche Raad an Beauftragten des Reichskommissars für die Stadt Amsterdam, Böhmcker, April 1, 1942.

37. G. Aalders, Geraubt!, 278–82; see also Jaap Barendregt, *Securities at Risk: The Restitution of Jewish Securities Stolen in the Netherlands during World War II* (Amsterdam: Aksant, 2004), 25–34.

38. Gerald Feldman, *Die Allianz und die deutsche Versicherungswirtschaft 1933–1945* (Munich: C. H. Beck, 2001), 463; see also R. Hilberg, *Die Vernichtung*, 2: 601.

39. A copy of the "Second LiRo Decree" can be found in BAL, R 177/214 VO 58/42, May 21, 1942; see also R 177/203, GkFW Abt. Feindvermögen an Ministerialrat von Böckh, enclosing report for Reichskommissar Seyss-Inquart, June 3, 1942.

40. BAL, R 177/213, Lammers an Seyss-Inquart, February 12, 1942.

41. LAB, B, Rep. 039–01/320, A. J. van der Leeuw, Gutachten, December 11, 1969, 22.

42. G. Aalders, *Geraubt!*, 245–47; Joods Historisch Museum Amsterdam, ed., *Documents of the Persecution of the Dutch Jewry* (Amsterdam: Polak and Van Genneo, 1979). 44.

43. See, for example, A. J. van der Leeuw, *"Der Griff"* 221.

44. G. Aalders, *Nazi Looting*, 187–88.

45. See, for example, BAL, R 177/203, ERR an LiRo, May 14, 1942.

46. G. Aalders, *Nazi Looting*, 187–89 and 213–16.

47. Ibid., 186–89; BAL, R 177/203; see also Peter Hayes, *From Cooperation to Complicity: Degussa in the Third Reich* (New York: Cambridge University Press, 2004), 187, noting the receipt of 225 kilograms of fine silver by Degussa from LiRo.

48. G. Aalders, *Nazi Looting*, 187–91; see also A. J. van der Leeuw, "Die Käufe des Generalkommissars z.b.V. Fritz Schmidt," in A. H. Paape, ed., *Studies over Nederland in oorlogstijd* ('s-Gravenhage: Martinus Nijhoff, 1972), 278–82.

49. G. Aalders, *Nazi Looting*, 120–22; J. Presser, *The Destruction*, 371–74.

50. G. Aalders, *Nazi Looting*, 120–22; A. J. van der Leeuw, "Die Aktion Bozenhardt und Co.," in A. H. Paape, ed., *Studies over Nederland in oorlogstijd*, 257–77.

51. A. J. van der Leeuw, "Die Aktion Bozenhardt," 270; J. Presser, *The Destruction*, 373–74.

52. G. Aalders, *Nazi Looting*, 180–83. The deadline can be found in an undated LiRo memo from 1942; see BAL, R 177/214.

53. BAL, R 177/209, Liro an GkFW, July 1 and December 12, 1942.

54. G. Aalders, *Nazi Looting*, 180–83; in both the German and English editions of Aalders's book there is some confusion about the date of "54/1943," which should be June 11, 1943. According to the conclusions of the various official Dutch investigations, insurance policies were the only sorts of Jewish assets not reported to LiRo on a large scale; see the Web site of the Dutch Ministry of Finance: http://www.niinfin.nl/ttw/english.htm, as of February 8. 2001.

55. According to VO 154/1941 (über den jüdischen Grundbesitz), Jewish real estate had to be registered with the NGV by September 15, 1941.

56. G. Aalders, *Geraubt!*, 210–11. The "Algemeen Nederlandsch Beheer van Onroerende," or General Dutch Management of Real Estate, also became involved in the management and sale of Jewish properties after a while. Like the NGV, it was staffed mainly by Dutch Nazis and claimed a commission of 5 percent for "management fees."

57. Ibid., 212–20.

58. Bob Moore, *Victims and Survivors: The Nazi Persecution of the Jews in the Netherlands 1940–1945* (London: Arnold, 1997), 88; J. Presser, *The Destruction*, 360–61.

59. Wolfgang Seibel, "Perpetrator Networks and the Holocaust: Resuming the 'Functionalism' versus 'Intentionalism' Debate," paper prepared for delivery at the 2000 Annual Meeting of the American Political Science Association, 19. Only about 5,200 Jews returned to the Netherlands after the war from the concentration and death camps; see G. Aalders, *Nazi Looting*, 228.

60. J. Presser, *The Destruction*, 361–62.

61. J. Presser, *The Destruction*, 359.

62. G. Aalders, *Nazi Looting*, 139–41.

63. NARA RG-23S, T-1139, Nbg. Doc. NG-2631, Reichskommissar an AA, Betr.: Abschiebung der Niederländischen Juden, March 26, 1943.

64. See Ad van Liempt, *Kopgeld: Nederlandse premiejagers op zoek naar joden 1943* (Amsterdam: Balans, 2002); for an example of an arrest report by W. C. H. Henneicke himself, see USHMM, RG-41, ACC.1997.A.0117 (NIOD), reel 392, Bericht Betr.: die Jüdin Mina Rubins und das Judenkind Rozette v/d Stam. A note on the file indicates they were gassed shortly afterward on September 3, 1943.

65. J. Presser, *The Destruction*, 366.

66. BAL. R 177/203, DSK memo, March 30, 1942.

67. J. Presser, *The Destruction*, 363.

68. See, for example, Eichmann Trial doc. T/536, Gestapo report on "The Development of the Jewish Problem in the Netherlands," December 31, 1942.

69. W. Seibel, ed., *Holocaust und 'Polykratie' in Westeuropa, 1940–1944: Nationale Berichte*, xxxvi and xlix. Seyss-Inquart was careful to insist on a unified approach toward Jewish policy at a meeting on October 8, 1941.

70. J. Michman, "Planning for the Final Solution," 167–69; B. Moore, *Victims and Survivors*, 76–79; the reference to "Aussiedlung" can be found in USHMM, RG-41 (ACC.1997.A.0117), reel 302 (NIOD Collections 77–85), File 53A, BdS den Haag, circular re. "Sonderreferat J," August 28, 1941.

71. BAL, R 177/214, Arbeitsbericht der "Inspectie," September 15, 1942, 3; the report also noted that hidden property was much harder to track down after the Jewish owners had gone.

72. G. Aalders, *Nazi Looting*, 224; see also, Helen B. Junz, *Where Did All the Money Go?: The Pre-Nazi Era Wealth of European Jewry* (Bern: Staempfli, 2002), 65; Second World War Assets Contact Group, ed., *Second World War: Theft and Restoration of Rights. Final Report of the Second World War Assets Contact Group* (Amsterdam, 2000), 84–87, gives a rough breakdown of known amounts: LiRo-fl. 370 million; businesses-fl. c. 300 million; real estate and mortgages-fl. 196 million; household effects—fl. c. 118 million; valuables and cash surrendered to the Security Police and others lor blackmail-fl. c. 43 million; noncommercial organizations—fl. 7 million.

73. Report by Seyss-Inquart in 1944, see Eichmann Trial doc. T-571, letter from Seyss-Inquart to Martin Bormann, February 28, 1944; see also G. Aalders, *Geraubt!*, 388–89.

74. H. B. Junz, *Where Did All the Money Go?*, 65.

75. G. Aalders, *Geraubt!*, 398–99. On June 7, 1940, the Dutch government in exile banned any transactions with the German occupation regime. On January 5, 1943, the "Inter-Allied Declaration against Acts of Dispossession Committed in Territories under Enemy Occupation and Control" specifically warned against offering any assistance to German looting policies.

76. J.-M. Dreyfus, "Die Enteignung der Juden in Westeuropa," 53–54.

6 The German Killers and Their Methods

12 After liberation, eyeglasses, clothing, footwear, and other personal effects taken from prisoners were found in warehouses at Auschwitz-Birkenau. October 14, 1945. (U.S. Holocaust Memorial Museum, courtesy Philip Vock.)

13. Auschwitz, Poland . . . 1940—With the outbreak of war, Jerzy Radwanek, a Polish Air Force pilot, prepared for a secret intelligence mission. But before his flight could depart, the Gestapo received information about the clandestine operation; Jerzy was arrested and deported to Auschwitz in the fall of 1940. Jerzy, along with other Polish inmates, established a secret military organization inside the camp, planning escape routes and documenting Nazi atrocities. Jerzy was given the job of camp electrician and was able to move around the grounds more freely than most other inmates. On several occasions the young Polish prisoner was sent to the Jewish barracks to repair wiring and install lights. He was greatly disturbed by the plight of the Jewish inmates and offered to help them in any way possible. Often Jerzy would secretly create short circuits in the Jewish compound's fuse box. When called in to "fix the light," Jerzy would smuggle food and medicine in his toolbox to distribute to the Jewish women and children. He befriended several of these women and visited them often, promising that if he survived, he would tell the world of Nazi brutality and Jewish suffering. As a result of his efforts, Jewish inmates referred to Jerzy as the "Jewish Uncle" of Auschwitz. (Courtesy JFR Photo Archives.)

Introduction

PETER HAYES

Once Nazi leaders began to use the word "annihilation" in connection with the Jews at the turn of 1938/39, the Reich began inching toward that policy. Indeed, death on a large scale was implicit in the ghettoization and deportation programs, even though they stopped short of aiming at comprehensive killing. Both undertakings involved transporting large numbers of people into inhospitable physical surroundings with minimum provision for their care and sustenance. Considerable attrition would be the inevitable consequence, the Nazi leaders knew. Still, as late as May 1940, Heinrich Himmler called "the Bolshevist method of the physical destruction of a people . . . un-German and impossible," though he made that remark in reference to the treatment of Poles, not Jews.

In 1941, however, a number of developments swept aside Himmler's and the regime's inhibitions. First, mounting frustration with the postponement of deportations of Jews from the Reich and the annexed regions led to increased pressure from the *Gauleiter* and Himmler's subordinates to do something to break the impasse. Similar grumbling arose from the SS officers charged with managing the supposedly temporary ghettos, which increasingly were depicted as menacing sources of epidemics and burdensome drains on food supplies. Second, Operation Barbarossa, the planned invasion of the Soviet Union, promised to compound these problems by adding more conquered territory in which Jews were numerous. Third, the perceived diplomatic value of holding Europe's Jews as hostages declined as Hitler

came to believe that the United States would enter the war sooner or later in any case. Finally, during the heady months that followed the invasion of the Soviet Union on June 22, Nazi racists recognized that the practical and political limits on action were fewer than previously thought. While military operations against supposed "partisans" provided ample pretexts for massacre, the regime already possessed the capacity to do away with large numbers of people by applying gassing techniques developed during the euthanasia program at home. During the euphoria of the advance on Moscow, Hitler, Himmler, and Heydrich concluded that Germany did not need to wait for complete victory to carry out a "final solution of the Jewish question."

The first three readings in this chapter detail the effects of these developments. In the second half of 1941, as Mark Roseman relates, the Nazi regime engaged in a gradual, two-track process of *deciding to kill* the Jews within its grasp. During the summer, the first track produced a program for *bringing death to Jews* in the path of the German advance, with limited exceptions of the most able-bodied potential workers among them. Richard Rhodes traces the escalation of this carnage, as *Einsatzgruppen*, Order Police, and local collaborators carried out increasingly comprehensive massacres, epitomized by the shooting at Babi Yar, outside of Kiev, of almost 34,000 Jewish men, women, and children over two days in late September, and then continuing throughout the following year. In the course of the autumn, the second track yielded a design for *bringing Jews to death* by transporting those in the rest of Nazi-occupied or -allied Europe to gassing installations on the territory of prewar Poland. Raul Hilberg's summary of the history of the concentration camp system points out that two designated sites already existed, Auschwitz and Majdanek, and they remained distinct from the new death factories the Nazis now began building in two respects: both continued to cage populations of potential slave laborers even as they murdered most people sent to the sites, and both killed by using Zyklon, a commercially available, inexpensive, and highly toxic fumigant routinely used to disinfest military bases, rather than the carbon monoxide gas previously employed in the euthanasia centers. Test gassings of Soviet prisoners of war occurred at Auschwitz in early September. Construction at Belzec, the first of four new locations, began in October. That was also the month in which Chelmno was selected as a second new site and Himmler banned all further emigration from Europe by Jews, thus signaling a turn away from that form of their "removal." By late November, when the first round of invitations to what later became known as the Wannsee Conference went out, the regime was committed to a program of mass murder, and Hitler passed the word personally to the assembled Gauleiter on December 12, 1941.

The result was a veritable orgy of violence that consumed perhaps two-thirds of the victims of the Holocaust (some 4 million people) in only 19 months, from July 1941 to February 1943, and fully half of them (3 million) in only the last eleven months of that time span, beginning in March 1942. That year marked the temporal epicenter of the slaughter, and Poland, Lithuania, and the occupied Soviet Union composed the geographical one, since three-quarters of the victims came

from those places and nearly all of them were murdered there. For the most part, the camps that devoured many of them were small, primitive, and ramshackle affairs, easily and swiftly dismantled when their work was done. By late 1943, only Auschwitz and Majdanek, the dual-purpose labor and death camps and thus the ones built to last, remained as the intended destinations for the Jews from other parts of the continent.

The Germans who perpetrated both the mobile and the stationary massacres seldom were mere bureaucrats carrying out their orders. Neither were they usually "ordinary men" plucked from civilian life and placed in unfamiliar situations. Rather, as Edward Westermann shows in discussing the Order Police who carried out many of the shootings in the occupied East, the great majority of these men were ideologically committed warriors who saw themselves as "political soldiers" carrying out an important military mission, the eradication of present and future enemies of the German people. Similarly, the German historian Michael Wildt has demonstrated that the SS officers who composed the Reich Security Main Office (RSHA) and commanded the *Einsatzgruppen* and the death camps were predominantly young (nearly all born after 1900), highly educated, upwardly mobile men who had long records of involvement in extreme nationalist and antisemitic politics. By 1941, they had long since internalized the notion that nothing could be allowed to stand in the way of the Reich's supposed needs; they thus composed what Wildt aptly dubbed a "generation without limits" (*Generation des Unbedingten*).

Among their victims were people other than Jews, though no other group experienced such comprehensive, relentless assault. Of the other people generally targeted by Nazism within Germany, gay men were usually left alone outside of it, and the slaughter of the mentally ill extended to the conquered eastern regions, but not to Nazi-allied states or Western Europe. Only the *fates of gypsies* approximated the treatment of Jews, in that Nazi animosity applied across the continent, yet as Yehuda Bauer's analysis makes clear, gypsies were not attacked uniformly, which allowed higher survival rates.

Among the German killers' methods were attrition through concentration *camp labor*, especially in constructing and operating a network of mines and factories around Auschwitz in Eastern Upper Silesia, the region Germans colloquially called the "Reich Air Raid Shelter" because it lay beyond the range of Allied bombers until mid-1944. Primo Levi describes the degradation and demoralization created by the conditions and practices at one of the most infamous of these labor sites, the Monowitz camp of IG Farben, later officially titled Auschwitz III, a few miles east of the main camp. As the Russians closed in on these and similar installations early in 1945, a *final frenzy* of murder took place. Daniel Blatman demonstrates that even though the ss's decision to evacuate rather than abandon the camps was an attempt to preserve its labor force, poor preparation, antisemitism, and fear of the camp populations turned evacuations into death marches on which often one-quarter to one-third of the evacuees died. Even the survivors of these treks faced long odds on survival because the conditions at their destinations were catastrophic as the Reich collapsed and because the practice of gassing prisoners now spread at camps where it had been infrequent and to camps where it had been unknown.

The Nazi murder machine carried off roughly two-thirds of the estimated population of European Jews in 1939, 6 out of 9 million people; in all probability, the 6 million constituted more than three-quarters of the Jews in the Nazi-occupied or Nazi-allied parts of the continent—that is, who did not inhabit the British Isles, the neutral countries, and the unconquered portions of the Soviet Union. This chapter explains how the Third Reich came so close to achieving Hitler's goal of a "Jew-free Europe."

Deciding to Kill

MARK ROSEMAN

From *The Wannsee Conference and the Final Solution*

In 1940–41, occupied Poland seethed with acts of brutality. In the little town of Izbica, the new ethnic-German mayor trained his dog to recognize the Jewish star. Women on their way to the well for water were brought down by the mayor's beloved Alsatian and murdered for sport. In Odilo Globocnik's labor camps, Jews constructing defensive fortifications along the Bug River died in droves. The guards amused themselves by making them leap from car to car on moving trains. There are thousands, even tens of thousands, of such examples, and they already convey an authentic Holocaust character. Yet at the highest level of planning genocide had still not become part of the agenda. It was the war against the Soviet Union that would make the decisive difference.

On June 22, 1941, German troops entered Soviet territory. Behind the troops swept in four motorized *Einsatzgruppen* of six hundred to a thousand men each. Karl Jäger, the head of one of the subcommandos operating within the northern group, *Einsatzgruppe* A, reported in December on the activities of his own unit:

> I can now state that the aim of solving the Jewish problem for Lithuania has been achieved by *Einsatzkommando* 3. There are no more Jews in Lithuania apart from the work-Jews and their families. . . . The carrying out of such actions is first and foremost a matter of organization. The decision to clear each district systemati-cally of Jews required a thorough preparation of every single action and the investigation of the conditions in the particular district. The Jews had to be concentrated in one place or in several places. The place for the pits that were required had to be found and dug out to suit the numbers involved. The distance from the place where the Jews were concentrated to the pits was on average 4–5km. The Jews were transported to the place of execution in groups of up to 500 with gaps of at least 2km. . . .[1]

By the time of his report, mass shootings by *Einsatzkommandos* and other killing units had led to the deaths of half a million Jews. The era of genocide had begun.

This was no ordinary war, Hitler told his generals, but a fight to the death between two ideologies. The Soviet state had to be destroyed; the Communist officials were all criminals and must be treated as such.[2] The latter demand was perhaps not very different from his instruction of August 1939 that the Polish leadership be eliminated. The disastrous difference as far as Jews were concerned was that Hitler believed they were at the heart of the Communist system. Hitler's aim was the elimination of the "Judeo-Bolshevik intelligentsia." In Russia, therefore, the campaign against the elites was to be from the beginning also a campaign against the Jews, with the limits of Jewish culpability and participation poorly defined.

Hitler could count on the enthusiastic endorsement of the Security Police and SD. The tasks of the four *Einsatzgruppen* sent into the Soviet Union had been planned by Reinhard Heydrich in the months before Barbarossa. The same highly educated elite in the higher echelons of the SD now provided the cool commanders of the *Einsatz* squads. The detailed head counts sent back to Berlin, listing carefully and separately the Jewish men, women, and children shot during the reporting period, reveal for the first time in its full horror the unique fusion of annihilatory ideology and bureaucratic fastidiousness that characterized Heydrich's staff. Striking, too, was the degree to which the army now accepted anti-Jewish measures as essential to the fight against the Soviet leadership. Sharing Hitler's anti-Bolshevism and antisemitism and having learned subservience in Poland, the army high command willingly plotted a new kind of war.[3] They accepted the infamous *Kommissarbefehl* (commissar order) of June 6, which ordered that all political commissars attached to the Red Army be shot.[4] They further agreed that Himmler's men would have "special tasks" within their zone of operation, and that they were entitled to act against the civilian population on Himmler's authority. For both the army and the *Einsatzkommandos*, anti-Bolshevism and antipartisan actions became the legitimation for action against Jewish civilians.[5] . . .

Barbarossa, then, created murderous imperatives and altered the whole tone of war. But does this mean that there was from the beginning a clear decision to murder all Soviet Jews or that a more limited strategic concept (eliminating the Judeo-Bolshevik intelligentsia) later widened into something more comprehensive? Unfortunately, much of Heydrich's planning is concealed from us. We know far less about the instructions given to the *Einsatzgruppen* commanders than we do about the *Wehrmacht*'s basic directives. All that has been preserved is a précis of Heydrich's instructions

handed on in June to the Higher SS and Police Leaders (HSSPF) in the Soviet Union.[6] This document indicates that "all Jews in the service of Party and state" should be targeted, an instruction not intrinsically genocidal though vague in the extreme. It seems quite possible that Heydrich's verbal instructions to the *Einsatzgruppen* went beyond the written orders.[7]

If we look at the actual practice of the killing squads, we see that they began by targeting a narrower group of state officials and Jews in leading positions but very rapidly began to include all Jewish men of military age.[8] A few weeks later, in July to August, women and children began to be included, and in August to September squads moved to eliminate entire communities.[9] Was this the stepwise implementation of a preexisting plan or did the instructions change over the summer? If they did, who ordered the more extensive killing? Postwar trial testimony of captured *Einsatzgruppen* and *-kommando* leaders is extremely contradictory, as are the progress reports they submitted during the war.[10] While confirming the general trend toward greater comprehensiveness, the reports also indicate considerable variations in local commanders' interpretations of their brief. As early as July 1941, the leader of *Einsatzgruppe* A believed that the special conditions in the Soviet Union made possible the murder of all Jews.[11] Yet even in September, *Einsatzgruppe* C did not seem to think that eliminating Jews was its principal task.[12]

Whatever instructions the group and local commanders had initially received, therefore, had been susceptible to narrower or broader interpretation. This suggests that the initial orders were not clearly genocidal but that their definition of the Jewish elite was so loose that it enabled something quite close to genocide—namely, the elimination of all Jewish men of working age. Once killings on that scale had been carried out, it often seemed but a small step to widen the scope of murder. The widows and children of the murdered men did not look like an economically viable community, particularly in view of the intensifying food shortages.

Hitler certainly established the general climate for this radicalization of policy. We know that he asked for regular reports on *Einsatzgruppen* activities, and a shooting may even have been filmed for him.[13] Moreover, at an important meeting on July 16, after which he gave Alfred Rosenberg, minister for the occupied eastern territories, jurisdiction over those areas no longer directly under military command, Hitler announced that Germany would never relinquish the conquered Soviet territories. All measures necessary for a final settlement— such as shooting and deportation—should be taken. Stalin's partisan war provided the excuse to "exterminate anything opposing us"—"anyone who even looks at us the wrong way should be shot."[14] Hitler made these statements in confident anticipation of a rapid victory. Toward the end of July, however, it became apparent that progress was slower than expected and that supplying the troops had become a major problem.

It was above all Himmler who conveyed the need for more radical measures. On July 17, 1941, Hitler made him responsible for security in the civilian regions in the East now under Rosenberg's jurisdiction. From July 15 to 20, Himmler was in the Führer's headquarters. We do not know what communications he had with Hitler, but whatever took place, Himmler rapidly moved from policies that still might be characterized as murderous security measures to ones that could only be seen as genocidal—solving the "Jewish problem" in large areas of the conquered Soviet Union by killing. Himmler's actions reflected not only his security mandate from Hitler but also his informal

(later official) quest to extend his role as Reich Commissar for the Strengthening of Germandom from Poland to the former Soviet territories. Within a week of his appointment, Himmler quadrupled the number of SS men operating behind army lines. He also assigned the police reserve battalions to his direct subordinates in the field, the Higher SS and Police Leaders (HSSPF). Through the HSSPF, Himmler began to press for the radical cleansing of huge swaths of territory for both security and settlement purposes. At the end of July there may still have been a little hesitation at ordering the killings of women and children— for example, in an operation to drive them into the Pripet Marshes—but only a little.[15] Increasingly, the HSSPF took the leading role in the killing process, and the SS brigades and police battalions under their direction eventually murdered far more Jews than the original *Einsatzgruppen*.[16]

Overall, the evidence does not support the idea that there was one single clear-cut order to murder all Jews. The point in time at which the individual *Einsatzgruppen* widened the scope of their killing varied considerably. What we can say is that in the murderous climate fostered by Hitler, a variety of agencies, with the Himmler-Heydrich axis at the center, worked together to push measures forward. The *Einsatzgruppen* leaders, most of them drawn from the educated, ideologically homogeneous upper ranks of the Security Police and SD, interpreted their brief liberally. In the latter half of July and first half of August, Himmler, perhaps under instructions from Hitler, moved toward a more openly genocidal line. As economic pressures increased, the SS-Security Police leadership found further support for their actions from civilian officials who complained about undesirable elements making claims on scarce resources. The civilian administration in Lithuania and some field commanders in the Wehrmacht drew up agreements with the SS to get rid of the useless eaters left alive after the first shootings. By August 1941 at the latest, the fate of Soviet Jewry was sealed.[17]

Hitler's Elusive Decision

The weeks following the outbreak of war against the Soviet Union had changed the climate irrevocably. Assumptions about what was feasible were reformulated, inhibitions about what was intolerable were progressively discarded. As early as July, Himmler's thoughts turned to gas as an alternative to shooting. At the same time, knowledge of the shootings spread among Nazi elites in Germany and elsewhere in occupied Europe, and their perception of what was possible also began to change. A psychological threshold was irrevocably crossed.

Yet widespread murder in the lawless conditions behind the military front line was still significantly different from the systematic killing of Jews all across Europe, the project expressed in the Wannsee Protocol. How and when was this transition effected? Unfortunately, our need for precise answers is greater than the ability of the documentation to supply them. Despite the absence of evidence, most historians continue to assume that, however twisted the road may have been, Hitler must at some point have made the ultimate decision to murder European Jewry. His role in redefining the character of warfare and introducing pacification through murder and social engineering had been crucial. But how closely did he now direct the killing of Jews? Was his approval given or merely presumed? Did the transition from mass killing to genocide involve a clear decision or was the program outlined at Wannsee more of a retrospective codification of a process already under way?

Even more than in peacetime, Hitler carefully concealed his involvement in the Jewish question.[18] The paucity of official records is not compensated by the existence of private ones. Hitler kept no diary and sent no letters expressing views on the Jewish question. A number of those close to him recorded his views, but often their notes are ambiguous too. The challenge, therefore, is to ascertain not only what Hitler's subordinates thought he said but also whether they got it right. In any case, we have virtually no record of probably the most important channel of communication on the Jewish question, Hitler's conversations with Himmler. The occasional pertinent entries in Himmler's appointment diary are abbreviated and cryptic.

Those statements of Hitler's that we do have are, of course, forthright enough. But Hitler's rhetoric, as we have seen, is deliberately inflammatory. There is a relationship between his brutal words and his brutal policies but it is not a direct one. Take Hitler's "prophecy" of January 1939 that a future world war would lead to the extermination of Jews in Europe. There is no doubt his warning was significant, not least in setting the rhetorical pitch for his subordinates. For some historians, it represents a clear threat of genocide. Yet there is no evidence that mass extermination was being planned in 1939, and Hitler himself made little reference to the prophecy throughout the whole of 1940. It's impossible to tell, then, whether his statements demonstrate clear intent or even to ascertain precisely what the intent might have been. Hitler warned that annihilation would follow if the Jews were to plunge Europe into *world* war. Is it possible that he did not yet see the conflict with Britain and the Commonwealth as world war? Something that might support such an idea is that in January 1941, when war with the Soviet Union was in the offing, Hitler recalled his prophecy of two years earlier and thereafter returned to it more often. Yet his timing then may have been a response to other developments that were changing his thinking rather than evidence of consistent understanding of what "world war" meant.

It is also uncertain whether the "annihilation" of Jews in Europe implied a clearly formulated desire for their death or simply for their complete banishment. Hitler repeatedly talked of the need to drive the Jews out of Germany by force. Brutal means were required to cleanse the racial state. But his pronouncements seldom unequivocally crossed the line from physical removal to physical extermination.

Altogether, Hitler's table talk sounds not like the clear goal setting of a policy maker but like the late-night ramblings of a know-nothing at a *Bierkeller*. The thought that this speaker was presiding over the fate of millions is almost inconceivable. With monologues as disjointed as these, how could even his closest confidants know his intentions? Were the issue not genocide, of course, we would not be interrogating his language so scrupulously. But the Holocaust is so monstrously innovative that we are obliged to understand precisely how the taboos could be broken.

Extending Murder: July 1941

Until recently, most historians would have chosen one of two moments as the most likely point at which Hitler committed himself to eliminating European Jewry. One occurred sometime in mid-July, just before Himmler moved to extend the killings in the Soviet Union, the other in mid-September, when Hitler approved the deportation of German Jews eastward.

In mid-July, as we have seen, Hitler, anticipating imminent victory over the Soviet Union, made some fundamental policy decisions, laying down harsh guidelines for the "pacification" and colonization of Soviet territory. It was in the wake of these decisions that Himmler radically widened the scope of the killings in the Soviet Union. Goebbels wrote in his diary at the beginning of August that "the Führer is convinced that his former prophecy in the Reichstag is being confirmed: if Jewry succeeded once more in provoking a world war, it would end with the annihilation of the Jews. It is being confirmed in these weeks and months with a certainty that seems almost uncanny."[19] The commandant of Auschwitz, Rudolf Hoss, stated after the war that he was summoned by Himmler in the summer of 1941 and told that Auschwitz, then an "ordinary" concentration camp, was going to be an extermination center for the Jews. On trial in Jerusalem, Adolf Eichmann, too, said he learned that summer about a fundamental Hitler decision. It was around this time that Himmler began thinking of using gas as an alternative to shooting.[20] Friedrich Suhr, a legal expert in the RSHA, was given an official title: "Official for the Final Solution of the European Jewish Question, Particularly Abroad." On July 28, 1941, Viktor Brack, the man in charge of T4, the so-called euthanasia operation, asked for support from the military economic administration for a major forthcoming action, yet as far as we know, no such action was planned within the euthanasia program.

Most significant, there is Göring's infamous *Ermächtigung* (authorization) to Heydrich of July 31, 1941, which many historians see as the authentic inception of genocide:[21]

In completion of the task entrusted to you in the edict dated January 24, 1939, of solving the Jewish question by means of migration or evacuation in the most convenient way possible, given the present conditions, I herewith charge you with making all necessary preparations with regard to organizational, practical, and financial aspects for an overall solution of the Jewish question in the German sphere of influence in Europe.

Insofar as the competencies of other central organizations are affected, these should be involved.

I further charge you with submitting to me promptly an overall plan of the preliminary organizational, practical, and financial measures for the execution of the intended final solution of the Jewish question.

Thanks to recent research in the former Soviet archives we now know a little more about the background to the Göring document. Heydrich himself produced the first draft in March 1941, noting at the time that he had submitted it to Göring for signature but that agreement with Rosenberg was required before it could be authorized.[22] Rosenberg was the minister designate for the occupied Soviet territories, and it would seem that Heydrich was seeking Göring's approval to develop a new deportation policy into Siberia or some eastern Soviet territory, now that the Polish deportations had failed.[23] Discussions clarified Rosenberg's attitude and involvement, enabling Heydrich to re-present the draft in July.[24] Of course, the terms in the authorization—"overall solution" (*Gesamtlösung*) and "final solution" (*Endlösung*) of the Jewish question—would soon be euphemisms for murder. By the end of November, when Heydrich attached this document to the invitations to the Wannsee Conference as proof of his authority, there is little doubt that "final solution" had lost any other meaning. But up to 1941, Heydrich, for one, regularly distinguished between "interim" and "final" solutions without meaning genocide in the latter case—for example, in relation to the future of the Protectorate.[25] We do not need to assume that the terms had attained their clear code meaning by July.

On closer inspection, the other evidence for a July decision for genocide also looks problematic. Both Höss's and Eichmann's testimonies lack credibility. Höss's meeting with Himmler almost certainly took place at least nine months later than he remembered.[26] Above all, Höss made clear that at the point when he learned about Auschwitz's new function, other extermination camps in Poland were already functioning—and that can only have been in 1942.[27] Eichmann, for his part, was at pains to establish a clear set of orders that absolved him of responsibility. In the interviews he gave in Argentina and in his first interrogation, he said that he learned about the Final Solution only at the end of 1941. But later he claimed to remember hearing of Hitler's order in the summer of that year. However, the details he attached to the memory, relating to a visit to the Belzec camp, meant that he could not have heard before November 1941.[28]

What we find in spring and summer 1941, in fact, is growing clamor from different groups hoping to use the Soviet territory as a dumping ground for German and other European Jews. Hitler himself made various pronouncements about the deportation of Europe's Jews. Before the start of the Russian campaign he had promised Hans Frank that the Jews would be removed from the *Generalgouvernement* in the foreseeable future.[29] On July 22, he announced to Croatian Marshal Slavko Kvaternik his intention to deport Jews, saying it was a matter of indifference to him whether they were sent to Madagascar or to Siberia.[30] Whether his talk of deportation was sincere or not, other Nazi officials certainly concluded from conversations with Hitler that European Jews were going to be sent to the East. Having failed in March 1941 to send Jews to the Polish *Generalgouvernement*, Goebbels noted delightedly in June that they were all looking forward to expelling their Jews. For Hans Frank, the governor of the *Generalgouvernement*, Russia represented the answer to his prayers.[31]

Doubts must remain. Did the Germans really intend to deport Jews to the Soviet Union when, even if Germany won the war, border skirmishes were certain to continue for some time? Were they likely to deposit their archenemy, the Jews, in an area where the Jews could make contact with Germany's other enemies? Possibly—if the borders were suitably policed.[32] What is certain is that the deportation plans had a new and consciously genocidal aspect. None of those seeking to drive Jews to the Pripet Marshes or to Siberia would have expected or hoped the deportees would thrive. As news of the events in the Soviet Union spread among the Nazi elite—and we know that in the course of the summer knowledge of what was happening to the Jews there became quite widespread—so the sense of what deportation to the Soviet Union meant must have changed too. When in August, for example, Nazi officials in France put forward the idea of deporting Europe's Jews to Russia, they were proposing not the separate existence of a Jewish people but its disappearance in hostile terrain. The acceptability of killing was spreading out from the Soviet Union, an invitation to key Nazis all across Europe.[33]

Death and Deportation: September 1941

In March 1941, Hitler had resisted initiatives by Heydrich and Goebbels to dispatch Jews to Poland. In July 1941, he rejected attempts by Governor Frank to claim the Pripet Marshes from the occupied Soviet territory and use them as a Jewish reservation. In August, he blocked a new deportation plan of Heydrich's. The war needed to be won before major deportations could be resumed.

A variety of figures continued to urge not only deportations but also other special measures—

above all forcing German Jews to wear a special star, as had long been required of Jews in Poland and was now being required in the Czech Protectorate. Goebbels, keen to liberate Berlin of its sizable Jewish presence, visited Hitler on August 18. Hitler agreed that German Jews should wear the yellow star—a considerable step and tacit recognition that voluntary emigration was no longer the anticipated fate of most German Jews. The star would make them easy to round up. Hitler promised, too, that Jews would be deported before the end of the war. But he still resisted any immediate action; the trains could be dispatched only after the eastern campaign was over.[34]

Sometime in mid-September 1941, however, Hitler changed his mind. After meeting Otto Abetz, the German ambassador to France, who requested that all Jews be deported from occupied France, and hearing from the *Gauleiter* of Hamburg, Karl Kaufmann, who requested that Jewish housing be made available to German victims of the recent British bombing raids, Hitler now said that German Jews and those from the Czech Protectorate could be deported immediately.[35] Other European Jews were also targeted: in the same month, the deportation of French Jews, initially limited to those in detention, was also announced.[36]

In contrast to the onset of Operation Barbarossa, where we can see an obvious stimulus to new actions, Hitler's reversal of his line on deportations seems less clearly motivated. The immediate trigger to act against Jews may have been the Soviets' sudden deportation of Volga Germans to Siberia on September 13–15.[37] Hitler was a vengeful man, and Goebbels's diary entry of September 9 (after Stalin's decision to deport the Volga Germans had been announced) makes evident that the regime regarded Stalin's announcement as legitimation to take more radical steps.[38] For

Hitler, it will have been a fitting part of his revenge to start the deportations of Jews in October, at exactly the point when the Soviets were to have been defeated in the Nazis' original plans. He may have been helped to his decision by Rosenberg, now minister for the eastern territories, who had concluded—no doubt on the basis of the Germans' own deportations—that most of the ethnic Germans would not survive those initiated by the Soviets. It was Rosenberg who on September 14 had passed on via his liaison officer at the army high command, Otto Bräutigam, the idea of deporting the Jews from Central Europe to the East as a "reprisal" to the Soviet action.[39]

At the very least, Hitler's decision on deportation was a significant radicalization of existing measures and moved him significantly closer to realizing his long-expressed desire to rid Europe of its Jews. But where were the Jews to go? Poland was no better equipped to take on the Jews than it had been in August. The Soviet campaign was not over. Hitler had given the green light for deportations under conditions no more favorable than those earlier, when he had blocked them. For some historians, this is crucial evidence that Hitler had now either already decided on genocide or was on the brink of that decision.[40]

Other developments reinforce the idea that September 1941 was the decisive turning point. The policy of mass shootings began to be extended beyond the borders of the Soviet Union into Serbia and Galicia. Experiments in gassing Jews took place in Mogilev and Minsk between September 3 and 18. In the *Warthegau*, the machinery of murder began to be put in place from October. In November, mobile gas vans were utilized in the *Warthegau* to murder Jews in the Kalisch district, while preparations at the Chelmno camp site date from the beginning of October. Farther east, within the *Generalgouvernement*, too, there were

moves toward creating at least one gas camp. And sometime in the autumn the first experiments were carried out with cyanide at Auschwitz, though to kill Soviet POWs.[41]

Hitler's command for deportation did not tie in with these various initiatives very neatly. Logically, if mass murder was already on the agenda, it would have made more sense to hold the Jews in Germany until the camps were ready.[42] Moreover, Hitler seemed very uncertain over the following weeks as to whether the timing for deportations was opportune. His hesitation adds credence to the view that, in a rage at Soviet deportations of Volga Germans, Hitler had given in to pressure without having formulated a new master plan. There is also evidence that Hitler still held to the belief that until the United States entered the war the Jews were useful as hostages. Four days after Hitler agreed to the deportations, Werner Koeppen, Rosenberg's personal aide, noted that the Führer had not yet made a decision about reprisals against German Jews; Koeppen had heard that Hitler would act if the United States entered the war.[43]

Thus when Hitler and Himmler agreed in September that, as a temporary step, sixty thousand Jews should be deported not to the *Generalgouvernement* but to the Lodz ghetto in the *Warthegau*, it seems that what they had in mind was deportation, not murder. As Himmler wrote to Arthur Greiser, *Gauleiter* of the *Warthegau*, on September 18, the plan was to deport Jews first to temporary quarters in the Lodz ghetto, then, in the spring, farther east.[44] (In late September Hitler was again so confident about the military situation in the Soviet Union that this timetable may have seemed realistic.)[45] After protests from Lodz, however, the figure was reduced to twenty-five thousand Jews and Gypsies. In early October, when Hitler called for the entire Czech Protectorate to be cleared, he suggested that the Czech Jews should not first be sent to Poland but should immediately be directed farther east, that is, to the Soviet Union. Although it is unknown whether Hitler expected the deportees to be murdered on Soviet soil, it seems clear, at the very least, that he had not yet arrived at a plan for exterminating the Jews on Polish territory.[46]

The Middle Managers of Murder

Over the last decade or so, our understanding of the events of these months has been transformed by a series of studies drawing on previously inaccessible German material held in Soviet bloc archives. These studies have shown that while regional leaders may have responded to common signals and pressures, their various initiatives in these months were probably not part of a central plan.

Starting in the summer of 1941 the notion spread that it was acceptable, even appropriate, to shoot Jews. Within the Soviet Union, all sorts of local units—including regular units of the German army—decided on their own to extend their killing operations.[47] Outside the Soviet Union, in Serbia, the newly arrived commander, General Franz Böhme, introduced a radical new policy of reprisal against partisan attacks: all Jewish men of arms-bearing age were placed in a "reservoir" of potential hostages and a hundred were shot for every German soldier killed. Böhme made no distinction between Jews or different patterns of behavior. The official explanation was that the Jews were linked to the partisan war, but it was clear that this was not the case. Even Jews who had been deported to Serbia from Austria, Bohemia, and Danzig before the beginning of the partisan uprisings and who had no conceivable part in them were included. Böhme referred to the killings as shooting hostages. But if these were "hostages," they were so only in the abstract sense

that the Germans were holding the conspiratorial force "World Jewry" ransom.[48]

The ratio of a hundred Jews for every German was not Böhme's own idea; it had been dictated from on high. Moreover, soon after his arrival in Serbia in September he had been approached by German officials urging a speedy resolution to the Jewish question. The officials, it seems, had been thinking of deportation. But though he undoubtedly responded to such signals, Böhme had no central instructions to make Jews his principal target. Instead, the historian Walter Manoschek has concluded, by the autumn of 1941 no special orders were necessary for such genocidal policy decisions to be made. Whatever their disagreements on other questions, when it came to the Jews, all the German authorities cooperated. What's more, the willingness to kill was not the result of special indoctrination, such as that given to ss men. It was the regular army that carried out most of the murders. By the end of the year, there were virtually no adult Jewish males left in Serbia. Following the murder of the women and children in early 1942, Serbia became one of the first countries to be "Jew free."[49]

Eastern Galicia offers a similar picture of regional initiative, drawing on the "lessons in shooting" provided by the Soviet experience. On October 12, the security forces embarked on a huge killing program, eliminating thousands of Jewish men, women, and children in the first two weeks, tens of thousands in the next couple of months.[50] Although Himmler had held meetings with regional officials in early September and some postwar testimony intimates that a killing order was passed down the line, the report submitted in 1942 by the principal instigator of murders in the region, the Galician district ss and police leader (sspf) Fritz Katzmann, does not support this contention. Himmler's direct orders to kill are clearly confirmed only much later—in July and October 1942 and May and October 1943. Of course, the Galician officials undoubtedly knew that Himmler and, above him, Hitler were willing to endorse mass murder. But the shootings seem to have been a regional initiative designed in the short term to thin out the population so that "manageable" ghettos could be created. Regional officials like Katzmann, it seems, were also thinking of the possibility of total eradication of the Jews through murder.[51]

Killings in the Soviet Union had other repercussions, too. Relatively early on Himmler concluded that some other form of murder might be preferable to shooting. The search for alternative methods probably began in July 1941—there is a cryptic memo from Himmler about gas installations, and there is other evidence, too, that plans were already afoot to gas Jews either on Soviet soil or in Eastern Europe.[52] Postwar testimony suggests that Himmler was so badly affected by witnessing a shooting in August that he commissioned Arthur Nebe (or perhaps the HSSPF in central Russia, Erich von dem Bach-Zelewksi, who in turn commissioned Nebe) to develop alternatives, so as to avoid the spiritual burdening of his men. Nebe, as well as being the head of *Einsatzgruppe* B, was in charge of the institute involved in developing mobile gas vans to kill mentally ill patients in Poland.

Perhaps in response to Himmler's concerns, perhaps independently, various local officials in the annexed Polish territories also began to wonder about other ways of getting rid of the Jews. A notorious memorandum sent to Eichmann on July 16 by the head of the SD in Posen, Rolf Heinz Höppner, summarized discussions under way among the advisers to *Gauleiter* Arthur Greiser. A series of proposals had been made for dealing with the Jewish problem: those who could work should be put in forced labor columns; women of childbearing age should be sterilized, so that with this generation the problem would be solved. In winter, however, there would not be enough food to feed all the Jews. "It should be seriously considered if the most humane solution would not be to kill those Jews not capable of work with some quick acting means. This would certainly be more pleasant than allowing them to starve to death," Höppner wrote. "The things sound in part fantastical," he added, "but in my view they are thoroughly practicable."[53]

On September 3, Höppner sent another memorandum, thirteen pages long, proposing that the organizations in the annexed territories that handled deportations to the *Generalgouvernement* be expanded into a body responsible for deportations from a much wider area—that is, the whole Reich. He understood that certain fundamental decisions had not yet been made. Nor did he know the intentions of top officials. He imagined nevertheless that the Soviet territory would provide adequate space. But the important thing, as he saw it, was to know the Jews' final fate, and here he asked a question: Was the goal to guarantee them permanently the promise of life or was it to exterminate them completely?[54]

This memorandum shows that there was still uncertainty but also that the unthinkable was now being thought, at least in the *Warthegau*. What is not clear is to what extent Höppner was picking up signals from on high. Whatever the case, Höppner was clearly responding to a growing sense in both the *Warthegau* (particularly with respect to Lodz) and the *Generalgouvernement* that in the absence of a program of immediate deportation the problems of food and epidemic raised by the Jewish population required drastic action.

In the late summer and early autumn two new factors influenced policy in the annexed territories and the *Generalgouvernement*. The first was Hitler's September decision to allow the deportation trains to run once more. Whatever Hitler's immediate intentions, the eastward deportation of German Jews created yet more pressures and challenges for the receiving territories. Until then, the lack of capacity (above all in the *Generalgouvernement*) had repeatedly stymied the deportation aspirations of Heydrich and Eichmann. Now, the deportations were not to be blocked, and the receiving authorities had to deal with the problem as best as they could. Despite fierce protest from the mayor of Lodz, from Commissar Wilhelm Kube in Minsk, and from authorities in Latvia and Lithuania, the deportation trains started rolling.

Construction of the Chelmno gas camp began within two weeks of Himmler's decision that the first deportations would be sent to Lodz, an already overcrowded ghetto. Looking back on events in a May 1942 letter to Himmler, Greiser indicated that the killing of a hundred thousand Polish Jews from the region was specifically authorized by Himmler, through Heydrich, as a quid pro quo for the willingness of the *Warthegau* authorities to receive deportees from Germany. While authorization for the killings came from the top, the initiative had come from the locality, and the goal was the solution of a regional "problem" rather than the implementation of a more comprehensive program.[55]

The second major development affected the *Generalgouvernement*, which unlike the annexed former Polish territory in the *Warthegau* was not directly affected by Hitler's deportation decision. Here, the biggest impact of the Soviet campaign was to disappoint earlier expectations of offloading the region's Jews. Over the course of 1941, the whole of the administration, from Hans Frank down, had been anticipating the Jews' rapid removal into the territory of the former Soviet Union. But in mid-October Frank learned that the slow progress of the war meant there was little prospect of such removals. The dragging Soviet campaign also had economic implications for his region. The failure to gain control of Soviet resources exacerbated the already severe food crisis in the *Generalgouvernement*—and on top of everything else there was a very poor harvest in 1941. Pressure grew for the removal of "useless mouths."[56] For Frank's staff the Jews represented a constant source of illegal activity. Not surprising given that the restrictions imposed on Polish Jews denied them any legal opportunity to earn enough even just to survive. A fatal two-pronged development ensued. The hardline radicals in Himmler's almost autonomous police empire in Poland undertook increasingly violent measures, while the civilian administration imposed exclusionary and persecutory measures on the Jewish population that made killing seem the only option.[57]

The Lublin district SS and police leader Odilo Globocnik had shown ruthless energy in developing murderous labor projects for Jews in the Bug region. In 1941 he unfolded far-reaching plans to Germanize Lublin, expelling all Poles and Jews from the area. On July 20, 1941, Himmler commissioned him to prepare the ground for German settlement of the Lublin district and then farther east. At the beginning of October, Globocnik urgently sought a meeting with Himmler to discuss proposals for clearing the Lublin area of its Jews. Globocnik's letter of October 1 suggests that up till then he had heard nothing of a comprehensive program of murder. His meeting with Himmler took place on October 13, the same day that Governor Frank discovered that no deportations were likely to take place in the near future. The outcome of Globocnik's consultation with Himmler was the decision to begin building an extermination camp at Belzec. At a meeting on October 17, Globocnik, Frank, and others agreed that the Lublin area should be cleared of Jews. Although they talked about "Jews being transferred across the Bug River," it is clear—since all participants knew by then that such deportations were impossible—that the "transfer" was a euphemism for murder.[58]

What remains in dispute is exactly what the camp's remit was. The rather limited initial scale of the construction may indicate that Belzec was more of an experiment than part of a comprehensive murder program. Belzec consisted of a few wooden buildings, staffed until the arrival of former euthanasia personnel in November by only three ss people. On the other hand, even camps that were quite small would prove capable of murdering extraordinarily large numbers of people, so the camp's size is not immediate proof of modest ambitions. At the very least, the murder of the hundreds of thousands of Lublin Jews was being contemplated. But there is some evidence that the authorities in the *Generalgouvernement* as a whole were now assuming that the Jewish population throughout that area would soon all be eliminated. In other words, even if the creation of the Belzec camp represents merely a response to Globocnik's initiative in Lublin, it seems possible that expectations within the wider *Generalgouvernement* were rapidly focusing on the murder of Polish Jews.[59]

The Crystallization of Genocide

The thrust of recent research, then, is to suggest that the transition from murderously neglectful and brutal occupation policies to genocidal measures occurred initially without a comprehensive set of commands from the top. The leadership, above all Himmler, was consulted in almost all the cases we have looked at. But neither Hitler nor Himmler provided a clear-cut plan or even a basic command for the lower echelons to carry out.

What precisely was the role of Hitler, Himmler, and Heydrich in these months? Without Hitler, none of the developments would have materialized. It was Hitler who foregrounded the agenda of antisemitism and, just as important, imposed the fundamental terms of warfare and occupation. The failure of humanitarian impulses to exercise any restraint on the regime's activity was due to him. Perhaps the last check fell when Hitler expressly overruled the army's humanitarian concerns in the Polish campaign.[60] Every action taken against Jews by lower-level officials was legitimated by their knowledge of Hitler's own radical antisemitic agenda. Hitler's public pronouncements against Jews were legion.[61] He repeatedly returned, for example, to his "prophecy."[62] Whatever Hitler's precise intentions, his rhetoric thus provided the justification for others' actions, assuring the perpetrators that murder was appropriate.

Moreover, though the evidence is less clear here, the regime was so focused on Hitler that it seems likely that any initiatives on the Jewish question had his imprimatur. When, for example, Wilhelm Koppe, a senior ss commander in the *Warthegau*, asked Himmler if thirty thousand Poles suffering from TB could be killed, he was told that the Führer's approval was required.[63] Even where Hitler concealed his involvement, therefore, we know that authority lay with him. As the Serbian case shows, however; there is some question as to what his subordinates believed was already covered by their existing remit and what required new authorization. Many historians assume that in October 1941 Hitler gave approval for the killings of *Warthegau* Jews at Chelmno and for the construction of Belzec. There is no evidence of Hitler's direct involvement, but the way the system functioned makes it highly probable.

In contrast to Hitler's ambiguous intention in authorizing resumption of deportations in September, Heydrich's approach to them bordered on the genocidal from the start. The preparations of the Security Police in Lodz suggest that Heydrich always assumed that a large percentage of the deportees would die though not necessarily that they would be shot outright. The Gestapo planned to divide the ghetto into two sections, one for working Jews and a much smaller one for the larger number of nonworking Jews. The clear implication was that the latter group would die of hunger and disease. In October, once it was plain that Lodz would receive only a small share of the envisaged deportees, Heydrich looked to the Baltic and Byelorussia as additional destinations. At a meeting on the tenth, Heydrich proposed a particularly radical approach to the deportation of Czech Jews.[64] Those to be deported to Riga, in the Baltic, and to Minsk, in Byelorussia, should be the most burdensome Jews (*lästigste Juden*), that is, the least capable of working. Some historians believe that he assumed these Jews would be shot by the *Einsatzgruppen*.[65] More recently, Christian Gerlach has raised the possibility that the preparations for an extermination camp at Mogilev, in Byelorussia, where gassing experiments had taken place in September, may have had some connection to these deportations.[66] Whatever he intended exactly, Heydrich seems to have been thinking of very low survival rates: for the Czech Jews not on the first deportation lists, Heydrich planned to create separate ghettos for those able to work and those dependent on assistance (*Versorgungslager*), so that the Jewish communities would be decimated before they were even shoved onto the trains.[67]

In other words, even though there was not yet a precise concept of killing the deportees by gas, the dividing line between the territorial solution and that of outright murder was becoming very thin indeed. On October 23, all Jewish emigration from the Reich was prohibited. On the twenty-fifth, Erhard Wetzel, the official in charge of race questions in Rosenberg's Ministry for the Occupied Eastern Territories, wrote to the Reich commissioner for the *Ostland* (the Baltic), Hinrich Lohse, recommending the deployment of the former euthanasia personnel to construct gas installations for eliminating deported Jews who were unfit to work.[68] The "territorial" policy of sending the Jews east was becoming more and more of a metaphor. Selection and attrition were becoming the central elements of the process rather than desirable by-products.

In mid-November, Himmler and Rosenberg had a lengthy meeting, after which Rosenberg provided a detailed press briefing. Here the distance between deportation and destruction had narrowed to nothing. Though the issue of killing Jews—as against allowing them to die—was not yet spelled out and Rosenberg still spoke of deportation, his reference to the "biological eradication of the entire Jewry of Europe" made absolutely explicit that the Reich's aim was the extinction, not just the removal, of the Jewish presence.[69] At almost exactly the same time, on November 16, in the journal *Das Reich*, Goebbels published a lead article that was excerpted in many of the German regional papers.[70] Entitled "The Jews Are Guilty," the piece provided one of the clearest communications to the German people that Jews were going to be exterminated. World Jewry, Goebbels wrote, was suffering a gradual process of annihilation. Jews were falling according to their own law—an eye for an eye, a tooth for a tooth. In December, Goebbels acknowledged in his diary that the deportation of Jews to the East was "in many cases synonymous with the death penalty."[71]

Although Hitler still occasionally spoke as though deportation to a reservation remained the policy, there are hints that he was now rejecting any kind of territorial solution. . . . Hitler's shift may have had something to do with his loss of interest in Jews as hostages, which, the historian Shlomo Aronson argues, occurred at around this time. Roosevelt's declaration on September 11 that the U.S. navy would shoot on sight Axis warships in waters essential for American defense was one turning point.[72] It is possible that Roosevelt's decision to extend Lend-Lease aid to Moscow on October 1 was the final straw.[73] In any case, on November 28, Hitler met with the Grand Mufti of Jerusalem. Hitler was seeking to court the Grand Mufti, who was no doubt aware that just a few years earlier the Nazis had been working together with Jewish agencies to "facilitate" Jewish emigration to Palestine. Some of what Hitler said will have been for effect. Still, Hitler's declaration, which he requested the Mufti to "lock deep into his heart," was striking.[74] To please the Grand Mufti, Hitler need only have specified that the Germans would deport the Jews to Siberia, much as he had told Croatian Marshal Slavko Kvaternik in the summer.[75] But he went much further. After a successful war, Hitler said, Germany would have only one remaining objective in the Middle East: the annihilation of the Jews living under British protection in Arab lands. Not even a shadow of a territorial solution remained.

Another index of the hardening of attitudes was the evolving treatment of the German Jewish deportees. Up to November 8, twenty thousand German, Austrian, and Czech Jews (and five thousand Gypsies) had been deported to Lodz. In response to the protests of the Lodz authorities, more than thirty thousand more were deported to Minsk, Kovno, and Riga in the course of the following three months. What happened to these Jews varied greatly. Those sent to Lodz were interned in the ghetto. Those dispatched to Minsk were similarly housed in ghettos—left empty by the murders of the previous inhabitants. Though living conditions were horrendous, indeed barely survivable, the deportees were not murdered. Train shortages meant that only seven of the eighteen Minsk transports planned for 1941 actually took place; the last left on November 19. The proposed camp in Riga was not yet ready, so in the following week, five transports were sent instead to Kovno, in Lithuania. All the occupants were murdered on arrival in the infamous Ninth Fort. The first deportees to Riga, arriving on November 30, were also massacred. Up to early December 1941, then, "only" six of the forty-one transports of Reich Jews had been murdered on arrival, and all the murders had taken place at the end of November.[76] . . .

There is considerable debate as to the reason for these murders, particularly the killing of Berlin Jews in Riga. On November 29–30, just before the deportees' arrival, four thousand Latvian Jews in the Riga ghettos had been murdered on the order of the HSSPF in the Baltic, Friedrich Jeckeln, and the local head of the Security Police, Rudolf Lange. On November 30, Himmler telephoned Heydrich from the Führer's headquarters with the message "Jewish transports from Berlin. No liquidation."[77] The message was duly sent on to Riga—but too late: the Berlin deportees had been included in the shooting.

What began as a Soviet experiment was thus disseminated and modified piecemeal, by improvisation and example, over the period from September to November 1941. Himmler and Heydrich were closely involved; Hitler's involvement is less well documented, though he would at the very least have known what was happening, and at the very least have decided not to prevent it. Himmler could not have stayed his course without Hitler's approving nod, though how emphatic that was we do not know. Statements made by Hitler, Himmler, and those around them in October and November show how rapidly the idea of a territorial solution was dissolving into metaphor. The territories were becoming holding bays for those condemned to death.

NOTES

1. Quoted in Jeremy Noakes and Geoffrey Pridham, eds., *Nazism, 1919–1945*, vol. 3 (Exeter: University of Exeter Press, 1995), 1094.

2. Burrin, *Hitler and the Jews*, 95.

3. At various times, Generals Manstein, Guderian, Hoth, Küchler, and Reichenau all endorsed the struggle against the Jewish subhumans. See Wilhelm, *Einsatzgruppe A*, 15–16, n. 9.

4. Reprinted in Yitzhak Arad, Yisrael Gutman, and Abraham Margaliot, eds., *Documents on the Holocaust* (Lincoln: University of Nebraska Press, 1999), 376. See also Krausnick and Wilhelm, *Truppe*, 136.

5. Walter Manoschek, *"Serbien ist judenfrei": Militärische Besatzungspolitik und Judenvernichtung in Serbien, 1941/42* (Munich: R. Oldenbourg Verlag, 1993), 191.

6. Arad, Gutman, and Margaliot, *Documents on the Holocaust*, 378.

7. Echoing the work of Alfred Streim, Ralf Ogorreck believes that the stress on cooperating with the military meant there would not have been secret instructions in the early weeks (*Einsatzgruppen*, 95–109). Helmut Krausnick believes that the actions that followed showed that the verbal orders must have exceeded written instructions (Krausnick and Wilhelm, *Truppe*, 161). Christian Gerlach, too, believes that some kind of exterminatory intention must have been voiced in premeetings at Pretzsch or in Berlin (*Kalkulierte Morde*, 629–30). In similar vein, see Breitman, *Architect*, 164. We know, for example,

that Heydrich distinguished between short-term and final goals, but it is not clear whether the final goal was to deport the purged remainder farther east—this would fit in with the European deportation plans he had been making since the spring—or to kill the remainder. See the Introduction in Peter Witte et al., eds., *Der Dienstkalender Heinrich Himmlers 1941/1942* (Hamburg: Christians Verlag, 1999), 70.

8. Longerich, *Politik der Vernichtung*, 321–52.

9. Christian Gerlach, "Die Einsatzgruppe B 1941/2," *Die Einsatzgruppen in der besetzten Sowjetunion 1941/2*, ed. Peter Klein, (Berlin: Edition Hentrich, 1997), 57–58.

10. Ogorreck, *Einsatzgruppen*, 95–109.

11. The October 1941 report from *Einsatzgruppe* A suggests that from the start "the goal of the cleansing operation of the Security Police, in accordance with the fundamental orders, was the most comprehensive elimination of the Jews possible" (Breitman, *Architect*, 169). See also the discussion of the response of Franz Stahlecker, head of *Einsatzgruppe* A, to *Reichkommisar* Hinrich Lohse's new directives in Browning, *Path to Genocide*, 109–10. Browning's interpretation, that Stahlecker's proposals to create single-sex ghettos were a cover for murder, seems to me more plausible than Longerich's more literal interpretation (see Longerich, *Politik der Vernichtung*, 394–95).

12. Christian Streit, "Wehrmacht, Einsatzgruppen, Soviet POWs, and Anti-Bolshevism in the Emergence of the Final Solution," Cesarani, *Final Solution*, 106.

13. Gerlach, *Kalkulierte Morde*, 573.

14. Kershaw, *Hitler, 1936–1945*, 469.

15. Browning, *Path to Genocide*, 105–6; Kershaw, *Hitler, 1936–1945*, 469; Witte et al., *Dienstkalender*, 185, n. 15.

16. Longerich, *Politik der Vernichtung*, 362–69; Ogorreck, *Einsatzgruppen*, 179–81; Gerlach, *Kalkulierte Morde*, 566ff., 648; Gerlach, "Einsatzgruppe B," 57–58.

17. Witte et al., *Dienstkalender*, 71.

18. Czeslaw Madajczyk, "Hitler's Direct Influence on Decisions Affecting Jews during World War II," *Yad Vashem Studies* 20 (1990): 53–68.

19. Cited in Evans, *Lying about Hitler*, 78.

20. Breitman, *Architect*, 159ff.; Gerlach, *Kalkulierte Morde*, 648–49.

21. Quoted in translation in Arad, Gutman, and Margaliot, *Documents on the Holocaust*, 233.

22. Aly, "'Judenumsiedlung,'" 91; Aly, "*Final Solution*," 171–72.

23. Longerich, *Politik der Vernichtung*, 288.

24. Ibid., 422.

25. Safrian, *Eichmann-Männer*, 108ff.

26. Karin Orth, "Rudolf Höss und die 'Endlösung der Judenfrage': Drei Argumente gegen die Datierung auf den Sommer 1941," *Werkstatt Geschichte* 18 (1997): 45–58.

27. Orth, "Rudolf Höss," 52.

28. Longerich, *Politik der Vernichtung*, 424.

29. Kershaw, *Hitler, 1936–1945*, 462.

30. Longerich, *Politik der Vernichtung*, 427

31. Burrin, *Hitler and the Jews*, 101; Pohl, "*Judenpolitik*," 87.

32. Kershaw, *Hitler, 1936–1945*, 476.

33. Pohl, *Von der Judenpolitik*, 91–92.

34. Peter Witte, "Two Decisions concerning the 'Final Solution to the Jewish Question': Deportations to Lodz and Mass Murder in Chelmno," *Holocaust and Genocide Studies* 9 (1995): 319, 323–34; Kershaw, *Hitler, 1936–1945*, 472–75.

35. Longerich, *Politik der Vernichtung*, 438; Witte, "Two Decisions," 321–25; Kershaw, *Hitler, 1936–1945*, 479.

36. Christian Gerlach, "The Wannsee Conference, the Fate of German Jews, and Hitler's Decision in Principle to Exterminate all European Jews," *The Holocaust: Origins, Implementation, Aftermath*, ed. Omer Bartov (London: Routledge, 2000), 110.

37. Christian Gerlach, "Die Ausweitung der deutschen Massenmorde in den besetzten sowjetischen Gebieten im Herbst 1941: Überlegungen zur Vernichtungspolitik gegen Juden und sowjetische Kriegsgefangene," *Krieg, Ernährung, Völkermord: Deutsche Vernichtungspolitik im Zweiten Weltkrieg* (Zurich: Pendo Verlag, 2001), 72.

38. Stalin had announced the decisions at the end of August. See Longerich, *Politik der Vernichtung*, 429–30.

39. See Witte, "Two Decisions," 321–26; Steur, *Theodor Dannecker*, 63–65; Longerich, *Politik der Vernichtung*, 430; Kershaw, *Hitler, 1936–1945*, 478.

40. See esp. Burrin, *Hitler and the Jews*.

41. Manoschek, "*Serbien ist Judenfrei*," 185–87; Pohl, "*Judenpolitik*," 94; Gerlach, *Kalkulierte Morde*, 646–51; Longerich, *Politik der Vernichtung*, 443; Witte, "Two Decisions," 322. Thomas Sandkuhler, "*Endlösung*" in Galizien: Der Judenmord in Ostpolen und die Rettungsinitiativen von Bertold Beitz, 1941–1944 (Bonn: J. H. W. Dietz Nachfolger, 1996). There is some dispute about the Auschwitz date. See Karin Orth, *Das System der nationalsozialistischen Konzentrationslager: Eine politische Organisationsgeschichte* (Hamburg: Hamburger Edition, 1999), 139.

42. Wolfgang Scheffler, "Chelmno, Sobibor, Belzec und Majdanek," Jäckel and Rohwer, *Der Mord*, 148.

43. Koeppen's information was indirect, and it is very possible that it dated back to before the deportation decision and that the deportation itself was the "reprisal." It is possible, too, that Hitler still held back with an eye to Roosevelt, even though he was losing faith in the chances of averting America's entry into the war (Lukacs, *Hitler of History*, 192; Longerich, *Politik der Vernichtung*, 431).

44. Kershaw, *Hitler, 1936–1945*, 479.

45. On Hitler's perception of the military situation, see Browning, *Path to Genocide*, 112–17.

46. Aly, "*Final Solution*," 231.

47. Gerlach, *Kalkulierte Morde*, 618–19.

48. Manoschek, "*Serbien ist Judenfrei*," 185–90.

49. Manoschek, "*Serbien ist Judenfrei*," 188.

50. Witte et al., *Dienstkalender*, 66; Gerlach, *Kalkulierte Morde*, 186; Dieter Pohl, *Nationalsozialistische Judenverfolgung in Ostgalizien, 1941–1944: Organ-*

*isation und Durchführung eines staatlichen Massen-
verbrechens* (Munich: Oldenbourg, 1996), 140ff.;
Sandkühler, *"Endlösung" in Galizien*, 138–40;
Longerich, *Politik der Vernichtung*, 455.

51. Witte et al., *Dienstkalender*, 201–2; Pohl, *Nationalsozialistische Judenverfolgung*, 140–43; Sandkühler,
"Endlosung" in Galizien, 151–52, 407.

52. On Himmler and gas, see Breitman, *Architect*,
160ff. On July 16, 1941, the police authorities
in the *Warthegau* requested the extermination of Jews unable to work (Madajczyk, "Hitler's Direct Influence," 56, n. 12). In Latvia there
were rumors in early August that the Germans
intended to gas Jewish women there. See Gerlach, *Kalkulierte Morde*, 648–49.

53. Raul Hilberg, *Documents of Destruction: Germany and Jewry, 1933-1945* (London: W. H. Allen,
1972), 87.

54. Cited in Burrin, *Hitler and the Jews*, 119.

55. Ian Kershaw, "Improvised Genocide? The Emergence of the 'Final Solution' in the Warthegau,"
Transactions of the Royal Historical Society, 6th
series (1992): 51–78; Deborah Dwork and Robert Jan van Pelt, *Auschwitz: 1270 to the Present*
(New York: Norton, 1996), 294.

56. Bogdan Musial, *Deutsche Zivilverwaltung und
Judenverfolgung im Generalgouvernement* (Wiesbaden: Harrassowitz, 1999), 195.

57. Sandkühler, *"Endlösung" in Galizien*, 138–40.

58. Pohl, *"Judenpolitik,"* 99–100; Witte et al., *Dienstkalender*, 233 and n. 35; Sandkühler, *"Endlösung"
in Galizien*, 136; Bogdan Musial, "The Origins
of 'Operation Reinhard': The Decision-Making
Process for the Mass Murder of the Jews in the
Generalgouvernement," *Yad Vashem Studies* 28
(2000): 116–18.

59. Pohl, *"Judenpolitik,"* 105–6; Aly, *"Final Solution,"*
232; Musial, "Origins," 145.

60. See Hitler's comments conveyed by Martin Bormann to Heinrich Lammers, head of the Reich
Chancellery, in Krausnick and Wilhelm, *Truppe*,
627.

61. See Evans, *Lying about Hitler*, 88.

62. Adler, *Verwaltete Mensch*, 62.

63. Kershaw, *Hitler, 1936–1945*, 484.

64. See Heydrich's statement in Hans-Günther
Adler, *Theresienstadt 1941–1945. Das Antlitz einer
Zwangsgemeinschaft: Geschichte, Soziologie, Psy-
chologie* (Tubingen: J. C. B. Mohr/Paul Siebeck,
1955). 720–22.

65. Heydrich said that Arthur Nebe and Emil Otto
Rasch (the commanders of *Einsatzgruppen* B and
C, respectively) could take Jews into the "camps
for communist prisoners in the operation area"
(Burrin, *Hitler and the Jews*, 128).

66. Gerlach, *Kalkulierte Morde*, 650.

67. Adler, *Theresienstadt*, 720–22; see also Sandkühler,
"Endlösung" in Galizien, 135.

68. The document is cited in Gerald Fleming, *Hitler
and the Final Solution* (Oxford: Oxford University Press, 1986), 70–71.

69. See Adam, *Judenpolitik*, 309, citing Serge Lang
and Ernst von Schenck, *Portrait eines Mensch-
heitsverbrechers: Nach den hinterlassenen Memoi-
ren des ehemaligen Reichsministers Alfred Rosenberg*
(St. Gallen: Zollikofer, 1947), 129, and the discussions in Christopher Browning, *Nazi Policy,
Jewish Workers, German Killers* (Cambridge:
Cambridge University Press, 2000), 48–49, and
Witte *et al., Dienstkalender*, 262, n. 46.

70. Cited in Adler, *Verwaltete Mensch*, 63.

71. Kershaw, *Hitler, 1936–1945*, 485, citing Goebbels's
diary.

72. Werner Jochmann, ed., *Adolf Hitler: Monologe
im Führer-Hauptquartier, 1941–1944* (Hamburg:
Albrecht Kanus Verlag, 1980), 30–31; see also the
discussion in Evans, *Lying about Hitler*, 72.

73. Kershaw, *Hitler, 1936–1945*, 478.

74. Shlomo Aronson, "Hitlers Judenpolitik, die Alliierten und die Juden," *Vierteljahreshefte für Zeitgeschichte* 32 (1984): 51–52.

75. Fleming, *Hitler and the Final Solution*, 104.

76. This point seems to me the weakness of Christian
Gerlach's otherwise pertinent questions about
Hitler's statement to the Grand Mufti. See Ger-
lach's *Krieg, Ernährung, Völkermord*, 147, n. 240.

77. Longerich, *Politik der Vemichtung*, 434, 449; Gerlach, *Kalkulierte Morde*, 751.

Bringing Death to Jews

RICHARD RHODES

From *Masters of Death*

In the spring of 1941 a police academy in Pretzsch, a town on the Elbe River about fifty miles southwest of Berlin, became the site of a sinister assembly. Several thousand men from the ranks of the ss—the Nazi Party's *Schutzstaffel*, or defense echelon, a police and security service that answered directly to Adolf Hitler and operated outside the constraints of German law—were ordered to report to Pretzsch for training and assignment. They were not told what their assignment would be, but their commonalities offered a clue: many of them had served in ss detachments in Poland, which Germany had invaded and occupied in 1939, and preference was given to men who spoke Russian.[1]

Assignment to Pretzsch emptied the ss leadership school in Berlin-Charlottenburg and depleted the professional examination course of an ss criminal division. It drew in lower- and middle-ranking officers of the Security Police (the Gestapo and the criminal police), some of them passed on gratefully by their home regiments because they were considered too wild. The *Waffen-ss*, the small but growing ss army, contributed enlisted men. High-ranking bureaucrats within the shadowy Reich Security Main Office, an internal ss security agency, were posted to Pretzsch as well. They had been handpicked for leadership positions by *Obergruppenführer* [Lieutenant General] Reinhard Heydrich, the head of the RSHA and the second most powerful man in the ss, and his

superior Heinrich Himmler, the *Reichsführer-ss*. Most of these handpicked leaders were lawyers, and a few were physicians or educators; most had earned doctoral degrees.[2] Among the more exotic specimens were Otto Ohlendorf, a handsome but argumentative young economist who had fallen into disfavor with Himmler; Paul Blobel, a raw-boned, high strung, frequently drunken architect; Arthur Nebe, a former vice squad detective and Gestapo head who had enthusiastically volunteered; and Karl Jäger, a brutal fifty-three-year-old secret police commander. A reserve battalion of the regular German Order Police (uniformed urban, rural and municipal police) completed the Pretzsch roster.[3]

Soon the men learned that they would be assigned to an *Einsatzgruppe*—a task force. *Einsatz* units—groups and commandos—had followed the German army into Austria, Czechoslovakia and Poland when Germany had invaded those countries successively in 1938 and 1939. *Einsatzgruppen* secured occupied territories in advance of civilian administrators. They confiscated weapons and gathered incriminating documents, tracked down and arrested people the ss considered politically unreliable, and systematically murdered the occupied country's political, educational, religious and intellectual leadership. Since Germany had concluded a nonaggression pact with the Soviet Union in August 1939, many of the candidates at Pretzsch assumed they would be assigned to follow the *Wehrmacht* into England.[4] Some of them had previously trained to just that end.

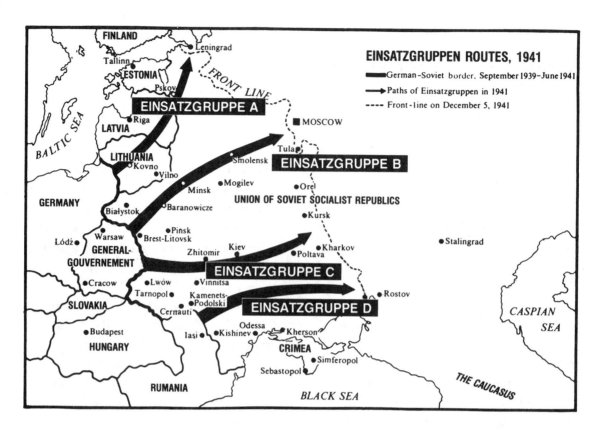

EINSATZGRUPPEN ROUTES, 1941

▬▬ German-Soviet border, September 1939–June 1941
➤ Paths of Einsatzgruppen in 1941
----- Front-line on December 5, 1941

FINLAND
Leningrad
Tallinn
ESTONIA
Pskov
FRONT LINE
EINSATZGRUPPE A
Riga
LATVIA
BALTIC SEA
LITHUANIA
Kovno
Vilno
■ MOSCOW
Tula
Smolensk
EINSATZGRUPPE B
GERMANY
Minsk
Mogilev
Orel
Białystok
Baranowicze
UNION OF SOVIET SOCIALIST REPUBLICS
Warsaw
Pinsk
Kursk
Łódź
Brest-Litovsk
Stalingrad
GENERAL-
GOUVERNEMENT
Zhitomir
Kiev
Kharkov
Poltava
EINSATZGRUPPE C
Cracow
Lwów
Vinnitsa
Rostov
Tarnopol
Kamenets-
Podolski
EINSATZGRUPPE D
CASPIAN
SEA
SLOVAKIA
Cernauti
Odessa
Budapest
Iasi
Kishinev
Kherson
HUNGARY
CRIMEA
Simferopol
Sebastopol
THE CAUCASUS
RUMANIA
BLACK SEA

Map 3. Einsatzgruppen routes, ca. 1940. Source: The Einsatzgruppen Reports, edited by Yitzak Arad et al., originally published by the Holocaust Library in 1989. Used with the permission from the U.S. Holocaust Memorial Museum.

The three-week course at Pretzsch in June 1941 involved only minimal training. Bruno Streckenbach, one man remembered, told the new *Einsatzgruppen* "that this was a war assignment which would be concluded by December at the latest."[5] Another recalled hearing from Stahlecker, the newly appointed chief of *Einsatzgruppe* A, that "we would be putting down resistance behind the troop lines, protecting and pacifying the rear army area (the word 'pacify' was used very frequently) and hence keeping the area behind the front clear. . . . Stahlecker also told us we would have to conquer our weaker selves and that what was needed were tough men who understood how to carry out orders. He also said to us that anyone who thought that he would not be able to withstand the stresses and psychological strains that lay ahead could report to him immediately afterwards."[6] The men sat through familiar lectures on honor and duty and the subhuman nature of the people they would be asked to corral. They conducted "terrain exercises," which one of them dismissed as "games of hide and seek."[7] The military training, another remembered, "was very brief. It was limited to firing of weapons. The men and the NCOs had the opportunity to go on a range and fire their weapons. At that time no intensive military training was possible, because the physical condition of the men didn't permit this in most cases; . . . all the men intended to be sent to an *Einsatz* were inoculated, and . . . this inoculation brought fever and weakness in its wake, so that military training was not possible."[8] Nor, evidently, was it necessary for accomplishing the work the *Einsatzgruppen* would do.

Only near the end of their time in Pretzsch, a few days before they would march, did the men learn where they were going: Russia.[9] The Third Reich was preparing a surprise attack against the Soviet Union, Operation Barbarossa, scheduled to begin on June 22, 1941. Behind the *Wehrmacht* as it invaded the USSR from the west would follow four *Einsatzgruppen*. *Einsatzgruppe* A, under forty-year-old SS-*Brigadeführer* [Brigadier General] Stahlecker, attached to Army Group North, would operate in the former Baltic states of Estonia, Latvia and Lithuania. *Einsatzgruppe* B, under forty-six-year-old SS-*Brigadeführer* Arthur Nebe, attached to Army Group Center, would "pacify" Byelorussia. *Einsatzgruppe* C, under forty-nine-year-old SS-*Brigadeführer* Dr. Otto Rasch, attached to Army Group South, would sweep northern and central Ukraine. *Einsatzgruppe* D, under thirty-four-year-old SS-*Standartenführer* [Colonel] Otto Ohlendorf, attached to Eleventh Army, would operate in southwestern Ukraine (Bessarabia), southern Ukraine, the Crimea, and the Caucasus.

The four task forces were further subdivided into a total of sixteen *Sonderkommandos* and *Ein-satzkommandos*, the real operational units of the formations, answerable to the task force leaders but functionally independent. Blobel, for example, led *Sonderkommando* 4a of Rasch's *Einsatzgruppe* C, operating through the Ukraine to Kiev and beyond; Jäger, the brutal, walrus-mustached secret policeman, led *Einsatzkommando* 3 of Stahlecker's *Einsatzgruppe* A, operating throughout Lithuania.

Einsatzgruppe A, the largest of the four task forces, counted 990 personnel (divided into two *Sonderkommandos* and two *Einsatzkommandos*), including 340 *Waffen-SS*, 172 motorcycle riders, 18 administrators, 35 Security Service (SD) personnel, 41 Criminal Police, 89 State Police, 87 Auxiliary Police, 133 Order Police, 13 female secretaries and clerks, 51 interpreters, 3 teletype operators and 8 radio operators.[10] Ohlendorf, whose *Einsatzgruppe* D, with a roll call of about 500, was the smallest of the four (but was subdivided into four *Sonderkommandos* and one *Einsatzkommando*), would testify that his task force "had 180 vehicles. . . . This large number of [trucks] shows that the *Einsatzgruppe* was fully motorized. The *Waffen-SS* . . . were equipped with automatic rifles. The others either had rifles or automatic rifles. I believe that is about the total equipment."[11] The fact that the *Einsatzgruppen* were fully motorized is significant: the *Wehrmacht* itself was only partly motorized in June 1941, with much of its artillery still horse-drawn. Himmler intended his *Einsatzgruppen* to succeed and made sure the units were properly outfitted. . . .

On June 17, 1941, a day or two after Streckenbach told the men in Pretzsch about Barbarossa, Heydrich ordered the chiefs of the *Einsatzgruppen* and their commandos to Berlin, to RSHA headquarters at No. 8 Prinz Albrechtstrasse, where he briefed them further on their impending mission. Erwin Schulz, who had led an *Einsatzkommando* in Czechoslovakia in 1938 and who had just been appointed to lead *Einsatzkommando* 5 (EG C), remembered Heydrich using many of the same arguments Hitler had used with the *Wehrmacht* leadership. "The fight which would soon take place would be the hardest and most bitter the German people have ever gone through," Schulz testified Heydrich told them. "In the fight to come not only were people fighting against other people, but for the first time ideology was fighting against another ideology. . . . He explained that Bolshevism would not stop from using every means of fighting, as Lenin had already written, emphasizing in particular the part the partisans were to play, which Lenin and others had written about, and this could not be misunderstood. [He said] that everyone should be sure to understand that in this fight Jews would definitely take their part, and that in this fight everything was at stake, and the side which gave in would be . . . overcome. For that reason all measures had to be taken against the Jews in particular. The experience in Poland had shown this."[12]

Schulz emphasized in this postwar testimony, however, that neither in Berlin nor in Pretzsch had Heydrich and Streckenbach mentioned . . . the extermination of the Jews.[13] At the outset of Barbarossa, at least, the work of the new *Einsatzgruppen* would be similar to the work of the *Einsatzgruppen* in Austria, Czechoslovakia and Poland—brutal enough work at that. Heydrich ordered four categories of enemies executed: "[1] All officials of the Comintern [the international organization of the Communist Party] (most of these will certainly be career politicians); [2] officials of senior and middle rank and 'extremists' in the [Communist] Party, the Central Committee, and the provincial and district committees; [3] the people's commissars; [4] Jews in the service of the party or the government; [as well as] other extremist elements (saboteurs,

propagandists, snipers, assassins, agitators, etc.)."[14] Heydrich also told the *Einsatzgruppen* leaders to secretly encourage and not to interfere with "any purges that may be initiated by anti-Communist or anti-Jewish elements in the newly occupied territories." Which meant that Jews who were not "in the service of the party or the government" were targeted from the outset; if the SS was not yet prepared to be seen murdering large numbers of Jews without at least minimal "political" justification, it was charged with the responsibility of organizing others to do so.[15] ("The aim of *Einsatzkommando* 2 from the beginning," commando leader Rudolf Lange would report from Latvia in January 1942, "was a radical solution of the Jewish problem through the execution of all Jews.")[16] . . . .

Barbarossa

When forward units of the German Army occupied Kaunas in central Lithuania on June 23, 1941, a small advance detachment of *Einsatzgruppe* A entered the city with them and set to work immediately organizing "spontaneous" attacks against Jews.[17] The town of stone buildings and chinked-log wooden houses at the junction of the Neris and Nemunas Rivers counted 35,000 Jews among its population of 120,000 people. Also known as Kovno, Kaunas had served as the Lithuanian capital under Soviet domination, and the occupying forces found four large groups of armed Lithuanian nationalists competing to help them harry the retreating Soviet garrison.[18]

Within a day or two of the occupation, several enlisted men in a bakers' company of the *Wehrmacht* Sixteenth Army encountered what was probably the first pogrom in Kaunas when they joined "a crowd of people gathered in a square somewhere in the center of the town."[19]

"We were quartered in an old Russian barracks," a sergeant recalled, "and immediately started to make bread for the troops. I think it must have been one day after we had arrived in Kovno that I was informed by a driver in my unit that Jews were being beaten to death in a nearby square. Upon hearing this I went to the said square [with] other members of our unit." On the cobbled square, lined with houses and opening onto a park, the sergeant "saw civilians, some in shirtsleeves . . . beating other civilians to death with iron bars." He heard someone say that "these were Jews who had swindled the Lithuanians before the Germans had arrived." The bystanders were mostly German soldiers. The sergeant questioned those nearest him, who told him that "the victims were being beaten to satisfy a personal desire for vengeance." His account continues:

> When I reached the square there were about fifteen to twenty bodies lying there. These were then cleared away by the Lithuanians and the pools of blood were washed away with water from a hose. . . . I saw the Lithuanians take hold of the bodies by their hands and legs and drag them away. Afterwards another group of offenders was herded and pushed onto the square and without further ado simply beaten to death by the civilians armed with iron bars. I watched as a group of offenders were beaten to death and then had to look away because I could not watch any longer. These actions seemed extremely cruel and brutal. . . . The Lithuanian civilians could be heard shouting out their approval and goading the men on.

A bakers' company grenadier remembered asking a medical-corps sergeant beside him "why these people were being beaten to death in such a cruel manner." The sergeant told him that they "were all Jews who had been apprehended by Lithuanians in the city and had been brought to this square. The killings were carried out by recently released Lithuanian convicts." The ss had released violent criminals from prison, that is, and put them to work, murdering Jewish victims to make the "pogrom" look spontaneous. The corporal counted five men wielding crowbars and "about fifteen dead or seriously injured people" collapsed on the cobblestones. Another enlisted man noticed that there were men guarding the square "wearing armbands and [carrying] carbines," and the grenadier identified them as "some members of the Lithuanian 'Freikorps'"—that is, irregulars. The irregulars were feeding victims to the killers, moving in and out of the square "with more Jews who were likewise beaten to death by the convicts." In the ten minutes the grenadier could bear to watch he "witnessed the beating to death of some ten to fifteen Jews." All the victims were men.

A similar scene confronted a colonel who was adjutant to the staff of Army Group North on his arrival in Kaunas on the morning of June 27, 1941. He passed a filling station surrounded by a dense crowd and noticed women in the crowd who had "lifted up their children or stood them on chairs or boxes so that they could see better." He thought he must be witnessing "a victory celebration or some type of sporting event because of the cheering, clapping and laughter that kept breaking out." But when he asked what was happening, he was told that "the 'Death-dealer of Kovno' was at work and that this was where collaborators and traitors were finally meted out their rightful punishment!" He moved closer and witnessed "probably the most frightful event that I had seen during the course of two world wars":

> On the concrete forecourt of the petrol station a blond man of medium height, aged about twenty-five, stood leaning on a wooden club, resting. The club was as thick as his arm and

came up to his chest: At his feet lay about fifteen to twenty dead or dying people. Water flowed continuously from a hose washing blood away into the drainage gully. Just a few steps behind this man some twenty men, guarded by armed civilians, stood waiting for their cruel execution in silent submission. In response to a cursory wave the next man stepped forward silently and was then beaten to death with the wooden club in the most bestial manner, each blow accompanied by enthusiastic shouts from the audience.[20]

A military photographer who photographed the scene (and who identified the murder weapon as an iron crowbar) nearly had his camera confiscated by a hovering ss officer, indicating just how "spontaneous" these early public massacres were. Bystanders he questioned claimed that the death-dealer's parents "had been taken from their beds two days earlier and immediately shot"—presumably by departing NKVD—"because they were suspected of being nationalists, and this was the young man's revenge." "The death-dealer," the photographer adds, "within three-quarters of an hour . . . had beaten to death the entire group of forty-five to fifty people in this way," after which "the young man put the crowbar to one side, fetched an accordion and went and stood on the mountain of corpses and played the Lithuanian national anthem."[21]

There were other murderers busy at the garage at other times that day. A Gentile Lithuanian, Julius Vainilavicius, described the scene:

I was returning home after angling. Going past the garage I saw some civilians working there. The Germans were treating them roughly. The Jews were removing [horse] dung with naked hands and putting it into a heap. Yielding to curiosity, I walked into the schoolyard and over

the fence kept on watching them. The work being finished, the people were ordered to wash themselves. . . . Here a great massacre began. The Germans and ten to fifteen Lithuanians, who happened to be in the garage at this time, swooped down on the Jews, belaboring them with rifle butts, spades, sticks and crowbars. About fifty people were wounded. They lay on the ground, groaning and crying. Then the water hose was brought and cold water turned onto them. Those who regained consciousness were beaten to death on the spot. After all the Jews were killed, a truck with a group of Jews [i.e., prisoners] came into the yard. They loaded the corpses onto the lorry and drove away. A few minutes later the Germans dispersed the onlookers.[22]

Between these public spectacles, the ss advance detachment organized the Lithuanian irregulars. *Einsatzgruppe* A leader Stahlecker explained in a follow-up report that "it was not easy at first to set any large-scale anti-Jewish pogrom in motion [in Kaunas]."[23] But the ss found early collaborators in Algirdas Klimaitis, a Lithuanian journalist who led one of the four groups of local irregulars, and a physician, Dr. Zigonys. Under Klimaitis's command, *Einsatzgruppe* A organized six hundred of the most reliable irregulars into an auxiliary police force; under Zigonys's command, another two hundred. On the night of June 25, 1941, the auxiliaries bombed or set fire to several Kaunas synagogues and burned down sixty houses in the Jewish quarter. That same night they began rounding up Jews, plundering their houses and murdering them—1,500 victims on the night of June 25; on succeeding nights another 2,300.[24] The *Wehrmacht* colonel reports seeing "long columns consisting of some forty to fifty men, women and children, who had been driven out of their homes . . . herded through the streets by armed civilians. . . . I was told that these people were being taken to the city prison. I assume, however, that the route they were taking led directly to their place of execution."[25]

"During the last three days," *Einsatzkommando* 1b reported to Berlin on June 30, 1941, "Lithuanian partisan groups have already killed several thousand Jews."[26]

The Lithuanian auxiliaries justified their arrests and executions by claiming that Jews had been shooting from their windows at the German troops. A Jewish eyewitness, William Mishell, a draftsman in an engineering office, dismisses the accusation as "utterly ridiculous: first of all, the Jews never had arms in Lithuania; and secondly, no German soldiers were present where most of the Jews were being arrested, beaten up and manhandled. Saturday [June 28, 1941], the Jewish Sabbath, only made the partisans' zeal higher. Groups of Jews were made to dance in front of jeering crowds and then were beaten in full view of the population, including Germans, but nobody intervened."[27]

From the prison, the victims were marched to a secure facility where their systematic murder could be concealed. Kaunas was ringed with massive forts built by the Czar on the hills above the city prior to World War I and subsequently converted to warehouses or jails. Mishell describes these numbered forts as having "heavy masonry walls . . . topped with barbed wire and observation towers."[28] Bunkered underground barracks and protective earthen berms made the interior compound of a fort "an artificial valley." Into one such valley of death, the Seventh Fort, located in the northeastern suburbs, the auxiliaries drove the crowds of Jewish civilians they had arrested, separating the men from the women and children. "Under heavy blows with the butts of the rifles,

we [men] were chased down the slopes into the large hole," a survivor of these early atrocities told Mishell soon after he escaped:

The entire area was full of humanity. The women and small children, we found out, were locked up in the underground barracks. Here we were now kept for days without even a piece of bread or a drink of water. On top of the slopes were hundreds of Lithuanian partisans with machine guns. Escape was totally impossible. We received strict orders to sit on the ground and not to talk. When somebody moved or was caught talking, the partisans would open automatic fire into the crowd. Not everyone was lucky enough to be killed outright. . . . Many of the wounded were twisting in agony and asking the bandits to kill them, but the bastards would laugh and say, "You were told to keep quiet," but would not shoot, and instead let them die in pain.[29]

There was an artesian well within the Seventh Fort compound, the survivor told Mishell, but they were forbidden to drink from it; people who approached it were shot. Finally, desperate after several days without water, "a group got up and tried to attack the guards. But without guns, weakened by hunger and thirst, they were no match and were mercilessly gunned down by the bandits." The guards gave the survivors some water and bread then, to prevent further mass revolts. After several more days, the stench of the corpses forced the guards to organize a Jewish burial team; when the dead had been removed and buried behind the artesian well, the guards shot the gravediggers.

Later that week, on July 4, 1941, the women and children were led out from the barracks and out of the fort. "They looked terrible," the survivor remembered: "bloody, torn clothes, pale, shaky, barely walking." As soon as the high iron gates closed behind the women and children, "without any warning the guards suddenly opened a murderous fire into the valley [where the men were confined] completely at random, just blanketing the area with bullets, covering the site with dead and injured." Abruptly the shooting stopped. A party of high-ranking Lithuanian army officers had arrived. Their representatives ordered Jewish men who had served in the Lithuanian army to assemble at the gate. The veterans, Mishell's informant among them, were taken to the Kaunas central prison to have their army records checked and to be set free. On July 6, 1941, the men left behind at the Seventh Fort, including Mishell's father, were murdered. About fifteen hundred people died at the Seventh Fort during the first week of July 1941.[30]

What became of the women and children? The survivor's wife described their ordeal at the fort:

> The women were immediately taken to the underground barracks, where we all lay down on the bare concrete, one on top of the other. For several days we had no food and no water. They would not even let us out. The children were crying and sobbing and were asking their mothers why they were not taking them back home. The weaker women fainted from the thirst and the horrible air. But the nights were even worse than the days. Partisans with flashlights would come in and rob the women of their jewelry. Then others would come and beat up the women because they had nothing to give them any more. A favorite sort of entertainment was to order the women to take off their clothes and dance. When they got sufficiently excited they picked up the more beautiful ones and took them out by force and raped them.[31]

Some of the women the guards raped they then murdered. But the ss was not yet ready to risk the mass killing of women and children. For the time being, dependents who survived their ordeal at the fort were released and returned to Kaunas.

"It was thought a good idea," Stahlecker wrote, summarizing these early Kaunas pogroms a few months later, "for the security police [that is, the ss] not to be seen to be involved, at least not immediately, in these unusually tough measures, which were also bound to attract attention in German circles. The impression had to be created that the local population itself had taken the first steps of its own accord as a natural reaction to decades of oppression by the Jews and the more recent terror exerted by the Communists."[32] Stahlecker's explanation parrots Heydrich's instructions to the *Einsatzgruppen* commanders before they departed Pretzsch, repeated on June 29, 1941, in a telegram:

> The attempts at self-cleansing on the part of anti-Communist or antisemitic elements in the areas to be occupied are not to be hindered. On the contrary, they are to be encouraged, but without leaving traces, so that these local "vigilantes" cannot say later that they were given orders or [offered] political concessions. . . . For obvious reasons, such actions are only possible during the initial period of military occupation.[33]

By his own admission, Stahlecker's *Einsatzgruppe* organized the early Lithuanian pogroms.[34] Why were locals in the western territories of the Soviet Union willing to do the ss's dirty work? Personal aggrandizement and enrichment, long-standing antisemitism, private scores to settle, jealousy and currying favor for national independence (a forlorn hope) were primary reasons, but "the more recent terror exerted by the Communists" was also a significant factor, especially in Lithuania and the Ukraine, where the ss's pogrom efforts were most successful.

"When Lithuanian and Latvian forces were attached to the execution units," Stahlecker wrote of the areas under his authority, "the first to be chosen were those who had had members of their families and relatives killed or deported by the Russians."[35] The deportations in particular had poisoned Jewish-Gentile relations in Lithuania. Jews were significantly underrepresented in the Lithuanian NKVD, not surprising given Russian antisemitism and Communist Party hostility to religion: of 279 Lithuanian NKVD senior officers, 148 were Russians and 111 were ethnic Lithuanians; the remaining 20 included Jews as well as other nationalities.[36] One week before Barbarossa, on the night of July 14, the NKVD had seized and deported to the Russian gulag some 35,000 Lithuanian citizens. Slightly more than half of the deportees were ethnic Lithuanians, the other half Jews and Poles, but the Lithuanian nationalists had blamed the deportations on the "Bolshevik" Jews.[37] On the night before Barbarossa, William Mishell and his friend Nahum Shoham had stayed up late discussing the impact of these deportations on the Kaunas Jewish community: "Our conversation inevitably turned to the deportations. It worried us, because these deportations had suddenly created enormous strains on the Lithuanian society and increased very perceptibly the antisemitic feelings."[38]

Despite the deportations, Barbarossa surprised the NKVD, whose jails and prisons in the invaded western territories were crowded with political prisoners. Rather than release their prisoners as they hastened to retreat during the first week of the war, the Soviet secret police had simply slaughtered them. NKVD prisoner executions in the first week after Barbarossa totaled some ten thousand in the western Ukraine and more than nine thousand in Vinnitsa, eastward toward Kiev; comparable numbers of prisoners were executed in eastern Poland, Byelorussia, Lithuania, Latvia, and Estonia.[39] These areas had already sustained losses numbering in the hundreds of thousands from the Stalinist purges of 1937–38. "It was not only the numbers of the executed," historian Yury Boshyk writes of the evacuation murders, "but also the manner in which they died that shocked the populace. When the families of the arrested rushed to the prisons after the Soviet evacuation, they were aghast to find bodies so badly mutilated that many could not be identified. It was evident that many of the prisoners had been tortured before death; others were killed en masse."[40] In some cases, cells crowded with prisoners had been dynamited, badly mutilating the remains.

The conquering Germans opened up the prisons and jails and invited the communities to collect their dead, organizing the events to implicate local Jewish citizens in the murders. "Jews were paraded out," historian John-Paul Himka confirms, "forced to clean the corpses and accused of responsibility for the atrocities."[41] ....

Babi Yar

Kiev fell on September 19, 1941. "Hold it at all costs," Stalin had ordered [Semyon] Budenny.[42] The dull-witted marshal had positioned more than a half million men in trenches and dugouts in its suburbs to defend it. But the *Luftwaffe* had dominated the air, and the *Wehrmacht* had ... encircled the city on its bluff above the Dnieper with a deadly ring of steel. Bombs and artillery barrages had destroyed its suburbs. "The whole horizon had been lit up by flashes and fire," twelve-year-old Anatoli Kuznetsov saw from his family's house on the western outskirts of the city. Then silence had replaced the din of cannons and air-raid sirens and the boy had noticed "the men of the Red Army in their faded khaki uniforms ... running in twos and threes through the courtyards and across the back gardens."[43] The *Wehrmacht* took Kiev itself largely intact, a city twelve centuries old graced with Parisian boulevards and gilded onion-domed churches, luxurious with chestnut and linden trees glowing yellow in the gathering autumn. . . .

The Germans . . . moved into the offices and hotels along the Kreshchatik, Kiev's fashionable main street, formed out of one of the many wide ravines, or yars, that centuries of runoff had cut down through the right bank of the Dnieper. . . . The first building to explode, on September 20, 1941, was the citadel where the *Wehrmacht* artillery staff was quartered. . . . Four days later the headquarters of the *Wehrmacht* field commander at the corner of Kreshchatik and Pjoreznaya exploded with such force that windows were blown out blocks away. The explosion set the building afire. As the Germans were seizing and beating anyone they happened to find in the vicinity, a second large explosion reduced the structure to rubble and dusted the Kreshchatik white. A third explosion blew up the offices across the street and started panic.

Explosions up and down the Kreshchatik continued throughout the night and intermittently for several days. The Soviets had stored crates of Molotov cocktails in the upper stories of buildings to defend the city and left them behind when they abandoned it; the explosions shattered the glass bottles and spilled jellied gasoline across the floors that ignited and poured down stairwells to fuel raging fires. "The Germans cordoned off the whole of the center of the city," Kuznetsov remembers. "But the fire was spreading: the two parallel streets, Pushkin and Mering, were already ablaze, as were the streets which crossed the Kreshchatik. . . . It seemed as though the whole city was being blown up." . . .

Blobel arrived on September 24 and the *Einsatzgruppe* C group staff followed the next day.[44]

Between his arrival and September 28, 1941, he reported the conditions in Kiev to Berlin, his training as an architect informing his comments:

> The ensuing fire has not yet been extinguished. Fire in the center of the town. Very valuable buildings destroyed. So far, firefighting practically without effect. Demolitions by blasting being carried out to bring the fire under control. Fire in the immediate neighborhood of this office. Had to be evacuated for this reason. . . . Up to now, 670 mines detected in buildings, according to a mine-laying plan that was discovered: all public buildings and squares are mined. . . . Buildings being searched most assiduously. . . . In the Lenin Museum, 1,000 pounds of dynamite discovered that were to be touched off by radio. It was repeatedly observed that fires broke out the moment buildings were taken over.[45]

In a more extensive report a week later Blobel would acknowledge that "there exists in Kiev a Red sabotage battalion as well as numerous members of the NKVD and of the Communist Party who have orders to commit continuous acts of sabotage,"[46] but inevitably he found it convenient to blame the mining of the Kreshchatik on the Jews: "As has been proved, Jews played a preeminent part. . . . During the first action, 1,600 arrests were made and measures undertaken for the arrest of all the Jews. Execution of at least 50,000 Jews is anticipated."[47]

Historians, crediting Blobel's claims, have presented the executions that followed in Kiev as retaliatory. The justification was nothing more than the usual window dressing; the Jews of Kiev would have been murdered anyway. Jeckeln's massacre of 23,600 refugees at Kamenets-Podolsky was a month old, and Ohlendorf's *Einsatzgruppe* D was busy slaughtering 22,467 "Jews and Communists" in the Nikolayev area, near Odessa, 250 miles south of Kiev, even as Blobel was radioing his report.[48]

Anatoli Kuznetsov saw the notice, "printed on cheap gray wrapping paper," posted throughout Kiev on September 28, 1941, and checked its wording, years later, in the Central State Archives in Moscow. As a twelve-year-old it made him shudder:

All Yids living in the city of Kiev and its vicinity are to report by 8 o'clock on the morning of Monday, September 29, 1941, at the corner of Melnikovsky [Melnikov] and Dokhturov [Degtyarev] Streets (near the cemetery). They are to take with them documents, money, valuables, as well as warm clothes, underwear, etc. Any Yid not carrying out this instruction and who is found elsewhere will be shot. Any civilian entering apartments evacuated by Yids and stealing property will be shot.[49]

"This summons was posted all over town by members of the newly organized Ukrainian militia," Blobel reported to Berlin. "At the same time it was passed around by word of mouth that all the Jews in Kiev were to be resettled."[50]

"They started arriving while it was still dark," Kuznetsov remembers of that cold, windy Monday morning, "to be in good time to get seats in the train." The ordinary Jews of Kiev believed that the Germans intended to deport them, especially since the assembly point was near the Lukyanovka railway freight yards. Word of the massacres to the west and in Poland had not reached many of them; the Soviet government had suppressed information about the Nazi treatment of the Jews during the period of the Nazi-Soviet Pact, and the confusion of war had limited communications after Barbarossa. Most of the people young Kuznetsov saw were poor, old, invalid—"sick and unfortunate," he says; many women and children walked to the assembly point unaccompanied. Able-bodied Jewish men had been drafted into the Red Army and anyone with money or influence had been evacuated eastward. People carried "bundles roughly tied together with string, worn-out cases made from plywood, woven baskets, boxes of carpenters' tools.... Some elderly women were wearing strings of onions hung around their necks like gigantic necklaces—food supplies for the journey."[51]

"Families baked bread for the journey," Soviet journalist Lev Ozerov writes, summarizing eyewitness testimony, "sewed knapsacks, rented wagons and two-wheeled carts. Old men and women supported each other while mothers carried their babies in their arms or pushed baby carriages. People were carrying sacks, packages, suitcases, boxes."[52] Some of them sang, moving through the streets in the brisk early morning. Russians and Ukrainians, friends and relatives, saw their neighbors off, waved from windows. "There were plenty of people on Turgenyev Street," an eyewitness told Kuznetsov, "and Artem Street was completely jammed. People with bundles, with prams, all sorts of trolleys and carts and even trucks—all standing there, then moving forward a little, then standing still again."[53] They flowed in crowds from their neighborhoods into Melnikov Street on what had been the old Zhitomir road.

Melnikov led past a Jewish cemetery in northwest Kiev, and immediately beyond the Jewish cemetery a mile-long ravine, a yawning pit, dropped away northeastward down to the Dnieper: Babi Yar. The *Einsatzgruppen* had become expert at picking killing sites; Babi Yar could have swallowed the entire population of Kiev.

Babi Yar—"babushka ravine," "grandmother ravine"—ran through Kuznetsov's neighborhood and had been his childhood playground:

The ravine was enormous, you might even say majestic: deep and wide, like a mountain gorge. If you stood on one side of it and shouted you would scarcely be heard on the other. It is . . . surrounded by cemeteries, woods and [garden] allotments. Down at the bottom ran a little stream with clear water. The sides of the ravine were steep, even overhanging in places; landslides were frequent at Babi Yar.[54]

. . . Jeckeln planned the Babi Yar *Aktion* along the same basic lines as the Kamenets-Podolsky massacre. When the first Jews approached the Jewish cemetery on the morning of September 29, 1941, *Sonderkommando* 4a, two commandos of Police Regiment South, and Ukrainian militia were waiting for them. Coming up Melnikov Street after their two-mile walk from central Kiev, the victims would begin passing the long brick wall of the cemetery.[55] "At that point," Kuznetsov writes, "there was a barbed-wire barrier across the street and anti-tank obstacles, with a passage left between them, and there were rows of Germans wearing badges on their chests as well as Ukrainian police in black uniforms with gray cuffs."[56] A tall Ukrainian in an embroidered shirt with a Cossack mustache gave instructions. A crowd grew in the street before the barrier: people milling, talking, craning to see, children crying, dogs barking somewhere and distant bursts of machine-gun fire. Armed Ukrainians counted out thirty or forty people at a time, watched while they deposited their belongings on the growing pile at streetside and led them through the passage and farther up the street. There, Ozerov reports, "an entire office operation with desks had been set up in an open area."[57] The headquarters staff of *Einsatzgruppe* C manned the desks, collecting valuables and documents. "The documents were immediately thrown to the ground," Ozerov adds, "and wit-

nesses have testified that the square was covered with a thick layer of discarded papers, torn passports and union identification cards."[58]

Beyond the desks waited a further gauntlet of soldiers with dogs. . . . As one of the few survivors, Dina Mironovna Pronicheva, a young mother who was an actress with the Kiev Children's Theater, saw it that day:

It was very narrow—some four or five feet across. The soldiers were lined up shoulder to shoulder with their sleeves rolled up, each of them brandishing a truncheon or a club. Blows rained down on the people as they passed through.

There was no question of being able to dodge or get away. Brutal blows, immediately drawing blood, descended on their heads, backs and shoulders from left and right. The soldiers kept shouting: "*Schnell, schnell!*" [fast, fast!], laughing happily, as if they were watching a circus act. . . . Everybody started shouting and the women began to scream. . . . The dogs were immediately set on them. One man managed to pick himself up, but others remained on the ground while people pressed forward behind them, and the crowd carried on, walking on the bodies and trampling them into the ground.

From this funnel into hell they debouched into an open field cordoned by Ukrainian militia—"not local people but from the western Ukraine," says Kuznetsov—piled with separated clothing. The militiamen rushed them. "Get your clothes off! Now! Hurry!" Brutally they ripped the clothes off anyone who hesitated and kicked and beat them with brass knuckles or clubs. A truck driver named Höfer who was loading clothes saw the disrobing process. "I don't think it was even a minute from the time each Jew took off his coat before he was standing there completely naked," he testified. "Most people put up a fight when they had to undress and there was a lot of screaming and shouting."[59] Kuznetsov thinks "all this was obviously being done so that the great mass of people should not come to their senses. There were many naked people covered in blood."

Beyond the disrobing area, Babi Yar dropped down steeply from the plateau of the green field to the sandy bed of the stream that had eroded the ravine. The Germans had cut entrances into the *yar* side canyons so the victims could descend toward the central channel, which was as wide as a two-lane road. Höfer, the truck driver, describes the killing process:

Once undressed, the Jews were led into [Babi Yar]. Two or three narrow entrances led to this ravine through which the Jews were channeled. When they reached the bottom of the ravine they were seized by members of the *Schutzpolizei* and made to lie down on top of Jews who had already been shot. This all happened very quickly. The corpses were literally in layers. A police marksman came along and shot each Jew in the neck with a submachine gun at the spot where he was lying. When the Jews reached the ravine they were so shocked by the horrifying scene that they completely lost their will. It may even have been that the Jews themselves lay down in rows to wait to be shot.... The moment one Jew had been killed, the marksman would walk across the bodies of the executed Jews to the next Jew, who had meanwhile lain down, and shoot him. It went on this way uninterruptedly, with no distinction being made between men, women, and children. The children were kept with their mothers and shot with them.

I only saw this scene briefly. When I got to the bottom of the ravine I was so shocked by the terrible sight that I could not bear to look for long. In the hollow I saw that there were already three rows of bodies lined up over a distance of about two hundred feet. How many layers of bodies there were on top of each other I could not see. I was so astonished and dazed by the sight of the twitching blood-smeared bodies that I could not properly register the details.... There was a "packer" at either entrance to the ravine. These "packers" were *Schutzpolizisten* whose job it was to lay the victim on top of the other corpses so that all the marksman had to do as he passed was fire a shot.

When the victims came along the paths to the ravine and at the last moment saw the terrible scene they cried out in terror. But at the very next moment they were already being knocked over by the "packers" and being made to lie down with the others. The next group of people could not see this terrible scene because it took place round a corner.

Höfer saw only two "marksmen" working. The level of bodies and piles of clothes suggest that he saw a late stage of the massacre. Kurt Werner, a member of *Sonderkommando* 4a, worked the killing floor on the first morning, even before the entrance paths had been cut and more accurately testifies to the killing system Blobel had organized:

As soon as I arrived at the execution area I was sent down to the bottom of the ravine with some of the other men. It was not long before the first Jews were brought to us over the side of the ravine. The Jews had to lie face down on the earth by the ravine walls. There were three groups of marksmen down at the bottom of the ravine, each made up of about twelve men. Groups of Jews were sent down to each of these execution squads simultaneously. Each successive group of Jews had to lie down on top of the bodies of those that had already been shot. The marksmen stood behind the Jews and killed them with a *Genickschüss* [shot in the back of the neck]. I still recall today the complete terror of the Jews when they first caught sight of the bodies as they reached the top edge of the ravine. Many Jews cried out in terror. It's almost impossible to imagine what nerves of steel it took to carry out that dirty work down there. It was horrible. . . .[60]

When Dina Pronicheva, whose husband was Russian, had reached the disrobing area and realized what was happening at Babi Yar she had shredded her identity card and told a Ukrainian militiaman she had been caught up by accident while seeing someone off. Her Russian name on her other papers convinced the man—she "didn't look at all Jewish," Kuznetsov says ironically or innocently—and the militiaman had moved her aside to wait among a small group of similar unfortunates. They waited all day, watching the bloodied, panicked people emerge from the gauntlet, undress, and disappear into the *yar*. Pronicheva especially noticed what the Germans did when mothers tried to hold back with their children: grab the child, drag it screaming to the bluff and throw it over the edge. At dusk an open car arrived bearing a German officer. He was tall and elegantly uniformed and carried a riding crop—Blobel? He questioned the Ukrainians about the group, a crowd by now, perhaps fifty people. Our own people, the Ukrainians explained. "Shoot the lot at once!" Pronicheva heard the officer shout. "If even one of them gets out of here and starts talking in the city, not a single Jew will turn up tomorrow."

The militiamen forced the group down into a side canyon. It opened onto Babi Yar well above the ravine floor. Pronicheva saw German soldiers at a bonfire, making coffee. She saw the carnage of bodies below. Before or after one of the soldiers began shooting—at different times she remembered the moment differently—she fell into the masses of the dead and lay still. "All around and beneath her," Kuznetsov writes, telling her story as she told it to him, "she could hear strange submerged sounds, groaning, choking and sobbing: many of the people were not dead yet. The whole mass of bodies kept moving slightly as they settled down and were pressed tighter by the movements of the ones who were still living." Pronicheva found herself unwounded. She waited for darkness. Lights flashed down. Shots were fired. Killers walked around on the dead finishing off the wounded. The air smelled of blood and opened bodies. Later sand rained down as workers began shoveling soil to cover the bodies. Pronicheva was lying face up and the sand choked her and gritted her eyes. She scraped it away, turned over and started crawling toward the ravine wall, out of Babi Yar. She made it, survived the war, testified at war trials, and went back to performing for children in puppet shows.

The *Aktion* continued through a second day. "As a result of a very clever piece of organization," Blobel bragged in a report, "[the Jews] still believed they were going to be resettled right up until the time they were executed."[61] On the third day, as Anton Heidborn, a member of SK 4a, testified, civilians shoveled sand to cover up the last bodies, and then Blobel's men dynamited the walls of that section of the ravine. "The next few days," Heidborn recalled, "were spent smoothing out banknotes belonging to the Jews who had been shot. I estimate these must have totaled millions."[62] Truckloads of clothing were donated to the NSV [National Socialist People's Welfare] "for the use of ethnic Germans" and to the Kiev city administration "for use of the needy population."[63]

An *Einsatzgruppen* report on October 2, 1941, summarized the Babi Yar *Aktion* brazenly, not even bothering to justify it as retaliation: "*Sonderkommando* 4a in collaboration with the group staff and two commandos of Police Regiment South on September 29 and 30, 1941, executed 33,771 Jews in Kiev."[64]

Executions continued at Babi Yar every Tuesday and Friday for the next year, by which time the German administration had set up a concentration camp that backed up to the *yar*.[65]

When Kiev fell, a German physician, Wilhelm Gustav Schüppe, was posted to the Kiev Pathological Institute assigned to destroy "life unworthy of life." His commando of about ten physicians and ten SS men dressed as medics used lethal injections to murder the disabled of the Kiev area as well as Jews, Gypsies, and Turkmen. Interrogated after the war, Schüppe estimated that in the space of six months, from September 1941 to March 1942, his commando killed more than one hundred thousand people—an average of more than five hundred per day.[66] "The executioners used to boast about their records," a doctor involved in similar executions at Auschwitz would testify. "'Three in a minute,'" he said, quoting their boast.[67] Schüppe had every reason to minimize rather than exaggerate his crimes. Since the Schüppe commando had no crematoria, the bodies were almost certainly dumped into Babi Yar. Anatoli Kuznetsov's childhood playground thus became the SS's largest single mass grave. . . .

By the end of 1942, the *Einsatzgruppen* and their SS cohorts had largely fulfilled their mission. *Einsatzgruppe* A had murdered, according to its own reports, 249,421 Jews. *Einsatzgruppe* B counted 126,195, surely only a fraction of its total in Byelorussia. *Einsatzgruppen* C and D had murdered 363,211 between September and December 1942 alone. Adding in other agencies—the

Higher SS and Police Leaders, the *Wehrmacht*, *Sonderkommando* Dirlewanger, the Romanian army and gendarmerie, Lithuanian and Ukrainian auxiliaries—and including the full period of the war, Raul Hilberg estimates that more than 1,300,000 Jewish men, women and children were murdered in the East after Barbarossa.[68] Adding non-Jewish victims would raise the total above two million, each one a name, a person, a kin, a soul, a loss.

NOTES

1. Krausnick (1981), 122.
2. Ibid.
3. Büchler (1989), 457.
4. According to Lothar Fendler, Nuremburg War Crimes Trials (1978) (hereafter EG [*Einsatzgruppen*] Trial Tr.), 3995.
5. Waldemar von Radetzky EG Trial Tr., 4142.
6. Quoted in Klee et al. (1988), 81.
7. Quoted in Reitlinger (1957), 182.
8. Lothar Fendler EG Trial Tr., 3993.
9. According to Lothar Fendler EG Trial Tr., 3995.
10. Hilberg (1985), 289.
11. Ohlendorf EG Trial Tr., 672.
12. EG Trial Tr., 934.
13. Other EG leaders on trial, of course, did make such a claim, but there is good evidence that they were lying. For a full discussion, see Alfred Streim, "The Tasks of the SS Einsatzgruppen," in Marrus (1989), vol. 2, 436 ff.
14. From Heydrich's July 2, 1941, minute to the Higher SS and Police Leaders, which "summarized" the "basic instructions" that he had already issued to the *Einsatzgruppen*. Quoted in Krausnik et al. (1968), 62–63.
15. Ibid.
16. Noakes and Pridham (1998), vol. 3, 1093.
17. According to Stahlecker Report, Gitelman (1997), 265.
18. Stahlecker Report, quoted in Klee (1991), 26.

19. Klee *et al.* (1991), 32–35, for this and the following quotations.

20. Ibid., 28ff.

21. Ibid., 31ff.

22. Baranauskas (1970) 194–95.

23. In variant translations in Klee et al. (1988), 24ff, and Gitelman (1997), 265ff.

24. OSR USSR No. 12, Arad et al. (1989), 7.

25. Klee et al. (1991), 29.

26. OSR USSR No. 8, Arad et al. (1989), 1.

27. Mishell (1988), 27.

28. Ibid., 38.

29. Ibid., 38ff.

30. MacQueen (1996), 47, n. 43.

31. Mishell (1988), 44.

32. Quoted in Klee et al. (1991), 24.

33. Quoted in Longerich (1997), 263.

34. The Stahlecker Report speaks specifically of "Klimatis" [*sic*] "starting a pogrom with the aid of instructions given him by a small advance detachment [of EG A] operating in Kovno." Gitelman (1997), 265.

35. Ibid., 266.

36. MacQueen (1996), 33.

37. Ibid., 34.

38. Mishell (1988), 10.

39. Boshyk (1986), 43.

40. Ibid., 11.

41. Himka (1997), 174.

42. Quoted in Clark (1965), 136.

43. Anatoli (1970), 21.

44. EG Trial Tr. 1; OSR USSR No. 106 NA RG 895, roll 11.

45. OSR USSR No. 97, Arad et al. (1989), 165; OSR USSR No. 106 NA RG 895, roll 11.

46. OSR USSR No. 106 NA RG 895, roll 11.

47. OSR USSR No. 97, Arad et al. (1989), 16; IMT NO-3145 evidence summary.

48. OSR USSR No. 101, Arad et al. (1989), 168.

49. Anatoli (1970), 90–91.

50. OSR USSR No. 106, Arad et al. (1989), 173 (translation modified).

51. Anatoli (1970), 93.

52. Ehrenburg (1981), 6–7.

53. Anatoli (1970), 100.

54. Anatoli (1970), 15.

55. This reconstruction is based on information in Anatoli (1970), 99ff; Ehrenburg and Grossman (1980), 3ff; Gitelman (1997), 275–78; Klee et al. (1988), 63–68; and interviews with members of the Kyiv Jewish Council, Kyiv, June 2.

56. Anatoli (1970), 101.

57. Ehrenburg and Grossman (1980), 7.

58. Ibid.

59. Klee et al. (1989), 63ff.

60. Werner testimony: Klee et al. (1989), 66–67.

61. OSR USSR No. 128, quoted in Klee et al. (1989), 68, and in Noakes and Pridham (1988), 1095.

62. Klee et al. (1989), 67–68.

63. OSR USSR No. 106 NA RG 895, roll 11.

64. IMT NO-3137.

65. Interview with Kyiv Jewish Council, June 2.

66. Friedlander (1995), 142.

67. Quoted in Padfield (1990), 345.

68. Hilberg (1985), 390; Headland (1992), 105.

Bringing Jews to Death

RAUL HILBERG

From *The Destruction of the European Jews*

Origins of the Killing Centers

The most secret operations of the destruction process were carried out in six camps located in Poland in an area stretching from the incorporated areas to the Bug [River]. These camps were the collecting points for thousands of transports converging from all directions. In three years the incoming traffic reached a total of close to three million Jews. As the transports turned back empty, their passengers disappeared inside.

The killing centers worked quickly and efficiently. A man would step off a train in the morning, and in the evening his corpse would be burned and his clothes packed away for shipment to Germany. Such an operation was the product of a great deal of planning, for the death camp was an intricate mechanism in which a whole army of specialists played their parts. Viewed superficially, this smoothly functioning apparatus is deceptively simple, but upon closer examination the operations of the killing center resemble in several respects the complex mass-production methods of a modern plant. It will therefore be necessary to explore, step by step, what made possible the final result.

A salient fact about the killing center operations is that, unlike the earlier phases of the destruction process, they were unprecedented. Never before in history had people been killed on an assembly-line basis.[1] The killing center as such had no prototype, no administrative ancestor. This is explained by the fact that it was a composite institution that consisted of two parts: the camp proper and the killing installations in the camp. Each of these two components had its own administrative history. Neither was entirely novel. As separate establishments, both the concentration camp and the gas chamber had been in existence for some time. The great innovation was effected when the two devices were fused. An examination of the death camp should therefore begin with its two basic components and how they were put together.

The German concentration camp was born and grew amid violent disputes and struggles between Nazi factions. Even in the earliest days of the Nazi regime, the importance of the concentration camp was fully recognized. Whoever gained possession of this weapon would wield a great deal of power.

In Prussia, Interior Minister (and later Prime Minister) Göring made his bid. He decided to round up the Communists. This was not an incarceration of convicted criminals but an arrest of a potentially dangerous group. "The prisons were not available for this purpose";[2] hence Göring established concentration camps, which he put under the control of his Gestapo (then, *Ministerialrat* Diels).

Almost simultaneously, rival camps appeared on the scene. One was set up at Stettin by *Gauleiter* Karpenstein, another was established at Breslau by SA leader Heines, a third was erected near Berlin by SA leader Ernst. Göring moved with all his might against these "unauthorized camps." Karpenstein lost his post, Ernst lost his life.

But a more powerful competitor emerged. In Munich the police president, Himmler, organized his own Gestapo, and near the town of Dachau he set up a concentration camp which he placed under the command of *ss-Oberführer* Eicke.[3] Soon Himmler's Gestapo covered the non-Prussian *Länder* [states], and in the spring of 1934 Himmler obtained through Hitler's graces the Prussian Gestapo (becoming its "deputy chief"). Along with Göring's Gestapo, Himmler captured the Prussian concentration camps. Henceforth all camps were under his control.[4]

Eicke, the first Dachau commander, now became the Inspector for Concentration Camps. His *Totenkopfverbände* (Death's Head Units) became the guards. Thus the camps were severed from the Gestapo, which retained in the administration of each camp only one foothold: the political division, with jurisdiction over executions and releases. After the outbreak of war, Eicke and most of his *Totenkopfverbände* moved into the field (he was killed in Russia), and his deputy, the later *Brigadeführer* Glücks, took over the inspectorate.

Eicke's departure marks the midpoint in the development of the concentration camps. Up to the outbreak of war the camps held three types of prisoners:[5]

1. Political prisoners: a. Communists, b. Active Social Democrats, c. Jehovah's Witnesses, d. Clergymen who made undesirable speeches or otherwise manifested opposition, e. People who made remarks against the regime and were sent to camps as an example to others, f. Purged Nazis, especially SA men
2. So-called asocials, consisting primarily of habitual criminals and sex offenders

3. Jews sent to camps in *Einzelaktionen* [apprehension of individuals].

After 1939 the camps were flooded with millions of people, including Jewish deportees, Poles, Soviet prisoners of war, members of the French resistance movements, and so on.

The inspectorate could not keep up with this influx. Therefore, from 1940 on the Higher SS and Police Leaders established camps of their own, specifically the transit camps in the west and the labor camps in Poland. During the last stage of the destruction process, the Higher SS and Police Leaders also put up killing centers.

At this point an office stepped in to centralize and unify the concentration camp network: the SS Economic-Administrative Main Office, the organization of *Obergruppenführer* Oswald Pohl. In a process that took several years, Pohl finally emerged as the dominant power in the camp apparatus. His organization incorporated the inspectorate and enveloped almost completely the camps of the Higher SS and Police Leaders....

With the inspectorate's incorporation into the Pohl machine, the administration of the concentration camps acquired an economic accent. The exploitation of the inmate labor supply, which had motivated Pohl to undertake this consolidation, now became the very reason for the existence of concentration camps. This factor brought into the killing center operations the same dilemma that had already surfaced in the mobile killing operations and the deportations, namely the need for labor versus the "Final Solution." This time the quandary was entirely an internal SS affair.

The consolidation process did not stop with the incorporation of the inspectorate, for Pohl also bit into the camps of the Higher SS and Police Leaders. He annexed some camps outright, controlled others by installing regional officials responsible to the WVHA[6] and invaded the killing centers in the *Generalgouvernement* by acquiring control over the entire camp confiscation machinery in the territory. Concentration camps had become the principal factor in the power structure of Pohl. He in turn had emerged as the dominant figure in the sea of concentration camps.[7]

While Pohl tightened his hold over the camps, the camps absorbed ever larger numbers of inmates. The following figures indicate the growth of the increasingly important army of slaves in concentration camp enclosures:

September 1939: 21,400[8]
April 19, 1943: over 160,000[9]
August 1, 1944: 524,286[10]

The compilations do not include the camps of the Higher SS and Police Leaders, nor do they show the millions of deaths.

To keep up with the influx of victims, the camp network had to be extended. In 1939 there were six relatively small camps.[11] In 1944 Pohl sent Himmler a map that showed 20 full-fledged concentration camps (*Konzentrationslager* or KL) and 165 satellite labor camps grouped in clusters around the big KLs. (Again the camps of the Higher SS and Police Leaders were not included.)[12] Himmler received the report with great satisfaction, remarking that "just such examples show how our business has grown" [*Gerade an solchen Beispielen kann man sehen, wie unsere Dinge gewachsen sind*].[13] Pohl's empire was thus characterized by a three-fold growth: the jurisdictional expansion, the increase in the number of camp slaves, and the extension of the camp network.

The six killing centers appeared in 1941–42, at a time of the greatest multiplication and expansion of concentration camp facilities. During this burst of activity, the construction and operation of the killing centers could proceed smoothly and unobtrusively.

The death camps operated with gas. There were three types of gassing installations, for the administrative evolution of the gas method had proceeded in three different channels. One development took place in the Technical *Referat* of the RSHA. This office produced the gas van. In Russia and Serbia, the vans were auxiliary devices used for the killing of women and children only. But there was to be one more application. In 1941 *Gauleiter* Greiser of the *Wartheland* obtained Himmler's permission to kill 100,000 Jews in his *Gau*.[14] Three vans were thereupon brought into the woods of Kulmhof (Chelmno), the area was closed off, and the first killing center came into being.[15]

The construction of another type of gassing apparatus was pursued in the *Führer* Chancellery, Hitler's personal office. For some time, thought had been given in Germany to doctrines about the quality of life, from the simple idea that a dying person may be helped to die (*Sterbehilfe*) to the notion that life not worth living may be unworthy of life. This move from concern for the individual to a preoccupation with society was accomplished by representing retarded or malfunctioning persons, especially those with problems perceived to be congenital, as sick or harmful cells in the healthy corpus of the nation. . . .

Not until after the outbreak of World War II, however, did Hitler sign an order (predated September 1, 1939) empowering the chief of the Führer Chancellery, *Reichsleiter* Bouhler, and his own personal physician, Dr. Brandt, "to widen the authority of individual doctors with a view to enabling them, after the most critical examination in the realm of human knowledge, to administer to incurably sick persons a mercy death."[16] . . . The administrative implementation of this psychiatric holocaust was in the hands of Bouhler's Führer Chancellery. The man actually in charge of the program was a subordinate of Bouhler, *Reichsamtsleiter* Brack.[17] For the technical aspects of the project, the *Reichsamtsleiter* obtained the services of *Kriminalkommissar* Wirth, chief of the Criminal Police office in Stuttgart and an expert in tracking down criminals.[18]

"Euthanasia" was a conceptual as well as technological and administrative prefiguration of the "Final Solution" in the death camps. In the summer of 1941, when the physical destruction of the Jews was in the offing for the whole of the European continent, Himmler consulted with the Chief Physician of the ss (*Reichsarzt-ss und Polizei*), *Gruppenführer* Dr. Grawitz, on the best way to undertake the mass-killing operation. Grawitz advised the use of gas chambers.[19]

On October 10, 1941, at a "final solution" conference of the RSHA, Heydrich alluded to Hitler's desire to free the Reich of Jews, if at all possible, by the end of the year. In that connection, the RSHA chief discussed the impending deportations to Lodz, and mentioned Riga and Minsk. He even considered the possibility of shipping Jews to concentration camps set up for Communists by *Einsatzgruppen* B and C in operational areas.[20] The *Ostland*, emerging as the center of gravity in this scheme, served to crystallize the idea of what was to be done to Reich deportees on their arrival.

By the end of the month the race expert (*Sonderdezernent für Rassenpolitik*) in Bräutigam's office in the East Ministry, *Amtsgerichtsrat* Wetzel, drafted a letter in which he stated that Brack was prepared to introduce his gassing apparatus in the East. Brack had offered to send his chemical expert, Dr. Kallmeyer, to Riga, and Eichmann had referred to Riga and Minsk in expressing agreement with the idea. "All things considered" wrote Wetzel, "one need have no reservation about doing away with those Jews who are unable to work, with the Brackian devices [*Nach Sachlage, bestehen keine Bedenken wenn diejenigen Juden, die nicht arbeitsfähig sind, mit den Brackschen Hilfsmitteln beseitigt werden*]."[21] There were, however, some second thoughts about directing a continuing flow of transports to the icy regions of the occupied USSR.[22] Dr. Kallmeyer, told to wait in Berlin because of the cold in the east, spent Christmas at home.[23] The scene of the action had already been shifted to the *Generalgouvernement*.

Under primitive conditions, three camps were built by *Amt Haushalt und Bauten* (after the reorganization of March 1942, the WVHA-C) and its regional machinery at Belzec, Sobibór, and Treblinka. The sites were chosen with a view to seclusion and access to railroad lines. In the planning there was some improvisation and much economizing; labor and material were procured locally at minimum cost.

Belzec, in the district of Lublin, was the prototype. Its construction, according to Polish witnesses, was begun as early as November 1941. A locksmith who worked in the camp while it was being built provides the following chronology:[24]

October 1941: SS men approach Polish administration in town of Belzec with demand for twenty workers. The Germans select the site.

November 1, 1941: Polish workers begin construction of three barracks: a waiting hall leading through a walkway to an anteroom, leading to a third building that had a corridor with three doors to three compartments, each of which had floor piping and an exit door. All six doors (entry and exit) in these three compartments were encased in thick rubber and opened to the outside.

November–December 1941: A contingent of about seventy black-uniformed eastern collaborators (Soviet prisoners of war released from captivity) lay narrow-gauge rail, dig pits, and erect a fence.

December 22, 1941: Polish workers are discharged.

January–February 1942: Watchtowers are built.

The Germans at the Belzec site who had requisitioned the Polish work force were members of an ss construction *Kommando*.[25] The work was supervised by a "master from Katowice," an unidentified German with some knowledge of Polish who was in possession of building plans. When one of the Poles asked about the purpose of the project, the German only smiled.[26] Sometime before Christmas, the construction chief (*Bauleiter*) showed the blueprints to an ss noncommissioned officer (Oberhauser) who was stationed in the area and who was going to be a functionary in the administration of the death camps. The drawings were plans of gassing installations (*Vergasungsanlagen*). By that time the construction of the buildings was substantially finished,[27] and shortly thereafter the chemist Dr. Kallmeyer arrived from Berlin.[28]

Sobibór, also in the Lublin District, was built, evidently more quickly, in March and April of 1942. Supervision of the construction was in the hands of *Obersturmführer* (later *Hauptsturmführer*) Thomalla, a master mason regularly assigned to the ss-*Zentralbauleitung* Lublin/*Bauleitung* Zamosc.[29] Thomalla had some professional help from *Baurat* Moser, employed by the *Kreishauptmann* of Chelm (Ansel), in whose territory Sobibór was located.[30] To speed the work, Jewish labor from the surrounding region was employed extensively during the construction phase.[31]

At Treblinka (within the Warsaw District), where euthanasia physician Dr. Eberl was in charge, the *Zentralbauleitung* of the district, together with two contractors, the firm Schönbrunn of Liegnitz and the Warsaw concern Schmidt und Münstermann (builders of the Warsaw Ghetto wall), were readying the camp.[32] Labor for construction was drawn from the Warsaw Ghetto.[33] Dr. Eberl also availed himself of the resources of the ghetto for supplies, including switches, nails, cables, and wallpaper.[34] Again, the Jews were to be the unwitting contributors to their own destruction.

Even while the three camps were being erected, transports with Jewish deportees from the Kraków District, the Reich, and the *Protektorat* were arriving in the Hrubieszów-Zamosc area. The director of the Population and Welfare Subdivision of the Interior Division in the Gouverneur's office of Lublin (Turk) was instructed by the *Generalgouvernement* Interior Main Division (Siebert) to assist Globocnik in making room for the Jews pouring into the district. Turk's deputy (Reuter) thereupon had a conversation with Globocnik's expert in Jewish "resettlement" affairs, *Hauptsturmführer* Höfle. The *Hauptsturmführer* made a few remarkable statements: A camp was being built at Belzec, near the *Generalgouvernement* border in subdistrict (*Kreis*) Zamosc. Where on the Deblin-Trawniki line could 60,000 Jews be unloaded in the meantime? Höfle was ready to receive four or five transports daily at Belzec. "These Jews would cross the border and would never return to the *Generalgouvernement* [*Diese Juden kämen über die Grenze und würden nie mehr ins Geneneralgouvernement zurück kommen*]?[35] The discussion, on the afternoon of March 16, 1942, was held a few days before the opening of Belzec. During the following month Sobibór was finished, and in July, Treblinka.

The terrain of each camp was only a few hundred yards in length and width. The layout was similar in all three camps. There were barracks for guard personnel, an area where the Jews were unloaded, an undressing station, and an S-shaped walkway, called the *Schlauch* (hose), two or three yards wide that was bordered by high barbed-wire fences covered with ivy. The *Schlauch* was traversed by the naked victims on their way to the gassing facilities. The entire arrangement was designed to convince the Jews that they were in a transit camp, where they would be required to clean themselves on the way to the "east." The gas chambers, disguised as showers, were not larger than medium-sized rooms, but during gassings they were filled to capacity. At the beginning, no camp had more than three of these chambers. The gas first used at Belzec was bottled, either the same preparation of carbon monoxide that had been shipped to the euthanasia stations or possibly hydrogen cyanide.[36] Later, Belzec is reported to have been equipped with a diesel motor; Treblinka is said to have had one from the start; and Sobibór began with a heavy, eight-cylinder, 200+ horsepower, water-cooled Russian gasoline engine that released a mixture of carbon monoxide and carbon dioxide into the gas chambers.[37] No crematoria were installed; the bodies were burned in mass graves.

The limited capacity of the camps troubled SS and Police Leader Globocnik; he did not wish to get "stuck."[38] During the summer of 1942 there was congestion of railway traffic in the *Generalgouvernement*, and the line to Sobibór was under repair. At Belzec operations were reduced and interrupted, and at Sobibór the stoppage was prolonged. But Treblinka received transports to the point of overflow, and mounds of unburned bodies in various stages of decay confronted new arrivals of deportees.[39]

Between July and September an expansion was undertaken in the three camps. Massive structures, of stone in Belzec and brick in Treblinka, containing at least six gas chambers in each camp, replaced the old facilities. In the new gas buildings the chambers were aligned on both sides of a corridor, and at Treblinka the engine room was situated at its far end. The front wall of the Treblinka gas house, underneath the gable, was decorated with a Star of David. At the entrance hung a heavy, dark curtain taken from a synagogue and still bearing the Hebrew words "This is the gate through which the righteous pass."[40]

The *Generalgouvernement* was the location also of a regular concentration camp of the WVHA, where Jewish transports were received from time to time. In German correspondence the camp was referred to as Lublin, whereas its common name after the war was Majdanek. Up to October 1942, the camp had facilities for men only. It had been built to hold prisoners of war (among them Jewish soldiers of the Polish army) under SS jurisdiction. Even during these early days, however, several thousand Jews, including men, women, and children, were brought into the camp from nearby localities. In September-October 1942, three small gas chambers, placed into a U-shaped building, were opened. Two of them were constructed for the interchangeable use of bottled carbon monoxide or hydrogen cyanide gas, the third for cyanide only. The area in front of the building was called *Rosengarten* and *Rosenfeld* (rose garden and rose field). No roses adorned the camp—rather, the SS managers associated the facility with a typical name of Jewish victims. The gassing phase, which resulted in about 500 to 600 deaths per week over a period of a year, came to an end with the decision to wipe out the entire Jewish inmate population in one blow.[41] After the Lublin camp acquired administrative control of the Trawniki and Poniatowa labor camps, mass shootings took place at all three sites in the beginning of November 1943.[42]

While Kulmhof in the Wartheland was being set up with gas vans and network of gas-chamber camps was established in the *Generalgouvernement*, a third development came to fruition in the incorporated territory of Upper Silesia. There, in the corner below the convergence of the Vistula and Sola rivers, the Polish army had maintained an artillery base encircled by stagnant fish ponds which permeated the compound with dampness, mist, and mud.[43] After the Polish collapse, the German army quartered a company of construction troops in this facility. At the beginning of 1940 the Inspectorate of Concentration Camps, making a survey of the area, decided that with proper sanitary and structural improvements the buildings might be used as a quarantine center.[44] A few months later the ss moved in.[45] Another concentration camp was born. Its name was Auschwitz. Its commander, a Nazi from the earliest days of the movement who had come up in the concentration camp world with experience in Dachau and Sachsenhausen, was Rudolf Höss.

The first inmates were Poles and the first distinct purpose of the camp was their local exploitation for economic purposes of the ss, including agriculture in the vicinity of the camp enclosure. To this end, the ss made a considerable effort to extend its influence into the surrounding territory. The land between the two rivers was consequently declared a "zone of interest" (*Interessengebiet*), and all the Polish peasants in the local villages were evicted. The aim was to establish a *Gutsbezirk* of the *Waffen-ss*, a district owned by the ss, and conferences to this end were held over a period of two years. The complicated land transfer process, comprising land of the Polish state, municipal property, ecclesiastical property, as well as property belonging to Germans, could not be mastered, and on March 3, 1943, the *Oberpräsident* of Upper Silesia, Bracht, issued a decree establishing, in lieu

of a *Gutsbezirk*, the administrative district (*Amtsbezirk*) of Auschwitz.[46] Höss also became the chief executive of this *Amtsbezirk*.[47]

This maneuvering for control was accompanied by plans for building in the area. A decision of the I. G. Farben Company to build a plant at Auschwitz led to an order by the ss construction chief Kammler to erect barracks for 18,000 inmates by the end of 1941.[48] A branch of Auschwitz was founded outside the interest zone. It was called the Buna camp, descriptive of the synthetic rubber (Buna) that was to be produced there. Later it was also named Monowitz. Now there was a shortage of labor, and when Höss made an agreement with the local *Landrat* for the seizure of Poles and Ethnic Germans who had refused work in the free market, the civilian prosecutor protested against this encroachment of his prerogatives.[49]

The invasion of the Soviet Union stirred Himmler into action. From the overflow of prisoners of war he wanted his share. The army agreed, and two sites were hurriedly styled ss prisoner-of-war camps: the Lublin camp (Majdanek) and Birkenau. The latter was a virtually empty expanse, about two miles from the main Auschwitz camp. Although Birkenau was "partially swampy," it was thought that 125,000 prisoners could be held there.[50] Such masses of men, however, did not materialize. Some 10,000 were marched from a nearby prisoner-of-war camp at Lamsdorf. Hoss had been told that they were the cream of the crop for hard labor, but by February 1942, almost all of them were already dead.[51]

In the midst of this ferment, a new development was introduced into Auschwitz: the final solution of the Jewish question. Höss recalled that in the summer of 1941 he was summoned to Berlin by Heinrich Himmler himself. In a few spare words, Himmler told him of Hitler's decision to annihilate the Jews. One of the factors in the choice of

Auschwitz, said Himmler, was its location near railways. The details of this assignment would be brought to Höss by Eichmann. Having placed this burden on the shoulders of Höss, Himmler added: "We, the ss, must carry out this order. If it is not carried out now, then the Jews will later on destroy the German people."[52] During the following weeks, Eichmann came to Auschwitz, and Höss attended a conference in Eichmann's office about railroads and arrangements for trains.[53]

One of the details to be resolved was the mode of killing. The solution to that problem was serendipitous. Auschwitz served as one of the concentration camps to which the Gestapo brought selected Soviet prisoners of war and Communist functionaries for "liquidation." One day, when Höss was away on business, his deputy, Fritzsch, locked some of the prisoners into a cellar and killed them with hydrogen cyanide, a gas in stock for fumigation. The experiment was repeated when Höss returned. The building (or "block" as it was called in Auschwitz), numbered 11, had to be aired out for two days, and the next gassing was therefore planned for a somewhat larger number of Russians in the crematory. Holes were made in the earth and in the concrete roof over the crematory's morgue. After the cyanide was introduced into the room, some of the Russians shouted, "Gas!" and tried to break down the door, but the bolts did not give way. Höss observed the corpses and listened to the explanations of the camp physician. The victims, he was assured, had not suffered in agony. He concluded that death from the gas was bloodless and that its use would spare his men a great psychological burden.[54]

The mortuary now became the first gas chamber. It was in operation, with an interruption for repair of the smokestack, for a year. Since the size of the chamber and the capacity of the two ovens were not sufficient for the task at hand, Höss looked for a new location to carry out additional gassings. Accompanied by Eichmann, he found two small farmhouses in Birkenau that seemed suitable. Work was begun to fill in their windows. The interior walls were removed and special airtight doors installed. The two gas buildings were placed in operation during 1942, the smaller one in March, the larger in June. They were called Bunker I and II.[55]

Himmler visited the camp on July 17 and 18, 1942, with *Gauleiter* Bracht and the Higher ss and Police Leader of Upper Silesia, Schmauser. He watched a procedure from the unloading of the living to the removal of the dead at Bunker II. At that time he made no comment. Later, he sat in Höss's office and said that Eichmann's transports would rise from month to month, that Jews incapable of work were to be annihilated ruthlessly, and that the Gypsies too were to be killed.[56]

The bodies of the people gassed in the two bunkers were buried in mass graves. A survivor reports that in the summer of 1942 the corpses swelled, and a "black, evil-smelling mass oozed out and polluted the ground water in the vicinity."[57] From the end of summer to November 1942, the accumulated decomposing bodies infested with maggots had to be uncovered and burned.[58]

In the meantime the entire camp was in ferment. Auschwitz was continually under construction. Most of the work was planned and supervised by the *ss-Zentralbauleitung* Auschwitz, an organization of barely one hundred, including engineers, architects, technicians, and other personnel.[59] The *Zentralbauleitung* was responsible for erecting all the ss installations and two plant halls that were to be used by the Krupp company. In addition, I. G. Farben had a construction commission for its buildings, and the construction office of the Auschwitz railway station laid tracks and set up its equipment.[60]

The *Zentralbauleitung* was not capable of carrying out its task by itself. The ss company *Deutsche Ausrüstungswerke* (DAW) could undertake only simple carpentry. Consequently, about two hundred private firms were engaged, many for construction in the camp, the others as suppliers of materials to Auschwitz. Most of the companies were in Upper Silesia and their volume of business was small, but several of them were in Düsseldorf, Cologne, or Vienna, and a few had branches in several cities.[61]

Almost all the firms had to wrestle with multiple problems caused by wartime conditions: the allocation of material, which was a concern of the Speer ministry; the availability of freight cars for shipment, which was determined by the *Reichsbahn*; and the assignment of labor for Auschwitz projects, which was subject to the control of labor offices. In these matters the *Zentralbauleitung* attempted to support applications in order to expedite the process,[62] but only the labor shortage could be alleviated on the spot by drawing on the inmate population. As of December 22, 1942, for example, the construction firms employed 905 of their own workers and 2,076 prisoners in the camp, while the *Zentralbauleitung* used an additional 5,751 inmates.[63] The search for professional and skilled labor was a special effort early on, when Auschwitz tried to find qualified engineers and architects among German inmates of other concentration camps.[64]

The Auschwitz construction projects were begun with the laying of streets, the importation of electricity, and the digging for water.[65] Then came hundreds of barracks, particularly in Birkenau. Most of these structures were prefabricated horse stables assembled on bare earth without floors, and used for inmate housing and latrines.[66] Temporary guard towers (without hygienic amenities) were to be replaced in April 1943 by 16 large,

45 medium, and 42 small structures.[67] Throughout these activities, tons of barbed wire were strung and electrified.[68]

It was in the course of all this construction that a new kind of edifice made its appearance. Four massive buildings containing gas chambers and crematoria were erected in Birkenau. They were to be the answer to Himmler's admonition that more and more transports would arrive in Auschwitz. While under construction they were designated *Bauwerke* (Building Projects) 30, 30a, 30b, and 30c, and this numeration indicates that they were planned, not all four at one time, but in sequence.[69]

Bauwerk 30, the first in the set, was to become Krematorium II: the second Krematorium of Auschwitz. It was put on the drawing board in late 1941 when there was still an expectation of the large-scale delivery of Soviet prisoners of war.[70] At that moment the *Zentralbauleitung* envisaged five ovens with three retorts each. After the flow of Soviet prisoners had stopped, the design was scaled back to two morgues in the cellar and only two furnaces on ground level. By February 27, 1942, however, the Jewish transports were in the offing. That day, *Oberführer* Kammler visited the camp and decided that the five furnaces should be installed.[71] Some time later several changes were made in the plans for the building. A chute for corpses was deleted and a staircase inserted. One of the morgues in the basement was turned into an undressing room. For the other the planners added a separate drainage system as well as ventilation—the transformation into a gas chamber.[72]

While these modifications were projected in a succession of drawings, a third Krematorium, identical to the final version of the second, was planned. This structure, 30a, was to become Krematorium III.[73] Finally, two more *Bauwerke*, 30b

TABLE 6. Numeration of Krematoria

NUMERATION OF KREMATORIA	START OF CONSTRUCTION	DATE OF TRANSFER TO CAMP ADMINISTRATION (*STANDORTVERWALTUNG*)
II	July 2, 1942	March 31, 1943
III	September 14, 1942	June 26, 1943
IV	October 9, 1942	March 22, 1943
V	November 20, 1942	April 4, 1943

and 30c, were added. These buildings, which were Krematoria IV and V, did not have a cellar. Their gas chambers were on the surface, and as an economy measure each Krematorium was to have a double furnace with two smokestacks.[74] The double ovens had been ordered by the ss Construction Inspectorate in the area of the Higher ss and Police Leader Russia Center von dem Bach for Mogilev on the Dnepr River, but they were diverted from that destination to Auschwitz.[75]

The hydrogen cyanide, solidified in pellets, was to be shaken into the cellars of Krematoria II and III through shafts, and into the surface chambers of Krematoria IV and V through side walls. In the gas chambers, the pellets would pass immediately into the gaseous stage. Thus an altogether more efficient system, which guaranteed much more rapid processing than in other camps, had been devised in Auschwitz.

There was one drawback. The construction of these elaborate buildings required much more time than the erection of their counterparts in the *Generalgouvernement* killing centers of Sobibór and Treblinka. Table 6 (above) shows the time spans in Auschwitz from start to finish.[76]

More than a dozen firms were contractors on the sites of the four Krematoria,[77]

—for crematory–gas chamber design and the supply of ovens: J. A. Topf und Söhne, Erfurt

—for erection of the buildings: HUTA Hoch- und Tiefbau, Breslau, branch Kattowitz; Hermann Hirt Nachf., Beuthen; W. Riedel und Sohn, Bielitz; VEDAG Vereinigte Dachpappen A. G., Breslau

—for drainage: Continentale Wasserwerksgesellschaft, Berlin; Tiefbauunternehmung "TRITON," Kattowitz

—for roofs: Baugeschaft Konrad Segnitz, Beuthen; Industrie-Bau A. G., Bielitz

—for smokestacks: Robert Koehler, Myslowitz

—for plumbing: Falck, Gleiwitz

—for ventilation: Josef Kluge, Alt Gleiwitz

—for electrical current: AEG (Allgemeine Elektrizitätsgesellschaft), branch Kattowitz.

Much of the work was plagued by shortages of products, delays in the completion of installations, and poor quality of workmanship. On January 29, 1943, for example, the AEG bluntly told the *Zentralbauleitung* that the company was unable to obtain the best components for the supply of electricity in time, that equipment would have to be cannibalized from other projects, and that this compromise would curtail simultaneous incineration and "special treatment" in Krematorium II.[78] A stoppage in the allocation of freight cars, in turn, delayed the installation of ventilation equipment through the concrete ceiling of the "special cellar" (*Sonderkeller*) of the Krematorium.[79] The

Zentralbauleitung complained to the ss company *Deutsche Ausrüstungswerke* on January 13, 1943, that carpentry work had not been completed and that doors for one of the units, "which was urgently needed for the implementation of special measures [*welches zur Durchführung der Sondermassnahmen dringend benötigt wird*]" were not finished.[80] On March 31, another note was sent about a door that was to have a peephole, with a reminder that this order was specially urgent.[81] After the Krematoria had been placed into operation, repairs were needed, particularly of the chimney in Krematorium II. On this occasion there was an argument between Engineer Prüfer of Topf, who was responsible for the plans, and the firm Koehler, which carried them out. In the fact-finding attempt, even the senior German inmate supervisor had to be consulted.[82] Finally, the two double ovens diverted from Mogilev to Krematoria IV and V did not function very well.[83]

There was a reason for the feverish attempts to ready the buildings and to use them even with faulty parts. Throughout 1942, Auschwitz had received barely 175,000 Jews. The *Generalgouvernement* camps had swallowed more than eight times as many. The burial pits in Birkenau and in the *Generalgouvernement* were filling up or they were already full. In the first few months of 1943, more Jews were arriving in Auschwitz, but additional tens of thousands, from Macedonia, Thrace, France, and the Netherlands, were directed on longer routes to Treblinka and Sobibór, where no industry was located and no selection of the fittest could be conducted. Consequently, Auschwitz was becoming the center of attention. Auschwitz had to come into its own.

The status of Auschwitz as a focal point was underscored in a report by Bischoff to Kammler on January 27, 1943. Referring specifically to the "implementation of the special action [*Durch-*

führung der Sonderaktion]" in Birkenau, Bischoff noted an intervention by Hitler himself: "Pursuant to a Führer order the completion of construction in the camp is to be carried out on a specially accelerated basis [*Durch einen Führerbefehl ist der Aufbau des Lagers besonders beschleunigt durchzuführen*]."[84] Two days later Bischoff wrote encouragingly to Kammler that after the commitment of all available manpower and in spite of tremendous difficulties (*unsagbare Schwierigkeiten*), Krematorium II was now ready but for minor construction details (*bauliche Kleinigkeiten*).[85] . . .

If the construction of the gas chambers was a drawn-out affair, the laying of railway tracks for transports coming to Birkenau took even longer. The Auschwitz station, as part of the Upper Silesian network, was under the jurisdiction of *Reichsbahndirektion* in Oppeln. This *Direktion*, which had various offices also in Katowice and Sosnowiec, was headed until October 14, 1942, by *Präsident* Pirath, who retired on that day, and then by *Präsident* Geitmann, an engineer. On frequent occasions, the ss *Zentralbauleitung* had direct dealings not only with functionaries of the Auschwitz station but with officials of the *Reichsbahndirektion* responsible for construction, operations, and traffic.

Trains arriving in Auschwitz carried building supplies and raw materials for production, as well as prisoners. As early as the spring of 1942, when the prisoners were still unloaded at the railway station, the *Zentralbauleitung* began to consider the laying of a spur to Birkenau.[86] Already then, Oppeln had warned the *Zentrabauleitung* of a possibility that trains might be barred (*Annahmesperre*).[87] The construction project, however, was not so simple. Under a law of 1892, any tracks, including those owned by official agencies, were defined as "private" if they were not open to general traffic.[88] The ss, therefore, had to have a budget, allocations of rails and ties, agreements with the *Reichsbahn*, and permission of the *Regierungspräsident* before it could proceed.

By the beginning of 1943, the *Zentralbauleitung* unloaded thirty cars a day for construction materials alone.[89] Höss had negotiated with the *Reichsbahn* for the use of an outside spur that had been put down by the railways themselves for their own construction projects.[90] The ss, however, wanted arriving transports to halt before the new gas chambers inside Birkenau. Tracks were to be laid through the guard building at the entrance, with gates that could be locked.[91] On March 19, 1943, Höss explained to *Oberreichsbahnrat* Stäbler that the tracks were needed "urgently" now that notification had been received of a heavier flow of transports.[92] The provisional ramp had to be moved when the *Reichsbahn* was expanding its construction, and the ss had some anxiety that congestion might limit its unloading capacity to five transports a day.[93]

Nevertheless, there were more complications and interim solutions.[94] Finally, the construction of the spur was started in early 1944, when a contractor, the firm Richard Reckmann of Cottbus, was engaged for the undertaking.[95] On April 19, 1944, the railway station of Auschwitz approved the use of the newly built tracks for locomotives of the *Reichsbahn*.[96] Barely one month later, the Hungarian transports began to roll in, and for the next half-year the camp was to receive more Jews than had arrived during the preceding two years.

Construction was one-half of the problem faced by the ss. The gas supply was the other half. Hydrogen cyanide or *Zyklon* was a powerful lethal agent—a deadly dose was 1 milligram per kilogram of body weight. Packed in containers, the *Zyklon* was put to use simply by opening the canister and pouring the pellets into the chamber; the solid material would then sublimate. The *Zyklon* had only one drawback: within three months it deteriorated in the container and thus could not be stockpiled.[97] Since Auschwitz was a receiving station, always on call, it was necessary to have a dependable gas supply.

The ss did not manufacture *Zyklon*, so the gas had to be procured from private firms. The enterprises that furnished it were part of the chemical industry. They specialized in the "combating of vermin" (*Schädlingsbekämpfung*) by means of poison gases. *Zyklon* was one of eight products manufactured by these firms,[98] which undertook large-scale fumigations of buildings, barracks, and ships; disinfected clothes in specially constructed gas chambers (*Entlausungsanlagen*); and deloused human beings, protected by gas masks.[99] In short, this industry used very powerful gases to exterminate rodents and insects in enclosed spaces. That it should now have become involved in an operation to kill off Jews by the hundreds of thousands is no mere accident. In German propaganda, Jews had frequently been portrayed as insects. Frank and Himmler had stated repeatedly that the Jews were parasites who had to be exterminated like vermin, and with the introduction of *Zyklon* into Auschwitz that thought had been translated into reality.

NOTES

1. The phrase was used by a camp doctor, Friedrich Entress, in his affidavit of April 14, 1949, NO-2368.
2. Testimony by Göring, International Military Tribunal, *Trial of the Major War Criminals* (Nuremberg, 1947) IX, 257.
3. See orders by Eicke, October 1, 1933, PS-778.
4. Camps for foreign laborers and prisoner-of-war camps were outside of Himmler's sphere. However, in October 1944 Himmler took over the POW camps in the rear.

5. By October 1943, 110,000 German prisoners, including 40,000 "political criminals" and 70,000 "asocials," had been sent to the concentration camps. Himmler speech before *Militärbefehlshaber*, October 14, 1943, L-70.

6. Order by Pohl, July 23, 1942, NO-2128. Pohl to Himmler, July 27, 1942, NO-2128.

7. See the essay by Martin Broszat, "The Concentration Camps 1933–45," in Helmut Krausnick, Hans Buchheim, Martin Broszat, and Hans-Adolf Jacobsen, *The Anatomy of the SS State* (New York, 1968), 397–504.

8. Pohl to Himmler, April 30, 1942, R-129.

9. Pohl to OStubaf. Brandt, April 19, 1942, Himmler Files, Folder 67.

10. WVHA D-IV (signed Stubaf. Burger) to WVHA-B (Gruf. Lörner), August 15, 1944, NO-399.

11. Pohl to Himmler, April 30, 1942, R-129.

12. Pohl to Himmler, April 5, 1944, NO-20.

13. Himmler to Pohl, April 22, 1944, NO-20.

14. Greiser to Himmler, May 1, 1942, NO-246.

15. Judge Wladyslaw Bednarz (Lodz), "Extermination Camp at Chelmno," Central Commission for Investigation of German Crimes in Poland, *German Crimes in Poland* (Warsaw, 1946–47), vol. 1, 107–17.

16. Order by Hitler, September 1, 1939, PS-630.

17. For the organization and personnel of this office, see Friedlander, *The Origins of Nazi Genocide*.

18. Affidavit by Morgen, July 13, 1946, SS(A)-65. The chief psychiatric examiner for asylums was an SS physician, Prof. Werner Heyde. Each euthanasia station had its own medical director. The term "psychiatric holocaust" was coined by Peter Roger Breggin, 'The Psychiatric Holocaust," *Penthouse*, January 1979, 81–84, 216. The stations were called "killing centers" by Leo Alexander, "Medical Science under Dictatorship" *New England Journal of Medicine* 24 (1949): 39–47. Alexander's designation is used here to describe the camps in which the gassings of the Jews took place.

19. Affidavit by Morgen, July 13, 1946, SS(A)-65.

20. Israel Police 1193.

21. Draft memorandum by Wetzel for Lohse and Rosenberg, October 25, 1941, NO-365.

22. When *Generalgouverneur* Frank was in Berlin (middle of December 1941), he was told that "nothing could be done with the Jews in the Ostland." Frank in GG conference, December 16, 1941, Frank Diary, PS-2233.

23. Helmut Kallmeyer (in Havana) to Dr. Stahmer (attorney), June 18, 1960, Oberhauser (Belzec) case, Landgericht München 1, 1 Js 278/60, vol. 5, 974–75. All volume numbers pertaining to the Belzec, Sobibór, and Treblinka cases refer to the collection in the Zentrale Stelle der Landesjustizverwaltungen in Ludwigsburg, 8 AR-Z 252/59.

24. Statement by Stanislaw Kozak, October 14, 1945, Belzec case, vol. 6, 1129–33. The November 1, 1941, date is mentioned also by Eustachy Ukrainski (principal of grade school in the town of Belzec), October 11, 1945, Belzec case, vol. 6, 1117–20. The presence of eastern collaborators at the end of 1941 is confirmed by Ludwig Obalek (mayor of Belzec) in his statement of October 10, 1945, Belzec case, vol. 6, 1112–14.

25. Statements by Josef Oberhauser, February 26 and September 15, 1960, Belzec case, vol. 4, 656–60, and vol. 6, 1036–40.

26. Statement by Kozak, and statement by Edward Ferens (also a locksmith), March 20, 1946, Belzec case, vol. 6, 1222–23.

27. Statement by Oberhauser, December 12, 1960, Belzec case, vol. 9, 1678–93.

28. Kallmeyer to Stahmer, June 18, 1960, Belzec case, vol. 5, 974–75. In the letter Kallmeyer asserts that he was not needed.

29. Statement by Georg Michalsen (Globocnik's *Aussiedlungsstab*), September 4, 1961, Sobibór case, Hagen, 45 Js 27/61, vol. 4, 723–25. See also Richard Thomalla's personnel record in the Berlin Document Center.

30. Statement by Landrat Dr. Werner Ansel, June 15, 1960, Sobibór case, vol. 3, 416. Moser is mentioned also by Sobibór commander Franz Stangl, June 26, 1967, Treblinka case, Düsseldorf, 8 Js 10904/59, vol. 13, 3712–22.

31. Statement by Jan Stefaniuk (a non-Jewish worker at Sobibór), February 26, 1966, Sobibór case, vol. 13, 2694–95. The gassing apparatus was tried out in the presence of an unnamed chemist. See Adalbert Rückerl, *NS-Vernichtungslager* (Munich, 1977), 165–66. Rückerl's book contains texts of German Federal Republic court judgments and selected testimony about all three of the *Generalgouvernement* camps as well as Kulmhof.

32. Indictment of Kurt Franz, enclosed by prosecutor Hühnerschulte to Landgericht in Düsseldorf, January 29, 1963, through the courtesy of the Israel police.

33. See entries by Czerniaków (chairman of Warsaw Ghetto Jewish Council) in his diary (January 17; February 4 and 20; March 10, 27, and 29; April 9 and 18; May 23; and June 1, 1942), in Raul Hilberg, Stanislaw Staron, and Josef Kermisz, eds., *The Warsaw Diary of Adam Czerniakow* (New York, 1979), 316, 322, 328, 333, 338, 339, 341, 344, 358, 361. A labor camp (Treblinka I) was already in existence not far from the site. Jewish labor from the Warsaw Ghetto was sent to Treblinka I, and its inmates, Poles as well as Jews, could be utilized for construction. Treblinka I, under *Hauptsturmführer* van Eupen, was not administratively joined to the death camp.

34. Eberl to Kommissar of Jewish district (Auerswald), June 26, 1942, facsimile in Jüdisches Historisches Institut Warschau, *Faschismus-Getto-Massenmord* (Berlin, 1961), 304. Eberl to Kommissar, July 7, 1942, facsimile in Alexander Donat, cd., *The Death Camp Treblinka* (New York, 1979), 255.

35. Memorandum by Reuter, March 17, 1942, in Jüdisches Historisches Institut *Faschismus-Getto-Massenmord*, 269–70.

36. Bottled gas (*Flaschengas*) is mentioned by Oberhauser (*Obersturmführer* at Belzec). See text of his statement in Rückerl, *NS-Vernichtungslager*, 136–37. The court judgment in the Oberhauser case identifies the gas as cyanide (Zyklon B). Ibid. 133.

37. Ibid., 133, 203, 165–66. Eugen Kogon *et al.*, *Nationalsozialistische Massentötungen durch Giftgas* (Frankfurt am Main, 1986), 154, 163, 158–59. The Sobibór engine is described by *Unterscharführer* Erich Fuchs in *Massentötungen*, 158–59. Fuchs helped install the engine and tried it out on a contingent of 30–40 Jewish women.

38. Brack to Himmler, June 23, 1942, NO-205.

39. Rückerl, *NS-Vernichtungslager*, 208–9.

40. Ibid., 204. Information about the number and size of gas chambers in each camp rests not on documentation but on recollection of witnesses. There is agreement that the new chambers were larger than the old (the capacity for simultaneous gassing in Belzec during the summer of 1942 was estimated at 1,500). Counts of gas chambers are given in the following ranges: Belzec 3, then 6; Sobibór 3, then 4, 5, or 6; Treblinka 3, then 6 or 10. It is likely that each facility was designed from the same basic plan; hence three is probably the initial capacity, and six the subsequent one. German defendants in Treblinka trial of 1965 (Franz *et al.*) indicated six chambers there after expansion. Ibid. A Jewish survivor, who was a carpenter at Treblinka, states that there were ten gas chambers. Jankiel Wiernik, "A Year in Treblinka," in Donat, *Treblinka*, 147–88, at 161. For a sketch drawn by Wiernik, see Filip Friedman, *This Was Oswiecim* (London, 1946), 81–84; and Główna Komisja, *Obozy*, 526. See, however, two different sketches, in Donat, *Treblinka*, 318–19; and *Stern*, May 17, 1970, 170.

41. For a history of the Lublin camp, see Jozef Marszalek, *Majdanek* (Hamburg, 1982), particularly 24–44,135–52; judgment of Landgericht Düsseldorf April 27, 1979, in the matter of Ernst Schmidt, 8 Ks 1/75; affidavit by Friedrich Wilhelm Ruppert (Director, Technical Division, Lublin camp from September 1942 to August 6, 1945, NO-1903; and Główna Komisja, *Obozy*, 302–12. On deliveries of *Zyklon* to the camp in 1943, see affidavit by Alfred Zaun (bookkeeper with *Tesch und Stabenow*, suppliers), October 18, 1947, NI-11937, and facsimiles of correspondence between Lublin camp and *Tesch und Stabenow* during June-July 1943, Glowna Komisja, *Obozy*,

appendix, items 18, 140, and 141. The gas was routinely used in camps also for fumigation.

42. According to Ruppert, about 17,000 Jews were shot in Lublin in November 1943. Franz Pantli, an SS man in the camp, estimates 12,000. Affidavit by Franz Pantli, May 24, 1945, NO-1903. *Obersturmführer* Offermann cited 15,000 killed in Lublin, another 15,000 in Poniatowa, and 10,000 in Trawniki. Jüdisches Historisches Institut, *Faschismus-Getto-Massenmord*, 366–67n. See also Marszale, *Majdanek*, 138.

43. Jan Sehn, "Concentration and Extermination Camp at Oswięçim," Central Commission for Investigation of German Crimes in Poland, *German Crimes in Poland* (Warsaw, 1946–47), vol. 1, 27–29. Certificate of the New Construction Directorate (*Neubauleitung*) in Birkenau, October 21, 1941, noting heavy clay soil and frequent rain, U.S. Holocaust Memorial Museum Archives Record Group 11.002 (Center for the Preservation of Historical Documentary Collections, Moscow), Roll 21, Fond 502, Opis 1, Folder 41.

44. Obf. Glücks to Himmler, copies to Pohl and Heydrich, February 21, 1940, NO-34.

45. Heeresamt Gleiwitz to IdS Breslau, April 27, 1940, and IdS to Hoss, May 31, 1940, U.S. Holocaust Memorial Museum Archives Record Group 11.001 (Center for Historical Collections, Moscow), Roll 21, Fond 502, Opis 1, Folder 55. No payment was made by the SS to the army for the camp. The owner was simply the Reich. Report by the Chief of the Zentralbauleitung in Auschwitz (Ostuf. Jothann), June 22, 1944, ibid., Roll 20, Fond 502, Opis 1, Folder 38. The goal was 10,000 prisoners. Hauptamt Haushalt und Bauten II c 5 to Neubauleitung Auschwitz, August 3, 1940, ibid., Roll 36, Fond 502, Opis 1, Folder 265.

46. Bodenamt Schlesien in Kattowitz (signed Kusche) to Director of Zentralbodenamt beim Reichsführer-SS/RKfdFdV (Gruf. Freiherr von Holzschuher), May 22, 1940, PS-1352. Brif. Lörner to Finance Ministry, October 1, 1941, NG-5545. Pohl to Finance Ministry, November 7, 1942, PS-

1643. Records of conferences, November 3 and December 17–18, 1942, under the chairmanship of Oberfinanzpräsident Dr. Casdorf of the Finance Ministry, PS-1643. Full power signed by Casdorf in agreement with the chief of the Main Trusteeship Office East (Winkler), January 12, 1943, PS-1643. Ministerialrat Hoffmann (Interior Ministry) to Regierungspräsident in Kattowitz, January 22, 1943, PS-1643. Order by Bracht establishing the *Amtsbezirk* of Auschwitz with detailed description of the area, May 31, 1943, PS-1643. Map in U.S. Holocaust Memorial Museum Archives Record Group 11.001 (Center for Historical Collections, Moscow), Roll 34, Fond 502, Opis 1, Folder 26.

47. *Kommandantur* Order (signed Höss), March 2, 1942, in which Höss refers to himself as *Amtskommissar*, U.S. Holocaust Memorial Museum Archives Record Group 11.001 (Center for Historical Collections, Moscow), Roll 20, Fond 502, Opis 1, Folder 32.

48. Kammler to Zentralbauleitung, June 27, 1941, ibid., Roll 54, Fond 502, Opis 1, Folder 215.

49. Weekly report by I. G. Farben (Auschwitz) engineer Faust, covering August 17–23, 1941, NI-15254.

50. Bauleitung Explanatory Report, October 30, 1941, U.S. Holocaust Memorial Museum Archives Record Group 11.001 (Center for Historical Collections, Moscow), Roll 35, Fond 502, Opis 1, Folder 233. Kammler to Bauleitung, November 1 1941, ibid. HStuf. Bischoff (*Zentralbauleitung*) to Rüstungskommando Weimar November 12, 1941, ibid., Roll 41, Fond 502, Opis 1, Folder 314. Construction Certificate by Neubauleitung, November 18, 1941, ibid., Roll 20, Fond 502, Opis 1 Folder 41.

51. Rudolf Höss, *Kommandant in Auschwitz* (Munich, 1978), 105–6. Danuta Czech, *Kalendarium der Ereignisse im Konzentrationslager Auschwitz-Birkenau 1939–1945* (Reinbek bei Hamburg, 1989), particularly 160, 166, 170, 177. Most of the prisoners had arrived in October.

52. Höss, *Kommandant*, 157, 180–81. See also his testimony in International Military Tribunal, *Trial of the Major War Criminals* (Nuremberg, 1947–49),

vol. 11, 398. Höss does not recall the precise date of the meeting with Himmler, although in one of his statements, which is also his most confused, he mentions June. See his affidavit of March 14, 1946, NO-1210. Given the development of the final solution, June is unlikely. July may also be ruled out. Richard Breitman, reviewing Himmler's traveling, specifies July 13–15 as the only time that month when Himmler was in Berlin. See his *Architect of Genocide* (New York, 1991), 295. Danuta Czech suggests that in July Höss was absent from Auschwitz on the 29th. See her *Kalendarium*, entry for July 29, 1941, 106–7.

53. Höss, *Kommandant*, 157–59. Dating the meetings with Eichmann is difficult. See Christopher Browning, *Fateful Months* (New York, 1985), 22–28.

54. Höss, *Kommandant*, 127, 159. Czech, *Kalendarium*, 115–18. On the basis of witness testimony, Czech proposes September 3 as the date of the gassing in Block 11. Franciszek Piper also chooses September 3–5. See his article, "Gas Chambers and Crematoria," in Yisrael Gutman and Michael Berenbaum, eds., *The Anatomy of the Auschwitz Death Camp* (Bloomington, Ind., 1994), 158–59. Soviet prisoners sent to Auschwitz before October were communists and Jews selected, not for labor, but killing. No precise date has been advanced for the second gassing in Auschwitz.

55. Jean-Claude Pressac, *Auschwitz: Technique and Operation of the Gas Chambers* (Auschwitz, 1989), 123–82, and (for information about the original Krematorium) his *Les crematoires d'Auschwitz* (Paris, 1993), 16–20. On the bunkers see also the affidavit by Friedrich Entress, April 14, 1947, NO-2368. The gassing of Jews in the Krematorium began on February 15, 1942, in Bunker I on March 20, 1942, and in Bunker II on June 30, 1942. Czech, *Kalendarium*, 174–75, 186–87, 238–39.

56. Höss, *Kommandant*, 161, 184.

57. Filip Müller, *Eyewitness Auschwitz* (New York, 1979), 50–51.

58. Höss, *Kommandant*, 161.

59. See the Zentralbauleitung's figure of 98 for the second quarter of 1943, U.S. Holocaust Memo-rial Museum Archives Record Group 11.001 (Center for Historical Collections, Moscow), Roll 21, Fond 502, Opis 1, Folder 46.

60. See the partially reconstructed figures of Reichs-bahndirektion Oppeln for Auschwitz and other localities in the area of the Direktion. Verkehrs-museum Nuremberg Archive, Folder mm.

61. For firms participating in the construction of the Auschwitz complex, see the files of the Zentral-bauleitung in the U.S. Holocaust Memorial Museum Archives Record Group 11.001 (Center for Historical Collections, Moscow), *passim*.

62. For allocations of material, see, for example, Himmler's Personal Staff/Raw Materials Office (Rohstoffamt) to Zentralbauleitung, May 11, 1944, regarding Speer Ministry's authoriza-tion to AEG/Kattowitz for relay station, ibid., Roll 21, Fond 502, Opis 1, Folder 38, and cor-respondence affecting other firms in ibid., Roll 41, Fond 502, Opis 1, Folder 307. For railroad freight embargo and priority problems, see 1943 correspondence in Folder 307, and with specific reference to crematory construction, Eng. Prüfer (Topf firm) to Zentralbauleitung, January 29, 1943, ibid., Roll 41, Fond 502, Opis 1, Folder 313. For approval of the Labor Office in Kattowitz (Katowice), see Wilhelm Kermel Kattowitz Elektrotechnisches Installationsge-schäft, September 8, 1942, seeking the help of the Zentralbauleitung, ibid., Roll 41, Fond 502, Opis 1, Folder 307.

63. Compilation of the Zentralbauleitung for December 22, 1942, ibid., Roll 21, Fond 502, Opis 1, Folder 57.

64. Bauleitung to Kommandantur Auschwitz, November 12, 1941, ibid., Roll 21, Fond 502, Opis 1, Folder 54.

65. See the proposed budget of the Zentralbauleit-ung, January 9, 1942, referring to budget pro-posal of October 20, 1941, ibid., Roll 20, Fond 502, Opis 1, Folder 24.

66. Bischoff to Kammler, January 27, 1943, and Zentralbauleitung audit report, February 2, 1943, ibid., Roll 20, Fond 502, Opis 1, Folder 28.

67. Notation by Untersturmführer Dejaco (Zentral-bauleitung), December 4, 1942, ibid., Roll 20, Fond 502, Opis 1, Folder 26. Höss to WVHA-D, April 12 1943, ibid., Roll 36, Fond 502, Opis 1, Folder 260. Bischoff to Kammler, April 27, 1943, ibid., Roll 20, Fond 502, Opis 1, Folder 28.

68. Special Order (Sonderbefehl) by Höss, November 10, 1940, ibid., Roll 20, Fond 502, Opis 1, Folder 32. Bauleitung to Festungspionierstab 12 (Fortification Engineers Staff 12 of the army), November 28, 1941, asking for 7 metric tons of barbed wire for Birkenau, ibid., Roll 21, Fond 502, Opis 1, Folder 55. Work card, Zentralbauleitung, July 10, 1943, ibid., Roll 41, Fond 502, Opis 1, Folder 316.

69. See construction correspondence in ibid., Roll 41, Fond 502, Opis 1, Folders 306–14. Contractors were sometimes confused by these designations.

70. Bischoff to Rüstungskommando Weimar, referring to the Russians, November 12, 1941, ibid., Roll 41, Fond 502, Opis 1, Folder 314.

71. As of October 22, 1941, the Krematorium was to have five ovens, each with three retorts. See the letter of the Bauleitung to the Topf firm on that day, with specification of time limits for delivery of plans and parts. Facsimile of an original copy (*Abschrift*) without signature in Pressac, *Auschwitz: Technique and Operation*, 187. A brief letter outlining a plan for substituting 150,000 Jews for the missing Soviet prisoners was sent by Himmler to Glücks on January 25, 1942, NO-500. Lacking exact word, the Zentralbauleitung placed an order orally for only two ovens on February 12, 1942. Bischoff to Topf, March 2, 1942, facsimile in Pressac, *Auschwitz: Technique and Operation*, 191. After Kammler's visit on February 27, 1942, the oral order was rescinded and the original one was reinstated. Bischoff's letter of March 5, 1942, ibid. See also Bischoff to WVHA-C III (Stubaf. Wirtz), March 30, 1942, U.S. Holocaust Memorial Museum Archives Record Group 11.001 (Center for Historical Collections, Moscow), Roll 41, Fond 502, Opis 1, Folder 313. Pressac assumes from the blueprints that Kre-

matorium II was at first intended for the main camp. See his discussion and facsimiles of drawings in his two books.

72. See the blueprints in Pressac with his analyses, *Auschwitz: Technique and Operation*, 183–84, 267–329 (particularly 284–303), 355–78, and his *Les crematoires d'Auschwitz*, 46–86 (*passim*), with blueprints and photographs on glossy pages. See also his article (with Robert-Jan van Pelt), "Machinery of Mass Murder," in Gutman and Berenbaum, eds., *Anatomy of the Auschwitz Death Camp*, 199–201.

73. See photographs of Krematorium III under construction and completed in Pressac, *Auschwitz: Technique and Operation*, 333, 336–37, 339, and 342.

74. See facsimiles of drawings, ibid., 392–403. The earliest of these drawings, by a prisoner, is dated August 14, 1942.

75. Memorandum by UStuf. Ertl (Zentralbauleitung), August 21, 1942, U.S. Holocaust Memorial Museum Archives Record Group 11.001 (Center for Historical Collections, Moscow), Roll 41, Fond 502, Opis 1, Folder 313. Liquidation post (in Poznan) of SS Construction Group Russia Center to Zentralbauleitung, August 11, 1944, and other correspondence in the same folder. Prüfer (Topf firm) to Zentralbauleitung, July 7, 1943, in Pressac, *Auschwitz: Technique and Operation*, 382–83.

76. Start of construction dates in timetable of Zentralbauleitung, U.S. Holocaust Memorial Museum Archives Record Group 11.001 (Center for Historical Collections, Moscow), Roll 34, Fond 502, Opis 1, Folder 210. Completion dates in Zentralbauleitung file, facsimile in Jadwiga Bezwinska, cd., *Amidst a Nightmare of Crime* (Auschwitz, 1973), 55.

77. Pressac, *Les crématoires d'Auschwitz*, 140–42, and documents of the Zentralbauleitung in U.S. Holocaust Memorial Museum Archives Record Group 11.00] (Center for Historical Collections, Moscow), Fond 502, *passim*.

78. Memorandum signed by engineer Tomitschek of AEG and Unterscharfuhrer Swoboda of the Zentralbauleitung, January 29, 1943, U.S. Holo-

caust Memorial Museum Archives Record Group 11.001 (Center for Historical Collections, Moscow), Roll 20, Fond 502, Opis 1, Folder 26.

79. Memorandum by UStuf. Wolter (Zentralbauleitung), November 27, 1942, ibid., Roll 41, Fond 502, Opis 1, Folder 313.

80. Zentralbauleitung to DAW, January 13, 1943, NO-4466.

81. Zentralbauleitung to DAW, March 31, 1943, NO-4465.

82. Memorandum by UStuf. Kirschncck (Zentralbauleitung) on discussion with Topf representative Prüfer and Ing. Koehler, September 14, 1943, U.S. Holocaust Memorial Museum Archives Record Group 11.001 (Center for Historical Collections, Moscow), Roll 20, Fond 501, Opis 1, Folder 26. The inmate, *Oberkapo* August Brück, had arrived from Buchenwald. Czech, *Kalendarium*, 431n.

83. Pressac, *Auschwitz: Technique and Operation*, 386–90.

84. Bischoff to Kammler, January 27, 1943, U.S. Holocaust Memorial Museum Archives, Record Group 11.001 (Center for Historical Collections, Moscow), Roll 20, Fond 502, Opis 1, Folder 28.

85. Zentralbauleitung to Kammler, January 29, 1943, NO-4473.

86. Zentralbauleitung to Reichsbahndirektion (RBD) Oppeln/Dezernat 47, July 30, 1942, U.S. Holocaust Memorial Museum Archives Record Group 11.001 (Center for Historical Collections, Moscow), Roll 32, Fond 502, Opis 1, Folder 186.

87. Reichsbahn Operations Office (Betriebsamt) Kattowitz 4 (signed Reichsbahnrat Mannl) to Zentraibauleitung, and RBD Oppeln to Zentraibauleitung, May 1942, ibid.

88. See the correspondence of 1943, the approval of March 6, 1944, by the office of the Regierungspräsident in Kattowitz (signed Scholz), and RBD Oppeln to Standortverwaltung of Auschwitz, February 5, 1944, ibid.

89. Bischoff to Höss, April 7, 1943, ibid. A single prefabricated barracks was carried by five cars. Army Construction Office/Barracks (Heeresbauamt/Barracken) to Zentralbauleitung, Feb-

ruary 18, 1943, ibid., Roll 35, Fond 502, Opis 1, Folder 236.

90. Memorandum by Zentralbauleitung, January 18, 1943, ibid., Roll 32, Fond 502, Opis 1, Folder 184. Bischof F to WVHA C-HI, May 4, 1943, ibid., Folder 186.

91. Bischoff to WVHA C-III, May 4, 1943, ibid., Folder 186.

92. Höss to Stabler, April 19, 1943, and Bischoff repeating the call for urgency in a letter to the Regierungsprasident, September 11, 1943, ibid.

93. Discussion between Oberreichsbahnrat Stäbler, Oberreichsbahnrat Doll (Dezernat 32), Reichsbahnrat Sander, Amtmann Löw, and Bischoff, Untersturmführer Jänisch, and Unterscharführer Dr. Kuchendorf (Zentralbauleitung), March 27, 1943, ibid.

94. See the note of a meeting between Möckel, Bischoff, and Jänisch, with Oberreichsbahnrat Fehling and two of his assistants, July 12, 1943, ibid., Roll 20, Fond 501, Opis 1, Folder 26, and other correspondence in ibid., Roll 32, Fond 510, Opis 1, Folder 186.

95. Zentralbauleitung to Standortverwaltung, February 10, 1944, ibid., Roll 32 Fond 501, Opis 1, Folder 186.

96. Railway station to Zentralbauleitung, April 19, 1944, ibid. Road crossings, heavily used, were a remaining problem, because warning signs and beams were still missing. Memorandum by Bauleitung, May 30, 1944, ibid.

97. Characteristics of Zyklon described in undated report by Health Institute of Protektorat: "Directive for Utilization of Zyklon for Extermination of Vermin" (*Ungeziefervertilgung*), NI-9912. For the toxic properties of the gas, see also Steven I. Baskin, "Zyklon B" in Walter Laqucr, ed., *The Holocaust Encyclopedia* (New Haven, 2001), 716–19.

98. Lectures by Dr. Gerhard Peters and Heinrich Sossenheimer (gas experts), February 27, 1942, NI-9098.

99. Ibid.

Political Soldiers

EDWARD B. WESTERMANN

From *Hitler's Police Battalions*

Christmas Eve 1941 was particularly cold for those serving on the Eastern Front, but for the men of the Third Company of Police Battalion (PB) 322 the evening offered a chance to celebrate as a group indoors, away from the frigid weather. The men assembled around a Christmas tree, enjoying the soft light cast by the candles adorning the branches. A senior police sergeant began the festivities by reading a Christmas poem that he had composed expressly for this gathering of his comrades. After the poem was finished, the company commander, First Lieutenant Gerhard Riebel, moved forward to address the group.[1] The men probably expected their commander, a man who at one time had intentions of becoming a Protestant theologian, to offer a prayer or words of encouragement to bolster the spirits of a unit that had spent the last five months conducting operations in the East.[2] In fact, Riebel had prepared a "homily" for his men; however, his words did not highlight the virtues of charity, forgiveness, and redemption. Instead, he spoke of "the necessity of the battle between Germandom and Jewishdom" that justified the sacrifices made by men separated from their families in the "great contest between two [opposing] worldviews." Riebel's words apparently had the desired effect as the unit diarist made note of "the good spirits" of the men and the fact that the celebration lasted until the early hours of Christmas Day.[3]

Riebel's words concerning the battle between "Germandom" and "Jewishdom" were not simply the empty platitudes of a commander parroting the orders of his superiors or the propaganda slogans of the Third Reich. He and the men of his company had done much to translate words into action during their brief stay in the East. . . . They had participated in the full spectrum of security, pacification, atrocity, and reprisal actions conducted by German SS and police forces on the Eastern Front. Their victims included almost the entire range of National Socialist racial, political, and social enemies, including Jews, POWs, Communist functionaries, "vagrants," Russian civilians, partisans, and irregulars.[4] Senior SS leaders, including [Heinrich] Himmler and [Kurt] Daluege, had visited the battalion on several occasions to emphasize the importance of its efforts, and Daluege himself sent at least one congratulatory message to Police Regiment Center. Furthermore, the *Wehrmacht* leadership in the army rear areas became more and more reliant on police assistance in support of their pacification efforts and even directly requested the employment of police forces in actions aimed at Jews.[5] During Hitler's "crusade" in the Soviet Union, Himmler's police emerged as one of the primary instruments for the conduct of racial war, and the transformation of these men from civil servants into political soldiers offers a key insight into the nature of how men became murderers in support of an atavistic and malevolent campaign of destruction.

The Role and Function of Ideology

... The historian cannot afford to ignore or minimize the role of ideology in creating the environment that framed and even catalyzed the actions of individuals and specific organizations during the Nazi dictatorship. Ideology played a central role in the creation of the National Socialist racial state, which is not to say that every German embraced the most radical implications of the antisemitic and national chauvinistic images that confronted them daily in classrooms, workplaces, and theaters or in the print media or over the airwaves.[6]

In earlier studies tracing the effect of Nazi ideology, historians have examined the actions and motivations of a diverse array of organizations. For example, Christopher Browning found that Foreign Office personnel "were primarily motivated by considerations of careerism, not racial ideology or fanatical and blind obedience to higher authority" in the pursuit of "*Judenpolitik*."[7] Similarly, Peter Hayes highlighted "amoral pragmatism and professionalism," not ideology, as the motive force guiding the actions of executives at IG Farben as German industry made its own contribution to the annihilation of the European Jews.[8] In a further example, according to Alfred Mierzejewski, as trains rolled toward Auschwitz, the leadership and operators of the German railway were motivated by professional competence and an "indifference" to the fate of the Jews trapped within *Reichsbahn* freight cars.[9]

If one accepts the premise that diplomats, businessmen, and railway personnel remained relatively immune to the poisonous influence of National Socialist ideology, can the same be said of the organizations of state control? In his work examining the motivations of the Security Police, Yaacov Lozowick reached the conclusion that these men were "a group of people completely aware of what they were doing, people with high ideological motivation, people of initiative and dexterity who contributed far beyond what was necessary. . . . [T]hey clearly understood that their deeds were not positive except in the value system of the Third Reich. They hated Jews and thought that getting rid of them would be to Germany's good."[10] Lozowick's contention is highly reminiscent of the explanation offered by Rudolf Höss, the commandant of the Auschwitz death camp, that the brutality of the ss concentration camp guards resulted from a "hate indoctrination" passed along from the senior leadership to the rank and file, a doctrine that was part and parcel of the National Socialist worldview.[11] Similarly, Michael Thad Allen's work on midlevel ss bureaucrats controlling the ss system of slave labor presents a picture of men with ideological commitment and not mechanical, amoral technocrats focused merely on the task at hand.[12]

Explaining the Behavior of the Uniformed Police

The recognition of the large-scale role of the Uniformed Police in the conduct of genocide has led to several competing explanations concerning the reasons why the men of the police battalions participated in the prosecution of racial war. In his innovative study of the activities of Reserve PB 101 in Poland, Christopher Browning paints a convincing portrait of "ordinary men" largely motivated by mundane concerns for acceptance and conformity within a larger group. According to Browning, the policemen of PB 101 were guided, not by ideological hatred or fanatical adherence to National Socialism, but by respect and deference to authority, concern for career advancement, and peer group pressure.[13] In contrast, the political scientist Daniel Goldhagen catalyzed an academic furor with the publication of *Hitler's Willing Executioners*. Although the actions of the police battalions were not the main focus of his work, Goldhagen devoted considerable attention to them, concluding: "The study of police battalions, finally, yields two fundamental facts: First, ordinary Germans easily became genocidal killers. Second, they did so even though they did not have to." For Goldhagen, what prepared German policemen for genocide was neither institutional affiliation nor professional background and experience but simply German culture itself with its existing atmosphere of "eliminationist antisemitism."[14] While Browning's explanation of police behavior minimizes the effect of ideology and indoctrination within the police, Goldhagen's model elevates ideology as the *sine qua non* of German social behavior.

More recently, the work of the German historian Klaus-Michael Mallmann has provided important insights into the activities and motivations of the Uniformed Police.[15] Likewise, Jürgen Matthäus examined the effects of SS indoctrination efforts on the Uniformed Police with a specific focus on the portrayal of the "Jewish question" in SS and police literature. Matthäus recognized the importance of ideological indoctrination, especially within the circles of the senior SS leadership, and detailed the initiatives and themes pursued by the leadership as well as the practical effect of organized entertainment activities and professional and social get-togethers or "fellowship evenings" (*Kameradschaftsabende*) on police behavior. He argues that these efforts were "from the beginning directed at the internalization of an attitude; an attitude with regard to the methods to be used in the Jewish question that remained flexible and situational allowing for different practices [in application]."[16] Matthäus is correct in looking for the impulse for genocide among the ideological initia-

tives pursued by Himmler and the senior SS and police leadership; however, the ambition of these men extended beyond the conditioning of the police as convinced antisemites. Instead, Himmler, Daluege, and the HSSPFs sought to create an organizational culture within the police corps that glorified the concept of uniquely defined military identity married with the precepts of an SS ethic that embraced National Socialist racial philosophy and stressed the special obligations of membership in an exclusive and hallowed order. In fact, it was the acceptance by the Uniformed Police of this martial attitude in conjunction with Nazi racial ideology that resulted in the emergence of a police apparatus more suitable for the conduct of war and atrocity than public service.

Creating an Organizational Culture

. . . Edgar H. Schein's pioneering work on organizational culture provides the foundation for relating this theoretical construct to the activities of the German Uniformed Police. Schein defines organizational culture as the "basic assumptions and beliefs that are shared by members of an organization, that operate unconsciously, and that define in a basic 'taken for granted' fashion an organization's view of itself and its environment."[17] In short, organizational culture sets the boundaries for accepted behavior, establishes institutional goals, and defines the standards of group membership.

The culture of an organization is formed and defined by the values, rituals, climate, and patterns of behavior of the organization's members; it is, however leadership, according to Schein, that "embeds and transmits" culture to the organization's members and acts as the key mechanism in the creation of an institutional identity.[18] Contemporary research also demonstrates the key role of leadership in defining the organizational culture of law enforcement agencies. One study concerning police organizations described leadership as the glue holding all parts of the organization together through the propagation of a shared vision.[19] And, in fact, the leadership of the Uniformed Police played a key role in establishing an organizational climate within the police that established the precepts of National Socialist racial thought as the institutional standard.

The Facilitators of Genocide

Without a doubt, Heinrich Himmler and Kurt Daluege shared a vision of the police and expended substantial effort in promulgating this vision among the members of the organization. In the prewar years, and, especially, as Hitler embarked on his quest for an empire in the East, the Uniformed Police battalions became a special target of Himmler's and Daluege's efforts and a ready instrument for the conduct of annihilation. Indeed, two dominant characteristics within the organizational culture of the police offer strong evidence for explaining the actions of the police battalions on the Eastern Front.

First, the "militarization" of the police constituted a central objective of the Uniformed Police leadership from the initial National Socialist "seizure of power" until the ultimate collapse of Hitler's Thousand-Year Reich. The concept of militarization was not simply limited to the establishment of a hierarchical police organization with military capabilities but also encompassed a specific worldview (*Weltanschauung*) that married the concept of military duty with absolute obedience and the vision of a "higher purpose." Second, the police leadership increasingly pursued efforts to inculcate the "police soldier" with National Socialist values by "merging" (*verschmelzen*) the police in a psychological and physical sense with the ss. It is, of course, impossible, when dealing with a large organization, to achieve a homogeneous and unified body all members of which think and act completely alike in consonance with a shared corporate mind-set. However, it is equally clear that the dominant organizational culture of a particular institution plays a vital role in establishing the parameters of both desired and accepted behavior to guide the actions of individuals. Likewise, the dual initiatives of militarization and the merging of the police with the ss go far to explain the manner in which individual policemen and the police battalions were shaped into instruments of annihilation.

The ss and Police Complex

After the National Socialist seizure of power, Hitler and his paladins recognized the importance of gaining control of the Uniformed and Political Police forces of the independent state governments (*Länder*). Heinrich Himmler's plans for creating a national police force or "*Reichspolizei*" included, not only the men of the police, but also a fusion of state and party organizations, specifically the merging of the organizations of the ss with the police.[20]

The creation of the Security Police Main Office and the Uniformed Police Main Office in June 1936 under the command of Reinhard Heydrich and Kurt Daluege, respectively, went far toward achieving both goals.[21] The former encompassed the two branches of the Security Police, the Criminal Police and the secret state police or Gestapo, as well as the Party's intelligence branch, the Security Service. The Criminal Police (*Kriminalpolizei*) consisted of the Reich's plainclothes detective forces charged with the investigation of "nonpolitical" crimes. In contrast, the Gestapo investigated "political" crimes, including charges of treason, subversion, and, significantly, those dealing with the racial and political enemies of the Third Reich.

The Security Service (SD) constituted the final element of the Security Police Main Office. Originally created as an intelligence-gathering network to support Party activities, the SD emerged as a key organization in the prosecution of Nazi racial policy in the occupied East, including the formation of the notorious *Einsatzgruppen*.[22]

The Uniformed Police Main Office under Kurt Daluege consisted of three branches of the police, including the *Schutzpolizei* (lit. "Protection Police"), the *Gendarmerie*, and the *Gemeindepolizei* (Community Police). The *Schutzpolizei* essentially resembled the beat cops of contemporary American society and were responsible for everyday law enforcement activities. The *Gendarmerie*, established on the French model in the first decade of the nineteenth century, conducted police duties in the countryside and in communities with fewer than two thousand inhabitants.[23] Finally, the men of the *Gemeindepolizei* with their motley collection of uniforms and rank insignia worked for the mayor in small towns and villages.[24]

In contrast to the police forces of the Reich, the SS under Himmler represented the soldiers of the Party. Established originally as an elite force charged with protecting Hitler, the black corps under Himmler emerged as the "ideological vanguard" of the National Socialist movement "invested with the responsibility for ensuring the racial renewal of the nation."[25] At the outbreak of World War II, the SS empire included the General SS (*Allgemeine-SS*), the SS Special Duty Troops (*SS-Verfügungstruppe* or SS-VT), and the SS Death's Head units (*SS-Totenkopfverbände*). The General SS provided the manpower base for the creation of the militarized SS units, including the SS-VT and the SS Death's Head formations. In turn, the garrisoned units of the SS-VT constituted the backbone of the *Waffen-SS* established in November 1939, while the Death's Head formations became

infamous for their duties as the administrators and guards of the concentration camps.[26]

Hitler's selection on June 17, 1936, of Himmler to head this SS and police empire provided evidence of the Führer's desire to see the police merged with the "Party's soldiers," the SS, in both an organizational and a philosophical sense.[27] At the official ceremony to mark Himmler's appointment, Daluege made exactly this point by exclaiming: "We can be proud that at this moment a dream is coming true, something I dreamed of as an SS Leader before the [National Socialist] revolution, that is, the unification of the police of the movement [the SS] with the police of the state in the person of Reich Leader of the SS Himmler."[28] For his part, Himmler made his expectations for the police absolutely clear:

> We are a land in the heart of Europe, surrounded by open borders, surrounded in a world that is becoming more and more Bolshevized in which the Jew in his worst form increasingly takes control through the all-destructive tyranny of Bolshevism. . . . We have to expect that this battle will be a battle of the generations, the primeval contest between men and subhumans [that] in its contemporary form is the battle of the Aryan peoples against Jewry and its organizational manifestation, Bolshevism.[29]

Near the end of his speech, Himmler noted that he would need the loyalty and the commitment to duty of each individual within the "soldierly corps" (*soldatisches Korps*) of the police to achieve his vision.

Without doubt, Himmler intended to use his authority to set the tone and direction of the unified Reich-wide police force. In September 1936, the desire to inculcate a stronger military character among the police resulted in an order for "the official basic and continued professional training" of the entire German police to be based on a "military foundation."[30] In line with the second objective of the Nazi conversion strategy, Daluege embraced the "merging" of the SS and the police, declaring: "It can be only a question of time before the entire police coalesces with the SS corps into a permanent unit."[31]

Not only did Himmler's words present his expectations of the police under his command, but they also created an organizational culture within the police in which antisemitism and anti-Bolshevism emerged as institutional norms. It is clear that not every policeman embraced the extreme implications of Himmler's rhetoric, but it is equally clear that the *Reichsführer's* vision established an atmosphere promoting the development of a distinct institutional mind-set, one that saw the police as the ideal of a soldierly corps locked in an apocalyptic battle with "Jewish-Bolshevism." Himmler's efforts found similar expression in what Claudia Koonz has described as the "Nazi conscience" or a "secular ethos that extended reciprocity only to members of the Aryan community."[32] If the "Nazi conscience" established the principles of National Socialist "theology," then Himmler's SS and policemen acted as the protectors and guarantors of the new order, charged with the task of safeguarding and enforcing the dogma of racial superiority.

The men of the Uniformed Police experienced the same hate indoctrination as their counterparts in the Security Police and the SD did, and they did not prove immune to its effects. This process rapidly accelerated after June 1936 with Himmler's exercise of overlapping authority over the SS, the Security Police, and the Uniformed Police. From this point on, Himmler's control of all the institutions of internal state control guaranteed that all three would exist in a symbiotic relationship in which the Reich leader's goal of merging the

SS with the police progressed in a physical and philosophical sense prior to 1939 and accelerated during the war years.

In fact, the entire SS and police complex existed as an interconnected and self-reflexive organization in which the initiatives taken by one affected the identity, attitudes, and actions of the whole. The patterns of influence in the SS and police complex operated in much the same way as the concentric rings produced by dropping a pebble into body of water. Initiatives pursued by Himmler with respect to the SS were bound to influence the behavior and actions of the Security and Uniformed Police through the mechanism of an intertwined leadership structure united in the persons of the HSSPFs as well as in the ranks of policemen holding SS membership. Likewise, the extensive collaboration between the Security Police and the Uniformed Police provided both an avenue for cooperation and an expression of an existing symbiotic relationship between the policemen in uniform and their plainclothes counterparts in the Gestapo, the Criminal Police, and the SD.

Ideology and Annihilation

In the prewar period, both Himmler and Daluege expended great effort to instill the Uniformed Police with a martial attitude and an SS ethic, and they brought this message to the police battalions during their repeated visits to the Eastern Front in 1941 in which they tasked these formations with the final annihilation of "Jewish-Bolshevism." The expression of antisemitism took several forms within the police, from the virulent to the taken for granted. In the case of the former, the police captain Erich Mehr, a company commander in Reserve PB 61, described by men in his unit after the war as a "fanatical Jew-hater," took delight in abusing Jews with his bayonet and randomly shooting at them in the Warsaw ghetto. Mehr told one of his platoon leaders: "The Führer said that the Jews must be exterminated, and I intend to see to it that the Jews will be exterminated."[33] In the case of the latter, another policeman, Kurt Mobius, provided an apt summary of the mindset of many of his colleagues during the war. Mobius reflected: "We police went by the phrase, 'Whatever serves the state is right, whatever harms the state is wrong.' . . . Although I am aware that it is the duty of the police to protect the innocent, I was at the time convinced that the Jewish people were not innocent but guilty." He continued: "I believed all the propaganda that Jews were criminals and subhuman. . . . The thought that one should oppose or evade the order to take part in the extermination of Jews never entered my head either."[34] This latter view was not unique or limited to the police. In her autobiography of life as a young woman in the Third Reich, Melita Maschmann recalled similarly taking for granted the depiction of Jews as the natural enemy of the Germans, a view that she held in spite of her close friendship with a Jewish girl.[35]

The words of Mehr and Mobius present two expressions of antisemitism within the police. Despite the degree of virulence separating the two, the practical manifestations of both were, in fact, the same, a belief in the necessity for the murder of Jews. Both men were, in fact, members of an institution whose leadership promoted an organizational culture that established antisemitism and anti-Bolshevism as organizational norms, a culture that extended the boundaries of desired and acceptable behavior within the ranks of the police, eventually facilitating countless acts of murder and atrocity throughout the occupied territories.

The effectiveness of these efforts can be seen in part in the responses of several of PB 322's members during a postwar criminal investigation into the unit's activities in Russia. One member of the battalion, Erich Holtzmeier (a pseudonym), provided the following response regarding the execution of defenseless persons: "Why the Jews? Because it was preached to us at every instructional period that one needed to exterminate this race. They [the Jews] were responsible for all the evil in the world and for the war." Concerning the Jews, another policeman from the unit stated: "Jews were in any event free game, and they were shot without mercy and without justification or the need to provide one."[36]

The open and frank statements of these policemen are somewhat unusual in the mass of postwar testimonies, in which, in the face of criminal prosecution, few men acknowledged that their units had conducted actions of atrocity and reprisal and even fewer admitted that they participated in these acts. The importance of these statements should not be minimized as they provide valuable insights into the mentality of the policemen and the unstated views and opinions of many of their colleagues both during their service and, in some cases, long after the end of the Second World War.

In addition to postwar testimony, policemen also gave vent to their feelings of antisemitism and anti-Bolshevism during their service in the East. For example, a policeman serving with a police regiment in Hungary in 1944 wrote a letter back to his colleagues in Flensburg contrasting the appearance of the Hungarian Jews with the Orthodox Jews (*Talmudjuden*) of the ghettos of the East. The writer noted his astonishment at the "marked Nordic characteristics" of the Hungarian Jews, an appearance that demonstrated the adaptability of these "parasites of humanity."[37] . . .

The manifestation of these prejudices also found expression in the personal and professional correspondence of the police. In his infamous speech to SS and Party leaders in October

1943, Himmler remarked: "Antisemitism is exactly the same as delousing. Getting rid of lice is not a question of ideology, it is a matter of cleanliness. In just the same way antisemitism for us has not been a question of ideology but a matter of cleanliness."[38] The metaphoric equation of Jews with filth, vermin, and disease also found expression in German theaters, where, in Fritz Hippler's *The Eternal Jew*, hordes of rats streaming across the movie screen symbolized the danger posed by Jews to the *Volk*.[39] The use of the terms *Pest* (plague) and *Seuche* (epidemic) within the police reports to describe both Jews and Bolshevists offers but one example. In this case, terms such as *ausrotten* (extermination) and *vernichten* (annihilation), used when the subject was the *Kampf* (combat) against a Jewish or Bolshevist *Pest* (pestilence), provided the perfect linguistic complement to this biologically prescribed threat.[40] . . .

Instruments for Annihilation

The policemen of PB 322 were not unique in training or composition from the majority of the police battalions that served in the occupied territories. PB 322 was one of twenty-four police battalions participating in the initial phase of the assault against the Soviet Union, including a battalion that had been split up in order to support the *Einsatzgruppen*.[41] The police battalions that entered the Soviet Union in the summer of 1941 were, for the most part, led by officers and senior enlisted men from the ranks of career policemen[42]—a group of men whose backgrounds, demographics, and training, as well as the organizational culture within the police, had prepared them for a war of extermination in the East.

Of the nine police battalions placed directly at the disposal of the HSSPFs during the invasion of the Soviet Union, seven were regular battal-

ions with numerical designations in the 300s. The enlisted ranks of these seven battalions consisted in large part of a pool of twenty thousand recruits mobilized from the 1909–1912 year groups. For example, the majority of the rank and file of PB 307 came from these year groups.[43] Likewise, the vast majority of the men of PB 310, another police battalion that cut a bloody path through the Soviet Union in 1942, came from the 1905–1915 year groups.[44] In his study of Party membership, Michael Kater found that National Socialism held its "greatest attraction" for those born between 1905 and 1912, precisely the age groups from which the 300-level battalions were drawn.[45] The relative youth of these policemen contrasts sharply with the age of the members of PB 101, who were, on average, thirty-nine years old.[46] Still, not all reserve police battalions followed this pattern, as the average age of thirty-one for the members of PB 61 demonstrates.[47] In fact, of the approximately one hundred police battalions mobilized during the Nazi dictatorship, only twenty came from the ranks of overage reservists.[48] . . .

The Uniformed Police formations and policemen who served in the occupied Eastern territories during World War II embarked on a premeditated campaign of annihilation sanctioned from the highest levels of political, civil, and military leadership. The very structure and premise on which Hitler's "racial state" rested promoted the creation of an apocalyptic mind-set in which "toughness and ruthlessness" became the acceptable and preferred standard for dealing with conquered populations and especially the European Jews. In turn, the police accepted their murderous mission as a "necessary evil" in the course of creating a German empire.[49] In this sense, Himmler's ss and policemen existed in an organizational environment that created a "new moral order," one in which principles of exclusion and enmity such as antisemitism and anti-Bolshevism reigned supreme.[50]

Killing Eye to Eye

In his study of Police Battalion (PB) 101, Christopher Browning discussed the experiment by Stanley Milgram concerning the willingness of "naive volunteer subjects" to inflict pain on fellow human beings when given orders from an "authority figure" and placed in a position of power over the "victim."[51] Certainly, Browning is correct in using this model to point out the effect of authority figures and disparate power relationships in influencing human behavior. However, does Milgram's model then account for the behavior of German policemen?

. . . There are important differences between the two situations. First, the policemen were not naive volunteers but, in most cases, and especially within the officer corps and senior enlisted ranks, experienced professionals whose choice of law enforcement as a career routinely faced them with hostile situations and violent behavior. Second, the men of the police generally knew beforehand the murderous nature of the actions that they were about to undertake. While some former policemen contended that the first killing may have come as a surprise, the many subsequent actions certainly did not. Likewise, the fact that the killings became an open secret within the units and that some units passed around photographs of killings to new arrivals also calls into question the supposed lack of cognizance of these men as they loaded onto trucks and drove to a local Jewish ghetto, prison, or nearby town.[52] Admittedly, some men experienced a period of desensitization, but this period often proved to be very short. Third, these men routinely killed their victims while standing next to them and after looking into their eyes. The standard pro-cedure for mass killings at the side of an open pit meant that the uniforms and boots of the shooters literally became covered with the blood and body matter of their victims. Stated another way, how much compliance would Milgram have received if his naive volunteers had been asked to kill up close and for an extended period of time? As Milgram found, . . . as the level of active participation and physical contact required between the "perpetrator" and the "victim" increased, so did the refusal of the former to administer punishment to the latter.[53]

The purpose of the preceding discussion is not to discount the influence of authority figures completely. However, Milgram's model does not explain the numerous examples of gendarmes serving at isolated outposts in the East who on their own initiative routinely and enthusiastically killed even when they had a choice not to. Nor does it explain the behavior of men like Helmuth Palm, whose suggestions for operations were intended to increase the number of murdered, all in accordance with the motto: "One Pole or Russian too many is better than one too few." . . .

Proving the Negative

Not every man was able to withstand the psychological strain of repeatedly being involved in murder, a fact recognized by Himmler and Daluege. In the end, policemen always had the choice of refusing to participate in murder.[54] At worst, this refusal led to some further additional duty, possibly verbal abuse by an officer, and snide comments from one's colleagues. It did not, however, carry with it the danger of execution or incarceration, as so many policemen claimed during postwar investigations. There is not a single documented case of a policeman being executed as a result of refusing to kill Jews in cold blood.[55] Likewise, of the literally millions of pages of documents recovered from Himmler's and Daluege's headquarters, there is not one mention of either man discussing a problem within the ranks of the police concerning a refusal to murder or an inability to find policemen willing to kill.[56] This is significant, especially when one considers Himmler's penchant for becoming involved in any problem, great or small, within his ss and police empire, including such mundane issues as the prevention of sexually transmitted diseases.[57] Given the attention that Himmler devoted to a marriage application rejected because the policeman's ethnic German fiancée remained "under the sway" of Polish influence, certainly policemen objecting to murder or refusing to kill would have received his attention had the issue been of any concern.[58] In the end, lack of evidence is not proof that it does not exist; it is, however, worth noting its implications for the general course of police behavior.

Ideology and Antisemitism

Despite its best efforts, the ss and police leadership was unable to establish a uniform and homogenous body of members; however, it did succeed in creating an organizational culture within the police, one built on the pillars of antisemitism and anti-Bolshevism, that progressively broadened the boundaries of acceptable and desired behavior. Himmler's rant against the danger posed by Jewish-Bolshevism during the ceremony appointing him as chief of the Police and Daluege's "statistical evidence" tying the Jews to the majority of crimes committed in Germany offer but two examples. Likewise, a directive preventing policemen from staying in a Berlin hotel because it was frequented by Jews or the prohibition on incarcerating Latvians with Jews on "ideological and racial political grounds" offer two seemingly minor but telling examples of the practical manifestations of this culture beyond the conduct of mass killings.[59]

Equipped with a new conception of crime and a vision of their role in ensuring the health of the peoples' community, the police emerged as an instrument par excellence for the conduct of murder and atrocity.... Writing a letter home in early July 1941, a member of Reserve Police Battalion 105 warned: "The Jews are free game.... One can only give the Jews some well intentioned advice: Bring no more children into the world. They no longer have a future."[60] Three years later, another policeman wrote to his hometown police commander in Oldenburg discussing the pleasure that he and his colleagues received from getting news from their old precinct. This policeman then boasted: "The comrades Sgt. Schulze, Wilken, and Sgt. of the Reserves Wemken and Stöver were very active in the cleansing of Hungary of the Jews. Riding the trains for days on end with the purpose of guarding the transports was the task and really did a number on my waistline [*hat stark am Fett gezehrt*]. But here we still have good provisions in the form of bacon, butter, and eggs." He then remarked: "Comrade Sergeant Wiemers is a platoon leader and with comrades Janacek, Kühl, Müller K., Uhlenhut, Bohle, Eisenhauer, and Osterthun is currently in the Carpathians for a special mission. I myself was attached to a special unit [*Sondereinsatzkommando*] of the sd and have traveled throughout most of Hungary with this unit."[61] Here again we see a man capable of discussing the mass murder of the Hungarian Jews and his waistline in the same paragraph. This matter-of-fact approach to genocide— exemplified, as previously seen, by men like Police Sergeant Helmuth Schmidt, the "Terror of Lemberg," who "could shoot a Jew in the head while eating a sandwich"—is perhaps, the most striking aspect uncovered by this research.[62] ...

"Ideological Soldiers" or "Ordinary Men"?

Historians should rightly be wary of treating the complexities of human motivation reductively and finding one single explanation so monstrously beyond human comprehension. However, to argue that organizational culture and the ideology underpinning it provided the environment that facilitated annihilation is not to paint the world of the police in simplistic Manichaen terms. Instead, it is to recognize that the impetus for genocide came from within an organization that established and promoted its own values, beliefs, and standards for behavior, that created an environment in which persecution, exploitation, and murder became both acceptable and desirable attributes of a police corps charged with preserving the German *Volk* and locked in an apocalyptic battle against the internal and external enemies of the Reich. In a January 1943 speech commemorating the tenth year of National Socialist rule, Daluege boasted of Himmler's success in building a "police combat troop of the National Socialist movement." He then exclaimed: "For Adolf Hitler, this corps of the ss and the police represents his struggle for a greater Germany, Europe, and the world. Its [the corps'] task is the annihilation of the eternal enemies of all folkish [*völkisch*] and racially conscious nations."[63] If annihilation was the goal then the men of the Uniformed Police more than met their quota—the ultimate testament to Himmler's and Daluege's efforts to create a corps of "political soldiers."

NOTES

1. "Auswärtiger Einsatz (War Diary of the Third Company of Police Battalion 322, December 24, 1941]," RG 48.004M, reel 2, frame 200851, U.S. Holocaust Memorial Museum Archive (hereafter USHMMA).

2. Heiner Lichtenstein, *Himmlers grüne Heifer: Die Schutz-und Ordnungspolizei im "Dritten Reich"* (Cologne: Bund, 1990), 61.

3. "Auswärtiger Einsatz [War Diary of the Third Company of Police Battalion 322, December 24, 1941]," RG 48.004M, reel 2, frames 200851–200852, USHMMA.

4. "III./Pol/Rgt.Mitte, Betrifft: Judenaktion der 8. Kompanie in Krassnopolje am 22.10.1941 [October 26, 1941]," RG 48.004M, reel 2, frames 201328–201335, USHMMA.

5. War Diary of Police Battalion 322 [October 16–17 and 22, 1941] RG 48.004M, reel 2, frames 200997 and 2,00100, USHMMA.

6. See Robert Gellately, *Backing Hitler: Consent and Coercion in Nazi Germany* (New York: Oxford University Press, 2001); and Gregory Wegner, *Anti-Semitism and Schooling under the Third Reich* (New York: Routledge Falmer, 2002). For one man's view of this issue, see Victor Klemperer, *I Will Bear Witness: A Diary of the Nazi Years, 1933–1941* (New York: Random House, 1998), and *I Will Bear Witness: A Diary of the Nazi Years, 1942–1945* (New York: Random House, 1999).

7. Christopher R. Browning, *The Final Solution and the German Foreign Office: A Study of Referat D III of Abteilung Deutschland, 1940–43* (New York: Holmes & Meier, 1978), 185.

8. Peter Hayes, *Industry and Ideology: IG Farben and the Nazi Era* (Cambridge: Cambridge University Press, 2001), xxvi.

9. Alfred Mierzejewski, "A Public Enterprise in the Service of Mass Murder: The Deutsche Reichsbahn and the Holocaust," *Holocaust and Genocide Studies* 15 (spring 2001): 41.

10. Yaacov Lozowick, *Hitler's Bureaucrats: The Nazi Security Police and the Banality of Evil* (London: Continuum, 2000), 8.

11. Rudolf Höss, *Commandant of Auschwitz: The Autobiography of Rudolf Höss* (Cleveland: World, 1959), 85.

12. Michael Thad Allen, *The Business of Genocide: The ss, Slave Labor, and the Concentration Camps* (Chapel Hill: University of North Carolina Press, 2002).

13. See Christopher R. Browning, *Ordinary Men: Reserve Police Battalion 101 and the Final Solution in Poland* (New York: Harper Collins, 1992).

14. Daniel J. Goldhagen, *Hitler's Willing Executioners: Ordinary Germans and the Holocaust* (New York: Knopf, 1996), 277, 416. A more thoughtful examination of this issue is provided by Jürgen Matthäus, "Ausbildungsziel Judenmord? Zum Stellenwert der 'weltanschaulichen Erziehung' von SS und Polizei im Rahmen der 'Endlösung,'" *Zeitschrift für Geschichtswissenschaft* 47 (1999): 673–99.

15. See, e.g., Klaus-Michael Mallmann, "Der qualitative Sprung im Vernichtungsprozeß: Das Massaker von Kamenez-Podolsk Ende August 1941," *Jahrbuch für Antisemitismusforschung* 10 (2001): 241, and ". . . Mißgeburten, die nicht auf diese Welt gehören': Die deutsche Ordnungspolizei in Polen, 1939–1941," in *Genesis des Genozids: Polen, 1939–1941*, ed. Klaus-Michael Mallmann and Bogdan Musial (Darmstadt: Wissenschaftliche Buchgesellschaft, 2004), 71–89; and Klaus-Michael Mallmann, Volker Rieß, and Wolfram Pyta, eds., *Deutscher Osten, 1939–1945: Der Weltanschauungskrieg in Photos und Texten* (Darmstadt: Wissenschaftliche Buchgesellschaft, 2003).

16. Jürgen Matthäus, Konrad Kwiet, Jürgen Förster, and Richard Breitman, *Ausbildungsziel Judenmord? "Weltanschauliche Erziehung" von SS, Polizei und Waffen-SS im Rahmen der "Endlösung"* (Frankfurt a.M.: Fischer Taschenbuch, 2003), 85.

17. Edgar H. Schein, *Organizational Culture and Leadership* (San Francisco: Jossey-Bass, 1985), 6.

18. Ibid., 223–43.

19. Stephen J. Harrison, "Police Organizational Culture: Using Ingrained Values to Build Positive Organizational Improvement," *Public Administration and Management: An Interactive Journal* 3, no. 2 (1998), http://www.pamij.com/harrison.html (accessed October 27, 2004).

20. International Military Tribunal (hereafter IMT), *Trials of the Major War Criminals before the International Military Tribunal*, vol. 29 (Nuremberg: Secretariat of the Military Tribunal, 1948), 227–28.

21. "Geschäftsverteilimg u. Geschäftsverkehr d. Chefs der Deutschen Polizei im Reichsministerium des Innern, RdErl. des RFSSuChdDtPol. im RMdI v. 26.6.1936, O/S Nr. 3/36 [June 26, 1936]," T580, reel 95, NARA.

22. For a detailed description of the activities of the Security Police and SD, see George C. Browder, *Foundations of the Nazi Police State: The Formation of SIPO and SD* (Lexington: University Press of Kentucky, 1990); and Michael Wildt, *Generation des Unbedingten: Das Führungskorps des Reichssicherheitshauptamtes* (Hamburg: Hamburger Edition, 2003).

23. Friederich Wilhelm, *Die Polizei im NS-Staat: Die Geschichte ihrer Organisation im Überblick* (Paderborn: Ferdinand Schoningh, 1997), 13–14, 85–87.

24. "Entwurf eines am 27. April 1939 vor dem Deutschen Gemeindetag zu haltenden Vortrages des Reichsführers SS und Chef der Deutschen Polizei über die Gemeindepolizei und das Feuerlöschwesens [April 1939]," T580, reel 37, NARA. See also "Disposition zum Vortrag General Daluege, Die Ordnungspolizei," T580, reel 216, file 5, NARA; and "Der Chef der Ordnungspolizei [September 5, 1939]," T580, reel 96, NARA.

25. Tom Segev, *Soldiers of Evil: The Commandants of the Nazi Concentration Camps* (New York: McGraw-Hill, 1987), 73. See also Robert Lewis Koehl, *The Black Corps: The Structure and Power Struggles of the Nazi SS* (Madison: University of Wisconsin Press, 1983), 48.

26. Bernd Wegner, *Hitlers politische Soldaten: Die Waffen-SS, 1933–1945*, 4th ed. (Paderborn: Ferdinand Schoningh, 1982), 79. See also Segev, *Soldiers of Evil*, 95–96; and Charles W. Sydnor Jr., *Soldiers of Destruction: The SS Death's Head Division, 1933–1945* (Princeton NJ: Princeton University Press, 1977). The Death's Head units also provided combat formations for duty at the front as part of the *Waffen-SS*.

27. Max Domarus, ed., *Hitler: Reden und Proklamationen, 1932–1945*, 2 vols. (Wiesbaden: R. Lowit, 1973), 1: 881. Hitler admitted this desire in a directive dealing with the SS dated August 17, 1938.

28. Speech by Kurt Daluege during the state ceremony naming Heinrich Himmler as chief of the German police [June 18, 1936], T580, reel 216, file 3, National Archives and Records Administration (hereafter NARA).

29. Speech by Heinrich Himmler during the state ceremony naming him as chief of the German police [June 18, 1936], T580, reel 216, file 3, NARA.

30. Gerd Rühle, *Das Dritte Reich: Dokumentarische Darstellung des Aufbaues der Nation, das vierte Jahr* (Berlin: Hummelverlag, 1937), 272.

31. "Der Weg der Ordnungspolizei von SS-Gruppenführer, General der Polizei, Kurt Daluege [January 23, 1939]," T580, reel 216, file 5, NARA.

32. Claudia Koonz, *The Nazi Conscience* (Cambridge MA: Harvard University Press, 2003), 6.

33. Stefan Klemp, *Freispruch für das "Mord-Bataillon": Die NS-Ordnungspolizei und die Nachkriegsjustiz* (Minister: Lit Verlag, 1998), 23–24.

34. Ernst Klee, Willi Dreßen, and Volker Rieß, eds., *"The Good Old Days": The Holocaust as Seen by Its Perpetrators and Bystanders* (New York: Free Press, 1991), 220–21. Testimony given by Möbius in 1961.

35. Melita Maschmann, *Fazit: Kein Rechtfertigungsversuch* (Stuttgart: Deutsche Verlags-Anstalt, 1963), 61.

36. Mallmann, Rieß, and Pyta, eds., *Deutscher Osten*, 137.

37. Stephan Linck, "'. . . schon allein wegen des Schmutzes . . .' Wie Polizisten über ihren Einsatz schreiben: Das Mitteilungsblatt der Schutzpolizei Flensburg, 1944/45," *Archiv für Polizeigeschichte* 9 (1998): 52.

38. IMT, *Trials of the Major War Criminals before the International Military Tribunal*, vol. 22 (Nuremberg: Secretariat of the Military Tribunal, 1948), 232.

39. Rolf Giesen, *Nazi Propaganda Films: A History and Filmography* (Jefferson NC: McFarland, 2003), 137–39.

40. "Der Kominandeur der Gendarmerie Shitomir, Kommandobefehl Nr. 27/43 [April 1 2, 1943]," RG 53.002M, fond 658, reel 5, file 3, USHMMA.

41. "Rede des Chefs der Ordnungspolizei bei der SS-Führertagung des RFSS, Der Winterkampf der Ordnungspolizei im Osten" (captured German documents microfilmed at the Berlin Document Center), T580, reel 217, file 6, NARA. See also "Der Chef der Ordnungspolizei, Vortrag über den Kräfte-und Kriegseinsatz der Ordnungspolizei im Jahre 1941," T580, reel 96, NARA.

42. Peter Longerich, *Politik der Vernichtung: Eine Gesamtdarstellung der nationalsozialistischen Judenverfolgung* (Munich: Piper, 1998), 306–7, 662.

43. Klaus-Michael Mallmann, "Der Einstieg in den Genozid: Das Lübecker Polizeibataillon 307 und das Massaker in Brest-Litowsk Anfang Juli 1941," *Archiv für Polizeigeschichte* 10 (1999): 83.

44. Edward B. Westermann, "'Ordinary Men' or 'Ideological Soldiers'? Police Battalion 310 in Russia, 1942," *German Studies Review* 21 (February 1998): 51.

45. Michael H. Kater, *The Nazi Party: A Social Profile of Members and Leaders, 1919–1945* (Cambridge MA: Harvard University Press, 1983), 141.

46. Browning, *Ordinary Men*, 48.

47. Klemp, "*Mord-Bataillon*," 30. Average age is based on the year 1940.

48. Longerich, *Vernichtung*, 306.

49. Mallmann, "Der qualitative Sprung im Vernichtungsprozeß," 253.

50. For one analysis of this process, see Koonz, *The Nazi Conscience*.

51. Browning, *Ordinary Men*, 171–76.

52. Testimony of Johann P., 204 AR-Z 1251/65, file 1, 38, ZStl.

53. Stanley Milgram, *Obedience to Authority: An Experimental View* (New York: Harper & Row, 1974), 36. Milgram's study found that *70 percent* of "perpetrators" defied the experimenter when they sat next to the "victim" and were forced to place the victim's hand on the shock plate.

54. Browning, *Ordinary Men*, 2, 56.

55. For a more detailed examination of this question, see David H. Kitterman, "Those Who Said 'No!': Germans Who Refused to Execute

Civilians during World War II," *German Studies Review* 11 (May 1988): 241–54.

56. I would like to thank Klaus-Michael Mallmann for sharing this insight during a conversation at the University of Stuttgart.

57. "Der Höhere SS-und Polizeiführer West, Betrifft: Verhütung von Geschlechtskrankheiten," T175, reel 224, frame 2762919, NARA.

58. "Der Kommandeur der Ordnungspolizei im Distrikt Lublin II a/b [March 13, 1943]," RG 15.011M, reel 20, file 274, USHMMA. This document contains an order forwarded under Daluege's signature with the following subject line: "Verwendung von polnisch versippten Angehörigen der Ordnungspolizei in den eingegliederten Ostgebieten und im Generalgouvernment [March 8, 1943]."

59. "Der Kommandeur der Orpo b. SS-u. Polizeiführer Weissruthenien, Tagesbefehl No. 16 [July 31, 1943]," RG 53.0c.zM, reel 3, fond 389, file 1, USHMMA.

60. Browning, *Origins*, 260.

61. Letter (*Feldpost*) from a policeman to his home unit commander in Oldenburg [August 6, 1944], Verschiedenes 301Ch, file 167, 178–79, ZStl.

62. Testimony of Schmidt's ex-wife, 204 AR-Z 12/61, file 1, 29–30, ZStl.

63. "Zum 10. Jahrestage der nationalsozialistischen Revolution SS und Polizei im großdeutschen Freiheitskampfe [January 30, 1943]," T580, reel 216, file 2, NARA.

The Fates of Gypsies

YEHUDA BAUER

From *Anatomy of the Auschwitz Death Camp*

For the Nazis, Gypsies posed first a social and subsequently an ideological problem. If ever there was an Aryan population, surely it was the Gypsies. Their Indo-European history can be traced to the fifth century, when their clans headed westward from northwest India. According to some researchers, one stop on their migratory journey, a settlement at Gype near Modon in what is now Greece, may have been the source of the term *Gypsy*.[1] European Gypsies now call themselves Roma (humans).

By the 14th century, Gypsies had arrived in Western Europe. They did not settle on land, an impossibility for newcomers to feudal Europe, but became itinerant craftsmen and petty traders: tinkers, iron-, silver-, and goldsmiths, horse traders, and so on. As landless wanderers, they were soon marginalized and persecuted in the most brutal fashion. The Central and West European Gypsy tribes who called themselves the Sinti (from the Sindh River in India) or the Manush (men, humans), were occasional targets of attempts to eliminate them or to kidnap their children to be raised as Christians. Gypsies were frequently subjected to eviction, criminalization, whipping, and forced labor. After the Diet of Freiburg in Germany in 1498, their lives were officially declared to be forfeit.

Over the centuries, anti-Gypsy prejudice in Central Europe and Germany resulted in both legal and illegal discrimination and persecution, partly forcing the Gypsies into a semicriminal existence. Large numbers must have perished in these persecutions between the 15th and 19th centuries, but others fled in search of relative security.

With the rise of the Third Reich, harassment of Gypsies continued. Gypsies were classified as "asocials." Being asocial was a serious crime in a Nazified society that insisted on regimentation based on settled existences. More important, the Nazis saw their "asocial" behavior as a genetically induced, unchangeable characteristic. They were defined as "parasites" or as "a peculiar form of the human species who are incapable of development and came about by mutation."[2]

These ideological quirks may have reflected practical problems as well. The Gypsy population was small; a report to SS chief Heinrich Himmler in 1941 indicated that there were 28,000 Sinti in Germany and 11,000 in Austria.[3] But they formed, from a bureaucratic point of view, an inefficiently used labor potential; local authorities had to pay for social help, educational facilities, and so forth for the wanderers. Gypsies were accused of petty crimes, reflecting the hostility of the settled German population. An administrative decree of the Prussian Ministry of the Interior in 1936 spoke of the Gypsy "plague" and of the Gypsies as thieves, beggars, and swindlers.[4] A number of racist Nazi authors wrote books and articles about the Gypsies and their unassimilability to the German Volk.

The solution Nazi ideology found for all these problems was to argue that the Gypsies were no longer "pure" Gypsy Aryans but *Mischlinge*, or mixed-bloods. The definition of who was a Gypsy often ran parallel to the definition of Jews.

In 1936, in the course of a roundup of so-called asocials, about 400 Gypsies were sent to Dachau concentration camp. Until 1938, however, Gypsies could follow their traditional occupations in Germany more or less unhindered, though after 1937 every effort was made to deport Gypsies who were not German subjects or to prevent such people from entering Germany.

A racist ideologue with medical background, Dr. Robert Ritter, was empowered to set up the Research Office for the Science of Inheritance, later the Research Office for Race Hygiene and Population Biology.[5] Ritter was to examine the whole German Gypsy population for its racial characteristics; his findings were to determine Nazi policy. Ritter examined some 20,000 Roma and determined that about 90 percent were *Mischlinge*. He proposed to separate the Gypsies from the German population, separate the *Mischlinge* from the "pure" Gypsies, and send the *Mischlinge* to forced-labor camps, where they would be sterilized. Still, both types of Gypsies were considered "asocial." These ideas were by no means kept secret. Ritter presented them in 1937 at an international population congress in Paris.

A decree by Himmler on December 14, 1937, provided for preventive arrest of people who had not committed any illegal act but were endangering the community by their asocial behavior. The list for administrative enforcement published April 4, 1938, included "vagabonds (Gypsies)" along with beggars and prostitutes. A further Himmler decree (issued later but predated to December 8, 1938) promised to solve the Gypsy question "in accordance with the essence of their race." On March 15, 1939, Himmler declared that while Germany respected other races, a strict separation should be enforced between the "Gypsy plague" and Germans and between half-breeds and "pure" Gypsies. The police would deal with the problem. These measures appear to have been related to the tendency of the SS to put a maximum of new asocial prisoners in its camps, which were being converted to economic enterprises employing slave labor.

Probably 8,000 of the 11,000 Gypsies in Austria were members of the so-called Ungrika (Lalleri) tribe in the Burgenland, the eastern Austrian province bordering on Hungary. They had been living there since the 18th century as a settled village proletariat, some of whom were musicians, helpers in hunts, etc. Relations with the Austrian peasants were generally good, because the Gypsies fulfilled an important social function. After the "*Anschluss*," Gypsy children were forbidden to go to school, and the Gypsies were disenfranchised. In November 1940, the Nazis established a family concentration camp for Gypsies at Lackenbach in the Burgenland. By October 1941, 2,335 people were interned there. In November 1941, two transports of 1,000 Gypsies each arrived in Lodz, where they met the fate of other Gypsies who were deported there. It is likely that most of the 8,000 Burgenland Gypsies were murdered during the war, but we do not have exact figures. Many were deported to Auschwitz in 1943.[6]

On September 21, 1939, in the course of the conquest of Poland, Reinhard Heydrich, chief of the RSHA (Reich Main Security Office), issued orders regarding Jews which also included the provision that 30,000 German Gypsies (along with Poles and Jews from the newly acquired west Polish territories) should be deported to Poland, an edict that would have included most of the Reich's Gypsies. Over time, the policy toward the Roma became more brutal. In the autumn of 1941, 5,007 Austrian Gypsies . . . were deported to the Lodz ghetto, then gassed at Chelmno in early 1942.

In April 1941, Ritter and his race hygiene office released their findings on Gypsies. Of the 18,922 Gypsies classified by Ritter, 1,079 were defined as "pure" Gypsies, 6,992 as "more Gypsy than German," 2,976 as half-breeds, 2,992 as more German than Gypsy, 2,231 as uncertain, and 2,652 as "Germans who behaved like Gypsies."[7] Ritter's definitions paralleled those applied to Jews: "A Gypsy is a person who, as a descendant of Gypsies, has at least three purely Gypsy grandparents. Moreover, a Gypsy half-breed is a person who has less than three Gypsies among his grandparents." Ritter defined these "half-breeds" as "highly unbalanced, characterless, unpredictable, unreliable, as well as lazy or disturbed and irritable, or in other words disinclined to work and asocial," especially if they carried within themselves "also from the local (i.e., German) side low-grade hereditary qualities."[8]

A year later, in May 1942, Gypsies were put under the same labor and social laws as the Jews.[9] Himmler issued a clarification on October 13, 1942, relating to Gypsy chiefs who would supervise the pure Sinti, for whom a certain freedom of movement would be allowed. According to a document of January 11, 1943, 13,000 Sinti and 1,017 Lalleri would be thus considered.[10]

As for all the other Gypsies, Himmler issued a decree on December 16, 1942, providing for their deportation to Auschwitz, with the exception of socially adapted former *Wehrmacht* soldiers (all Gypsies were supposed to have been discharged from the army after 1940, but practical implementation did not come on a large scale until 1942–43) and war industry workers in important positions. The RSHA issued an administrative order to implement this decree on January 29, 1943.

Orders regarding Gypsies, especially orders to be executed by organizations such as the *Wehrmacht*, were not always followed. There is evidence that some Gypsies, or part-Gypsies, were

let alone. Others managed to hide their identity, which was easier for Gypsies than for Jews. In addition, the definitions contained in the decree were rather confusing. The order was to apply to "Gypsy *Mischlinge*, Roma Gypsies, and members of clans of Balkan origins who are not of German blood." This apparently meant that all non-Sinti Gypsies and all Mischlinge in Germany should be deported. Whether the order was to apply to Gypsies outside the official Reich boundaries—in Western Europe, Poland, Yugoslavia, Russia, etc.—was unclear.

Treatment of Gypsies in the various European countries differed considerably. In Bohemia and Moravia, which were part of the Reich, Gypsies shared the fate of the German Gypsies: discrimination, concentration, and annihilation. The number of Gypsies who were not caught in this process remains undetermined. In Slovakia, which was half-independent, only desultory attempts were made to concentrate some of the wandering Gypsies in forced labor camps. As far as one can tell, Slovakian Gypsies were not deported. Hundreds were brutally murdered in a number of villages during the occupation of Slovakia by German troops after the failure of the Slovak national uprising in October 1944.[11]

For France, there is testimony that some 30,000 were interned under the supervision of the Secretariat for Jewish Affairs of the Vichy government. Many or most of them were later sent to camps, including Dachau, Ravensbrück, and Buchenwald. One estimate claims that 15,150 of them died, while 40,000 appear to have survived in French camps. Five hundred of the 600 Gypsies in Belgium are reported to have died in Polish camps.[12] The situation in Holland is instructive. After the failure of the local Nazi police to concentrate the Gypsies in late March 1943 as they had been ordered, they received new orders in May to concentrate all "wandering" Gypsies. Because of exceptions, only 1,150 out of 2,700–3,000 wandering Gypsies were affected. Many of them fled in time or sold their wagons and thus were no longer considered wanderers. On May 16, 1944, 565 persons were arrested in their wagons, of whom 245 were deported to Birkenau via the Jewish camp of Westerbork.[13]

Some figures for Croatia, where the local *Ustasha* movement targeted Gypsies along with Serbs and Jews, report 90,000 Roma victims in local *Ustasha* murder camps, but another source puts the number at 26,000 (out of 27,000). In Serbia, there is no doubt that Gypsies, along with Jews, were murdered in retaliation for the Serb uprising against the Nazis.[14] Some Italian Roma were sent to camps in Germany after the German occupation of the country in September 1943, but most escaped. For Hungary, one source claims that 30,000 were sent to German death camps, and only 3,000 returned.[15] While no evidence exists to substantiate that figure, there is evidence that in the last stages of the war, the fascist government of Ferenc Szalasi did try to concentrate and deport Gypsies in some provinces, without much success. The large Gypsy contingent in Romania (at least 280,000) was not attacked en masse, but about 25,000 of them were dumped in Transnistria, according to one source.[16]

In the Baltic States and the Soviet Union, Roma were murdered by some of the *Einsatzgruppen*, according to their reports. The *Wehrmacht* Field Police, in a communication of August 25, 1942, stressed the need to ruthlessly "exterminate" bands of wandering Gypsies.[17] In May 1943, Alfred Rosenberg, in charge of the Eastern Territories, suggested that Roma should be concentrated in camps and settlements but not treated the same as Jews. But Himmler would not permit the intrusion of another authority in what he considered to be his own area of competence. His order of Novem-

ber 15, 1943, determined that "sedentary Gypsies and part-Gypsies are to be treated as citizens of the country. Nomadic Gypsies and part-Gypsies are to be placed on the same level as Jews and placed in concentration camps. The police commanders will decide in cases of doubt who is a Gypsy."[18]

While the order applied only to the occupied Soviet areas, it seems to indicate a trend of thinking among top-level Nazi officials. Some sedentary Roma were drafted into labor brigades or sent to concentration camps, but the same fate befell other Soviet citizens as well. Kenrick estimates the number of Roma murdered in the USSR at about 35,000. That excludes Gypsies who were murdered by the *Einsatzgruppen*, especially in the south (*Einsatzgruppe* D under Otto Ohlendorf, who stated in his postwar trial that his group murdered tens of thousands of Gypsies). As far as we know, only a few Soviet Gypsies were sent to Auschwitz.[19] There is information about Roma being sent to Jewish ghettos but kept separate from the Jews. We do not know whether they were sedentary or not, nor what their numbers were; nor do we know anything about their lives while in the ghettos. In most cases, we also have no information about their ultimate fate. They apparently constituted a small percentage of Polish Gypsies. It is possible that they were the wandering Gypsies Himmler referred to in the case of the USSR.[20]

Himmler's order regarding the USSR and the possibility that a similar policy might have been followed elsewhere contradict the other Himmler policy of allowing the "pure" Gypsies a wandering existence of sorts within the Reich confines. This latter policy, however, was challenged by Martin Bormann, Hitler's secretary, who was appalled at the possibility that wandering Gypsies would continue to be part of the German landscape. It seems that the problem was not discussed further and that the whole Gypsy "problem" was for Himmler and most other Nazis only a minor irritant. Since Nazis often solved minor social irritants by murder, this is apparently what happened to many of the Gypsies.

If this analysis is correct, a picture emerges of the Nazi policy toward the Gypsies. An originally Aryan population, so the policy went, had been spoiled by admixture of non-Gypsy blood and had therefore acquired hereditary asocial characteristics. In the Reich, their asocial behavior constituted a problem to be solved by police means, sterilization, and murder, primarily of those defined as half-breeds. What would happen to the "pure" minority was a matter for further discussion. In the territories controlled by the Reich, wandering Gypsies constituted an irritant that would be often removed by murder. Sedentary Gypsies, by and large, were not important enough to bother about. Gypsies caught by police would be shipped to concentration camps. As German power declined, there was a tendency to utilize Gypsy manpower for military means, and some Gypsies interned in camps were used for this purpose, just as Nazi policy dictated the same use for German criminals interned in camps.

How was this policy implemented in Auschwitz? There is no evidence that Roma were sent to the Auschwitz concentration camp complex (or the gassing establishment at Auschwitz-Birkenau) before 1943. In the agreement signed on September 18, 1942, between Himmler and Nazi Justice Minister Otto Thierack, Gypsies were included among those groups whose members, if sentenced by regular German courts, were to be handed over to the SS for "annihilation through labor"; they appeared in third place, after security cases and Jews.[21] But during the remainder of 1942, this agreement apparently did not lead to any large-scale deportations to Auschwitz.

The Auschwitz *Kalendarium*[22] contains a notation for July 1942 that the total of those who had been killed in the camp was 4,124, of whom one was a Gypsy. On December 7, 1942, two Czech Gypsies escaped; one, Ignatz Mrnka of Banova, was recaptured on January 12, 1943, and the other, Franz Denhel, apparently managed to hide. Both had arrived at Auschwitz in a transport of 59 males from Bohemia, and it is unclear whether the others were Gypsies. The two escapees apparently had been marked as "asocials" by the SS because they were Gypsies. On April 7, a Polish woman, Stefania Ciuron, a Gypsy who had been sent to Auschwitz on February 12, fled from the camp and was apparently never caught.[23]

On January 29, 1943, an RSHA decree ordered the deportation of German Gypsies to Auschwitz. It is unclear whether this decree abolished the former provision by Himmler to preserve the racially "pure" Sinti and Roma of Germany. The general impression remains of a lack of clarity in Nazi thinking regarding the Gypsy "problem." On February 26, 1943, the first transport of German Gypsies arrived in Auschwitz, containing a few families. They were placed in Birkenau IIe, a section of the Birkenau extension of Auschwitz that was to become the Gypsy family camp but which at that stage had not been completed. A second transport arrived on March 1. These two were followed by transports on March 3 and 5 (two transports). In these four transports, 828 Sinti and Roma from Germany were included, 391 males and 437 females.[24]

The major transports of Gypsies arrived in Auschwitz between March and May 1943, but smaller groups and a couple of larger ones were sent intermittently in the autumn of 1943 and until May 1944. Smaller groups and individuals were sent to Auschwitz in between these dates. One last group (18 persons from Vitebsk in Russia) arrived on June 17, 1944. According to the *Kalendarium*, the larger groups consisted of 32 transports from Germany, four from what the *Kalendarium* calls Czechoslovakia, three from Poland (among them, on May 12, 1943, a transport with 971 persons), one from Germany and Hungary, one from Yugoslavia (on December 2, with 77 persons), and three mixed transports (on March 7 from Germany, Yugoslavia, Poland, and Czechoslovakia; on March 17 from Germany, Czechoslovakia, and Poland; and on January 17, 1944, from France, Belgium, Holland, Germany, and Norway). With no evidence that any Roma were deported from Slovakia to Auschwitz, it would seem that when Czechoslovakia is mentioned, Bohemia and Moravia are meant. These areas were under a German protectorate and were considered by the Nazis as part of the Reich.[25]

The great majority of the Roma sent to Auschwitz—13,080, according to one source[26]—were Sinti from Germany and Lalleri and others from Austria and the Protectorate. Numbers from each of the other countries were small, with the exception of one large transport from Poland. There is no indication how or why these Gypsies were arrested or whether there was a policy of seeking them out, and if so, why this policy did not succeed or was not executed energetically. While a large proportion of the Gypsy population of the extended Reich was sent to Auschwitz, only very small numbers of Gypsies from the rest of Europe were affected. On the other hand, that these small numbers were included seems to indicate a trend toward an emerging policy on all Gypsies.

Almost all the Roma were interned in the BIIe Gypsy family camp at Birkenau. Writings on the subject do not explain why the Nazis treated the Gypsies differently from other arrestees, who were not housed in family camps, with the exception of the Theresienstadt Jewish family camp. As to the Theresienstadt Jews, there is sufficient documentary evidence that Nazis considered a possible Red Cross visit to Auschwitz in their decision-making. As far as the Roma are concerned, such considerations played no part. No documentary evidence is available to help solve the question. But it would be a mistake to assume that the Gypsy family camp was unaffected by "normal" procedures at Auschwitz. On March 22, 1943, 1,700 Roma men, women, and children who had arrived in transports in the previous few weeks but had not been registered because of illness (mainly typhoid) were murdered by gassing. A second mass gassing of Roma occurred on May 25, 1943, when 1,035 persons were murdered; they were ill, mostly with typhoid. Others continued to be kept in the family camp. Perhaps this policy was adopted due to a lack of clarity among Nazi bureaucrats about the Roma. They were obviously viewed as hereditary asocials, yet hesitation about them continued. By the end of 1943, 18,736 Roma had been interned in the BIIe camp, of whom at least 2,735 were later murdered by gassing.

Danuta Czech argues in the Kalendarium[27] that Himmler decided on the liquidation of the Gypsy family camp during his visit to Auschwitz in the summer of 1943, a visit that ended with the removal of Rudolf Höss as camp commandant. However, the first major attempt at liquidating the family camp did not occur until May 1944, or about nine months later. If Himmler said something about the Gypsies in the summer of 1943, it was not followed through on. . . . In the spring of 1944, a number of Roma in Auschwitz were sent elsewhere. Thus on April 15, 1,357 men and women were sent to Buchenwald and Ravensbrück (the women's camp). Others were transferred to the main labor camps.

Accommodations in the Gypsy camp were in long, primitive wooden barracks, each of which had a smokestack at either end. Between the smokestacks, running the whole length of the barrack, was a thick pipe, which also served as a kind of table. On both sides of the pipe stood three-tiered wooden beds, on each of which a Gypsy family was accommodated. The inmates separated the beds with blankets which they had brought with them. . . . Apparently the inmates organized in accordance with Roma custom in clans and families, trying to keep their culture intact as much as possible. ss attempts to make the Gypsies adjust to German order met with little success, and the Germans desisted from trying to turn the families into ordinary Auschwitz camp "material." The Gypsies played music and had circuslike performances, despite the hunger, disease, and deprivation. Under the deplorably unhygienic conditions, a rare sickness prevailed—noma—whose symptoms are somewhat akin to leprosy. The main sufferers were children and the aged.

On May 15, 1944, for unknown reasons, the camp command decided to murder the remaining 6,000 Roma in BIIe. The German commander of the family camp, Georg Bonigut, apparently disagreed with the decision and informed some of his Roma acquaintances of the fate that was awaiting them. On May 16, the ss surrounded the camp, intending to lead the inmates to the gas chambers. They were met by Roma armed with knives, iron pipes, and the like, and it was clear that there would be a fight. The Germans retreated, and the liquidation was temporarily postponed. On other occasions, when they met with organized resistance, the ss never hesitated to use brute force. Clearly, the weapons in the hands of the inmates did not pose any major threat to the well-armed Germans. Yet they desisted, perhaps owing to the general uncertainty and hesitancy surrounding the whole Gypsy "problem."[28]

On May 25, the ss separated out 1,500 Roma for work, and removed them from the family camp. On August 2, 1,408 more men and women were selected for work, and most of the remaining Gypsy men, women, and children were gassed. Only a few Roma were housed in Auschwitz after that. Camp records show that on September 9, 1944, one Roma was sent from Auschwitz to Buchenwald. On October 5, 1,188 Gypsy inmates were transferred to Auschwitz from Buchenwald, apparently persons who were physically exhausted and destined to be killed. Most likely, all were gassed.

It appears that 2,735 Gypsies were murdered at Auschwitz in March and May 1943; 2,897 on August 2, 1944; and 800 probably on October 5, for a total of 6,432, out of 20,946 Gypsies registered in the two main books (Hauptbücher) covering the Gypsies that were found in Auschwitz after liberation. Subtracting the number gassed and those transferred elsewhere (probably at least 4,000) from the total registered, some 10,000 Gypsies remain unaccounted for. The most likely explanation is that illness, deprivation, and individual or small-scale acts of murder caused their demise. This supposition appears to be borne out by the few Gypsy postwar testimonies. The number of survivors, those transferred out of Auschwitz and alive at the war's end, is unknown.

An additional question arises: what happened to the German and Austrian Gypsies who were not deported to Auschwitz? According to Ritter's figures, there were 25,955 German Sinti Gypsies (not including 2,652 Germans "behaving like Gypsies"), and the number of Austrian Gypsies was estimated at 11,000, for a total of some 37,000. With 2,500 of these Gypsies deported to Poland in 1938–40 and 3,000 interned in Austrian camps (most all of whom were eventually killed), 5,000 sent to Lodz and gassed at Chelmno, and 13,000 deported to Auschwitz and killed there, we derive a total of up to 23,500 German and Austrian Gypsies killed. That would leave 13,500 unaccounted for. They may be the 14,017 Sinti and Lalleri defined by Himmler as pure or nearly pure Gypsies who would be spared.

As the war drew to its close and the German military situation became more and more desperate, the Nazis used some of the concentration camp inmates, as well as German criminal prisoners and Gypsies, as cannon fodder. According to one testimony, some 4,000 Gypsies were recruited into the *Wehrmacht* in these last stages. Only 700 survived.[29] One must regard this testimony with great caution until more documentary evidence emerges.

The murder of Gypsies in Auschwitz must be viewed from two perspectives: the fate that the Nazis prepared for the Gypsies generally and the fate of the Gypsies in the framework of Auschwitz.

While clear parallels existed with the plight of the Jews, it is precisely these parallels that also point to the major differences between the fate of the two groups. The Gypsies were defined in much the same way as the Jews were, but for opposite purposes, at least in theory. The "pure" Gypsies were, initially, to be spared as a separate, originally Aryan group, while the *Mischlinge* were destined for extermination. In the case of the Jews, all were to be murdered, except some grades of *Mischlinge*, who were to be sterilized or even let alone. There was logic in this, from a National Socialist ideological point of view, as the Jewish "race" had to be completely eliminated but not the "pure" Aryan Gypsies.

But Nazi thinking about the Gypsy problem was hopelessly muddled. "Pure" as well as *Mischlinge* Gypsies in Germany were considered genetically "asocial." Ritter and others argued in favor of their sterilization. The Nazis' Gypsy "problem" thus had both racial and social aspects. In the case

of the wandering Gypsies, there was the additional irritant of old prejudices and practical considerations of administrators and soldiers who did not like groups of wanderers threatening their communications. To them, differentiations between racially pure and less pure wanderers must have been unimportant. In a social-psychological environment such as that, irritations were solved by murder. When wanderers were encountered, they were often annihilated; settled Gypsies were not disturbed. Nazis also differentiated between Gypsies in Germany and those elsewhere, because Gypsies in the occupied countries, especially in the East, did not pose a "racial" danger to Germans.

The second perspective is that of the fate of the Gypsies in Auschwitz. Only a minority of German, Austrian, and Czech Gypsies and a tiny minority of non-German Gypsies were sent to Auschwitz, but their fate became a symbol for the general fate of the Gypsies. That the Germans kept the Gypsies alive in family groups for almost a year and a half without separating men from women indicates that no decision as to their fate had been made when they were sent to the camp. If there had been a plan to murder them, it would not have taken the ss that long to do so.

Yet, while the fate of the Gypsies at camp BIIe hung in the balance, they were treated just as badly as the other prisoners, and in some ways worse. There were very few privileged Gypsies. Most suffered from the terrible deprivation, hunger, disease, and humiliation. Evidence shows that in camps such as Ravensbrück, Gypsies were also subjects of medical experiments. An unknown number of men and women were sterilized. In Auschwitz, Dr. Josef Mengele conducted his notorious experiments on Gypsies as well as Jews. All or most of the Gypsy twins used in his experiments were killed, whereas at least some Jewish twins survived. Dr. Carl Clauberg's medical experiments at Auschwitz involved Gypsy women.

While Jews were the lowest group in Auschwitz, Gypsies were a very close second. . . . One of the few Gypsy testimonies may provide insight. . . .[30] The witness was deported to Auschwitz in the early spring of 1943 and received the number z-3890. She was put into the women's camp, along with her mother and sister. She had blood in her lungs and was put into the hospital, "which was worse than a stable. The lice crawled all over our faces; I have never seen so many lice. In the blankets with which we had to cover ourselves they were as thick as nuts. I suddenly saw that my mother had come . . . She wasn't there long. . . . She cried for water. I couldn't give her any; I was forbidden to get near the water. My mother then lay in my bed with me; they brought her to me, [she had] high fever, and then my mother died."

Her brothers, her father, her husband, and her three children—aged ten, eight, and six— were in the family camp. Another Gypsy woman suggested to her that she should volunteer to be a nurse in the family camp, where the woman prisoner-doctor was a Gypsy, too. Though she could hardly stand on her feet, the witness asked the other woman to help her get the job. She managed somehow to pass the examination by an ss doctor and became a nurse. When she was taken to the family camp, she saw her father.

So I asked where the children were. So he said, they are in block 30. . . . And the ss came and tore me away from my father and brought me to the block . . . and so I worked with the camp doctors, they were prisoners, too, Jews. And they were good to us, yes, they helped us a lot. I was in there for a day, not quite, I went out again and went to the block where my children were. They were only skin and bone, unrecognizable.

They lay there, one can say, already dying. And so I said to my father, bring the children to the sick bay, bring the children in, I said, I will see what I can do. Had they come in there earlier, it might have made a difference. And so my father brought in the eldest the next day, she was ten. And when I saw her, she could not speak a word anymore. She only lay there, her eyes open, and not a word. Could only lie there, was more dead than . . . only breathed. So I spoke to her . . . then she died. They simply threw her there, with the other corpses. My own child. And so one after the other. . . . They were only skin and bones. Skin and bones, nothing else, one could count the ribs. The eyes so deep in the head. The children were dead, all three.

My father came into the sick bay, also died. Two uncles were in there, a cousin; and one of the uncles with all his family, and Mrs. Wagner, she had nine children, seven of them died in there. . . . I saw it myself. One of them was my sister-in-law, she was married to my brother. And then . . . I was just skin and bones, I could hardly stand. I only prayed that I should die, I could hardly live anymore. And if I had not had my strong religion, I would have killed myself. . . . But I couldn't. Well, so I recovered a bit through the other women who spoke to me, "you have still siblings who need you," and so on.

In reading testimonies, it becomes clear that the fate of individual Roma deported to Auschwitz paralleled that of the Jews. However, it was not the same. There were no young Jewish children in the camp, with a few exceptions, as they and a large proportion of the women and the elderly were murdered upon arrival. The Gypsies saw their helpless family members die in the family camp one by one, from hunger and disease. Others were mutilated by sterilization or tortured in medical experiments.

The fate of the Gypsies in Auschwitz and elsewhere has been little reported, and the reports have often been stereotyped. Most researchers note that lack of information can be attributed to the suspicion and distrust with which the Gypsies, based on their collective experience, view the *Gadja* [non-Gypsies]. Gypsies also would have had difficulty discussing aspects of their experience, since some of the basic taboos in Gypsy culture were violated at Auschwitz and elsewhere regarding standards of cleanliness and sexual contact. The sterilizations performed on many Gypsies were part of this violation. Most Gypsies could not relate their stories involving these tortures; as a result, most kept silent and thus increased the effects of the massive trauma they had undergone. In addition, very few Gypsies became members of the intellectual community, in Germany or elsewhere, so that too few from among their own number sought information about what happened to them. Even today, most of the research done on the fate of Gypsies is the work of non-Gypsies, especially Jews.

NOTES

1. Rüdiger Vossen, ed., *Zigeuner* (Frankfurt am Main, 1983), 22–23.
2. Dr. Robert Ritter, quoted in Joachim Hohmann, "Der Völkermord an Zigeunern," lecture delivered at the Paris conference "La Politique Nazis d'Extermination," 3.
3. Statistics here closely follow my article "Jews, Gypsies and Slavs," in UNESCO *Yearbook on Peace and Conflict Studies* (Paris, 1985), esp. 81–86, and the literature cited therein.
4. Ibid., 5.

5. "Rassenhygienische und bevölkerungsbiologische Forschungsstätte," *Gesellschaft für bedrohte Völker* (Göttingen-Vienna, 1981).
6. Claudia Mayerhofer, *Dorfzigeuner* (Vienna, 1987); Erika Thurner, *Nationalsozialismus und Zigeuner in Osterreich* (Vienna-Salzburg, 1983).
7. Cf. Tilman Zülch, ed., *In Auschwitz vergast, bis heute verfolgt* (Hamburg, 1979), 67.
8. Hohmann lecture, 17, quoting the Informationsdienst des Rassenpolitischen Amtes der NSDAP, April 20, 1941.
9. Ibid., 23, quoting the Informationsdienst des Rassenpolitischen Amtes der NSDAP, May 20, 1942.
10. Ibid., 85–86.
11. Ctibor Necas, *Nad osudem céskych a slovenskych Cikanu v letech 1939–1945* (Brno, 1981).
12. Donald Kenrick and Grattan Puxon, *The Destiny of Europe's Gypsies* (London, 1972), 103–7; Vossen, 85; Sybil Milton, "Occupation Policy in Belgium and France," in Michael Berenbaum, ed., *A Mosaic of Victims: Non-Jews Persecuted and Murdered by the Nazis* (New York, 1990), 80–87.
13. Michael Zimmermann, *Verfolgt, vertrieben, vernichtet* (Essen, 1989), 62–63.
14. Menachem Shelah, "Genocide in Satellite Croatia during the Second World War," in Berenbaum, 20–36; Christopher R. Browning, "Germans and Serbs: The Emergence of Nazi Antipartisan Policies in 1941," in ibid., 64–73.
15. Kenrick and Puxon, 125–27; Joachim S. Hohmann, *Geschichte der Zigeunerverfolgung in Deutschland* (Frankfurt, 1988), 171–72. Hohmann states that there were 275,000 Gypsies in Hungary and Hungarian Transylvania and that there was a sterilization program in place in Hungary starting in 1942. The evidence is not convincing.
16. Kenrick and Puxon, 128–30; Hohmann, *Geschichte*, 171.
17. Kenrick and Puxon, 146–50.
18. Ibid., 150. Hohmann. *Geschichte*, 172, claims that East European Gypsies were included in the genocide wholesale, with the deportation east-

ward of the German Gypsies. I can find no proof
of this.

19. Kenrick and Puxon, 149.

20. Jerzy Ficowski, a Polish writer who has tried to
trace the fate of the Polish Gypsies, tells us that
most of them fell victim to mass murders outside the concentration camps, committed by
the *Feldgendarmerie*, the Gestapo, the ss, and
Ukrainian fascists (Ficowski, "Die Vernichtung," in Zulch, 91–112). This is a rather inexact
description. Gypsies brought into the Warsaw
ghetto were murdered at Treblinka, but we have
no list of ghettos in which Gypsies lived alongside Jews (with the exception of Lodz). Interestingly, Ficowski says (93) that in Volhynia,
formerly in eastern Poland, where there was a
Ukrainian majority, "only" Polish Gypsies were
murdered (some 3,000–4,000); Ukrainian Gypsies were left alone. Small groups of Gypsies
were brought to Majdanek and to the extermination camp of Belzec (a group of 20 persons is mentioned). The upshot is, according
to Ficowski, that of the 18,000–20,000 Gypsies
living in prewar Poland, only 5,000–6,000 survived. Ficowski's claim is, it seems, not conclusive, as there are many more Gypsies in Poland
today than there would be if only 5,000–6,000
had survived the war. Cf. Jerzy Ficowski, "The
Fate of the Polish Gypsies," in Jack N. Porter,
ed., *Genocide and Human Rights* (Washington
DC, 1982,) 166–77.

21. PS-654, Nuremberg Trial Documents. In the
future, Gypsies and others who had transgressed
would be handed over not to the courts but to
the ss directly.

22. Danuta Czech, ed., *Kalendarium der Ereignisse im
Konzentrationslager Auschwitz Birkenau 1939–1945*
(Hamburg, 1989), 263. The material on which
the *Kalendarium* was based includes lists prepared at the behest of the Nazis, lists and reports
illegally copied by inmate clerks and preserved,
documents abandoned when the Nazis retreated
from Auschwitz in January 1945, and other materials, including testimonies of survivors. See the
editor's introduction, 7–14.

23. Ibid., 354.

24. Ibid., 423, 426, 429, 432, 433.

25. Ibid., passim.

26. Zülch, 315.

27. Czech, 374–75.

28. Ibid., 774–75.

29. Testimony of Julius Hadosi, in Anita Geigges
and Bernhard W. Witte, *Zigeuner Heute* (Bernheim, 1979), 276; see also Kenrick and Puxon,
162–65.

30. The testimony was published by Roland Schopf
in Joachim S. Hohmann and Ronald Schopf,
Ziegeunerleben (Darmstadt, 1980), 125–41.

Camp Labor

PRIMO LEVI

From *If This Is a Man (Survival in Auschwitz)*

The journey did not last more than twenty minutes. Then the lorry stopped, and we saw a large door, and above it a sign, brightly illuminated (its memory still strikes me in my dreams): *Arbeit Macht Frei*, work gives freedom. . . . We are at Monowitz, near Auschwitz, in Upper Silesia, a region inhabited by both Poles and Germans. This camp is a work-camp, in German one says *Arbeitslager*; all the prisoners (there are about ten thousand) work in a factory which produces a type of rubber called Buna, so that the camp itself is called Buna. . . . At the sound of the bell, we can hear the still dark camp waking up. Unexpectedly the water gushes out boiling from the showers-five minutes of bliss; but immediately after, four men (perhaps they are the barbers) burst in yelling and shoving and drive us out, wet and steaming, into the adjoining room which is freezing; here other shouting people throw at us unrecognizable rags and thrust into our hands a pair of broken-down boots with wooden soles; we have no time to understand and we already find ourselves in the open, in the blue and icy snow of dawn, barefoot and naked, with all our clothing in our hands, with a hundred yards to run to the next hut. There we are finally allowed to get dressed.

When we finish, everyone remains in his own corner and we do not dare lift our eyes to look at one another. There is nowhere to look in a mirror, but our appearance stands in front of us, reflected in a hundred livid faces, in a hundred miserable and sordid puppets. We are transformed into the phantoms glimpsed yesterday evening.

Then for the first time we became aware that our language lacks words to express this offence, the demolition of a man. In a moment, with almost prophetic intuition, the reality was revealed to us: we had reached the bottom. It is not possible to sink lower than this; no human condition is more miserable than this, nor could it conceivably be so. Nothing belongs to us any more; they have taken away our clothes, our shoes, even our hair; if we speak, they will not listen to us, and if they listen, they will not understand. They will even take away our name: and if we want to keep it, we will have to find ourselves the strength to do so, to manage somehow so that behind the name something of us, of us as we were, still remains. . . .

Imagine now a man who is deprived of everyone he loves, and at the same time of his house, his habits, his clothes, in short, of everything he possesses: he will be a hollow man, reduced to suffering and needs, forgetful of dignity and restraint, for he who loses all often easily loses himself. He will be a man whose life or death can be lightly decided with no sense of human affinity, in the most fortunate of cases, on the basis of a pure judgment of utility. It is in this way that one can understand the double sense of the term "extermination camp," and it is now clear what we seek to express with the phrase: "to lie on the bottom."

Häftling [prisoner]: I have learnt that I am *Häftling*. My number is 174517; we have been baptized, we will carry the tattoo on our left arm until we die. The operation was slightly painful and extraordinarily rapid: they placed us all in a row, and one by one, according to the alphabetical order of our names, we filed past a skilful official, armed with a sort of pointed tool with a very short needle. It seems that this is the real, true initiation: only by "showing one's number" can one get bread and soup. Several days passed and not a few cuffs and punches before we became used to showing our number promptly enough not to disorder the daily operation of food-distribution; weeks and months were needed to learn its sound in the German language. And for many days, while the habits of freedom still led me to look for the time on my wristwatch, my new name ironically appeared instead, a number tattooed in bluish characters under the skin.

Only much later and slowly, a few of us learnt something of the funereal science of the numbers of Auschwitz, which epitomize the stages of destruction of European Judaism. To the old hands of the camp, the numbers told everything: the period of entry into the camp, the convoy of which one formed a part, and consequently the nationality. Everyone will treat with respect the numbers from 30,000 to 80,000: there are only a few hundred left, and they represented the few survivals from the Polish ghettos. It is as well to watch out in commercial dealings with a 116,000 or a 117,000: they now number only about forty, but they represent the Greeks of Salonica, so take care they do not pull the wool over your eyes. As for the high numbers they carry an essentially comic air about them, like the words "freshman" or "conscript" in ordinary life. The typical high number is a corpulent, docile and stupid fellow: he can be convinced that leather shoes are distributed at the infirmary to all those with delicate feet, and can be persuaded to run there and leave his bowl of soup "in your custody"; you can sell him a spoon for three rations of bread; you can send him to the most ferocious of the *Kapos* to ask him (as happened to me!) if it is true that his is the *Kartoffelschalenkommando*, the "Potato Peeling Command," and if one can be enrolled in it.

In fact, the whole process of introduction to what was for us a new order took place in a grotesque and sarcastic manner. When the tattooing operation was finished, they shut us in a vacant hut. The bunks are made, but we are severely forbidden to touch or sit on them: so we wander around aimlessly for half the day in the limited space available, still tormented by the parching thirst of the journey. Then the door opens and a boy in a striped suit comes in, with a fairly civilized air, small, thin, and blond. He speaks French and we throng around him with a flood of questions which till now we had asked each other in vain.

But he does not speak willingly; no one here speaks willingly. We are new, we have nothing and we know nothing; why waste time on us? He reluctantly explains to us that all the others are out at work and will come back in the evening. He has come out of the infirmary this morning and is exempt from work for today. I asked him (with an ingenuousness that only a few days later already seemed incredible to me) if at least they would give us back our toothbrushes. He did not laugh, but with his face animated by fierce contempt, he, threw at me *"Vous n'étes pas à la maison."* And it is this refrain that we hear repeated by everyone: you are not at home, this is not a sanatorium, the only exit is by way of the Chimney. (What did it mean? Soon we were all to learn what it meant.)

And it was in fact so. Driven by thirst, I eyed a fine icicle outside the window, within hand's reach. I opened the window and broke off the icicle but at once a large, heavy guard prowling outside brutally snatched it away from me. "*Warum*?" I asked, him in my poor German. "*Hier ist kein warum*" (there is no why here), he replied, pushing me inside with a shove.

The explanation is repugnant but simple: in this place everything is forbidden, not for hidden reasons, but because the camp has been created for that purpose. If one wants to live one must learn this quickly and well: "No Sacred Face will help thee here! It's not//A Serchio bathing-party" . . .

Hour after hour, this first long day of limbo draws to its end. While the sun sets in a tumult of fierce, blood-red clouds, they finally make us come out of the hut. Will they give us something to drink? No, they place us in line again, they lead us to a huge square that takes up the centre of the camp, and they arrange us meticulously in squads. Then nothing happens for another hour: it seems that we are waiting for someone.

A band begins to play, next to the entrance of the camp: it plays *Rosamunda*, the well known sentimental song, and this seems so strange to us that we look sniggering at each other; we feel a shadow of relief, perhaps all these ceremonies are nothing but a colossal farce in Teutonic taste. But the band, on finishing *Rosamunda*, continues to play other marches, one after the other, and suddenly the squads of our comrades appear, returning from work. They walk in columns of five with a strange, unnatural hard gait, like stiff puppets made of jointless bones; but they walk scrupulously in time to the band.

They also arrange themselves like us in the huge square, according to a precise order; when the last squad has returned, they count and recount us for over an hour. Long checks are made which all seem to go to a man dressed in stripes, who accounts for them to a group of ss men in full battle dress.

Finally (it is dark by now, but the camp is brightly lit by headlamps and reflectors) one hears the shout *"Absperre!"* at which all the squads break up in a confused and turbulent movement. They no longer walk stiffly and erectly as before: each one drags himself along with obvious effort. I see that all of them carry in their hand or attached to their belt a steel bowl as large as a basin.

We new arrivals also wander among the crowd, searching for a voice, a friendly face or a guide. Against the wooden wall of a hut two boys are seated on the ground: they seem very young, sixteen years old at the outside, both with their face and hands dirty with soot. One of the two, as we are passing by, calls me and asks me in German some questions which I do not understand; then he asks where we come from. *"Italien,"* I reply; I want to ask him many things, but my German vocabulary is very limited.

"Are you a Jew?" I asked him.

"Yes, a Polish Jew."

"How long have you been in the *Lager*?"

"Three years," and he lifts up three fingers. He must have been a child when he entered, I think with horror; on the other hand this means that at least some manage to live here.

"What is your work?"

"*Schlosser*," he replies. I do not understand. *"Eisen, Feuer"* (iron, fire), he insists, and makes a play with his hands of someone beating with a hammer on an anvil. So he is an ironsmith.

"Ich Chemiker," I state; and he nods earnestly with his head, *"Chemiker gut."* But all this has to do with the distant future: what torments me at the moment is my thirst.

"Drink, water. We no water," I tell him.

He looks at me with a serious face, almost severe, and states clearly: "Do not drink water, comrade," and then other words that I do not understand.

"*Warum?*"

"*Geschwollen,*" he replies cryptically. I shake my head, I have not understood. "Swollen," he makes me understand, blowing out his cheeks and sketching with his hands a monstrous tumefaction of the face and belly. "*Warten bis heute Abend.*" "Wait until this evening," I translate word by word.

Then he says: "*Ich Schlome. Du?*" I tell him my name, and he asks me: "Where your mother?"

"In Italy." Schlome is amazed: a Jew in Italy? "Yes," I explain as best I can, "hidden, no one knows, run away, does not speak, no one sees her." He has understood; he now gets up, approaches me and timidly embraces me. The adventure is over, and I feel filled with a serene sadness that is almost joy. I have never seen Schlome since, but I have not forgotten his serious and gentle face of a child, which welcomed me on the threshold of the house of the dead.

We have a great number of things to learn, but we have learnt many already. We already have a certain idea of the topography of the *Lager*, a square of about six hundred yards in length, surrounded by two fences of barbed wire, the inner one carrying a high tension current. It consists of sixty wooden huts, which are called Blocks, ten of which are in construction. In addition, there is the body of the kitchens, which are in brick; an experimental farm, run by a detachment of privileged *Häftlinge*; the huts with the showers and the latrines, one for each group of six or eight Blocks. Besides these, certain Blocks are reserved for specific purposes. First of all, a group of eight, at the extreme eastern end of the camp, forms the infirmary and clinic; then there is Block 24 which is the *Krätzeblock*, reserved for infectious skin-diseases; Block 7 which no ordinary *Häftling* has ever entered, reserved for the "*Prominenz,*" that is, the aristocracy, the internees holding the highest posts; Block 47, reserved for the *Reichsdeutsche* (the Aryan Germans, "politicals" or criminals); Block 49, for the *Kapos* alone; Block 12, half of which, for use of the *Reichsdeutsche* and the *Kapos*, serves as canteen, that is, a distribution centre for tobacco, insect powder, and occasionally other articles; Block 37, which formed the Quartermaster's office and the Office for Work; and finally, Block 29, which always has its windows closed as it is the *Frauenblock*, the camp brothel, served by Polish *Häftling* girls and reserved for the *Reichsdeutsche*.

The ordinary living Blocks are divided into two parts. In one *Tagesraum* lives the head of the hut with his friends. There is a long table, seats, benches, and on all sides a heap of strange objects in bright colors, photographs, cuttings from magazines, sketches, imitation flowers, ornaments; on the walls, great sayings, proverbs and rhymes in praise of order, discipline and hygiene; in one corner, a shelf with the tools of the *Blockfrisör* (official barber), the ladles to distribute the soup, and two rubber truncheons, one solid and one hollow, to enforce discipline should the proverbs prove insufficient. The other part is the dormitory: there are only one hundred and forty-eight bunks on three levels, fitted close to each other like the cells of a beehive, and divided by three corridors so as to utilize without wastage all the space in the room up to the roof. Here all the ordinary *Häftlinge* live, about two hundred to two hundred and fifty per hut. Consequently there are two men in most of the bunks, which are portable planks of wood, each covered by a thin straw sack and two blankets.

The corridors are so narrow that two people can barely pass together; the total area of the floor is so small that the inhabitants of the same Block cannot all stay there at the same time unless at least half are lying on their bunks. Hence the prohibition to enter a Block to which one does not belong.

In the middle of the *Lager* is the roll-call square, enormous, where we collect in the morning to form the work squads and in the evening to be counted. Facing the roll-call square there is a bed of grass, carefully mown, where the gallows are erected when necessary.

We had soon learned that the guests of the *Lager* are divided into three categories; the criminals, the politicals, and the Jews. All are clothed in stripes, all are *Häftlinge*, but the criminals wear a green triangle next to the number sewn on the jacket; the politicals wear a red triangle; and the Jews, who form the large majority, wear the Jewish star, red and yellow. ss men exist but are few and outside the camp and seen relatively infrequently. Our effective masters in practice are the green triangles, who have a free hand over us, as well as those of the other two categories who are ready to help them—and they are not few.

And we have learnt other things, more or less quickly, according to our intelligence: to reply "*Jawohl*," never to ask questions, always to pretend to understand. We have learnt the value of food; now we also diligently scrape the bottom of the bowl after the ration and we hold it under our chins when we eat bread so as not to lose the crumbs. We, too, know that it is not the same thing to be given a ladleful of soup from the top or from the bottom of the vat, and we are already able to judge, according to the capacity of the various vats, what is the most suitable place to try to reach in the queue when we line up.

We have learnt that everything is useful: the wire to tie up our shoes, the rags to wrap around our feet, waste paper to (illegally) pad out our jacket against the cold. We have learnt, on the other hand, that everything can be stolen, in fact is automatically stolen as soon as attention is relaxed; and to avoid this, we had to learn the art of sleeping, with our head on a bundle, made up

of our jacket and containing all our belongings, from the bowl to the shoes.

We already know in good part the rules of the camp, which are incredibly complicated. The prohibitions are innumerable: to approach nearer to the barbed wire than two yards; to sleep with one's jacket or without one's pants or with one's cap on one's head; to use certain washrooms or latrines which are "*nur für Kapos*" or "*nur für Reichdeutsche*," not to go for the shower on the prescribed day or to go there on a day not prescribed; to leave the hut with one's jacket unbuttoned or with the collar raised; to carry paper or straw under one's clothes against the cold; to wash except stripped to the waist.

The rites to be carried out were infinite and senseless: every morning one had to make the "bed" perfectly flat and smooth; smear one's muddy and repellent wooden shoes with the appropriate machine grease; scrape the mud stains off one's clothes (paint, grease and rust-stains were, however, permitted); in the evening one had to undergo the control for lice and the control of washing one's feet; on Saturday, have one's beard and hair shaved, mend or have mended one's rags; on Sunday, undergo the general control for skin diseases and the control of buttons on one's jacket, which had to be five.

In addition, there are innumerable circumstances, normally irrelevant, which here become problems. When one's nails grow long, they have to be shortened, which can only be done with one's teeth (for the toenails, the friction of the shoes is sufficient); if a button comes off, one has to tie it on with a piece of wire; if one goes to the latrine or the washroom, everything has to be carried along, always and everywhere, and while one washes one's face, the bundle of clothes has to be held tightly between one's knees: in any other manner it will be stolen in that second. If a shoe hurts, one has to go in the evening to the ceremony of the changing of the shoes: this tests the skill of the individual who, in the middle of the incredible crowd, has to be able to choose at an eye's glance one (not a pair, one) shoe, which fits. Because once the choice is made, there can be no second change.

And do not think that shoes form a factor of secondary importance in the life of the *Lager*. Death begins with the shoes; for most of us, they show themselves to be instruments of torture, which after a few hours of marching cause painful sores which become fatally infected. Whoever has them is forced to walk as if he was dragging a convict's chain (this explains the strange gait of the army which returns every evening on parade); he arrives last everywhere, and everywhere he receives blows. He cannot escape if they run after him; his feet swell and the more they swell, the more the friction with the wood and the cloth of the shoes becomes insupportable. Then only the hospital is left: but to enter the hospital with a diagnosis of "*dicke Füsse*" (swollen feet) is extremely dangerous, because it is well known to all, and especially to the ss, that here there is no cure for that complaint.

And in all this we have not yet mentioned the work, which in its turn is a Gordian knot of laws, taboos, and problems.

We all work, except those who are ill (to be recognized as ill implies in itself an important equipment of knowledge and experience). Every morning we leave the camp in squads for the Buna; every evening, in squads, we return. As regards the work, we are divided into about two hundred *Kommandos*, each of which consists of between fifteen and one hundred and fifty men and is commanded by a *Kapo*. There are good and bad *Kommandos*; for the most part they are used as transport and the work is quite hard; especially in the winter, if for no other reason merely because it always takes place in the open. There are also skilled *Kommandos* (electricians, smiths, bricklayers, welders, mechanics, concrete-layers, etc.), each attached to a certain workshop or department of the Buna, and depending more directly on civilian foremen, mostly German and Polish. This naturally only applies to the hours of work; for the rest of the day the skilled workers (there are no more than three or four hundred in all) receive no different treatment from the ordinary workers. The detailing of individuals to the various *Kommandos* is organized by a special office of the *Lager*, the *Arbeitsdienst*, which is in continual touch with the civilian direction of the Buna. The *Arbeitsdienst* decides on the basis of unknown criteria, often openly on the basis of protection or corruption, so that if anyone manages to find enough to eat, he is practically certain to get a good post at Buna.

The hours of work vary with the season. All hours of light are working hours: so that from a minimum winter working day (8–12 a.m. and 12.30–4 p.m.) one rises to a maximum summer one (6.30–12 a.m. and 1–6 p.m.). Under no excuse are the *Häftlinge* allowed to be at work during the hours of darkness or when there is a thick fog, but they work regularly even if it rains or snows or (as occurs quite frequently) if the fierce wind of the Carpathians blows; the reason being that the darkness or fog might provide opportunities to escape.

One Sunday in every two is a regular working day; on the so-called holiday Sundays, instead of working at Buna, one works normally on the upkeep of the *Lager*, so that days of real rest are extremely rare.

Such will be our life. Every day, according to the established rhythm, *Ausrücken* and *Einrücken*, go out and come in; work, sleep and eat; fall ill, get better or die.

. . . And for how long? But the old ones laugh at this question: they recognize the new arrivals by this question. They laugh and they do not reply. For months and years, the problem of the remote future has grown pale to them and has lost all intensity in face of the far more urgent and concrete problems of the near future: how much one will eat today, if it will snow, if there will be coal to unload.

If we were logical, we would resign ourselves to the evidence that our fate is beyond knowledge, that every conjecture is arbitrary and demonstrably devoid of foundation. But men are rarely logical when their own fate is at stake; on every occasion, they prefer the extreme positions. According to our character, some of us are immediately convinced that all is lost, that one cannot live here, that the end is near and sure; others are convinced that however hard the present life may be, salvation is probable and not far off, and if we have faith and strength, we will see our houses and our dear ones again. The two classes of pessimists and optimists are not so clearly defined, however, not because there are many agnostics, but because the majority, without memory or coherence, drift between the two extremes, according to the moment and the mood of the person they happen to meet.

Here I am, then, on the bottom. One learns quickly enough to wipe out the past and the future when one is forced to. A fortnight after my arrival I already had the prescribed hunger, that chronic hunger unknown to free men, which makes one dream at night, and settles in all the limbs of one's body. I have already learnt not to let myself be robbed, and in fact if I find a spoon lying around, a piece of string, a button which I can acquire without danger of punishment, I pocket them and consider them mine by full right. On the back of my feet I already have those numb sores that will not heal. I push wagons, I work with a shovel, I turn rotten in the rain, I shiver in the wind; already my own body is no longer mine: my belly is swollen, my limbs emaciated, my face is thick in the morning, hollow in the evening; some of us have yellow skin, others grey. When we do not meet for a few days we hardly recognize each other.

We Italians had decided to meet every Sunday evening in a corner of the *Lager*, but we stopped it at once, because it was too sad to count our numbers and find fewer each time, and to see each other ever more deformed and more squalid. And it was so tiring to walk those few steps and then, meeting each other, to remember and to think. It was better not to think.

The Final Frenzy

DANIEL BLATMAN

From *The Death Marches*

On January 18, 1945, the evacuation of some 56,000 Auschwitz prisoners was set in motion. About 2,200 inmates from several of the subcamps were transported by rail directly to camps in the Reich. Another 8,000 were left in the main camp and in Birkenau, and another 500 or so, mainly sick inmates, were left in several subcamps that were not evacuated. Many were dying and all were unfit for marching. The prisoners left behind were convinced that they were fated to be murdered within the next few hours by the SS men. For this reason, quite a few made the effort to join the convoys of evacuees despite their poor physical condition and consequently collapsed en route.[1] ... In such remote subcamps as Golleschau, ... the 37 sick prisoners left behind were also certain that the guards would slaughter them all as soon as the convoy had left the camp. But it was precisely this small group that was liberated several days later by the Russians.[2] ...

Despite the evacuation, the extermination of the Jewish camp inmates was not yet over and done with. The last massacre of Jews in Birkenau took place between January 20 and 25. After most of the prisoners had been evacuated and only the sick and frail were left, a small group of SS and SD men from the Political Section (Gestapo) continued to destroy the remaining documents and other evidence that needed to be obliterated before the Russians arrived. They apparently completed the job during the afternoon of January 25, some 48 hours before the Red Army arrived, and made plans to leave. But before they left, they murdered some 300 sick Jews in Birkenau. The SD personnel separated the Jews from the other sick prisoners, who were not harmed. This was the last group of Jews murdered in Auschwitz.[3]

... None of the written or oral instructions issued by Himmler or Pohl from summer 1944 onward hinted in any fashion whatsoever that the evacuated prisoners were to be exterminated. Rather, they suggested the contrary; they generally emphasized their importance to the German war effort and the need to transport them in good shape to the various labor camps. And yet the period of the death marches, which began in January 1945 and lasted about five months, was marked by a bloodthirstiness that reached unprecedented heights of brutality and horror. ...

As the evacuation proceeded and the columns of prisoners began to move toward the place where they were scheduled to board trains, it developed into a scenario of unceasing slaughter. The columns stretched for miles. The guards at the tail of the column often lost contact with those at its head, and when they wanted to convey a message or to halt the column, they often fired into the air by agreed signal.[4] Once they left the camp, the prisoners were under the total responsibility of the guards, who had received no clear instructions, although in general they realized that the killing of problematic prisoners or failed escapees would not cause problems for them. This state of havoc generated the conditions that transformed

513

the evacuations into gruesome death marches. The aimless wandering that often characterized the evacuation gradually took on an absurd and threatening aspect. The prisoners grasped immediately that the longer the march, the slimmer their prospects for survival. They also soon realized that often their guards had not received instructions as to what to do with them. A survivor of one of the Auschwitz subcamps described the situation:

> After a day's marching the order was given to go back. We waited for seven hours at night back at the place we had left. Why? What was the reason? We learned that the Russians had attacked and cut off the passes and so, once again, we turned back. Then we turned again in a different direction. Three times we were given orders after a few kilometers to turn back and try another direction.[5]

Conditions along the way were appalling. In many cases, the prisoners had wolfed down the ration they had been allotted in the camp, consisting of a hunk of bread and a can of food, as soon as they received it. They were given no more food along the way. Their constant fear that the trek along the densely crowded roads would eventually end in their extermination was heightened by the difficulty of walking at a rapid pace in harsh weather, while hunger gnawed at them:

> No food had touched my lips all the day before. Others "snatched" whatever they could—grass, snails, potatoes left in the fields—but my throat was blocked, although my stomach was growling with hunger. I had nothing else, so I ate snow. My whole body shook with cold. . . .
> The march went on for days and nights and nobody knew where we were being taken. If they want to mow us down somewhere with machineguns, why don't they do it immedi-

ately? Or, perhaps there are special installations for that? Perhaps they are taking us again to some new installation for killing by gas? But it seemed that there was no need for any of that; at least two-thirds of the prisoners were already lying lifeless by the roadside. In a few days all of us would suffer the same fate.[6]

The ability to survive the death march often depended on whether the prisoner had succeeded in procuring comfortable shoes and a warm garment before leaving. Those who set out into the icy cold wearing wooden clogs soon found it hard to keep up with the column. In some cases, as the column advanced through the snow and ice, prisoners threw away the few belongings they had brought with them from the camp, including bundles of blankets and clothes that weighed them down and made it impossible for them to keep up the pace dictated by the guards.[7] The idea of escape was not inviting because most of the prisoners, in particular the Jews, were not familiar with the region and did not know how the local villagers would respond to requests for shelter.[8] Only a few hours after they left the camp, the guards began to shoot at prisoners who stumbled. So many of the prisoners who set out on the march were sick, wounded, and too feeble to stand that the guards regarded it as a minor problem to rid themselves of those who straggled or fell.[9] Some prisoners recalled vividly that the guards did not differentiate between men and women.

> Those who stopped, everyone who would fall on the road, was shot, no difference whether it was a man or a woman. You see, we left after the women . . . and we saw en route many dead bodies of women lying on the ground. We marched at night and we had to rest during the day, so that the people should not see

us being led through, and evenings when it was dark we marched on again.[10]

The story of one of the columns of prisoners is typical of what occurred. They left Auschwitz-Birkenau on January 18, 1945, in a group of some 14,000 prisoners in all. The column consisted of 2,500–3,000 prisoners, almost all of them Jews from Hungary, France, and Poland.[11] There are few known details about the first lap of this death march from the camp to Mikolow, a distance of 20 miles (32 kilometers). After marching about 12 miles (20 kilometers) they reached Gliwice on January 20. The next day they were loaded onto a train and transported southward to the town of Rzedowka-Leszczyny, where additional small groups of prisoners from several subcamps were already waiting. Thirteen years later, in 1958, a mass grave was uncovered there, containing about 290 corpses. These were apparently the bodies of prisoners who had died aboard the train and others who died or were liquidated while in the town.[12] From there the prisoners set out on a 124-mile (200-kilometer)-long death march that passed through a series of small towns and villages on the roads stretching westward to Groß-Rosen. They entered the Protectorate (Nazi-annexed territories of Bohemia and Moravia, 1939–1945), returned to Silesia, and advanced northward toward Dzierzoniow and from there to Groß-Rosen. At least a thousand of them died or were murdered in this death march. . . . In other words, about 30 percent of the prisoners perished or were murdered in less than a week. . . .

The guards were tense and nervous because of the haste of the retreat, particularly in small and remote places. This heightened their murderous instincts to a degree that astounded even those veteran prisoners who were only too familiar with the dimensions of brutality in the camps.

And that's how it was, and anyone who lingered and didn't go back in very fast, was shot. And there was a shot and then another shot, real shots; they shot like you shoot stray dogs. And till then we hadn't seen anything like that. We'd seen hangings and we'd seen all kinds of things because of some crimes people were supposed to have committed. But suddenly we saw that people were simply abandoned to their fate, defenseless. They didn't pay attention and fired right and left without consideration for anything. And we saw the blood on the white snow, and we walked on.[13]

Joachim Neander defined these orders as "local liquidation orders" (*lokale Vernichtungsbefehle*).[14] . . . These local decisions transformed the evacuations into murder routes and death marches. Issuing instructions to kill did not require a prior order from the senior command. Any junior sergeant or guard marching alongside the prisoners had sufficient authority to give such an order and carry it out. The fact that in many camps, particularly the subcamps, there was a high proportion of Jews among the prisoners during the evacuation undoubtedly helps explain the ease with which such local decisions were taken and must have rendered them self-evident to the perpetrators.

The evacuees from Auschwitz and the subcamps advanced along two main evacuation routes. The first stretched 34 miles (55 kilometers) from Auschwitz and Birkenau to the northwest as far as Gliwice; the second, a 39-mile (63-kilometer)-long southwesterly route, led to Wodzislaw-Slaski. Those who arrived at the destination were loaded onto open freight cars and transported to various concentration camps in Germany. About 400 of the women prisoners from Auschwitz arrived in Bergen-Belsen, and another 7,000 were taken to Ravensbrück. Fourteen hundred prisoners reached Dachau; 500 Auschwitz evacuees were brought to Neuengamme; and about 9,000 ended up in Mauthausen[15] and 2,000 in Flossenbürg. The largest number, 14,000, were absorbed by Buchenwald.[16] At least 4,000 of these were transferred soon after to Mittelbau-Dora. Another 15,000 Auschwitz prisoners survived the march to Groß-Rosen, from which they were evacuated soon after.[17] . . .

The journey by rail from the concentration sites in Auschwitz and Groß-Rosen to camps in the heart of Germany, which lasted for several days, was an additional chapter in the lethal history of this period of evacuations and death marches. The congestion and lack of food and water in the densely packed freight cars killed hundreds of prisoners and threatened the sanity of the survivors:

The doors were shut. We had no food with us, and now we tried to sit down. When eighty people sat down the others had no place where to stand, and there were many people who were very tired. . . . We trampled on other people's fingers, and these people, of course, resisted and were striking at others, and so a panic ensued. It was so terrible that people went crazy during the trip and soon we had the first death among us. And we didn't know where to put the dead—on the floor they were taking up space—because they had to lie stretched out. And there it occurred to us—we had a blanket with us, so we wrapped the dead man into the blanket, and there were two iron bars in the car and so we tied him on above us.

[It was] like in a hammock. But soon we understood that that won't do because we had more and more dead due to the heat in the car, and the bodies began to smell. And that is

how we were travelling. There were the German troop transports retreating from the front because the front was receding, and they had to retreat further. All the tracks were blocked and we had to stand for days to let the troop transports through first, and at night one could not see a thing. And one was beaten and trampled. In my case it was so that my trousers, my prisoner's trousers, were torn longwise and I couldn't wear my trousers any more. And I remained in my underpants. And so without any nourishment, without a drop of water, and there was snow outside, the ss gave us nothing. And we—there was a mass of insane and dead people in the car and after continuous travelling for five days we arrived in Regensburg. And it was already night and the ss opened the doors and said: If we throw out the dead bodies we shall get some food. And so I myself, together with a friend, removed twenty-five dead bodies from this car and laid them outside in the snow, you see? And then we were given a piece of bread and a little beaker of soup.

I had been standing all the way during this trip and I saved my life only because I had fastened to the car a piece of rope and held on tight. It was indeed utterly impossible. For instance, a friend of mine who withstood all these years in Auschwitz, went insane during the trip and attempted to attack us with a knife and four of use [sic], even five, had to hold him, otherwise he would have killed somebody. It was decidedly a panic. The whole car was in a tumult, and . . . when we arrived in Dachau there were more dead bodies than survivors.[18]

Conditions in the open wagons in which many of the prisoners were transported were no better than in the closed freight cars. One of the prisoners who endured the death march from Auschwitz to Groß-Rosen described the scene in the wagon in which he was transported:

> We entered the wagons naked, nearly naked, with the thin trousers, no . . . no overcoat, in the snow. Food we did not get. And so in these wagons we traveled for six days and six nights without food. . . . I myself can't believe that I have endured it! In every wagon there were every morning from ten to fifteen dead. . . . We slept on the dead. We lay on top of the dead. One took off the shoes from the dead if he had other, worn out shoes. We sat on top of the dead. . . . The Greeks were more terrible. They wanted to commit a dreadful deed. We didn't permit them. They wanted to cut off flesh from . . . the dead and roast it . . . and eat it, simply eat it. They asked if anybody has matches. . . . We did not permit them to do it. It was eaten in several wagons. It was eaten.[19]

The prisoners evacuated from Groß-Rosen were brought to several camps in Germany. About 2,300 reached Dachau, 4,000 reached Bergen-Belsen, 4,800 reached Mauthausen, and some 6,000 reached Buchenwald. About 9,500 of the evacuees from Groß-Rosen and its subcamps were brought to Flossenbürg. The camp that took in the largest number, more than 11,000, was Mittelbau-Dora. Several dozen apparently also reached Sachsenhausen.[20] . . .

Written Instructions and Verbal Realities: Stutthof

In January 1945 the Stutthof camp network was also in danger of falling into the hands of the Red Army. Stutthof had developed somewhat differently from other camps established in Poland after 1940. Until the beginning of 1942, its inmates were almost all Polish prisoners from the Gdansk area and Western Prussia. . . . From the beginning of 1942, it began to serve as a center for the supply of forced labor for the war effort.[21] The number of prisoners in the camp and its subcamps increased significantly in 1944. In Stutthof, as in other camps at that time, the Jews were a prominent national group among the incoming prisoners. The first transport of 2,500 Jews arrived from Auschwitz on July 9, 1944. During summer and fall 1944 tens of thousands of Jews evacuated from camps in the Kovno region and from Riga and Auschwitz arrived at Stutthof. The last transport arrived on October 28, 1944, and included 1,500 Jews. All in all, 23,566 Jewish prisoners were brought from Auschwitz; 21,817 of them were women and the great majority from Hungary. Another 25,043 Jews were transported from the Baltic states, and here too a large proportion were women: 16,123. Among the evacuees from the camps in the Baltic states were some 150 children and adolescents. Other Jews arrived in smaller numbers in transports from other camps.[22] . . .

The evacuation of the remoter subcamps of Stutthof began on January 20 and the prisoners were transported by road to the main camp. By January 23–24 the Red Army was less than 31 miles (50 kilometers) from the main camp. The area around the camp, not far from Danzig port, was teeming with more than 60,000 civilians and soldiers, heading for the port in order to leave by sea for Germany.[23] This disorder was at its height precisely at the time the prisoners were to be evacuated.

On January 25, 1945, Paul Werner Hoppe, commandant of Stutthof, sent out a detailed directive on the evacuation of the camp. . . . There were 46,331 prisoners in the main camp and 22,521 in the sub-camp when Hoppe sent out his order.[24] Concomitantly he circulated another order, headed Operational Plan (*Ablaufplan*), which included a detailed plan of the evacuation routes. It also specified the routes and the time of departure of each column of evacuated prisoners. The first left at 6 a.m. as planned, followed by Column 2, Column 3, and so on. Column 6 was scheduled to leave Stutthof at 10 a.m. The columns were heading for the town of Nickelswalde, west of Stutthof, and from there were to continue to northwestern Pomerania toward Lauenburg. Several of the columns were later directed to the Baltic coast, most of them to the town of Puck.[25]

The fact that plans had been drawn up ahead of time ostensibly ensured an orderly and organized evacuation. On January 25, 1945, at 4 a.m., the prisoners were called out to the parade ground and divided up by block into columns that left one after the other. Among them were Poles, Russians, Lithuanians, Czechs, Hungarians, Norwegians, Italians, Germans, and Jews. Each prisoner was allocated 18 ounces (500 grams) of bread and 4 ounces (120 grams) of margarine.[26] . . .

A large number of Jews made up at least three of the columns of prisoners that set out from Stutthof.[27] None of the evacuees were wearing clothes that could protect them against the wintry conditions, and many were barefoot. Every day the guards killed dozens of prisoners who were too weak to march on. On the other hand, at least some of the guards did not object when civilians at the roadside offered food to the prisoners. The guards and prisoners even conversed at times, speculating together about what the future held in store. A Lithuanian prisoner found himself exchanging views with a Lithuanian guard who had volunteered for the ss and served at Stutthof as to who was in a better position: the prisoner who was about to be liberated or the guard who had to contemplate his future after the war. Neither of them was willing to change places with the other. In some cases, the guards even tried to persuade German civilians that these prisoners

were not a gang of criminals whose only desire was to murder innocent citizens and that they could allow them to spend the night in a barn in the farmyard.[28]

An entirely different scenario was played out in the dozens of small camps stretching from Eastern Prussia to the south of Danzig district and central Pomerania. Thousands of prisoners perished during these evacuations, among them a large number of Jewish women who had arrived in those camps in summer and fall 1944.

In August 1944 a labor camp was established near the little Polish village of Szerokopas in Pomerania; it housed 500 to 600 Jewish women, about 450 of them Hungarian and the others from Poland and Lithuania. As was the case in other subcamps of Stutthof, winter took a devastating toll on the prisoners, and many of them died of hunger, cold, and hard labor. This camp was evacuated around January 13, 1945, with 150 of the surviving women prisoners beginning the march northward toward Danzig. Thirty women remained behind because they were too weak to leave. Apparently, one guard stayed with them, his task being to liquidate them. According to one version, these wretched women were killed by injections of poison. Later, people from the neighboring village saw the dead prisoners heaped on a wagon that was transporting their corpses out of the camp for burial.[29]

This policy of liquidating women too feeble to be evacuated was repeated in a number of places. Killings also occurred in the Gutowo subcamp in Western Prussia, where 1,200–1,500 Jewish women from Hungary, Czechoslovakia, France, Germany, Holland, Poland, and the Baltic states were incarcerated. Only about 1,000 of them lived to see the day of evacuation, January 17, 1945. The others perished from the backbreaking labor: digging antitank trenches in the frozen soil. About 200 to 300, who were too infirm to set out on the trek to the town of Nowo Miasto, which began in the early morning, were murdered by injections of kerosene, strychnine, or Lysol.[30] Similar liquidations also took place at the Hopeehill camps where approximately 50 women were selected and shot shortly before the evacuation began early in January.[31] Thirty sick inmates of the Kzremieniewo subcamp not far from Gotowo suffered a similar fate. On January 19, 1945, they were executed by poison injections on the eve of the evacuation.[32]

The liquidation of prisoners too infirm to march was common in the more remote subcamps south of the main camp, in the heart of Pomerania. These camps were located at a considerable distance from the main evacuation routes to the north, in the Baltic Sea area, and were evacuated as the Red Army came closer. The scope of the murders perpetrated in these small camps, where many of the inmates were Jewish women, was greater than that in the subcamps of Auschwitz and Groß-Rosen, where the sick were often left to their own devices. This liquidation activity can be explained in part by the very restricted opportunities for evacuation in those areas, the fact that the inmates were Jewish, and the lack of instructions from the camp command as to evacuation procedures. In any event, without doubt every effort was made to leave no living prisoners behind. . . .

In the havoc of the evacuation from Western Prussia and Pomerania, where most of the Stutthof subcamps were located, the columns of prisoners trudging westward for hundreds of miles were a hallucinatory sight. A large proportion of the prisoners were Jewish women. When one of them collapsed and died, her fellow prisoners would rapidly strip off the rags she was wearing so as to add a little warmth to their own bodies. The sight of the corpses scattered along the evacuation route was branded forever on their minds.

The guards, generally middle-aged men, walked over to prostrate prisoners and coolly shot them in the head. At night the evacuees were lodged in a barn, if one was accessible, or in other buildings that could be used for the same purpose. Sometimes they were given rations of food, organized haphazardly. In the morning they often discovered that they were lying on the corpses of those who had died during the night. This nightmare lasted for several weeks until the Soviet tanks caught up with the death marchers of the subcamps, particularly in Pomerania.[33] . . .

Other Camps

The liquidation of "dangerous prisoners" began almost simultaneously at Sachsenhausen and Ravensbrück. Parzifal Triete, an ss physician who served in Ravensbrück camp, said after the war that executions were carried out beside the crematorium and estimated that 50 prisoners at a time were liquidated. Two members of the camp staff executed the victims by pistol shots to the back of the head, and the corpses were then carried to the crematorium.[34] Schwarzhuber, who was the main figure behind the winter 1945 liquidation operation, reckoned that 150 to 200 prisoners were murdered by the Kommando Moll in that period.[35] In its final months of existence, Ravensbrück was transformed into an extermination camp. Between 150 and 180 male prisoners were liquidated in January 1945 in an improvised gas chamber as the overture to a wave of murderous activity. In the course of three months, until close to the date of evacuation of the camp, 5,000 to 6,000 prisoners were gassed.[36] Experts, who had gained their experience in operating extermination installations at Auschwitz, contributed their expertise to the construction of the gas chamber and to the mass extermination project at Ravensbrück in January–February 1945.[37] Almost all the victims were women.[38] The gas chamber was not large, about 10 yards by 5 yards (9 meters by 4.5 meters), and its capacity was a mere 150 prisoners at a time. It was built about 5.5 yards (5 meters) from the crematorium.[39]

However, the proficiency of the extermination experts from Auschwitz did not apparently extend to the ability to draw subtle distinctions between sick and unfit prisoners and those who could still be of some use to the system. Not all the victims were sick and elderly men, and among them were quite a few young women still capable of working.[40] The selections conducted in the camp were a daily nightmare for the women prisoners. The older women and the sick who were hospitalized in the revier or who lay prostrate in the barracks, lived in constant terror of being dispatched to the gas chamber in the next selection. Every day that passed without selection for death was a miracle.[41]

Quite a few women prisoners from the sub-camps were liquidated in the gas chamber at Ravensbrück. One such camp, Uckermark, operative from 1942, changed its function in December 1944, when thousands of women were evacuated from Auschwitz. It was, essentially, no more than a provisional transit camp for thousands of women prisoners from the East who were earmarked for extermination. Their physical condition was particularly pitiable since they had already undergone one evacuation from the East. Many of them fell victim to the devastating terror campaign, which lasted a few weeks.[42] One of the supervisors of the women SS guards, Ruth Closius-Neudeck, who was transferred to Uckermark from Ravensbrück in January 1945, explained:

When I took over the Uckermark camp, there were about 4,000 prisoners of all nationalities there. When I left Uckermark, apprx. six weeks later, there were only apprx. 1,000 prisoners left.

About 3,000 women were selected for gassing during my activities in Uckermark.[43]

Dr. Adolf Winkelmann, one of the physicians who carried out the selections, described them as follows:

I selected for removal the prisoners unfit to work. I always did this together with Dr. Trommer. . . . The prisoners marched in single file past Dr. Trommer and me. We could, of course, conduct only a very superficial examination, and people who were obviously sick, unfit to work or unfit to march, were picked out. The prisoners had their legs bare, so that we could see whether they were fit to march. It is possible that prisoners were examined in a barrack stripped to the waist. The barracks were unheated, and the last prisoners would have to wait about an hour. During my time at Ravensbrück, Dr. Trommer and I selected about 1,500 to 2,000 prisoners for outward drafts.[44]

Schwarzhuber, who claimed to have attended only one *Aktion* (assembly and deportation of prisoners for extermination) of women prisoners who underwent selections in the final period at Ravensbrück, described what he had witnessed:

I attended the gassing. 150 women at a time were forced into the gas-chamber. *Hauptscharführer* Moll ordered the women to undress as they were to be de-loused. They were then taken into the gas chamber and the door was closed. A male internee with gasmask climbed on the roof and threw a gas container into the room through the window, which he again closed immediately. I heard groaning and whispering in the room. After two or three minutes it grew quiet. Whether the women were dead or just senseless, I cannot say. I was not present when the room was cleaned out. I have only been told by Moll that the bodies were taken straight to the crematorium.[45]

Thus it was that Auschwitz, whose gas chambers and crematoria had been out of action for several months, stretched out a tentacle in spring 1945 to a veteran concentration camp in the very heart of the old Reich. . . .

Concurrently with the selections at Ravensbrück and the dispatch of the prisoners to the gas chamber, the Sachsenhausen command began to liquidate inmates "unfit to march." In February—March 1945 about 4,000 infirm prisoners were selected; some were shot and others gassed.[46] It is evident that the planned liquidation of prisoners classified by the camp command as sick, dangerous, or unfit for marching was carried out in spring 1945 in almost all the concentration camps. The killings were perpetrated by shooting, in gas chambers if such existed in the camp, or by injection of poison.[47]

In Dachau, a gas chamber was constructed in February 1945, and there too experts evacuated from Auschwitz played a significant part in the extermination project. Heinrich Schuster was an Austrian prisoner who had been interned in Auschwitz, where he assisted the camp's physicians. After the evacuation of Auschwitz in January 1945 he arrived at Dachau, and there he volunteered to help in dealing with the numerous cases of typhus in the camp. He was not a full-fledged physician since he had not completed his medical studies, but his partial qualifications sufficed for his tasks at Dachau. He continued to send sick prisoners to the gas chambers, as he had at Auschwitz.[48] . . . As was the case in other camps, Zyklon B gas was used in the gas chamber at Dachau.[49]

The situation at Flossenbürg was similar. The arrival of transports of prisoners from the camps in the East led to a steep rise in the mortality rate in the camp. Between mid-January and April 13, 1945, 3,370 prisoners perished, an average of 42 daily. The peak month was February, when most of the transports arrived; 59 prisoners on average died each day. At the same time there was a considerable increase in the selective liquidation of prisoners designated for "special treatment" (*Sonderbehandlung*), namely, those who were considered potentially dangerous, since it was feared that they might attempt to escape or foment resistance. Most of these were Russians.[50]

In Mauthausen, mass murders of prisoners had taken place even before early spring 1945. A regular gas chamber was constructed in fall 1941 in the cellar of one of the buildings, and there too Zyklon B was the accepted murder method. The chamber was small: 4.1 yards by 3.8 yards (3.8 meters by 3.5 meters). Only 80 prisoners at a time could be gassed. The victims were almost always camp inmates, excluding one case in 1942 when a group of Soviet POWs were gassed.[51]

At least nine cases of liquidation by gassing of large groups took place at Mauthausen in April 1945. Some of the victims, arrested for political reasons, were sent to the camp for execution there by the Vienna, Graz, or Linz Gestapos. They were taken directly to the gas chamber without any record being made of their names. On April 20, 1945, Dr. Waldemar Wolter SS physician in the camp, gave instructions that at least 3,000 of the 7,782 sick inmates should be transferred to Camp III (a section of the camp constructed in spring 1944, where most of the inmates were infirm and earmarked for liquidation) because they were feeble, sick, and nonfunctioning. In the end, 1,500 prisoners were sent to Camp III, and about 650 of them were dispatched to the gas chamber between April 22 and 25. The mass extermination continued until the end of the month, and some 1,200 to 1,400 men and women were gassed.[52] This was in addition to the 3,000 or so other prisoners who perished in the camp in the final weeks of the war as a result of the camp's inhuman conditions.[53] In Neuengamme as well, the massacre of sick prisoners began in fall 1944 and continued in the first few months of 1945. Between January and March, 6,224 sick prisoners were executed by poison injections administered by the camp physicians. In the first two weeks of April, another 1,800 prisoners were liquidated.[54]

In the same period, prisoners were liquidated in other camps by different means. In Buchenwald, for example, a section of the camp known as the "Little Camp," which had been a tent camp until 1944, was expanded to contain 17 prisoners' barracks. Thousands of prisoners evacuated from camps in the East soon filled those barracks. Each was intended to hold between 500 and 600 inmates, but 1,000 (and, in some cases, even 1,800–1,900) were packed in. The Little Camp was closed off and isolated from the rest of the camp. Hunger, disease, and death reigned there, and countless corpses lay sprawled between the barracks. The Jews who arrived from Auschwitz and Groß-Rosen on February 10, 1945, were thrown like discarded objects into a site that resembled a vast pigsty.[55] At the beginning of January there had been 6,000 prisoners in the Little Camp; by early April the number had swelled to 17,000. Extermination through starvation and disease produced results similar to active initiatives such as gas and poison injections adopted in other camps: about 5,200 prisoners died in the Little Camp at Buchenwald in less than 100 days. In all, more than 13,000 inmates perished in the camp and its subcamps in January—April 1945.[56]

However, the most blatant example of extermination through epidemic and disease, as practiced in 1945, was Bergen-Belsen. It had started out as a small camp for the internment of groups of "Jews for exchange" (Austauschjuden)—that is, those who were to be exchanged for groups of Germans living in Palestine or other countries under Allied protection. With time it expanded into the camp where Himmler intended to hold 30,000 Jews as a bargaining card in the negotiations. In the last weeks of the war it was transformed into one of the most atrocious murder sites for Jews and other concentration camp prisoners.[57]

In early 1944, Oswald Pohl and other officials in the WVHA came to the conclusion that Bergen-Belsen was being underexploited and should be used more efficiently. As a result the camp was assigned a new series of tasks in March 1944: it became an absorption camp for sick prisoners from concentration and labor camps administered by the WVHA. In the cynical coded language of the WVHA, the camp was denoted a "rehabilitation camp" (Erholungslager) whose task was to rehabilitate sick prisoners in order to restore their capacity for work. By spring 1944, groups of prisoners from Mittelbau-Dora who could no longer keep up the pace required by the intensive construction work began to arrive at Bergen-Belsen.[58] They were housed in empty barracks without reasonable sleeping arrangements, received very little food, and were given no medical treatment. Its high mortality rate became a constant feature of the "rehabilitation camp." In the course of 1944 Bergen-Belsen rapidly became a vital cog in the "extermination through labor" machine, which was then approaching maximal production. In summer 1944 the camp was expanded to include a women's camp, and in the fall large transports of women prisoners from Auschwitz arrived in order to become slave laborers.[59]

In view of the anticipated large-scale evacuations from the East and the planned expansion of the camp, Josef Kramer was appointed commandant of Bergen-Belsen. Kramer had acquired considerable experience in the system. His career was launched in April 1936 at Dachau; he moved on in 1938 to Mauthausen, and in 1940 to Natzweiler-Struthof, where he was promoted to camp commandant in 1942. In May 1944 Glücks appointed him commandant of Auschwitz II (Birkenau), but he held this position for only a few months. By fall 1944 Auschwitz was being dismantled and Bergen-Belsen was growing. In late November 1944, Glücks ordered Kramer to take up the position of commandant of Bergen-Belsen.[60] There were 15,257 inmates when Kramer arrived in the camp, and the number expanded rapidly in the last few months of the war. Prisoners were sent there from all over Germany. . . . Bergen-Belsen became the main center for extermination of prisoners who were of no further economic value. By March 31, 1945, the number of prisoners had reached 44,060. Kramer realized that matters were spiralling out of control after he received instructions to absorb another 2,500 sick women from Ravensbrück. He appealed to Glücks that month to take immediate action in light of the situation:

At the end of January it was decided that an occupation of the camp by over 35,000 detainees must be considered too great. In the meantime, this number has been exceeded by 7,000 and a further 6,200 are at this time on their way. The consequence of this is that all barracks are overcrowded by at least 30 per cent. The detainees cannot lie down to sleep, but must sleep in a sitting position on the floor. . . . In addition to this question, a spotted fever and typhus epidemic has now begun, which increases in extent every day. The daily mortality rate, which was still in the region of 60–70 at the beginning of February, has in the meantime attained a daily average of 250–300 and will still further

increase in view of the conditions that at present prevail. . . .

The number of sick has greatly increased, particularly on account of the transports of detainees, which have arrived from the east in recent times—these transports have sometimes spent eight to fourteen days in open trucks. An improvement in their condition, and particularly a return of those detainees to work, is under present conditions quite out of the question. The sick here gradually pine away till they die of weakness of the heart and general debility . . . On one occasion, out of a transport of 1,900 detainees, over 500 arrived dead. The fight against the spotted fever is made exactly difficult by the lack of means of disinfection. . . .[61]

The number of prisoners who perished at Bergen-Belsen in the last four and a half months of the war, namely, from early 1945 until the liberation, has been estimated as approximately 35,000. When British troops reached the camp on April 15 there were about 60,000 inmates there, most of them suffering from typhus. Many of them died after being liberated.[62]

Bergen-Belsen's evolution in the final months of the war from a transit camp of secondary importance to the site of mass extermination cannot be explained solely on the basis of the conditions in the camp system after the large-scale evacuations from the East. Eberhard Kolb regarded this development as an intrinsic component of the Nazi concentration camp system. It converted a concentration camp, which had been established as an installation for imprisonment, punishment, and later, for labor supply, into an installation for mass extermination. Although this extermination was not preplanned, its scope was no smaller than that of installations established specifically for liquidating target populations, first and foremost among them the Jews. Bergen-Belsen is the prime example of this development.[63] . . .

The situation at Bergen-Belsen and other camps was the direct outcome of the need for slave laborers, and of the inability and impossibility of maintaining them, the lack of places to which to transfer them, and the overall system rationale that it was preferable to be rid of and even to murder sick, feeble, and worn-out prisoners who were of no further value. In no other camp were the Jews so prominent a presence as in Bergen-Belsen in early 1945, and this fact undoubtedly exacerbated this unique situation. These were indeed unparalleled circumstances, a combination of planned and spontaneous extermination that existed in all the camps in Germany but took on monstrous proportions at Bergen-Belsen. The extermination activity in the concentration camps in the weeks and days before the evacuations was an inseparable part of the death marches chapter that began in January 1945 in camps in Poland, continued in the camps in Germany, and was to end in April-May.

NOTES

1. Hans-Peter Messerschmidt, "Bericht über meine KZ-Zeit 1943–1945" [Report on my days in the camp, 1943–1945], June 1945, YVA, 033/1692, 37–38.
2. Strafverfahren gegen Helmrich Heilmann, Josef Kierspel, and Johann Mirbeth, Staatsarchiv Bremen (hereafter StaB), 3 Js 1263/50, vol. 14, 2942–44.
3. Témoignage de Samuel Steinberg AN, 72 AJ 318–21; Strzelecki, *The Evacuation*, 211.
4. Testimony of Alexander Gertner, August 26, 1946, Boder Collection.
5. Memoirs of Avraham Baruch, January 1965, YVA, 033/1397, 31.
6. Beny Wirtzberg, *MiGai HaHariga LeShaar HaGai* [From the valley of death to the valley gateway] (Ramat Gan: Massada, 1967), 72–73.
7. Testimony of Hadassa Marcus, September 13, 1946, Boder Collection.
8. Testimony of Simcha Appelbaum, March 25, 1988, YVA, 03/4561.
9. "A gruss fun a geheynem," 32.
10. Testimony of Juergen Bassfreund, September 20, 1946.
11. *Death Marches*, UNRRA/Arolsen II, 9–9a.
12. Delowicz, *Sladem krwi*, 23; and see Gmina Leszczyny pow. Rybnik, September 29, 1945, USHMMA, RG-15.019M, reel 12, no. 247.
13. Testimony of Yitzhak Grabowsky, July 8, 1993.
14. Neander, *Konzentrationslager Mittelbau*, 100.
15. On the evacuation route from Auschwitz to Mauthausen, see *Death Marches*, UNRRA/Arolsen II, 42.
16. On the evacuation route from Auschwitz to Buchenwald, see ibid., 8.
17. See Strzelecki, "The Liquidation of the Camp," in Dlugborski and Piper, *Auschwitz 1940–1945*, vol. V, 31–33, and Appendix 18, 322; and Strzelecki, *The Evacuation*, 47.
18. Testimony of Juergen Bassfreund, September 20, 1946.
19. Testimony of Alexander Gertner, August 26, 1946.
20. Mieczyslaw Moldawa, *Groß Rosen: Oboz koncentracyjny na Slasku* (Warsaw: Wydawnictwo Ministerstwa Obrony Narodowej, 1980), 28. For a detailed list of the transports from Groß-Rosen to German camps in January—April 1945, see Sprenger, *Groß-Rosen*, 353–59.
21. Krzysztof Dunin-Wasowicz, *Oboz koncentracyjny Stutthof* (Gdansk: Wydawnictwo Morskie, 1970), 34–42; Glinski, "Organizacja obozu," 54–65; *Stutthof: Hitlerowski oboz koncentracyjny* (Warsaw: Wydawnictwo Interpress, 1988), 116–19.
22. Drywa, *Zaglada Zydow*, 83–92. For details of the transports that brought Jewish prisoners to Stutthof in 1944, see Drywa, "Ruch transportów," 29–30.
23. Goinski, "Organizacja obuzu," 184.
24. Report on number of prisoners in Stutthof and subcamps, January 24, 1945, USHMMA, RG-04.058M, reel 223.

25. Ablaufplan, January 25, 1945, USHMMA, RG-04.058M, reel 209.

26. Grabovvska, *Marsz smierci*, 15–16.

27. Drywa, *Zaglada Zydow*, 282.

28. Ralys Sruoga, *Forest of the Gods: Memoirs* (Vilnius: Vaga, 1996), 281, 290–91.

29. Testimonies of Guta Lev, July 29, 1968; Bernard Bugun, November 12, 1969; Henrik Libera, November 12, 1969; and Bronislav Gurlej, September 1, 1970, ZStL, 407 AR-Z, 44/7, vol. 1.

30. Testimonies of Blanka Szabo, October 26/27, 1961; Leslie Keller, December 10, 1968; and Sara Alter, September 19, 1972, ZStL, 407 AR-Z 51/69, vol. 11.

31. Summary of the conclusions of the investigation regarding Hopeehill, September 25, 1972, ZStL, 407 AR-Z, 182/72, vol. 1.

32. Summary of conclusions of investigation of Krzemieniewo, November 17, 1972, ZStL, 407, AR-Z 242/72, vol. 1.

33. Testimony of Rochel Blackman-Slivka, June 15, 1990, USHMMA, RG-50.030# 216; testimony of Ruth Kenet, August 7, 1984, USHMMA, RG-50.155#03; memoirs of Sonia Heyd-Green, 1992, USHMMA, RG-02.112#01.

34. Depositions of Dr. Parzifal Triete, May 5, 1945, August 14, 1945, and October 3, 1946, Ravensbrück trial, TNA WO 235/309.

35. Depositions of Johann Schwarzhuber, August 15 and 30, 1946, Ravensbrück trial, TNA WO 235/309.

36. Suhren gave a much lower estimate [of] no more than 1,500 prisoners liquidated (deposition of Fritz Suhren, December 30, 1945, IMT, NO-3647). Schwarzhuber referred to 2,300–2,400 (deposition of Johann Schwarzhuber, August 30, 1946, Ravensbrück trial). On the number of prisoners murdered in the camp in the final months, see Erpel, *Zwischen Vernichtung und Befreiung*, 75; Strebel, *Das KZ Ravensbrück*, 485–86; Orth, *Das System*, 291.

37. Testimony of Dr. Adolf Winkelmann, January 22, 1947, Ravensbrück trial, TNA WO 235/303, 311.

38. Bernard Strebel, "Das Männerlager im KZ Ravensbrück 1941–1945," *Dachauer Hefte* 14 (1998), 167.

39. Deposition of Johann Schwarzhuber, August 30, 1946, Ravensbrück trial. On extermination in the gas chamber at Ravensbrück in 1945, see Strebel, *Das KZ Ravensbrück*, 476–86.

40. Deposition of Dr. Parzifal Triete, May 5, 1945, Ravensbrück trial.

41. Depositions of Lotte Sontag, August 17, 1947, and Marta-Elizabet Ruthenberg, December 18, 1947, Ravensbrück trial, TNA WO, 235/516A; Lucia Schmidt-Fels, *Deportation nach Ravensbrück* (Essen: Plöger, 2004), 109–10; Gorce, *Journal de Ravensbrück*, 107, 111.

42. Summary of the findings of the investigation in the trial of three women guards at Uckermark, Ravensbrück trial, the Deputy Judge Advocate General, British Army of the Rhine, May 18, 1948, TNA WO 235/516A.

43. Deposition of Ruth Closius-Neudeck, December 2, 1947, Ravensbrück trial, TNA WO 235/516A.

44. Deposition of Dr. Alfred Winkelmann, November 4, 1946, Ravensbrück trial, TNA WO, 235/310.

45. Deposition of Johann Schwarzhuber, August 15, 1946, Ravensbrück trial.

46. *Justiz und NS-Verbrechen*, vol. 18, 299–306.

47. Orth, *Das System*, 299.

48. Stanislav Zamecnik, *C'etait ça, Dachau 1933–1945* (Paris: Fondation international de Dachau, 2003), 408–9; Michael W. Perry, ed., *Dachau Liberated: The Official Report by the U.S. Seventh Army* (Seattle WA: Inkling Books, 2000), 94.

49. Zamecnik, "Dachau-Stammlager," 266.

50. Toni Siegert, "Das Konzentrationslager Flossenbürg: Ein Lager für sogenannte Asoziale und Kriminelle," in Martin Broszat and Elke Fröhlich, eds., *Bayern in der NS-Zeit*, vol. II (Munich: R. Oldenbourg, 1979), 476–77.

51. Hans Marsalek, *The History of Mauthausen Concentration Camp: Documentation* (Linz: Gutenberg-Werbering, 1995), 198–99.

52. Hans Marsalek, *Die Vergasungsaktionen im Konzentrationslager Mauthausen: Dokumentation* (Vienna: Steinde-Druck, 1988, 13–15; Michel Fabréguet, *Mauthausen: Camp de concentration*

national-socialiste en Autriche rattachée (1938–1945) (Paris: Champion, 1999), 490–98.

53. David W. Pike, *Mauthausen: L'enfer nazi en Autriche* (Toulouse: Privat, 2004), 231.

54. Kaienburg, *Vernichtung durch Arbeit*, 381–82.

55. "A gruss fun a geheynem," 43–44.

56. *Buchenwald Concentration Camp 1937–1945: A Guide to the Permanent Historical Exhibition* (Göttingen: Wallstein Verlag, 2004), 224; Kogon, *The Theory and Practice of Hell*, 250.

57. On the development of Bergen-Belsen in 1943–1945, see Wenke, *Zwischen Menschenhandel*, 94ff.; Kolb, *Bergen Belsen*, 44ff.

58. Wagner, *Produktion des Todes*, 89.

59. Wenke, *Zwischen Menschenhandel*, 338–47; Joanne Reilly, *Belsen: The Liberation of a Concentration Camp* (London: Routledge, 1998), 15–17.

60. Deposition of Josef Kramer, July 23, 1945, USHMMA, RG-04.03M, reel 1.

61. Report of Josef Kramer to Richard Glücks, March 1, 1945, TNA WO 309/17, in Raymond Phillips, ed., *The Trial of Josef Kramer and Forty-Four Others (The Bergen Trial)* (London: William Hodge & Co., 1949), 164–66.

62. Wenke, *Zwischen Menschenhandel*, 362; Reilly, Belsen, 17.

63. Kolb, *Bergen Belsen*, 9–10.

7 Collaboration and Its Limits

14. Hungarian police arresting Robert Mandel in Budapest, December 1944. (U.S. Holocaust Memorial Museum, courtesy of Eva Hevesi Ehrlich.)

15. Rescuer Vladimir Chernovol, Vodiana, Ukraine, 1942. Gregory Lantsman was a Jewish pilot in the Soviet army when his plane was shot down over Ukraine. Surviving the crash, Gregory wandered the countryside seeking shelter. The Germans had already killed his family and wiped out his regiment. By chance, Gregory met Vladimir Chernovol, a Ukrainian teacher, who was out for a walk. Gregory told Vladimir that he was Jewish. Vladimir understood that without assistance Gregory would surely be caught and killed. He offered to take him in. With great difficulty Vladimir was able to obtain Ukrainian identity papers for Gregory. But soon the Germans were forcibly taking young Ukrainian men for hard labor. Gregory was one of those selected. He managed to escape from the train and returned to the safety of Vladimir's home. Though there were many close calls, Vladimir was able to hide Gregory until liberation in May 1944. (Courtesy JFR Photo Archives.)

Introduction

PETER HAYES

The Nazi regime could not carry out the dispossession and murder of Europe's Jews alone. For that, it lacked sufficient personnel, local knowledge, and sometimes even jurisdiction. Hitler's henchmen therefore often depended on the active or passive cooperation of collaborators: individuals, organizations, and governments that chose to aid or, at least, not impede the killing. In the early, most mortal phase of the Holocaust, the period between June 1941 and February 1943, their conduct extended the Reich's reach and added to the death toll; later, their gradual defection had the ironic consequence that, when the Holocaust ended, the largest numbers of Jewish survivors inhabited countries that earlier had allied with Nazi Germany.

The table below distributes the German-administered or -allied territories of Europe in 1941–45 according to whether the mortality rate of Jews in each region ultimately exceeded or fell below the continent-wide average of two-thirds.

That the most lethal parts of the continent were those directly occupied and administered by German officials does not mean that collaboration there was unimportant. In nearly all these places, local police forces and/or militias continued to function and often to participate in rounding up Jews, and denizens eager to denounce Jews in hiding were numerous. Conversely, the generally lower death rates under indigenous collaborating governments do not imply that their personnel or citizens refrained from persecuting Jews. On the contrary, Vichy France under Philippe Pétain, Hungary under Regent Miklos Horthy, Romania under Marshall Ion Antonescu, and Bulgaria under Tsar Boris III independently enacted virulently antisemitic legislation, stripped many Jews of citizenship, and delivered certain groups of Jews to Germany and/or engaged in killing them.

The decisive variable that determined the mortality rate in any given country was usually time, more specifically, whether the Nazi state

TABLE 7. Death rates

	UNDER GERMAN ADMINISTRATION	UNDER COLLABORATING GOVERNMENTS
Over two-thirds	Baltic states, Belarus, Ukraine, Holland, Germany, Luxembourg, Bohemia-Moravia, Poland, Serbia, Greece	Slovakia, Croatia, Hungary after May 1944
Under two-thirds	Belgium	Bulgaria, Romania, Denmark, Finland, Norway, France, Italy, Hungary until May 1944

attacked the resident Jews in 1941–42. Where Germans ruled directly, they almost always mobilized in pursuit of Jews promptly and thoroughly, unencumbered by an interest in preserving smooth working relations with local governments and populations. Where local administrations remained in place, however, the Germans at first preferred to let native antisemitism run its course while they concentrated on the Jews in their grasp elsewhere. By late 1942, when most of those Jews were dead and the Reich became insistent, the tide of war was turning and affiliated governments were growing wary of further persecution. Emblematic of the changing climate are the deportation statistics from two countries where the final death toll proved relatively low: 50% of the Jews ever deported from France and 60% of those from Belgium departed in 1942, and then the pace slowed from both places. Equally telling was the behavior of Hitler's Balkan allies. Bulgaria, Hungary, and Romania each handed over to the Nazis the Jewish populations of regions taken in 1939–41 from neighboring states under German auspices, but declined to turn over the Jewish inhabitants of their core territories in 1942–43.

If chapter 6 sought to explain how the Nazi regime came so close to its goal of eradicating the Jews of Europe, this chapter both continues that story and shows why the Third Reich in the end fell short of its objective. Jan Grabowski's description of killings by *the Polish "Blue" Police* in Dabrowa county, a part of the occupied General Government near Krakow, reveal how greed, prejudice, group bonding, and fear of German punishment turned local lawmen into executioners of Jews in hiding. Jean Ancel traces the *aborted annihilation* that stemmed from the Romanian government's mixture of crazed and cynical antisemitism. Virulent racism led that regime in

1941–42, on the one hand, to slaughter the Jewish inhabitants of regions conquered from the Soviet Union and to dream of dumping Romania's own Jews beyond these territories, but on the other hand, to renege on a promise to deliver these indigenous Jews to the Nazis, largely because doing so seemed by late 1942 to entail greater costs than benefits. Saul Friedländer, the orphaned son of Jewish refugees in France who were handed over to the Germans and gassed at Auschwitz, delineates the sad, semi-delusional, but ultimately statistically successful story of the efforts of both the Vichy French government and the main association of Jews in France to draw a distinction between *"our" Jews and the rest* and thus to buy the lives of most native-born Jews by accepting and abetting the deportation of foreign ones. Susan Zuccotti ponders *the Italian paradox*, tracing and seeking to account for the contradiction prior to Mussolini's fall in September 1943 between Italy's official, sometimes violently antisemitic policies and its protection of Jews from deportation in Italian-occupied regions, such as southeastern France, the Dalmatian coast, and central Greece. Randolph Braham describes how a similar, long-standing paradox between official antisemitism and refusal to surrender Jews to Germany ended in *the Hungarian paroxysm* of 1944, when the pent up hatreds of that nation's right wing were unleashed by the onset of German military occupation. Within less than two months, Hungarian army and police forces, advised and aided by only 200 German personnel, carried out the deportation of more than 400,000 people to Auschwitz, where some three-quarters of them perished. By the time Horthy withdrew his government's cooperation in July, virtually the only Jews left alive in Hungary were in Budapest.

Others forms of collaboration with the Holocaust were less bloody, but equally fraught with moral compromise. Two cases in point stand out, the Vatican and Swiss financial institutions. Michael Phayer analyzes the unfortunate *papal priorities* that prompted Pope Pius XII, a diplomat by training and a Roman aristocrat by descent, to rank his aspirations to broker a peace that would check the influence of communism in Europe and to avert the bombing of Rome ahead of using the Church's intelligence network and influence to check the carnage. Not until mid-1944, following both the liberation of Rome and the Allies' repeated reiteration that they would accept nothing short of unconditional surrender by the Germans, did the Pope publically intervene to save the lives of Jews by calling on Horthy to stop the Hungarian deportations. The pontiff's record of private, behind the scenes action was little better. The role of a *self-serving Switzerland* in facilitating both Nazi aggression and the Holocaust is laid bare in the sober, authoritative prose of the report of an international historians' commission appointed by the Swiss government. That document reveals that the Swiss National Bank, along initially with a few privately owned Swiss banks, knowingly accepted gold stolen by the Nazis from the treasuries of occupied countries and from Jews, including from the mouths of corpses, and that several of these commercial banks later quietly and wittingly pocketed "dormant" bank accounts, that is, sums deposited in Swiss banks by people who had been killed in the Holocaust.

The Vatican and Swiss examples serve as fitting final entries in this chapter because each reflects the degree to which the German perpetrators of the Holocaust benefitted from the self-interest of others. Whether it took the form of assuring one's own or one's neighbors' survival, as in the conduct of the Blue Police, or in asserting a perceived national goal at the expense of some Jews, as in the French, Bulgarian, Romanian, and Hun-

garian cases, or in pursuing putatively grander purposes, such as the Pope's, or more venal ones, such as those of the Swiss banks, the Nazis generally could rely on individual or institutional self-interest to work in their favor, at least as long as they seemed to be winning the war, and sometimes even longer.

Poland: The Blue Police

JAN GRABOWSKI

From *Hunt for the Jews*

An important and, as it seems, largely unknown role in the hunting down and killing of Jewish refugees between 1942 and 1945 was performed by the Polish "blue" police. The only book that takes up the topic of the history of the "blue" police, surprising as it may seem, fails even to mention this problem.[1] Nevertheless, the deadly efficiency of the Polish "blue" police operating in Dąbrowa Tarnowska County at least matched that of their colleagues, the German gendarmes. Although our analysis concerns only one county, there is no reason to think that the activities of Polish policemen from Dąbrowa differed from the working habits of their counterparts from other rural areas of occupied Poland with similar ethnic composition. Detachments of Polish and German police were spread throughout the county. Some of them were closed after 1942 (when the security situation deteriorated considerably) but other, reinforced, stations lasted until the end of the occupation. As noted, police stations were located in all larger villages, and definitely in the administrative centers of the communes (*gminy*) of the county.

Who were the "blue" policemen stationed in Dąbrowa and in the area? Most of them were prewar Polish policemen, mobilized by the Germans in the fall of 1939. The rest were new officers recruited under the occupation and trained in the police school in Nowy Sącz (Neu-Sandetz). Some of the new wartime recruits failed to meet even the modest prewar police selection criteria, having completed less than the four classes of primary school normally required for future officers. Finally, there were many policemen from northern and western Poland.[2] These areas had been incorporated directly into the Reich, and consequently the local police forces had been entirely replaced by the German authorities, with personnel brought in from the Reich. At this point, the former Polish policemen were offered a chance to continue to serve—but in the *Generalgouvernement*. According to numerous contemporary testimonies and to reports of the underground press, these "imported" policemen lacked ties to the local population, tended to be loyal to the occupation authorities, and were eager to fulfill German orders.

In the eyes of the Polish policemen, the Jews, or rather their goods, were a prized catch. . . . In the period before the liquidation of Dąbrowa-area ghettos, the "blues" had perfected the methods of robbing the Jews who moved between the Jewish communities. The memoirs of a "blue" policeman from Dąbrowa provide a detailed description of this practice, which most often targeted Jewish village merchants.[3] In the beginning the "blues," unwilling to kill the goose which laid golden eggs, simply requested their "cut." Jewish merchants were forced to hand over a part of their merchandise or some of their cash. Those reluctant to follow the orders of bandits in blue uniforms were arrested, severely beaten, or both. And in the end, they were always robbed. Chaja Rosenblatt observed the "officers in blue" in action from her home, in Radomyśl Wielki:

Until then [December 1941] some Radomyśl Jews drove their carts to Tarnów, to the market. Thanks to this trade they were able to keep their families alive. Theirs was a very difficult and very dangerous profession. The carts left before dawn, and the merchants hid their modest goods in their clothing, on their bodies, in the pockets of their overcoats. Meat and other foodstuffs were being hidden in special concealed compartments inside the carts. On the way back, they would bring cloth and fabric. Jews engaged in this trade risked the penalty of death, and the roads were often watched by the Polish Police. Hopefully, the Polish policemen could be bought with money.[4]

Later, when the ghettos had been liquidated, the Polish policemen continued to stop the Jews, but this time the price was life:

Kazimierz Ł. promised Mrs. Kupelman to guide her to a safe location. He went to Tarnów to pick her up and told her to take along all her valuables. He then asked a "blue" policeman, his partner, to wait in ambush. Close to Bolesław they raped the poor woman and later brutally murdered her. It was not the only crime of this kind—Ł. frequently offered help to the Jews who tried to cross Vistula River and flee to the north. Then he robbed and killed them; none of them have ever been seen alive again.[5]

Given the potential profits, it is hardly surprising that "Jewish affairs" occupied an important place in the schedule of work of Polish "blue" police. The testimonies of policemen from Radgoszcz station are particularly revealing. The officers described in minute detail the successive steps of the hunt for Jews, the importance of local inform-

ers, and the cooperation with German gendarmerie. They also tried to shift some of the blame onto their German colleagues. Officer Stanisław Młynarczyk from Radgoszcz police station testified as follows:

In the fall of 1942, together with officers Gordziejczyk and Heinberger, we went to the village of Żdzary where we caught four Jews (among them one Jewess), who were hiding in the house of one Szkotak. The Jews were later brought to Radgoszcz and shot by the Germans. Gordziejczyk, who went on horseback to alert the police in Radgoszcz, returned with Gestapo agents, and they shot Szkotak and his wife for having kept the Jews. Also in the fall of 1942, in Radgoszcz, I caught one Jewess and her small child. They were hiding in the house of Władyslaw Odoki, and it was Odoki himself who informed us about the Jews in his house. I went along with Hajnberger from the *Sonderdienst*. When we were some 200 meters away from Odoki's farm, Hajnberger took them aside, and first shot the woman, and then her child. I took no part in the shooting. Sometime later the same Odoki betrayed other two Jews who were hidden at his farm. They also were shot by the German Gestapo agents.[6]

The deadly efficiency of the "blue" police in the process [of] exterminating the Jews was linked, on the one hand, to their excellent knowledge of the area and, on the other, to the dense network of available informers. Unlike gendarmes, who appeared rarely, if ever, in remote areas, the "blues" were constantly present in rural communities. Dąbrowa County was not only their place of work, but they often hailed from this area and had spouses and children in the villages nearby. The existence of intimate links between the rural population and hunters in police uniforms often had fatal consequences for the Jews in hiding. One survivor from the Mielec area made [the] following observation: "Normally, Poles who betrayed Jews notified the Blue Police, who either shot the Jews or handed them over to the Germans, claiming that they had been caught in the fields. Such stories were unlikely to be challenged, since the Gestapo wanted to make it easier for Poles to get rid of any Jewish families they were sheltering."[7]

The police action was usually triggered by "confidential information" communicated personally or sent anonymously through the mail. The scale of denunciation has been discussed before in the historical literature.[8] Although the studies looked at the urban side of this phenomenon, there is nothing to indicate that in the rural context the informers were any less dangerous. Władysław Reiter, a Kripo agent from Mielec and, at the same time, an intelligence officer for the underground Home Army (AK), testified that he "had helped Poles who had been denounced for sheltering Jews. He warned these Poles of impending danger."[9] Sometimes, fear of official reprisals pushed people to inform on their neighbors. In Miroszów (close to the town of Miechów), a group of Polish policemen on the so-called quota patrol (looking for "unlicensed" cattle, or for peasants who failed to fulfill their quotas of deliveries to the state) entered the house of one Piotr Jaworski. Jaworski "brought forth half a liter of vodka and told the officers that there were Jews hiding in Bielawski's house."[10] This information was intended to draw the officers' attention away from unfulfilled quotas and possible penalties and toward a more inviting target. Indeed, a quick search of Bielawski's house revealed the presence of four Jews. The Jews were searched, and all their valuables were seized by the policemen. Finally, the officers took the Jews outside the village and executed all of them with shots to the back of the head. "Consider yourself lucky," said Officer Krawczyk to Bielawski. "Had we taken them to the police station, the Germans would have shot you, and your family."[11]

Indeed, although the locals from time to time delivered Jews into the hands of the Germans, they did it much more willingly if the "blue" policemen were involved. The reason was simple: the officers of the Polish police did not inspire such fear as the dreaded German gendarmes. The "blues" belonged, after all, to the same "universe of moral obligation."[12] Unlike Germans, they were predictable (at least they seemed predictable to the peasants) and, as far as the "Jewish cases" were concerned, one could hope for their leniency and a sense of national, ethnic, or racial (depending on the circumstances) solidarity. Furthermore, the "blue" policemen in many cases were officers remembered from the better, prewar times, representing continuity of familiar authority. In Kaszowice, in the spring of 1943, a group of local boys, shepherds tending the cattle, caught Józef Goldfeier (or Goldfinger—the peasants were not sure of his name) and brought him to the village elder.[13] The elder sent for the "blue" policemen from the nearby Liszki detachment. Some time later the peasants met in front of the elder's house to discuss the situation. The people who at one point or another had given assistance to the unfortunate Jewish captive were most upset. Now, should he talk, their own lives would be at risk. A tumultuous debate ensued in order to decide whether the captured Jew should die or be set free. The first option carried the day and Goldfeier (or Goldfinger) was soon executed by Officer Kożuch, on the orders of his superior, Lieutenant Stanisław Habdas. "Despite repeated warnings, the Jew tried to flee," said Habdas during his interrogation in 1949.

In other cases, peasants would try to reach an understanding with the "blues," in order to solve—with the assistance of the police—their "Jewish problem." Icek Mendel before fleeing his native village of Dulcza Wielka left a considerable amount of money for safekeeping with Jan J., his gentile neighbor. In the winter of 1942–1943, Mendel reappeared in the village and requested his money back. Jan J., unwilling to hand over the 30,000 zlotys that he had in the meantime started to consider his own, contacted the local "blue" policemen.[14] We have no information as to the precise nature of the deal reached between the two parties, but its results were dramatic and immediate. Józef Kozub, whose house was situated on the outskirts of Dulcza close to the forest, testified after the war:

> There were three Jewboys and a Jewess in my house. They came in to dry their shoes and to warm up by the oven. One of them was Icek Mendel from Radomyśl, whom I knew well. In the afternoon, around 3 p.m., the Polish Police surrounded my house and found inside all these four Jews. There were three police officers, although I do not recall their names because they beat me up like savages. My wife told me that one of them was officer Strzępka but she didn't know the two others. They shot the Jews and later told me to bury them.[15]

There were better policemen and there were worse policemen. Some of them wanted to have nothing to do with the implementation of the "Final Solution." One P. who (together with his wife) performed something akin to "citizens' arrest" and delivered two Jewish women to the police, encountered hostility instead of gratitude. One witness said,

> I have heard with my own ears how the Jewesses begged P. to let them go. But P.'s wife said, "you deserve it, and now you will suffer, and there is

nothing that you can do about it!" So the pleas and begging were for nothing, and the women were brought to the police. Later P. came to me and said that he hoped for an award: "But instead I received a reprimand. Gromala, one of the 'blue' policemen, asked me why I had delivered the Jewesses to his station. He even said to me, 'Well, if you have already brought them here, you can just as well shoot them yourself!'"[16]

Another "blue" policeman, one Stanisław, offered to help Rivka Shenker, who had been caught hiding in the forest, in November 1944:

> He came up to me and asked: "What is your name? It seems to me that I know you from somewhere." . . . So I gave him my name, and he went pale and said: 'Do you know who I am?' So I said: "You look very much like Stanisław, the policeman I used to know." He was silent for a moment and then said: "Because I am this Stanisław. What do you do here? Where did they catch you? Dear Lord, I want to help you, I knew your grandmother very well. She was always so good to me, so now I want to pay it back. I hope you don't hold it against me that I work with the Germans; I had no other choice."[17]

Distrustful and suspecting treason, Shenker rejected the offer of help. "I was sure that if I accepted his offer, I would be doomed because I was young and attractive and he would first take advantage of me and later he would shoot me."[18] Only much later, after the war, did Shenker learn that, indeed, Stanisław the "blue" policeman had sheltered another Jewish woman under his roof. In the first case, Gromala's decision could have had serious implications (from the point of view of the Germans, setting Jews free was tantamount to sabotage) and could result in various disciplinary measures. Officer Stanisław, who decided to shelter Jews, was quite obviously ready to put his own life on the line.

Unfortunately, much more numerous were officers who arrested and killed Jews without a second thought. In the case of Dąbrowa, many names come to mind: Lewandowicz, Niechciał, Mądry, Szewczyk or policeman Piotr Bińczycki who served in the Ujście Jezuickie detachment, to name but a few. Aleksander Kampf, a Jewish survivor, wrote a brief note after the war: "On April 12, 1943, Bińczycki, with two other Polish officers, barged into the barn and pulled out my wife and children. He shot my wife on the spot, and took the children to the police station. He tortured them the whole day and night and killed them the next day."[19] Bińczycki continued his career after the war under communism as an agent of the State Security in Kraków.[20] These policemen seem to have been average representatives of their profession, rather well liked by the locals and in many cases fine-tuned to the needs of their community. Once under investigation, the "blue" policemen, murderers of the Jews, received massive support from the peasants, who petitioned the Kraków Appellate Court to set the accused free or at least to show them leniency. Some of these open letters, itself a rare phenomenon in postwar Stalinist times, bear hundreds of signatures!

Once a "confidential report" indicated the location of the Jews, the chief of the "blue" police station ordered two or three officers to apprehend the fugitives. The gendarmes were rarely asked to assist; assistance was mostly required when the "blues" anticipated armed resistance or when the German liaison officers themselves expressed interest in taking part in the expedition. On quite exceptional occasions, the Tarnów Gestapo also appeared on the scene. Once in the village, the "blues" summoned the elder, his deputy, village courier, hostages, or the local informer and surrounded the house (or farm) where they expected to find their victims. Then they started the search. The searches were brutal and intimidating. The officers often used physical violence, beating up the peasants and taking apart the houses. In Gorzyce (Otfinów commune), the "blues" searched a number of dwellings because their information was incomplete and there were many peasants with the same surname as the suspect. One of them woke up hearing shouts: "Police, open up!" The peasant, expecting nothing good, pulled on his pants and jumped through the window, trying to flee. He did not get far, because one of the officers was already waiting for him outside: "One of them pulled out his revolver," testified the peasant shortly after the war, "pointed it at me, and said 'stand still, you son of a bitch, hands up, in the air!' The same individual ordered me to climb back home, through the window; I did as I had been told." Once inside, the policemen pulled off his pants and applied seventy strikes with a baton to his bare buttocks. "When I fainted, they threw water in my face"—he finished his deposition.[21] In another house, policemen from Otfinów looked for Jews with such zeal that they tore out the planks from the floor.[22] The arrested Jews were usually interrogated in the village holding pen, or in the house of the informer. The point was to quickly extract information about the fabled Jewish gold.

According to the deep conviction of peasants in the Tarnów area, Jews had gold. All Jews. From today's perspective, the strength of this conviction may seem surprising. After all, before the war the local Jews were often just as poor as their Aryan neighbors. The victims of *Judenjagd* (Jew Hunt) came from the same villages as their hunters, and there was no doubt that they had no fortunes to speak of. Berl Fischman, who survived the war in Auschwitz and returned to Dąbrowa in 1945, found his house occupied by a Polish family and the area around the house dug up by the new owners who searched in vain for the "Jewish treasures."[23] The absolute conviction and deep belief about the universality of "Jewish gold" is, therefore, a powerful tribute to the influence of prewar nationalist and Church-led antisemitic propaganda and the German efforts in the same direction.

The interrogation of victims sometimes allowed hidden valuables to be retrieved, but much more often it enabled officers to establish a list of peasants who had accepted "Jewish items" for safekeeping. The sought "items" usually meant linens, bed covers, duvets, cutlery, furniture, or even cattle.[24] One witness left a description of a "search for Jewish things" carried out by peasants in Gniewczyna, a village close to Łańcut. In 1942, shortly after the Germans initiated deportations of Jews in the area, a group of inhabitants seized three local Jewish families and locked all of them in one of the houses. Over several days, the women were gang-raped and the men were tortured and questioned. The tormentors wanted to learn where the "Jewish items" were hidden. Afterward, they

> knocked from door to door and took back Jewish winter clothes which had been left for safekeeping. If someone refused [to give back the clothes] they were threatened with the Gestapo. So it was in the case of good Mary Kulp: "Blessed be Jesus, is John at home?" 'Lord be praised, he will soon be back." "Oh, well, I am in a rush." "And what do you want?' "Nothing much, just these Jewish rags." "What rags? We have nothing," "Mary, Mary, think real well, these rags, you have them. . . ." "I swear, we have nothing!" "Lejba admitted that you have them." "So let Lejba come and pick them up himself!"

"Give back this winter coat and hat!" "You have no conscience!"[25]

The peasants, while highly motivated, were not as experienced as "blue" police officers. Kubala, a policeman from the village of Skrzydlna, made fun of the peasants who a day earlier had killed two Jews but left behind, in the pocket of one of their victims, a valuable watch. One of the peasants, questioned later about the murders, said, "We should have taken the watch, it was worth at least a good cow, and now the police have taken it."[26] The officers were very thorough. Having shot two young Jewish girls close to Radgoszcz, they left the bodies practically naked.[27] The reason why the bodies of the executed Jews were left naked was simple: some of the victims tried to hide their last valuables in body cavities or in their underwear. In the case of Szmulek Brewerman, delivered to the police by peasants from village of Walizka, the "blues" went even further. After some time the elder received a list of names of peasants who during the last few months offered assistance to Brewerman. The peasants were ordered to report to the police, were lectured about their irresponsible behavior and were fined 500 zlotys each. Szmulek, after a thorough interrogation, was shot behind the police station.[28]

After the searches and interrogations, the "blues" could follow several courses of action. First, they could transfer the Jews for execution to the nearest German police station. This option, however, was fraught with risks: once in German hands and before the execution, the Jews could talk and reveal the names of their Polish helpers. They could also accuse the "blue" policemen of theft—in the eyes of the Germans and according to the German laws, stealing from Jews was equivalent to stealing from the Reich, the sole owner of the "former Jewish property." The policemen had also to think about other administrative hurdles: one had to deliver the Jews into the hands of the Germans (and this sometimes meant a night-long journey) and to prepare a written report for the authorities. In these circumstances in the eyes of the "blue" policemen, shooting the Jews often appeared to be the easiest solution.

In order to better understand this area of "blue" policemen's work, one can take advantage of an extraordinary book—the recently published memoirs of Tadeusz Krasnodębski, an officer attached to the Otfinów detachment of the "blue" police from 1940 to 1944. This is the only, as far as I know, published memoir of a Polish "blue" policeman. Krasnodębski's book is self-serving and full of vicious antisemitic remarks, but with several reservations it can still be considered a useful tool to study the role of the Polish police in the implementation of the "Final Solution." One can look, for instance, at the description of the capture and the murder of Kalm Wilk, a Jewish policeman from Żabno who went into hiding after the liquidation of the ghetto. According to Krasnodębski, "Wilk was hiding for some time in the village of Diament, where he met the fiancée of Niechciał [a policeman from Otfinów], and she told her boyfriend about the meeting. Niechciał and Lewandowicz went to Diament and caught Wilk, who promised to show them where he had buried his valuables. It didn't help him one bit, because the policemen took away the valuables and shot the Jew all the same."[29] Albin B., one of the witnesses testifying just after the war in a Kraków court, had a slightly different recollection of the same event: "When the Jew Wilk came to my house, one of the five local boys [who saw him] went to report him to the police. A short while later I saw four officers on bicycles: Tadeusz Krasnodębski, Lewandowicz, Lesiński, and Mądry. They took the Jews straight from my house, and they led

him to the police station. The Jew asked them to let him go, and promised them to show where he had hidden the gold and cash. So the policemen took him to Żabno, where he had hidden his gold and money, and then they shot the Jew and split the gold and money between themselves, these four policemen." Perhaps Krasnodębski was less than forthcoming about his own involvement in the murder, but he certainly had first-hand knowledge of the described events.

Krasnodębski also gave an account of the death of Mendel Kapelner:[30] "The Jew showed up one day in our police station. He looked hardly human, he had been hiding since the fall of last year and now was completely exhausted both physically and mentally. He stood in the door and said, 'Please, shoot me, I can't stand it anymore.'" The author, if we are to believe him, found an excuse but his colleague obliged Kapelner and shot him in front of the station. Józef Dybała, who testified a few years after the war, had, however, a very different recollection of Mendel Kapelner's death. "Władysław Nagórzański, the village elder, told us, 'Let's go and catch this Jew-boy Mendel Kapelner, who's hiding in Władysław Migała's barn.' I said, 'I didn't give him life, so I won't take it away.' But we had to go to the barn, and the elder told us that Migała had already reported the Jew to the German police in Otfinów, and the police ordered him to hold the Jew. So the elder told us to catch the Jew-boy, and we all went into the barn."[31] Józef Migała said, "In 1943, in the month of May, the people caught the Jew-boy Mendel Kapelner and brought him to the Polish police officers, who shot him."[32] Indeed, it is true (however horrible it might sound) that some Jews, having lost all hope, asked the police for a speedy execution, but it seems that Mendel Kapelner from Siedliszowice was not one of them. One can add that similar fate befell Mendel's cousin,

Pejka (Pearl) Kapelner. Pejka was hiding in Bieniaszowice, a village nearby. Together with one Jacob "Black," a Jew from Opatowiec, she stayed in the barn of an "Aryan" friend. Unfortunately, Karol Motyka, one of the neighbors, found out about them, and—with the help of a few others—delivered the Jews to the police in Gręboszów, where they were executed.[33]

We know little about what happened to "hidden" Jews once they had been brought to the nearest police station; very few lived to tell the story. In the fall of 1942, Krasnodębski's colleagues from the nearby Wietrzychowice detachment arrested Rozalia Polanecka, a Jewish woman who had been hiding in the village of Wola Przemykowska. Held in police custody in Wietrzychowice, she managed to smuggle a short note from her cell. The letter survived the war:

> Wietrzychowice, September 18, 1942.[34] This letter is written by Rozalia Polanecka (née Berl) from Ujście Jezuickie, parish Gręboszów, who has been sentenced to death. I leave this world grateful to people who dared to act decently. I thank you, reverend father, for all the good you have done. Perhaps, by chance, one of the Polaneckis will survive? Please, let them have this last whisper of mine. And don't worry about this life—one day we will [all] be reborn as spirits. Farewell, beloved people and beloved world, wonderful world! We need to love even those, who do not know what they do. My hideout was betrayed by one Szywała, a deportee from Kolbuszowa, now resident of Miechowice Wielkie. May Lord be with you. [May] all [have] a better future. Once the war is over, please write to America, to Jack Lippel, 94–96 Ave. C.D., N.Y. America, USA, I say goodbye to those who wish other people well. (Signed) Rozalia Polanecka.

In Radgoszcz, the "blue" policemen worked under the authority of two German gendarmes attached to their unit. The holding cells at the station were often used to interrogate Jews who had been caught in the area. According to the testimony of a local "blue" policeman, a notorious and fear-inspiring gendarme named Engelbert Guzdek would torture the Jewish prisoners in order to force them to name the people who had given them food. The officer added: "Gendarme Guzdek, I, and several other said 'blue' policemen, we brought the Jewboys to the police station in Radgoszcz. Once inside, Guzdek with another Gestapo-man from Tarnów interrogated these Jewboys, torturing and beating them. I and the other 'blue' policemen who captured these Jewboys, we went to sleep."[35]

According to abundant and unequivocal historical evidence, the Polish "blue" police from the Tarnów area murdered Jews often and routinely. It even seems that the executions were done in a matter-of-fact way. One day, local peasants brought a Jew to a police station, whom they had caught in a nearby forest. Marian Czerniewski, the officer on duty, led the anonymous Jew (whose hands had been tied with wire) 100 yards away from the station: "Then Officer Czerniewski said, 'I won't take him any further' and shot him through the head, killing him on the spot."[36] The execution of Jews also served as a form of initiation, an act of deeper friendship between officers, and a way to prove loyalty to the "blue" collective. Participation in the shootings reinforced professional and social bonds and, of course, guaranteed loyalty and silence in the future. Jan Szewczyk, another policeman from the Otfinów detachment, described the last moments of eighteen-year-old Salomea Süss and her twenty-year-old sister, who had earlier been betrayed by Jan A. from Gorzyce:

Commander [of our detachment] Lewandowicz said to me, and to the young Officer Stachowicz, "Since you done nothing yet, now you have to fix them," which meant that I and Stachowicz had to kill the Jewesses. I told him that since I hadn't shot anyone yet, I didn't want to shoot the Jewesses now. So then he told me that I was an arse and not a policeman. Then he turned to the Jewesses and ordered them to get off the road and to go to the bushes nearby. So at this point the young policeman Stachowicz fired off one round from his carbine. One of the girls fell to the ground, and the other cried out and rushed towards the lying Jewess. At this point I fired a shot and this second Jewess shouted even louder and fell next to the other Jewess, who had been wounded before. Seeing this, Commander Lewandowicz said with irony, "What are you screwing around!?" It meant, why hadn't we finished the Jewesses off right away. So the commander approached the lying Jewesses, took out his pistol, and shot them twice, and they were still. I would also like to add that before the shooting, the commander told Dulka, one of the peasants, to dig a grave for the Jewesses.[37]

Not surprisingly, the officers justified the murder of the Süss sisters in terms of protecting the peasants and shielding the village of Gorzyce from the vengeance of the Germans. Had both Jewish girls been caught by the Germans, all the inhabitants of this hamlet would have paid the price, argued the "blue" policemen.[38]

The same patriotic argument was used by two "blue" policemen called by the elder to the village of Kłyż to "do something with a Jewess." One of the witnesses later testified as follows: "The policemen arrived, and they took [the Jewish girl] 300 yards away from my house and shot her behind a barn. She was later buried behind this barn, but I have no idea who took away her clothes or what happened to them."[39] A few days after the execution, the "blue" policemen appeared again in Kłyż and told the locals that "had the Jewess been caught by the Germans, they would have shot several families."[40]

Józef Górski, an estate owner and a fervent nationalist from Podlasie, agreed:

Most of all, the Jews hated us. I saw many examples of it during the war. There was one Całka, a glassmaker in Sterdynia. He had been in hiding in Ceranów but, finally, he was caught and a "blue" policeman led him to the police station in Kossowo. That's when Całka shook his fists at Ceranów, and started making threats that he would give the Germans the names of all those who had helped him. The officer shot the Jew under the bridge and later told [the Germans] that the prisoner had tried to escape. "I couldn't allow the whole village to be turned to ashes just because of one scoundrel!" he explained to me in a later conversation.[41]

This attitude and similar comments come across strongly in reports sent to Warsaw commanders of the Home Army by the regional intelligence officers. In 1943, one of them warned his superiors, "The Jews hiding in the forests are hated by the [local] population. They are at the root of many problems of the Polish population, they steal, and they are usually communists. These 'forest Jews,' when caught by the gendarmes, practically always accuse innocent inhabitants of the nearby villages. It is either revenge for having received no assistance, or the principle 'since I have to die, you shall die too!'"[42] Another intelligence report from the same period stated flatly that "the attitudes towards Jews are hostile, often even hateful. There are many cases of liquidations of Jews who wander in the area. This month alone eight Jews were liquidated in such a way. Execution usually takes place right there where a Jew has been found. We have to note the cases when peasants who have already taken advantage of a Jew give him away to the gendarmes."[43]

The murders and executions were usually done in a business-like, routine fashion. The arrested Jews were later marched toward the nearest forest or to the bush and executed. Officer Wesołowski from Racławice said, "Krawczyk, my commanding officer, ordered me to shoot, so I shot one Jew, and I wounded the other one in the neck. [Officer] Faryński finished that one off. Faryński also killed two other Jews, and finished off the third one. Those [killed] ones were two men and one woman."[44] Sometimes the Jews on their way to the execution tried to beg for mercy and in quite exceptional cases even tried to flee. "I saw these young Jewesses"—testified a "blue" policeman from Otfinów—"I remember how they asked us to set them free. They told us that the Germans would kill them, but the commanding officer refused to even listen to them."[45] Most often, however, they had already been so badly beaten that they had lost the will to struggle. Sometimes the executions did not follow the "impersonal" routine, but erupted in a spectacle of sadistic violence of murderers in dark blue uniforms. In the late fall of 1942, in Radgoszcz, the locals delivered a young Jewish woman and her infant child into the hands of the Polish police. Led to the place of the execution, the woman begged the "blue" policeman to show her mercy and to shoot her first, so that she would not have to watch the death of her child. It did not happen that way, "because the officer did something quite the opposite: first he shot her child and only then finished her off."[46]

Before the killings, the "blue" policemen liked to fortify themselves with vodka. Officer Ryczek from Pilzno detachment, shortly before shooting a captive in Słotowa commune, requested "a quart of vodka because they have a Jew who has to be shot, and shooting without vodka is no good."[47] Before the killings, the officers would raise a glass or two. Another drinking session usually followed the executions, indicating a ritual or a pattern of behavior of "blue" policemen from the Tarnów area. This is not to suggest that the officers of the Polish "blue" police in other areas drank any less. The tradition was known in all other districts, and in some cases the officers facing the court after the war mentioned their intoxication as an extenuating circumstance. "I killed the person of Jewish nationality because I was drunk," argued an officer accused of killing Lejba Syjak, his Jewish neighbor from Stanisławów. "Had I been sober, I would have never done it."[48]

The executions opened the way to the next stage of "police work"—to robbery and burial of the bodies. These stages need to be discussed in some detail. As already noted, the first robbery took place immediately after the arrest, with peasants or policemen torturing the Jews to extract information about the hidden "Jewish goods." After the execution it was time to search the bodies for cash, gold coins, or jewelry that could have been sewn into the seams of underwear. "Together with Franciszek Owsiak we placed the two bodies in the grave and covered it with earth. The Jewess had some clothes on, and the Jew was in long johns only. I have no idea who took away the clothes of this Jew, but I remember that Owsiak took off the long johns too, so that we buried the Jew naked," testified Piotr Skrzyniarz from Brnik.[49] The bodies were usually buried at the site of the execution. Some time earlier, the police (or the village elder, depending on the circumstances) selected peasants responsible for digging graves. The grave-diggers received a small compensation for their trouble, most often some of the Jewish clothes. One of these peasants gave the following account: "So he tore all the clothes and underwear off the bodies, so that these two Jewesses were completely naked, and he buried them like that. Franciszek Wróbel told me that Dudek took off these clothes from their dead bodies."[50] Another peasant assigned to a burial detail recalled that "the police officers were at the scene, they tore the clothes off the bodies, and they searched them piece by piece. The bodies were left in underwear only. Lewandowicz put aside one skirt, one pair of shoes, and a head scarf, and told me to take these items. The rest of the clothing was placed on the [police] cart. Later we buried them [Jews] in a pit."

In extreme cases, unlucky rescuers were threatened with having "their" Jews buried next to or within the walls of their own houses. This was the plan of Stanisław Nawrocki, the village elder from Swiebodzin (south of Tarnów), who "instructed the people to bury [the Jews killed by the police] next to the house."[51] The plan was aborted, however, when it became known that the rescuers were at the same time informers who "rendered" their Jews to the Germans. The treacherous rescuers turned the tables on the elder, threatened him with possible German reprisals, and the Jewish victims were finally buried in the woods nearby. This horrible kind of burial was known in other areas of the Kraków District too. A Jewish woman, hiding in the Miechów area, noted in her diary, "I happened to listen to one peasant, who told us that the Germans had found a Jew in the village of Kazimierza. The Jew had been shot, and the body was buried in the same room where he had been discovered. There were no wooden floors in the room, just an earth floor, so they buried the Jew in such a way that his legs, from the knees down, stuck out in the air."[52] It is hard to say how much these stories were prod-

ucts of horrified imagination, but they certainly instilled fear into the minds and hearts of people who were hiding Jews and had a chilling effect on those who were contemplating such a move. Finally, the macabre rituals of murder and burial were not only a "Galician" phenomenon. Similar accounts were reported from other districts of the *Generalgouvernement*. In the night of November 1, 1943, in Rechta, a small village close to Lublin, local peasants committed mass murder of Jews who were hiding in their community. One Polish women from Rechta recalled these events: "Michał Rymarz, our elder, came to our house and told my husband to take a spade and to go and bury the bodies. . . . In the meantime I was in the house of Kułaga, and his wife told me to take their axe and a bed cover, because her husband had been taken away by the Germans to Majdanek [concentration camp]. Then Józef Teter showed up and said the Kułaga's wife had to go and dig a grave for the killed [Jews] because she was guilty of keeping Jews. And then he ordered three bodies to be buried—next to Kułaga's window—and even wanted to bury them inside the house, but the neighbors protested, so the Jews were finally buried by the window."[53]

NOTES

1. Adam Hempel, *Pogrobowcy klęski, rzecz o policji "granatowej" w Generalnym Gubernatorstwie* (Warsaw: PWN, 1990).

2. The areas in question were, in the south: Silesia (Schlesien), in the north: Pomorze (Pommern) and, in the west: Wielkopolska (Warthegau).

3. Tadeusz, S. Krasnodębski, *Policjant konspiratorem. Szesnaście lat na celowniku gestapo I bezpieki.* Mięidzyzdroje-Kraków: Arkadiusz Wingiert, Projekt Galicja, 2008, 132.

4. AŻIH, 302/318, testimony of Chaja Rosenblatt (b. Garn).

5. Adam Kazimierz Musiał, *Krwawe upiory. Dzieje powiatu Dąbrowa Tarnowska w okresie okupacji hitlerowskiej*. Tarnów: Karat, 1993, 38.

6. APK, SAKr 1025 IVK 164/50.

7. Mark Verstandig, *I Rest My Case* (Evanston IL: Northwestern University Press, 2002), 187.

8. The plague of denunciations in Kraków was commented upon by Edward Kubalski, a prominent citizen of that city and author of a diary of everyday life under the occupation. According to Kubalski, the epidemic of denunciations in the capital city of the *Generalgouvernement* took on such proportions that it started to overwhelm the German institutions. During special meetings, German officials called in Polish priests and *voits* and ordered them to use their influence with the Polish population in order to stem the flow of anonymous letters to the police. See Edward Kubalski, *Niemcy w Krakowie* (Germans in Kraków) (Kraków: Austeria, 2010), entry for May 23, 1941. For more about denunciations in Warsaw, see Barbara Engelking, *Szanowny Panie Gistapo* (Warsaw, IFiS PAN, 2003).

9. APK, SAKr, 1013 IVK 109/50.

10. APK, SAKr, 1014/IVK/116/50, 10–10v.

11. Ibid., 11–11v. The dead included three Jews named Spokojny and one more person whose name was not known.

12. This term was coined by Helen Fein in her important book *Accounting for Genocide: Victims and Survivors of the Holocaust* (New York: Free Press, 1979).

13. APK, SAKr, 1042/IVK/252/50.

14. APK, SAKr, 967 IVK 158/49, deposition of Wojciech Salej.

15. APK, SAKr, 967 IVK 158/49, testimony of witness Józef Kozub.

16. Archive of the IPN (Warsaw), AIPN, SOKr, 552 trial of Zbigniew P.

17. Memoir of Regina Goldfinger (b. Rivka Shenker).

18. Ibid., 81.

19. AŻIH, 301/1908, testimony of Aleksander Kampf.

20. It was not infrequent to see the murderers of Jews join the communist security apparatus. Membership in the "People's Militia" guaranteed a degree of immunity and often gave license to commit further act of violence. For a particularly heinous crime committed by local peasants, soon to become officers of "People's Militia," see the deposition of Baruch Mehl, concerning the murder of his entire family in July 1944. YVA, 033 dossier 1943.

21. APK, SAKr 1034/IV K/ 204/50, 9–9v.

22. Ibid., 4–4v; 8–8v, "The policeman came to me with a loaded carbine and said, 'You keep Jews!' So I told him that I didn't, but then another policeman came to me and said, 'You are sheltering Jews!'"

23. Personal account obtained from Stuart Fischman, son of Berl Fischman.

24. SAKr 1025 IV K 164/50. "In July of 1942 they took away my cow, which I had left for safekeeping with Stefan Dobrowolski in Radwan, commune Mędrzychów" —testified Benek Grün.

25. Tadeusz Markiel, "Zagłada domu Trynczerów" (The Destruction of the House of Trynczer), *Znak* 4 (2008): 133. Once the "Jewish items" had been retrieved, the peasants called in the gendarmes, who shot all of the eighteen Jews from Gniewczyna on the main road, in full view of the inhabitants.

26. APK, SAKr 1020/ IV K/147/50, 8.

27. APK, SAKr 1034 IV K/204/50, 56v.

28. AIPN, SWWW, 318/322.

29. Tadeusz S. Krasnodębski, *Policjant konspiratorem, Szesnaście lat na celowniku gestapo i bezpieki* (Międzyzdroje-Kraków: Arkadiusz Wingiert, Projekt Galicja, 2008), 116–17.

30. Mendel Kapelner (b. 1887) was a wealthy Jewish merchant who had been hiding in the Siedliszowice area since the summer of 1942.

31. APK, SAKr 1023/IV K/ 155/50, deposition of witness Józef Dybała, 6–6v.

32. Ibid., deposition of witness Józef Migał, 7–7v.

33. APK, SAKr 1001/k IV/44/50.

34. AŻIH, collection 301/1365, transcribed at the District Jewish Historical Commission in Kraków.

35. APK, SAKr, 1014, IVK, 118/50, 20 and 23. Service note by officer Henryk Dudak and the deposition of officer Andrzej Szypulski.

36. AIPN, SWWW, 318/293.

37. APK, SAKr, 1055 IV K 344/50. Apart from Szewczyk's testimony, we also have the deposition of Eugeniusz Niechciał, another policeman who is often mentioned in this text. See APK, SKKr, 1055 IV K 344/50, 25–26. The Süss sisters managed to survive almost a year in hiding. Some more information about their life and fate can be found in APK, SAKr 1034/IV K/204/50.

38. Musiał, 197.

39. APK, K 122/49, SAKr 965, interrogation of the suspect, December 12, 1947.

40. Ibid., minutes of the sentencing proceedings, November 8, 1949.

41. Józef Górski, manuscript "Na przełomie dziejów," National Library, Warsaw, Manuscript Section, III 9776. An English translation of parts of Górski's memoirs appears in *Holocaust: Studies and Materials* (Warsaw: Polish Center for Holocaust Research, 2008), 300–312.

42. AAN AK, 203/x-68, 31.

43. AAN AK 203/X-69, report from June 1943.

44. APK, SAKr, 1014 IV K/116/50 9v.

45. PK, SAKr 1055, 1vk/344/50, 38.

46. APK, SAKr 1025 IV K 164/50, testimony of Beniek Grün, January 2, 1950.

47. APK, SAKr 1011 IV K 102/50, 26.

48. AIPN, Sąd Wojewódzki dla Województwa Warszawskiego GK 318\574 k. 17, interrogation of Stefan Pragacz, December 17, 1954. For another description of a "drinking session" after the execution of Jews, see APK, SAKr, 1014 IV K/110/50, 11v.

49. APK, SAKr 967 K 153/49, 77–78.

50. APK, SAKr, 1034/ IVK 204/50, testimony of Bronisław Rajski.

51. APK, SAKr, 1022 IV K, 151/50.

52. AŻIH, collection 302/66, testimony of "Maria Steczko," February 25, 1946.

53. Dariusz Libionka and Paweł P. Reszka, "Swięto Zmarłych w Rechcie" (Feast of All Saints in Rechta), *Karta* 46 (2005): 131.

Romania: Annihilation Aborted

JEAN ANCEL

From *The History of the Holocaust in Romania*

In Romania the murder of Jews merely for being Jews began in June 1940, after the Romanian army's withdrawal from the areas ceded to the Soviet Union [Bessarabia and Bukovina]. These murders were isolated events and would have remained so but for explicit instructions for the implementation of an overt Romanian policy of genocide. This policy was devised under Nazi influence, probably in March—April 1941 after the arrival of special emissaries of the Reich and Himmler. . . . After their arrival, [Prime Minister] Mihai Antonescu concluded "understandings" with the SS, or rather with the Reich Central Security Office (RSHA). Although we know little of the true nature of these understandings, practical preparations for the liquidation of the Jews evidently began in late May or early June, shortly before Antonescu was informed of the exact date of Operation Barbarossa. Since the late thirties, conditions in Romania had been ripe for the implementation of an extermination policy, although this was not obvious. Therefore, the orders for the liquidation of Jews neither shocked nor elicited any form of opposition among members of the army or the Romanian establishment. The Romanian army's General Staff drew up a plan to incite the Romanian population of Bessarabia to perpetrate riots against the Jews prior to the arrival of the Romanian forces.

[*Conducator* (Leader)] Ion Antonescu himself gave the order to liquidate a part of Bessarabian and Bukovinian Jewry. He entrusted the implementation of this order to the gendarmerie (which was attached to the Ministry of the Interior) and the army, particularly the *pretors* (types of military governors). Anticipating Germany's victory, Romania's leaders informed the government on June 17–18, 1941, of their plans for the Jewish population in the two provinces. The leadership left no doubt about the significance of the order to "cleanse the ground." Mihai Antonescu's speech of July 3, 1941, at the Ministry of Interior was distributed in limited-edition brochures titled "Guidelines and Instructions for the Liberation Administration." Guideline ten revealed the regime's intentions regarding the Jews: "This is the . . . most favorable opportunity in our history . . . for cleansing our people of all those elements foreign to its soul, which have grown like weeds to darken its future."[1] Mihai Antonescu elaborated on this theme during the cabinet session of July 8, 1941:

> At the risk of not being understood by traditionalists . . . I am all for the forced migration of the entire Jewish element of Bessarabia and Bukovina, which must be dumped across the border. . . . You must be merciless to them. . . . I don't know how many centuries must pass before the Romanian people shall again encounter such total liberty of action, such opportunity for ethnic cleansing and national

revision. . . . If necessary, use your machine guns. I couldn't care less if history remembers us as barbarians. . . . I take formal responsibility in telling you there is no law. . . . So, no formalities, complete freedom.[2]

On June 19, Ilie Steflea . . . sent a secret circular to the army informing it of Antonescu's instructions: "All Yids, Communist agents, and their sympathizers must be identified . . . to enable the Ministry of Interior to track them down, restrict their freedom of movement, and apply future directives."[3] This order resembled a similar instruction given by Field Marshal Wilhelm Keitel to the *Wehrmacht*.[4] Gen. Ion Topor, the grand *pretor* and commander of the gendarmerie units in the liberated territories, was given explicit orders regarding the Jews and Communist and Soviet functionaries in Romanian territories: "All pro-Communist Romanians and Ukrainians shall be sent across the Dniester, and all pro-Communist members of the minorities [a euphemism for Jew] shall be eliminated."[5]

The *pretors* implemented these orders with the army's full collaboration and with the tacit agreement of the High Command. Since the special orders issued to the army were not written down, very little is known about them today. These orders were usually given to officers, albeit not necessarily those of the highest rank, although almost all senior officers knew of them.[6] The special orders were invoked every time military or civil authorities were reluctant to kill Jews, whether out of fear of the consequences or because they did not believe such orders existed. In Cetatea Alba, for example, Major Frigan of the local garrison requested written instructions to execute the Jews. The *pretor* of the Third Army, Col. Marcel Petala, traveled to Cetatea Alba to inform the major of the

directives concerning the Jews in the ghetto. The next day 3,500 Jews who had survived the main offensive were killed.[7] . . .

The orders to kill Jews soon became an open secret, and all Christians in Bessarabia and Bukovina knew that the Jews were doomed.[8] Soldiers as well as local citizens knew of the directive, or rather special dispensation, issued by the army to do with the Jews' lives and property as they saw fit "within the first 24 hours of the occupation."[9] Although this written order was not discovered after the war, we know that it was circulated among both military and civilian officials. It was mentioned in the testimonies of Jews and non-Jews alike (the latter referred to a dispensation of three days rather than twenty-four hours) and was likewise referred to in the trials of Romanian war criminals. . . .

The Stages of Genocide

The destruction of the Jews of northern Romania took place in two stages: the spontaneous stage and the planned stage. Before we embark on a discussion of the various techniques the Romanians employed to liquidate the Jews, it is worth noting that the methods used in rural areas differed vastly from those used in urban centers. In rural and semirural areas (including some towns), the period between the withdrawal of the Soviet army and the entry of the Romanian and German forces was characterized by spontaneous waves of killing. Sometimes the local population exploited this interregnum to form gangs of terrorists, "whose main aim was to kill Jews."[10] Most of these spontaneous killings occurred in areas where no real tensions had existed between Jews and gentiles and where, on the contrary, a tradition of more or less peaceful coexistence had been characteristic for a century. This fact

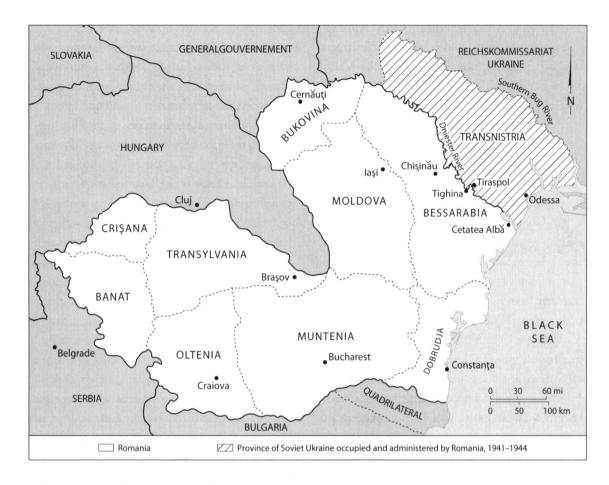

Map 4. Romania, ca. 1941–1944. From Vladimir Solonari, *Purifying the Nation: Population Exchange and Ethnic Cleansing in Nazi-Allied Romania.* © 2009 by the Woodrow Wilson International Center for Scholars. Reprinted with permission of Johns Hopkins University Press.

alone explains why, all in all, so few Jews tried to escape. In Bessarabia, however, many rural Jews did try to escape the first wave of killings, seeking refuge in towns, fields, or hiding places or with their Christian neighbors.

Almost overnight the feelings and attitudes of Romanian society underwent a sea change, as Romanians and Ukrainians turned against their former friends, comrades-in-arms, and fellow employees. The change was so swift that the Jews had no time to fully absorb what was happening. We now know that this change of heart was not entirely spontaneous but was preceded by a detailed plan drawn up by the chief of the General Staff's Second Bureau to incite the Romanian population against the Jews.

In Bessarabia and in parts of northern Bukovina, the acts of pillage and murder evolved into a kind of popular uprising of sorts against Jews, both as Jews and as "allies" of the Soviets, the foreign occupier. This explains why the attacks on Jews occurred immediately after the withdrawal of the Soviet forces. Although there is no way of knowing the extent of the carnage against Jews during this period, we do know that their numbers [of dead] ran into the tens of thousands.

On July 8, Iosif Iacobici, the chief of the General Staff, ordered the commander of the General Staff's Second Bureau, Lt. Col. Alexandru Ionescu, to implement a plan "for the removal of the Judaic element from Bessarabian territory . . . by organizing teams to act in advance of the Romanian troops." Implementation began on July 9. "The mission of these teams is to create an unfavorable atmosphere toward the Judaic elements in the villages, thereby encouraging the population to remove them on its own, by whatever means it finds most appropriate and suited to the circumstances. Upon the arrival of the Romanian troops, the feeling must already be in place and even acted upon."[11]

Attached to the report was a detailed plan of the instructions given to the General Staff's Second Bureau and a map of the distribution of the teams. The special teams recruited Romanians from Bessarabia who "had proved their mettle," possessed valid Soviet documents, and had left their families behind in Romania—"an additional guarantee that they would carry out the assignment." These teams, duly reinforced, were dispatched to incite the peasants against the Jews and encourage them to loot, rape, and kill. They were sent along nine parallel itineraries from the central and southern sections of the Romanian-Bessarabian border toward the Dniester and spread from the Danube and Cetatea Alba in the south to Bucovici and Kishinev in the north. Each team comprised two to four men and was headed by an agent of the Second Bureau. After being provided with money, the members of the team were ordered "to exploit relatives, acquaintances, and anti-Communist elements, in order to disseminate the idea of joint resistance to the Jewish danger."[12]

The first killings took place at Siret, in southern Bukovina, five kilometers from the new Soviet border and home to many Vizhnitz and Sadagura *Hasidim*. Fifteen hundred local Jews were marched to Dornesti, twelve kilometers away, where trains waited to deport them to southern Romania. That same day, all of the Jews who remained behind were shot near the bridge over the River Prut in the presence of the inhabitants of Siret, who had been invited along to witness the proceedings.[13] In Herta the shooting of large groups of Jews posed certain technical problems, as no thought had been given to burial requirements. After the execution a heap of corpses lay in pools of blood, guarded by a soldier who "from time to time fired his rifle at one of the bodies that twitched."[14]

On July 7, 1941, the Sixteenth Regiment, followed closely by the Ninth and Tenth Regiments, occupied Noua Sulita. Although members of the Tenth and Sixteenth Regiments killed "only" 50 Jews, the members of the Ninth Regiment more than made up for it. As soon as they entered the city they accused the Jews of shooting at the army and raided their homes. The next day 880 Jews and 5 Christians were found dead in the courtyards and streets.[15] An additional 45 Jews were shot at the behest of the regiment's commander, Colonel Carlan, who took an active part in their murder.[16] . . . On July 3, 450 local Jews were gunned down in the Bukovinian village of Ciudei.[17] Later that day 200 Jews in Storojinet were gunned down in their homes. On July 4, nearly all Jews in the villages of Ropcea, Iordanesti, Patrauti, Panca, and Broscauti, near Storojinet, were massacred with the active collaboration of local Romanians and Ukrainians.[18] On July 5, the wave of murder expanded to include thousands of Jews in the villages [nearby].[19]

On July 4, after the combined German-Romanian armies entered Czernowitz, they began killing operations among the city's fifty thousand Jews—operations that continued for four days. Despite Russian resistance, the scope of the task, and challenging physical terrain, Bessarabian Jewry suffered the greatest losses in the Romanian campaign to "cleanse the ground." On July 6, a day after the Romanian occupation of Edineti, about a thousand Jews were shot by Romanian troops, and sixty more were murdered at Noua Sulita. The next day it was the turn of those Jews who had buried their relatives in Edineji to be slaughtered. . . . By July 9, the wave of exterminations implemented by the combined German-Romanian forces reached the Jewish settlements of Plasa Nistrului (near Czernowitz), Zoniache, Rapujinet, and Copnani in northern Bukovina, and dozens of small villages became *Judenrein* (cleansed of Jews).[20] The seventeenth of July marked the beginning of the liquidation and deportation of Kishinev's fifty thousand Jews. On that day alone several thousand Jews— perhaps as many as ten thousand—were killed.[21] The destruction of this large Jewish center—the largest in Bessarabia—continued until the last of its Jews were killed or sent to camps in Transnistria in November 1941. The slaughter of the Jews of Cetatea Alba in southern Bessarabia followed a similar pattern.

Thus the first stage of the Romanian Holocaust was implemented with the help, but not under the coercion, of the German Eleventh Army and *Einsatzgruppe* D. This first stage spanned the period between the occupation of Bessarabia and northern Bukovina by the Romanian and German forces (Balti, Czernowitz, and Kishinev, for example) and the partial or complete replacement of these forces by a civil Romanian administration (in large cities, by a garrison). From this point on the lives of urban Jews depended on not one but several, usually competing, civilian Romanian authorities. This meant further suffering for the Jews, as each authority attempted to outdo the other. These authorities were the regular police, the *Siguranta*, the prefect and mayor, and sometimes—as in the case of Balti and Kishinev—even *Einsatzkommando* 10a, which stayed in these cities for short periods. In rural areas this stage ended with the arrival of the gendarmes. . . .

Shortly before June 21, 1941, Antonescu [had] ordered the Romanian Special Intelligence Service (ssi) to establish a special unit of about 160 men to "obtain intelligence and protect the home front from acts of espionage, sabotage, and terror."[22] This unit, Operational Echelon no. 1, known as the Operational Echelon or the Special Echelon, belonged to the ssi and in some ways resembled the German *Einsatzgruppe*. Although the Operational Echelon was established on an *ad hoc* basis shortly before the invasion of the Soviet Union and its members had not undergone formal training, it was undeniably antisemitic. Like the *Einsatzgruppe*, the Operational Echelon was divided into smaller teams (*echipe*).[23]

The echelon's first operation was carried out in Iasi along with the Romanian army and police and with the assistance of German military units. More than fourteen thousand Jews were murdered there on June 29–30, 1941. From Iasi the echelon continued with the Fourth Romanian Army to Bessarabia. In Kishinev it collaborated with *Einsatzkommando* 11b in the pogrom described in its reports of August 4 and 7.[24] As soon as the echelon and the Romanian police units crossed the River Prut they collaborated with *Einsatzgruppe* units and in most cases were under their direct influence and acted under their guidance.

Such collaboration notwithstanding, the relationship between the various units of *Einsatzgruppe* D, on the one hand, and the Romanian army, gendarmerie, police, and Operational Echelon, on the other, left much to be desired. The Germans were content only when the Romanians acted according to their directives. In Kishinev, for example, the ghetto was erected after *Sonderkommando* 11 a and Antonescu ordered the Romanian military commander of the town to do so.[25] In Balti cooperation between the Romanian police and *Einsatzkommando* 10a was successful, as reflected in a German report of July 29 that stated that the Romanian police acted "in accordance with the commando's directives"—that is, with a brutality toward the Jews that was already commonplace in Balfi and in Bessarabia in general.[26]

If, however, the Romanians acted in an impulsive or unplanned manner, failed to remove the evidence of their mass murder operations (massacres, looting, and rape), or accepted bribes from Jews, they elicited the wrath of their Nazi counterparts. The exchange of letters among German and Romanian army commanders reflects the Germans' displeasure with the way things were proceeding. They were not displeased with the crimes themselves but rather with the inefficient way in which they were carried out. In a letter dated July 14, 1941, sent to Romanian army headquarters, General von Schobert, commander of the Eleventh Army, criticized the way in which the Romanian soldiers killed Jews near the village of Taura in the Balti district, allowing two Jews to escape and failing to bury their victims' corpses. Their behavior, he complained, "has lowered the prestige of the Romanian army, and at the same time, that of the German army in the eyes of world opinion." He demanded that steps be taken to prevent the repetition of such incidents.[27]

Death Toll (Stage 1 of the Liquidation)

As of December 29, 1930, the Jews of Bessarabia (including Hotin) had numbered 206,958 and of Bukovina, 107,975.[28] Under the Soviets (June 1940–July 1941) their numbers increased, especially in the large cities of Kishinev and Czernowitz. Jewish survivors from Czernowitz, some of them officials of the Jewish community, also noted the increase in the number of the Jews, estimating the number in the city at some 70,000–75,000 during the Soviet regime.[29] ... On September 1, 1941, the Romanian army conducted a special population census in the areas recaptured from the Russians.[30] Following this census, the Romanian authorities declared, "On that date, there were 126,434 citizens of Jewish nationality in the two provinces, some of them free, and some in camps."[31] The total number of Jews deported by the Soviet authorities before the war or recruited to the Red Army or who fled from the Romanian-German invasion did not exceed 30,000–40,000. On September 4, 1941, the Romanian army reported that 64,176 Jews had been interned in camps before being sent to their deaths.[32] On September 25, another 44,397 Jews remained in these camps.[33] On January 15, 1942, the Inspectorate of the Transnistrian Gendarmerie reported that 118,347 Jews from Bessarabia, Bukovina, and the Dorohoi district had been deported to Transnistria.[34] Extrapolating from the above data, we see that in the space of two months (July—August 1941), at least 100,000 Jews perished or disappeared in these areas (including Herta and its surroundings).[35]

It was Ion Antonescu who sealed the fate of the survivors of the first wave of killings in the two provinces. Antonescu himself relayed his decision to the Operational Echelon, while Mihai Antonescu relayed it to the Civil Administration Echelon. Like previous operations, this one was supposed to be conducted without written orders so as to leave no trace of the crimes and preclude Jews' demands for compensation or the return of property. The corrupt nature of the Romanian administration, however—both military and civil—occasionally prompted Antonescu and other high-ranking officers to set up committees of inquiry to investigate alleged irregularities. The reports of these committees of inquiry contained almost all the secret orders, even the ones transmitted orally, thereby exposing the Antonescu regime's responsibility for imprisoning the survivors of the first waves of murder in ghettos and camps, subjecting them to a reign of terror in the ghettos and camps, and subsequently deporting them.

Before leaving for Kishinev Gen. Gheorghe Voiculescu, governor general of Bessarabia, was summoned to meet with Antonescu for a briefing on the *Conductor*'s policy in Bessarabia and Bukovina.[36] Among the unwritten prerogatives Antonescu gave Voiculescu was one empowering him "to mercilessly punish those who did not fit into the framework of his basic ideas." These basic ideas, as reflected in the verbal commands, determined that the first problem the governor general had to resolve was the Jewish problem. As the *Conductor* put it, "the Jews had to be disciplined for their attitudes and actions" during the withdrawal from Bessarabia in June 1940, during Soviet rule, and in the early stages of the war (June–July 1941). "Accordingly, and taking cognizance of the fact that Bessarabia and especially Kishinev is teeming with Jews," Voiculescu later reported, "I have issued, a mere five days after my arrival in Kishinev, Ordinance No. 61 of July 24, 1941 . . . concerning the establishment of camps

and ghettos. The same ordinance states that a ghetto must be set up in Kishinev forthwith."[37]

Voiculescu's reports to Antonescu in the months following the occupation of Bessarabia, as well as other sources, show beyond a shadow of a doubt that the initiative for the establishment of camps and ghettos—and the subsequent deportation of Jews to Transnistria—came from Bucharest, and the actions were not prompted by German pressure. Indeed, such pressure was unnecessary, given that Romania's policy toward the Jews of Bessarabia and Bukovina corresponded in every respect to Germany's. . . .

. . . The Romanian army began deporting tens of thousands of Jews across the Dniester—the Romanian-Soviet border until June 1940—to what later became known as Transnistria, based on the talks between Hitler and Antonescu in Munich on June 12, 1941, [but] without any coordination with the German army. The operation began when the Romanian army reached the Dniester River and completed the occupation of the territories that had been annexed to the Soviet Union the previous year.

The deportations were Antonescu's brainchild, prompted by his wish to purge the liberated territories of Jews. On October 16, 1943, the minister of the interior wrote a memorandum on the repatriation of some of the survivors in Transnistria in which he claimed that the Jews had brought the deportations on themselves "because of their attitude toward the Romanian Army when it had retreated from the Soviet-annexed territories and toward the Romanians during the Soviet occupation."[38] There was not one verbal or written reference to German pressure as a predisposing factor in the deportations.

Likewise, in a special memorandum issued by Antonescu, the Presidency of the Council of Ministers claimed that the deportation of the Jews from

Bessarabia and Bukovina was intended "to restore the dignity of the Romanian people," which had been hurt by the Jews' attitude toward the army and the Romanian people.[39] At the height of the deportation campaign Ion Antonescu informed the nation of his resolve "to punish the Jews for the crimes they have committed against the nation, the army, and our recaptured fatherland." In his idiosyncratic style, he added, "As long as I live, no one and nothing can stop me from completing the cleansing operation."[40]

At this stage Antonescu was planning the deportation of Jews not only from Bessarabia and Bukovina but also from the Regat [the core provinces of Romania when it achieved statehood in 1878]. In his trial, Alexianu, the governor of Transnistria, testified that Marshal Antonescu had dispatched two colonels to Tiraspol (his temporary headquarters until the occupation of Odessa) in September 1941 "to prepare Transnistria for the deportation of Bessarabian and Bukovinian Jewry, to be followed by the deportation of the Jews of the Regat."[41]

Transnistria under Romanian Occupation

Transnistria was the name given to the part of the Ukraine that Hitler awarded Antonescu as a prize for Romania's participation in the war against the Soviet Union. The territory stretched over forty thousand square kilometers and was bordered by the Dniester in the west, the Bug in the northeast, the Black Sea in the south, and the Liadova River in the west (from the Dniester north to Zhmerinca and then east to the Bug). The 1939 Soviet population census reported 3 million people in the area, most of whom were Ukrainians and Russians, and a few Jews (about 331,000), Romanians (300,000), and Germans (125,000).[42] . . . Transnistria (meaning "across the Dniester") was a special, *ad hoc* term coined during the period of

Romanian-German occupation of the area. For many Romanians the name was reminiscent of northern Transylvania (meaning "beyond the forests"), which had been annexed to Hungary.

The Romanian government favored annexing Transnistria to Romania. However, the opposition, headed by Iuliu Maniu, strongly opposed the expansion of Romania beyond its ethnic borders. In particular, it feared that the annexation of this area could be interpreted as a renunciation of northern Transylvania. Consequently, Transnistria remained an occupation zone held by the Romanians.

From a geographical standpoint Transnistria was part of the fertile Podolian plateau, most (70 percent) of which was rich arable land used to grow wheat, corn, vines, fruit trees, and tobacco. Odessa, southern Transnistria's largest city, was its natural capital. In 1939, it had six hundred thousand inhabitants, most of them Russians; the rural areas were populated mainly by Ukrainians. Transnistria had many towns with populations ranging from four thousand to thirty thousand. . . . Some of them, such as Tiraspol, Rybnitsa, and Dubossary, had a sizeable Romanian minority. These towns were, at the time of the occupation, undergoing the initial stages of Soviet industrialization and had simple factories and many workshops.

About 30 percent of Odessa's population was Jewish—200,961 people, according to the 1939 census.[43] In the early months of the war, this number rose by tens of thousands due to the influx of refugees from the surrounding area and from southern Bessarabia. The remaining Transnistrian Jews lived mainly in towns, particularly in the north and the central area. Some of these towns had a Jewish majority. When German and Romanian troops entered Transnistria, there were an estimated 331,000 Jews there.

Generally speaking, events in Transnistria were a replay of events in Bessarabia and Bukovina. The main differences were that more youth and men in general [had been] conscripted into the Red Army and thousands of Jews managed to escape from Odessa, mainly by sea, before and during the four-month siege. . . .

The first stage of the murder of Transnistrian Jewry was carried out by *Einsatzgruppe* D, which arrived with the soldiers of the German Eleventh Army and the Romanian Third and Fourth Armies. Both German and Romanian soldiers participated in the murders. . . . According to Otto Ohlendorf, the *Einsatzgruppe* commander, tens of thousands and possibly over one hundred thousand Jews were murdered.[44] The murderers of *Einsatzgruppe* D did not manage to kill all the Jews of Transnistria because of the huge tracts of land in which they operated and because of the need to stay close to the [advancing armies]. Their failure to complete their mission may also have been due to the fact that they left Transnistria after the signing of the Tighina Agreement that transferred responsibility for the Jews to the Romanians. Ohlendorf had to leave his headquarters in Ananyev in early September 1941. Apparently the Romanians even prevented him from helping them deal with the Jews of Odessa after it was captured on October 16, 1941.

With the lull in the first wave of massacres perpetrated by the *Einsatzgruppe* units and after their retreat across the Bug, the remaining local Jews who had hidden among the Ukrainians or in the forests returned to their homes, which had been looted and destroyed. According to estimates based on the reports of the gendarmerie and the Romanian authorities and on personal testimonies, approximately thirty-five thousand Jews remained in the northern and central districts of Transnistria—Mogilev, Tulchin, Yampol, Balta,

and Rybnitsa. At that time there were still over seventy thousand Jews living in other districts in southern Transnistria and approximately another one hundred thousand Jews in Odessa.[45]

The governor of Transnistria issued a directive requiring residents to report and register with their municipality, which would issue them identity cards. This order, however, did not apply to Jews, who had ceased to be free human beings.[46] The gendarmerie commanders, armed with Directive no. 1 of September 8, 1941, sent out their men to comb the villages of Transnistria. This directive ordered them "to ascertain the number of Yids in each locality, to set up ghettos, [and] to place Yids who are caught in the ghettos . . . under strict surveillance to ensure that they do not escape across the Dniester (westward). Suspects or those liable to carry out acts of terrorism are to be sent, following interrogation . . . to the nearest detention center."[47]

The incarceration of the local Jews in the northern and central districts of Transnistria was completed in October with the deployment of the Romanian authorities up to the banks of the Bug. The gendarmes established a network of informers in the villages and gathered whatever information they could about the whereabouts of Jews, half-Jews, and Jewish children, even those who had been baptized at birth. Most of them were arrested and sent to camps.[48] In mid-October 1941 the inspector general of the gendarmerie in Transnistria, Colonel Brosteanu, reported to the governor that the roundup of the local Jews had been completed and that "the Jews have been concentrated in ghettos and camps and are extremely upset by the measures that are being adopted against them. . . ."[49] On September 9, 1942, the Gendarmerie Inspectorate of Transnistria informed the Transnistrian administration that there were sixty-five thousand local Jews in the Odessa district and four thousand in the Mogilev district and that all the Jews of the Berezovka, Ananyev, Ovidopol, and Ochakov districts had "disappeared" (disparuti)—that is, had been exterminated.[50]

The Convoys

From late July 1941 to the spring of 1943 approximately three hundred thousand Romanian Jewish citizens and local Jews were moved from place to place in convoys that wandered throughout Transnistria. This was part of an overall plan consolidated by the Romanian General Staff and the result of verbal instructions by Ion Antonescu to Alexianu at their meeting in Tighina in late August 1941, prior to the signing of the Tighina Agreement between the Romanian and German armies. Antonescu presented this policy on October 11, 1941, to the district prefects in Romania at a session attended also by the interior minister, Gen. Dumitru Popescu, and the deputy interior minister, Gen. Ion Popescu:

> Gentlemen, you are aware that one of the campaigns I have taken on is to change this people. I will turn the Romanian nation into a homogeneous body. Anything alien to it shall have to go. I have begun to implement this wish by removing the Jews. If the Jews still continue to move around freely and go about their business, this is due to the weakness and duplicity of our Administration. . . . I have begun with Bessarabia. No trace of the Jews shall remain in Bessarabia. Bukovina shall also be purged of eighty percent of the Jews who live there. The entire suspect Jewish element, all Jewish Communists, shall be sent back to where they came from. I shall drive them to the Bug, and they will carry on from there.[51]

The ultimate objective was to transfer all Jews in Romania and Transnistria who were still alive after the first wave of massacres to improvised—as yet non-existent—camps in the vicinity of the River Bug, until the time was ripe for dispatching them across the Bug, in order to cleanse Transnistria, too, of Jews. To this end the General Staff established five crossing points over the Dniester and four transit points along the Bug.

The roads were practically impassable, and the gendarmes ruthlessly shot to death anyone who lagged behind, leaving trails of corpses all the way to the Bug, which they did not bother to bury, thereby angering the Germans. The gendarmes led the convoys of thousands of starving and exhausted Jews on a wild goose chase, searching for bridges that had disappeared in floods or crossing-points over frozen rivers. Many of the Jews reached the breaking point and collapsed in the knowledge that they would be shot. Children were orphaned en route and adopted by other families or they insisted on staying with their dying parents and were shot to death along with them. Gangs of Ukrainians operated throughout Transnistria, particularly in the Mogilev district, falling upon the convoys of Jews to rob and kill them and often leaving hundreds of naked Jews in their wake, who subsequently froze to death. Many Jews, especially the elderly, were too weak to lift their feet out of the deep mud and remained where they were until they were shot by the gendarmes who brought up the rear of the convoy. Each convoy was robbed first by the gendarmes—who usually were furious at the meager spoils—and then by the Ukrainian escorts and citizens. In each convoy young women were raped by ordinary gendarmes and especially by gendarmerie officers, who ordered nightly stopovers in places suitable for conducting orgies. The convoy commanders were not required to be responsible for the lives of the Jews. Their job was simply to transfer them from place to place, without names or identities. The gendarmes, who were as yet unfamiliar with the terrain, were assisted by local policemen, whom they partially entrusted with the task of guarding and accompanying the convoys. Many of these Ukrainians had already been armed by members of *Einsatzgruppe* D during July and August, when they had helped them murder tens of thousands of Jews.

About fifteen days after the start of the deportation, the inspector general of the gendarmerie in Transnistria, Colonel Brosteanu, informed the Transnistrian administration that the deportation plan had collapsed due to disorganization and the lack of guards, accommodation, and food for the deportees. Moreover, he stated, Romanian and German army units were also involved in the operation, as well as the gendarmes, and "constantly brought over new groups of Jews for whom there was no room." The gendarmerie companies were forced to set up provisional ghettos pending further instructions. "We received no instructions concerning the feeding and upkeep of these Jews, and the prefectures we turned to could not give us any constructive answer." The gendarmerie commander asked the governor for instructions as to how to feed and maintain "these Jews."[52] The prefectures used to cable the administration in Tiraspol regarding the progress of the convoys toward the River Bug. On October 2, 1941, the prefect of Rybnitsa, Colonel Popescu, reported to the administration that "the convoys of Jews continue as per schedule. To date, I have dispatched 3,764 [Jews]."[53]

The transfer of the convoys of Jews to the Bug continued, in total disarray, during October and November [1941]. No attempt was made to keep to the original plan of directing the convoys to specific localities along the Bug. Thousands of Jews were left in towns and villages that had never been intended to serve as ghettos or labor camps.

The final destinations remained unchanged, however, and from time to time a convoy that had been abandoned in a certain locality was collected and taken to the Bug. The deportation routine was shattered in early October when the gendarmerie escorts contracted typhus from the Jews, who had contracted it already in Bessarabia. The gendarmerie reported that "dozens of case[s] of typhus" had been identified among the gendarmes, who had caught it "from the Jews in the convoys they escorted across the Dniester."[54] . . .

Antonescu, who followed the deportation of the Jews as if it were a military campaign, pointed out at a cabinet session on November 13, 1941, that Iasi's Jewish population had been downsized due to "congestion." He had had many problems, he added, "with those I sent to the Bug. *Only I know how many died on the way.*"[55] This statement confirms that Antonescu knew about the murder of the freezing and starving Jews in the convoys. Statistical data that he ordered provided him with an accurate picture of the scope of the extermination.

Odessa and "The Kingdom of Terror"

From October 18, 1941, until the middle of March 1942, the Romanian military authorities in Odessa—helped by the gendarmerie, the police, and the civil authorities—waged a campaign of terror, execution, and deportation against the city's Jews, resulting in the murder of at least twenty-five thousand Jews and the deportation of another sixty thousand. This campaign was planned and executed by the Romanians alone— the German army and *Einsatzgruppe* D never even set foot in the city.[56]

On the evening of October 22, the Romanian military general headquarters exploded, killing sixty-six Romanian officers (including the city's military commander, Gen. Ion Glogojanu). Tenth Division headquarters took over the building that had formerly served as headquarters of the NKVD (the Soviet secret police). Immediately upon learning of the disaster, Antonescu ordered Gen. Iosif Iacobici, chief of staff and commander of the Fourth Army, to "take drastic punitive measures."[57] Meanwhile, Gen. Nicolae Tataranu's deputy, Col. Ion Stanculescu, deputy chief of the General Staff and chief of staff of the Fourth Army, reached Odessa in the morning with a secret order from Antonescu, which he personally handed to Gen. Nicolae Trestioreanu, deputy commander of the Tenth Division. Antonescu ordered "immediate retaliatory action, including the liquidation of 18,000 Jews in the ghettos and the hanging in the town squares of at least 100 Jews for every regimental sector."[58] The same day (October 23) Stanculescu again cabled Tataranu, with details of the punitive measures: "Retaliatory action has been taken within the city via shooting [and] hanging. . . . The execution of the Jews in the ghettos is well on the way to reaching the aforementioned number."[59] Stanculescu also reported that although the German liaison officer had offered the help of an SS regiment to rid Odessa of "Jews and Bolsheviks," the Romanian authorities chose to act alone. Soldiers from the Tenth Division and from the Tenth Machine Gun Battalion and military gendarmes shot at Jews in the streets and hung them on tram posts, on improvised planks on street corners, on balconies overlooking the main streets, or simply on streets, after first conducting a hasty search.[60] The main executions took place in the municipal penitentiary and in Dalnic—a village near Odessa that was designated as a ghetto and to which tens of thousands of Jews were taken. According to Gherman Pantea, the Romanian mayor of Odessa, the convoy to Dalnic consisted of some fifty thousand Jews.[61] Thirty thousand or more Jews were rounded up by the gendarmes, some of whom

were mounted. Shooting into the air and at people and lashing their whips, they led the massive convoy northward along the Odessa-Katarzi highway to an improvised camp in Berezovka. The deportees were then marched for about two weeks to the Bogdanovka camp, where they were liquidated.

The twenty-five thousand Jews who were the first to reach Dalnic were lined up near the anti-tank trenches that had been dug during the siege and shot in the head. About forty to fifty Jews were shot in one go. The operation was carried out in total chaos and disorder. Although we do not know the exact number of Jews shot, it ran into the thousands.[62] The method they used was slow and inefficient. On the afternoon of October 24, when the liquidation operation was at its height, Personal Order no. 563 arrived, determining new punitive measures. Antonescu ordered General Tataranu "to execute all Bessarabian Jews who had fled to Odessa" and herd all Jews "who had not yet been executed [by the previous order]" into a mined building and explode it.[63] About twenty-two thousand Jews of all ages who had been taken to Dalnic were packed like sardines into nine huge stone warehouses and slaughtered: "One by one, the warehouses were riddled with machine gun and rifle fire, doused with gasoline and ignited, except for the last warehouse, which was blown up. The chaos and the horrifying sights that followed defy description: wounded people burning alive, women with their hair on fire coming out through the roof or through openings in the burning storehouses in a desperate search for salvation. . . . Others tried to escape, climbed on to window ledges or on to the roof amidst the flames, and begged to be shot."[64] The operation continued all night and over the next day. Of about twenty-two thousand Jews, there remained only charred or blown up body parts that were collected and buried in late November by Soviet prisoners of war.[65] . . .

Toward the Implementation of the Final Solution

In early 1942 Ion Antonescu decided that, having liquidated most of the Jews of Bessarabia and Bukovina, it was now the turn of the Jews of the Regat. On February 12, he met in Berlin with Hitler, who praised him generously for the Romanian army's contribution and bravery in the war and attempted to explain away the defeat on the outskirts of Moscow. He further promised that "he was resolved to complete the destruction and final rout of the Russians from the battlefield that summer."[66] Antonescu agreed to send three-quarters of the Romanian army, most of which had already been demobilized after the 1941 campaign, to fight on the eastern front. As a token of his gratitude the führer presented Antonescu with a Mercedes-Benz. In the summer of 1942 Antonescu truly believed that victory was around the corner and that all that was needed was one final effort to defeat the Soviet Union.

It was this belief that fueled his policy toward the Jews. His desire to turn Romania into a homogeneous nation, as he had promised his ministers, affected not only the Jews but Slavs, Gypsies, and other minority groups, too. Believing that he was serving the highest interests of the Romanian nation, he was determined to forge ahead with his plans, irrespective even of the Nazis' plans. As far as the Jews were concerned, Antonescu went berserk. He constantly—sometimes even daily—issued orders to deport, detain, shoot, punish, or rob Jews in the Regat and southern Transylvania, as well as Gypsies, members of Christian sects, or any Jew who happened to irritate him at the time.

On the face of it Antonescu was bound by his promise to [Wilhelm] Filderman [the leader of Romanian Jewry] of September 2, 1941, to grant the Jews of the Regat preferred status. Before the start of the battle of Odessa, he agreed to abolish the yellow badge and, believing he would shortly capture Odessa, issued vague promises to the effect that he would grant a privileged status to the Jews of the Regat. "He draws a distinction between the Jews of the Regat [and other Jews], and he plans a privileged status for them."[67]

Only a month later the marshal broke his promise by ordering the deportation of the Jews of the Dorohoi district and most of the Jews of the city of Dorohoi (Dorohoi had always belonged to the Regat). In the last months of 1941 the Romanian press, under directives from Mihai Antonescu's Ministry of Propaganda, published daily announcements about the impending deportation of the Jews of the Regat. It is clear from these activities that Antonescu's promise was not made in good faith. As a despot who did not have to account for his behavior, Antonescu was free to do as he pleased. On December 10, 1941, he decided to dismiss Filderman from his post and from that point on refused to grant him an audience.

As a preliminary step to the deportations of 1942 Antonescu drew up "categories" of Jews earmarked for deportation, such as so-called lawbreakers, enemies of the state, and evaders of forced labor. By the end of the summer, however, he had drawn up a plan to deport all the Jews of southern Transylvania, irrespective of category. The introduction of categories led, in the final analysis, to the attempted deportation of ninety-five thousand to one hundred thousand Jews in 1942. In late February 1942, Antonescu informed his ministers that circumstances had never been so ripe for implementing Romanization, and "we would be wrong not to exploit them." Romanization, however, was merely one aspect of the struggle he waged on the battlefront and against the Jews. "No one was so naive as to believe, when the struggle against the Yids began, that it would be easy. Just as no one was so naive as to believe, when we launched [the war] against Russia, that ten bullets over the Prut [would be enough] to end the war without bloodshed. Through this battle, we shall build a new path for the Romanian nation and new life for the coming generations. Romanian society will be built on this struggle and on the victims we are sacrificing today."[68]

Antonescu's message was clear: the war against the Soviet Union and the war against the Jews were one and the same thing. The new Romanian society would be built on the ashes of these two enemies. . . . Both his actions and his decisions until October 1942 (and in certain cases even after that) clearly showed, as he himself admitted, that his aim was to deport as many Jews as possible in 1942.

On July 10, 1942, Antonescu introduced measures that indicated the start of the deportation from Romania proper. About thirty thousand Jews from southern Transylvania were to be deported to the Kingdom of Death in Transnistria.[69] On July 16 and 17, in an uncontrollable but not random burst of rage, Antonescu decided to deport tens of thousands of Jews from the Regat, depending on the various categories of real or imaginary offenses they had committed. The military cabinet opened a special file titled "The Problem of the Deportation of the Jews to the Bug."[70] From his villa in Predeal, where he was recovering from a new bout of his mysterious disease (syphilis), Antonescu ordered Radu Davidescu, head of the military cabinet, to deport "all Jews who had infringed current price regulations, restrictions on the sale of certain products . . . and similar offenses . . . over the Bug." Antonescu added a number of explanations that shed light on the impulsive nature of his anti-Jewish decisions. . . . "These measures are designed not only for criminals, but also to rid densely populated areas of parasitic Jewish ele-

ments that violate economic laws and [disrupt] internal order." Antonescu ordered a report on the progress of the deportation of Jews in the Regat and southern Transylvania by category as well as a report on "proposals for future deportations." He added that next on the list were "the [remaining] Jews of Bukovina, Jews who violate trade restrictions, and the Jews of Transylvania who are being relocated [i.e., deported] in order to make room for Romanian refugees, and the like."[71]

The following day (July 17), giving full vent to his rage, Antonescu sent yet another order from Predeal via teleprinter to the military cabinet and minister of the interior for implementation. He expanded his previous directives and broadened the eligibility criteria for deportation by ordering the deportation of all Jews and foreigners who infringed economic laws: "anyone hiding medicines, fabrics, footwear, cotton, couponed goods, and food products, as well as middlemen, saboteurs of the economy, and those who fail to respect price ceilings." Antonescu ordered the Ministry of the Economy and the Ministry of the Interior to issue a formal decision regarding the new deportations and to send it to him in his villa in Predeal for signature by July 25. "Due process shall be reduced to a minimum. Offenders shall be deported to Transnistria without trial, together with their families. This decision shall be valid retroactively." The immediate cause of the marshal's mounting rage was apparent in an order of July 17, 1942: "We must not agree to the violation of our laws . . . while Romanian officers and soldiers risk their lives on the front. Understanding and tolerance toward these monopolizing and disruptive elements is unthinkable."[72] The second order turned all Jews who were still wage earners into prospective deportees, without recourse to due process. The order empowered the corrupt and antisemitic Romanian administration to immediately deport all offenders and their families. While implementation of the first order would have resulted in the deportation of ninety-five thousand to one hundred thousand Jews (about nineteen thousand from Czernowitz and Dorohoi; thirty thousand from southern Transylvania; forty thousand deemed to have evaded forced labor; and five thousand who fit in other categories), implementation of the second order signified the gradual deportation to Transnistria of all Romanian Jews.

Once the decision had been made to deport all Romanian Jews, the fate of Romanian Jews residing in Nazi-occupied Europe became irrelevant. The consuls in Germany "received orders on August 21, 1942, to no longer protest the measures adopted by the Germans against Romanian Jews and their property," but to monitor the confiscation of property and to draw up an inventory of items seized by the German authorities.[73] Gheorge Davidescu, secretary general of the Foreign Ministry, sent all Romanian ambassadors a clarification concerning the government's policy toward Jews whose passports had expired. He informed the Romanian ambassador in Switzerland that, regarding the Jews who had fled to Switzerland to renew their Romanian passports: "It is our country's policy to get rid of as many members of the Jewish minority as possible." He recommended that the passports of Jews be confiscated and that they be left to deal with the Swiss authorities alone.[74]

In early September, Antonescu decided to deport Jews to Transnistria after reading reports on the economy in the Romanian press that groundlessly accused Jews of economic sabotage. For example, after reading such an article in *Curentul* he ordered the confiscation of the property, internment, and deportation of the "Yids and their families" whom the newspaper had accused

of sabotaging the economy. Antonescu's adoption of the final solution was reflected in his vocabulary when speaking of the Jews. It was as if a mutation had taken place; whereas until June 1941 he was merely antisemitic, after June 1941 his antisemitic outlook assumed an unmistakably Nazi-racist character.

On August 31, 1942, about two weeks before the beginning of the deportation to Poland and Transnistria, Antonescu was infuriated by reading a detailed survey he had commissioned on the size and distribution of the Jewish population in Romania, and he ordered that steps be taken to prepare the general public for the deportation of Romanian Jews:

> The [data] on the population breakdown in the cities must be published in order for the country to realize the enormity of the danger facing Romania's economic life and development, due to the crimes of the Jewish-Masonic policy, as represented through parties that call themselves "nationalist" in Transylvania and the Regat. By leaving things the way they are for my heirs, I would be turning my regime into an accomplice, too. No one and no obstacle shall alter my resolve to completely purge the nation of this pest. When the time comes, I shall condemn all those who tried (most recently Mr. Maniu), and are trying, to prevent me from carrying out the wish of the vast majority of this nation. . . . This decision should be published in its entirety together with the statistics and the present survey . . . by September 10.[75]

The Deportation in the Autumn of 1942

In the autumn of 1942, most Jews in Bukovina (Czernowitz) and southern Transylvania, offenders and evaders of forced labor, Communists and their sympathizers, new converts, Jews who tried to return to Bessarabia after its annexation to the Soviet Union, and Gypsies were about to be deported. A total of ninety-five thousand to one hundred thousand Jews faced deportation to Transnistria. At the same time, secret negotiations with the German government concerning the wholesale deportation of Romanian Jewry to the Belzec camp in Poland approached their final stages. Everything was proceeding as planned. In late August Antonescu's rage reached a pinnacle. The Ministry of the Interior received a list of Communists whom the police and gendarmerie had marked variously as dangerous, undercover Communists, or Communist sympathizers, as they saw fit. The General Staff drew up a list of Jews who failed to report for forced labor or whom they labeled "work-shy" (even if they had died or been murdered), who had escaped from forced labor detachments, or who simply were absent when Gen. Constantin Cepleanu, the new inspector of forced labor, conducted his impromptu raids, even if they had been granted leave of absence. The Jewish Center, as ordered, supplied the authorities with the latest addresses of Jews, including relatives and converts. In the Targu Jiu camp, which held Communists who had been arrested without trial, preliminary preparations were made for deportation.

The Gendarmerie Inspectorate General, under General Vasiliu, was responsible for organizing the transports to Transnistria. Vasiliu instructed the General Police Inspectorate to oversee the confiscation of the deportees' (Jews and Gypsies) belongings, the arrest of those slated for deportation, and their transfer to the gendarmerie authorities. The gendarmerie legions throughout Romania were provided with timetables of the deportation trains.[76] ...

On the night of September 15–16 the General Staff unleashed its deportation operation. On September 22, some 160 Bucharest Jews and their families were arrested and deported to Transnistria via Tiraspol. At stations en route the train picked up several hundred more Jews from all over Romania who had been arrested under the General Staff's deportation plan.[77] The Jewish author Mihail Sebastian noted in his diary on September 22: "The deportation plan is being implemented slowly but surely."[78] On October 2, several hundred Jews—General Cepleanu's victims—were imprisoned in two Jewish schools in Bucharest prior to their deportation, this time without their families.

The deportation operation was huge and required careful organization and planning as well as the cooperation of the various authorities, such as the Ministry of the Interior, the Finance Ministry, the National Romanization Center, the municipalities, and the Jewish Center, which supplied the addresses of the Jews and their families. The General Staff assigned the Jewish Center the task of guarding the families until the arrest of the family heads and of loading them onto the trains. The number of those accused of evading forced labor totaled 14,247 (about 40,000 with their families). The General Staff, with Ion Antonescu's approval, planned to deport most of them in the autumn of 1942 to the Golta and Berezovka districts, where they were to be liquidated.

In early October 1942 the Antonescu regime's resolve to deport Romanian Jewry to the camps and ghettos of Transnistria appeared inevitable and irrevocable. They were not, however, the only actors on the scene. The Nazis were also competing for the privilege of liquidating Romanian Jewry, and their methods were far more organized and efficient.

Destination Belzec

The Belzec concentration camp in the Lublin district, in which Jews were asphyxiated by carbon monoxide generated by a diesel engine, was chosen by the RSHA and the German Foreign Ministry to serve as a mass grave for Romanian Jewry. In June 1942, the camp was renovated and its extermination capacity enhanced. Six large, new gas chambers were added, capable of killing 1,000–1,200 deportees at a time (half of a daily transport of 2,000) within twenty to thirty minutes. The entire procedure, from the arrival of the deportees in the camp to the removal of the corpses via the rear doors of the gas chambers for burial, took an hour to an hour and a half. This extermination method was shrouded in secrecy and duplicity. From the moment they boarded the trains until they were forced into the gas chambers, the victims were told that they were being taken to labor camps.[79]

Access to the Belzec camp was easy. It was the terminal station on the Czernowitz-Sniatyn-Belzec railroad (Sniatyn was on the former Polish border). It was necessary to persuade the Jews that they were being taken to a labor camp, where they would be treated in a civilized manner, in order to facilitate matters. Mihai Antonescu was fed the same story when [SS officer Gustav] Richter insisted that the Romanian Jews be deported to occupied Poland, not Transnistria: "Mr. Richter informed me that the Jews from Romania and other countries were being taken to Poland where they were organized into work camps, and that while the regime in these camps could hardly be called comfortable, it was nevertheless reasonable in terms of physical preservation."[80] Although Richter was aware that he was dealing with criminals and murderers like himself, he did not realize that they had already learned about the Final Solution from Hitler himself and that the liquidation of the Jews in the "labor camps" of Poland was no secret for them (although the actual method of extermination may have been). Nor did he realize that even

the Romanian diplomatic legations in the Reich and in German-occupied countries were aware of what was going on, as their reports indicated. . . .

On July 26 Heinrich Müller, Gestapo head, informed Martin Luther, undersecretary for foreign affairs, that the deportation of Romanian Jews in special trains "to the east" would begin on September 10, 1942.[81] Luther drew up a memorandum describing the important landmarks in the negotiations with the Romanians concerning the deportation, starting with the Romanian government's agreement in November 1941 to the deportation of its Jewish citizens living in the Reich and in the Protectorate, [and adding]: "The deputy President of the Council of Ministers has given us his approval in writing, in accordance with Marshal Antonescu's wishes, for the German authorities to carry out the evacuation of the Jews from Romania.[82] At the same time, [Emil von] Rintelen from the [German] Foreign Ministry drew up a memorandum . . . outlining preparations for the deportation of Romanian Jewry. . . . In accordance with the plan, transports were to leave for the Lublin area beginning around September 10 in groups of two thousand Jews per transport. Those unfit for work were to be given "special treatment." After crossing the border the deportees were to be deprived of their Romanian nationality. The Foreign Ministry was still negotiating the settlement of certain issues in Romania. Talks with the Reich Ministry of Transport had still to be finalized but were progressing smoothly. At the RSHA'S behest Richter received written confirmation from Mihai Antonescu that he consented to the deportation, and Rintelen enclosed a copy of the agreement.[83] . . .

The Postponement of the Nazi Final Solution

In the government session of October 13, 1942, Mihai Antonescu announced a change of policy toward the Jews: "For the time being, the transports of Jews across the Dniester are being halted."[84] ... Mihai Antonescu stressed that one of the reasons for halting the deportations was rampant corruption among Romanian officials: "Not only do the police agents receive bribes in order to save [people earmarked] for deportation to Transnistria ... they also threaten others who do not come under this category, earning a tidy income and tainting our Administration ... because of their brazen and unseemly bribery operations."[85] ...

The change in policy toward the Jews occurred only when Ion and Mihai Antonescu came to the gradual realization that they were unlikely to be rewarded for the many human and material sacrifices they had made (and were still making) for the realization of Hitler's dream to conquer the world. The reward they expected was the return of northern Transylvania. In 1942 Antonescu and the entire Romanian nation were prepared to pay with blood, oil, food ... and Jews, in return for northern Transylvania. In September 1942, before the defeat at Stalingrad but closely linked to the situation on the fronts, the two leaders began to wonder if they had made the right choices, after realizing that their expectation that Hitler would return northern Transylvania to Romania was unrealistic. Later in September, Mihai Antonescu realized that the Romanian soldiers on the front were serving as cannon fodder and that Germany was unable to defeat the Soviet Union. By 1942, three-quarters of the Romanian army had been sent to Russia, almost all Romania's oil had been sent to fuel the German war machine, and huge quantities of food had been transferred to the Reich, at a time when Romania itself was suffering shortages, and all this to what end and for what purpose? ...

Unlike the Nazi plan to deport the Jews to occupied Poland, which was revoked in October 1942,

Antonescu's plan to deport the Jews to Transnistria was never abolished. Antonescu's intention to deport most of Romanian Jewry remained intact and served as a guiding principle for Vasiliu, the minister of internal affairs (who, together with the marshal and the head of the SSI, directed Romania's internal security), and was occasionally translated into decisions. Antonescu's insistence on doing with Romanian Jewry as he saw fit, despite changes in political and military circumstances, even when it was clear that Germany would be defeated, was a reflection of his character. Common sense could not prevail against his inflated self-esteem, his total identification with Romania's national goals, and his absorption of all the negative stereotypes that had been attributed to Jews since the days of the founding fathers of Romanian antisemitism.

The Presidency of the Council of Ministers, the General Staff, and Vasiliu acted in the knowledge that the deportations to Transnistria would resume whenever the *Conducator* decided that the time was ripe. On October 22, 1942, for example, Ovidiu Vladescu, secretary-general of the Presidency of the Council of Ministers, issued a general directive ordering the deportation to Transnistria of all Jews who were petitioning the courts in the hope of receiving a provisional exemption from deportation pending the courts' decisions.[86] ...

In March 1943, the plan to deport the Jews of Czernowitz was still valid, as Vasiliu's refusal to allow a Jewish family to move from Czernowitz to Bucharest indicates: "Marshal Antonescu forbids any relocation of Jews from Czernowitz to the country [Regat]. Moreover, the petitioner and his family belong to the group of Jews who are shortly to be deported."[87] The plan to deport the Jews of Czernowitz was still valid in August 1943, although by then the Interior Ministry realized that it might not be implemented. The Interior

Ministry rejected a request by the Presidency of the Council of Ministers to grant a special travel permit to a Jew from Czernowitz who had converted to Christianity, on the grounds that they could not allow exceptions, "especially in the case of the remainder of the Jews of Czernowitz, whose are simply there on sufferance instead of being in Transnistria."[88]

Antonescu continued his policy of concentrating the Jews of Moldova into the main cities in order to facilitate their subsequent deportation or forced emigration when the time came.... On April 17, 1943, Antonescu ordered "the Jews to be evacuated from cities that were not district capitals to cities that served as district capitals." For many this was a second evacuation, since in June 1941 they had been relocated from their villages and towns under another order issued by Antonescu. The interior minister ordered all Romanian police inspectorates to assess the number of Jews still in these cities and the advantages and disadvantages of the proposed evacuation and to facilitate the "transfer [of their businesses] to Christian hands."[89] ...

Antonescu never came to terms with the fact that he had to relinquish his dream of purging the country of Jews. However, unlike the Nazis, he no longer insisted on killing them and, from October 1942, agreed to let them emigrate anywhere they wished, provided they left all their possessions behind. On March 26, 1943, the Romanian government submitted a memorandum to the German ambassador stating, "The only solution to the Jewish problem in Romania is emigration."[90] In the same month, in an interview with his friend, the antisemitic author Ioan Bratescu-Voinesti, Antonescu thanked the Germans for their support in efforts to purge the country of parasites and internal enemies. These enemies, Antonescu added, "are more dangerous in my eyes than exter-nal enemies, because while external enemies may lop off parts of the homeland, internal enemies bring about the cultural and moral poisoning of our people's soul." In the interview Antonescu promised to continue the struggle until "Jewish Bolshevism was totally eradicated."[91]

On September 26, 1943, after the collapse of Mussolini's regime, Antonescu realized that the Soviet army could not be checked and began to plan the withdrawal of troops, the administration, and local collaborators from Transnistria to Romania. It was at this juncture that the marshal informed his military secretary of the necessity of examining "in parallel" the possibility of relocating (i.e., deporting) Romanian Jews to Transnistria."[92] Thanks to the rapid advance of the Soviet forces and Mihai Antonescu's (and perhaps also the opposition's) political logic, this program remained a historical document only, one that, more than anything, revealed Antonescu's intentions toward the Jews of the Regat.

In a letter he sent Nicolae Clejan, his Jewish architect, on February 4, 1944, Antonescu expressed his regret at not having managed to deport all the Jews from Bessarabia and Bukovina (14,000 Jews were left in Czernowitz and 101 in the whole of Bessarabia) and hypocritically claimed that he had been forced to carry out the deportations in order to protect these Jews from pogroms. He threatened to settle the score with the remaining Jews and the Jews of Romania: "I again draw the Jews' attention to the fact that if they continue to subvert the State, which is too tolerant by far, they will suffer even more serious consequences than those they have suffered so far."[93]

The Alibi

In late March 1943 Mihai Antonescu tried to persuade the Swiss ambassador in Romania, René de Weck, who since December 13, 1941, had also represented the interests of Britain, the United States, Belgium, Greece, and Yugoslavia, "that he had finally relinquished the persecution of the Children of Israel" and that the dissemination of the latest antisemitic leaflets was perpetrated by the German embassy and its Romanian lackeys.[94] Following this, Mihai Antonescu set about building a national alibi for the regime, the Romanian people, and himself for the crimes they had committed against the Jewish people. General antisemitic and racist propaganda stopped. The greater the defeats on the front, the greater Mihai Antonescu's belief in the omnipotence of world Jewry, which, he was convinced, ruled the world in one way of another—whether in the guise of Soviet Bolshevism or in the guise of the Anglo-American plutocracy. Mihai Antonescu developed totally unrealistic and almost insane expectations concerning the ability of Jewish leaders to influence the democratic powers in his favor and in favor of Romania. . . .

Summary

. . . The number of victims in the territory that remained under Romanian sovereignty on the eve of the war against the Soviet Union was relatively small. About 200 Jews were killed in the Dorohoi pogrom in July 1940, several hundred were pushed off moving trains, about 400 were shot to death during the Galati pogrom in July 1940, about 150 were killed before and during the Bucharest pogrom, about 15,000 were killed in the Iasi pogrom or died from asphyxiation in the death trains, about 1,300 who were deported from Romania in the autumn of 1942 were executed or met their death in Transnistria, and several hundred more from the forced labor detachments perished in work-related accidents, from disease, or from the terrible living conditions—bringing the total up to about 20,000 Jews.

The extermination and deportation operations took place mainly in areas that Romania [retook from] the Soviet Union in June 1941—Bessarabia and northern Bukovina—as well as in southern Bukovina and in the Dorohoi district of the Regat, in accordance with Ion Antonescu's decision to deport Jews from these areas. In 1930, 300,059 Jews lived in these territories, excluding the Dorohoi district, and 312,991 including Dorohoi. Under Soviet rule (July 1940–July 1941) the number of Jews in these regions grew by several tens of thousands, but this estimate cannot be corroborated due to the lack of relevant data. Consequently, this population increase was not taken into account in the calculations made in this study.

The discovery of classified Romanian documents showed that fewer Jews were murdered in the first wave of killings than was originally thought. In July 1941 there were at least 112,000 Bessarabian Jews and 82,478 Jews in Bukovina (excluding the Dorohoi district)—a total of 195,000. About 105,000 Romanian Jews of the 300,059 Jews who lived in Bessarabia and Bukovina in 1930 disappeared in July—August 1941, during and immediately after the battles to recapture the area. In Bessarabia, 25,000 were murdered.[95] . . .

The tens of thousands of Jews who tried to escape suffered the same fate as those who remained, because of the rapid advance of the German army and the explicit order to shoot them. About 76,000 Jews who survived the massacres perpetrated by the Romanian authorities and the local population in Bessarabia were deported to Transnistria (55,867 plus 20,000 killed by the German ss in the Ukraine during the hasty deportations). It has been proved that most of the Jewish population in northern Bukovina did not try to escape and that most of the Jews in the small towns and villages were slaughtered. A total of 86,408 Jews were deported from Bukovina in 1941 and 1942 and a further 11,667 from the Dorohoi district, bringing the total number of deportees to Transnistria to 174,249. In November 1943 there were about 50,000 survivors from all the deportation areas, including the Jews of Dorohoi. Thus, a total of 129,000 Romanian Jews were killed or perished in or en route to Transnistria. The Romanian occupation authority found at least 200,000 local Jews alive in Transnistria. The massive killing operations launched by the Romanian occupation regime in Odessa and the Kingdom of Death and during the deportation campaigns and the delivery of Jews to the German killing squads resulted in the death of about 180,000 of these Jews. Thus, altogether, the Romanian authorities were responsible for the disappearance of at least 400,000 Jews.

The secret documents that were discovered in the Foreign Ministry and Interior Ministry archives indicate the scale of the deportation and killing operations and prove that the Romanian government kept accurate statistics of the number of Jews, including Ukrainian Jews, it liquidated or deported.

NOTES

1. M. Antonescu, *Pentru Basarabia si Bucovina*, 60–61.
2. Ancel, *Documents*, vol. 6, doc. 15, 199–201.
3. Ancel, *Documents*, vol. 5, doc. 1, 1.4.
4. Special orders for Operation Barbarossa issued by the German army Supreme Command on May 19, 1941, together with guidelines for the behavior of soldiers in Russia, in *Trials of War Criminals*, 10: 990–94.
5. This order was reconstructed in the indictment of the People's Court against nineteen commanders, officers, and low-ranking officers of the gendarmerie sections of Czernowitz, Hotin,

Orhei, Cetatea-Alba, Ismail, and Kishinev who were accused of massacring the Jewish population (hereafter indictment against nineteen commanders), in Ancel, *Documents*, vol. 6, doc. 15, 202.
6. Indictment against Stavrat, in Ancel, *Documents*, vol. 6, doc. 40, 428. General Doncea asked General Stavrat, Vartic's commander, to stay the execution of eighty Jews. In his answer Stavrat explained that Vartic had been "given personal orders" and asked the general "not to interfere," since these orders were meant specifically for the pretors.
7. Indictment against nineteen commanders, in Ancel, *Documents*, vol. 6, doc. 15, 214.
8. Indictment against Stavrat, in Ancel, *Documents*, vol. 6, doc. 40, 434. In Hotin, for example, a junior employee at the municipality entered "a Jewish woman's home and told her that she would have no more need of her property since she was going to die anyway. He then proceeded to load carpets, linen, curtains and quilts onto carts" (436).
9. Mircu, *Pogromurile din Bucovina si Dorohoi*, 24, 32–33, 39, 44.
10. Arrest warrant against Vladimir Clem and Sofia Loy, village of Banila on Ceremus, May 1948, in Ancel, *Documents*, vol. 6, doc. 29, 301. In July 1941 Clem and Loy informed terrorist gangs of the whereabouts of the Katz family, resulting in the murder of the family and the looting of its property.
11. Commander of the General Staff's Second Bureau Lt. Col. Alexandru Ionescu to the General Staff, July 11, 1942, USIIMM/MSM, RG-25.003M, reel 11, file 781, 0144.
12. "The Plan to Remove the Judaic Element from Bessarabian Ground Still under Soviet Control by Organizing Teams that Will Precede the Romanian Forces," USHMM/MSM, RG-25.003M, reel 11, file 781, 145–46.
13. Indictment against Stavrat, in Ancel, *Documents*, vol. 6, doc. 40, 425. See also Gold, *Geschichte der Juden*, 2: 105–8.

14. Indictment against Stavrat, in Ancel, *Documents*, vol. 6, doc. 40, 425.

15. Ibid., 429.

16. Ibid.

17. On Sunday, July 6, two days after the pogrom, Rabbi Horovitz of Banila was forced to march to Ciudei with the remnants of his community. He testified, "A sorry sight awaited us at Ciudei. The vile objective of liquidating the Jews had been accomplished. Of the 500 Jews who had lived there, not one remained alive. This Jewish community was liquidated at the order of the criminal, Major Carp." Testimony of Rabbi Horovitz from Banila before the People's Court, in Ancel, Documents, vol. 6, doc. 12, 145–53. See also Carp, *Cartea neagra*, 3: 29.

18. Carp, *Cartea neagra*, 3: 30. Carp describes how Romanian soldiers "derived pleasure" from killing Jews in Ropcea.

19. Carp, *Cartea neagra*, 3: 30–31, and Mircu, *Pogromurile din Bucovina si Dorohoi*, 23–51. In Hlinifa soldiers killed five Jews. The synagogues were desecrated, and the local citizens used the parchment of fifteen Torah scrolls to make shoes. Rabbi Horovitz was deported with the remnants of the Banila community to Transnistria. . . . The rabbi pointed out that "in the villages of Costesti, Hlinita and Drosnifa, 90 per cent of the Jewish population was destroyed. The only survivor of about 400 Jewish citizens of Costesti was an orphan boy." Testimony of Rabbi Horovitz from Banila before the People's Court, in Ancel, *Documents*, vol. 6, doc. 12, 148.

20. We know nothing of the last moments of the Jews of the Bukovinian villages near the Dniester, in the area known as Plasa Nistrului, since there were almost no survivors from these villages. The massacres were carried out by Romanian and German soldiers, who shot 30 Jews in the village of Zoniache and 32 in Rapujinet. See Carp, *Cartea neagra*, 3: 35; appendix to the testimony of Jacob Stenzler, YVA, 0–11/89, PKR III, 261–62.

21. Carp, *Cartea neagra*, 2: 36. See also Ancel, "Kishinev," in *Pinkas Hakehilot, Rumania*, 2: 411–16.

22. Testimony of Eugen Cristescu, former head of the SSI, in Carp, *Cartea neagra*, 2: 43.

23. Testimony of Eugen Cristescu, in Carp, *Cartea neagra*, 2: 43, 51.

24. Nuremberg Documents, NO-2851.

25. Nuremberg Documents, NO-2952, NOKW-3233.

26. Nuremberg Documents, NO-2952.

27. Carp, *Cartea neagra*, no. 14, 3: 55–56.

28. *Buletinul Demografic*, 345–46; Centrala Evreilor din Romania, *Breviarul statistic*, 25, 145; copy in Ancel, *Documents*, vol. 1, docs. 37, 45, 274–76, 305–22.

29. See YVA, testimonies, 03–1452, 3; 03–1456, 5; 03–1536, 2; and 03–1537, 45.

30. *Die Bevölkerungszählung*.

31. I. Calafeteanu and M. Covaci, "Situation of the Jews in Bessarabia, Bukovina and 'Transnistria' in the 1941–1944 Years," mimeograph, 1983, 8; copy in Ancel, *Documents*, vol. 10, doc. 182, 487.

32. I. Calafeteanu and M. Covaci, "Situation of the Jews in Bessarabia, Bukovina and 'Transnistria' in the 1941–1944 Years," mimeograph, 1983, 8; copy in Ancel, *Documents*, vol. 10, doc. 182, 486–87.

33. See graph showing the situation of Bessarabian Jewry on September 25, 1941, in Ancel, *Documents*, vol. 10, doc. 43, 100.

34. Gendarmerie Inspectorate, "Bulletin of Transnistria," referring to the 118,847 deportees from Bessarabia and Bukovina, in Ancel, *Documents*, vol. 5, doc. 128, 220. See also Zaharia and Copoiu, "Le probleme," 9; copy in Ancel, *Documents*, vol. 10, doc. 181, 481. In fact, over 170,000 Jews were deported.

35. The statistical data compiled by the Jewish Center's Statistical Department, based on data provided by the Romanian Central Bureau of Statistics, present an accurate picture of the Jewish demographic situation in the two provinces. See also *Die Bevölkerungszählung*; official census of the Jewish population in the provinces of Bessarabia and Bukovina and in the Doro-

hoi region, 1930–42, in Ancel, *Documents*, vol. 1, doc. 40, 324; Carp, *Cartea neagra*, no. 1, 3: 41–42; Ancel, *Transnistria*, 1Q41–1Q42, vol. 1, chap. 8.

36. Memorandum by Voiculescu, governor of Bessarabia, to Antonescu, undated [late 1941] (hereafter Voiculescu report), in Ancel, *Documents*, vol. 10, doc. 61, 137, 142.

37. Voiculescu report, in Ancel, *Documents*, vol. 10, doc. 61, 137, 143.

38. Ministry of the Interior memorandum on the problem of the repatriation of deported Jews to Romania, October 12, 1943, in Ancel, *Documents*, vol. 4, doc. 356, 666.

39. Memorandum from the Presidency of the Council of Ministers, submitted to Antonescu for inspection, concerning the interventions made on behalf of Bukovinian Jewry, January 24, 1944, in Ancel, *Documents*, vol. 10, doc. 131, 351.

40. "Raspunsul d-lui Maresal Antonescu la scrisoarea profesorului I. Gavanescu" [Antonescu's response to Professor Gavanescu's letter], *Curentul*, November 3, 1941.

41. *Procesul marei tradari nationale*, 144.

42. Altshuler, *Distribution of the Jewish Population*.

43. According to Ibid., table 1, Odessa had 233,155 Jews.

44. On the murder of the Jews of Transnistria, see Arad, Krakowski, and Spector, *Einsatzgruppen Reports*, 72–74, 86–87, 105–11, 119, 141–43, 166–70, 194–95, 221.

45. These calculations are based on documents I discovered in archives in Russia, Ukraine, Moldova, and the United States.

46. Ordinance no. 16 by Governor Alexianu, issued in Tiraspol on September 25, 1941, Odessa Archives, 2359–1–6, 15.

47. Ordinance no. 1 of the gendarmerie, September 8, 1941, copied by hand by the commander of the Fifth Gendarmerie Battalion deployed in the Golta district, USHMM, NOA, RG-31.008M, microfiche 2178, fond 2178, opis 1, delo 42.

48. See report of the commander of the gendarmerie company in Ovidopol, November 28, 1941, Odessa Archives, 2357–1C–356, 3.

49. Report of the Gendarmerie Inspectorate on the activities of the gendarmerie in Transnistria, October 15–31, 1941, Odessa Archives, 2242–4C–2, 187.

50. Inspector of the gendarmerie in Transnistria to the Secretarial General of the Transnistrian administration, data relating to the scope of the deportations from Romania and the "movement" [i.e., extermination] of local Jews, September 9, 1942, USHMM/RMFA, RG-25.006M, reel 10, "The Jewish Problem," vol. 21, 152.

51. Excerpt from the transcript of a speech by Antonescu at a meeting with the prefects, October 11, 1941, USHMM/SRI, RG-25004.M, reel 25b, investigation file of Dumitru Popescu, vol. 11, no. 47/1945, 47 (author's emphasis).

52. Gendarmerie Inspectorate to the governor, September 30, 1941, Odessa Archives, 2242–1–1067.

53. Telegram by Prefect Popescu on the progress of the convoys, October 2, 1941, Odessa Archives, 2242–1–1067, 33.

54. See report by the Gendarmerie Inspectorate, October 15–31, 1941, Odessa Archives, 2242–1–2, 184.

55. Minutes of cabinet session of November 13, 1941, in Benjamin, *Problema evreiasca*, doc. 119, 337.

56. Dallin, *Odessa*, 310.

57. Telegram from the military cabinet to Fourth Army headquarters, signed by the head of the military cabinet, Colonel Davidescu, October 22, 1941, USHMM/AMD, RG-25.003M, reel 12, fond: Armata 4a, file 870, 634.

58. Telegram from Colonel Stanculescu to General Tataranu, October 23, 1941, 7:45 a.m., USHMM/AMD, RG-25.003M, reel 12, fond: Armata 4a, file 870, 651–53.

59. Telegram from Colonel Stanculescu to General Tataranu, October 23, 1941, 23:00, USHMM/AMD, RG-25.003M, reel 12, fond: Armata 4a, file 870, 640.

60. *Actul de acuzare*, 52–53; Ehrenburg *et al.*, *Cartea neagra*, 96.

61. Certified court copy (1945) of Gherman Pantea's memorandum to Ion Antonescu on the punitive

measures adopted against the Jews of Odessa, USHMM/SRI, RG-25.004M, reel 30, file 21401, vol. 2, 119b-200.

62. *Actul de acuzare*, 48. Dallin mentions two thousand who were murdered in the antitank trenches. Dallin, *Odessa*, 77.

63. Order no. 563, October 24, 1941, USHMM/AMD, RG-25.003M, reel 12, fond: Armata 4a, file S70, 688.

64. Arrest order of May 10, 1948, in Ancel, *Documents*, vol. 6, doc. 26, 281–82.

65. Obkom report, Partinii Arhiv, Odescovo obkoma Kompartii Ukraini, fond 2, opis 2, delo 52, 22.

66. Protocol of the meeting between Ion Antonescu and Hitler in Berlin, February 11, 1942 (Romanian version), in Armin, Ardeleanu, and Lache, *Antonescu-Hitler*, doc. 40, 1: 179.

67. Note by Filderman and Clejan on their meeting with Ion Antonescu on September 8, 1941, in Ancel, *Documents*, vol. 3, doc. 74, 132.

68. Minutes of the government session of February 26, 1942, in National Romanian Archives, *Shorthand Notes*, vol. 6, doc. 6, 185.

69. Col. Radu Davidescu, head of Antonescu's military cabinet, to the minister of the interior, July 10, 1942, USHMM/RSA, RG-25.002M, reel 18, file 104/1941, 61.

70. Heading of file no. 55, Antonescu's military cabinet, office no. 2 [last document in file, dated October 6, 1942], USHMM/RSA, RG-25.002M, reel 18, file 104/1941, 12.

71. Order no. 35 issued by Antonescu on July 16, 1942, to the minister of the interior, signed by Davidescu, head of the military cabinet, USHMM/RSA, RG-25.002M, reel 18, file 104/1941, 20. See also the order as dictated by Antonescu and written down by Davidescu, 22–24.

72. Addendum to Antonescu's Order no. 35, July 17, 1942, USHMM/RSA, RG-25.002M, reel 18, file 104/1941, 25–26.

73. Top secret report by Constantin Caragea, "concerning the property that had been confiscated from Romanian Jews in Germany," January 4, 1943, USHMM/RMFA, RG-25.006M, reel 7, "Jewish Problem," vol. 16, 472–72b.

74. Foreign Ministry directives on Jews holding expired Romanian passports, October 12, 1942, in Federation of Jewish Communities in Romania, Evreiidin Romania., doc. 621, 3: 372.

75. Internal memo of the Presidency of the Council of Ministers on the Jewish population in Romania, August 31, 1942, in Ancel, *Documents*, vol. 10, doc. 91, 210–15.

76. Interior Minister C. Z. Vasiliu to the General Police Inspectorate, September 1, 1942, USHMM/SRI, RG-25.004M, reel 32, file 40010, vol. n, 93.

77. Carp, *Cartea neagra*, 3: 241; Ancel, *Documents*, vol. 5, doc. 205, 383–89.

78. Sebastian, *Jurnal*, 471.

79. *Encyclopedia of the Holocaust*, 1: 190–93.

80. Note of M. Antonescu's talk with G. Richter, November 11, 1942, in Ancel, *Documents*, vol. 10, doc. 99, 242.

81. Luther to Müller, August 11, 1942, in Ancel, *Documents*, vol. 4, doc. 56, 104–5.

82. Memo by Luther, August 17, 1942, in Ancel, *Documents*, vol. 4, doc. 60, 111.

83. Rintelen to Luther, August 19, 1942, in Ancel, *Documents*, vol. 4, doc. 65, 120.

84. Protocol of government session of October 13, 1942, USUMM/RSA, RG-25.002M, reel 16, Presidency of the Council of Ministers, file 473/1942 (II), 859–60.

85. Ibid., 860–61.

86. Directive by the Presidency of the Council of Ministers, October 22, 1942, copy in ic Kishinev Police Inspectorate, October 28, 1942, USIIMM/SSARM, RG-54001, reel 5, 696–I–32, 216.

87. Interior Ministry to the Presidency of the Council of Ministers, March 18, 1943, USHMM/RMFA, RG-25.006M, reel 13, "Jewish Problem," vol. 24, 297.

88. Interior Ministry to the Presidency of the Council of Ministers, August 27, 1943, USHMM/RMFA, RG-25.006M, reel 14, "Jewish Problem," vol. 25, 487.

89. Order issued by Marshal Antonescu on April 17, 1943, on the evacuation of Jews from cities that were not district capitals, copy in the Kishinev

Police Inspectorate, April 22, 1943, USHMM/
SSARM, RG-54001, reel 6, 696–1–84, 21.

90. Memorandum by the Romanian government
concerning measures it adopted to solve the
Jewish problem, March 26, 1943, in Ancel, *Documents*, vol. 4, doc. 285, 524–25.

91. Ion Bratescu-Voinesti, "Am vazut pe Maresal" [I
saw the marshal], *Porunca Vremii*, March 5, 1943,
copy in Ancel, *Documents*, vol. 4, doc. 266, 491–92.

92. Directive by Ion Antonescu to the General Staff
to draw up plans in the event of an evacuation
from Transnistria, Bessarabia, and Bukovina,
September 23, 1943, YVA, Romanian Collection,
0–11/48.

93. Antonescu's letter to architect Nicolae Clejan,
February 4, 1944, in Ancel, Documents, vol. 8,
doc. 13, 19.

94. De Weck, "Journal," entry for late March 1943.

95. Niculescu report, USHMM/RMFA, RG-25.006M,
reel 11, "Jewish Problem," vol. 20.

Vichy France: "Our" Jews and the Rest

SAUL FRIEDLÄNDER

From *The Years of Extermination: Nazi Germany and the Jews, 1939–1945*

A month after signing the armistice [on June 22, 1940], seven days after the demise of the Third Republic, Marshal [Philippe] Pétain's new regime, on its own initiative, introduced its first anti-Jewish measure. One hundred fifty years after the emancipation of the Jews of France, the rollback had started. Of the approximately 330,000 Jews in prewar France almost half were either foreigners or born of foreign parents. And among the foreigners, 55,000 had arrived between 1933 and 1939 (40,000 since 1935).[1] . . .

Strident collaborationism was rarely heard in Vichy during the summer of 1940, but traditional native antisemitism was rife from the very first days. After reporting on August 16, 1940, about an expulsion campaign from Vichy on orders of the new government, the American chargé d'affaires in Pétain's capital, Robert Murphy, added: "There is no question that one of its objectives is to cause the departure of Jews. These, Laval [the deputy prime minister] told me recently, were congregating in Vichy to an alarming extent. He believed they would foment trouble and give the place a bad name. He said he would get rid of them."[2]

Vichy's first anti-Jewish decree was issued on July 17. The new law limited civil service appointments to citizens born of a French father. On July 22, a commission chaired by Justice Minister Raphael Alibert started checking all post-1927 naturalizations.[3] On August 27, Vichy repealed the Marchandeau Law of April 21, 1939, which forbade incitement on racial or religious grounds: The floodgates of antisemitic propaganda reopened. On August 16, a National Association of Physicians was established, whose members had to be born of French fathers. On September 10, the same limitation was applied to the legal profession.[4] And, on October 3, 1940, Vichy, again on its own initiative, issued its *Statut des juifs* (Jewish Statute.)

In the opening paragraph of the statute, a Jew was defined as any person descending from at least three grandparents of the "Jewish race" or of two grandparents of the "Jewish race" if the spouse too was Jewish (the German definition referred to the grandparents' religion; the French, to their race). The next paragraphs listed all the public functions from which Jews were barred. Paragraph 5 excluded Jews from all positions of ownership or responsibility in the press, theater, and film. The statute, drafted under Alibert's supervision, was signed by Pétain and by all the members of his cabinet. The next day, October 4, a law allowed the internment of foreign Jews in special camps, if the administration of their department so decided. A commission responsible for these camps was established. The same regional administration could also compel foreign Jews to reside in places defined by the authorities.[5]

The October 1940 statute was approved by all members of the French government, with some individual nuances. Neither before nor later did Pétain publicly attack the Jews as such, yet he alluded to an "anti-France" that in common ideological parlance also meant "the Jews"; moreover he strongly supported the new measures during the cabinet discussions.[6] It seems that Laval, arguably the most influential member of the cabinet, although not a declared antisemite either, mainly thought of the benefits to be reaped in exchange from Germany; Admiral Francois Darlan, on the other hand, displayed open antisemitism in the French Catholic conservative tradition; as for Alibert, his hatred of Jews was closer to the Paris collaborationist brand than to the traditional Vichy mold.[7]

In a cable sent on October 18 to Gaston Henry-Haye, Vichy's ambassador in Washington, the secretary general of Vichy's Foreign Ministry presented the arguments that could be used to explain the new statute to the Americans. The responsibility was, of course, that of the Jews themselves. A Léon Blum or a Jean Zay (the minister of education in Blum's government) was accused of having propagated antinational or amoral principles; moreover they helped "hundreds of thousands of their own" to enter the country, and the like. The new legislation, it was said, neither targeted the basic rights of individuals nor threatened their private property. "The new legislation merely aims at solving definitively and without passion a problem that had become critical and to allow the peaceful existence in France of elements whom the characteristics of their race turn into a danger when they are too intimately present in the political and administrative life of the country."[8]

Vichy's anti-Jewish legislation was generally well received by a majority of the population in the non-occupied zone. French popular antisemitism grew as a result of the defeat and during the following years. On October 9, 1940, the Central Agency for the Control of Telephone Communications—a listening service, in other words—

reported that "hostility against the Jews remains"; on November 2 it indicated that the statute had been widely approved and even that for some it did not go far enough.[9] Although only fourteen *préfets* (district governors appointed by the state) out of forty-two reported on public reactions to the statute, nine indicated positive responses and one reported mixed ones.[10] In the midst of such a dire general situation, public opinion would of course tend to follow the measures taken by the savior and protector, the old *maréchal* [Pétain]. Moreover, a large segment of the population remained attentive to the spiritual guidance offered, now more than ever, by the Catholic Church. . . .

During the summer of 1940 the Catholic hierarchy had been informed of the forthcoming statute. When the assembly of cardinals and archbishops met in Lyon, on August 31, 1940, the "Jewish question" was on the agenda. Emile Guerry, adjunct bishop of Cambrai, summed up the assembly's official stand: "In political terms, the problem is caused by a community [the Jews] that has resisted all assimilation, dispersion, and the national integration of its members taken individually. The State has the right and the duty to remain actively vigilant in order to make sure that the persistence of this unity [of the Jews] does not cause any harm to the common good of the nation, as one would do in regard to an ethnic minority or an international cartel. . . ."[11] In other words the assembled leaders of the French Catholic Church gave their agreement to the statute that, a month later, would be announced by the government. Of course when the official announcement came, no Catholic prelate protested. Some bishops even openly supported the anti-Jewish measures.[12]

The most immediate reason for the French Church's attitude stemmed from the unmitigated support granted by Pétain and the new *État fran-*

çais to the reinsertion of Catholicism into French public life, particularly in education. Whereas the republic had established the separation of church and state and thus banned the use of state funds for the support of religious schools, Vichy canceled the separation and all its practical sequels: In many ways Catholicism had become the official religion of the new regime.[13] There was more, however.

Since the French Revolution a segment of French Catholicism had remained obdurately hostile to the "ideas of 1789," which they considered to be a Judeo-Masonic plot intent upon the destruction of Christianity. . . . The ultranationalist and antisemitic party created by Charles Maurras, the *Action Française*, had been excommunicated in the 1920s, but many Catholics remained strongly attached to it, and the ban was lifted by Pius XII on the eve of the war. The *Action Française* inspired Vichy's *Statut des Juifs*, and its antisemitism belonged to the ideological profile of an influential part of the French church in 1940.

Finally, some of the most fundamental tenets of Christian religious antisemitism resurfaced among French Catholics. Thus the newspaper *La Croix*, which during the 1920s and 1930s had abandoned its violent anti-Jewish diatribes of the turn of the century (mainly during the Dreyfus affair), could not resist the temptation offered by the new circumstances. "Are the Jews Cursed by God?" was the title of an article published on November 30, 1940. Having justified the new statute, the author, who wrote under the pseudonym C. Martel [the name of the Frankish commander who defeated the Moorish invasion of France in 732 C.E.], reminded his readers that since the Jews themselves had called Jesus' blood "upon their heads and those of their children," a curse indeed existed. There was only one way of escaping it: conversion.[14]

The small French Reformed (Calvinist) Church was influenced by the general cultural-ideological stance shared by most of the country, although Pastor Marc Boegner, its leader, was to become an outspoken critic of Vichy's anti-Jewish laws. Yet, in the summer of 1941, Boegner himself would emphasize on several occasions that his support was granted to French Jews only and that, in his opinion, the influx of Jewish immigrants had created a major problem.[15] . . .

In September 1940, the association of French publishers promised the German embassy in Paris that no Jewish authors, among other excluded groups, would be published or reprinted any longer: The publishers would, from then on, exercise strict self-censorship. Within days, a first list of banned books, the "*liste Bernhard*," was made public, soon followed by a "*liste Otto*." It was preceded by a short declaration from the association: "These are the books which by their lying and tendentious spirit have systematically poisoned French public opinion; particularly the publications of political refugees or of Jewish writers who, having betrayed the hospitality that France had granted to them, unscrupulously agitated in favor of a war from which they hoped to take advantage for their own egoistic aims."[16] . . .

As a result of the Vichy laws of the summer and fall of 1940, 140 faculty members of Jewish origin, around 10 percent of the teaching body nationwide, were banned from the universities. Fourteen particularly eminent Jewish scholars were exempted from the ban on condition that they continue teaching in the Vichy zone only. The French academic community acquiesced.[17] At the *Collège de France*, the most prestigious academic institution in the country, its four Jewish professors were dismissed, according to the new regulations.

The director of the *Collège*, Edmond Faral, had not waited for the new laws. In a January 1941 report to Vichy's delegation in occupied France, Faral eagerly mentioned his own initiative: "The Jewish question: no Jew has taught at the *Collège de France* since the beginning of the academic year. That decision was taken even before the law of October 3, 1940." In the draft of the report, the last sentence, later deleted, read as follows: "The administration had taken that decision." When the Jews were no longer allowed to teach at the College, none of their "Aryan" colleagues protested. The same happened in all French institutions of higher learning. At the prestigious *École Libre des Sciences Politiques*, the assistant director, Roger Seydoux, expelled all Jewish professors when asked to do so by Karl Epting, the head of the cultural section of the German embassy in Paris. No attempts were made to obtain exemptions.[18] . . . .

A Hitler-Pétain meeting took place in the little town of Montoire, on October 24, 1940: "Collaboration" between Vichy France and the Reich was officially proclaimed. . . . In early 1941, Darlan replaced the moderate Pierre-Étienne Flandin as the head of government, and the collaboration with Germany tightened. Anti-Jewish measures spread. In February 1941, out of the 47,000 foreigners imprisoned in French concentration camps, 40,000 were Jews.[19] Aryanization progressed apace. Jewish businesses were increasingly put under the control of "French" supervisors (*commissaires-gérants*) who had, in fact, full power to decide the businesses' fate. . . . In April 1941, the Jews were forbidden to fill any position—from selling lottery tickets to any form of teaching— that would put them in contact with the public. Only a few "particularly deserving intellectuals" were exempted from this total professional segregation. As for the vast majority of the French population, it did not react. Anti-Jewish propaganda intensified, as did the number of acts of anti-Jewish violence. Individual expressions of sympathy were not rare, but they were volunteered in private, far from any public notice. . . .

At the beginning of 1941 the Germans decided that further coordination of the anti-Jewish measures throughout both French zones was necessary. In a January 30 meeting at military headquarters in Paris under the chairmanship of Werner Best, Kurt Lischka and Theodor Dannecker informed the participants that a central office for Jewish affairs had to be set up in France to implement the measures decided on to solve the Jewish problem in Europe. The functions of the office would be to deal with all police matters regarding the arrest, surveillance, and registration of Jews; to exercise economic control (exclusion of Jews from economic life and participation in the "restitution" of Jewish businesses into Aryan hands); to organize propaganda activities (dissemination of anti-Jewish propaganda among the French population), and to set up an anti-Jewish research institute. In the meantime the Paris *Préfecture de Police* was ready to assume these functions. The establishment of the new office should be left to the French authorities to avoid opposition to a German initiative; the Germans should limit themselves to "suggestions." Everyone agreed.[20]

The Germans were confident that even if the new office turned out to be less forceful than they wished (mainly in its dealings with native Jews), they would be able in due time to ensnare it in the full scope of their own policies. In reporting to Berlin on March 6, 1941, about a conversation with Darlan regarding the new office and Pétain's wish to protect native Jews, Abetz indicated how any French reservations would be overcome: "It would be advisable," the ambassador wrote, "to have the French Government establish this office. . . . It would thus have a valid legal foundation and its activity could then be stimulated through German influence in the occupied territory to such an extent that the unoccupied territory would be forced to join in the measures taken."[21]

On March 29, 1941, the Vichy government established the Central Office for Jewish Affairs (*Commissariat Général aux Questions Juives*, or CGQJ); its first chief was Xavier Vallat.[22] Vallat belonged to the nationalist anti-Jewish tradition of the *Action Française* and did not share the racial antisemitism of the Nazis. Nonetheless the CGQJ soon became the hub of rapidly expanding anti-Jewish activity. Its main immediate "achievement" was the reworking of the Jewish statute of October 3, 1940. The new *Statut des Juifs* was accepted by the government and became law on June 2, 1941.[23] Strangely enough, for the staunchly Catholic Vallat, baptism seemed inconsequential and, implicitly, inherited cultural-racial elements were at the core of his conception of the Jew. . . . Only the CGQJ would be entitled to issue certificates of non-membership of the Jewish race.[24]

It has occasionally been argued that Vichy's anti-Jewish measures and its ready cooperation with the Germans were a "rational" maneuver within the general framework of collaboration in order to maintain as much control as possible over developments in the occupied zone and to obtain a favorable bargaining position for the future status of France in Hitler's new Europe. In other words, Vichy supposedly displayed a non-ideological acceptance of Nazi goals (a "*collaboration d'État*" as opposed to some wild "collaborationism") in the hope of harvesting some tangible benefits in return.[25] Political calculation was undoubtedly part of the overall picture, but Vichy's policy was also determined by the right-wing antisemitic tradition that was part and parcel of the "*Revolution nationale.*" Moreover, *collaboration d'État* does not account for the facts that

the French episcopate welcomed the exclusion of Jews from public life as early as August 1940 and that mainly among the rural population and the provincial Catholic middle classes antisemitism was not limited to a tiny minority but widespread. Thus, although the Vichy legislation was not dictated by the passions of French "collaborationists," it was nonetheless a calculated response both to a public mood and to ideological-institutional interests, such as those of the church.

In general, antisemitism may well have been outweighed by sheer indifference, but not to the point of forgoing tangible advantages. As [ss-*Obersturmführer*] Helmut Knochen put it in January 1941, "It is almost impossible to cultivate among the French an anti-Jewish sentiment that rests on an ideological foundation, while the offer of economic advantages much more easily excites sympathy for the anti-Jewish struggle."[26]

There was a striking (yet possibly unperceived at the time) relation between French attitudes toward the Jews and the behavior of representatives of native Jewry toward the foreign or recently naturalized Jews living in the country. While native Jews affiliated to the community were represented by the *Consistoire* [*des Israelites de France*] and its local branches, foreign Jews—and the recently naturalized ones—were loosely affiliated to an umbrella organization, the *Féderation des Societés Juives de France*, comprising various political associations and their related network of welfare organizations. Part of the umbrella organization came to be known as "*Rue Amelot*" (the Paris address of the main office of its leading committee).

After the Rothschilds had fled the country. Jacques Helbronner, the acting vice-president of the *Consistoire*, became the de facto leader of native French Jewry (*Rue Amelot* was more collectively run by the heads of its various associations). In many ways Helbronner was a typical representative of the old-stock French Jewish elite: a brilliant officer during World War I, a sharp legal mind who at a young age was appointed to the *Conseil d'État* (the highest civil service institution in France), Helbronner married into old (and substantial) French Jewish money. He belonged, quintessentially, to the French Jewish *haute bourgeoisie*, a group considered almost French by its non-Jewish surroundings. And despite his own genuine interest in Jewish matters—which led him to become active in the *Consistoire*—Helbronner, like all his peers, saw himself first and foremost as French. Typically enough, he was close to Philippe Pétain, since the day during World War I when, as head of the personal staff (*chef de cabinet*) of the minister of war, he was sent to inform Pétain of his appointment as *generalissime* (commander in chief of all French forces). Another friend of Helbronner's was Jules-Marie Cardinal Gerlier, cardinal-archbishop of Lyon and head of the French episcopate. In March 1941 Helbronner was appointed president of the *Consistoire*.[27]

Few native French Jews achieved the exalted status of a Helbronner, but the great majority felt as deeply integrated in French society as he did and were to share the positions he adopted: France was their only conceivable national and cultural home, notwithstanding the injustice of the new laws. The growing antisemitism of the thirties and its most violent outbursts following the defeat were, in their opinion, caused in large part by the influx of foreign Jews; the situation thus created could be mitigated by a strict distinction between native French "separation" Jews and the foreign Jews living in the country.

It was precisely this difference that Helbronner attempted to convey to Pétain in a memorandum he sent him in November 1940, after the first statute and its corollaries had sunk in. In this statement, titled *Note sur la question juive*, the future

president of the *Consistoire* argued that the Jews were not a race and did not descend from the Jews who had lived in Palestine two thousand years before. Rather, they were a community composed of many races and, as far as France was concerned, a community entirely integrated in its homeland. The problems began with the arrival of foreign Jews "who started to invade our soil." The open-door policies of the postwar governments had been a mistake, and they resulted "in a normal antisemitism the victims of which were now the old French Israelite families." Helbronner then suggested a series of measures that would free the native Jews from the limitations of the statute *but not the foreign or recently naturalized Jews . . .*[28] Helbronner's message went unanswered.

Over the following months the head of the *Consistoire* and a number of his colleagues pursued their futile and demeaning entreaties. The messages and visits to Vichy pointedly continued to ignore the fate of the foreign Jews and to plead for the French Israelites only. The epitome of this course of action was probably the solemn petition sent to the *maréchal* by the entire leadership of the *Consistoire*, including the chief rabbi of France. The closing paragraph was unambiguous in its omission of any reference to the non-French Jews:

> Jewish Frenchmen still wish to believe that the persecutions of which they are the object are entirely imposed on the French State by the occupying authorities and that the representatives of France have tried their best to attenuate their rigors . . . Jewish Frenchmen, if they cannot safeguard the future and perhaps even the life of their children and grandchildren, but seeking above all to leave them honorable names, demand of the head of state who, as a great soldier and a fervent Christian, incarnates in their eyes the fatherland in all its purity, that

he should recognize this solemn protest, which is their only weapon in their weakness. Jewish Frenchmen, more than ever attached to their faith, keep intact their hope and their confidence in France and its destiny."[29]

The second Jewish statute was to be Vichy's answer to the petitions.

Time and again some of the most prestigious names of French Jewry confirmed that, in their view, the fate of the foreign Jews was none of their concern. Thus, when, during the spring of 1941, Dannecker started using pressure for the establishment of a unified Jewish Council, René Mayer, also a prominent member of the *Consistoire* (he would become a postwar French prime minister), asked Vallat to encourage the foreign Jews to emigrate.[30] So did Marc Bloch, one of the most eminent historians of his time.

In April 1941, in response to a project promoted by the *Consistoire* envisioning the establishment of a center for Jewish studies, Bloch demanded that all trends within French Jewry be taken into account, but regarding the foreign Jews living in France, his stand was clear: "Their cause is not exactly our own." Though unable to participate actively in the planning of the center, Bloch suggested that one of the main aims should be to counter the dangerous notion that "all Jews formed a solid homogeneous mass, endowed with identical traits, and subject to the same destiny." In Bloch's view the planners of the center should recognize two distinct Jewish communities, the assimilated (French) and the nonassimilated (foreign). While the fate of the former depended on its complete integration and the preservation of its legal guarantees, the survival of the latter might well depend on "some form of emigration."[31] . . .

After the proclamation of the new statute of June 1941, the Vichy government forged ahead.

On July 22, "Aryanization" was introduced in the non-occupied zone according to the same criteria and methods used in the north. Businesses were liquidated or put under "French" control, assets were seized, and the proceeds were deposited in a special government bank, the *Caisse des Dépôts et Consignations.*[32] . . .

For Darlan and Vallat this did not suffice. On the day the June statute was published, the registration of all Jews (according to the new definition) in the Vichy zone was mandated. According to Vallat's estimate, approximately 140,000 Jews had been registered by the spring of 1942, although the head of the national office of statistics, René Carmille, had reached the much lower total of 109,000. The exact number of Jews living in the Vichy zone at that time is not clear. More immediately ominous was Darlan's order of December 1941, to register all Jews who had entered France after January 1, 1936 (even those who had in the meantime acquired French citizenship); this identification was to become an essential element of the Franco-German agreements concerning the round-ups and deportations that were to come.[33]

On the morrow of the June statute, [Raymond-Raoul] Lambert [the head of the General Union of the Jews of France] noted that Pétain had met Helbronner and told him that all the measures had been ordered by the Germans. The marshal supposedly commented: "These are horrible people!" (*Ce sont des gens épouvantables!*). After some further remarks about the new measures, Lambert naively added: "One gets the feeling that even the details of the law have been inspired or dictated by the German authorities—as the Reich now considers the way France will solve the Jewish question as a test of its sincerity in the policies of collaboration."[34] Lambert did not yet dare to acknowledge that the initiative was French and the anti-Jewish decrees were indeed meant as a proof—but one volunteered by Vichy—of its will to collaborate.

And while, during the summer and fall of 1941, the situation of the Jews in France looked more precarious by the month, the Germans made further attempts to convince the French population that the struggle against Jewry was a vital necessity. On September 5, a major antisemitic exhibition opened its doors in Paris. Officially it was organized by [Paul] Sézille's "Institute for the Study of Jewish Questions." Thus, it appeared as a French exhibition organized by a purely French institution. On the seventh Biélinky commented: "An antisemitic exhibition has just opened at the Palais Berlitz, on the Boulevards; a blustering advertisement campaign promotes it in the newspapers and on the walls. A Jewish female friend who does not look Semitic went to the opening and heard in the crowd: 'here at least, one is sure not to meet any Jews.'"[35] The exhibition remained open through January 3, 1942, and drew more than three hundred thousand visitors (most of whom had to buy tickets), with indeed a few Jews among them. Apparently some of the Jewish visitors even dared to express open criticism.[36]

The Germans however, did not stop at propaganda campaigns. On August 20, 1941, on German instructions, the Paris police arrested a further 4,230 Jews, mainly in the eleventh *arrondissement*; they were sent to Drancy, the newly established concentration camp near the French capital. This second roundup was probably undertaken in reprisal for the anti-German demonstrations organized in the city on August 13 by communist youth organizations; the police had supposedly noticed a substantial number of Jews among the demonstrators (the French police had ready lists of these Jews, as many had served in the French army in 1939–40). This time some French Jews, mainly communists, were also arrested.[37] . . .

[On March 27, 1942,] a day after the departure of the first transport from Slovakia to Auschwitz, a transport of 1,000 Jews detained in Compiègne left France for the Upper Silesian camp. . . . The early deportations from France did not encounter any difficulties, either in the occupied zone or in Vichy. In the occupied zone French authorities were far more worried about the increasing number of attacks on *Wehrmacht* personnel. The execution of hostages did not have the desired effect (in December 1941, ninety-five hostages had been shot, among them fifty-eight Jews). In early 1942, the commander in chief, Otto von Stülpnagel, deemed too lenient, was replaced by his cousin, Karl-Heinrich von Stülpnagel, a brutal antisemite who showed his colors on the Eastern front; on June 1 ss general Karl Oberg, previously posted in Radom in the General Government, arrived in France as higher ss and police leader.

Before taking office, Oberg had paid a visit to the French capital on May 7, in the company of Heydrich. The atmosphere was favorable for closer collaboration between France and the Reich, as, since the end of April, Laval was back at the head of the Vichy government. Vallat had been replaced at the head of the CGQJ by a much fiercer Jew hater, Louis Darquier de Pellepoix, and the French police in the occupied zone were now headed by a brilliant and ambitious newcomer, René Bousquet, all too ready to play his part in the German-French rapprochement. During Heydrich's visit Bousquet again requested the further deportation of some 5,000 Jews from Drancy to the East. Although Heydrich made his agreement conditional on the availability of transportation, four trains with approximately 1,000 Jews each left for Auschwitz in the course of June.[38]

Two major points of contention between the Germans and Vichy remained unresolved at the end of spring: the inclusion of French Jews in the deportations and the use of French police in the roundups. As Vichy did not appear ready to agree to either German demand, a serious crisis loomed during the last week of June; it brought Eichmann to Paris on June 30 for a reassessment. Finally, in a July 2 meeting with Oberg and his acolytes, Bousquet gave in to the Germans, and, on the fourth he conveyed Vichy's official stand. According to Dannecker's notes, "Bousquet declared that, at the recent cabinet meeting, Marshal Pétain, the head of the state, and Pierre Laval, the head of the government, agreed to the deportation, *as a first step* [*dans un premier temps*] of all stateless Jews from the Occupied and Unoccupied zones." French police forces would arrest the Jews in both zones. Moreover, as Dannecker reported on July 6, in a conversation with Eichmann, while all "stateless" Jews (that is, formerly German, Polish, Czechoslovak, Russian, Lithuanian, Latvian, or Estonian Jews) were to be deported, Laval had also suggested, on his own initiative, the deportation of children under age sixteen from the unoccupied zone. As for children in the occupied zone, Laval declared that their fate was of no interest to him. Dannecker added that in a second phase, Jews naturalized after 1919 or after 1927 would be included in the deportations.[39]

In this deal each party had its own agenda. The Germans were intent on achieving complete success both in Holland and in France, the first mass deportations from the West. They did not have sufficient police forces of their own on hand and had to rely on the full participation of each national police. For Laval, full collaboration had become his unquestioned policy in the hope of extracting a peace treaty from Germany and ensuring a rightful place for France within the new German-led Europe. And, in the late spring of 1942, as the head of the French government was maneuvering to deliver enough foreign Jews to postpone any

decision regarding the fate of French Jews (whose deportation, he thought, French opinion would not readily accept), Hitler seemed, once more, to march on the road to victory. . . .

On June 7, the star [i.e., Jews' wearing of the Star of David on clothing] became mandatory in the occupied zone of France. Vichy refused to enforce the decree on its territory, in order to avoid the accusation that a French government stigmatized Jews of French citizenship (the more so because Jewish nationals of countries allied with Germany, as well as of neutral or even enemy countries, were exempted from the star decree by the Germans). There was some irony and much embarrassment in the fact that Vichy had to beg the Germans to exempt the Jewish spouses of some of its highest officials in the occupied zone. Thus, Pétain's delegate in Paris, the antisemitic and actively collaborationist Fernand de Brinon, had to ask the favor for his wife, née Frank.[40] Among Catholic intellectuals, communists, and many students, reactions to the German measure were particularly negative. The Jews themselves quickly recognized the mood of part of the population and, at the outset at least, the star was worn with a measure of pride and defiance.[41]

In fact, indications about French attitudes were contradictory: "Lazare Lévy, professor at the Conservatory, has been dismissed," Biélinky noted on February 20. "If his non-Jewish colleagues had expressed the wish to keep him, he would have remained as professor, as he was the only Jew at the Conservatory. But they did not make the move; cowardice has become a civic virtue." On May 16, Biélinky noted some strange inconsistencies in Parisian cultural life: "The Jews are eliminated from everywhere and yet René Julliard published a new book by Elian J. Finbert, *La Vie Pastorale*. Finbert is a Jew of Russian origin raised in Egypt. He is even young enough to inhabit a concentration camp. . . . Although Jews are not allowed to exhibit their work anywhere, one finds Jewish artists at the Salon [the largest biannual painting exhibition in Paris]. They had to sign that they did not belong to the 'Jewish race'. . . . A concert by Boris Zadri, a Romanian Jew, is announced for May 18, at the *Salle Gaveau* [a well-known Paris concert hall]." On May 19, Biélinky recorded the opinion voiced by a concierge: "What is done to the Jews is really disgusting. . . . If one didn't want them, one should not have let them enter France; if they have been accepted for many years, one has to let them live as everybody else. . . . Moreover, they are no worse than we Catholics."And, from early June on, Biélinky's diary indeed recorded numerous expressions of sympathy addressed to him and to other Jews tagged with the star, in various everyday encounters.[42]

Yet individual manifestations of sympathy were not indicative of any basic shifts in public opinion regarding the anti-Jewish measures. Despite the negative response to the introduction of the star and soon thereafter to the deportations, an undercurrent of traditional antisemitism persisted in both zones. However, both the Germans and Vichy recognized that the population reacted differently to foreign and to French Jews. Thus in a survey that Abetz sent to Berlin on July 2, 1942, he emphasized "the surge of antisemitism" due to the influx of foreign Jews and recommended, along the lines of the agreement reached on the same day between Oberg and Bousquet, that the deportations should start with the foreign Jews in order to achieve "the right psychological effect" among the population.[43]

"I hate the Jews," the writer Pierre Drieu la Rochelle was to confide to his diary on November 8, 1942. "I always knew that I hated them."[44] In this case at least, Drieu's outburst remained hidden in his diary. On the eve of the war, however,

he had been less discreet (but far less extreme) in *Gilles*, an autobiographical novel that became a classic of French literature. Compared to some of his literary peers, Drieu was in fact relatively moderate. In *Les Décombres*, published in the spring of 1942, Lucien Rebatet showed a more Nazi-like anti-Jewish rage: "Jewish spirit is in the intellectual life of France a poisonous weed that must be pulled out right to its most minuscule roots. . . . Auto-da-fés will be ordered for the greatest number of Jewish or Judaic works of literature, paintings, or musical compositions that have worked toward the decadence of our people." Rebatet's stand regarding the Jews was part and parcel of an unconditional allegiance to Hitler's Reich: "I wish for the the victory of Germany because the war it is waging is my war, our war. . . . I don't admire Germany for being Germany but for having produced Hitler. I praise it for having known how . . . to create for itself the political leader in whom I recognize my desires. I think that Hitler has conceived of a magnificent future for our continent, and I passionately want him to realize it."[45]

Céline, possibly the most significant writer (in terms of literary importance) of this antisemitic phalanx, took up the same themes in an even more vitriolic form; however, his manic style and his insane outbursts marginalized him to a point. In December 1941, the German novelist Ernst Jünger encountered Céline at the German Institute in Paris: "He says," Jünger noted, "how surprised and stupefied he is that we soldiers do not shoot, hang, exterminate the Jews—he is stupefied that someone availed of a bayonet should not make unrestricted use of it." Jünger, no Nazi himself but nonetheless quite a connoisseur in matters of violence, strikingly defined Céline and—undoubtedly—also a vast category of his own compatriots: "Such men hear only one melody, but that is singularly insistent. They're like those machines that go about their business until somebody smashes them. It is curious to hear such minds speak of science—of biology, for instance. They use it the way the Stone Age man would; for them, it is exclusively a means of killing others."[46]

Robert Brasillach was outwardly more polished, but his anti-Jewish hatred was no less extreme and persistent than that of Céline or Rebatet. His anti-Jewish tirades in *Je Suis Partout* had started in the 1930s, and for him the ecstatic admiration of German victories and German dominance had a clearly erotic dimension: "The French of different persuasions have all more or less been sleeping with the Germans during these last years," he wrote in 1944, "and the memory will remain sweet." As for the French and German policies regarding the Jews, Brasillach applauded at each step but, as far as the French measures went, they appeared to him at times too incomplete: "Families should be kept together and Jewish children deported with their parents," he demanded in a notorious *Je Suis Partout* article on September 25, 1942.[47]

How far the virulent antisemitism spewed by the Paris collaborationists influenced public opinion beyond the rather limited segment of French society that supported them politically is hard to assess. Be that as it may, Rebatet's *Les Décombres* became a runaway bestseller . . . , the greatest publishing success in occupied France.[48] . . .

"The papers announce new measures against the Jews," Jacques Biélinky recorded on July 15, 1942: "They are forbidden access to restaurants, coffeehouses, movie theaters, theaters, concert halls, music halls, pools, beaches, museums, libraries, exhibitions, castles, historical monuments, sports events, races, parks, camping sites and even phone booths, fairs, etc. Rumor has it that Jewish men and women between ages eighteen and forty-five will be sent to forced labor in Germany."[49]

That same day the roundups of "stateless" Jews started in the provinces of the occupied zone, on the eve of the operation in Paris.

According to a July 15 report from the police chief of the *Loire-Inférieure*, French gendarmes were accompanying German soldiers on their way to arrest Jews in the department; according to another report of the same day, the French authorities were providing police officers to guard fifty-four Jews on the request of the SS chief of Saint-Nazaire. Jews arrested throughout the west of the country—among them some two hundred arrested in Tours, again on July 15—were taken to an assembly point in Angers (some were selected from French camps in the region) and, a few days later, a train carried 824 of them directly from Angers to Auschwitz.[50]

On July 16, at 4:00 a.m., the Germano-French roundup of 27,000 "stateless" Jews living in the capital and its suburbs began. The index cards prepared by the French police had become essential: 25,334 cards were ready for Paris, and 2,027 for the immediate suburbs.[51] Every technical detail had been jointly prepared by French and German officials in their meetings on July 7 and 11. On the sixteenth fifty municipal buses were ready, and so were 4,500 French policemen.[52] No German units participated in the arrests. The manhunt received a code name: *Vent printanier* (Spring Wind).

As rumors about the forthcoming raids had spread, many potential victims (mostly men) had gone into hiding.[53] The origins of these rumors? To this day they remain uncertain, but as historian André Kaspi noted, "a roundup such as had never taken place in France, could not remain secret for long."[54] UGIF employees, resistance groups, police personnel must all have been involved in some way in spreading warnings.

Nine hundred groups, each including three police officials and volunteers, were in charge of the arrests. "Suddenly, I heard terrible banging on the front door . . . ," Annette Müller, then nine years old, recalled. "Two men entered the room; they were tall and wore beige raincoats. 'Hurry up, get dressed,' they ordered, 'we are taking you with us.' I saw my mother get on her knees and embrace their legs, crying, begging: 'Take me but, I beseech you, don't take the children.' They pulled her up. 'Come on, madam, don't make it more difficult and all will be well.' My mother spread a large sheet on the floor, and threw in clothes, underwear. . . . She worked in a panic, throwing in things, then taking them out. 'Hurry up!' the policemen shouted. She wanted to take dried vegetables. 'No, you don't need that,' the men said, just take food for two days; there, you will get food.'"[55]

By the afternoon of July 17, 3,031 Jewish men, 5,802 women, and 4,051 children had been arrested; the number of Jews finally caught in *Vent printanier* totaled 13,152. Unmarried people or childless couples were sent directly to Drancy; the others, 8,160 men, women, and children, were assembled in a large indoor sports arena known mainly for its bicycle races, the *Vélodrome d'Hiver* (*Vel d'Hiv*). At the *Vel d'Hiv*, nothing was ready—neither food, water, toilets, nor beds or bedding of any sort. For three to six days, thousands of hapless beings received one to two portions of soup per day. Two Jewish physicians and one Red Cross physician were in attendance. The temperature never fell below one hundred degrees Fahrenheit. Finally, group after group, the *Vel d'Hiv* Jews were temporarily sent to Pithiviers and Beaune-la-Rolande camps just vacated by the inmates deported in June.[56]

Vent printanier had not achieved the expected results. In order to keep Drancy stacked with Jews ready for deportation, the arrests of stateless Jews had to extend to the Vichy zone, as agreed by the French government. The major operation,

again exclusively implemented by French forces (police, gendarmes, firemen, and soldiers), took place from August 26 to 28; some 7,100 Jews were seized. Although Laval had promised in early September to cancel the naturalization of Jews who had entered the country after January 1933, the roundups in the Vichy zone were aimed at filling the German quotas without having to start denaturalizing French citizens. By the end of the year 42,500 Jews had been deported from France to Auschwitz.[57] . . .

Until mid-1943 Drancy remained under French authority. The main goal for the camp administration remained filling the quotas imposed by the Germans for each departing transport. "Under our current obligation to come up with one thousand deportees on Monday," a French police officer noted on September 12, 1942, "we must include in these departures, at least in reserve, the parents of sick [children] and advise them that they could be deported without their children remaining in the infirmary."[58]

On August 11, *Untersturmführer* Horst Ahnert, from Dannecker's office, informed the RSHA that due to the temporary halt in the roundups, he planned to send the children assembled in the camps Beaune-la-Rolande and Pithiviers to Drancy, and asked for Berlin's authorization. On the thirteenth, Gunther gave his approval but warned Ahnert not to send transports filled with children only.[59]

It was probably the arrival of these children, aged two to twelve, that Drancy inmate George Wellers described after the war: "They were disembarked from the buses in the midst of the courtyard like small animals. . . . The elder children held the younger ones and did not let go of them until they reached their allocated places. On the stairs the bigger children carried the smaller ones, panting, to the fourth floor. There, they remained fearfully huddled together. . . . Once the luggage had been unloaded the children returned to the courtyard, but most of the younger ones could not find their belongings; when, after their unsuccessful search they wished to get back to their rooms, they could not remember where they had been assigned."[60]

On August 24, transport number 23 left Drancy for Auschwitz with its load of 1,000 Jews, including 553 children under age seventeen (288 boys and 265 girls). Among the children, 465 were under twelve, of whom 131 were under six. On arrival in Auschwitz, 92 men aged from twenty to forty-five were selected for work. All the other deportees were immediately gassed. Three Jews from this transport survived the war.[61]

As a result of the only petition sent to Vichy by UGIF-North shortly after the Paris roundup, some relatives of war veterans and some "French children of foreign parents" (these were the words used in the petition) were released. André Baur, the president of UGIF-North, thanked Laval for his gesture.[62]

On August 2, Lambert met Helbronner. Despite the ongoing roundups and deportations, the head of the *Consistoire* was not ready to share his contacts at Vichy with any member of UGIF nor to tell Lambert that in fact Laval was refusing to see him. In the course of the conversation, Helbronner declared to a stupefied Lambert that on August 8 he was going on vacation and that "nothing in the world would bring me back." This declaration, quoted by Lambert only, has to be taken guardedly given the tense relations between the author and the *Consistoire*. "The president of the *Consistoire* seems to me to be more deaf, more pompous, and older than ever. The fate of the foreign Jews does not touch him at all," Lambert added on September 6, describing another meeting with Helbronner, on July 30.[63] The remark about

Helbronner's attitude toward *les juifs étrangers* was probably on target.

In August, the *Consistoire* prepared two drafts of a protest letter. The milder version, not alluding to "extermination" (mentioned in the other draft) or to the participation of the French police or to that of the Germans, was delivered in Vichy on August 25, not to Laval to whom it was addressed and who once again refused to meet with the delegate of French Jewry, but to some low-ranking official.[64] That was all. . . .

Then, as in early 1943 the number of foreign Jews in France was rapidly dwindling and the weekly quotas of deportees were no longer met, the Germans decided to move to the next step: Pétain and Laval were now prodded to cancel the naturalizations of Jews that had taken place after 1927. It was at this point that unexpectedly, after first agreeing, Laval changed his mind.

The immediate reaction of the majority of ordinary French people to the roundups was unmistakably negative in both zones.[65] Although it did not lead to any organized protest, it did enhance readiness to help Jews on the run. Feelings of pity at the sight of the unfortunate victims, particularly women and children, spread, albeit briefly; but, as already mentioned, basic prejudice toward the Jews did not disappear. "The persecution of the Jews," a February 1943 report from a Resistance agent stated, "has profoundly wounded the French in their humane principles; it has even, at times, made the Jews almost sympathetic. One cannot deny, however, that there is a Jewish question: the present circumstances have even helped plant it firmly. The Blum ministry, which was overflowing with Jewish elements, and the penetration of tens of thousands of foreign Jews into France, provoked a defensive mechanism in France. People would pay any price not to see a similar invasion repeated." A March report from another agent was almost identical in its main assessment. "The persecutions directed against the Jews have not stopped stirring and angering the population. Public opinion is nevertheless somewhat suspicious of them. It is feared that after the war some leading professions (banking, broadcasting, journalism, cinema) will be invaded again and in some fashion controlled by the Jews. Certainly, no one wants the Jews to be victimized and even less that they be molested. People sincerely want them to be as free as possible, in possession of their rights and property. But no one wants them to be supreme in any domain."[66]

Within the Resistance itself, the same kind of low-key antisemitism was present, even explicitly so. In June 1942, the first issue of *Cahiers*, published by the central body of the French underground, the OCM (*Organisation Civile et Militaire*), carried a study on ethnic minorities in France. The author, Maxime Blocq-Mascart, singled out the Jews as the group that caused "ongoing controversies": "Antisemitism in its moderate form was quasi universal, even in the most liberal societies. This indicates that its foundation is not imaginary." Blocq-Mascart 's analysis brought up the usual repertory of anti-Jewish arguments and suggested the usual measures: "stopping Jewish immigration, avoiding the concentration of Jews in a small number of cities, encouraging complete assimilation." The article was widely debated and denounced by some high-ranking members of the underground; it nonetheless represented the opinion of a great majority of the French people.[67]

The Assembly of French cardinals and archbishops met in Paris on July 21, 1942, less than a week after the raid. A minority was in favor of some form of protest, but the majority, headed by Archbishop Achille Lienart of Lille and Cardinal Emmanuel Suhard of Paris, opposed it. Unsigned notes, drafted after the assembly, most probably by Lienart, indicate the main points of the discussion and the views of the majority. "Fated to disappear from the Continent. Those who support them are against us. The expulsions have been ordered. The answers: some belong to us; we keep them; the others, foreigners—we give them back. No, all have to leave by the action of our agencies, in both zones. Individualist project. Letter to our government out of sense of humanity. Help of social services to children in centers. They themselves ask only for charity from us. Letter addressed in name of humanity and religion."[68]

In other words the notes indicated that the French episcopate knew (probably on information received from the government or the Vatican) the Jews were fated to disappear from the Continent; whether this disappearance was understood as extermination is unclear. Support for the Jews, the note further mentioned, came mainly from segments of the population that were hostile to the church (communists? Gaullists?). The deportations have been ordered by the Germans; Vichy wants to keep the French Jews and have the foreigners expelled; the Germans insist on generalized deportation from both zones and demand the help of French agencies (mainly the police). The meaning of the words "individualist project" (*Projet individualiste*) is unclear but it could be that assistance to individuals was discussed. The bishops apparently believed that the caretaking of children would be implemented by French welfare agencies. The Jews, according to the notes, did not ask for anything else but charitable help (not for political intervention or public protest). A letter would be sent to the government in the spirit of the declaration issued by the assembly.

On July 22, Cardinal Suhard, in the name of the assembly, sent the letter to the *maréchal*. It was the first official protest of the Catholic church of France regarding the persecution of the Jews:

"Deeply moved by the information reaching us about the massive arrests of Israelites that took place last week and by the harsh treatment inflicted upon them, particularly at the *Vélodrome d'Hiver*, we cannot suppress the call of our conscience. It is in the name of humanity and of Christian principles that our voice is raised to protest in favor of the unalienable rights of human beings. It is also an anguished call for pity for this immense suffering, mainly for that of mothers and children. We ask you, Monsieur le Maréchal, to accept to take [our call] into account, so that the demand of justice and the right to charity be respected."[69]

The papal nuncio in Vichy, Monsignor Valeri, considered the letter as rather "platonic."[70] Helbronner thought so as well and beseeched his friend Gerlier to intervene personally with Pétain. After obfuscating for a while, the cardinal of Lyons (also prodded by Pastor Boegner) agreed to send a letter to the maréchal, and did so on August 19. But, like Suhard before him, Gerlier wrote in convoluted terms that could only indicate to Pétain and Laval that the French church would ultimately abstain from any forceful confrontation. Despite his promise to Helbronner, the cardinal did not ask for a meeting with Pétain.[71] ...

In order to increase the number of deportees from France, the Germans were now pushing Vichy to adopt a law revoking the citizenship of Jews naturalized since 1927. But, after seemingly going along with the German scheme in the early summer of 1943, Laval rejected the new demand in August. Reports from the prefects had convinced the head of the Vichy government that public opinion would resent the handing over of French citizens (even recently naturalized ones) to the Germans.[72]

Due to the importance of the issue, Laval informed Eichmann's men, the decision would have to be taken by the head of state himself.

Pétain was of course aware of the possible reactions of the population. Moreover, he had been warned by the delegate of the Assembly of Cardinals and Archbishops, Henri Chappoulie, that the church would react negatively to any collective cancellation of the naturalization of Jews who had become French citizens after 1927.[73] Finally, it is likely that by August 1943, when Pétain and Laval rejected the German demand, both—like everybody else beyond the borders of the Reich—simply perceived that the Germans were undoubtedly losing the war.

It is hard to assess which of these elements played a decisive role in determining Vichy's decision. A public opinion poll completed by the CGQJ in the spring of 1943 on the demand of the government pointed to the existence of an absolute majority (more than 50 percent) of antisemites in the country.[74] These results, which may have been manipulated by the *Commissariat*, have of course to be regarded cautiously; they did, however, confirm trends previously mentioned, although they did not tally with the prefects' reports about potential reactions to the cancellation of naturalizations.

The Germans were not deterred: They would start the deportation of French Jews. To that effect, Dannecker's successor, *Obersturmbannführer* Heinz Rothke, got reinforcement: Eichmann's special delegate, Alois Brunner, arrived directly from Salonika, where the deportation of almost the entire Jewish population had just been successfully completed. Accompanied by a special group of some twenty-five SS officers, Brunner would be in direct contact with Berlin. He immediately replaced the French officials in charge of Drancy with his own men. . . .

On August 21, Lambert, his wife, and their four children were arrested and sent to Drancy; on December 7, they were deported to Auschwitz and murdered. Helbronner's turn followed. On October 28, the Gestapo arrested the president of the *Consistoire*, Pétain's and Gerlier's friend, the most thoroughly French of all French Jews. Vichy was immediately informed, and so was Cardinal Gerlier. Helbronner and his wife were deported from Drancy to Auschwitz in transport number 62 that left French territory on November 20, 1943; they were gassed on arrival. Between October 28 and November 20, neither the Vichy authorities nor the head of the French Catholic Church intervened in any way.[75] That Pétain did not intervene is not astonishing; that Gerlier abstained demonstrates that to the very end the leaders of the French church maintained their ambiguous attitude even toward those French Jews who were the closest to them.

NOTES

1. These numbers, all based on post—June 1940 computations, do not include some 10,000 to 15,000 Jewish prisoners of war, nor do they take into account that in the various censuses, a few thousand foreign Jews did not register. See André Kaspi, *Les Juifs pendant l'occupation* (Paris, 1991), 18ff.
2. *Foreign Relations of the United States, General and Europe 1940*, vol. 2 (Washington DC, 1957), 565.
3. A 1927 law had eased the naturalization process. The intention of Alibert's commission was clear: Forty percent of the naturalizations that were cancelled were those of Jews. See Robert O. Paxton, *Vichy France: Old Guard and New Order, 1940–1944* (New York, 2001), 171.
4. Michael R. Marrus and Robert O. Paxton, *Vichy et les juifs* (Paris, 1990), 17–18.
5. For the full text of both laws, see ibid., 399–401.
6. Pétain's own antisemitism was apparently fed by his wife (*La Maréchale*) and by his physician, Dr. Bernard Menetrel. See Denis Peschanski, *Vichy, 1940–1944: Contrôle et exclusion* (Bruxelles, 1997), 78.

7. See in particular Denis Peschanski, "The Statutes on Jews, October 3, 1940, and June 2, 1941," *Yad Vashem Studies* 22 (1992), 65ff.; Pierre Laborie, "The Jewish Statutes in Vichy France and Public Opinion," *Yad Vashem Studies* 22 (1992), 89ff; Renee Poznanski, "The Jews of France and the Statutes on Jews, 1940–1941," *Yad Vashem Studies* 22 (1992), 115ff.
8. Quoted in Kaspi, *Les Juifs pendant l'occupation*, 61–62.
9. Peschanski, *Vichy, 1940–1944: Contrôle et exclusion*, 180.
10. Marrus and Paxton, *Vichy et les juifs*, 28.
11. In a book published in 1947, *L'Église Catholique en France sous l'occupation*, Monsignor Guerry himself reproduced the gist of the declaration, possibly without even perceiving its problematic aspect.
12. For example, the bishop of Grenoble and the archbishop of Chambery, ibid., 143 n. 11.
13. For a good summary of these attitudes, see Francois Delpech, "L'Episcopat et la persecution des juifs et des étrangers," in *Églises et chrétiens dans la IIe Guerre mondiale* (Lyon, 1978).
14. Quoted in Michèle Cointet, *L'Église Sous Vichy, 1940–1945. La repentance en question* (Paris, 1998), 187–88.
15. Marrus and Paxton, *Vichy et les juifs*, 203–4.
16. Herbert R. Lottman, *La Rive gauche: Du Front populaire à la guerre froide* (Paris, 1981), 303–4; Verdes-Leroux, *Refus et violences*, 149. All Jewish authors were excluded, whereas in many other cases the exclusion targeted only specific books.
17. See Lutz Raphael, "Die Pariser Universität unter deutscher Besatzung 1940–1944," in *Universitäten im nationalsozialistisch beherrschten Europa*, ed. Dieter Langewiesche, *Geschichte und Gesellschaft* 23, no 4. (1997), 511–12, 522. Some protests against the anti-Jewish measures were expressed by a few faculty members . . . (ibid., 523).
18. Burrin, *France under the Germans*, 307–8.
19. Anne Grynberg, *Les Camps de la honte: Les internés juifs des camps français, 1939–1944* (Paris, 1991), 12. In a meeting at the German embassy

on February 2, 1941, Dannecker confirmed these data. See Serge Klarsfeld, ed., *Die Endlösung der Judenfrage in Frankreich: Deutsche Dokumente 1941–1944* (Paris, 1977), 17.

20. Pätzold, *Verfolgung*, 281–82.
21. *DGFP: Series D*, vol. 12 (Washington DC, 1962), 228.
22. For details on the establishment of the CGQJ and on Vallat's activities, see Marrus and Paxton, *Vichy et les juifs*, 79ff.
23. Ibid., 92ff.
24. For the full text of the law summed up here, see ibid., 402.
25. See among others Claude Singer, *Vichy, l'université et les juifs: Les silences et la mémoire* (Paris, 1992), 136ff, and Stanley Hoffmann, "Collaborationism in France during World War II," *Journal of Modem History* 40 (September 1968).
26. Marrus and Paxton, *Vichy et les juifs*, 209.
27. For Helbronner's career, see mainly Simon Schwarzfuchs, *Aux prises avec Vichy: Histoire politique des juifs de France, 1940–1944* (Paris, 1998), 94ff.
28. Ibid., 90ff.
29. Paula Hyman, *The Jews of Modern France* (Berkeley, 1998), 167.
30. Adler, *The Jews of Paris*, 84.
31. Carole Fink, *Marc Bloch: A Life in History* (Cambridge, 1989), 272.
32. Poznanski, *Yad Vashem Studies* 22 (1992), 115–16.
33. René Rémond, *Le "Fichier juif"* (Paris, 1996), 67–68, 74.
34. Raymond-Raoul Lambert, *Carnet d'un témoin: 1940–1943*, ed. Richard I. Cohen (Paris, 1985), 105, 187.
35. Jacques Biélinky, *Journal, 1940–1942: Un journaliste juif à Paris sous l'Occupation*, ed. Renee Poznanski (Paris, 1992), 146.
36. See Joseph Billig, *L'Institut d'étude des questions Juives* (Paris, 1974), 160fF.
37. Lucien Steinberg and Jean Marie Fitère, *Les Allemands en France: 1940–1944* (Paris, 1980), 75–76. Adler, *The Jews of Paris and the Final Solution*, 75ff; Poznanski, *Etre juif en France*, 311.

38. For the chronology and most of the relevant documents see mainly Klarsfeld, *Vichy-Auschwitz*, vol. 1 (Paris, 1983).
39. Ibid., vol. 1, 236–37.
40. Marrus and Paxton, *Vichy et les juifs*, 236–37.
41. Poznanski, *Etre juif en France*, 358.
42. Biélinky, *Journal*, 191, 209–10, 214ff.
43. Nuremberg doc. NG-183, *The Ministries Case*, 235.
44. Pierre Drieu la Rochelle, *Journal, 1939–1945*, ed. Julien Hervier (Paris, 1992), 302.
45. quoted in David Carroll, *French Literary Fascism: Nationalism, Antisemitism, and the Ideology of Culture* (Princeton, 1995), 211–12).
46. Quoted in Frédéric Vitoux, *Céline: A Biography* (New York, 1992), 378.
47. Quoted in Carroll, *French Literary Fascism*, 121.
48. See in particular Robert Belot, "Lucien Rebatet, ou L'Antisémitisme comme Evénement Littéraire," in *L'Antisémitisme de plume, 1940–1944: Etudes et documents*, ed. Pierre-andré Taguieff (Paris, 1999), 217ff. See also Robert Belot, *Lucien Rebatet: Un itinéraire fasciste* (Paris, 1994).
49. Biélinky, *Journal*, 232–33.
50. Robert Gildea, *Marianne in Chains* (New York, 2003), 259–60.
51. André Kaspi, *Les Juifs pendant l'occupation* (Paris, 1991), 222.
52. Poznanski, *Etre juif en France*, 385.
53. On July 15, Bielinky noted in his diary: "It appears that Jews and Jewesses aged eighteen to forty-five are going to be arrested and sent to forced labor in Germany." *Journal*, 233.
54. Kaspi, *Les Juifs pendant l'occupation*, 224.
55. Quoted in ibid., 226–27.
56. Poznanski, *Etre juif*, 385–86.
57. Marrus and Paxton, *Vichy et les juifs*, 258, 260–61.
58. Ibid., 255.
59. Serge Klarsfeld, *Vichy-Auschwitz: Le rôle de Vichy dans la solution finale de la question juive en France*, 2 vols. (Paris, 1983–85), vol. 1, 328, 330.
60. Georges Wellers, *De Drancy à Auschwitz* (Paris, 1946), 55ff.
61. Klarsfeld, *Vichy-Auschwitz*, vol. 1, 355.

62. Richard I. Cohen, *The Burden of Conscience: French Jewish Leadership during the Holocaust* (Bloomington, 1987), 79.

63. Raymond-Raoul Lambert, *Carnet d'un témoin: 1940–1943*, ed. Richard I. Cohen (Paris, 1985), 178, 180.

64. Schwarzfuchs, *Aux prises avec Vichy*, 253–56. For the text of a draft of July 28, see Klarsfeld, *Vichy-Auschwitz*, vol. 1, 295.

65. For some of the *préfets'* reports about reactions in their districts, see Klarsfeld, *Vichy-Auschwitz*, vol. 1, 305ff.

66. Renée Poznanski, "Jews and non-Jews in France During World War II: A Daily Life Perspective," in *Lessons and Legacies V: The Holocaust and Justice*, ed. Ronald M. Smelser (Evanston IL, 2002), 306.

67. Kaspi, *Les Juifs pendant l'occupation*, 306–7; Renée Bedarida, *Les Catholiques dans la guerre, 1939–1945: Entre Vichy et la Resistance* (Paris, 1998), 176.

68. The notes are published in Cointet, *L'Église Sous Vichy*, 224.

69. For the French original see Klarsfeld, *Vichy-Auschwitz*, vol. 1, 280. See also Cointet, *L'Église Sous Vichy, 1940–1945*, 225. On Cardinal Suhard, see Bedarida, *Les Catholiques dans la guerre*, 78.

70. Cointet, *L'Église Sous Vichy*, 266. For Valerio Valeri's letter to Maglione, where the expression is used, see Klarsfeld, *Vichy-Auschwitz*, vol. 1, 297.

71. Schwarzfuchs, *Aux prises avec Vichy*, 209–10.

72. Marrus and Paxton, *Vichy et les juifs*, 325ff.

73. Klarsfeld, *Vichy-Auschwitz*, vol. 2, 331.

74. Jacques Adler, "The Changing Attitude of the 'Bystanders' Toward the Jews in France, 1940–1943," in John Milfull, *Why Germany?: National Socialist Antisemitism and the European Context* (Providence RI, 1993), 184ff.

75. Schwarzfuchs, *Aux Prises avec Vichy*, 304–6.

The Italian Paradox

SUSAN ZUCCOTTI

From *The Italians and the Holocaust*

In his memoirs, Primo Levi recalled Olga, the Yugoslavian Jewish refugee who found temporary peace in "paradoxical Italy, officially antisemitic."[1] He did not exaggerate. Wartime Italy was indeed a paradox. Italian Jewish citizens could be arrested for no apparent cause in their own country, while their government protected them in German-occupied areas. Italian Jewish doctors, lawyers, and teachers could not practice and were forced to perform manual labor, yet foreign Jewish refugees received rudimentary shelter and living allowances from the same government. Synagogues were sacked with impunity, while Jewish relief agencies were allowed to collect funds abroad and aid refugees.

Nothing demonstrates the paradox more clearly than the exceptional measures of the Italian army, Foreign Ministry, and entire diplomatic corps to protect Jews in Italian-occupied territories. Italy occupied much of Greece in 1941, part of Croatia at about the same time, and eight departments in southern France in November 1942. In all three areas, military and diplomatic personnel, often without instructions or coordination, acted similarly. They resorted to innumerable schemes and subterfuges to resist repeated German demands for the deportation of Jews. They ignored Mussolini's directives, occasionally with his tacit consent. They neglected to pass on instructions, made orders deliberately vague and imprecise, invented absurd bureaucratic excuses, lied, and totally mis-

led the Germans. If the subject had not been so serious and the stakes so desperately high, the story might have acquired the dimensions of a comic opera, with befuddled Germans concluding, as usual, that Italians were blatant liars and hopelessly incompetent administrators. But thousands of lives were at stake, and the game was stark and deadly.

The game was also unique, for the behavior of the players bore little resemblance to activities in other nations. In most European countries, but especially in Denmark and in Italy itself somewhat later, individuals tried to save local Jews who were their friends, neighbors, and compatriots. Even in areas friendly to Nazi Germany such as Vichy France, Bulgaria, and Romania, local authorities resisted German demands for the deportation of native Jews. But they rarely extended their protection to foreign Jews. In contrast, the occupying forces in the Italian-controlled territories of Croatia, Greece, and southern France protected total strangers—neither Italian citizens nor, in many cases, even citizens of the occupied country. The only link between protector and victim was their common humanity.

Chronologically, the story of the Italian rescue of foreign Jews begins in Croatia. After a military resistance of eleven days, the kingdom of Yugoslavia capitulated on April 17, 1941, to the invading German army and its Italian, Bulgarian, and Hungarian allies. The Germans immediately occupied Serbia, with its capital at Belgrade, and the Italians seized most of the Dalmatian coast. In

Croatia, a nominally independent government was established at Zagreb under the leadership of Ante Pavelic, chief of the *Ustasha*, or Croatian Fascist party. Because Pavelic had close ties with Italian Fascists, Croatia was expected to remain within the Italian sphere of influence. In fact, independent Croatia was almost immediately divided into an Italian and a German military occupation zone, to last for the duration of the war.

During the terrible summer of 1941, *Ustasha* assassins ran wild in Croatia, destroying entire villages and murdering thousands of Jews and Serbs. Italian policies toward refugees were initially harsh, and unknown numbers of asylum-seekers were turned back at the borders to face certain death. But the attitudes of many occupiers within the Italian zone gradually softened with the horrors they witnessed. While the Germans tended to give the *Ustasha* free rein in their zone, individual Italian soldiers refused to look the other way. Without instructions from above, they simply gathered up Jews in military trucks, cars, and even tanks and moved them to protected areas. Their officers, soon aware of events, did nothing to interfere. Many lives were saved, and the infuriated *Ustasha* ceased operations in most of the Italian zone. Meanwhile, word spread, and thousands of other Jews and Serbs fled from German to Italian territory.[2]

Julia Hirschl, a Croatian Jew, and her Viennese husband were among the many refugees who came under Italian protection. Desperately fleeing Croatian terrorists, the Hirschls found themselves in a burned-out village in Herzegovina, 1,100 meters above sea level, in the middle of a battle between the *Ustasha* and Tito's partisans. "Fortunately the Italians arrived," she recalls, "naturally to help the *Ustasha*, but at the same time they helped us refugees." The Italians protected them and helped them reach Kupari, near Dubrovnik in the Italian zone.[3]

Of a prewar total of about thirty thousand Jews in Croatia, only a few thousand remained alive in 1942. These survivors faced a new threat that summer, when Ante Pavelic agreed to restrain his *Ustasha* terrorists and allow the Germans to deport the Jews instead. The Croatian leader even promised to pay thirty marks for every Jew deported. This grisly deal had one serious drawback, however, for three to five thousand Jews had taken refuge in the Italian zone, where the authorities refused to give them up. Croatian and German officials were more than a little embarrassed. Italian occupying forces were playing the role of noble savior amid much popular approval.

For the first time in the history of Nazi-Fascist relations, the Germans began to interfere with Italian policy toward the Jews. They had not pressed for antisemitic measures in Italy itself, but now in Croatia in 1942, they did. Italians at all levels of command refused to budge. Finally in August 1942, the frustrated Germans appealed to Mussolini himself. The obliging prime minister replied that he had no objections to the deportations. He communicated this position to the Army General Staff clearly, but without detailed instructions or a timetable. Nothing happened.

The Italian response to Mussolini's communication was masterful. Foreign Ministry officials concerned with Croatia met and decided to ignore it. They made careful arrangements with army liaison officers to delay and obfuscate matters as much as possible. Bureaucratic reports began to flow, explaining that while military authorities would hand over some Jews as soon as possible, the matter was immensely complicated. Croatian Jews subject to deportation had to be separated from foreign Jews who were exempt. Criteria needed to be established. Was place of birth to be the defining characteristic of a Croatian Jew or should place of residence, citizenship, and family connections be considered? The army needed time.

Such evasion was not easy. With Croatians and Germans constantly complaining, most high-level Italian officials were anxious to avoid personal responsibility for the delay. A reputation as a "pietist," after all, was not good for one's career. Furthermore, military and diplomatic officers wanted to prevent the involvement of Ministry of the Interior personnel, notoriously less sympathetic to Jews than themselves. In October, the Italian Army General Staff finally decided that some concrete action was needed.

Without warning and within a very few days, soldiers rounded up about three thousand Jews in the Italian zone, settled them in a confined area, and began a census.[4] The roundup was traumatic for the victims, who were certain that they were about to be delivered to the Nazis. Tragically, there were even a few suicides. The roundup also prompted a furious response from many Italian army officers who similarly misunderstood the policy. Everyone soon realized, however, that the roundup and census were simply another ruse. The Italians could now show the Germans they were trying, and the Germans could no longer argue that the Jews constituted a security risk.

Diplomatic pressure did not cease with the roundup. After many less formal appeals, Foreign Minister Joachim von Ribbentrop himself met with Mussolini in Rome in late February 1943. The prime minister again agreed to deliver the Croatian Jews. When he conveyed that decision to General Mario Robotti, commander of the Second Army in Yugoslavia, however, Robotti protested strongly. Mussolini's response, confirmed by several sources, is classic. "O.K., O.K.," he is reported to have told Robotti, "I was forced to give my consent to the extradition, but you can produce all the excuses you want so that not even one Jew will be extradited. Say that we simply have no boats available to transport them by sea and that by land there is no possibility of doing so."[5]

As the spring and early summer of 1943 passed, the Italian problem became less one of German diplomatic pressure than one of the physical inability to protect Jews in Croatia. An Allied invasion of Italy itself seemed imminent, involving the probability that Italian troops based in Yugoslavia would be withdrawn for defense of the homeland. Foreseeing disaster, many Italian authorities again did everything in their power to save the Jews in their zone. By July 1943, roughly three thousand people had been transferred to the Island of Arbe in the Gulf of Carnero, just a few miles from the Italian mainland. After the fall of Mussolini on July 25, the Foreign Ministry repeatedly instructed the General Staff that the Jews on Arbe should not be released unless they themselves requested it. The same ministry also began desperate negotiations with other Italian agencies to arrange for the transfer of the Jews to Italy itself.

Fortunately, because Jews in Italy were soon to be hunted and deported also, those negotiations proceeded too slowly. On September 8, 1943, General Eisenhower announced the armistice, and the Italian army in Yugoslavia laid down its arms. In the resulting confusion, all but 204 mostly sick or elderly Jews on Arbe were able to go into hiding or join Tito's partisans before the Germans occupied the island. The 204 were immediately deported to Auschwitz. Roughly 275 of those who joined the partisans also died before liberation. The rest survived—roughly 2,200 out of 2,661 according to one set of figures; about 3,000 out of 3,500 according to another. The numbers are not high relative to other Holocaust statistics. Perhaps for that very reason, the exceptional effort of Italian officials to protect so few Jewish refugees in their Croatian zone of occupation was indeed impressive.[6]

Julia Hirschl and her husband were among the Jews transferred to Arbe. She relates that after the armistice, partisans helped her move to the island of Lissa. From there, a British convoy took her and many others to a huge refugee complex in the Sinai. Twelve hours after she left Arbe, the Germans arrived there and deported all remaining Jews—the men, women, and children the Italians had been protecting for so long.[7] . . .

Like Yugoslavia, a defeated Greece had been divided into occupation zones in the spring of 1941. Bulgaria received most of Thrace. Germany controlled Crete, Macedonia, a narrow strip of Thrace bordering Turkey, and the city of Salonika with its 53,000 Jews. Italy occupied what remained: the Ionic islands and much of the Greek peninsula, including Athens. The German zone contained a total of 55,000 Jews. The much larger Italian zone had only 13,000.[8]

The brutal Nazi roundup and deportation of the Jews of Salonika began early in 1943. At that time, officers of the German General Staff invited the Italian General Staff to follow the Nazi example. The Italians not only refused, but insisted that the Germans spare all Jews of Italian origin. In a brief comic scene in an otherwise tragic setting, Italian consulate officials in Salonika then proceeded to define "Italianness" in the broadest possible way. They issued naturalization papers to Jews married to Greeks in the Italian zone and to their children—"minors" often as old as thirty. Any remote relationship to an Italian was sufficient, as was an Italian-sounding name. Indeed, they often demanded no pretext at all.[9] All this was done by representatives of the same government that, at home, had revoked the citizenship of Jews who had lived in Italy for years and had been naturalized as long ago as 1919.

During the Salonika roundups, Italian consulate officials presented the Nazis with daily lists of newly naturalized Italian subjects being detained awaiting deportation. In most cases, detainees were promptly released. Furthermore, scores of Italian soldiers went to detention areas each day to insist that particular female detainees were their wives. These, too, were often released.[10] The Nazis were undoubtedly not fooled. Perhaps they already assumed they would soon reach into Italian-occupied Greece as well. In any case, they were obliging. Italian military trains carried the released Jews to Athens, where they were fed, sheltered, and protected.

Their respite was short. Unlike the Jews in Italian-occupied Croatia, most Jews in Greece did not survive. When the Germans occupied all of Greece after the Italian armistice, brutal manhunts began immediately. Nearly half of the 3,500 Jews in Athens were deported in 1944. Over 5,000 from the remaining Greek mainland, and several thousand from Rhodes, Corfu, and Crete soon joined them.[11] The Italians who had protected them until the armistice were gone. There was no one to help.

In France, the story of the Jews and the Italian occupation began about a year and a half later than in Croatia and Greece. Vichy France before occupation was, like Croatia and Italy, an antisemitic state. . . . On November 11, 1942, shortly after the Allied landings in Morocco and Algeria, the German army moved into southern France. The Italians, in turn, occupied eight French departments east of the Rhone. Technically, as in "independent" Croatia, the indigenous government remained in place, but in fact, occupying forces controlled events. In the German zone, the French police were encouraged to continue their manhunts for foreign Jews, while the Nazis watched. In the Italian zone, arrests ceased, and Jews already captured but not yet deported were released. Jews actually found themselves better off than before the Italian occupation.

The first direct confrontation between Italian occupation authorities and Vichy administrators occurred in December. The prefect of Alpes-Maritimes, a close friend of Vichy head of state Philippe Pétain and an ardent collaborator, ordered that all foreign Jews in his department be sent for security reasons to enforced residence in the departments of Drôme and Ardèche. Drôme was partially occupied by the Germans, and Ardèche, west of the Rhône, was entirely in the German zone. Jews sent there would certainly be deported. Italian Foreign Ministry officials immediately canceled the order, explaining that non-French Jews including Italians, of whom there were comparatively few, were under Italian, not French, jurisdiction. By implication, the Vichy administrators could do what they liked with French Jews, but they could not touch the foreigners.[12]

Laval immediately protested. He could understand, he said, why the Italians might want to protect Italian Jews, but why were they concerned about foreigners?[13] Why, indeed, he might have added, after having interned foreign Jews at home? The Italians, however, had placed Laval in an untenable position. He had promised to protect French Jews; how could he arrest them while allowing foreign Jews to go free? As in Croatia, but even more so in a nation with less pervasive anti-Jewish hostility, native authorities did not wish to place the Italians in the role of noble savior. The Italian action, soon extended to all eight occupied departments, in effect protected French and foreign Jews alike.

In the weeks that followed, Italian occupying forces prevented other anti-Jewish measures. They forbade the stamping of identification papers or ration books with the word "Jew," as required by a recent French law. In March, they ordered the French government to annul all arrests and internments of Jews in their zone, including French Jews. French police had arrested well over a hundred Jews in February and were holding them for deportation. In Grenoble and Annecy, Italian soldiers actually surrounded the prisons where they were being held to insure their release.

As in Croatia and Greece, reports of Italian policies toward the Jews spread rapidly, and thousands of refugees fled into the Italian zone. According to a German report, an area that before the war had contained 15,000 to 20,000 Jews held 50,000 in July 1943.[14] Of these, 20,000 to 30,000 were foreigners. Most refugees gravitated to Nice, where they received the necessary residence permits and ration cards. From Nice, many were sent to enforced residence in villages in the interior.

Enforced residence was not necessarily unpleasant. Most refugees were sent to resort areas where hotel space and vacation homes were available because of the war; . . . These villages had the added advantage of being near the Swiss and Italian frontiers, "just in case." Refugees in enforced residence had to report to the Italian authorities twice a day, observe a 9:00 P.M. curfew, and remain within the limits of their village. But social contacts were not limited, and they were free to visit restaurants and cafes and organize schools, cultural centers, and clubs. For Jews who had been eluding the Nazis for years, enforced residence in the Italian zone seemed almost like freedom. . . .

Needless to say, Italian protection of the Jews in their zone enraged the Nazis, and the German Foreign Ministry exerted considerable pressure for the delivery of refugees for deportation. Foreign Minister Joachim von Ribbentrop added the issue to his discussion of Croatian Jews when he met Mussolini in Rome in late February 1943. Hans Georg von Mackensen, German ambassador to

Italy, also had at least two conversations with the prime minister on the subject. As with the Croatians, Mussolini apparently told the Germans everything they wanted to hear. In a telegram on March 18, 1943, Mackensen reported that Mussolini had said, "This is a question with which the [Italian] Generals must not meddle. Their attitude is the result not only of lack of understanding, but also of sentimental humanitarianism, which is not in accord with our harsh epoch. The necessary instructions will therefore be issued this very day to General Ambrosio, giving a completely free hand to the French police in this matter."[15]

As proof of his intentions, Mussolini subsequently sent Guido Lospinoso, a former police inspector from Bari, to establish a Commissariat for Jewish Affairs at Nice. Lospinoso was a personal acquaintance of the prime minister, with a reputation for efficiency and energy. The Italian message to the Germans was clear. If Italian Foreign Ministry and military officials were reluctant to cooperate with German demands, the Italian police and the notoriously more antisemitic Ministry of the Interior would simply bypass them. The Germans were delighted. Heinrich Müller, chief of the Gestapo, stated from Berlin on April 2 that Lospinoso would "regulate the Jewish problems . . . in accordance with the German conception and in the closest collaboration with the German police." Lospinoso had, Müller added, already been in France for several days.[16]

Another brief comedy began. On April 5 ss Colonel Dr. Helmut Knochen, chief of German security police in Paris, informed Berlin that "nothing is known of [Lospinoso's] journey." On April 7, Müller in Berlin insisted that "Lospinoso has been in France for some days." By April 8, Knochen had finally learned that Lospinoso had been in Menton for three days, but had returned to Rome. A month and a half later, on May 24, Knochen was still complaining that "we know nothing of [Lospinoso's] possible presence in the Italian zone."[17]

On May 26, relieved ss agents in France finally discovered that Lospinoso had set up headquarters in a villa near Nice. The man himself, however, remained elusive. As late as June 23, Knochen complained that Lospinoso was still "evading a visit to the Supreme Chief of the ss . . . yet at the same time establishing contact with the Chief of the French Police about the application of the anti-Jewish measures." Then on July 7, Lospinoso failed to appear at an arranged meeting with German security police in Marseilles. He sent a representative, who immediately declared that he had no authority to make decisions about the Jewish question. The Germans would have to speak with Lospinoso himself.[18]

As in Croatia, however, Italian authorities realized that some action was required to appease German wrath. Thus between May and the September 8 armistice, they intensified their efforts to send Jews away from coastal areas to enforced residence in the interior. The Nazis were far from satisfied. They complained that the transferred Jews were lodged in luxury hotels in fashionable spas, while the thousands remaining along the Cote d'Azur dined in the best restaurants, lived comfortably, and attempted to undermine Italian-German friendship. There was an element of truth in their charges, but Italian authorities could again claim that they were trying.

Mussolini's fall in July did not alter Lospinoso's official status, but it did provide him with a welcome excuse for further delay. He carefully informed the Germans on August 18 that he would have to return to Rome for new instructions. In fact, however, the nature of his problems had changed, for the Badoglio government, anticipating the still secret armistice, decided in August to withdraw from most of occupied France. The

Italian army would attempt to hold only a vastly reduced area around Nice. On August 28, Italian officials agreed that the Jews should be allowed to accompany the army when it withdrew. Jewish relief agencies hired fifty trucks to bring refugees in Haute Savoy back to Nice and, they believed, to safety.

The Badoglio period also witnessed the Herculean efforts of Angelo Donati, a Jewish Italian from Modena, to organize a massive rescue operation. Donati had served as a liaison officer between the French and Italian armies during World War I. After the war, he had helped found and direct a French-Italian bank in Paris. He became involved with German Jewish refugee relief after 1933. When the Germans occupied northern France in 1940, he moved to Nice and dedicated his considerable talents to refugee assistance.[19]

Donati's activities span the entire period of Italian occupation in southern France. In December 1942, when the prefect of Alpes-Maritimes wanted to evacuate foreign Jews into a German-occupied department, Donati first alerted Italian authorities. In March 1943, when Lospinoso arrived in Nice to begin his duties as commissar for Jewish affairs, Donati met, befriended, and advised him. Donati cooperated fully in the transfer of foreign Jews from Nice to enforced residence in Haute Savoy—a move that temporarily stalled the Germans and located Jews near the Swiss and Italian frontiers. Donati subsequently petitioned the Badoglio government to permit those same Jews to withdraw with the Italian army back into the soon-to-be reduced occupation zone around Nice.

Donati knew that thousands of Jews could not remain permanently concentrated around Nice, practically surrounded by Germans and totally dependent on the protection of the crumbling Italian army. During the last days of August and the first week of September, he made a last heroic effort to save his people. On the morning of September 8, after desperate negotiations with Italian officials, British and U.S. representatives at the Vatican, and the American Joint Distribution Committee, he finalized his rescue plan: the Badoglio government was to provide four ships, the British and Americans would permit thirty thousand Jews from France to land in North Africa, and the "Joint" would finance the vast move. The armistice, signed by Badoglio, was not scheduled to be made public until the end of the month. The ships would sail well before then.[20]

The premature announcement of the armistice caught everyone but the Germans unprepared, destroying all hope of implementing Donati's plan. The Italians clearly could not hold Nice, or even keep the Germans out of their own country. The army immediately disintegrated and Italian soldiers scrambled back across their frontier. As in Croatia and Greece during the same period, the Jews were left unprotected.

The Nazis entered Nice on September 9, angry and determined to take revenge for the ten months of Italian interference with their Final Solution. In addition to more than five thousand French Jews living in Nice at the time, there were at least sixteen thousand Jewish refugees in the city officially, and probably another two thousand there unofficially. At least another two thousand had left their enforced residences and descended on Nice in the early days of September, as rumors of the reduced Italian zone and Donati's escape plan filtered through the countryside. Most of the refugees were foreigners. They did not speak French. They knew no one in Nice. They had no plans, no hiding places, no documents, and with the disintegration of the Jewish relief agencies, no money. They were totally helpless.

The Jews of Nice, French and foreign alike, were caught in one of the most ruthless manhunts of the war in Western Europe. For more than a week, the Nazis searched every hotel and boarding house in the city, room by room. They also searched all trains leaving the city, so no one could escape. They ignored even valid documents, arresting and beating people who simply "looked Jewish." They physically searched every male, and sent every circumcised victim, together with all the men, women, and children in his household, to the notorious French holding camp at Drancy. From there, the trains left for Auschwitz. For 1,326 desperate refugees and 494 Jews born in France, a long odyssey of escape reached a terrible conclusion. The Italians had given them only a brief respite.[21]

Jews still in the French countryside on September 8 fared somewhat better. While many were caught and deported when the Germans entered the Italian zone, some escaped into the mountains and joined the French partisans. Others hid with French families or crossed the border to Switzerland. About 1,100 others, too far from Switzerland, followed the retreating Italian army across another frontier, hoping to find an Italy at peace. They entered, instead, a country as strictly occupied as the one they had left. In the next year and a half, their fate became linked with that of the Jews of Italy. . . .

Leaving aside for the moment the many Italians at home who aided or failed to aid Jews, the behavior of Italian officials in occupied territories remains to be explained. Why did they act as they did? The Jews they helped were not friends, neighbors, or even conationals. Their own government was officially antisemitic. They themselves had shown no heroic tendency to protest when Italian Jews were forced out of the army or the Foreign Ministry. They had stood by when police shipped foreign Jews in Italy to internment camps within the country. Why, when Germans tried to deport foreign Jews from Italian-occupied territories, did they behave differently?

It should be noted that most Italians dealing with Jews abroad probably had no direct experience with antisemitism at home. The tiny size of the Jewish community—one-tenth of 1 percent of the population—and its concentration in larger cities meant that most Italian soldiers and diplomats, like most Italians generally, knew almost no Jews at all. They may or may not have found the racial laws distasteful and the Ministry of the Interior bureaucrats who enforced them reprehensible. But one rarely risks a career to protest something one has not directly experienced.

On the other hand, Italians in the occupied territories faced an enormous "Jewish problem" every single day. They could not ignore the massacres of Jews and Serbs in Croatia, the roundups and deportations in Croatia and Greece, or the manhunts for thousands of destitute refugees in southern France. Furthermore, the implications of the problem were overwhelmingly different, for if in Italy before September 1943 Jews were being persecuted, in the occupied territories they were clearly being murdered. In 1941 and early 1942, Italian soldiers in Croatia acted spontaneously to save Jews and Serbs from murder on the spot. By mid-1942, when Nazis began to demand Croatian and Greek Jews for "resettlement in the East," most Italian diplomats and officers understood that deportation also meant murder.[22] The distinction between internment camps in southern Italy and "resettlement in the East" was a distinction between hardship and death. While Italians might overlook the first, it was more difficult to abet the second.

The peculiar blend of little direct experience of antisemitism at home and daily contact with persecution and murder abroad explains statements by Italian officials that would otherwise smack of hypocrisy or outright lying. For example, an Italian chief of staff in Mostar, near the Dalmatian coast, refused to permit deportation of Jews from that city on the grounds that Italians granted full equality to all residents.[23] After 1938, that clearly was not true. An Italian consul general in southern France, when denying a similar demand, stated that he would apply the same legislation as at home, for it was "a humane legislation."[24] It is hard to label internment camps, expulsion from professions and schools, and denial of nationality "humane," but that official may never have seen his country's racial laws at work. He had surely seen victims of antisemitism in southern France.

Nevertheless, Italian officials might have stood aside. After all, French bureaucrats, German army officers, and thousands of frightened, ambitious, or merely indifferent public officials in other occupied countries simply pretended they did not know about, or could not influence, events. Even most Italians, when the Germans in turn occupied their country, chose to ignore the deportations. Why did so many Italians abroad act differently?

The Jewish question in the occupied territories was intricately related to Italian perceptions of their own honor, prestige, and independence in the Axis partnership. That image had suffered greatly since the beginning of the war and the revelation of Italian military weakness. The German army had bailed out the Italians twice, in Greece in April 1941, and in North Africa later the same year. Italian pride had been hurt, and public officials were sensitive to challenges to Italian sovereignty.

Nor were the challenges imaginary. In all areas where Italians ultimately resisted German demands for the Jews, they already nursed grievances against their ally. In Croatia, Italians had expected to occupy the entire new state, only to be forced to divide it with the Germans. Adding insult to injury, the Germans and the Croats then made a deal to deport Croatian Jews without consulting the Italians. In Greece, the Germans had easily taken Athens in April 1941, after the Italian military stalemate. They then delivered it to the Italians for occupation. Humiliating Nazi interference in Athens continued, and German-sponsored groups of Greek students attacked Jews there throughout the period of Italian occupation. In southern France after November 1942, Italy had occupied most of the region east of the Rhone with little difficulty, but actual jurisdiction in the departments nearest the German zone was often unclear. Significantly, it was in this border area, in Ardèche and Drôme, that Italian, German, and French differences over the treatment of Jews in France first emerged.

Italian diplomats and military officers, with their injured pride and their grievances against the Germans, were determined to resist any demand that appeared as an encroachment upon their sovereignty. German demands for the Jews clearly fell into that category. Furthermore, many Italians feared that submission to those demands would weaken their authority over the occupied peoples and complicate the job of maintaining order. In both Croatia and southern France, they were dealing with nominally autonomous governments that wanted to cooperate with German deportation decrees. Italian acquiescence would have reduced their own role to that of a mere accomplice. In addition, in Greece and southern France, where a majority of the population remained mildly sympathetic to the Jews, Italian opposition to deportations could serve as a wedge between citizens and local pro-Nazi contenders for power. In all areas, Italian submission to German deportation demands would have made them look like weak junior partners in the Axis alliance, unworthy of the respect of those they meant to rule.

To some extent, their first spontaneous responses to the Jewish question also committed Italians to consistent resistance to German demands. Thus, in Croatia, after Italian soldiers rescued Jews from *Ustasha* terrorists, it would have been difficult for Italian officers to deliver them up for deportation later. Local Croatians would have concluded that the Italians were afraid of the Germans. Similarly, in southern France, after Italian officials publicly opposed the transfer of foreign Jews from the Italian to the German-occupied zone for internment—a decision probably made as much to insure Italian authority over Nazi and French police as to safeguard Jews—it was difficult to alter that policy. Concessions or changes would appear as weakness.

Finally, some evidence exists that with regard to Jews in the occupied territories, Italian officials acted with an eye on a future reckoning of accounts. By early 1943, many knew the horrors that resettlement in the East entailed. By about the same time, German defeats at Stalingrad and in Africa left little doubt about the outcome of the war to all but the most fanatic. Italy shared with Germany an ideology and a responsibility for an aggressive war. Many of her less fanatic leaders did not wish to share responsibility for the Holocaust as well.

But when all is said, something still seems missing. Bureaucrats in other nations suffered wounded pride, yet often hastened to ingratiate themselves with those in power. As late as 1944, Hungarian bureaucrats who knew the war was lost and were not yet implicated in Nazi atrocities did not hesitate to deliver their own, not foreign, Jews for deportation. Furthermore, from the Italian point of view there were often good reasons why protection of the Jews was not in the best interest of officials or of the country at large. Resistance to German demands not only jeopardized personal careers, but weakened the whole alliance on which Italian security during the war depended.

When all the logical reasons for and against cooperation in the Holocaust are weighed and measured, it is apparent that decency, courage, and humanity often tipped the balance. The soldiers who instinctively saved Jews and Serbs from the *Ustasha* did not act merely from calculation or a dislike of Germans. Italians who issued passports to Greek Jews with Italian-sounding names in Salonika or went to internment camps to claim their "wives" were not motivated by threats to their nation's sovereignty, for Salonika was clearly in the German zone. Italian officials during the confused Badoglio period who remembered to instruct authorities on Arbe not to release interned Jews to the Croats unless Jews themselves requested it, and who negotiated frantically to find places for those same Jews in Italy, were no longer motivated by injured pride or concerns of sovereignty. They were preparing to abandon Croatia, and were acting to save lives. Italian peasant soldiers who carried Jewish children over the Alps from France to Italy would not have understood complicated behavioral analysis. They too were acting to save lives. Not the lives of friends, neighbors, coreligionists, or countrymen. Just lives.

NOTES

1. Primo Levi, *The Reawakening: A Liberated Prisoner's Long March Home Through East Europe*, trans. Stuart Woolf (Boston: Little, Brown, 1965), 30–31.

2. Daniel Carpi, "The Rescue of Jews in the Italian Zone of Occupied Croatia," *Rescue Attempts during the Holocaust*, ed. Yisrael Gutman and Efraim Zuroff (Jerusalem: "Ahva" Cooperative Press, 1977), 465–525; and Jacques Sabille, "Attitude of the Italians to the Persecuted Jews in Croatia" in Leon Poliakov and Jacques Sabille, *Jews under the*

Italian Occupation (Paris: Centre de Documentation Juive Contemporaine, 1954), 131–50.

3. CDEC, Milan, 5-H—b: *Vicissitudini dei singoli— particolare*, f. H, s.f. Julia Hirschl, letter from Hirschl, November 3, 1980.

4. Carpi, 488.

5. Ibid., 496.

6. Ibid., 502–3.

7. Hirschl. Mrs. Hirschl estimates the number of Jews caught on Arbe at 400, rather than the 204 cited earlier.

8. Jacques Sabille, "Attitude of the Italians to the Jews in Occupied Greece" in Poliakov and Sabille, 153–60; and Raul Hilberg, *The Destruction of the European Jews* (1961; New York: New Viewpoints, 1973), 442.

9. Sabille, 157.

10. Ibid.

11. Hilberg, 451–53; and Nora Levin, *The Holocaust The Destruction of European Jewry 1913–1945* (1968; New York: Schocken Books, 1973), 523.

12. Italian Foreign Ministry order, telegram 34/R 12825, December 29, 1942, cited in English translation in Leon Poliakov, "The Jews under the Italian Occupation in France," in Poliakov and Sabille, 23. A photographic reproduction of the Italian original is printed on 183.

13. Ibid., 25.

14. "Present State of the Jewish Question in France," report by SS Obersturmführer Röthke, Paris, July 21, 1943, printed in English translation in Poliakov and Sabiile [note 2], doc. 25, 104–6.

15. Poliakov, doc. 8, 68–70.

16. Ibid., doc. 9, 73.

17. Ibid., doc. 10, 74; doc. 12, 76; doc. 13,77–78; photographic reproduction of German original, 189–90; and doc. 18, 84–85.

18. Ibid., doc. 22, 97–98; doc. 24, 101–3; photographic reproduction of German original, 195–96.

19. Renzo De Felice, *Storia degli ebrei italiani sotto il fascismo* (1961; Turin: Giulio Einaudi, 1972), 432. See also "General Considerations on the Jewish Question in Southern France," doc. 21, Poliakov, 93–96.

20. Poliakov, 39–42; De Felice, *Storia degli ebrei* [note 19], 432–33.

21. Poliakov, 40–44; and Serge Klarsfeld, *Vichy-Auschwitz: Le Rôle de Vichy dans la solution finale de la question juive en France-1942* II (Paris: Librarie Arthème Fayard, 1983), 117–26. . . . Serge Klarsfeld himself was an eight-year-old refugee living with his family in a hotel in Nice at the time of the roundups. His father hid the family but allowed himself to be arrested to protect their hiding place. The elder Mr. Klarsfeld did not survive.

22. See a copy of an Italian Foreign Ministry memorandum relaying Pieche's message to Mussolini, stamped "Seen by Duce," reproduced as doc. 9 in Carpi, 520. General Pieche was honored by the Italian Jewish Community in 1955 for his rescue work. See CDEC, Milan, 9/2 (42), f. Benemeriti (medaglia d'oro), s.f. Pièche gen. Giuseppe.

23. Carpi, 473.

24. Italian Consul General M. Calisse, quoted by French Prefect Ribière, January 14, 1943, doc. 2, Poliakov, 5.

The Hungarian Paroxysm

RANDOLPH L. BRAHAM

From *Studies on the Holocaust*

It is almost universally assumed by historians and laymen alike that the destruction of Hungarian Jewry was solely the consequence of the German occupation of Hungary on March 19, 1944. While it is true that mass deportation of Jews took place only during the occupation, the role played by the Hungarian radical Right in precipitating the catastrophe has been ignored or at best underestimated in both the general and the Jewish historiography of the postwar period. This article aims to demonstrate the link between the destruction of Hungarian Jewry and the initiatives that were taken by the radical Right of the Hungarian military and political establishment years before the occupation. A close investigation of the available evidence indicates that one of the determining factors underlying the destruction of the Jewish community was the desire of the Hungarian radical Right to rid the country of its "alien" Jews.

Although these elements of the radical Right were relatively unknown and played only a secondary role in the country's military and political establishment, their position on the Jewish question had been accepted by the Nazis immediately concerned with the "Final Solution" as the position of "Hungarian statesmen." Notwithstanding the Hungarian government's official opposition to the "Final Solution," the Nazis looked upon these radical Rightists as pawns to be used for the implementation of sinister designs in the country.

The category of alien Jews which the radical Right wanted to eliminate consisted basically of the following three groups: (1) The refugees, who had found a haven in Hungary from persecution in Nazi-occupied territories and Slovakia; (2) The Jews of foreign background—mostly Galician Jews who had fled to Hungary during World War I—and who had lived there for several decades but been refused naturalization; and (3) A large percentage of the Jews inhabiting the areas which were acquired by Hungary during the 1938–1941 period.[1] Unlike many of their brethren of Trianon Hungary [the territory demarcated by the Trianon Treaty of 1920], who tended toward assimilation and acculturation, a large percentage of these Jews refused to identify themselves as "Magyars of the Israelite faith" and continued to cling to their own traditions. In addition to suffering the consequences of the discriminatory anti-Jewish laws that affected all of Hungary's Jewry since 1938, many of these alien Jews also suffered the crushing burden of poverty and the special police measures that were enacted against them. Nevertheless, they continued to live in relative physical safety until shortly after Hungary's entry into the war against the Soviet Union on June 27, 1941.

However, the ambiguously antisemitic policies of Admiral Miklós Horthy's conservative, aristocratic, gentry-dominated, semi-fascist regime . . . slipped logically and inevitably toward the open, though at first only partial adoption of the Nazi solution to the Jewish question. Soon after the outbreak of hostilities, there arose the desire to emulate the Third Reich by transcending the legal solution of the problem of the alien Jews by a physical one that would involve their arrest, internment, and "resettlement." This solution, at first designed for and successfully employed only against alien Jews, came to be applied three years later against the entire community with almost equal success.

Emboldened by the initial successes of the anti-Soviet military campaign, and reports on the effective "dejudaification" of the occupied territories, a plan for the resettlement of alien Jews in Galicia originated with the KEOKH (National Central Alien Control Office). Empowered to act by the Council of Ministers, the KEOKH began, in July, 1941, a round-up of such Jews, together with a number of Hungarian Jews who could not prove their citizenship. About 15,000 to 18,000 of them were deported, most of them subsequently slaughtered by the SS and their Hungarian and Ukrainian hirelings near Kamenets Podolsk on August 27–28, 1941.[2]

The success of this first mission encouraged a number of high-ranking military officers and ambitious political figures of the Right to pursue the "purification" of the country. . . . Among the most prominent of them were Major-General Jozsef Heszlenyi,[3] commander of the Fourth Army Corps, and Lieutenant-General Sandor Homlok,[4] the Hungarian military attaché in Berlin. Acting, presumably without authorization, in the name of the Hungarian government,[5] Heszlényi took the initiative in proposing to the Germans that a second, larger group of alien Jews be deported to the then Romanian-occupied part of the Soviet Union "east of the Dniester," namely Transnistria. He submitted his proposal to Dr. Karl Clodius, deputy chief of the Economic Policy Division of the German Foreign Office, early in January 1942. Clodius was quite a familiar figure in Budapest, for

he visited Hungary frequently in connection with foreign trade relations between the two countries. Clodius dutifully forwarded the proposal to the OKW (*Oberkommmando der Wehrmacht*). Attractive as the proposal must have appeared, it had to be shelved for a few months—until later in the spring—because of transportation difficulties.[6]

In the interim, the [Laszlo] Bardossy ministry was replaced, on March 7, 1942, by that of Miklos Kallay and the Rightist-inspired deportation project was temporarily allowed to lapse. Kallay's position in connection with the Jewish question was as ambivalent as his general policy. . . . Although he consistently opposed the physical solution of the Jewish question, he was an advocate of the "civilized" form of antisemitism, which aimed, *inter alia*, at the gradual elimination of Jews from the country's economic and intellectual life. Kállay exacerbated their legal position and tolerated the virulent antisemitic agitation and propaganda, which played into the hands of the Nazis during the occupation.

Kállay's position on the Third Reich, as on the Jewish question in general, tended to fluctuate with the fortunes of the war. While during his first year in office, convinced of Nazi military supremacy, he pursued a consistently pro-German policy, during his second year, that is to say, after the destruction of the Hungarian army at Voronezh on January 12, 1943, and the defeat of the Germans at Stalingrad on February 2, 1943, he began to reorient his policies toward a possible extrication of Hungary from the Axis Alliance.

Although eager to free Hungary from the clutches of Nazism before its final defeat, Kallay, like Horthy and the other representatives of his class, was paralyzed by his fear of Russia and communism. He tried unrealistically to solve his dilemma by maneuvering secretly for the possible surrender of Hungary to the Western Powers exclusively. . . . Preoccupied as he was with his efforts to avoid a Soviet occupation, he failed to take the necessary precautionary measures to forestall a possible German attack from without and a pro-Nazi coup from within. It was this vacillating policy and the open courting of the West that induced the Germans to occupy the country in order to prevent it from emulating Italy. The extrication of Hungary at the time the Soviet forces were already crossing the Dniester would have exposed the Nazis in the central and southern parts of Europe to encirclement and possibly to a crushing defeat. The destruction of Hungarian Jewry was to a large extent a concomitant of this German military decision.

Although Kállay was consistently opposed to any physical solution of the Jewish question, he was not, in 1942 at least, politically averse to the advancement of proposals for the "humane" resettlement of the Jews. In a policy statement delivered on April 20, 1942, and calculated to a large extent to appease the pro-Nazi elements at home and abroad just prior to his scheduled visit with Hitler on June 5, Kállay in fact mentioned the desirability of solving the Jewish question in Hungary by expelling the approximately 800,000 Jews who lived there. However, he merely identified this as a goal to be implemented eventually after the war.[7]

Some of his military and political subordinates manifested greater impatience on the Jewish question and demanded and worked for an immediate solution. They planned to solve the problem by the resettlement of the Jews in several phases, with the first installment designed to include 100,000 alien Jews. Thus, about four months after Kallay came into office, the initiative undertaken by Major-General Heszlenyi was revived. In the interim, the policies of the new government crystallized . . . and many thousands of Hungarian-

speaking Jews had already perished together with their Slovakian brethren in Auschwitz.[8]

The initiative for the resettlement of the alien Jews was now assumed by Sándor Homlok. In a letter dated July 2, 1942, he reminded the OKW about the request submitted by Heszlenyi and demanded a definitive solution.[9] Toward the end of the same month, Karl Klingenfuss, legation counselor in the *Deutschland* (later *Inland*) section of the German Foreign Office, expressed his section's concurrence with Hungary's desire to get rid of its unwanted Jews and promised to look into the problem of transportation, which had prevented the implementation of the plan by OKW in January. He also promised to investigate the feasibility of using Transnistria as the destination for the deportees.[10] Early in August, he informed the OKW that the entire matter was being transferred for a final decision to the RSHA (*Reichssicherheitshauptamt*; Reich Security Main Office), Heinrich Himmler's agency in charge of resettlements.[11] Since Himmler's resettlement areas, such as Auschwitz and Treblinka, were in German-occupied Poland, Klingenfuss hastened on August 5, 1942, to inform Adolf Eichmann about the good news that the Romanians had shelved the idea of transferring the Hungarian Jews to the "area between the Bug and Moldavia."[12] In his letter of September 25, 1942, Eichmann, citing technical reasons, rejected the idea of mobilizing the entire deportation apparatus merely for the expulsion of the Jewish refugees. He contended that it would be better to delay this action until Hungary was ready to bring about the total solution of the Jewish question.[13]

The scheme to bring about the resettlement of 100,000 Jews as a first installment of the solution of the Jewish question in Hungary was known not only to the higher German authorities and generals Heszlenyi and Homlok, but, as the evi-

dence clearly shows, also to a number of leading Hungarian political figures. Gyorgy Ottlik, a
member of the influential Foreign Affairs Committee of the Upper House of Parliament and the
chief editor of the German-language newspaper
Pester Lloyd of Budapest, the semiofficial organ of
the government, visited Germany in the course
of his West European tour made during August
and September 1942. Upon his return on October
10, he submitted a lengthy memorandum to the
Foreign Ministry, then headed by Prime Minister Kallay. Based on a three-hour conversation he
had had with Sztojay, the Hungarian minister in
Berlin, during the first day of his visit to the German capital, the memorandum reveals that Sztójay knew about the German decision to solve the
Jewish question in a radical manner during the
course of the war. Ottlik further contended that,
according to Sztójay, only two elements strained
Hungarian-German relations: One was the Hungarian attitude toward the German *Volksgruppe*
living in the country, a problem which was being
solved. The other, to quote Sztójay's statement
to Ottlik, was "the incomparably graver one, the
great influence and role played by the Jews in Hungary." The memorandum continues:

> As long as this is condoned, one cannot trust
> in the Hungarians. Sztójay consequently would
> find it appropriate if Hungary did not wait until
> (the Germans) raised this issue sharply, but
> would expedite the tempo of the changing of
> the guards and resettle a sizeable portion of
> our Jewish population in occupied Russia. Our
> Minister first spoke of about 300,000 [roughly
> the number of Jews in the territories added to
> Hungary in 1938–41], but then bargained him-
> self down to 100,000. On my interjected remark
> he did not keep it a secret that resettlement
> meant execution.[14]

About the same time, that is, in early October 1942, *ss-Hauptsturmführer* Dieter Wisliceny,
then serving in Bratislava and in charge of the
deportation of Slovak Jews, visited Budapest. In
his report to Han[n]s Elard Ludin, the German
minister in Bratislava, dated October 8, 1942, Wisliceny stated that two days earlier he had been
introduced to a certain Fáy, whom he identified
as Kállay's personal secretary.[15] . . . Immediately
after lunch at the Golf Club in Budapest on October 6, Fáy inquired closely about the solution of
the Jewish question in Slovakia and solicited his
(Wisliceny's) views on the question in Hungary.
The report continues:

> Fay mentioned that the existing laws were inad-
> equate and that the concept of Jews was also
> not specified in sufficiently clear form. The eco-
> nomic 'dejudaification' was also said not to have
> led to the desired results. The problem was very
> difficult, since the Jews represented an enor-
> mous economic factor and their large num-
> ber also was important. A resettlement of the
> Jews from Hungary, as was being carried out at
> this time in all Europe, could be realized only
> in stages [in Hungary]. Fay asked me whether
> it was a fact that the Jews were being resettled
> out of Romania as well. I answered him that to
> my knowledge preparations to that effect were
> being made. Suddenly Fay asked if Hungary
> would also be considered in a resettlement pro-
> gram. It was a matter of about 100,000 Jews in
> Carpatho-Ukraine and the territories acquired
> from Romania, which Hungary would like to
> resettle. As a second stage, one would have to
> handle the [Jews in the Hungarian Plains], and
> finally [those in] the capital city of Budapest. I
> then told him that I was in Budapest merely for
> private reasons and that I could not answer this
> question. I had no clear picture whether there

were reception possibilities for Hungarian Jews in the Eastern Territories.[16]

This document is extremely important, for it not only identifies for the first time the intended composition of the first 100,000 Jews to be resettled, namely Jews from Carpatho-Ruthenia and Northern Transylvania, but also reveals that it was designed merely as the first of several phases of the resettlement program calculated to bring about the total solution of the Jewish question in Hungary. . . .

Ludin dutifully forwarded Wisliceny's report to the German Foreign Office with a covering letter dated October 13.[17] It must have reached the RSHA shortly thereafter, for Himmler himself suddenly took a personal interest in the affair. He approached Joachim von Ribbentrop, the Foreign Minister of the Third Reich, in a lengthy letter dated November 30, 1942, in which he reviewed the Heszlenyi offer to the OKW as expressed in the name of the Hungarian government. Himmler further reminded Ribbentrop of the recent demands advanced by Hungarian statesmen for the solution of the Jewish question in that nation. Almost paraphrasing Fay's assertion as stated in Wisliceny's report, Himmler informed Ribbentrop that the solution of the Jewish question in Hungary was envisioned to be carried out in several phases, with the first phase to involve the evacuation of 100,000 Jews from the eastern part of the country. He stressed that although at first he had been against a partial solution of the question in Hungary, he was now ready to assign Wisliceny, the expert responsible for clearing Slovakia of its Jews, to the German legation in Budapest, where he could act as a "scientific adviser." Himmler further claimed that the elimination of this "burning problem" in Hungary would undoubtedly also affect the Bulgarian and Romanian governments

inducing them to solve their respective Jewish questions as well.[18]

At Ribbentrop's request, Martin Luther, the chief of the *Deutschland* section of the German Foreign Office, instructed Dietrich von Jagow, the German minister in Budapest, to inquire whether the Hungarian authorities were ready to effectuate the deportation of the 100,000 alien Jews or perhaps all of the Jews of Hungary.[19] In his answer of February 18, 1943, Jagow informed the Foreign Office that he had instructed the German military attaché in Budapest to contact the Hungarian General Staff and ascertain whether Heszlenyi and Homlok were actually empowered by their government to make the request for the deportation of the alien Jews. The text of Jagow's final report remains a mystery, for the archives of the German Foreign Office contain no record of it.

The Hungarian initiative announced by Wisliceny, however, received new impetus [from] Baron László Vay, a leading member of the Rightist radical wing of MEP (*Magyar Elet Partja*; Party of Hungarian Life), the government party, which he headed until November 1940, when Béla Lukács, another member of the same wing, took over leadership. . . . Vay was one of the prominent members of the Lukacs-led Hungarian delegation that visited *Reichsleiter* Martin Bormann, the chief of the Nazi Party Chancellery, in Munich on March 12, 1943. About two weeks before his departure, Vay sought out Jagow and expressed his hope that the Jewish question would also be discussed in Munich, "for there was much to be done yet in this area in Hungary." He was particularly anxious that Lukács and his colleagues be briefed on this question in depth and in an authoritative fashion. Jagow alerted the Foreign Office that the initiative must not be revealed as having come from Vay.[20]

In response to this initiative, Bergmann of the Foreign Office prepared with Ribbentrop's concurrence a lengthy memorandum dated March 9, 1943, to guide Bormann in his discussion with Lukács and his colleagues. Specifically, the Hungarian government was to be advised: (1) To exclude all Jews forthwith and without exception by appropriate legislation from the country's intellectual and economic life and to dispossess them immediately without compensation; (2) To mark all Jews without delay in order to facilitate governmental measures against them and to enable the [Hungarian] people to hold themselves aloof from them; and (3) To concur with the prompt beginning of the deportation and transportation [of the Jews] to the East by the appropriate German organization.[21]

At this time Regent Horthy was invited to visit Hitler at *Schloss Klessheim*, near Salzburg. At the meeting, which took place on April 17, 1943, the Regent was advised by the Führer that Hungary ought to follow the example of Poland where "if the Jews did not want to work they were simply shot." Upon Horthy's alleged assertion that he could not have Jews killed after they were deprived of a livelihood, Ribbentrop, who also attended the conference, replied that they should "either be killed or sent to concentration camps."[22] Ribbentrop's views on the Jewish question were further detailed by Sztójay in a lengthy memorandum dated April 28, in which he proposed that this problem "should be solved in a way that will avert a third [German] intervention."[23] About a month later, on May 21, Sztójay was already in a position to inform Horst Wagner, Luther's successor as chief of the *Inland II* section of the German Foreign Office, that in the wake of the Hitler-Horthy discussions on the Jewish question at Klessheim, Kállay was about "to consider seriously the initiation of decisive measures against the Jews."[24] . . .

But by this time, four months after the Voronezh and Stalingrad disasters, the Prime Minister was already groping, however unrealistically, for an honorable way out of the war. The search for peace gathered momentum after Italy's surrender late in the summer and in consequence of the military victories of the Anglo-American forces in Italy, North Africa, and the Far East, and the inexorable advance of the Red Army in eastern Europe. The establishment of contacts with representatives of the Western Allies was accompanied in fact by a relative easing of the position of the Jews, which was felt especially by those in labor battalions. But while Kállay became increasingly involved in his inauspicious secret negotiations, he, like Horthy on October 15, 1944, failed to take the most elementary military precautionary measures. The General Staff, like the officer corps on the whole, continued to be composed almost exclusively of Germanophiles of Homlok's and Heszlenyi's ilk, and the press with a few exceptions continued to feed the anti-Jewish psychosis that preoccupied the people. Because of Hungary's strategic position and Hitler's well-based fear of another impending Italian-type surrender, the German General Staff finalized the plans for the country's occupation as early as September 1943.[25] The actual invasion, however, took place on March 19, 1944, during Horthy's second visit to Klessheim.

In the interim, Hitler's suspicions were reinforced by a lengthy memorandum that Edmund Veesenmayer, an SS Brigadier General who later became the German minister and Reich plenipotentiary in Budapest, sent to the German Foreign Office in December 1943.[26] Veesenmayer presented a very bleak picture of Hungary's performance as an ally and submitted a series of proposals to correct the situation. The changes were to be brought about by keeping Horthy in power in spite of his weaknesses. Veesenmayer was not far from the mark when he characterized the

Regent as basically a good soldier, but "a miserable politician," who "understands nothing about either domestic or foreign policy." ...

After a stormy encounter with the Führer on March 18, Horthy and his entourage left Klessheim with no written agreement but with Hitler's assurances that German troops would leave Hungary as soon as an acceptable government was formed and that no satellite, that is Croatian, Romanian, or Slovak, troops would be involved in the occupation. However, the assurances did not specifically include the withdrawal of SS units. Although no formal agreement was signed at Klessheim,[27] there is absolutely no doubt that the question of the treatment of the Jews was also discussed and that Horthy made certain concessions that proved disastrous for them.

In his report to the Crown Council that convened shortly after his return on March 19, the Regent made no reference to these concessions, but merely reported Hitler's complaint that "Hungary did nothing in the matter of the Jewish problem, and was not prepared to settle accounts with the large Jewry in Hungary. . . ." Laconic as the report was on the Jewish question, the minutes of the Crown Council meeting clearly reveal that the Regent, while anticipating many German demands, considered the Nazi occupation less of an evil than a possible Russian invasion.[28] It [also] appears that Horthy deliberately failed to inform the Crown Council about [his] agreement ... to the delivery of a considerable number of "Jewish workers for German war production purposes." ... The Germans were suffering terrible losses on the eastern front and the aircraft industry was heavily damaged by the American Eighth and Fifteenth Air Forces. Field Marshall Erhard Milch, then state secretary in the Air Ministry and armaments chief of the *Luftwaffe*, approached Albert Speer, Minister of Armaments and War

Production, on February 23, 1944, with the idea that a Fighter Aircraft Staff [*Jägerstab*] be established ... "in order to overcome the crisis in aircraft production." The plan, as worked out in detail by a department head in Speer's ministry, called for the construction of six underground industrial plants, each with an area of over one million square feet, to be completed by November 1944. One of these was to be built in the Protectorate of Bohemia and Moravia with the aid of Jewish workers from Hungary. To head the Fighter Aircraft Staff, Hitler appointed Karl Saur, a department chief in the Armaments Ministry of whom Milch and Speer also approved.[29]

Hitler and Speer again reviewed the manpower needs of the *Jägerstab* project in the first week of April and agreed to request that the 100,000 Jews be sent from Hungary.[30] In response to this review and Horthy's apparent concurrence, Hitler informed Milch on April 9 that 100,000 Hungarian Jews "were to be found for the construction of underground aircraft factories in the Reich."[31]

Duly appointed to his new position, Saur called a top-secret meeting of the Fighter Aircraft Staff on April 14, 1944, and revealed that the details relating to the employment of 100,000 Hungarian Jews in the Protectorate project were being finalized.[32] On the same day, Veesenmayer informed Ribbentrop that Sztojay had given him a "binding assurance" that 50,000 able-bodied Jews would be placed at the disposal of the Reich by the end of the same month, and that 50,000 more would be made available before the end of May. He further reported that practical measures for the implementation of Sztojay's assurances were already under way through the action initiated by the SD (*Sicherheitsdienst*; Security Service) and the Hungarian police. He also revealed that he had the concurrence of the Regent and that the *Honvédség* (Hungarian Armed Forces) and the Ministry

of the Interior had expressed readiness to cooperate. The following day, Veesenmayer reported
to the German Foreign Office that the *Honvédség*
was ready to provide 5,000 Jews at once, to be followed by an additional 5,000 every three or four
days until the figure of 50,000 was reached. With
the Jews now at his disposal, Veesenmayer asked
for instructions as to where in Germany the transports should be directed.[33] The news about the
availability of Hungarian Jews was immediately
relayed to Eichmann. Veesenmayer pressed for
freight cars and was assured that all the details
relating to the time and means of shipping them
were being worked out by the RSHA in close cooperation with Eichmann and his staff and Ernst
Kaltenbrunner.[34]

In the meantime, the newly established government headed by Sztójay issued a series of anti-
Jewish decrees, including one requiring Jews to
wear the distinctive yellow Star of David while
the Jewish Council that was established under the
order of and for a while made responsible exclusively to the Germans was busy organizing the
Jewish community on a national basis.

The northeastern parts of the country, namely
Carpatho-Ruthenia and Transylvania, were
declared "operational zones" on April 13, and
three days later, on the eve of Passover, the Jews of
Carpatho-Ruthenia were rounded up as a "precautionary measure." They were driven into ghettos
about two weeks before the actual "ghettoization"
decree was promulgated on April 28. The plans for
their deportation were being finalized in accordance with a decision of the Council of Ministers
of April 26, under which 50,000 labor service men
were authorized to be sent to Germany together
with their families.[35]

On April 29, Veesenmayer reported that the
first transport, including 1,800 able-bodied Jews
between the ages of 16 and 50, had been shipped
from Budapest (Kistarcsa) and that 2,000 more
would be sent from Topolya the following day.[36]
In his testimony during his trial in 1948, Veesenmayer stated:

> Horthy himself told me that he was interested
> only in protecting the prosperous, the economi-
> cally valuable Jews in Budapest, those who were
> well off. However, as to the remaining Jewry—
> and he used a very ugly term there—he had no
> interest in them and was quite prepared to have
> them go to the Reich or elsewhere for labor. He
> approved that; and he did not approve it after
> a demand made by me but he approved it after
> agreements and discussions with his premier
> and his ministries. The fact has been proved
> that he later moderated the deportations, and
> then stopped them. Somebody who forbids
> something later on must have given permis-
> sion for it earlier.[37]

This assessment of Horthy was also corroborated by László Baky. In his statement written
while in prison, Baky claimed that he had issued
the decree of April 7, 1944, that called for the
"ghettoization" of Jews because László Endre, state
secretary in charge of political (that is, Jewish)
affairs in the Ministry of the Interior, and as such
one of those chiefly responsible for the destruction of the Jews, had requested it on the basis that
"the Regent agreed to the delivery of the Jews to
the Germans for purposes of labor." He believed
this, he claimed, because during his own previous
audience with the Regent, Horthy had told him:

> The Germans have cheated me. Now they want
> to deport the Jews. I don't mind. I hate the Gali-
> cian Jews and the Communists. Out with them,
> out of the country! But you must see, Baky, that
> there are some Jews who are as good Hungar-
> ians as you and I. For example, here are little

Chorin and Vida—aren't they good Hungarians? I can't allow these to be taken away. But they can take the rest.[38]

Baky's identification of Horthy's attitude toward the Jews was also corroborated by Haller, Veesenmayer's secretary. In his view "Horthy considered the assimilated Jews of Budapest as Hungarians, but the poorer ones of the provinces only as rabble for whom he had done nothing for a long time."[39]

Endre also stated in his testimony that "the Regent raised no objection to the deportations, saying that the sooner the operation was concluded, the sooner the Germans would leave the country." Perhaps the most convincing evidence for Horthy's consent was offered by Bishop Laszlo Ravasz. He claimed that when he was informed about the atrocities committed during the "ghettoization" in Carpatho-Ruthenia, he contacted Horthy to express his misgivings. At a meeting held on April 28, the Regent told him that "a large number of labor draftees were requested of Hungary. . . . A few hundred thousand Jews will in this manner leave the country's frontier, but not a single hair of their heads will be touched, just as is the case with the many hundreds of thousands of Hungarian laborers, who have been working in Germany since the beginning of the war."[40] . . .

With the green light provided by the legal agreement under which Horthy and his government consented to the delivery of one hundred thousand or several hundred thousands of Jews to Germany "for war production purposes," the Nazi elements—both German and Hungarian—who saw in this merely the first of several phases in the total solution of the Jewish question in Hungary, involving not only the alien but also the assimilated Jews, got busy to take full advantage of the opportunity.

The master plan for the total solution of the Jewish question in Hungary was worked out at the RSHA with the direct involvement of Himmler, Kaltenbrunner, and Eichmann and his staff. It was based, *inter alia*, on the Heszlényi-Homlok-Fáy idea as detailed in Himmler's letter to Ribbentrop of November 30, 1942, and on Germany's immediate needs for labor. On the Hungarian side, it involved the wholehearted cooperation of the ultra-Rightist elements of the Sztójay government and above all of those associated with the Ministry of the Interior, Baky, Endre, and Andor Jaross, who became Minister on March 22, 1944, and had immediate control over the state apparatus and the instruments of coercion: the police and the gendarmerie. Baky, Endre, and their immediate collaborators were briefed by Kaltenbrunner, who arrived in Hungary together with Horthy on March 19, and was instrumental in their appointment.

In the finalization of the master plan, the German and the Hungarian leaders had to consider: (1) The rapid advance of the Soviet forces in eastern Europe; (2) The limited German forces available for the operation;[41] (3) The necessity of acquiring the Hungarian government's help to carry out the operation; (4) The desirability to lull the large Jewish community into a false sense of security and optimism in order to minimize the risk of resistance and to induce its leadership to collaborate; and (5) The need to implement the plan with lightning speed.

The scenario as worked out by those directly involved in the operation called for a two-pronged approach: (1) The legal, political, formalistic one to provide the facade of bona fide actions authorized by Horthy and the German and the Hungarian governments; and (2) The covert, technical operation based on the master plan. Each of the many elements and agencies involved—German,

Hungarian, and Jewish—had and was to play a preassigned role, though this was not known to many of them at the time.

To satisfy the requirements of the former, Horthy was to remain in office to provide legitimacy; Veesenmayer and his staff were to provide the camouflage of international law; the Hungarian government was to provide the civil service, the police, and the gendarmerie to make possible the satisfaction of "Germany's legitimate labor needs" and the clearing of "military operational zones" of potential "saboteurs"; the Jewish Council was to be induced to collaborate by organizing the entire Jewish community and by exercising sole leadership over it; and, last but not least, the Hungarian masses, already mesmerized by decades of antisemitic propaganda, were to be persuaded that, finally, their "legitimate" demands were being fulfilled.

The covert, technical operational plan called for the: (1) Separation of Jews from the rest of the population by marking them by means of the compulsory wearing of the yellow Star of David; (2) Expropriation of their property; (3) Their systematic and accelerated internment and deportation to be effectuated on a territorial basis; (4) Deportation was to be requested by the Hungarian authorities "in view of the danger of epidemics and other hardships in the overcrowded ghettos"; (5) Lulling of the Jewish masses into submission in order to avoid the repetition of the Warsaw Ghetto uprising by trapping the leadership into unintended collaboration through a variety of reassurances and rescue and emigration schemes;[42] and (6) Total silence of the press and other media of mass communication concerning the deportations.

In accordance with this scenario, Veesenmayer's earlier request as to where in Germany the transports of Jewish laborers should be sent was duly answered by the RSHA on April 24. As relayed to Veesenmayer on April 27, the reply revealed the objection of the Sipo (*Sicherheitspolizei*; Security Police) and SD chief Ernst Kaltenbrunner to the direct assignment of Jews to work in German factories, because that would render Germany's cleansing of Jews "illusory." He saw no objection, however, to their transportation to the labor camps operating under the jurisdiction of the Reichsführer-SS, that is, to the concentration camps.[43]

The master plan, in other words, called for the selection of able-bodied Jews for labor in the Reich only after the mass arrival of the deportees in Auschwitz. As Veesenmayer stated in his telegram of May 8, 1944, the "100,000 Hungarian workers required by the Todt Organization for labor allocation in the Reich would have to be requested from the SS Main Administrative and Economic Office [*SS-Gruppenführer* Richard Glücks], which is in charge of Jews to be deported from Hungary."[44]

Under the plan worked out by the RSHA, the 100,000 able-bodied Jews represented about ten percent of the 1,000,000 Jews the Nazis expected to deport from Hungary. It was this percentage target that most probably guided Dr. Josef Mengele and the other "physicians" on the Auschwitz railway station ramp when they made their selections upon the arrival of the transports. . . .

The master plan was carried out with lightning speed thanks to the unique combination of Germanic efficiency and Hungarian brutality. Within three months the provinces were cleared of Jews by means of the deportation to Auschwitz of 437,402 persons.[45]

As the evidence clearly proves, the destruction of Hungarian Jewry was the consequence of both the German occupation and the initiatives taken by and the wholehearted cooperation of the radical Right elements in the country. The speed and efficiency with which the Final Solution was implemented are explained by the high priority the Germans attached to the military projects that were to employ 100,000 Jewish workers from Hungary. It appears that the figure of 100,000 was based upon the offer the Hungarian Right, advanced through Heszlényi, Homlok, and Fáy since January 1942, and to whose delivery Horthy agreed apparently under pressure at Klessheim in March 1944. It is probable that the Germans would have been satisfied with the delivery of 100,000 able-bodied Jewish workers, had the Hungarians—like the Bulgarians and Romanians, not to speak of the Danes and Italians—resisted the total solution of the Jewish question, which, of course, the Nazis preferred. But the first and foremost objective of the Germans in Hungary in 1944 was to keep the Magyars in line and to exploit to the maximum the country's military and economic resources in the death struggle of the Reich with the Grand Alliance. A great share of the responsibility for the extermination of the Jews must therefore be borne by the Magyars themselves. In the words of Jeno Levai, the noted Hungarian Jewish journalist and one of the foremost experts on the Holocaust in Hungary:

> Owing to their insignificant numbers, the Nazis were practically unable even to supervise the deportations, let alone to carry them out. The marking of the Jews with the Star of David, their "roundup" into ghettos and concentration camps, were made possible only by the fact that the gendarmerie—although well-acquainted with the situation and numbering some 20,000 men—could everywhere be sure of the aid of the local police. Even then the procedure could not have been carried through if the Christian population had shown resistance.

Thus it must be assumed that, quite apart from the part played by the Regent and the Sztójay Government, the chief causes for the complete sellout of the Jews were the antisemitic propaganda with which the Hungarian population had been inundated for scores of years, the stirring up of their hatred and, last but not least, the rousing of the rabble's rapacious instincts.[46]

Veesenmayer was basically correct, then, when he confessed after the war that:

> Had the Hungarians consistently refused to meet the German demands concerning the solution of the Jewish question, this could not have taken place! There would certainly have been "pressure," but as 1944 was already a year of "crisis," we would not have had sufficient power to bring about the roundup and deportation of 1,000,000 people. This is such a grandiose police task that it could have been implemented within three months only with the total and enthusiastic support of the entire military and administrative apparatus. We could not have brought in suitable forces from outside, for this job could be performed only by those who knew the country, its people, and spoke its language. Eichmann had only a small staff. The deportation could be effectuated so quickly and so smoothly only with the total help of the Hungarian Government.[47]

Nevertheless, one must keep in mind that the military and administrative apparatus, which Veesenmayer correctly identified as having enthusiastically supported the deportation program, was provided by the government which he and his Nazi colleagues imposed upon Hungary in the wake of the occupation. Consequently, first and foremost responsibility for the destruction of Hungarian Jewry must rest with the Germans, for while the Hungarian radical Rightists were eager to solve the Jewish question and whole-heartedly collaborated in the deportation program, their plans could not have been carried out in the absence of the occupation.

NOTES

1. The number of Jewish refugees in Hungary at the start of the war (June 1941) was between 30,000 and 35,000; Ernest Landau, ed., *Der Kastner-Bericht über Eichmanns Menschenhandel in Ungarn* (Munich, 1961), 45. In November 1938, Hungary acquired the so-called Upper Province (*Felvidék*), including the southern part of Slovakia, with 67,876 Jews; in March, 1939, Hungary forcibly incorporated Carpatho-Ruthenia or Sub-Carpathia (*Kárpátalja*) with 78,087 Jews; in August 1940, Hungary obtained Northern Transylvania (*Eszak Erdély*) with 164,052 Jews; and in April 1941, Hungary conquered the Backa (*Bácska*) and the adjacent areas of Yugoslavia with 14,202 Jews. Ernö László, "Hungary's Jewry: A Demographic Overview, 1918–1945," *Hungarian-Jewish Studies*, Randolph L. Braham, ed., (New York, 1969), 2: 137–82.

2. For further details, see Randolph L. Braham, "The Kamenets Podolsk and Délvidék Massacres: Prelude to the Holocaust in Hungary," in *Yad Vashem Studies*, Livia Rothkirchen, ed. (Jerusalem, 1972) IX.

3. Very little verifiable biographical data is available on Heszlényi. Recognized as one of the leading Germanophile officers, he was recommended on May 13, 1944, by Edmund Veesenmayer, German Minister and Reich Plenipotentiary in Hungary, as the best possible candidate for the position of Deputy Minister of Defense. Veesenmayer identified him as "one of the best officers enjoying great prestige in the army," who "is unimpeachable from the political point of view." György Ránki, et al., eds. and comps., *A Wilhelmstrasse és Magyarország. Német diplomáciai iratok Magyarországról, 1933–1944* (The Wilhelmstrasse and Hungary. German Diplomatic Papers About Hungary, 1933–1944) (Budapest, 1968), 847 (hereafter, *A Wilhelmstrasse és Magyarország*). . . . In connection with the Jewish question, he came into prominence again in September 1944, when as commander of the Hungarian forces that had occupied a part of southern Transylvania, he issued a series of and-Jewish edicts. A month later, he became one of the chief supporters of Ferenc Szálasi, leader of the Arrow Cross (*Nyilas Keresztes*) movement, in the coup that ousted Admiral Horthy. Professor Macartney claims that Heszlényi "killed himself on the frontier when the troops retreated into Austria." C. A. Macartney, *October Fifteenth: A History of Modern Hungary, 1929–1945* (Edinburgh, 1957) II, 340 (hereafter, Macartney). His name was listed in 1946, however, among Hungarian war criminals held by American authorities in Germany. See the letter of Major-General William S. Key to Lieutenant-General Sviridov, chairman of the Allied Control Commission in Hungary, June 12, 1946, in István Pintér and László Szabó, eds., *Criminals at Large* (Budapest, 1961), 298–99.

4. In his dispatches [from Berlin, Homlok], warned about the imminence of the Russo-German war and insisted on the necessity of Hungary's military participation on the side of the Third Reich. Following the collapse of Germany, Homlok fled to Austria, where he was "liberated" by the Americans. Shortly thereafter he was employed by the International Refugee Organization (IRO) of the United Nations in Austria and came to the United States in 1951. From 1952 to 1956, he worked for the Hungarian National Committee in New York. He retired in 1956 and died in New York in April 1963. For further details on Homlok, László Zsigmond, *et al.*, eds. and comps., *Magyarország és a második világháború* (Hungary and the Second World War) (Budapest, 1961); *A Wilhelmstrasse és Magyarország*; Elek Karsai, *A budai Sándor palotában történt* (It Happened in

the Sándor Palace of Buda) (Budapest, 1963);
and Macartney.

5. Though this proposal was apparently kept alive
until its implementation in the wake of the
German occupation in 1944, neither Admiral
Horthy nor Prime Minister Kállay made any reference to it in their memoirs. During an interview with the author on January 26, 1956, Kállay
denied having even heard of Heszlenyi.

6. See letter of Alfred Jodl, Chief of the OKW, to the
German Foreign Office, July 21, 1942, in Randolph
L. Braham, *The Destruction of Hungarian Jewry*
(New York, 1963), Document 46 (hereafter RLB).

7. Nicholas Kállay, *Hungarian Premier: A Personal
Account of a Nation's Struggle in the Second World
War* (New York, 1954), 99.

8. The roundup of the Jews of Slovakia began in
March 1942. The first transport of 999 girls was
taken to Auschwitz on March 26. By late May
1942, about 40,000 persons had been deported
from the country. Livia Rothkirchen, *The
Destruction of Slovak Jewry* (Jerusalem, 1961),
xxii–xxiii.

9. RLB, Doc. No. 46.

10. *Inland II, Geheim 58/1, 208/K213390. Auswärtiges
Amt, Akten betreffend Juden in Ungarn von August
1942 bis März 1948* (Politisches Archiv, Bonn)
[hereafter *Inl.IIg*].

11. *Inl.IIg.* 208/K213391.

12. *Inl.IIg.* 208/K213, 388–89.

13. RLB, Doc. No. 47.

14. Elek Karsai, *A budai vártól a gyepüig, 1941–1945*
(From the Fort of Buda to the Borderland, 1941–
1945) (Budapest, 1965), 203–6.

15. Jenö Levai, the noted expert on the Hungarian
Jewish catastrophe, in a personal communication dated August 25, 1971, claims that the Fay
in question was Gedeon Fáy. His full name is
Gedeon Fáy-Halasz, and in fact he served in the
Ministry of Foreign Affairs, when Prime Minister Kallay was its head. Fay served in "the Minister's Cabinet" and his title was identified in the
official register of the government as "*dr. min. s.
titk.*" (Dr. Ministerial Assistant Secretary). *Mag-

yarország tiszti cim-és névtára II, 36. In 1943, he
was promoted to head the Minister's cabinet.
Magyarország is a második világháború, 498. In
a letter to this author dated November 3, 1971,
Dr. Aladár Szegedy-Maszák, the former head
of the Political Section of the Hungarian Foreign Ministry (1943–1944), asserts that when he
was attached to the Minister's Cabinet Fáy was
"technically and administratively the personal
secretary of Kallay in his capacity as Foreign
Minister."

16. RLB, Doc. No. 74.

17. Ibid.

18. Ibid., Doc. No. 48.

19. Ibid., Docs. No. 49–50.

20. RLB, Doc. No. 96. Shortly after the German
occupation, Vay was entrusted on April 5, 1944,
by the caucus of the government party headed
by Lukacs to bring about the union of all the
Rightist forces "willing to cooperate with the
government party" in order to assure national
unity. *A Wilhelmstrasse és Magyarország*, 814.

21. RLB, Docs. No. 97, 98.

22. Ibid., Doc. No. 103.

23. Jenö Lévai, *Eichmann in Hungary* (Budapest,
1961), 55–57.

24. RLB, Doc. No. 106.

25. György Ránki, *1944. március 19* (March 19, 1944)
(Budapest, 1968), 30.

26. RLB, Doc. No. 110.

27. The Germans prepared a draft communique,
which, however, was not signed. For the text of
the communique, see *A Wilhelmstrasse es Magyarország*, 782–83.

28. For the minutes of the Crown Council meeting, see *The Confidential Papers of Admiral Horthy*,
278–90.

29. Albert Speer, *Inside the Third Reich* (New York,
1970), 395; PS-1584 reproduced in International
Military Tribunal, *Trial of the Major War Criminals Before the International Military Tribunal*
(Nuremberg, 1947–1949), 37: 351–64, 396.

30. Elek Karsai, *A budai vártól a gyepüig*, 689. See
also Speer's summary (dated April 9, 1944) of

his discussions with the Führer on April 6 and 7 relating to the employment of Jewish workers from Hungary, in Levai, *Eichmann in Hungary*, 81.

31. Macartney II, 280.

32. RLB, Doc. No. 133.

33. Ibid., Docs. No. 134–35.

34. Ibid., Docs. No. 138–41. Eichmann managed to acquire the trains from the German military authorities because of the high priority the Nazis attached to the building of the underground aircraft factories that required Hungarian Jewish labor.

35. See excerpts from the minutes of the meeting of the Council of Ministers of April 26, 1944, in Lévai, *Eichmann in Hungary*, 82.

36. RLB, Doc. No. 150. These first transports were put together not by Eichmann's *Sonderkommando* but by the *Honvédség*.

37. Veesenmayer's testimony on July 22, 1948, transcript version of Ministries Trial, 13260.

38. Levai, *Fekete könyv a magyar zsidóság szenvedéseiröl*, 128.

39. Ranki, *1944. március 19*, 175.

40. Macartney II, 283.

41. The *Einsatzgruppe* was composed of only 500 to 600 *Gestapo* and SD members who operated under the immediate command of SS-*Standartenführer* Hans Geschke, the *BdS* (*Befehlshaber der Sicherheitspolizei*, Commander of the Security Police) in Hungary. Eichmann's *Sonderkommando* had only 200 to 300 men available for the Final Solution. Macartney II, 228.

42. Among these schemes one can cite the techniques employed by the Nazis to reassure the leaders of Hungarian Jewry about the "safety" of their community; the mailing of "arrived safely" cards by the first deportees to "Waldsee" (Auschwitz) written just before they were sent into the gas chambers; the offer to sell lives for trucks and other goods (the Kasztner-Brand mission); and the saving of a handful of Jews as evidence of goodwill (the Kasztner deal).

43. RLB, Docs. No. 147 and 149.

44. Ibid., Doc. No. 158.

45. This is merely the official figure given by Veesenmayer concerning the deportations from May 15 through July 9, 1944. RLB, Docs. No. 174, 182, 193.

46. Eugene (Jenö) Lévai, *Black Book on the Martyrdom of Hungarian Jewry* (Zurich, 1948), 139.

47. Jenö Lévai, *Zsidósors Magyarországon* (Jewish Fate in Hungary) (Budapest, 1948), 101.

Papal Priorities

MICHAEL PHAYER

From *The Catholic Church and the Holocaust, 1930–1965*

Between July and October of 1941, a mobile killing squad murdered more than 18,000 Kovno Jews, including more than 5,000 children, with the help of Lithuanian Christian partisans. Before this tragedy occurred, the Jews had appealed for help to the Catholic archbishop of the city without success. The doomed Jews were walked from a ghetto of the city of Kovno to pits located about three miles out in the country, where they were shot in groups of about 500.[1] Unimaginable brutality took place. In an attempt to save her baby while en route to the killing pits, a mother tried to throw "her child over the fence [to safety], but missed her aim and the child remained hanging on the barbed wire [enclosing the ghetto]. Its screams were quickly silenced by bullets [of the guards]."[2]

Just slightly more than three months after the Kovno massacre, a member of the Berlin Catholic resistance circle, Margarete Sommer, filed this timely and accurate report:

> The Jews had to undress (it could have been eighteen degrees below freezing), then climb into "graves" previously dug by Russian prisoners of war. They were then shot with a machine gun; then grenades were tossed in. Without checking to see if all were dead, the Kommando ordered the grave filled in.[3]

Sommer's report circulated among German bishops.

Konrad Preysing, Sommer's collaborator and the bishop of Berlin, would have seen to it that Nuncio Eugenio Orsenigo became privy to the information about the work of the mobile killing squad. Preysing, the leader of those bishops who wanted the church to take a stronger stand against Hitler, also wanted the pope to know about the atrocity at Kovno. But the report never reached the Vatican. The explanation for this breakdown in communication is to be found in the special relationship between Pope Pius and Germany.

At the outset of his reign, Pius told Vatican officials that "to me the German question is the most important; I will reserve handling it to myself." He added, "Naturally I will follow German matters closer than all others."[4] The new pope appointed Luigi Maglione, a specialist in French affairs, as his secretary of state, and kept Orsenigo in Berlin as his nuncio. For the Berlin appointment, the pope wanted a person who would not undo the work he had done as nuncio and later as secretary of state, namely, maintaining the Concordat [the Treaty signed in July 1933 between the Vatican and the Reich] and German-Vatican relations. In Orsenigo, Pius had the right man for the job. A pro-German, pro-Nazi, antisemitic fascist, Orsenigo would have no trouble adjusting to the Nazi regime in Berlin.[5] In addition, Orsenigo, who hankered after a cardinal's hat, could be trusted not to interfere with Pius's own well-known intention to deal with Germany himself. Although the pope was well aware of Orsenigo's limitations and would hear more about them during the Holocaust from Bishop Konrad Preysing, he could be sure that in matters concerning Jews the nuncio would not rashly overstep Vatican policy.

Ensconced in his Berlin residence, Orsenigo took on a priest-assistant who was, secretly, a member of the Nazi party.[6] After the Concordat was signed in 1933, the nuncio urged German bishops to support Hitler's regime. Bishop Kaller (Ermland) later complained that the nuncio had "put the skids under me" by telling him to patch things up with the Nazis. Kaller, assuming that the nuncio spoke for the pope, did as he was told.[7] Later, when Bishop Clemens August von Galen publicly confronted the Nazis regarding their illegal euthanasia program, Orsenigo's report to Rome was critical of him, and when the war began, the nuncio complained that Catholics did not support it as strongly as Protestants.[8] On the occasion of Hitler's fiftieth birthday, Pope Pius told Orsenigo to congratulate the Führer warmly and publicly.[9]

Under the circumstances, it was unlikely that Nuncio Orsenigo would relay unfavorable information to Rome, especially if the information was not common knowledge. The nuncio seldom intervened on behalf of Jews.[10] Sommer's report on the Kovno massacre, which did not find its way to the Vatican, was no exception. Orsenigo became impassioned on one occasion about Nazi treatment of Jews, when a plan developed to "resettle" Jews married to Christians, but his concern actually extended more to the Christian spouses, especially if they were the wives, because of the likely impoverishment of their families.[11] At other times, when the nuncio was directed by the Holy See to discuss incidents concerning Jewish victims with Nazi officials, he did so timidly and with embarrassment.[12]

A few months after the news about the Kovno massacre ss officer Kurt Gerstein paid a surprise visit to Nuncio Orsenigo. Gerstein had just come from Belzec, where he had observed firsthand how a death camp functioned. He watched as 700 to 800 Jews were squeezed into four rooms of the Belzec gas chamber, into which the exhaust from a diesel engine was vented. Before the fumes could do their work, the motor malfunctioned and stopped. "For two hours and forty-nine minutes" (Gerstein used a stopwatch), the victims "were kept standing naked in the four chambers measuring five square yards each. When the motor was finally activated, it took thirty-two minutes to kill all of the victims."[13] Gerstein was a man with a troubled conscience. Although he served in the apparatus of the Holocaust, he wanted to end it. This is why he sought out the papal nuncio in Berlin to tell him about the Holocaust so that he could tell the pope. Not wanting to hear what Gerstein had to say about the murder of the Jews, Nuncio Orsenigo refused to see him.

Officer Gerstein turned next to the auxiliary bishop of Berlin, a member of the city's anti-Nazi clique, who received him warmly and heard him out.[14] The bishop found Gerstein's report entirely credible, as did others with whom he communicated, such as Protestant bishop Otto Dibelius. Gerstein's request that his report be sent on to Rome was fulfilled, but not, of course, by the nuncio's office. The Vatican, however, allowed Gerstein's information about the Holocaust to die; that is, it was not relayed to other countries, such as France, whose Jews had not yet been "resettled."[15] The Vatican was a dead end for information about genocide.

The lack of communication about the Holocaust between the Berlin nuncio and the Holy See also characterized the Vatican secretariat's dispatches to its nuncios and the European hierarchy. Father Josef Tiso, president of the Slovakian government when his People's Party persecuted Jews in 1941 and again in 1944, serves as an example.

When the Jewish community reacted to imminent deportations by appealing to Tiso as a priest and civic leader to intervene, his reply was to launch an investigation into how the Jews had found out about the plan.[16] The Vatican disapproved of Tiso and demoted him. Monsignor Tardini of the secretariat of state remarked that although everyone understands that the Holy See cannot displace Hitler, that it is unable to restrain a priest, no one will understand.[17]

But the Vatican never informed other European bishops of Tiso's involvement in the Holocaust. Cardinal Michael Faulhaber of Munich embarrassed himself after the war by pleading for Tiso, who had fled to Germany, to the American occupational forces: "I feel duty bound to notify the Holy Father of [your] arrest of Dr. Tiso, since as a prelate in good standing he is a member of the papal family."[18] When Tiso was returned to Slovakia, tried, and hanged, Vatican radio refused to defend him, saying, "There are certain laws that must be obeyed no matter how much one loves his country."[19] The world learned too late of the Holy See's disapproval of Tiso's involvement in the Holocaust.

Bishop Alojzije Stepinac of Zagreb provides the opposite type of illustration. The Vatican was constantly in touch with him and with Pope Pius's representative to the fascist *Ustasha* government in Croatia, Abbot Marcone. For the most part, the Holy See left it to the bishop to figure out how to censure the *Ustasha* genocide and still remain on good terms with its fascist leader, Ante Pavelic. In July and October of 1943, Stepinac condemned racial killing explicitly and bluntly. His denunciation was read from pulpits across the land. German authorities in Croatia, who took Stepinac's words as a condemnation of their Jewish policy as well as of Ustasha's anti-Serb policy, arrested thirty-one priests.[20] No leader of a national

church ever spoke about genocide as pointedly as Stepinac. His words were courageous and principled, because he—a Croat—denounced Croatian nationals at a time when Germany's war fortunes suggested that they would soon no longer be able to prop up the murderous *Ustashi*. Stepinac had no illusions about his fate should Marshal Josip Tito's Communists come to power.

Unfortunately, the Holy See let no one know that Archbishop Stepinac had dared to speak out against racism and genocide or whether it approved of his conduct. Based on Stepinac's words, the Holy See might have established guidelines for the bishops to follow regarding genocide, and based on Stepinac's actions—he gave refuge to endangered Jews and Serbs—the papacy might have held him up as a model for Catholics to emulate. But until the Cold War era, the world never heard of Stepinac.

Tiso's and Stepinac's actions were directly related to the Holocaust, but their original involvement with fascist racism antedated it. When exactly did Vatican personnel become aware of the Holocaust itself?

In October of 1941, the Vatican got reports from Charge d'Affaires Giuseppe Burzio, Slovakia, about Jews being immediately shot by Germans.[21]

In March of 1942, Burzio informed Secretary of State Maglione that 80,000 Jews were likely to be deported to a certain death, and in May he reported that they had been deported.[22]

Gerhart Riegner of the World Jewish Congress sent a memo in March 1942 to the nuncio in Bern, Monsignor Filippi Bernardini, stating that there was sufficient information from a number of sources to verify Jewish extermination.[23] (Document omitted from Vatican collection *Actes et Documents*.)

On May 12, 1942, Italian priest Pirro Scavizzi wrote to Pope Pius informing him of the mass murder of Jews; some details were inaccurate.[24]

In the summer of 1942, Abbot Ramiro Marcone wrote to Maglione telling him that Croatian Jews were to be deported to Germany and killed, and that 2 million Jews had already met this fate.[25]

Bishop Szeptyckyj of Lwow, Poland, notified the Holy See that "the number of Jews killed in this small region has certainly passed two hundred thousand."[26]

Memos of Ambassador Kazimierz Papée (Poland) and Envoy Myron C. Taylor to Secretary of State Maglione dated September 26, 1942, reported on the liquidation of the Warsaw ghetto, mass executions at special killing centers, and mass deportations of Jews from various European countries.[27]

On October 3, 1942, the Polish ambassador to the Vatican reported that all over Poland Jews were being put in camps to be murdered.[28]

Sometime in mid to late 1942, SS officer Gerstein's eyewitness report on the Belzec death camp operation became known in the Vatican. (Document omitted from the *Actes et Documents*.)

Chargé d'Affaires Tittman filed a memo on November 23, 1942, reporting on mass extermination of Jews in occupied Poland by poison gas in chambers especially prepared for that purpose and by machine-gun fire.[29]

In December of 1942, the British minister to the Vatican, Francis d'Arcy Osborne, had an audience with Pius XII in which he gave the pope the English-American-Soviet report on the systematic starvation and massacre of Jews.

Archbishop Anthony Springovics wrote Pius XII on December 12, 1942, that most of the Jews of Riga, Latvia, had been killed.[30]

An estimate of the quality of the information that flowed into the Vatican may be deduced from reports on the fate of some 80,000 Slovak Jews. In the spring of 1942, the Vatican heard from three sources—Nuncio Rotta (Hungary), Nuncio Bernardini (Switzerland), and Chargé d'Affaires Burzio (Slovakia)—that these Jews would be deported and killed. In June, confirmation of these reports came from the Polish government in exile in London. By the end of 1942, the Holy See had received accounts about the ongoing murder of Jews from at least nine different countries where the Holocaust took place, including occupied Poland itself.

Yet the Vatican avoided coming to the conclusion that genocide was occurring in Europe. In response to Taylor's September genocide memo, Secretary Maglione responded that the papacy had also heard of "reports of severe measures taken against non-Aryans" from sources other than Taylor, "but that up to the present time it has not been possible to verify the accuracy" of the reports.[31] What kind of confirmation, beyond the tracking of Slovak Jews, was Cardinal Maglione looking for? In fact, Taylor's memo verified a report that the secretariat had received just a few days previously from an Italian source: "The massacres of the Jews have reached proportions and forms which are horribly frightful. Incredible killings take place every day."[32] Secretary Maglione's response to Taylor appears to have been less than truthful. The fact was that the Holy See did not make public the reliable Holocaust reports of church leaders or members of its diplomatic corps; nor did it circulate them privately among Vatican diplomats and church leaders in Europe.

In the final months of 1942, President Roosevelt's personal envoy to the Vatican, Myron C. Taylor, and England's Minister Francis d'Arcy Osborne put considerable pressure on the pope to denounce the Holocaust. Osborne was outraged: "Is there not a moral issue at stake which does not admit of neutrality?"[33] After his audience with the Holy Father, Taylor had a more explicit discussion with Monsignor Tardini, during which Taylor said, "I'm not asking the pope to speak out against Hitler, just about the atrocities." Tardini wrote in his diary, "I could not but agree."[34]

The failure of the Vatican to exchange atrocity information with Taylor was critical because it came at a time when England and the United States were attempting to verify what turned out to be very reliable information about ongoing ethnic cleansing and about Nazi plans to exterminate all Jews. U.S. Undersecretary of State Sumner Welles and Rabbi Stephen S. Wise worked intensely to verify rumors about the atrocities, but, as historian Richard Breitman has noted, Myron Taylor "was unable to gather much information" at the Vatican.[35]

The pressure on the Holy See from the United States, England, and a host of other countries to break out of its silence about the Holocaust led Secretary Maglione to promise that the pope would speak about the issue. This he did in his 1942 Christmas address. Pope Pius's radio talk contained twenty-seven words about the Holocaust out of twenty-six pages of text. The part about the Holocaust, buried in a sea of verbosity, did not mention Jews. A few months later, Pius wrote to Bishop Preysing in Berlin saying that his address was well understood. In reality, very few people understood him, and no one, certainly not the Germans, took it as a protest against their slaughter of the Jews.[36]

In the following year, 1943, more Holocaust news and events came into the Vatican.

In January, Pius XII received a letter from Wladislas Raczkiewicz, president of the Polish government in exile, detailing Nazi horrors in Poland.[37]

Bishop Preysing wrote to Pope Pius on March 6, 1943, to tell him of the roundup of Jews in Berlin that had taken place from February 27th to March 1st. Preysing indicated that their deportation probably meant their death. They were in fact sent directly from their workplaces in Berlin to Auschwitz and gassed immediately, without even being registered.

Just as Pius received Preysing's appeal for intervention regarding Berlin Jews, Hungarian Catholic activist Margit Slachta asked him in a personal audience to intervene to save Slovakian Jews.

On July 16, 1943, Father Marie-Benoit Peteul of Marseilles had an audience with the pope to plead for his help in rescuing Jews in the Italian-occupied part of France.

The Holy See was itself a witness to the October 1943 roundup of the Jews of Rome.

From April to June 1944, the nuncio to Hungary, Angelo Rotta, notified the Holy See of the deportations of Jews to Auschwitz.[38]

By the end of 1943, it was simply no longer possible for the Vatican to deny that Germany was perpetrating a genocide. Already in the spring of that year, Secretary Maglione himself wrote that of the 4.5 million Polish Jews (his figure) living in Poland before the war, only 100,000 remained:

After months and months of transports of thousands and thousands of persons about whom nothing more is known, this can be explained in no other way than death. . . . Special death camps near Lublin and near Brest Litovsk. It is told that they are locked up several hundred at a time in chambers where they are finished off with gas.[39]

At approximately the same time that Maglione made this admission, Monsignor Antoni Czarnecki, pastor of a Warsaw parish, sent the Vatican details concerning the mass deportations and gassings at nearby Treblinka and of the ghetto uprising.[40]

The realization that genocide was taking place did not spur the Vatican to change its policies regarding the Holy Land. It was Catholics and their rights that Pius thought about when the question of Jewish escape to Palestine arose. Historian John Conway has pointed out that the Vatican never wavered from its path regarding Palestine, even in the middle of the Holocaust, when that land offered Jews one of the last hopes of escape. In May of 1943, Cardinal Secretary of State Maglione said that Catholics had a right to the holy places, and that their "religious feelings would be injured and they would justly feel for their rights if Palestine belonged exclusively to the Jews."[41] The Vatican repeated this position even when the failure of the Allies at the Bermuda conference to deal specifically with the rescue of Jews at the height of the Holocaust doomed them.

The Silence of the Holy See

Secretary Maglione did not share his terrible knowledge about the murder of the Jews with anyone outside the Vatican; nor were any of the other details about the Holocaust made known to the world. Thus, the policy to conceal information about genocide, which began in Croatia and Slovakia, continued when all European Jews began to be murdered. The reports about the Holocaust that the Vatican would continue to receive from the middle of 1943 to the end of 1944 it kept to itself. The German ambassador to the Vatican wrote that although Rome had always been considered a good listening post for diplomats, there was actually little current informa-

tion. This was true; an absence of communication characterized the highest levels of the hierarchy. A German bishop complained in 1941 that the country's bishops had heard nothing from Rome, nothing from Nuncio Orsenigo, and little from each other.[42] In the same year, two other German bishops, having heard that 10,000 Jews would be sent from Austria to the General Government in Poland, asked each other "whether the episcopacy should intervene for them out of humanitarian concern or whether this must be left up to Rome to do."[43] Catholic bishops felt the need of a coordinated policy.

It was not as if Germany's bishops were out of touch with the Holy See. Pius's letters to individual prelates during the war years number well over a hundred. He wrote eighteen times to Bishop Preysing alone, eleven times to Cardinal Bertram, and nine times to Cardinal Faulhaber.[44] But Pius never divulged to them the horrible news that the Vatican had learned in 1942 and confirmed in 1943, namely, that Germany had built extermination centers in occupied Poland where millions were being murdered. Rather, Pius commiserated with German bishops about their bombed-out cities and churches, recalling with fondness his years in Germany and the particular churches, now in ruins, where he had celebrated this or that holy day liturgy.[45] When the war turned against Germany, Pius assured its church leaders that he was praying daily, almost hourly, for peace.

But he almost never said a word about the Jews. Writing to Bishop Preysing, Pius said in April of 1943 that he was heartened to hear that Berlin Catholics were showing empathy for the city's Jews. To fend off Preysing, who pressured him more than any other Catholic bishop to speak out about the Holocaust, Pius adroitly put the blame on the United States. Recalling that a few years earlier in 1939 Bishop Preysing had urged him to assist emigrating Jews, Pius said that he "didn't want to mention all the difficulties the United States made for Jewish immigration."[46] Of course, it is true that the United States had been painfully negligent in the matter, not even admitting the allowed quota of Jews. But the difference between disallowing immigration of foreign nationals and persecuting and killing one's own citizens need not be belabored. The pope used the United States as a dodge for failing in what Bishop Preysing believed was his responsibility.

At times, lack of communication became miscommunication. In November 1943, Cardinal Bertram of Breslau wrote the Vatican secretary of state asking what could be done to provide the last sacraments for those being condemned to death and summarily executed in occupied Poland. Instead of telling Bertram that it would be impossible to get permission to provide the last sacraments for the victims because Germans were murdering them by the tens and hundreds of thousands, Maglione assured him that the Vatican was doing everything it could through local church officials (in Poland) to get permission to spend the sacraments.[47] There was clear intent here to conceal the facts about genocide.

Nor did the Holy See share its information about the Holocaust with Catholic resistance movements that were trying to save Jews. Volume eight of the Vatican's World War II documents contains numerous reports from French bishops and Nuncio Valerio Valeri that briefed the Holy See on their statements opposing Vichy antisemitic policies, made known the courageous rescue work of the *Témoignage Chrétien* group, and gave voice to their fears for the Jews. But one looks in vain in this and subsequent volumes of the documents for any kind of response from the Vatican regarding Jews.[48] It would have been quite possible to share information about the Holocaust with

Zegota in Poland, with Catholic resistance movements in greater Germany that were centered in Berlin and Vienna, and with the *Témoignage Chrétien* circle in France. Historian Gerhard Weinberg believes that had Pope Pius spoken out about the murder of the Jews, many more Catholics would have had the courage to hide them.[49] Such encouragement, even given privately, would certainly have bolstered the work of the four groups mentioned here.

How could the Holy See have supported the work of these groups? Rescue work required organization and numbers as much as courage. Because of food rationing and the frequent relocation of refugees, rescue work was more of a group than an individual activity. The French newsletter *Cahiers du Témoignage Chrétien* sought to inspire people to become active by reminding readers of Pius XI's "Spiritually we are Semites" statement and by urging action. "The church cannot disinterest itself in the fate of man, wherever his inviolable rights are unjustly threatened."[50] The *Cahiers* was clandestinely delivered to all French bishops and to thousands of priests and laypeople—even Pétainists read it. As early as the end of 1942 the *Cahiers* affirmed, based on information from Cardinal Hlond, that hundreds of thousands of Jews had been murdered in gas chambers; in 1943, it reported that Hitler intended to exterminate all the Jews of Europe. Had the newsletter received confirmation of this information from the Holy See, or had it received encouragement from Pius XII similar to that of his predecessor, some French bishops would have continued after 1942 to protest the deportation of Jews, and more French Catholics would have become involved in rescue work. No, the Holocaust would not have been stopped, but as Elie Wiesel has written, "the trains rolling toward [Auschwitz] would have been less crowded."[51]

The *Zegota* rescue circle in Poland had no need of Holocaust information; they had first-hand knowledge of the gruesome details. But the papacy could have assisted them with money. Since Polish Catholics had been the first victims of Nazi aggression and had felt totally abandoned by the papacy, any Vatican support of Jews, when their hour of desperation came, may have angered Poles. As we have seen, however, after the battle of Stalingrad, Polish church leaders became reconciled to Pius's ways. Certainly, more Poles would have been swayed to help rescue Jews if they had known the work had Rome's blessing. *Zegota* had need of money because Polish Catholics would not always harbor a Jew altruistically, and even if they would, they often did not have the money needed to feed extra mouths.

Could the Vatican have given financial support to resistance groups such as *Zegota* and *Témoignage Chrétien*? Early in the war, the Vatican transferred all or nearly all of its liquid assets to the Chase Manhattan Bank of New York and converted them to dollars. The Holy See then requested that some of the money be used to buy Swiss currency to allow it to carry out its work in various European countries. The U.S. Treasury Department hesitated to allow this, since some of the countries in question were occupied by Germany. Permission was nevertheless given, because the money would be used for charitable purposes and would not benefit the Nazi regime to any significant degree. During the war years, the Vatican budget for its operations in Europe fluctuated between 1.3 and 2.2 million dollars. By converting some of the dollars into Swiss franks, the Vatican could finance its work in Nazi-occupied Europe.[52] Clearly, the Holy See could have supported rescue operations. As it was, *Zegota* and *Témoignage Chrétien* depended solely on the Polish government-in-

exile and on American Jewish organizations for infusions of cash.

Pius XII's Hope for a Diplomatic Role

A second important theme to consider is the reasons that the Holy See gave for not speaking out about the Holocaust. One such explanation was that it was unnecessary because whenever and wherever cardinals and bishops denounced Nazi crimes, or other crimes throughout the world, they spoke for the pope. This is precisely what American Chargé d'Affaires Tittman was told in September of 1942.[53] On this occasion the Holy See specified France and Germany, among other countries, but as we have seen, Pope Pius failed to tell German bishops what their country was doing to the Jews. It was disingenuous for the Holy See to make the claim that bishops spoke for the Vatican when the pope withheld the very information from them that would have disposed them to speak out more explicitly. This was particularly true of France, because of the *Témoignage Chrétien* circle, but was even more critical in Germany's case.

With the exception of the very guarded terms of the 1942 Christmas message, Pope Pius did not speak out publicly about the Holocaust; nor did he disseminate information about it privately through the Vatican's effective network of nuncios. At various times the Holy See gave different reasons for papal silence, some of which ring true and some of which ring hollow. Pius XII often repeated what he had told the Italian ambassador to the Vatican in 1940: "We would like to utter words of fire against such actions [German atrocities] and the only thing restraining Us from speaking is the fear of making the plight of the victims even worse."[54] This justification cannot be taken seriously. The statement made to the Italian ambassador referred to Polish Catholic victims whose church leaders—both those in occupied Poland and those in exile—repeatedly begged the pope to condemn German aggression. Pius reiterated the argument that he had given the Italian ambassador in an address to the College of Cardinals in June 1943. By this time—post-Stalingrad—church leaders in Poland had reversed themselves and agreed that it was better for the pope not to speak out.

Taking this argument seriously, apologists for Pope Pius point to the Dutch case. After Archbishop of Utrecht Johannes de Jong publicly protested against Nazi treatment of Jews in July 1942, the Germans retaliated by seizing Catholics of Jewish descent, including Edith Stein (Sister Benedicta).[55] The Vatican often reverted to Holland's experience to explain its own silence during the years of the Holocaust. Pius XII's housekeeper and sometime confidante, Sister M. Pasqualina Lehnert, recalled after the war that after the pope found out about the roundup of Catholic Jews in Holland, he quickly formulated a sharp protest condemning the Nazi action on two large sheets of paper. Then, almost immediately, the pope had second thoughts. Fearing further Nazi retaliation against the Dutch, Pius destroyed his statements, burning them in the kitchen of the Vatican's papal quarters (and, Sister Pasqualina emphasized, remaining there until the flames had completely consumed the document).[56]

Is this story credible? Even assuming that Sister Pasqualina's memory served her correctly (her memoirs were not published until 1983), several problems or questions arise in connection with the Dutch pretext. Earlier, during the Croatian genocide, when Pius might have assumed that he could have restrained the country's Catholic regime from slaughtering Jews and Orthodox Serbs, he said nothing. After January 1940,

Pius said nothing about atrocities against Poles even when the victims themselves begged him to, thereby relieving him of his concern about worsening their plight. About the October 1943 roundup of Roman Jews—much closer to home than the roundup in Holland—Sister Pasqualina has no recollection at all of her beloved mentor's reaction. Finally, if Pope Pius refrained from speaking out so as not to endanger Christians of Jewish descent in Europe, why did he not speak out after the Nazis murdered them? In short, although the Vatican frequently used the Dutch case to explain papal silence, we must look elsewhere for the actual explanations.

A second reason for not condemning the Holocaust—one more imputed than asserted—concerns Pius XII's fondness for Germans. That Pius was a Germanophile there can be no doubt. He had made his mark as a young diplomat in Germany by skillfully concluding concordats with several states. As we have seen, when he became pope, he insisted on having hands-on control when it came to German matters. Pope Pius chose German nationals as his closest advisers, and he delighted in charming Germans with his facility with their language and knowledge of minutiae about their country.[57]

But it is difficult to conclude that Pius's love of Germany weighed heavily in his consideration not to speak out about the Holocaust. Although both Belgian and German historians have accused Pius of letting his attitude toward Germany lead to bias in his diplomacy, the pope retained sufficient impartiality to send messages of sympathy to Belgium, Luxembourg, and Holland when Germany invaded them, even if he did not condemn Hitler's aggression.[58] Pius also knew, as did German bishops, that if Hitler won the war and succeeded in nazifying Europe, a final and decisive showdown would be launched against Christianity and the Catholic church. Pius was pro-German, not pro-Hitler.

Two other facets of the question of the pope's love of Germany deserve mention. Pius apparently expressed his apprehension that by denouncing exterminations in occupied Poland he would bring German Catholics into a conflict of conscience, since they served in Hitler's army or supported the war effort on the home front.[59] If this is to be taken seriously, it would mean, first, that the pope was prepared to sacrifice Polish Catholics for German Catholics and, second, that Pius feared that Germans, forced to choose between Hitler and their church, would follow their Führer. Pope Pius is in fact on record as telling Chargé d'Affaires Tittman that he could not speak out early fall 1942 because the "German people, in the bitterness of their defeat, will reproach him later on for having contributed, if only indirectly, to this defeat."[60] The statement is surprising and disconcerting—surprising because in the fall of 1942 Germany's ultimate defeat could not be predicted, and disconcerting because of the warped standard that is implied—German disappointment with the pope as opposed to millions of innocently murdered Jews.

While these statements are not to be denied, we should beware of placing too much value on isolated individual remarks. From time to time Pope Pius or his secretary of state would, under pressure, respond variously about why the Holy See had not spoken out. It is clear from Pius's correspondence with German bishops that he would not have objected to their challenging Hitler about the Holocaust, although he did not advise them to do this. Thus, the remark made to Tittman cannot be taken as the entire reason for the pope's silence or as the sum total of the Vatican's position on the question of the murder of the Jews.

Pius XII's assertion to Tittman in December of 1942 can be viewed similarly. Pius said that he could not condemn Nazi atrocities without also condemning Soviet atrocities, "which might not be wholly pleasing to the Allies."[61] It is completely unclear to what Soviet atrocities Pius was referring. Was it to the Stalin purges? They had occurred five years earlier, well before the beginning of the Second World War and were already well known. Was it to the Katyn Forest massacre of German officers? Germany had not yet even charged the Soviets with this atrocity. Thus, the remark appears to be a temporizing exercise. Tittman was put off for the time being.

To find the actual reasons for Pius XII's silence about the Holocaust, we must look beyond these occasional stopgap statements and objections toward two concerns of utmost importance to the pope: his desire to play the role of a diplomatic peacemaker, savior of western Europe from communism, and his fear that Rome and the Vatican, entirely defenseless, would be obliterated by aerial attacks before the war came to an end.

Years after the end of the war, Robert Leiber, the German Jesuit who was one of Pius's closest confidants, made clear the connection between the pope's silence about the Holocaust and his diplomacy. The reason that Pius XII did not speak out about the murder of the Jews, Leiber confided to the Dutch historian Ger van Roon, was that he wanted to play the peacemaker during the war.[62] To safeguard his credentials for such a role, the Holy See had to preserve Vatican City's status as an independent state and neutral government. Pius's role model in this respect was Pope Benedict XV, whose efforts to negotiate a European peace during World War I had impressed a younger Eugenio Pacelli.[63] There would have been nothing negligent about this policy had it not kept Pius from dealing adequately with the Holocaust. In his postwar report to the British Home Office, Minister Francis Osborne said that Pius had at his disposal two strong weapons against Nazi criminality—"excommunication and martyrdom."[64] Pius did not use these, Osborne said, because he wanted to be the mediator of a negotiated peace. Thus, the Englishman, Osborne, a close observer of Pius, and the German, Leiber, his trusted adviser, are in full agreement on this point.

An effort to explain Pius's preoccupation with diplomacy would be somewhat speculative, but the consistency of this preoccupation lies beyond doubt. Because Pius wanted to see a Catholic state in place of Yugoslavia, he did not condemn the Catholic fascists in Croatia when they perpetrated genocide against Orthodox Christians. The Vatican secretariat of state actually treated the murderous *Ustashi* like children who "make mistakes" and who would have to learn to behave if they wanted the pope to recognize their state. . . . Croatian bishop Stepinac's tardy condemnation of the *Ustasha* genocide may be explained by the priority the Holy See gave to diplomatic negotiations. Nor did Pius condemn the Nazis for murdering Catholic Poles. Rather, his preference was to have Nuncio Orsenigo press Hitler to recognize the Polish-Vatican Concordat. The next major genocidal victims during the war years were the Jews. Bishop Konrad Preysing of Berlin wanted Pope Pius to recall his nuncio to Germany, break off diplomatic relations with the murderous Nazi regime, and condemn the Holocaust. Acting with consistency, Pius declined to do so.

In the latter case there were additional reasons for Pius XII's reluctance to part company diplomatically with Germany. The pontiff viewed Germany as the key to the European chessboard that pitted Bolshevism against Christianity. In his mind, Germany was and would remain the European bulwark against Russian communism; he wished, therefore, to preserve the country intact. From the beginning of the war to its very end, Pius sought to undo the consequences of the First World War by enlarging Germany. Even as Germany's fate became clear late in the war, Pius wrote to Cardinal Michael Faulhaber of Munich in 1944 indicating that in a negotiated peace Germany should not have to give up Austria and the Sudeten province of Czechoslovakia![65]

Historian Klemens von Klemperer has reviewed the Holy See's contacts with German anti-Nazi resistance and Pius's efforts to negotiate between them and England to overthrow Hitler. Although both sides were unclear about the details of a possible understanding, the status quo following the Munich Conference, which had awarded the Sudetenland to Germany, was the point of departure.[66] Pius wanted a powerful Germany without Hitler, and he seriously underestimated German ambitions, even of those Germans who opposed their dictator.[67]

Pius's concentration on diplomacy persisted. When the United States and Germany became World War II belligerents in 1941, Pius was disappointed. He had hoped to team up with President Roosevelt to negotiate a peace.[68] But a negotiated peace was precisely what the Allies did not want. The American president made the mistake of sending his envoy to the pope in 1942 to ask him not to seek a negotiated peace, and to tell him that the Allies would win the war as a moral crusade against evil. Pope Pius would naturally have taken exception to this, because in his mind the "moral crusade" should be directed against Communist Russia, and because he wanted to display world leadership himself by negotiating a peace. When President Roosevelt and Prime Minister Winston Churchill called for an unconditional surrender in their 1942 declaration at Casablanca, Pope Pius found himself cut out of the picture altogether.

A negotiated peace became an overriding concern for the Holy See. Before Stalingrad, Pius believed that the Americans should help the Russians, but with reservations, so that hostilities on the eastern front remained far from Germany. After the battle of Stalingrad and the successful Allied invasion of southern Italy in July 1943, Pius hoped that England and the United States would abandon the Russians so that Germany could deal with the Communist threat. Ideally, he hoped England would recognize the danger to the Christian west that communism posed, and conclude a separate peace with the Axis powers.[69] This would pay a second dividend: Rome would no longer be threatened with air raids.

When Germany switched ambassadors to the Vatican in 1943, Pius tried to impress the departing Diego von Bergen and the newly appointed Ernst von Weizsäcker with his belief in a powerful Germany to withstand the Marxist threat from the east. If the Nazis would just live up to the terms of the Concordat, Pope Pius could support a German mission against Russia.[70] After his first private audience with the pope, Weizsäcker reported to Berlin that "hostility to Bolshevism is, in fact, the most stable component of Vatican foreign policy," and that "the Anglo-American link with the Soviet Russia is detested by the [Holy See]."[71]

The combination of Russian successes on the eastern front, the invasion of Italy by Anglo-American forces, and the fall of Mussolini (July 1943) led to a very noticeable increase in Communist activity in Rome and northern Italy, where a number of Catholic priests were murdered by Communist guerrillas. This disturbed Pope Pius, particularly because of vehement antichurch Communist propaganda. Still, the Vatican refrained from promoting a separate Italian peace with the Allies, because it would necessarily weaken Germany. The radical cure for Italian communism lay in the defeat of Communist Russia.

But Communist agitation in Rome was close to home, and it rested uneasily on Pius's mind. It would necessarily have reminded him of the tumultuous days in Munich at the end of the Great War when he had himself faced down a gun-toting Red revolutionary. Pius's concern over Italian Communist activity coincided with Germany's concern about Rome's Jews, whom they wished to "resettle." When the roundup of hundreds of Jews took place in October 1943 just outside Vatican city, Ambassador Weizsäcker and other Germans held their breath to see if the pope would protest. He did not, but three days later he requested that Germany increase its police manpower in Rome in order to cut down on Communist agitation.[72]

The same priority of concerns was reflected several months later, in December 1943, when a Vatican consultation about Germany was intercepted by Berlin or allowed to leak out by the Holy See. *Reichssicherheitshauptamt* (Reich Security Main Office) chief Ernst Kaltenbrunner sent a memorandum to Joachim von Ribbentrop, German minister for foreign affairs, which reported that the main obstacles to a loyal relationship between the church and National Socialism lay in the latter's euthanasia and sterilization policies. The murder of the Jews was left out of the equation.[73]

Pius XII's response to the Allies' Casablanca ultimatum for an unconditional surrender was to call for a peace of justice rather than a peace of force in his 1943 Christmas address.[74] Sitting on the diplomatic sidelines, Pius referred derisively to the "Big Three" in conversation with Germany's Ambassador Weizsäcker.[75] Pius had been upset with Germany when Hitler negotiated a non-aggression pact with Russia and invaded western Europe, but when the dictator returned to his quest for *Lebensraum* and invaded Russia in 1941, the pope became visibly emotional in conversation with the Spanish ambassador about what appeared to be the German defeat of the Communist menace.[76] Because in Pius's mind Germany remained the last line of defense against Russian communism, the pope frequently discussed schemes for a negotiated peace with Weizsäcker.[77]

The troubling aspect of Pius's preoccupation with diplomacy was that Jews would continue to be murdered as peace negotiations were under way. Hundreds of thousands of Jews were murdered during the time period between the battle of Stalingrad and the end of the war. Instead of confronting Weizsäcker with these crimes, Pius discussed peace negotiations with him. The subject of the Jews and their fate never came up. During 1943, Pius's attention remained riveted on his church and the potential danger to it from aerial attacks and from communism. Historian Saul Friedländer asks, "How is it conceivable that at the end of 1943 the pope and the highest dignitaries of the church were still wishing for victorious resistance by the Nazis in the east and therefore seemingly accepted by implication the maintenance, however temporary, of the entire Nazi extermination machine?"[78] . . .

Although Catholics and non-Catholics inside and outside the diplomatic corps reminded Pius of his role as a moral leader with reference to the Holocaust, he concentrated on diplomacy, often to the exclusion of genocide. The pope allowed the Vatican to become involved with German resistance in an attempt to overthrow Hitler. Later, when Italy wearied of the war, Pius again violated the Vatican's neutrality by allowing England's minister to the Holy See to be an intermediary between England and Italy.[79] But when it came to the Holocaust, strict diplomatic rules were adhered to. The Holy See did not allow its diplomatic offices to involve themselves in the negotiations with England and the United States that

were necessary to ensure safe passage across the Mediterranean for the Jews in the Italian zone of France, who were desperately seeking to avoid deportation to Auschwitz.[80]

As the Holocaust lingered on into the latter years of the war, Pius wearied of hearing about the Jews. "I remember," Polish ambassador to the Vatican Kazimierz Papée recalled, "when I came to see the Holy Father for . . . perhaps the tenth time in 1944; he was angry. When he saw me as I entered the room and stood at the door awaiting permission to approach, he raised both his arms in a gesture of exasperation. 'I have listened again and again to your representations about Our unhappy children in Poland,' he said. 'Must I be given the same story yet again?'"[81] Even though ambassador Papée and western diplomats repeatedly pressed Pius about the Holocaust, the pope omitted time and again to discuss it with Germany's Ambassador Weizsäcker, who would later be found guilty of war crimes against Jews at the Nuremberg Trials.

Pope Pius's Concern about the Possible Bombardment of Rome

The correspondence and dispatches of the German ambassador and the American envoy to the Vatican make it clear that Pope Pius's second great concern was the possible bombing of Rome, not the murder of the Jews. With the Holocaust in full force, the Vatican's diplomatic staff and the pope himself devoted most of their energy to ensuring that neither Germany nor the Allies would bomb Rome. This became possible for the Allies after General Erwin Rommel's *Panzerkorps* had been pushed out of northern Africa, allowing English and American troops to cross the Mediterranean and occupy Sicily. Driving German forces from mountainous southern Italy proved a more difficult task, one that lasted from the summer of 1943 to the summer of 1944. During these months of acute danger, the Holy See communicated directly with Envoy Taylor or Chargé d'Affaires Tittman no fewer than thirty-four times in an effort to forestall the bombing of Rome.[82]

The problem facing Pius XII was that he had failed to condemn the German bombing of England during 1940 and 1941, but then spoke out against the bombing of civilians when the Allies gained aerial superiority. Perhaps Pius's words of affection for German air-raid victims resulted from the ferocity and duration of allied attacks after Marshal Hermann Göring's air force had become totally defenseless. Still, by expressing sympathy and concern for Germany's bombed-out churches after not having regretted the Nazi destruction of Coventry Cathedral in England, the pope had made a serious tactical mistake.[83]

In October 1942, when Taylor attempted to extract a promise from Winston Churchill not to bomb Rome, the prime minister refused to commit himself. Pius continued to hope that he could get the Americans to persuade the English not to bomb Rome, but Myron Taylor delicately pointed out that this might be difficult: "I am not clear," he told Monsignor Montini, "whether the Holy See has condemned the bombing of London, Warsaw, Rotterdam, Belgrade, Coventry, Manila, Pearl Harbor, and places in the South Pacific."[84] Early in 1943, Foreign Secretary Anthony Eden, addressing Parliament, stoked Pope Pius's anxiety when he said that "we have as much right to bomb Rome as the Italians had to bomb London. We shall not hesitate to do so to the best of our ability and as heavily as possible if the course of the war should render such bombing convenient and helpful."[85]

President Roosevelt tried to be more conciliatory. He promised that no American aircraft would drop bombs over the Vatican. The Holy See continued to press the issue relentlessly, both through Envoy Taylor and through the apostolic delegate to the United States, trying to exact promises that Vatican property outside Vatican City would also not be harmed. Roosevelt, somewhat exasperated, finally gave instructions that the apostolic delegate should be informed that "war is war," and that with the Germans in charge of the city of Rome, no further promises would be forthcoming.[86] The Holy See responded that if Vatican property were indeed bombed, the pope would protest publicly.[87] No such threat was ever made regarding the murder of the Jews.

It exasperated observers, both inside and outside the Vatican, that the pope would be so concerned over what had not yet taken place and so little concerned over the ongoing murder of the Jews. Cardinal Tisserant remarked as early as 1940 that the pope dwelt too much on the danger of Rome's being bombed and not enough on the affairs of the church.[88] In September, Myron Taylor told Montini that the "deplorable inhumanities in Germany against civilian populations are even more reprehensible than the attacks on all her neighbors whom she invaded."[89] Minister Osborne put it to the Vatican secretary of state more bluntly on December 14, 1942: "Instead of thinking of nothing but the bombing of Rome, [the Holy See] should consider [its] duties in respect to the unprecedented crime against humanity of Hitler's campaign of extermination of the Jews."[90]

Bishop Preysing, writing to Pius from heavily bombed Berlin, adopted the perspective that Minister Osborne found lacking in the pope. "Even more bitter [events than the air raids] face us here in Berlin with the new wave of Jewish deportations that were put in motion just before the first of March [1943]." Preysing then asked the pope to speak out again about the Holocaust.[91] Six months later, in October 1943, Pope Pius was confronted with the precise choice that Bishop Preysing had put to him so pointedly—deportation of Jews versus aerial bombardment. It was at that time that the Reich Security Main Office moved to deport the Jews of Rome to Auschwitz.

When the catastrophe struck the Roman Jews, the bombing of the Basilica of San Lorenzo, which took place in July, still weighed heavily on the pope's mind. Although President Roosevelt had assured Pope Pius in May 1943 that no American planes would drop bombs over the Vatican, the city of Rome was hit on numerous occasions. The Basilica of San Lorenzo was badly damaged. Pius wrote President Roosevelt expressing his anguish: "In person We have visited and with sorrow contemplated the gaping ruins of that ancient and priceless Papal Basilica of St. Laurence."[92] Later, Undersecretary Montini called Taylor's assistant, Tittmann, on the carpet for not expressing promptly enough his regrets about the bombing to the Holy Father.

In November, bombs fell on Vatican City itself, slightly damaging St. Peter's Basilica and other structures. These attacks, together with the unnecessary destruction by the Allies of the Abbey of Montecassino south of Rome, chagrined Vatican personnel. Pope Pius visited the damaged churches of Rome, commiserated with the Romans, and took the unprecedented step of granting a plenary indulgence for victims of air raids.[93] The evening of the day on which San Lorenzo was bombed, Pope Pius wept as he prayed the rosary while looking out over the city of Rome from his Vatican quarters.[94] When Vatican City itself became the victim of an air raid, the Holy See assumed, incorrectly as it turned out, that an American plane was to blame.[95] Because of all of the destruction by the Allies, Ambassador Weizsäcker could report to Berlin that Germany was winning the propaganda war.[96] How could

this be, survivor and historian Saul Friedländer has asked, at a time when the pope was aware of the nature of Hitler's regime?[97]

In his correspondence with Bishop Preysing, Pope Pius made no secret of his priorities. Responding to the Berlin prelate, who had urged the pope to address the Holocaust, Pius asserted that the most pressing problem facing him lay in maintaining the absolute trust of Catholics, regardless of which side they fought for, so as to ensure the church's unity. Pius felt that if Rome became contested by Germans on one side and Anglo-Americans on the other, this trust would be in jeopardy.[98] Pius also defended his policy by saying that he was conscience bound to bring all the pressure he could muster on the Allies not to bomb Rome. Catholics the world over, he said, saw the Eternal City as the center of Christendom and the birthplace of the church. As such, Rome symbolized the universal nature of the church. Should this symbol be destroyed, Pius affirmed, faith and hope among Catholics would be shaken.

What Pope Pius told Bishop Preysing, he could not tell the rest of the world. The fortunes of the war made the threat of Allied bombardment greater than bombardment by Germany so long as Pius remained silent about the murder of the Jews. The Holy See dared not link its concern over the possible bombing of Rome to its silence about the Holocaust because of the implication that the murder of Europe's Jews was a lesser priority.

Earlier Pius had assured Bishop Preysing that he was doing all that he could for the persecuted Jews, that he deeply sympathized with them, and that he prayed for them. The pontiff asserted that what he had said about the persecution of the Jews in his 1942 Christmas address "was short but well understood," and he said that he intended to speak out again when the circumstances were right.[99]

Whatever circumstances the pope had in mind evidently never came to pass.

The inconsistencies of papal policy relative to the Holocaust may best be understood in the light of Pius's assumptions and priorities. These were, first, that the welfare of Catholic states took precedence over the interests of Jews. The Holy See used diplomacy rather than (public) moral strictures to attempt to curtail the involvement of Slovakia and Croatia in genocide. Pius XII did not want to undercut popular support for the fledgling governments of these new Catholic countries by threatening their leaders with excommunication. The same policy held in western Europe for Catholic Vichy France. The Vatican avoided interfering with the "resettlement" of Jews after a sharp government warning following the courageous statements of a number of French bishops.

Second, the long-term danger that communism potentially held for the church preoccupied Pope Pius.[100] His assumption that Germany would be the west's defense against bolshevism ensured that Pius's diplomatic course would be rocky, since Hitler instigated both the Second World War and the Holocaust. But Pius stayed his course inflexibly. The Vatican warned Slovakian leaders that "resettlement" meant perdition for its Jews, but only months later Pius allowed the Germans to "resettle" the Jews of Rome without uttering a word. Earlier, before the German occupation of Italy, the Vatican and officials in Mussolini's government had cooperated smoothly to save Jews. When the Germans took control of the country, the Vatican refrained from even approaching them on behalf of Jews.[101]

Pius's assumptions and priorities are clearly set forth in his letters to Bishop Preysing in 1943 and 1944. He wanted his German friend from Weimar years to know that he cared about the Jews, but

that his first concern was for the Catholic church, its universality and unity. Pius may have feared that communicating throughout the church word of the murders perpetrated by the Catholic *Ustasha*, the complicity in genocide of Catholic Slovak priest Tiso, and the crimes of Catholic Austrians and Germans committed against Catholics in Poland would deeply divide the church. But this apprehension does not explain the Vatican's deceleration of information about the murder of the Jews.

Pius XII harbored a personal ambition to play an important role in world diplomacy, and he felt duty bound to shield the visible center of Catholicism from destruction. Standing amid the ruins of the Basilica of San Lorenzo, Pope Pius said, "Almost in the center of Rome . . . is our Vatican City, an independent state and an independent neutral state, which shelters priceless treasures, sacred not only to the Apostolic See but to the whole Catholic world."[102] The Vatican's "priceless treasures" were not worth the lives of millions of Jewish men, women, and children, but in Pius's view what those treasures stood for were worth those lives.

Pius XII's priorities put Jews at mortal risk. Thousands, perhaps tens of thousands, of additional Jews would have eluded Hitler's death camps had the Holy See accelerated rather than decelerated information about genocide. Did Pope Pius think the church so fragile that, should he speak out, it would not survive the war, even though it had survived the fratricidal Great War intact? Should the possible bombardment of Rome have been Pius's primary concern or, as Bishop Preysing pointed out, should not the moral issue of the murder of the Jews have taken precedence? Were the churches and other structures of Rome and the Vatican really the nerve center of Catholic faith that Pius believed them to be? Was the possible future clash between Christianity and atheistic communism more important than the slaughter of the Jews who were being murdered in eastern Europe, and who would continue to be murdered while Pius hoped for a negotiated settlement to the war that would favor genocidal Germany, the church's defender from Russian communism?

NOTES

1. Yahil, *The Holocaust*, 282–83.
2. Avraham Tory, *Surviving the Holocaust: The Kovno Ghetto Diary*, trans. Jerzy Michalowicz (Cambridge MA: Harvard University Press, 1990), 56.
3. VKZ, Series A, vol. 34, 675–78.
4. Schneider, *Pius XII*, 32; see also Papeleux, *Les silences de Pie XII*, 58.
5. A memo that Orsenigo sent to the Vatican secretariat on the eve of World War II makes his antisemitism apparent: "The 4 million Jews will certainly do their utmost to excite and to help the others fight against Germany, but they . . . will not fight because the Jew is selfish and does not like fighting." ADSS, I, 141.
6. Leiber to Preysing, Rome, October 28, 1945, Diözesanarchiv Berlin (henceforth DAB) V/16-4, Nachlass Preysing. It is not known whether Orsenigo knew of his assistant's party membership. Fr. Leiber found out about it from Ernst von Weizsäcker, the German ambassador to the Vatican.
7. Reifferscheid, *Das Bistum Ermland*, 270–76.
8. Papeleux, *Les silences de Pie XII*, 72.
9. Rolf Steininger, "Katholische Kirche und NS-Judenpolitik," *Zeitschrift für katholische Theologie* 114 (1992): 164.
10. John Morley writes that he *never* intervened on behalf of Jews; Morley, *Vatican Diplomacy and the Jews during the Holocaust*, 178. The German scholar Martin Hollen says that the nuncio helped in arranging visas for emigrating Jews; *Heinrich Wienken. Der 'Unpolitische' Kirchenpoli-*
tiker (Mainz: Grünewald, 1981), 105, VKZ, Series B, vol. 33.
11. Morley, *Vatican Diplomacy and the Jews during the Holocaust*, 115. Orsenigo's concern was probably sparked by Margarete Sommer.
12. *Pie XII et le IIIe Reich* (Paris: Editions de Seuil, 1964), see the conclusion.
13. Yahil, *The Holocaust*, 357.
14. Hollen, *Heinrich Wienken*, 108–9.
15. Zuccotti, *The Italians and the Holocaust*, 127–28. Pages 129–35 of *Freiburger Rundbrief* 30 (1978) give the full Gerstein report.
16. Lipscher, "The Jews of Slovakia," 206.
17. ADSS, 8, 598 (July 13, 1942).
18. Faulhaber to the Military Administration, Munich, June 9, 1945, BAM File 7500.
19. Lipscher, "The Jews of Slovakia," 256.
20. Shelah, "The Catholic Church in Croatia," 272–76.
21. Morley, *Vatican Diplomacy and the Jews*, 78.
22. John S. Conway, "Catholicism and the Jews," in *Judaism and Christianity*, 441.
23. *Freiburger Rundbrief* 37 (1980): 124. Subsequent scrutiny of Riegner's famous telegram of August 8, 1942, in which he outlines the intent to kill all Jews, indicates that it was amazingly accurate; see C. R. Browning, "A Final Hitler Decision for the 'Final Solution'? The Riegner Telegram Reconsidered," *Holocaust and Genocide Studies* 10, no. 1 (Spring 1996): 3–10.
24. ADSS, 8, 534.
25. ADSS, 8, 431; Morley, *Vatican Diplomacy and the Jews*, 153–54.
26. Ibid., 136.
27. *Foreign Relations of the United States* (hereafter FRUS), 1939 (Washington DC: Government Printing Office, 1961), III, 772.
28. ADSS, 8, 497.
29. Tittman Report of November 23, 1942, on illegal and inhumane warfare RG 59, Box 39, NARA.
30. Morley, *Vatican Diplomacy and the Jews*, 137.
31. FRUS, III, 777.
32. Morley, *Vatican Diplomacy and the Jews*, 87.
33. Chadwick, *Britain and the Vatican*, 199.

34. Ibid., 213.
35. Richard Breitman, *Official Secrets: What the Nazis Planned, What the British and Americans Knew* (New York, 1998), 145.
36. Friedländer, *Nazi Germany and the Jews*, 75.
37. *ADSS*, 7, 180.
38. *ADSS*, 10, 328.
39. *ADSS*, 9, 274; the date was May 5, 1943. In the passage, Maglione incorrectly places the Treblinka death camp near Lublin.
40. Dan Kurzman, *The Race for Rome* (New York: Doubleday, 1975), 64.
41. Godfrey to Maglione, March 13, 1943, *ADSS*, 9, 104.
42. Ludwig Volk, "Der Fuldauer Bischofskonferenz von der Enzyklika 'Mit Brennender Sorge' bis zum Ende der NS Herrschaft," in *Katholische Kirche im Dritten Reich*, ed. Dieter Albrecht (Mainz: Grünewald, 1976), 79.
43. Höllen, *Heinrich Wienken*, 107.
44. Burkhart Schneider, ed., *Die Briefe Pius XII. an die deutschen Bischöfe 1939–1944* (Mainz: Grünewald, 1966), VKZ, Series A, vol. 4.
45. Schneider, *Pius XII*, 237–40.
46. Ibid., 242.
47. *Akten Deutscher Bischöfe über die Lage der Kirche 1933–1945*, ed. Ludwig Volk and Bernhard Stasiewski (Mainz: Grünewald Press, 1972), 902, VKZ, Series A, vol. 38, 269–72. Maglione's reply is in the footnote.
48. *ADSS*. See vols. 8 through 11.
49. Gerhard L. Weinberg, *Germany, Hitler, and World War II* (New York: Cambridge University Press, 1995), 243.
50. Susan Zuccotti, *The Holocaust, the French, and the Jews* (New York: Basic Books, 1993), 141–42.
51. Elie Wiesel, *Memoirs* (New York: Knopf, 1996), 69.
52. Foreign Funds Control Subject Files RG 131, Box 487, NARA. See file marked Vatican City Funds in the U.S.
53. Tittman Memorandum no. 109, September 8, 1942, RG 59, 740.00119, NARA.
54. *ADSS*, I, 423.
55. Jacob Presser, *The Destruction of the Dutch Jews*, trans. Arnold Pomerans (New York: Dutton, 1969), 148.
56. Sister M. Pasqualina Lehnert, *Ich dürfte Ihm Dienen* (Würzburg: n.p., 1983), 117–18.
57. This theme comes up frequently in the notes of Ernst von Weizsäcker; see Leonidas E. Hill, *Die Weizsäcker Papiere 1933–1950* (Frankfurt: Allstein, 1974), *passim*.
58. Hansjakob Stehle, generally critical of Pope Pius, notes this; see Hansjakob Stehle, *Geheimdiplomatie im Vatikan. Die Päpste und die Kommunisten* (Zurich: Benzinger, 1993), 194. Regarding Pius's decision to send only messages of condolence, see Coppa, "The Vatican and the Dictators," 215.
59. Lewy, *The Catholic Church and Nazi Germany*, 32.
60. Tittman to Hull, October 6, 1942, *FRUS*, 1942, III, 777.
61. George O. Kent, "Pope Pius XII and Germany: Some Aspects of German-Vatican Relations, 1933–1943," *American Historical Review* 70, no. 1 (October 1964): 74–75.
62. Confided to the author by Ger van Roon at the 21st Annual Scholars Conference on the Holocaust and the Churches in March 1991.
63. Leiber also confided to van Roon that he destroyed his own papers. Since this is a remarkable thing for a historian to do, one assumes that Leiber feared this material would cast Pius in an unfavorable light.
64. Osborne's 1945 Annual Report, Rome, February 22, 1946; reproduced in *Akten Deutscher Bischöfe*, 902.
65. Papeleux, *Les silences de Pie XII*, 68–69.
66. von Klemperer, *German Resistance against Hitler*, 170ff. See also "American Jesuit in Wartime Rome: The Diary of Vincent A. McCormick, S.J., 1942–1945," *Mid-America* 56, no. 1 (January 1974): 32–33.
67. See Volker Berghahn, "Resisting the Pax Americana?" in *America and the Shaping of German Society, 1945–1955*, ed. Michael Ermarth (Providence RI: Berg, 1993), 95–96.
68. Conway, "Catholicism and the Jews," 439–40.

69. Stehle, *Geheimdiplomatie im Vatikan*, 200ff. Although Stehle's analysis of Vatican diplomacy seems realistic, it is surely speculative to conclude that the Holy See's position of neutrality was nothing but a facade hiding "weakness, indecisiveness and undiluted fear." See 202.

70. Saul Friedländer, *Pius XII and the Third Reich: A Documentation* (New York: Knopf).

71. Ibid., 195.

72. Zuccotti, *The Italians and the Holocaust*, 133.

73. Friedländer, *Pius XII and the Third Reich*, 21 Iff.

74. Historian Peter Hoffmann writes that Roosevelt's personal envoy to the Vatican, Myron Taylor, was primarily concerned with preventing Pius from making proposals for a compromise peace after the Allies had made unconditional surrender their announced objective in 1942. See "Roncalli in the Second World War: Peace Initiatives, the Greek Famine and the Persecution of the Jews," *Journal of Ecclesiastical History* 40, no. 1 (January 1989): 77.

75. Hill, *Die Weizsäcker Papiere*, 398.

76. José M. Sánchez, "The Popes and Nazi Germany: The View from Madrid" (paper at the 1995 spring meeting of the American Catholic Historical Association), 17.

77. See Hill, *Die Weizsäcker Papiere*, 343, 365, 369, 375, 383–85, and 398.

78. Friedländer, *Pius XII and the Third Reich*, 237.

79. Chadwick, *Britain and the Vatican*, 265–66.

80. Daniel Carpi, *Between Mussolini and Hitler* (Hanover NH: Brandeis University Press, 1994), 175–78.

81. Gitta Sereny, *Into That Darkness* (New York: Vintage Press, 1983), 333.

82. Boxes 2433–35, 2439, 2441, 2448–49, 2451–54, 2457–58, 2461–63, 2465, 2467, 2469, 2470–77 RG 59 740.0011, NARA.

83. Papeleux, *Les silences de Pie XII*, 58–65.

84. Informal Notes of Taylor for September 27, 1942, of discussion with Mgr. Montini, Myron C. Taylor Papers, 121.866A/302 RG 59. Complete Taylor collection is in Boxes 2433–77, NARA.

85. RG 982, microfilm reel 165, NARA.

86. FDR to Secretary of State, June 28, 1943, RG 982, microfilm reel 164, NARA.

87. Apostolic Delegate to Myron C. Taylor, Washington DC, June 15, 1943, RG 982, microfilm reel 164, NARA.

88. Clauss, *Die Bezeihungen des Vatikans*, 172.

89. Informal Notes of Taylor for September 27, 1942.

90. Chadwick, *Britain and the Vatican*, 216.

91. ADSS, 9, 127.

92. Pius XII to FDR, July 20, 1943, RG 982, microfilm reel 170, NARA.

93. Tittman to State Department, December 29, 1943, Myron C. Taylor Papers, 121.866A/302, NARA. A plenary indulgence was one that dispensed all punishment in purgatory for sins that a person had confessed.

94. Lehnert, *Ich durfter Ihm Dienen*, 116.

95. Tittmann telegram to the U.S. Department of State, Bern, January 3, 1944, RG 982, reel 178, NARA.

96. Hill, *Die Weizsäcker Papiere*, 352.

97. Friedländer, *Pie XII et le IIIe Reich*, 238.

98. Pius XII to Preysing, March 21, 1944, Korrespondenz 1944–45, DAB V/16-4.

99. Pius XII to Preysing, April 30, 1943, Korrespondenz 1944–1945, DAB V/16-4.

100. Regarding Pius's fixation with communism, see Coppa, "The Vatican and the Dictators," 199–203.

101. The one exception to this statement came when the Vatican hinted that it might break its silence if Rome's Jews were deported.

102. Reginald F. Walker, ed., *Pius of Peace* (Dublin: Gill and Sons, 1945), 58.

Self-Serving Switzerland

INDEPENDENT COMMISSION OF EXPERTS
SWITZERLAND—SECOND WORLD WAR

From *Switzerland, National Socialism and the Second World War*

During the Second World War, Switzerland was the most important market for gold from the territories controlled by the Third Reich.[1] Almost four-fifths of the Reichsbank's gold shipments abroad were arranged via Switzerland. Between 1940 and 1945, the Reichsbank sold gold for a value of 101.2 million francs to Swiss commercial banks and 1,231.1 million francs to the Swiss National Bank (SNB). . . . Even before the war, the Third Reich had supplied gold obtained through coercive measures to the German monetary institute. After war broke out, looted gold was used to acquire foreign currency. These transactions were highly problematical for political and legal reasons. Accordingly, they are a focal point of the debate about Switzerland's role in the Second World War and the issue of economic collaboration with Nazi Germany.

The Chronology of Gold Transactions

After the outbreak of the Second World War, the SNB continued to treat gold from the Reichsbank in the same way as gold from any other central bank, exchanging it for francs and other foreign currency. The first of these wartime-gold transactions took place between March and May 1940, with purchases totaling 27.3 million francs. In July, the SNB also sold a smaller amount (19.5 million francs) to the Reichsbank. These early transactions were relatively insignificant in numerical

terms, but signaled that the SNB was willing to maintain the convertibility of the franc. . . . [The SNB] accepted gold in ever-larger quantities in the years that followed.

During the first years of the war, most of the German gold was sold to Swiss commercial banks. . . . In these and other transactions with Germany, the Swiss banks sold francs and, to a lesser extent, other currencies, especially [Portuguese] escudos, in exchange for gold. The francs were then used by the German war economy to make payments to third parties. The Swiss francs entered the currency reserves held by foreign central banks—either via the Reichsbank or via the commercial banks as a means to obtain foreign exchange—and were then offered back to the SNB in exchange for gold. In this way, the gold available to the Reichsbank in increasingly substantial quantities due to the war and Germany's persecution policy flowed via the Swiss "hub" to other central banks. The major net purchasers were Portugal, Spain, Romania and, to a lesser extent, Hungary, Slovakia and Turkey. As a result, the gold acquired unlawfully by the Third Reich entered the reserves of freely available monetary gold. . . .

The SNB attempted to centralize the gold trade in October 1941. At this point, it considered imposing exchange controls, but then rejected this measure in favor of "gentlemen's agreements" with the banks. The Reichsbank was requested to deal with the SNB instead of the commercial banks as before. From then on, the commercial banks only engaged in smaller-scale gold transactions abroad. A further tightening of the regulations governing the Swiss gold trade occurred on December 7, 1942, when the Federal Council established maximum prices for gold coins and bars, thus restricting the opportunities for the banks to profit from the sharp rise in the price of gold. In addition, SNB permission was henceforth required for the import or export of gold. Credit Suisse (*Schweizerische Kreditanstalt*, SKA) was given a license to import small amounts of gold; however, in September 1943, it was refused permission to accept the delivery of gold from the suspect operations of Deutsche Bank's Istanbul branch.[2]

The largest transactions in the context of the "escudo business" (*Escudo-Geschäft*) took place up until the summer of 1942. These transactions enabled the Reichsbank to sell gold to the SNB for francs or Portuguese escudos in order to pay for strategically important raw materials and other key imports for the German war economy. The Banco de Portugal then bought gold from the SNB with the francs accumulated in its foreign currency reserves. Such transactions with the Reichsbank reached their peak in the winter of 1941/42. From the summer of 1942, Germany began to sell gold directly to Portugal via the deposit account in Bern, and the escudo deals became less significant for the Swiss financial center. Nonetheless, the associated gold shipments by the Reichsbank continued to be channeled through Switzerland.

The substantial purchases from Germany included coins (mostly from the Latin Monetary Union that included Belgium, France, and Italy, as well as Switzerland), and continued for some time. It was later revealed that all these coins had come from the holdings of the Belgian Central Bank. At the same time, the SNB sold a large quantity of gold coins on the market, including

those acquired from the Reichsbank. These transactions were an attractive source of revenue: the SNB earned 12.3 million francs from the purchase and sale of foreign-minted gold coins during the war. A significant proportion of these coins eventually may have been exported by private individuals, especially to France, where they are likely to have sustained an active underground or black market economy.

In addition to these purchases, consignments from the Reichsbank to the SNB amounted to around 500 million francs. This gold went to the depositories maintained in Bern by other monetary institutes or by the Reichsbank itself. Switzerland thus became the center of complex gold transactions, for in addition to the Reichsbank and the Bank for International Settlements (BIS), more than a dozen other central banks availed themselves of the SNB's services. The gold sales by the Reichsbank to Switzerland began to assume unprecedented dimensions in the last quarter of 1941 and remained at a high level throughout 1942 and 1943. It was only in the second quarter of 1944 that the volume of these transactions declined significantly, although they continued until the last month of the war in Europe.

From the beginning of 1943, Switzerland came under increasing pressure from the Allies to curtail the gold transactions with Germany. Due to the Allies' knowledge about the gold's origin, the British and Americans, in their declarations, raised the prospect of full restitution of the purchased gold after the end of the war. Although these warnings increasingly preoccupied the SNB Governing Board and prompted the adoption of various safeguards, it was not until the Agreement of March 8, 1945, with the Western Allies' mission, headed by Laughlin Currie, that the Swiss National Bank halted its purchases of gold from the Reichsbank, with the exception of consignments intended to cover German diplomatic expenses, payments for prisoners of war, and contributions for the International Committee of the Red Cross. Nevertheless, an agreement with the Reichsbank on April 11, 1945, established a far broader framework for German gold sales, partly as a result of pressure from the insurance industry which insisted on obtaining payment for insurance services to Germany. Reichsbank gold therefore continued to be shipped to Switzerland even during the last weeks of the war in Europe, factually circumventing the Currie Agreement. . . .

Examining Switzerland's role in these gold transactions raises two sets of problems. The first . . . centers on the way in which the SNB and the private banks appeared to regard these transactions as "*business as usual.*" Central banks adhering to the gold standard regularly bought and sold gold from other central banks; this was the basis of the international monetary system. However, the circumstances prevailing between 1939 and 1945 were exceptional. The gold transactions enabled Germany, whose national currency was no longer accepted as a means of payment in the international markets, to acquire foreign currency that then could be used to obtain essential goods for its war economy. The German armaments industry thus obtained strategically important raw materials and other key resources for the war effort, especially tungsten, manganese, and other ores from Spain, Portugal, and South America, but also crude oil from Romania and bauxite from Yugoslavia. This fact alone would not constitute grounds to describe the gold trade as an illegal activity that violated Swiss or international law. But even if this were all that could be said about the impact of these gold transactions, political objections would and do still arise, since the trade served the interests of Nazi Germany and undermined the objectives of the Allies' economic war.

The SNB was well aware of the political dimension of this issue from the outset. As early as October 1940, the SNB's directors were aware of accusations in U.S. newspapers that Switzerland was assisting the Axis powers. The directors raised this issue with the Swiss Government and approached the Federal Political Department to discuss the Swiss response to possible Allied counter-measures. At that time, the SNB argued that the U.S. had not imposed a blockade on German or Italian accounts, so America could hardly object to Swiss transactions with the Reichsbank. At the same time, the transactions appeared to offer some protection against German attack. In November 1940, a letter from Per Jacobsson, chief economist of the Bank for International Settlements (BIS), was forwarded by the Chairman of the SNB's Governing Board, Ernst Weber, to the Federal Council. In this letter, Jacobsson refers to Reichsbank Vice-President Emil Puhl's view that the convertibility of the Swiss franc "constitutes a reason for leaving Switzerland free."[3] In his accompanying letter to Federal Councillors Wetter and Pilet-Golaz, however, Weber made no reference to this dissuasive aspect; instead, he emphasized "Switzerland's needs" and raised the prospect of wide-ranging opportunities: "Nonetheless, there is practically no doubt that the existence of a free currency, such as the Swiss franc whose status is unique in Europe, can be of benefit to other countries on our continent as well."[4] It was only after the war, especially during preparations for the Washington negotiations of spring 1946, that the SNB directors claimed that their gold transactions and positive relations with Germany had prevented Germany from seriously considering the option of military operations against Switzerland. In other words, they argued that by providing financial services, Switzerland in effect had bought its freedom from German attack. This shifting of arguments retrospectively (for the purpose of self-justification) shows how important it is to differentiate analytically between intention and effect. It is quite possible that these economic relations and especially the provision of financial services had a "security effect" for Switzerland, but the argument that this outcome had been the chief motive for engaging in these transactions is based on twisted logic. One might just as well claim that with its "business as usual" approach, the SNB had effectively prevented Switzerland from using the convertibility of its currency as a trump card in the economic negotiations with Germany.[5]

The second set of problems relates to the legality of the transactions; it thus concerns the Reichsbank's dubious legal claim to a large part of the gold. The Reichsbank claimed that it was using its prewar reserves for its sales to Switzerland, but the quantity of gold sold exceeded these holdings substantially. The Reichsbank's published figure for its reserves on the eve of the war was just 124 million francs. However, informed observers pointed out that the actual holdings were much higher. There was an additional 358 million francs in "secret reserves" (*"stille Reserven"*), and the Reichsbank had also acquired the gold owned by the Austrian and Czech national banks either just before or in the immediate aftermath of Germany's annexation of these countries. A realistic estimate of the amount of gold held by the Reichsbank in September 1939 (including the stocks of Austrian and Czech origin) is around 1,100 million francs—in other words, less than the amount of 1.6 to 1.7 billion francs sold to Switzerland. Germany also bought gold during the war (mostly from the Soviet Union), but this was not the major source of supply. Based on simple arithmetic and without any detailed investigation into the route taken by specific amounts of the precious metal, it is clear that some of the

gold sold by the Reichsbank during the war could only have been acquired through the expropriation of central bank reserves, especially from Belgium, the Netherlands, and Luxembourg (totaling 1,582,000 francs). The Reichsbank also boosted its stocks of gold through looting and expropriation of individuals: the Four-Year Plan authorities who supervised the draconian exchange and currency controls acquired gold worth 311 million francs. Gold expropriated from Holocaust victims in Eastern Europe and transferred to the Reichsbank in the 76 so-called Melmer consignments totaled 2,577 kg fine weight (with a value of 12,549,442 francs).

The Fate of Individual Gold Bars

The detailed entries in the Reichsbank gold ledgers allow a reconstruction of the path taken by individual gold bars. Immediately after the war, U.S. researchers used these ledgers and the detailed weights they provided (which act as a kind of fingerprint for specific recast bars) to show that the consignments to the SNB came from recast gold belonging to the National Bank of Belgium that had been taken via Paris to Berlin. The same process for the identification of bars also allows the reconstruction of the path taken by Holocaust victim gold, especially the consignments of gold labeled by the Reichsbank as "Melmer"— sealed boxes delivered from August 1942 by SS-*Hauptsturmführer* Bruno Melmer and containing foreign exchange, precious metals, coins, and jewelry. This included dental gold, which until mid-1942 had been reused by the SS medical office (*Sanitätsamt*) for dental treatment of the SS; however, the quantities became too large to continue this use. There were 76 of these consignments in all.

Three "Melmer" bars (numbered 36903, 36904 and 36905) with a total weight of 37.5411 kilograms of fine gold (kgf) came from the seventh "Melmer" delivery on November 27, 1942, and were shipped by the Reichsbank to the SNB in Bern on January 5, 1943. Other "Melmer" bars came to Switzerland by a more circuitous route. Bars 36873 and 36874 from the second consignment (October 18, 1942) and bars 36902 and 36907 from the seventh consignment (November 27 and December 2, 1942) were recast together with German coins; they formed part of the 762 bars that were sold to the SNB. Four bars (37192, 37193, 37194, 37195) that arrived at the Reichsbank on November 1, 1943, were recast at the Prussian mint with coins and bars from Belgium and the Netherlands, and sold to Switzerland between February 23, 1944, and June 8, 1944. Bar 37198 was brought to the Reichsbank on November 11, 1943, recast with Dutch coins, and delivered to the SNB on February 23, 1944. In total, just under 120 kg of "Melmer" gold, with a value of 581,899 francs, was sold by the Reichsbank to Switzerland. In fact, this is a surprisingly low proportion of the total quantity of "Melmer" gold, which amounted to at least 2,580 kgf, most of which was sold through Germany's two largest commercial banks, Deutsche Bank and Dresdner Bank.

In a sense, this provides the clearest material link between Swiss banking and Nazi genocide. Except for the first three bars, the bars were recast and mixed with gold from Western European sources—looted both from natural persons and from central bank reserves—at the Prussian mint, which could recast bars, but not refine them. The refining had been done previously, almost certainly by Degussa, which issued refined gold of an equivalent weight to customers (such as the Reichsbank) that brought gold in an impure or unrefined state (such as dental or jewelry gold). It is therefore impossible to determine what happened to the physical atoms of gold extracted from the victims of Nazi genocide.

In the second half of 1940, as Jacobsson, Weber, and Wetter were contemplating the political implications of the gold transactions, the SNB received the first indications that gold was being taken from individuals as well as from the national banks in occupied countries. Evidence that German gold had been stolen was later presented in Swiss newspapers (in particular, in the *Neue Zürcher Zeitung* in August 1942).[6] In its report to the Federal Council on May 16, 1946, however, the SNB claimed that Allied warnings had only made it clear in January 1943 that gold sold by Germany to the neutral countries might have been stolen (a statement which was factually incorrect, since unofficial warning voices had been heard earlier on). The clearest indication . . . was presented by the Governor of the *Banque de France*, Yves de Boisanger, in the summer of 1943, when he provided information underpinning the suspicion that the stolen Belgian gold had been taken to Berlin and was being used in international transactions. In fact, de Boisanger played a key role in the transfer of the Belgian gold to Berlin: the gold, which had been entrusted to France at the outbreak of the war, was shipped from Bordeaux to Dakar and then taken across the Sahara back to France. Pierre-Eugene Fournier, the former Governor of the *Banque de France*, had refused to release it to the Germans without Belgian consent; the Vichy Government dismissed him and the more compliant de Boisanger was appointed in his place.

The warnings in January 1943 prompted a new round of discussions between the SNB general directors and the political authorities, especially in the SNB's supervisory body, the Bank Committee (*Bankausschuß*) (meetings of July 22–23 and August 26–27, 1943). At these meetings, there was a difference of opinion between Chairman of the SNB Governing Board Ernst Weber and President of the Bank Council and the Bank Committee

Gottlieb Bachmann, who had been Weber's predecessor as Chairman of the Governing Board from 1925 to 1939. Weber argued that adherence to the gold standard necessitated purchases of gold from other countries, whereas Bachmann emphasized the political dimension of this issue and explained that during the First World War, Sweden and the Netherlands had refused to purchase gold on technical grounds. . . . During the course of the debate, SNB Director General Paul Rossy stated that the bank had not been informed that Germans had looted any gold and that international law permitted the authorities of occupying powers to seize gold reserves. The SNB's motives for engaging in these transactions were never entirely clear. Indeed, it could be argued that the bank was under no obligation during the war to explain its conduct [and] . . . it would be misleading to assume that the bank's motives had remained the same throughout the course of the conflict.

In the summer of 1940, in view of the military threat posed by Germany and its apparent domination of the entire European continent, political factors (along the lines indicated in Jacobsson's letter) may well have been important, prompting the SNB to consult the political authorities at this time. As the volume of German business with the commercial banks increased and a significant proportion of Swiss reserves was frozen due to the U.S. blockade, centralizing the gold transactions offered a convenient source of gold, which seemed important in order to maintain the international stability and convertibility of the franc after the war. In the summer of 1943, when irrefutable evidence that the German gold had been looted made it clear that the SNB had already purchased gold which had been acquired unlawfully by Germany, a new type of reasoning emerged: putting a stop to the transactions or even simply demanding "an explicit statement" from Germany attesting to the lawful origins of the gold would cast doubt on the SNB's "good faith" and lay the bank open to postwar claims from parties who had lost their gold. It was also claimed that the continuing purchases of gold from Germany were justified by Switzerland's legal status as a neutral country, obliged to accept gold regardless of who was offering it. In January 1944, Weber argued that due to this obligation under international law, the purchase of Reichsbank gold could not be rejected.

The right of seizure, on which the SNB's Governing Board had apparently based its decision to accept the legality of German gold in the summer of 1943, was problematical. This had been made clear by legal opinions to both the SNB and the Reichsbank at the time.[7] Under Article 53 of the Hague Convention Respecting the Laws and Customs of War on Land of 1907, this right applied only to property of the State (although the Convention also permitted the seizure, during a conflict, of appliances for the transmission of news or the transport of persons even if these appliances belonged to private individuals, on condition that they were restored and compensation fixed when peace was made). Article 46 (1) of the Convention stated that private property had to be respected (as were to be the lives of civilians as well as their religious convictions and practice). Article 46 (2) explicitly stated that private property could not be confiscated. The expropriation of gold from private individuals or private corporations could therefore not constitute lawful seizure under the international law in force at the time (and, indeed, ever since). At that time many national banks (including the Belgian and Swiss national banks) were privately owned, [and] . . . such private ownership of central banks was frequently justified on the grounds that it protected the bank's gold reserves in the event of war, invasion, or occupation. The principles underlying these Articles of the Hague Convention had been widely endorsed during the final three decades of the nineteenth century, and in a famous precedent, the Prussian armies of 1870/71 had left the gold held by the *Banque de France* untouched.

The most extensive discussions with the political authorities and within the SNB's supervisory bodies thus occurred in 1943, at a moment when neither the defense argument ("deterrence" or "dissuasion") put forward in 1940, nor the debate about protecting the currency that had emerged during the second half of 1941 had much weight. At the same time, the legal basis was extremely tenuous. The SNB continued to purchase gold regardless of its problematical origins simply because its previous conduct had created a logic and momentum of its own. The bank was a prisoner of its earlier actions. . . .

The Banks and Assets Belonging to Nazi Victims

Among the customers who had confided their assets to Swiss banks in the 1920s, there were many who were to become victims of the Nazi policy of confiscation and extermination. In the 1930s too, many people who came under the threat of National Socialism or were already being persecuted, relied on the security of Swiss financial institutions. Many of these customers were later deported and killed.

In the 1930s various countries instituted ever more drastic measures to prevent the influx of flight capital and exerted pressure on the Swiss banks to stop them providing their facilities for such transactions. The banks thus faced the basic dilemma of either looking after the interests of their foreign customers or giving in to pressure from Germany and other countries. After the banking and currency crisis of 1931, German for-

eign exchange controls became even more draconian. Non-declaration of assets in foreign currencies was already being severely punished before the Nazis came to power. Afterward, penalties were increased. Under the Law on Treason against the German Economy (*Gesetz gegen den Verrat der Deutschen Volkswirtschaft*) passed on June 12, 1933, all German citizens as well as all foreigners living in Germany were obliged to register the foreign currencies and securities they held abroad. In 1934, a similar law was passed in Italy. In 1938, all Jewish property in Germany had to be registered. At the same time, many special taxes and levies were introduced such as the so-called *Sühneleistung* (atonement fine) instituted after the pogrom in November 1938, and the *Reichsfluchtsteuer* (emigration tax) was extended. To avoid the high penalties and meet the financial burden, many Jews and others who were persecuted had to withdraw their assets and securities from Switzerland. The machinery of Nazi legislation also specifically targeted assets abroad. According to a law passed on November 1936, all people resident in Germany had to deposit their foreign shares with a designated German foreign exchange bank. In order to ensure that this regulation was respected, a further law against economic sabotage was passed shortly afterward, according to which flight of capital could entail the death penalty. At the same time, the Nazi authorities subjected their victims to physical and psychological pressure in order to force them to turn over their assets. The Swiss banks complied with the instructions of their German customers, signed at times under duress, and transferred securities to the German banks indicated. Between 1933 and 1939 Credit Suisse, for example, transferred securities valued at around 8 million francs to Deutsche Bank,[8] while the Zurich office of the Swiss Bank Corporation transferred securities totaling over 6 million francs in value in accordance with the 1936 Law on Compulsory Deposits (*Depotzwangsgesetz*). Furthermore, the Swiss Bank Corporation sold shares quoted in Switzerland for a total market value of 8 million francs on behalf of German customers who probably had to transfer these proceeds too to banks designated by the Reichsbank. A considerable number of such transfers took place in 1936, but transactions of this sort also continued during the war.

Even though many of those persecuted had to withdraw their assets from the banks and despite the fact that Switzerland did not always prove to be an entirely safe haven, persecuted Jews were still well advised to seek a safe destination for their assets if possible in or via Switzerland. Ever more frequently, they opened accounts that were then managed by bank employees or lawyers. Although the asset management mandates were seen as a problem by the banks, they did not take any effective measures against this development. The Swiss Bank Corporation drew up a list of such trustee accounts in November 1938 in an attempt to gain a clear view of the situation. Other banks later followed suit in 1942.

After the *Anschluss* (annexation of Austria) in 1938 and the introduction of Nazi legislation, Austrian capital and securities started to be withdrawn rapidly from Swiss accounts.[9] The Jewish population, which was subjected to persecution and pressure, handed over considerable assets to the Reichsbank. Some were also forced by local authorities to declare the existence of accounts in Switzerland. The banks transferred the corresponding amounts directly to the Nazi Treasury. At the same time, the banks were confronted with requests from the provisional administrators (*kommissarische Verwalter*) of "Aryanised" Jewish firms who wanted to take possession of the assets of the corresponding companies. The

banks agreed on a common procedure and complied with the requests of the Austrian administrators if they bore the signature of the Jewish company owners. In cases where the company's owner was able to take legal action in Switzerland, the requests made by the provisional administrators were rejected by the judges and the blocked assets deposited with the court.

Assets of subsequent Nazi victims were also included in the flow of capital from France into Switzerland, in particular after the Popular Front's election victory in 1936. The assets held by the main Swiss banks (excluding the private banks) on behalf of French customers thus rose from 241.6 million francs to 520.4 million francs between December 31, 1935, and December 31, 1937. While assets were later transferred back to France or invested in the UK or the U.S.A, many French customers deposited their assets in bank safes, invested them in Swiss property, or handed them over to be managed by lawyers and trustees. The flow of capital from Hungary into Switzerland also increased dramatically. The total capital held in Switzerland on behalf of Hungarian banks and individuals, also including subsequent victims of Nazi extermination policy, rose from 15.5 million francs in 1937 to 37.7 million francs in 1943, a year before Hungarian Jews started being deported to Auschwitz.

Poland was another country from which large sums belonging to later Nazi victims were transferred to Switzerland. After overrunning Poland in September 1939, the new ruling power endeavored to acquire Polish assets deposited in Switzerland. As early as November 20, 1939, the Polish bank *Lodzer Industrieller GmbH* asked Credit Suisse to transfer assets deposited with it to an account at the German Reichsbank in Berlin. The bank saw a fundamental problem in this procedure and asked its legal affairs department to examine the matter. The latter recommended not complying with the request since the customer's signature had most likely been obtained under duress by the occupying authorities. A further reason for refusing the request was that it had come from Berlin and contained incorrect information about the amount deposited with Credit Suisse. The legal affairs department also pointed out that for Poland, German foreign exchange regulations represented a war measure taken by an occupying force and that Switzerland had not yet recognized the new political situation. Managing Director Peter Vieli subsequently discussed the issue with Rudolf Speich, his counterpart at the Swiss Bank Corporation. The latter contacted the Reichsbank, which agreed that in view of the unclear constitutional situation in Poland, Swiss banks were not obliged to comply with requests from German administrators (*Reichskommissäre*). Nevertheless, according to a file note "the directors of the Reichsbank and Dr. Speich were of the opinion that duly signed requests from customers for their assets held in Switzerland to be transferred to an account with the Reichsbank must be executed, since absolutely no justification could be found for not doing so."[10] Although there were legal and moral objections to transferring the funds, the consideration that they "still had important interests in Germany, and should avoid friction and unpleasantness whenever possible" prevailed at CS. It complied with the request and opted for the principle of carrying out legally signed orders even when they were not received directly from customers, but via the Reichsbank in Berlin. Their comportment in Poland was in this respect typical of how the banks dealt with the assets of Nazi victims: as a rule, they complied with transfer orders from foreign customers without properly checking whether the signatures they bore had been obtained under duress by the Nazi authorities

and whether the orders were in fact in the customer's interest. On the other hand, the Swiss banks also took measures that were sometimes to the advantage of those subject to persecution. For instance, they instituted special security measures for assets that were not declared to the German foreign exchange authority . . . and sponsored applications to the Swiss authorities for residence permits lodged by those being persecuted by the Nazi regime.

Many foreign customers of Swiss financial institutions were killed by the Nazi regime. An unknown part of their assets was handed over directly or indirectly to the Nazi authorities; the rest remained with the Swiss banks. So-called dormant accounts arose from both measures, in that descendants and heirs were either not aware of the existence of the accounts or not aware that the funds had been transferred to the Nazi regime. Thus, after the end of the war, the question of the fate of this capital and of these securities was by no means solved. The banks were able to use the amounts remaining in the accounts and to earn income from them. They showed little interest in actively seeking accounts of Nazi victims, justifying their inaction with the confidentiality desired by their customers. What the victims of National Socialism and their heirs thought to be the advantages of the Swiss banking system turned out to be disadvantageous for them. During the Third Reich, the principle of discretion that characterized the Swiss banking system and that, together with the tradition of stability and security, had been exploited as a competitive advantage over foreign competitors had made Switzerland particularly attractive as a financial center for those persecuted by the Nazi regime. Later, the question of the whereabouts of assets of Nazi victims became a highly topical issue, but the banks, invoking this tradition, did little to resolve the problem. The unwillingness of the Swiss financial institutions in the immediate postwar period to find the legal owners of unclaimed assets or to support rightful claimants in their search, constitutes the main point of criticism of the banks' behavior.

NOTES

1. Unless otherwise stated, this section is based on UEK, *Goldtransaktionnen*, 2002 (Publication of the ICE); Grossen, *Transsactions*, 2001 (Publications of the ICE).

2. Steinberg, *Deutsche Bank*, 1999, 56.

3. SNB Archives, 2224, Jacobsson to Weber, November 25, 1940 (original German); see also Perrenoud, *Banques*, 1987/88, 53–54; DDS, vol. 13, No. 419; Marguerat, *Suisse*, 1991, 113; Fior, *Schweiz*, 1997, 73–74.

4. Quoted in Perrenoud, *Banques*, 1987/88, 53 (original German). See also Basel University Library, Manuscript Department NL Per Jacobsson, Diary, November 27, 1940.

5. This is the argument put forward by Maissen, *Nationalbank*, 1999, 539.

6. Salomon Wolff, "Das Gold in der Kriegswirtschaft," *Neue Zürcher Zeitung*, No. 1291, August 16, 1942, 4.

7. SNB Legal Service, note of April 5, 1944; Schindler, expert opinion of July 22, 1944, which was commissioned by the SNB, and Sauser-Hall, expert opinion of March 28, 1946. Astonishingly, the Reichsbank lawyers in Berlin came to the same conclusion.

8. Jung, *Kreditanstalt*, 2000, 83.

9. Following the "Foreign Exchange Law concerning Austria" ("Devisengesetz für das Land Österreich") of March 23, 1938, securities valued at 4 million francs and capital amounting to 1.5 million francs belonging to Austrian customers of the SBC in Zurich were transferred to the Third Reich.

10. CSG Archives, SKA Fund, 11.105.208.301–0165, Legal affairs department file note, December 5, 1939 (original German).

8 Rescuing Jews—Means and Obstacles

16. A group of Jewish youth hiding from the Germans in the French village of Le Chambon-sur-Lignon pose for a picture in the snow, ca. 1941. The people of this small village of just 5,000, led by their Protestant ministers André Trocmé and Edouard Theis, opened their homes and rescued several thousand Jews. (U.S. Holocaust Memorial Museum, courtesy of Elizabeth Kaufmann Koenig.)

17. Rescuer Irena Sendler, Warsaw, Poland, 1942. During the Holocaust, Irena Sendler worked for Zegota, a unit within the Polish underground established specifically to help Jews in hiding. As a health worker she had access to the Warsaw ghetto, and between 1942 and 1943 she led hundreds of Jewish children out of the ghetto to safe hiding places. Some children were sedated and carried out in potato sacks or coffins. A church located at the edge of the ghetto had two entrances, one inside the ghetto and one on the Christian side of Warsaw. With Zegota's help some children entered the church as Jews and exited as "Christians." The Germans learned of Irena's activities. On October 20, 1943, she was arrested by the Gestapo and taken to Pawiak prison. Irena was tortured brutally but she refused to give any information about Zegota or about the children she had placed in hiding. She was sentenced to death. Members of Zegota bribed one of the Gestapo agents, and on the day Irena was to be executed she was permitted to escape. She had to go into hiding for the remainder of the war but continued to coordinate her rescue work. By January 1945, when Warsaw was liberated by Soviet troops, the Children's Bureau of Zegota had helped more than 2,500 Jewish children. The exact number of children saved by Irena and her partners is unknown. (Courtesy JFR Photo Archives.)

Introduction

PETER HAYES

Almost everywhere in Nazi-occupied or allied Europe, rare and brave individuals and groups risked their lives to rescue Jews. Sometimes people did so for material gain, but others were moved by human sympathy or solidarity, frequently though not always born of religious conviction. Most studies of these "righteous Gentiles" stress their prewar involvement in benevolent activity and/or the high incidence among them of minority confessional or ethnic status that fostered identification with persecuted Jews—e.g., Catholics in predominantly Protestant Holland and Polish Catholics in predominantly Ukrainian Orthodox Eastern Galicia, Baptists and Quakers in mostly Lutheran Germany, and Protestants in overwhelmingly Catholic France. Often because they possessed such characteristics, most rescuers appear to have acted spontaneously and automatically when their help was sought, just as, conversely, most of the vast majority of people who declined to aid Jews did so almost reflexively. In so acting, the former group defied and the latter group deferred to the considerable dangers that Germany imposed on anyone who concealed or otherwise sustained Jews. In occupied northern and western Europe, the penalties included time in a concentration camp; in eastern Europe, they extended to a bullet or the noose for offenders and their families.

Despite such perils, the readiness of non-Jews to rise to the defense of Jews increased over time in occupied Europe. In part, this occurred in response to the onset of the murders; until the Nazis began the slaughters in the East in 1941–42, the need for protective action did not seem urgent. The spread of knowledge about the killing also coincided with other developments that strengthened opposition to German policies in general, notably the reversal of the Reich's military fortunes after November 1942 and the concurrent beginning in Western Europe and intensification in Eastern Europe of the Nazis' forced labor drafts. Even at the level of individual behavior, the prospect of a German defeat and the sense of also being subject to German round ups emboldened growing numbers of would-be helpers.

Still, solidarity saved fewer people than politics: at most, 5 to 10% of the Jews who survived the Holocaust in Europe did so because a non-Jew or a non-Jewish organization (other than an indigenous government) concealed and sustained them. Disappointing and depressing as that statistic may be in retrospect, it underlines something much more heartening: the bravery of those relatively few people who refused to abandon their fellow human beings at a time when doing precisely that appeared "the better part of valor."

The excerpts in this chapter examine four different forms that rescue could take during the Holocaust—individual, collective, organizational, and national—and the achievements and limitations of each. As the Nazis were sweeping over Europe, virtually the only effective rescue stemmed from the swift and unauthorized decisions of foreign diplomats to issue entry visas to their homelands to fleeing Jews. A notable example from mid-1940 was Aristide de Sousa Mendes, the Portuguese Consul in Bordeaux who signed thousands of such documents as the German army bore down on that city. Jonathan Goldstein's essay analyzes a similar, almost simultaneous, and remarkable tag-team effort just beyond the opposite end of the Nazi empire. This was *the Kovno connection* by which the Dutch and Japanese consuls in that city, which the Soviets recently had occupied, provided partially specious documentation that enabled some 2,500 Jews to escape across the USSR to Shanghai and other destinations. Another celebrated individual, quasi-official rescue effort was that of the American journalist Varian Fry, who went to Europe on behalf of the newly formed Emergency Rescue Committee and funded the escapes of some 2,000 people, most of them Jews and many of them famous artists and intellectuals, in 1940–41.

Even prior to the Nazi ban on further emigration from Europe in October 1941, the scope of such efforts was necessarily limited, and the same has to be said for another kind of individual rescue attempt, exemplified here by Michael Good's discoveries about *the good German of Vilna*. The case of Major Karl Plagge, the commander of a military vehicle repair shop that employed some 1,000 Jews, shows what decency and imagination on the part of a humane German manager could and could not accomplish. Like the more famous Berthold Beitz, after the war the head of the Krupp Corporation and in 1941–44 the manager of Karpathian Oil Corporation's drilling in Boryslaw in Eastern Galicia, Plagge managed for an extended period to feed and treat his Jewish workers well and even to prevent most of them from being rounded up and/or killed. But, unlike the business owner Oskar Schindler, both Plagge and Beitz worked for others and could not arrange for their workers to retreat with them when the front closed in. The most they ultimately could do was provide sufficient warning of the impending end to enable several hundred of their respective charges to escape liquidation.

Networks of collective effort were likely to save more people, though also much more vulnerable to exposure. One that remained almost invulnerable is the subject of Patrick Henry's vivid portrait of *collective action in Vivarais-Lignon*, a high plateau in central France with a long tradition of defying authority and convention. Here a variety of religious and humanistic inspirations combined to assure the concealment and rescue of 5,000 persecuted people, including about 3,500 Jews. Perhaps even more surprising than this accomplishment in a remote region was the success of overlapping networks of helpers in protecting *the hidden Jews of Warsaw*. Gunnar S. Paulsson maintains that an entire "secret city" developed in the former Polish capital, containing some 28,000 Jews in hiding, some 3,000–4,000 blackmailers and "finders" who preyed on them, and some 70,000–90,000 people who aided them one way or another. Though the mortality rate of the hidden Jews was substantial—probably only about 11,500 survived the war—Paulsson's careful comparative accounting fruitfully complicates our understanding of both Polish-Jewish relations during the Holocaust and the determinants of successful rescue.

Whereas the preceding reading selections demonstrate the role in rescue of individuals and networks, the excerpt by Bob Moore underscores the importance of organizations, some new but most antedating the German onslaught, in *saving Jewish children in Belgium*. This reading also lays bare the ambiguity of the Catholic Church's conduct by documenting not only in the marked variation between Papal passivity and the numerous and vigorous helping actions at the lower levels of the hierarchy, but also the combination of generosity in hiding children with the Church's later resistance to returning them to the faith of their parents.

On the whole, the story of national rescue efforts during the Holocaust is a dismal one, typified by the failure of the Anglo-American Bermuda Conference of April 1943 to produce concrete proposals for helping victims of Nazi persecution. Richard Breitman and Alan Kraut provide a balanced depiction of the *American inhibitions* that stood in the way of greater activism. As at the beginning of the war, the exceptions to this pattern came from courageous diplomats, especially Carl Lutz, the Swiss consul in Budapest who invented the *Schutzpass*, a document placing a Jew under the protection of his embassy, as early as 1942. Even more efficacious eventually was the process in 1942–43 by which *Sweden expanded asylum* to cover ever larger groups of Jews, not only to those who reached its shores from Norway and Denmark, but also extraterritorially, to thousands of inhabitants of Budapest. To be sure, the turning point in Swedish policy coincided with the turning point in the war, but Paul Levine's thorough research in the Swedish archives reveals the steady growth in that country's Foreign Ministry of a genuine sense of obligation to help minimize a humanitarian disaster. This trend preceded and produced the rescue efforts in late 1944 popularly associated with the name of Raoul Wallenberg that contributed to the survival of tens of thousands of Hungarian Jews.

Although researchers have tried, no one has succeeded in identifying reliable predictors of willingness on the part of non-Jews to help the afflicted during the Holocaust. A few diplomats rose to the occasion, but most did not. More clergy accepted the challenge, but a majority did not. Minority group members expressed solidarity with Jews more frequently than the surrounding populations, but not reliably or uniformly. Cosmopolitan residents of Warsaw may have been more inclined to aid Jews than Poles in the countryside, but not dependably so. Rescue was always the choice of the relative few. Given the odds against the effort, one can only marvel at those who undertook it and rejoice at their existence.

The Kovno Connection

JONATHAN GOLDSTEIN

From *Lessons and Legacies VI*

By early 1940, as a result of both Nazi and Soviet oppression, many thousands of Polish and Lithuanian Jews had fled into unoccupied Lithuania from Memel, from the regions of Poland that had formally been annexed into the Third Reich, and from the German-controlled but unannexed General Government region of Poland. Some even had fled from as far away as Königsberg in East Prussia. The refugees concentrated in or near Vilna, which had been incorporated into independent Lithuania on October 10, 1939. [M. W.] Beckelman [the representative of the Joint Distribution Committee (JDC) in Vilna] reported that of the 9,824 Jewish refugees registered with his committee as of January 31, 1940, "3153 came from territory now occupied by the Russians [and] 6671 from German-occupied Poland."[1]

On June 15, 1940, the Soviet Union annexed all of unoccupied Lithuania. Jews who had fled [there] . . . precisely to escape Nazi and/or Soviet cruelty felt especially vulnerable during the annexation process. Those who had fled Soviet rule once now found themselves under Soviet rule a second time. By July, virtually all the foreign embassies and consulates in the now ex-Lithuanian capital of Kovno were closing, and therewith the refugees' last probable hope of getting documents to settle abroad. At this point [Jan] Zwartendijk took on a role that quickly evolved into the unpredictable business of rescuing Jews.

Since May 1939, Zwartendijk had been representing Philips, the Dutch electronics manufacturer, in Lithuania. In May 1940, when the Germans overran the Netherlands, a Dutch government-in-exile was established in London. L. P. J. de Decker, based in Riga, Latvia, represented this government in all of the Baltic states. Ambassador de Decker, suspecting the Dutch consul in Kovno (a Lithuanian citizen but ethnic German named Dr. Tillmanns) of pro-Nazi sympathies, dismissed him and in June 1940, only days before the Soviets occupied Lithuania, asked Zwartendijk to take over as consul in Kovno. In spite of the fact that Zwartendijk had no diplomatic experience, he accepted this assignment, expecting only such minor chores as occasionally extending some Dutch resident's passport.[2]

Zwartendijk's work quickly evolved into the rescue of Jews. In July 1940, Pessla Lewin, a former Dutch citizen who was then a Polish-Jewish refugee living in Lithuania with her husband Isaac and son Nathan, wrote to de Decker, who was still the Dutch ambassador, requesting immigration authorization for the Dutch West Indies. She learned that no immigration visas were required for that area, but she would need a landing permit from the local governor. Such permits were rarely issued. Nevertheless the ambassador tried to help by inscribing in her Polish passport a French-language statement that "for the admission of aliens to Surinam, Curaçao, and other Dutch possessions in the Americas, an entry visa is not required."

This stipulation, dated July 11, 1940, came to be known among the refugees as a "Curaçao visa." It gave the impression of being as good as a visa since it omitted the key phrase that a landing permit was required. On July 22, Isaac Lewin approached Zwartendijk in Kovno. Lewin writes in his 1994 memoir that Zwartendijk, after seeing what Ambassador de Decker had done, "copied [the "Curaçao visa'] into my Lithuanian safe-conduct pass."[3] This "visa" also covered the Lewins's three-year-old son, Nathan. Armed with this documentation, Pessla and Isaac Lewin, plus her mother and brother, who were still Dutch citizens, went to the Japanese consulate in Kovno, where they were issued seven- to fifteen-day transit visas to travel through Japan en route to Curaçao. They also went to the Soviet authorities, where they were issued permission to travel by train across the Soviet Union to Vladivostok, where they would leave the country for Japan.

The Japanese consul, far better known in the twentieth and twenty-first centuries than Zwartendijk, was Sugihara Chiune (1900–1986), who later changed his name to Sugihara Senpo. He has been featured in the movies *Escape to the Rising Sun*, *Sugihara: Conspiracy of Silence*, and *Visas That Saved Lives*; in the play *Virtue: Senpo Sugihara*; and in a published imaginary dialogue with Boston University Judaic Studies Professor Hillel Levine.[4] Nevertheless, apart from a relatively small number of genuine destination visas for entry into the United States, Palestine, Canada, and elsewhere, it was the 2,345 fictitious "Curaçao visas" that would be issued by Zwartendijk that enabled Sugihara to issue correspondingly large numbers of Japanese transit visas. Zwartendijk's action also would enable the Soviet authorities to issue correspondingly large numbers of their necessary travel permits.

How did the Lewins' single-family trip turn into a mass exodus of beleaguered Jews? Unaware of the Lewins' experience, Nathan Gutwirth, a legitimate Dutch citizen who was then a student at the Yeshiva of Telz (Telsiai), Lithuania, asked Zwartendijk if several of his fellow students, non-Dutch citizens, could accompany him to Curaçao. Zwartendijk said he was willing to provide Gutwirth's several friends with the same helpful notation he had given the Lewin family. According to Gutwirth, this help to his friends had de Decker's concurrence. Gutwirth then told Zorach Warhaftig what had been accomplished. When Warhaftig inquired of Zwartendijk, he let it be known that he was willing to give a Curaçao visa to anyone who asked. There is no evidence whether Zwartendijk sought or received authorization to issue Curaçao visas en masse.

Word of this possible escape mechanism spread quickly through the religious Zionist community in Lithuania and eventually to the broader Jewish refugee communities in Kovno and Vilna. It did not reach some of the more isolated Lithuanian Jewish communities.[5] Within hours, dozens of petitioners lined up at Zwartendijk's Kovno office. Zwartendijk issued 2,345 visas between July 24 and August 3, when the Soviets commandeered his office, obligating him and his family to return to the Netherlands in September.

Ultimately, not a single Jew to whom Zwartendijk issued a phony visa showed up in Curaçao. Armed with these notations, which could masquerade as the equivalent of end visas, about half of the roughly 2,200 refugees who reached Japan succeeded in moving on to the United States, Palestine, Canada, and other final destinations. It is unclear precisely how many of the 2,345 visas issued by Zwartendijk were actually used, and how many people actually travelled on each visa. Infants, for example, could travel on a parent's visa, as happened with the Levin family. What is clear is that after December 7, 1941, due to wartime conditions, very few of the refugees already in Japan were able to exit Japanese-held territory. The Japanese government interned approximately 1,000 of these stranded individuals in Japanese-occupied Shanghai for the duration of the war, including 250 faculty and students from the Yeshiva of Mir, Poland. That academy, through its own efforts and a sequence of events beyond its own control, is the only Eastern European Jewish institute of higher learning whose members escaped the Holocaust virtually intact.[6]

Dutch Governor Kasteel, in 1942 of Curaçao and Surinam, much later became ambassador to the state of Israel when Warhaftig was minister of religious affairs. Warhaftig records the following interview with Kasteel:

> After describing to him the type of visas we had received in 1940 for Curaçao, I asked him how he would have reacted had a ship actually arrived in Curaçao with hundreds of Jewish refugees aboard holding such "visas." Would he have accorded them asylum? "Nothing of the sort," he answered promptly. He would have forced the ship back into mid-ocean as had the American and Cuban authorities in the case of the *St. Louis*.[7]

On June 22, 1941, less than a year after the Kovno exodus, the Nazis overran Lithuania as part of their overall attack on the Soviet Union. The remaining Jews of Lithuania were almost entirely annihilated. Zwartendijk's action thus saved approximately 2,200 Jews from almost certain destruction.

It is clear that the Lewins, Gutwirths, Warhaftigs, and many others with direct knowledge of life under the Nazis and/or Soviets were determined to leave no stone unturned in their efforts to locate avenues of escape. For many of the Jews who ultimately fled across Siberia in 1940 or 1941, that trip would be their second, and in some cases, third, desperate exodus within a period of twelve to twenty-four months. But how to explain the behavior of other Jews who did not make vigorous efforts to leave? Were those individuals firmly rooted by a feeling of home and security that they did not wish to jeopardize? Did they underestimate the diabolical, ultimately genocidal nature of European antisemitism in spite of impassioned warnings from Vladimir (Zev) Jabotinsky and other Zionist leaders that Europe was not safe for a Jew? With respect to Zwartendijk's specific exit scheme, were some terrified by the idea of having to cross Siberia to get to Japan? Were some convinced they would end up as slave laborers in Siberia? Were some simply unaware that an avenue of escape was available? Mrs. Betty Goodfriend lived in the *shtetl* of Velki (Vilkija), approximately thirty kilometers from Kovno, during the Zwartendijk episode. In a 1999 interview she reminded me that "we never heard of Sugihara. We never heard of Zwartendijk."[8]

Quite remarkably, in the remaining war years Zwartendijk and his family escaped repercussions from the Kovno incident. As already noted, the family returned to the Nazi-occupied Netherlands in September 1940. Once the Germans had decided upon their "Final Solution to the Jewish Question," German High Commissioner Artur von Seyss-Inquart (1892–1946) set about the systematic extermination of the Dutch Jews. The Gestapo might well have come across a file mentioning Zwartendijk's name as the signer of 2,345 sham declarations that had in 1940 enabled many Polish and Lithuanian Jews to flee. Zwartendijk would then have been in deep trouble. In fact, in 1941 or 1942 Zwartendijk was interrogated by the Gestapo about an unrelated matter. He was released, to his great relief. As his elder son Jan recalls and records the incident:

> Two Gestapo officers came to see him at home. He feared the worst—that they had found out about the Kaunas affair. But it turned out that the Germans had killed an old friend of his from Prague "trying to escape" in Romania ["auf der Flucht erschossen"—a common German euphemism for tortured to death during interrogation]. This man had Zwartendijk's name and address in his pocket. There was no connection with Kaunas and there were no further consequences of this visit. It was nerve-wracking because drawing attention for any reason meant scrutiny of Gestapo files. Miraculously, his Kaunas activities must have escaped their intelligence. But Zwartendijk did not feel safe until the Allied liberators arrived in southern Holland in September 1944.[9]

In summation, Zwartendijk accepted what he thought would be a routine, quasi-diplomatic assignment. Very shortly thereafter he became involved in the rescue of Jews, endangering himself, his wife, and their three small children. The text beneath which he put his signature 2,345 times was a deliberately deceptive declaration. The nature of the inscription plus the number of times he issued it on his own volition could certainly qualify as an abuse of his consular authority. At the time he signed the "visas" no one knew how the ever-unpredictable Soviets would react, not to mention the Nazis once he returned to the Netherlands. Germany did not recognize the Dutch government-in-exile, and the Soviet Union and the Netherlands had no diplomatic relations; so Zwartendijk could not hope for diplomatic protection. As it turned out, against expectations at the time and for reasons that remain unclear, the Germans never caught onto his scheme and the Soviets decided to permit Jewish refugees to leave Lithuania. The "visas," valid or invalid, turned out not to constitute an irritation for the Soviets. But that was not foreseeable and it was always dangerous to stick one's neck out in the Soviet Union.

What Motivated Zwartendijk?

What motivated a Dutch businessman with a wife and three young children to almost instinctively partake in a dangerous scheme to rescue Jews when his own country was already overrun by the Nazis? Although Philips Company president Dr. Frederik Philips took the initiative in sheltering some 500 Jewish employees from the Nazis and ultimately went into hiding himself, neither Dr. Philips nor his company was even aware until 1997 of Zwartendijk's activities to rescue Jews.[10] Because Zwartendijk had to destroy all his consular files before leaving Kovno, there are few documents that can cast light on the key question of his motivation. One clue emerges in a July 5, 1940, letter from Zwartendijk in Kovno to Philips headquarters in Eindhoven in the Nazi-occupied Netherlands. Zwartendijk writes obliquely of trying to help folk who were "*in de puree*" colloquial Dutch for "in hot water" or literally "in the soup." Even this reference, however, casts little light on the motivation behind Zwartendijk's altruism.[11]

One possible motivation would be religious faith. Carl Lutz, the Swiss consul in Budapest from 1942 until the end of the war, protected Jews through legal and illegal channels. According to his stepdaughter, "he was a committed Christian and felt that he had been sent to Budapest for a purpose."[12] The Calvinist citizens of Le Chambon sur Lignon, almost in the shadow of Vichy, the capital of unoccupied but pro-Nazi France, sheltered many thousands of Jews throughout the war due to a deeply held Calvinist faith and historical acquaintance with religious intolerance.[13]

Was Zwartendijk also motivated by a religious belief system? According to his oldest son, Jan, who witnessed the events in Kovno, that was not the case. That son wrote in 1998:

> My father was not religious in the sense of participating in religious activities or going to church. His parents had been strong Protestants, inclined toward the socially-liberal side. He himself never felt comfortable with organized religion and never went to church. I think he could be described as a "humanist seeker" in his beliefs. I believe that what guided him in Kaunas was a set of strong personal convictions about what for him was right and what wasn't. He always stuck to his own code without hesitation or compromise, even if that occasionally got him into trouble. But he did not have the slightest inclination to lecture anybody about his values, nor even to discuss them. He just did what he felt he ought to do, period. No discussion or commentary called for, before or after.[14]

Zwartendijk's younger son Robert, although only an infant during the Kovno episode, has corroborated his brother's version of events. Robert stated categorically that Jan Sr. "did what he felt he had to do as a human being, nothing more and nothing less."[15] Perhaps the most telling evidence of Zwartendijk's selflessness is that between 1945 and his death on September 17, 1976, he never spoke about or made any attempt to publicize or glorify his role. Nor did he know how many people he aided had actually made it out of Lithuania. Indeed, he did not know that anyone at all had made it out until 1963, when he learned that there were survivors living in the Los Angeles area. Conversely, most of those whom he rescued did not know his name and referred to him as "Mr. Philips Radio" or "The Angel of Curaçao." Some thought "Philips Radio" was his actual name. In March 1976, through the efforts of Shanghai survivor Ernest G. Heppner and others, Zwartendijk was finally located.[16] Pinhas Hirschprung, *Av Beth Din* (Chief Judge) of the Montreal Rabbinical Court, wrote Zwartendijk in June 1976 that "not only have you saved us, but you literally saved the generations coming from us."[17] Several months before Zwartendijk's death he was notified by historian David Kranzler about the magnitude of his rescue mission.[18] Survivor Samuel Orlansky, of Bene Berak, Israel, wrote Jan Zwartendyk in 1996: "Our first aider and supporter was your late father. . . . What a great feeling it must be if one is privileged to save the life of even one person. And what great merit more was it to save a whole community from the clutches of death."[19]

Finally, in October 1997, through the efforts of Kranzler, Heppner, Israeli diplomat Moshe Yegar, this author, and others, Jan Sr. was recognized as "Righteous among the Nations" by Yad Vashem, the state of Israel's official Holocaust Martyrs' and Heroes' Remembrance Authority. Dr. Mordecai Paldiel, the head of the Department of the Righteous and arguably the individual with the most intimate knowledge of the motivation of some 18,000 other righteous gentiles, has drawn the following conclusion about motivation in the majority of cases he has examined. It would also seem to apply to Zwartendijk:

> The exceptional response of the rescuers to the plight of the Jews is predicated upon the presence of a deeper and more primal disposition, perhaps rooted in our genes, which causes some of us to respond instinctively and instantaneously when confronted with a situation that is so upsetting to our senses as to constitute a traumatic experience. This is especially the case when the potential rescuer is witness to a situation in which the principle of the right to

life is called into question, as it was for Jews on the European continent during the Nazi reign of terror.[20]

What Motivated the Dutch, Japanese, and Soviet Governments?

With respect to the motivations of governments, the Dutch government-in-exile had been in existence only a matter of weeks when its ambassador to the Baltic States asked Zwartendijk to take the place of the suspected pro-Nazi Dutch consul in Kovno—clearly a conscious, antifascist choice. The ambassador also, without asking or informing his government, acquiesced in the issuance of phony visas for the Lewin family and for Gutwirth's friends. In addition to Zwartendijk's voluminous visa-writing, Dutch diplomats in Stockholm (A. M. de Jong) and Kobe (N. A. G. de Voogt) later on issued identical Curaçao visas to Jewish refugees. The issuance of such "visas" was a heroic and commendable act but in all cases the individual decision of the diplomat himself. There was no governmental policy to issue phony documents to Jewish refugees. Indeed, the Dutch government did not know about the Kovno rescue scheme until about 1963 . . . and asked Zwartendijk for an explanation. He privately provided the information requested without seeking any broader publicity or recognition.

What motivated Sugihara? Unlike Zwartendijk, he was a professionally trained diplomat and intelligence officer. His granting of transit visas to Jews should be seen in that context, as has been suggested in several articles by Boris Bresler, archivist of the Tel Aviv—based Association of Former Jewish Residents of China (*Igud Yotzei Sin*).[21] In an unpublished memoir, Sugihara explained that he was assigned to open a new Japanese consulate in Kovno in 1939 because "General [Hiroshi] Oshima [the Japanese ambassador in Berlin] wanted to know whether the German army would really attack the Soviet Union." The Japanese General Staff wanted to withdraw its army from the Soviet-Manchurian border and move it to the South Pacific. Therefore, in Sugihara's words, his primary task in Kovno was to establish the foreseeable date of a German attack on Russia. He wrote:

> It was obvious why the Staff had insisted that the Foreign Office open a consulate in Kaunas. As a consul in Kaunas, where there was no Japanese colony, I understood that my main task was to inform the General Staff and the Foreign Ministry about the concentration of German troops near the border.[22]

Upon his arrival in Kovno, Sugihara set about establishing an intelligence-gathering network to ascertain regional troop movements. His activities received a major boost in the autumn of 1939 when agents from the Polish underground and the London-based Polish government-in-exile, along with many other Poles, crossed into unoccupied Lithuania while Poland was overrun. Large numbers of Polish troops were interned by the Lithuanian government in camps in Kolotowo, Birsztany, and Polaga. Sugihara helped get some key Polish officers and operatives out of internment and indeed out of Lithuania and into third countries, in several cases issuing them Japanese identity documents and loaning them his official vehicle. One of Sugihara's closest informants was Polish Lieutenant Leszek Daszkiewicz, whose memoir reveals the close connection between Sugihara's intelligence operations and his rescue of Polish Jews. Daszkiewicz wrote:

> Apart from supplying the Japanese consul with information from the territory of the U.S.S.R., I was to receive a reply from him as to the deci-

sion concerning the issue of Japanese transit visas to enable Polish refugees to travel via Russia and Japan to America or to one of the islands off the South American coast. . . . When the time came and the Japanese Consulate started issuing visas, it was the Jews who came in great numbers, while there were very few [ethnic] Poles. Only a dozen or so applied and I arranged for them to be treated as priority in all matters. . . . Sugihara told me that it was quite difficult for him to write the customary formula in Japanese in all passports and that caused delays. I suggested making a rubber stamp. He agreed and gave me a master copy. I then gave this to [Polish Army intelligence officer] Captain Jakubianiec who ordered a stamp to be made from it. However, we had two copies made and one sent to Vilnius where Japanese transit visas were issued later following the departure of the consul from Kaunas, but backdated.[23]

Polish documents make clear, then, that apart from any humanitarian motives, Sugihara's involvement with Polish Jewish refugees was part of a coordinated operation to get Jewish and non-Jewish Poles out of Lithuania. It was a by-product of his intelligence-gathering operations with the Polish government-in-exile. That cooperative effort was endorsed by the Japanese Foreign Office and military. After the Soviets closed Sugihara's consulate in Kovno, he went on to equally sensitive postings in Berlin and Königsberg and then went on to become Japanese consul general in Prague, an even more prestigious posting than the job he had held in Kovno.[24] The motivation for Sugihara's activities was fundamentally different from that of Zwartendijk, who was not a salaried or professional diplomat and who was certainly not acting in conjunction with an intelligence-gathering operation.

The Soviet Union's motives in the Kovno rescue are far more complex. Here we are no longer dealing with an individual's choice or even the collective choice of a family or a small community. Instead, we are dealing with the machinations of what was at that time one of the world's two largest totalitarian states. Who permitted approximately 2,200 Polish and Lithuanian Jews to travel thousands of miles across Siberia in order to leave the "paradise" of the Soviet Union? These highly unusual activities almost certainly could not have been authorized by local party functionaries in Kovno or even by Pozdniakov, the Russian representative in Kovno, whose task was to implement the incorporation of Lithuania into the Soviet Union.[25] Who were the higher authorities, and why might they have gone along with the scheme?

According to former USSR United Nations Ambassador Victor Israelyan, who is also a historian of the Soviet Union in the World War II period, one individual, Vladimir Dekanozov, would have been responsible in 1940 for approving exit visas for Polish and Lithuanian Jews and allowing them to travel across the Soviet Union to Vladivostok. Dekanozov was Lavrenti Beria's man when both were still in Soviet Georgia in the mid-1930s. When both were called to Moscow, Dekanozov became Foreign Minister Vyacheslav Molotov's long-time deputy (1939 to November 1940, and 1941–48) with a short stint as the Soviet Union's ambassador to Germany (November 1940–41). In 1938, Beria became head of the NKVD (the Soviet secret police, later named the KGB). Dekanozov became Beria's deputy in March 1953. Both were executed in December 1953.

The broader context in which Dekanozov had to decide about the visas was the August 1939 Hitler-Stalin nonaggression agreement, which Victor Israelyan calls "the pact between two scorpions in a bottle."[26] That treaty stipulated that the

Baltic republics were to be within the sphere of influence of the Soviet Union and not that they were to be annexed by the Soviet Union. Nevertheless, the Soviet Union annexed the Baltic republics in 1940 while Hitler was preoccupied overrunning France and the Low Countries on his way to invading Britain.[27] Stalin thought he could get away without a German reaction, and he did. Still, Stalin did not want to push his luck. According to Victor Israelyan, it would have been inconceivable for Dekanozov to allow 2,200 Polish and Lithuanian Jews to escape across Siberia without Molotov's approval, and Molotov would not have approved it without Stalin's approval.[28]

The question then becomes: why would Stalin have approved this? Humanitarian sentiments can be ruled out. What was the deal? With whom? One possible Soviet motive was that permitting the rescue mission was a convenient way of eliminating the burden of several thousand desperate and impoverished Jews in freshly annexed Lithuania. Warhaftig wrote that "the local government was interested in ridding itself of the refugee burden with maximum speed and was prepared to assist us, mainly in issuing passports and travel documents."[29] A second possible motive was that the escape scheme provided a good opportunity to induce some of the more desperate refugees, through intimidation or blackmail, to spy for the Soviets in the United States, Canada, Palestine, Japan, Shanghai, or elsewhere. (No one realistically expected the refugees to wind up in Curaçao.) Warhaftig writes that some of the applicants for Soviet transit and exit permits

> were called in for screening by an official of the NKVD. Two of the students from the Grodno yeshivah informed me [about] their screening. The NKVD suggested [to one of the students] that he might act as their agent, whatever his

destination. The issue of an exit permit was made dependent on his acceptance of the offer, but he claimed to have declined.[30]

Yet another possible Soviet motive was that this was an easy way to raise more than half a million dollars for Intourist, the Soviet state travel agency. Each refugee was charged between 170 and 240 U.S. dollars. The money was collected and the tickets bought with the assistance of American Jewish relatives, the JDC, and the *Vaad ha-Hatzala*, an Orthodox Jewish relief and rescue organization based in New York City.[31] Perhaps all three factors played a part.

According to Israelyan, there are probably no Soviet Foreign Office officials left alive who were involved in the authorization. Dekanozov's name was purged from all official Soviet histories and published Foreign Office documents. He "never existed." Only surviving KGB agents or KGB or Foreign Office files could tell us more.[32]

NOTES

1. "Beckelman," "Refugee," 2.
2. See Jan Zwartendijk to Benjamin Gray, August 21, 1963, and to H. Shapiro, January 22, 1967; both courtesy of Jan Zwartendyk.
3. Isaac Lewin, *Remembering Days of Old: Historical Essays* (New York: Research Institute of Religious Jewry, 1994), 171–76; Nathan Lewin, "Memories of My Father," *Washington Jewish Week*, September 7, 1995, 53.
4. Sugihara told Warhaftig in 1969 that he had been aware of the fictitious nature of the Curaçao visas. But, as long as his action was not in any way illegal, he was prepared to aid the refugees. Warhaftig, *Refugee*, 110 and *passim*. Other accounts about Sugihara include Hillel Levine, *In Search of Sugihara* (New York: Free Press, 1996); Christopher Lehmann-Haupt, "Tackling a Mysterious Mass Rescuer," *New York Times*,

December 23, 1996, C16; Ernest G. Heppner, "Sine Qua Non," *Hadassah Magazine*, November 1997, 41; and Mel Gussow, "Sugiharas List: A Play about 6,000 Saved Jews," *New York Times*, January 21, 1998, B3. A widely published but unsourced account about Sugihara appears in Marvin Tokayer and Mary Swartz, *The Fugu Plan: The Untold Story of the Japanese and the Jews during World War II* (New York: Paddington Press, 1979; reprint, New York: Weatherhill, 1996), also published under the title Desperate Voyagers (New York: Dell, 1980). . . .

5. Jan Zwartendijk to Gray, August 21, 1963; to Shapiro, January 22, 1967; Nathan Gutwirth, to Mordecai Paldiel, May 28, 1996; to Jan Zwartendijk, July 16, 1996; all courtesy of Jan Zwartendijk. Kranzler, *Japanese*, 311–12; Zuroff, *Response*, 80–87.

6. Until 1941, when the Japanese occupiers shut the gates of Shanghai (having earlier kept them open), Shanghai was the only place on earth just prior to the Holocaust where a foreigner could legally walk ashore without any documentation whatsoever. . . . On how intricacies of governance and nongovernance in Shanghai created a haven for Jews, see Ernest G. Heppner, *Shanghai Refuge: A Memoir of the World War II Jewish Ghetto* (Lincoln: University of Nebraska Press, 1993), 40 and *passim* . . . . Altman and Eber, "Flight," 51–86.

7. Warhaftig, *Refugee*, 104–5. There is at least one recorded instance of Jewish refugees' being admitted to Curaçao and not being turned back to sea. After the German invasion of the Netherlands in May 1940, several Jews with Austrian and German passports were interned on the Dutch West Indian island of Bonaire. In late 1941, a League of Nations refugee official in London prevailed upon the Dutch government-in-exile in London to cable the governor of Curaçao to admit to Curaçao an additional eighty-two Jewish refugees aboard the Spanish ship *Cabo de Hornos*, and the refugees were admitted. . . . Beckelman, then stationed in

Asuncion, Paraguay, to JDC, New York, December 13 and 23, 1941, JDC Archives; "High Seas," *Time Magazine*, December 1, 1941, 30; Pamela Rotner Sakamoto, "The Policy of the Japanese Ministry of Foreign Affairs toward Jewish Refugees" (doctoral diss., Fletcher School of Law and Diplomacy, Tufts University, 1996), 297–300; Walter Laqueur, *Generation Exodus* (Hanover NH: Brandeis University Press, 2001), 219.

8. Betty Goodfriend, interview with author, Atlanta, Georgia, October 1999. On Jewish fears of deportation to Siberia, see Menachem Begin, *White Nights* (New York: Harper and Row, 1977), *passim*.

9. Jan Zwartendijk, "Jan Zwartendijk: His Activities as Dutch Consul in Lithuania, 1940" (Ms., October 1, 1996), 7; courtesy of Jan Zwartendijk.

10. Even though the Holocaust rescue activities of Zwartendijk and Dr. Philips were unrelated, on November 4, 1997, the Israeli charitable organization Boys Town Jerusalem sponsored a dinner in Amsterdam to jointly honor both. At this event, Zwartendijk's children received his posthumous "Righteous among the Nations" medal from Yad Vashem. The same honor had been bestowed on Dr. Philips earlier that year. Letter: Mordecai Paldiel, Jerusalem, to Jan Zwartendijk, State College, Pennsylvania, October 7, 1997, copy to author.

11. J. Zwartendijk to Philips, Eindhoven, July 5, 1940; courtesy Jan Zwartendijk.

12. Ruth Rothenberg, "Belated Honor for Swiss Diplomat Who Saved Jews," *Jewish Chronicle* (London), April 7, 2000, 19.

13. See interviews with wartime survivors of Le Chambon in Pierre Sauvage's documentary film *Weapons of the Spirit*, produced by Friends of Le Chambon. For general background, see Gilbert, *Holocaust*, 403–4 and Yahil, *Holocaust*, 589–90.

14. Jan Zwartendijk to the author, December 29, 1998; courtesy Jan Zwartendijk.

15. Robert Zwartendijk, quoted in "The Man Who Saved Judaism," *Jerusalem Post International Edition No. 1860* (June 29, 1996), 1.

16. Jan Zwartendyk to author, September 23, 2001. On the efforts of Heppner, Kranzler, and others, see letters from J. Zwartendyk and Ernest G. Heppner in *The Jewish Post and Opinion*, April 30, 1976, 2; Ed Stattman, "Japanese Granted Dutch Denied Laurels for Saving Jews," *Jewish Post and Opinion*, June 21, 1995, NAT 4; Ed Stattman, "Dutchman to be Honored for 1940 Rescues? *Jewish Post and Opinion*, May 8, 1996, NAT 2; Steve Lipman, "The Decent Thing," Jewish Week (New York), May 10, 1996, 1; Letter: Paldiel to Jan Zwartendyk, October 7, 1997; and Phyllis Braun, "Yad Vashem Gives Righteous Gentile His Due," *Arizona Jewish Post* (Tucson), May 1, 1998, 1, 8.

17. Pinhas Hirschprung to Jan Zwartendyk, June 12, 1976, in Boys Town Jerusalem testimonial volume to Jan Zwartendijk, New York City, September 9, 1996, n.p.

18. Jan Zwartendyk to author, September 23, 2001.

19. Samuel Orlansky to Jan Zwartendyk, May 19, 1996, in Boys Town volume, n.p.

20. Mordecai Paldiel, "The Face of the Other: Reflections on the Motivations of Gentile Rescuers of Jews," in *Remembering for the Future: The Holocaust in an Age of Genocide*, vol. 2, ed. John K. Roth and Elisabeth Maxwell (Basingstoke, UK: Palgrave, 2001), 334.

21. Boris Bresler, "Sugihara Story: Facts, Mystery, Myth," *Bulletin of the Igud Yotzei Sin* (Tel Aviv) no. 350 (June—July 1997): 12–14, no. 351 (September—October 1997): 8–11; reprinted in Points East (Menlo Park, Calif.) 13, no. 2 (July 1998): 1, 6–10.

22. Sugihara Chiune, "Report on the Activity in Kovno and on Cooperation with the Polish Forces" (unpublished report, in Russian), 1–2, cited in Ewa Palasz-Rutkowska and Andrzej T. Romer, "Polish-Japanese Cooperation during World War II," *Japan Forum* (London) 7, no. 2 (Autumn 1995): 287–88.

23. Sugihara, "Report," 5, in Palasz-Rutkowska, "Polish," 289; Leszek Daszkiewicz, *Placowka wywiadowcza "G" Sprawodania i dokumenty* (Polish: Intelligence Agency "G." Reports and Documents), unpublished, England, 1948, in Palasz-Rutkowska, "Polish," 292–93.

24. Sugihara Yukiko, *Rokusennin-inochi-no biza* (Life Visas for 6,000 People) (Tokyo: Asahi-sonorama, 1990), 73, in Palasz-Rutkowska, "Polish," 293–4.

25. Warhaftig met with Pozdniakov on at least one occasion. Zuroff, *Response*, 85.

26. Jan Zwartendyk, notes on a conversation with Victor Israelyan, June 4, 1996; courtesy of Jan Zwartendyk.

27. Gerhard L. Weinberg, *A World at Arms* (Cambridge: Cambridge University Press, 1999), 100–107.

28. Zwartendyk, notes on Israelyan, June 4, 1996.

29. Warhaftig, *Refugee*, 92.

30. Ibid., 104–5.

31. Kranzler, *Japanese*, 312, 338.

32. Zwartendyk, notes on Israelyan, June 4, 1996.

The Good German of Vilna

MICHAEL GOOD

From *The Search for Major Plagge*

By September 25, 1943, only 2,300 Jews remained in Vilna: 1,200 were in a protected furrier's camp called "*Kailis*," 70 worked in a military hospital, and 70 worked at Gestapo headquarters. Additionally, just one week before the liquidation of the ghetto, 1,000 Jews were moved out to a small camp located at 37 Subocz Street, due to the insistence of an obscure Wehrmacht officer named Plagge who was in charge of Vilna's vehicle repair unit (HKP [*Heereskraftfuhrpark*])....My mother and her parents were among the lucky few transferred to the HKP camp.

For the lucky Jews working for HKP 562, it appeared that Major Plagge . . . had performed a miracle. It was said that he had traveled first to Kovno and then all the way to Berlin to demand that his workers be spared from the approaching liquidation. He had arranged for them to be transferred to a freestanding camp, separate from the rest of the ghetto. The camp was situated in what had previously been a subsidized housing complex on the far edge of town. . . . Originally built for the Jewish poor, these large apartment houses standing in the middle of grassy fields were now a refuge . . . On September 16th, 250 HKP workers and their families . . . left the ghetto and traveled to the newly formed HKP camp. It was none too soon. One week later, on September 23, 1943, the SS began the final liquidation of the Vilna ghetto. . . . My mother's uncle Mula Gerstein and aunt Nina, along with their son Gary, hid in a maline [prepared hiding place] during the liquidation. After many close brushes with death, Mula and his family eventually made their way into HKP with the help of my grandparents. Additionally, my grandfather managed to save his niece Eva and her husband Lolek by getting him inscribed on the HKP work list. Thus of the 33 members of my mother's family, eleven clung to life after the liquidation of the Vilna ghetto. Of those, eight were saved, for the time being, by Major Plagge's success in forming a camp for his workers.

While the Jews in the HKP camp were ultimately under the jurisdiction of the SS, the details of their day to day circumstances were delegated to Major Plagge and his unit. Plagge himself was somewhat of a mystery to the Jews working for HKP. While death and murder seemed to descend from all sides in the Vilna ghetto, Plagge's workers always seemed to be spared. Many of the HKP workers attributed their good fortune to the efforts of Plagge himself, although how and why he managed to protect his workers was totally unknown. Interestingly, shortly before his own death at the hands of the SS, Jacob Gens [head of the Vilna ghetto Jewish Council, 1941–43] advised our family friend and HKP survivor Bill Begell to try to get into the HKP camp as "Plagge can keep you safer than I can." My mother recalls seeing Major Plagge from a distance, a thin man who walked with a limp, always neat and proper in his *Wehrmacht* uniform. She thought that he was an older man as gray hair showed under his officer's cap. Even years later, it is hard for HKP survivors to explain why, but they say they were never afraid when they were around Plagge; to the contrary, they actually felt safe.

Unlike the notorious conditions in concentration camps and slave labor camps throughout Europe, conditions in Plagge's HKP camp were relatively benign. Work hours were reasonable, and:

> The sympathy toward us of Major Plagge, the chief of HKP, had put its stamp not only on our working conditions but on the whole way we lived. Personally I worked not too laboriously as the stockroom keeper of the workshop for vehicle seat-repair. We worked from 6 a.m. to 6 p.m. with a one hour interruption for dinner, which I ate in our room with my family.
>
> In the room, which we shared with other prisoners, there was running water and a kitchen stove. We slept in beds and were able to wash ourselves and to cook. We were frequently able to change our personal and bed linen and even had a carry-out privy which we placed in a cubbyhole under the staircase— thus we did not have to use the filthy, stinking enclosed pit in the courtyard. As in the ghetto, the HKP workshops serviced the needs of the German army. My wife worked in the workshop that repaired German army coats, and our fourteen-year-old daughter worked in the one where heels were knitted onto the torn and dirty socks of the German soldiers.[1]

. . . The HKP Jews initially felt safe under the protection of Major Plagge. They set up a system of smuggling food and essentials, which the *Wehrmacht* guards tolerated and benefited from monetarily. Within a few weeks, a camp routine, complete with black market economy, was established.

Listening secretly to the BBC via a homemade radio during the winter of 1943–44, the inmates could tell that the war was turning against the Germans. Their advances into Russia had been stopped and now the Red Army was moving west. However, they also heard from the BBC that the Nazi policy of extermination of the Jews was accelerating even as the fortunes of war changed. Tension mounted as everyone tried to calculate whether there was a chance for liberation by the Russians before the SS finished off the final remnants of Vilna's Jews. . . . Those who survived thirsted for life. They spent much of their energy trying to engineer plans of escape or preparing hiding places for the time when the SS returned to the camp. . . .

As the front-line fighting between the Russians and Germans approached Vilna, tension mounted within the camp. No one knew exactly what the military situation was. The Jews could not tell when the precise moment would be that they should go into hiding before the SS arrived. Having provisions to last only a few days, timing was of the essence if they were to survive. Once again, just as before the liquidation of the Vilna Ghetto, Major Plagge acted in a lifesaving manner. My mother recounts what happened next:

> On Saturday, July 1st, 1944, Major Plagge . . . came to talk to us. We clustered around him, eager to hear what he would tell us about what lay before us. Major Plagge warned us that the German army was leaving Vilna and our camp would be evacuated westward in connection with the nearing of the Russians. To emphasize his warning Major Plagge informed us in his speech that we would stop being a HKP work camp and would be entirely in the hands of the S.S.—he then carefully commented: "And you all know how well the S.S. takes care of their Jewish prisoners." This speech of Major Plagge aroused terrible fear in us. . . . The vast majority

of us understood, especially after Major Plagge's veiled warning, that for our camp the moment had come that we all feared. . . .[2]

Plagge indicated that the evacuation would occur on Monday, July 3. To prevent any escape, the SS posted more guards around the camp. Those inmates with prepared *malines* tried to slip into them without attracting attention. . . . The liquidation of the camp ensued. Special SS troops wearing black uniforms and a skull insignia on their caps arrived for roll call on Monday, July 3. The 500 inmates who, having nowhere to hide, appeared at roll call were taken to [the suburban village of] Ponary and killed. Seeing that there were almost 500 missing prisoners, the Germans began a systematic search and captured an additional 200 Jews, who were executed in the camp courtyard. Included in this number were my mother's cousin Eva and her husband Lolek. . . . For those hiding in the suffocating conditions in the *maline*, uncertainty reigned. Unable to stand the inhuman conditions below, some emerged from the hiding place too soon and were killed by the German troops who were scouring the camp. Those hidden in the *maline* suffered not only from lack of oxygen, but also from thirst. Becoming dehydrated, they were forced to drink sewer water strained through a handkerchief. . . .

Another day passed. Outside the camp, the Gentile population had heard that the Jews of HKP had been killed and came to the camp to loot their belongings. Taking clothes, bed linens, comforters, pots, and kitchen utensils, the Poles were disappointed that they were unable to find any of the gold and jewelry that they anticipated finding among the possessions of the "rich Jews." Groups of looters began to tear up the floors of the camp buildings in search of the hidden treasure. After a time, they found and removed the cover to [my family's] hidden *maline* . . . . Staggering out of their hiding place and extricating themselves from the looters, my mother and her parents quickly exited the HKP building. In the camp courtyard they passed the partially buried bodies of their neighbors and family members who had been captured and killed by the Germans the day before. They decided to leave the camp and try to get to their old apartment building on Zawalna 2, where they knew the janitor was trustworthy. Traveling across the fields that surrounded the camp, they encountered Poles who informed them that the center of town was still under German control. They were at a loss as to what to do, when suddenly a Lithuanian man appeared, offering to shelter them at his apartment in town. Frightened at the prospect of trusting a stranger, but having no other options, they decided to go with him. Before they could proceed, they tried as best they could to wash their filthy clothes, which were covered with mud and water from their stay in the hiding place over the previous three days. They then followed the Lithuanian into town. . . .

During the summer of 1999, I decided to attempt to uncover the full identity and fate of Major Plagge. My hope was to try to contact his family and make sure they knew of his role during the war and to express our family's gratitude for his good deeds. I do admit to some doubts in the beginning. I did not know if it was possible to find someone who had vanished into the chaos of war over half a century in the past. I also did not know exactly who or what I would find even if successful. While I knew that my mother and grandfather felt strongly that Plagge had saved their lives, it was not clear to me how he had helped Jews, nor why. . . . Who really knew how big a role this Plagge character played in the survival of such a large number of HKP Jews? In spite of all these questions, the fact remained that my mother (who is not exactly sentimental when it comes to Germans) was quite adamant that Plagge had saved her life along with her parents and many other Jews. In the end, it was my blind belief in what my mother told me that carried me forward to begin a search spanning thousands of miles across continents and half a century into the past.

I began by talking to my mother and reading my grandfather's memoirs, looking for clues as to Plagge's identity. I did not find much to go on. His workers knew him only as "Major Plagge," the commander of the HKP unit in Vilna. My mother remembered him as an older man; she could see that under his officer's cap he had gray hair. She did not know of anyone who had actually conversed with him, but she did note that, unlike the other Germans, the Jewish workers felt safe in his presence. My grandfather specifically mentioned in his memoirs that Plagge, ". . . according to those who had personal contact with him, was a man of the highest moral character." Yet no one knew for sure what he was his thinking when he formed the HKP camp or when he made his speech to the prisoners informing them of the coming of the SS. What were his motivations? Some of our survivor friends could think of self-serving reasons for his actions. . . . My mother did not agree with these hypotheses. She thought Plagge was motivated by a true desire to help his workers. She remembers that when some older women were discussing Plagge in the camp, they said they wished they could repay his kindness. Perhaps, they said, giving him a foot massage and pedicure would be a small token of appreciation that bespoke their warm feelings toward him. These were not the feelings that Jewish prisoners would have had toward a conniving, self-serving German. . . .

In October 2000, thirteen months after I had started my search, I received an innocent-appearing note from a Jewish genealogist specializing in the Vilna area named Joel Ratner, who forwarded an email from a man in Hamburg, Germany:

Subj: S. Klaczko
From: Joel Ratner
To: Michael Good

It looks like this gentleman may have some promising avenues you can pursue. I think his partner with the military background might be a good place to start, especially with his knowledge of logistics. Please keep in touch—I'm interested in how this proceeds. Joel

MONDAY, 09 OCTOBER 2000

From: "Dr. Salomon Klaczko-Ryndziun"
To: "Joel Ratner" and "Dr. Michael Good"
Dear Joel,

I read the letter you sent prepared by Dr. Michael Good on behalf of his family. I am living and working in Hamburg, where I own a small hitech company . . .

One of my co-owners is a retired lieutenant colonel of the German army and he teaches at the Hamburg Military Academy. Since he is a specialist in Logistics, he may know how to approach the military archives in Germany, in order to localize *Major Plagge*. I will try also at the national telephone directory of Germany, to look, if there is somebody there with the same family name. Maybe, we will succeed in localizing a son or daughter or grandchild of Major Plagge. There are not too many people in Germany who really risked to help Jews during the Nazi times. These few people are the real heroes of the German nation. I will therefore do my best in order to help. Sincerely yours, Salomon Klaczko

I immediately wrote to Mr. Klaczko, thanking him for his offer to help and telling him I would very much appreciate any assistance that his business partner could offer. I soon heard from Joerg Fiebelkorn, Klaczko's business associate:

Subj: your request—Maj. Plagge
DATE: 10/13/2000 10:01:10 A.M.
EASTERN DAYLIGHT TIME

From: Joerg Fiebelkorn
To: Michael Good

I have forwarded your request to the "Bundesarchiv—Zentralnachweisstelle" (Federal Archive—Central [Record] Bureau) in Aachen/Germany, where all personal files of the *Wehrmacht* are registered. If the name and unit is correct, you will have an answer about the where and when and further personal details such as the original address of Major Plagge within the next weeks. Then it should be no problem to trace his family—if he had one. I wonder, why there has not been any report about Major Plagge before? Especially in these days such an example of individual courage and humanity seems to be of some interest to the German public. With kind regards, J. Fiebelkorn. . . .

On November 13, 2000, I received an electrifying email from Joerg Fiebelkorn:

Subj: Plagge
From: Joerg Fiebelkorn
To: Michael Good

There has been a positive response from the Bundesarchiv about Major Plagge. They have found—as you may have heard from them as well—the date of birth, the home-address in Darmstadt and the correct name of his unit in Vilna. The letter from the Bundesarchiv will

need a few days more to reach the U.S. than to me. So, here is a brief translation:

Dear Mr. Fiebelkorn,

Following the research as done here, the person sought is Major (Reserve) Karl Plagge, born July 10th 1897. A place of birth is not mentioned. Since 1941 he was the commander of the "Heeresfuhrpark 562" (Army Repair Shop).

The home address was: Hoffmannstrasse 22, Darmstadt. The archive notes that he was married. Further details, especially about children, are not noted. To his further life we are unable to give any details. For this reason we suggest another request to the "Deutsche Dienststelle, Eichborndamm 179, D-13403 Berlin" (see attached form) and contact the personal register in Darmstadt as well.

I have sent a copy of this letter to Mr. Michael Good, in Durham CT, USA, who has contacted us directly as well. I assume you will proceed with your research and wish you all the success.

Now it is the question how to proceed:

I would suggest to write to the town mayor of Darmstadt directly, as this would be the most promising way to get more informations about his family. . . .

Soon the long awaited answer from Darmstadt arrived via Joerg Fiebelkorn:

Dear Michael,

The Darmstadt archive has responded. Here is the "raw" translation:

The requested Karl Plagge, borne 10.07.1897 in Darmstadt, by profession civil engineer ("Diplom-Ingenieur"), has died in Darmstadt on June 19th 1957. His wife Anke Dorothea, born Madsen on February 15th 1905 in Trier, moved on June 12th 1969 to Widdersdorf, Leonhardgasse 32 (now suburb of Cologne). Whether she is alive, is not known here. The Plagges had no children; the address known to you (Hoffmannstraße 22) is the address of the parents, where the Plagges lived before the war. He had a sister Marie Plagge, born September 28th 1893; to our records she stayed unmarried, had no children and was living in Hoffmannstraße 22 as well. Possibly she became one of the victims of the destruction of Darmstadt in 1944, when all buildings were destroyed (by allied bombing).

The Discoveries

When I became head of the *Kraftfuhrpark* (HKP) in Poland and Russia, I saw the civil population there in a very poor condition, without any rights or legal protection. There existed "soldier's letters" that informed the members of the German army that the Polish people were inferior and that the German soldier had to act as a *Herrenmensch*, a superior human being. I never understood this kind of behavior and never acted in the manner as specified in our orders. I took the decision to always act against the Nazi rules and to also give my subordinates the order to act in a very humane manner towards the civilian population . . . I did that because I thought it was my duty. There needed to be German people who could be seen by foreign countries as doing good. I was ashamed.[3]

—Testimony of Karl Plagge at his denazification trial, Darmstadt, Germany, 1947

In Darmstadt, Germany, Dr. Marianne Viefhaus was in earnest pursuit of Karl Plagge. In the university archives, she found his school records with a graduation date in 1924 with a degree in mechanical and chemical engineering. She also found records that he had been employed by an engineering firm called *Hessenwerke* in Darmstadt during the 1930s. [It] was no longer in business, but by looking in the Darmstadt Chamber of Commerce archives she found that the company had been owned and run by a family named Hesse. Checking the modern Darmstadt phone book, she saw that there was still a family named Hesse living at the same address that was listed for the owners of *Hessenwerke* in the archives. She gave the number a call and was able to talk to an elderly woman named Irma Freese who was the daughter of the now deceased head of *Hessenwerke*, Kurt Hesse. Mrs. Freese remembered Karl Plagge well as he and her father had been good friends. She said that after the war, German families did not discuss their wartime experiences. Whether it was due to guilt for unspeakable deeds or the general horror of the war experience for all Germans, talking about the war was not an acceptable topic of conversation in postwar German society. However, before finishing her conversation with Marianne, she did say that after the war, "Karl Plagge became cleared from incrimination because he saved many Jews."

This last comment loomed large in Marianne's mind. First of all, it would appear that some of his friends knew of his actions on behalf of Jews during the war. Secondly, this statement implied that Plagge may have had to defend himself against the common postwar accusation by the Allies that he had participated in war crimes. If this were the case, he may have had a denazification trial. Denazification in Germany was a process in which the victorious Allies attempted to identify and purge all Nazi war criminals from positions of power in postwar Germany. First, all Nazi Party members were required to fill out a lengthy questionnaire about their activities in the Nazi party and conduct during the war. If anything about their history implied a possible role in war crimes, they had to undergo a trial in a *Spruchkammer* or Denazification Court. Looking in the State of Hesse archives in Wiesbaden, Marianne found that Karl Plagge had indeed had a denazification trial. Most importantly, she found the trial transcript.

As Marianne read the court's file, she discovered that Karl Plagge had been a member of the Nazi Party. He had joined the party before most Germans—in 1931, two years before Hitler came to power. This implied that he did not join due to social pressures or career aspirations. People who joined the party at such an early date generally did so out of conviction. Because of this early date of party membership, as well as the fact that he had commanded a German labor camp where many Jews were killed, Karl Plagge was ordered to undergo a trial and had to defend himself from the charge of being a war criminal. He hired a lawyer and then proceeded to enlist friends and colleagues who had not been members of the Nazi Party to speak on his behalf. This dusty old file, . . . stored unread since 1947, contained testimonies by Plagge's subordinates from HKP, his employer Kurt Hesse, and from Karl Plagge himself. Additionally, there was testimony from a representative of Jewish survivors of the HKP camp who were living in the Ludwigsburg DP camp near Stuttgart, Germany, at the time. . . .

One of Plagge's Lieutenants, Alfred Stumpff, describes the tone that Plagge set within the HKP unit:

Karl Plagge . . . was my direct superior in the motor vehicle repair park in Vilna from June 16th 1942 until October 2nd 1942 where I served as a high lieutenant. During that time, I found that Major Plagge had an honorable and human mentality and strongly rejected the German policy of full extermination of the whole Jewish population in the occupied Eastern territories. He openly explained this to me in our discussions. Major Plagge demonstrated his opinions by really helping the endangered people; this not only took great courage but was also very dangerous for his position and himself.

Mr. Plagge himself always treated the Jews in a very proper and humane way and wanted his subordinates to do so as well. A good example is the following incident that represented a rare violation of Plagge's rules towards a Jewish worker.

One day I saw by chance how a sergeant from Wiesbaden, who was very proud to be a member of the SS, assaulted a Jewish worker, hitting and kicking him. When I confronted the sergeant with the incorrectness of his behavior, he excused himself by saying the Jew lied to him. He then used the common National Socialist phrases that the Jews are our enemies and aren't worthy of protection from a German. . . . I reported the incident to Plagge, and he had an even more serious discussion with the sergeant and ordered him to report to the front. Normally Plagge didn't have the right to do that, but afterwards the sergeant himself filed an application for going to the front and so he disappeared from the park very quickly after the incident.[4]

Plagge had learned from his experience in Darmstadt before the war that to be openly antagonistic toward the Nazis would cause him to be demoted or even arrested, which would not allow him to accomplish any of his goals. Five years later, in Vilna, he moved more subtly, encouraging those who secretly disagreed with the party, and transferring party stalwarts and "big Nazis" out of the unit. While Plagge was not publicly vocal about his political views, his men understood his inner leanings. The following is testimony given by Friedrich Asmus, one of Plagge's subordinates in Vilna:

The former major of the *Wehrmacht* Plagge was my direct superior during the war for about three and a half years. During this time he never . . . made any kind of provocative speech. It was known in our unit that comrades who were opponents of National Socialism were never disadvantaged but found a like-minded man in Major Plagge. "Big Nazis, Jew-eaters, and harassing people" were neutralized, displaced, or removed from the unit. I know about people, of higher rank than I, who acted in a too National Socialist way and were forced to leave the unit. Slave-driving methods were not tolerated.[5]

Plagge's main method of resistance against the genocide was to give work permits to Jewish workers, allowing them to save themselves and their family members from the aktions that swept the Vilna ghetto. To the outside authorities, he kept up the guise that he needed these skilled Jewish workers to carry out his duty of running an efficient vehicle repair operation. However, in reality, many of the Jews were unskilled and owed their jobs to Plagge's benevolence. Here again is Lieutenant Stumpff:

The large Jewish population of Vilna was herded into a ghetto. There the German administration distinguished between the "usable Jews" with their wives and children who could work for the *Deutsche Wehrmacht* or the war economy and who lived in a special part (after my memory it was called Ghetto A). The rest of the "unus-able Jews" became victims of extermination *Aktionen* and lived for a while in another part (Ghetto B). The employment in a factory of the *Wehrmacht* meant longer survival for the Jews during that time. Mr. Plagge employed in his factory Jewish workers in great numbers. There were many Jews who weren't really useful or necessary for the work that had to be done. The park employed, for example, Jews as barbers, shoemakers, tailors, and cooks. Jewish women and girls worked as cleaning workers and garden workers. Additionally, there was a Jewish doctor for the observation of the civil workers' health. Naturally, the park wasn't allowed to employ such people and Mr. Plagge could have gotten in serious trouble by doing so. These people were camouflaged to the outside as professional workers of the motor vehicle repair park. I knew from personal discussions with Mr. Plagge that he employed the majority of these Jews only to save them from extermination.[6]

Plagge did not worry too much about the real efficiency of his unit; his main goal was to protect as many workers as possible. At his trial, he stated, "I did not volunteer for this war and did not want to prolong the conflict by spurring on my labor to produce the needed resources with even greater efficiency."[7]

Plagge was also quite concerned with the nutritional status of his workers and their families. . . . [He] took several measures to try to ameliorate the hunger among both his Jewish and Polish workers. His quartermaster, Heinz Zeuner, testified about Plagge's concerns at his denazification trial: "I was the sub-superior of food administration in the motor vehicle repair park that he commanded. . . . He was especially concerned about the civilian workers, and I had to get extra rations for them (potatoes, flour, vegetables, . . .). For example, he ordered weekly observations about his workers' weight to convince himself that they got enough food."[8] Lieutenant Stumpff also recalled the efforts that Plagge made to feed his workers:

> The Jews got their food rations in the ghetto and didn't have any right to get them from our park administration. Even so, they got an extra lunch during the time I served there, just like the Polish workers; it was mostly a warm soup or another warm meal. Because the park didn't have any right to obtain extra food, the whole administration and particularly Major Plagge was always worried about how to get food like potatoes, vegetables, and horse meat. . . .[9]

During the war a variety of factors were at play, threatening the survival of both Poles and Jews in Lithuania. While the ss was actively murdering Jews in the forest of Ponary, the rest of both the Jewish and Polish population was threatened by the lack of basic social institutions needed for a population's survival. Plagge carefully analyzed the living situation of the civilians in Vilna and, with the precision of an engineer, carefully laid plans to provide them with life saving necessities. Here Staff Sergeant George Raab enumerates Plagge's efforts:

> During my service at the motor vehicle repair park I was in the rank of a staff sergeant and my duty was to work on personal affairs. I frequently talked with Major Plagge about the discriminating treatment the civilians had to endure by the German civil offices, the SD [Security Service of the ss] and the military police. I always knew that he hated the Nazi methods of handling civilian affairs, and he did everything in his power to help, defend and protect these miserable people.

Major Plagge created the following social institutions for the well being of his civil workers:

a) A park kitchen that served a wholesome lunch for the park workers and also to the workers who worked in faraway workshops belonging to the park

b) Creation of park-owned stores that supplied the workers and their families with food and meat

c) Creation of a park-owned hospital for the workers and their families (about 40 beds) supplied by army supplied medications

d) Creation of a "Unterstützungskasse" that supported civil workers who were in debt

e) Workers' supply of shoes, underwear, and working clothing, accomplished through a lot of negotiation with the Lithuanian offices

f) Workers' supply of winter potatoes and wood accomplished through a lot of negotiations with offices and distribution centers, but also through his own wood-cutting program.[10]

In addition to creating a basic infrastructure that sheltered both Jews and Poles from the life threatening hardships they encountered during the war, Plagge was frequently called on to rescue workers and their families who were caught in the Aktionen that swept through the ghetto. During the summer of 1941, the Lithuanian police or Khapuny (grabbers) would snatch Jews off the streets of Vilna and take them to Lukishki prison. They would be kept there for a day or two and then taken to Ponary for execution. Later, a similar pattern continued when the ss and Gestapo carried out Aktionen within the ghetto: first arrest and imprisonment in the Lukishki prison followed by transport to Ponary and execution. Survivors recall that while German soldiers usually scrutinized a worker's papers and respected the protection given by a valid work permit in a Wehrmacht workshop, the Lithuanian *Khapuny* would often arrest any Jew they encountered, ignoring their papers altogether. Once taken to Lukishki and placed in the hands of the Gestapo, an arrested Jew was doomed unless a German authority from a workshop came to claim him as an essential worker. Even the intervention of the *Wehrmacht* . . . was no guarantee, as the SD was always inclined to kill Jews rather that spare them. During the denazification trial, Plagge's men described how he struggled to keep ahead of the killing machine. Here again is Sergeant Raab:

> Mr. Plagge freed a large number of Jews (about 70) from the Lukishki prison. These Jews were to be deported to extermination camps, but were saved because of his protest at the SD office. He knew those workers personally and told the SD officials that they were indispensable for his park, but in reality they weren't and he knew that. He was allowed to enter the prison, and he not only freed the workers but also their family members. All those people really loved him from then on . . . I also knew that he knowingly allowed a number of Jews to hide on park territory during the persecutions until the end of the SD *Aktionen*.[11]

Plagge's men also described numerous individuals who Plagge personally saved from execution. There was the physician Dr. Baluk, who was arrested during the "provocation *Aktion*" in 1941 but freed at the last moment before execution due to Plagge's intervention. Another physician, Dr. Wolfsohn, and his elderly father were arrested during an *Aktion* carried out by the SS in the ghetto. Dr. Wolfsohn sent word to Plagge of his arrest and Plagge provided HKP work permits for both him and his father, even though neither of them were qualified workers. Here Lieutenant Stumpff describes a similar episode:

The wife and children of one of our Jewish workers visited relatives in the so-called Ghetto B ("unusable Jews"), where they were arrested during a military police raid and brought to an extermination camp. In his despair, the Jewish worker beseeched Major Plagge to save his family. He immediately went to the camp and after a long discussion with the commandant freed the worker's wife and children.[12]

HKP survivor Marek Swirski, who now lives in Israel, tells a dramatic story of how Plagge used deception to save his father David from the SS:

> . . . When leaving the kitchen after work one day, an SS officer searched a few Jews and found on my father and one other some food hidden in their trousers. The SS man became furious and started screaming. He took out his pistol either to kill them or only to frighten them when suddenly Plagge saw the scene and came with his driver and asked the SS to hand the Jews over to him. He said he intended to give them a proper lesson. The SS man accepted Plagge's offer. Plagge and his driver took the two Jews into a nearby barracks. He struck his whip on a table and asked the Jews to cry loudly and then had them cut their faces with a razor to draw blood. The two Jews, one of them my father, were then presented to the SS [man], who allowed them to leave and return to the Ghetto.
>
> This episode really traumatized my father. He was very grateful to Karl Plagge, who again enabled him to escape the SS murderers with his life.[13]

During the two years of the Vilna ghetto from fall 1941 until September 1943, Plagge continued to engage in these life-and-death struggles with the SS and Gestapo over his workers and their families. He manipulated the rules established by the German bureaucracy to protect his workers. He gave them work permits, he freed them from prison, and he fed them, all under the guise of trying to run an efficient vehicle repair operation. To the outside world he presented himself as a stern, earnest Prussian, intent on fulfilling his orders. Neither the SS nor many of his workers understood his true feelings and intentions; the latter seemed to sense that he was different, but unless they were among those who Plagge personally saved, they did not know for sure what he was up to. Plagge usually tried to act according to the regulations set up by the German occupying administration to protect himself from any potentially fatal accusations that he was working against the authorities. . . .

Through the years of the Vilna Ghetto, Plagge's manipulations were quite successful. He was able to establish a series of vehicle repair shops throughout Vilna as well as support services to keep his workers fed, clothed, and cared for medically. However, in the fall of 1943, the rules changed and Plagge's plans began to unravel when the SS decided to liquidate the Jews in the Vilna Ghetto. They began with the Estonian *Aktion* on September 1. Suddenly, no Jewish work permits were honored. Plagge discovered that not even he could safeguard his workers. Here is Sergeant Raab's description of that day:

The military administration planned to deport about 100 people (men, women and children) to the slate mines in Estonia. They were already in a transport train when a friend of theirs informed Mr. Plagge. He immediately went to the train station and ordered them to leave the train, even giving them military protection. The highest SD officer of Vilna then arrived after Plagge left and ordered the military

escort to bring them back in the train. They left for Estonia. Subsequently, there was a serious clash between Plagge and the SD officer. Plagge was very furious and desperate.[14]

Plagge could see that his methods of the previous two years were no longer sufficient. It was during this perilous time, just before the SS swept into the ghetto to deport the remaining Jews of Vilna, that Plagge achieved his biggest triumph on behalf of the HKP workers and their families: he formed a separate HKP labor camp on Subocz Street outside of the ghetto at the outskirts of town.

For years, HKP survivors have wondered how Plagge managed this miracle. Some HKP survivors thought that he traveled to the Lithuanian capital of Kovno to argue his case, others said that he went all the way to Berlin to lobby on behalf of his workers. The stories all agreed that Plagge spoke to his superiors to protest the planned killing of his skilled Jewish workers by the SS and proposed that he be allowed to form a special labor camp outside of the ghetto.

It was not until 2003, sixty years after the liquidation of the Vilna Ghetto that Marianne Viefhaus found testimony by Plagge that illuminates his methods:

When I learned that the Ghetto should be liquidated . . . I immediately consulted the SD and argued that the Jewish workers must be preserved for HKP. After consultation with the SD in Riga, this [HKP camp] was approved. I was obliged to accommodate them [the Jewish HKP workers] safely . . . I heard that the Ghetto was already surrounded. I therefore drove at night with trucks to the Ghetto entrance and, with the help of the *Judenrat*, succeeded in bringing out a large number of Jews from the Ghetto. A selection was not possible. About 800 Jews—men, women and children—were taken to HKP.[15] . . .

During the ensuing nine months that the HKP camp on Subocz Street was operating under his command, Plagge managed to keep the majority of his inmates relatively safe from the SS. There were notable exceptions, namely when the runaway prisoners David Zalkind, his wife, and his child were killed in November 1943, followed by the killing of thirty-six Jewish women by Bruno Kittel and his SS troops. Most significantly, he was unable to prevent the "children's *Aktion*" that occurred on March 27, 1944, while Plagge was on leave in Germany. Upon returning to his post in Vilna, he reportedly told the head Jewish representative in the camp, Nyona Kolysh, that if he had been present he might have been able to prevent this terrible *Aktion*. This may have been wishful thinking on his part, as the children's *Aktion* was carried out simultaneously throughout Lithuania. It is clear that, as the fortunes of war turned against the German *Wehrmacht*, its relative strength in power struggles with the SS declined. Indeed, after the September 1943 formation of the HKP camp, there is no evidence that Plagge was able to prevent the SS from carrying out any of their deadly activities against his workers once they chose to act. Plagge commented on this in the following passage:

> I took upon myself a great deal of risk because I hindered the SD and the party in their actions. There were some serious clashes between the SD leadership and me. My superior officer also reproached me for being too emotional and sentimental in my behavior towards the civil population. Because of my social actions, toward the end, they forbade all new measures I wanted to take.[16]

By fall and winter of 1943–44, it appears that Plagge had pushed the SS as far as he could without crossing the line into obvious treason. . . . At his trial many of his former officers wondered aloud how he managed to avoid accusations from the Gestapo. Sergeant Raab commented [that] "His actions in favor of Jews and foreign workers (Poles, Lithuanians) carried a high risk for him, because he often had serious conflicts with the dangerous SD. There was also the risk that different people were aware that he was helping and supporting enemies of the state."[17] Plagge himself said only, "I myself was not in contact with the SD but had many difficulties with it. I wasn't liked very well there. But they didn't persecute me. When I spoke with some of them personally they admitted the cruel things they were doing . . . all of them said they had orders to follow and they wouldn't act against orders."[18] . . .

By the time the Red army approached Vilna in July 1944, Plagge was unable to maneuver any longer within the Nazi hierarchy. He described his situation [thusly]: "Due to the collapse of the front, the military administration dissolved the park, and I was transferred to a military workshop, which I took as a personal slight. I think the reason for the closing of the motor vehicle repair park had to do with the fact that my regiment commander accused me of being too soft in the treatment of my workers."[19]

In the end, all he could do was warn his workers about the dissolution of the HKP camp and the danger they faced from the SS once his unit was evacuated from Vilna. In a characteristic manner, he made his warning in broad daylight, in the very presence of *Oberscharführer* Richter, the SS representative in the HKP camp. For approximately 250 of his prisoners, this warning would be lifesaving. Plagge's frustration at being unable to intervene to save his prisoners at the final hour is evident in the following testimony, given in 1959: "When, in the summer of 1944, HKP was ordered to relocate to Eastern Prussia, we wanted to take the Jews with us. . . . In the middle of the chaotic retreat I learned that there was a clearance gang of SD in the camp and that there was shooting . . . When I drove there, they refused me admission."[20]

At his denazification trial, Plagge was surrounded by his men, who testified to his exemplary conduct toward them and his prisoners. His men talked of their personal gratitude to Plagge, how he had protected them during the war. Then, unexpectedly, a woman arrived at the courthouse wanting to testify on behalf of some Jewish residents of the Displaced Persons camp at Ludwigsburg who were survivors of the HKP camp. The witness's name was Maria Eichamueller:

> I have to say the following words: Last Christmas I was in the DP camp at Ludwigsburg near Stuttgart. My girlfriend, whom I visited, knows the Jewish lawyer Dr. Paula Zanker who is in charge of the Jews in the camp. Through the help of my girlfriend, Dr. Zanker asked me to look for a Mr. Plagge here in Darmstadt with the reason that there are different Jews in her camp who want to thank Mr. Plagge. They told her that Plagge had always cared about them and that he helped them in a difficult time. They want to support him with their food and money if he lived in misery. There is also a Jewish father in Stuttgart who says that Plagge saved his son's life. I immediately went to the police in Darmstadt to find Mr. Plagge when I came home. I found different Plagges but not the one I looked for. On Saturday I accidentally read in the newspaper that there is a trial with a Mr. Plagge going on. I immediately came here.[21]

According to witnesses of the trial who were later interviewed by Marianne Viefhaus, the court was initially quite skeptical of the testimony of Plagge and his men. The witnesses said that the unexpected entrance of Mrs. Eichamueller to tes-tify on behalf of Jewish HKP survivors was "like in a film" and had a dramatic effect on the judges and those present in the courtroom.[22] . . .

Following the testimony of Plagge, his men, his friends from Darmstadt, and the representative of the Jewish prisoners in the Ludwigsburg DP camp, the court had to decide how to rule in the Plagge case. During denazification proceedings, the court could give one of five designations to the accused. Each designation had a corresponding level of punishment: (1) main war criminals, (2) activists, (3) less burdened by guilt, (4) fellow travelers (hangers-on), (5) Not guilty. . . . The prosecutor made no recommendation as to how the court should find the defendant, leaving it up to the court to decide. This implies that the prosecutor (whose job was to pursue and press charges against those responsible for the Nazi war crimes) felt that this defendant was innocent. However, in a most puzzling turn of events, Plagge himself, through his lawyer, asks for a designation of group 4, "Fellow Travelers, Hangers-On."[23]

Was it possible that he was just being humble? Those of us reviewing the file suspected that it was something more than mere modesty that prompted him to request this sentence. The designation of "fellow traveler" carried with it fines and court costs, not trivial matters in the impoverished days after the war. In order for us to understand Plagge, his conduct during the war and his actions during the trial, we needed to learn more about Plagge's own thoughts, his motivations and feelings regarding what happened during the war. Fortunately for our research group, Marianne Viefhaus was still hard at work at the Technical University of Darmstadt. On March 16, 2001, she announced another important find: "Another piece of good news: I discovered the godson of Karl Plagge who is mentioned in the denazification file as born just after the pogrom of 1938, son of the friend and witness Kurt Hesse and his wife. Yesterday I called him." . . .

Konrad Hesse remembered Plagge very well. He was 19 years old in 1957 when his godfather had suddenly died of a heart attack, old enough to have personal recollections about Plagge's personality. It seemed to me that Konrad Hesse was as close as I was going to get to my dream of speaking with Plagge's family. I wrote him a letter, telling him of our search for Plagge and the many grateful people who owed their lives to his godfather. . . .

Marianne told me that Konrad was very moved by my letter and the story of HKP survivors searching for Major Plagge and his descendants. He wrote back, speaking of his memories of Plagge and the lasting impression that his godfather made on him while he was growing up. Here are some excerpts of his letter:

Dear Mr. Good,

My name is Konrad Otto Karl Hesse. I was born on 19th December 1938 in Darmstadt . . . My third given name "Karl" refers to my godfather, Karl Plagge. The photograph, which you received via Mrs. Viefhaus, was made at the celebration of my confirmation in 1952.

Mr. Karl Plagge was, apart from Dr. Bruno Guenther, one of the two real friends of my parents. Before the war, my parents had a large circle of friends and acquaintances. However, in 1936, my father was confronted with the question as to whether he should separate himself from his non-Aryan wife or whether he would accept being excluded from all public offices, associations, and clubs. My father decided for his wife.

This caused the loss of his "friends" and "acquaintances" with the exception of the two friends mentioned above, i.e. Plagge and

Guenther. My mother later explained to me what she had recognized in the following way, "People usually act cowardly, one like all, all like one. They only pretend to stand for the ideal of life, one for all, all for one . . ."

Mr. Karl Plagge personified the man who was carrying a heavy burden in respect of his subjectively felt, assumed guilt. During the initial years of the National Socialist movement he had joined the party in good faith. The slogans of a romantic and idealistic character were tempting. In the misery of the German Reich the NSDAP seemed the only positive force for a new beginning. The reality, i.e. that criminals were acting for their own benefit and for criminal goals, became visible only at a later point in time. Even though Mr. Karl Plagge did everything in his power to limit damages by a human attitude once he had recognized this fraud and the reality, he was tortured by his conscience. In his view, it was not enough! He suffered because of this until his death. . . .

Now we could understand his actions at the denazification trial. Plagge asked for the designation of "fellow traveler" because of his deep sense of guilt for having helped create the genocidal monster that he later struggled against. Thus we see that in the years after the war, in spite of all the testimony of his subordinates and friends, Plagge did not consider himself "innocent." . . .

A year passed after Marianne's unveiling of the denazification file, the discovery of Konrad Hesse and the interviewing of the HKP survivors. The members of the Plagge research group and I digested the material we had and reflected on our findings. Over time I began to think that we had found all there was to uncover about Plagge. All known archives had been searched, it seemed all of Plagge's living relatives had been identified, most of the HKP survivors that my parents knew had been interviewed. I thought our research was largely complete and began to write the first draft of "The Search for Major Plagge." However, unexpectedly, yet another discovery was made that would allow us to see deeper into the mind of Karl Plagge. This new breakthrough was made possible by a man in Canada who, as a young boy in the HKP camp, had spent four months following the Children's *Aktion* hiding in a trunk.

Eliezer Greisdorf was eight years old when he, along with his older brother, parents, and uncle, went to the HKP camp on Subocz Street. He was hidden during the Children's *Aktion* by his uncle Leibl Greisdorf and then kept concealed each work day in a trunk so that, being an illegal child, he would not be discovered. He was able to leave his confinement only in the evening when the grownups returned from the HKP workshops and allowed him to move about under careful supervision. . . . Eliezer recalls that after they had been at HKP for a time, his family began to see that in many ways, Major Plagge seemed different:

> It was during our incarceration in HKP that my family became aware of Major Plagge as an unusually decent soldier. On several occasions, he came to inspect the camp and to speak to us. Why he took an interest in us, only he knew. During those visits, it became known that he always instructed the camp administrator that he wanted no cruelties or punishments to take place while he was there.[24]

Eliezer also tells the story of Plagge's warning, a deed that prompted his family to immediately enter a hiding place: "On his last visit he came to say good bye, some days before HKP was closed. During his speech he emphasized several times that the evacuation would be carried out by the SS.

Consequently, anyone who was still able to think clearly knew that this was the end."[25]

Eliezer and his family ended up in a DP camp in Stuttgart, Germany, after the war. One day in 1946, his father and uncle learned that the American authorities were looking for witnesses to testify for or against a list of Germans who were being tried for possible war crimes. They saw Karl Plagge's name on this list and immediately volunteered to testify on his behalf. As we now know, it was because of testimony like theirs that Karl Plagge was not convicted of being a war criminal. After his trial, Karl Plagge apparently made contact with some of his former prisoners, many of whom were living in DP camps. . . . Using an intermediary named Dr. Paula Zanker, who was the lawyer for the inmates of the DP Camp in Ludwigsburg, Germany, Plagge wrote letters to Eliezer's father and uncle, David and Leibl Greisdorf. He then arranged a visit with the family while he was on a business trip for *Hessenwerke* in Stuttgart in March of 1948.

After his father died, Eliezer found among his belongings three letters written in 1948, all in German, from Karl Plagge to his father. Here [is] Plagge's letter to the Greisdorfs . . . written before their visit:

FEBRUARY 20, 1948

Dear Herr Greisdorf:

How strange and puzzling are the ways we are led in life! Always and ever more my dreams and thoughts are engaged by the thought, where could those people be now who grew into my heart while close to me during that dreadful time. Who among all those friends might have survived the cruelty and the hell of this war and got out of it alive? Who could escape the demons of those tormented, cruel years we were forced to witness? With deep inner distress I read the book: Passover Book 5706 (1946),"The Confessions of a Survivor" by Dr. Mark Dworzecki, who also came from Vilna and was finally rescued by some miracle from many extermination camps. How much bravery and greatness of heart was responsible for the fact that in those days they did not despair and give up on life. How often back then I admired them and almost envied them for their courage and their mutual trust.

You yourself, my dear Herr Greisdorf, are known to me by name but no longer by your physical appearance. How miraculous it is that we will now once again be brought in contact with one another! And it would for me be a profound and heartfelt joy to meet with you once again, that is if you are not all too sorely reminded of what surely must have been the most terrifying time of your life. Since I discovered through Dr. Zanker and Frau Eichamueller that you had been searching for me to thank me for the regrettably inadequate help I was able to give you, then let me say this to you:

What I was able and permitted to do for you and your friends was only the obvious duty of any feeling person towards his fellow human beings in distress. It was also at the same time much too little when measured against the horrific situation in which all of you found yourselves at the time. It needs no thanks. But there exists—I am convinced—an inner bond between people suffering distress whose destinies have crossed with one another. Though you and yours suffered a fate a thousand times worse than mine, I also was subjected to much suffering during the war and in the postwar time. I believe that people

tested by suffering can really understand each other. In this sense, dear Mr Greisdorf, our getting together could bring us both a great inner joy. . . .

Yours very truly,
Karl Plagge

It is a testament to his own humility that after visiting with the Greisdorfs, Plagge quietly went back home. Without fanfare, he lived the final ten years of his life in Darmstadt, slipping into obscurity and almost vanishing from history's view.

NOTES

1. Memoirs of Samuel Esterowicz, 339–43.
2. Memoirs of Pearl Good, 75.
3. Plagge denazification file: Hessisches Hauptstaatsarchiv Wiesbaden 4.1.3. / 520 / Spruchkammern / Dl / Plagge, Karl. English translation can be found in Appendix A, 201, 212.
4. Ibid., appendix A, 224, 244.
5. Ibid., 235.
6. Ibid., 223–24.
7. Ibid., appendix A, 230.
8. Ibid., 221.
9. Ibid., 225.
10. Ibid., 231–33.
11. Ibid., 233.
12. Ibid., 225.
13. Marek Swirski submitted this testimony to Yad Vashem.
14. Plagge denazification file, appendix A, 232.
15. Bundesarchiv–Ludwigsburg, 204 AR 332/71. Plagge's testimony regarding this crucial period was found buried in the 1956 [sic: 1959] trial transcript of Nazi war criminal Karl Jäger. Jaeger was the commander of *Einsatzkommando* 3 and head of the Security Police in Lithuania. His forces carried out most of the killing of Lithuania's Jews during the war.
16. Plagge denazification file, appendix A, 229–30.
17. Ibid. A, 233.

18. Ibid., 240.

19. Ibid., 230.

20. Bundesarchiv—Ludwigsburg, 204 AR 332/ 71.

21. Plagge denazification file, appendix A, 245–46.

22. Marianne Viefhaus interview with Dr. Hans Madsen, Plagge's brother-in-law, 2004.

23. Plagge denazification file, appendix A, 247.

24. From cover letter accompanying the "Plagge Letters" written by Eliezer Greisdorf to Fanie Brancovskaja.

25. Ibid.

Collective Action in Vivarais-Lignon

PATRICK HENRY

From *We Only Know Men*

The Protestant pastors André Trocmé and Edouard Theis were the catalysts for much of what happened in and around the village of Le Chambon-sur-Lignon between 1940 and 1944, but the rescue mission was a collective effort that involved not only thirteen other Protestant ministers and their followers in all twelve Protestant parishes on the plateau, but also Darbyites, Catholics, Swiss Protestants, American Quakers, Evangelicals, Jewish organizations such as *Oeuvre de secours aux enfants* (Children's Rescue Network, OSE), other organizations such as *La Cimade* and *Secours Suisse aux enfants*, nonbelievers, students, Boy Scouts, underground railroad workers, farmers, city people themselves refugees, and other people from all walks of life. To a large degree, it was an ecumenical effort uniting Catholics, Protestants of many denominations, and Jews in a collective struggle against a powerful common enemy. No similar ecumenical endeavor has ever been undertaken on French soil.

Because the rescue operations included non-Protestants and nonbelievers, in 1979 the pastor in Le Chambon-sur-Lignon and his presbyterial council decided not to affix the [commemorative] plaque on the wall of the Protestant church but rather on a municipal building.[1] In a recent letter, Olivier Hatzfeld, a young historian in hiding who taught at the *École Nouvelle Cévenole* in Le Chambon-sur-Lignon from 1942 to 1944, captures the remarkable solidarity on the plateau at the time that seemed to unite, beyond religious convictions, all those who believed in the human dignity of all individuals: "The first word that comes to mind when I try to express what we felt . . . in Le Chambon-sur-Lignon is solidarity among everyone, longtime Chambonnais, yearly tourists, families looking for refuge, . . . students, teachers, shopkeepers, farmers."[2] This same solidarity existed across the plateau, where refugees were absorbed into the communal life and where not a single refugee was ever betrayed.

The collective nonviolent rescue mission on the plateau was truly remarkable. This is why Yad Vashem decided to honor the people of the plateau collectively as well as individually. It would have been impossible to find out the names of all the people who helped in the area, but by bestowing honor communally Yad Vashem would publicly recognize everyone who had helped in any way, even if not mentioned by name. In this regard, Le Chambon-sur-Lignon researcher Annik Flaud remarks: "This corresponds exactly to what the people on the plateau expected: collective recognition, not just individual recognition, for their parents' actions."[3]

This rescue mission took place in a Europe where, generally speaking, the gates of compassion for Jews were locked. Most people looked the other way or actively collaborated with the Nazis. Except in Denmark and Bulgaria, most churches remained silent. An immense bureaucracy, in the tens of thousands, from local police and railroad clerks to lawyers, soldiers, and physicians, was involved in the rounding up, transportation, confinement, registration, deportation, and extermination of, among others, six million Jews—two-thirds of European Jewry.

This rescue mission occurred, too, not in a country like Denmark, where it was not a crime to hide a Jew and where 93 percent of the Jewish population was saved, but in France, whose Vichy government created a climate of extensive collaboration and accommodation with the Germans and where antisemitism and informing on Jews were deemed not only acceptable but patriotic.[4] . . .

The earliest sustained Christian voice of opposition to Vichy's antisemitism came at the outset in June 1940 from individual French Protestants throughout the country—members of the hierarchy, lower clergy, and laity. The villagers on the plateau Vivarais-Lignon, armed only with the strength of their beliefs, in full view of the Vichy government and, eventually, neighboring storm troopers, were among those who refused to accept the invincibility of evil and brute power. They saved the lives of about five thousand refugees, approximately 3,500 of whom were Jewish, many of them children.

In 1936, 95 percent of Le Chambon-sur-Lignon's 2,721 people were Protestant and roughly half of them were poor peasants living on farms or in small hamlets scattered over many square miles around the village. Although throughout France no more than 2 percent of the overall population was Protestant, here, on the plateau Vivarais-Lignon, 38 percent of the population (24,058) was Protestant.[5] This Protestant enclave was on a high plateau with less than forty inhabitants per square kilometer whose twelve parishes covered an extremely isolated area of small villages and remote farms.

One of the most inspiring leaders of the nonviolent rescue mission was André Trocmé, the pastor of the Reformed Church of France in Le Chambon-sur-Lignon who, with his assistant pastor, Edouard Theis, founded a private coeducational school, the *École Nouvelle Cévenole*, on the principles of nonviolence, conscientious objection, internationalism, fellowship, and peace. Trocmé and Theis thus became catalysts in the rescue mission in and around Le Chambon-sur-Lignon. But, once begun, that mission developed on its own, with numerous individuals working independently. Each of the twelve parishes on the plateau had its own minister and rescue operation. Gerard Bollon, a major historian of the plateau, maintains that "fifteen pastors with seven foreign pastors, principally Swiss, did the same rescue work in their parishes as Trocmé did in his."[6]

While these other ministers headed rescue missions in their villages, in the area of Le Chambon-sur-Lignon Trocmé and Theis preached resistance against the hatred and naked destruction of the Third Reich. They rallied their flock against appeasement, violence, and violation of the Gospels . . . The official handbook of the Hitler Youth organization states that "the foundation of the National Socialist outlook on life is the perception of the unlikeness of men." Trocmé and Theis taught the absolute equality and dignity of all human beings. Their aggressive nonviolence and active pacifism helped to make the plateau the safest place in France for Jewish children, even during the last year of the Occupation when, sought by the German police, Trocmé and Theis were forced to go into hiding. . . .

It is time to jettison all myths, positive and negative, regarding all the people on the plateau. In the aftermath of the misrepresentations regarding André Trocmé, it is also time to give him his due. Sixty-two years after the end of the war, Trocmé is remembered as one of the principal architects of the rescue mission on the plateau. Before writing the second published version of his "André Trocmé: un violent vaincu par Dieu," which appeared in 1995, Georges Menut spoke to thirty people who knew Trocmé during the 1939–44 period and sent out a questionnaire to 130 others who knew him at that time. Seventy-five percent responded. Trocmé is characterized as "a superactive individual capable of mobilizing an entire region" who "encouraged [the other pastors] to help out the Jewish people" and the other refugees on the plateau. "He incited them to act and to offer shelter."[7] When asked why they sheltered Jewish people in their homes, Protestants on the plateau frequently responded: "because Pastor Trocmé asked us to do so and we couldn't refuse him."[8]

Menut is hardly alone in reporting the major influence of Trocmé on the rescue mission on the plateau. Olivier Hatzfeld calls Trocmé "a man of action" who, with Magda, was considered "the leader of the community." Local Resistance leader Pierre Fayol saw him in the same light.[9] Gerard Bollon credits all the ministers on the plateau for their rescue work, but singles out Trocmé as "a leader," "a visionary," "perhaps the principal organizer," "the soul of Le Chambon-sur-Lignon" with "a stature that went beyond a single parish."[10]

From the very beginning, June 23, 1940, the day after the armistice, more than two years before the official September 22, 1942, letter of protest from French Protestant leader Marc Boegner, Trocmé and Theis encouraged resistance to Vichy and spoke out publicly against Vichy's treatment of the Jews. They were influenced and inspired by Pastor Martin Niemöller and the Confessing Church, and as Christian pacifist conscientious objectors, they were dedicated to fighting the Nazis nonviolently. Trocmé, who believed that "the role of the Church was to struggle for social justice,"[11] led by

example. In a letter, most probably written in February 1943, to his older brother Robert, who lived in the original Occupied Zone, but addressed, for precautionary reasons, to the fictitious Simone, Trocmé explains the rescue work going on in his home:

> You know, perhaps, that this past summer we were able to help out about sixty Jewish people who had taken refuge in our home: we hid them, provided them with fresh supplies, rescued them from deportation groups and often led them to a safe country. . . . By the tens, by the hundreds, Jews are being directed toward Le Chambon. My usual ministry has ceased completely because of this situation. Normally, in the summer, my dining room has been transformed into a waiting room (10–15 people a day). Now that's the situation all year round.[12]

Trocmé's imagery here justifies Sabine Zeitoun's observation that "the presbytery became the heart of the village for the reception and then the dispersion of the refugees into the homes of the villagers and the peasants."[13] The Hotel May and Mme Barraud's boarding house, Beau Soleil, were two other such places.

In his unpublished "Mémoires," which were mainly written twenty to twenty-five years after the events and were conceived of as a private document composed solely for his children and grandchildren, Trocmé says that one should not speak of the rescue work one has done: "Haven't others also resisted? That Salvationist, that pastor, didn't he die in a concentration camp? Are you still among the living? Then keep quiet about it."[14] When in early March 1971, Trocmé, who was living in Geneva, learned that he was to be recognized by Yad Vashem as a "Righteous Gentile," he wrote to the Jewish historian Anny Latour:

Why me and not the host of humble peasants of the Haute-Loire region, who did as much and more than I did? Why not my wife whose behavior was much more heroic than mine? Why not my colleague Edouard Theis with whom I shared all responsibilities? I can only accept the Righteous Gentile medal in the name of all those who stuck their necks out and risked death for our unjustly persecuted brothers and sisters. Despite everything, I still feel guilty for what was not done for them.

Trocmé then asks Mme Latour to intervene so that the ceremony, originally planned for the Israeli embassy in Bern, can take place in Le Chambon-sur-Lignon. Later in the month, when he learns that the ceremony will take place in Le Chambon-sur-Lignon, Trocmé writes to the Israeli General Consul in Paris: "The ceremony should be held at the town hall so as to bring together all those who helped shelter and save Jewish refugees during the war. The inhabitants of the neighboring villages: Le Mazet, Tence, Mars, Saint-Agrève, Devesset should also be invited." These letters alone refute the ill-founded charges regarding the so-called propensity in Andre Trocmé to exaggerate the role he played in the rescue mission on the plateau.[15]

Georges Menut's advice regarding Trocmé is sagacious: "Let's remember him without making him either a god or a monument."[16] While Trocmé and Theis were extremely influential, very little if anything could have been accomplished without the people on the plateau. The congregation in Le Chambon-sur-Lignon, for example, was indeed up to the task. The scattered groups formerly created for Bible study in the distant areas of the parish became one of the important communication networks for locating hiding places and guiding the terrified foreigners to safety. Not everyone in Le Chambon hid refugees, but a great

majority of the village was actively involved in the rescue mission, including, among others, teachers who enrolled foreign students with obviously false papers in their classes, town hall employees who issued additional food tickets to families who were hiding Jews, and storekeepers who "forgot" to ask for rationing tickets. In fact, after the summer of 1942, sheltering Jews on the plateau was the norm, not the exception. Once the rescue operation began, it seemed to spread indiscriminately everywhere on the plateau. There was a constant flow of refugees, some staying only a few days, others for months or for years. The countryside somehow absorbed thousands of refugees over the war years.

The pastors, with help from national and international organizations, established houses of refuge to feed, clothe, protect, and educate young children who had been removed from internment camps in southern France, sometimes just before their parents were deported. By the middle of the Occupation, there were seven such houses near or in Le Chambon. They were financed by Quakers, American Congregationalists, the Swiss Red Cross, and even national governments like Sweden. In addition, there were more than a dozen pensions, or boarding houses, toward the center of the village that housed children and adolescent refugees of both sexes. Finally, in addition to the many private homes that sheltered Jews, some keeping children for years, there was the *École Nouvelle Cévenole*, where a fair portion of the student population on scholarship was Jewish and whose enrollment grew annually, from 18 in 1938 to 350 in 1944.[17] Whereas others have spoken perceptively of the "banality of evil" during the Holocaust, we can speak of the "ordinariness of goodness" on the plateau. Based on simple notions of common decency—strangers who came to the door were housed and fed—

goodness spread from farm to farm, from person to person, from one act to the next.[18]

In addition to sheltering Jews, the people on the plateau also hid Communists, antifascist Germans, Spanish republicans, other stateless people, and, as of February 1943, *Service du travail obligatoire* (STO) [compulsory labor service] defaulters. They also practiced noncooperation with the Vichy government. In Le Chambon, the ministers disobeyed orders to ring the church bell in honor of the chief of state. At the *École Nouvelle Cévenole*, they refused to put a picture of Pétain on the wall and would not enforce the mandatory saluting of the flag. In August 1942, three weeks after the Vel d'Hiv roundup, a group of students from the school protested the shocking treatment of Parisian Jews in a letter, at least inspired if not written by André Trocmé, that they presented to the visiting Vichy Minister of Youth, Georges Lamirand. The letter informed him that there were Jews among them, but that the villagers did not differentiate between Jews and non-Jews and in any event would never turn them in if asked to do so because that would violate Gospel teachings. Lamirand claimed this was not his affair and that they would have to speak to Prefect Bach, who promptly threatened to have Trocmé arrested if he were to disobey orders. Two weeks later, Trocmé was summoned to the town hall, where he was once again menaced with arrest, this time by the Vichy police chief, if he failed to turn over Jews hiding in the village.[19]

Trocmé was finally arrested, with Theis and Roger Darcissac, the director of the public school in Le Chambon-sur-Lignon, in the early evening of February 13, 1943. They spent almost five weeks in the internment camp Saint-Paul d'Eyjeaux, near Limoges, a political reeducation camp, not a forced labor camp, where 75 percent of the inmates were Communists. They were released unexpectedly on March 16 after a telegram arrived from Vichy, just before the camp was liquidated and the prisoners deported.[20] Later, both Trocmé and Theis spent ten months in hiding. It was not, however, "the fear of being harassed" that sent Andre Trocmé into hiding [because] "the Reformed Church (in the person of Maurice Rohr) asked them [Trocmé and Theis] to leave the village."[21] . . .

While there were openly collective actions undertaken on the plateau, much that happened there was done under a cloak of secrecy. People in the area often did not know about the rescue efforts of their neighbors. They suspected that others must have agreed to shelter the latest arrivals but did not know who or where. They did not talk about it much either during the war, when they used passwords and codes to do so,[22] or after the war. Furthermore, no permanent records were kept. Although many people never procured them, there were several suppliers of false identity papers on the plateau. Oscar Rosowsky, a teenager in hiding under the name of Jean-Claude Plunne, was the main provider of false papers but several others, including Roger Darcissac, also fabricated them. The rescue mission involved a mixture of candor and evasiveness. The people on the plateau did not conceal the fact that they sheltered Jews, but when the Vichy police came looking for them, the refugees had disappeared into their hiding places. The reticent nature of these isolated mountain people was a definite asset in a system where privacy and unspoken consensus, candor and concealment, were necessary. It worked well in the village known to the Germans and the Vichy officials as "that nest of Jews in Protestant country."[23] In this ecumenical village, no villager ever denounced a single refugee or a person concealing refugees.

It is important to know something about Protestantism and its history in Catholic France to understand not only why the Huguenots, in particular, identified with the persecuted Jews, but also why they were so successful in sheltering them. Protestants were persecuted in France from the 1530s until 1598, when Henri IV signed the Edict of Nantes, giving them the right to practice their religion openly. Louis XIV revoked that edict in 1685 and Protestants were again persecuted until the revolution in 1789. In 1560, there were sixteen million French people, one million of whom were Protestant. In 1940, there were forty million French people but at most only eight hundred thousand Protestants. During the times of persecution, there were huge emigrations into Holland, Germany, northern Italy, England, Canada, and the United States. Following the revocation of the Edict of Nantes, for example, roughly 200,000 Huguenots left the country.[24] Those who could not afford to flee to foreign countries and who hid in the most inhospitable areas of the country survived on cunning, secrecy, and silence. Living clandestinely, they cultivated a strong distrust of governments.

As daily readers of the Bible, French Protestants knew the Hebrew Bible well and were therefore familiar with Jewish history. A persecuted minority throughout the greater portion of their own history, they felt close to marginalized peoples, and many of them particularly identified with the Jews, whom they recognized as the chosen people of God. Patrick Cabanel notes magnificently regarding the plateau Vivarais-Lignon: "The Hebrews had been there for four centuries, when the Jews arrived."[25] If the Hebrew Bible is such a source of inspiration for the Protestants of France, why did it not rouse the Protestants in Germany against Hitler? For one reason, the Protestants of Germany . . . were not a minority. Then, as Patrick Cabanel points out, there is a radical difference between Luther's view of the Jews and that of Calvin. Whereas Luther's anti-Judaism was notorious, "Calvin insists on continuity between the two testaments and envisages that God's plan for humanity, distinguishing between the elect and the damned, held for the salvation of the Jews as well as that of Christians." For Cabanel, then, Calvin was the first "to call into question the teaching of scorn" for the Jews that continued in other Christian faiths into the twentieth century.[26] French Protestants refer to the 1685–1789 period of their history as "the desert," which is a clear indication of their identification and solidarity with the Jews. When the Jewish refugees were taken on the three-hundred-kilometer journey from Le Chambon-sur-Lignon to Switzerland, as Pierre Sauvage portrays beautifully in [his documentary film,] *Weapons of the Spirit*, they were following the same route taken by refugee Protestants hundreds of years earlier.

Roughly one-third of the Protestants in the area of Le Chambon-sur-Lignon were not Huguenots but Darbyites, evangelical followers of the nineteenth-century English preacher John Darby. They were radical fundamentalists who did not believe in the clergy and were obviously not parishioners of Trocmé and Theis. They held their own religious meetings and simply read the Scriptures and tried to live by them. Given the solidarity between the two persecuted minorities, the French Huguenots and the Jewish people, it is striking that the Darbyites responded more promptly to Trocmé's call to shelter the Jews than did the members of his own church. Also odd, for the same reason, is *not* the September 1942 public condemnation by National Protestant Federation President Marc Boegner of Vichy's antisemitism and outrageous treatment of Jews, but rather its date. Why did this public objection not take place two years earlier?[27]

Be that as it may, there was a long tradition of sheltering the persecuted on the plateau Vivarais-Lignon. Not only had the plateau served as a place of refuge for victimized Huguenots throughout the centuries of their persecution in Catholic France but it had sheltered Catholic priests during the period of the French Revolution and had also taken in, among others, Alsatian refugees in 1914 and refugees from Spain beginning in 1936.[28] This proud tradition of sanctuary extended to children. From the end of the nineteenth century onward, thanks in large measure to Pastor Louis Comte, undernourished and underprivileged children, mostly from the poor mining area of Saint Étienne, came to the plateau for health reasons. A former history and geography teacher at the École Nouvelle Cévenole, Bernard Galland, also explains that before there were summer camps in the area, many undernourished children (3,734 in 1935 alone, Bollon notes) came to live on farms to play, guard sheep, run errands, and build up their health.[29] As a result, by the late 1930s, many boarding houses for children and vacation camps had long been established in the area. The plateau was then, in a sense, ready to receive the Jewish children when they arrived. But everything regarding their arrival, lodging, and the nature of their residency would be quite different.

There has been much debate as to when the refugees arrived on the plateau. Despite the rather common belief, even among scholars,[30] that the Jewish refugees came after the Vel d'Hiv roundup in July 1942, in reality they came much earlier. Although it is true that there was more sympathy for the plight of Jews in France after July 1942 and evidence of much more rescue activity after that date in Le Chambon-sur-Lignon and more generally throughout the country, spiritual resistance to the Nazis began much earlier on the plateau and lasted through the entire length of time Hit-

ler was in power. According to Annik Flaud, for example, "there were three or four German political refugees in Mme Barraud's boarding house in 1934."[31] The enrollment records at the École Nouvelle Cévenole show an amazing increase in student numbers: 18 in 1938, 40 in 1939, 150 in 1940, and 250 in 1941.[32] Many of these students were Jewish refugees in hiding. In the winter of 1940–41, several pastors began relations with organizations such as La Cimade and the Quakers that were already working in the internment camps in the south of France and would eventually bring refugees to the plateau. In May 1941, for example, the house called La Guespy opened its doors to welcome eighteen children from these camps.[33] All the evidence indicates that there were Jews hiding on the plateau in the late 1930s, many more in 1941 and the first half of 1942, and much greater numbers after July 1942. . . .

The people on the plateau did what they did because these particular Christians believed that to do otherwise would be to act against their religious conscience. In the winter of 1940–41, André Trocmé went to the offices of the American Friends Service Committee in Marseille because he wanted to work with them to bring desperately needed supplies and consolation to Jews being held in internment camps in southern France. As soon as the Germans took over in June 1940, foreign Jews were rounded up and interned in concentration camps throughout the country. By the end of 1940, there were roughly 30,000 foreign Jews in these camps, three thousand of whom would die there. The conditions in these camps, entirely run by French personnel, were deplorable. Christian groups, such as La Cimade, the YMCA, the Quakers, and the Jewish group Oeuvre de secours aux enfants (OSE), rushed to the camps to provide food, clothing, medical care, libraries, and cultural services. Perhaps no one did more to alleviate suffering there than Madeleine Barot, the head of *La Cimade*, which she founded in 1939. This Protestant organization worked in the camps from August 1940 until the end of the war and played a large role in the evacuation of children from the camps, the placing of these children in homes throughout the south of France, and in many cases the smuggling of children into Switzerland.

Gurs was one of the first and largest of the internment camps established in the south of France. Situated on a high plain at the foot of the lower Pyrenees ten miles from the town of Oloron-Sainte-Marie, it was constructed to impound Spanish republicans who crossed the mountains into France after Franco's victory. When foreign Jews were rounded up and held there during the summer of 1940, the various charitable groups came to Gurs in an attempt to improve the situation. The Quakers brought large quantities of food. *La Cimade* established a five-thousand-volume library and brought musical instruments for recitals. OSE offered much needed psychological counseling to all internees, especially children.[34] But the conditions remained horrible. Survivors speak of constant hunger, head lice, rats, mud, jaundice, dysentery, infectious hepatitis, and typhus. Approximately 1,100 foreign Jews died in Gurs between 1940 and 1944.

André Trocmé's trip to the Quakers in Marseille began his relationship with a leading Quaker named Burns Chalmers, who told him at a subsequent meeting in Nimes: "We can get people out of the camps but nobody wants them. It is dangerous to take them. Is your village prepared to do such a thing? Do you wish to be that community?" Trocmé assured him that Le Chambon would be willing to serve in that capacity. Chalmers told him to find houses of refuge and the people to run them and the Quakers and the Fellowship

of Reconciliation would support them financially. Trocmé returned home, where the elders of the church voted immediately to commit the parish to this action. Le Chambon-sur-Lignon was designated as a place of refuge primarily for children. Even after America's entrance into the war, funds used to run the houses and to establish scholarships for refugee students continued to arrive from Geneva, from the Quakers, the Fellowship of Reconciliation, and the Congregationalists.[35] In his September 13, 2003, letter to Patrick Cabanel, Olivier Hatzfeld insists on the central role played by Trocmé "in the decision made by *La Cimade* and other organizations to entrust the children from the camps to Le Chambon-sur-Lignon"[36] and Gerard Bollon remarks that, when Trocmé returned from his meeting with Burns Chalmers in Marseille, he told his parishioners: "You must accommodate; you must protect; you must save these refugees."[37] In large measure, things happened the way they did in Le Chambon-sur-Lignon because of Trocmé and Theis, but elsewhere on the plateau others were harboring refugees on their own. Since the plateau Vivarais-Lignon had been a place of sanctuary for hundreds of years, it was only normal that, once again, the deeply held inner values of the inhabitants would result in the offering of shelter and passage to persecuted refugees.

The idea of a city of refuge originates in the Hebrew Bible and is described in some detail in Joshua 20:1–9, Numbers 35:9–31, and Deuteronomy 19:1–13, where the Jewish people were commanded to set up cities of refuge to which anyone who killed a person unintentionally could flee so as not to die by the hand of a blood avenger until there was a trial before the congregation. Perhaps because the situation in Le Chambon was different—a city of refuge was set up there for those being persecuted for no other crime than

that of being Jewish—the pastors and their followers took most seriously the command of Deuteronomy 19:10: "I command you [to protect the
refugee] lest innocent blood be shed in [your]
land . . . thereby bringing the guilt of bloodshed
upon you." Once Le Chambon became "a city of
refuge," for Trocmé, Theis, and the villagers, it was
not enough simply not to do evil, it was also necessary to keep others from doing harm to those
who came within the city gates.

The ministers and their followers accepted
the negative commandments of Exodus 20 that
require us to avoid doing harm (thou shalt not
kill, steal, commit adultery, etc.). Most people feel
that, most of the time, this ethic of the nondoing
of evil is all that is required of them. The people of
Le Chambon, however, heard other voices in the
Hebrew Bible, that of First Isaiah for example, urging them in addition to perform positive actions.
Responding affirmatively to Cain's question—
"Am I my brother's keeper?" (Genesis 4:9)—First
Isaiah tells Jewish people who their brothers and
sisters are: "seek justice / rescue the oppressed /
defend the orphan / plead for the widow" (Isaiah
1:17), while Second Isaiah urges them "to share
[their] bread with the hungry [and] bring the
homeless poor into [their] house" (Isaiah 58:7).
The Protestant population understood these commands, and it became known that refugees could
find shelter on the plateau.[38]

The people of the area found no difference
between the practical ethic emanating from the
Hebrew Bible and that of the Gospels. When
asked, after the war, why they did what they did,
many would invariably refer to the gospel of Luke
(10:25–37), where Christ cites the two great commandments in the Torah which require obedience
in order to gain eternal life, the second being to
love one's neighbor as oneself. Christ is then asked
"Who is my neighbor?" and he responds with

the parable of the Good Samaritan, in which the
Jew "who has fallen into the hands of robbers" is
helped by the Samaritan, a foreigner not expected
to show sympathy to Jews. The substance of these
references to the gospel of Luke constitute a leit-
motif in Sauvage's masterful *Weapons of the Spirit*.
Mme Brottes and Edouard Theis cite these gospel
passages explicitly in their interviews. The universal maxim "Love One Another," inscribed on
the pediment of the front wall of the Protestant
church in Le Chambon, had long been the guiding principle of the people in the area.

Theologically, then, the people of the plateau
believed that faith without works is dead. They
felt compelled to act for others, to diminish suffering, and to put into action the principles in
which they believed. Although a good number
of villagers were in fact part of the violent resistance, Trocmé and Theis conscientiously objected
to all violence and told their flock from the pulpit
in the famous sermon preached the day after the
armistice: "The duty of Christians is to use the
weapons of the Spirit to resist the violence that
will be brought to bear on their consciences. We
will resist whenever our adversaries will demand
of us obedience contrary to the orders of the Gospel. We will do so without fear, but also without
pride and without hate."[39] As Christian pacifists,
they justified no violence whatsoever, not even the
violence needed to defeat Hitler. Killing Germans,
for whatever reason, was absolutely incompatible
with being a Christian. Explaining what his purpose was in writing his "*Mémoires*," Trocmé notes:
"I'm not a novelist but I'm 'charged with a mission.' My goal is not to do the work of a historian
but to demonstrate that one can go through a war
practicing nonviolence."[40]

Trocmé and Theis did what they did because
they believed that hatred of other human beings
brings only destruction. They hated war as a

means of resolving conflict. They did not hate the so-called enemy. They were trying to prevent the Germans from doing more evil and were always ready to forgive them. In the last weeks of the war, when Frenchmen were finally getting revenge and Germans were being assassinated everywhere, still teaching the absolute uselessness of all hatred and the need for forgiveness, accompanied by August Bohny, Trocmé preached in German on Sundays in the nearby German prisoner of war camp, repeating the same sermon he had given that morning in French in his own church, offering the opportunity to repent, hoping to end all cycles of vengeance.

The people on the plateau, Christians, Jews, and unbelievers alike, did what they did because they believed in the dignity of all human life and the integrity of every individual. Despite their differences, they shared this vision. Never did the Protestants among them try to use their position to coerce refugee children to embrace their religion. As a survivor named Rudy Appel attests: "With the help of Pastor Trocmé, we held our own religious services on Jewish Holy Days, either in the Protestant temple or in the school."[41] . . . Other survivors note that Jewish children were encouraged to have their own services and that sometimes Protestant services would consist only of readings from the Hebrew Bible so the Jewish children could take part without betraying their faith. These people were fully cognizant of and perfectly comfortable with the Jewish origins of their faith. Being a Christian here had nothing to do with not being Jewish and whether or not Jews accepted the Gospels—they were still considered the chosen people of God. The only real distinction that mattered on the plateau was between those who believed and those who did not believe that people "who had fallen into the hands of robbers" were as precious as themselves.

Although the fundamental basis for this ethical community was largely biblical, there was an enormous amount of diversity among its members, many of whom, integral agents of the rescue operation, when asked after the war why they did what they did, responded outside of any religious context.[42] There was also, in the very household of the presbytery, an interesting dichotomy between the pastor and his wife, neither of whom was native to the plateau but each of whom was an equally important catalyst in the rescue mission. André, whose mother was German, was raised in a strict Calvinist home in northern France, while Magda Trocmé Grilli di Cortona, whom André referred to as "my primitive, authentic, and creative Florentine"[43] and whose grandmother was Russian, was raised in a Catholic convent in Italy from the age of ten to eighteen.

Although she ultimately renounced Catholicism, Magda never really embraced Protestantism: "I am not a Protestant," she told André (who claimed that she remained "on the edge of faith"), "I have never been able to declare that I believe a thing of which I am not sure. I prefer not to define what I believe."[44] In fact, Magda was never deeply religious. Unlike her husband, she rarely spoke of God or even of love. "But I never close my door," she told Hallie, "never refuse to help somebody who comes to me and asks for something. This, I think, is my kind of religion." Georges Menut also viewed her in nonreligious terms: "She was above all 100 percent humanist, not in the least mystical, fleeing abstract theories ('I have other things to do'), with a very well-developed practical sense and unlimited energy."[45] . . . In her "*Souvenirs Autobiographiques,*" Magda asserts that, in her life as the wife of a Protestant pastor, she collaborated with her husband "above all on social matters." Yet, on the same page, she insists that "my children were wrong to think that I was an unbeliever." Magda then offers a simple statement of her beliefs: "If there weren't somewhere a source of hope, justice, truth, and love, we would not have rooted in us the hope of justice, truth, and love that we find in every religion and every degree of civilization. It's that source that I call God."[46] Unlike his wife's essentially "horizontal" ethic of humanitarian conviction, André Trocmé's was a "vertical" ethic emanating directly from God's commands. Yet Trocmé had no doctrine of hell and was uncertain about the existence of an afterlife. As Trocmé told the inmates of the internment camp where he was held after his arrest in February 1943: "Faith works on earth; I do not know about Heaven."[47]

A "common union" brought together on this plateau a variety of people who differed politically and religiously to achieve a mutual end. It was a group of people who embodied the ethic of Scripture, whether they were believers or not. In all that they did, Trocmé, Theis, and the firmly resolved and independent-minded mountain people demonstrated that, for them, the kingdom of God means the complete and definitive elimination of every form of vengeance and reprisal in relations between human beings on earth.

NOTES

1. E-mail from Le Chambon-sur-Lignon researcher Annik Flaud to author, December 1, 2003.

2. Letter of September 13, 2003, from Olivier Hatzfeld to Patrick Cabanel. A copy of this letter is in my possession.

3. E-mail from Annik Flaud to author, December 2, 2003.

4. In addition to Ousby, Jackson, Burrin, and Gildea on Vichy and its treatment of the Jews, I have read with profit Robert O. Paxton, *Vichy France: Old Guard and New Order, 1940–1944* (New York: Columbia University Press, 1972); Richard J. Golsan, ed., *Memory, The Holocaust,*

and French Justice: The Bousquet and Touvier Affairs (Hanover NH: University Press of New England, 1996); Susan Zuccotti, *The Holocaust, the French, and the Jews* (New York: Harper Collins, 1993); Richard Weisberg, *Vichy Law and the Holocaust in France* (New York: New York University Press, 1996). I have relied most heavily on Michael R. Marrus and Robert O. Paxton, *Vichy France and the Jews* (Stanford CA: Stanford University Press, 1981).

5. Francois Boulet, "Quelques éléments statistiques," in Bolle et al., *Le Plateau Vivarais-Lignon,* 287.

6. Unpublished interview with Barbara Barnett (July 1993). A copy of this interview is in my possession.

7. Georges Menut, "Andre Trocmé: un violent vaincu par Dieu," *Le Chambon-sur-Lignon: Un village pas comme les autres* (Le Chambon-sur-Lignon: Société d'Histoire de la Montagne, 1995), 67–68; 84; 69. The first version, with the same title, appeared in 1992 in *Le Plateau Vivarais-Lignon,* 378–400.

8. Georges Menut, "Accueillir ou rejeter l'étranger," in *Le Chambon-sur-Lignon: un village pas comme les autres,* 58.

9. Letter of September 13, 2003, from Olivier Hatzfeld to Patrick Cabanel.

10. Unpublished interview with Barbara Barnett (July 1993).

11. André Trocmé, "Memoires," 269. On the influence of Niemöller, see 339.

12. Magda Trocmé, "Souvenirs Autobiographiques," 247. Although it appears in Magda's text, the letter was written by André Trocmé.

13. Sabine Zeitoun, *Ces enfants qu'il fallait sauver* (Paris: Albin Michel, 1989), 218.

14. Andre Trocmé, "Mémoires," 530.

15. Letter from André Trocmé to Mme A. Latour (March 8, 1971); undated letter from Andre Trocmé to the Israeli General Consul in Paris. Copies of both of these letters are in my possession.

16. Georges Menut, "André Trocmé: un violent vaincu par Dieu," 95.

17. See Francois Boulet, "Quelques éléments statistiques," in Bolle et al., *Le Plateau Vivarais-Lignon*, 288.

18. Along these lines, see Francois Rochat and André Modigliani, "The Ordinary Quality of Resistance: From Milgram's Laboratory to the Village of Le Chambon," *Journal of Social Issues* 51 (1995): 195–212, and David R. Blumenthal, *The Banality of Good and Evil: Moral Lessons from the Shoah and Jewish Tradition* (Washington DC: Georgetown University Press, 1999).

19. André Trocmé, "Mémoires," 361–66.

20. Ibid., 231–33.

21. E-mail to author from Annik Flaud, November 15, 2003, citing a letter from Edouard Theis's daughter, Jeanne, to Nevin Sayre. See too André Trocmé, "Mémoires," 402.

22. See Daniel Curtet, "Témoignage d'un ancien Pasteur," in Bolle et al., *Le Plateau Vivarais-Lignon*, 54–67.

23. Philip Halie, *Lest Innocent Blood Be Shed* (New York: Harper & Row, 1994).

24. On the history of Protestant emigration from France in times of persecution, see *La Diaspora des Huguenots: les réfugiés protestants de France et leur dispersion dans le monde (16e-18e siècles),* ed. Eckart Birnstiel and Chrystel Bernat (Paris: Champion, 2001), and *Memory and Identity: The Huguenots in France and the Atlantic Diaspora*, ed. Bertrand Van Ruymbeke and Randy J. Sparks (Columbia: University of South Carolina Press, 2003).

25. Patrick Cabanel, "L'Israel des Cévennes, reflexions sur une "exception huguenote" face aux juifs," in Cabanel and Gervereau, *La Deuxième Guerre mondiale*, 212.

26. Ibid., 217–18.

27. See, for example, Hallie, *Lest Innocent Blood Be Shed*, 95–98; 182–83, and Daniel Besson, "Les Assemblées des Frères, darbystes et ravinistes, et l'accueil des Juifs," in Bolle et al., *Le Plateau Vivarais-Lignon*, 86–89.

28. Gerard Bollon, "La tradition d'accueil avant la guerre," in Bolle et al., *Le Plateau Vivarais-Lignon*, 151–60.

29. Ibid., 154. For Bernard Galland, I refer to his unpublished interview with Barbara Barnett (July 1993), a copy of which is in my possession.

30. Jean-Pierre Houssel, "La résistance civile sur le Plateau: paysans et patriotes," 113.

31. E-mail to author from Annik Flaud, October 9, 2003.

32. Francois Boulet, "Quelques elements statistiques," in Bolle et al., *Le Plateau Vivarais-Lignon*, 288.

33. E-mail to author from Annik Flaud, September 2, 2003.

34. Jeanne Merle d'Aubigné, "Souvenirs de quelques camps en France, 1940–1947." *Quelques Actions des Protestants de France en faveur des Juifs persécutés sous l'Occupation Allemande 1940–1944* (Paris: La Cimade), ed. Violette Mouchon, 33; 40–41. Typescript in my possession.

35. André Trocmé "Mémoires," 351–53. Magda Trocmé, "Le Chambon," in *The Courage to Care*, ed. Carol Rittner and Sondra Myers (New York: New York University Press, 1986), 103. Philip Hallie, *Lest Innocent Blood Be Shed*, 129–38.

36. Letter of September 13, 2003, from Olivier Hatzfeld to Patrick Cabanel.

37. Unpublished interview with Barbara Barnett (July 1993).

38. Some pastors made precise reference to these passages in Isaiah. See in particular Andre Bettex, "Témoignage d'un ancien Pasteur," in Bolle et al., *Le Plateau Vivarais-Lignon*, 68. See in the same volume 12 and 434.

39. Edouard Theis and André Trocmé, "Message des deux pasteurs du Chambon à leur paroisse," in Bolle et al., *Le Plateau Vivarais-Lignon*, 599.

40. Andre Trocmé, "Mémoires," 371.

41. Carol Rittner and Sondra Myers, eds., *The Courage to Care*, 119. On this same issue, see Olivier Hatzfeld, "L'École Nouvelle Cévenole: nouvelle approche," and Francois Boulet, "L'attitude spirituelle des protestants devant les Juifs réfugiés," in Bolle et al., *Le Plateau Vivarais-Lignon*, 164 and 407.

42. For an analysis of the Catholic participation in the rescue mission, see Henri Dubois, "Les com-

munautés catholiques du Plateau," and Francois
Boulet, "L'attitude spirituelle des protestants
devant les Juifs réfugiés," in Bolle et al., *Le Plateau Vivarais-Lignon*, 82–85 and 412–13 respectively.

43. André Trocmé, "Mémoires," 50.

44. Ibid., 236.

45. Georges Menut, "Andre Trocmé: un violent vaincu par Dieu," 74.

46. Magda Trocmé, "Souvenirs Autobiographiques," 56 and 56–57.

47. Hallie, *Lest Innocent Blood Be Shed*, 37.

The Hidden Jews of Warsaw

GUNNAR S. PAULSSON

From *Secret City*

Ninety-eight per cent of the Jewish population of Warsaw perished in the Second World War, together with one-quarter of the Polish population: in all, some 720,000 souls, a number that dwarfs the destruction of life in Hiroshima and Nagasaki combined and is undoubtedly the greatest slaughter perpetrated within a single city in human history.[1] The flight of twenty-odd thousand Jews from the Warsaw ghetto seems by comparison a negligible phenomenon, and has passed along almost unnoticed by historians. Yet it was probably the greatest mass escape from confinement in history, and the life of these fugitives in hiding for anything from one-and-a-half to more than four years is a dramatic story that has few parallels. . . . A close analysis of a broad variety of sources shows that about 28,000 Jews lived "on the Aryan side" in Warsaw at one time or another, having stayed out of the Warsaw ghetto when it was formed or escaped from it or come to Warsaw to hide. . . . I have characterized these 28,000 Jews—together with the many non-Jews who helped to hide them, and the criminal element that ceaselessly hunted them—as not merely a collection of isolated individuals, but a "secret city." Secret it certainly was, of course: not only did it have to be concealed from the Polish population at large as well as the Germans and their minions, but its inhabitants themselves were barely aware of its existence. Each Jew in hiding knew of a few others—family, friends, people with whom they were sharing hiding places—and also of a few Polish friends who could be counted on to help. Each Jew had to deal with various strangers, perhaps friendly and perhaps not, who provided services usually for money. Each Jew was also confronted with an army of blackmailers, denouncers, policemen, and so forth, and faced a huge, impassive city of strangers who had to be presumed hostile until proven otherwise. Jews in hiding therefore felt themselves to be isolated and alone, with few friends and many enemies, and this is the impression that prevails in the many memoirs of the period.

Unbeknownst to the Jews, however, these various groups of friends, paid helpers and other Jews in hiding intertwined to form a large network, connecting every Jew in hiding to every other. No one was fully aware of this network, which came into being spontaneously through personal contacts rather than any organized effort, but there are many strands of evidence that testify to its existence. For one thing, nearly all the Jews in hiding were victimized by *szmalcowniks* (extortionists and blackmailers), showing immediately that their isolation was not so great as it seemed. For another, a common language developed: a hiding place was called a *melina*; if it was discovered, it was said to be "burnt;" Jews in hiding were called "cats." The word *szmalcownik* was itself a coinage of the time. 3,500 Jews fell into the Hotel Polski trap [a ruse by which Jews were lured out of hiding by a promise of buyable visas to Latin American countries]: about one in seven of the Jews in hiding at the time. Nearly all the Jews heard about this scheme, which was advertised strictly through word of mouth. The speed and thoroughness with which the news spread is testimony to the extensive communications networks that linked the secret city, just as the number of victims helps to demonstrate its scale.

The secret city also had its institutions, consisting mainly of a group of charitable organizations devoted to bringing aid to the Jews: the joint Polish and Jewish Council to Aid Jews (codenamed *Zegota*), its member Jewish organizations, the Jewish National Committee (ZKN), representing the Zionist parties, and the Bund. These organizations between them eventually reached about 8,900 of the Jews in hiding, and formed the single most important link in the network. There were also a number of other institutions: the Socialist (PPS), Communist (PPR) and Democratic (SD) parties, which helped their Jewish members directly; the Social Self-Help Organization (SOS), founded by the Democratic Party, which acted as a liaison between Zegota and Catholic welfare institutions; the Warsaw Housing Co-operative (WSM), run by the PPS, which harbored a large number of Jews and gave employment to a few; the Coordinating Committee of Democratic and Socialist Physicians (PPR, PPS and SD), which provided medical assistance to Jews in hiding; and even the tiny Association of Tartar-Muslims [descendants of Polish allies against the Teutonic Knights in the 15th century, this community was large enough to support a mosque in Warsaw], which provided a few Jews with false documents ("Aryan papers") and an explanation for being circumcised. The provision of false documents was not of course limited to the Muslims: *Zegota* and the mainstream Polish underground operated a vastly larger "legalization" enterprise, which produced documents for people in hiding in general, including Jews.

Besides institutions, the secret city had a cultural life of sorts, and literary achievements. These include four important books: Ludwik Landau's chronicles, *Kronika lot wojny i okupacji*, a fundamental source for the period; Emmanuel Ringelblum's *Polish-Jewish Relations during the Second World War*, a volume of poetry, *Z otchlani* (From the Abyss); and Jakub Wiernik's memoirs, *Rok w Treblince* (A Year in Treblinka). The latter two were published during the war and even smuggled out of the country and published in London and New York in 1944. Ringelblum also wrote other manuscripts: a series of biographical sketches of prominent Warsaw Jews, which was published after the war, and a history of the Trawniki labor camp, which has unfortunately been lost. In addition, he carried on a correspondence with Adolf Berman, which has been preserved. . . . Besides these "official" efforts, many diaries were kept in hiding, some of which survived, and some of which formed the basis of subsequent memoirs. There were also Polish literary works on the plight of the Jews, such as Maria Kann's *Przed oczyma swiata* (Before the Eyes of the World), also published during the war, and Czeslaw Milosz's poems *Campo di Fiori* and *Biedny polak patrzy na ghetto* (A Poor Pole Looks at the Ghetto) which appeared in the *Z otchlani* volume. There was a social life of a kind, too: there were restaurants and cafés whose clientele included Jews in hiding, and the activists' circles provided a social milieu as well as a working group.

The secret city's criminal element consisted not only of *szmalcowniks* and police agents, but of people who were prepared to cheat and rob Jews in other ways. These elements were also intertwined with the network that formed the city: that is how they found their victims. Some of the more sophisticated *szmalcowniks* infiltrated the city by playing a double game, helping Jews and providing hiding places, and then blackmailing them. Dishonest landlords and people who stole property that Jews had entrusted to them were also an integral part of it. Conversely, the secret city had a rudimentary justice system, arising late in the day and necessarily small and limited in power, which passed and carried out death sentences on collaborators, including a few of the *szmalcowniks*.

The secret city also carried out military operations. The Jewish Combat Organization (ZOB) continued in hiding after the Ghetto Uprising, with satellite partisan operations in the Wyszkow and Lomianki woods. There was a ZOB cell in the tractor factory in Ursus, to the west, and another in the southern suburb of Okecie. The fighters of the Revisionist ZZW [Jewish Military Union], who had made their way out of the ghetto during the uprising, took their weapons into hiding with them. One group died in a gun battle with German police on June 16, 1943, when its hiding place was discovered; another joined Polish Communist partisans in Michalin and was also killed in battle. When the Warsaw Uprising broke out in August 1944, both ZOB and ZZW fighters took part, as well as hundreds of Jews who had been in hiding or were liberated from German prisons.

The secret city of the Jews in hiding in Warsaw was thus a unique and extraordinary phenomenon.

A Case Study

The case study that follows will serve to illustrate the nature and extent of the relationships that crossed the ghetto wall.... This study is based on two longer accounts, one Polish and one Jewish, and a number of shorter ones, which, as we shall see, mesh together into a common story. This story is not about people who were part of the organized underground, and whose networks therefore spread, as it were, automatically, through their organizations, but concerns fairly ordinary people, with the sorts of contacts that ordinary people might have: they were people who happened to meet, some of whom happened to survive and happened to write their stories down. We will, in the telling, run into some prominent people and activists, but this should not, by itself, cause us to doubt that this story is typical. When we trace connections, we inevitably find our way to the well-connected. But the nature of these connections is usually unremarkable, even when the people are not. We shall begin, for example, with a national boxing champion, and soon be led to the director of the Warsaw zoo, who later was deeply involved in *Zegota*. But the link between these men has nothing to do with their membership in an elite (even supposing that boxers and zoo directors tended to move in the same circles)—rather, the boxer had a friend whose father-in-law did business with the zoo. Our two prominent individuals thus immediately lead us to two others, the friend and the father-in-law, who were quite average members of the Jewish middle class and quite representative of the kind of people who escaped from the ghetto. Both the people we are about to meet, and the relationships between them, are on the whole typical of those reported in the memoirs generally.

Szapse Rotholc was a national boxing champion before the war, and a member of the Bundist *Shtern* sports club. Together with his friend and fellow-boxer Shmuel Kenigswein, he became a member of the ghetto police and participated in smuggling, in the process forming contacts with German and Polish policemen and with smugglers on the Polish side.[2] ... Rotholc claims that he used his position as a policeman to help his nephew and several other Jews escape from the ghetto; and he himself, with his immediate family, escaped with the aid of a Pole, another boxer who was later killed together with Rotholc's wife after a betrayal. Rotholc also had a good Polish friend named Stanistaw Chmielewski. Kenigswein's father-in-law had been a supplier to the Warsaw zoo, so that Kenigswein knew the zoo's director, Dr. Jan Zabinski. Both Chmielewski and Zabinski became involved in bringing aid to their friends in the ghetto and later in hiding fugitives on the Aryan side. Chmielewski had twenty-four Jews under his direct care, keeping some in his own flat and helping many others, while Zabinski hid more than twenty-five Jews in the zoo, and again helped many others. Zabinski, in turn, knew the engineer Feliks Cywiniski, passing a number of people on to him. Cywinski arranged hiding places and documents for dozens of Jews and kept seven in his own flat at Sapiezynska 19. Cywinski was drawn into these activities by his friend Jan Bochenski, who had asked him for help in finding places for two Jewish friends. Both Cywinski and Bochenski sold family land to raise money, which they used to rent four additional apartments where Jews could be hidden. Cywinski and Bochenski are credited with having twenty-six Jews under their direct care, of whom twenty-three survived. . . .[3] In this way, this network was connected to Jewish activist circles, while Zabinski and Cywinski later also acted in *Zegota* . . . . Kenigswein, with his family, stayed with both Zabinski and Cywinski; during the Warsaw Uprising in 1944, he became the leader of a Jewish platoon, organized by Cywinski, in the "Wigry" battalion of the Home Army [the armed Polish resistance].[4] Another of the Jews under Cywinski's care, the lawyer Mieczyslaw Goldstein, was passed on to him by Stefan and Marta Koper, the caretakers of a building in the right-bank suburb of Praga, who hid thirteen Jews in their flat.[5] It should be noted that in all these cases aid was extended without payment.

Chmielewski, described by Ber Mark, then director of the ZIH [Jewish Historical Institute], as a "one-man underground organization," was apparently a homosexual, who was drawn into helping Jews through his relationship with his Jewish lover "Karol" (Wladyslaw Bergman).[6] Early in the war, Chmielewski and Bergman fled to the Soviet-occupied sector; once there, Bergman decided to flee deeper into Soviet territory, while Chmielewski promised to return to Warsaw to look after Bergman's mother Stefania as well as his own. . . . Late in October 1939, Chmielewski smuggled himself into the German-occupied part of Poland, carrying with him letters and messages from his Jewish friends in Vilna. "Crossing the border that night," he relates, "I knew how I would fight against the Hitlerite invaders. Not with weapons, which I did not have, but with a weapon that was given to me at birth: God's commandment, love thy neighbor as thyself. [. . .] So began my fight with the Nazi invader, the daily battle against Fascist racism."[7] Thus Chmielewski was moved by idealism as well as personal friendships to devote himself specifically to helping Jews. Perhaps as a homosexual he was also sympathetic to Jews as fellow-victims of persecution, and his own family obligations were few.

The letters that he delivered put Chmielewski in contact with a wider group of Jews, a number of whom he helped to escape to the Soviet zone. He was also introduced to wider Jewish circles by Mrs. Bergman, who drew him into the work of aiding Jewish refugees from Lodz. Chmielewski in turn recruited his own mother, and also a young Polish engineer, Andrzej Szawernowski, who "throughout the occupation bravely helped me with my daily difficulties," particularly with arranging documents and finding hiding places for the Jews under Chmielewski's care. Chmielewski insists that he also had help from other quarters:

"even the most stubborn 'Polish fascists,' from the Camp of Great Poland [OWP] or even the National Radical Camp [ONR], for the most part renounced their youthful ideology, and in an honest, real, brotherly fashion helped first of all me, and later even directly the Jews themselves. The Christian idea, 'love thy neighbor as thyself,' eroded the ideology 'beat the Jew.'"[8] There are indeed documented instances of members of the far right who devoted themselves to helping Jews—the case of Jan Mosdorf is well known.[9] . . . In general, however, the far right did not "renounce its former ideology": its underground press maintained an uninterrupted barrage of antisemitic propaganda, and partisan groups of the NSZ [National Armed Forces], the military organization of the OWP and ONR, carried on an internecine war against what it regarded as the nation's enemies, including Communists, liberals, and Jews. The NSZ carried out a series of assassinations, among others of the Jewish historian Marceli Handelsman, and some of its partisan groups carried out attacks on Jewish partisans. Another organization of the far right, *Miecz i Plug* (Sword and Plough), was widely regarded as collaborationist. . . . There is at least reason to think that Chmielewski's optimism is misplaced. He accurately reports the contradictory aspects of right-wing Christian ideology that warred in the breasts of such people, but certainly "love thy neighbor" did not always, or even very often, win out over "beat the Jew." . . .

With the closing of the ghetto, Chmielewski resolved to maintain contact with his Jewish friends and bring them aid. But as he writes, "Acting almost alone, I could not of course reach most of the prisoners of the ghetto, so that of necessity, of tragic necessity, my aid had to restrict itself to the narrow group of people who were my friends. I knew, in any case, that I was not isolated in my action, I believed that there must be others like me, who had friends among the Jews. This thought and faith gave me strength." Indeed, there are a number of accounts of Poles who maintained contact with their Jewish friends in the ghetto, and also of Jews who elected to remain outside the ghetto and smuggled food and other necessities in to their relatives. . . . Ringelblum reports that, in the last few days before Christians were excluded from the ghetto, there was "a mass phenomenon: Poles come to their Jewish friends . . . with packages of food, with flowers."[10] How many of these people kept up contact later on is hard to say, but certainly some of them did. As a policeman who participated in the illegal traffic through the ghetto gates, Rotholc noticed that "[t]here were also Poles who went into the ghetto. . . . . These Poles also arranged things for the Jews. Jews entrusted them with their fortunes. These Poles brought the Jews money. They took all sorts of things out of the ghetto. Those Jews who didn't have the possibility of smuggling food not seldom got money from Poles, which they used to buy food from the smugglers."[11] . . .

Chmielewski's action during the ghetto period consisted of arranging the sale of his friends' possessions to raise money for them (he could get a better price on the Aryan side than they could in the ghetto), and smuggling food and medicine across to them. In this work, he says, he had the help of a "small, but faithful and reliable group of friends." Among these was a German member of the Nazi party, Erich Horst, who "hated Hitler, and did whatever he could and however he could, always with dedication, to save the victims of persecution, Poles and Jews alike."[12] Horst gave Chmielewski's group access to German gendarmes who could be bribed. Later, Chmielewski found a less expensive and less dangerous method of smuggling. The ghetto's garbagemen, who dumped their refuse outside the ghetto, could be persuaded (for a price) to carry food back with them, concealed in their empty wagons. Still another method was to throw food over the ghetto wall, at prearranged times and places. Chmielewski's mother helped in this work, together with a friend of hers whose daughter-in-law was in the ghetto. . . .

With time, contact with the ghetto became more and more difficult and dangerous. Even the court building in Leszno Street, where Jews and Poles could legally mingle, became a favorite place for *lapanki* (hostage-takings and roundups for forced labor). Furthermore, access to the court building became restricted to those on court business, so that heavy bribes had to be paid to get in.

Money, in general, was the lubricating fluid of all transactions, according to Chmielewski. Now less sanguine about his countrymen, he complains that "during the occupation, unfortunately—today we have to be completely honest about this—money decided everything. You could look for sentiment with a candle in your hand. Or you could dream or daydream about it."[13] Raising money therefore became an increasing problem for Chmielewski, a man of modest means, especially as his work multiplied with the liquidation of the ghetto. He recounts that:

> During that feverish period I was once at a kind of reception. The home was cultured, the company select. [. . .] It started with cold snacks, prepared in the traditional Polish way; there were two green tables for bridge, and in the living room they were getting ready for a concert. The host was a man of inherited wealth, a member of the typical West-Polish bourgeoisie, the guests included wealthy landowners. *Nota bene*: the hostess was hiding two Jews in her house. One of them was a doctor. Both took an

active part in the reception, in the discussion, in the numerous disputes and controversies that usually take place under such circumstances.

> This was a typical social gathering of that tragic period, [. . .] which in effect not only brought together the representatives of the two nations but, the most important thing then, produced a greater or lesser income. Because all the participants in such gatherings [. . .] had to make a donation to a fund to aid the victims of the ghetto.[14]

Jewish sources do not mention such receptions, but it must be kept in mind that the recorded testimony represents only a small part of the whole reality. It seems, at any rate, that financial help to the Jewish fugitives was not limited to the money officially channelled to the aid organizations by the Government-in-Exile and Jewish groups abroad, but that money was raised within Poland as well. . . .

Chmielewski also mentions the Berson family, wealthy bankers long ago converted to Christianity, who nevertheless retained a sympathetic attitude to Jews. Among their philanthropies, for example, was the Bersons' and Baumans' Children's Hospital, which was incorporated into the ghetto. The Bersons maintained two estates, in Boglowice and Leszno. According to Chmielewski, both gave employment and hiding places to Jews who had escaped from the ghetto, and both contributed money and food to the relief of the ghetto. . . .

Besides raising money to cope with the flood of refugees, Chmielewski also needed to recruit more helpers. One of these was a Dr. Karlsbader of Zelazna 31, a woman who "gave aid and shelter to many people from the ghetto"; another was a Mrs. Gerzabek of Natolinska 3: their houses served as temporary shelters for Jewish fugitives. From there, Chmielewski and his friend Szawernowski found them more permanent places.

One of Chmielewski's Jewish friends, the professor of medicine Dr. Leo Plocker, was assigned to a *placówka* (work detail) outside the ghetto, where he had to perform heavy physical labor for which he was unfit. Chmielewski rescued him from this otherwise probably fatal situation by arranging for him to sneak away from the *placówka* and spend his days with another friend. In the evenings, Plocker would rejoin the work party and return to the ghetto. After Plocker escaped from the ghetto, Chmielewski found him a place with Dr. Karlsbader and placed Plocker's wife . . . in Mokotowska Street. Mrs. Plocker was a concert pianist, a gold-medalist of the Leipzig Conservatory, and of Aryan appearance. She could therefore appear in public and gave fund-raising concerts, often at the home of a couple called Andrzejewski, who had an excellent Bechstein. Chmielewski placed Dr. Plocker's mother with yet another friend, a Mrs. Wala, in Wilcza Street. Chmielewski also placed with Wala some relatives of his lover Wladyslaw Bergman, Alina Lewinson and her daughters, Janina and Sophie. Janina Lewinson, under her married name of Janina Bauman, is the author of *Winter in the Morning*, one of the outstanding memoirs of the period, from which we learn a good deal more about Chmielewski, Wala, and many other people. . . .

Chmielewski placed Stefania Bergman somewhere in Wesola Street, and after that *melina* was "burnt," with a Mr. and Mrs. Henrychów in Kopernika Street. This couple was also looking after a Mrs. Kasman. Mrs Kasman's daughter-in-law had been caught while hiding and shot, leaving a small son, whom Chmielewski took into his own flat. At that time, he was also hiding Mieczyslaw Goldstein, the lawyer.

Thus we come full circle, with Chmielewski's network connecting with that of the Kopers, and thereby to Cywinski, Zabinski, and the mainstream Polish underground. These various networks on the Polish side arose spontaneously as a result of the personal contacts and humanitarian impulses of such people, and eventually merged into a single large network, connected to the Polish underground and eventually also to the aid agencies when they arose. As it grew beyond its humanitarian nucleus, it came to include, as Chmielewski tells us, those for whom "money decided everything" and was infiltrated by more sinister elements as well.

Chmielewski's relatively short memoir (twenty-six typed pages) only skims the surface of his wartime activities. Writing a quarter of a century after the events, he admits that he has forgotten the names of many of the people in his circle, and can tell us little more about the Jews in his care. Janina Bauman's memory is more vivid: her extraordinarily detailed account puts the experiences of at least one of the families whom Chmielewski helped under the microscope and provides more details of his activities.

Chmielewski's lover, Wladyslaw Bergman, was Bauman's rather distant cousin. Her main "angel" throughout the occupation, however, was not Chmielewski but "Aunt Maria," Maria Bulat, her mother's former nanny and her grandparents' housekeeper. Bulat was recognized as a "Righteous Gentile" in 1993.[15] Sharing a single room with her sister and brother-in-law, Aunt Maria was unable to give shelter to Jews in her own home, but extended help in many other ways. During the ghetto period, she maintained contact with Bauman's family, by telephone, through the courthouse in Leszno Street and also through her brother-in-law, who as an electrician had a pass that allowed him to enter the ghetto freely.

He would bring "letters, money, and all sorts of useful things from her."[16] In January 1943, Aunt Maria arranged for the Lewinsons—Janina, her mother, and her sister—to escape from the ghetto and escorted them to their first *melina*. This was a large flat in the center of Warsaw belonging to the aristocratic family of Chmielewski's friend, Andrzej Szawernowski.

Eight Poles stayed at the Szawernowskis,' as well as four Jews—"Aunt Maryla" (Stefania Bergman) and the three Lewinsons. Not all the Poles were equally generous or courageous. The Szawernowskis' daughter, Mrs. Simonis, was nervous about "keeping cats" (the wartime slang for hiding Jews): she was cool toward them, demanded large payments, and refused to take in Jews after the flat had been visited by blackmailers in June 1943. The Szawernowskis themselves, on the other hand, would later take the Lewinsons in without payment while their daughter was away on holidays.

Forced out of the Szawernowskis' flat by the blackmailers, the Lewinsons next turned to Zena Ziegler, the ex-wife of their grandfather's former chauffeur, who was already giving shelter to Janina's uncle Stefan and his fiancée, Jadwiga. But Ziegler was a morphine addict and indiscreetly told her boyfriend, so that the Lewinsons had to find another hiding place after only a few days. Stefan and Jadwiga found shelter with Ziegler's sister, Mrs. Kulesza, while Mrs. Simonis arranged a temporary place for the Lewinsons with a prostitute named Lily who entertained German soldiers in her flat and whose brother was a *Reichsdeutsche* [native-born German] working with the railway police (*Bahnschutz*), whose job included catching Jews. Clearly this *melina* was unsuitable, and Aunt Maria next placed them with her sister Helena. Helena was not supposed to take such risks because her son was a high-ranking member of the AK [*Armja Krajowa*, the Polish nationalist resis-

tance force], whose arrest could therefore have serious implications for the movement. Again, therefore, the Lewinsons were able to stay for only a few days.

After this, Janina . . . speaks of wandering on the outskirts of Warsaw, staying in "somebody's cousin's flat; somebody else's friend's flat."[17] Chmielewski then came to the rescue, finding a place for her in the city center. This was a sophisticated, specially constructed hiding place on the burnt-out first floor of a building above a German trading company. Here the porter of a neighboring building, whom Bauman identifies only as "Kazik," and his mother hid "dozens" of Jews: fifteen were there when the Lewinsons arrived, eight others had just left. Kazik appears to have been middle-class, not the usual sort to be a building porter; Bauman thinks he was a member of the AK, using the porter's job as cover.

It was now the late summer of 1943 and the Lewinsons had lived in at least seven *melinas* in perhaps as many months. . . . Very soon, Kazik's *melina*, too, became "burnt." when a pair of blackmailers robbed the six remaining people of everything they could find. The Lewinsons found temporary refuge with Kazik's mother, who was also looking after a Jewish woman and her baby (Bauman thinks that the child was Kazik's). Kazik now placed the Lewinsons with his friends Tom and Wanda, who printed underground pamphlets, forged documents, and banknotes in their cellar. But Tom was soon arrested on the street. Since such arrests were invariably followed by a house search, the Lewinsons had to clear out quickly. They returned to the Szawernowskis.' The Szawernowskis could offer a place only until the unsympathetic Mrs. Simonis came back from holiday, and the search for a hiding place therefore resumed immediately. Alina Lewinson and her younger daughter,

Sophie, were put up in the suburb of Rembertow by another sister of Zena Ziegler's, Janka Zielinska, while Janina was placed in another suburb, Radosc, with a family whom she calls the Majewskis.[18] . . . [T]hey required the payment of a large sum in advance, were rude and uncouth, starved Janina and then invented a story that a stranger had been nosing about, in order to get rid of her and keep the money. Janina then joined the rest of her family at the Zielinskis, a family of four. Here, at last, the Lewinsons found some stability, staying for six months until January 1944. Between them they had had to move at least thirteen times in eight months.

Like the Majewskis, the Zielinski household also charged for keeping the Lewinsons, but Bauman writes that the amount was reasonable and they were well looked after. A working-class family, the Zielinskis could not get by during the occupation without supplementing their income by illegal activities. Mrs. Zielinska, a midwife, performed abortions and traded on the black market: keeping the Jews, says Bauman, was no more risky and less exhausting. But living with another family at close quarters and under such conditions could not remain just a commercial enterprise: "for the people who sheltered us our presence also meant more than great danger, nuisance, or extra income. Somehow it affected them, too. It boosted what was noble in them or what was base. Sometimes it divided the family; at other times it brought the family together in a shared endeavor to help survive."[19] Thus Janka generously gave up her double bed to Janina and her mother, sleeping in a single bed with her own daughter while her husband slept with their son.

Eventually, this hiding place, too, was discovered by blackmailers, and after they had been paid off there was no money left. To help out, Aunt Maria sold a plot of land that Janina's grandparents had given her. Chmielewski placed Janina with an elderly woman who was also looking after Stefania Bergman; her mother and sister in the meantime "were going through terrible ordeals. For various reasons they had to leave one shelter after another, to hide in wardrobes and chests, often to walk along the streets in full daylight."[20] Since all three had a "bad: appearance (Chmielewski thinks that the younger daughter, Sophie, could safely pass as a non-Jew, but Bauman thinks otherwise), appearing in public was highly dangerous. They disguised themselves by wearing mourning, but such disguises could often draw the very attention they were meant to deflect. Briefly, they sought refuge in a church, where the priest, suspecting who they were, offered food and consolation. Chmielewski then found lodgings for all three of them with Mrs. Wala. . . . This *melina*, too, had to be abandoned when Wala died in hospital. . . . With her death her flat reverted to the city and all the tenants had to leave. Finally, Aunt Maria found a place for them with a neighbor of hers, where they stayed until the 1944 uprising.

Bauman's story, though told with exceptional clarity and detail, is otherwise not untypical of the memoir literature: the constant moving from place to place, the repeated threat of blackmail and denunciation, the problem of money, the dependence on the goodwill of large numbers of people who were essentially strangers . . . are all quite typical. The Lewinson family were also rather typical of the assimilated Warsaw intelligentsia. Janina's father was a urologist, one grandfather was also a doctor, the other owned a music shop. Her family adhered nominally to the Jewish faith, but were non-observant and had adopted such Christian customs as putting up a Christmas tree. She received her primary education at *Nasza Szkolct* and then entered a state *gimnazjum*. She was the only Jewish girl in the whole school, the result of the unofficial *numerus clausus* that kept out all but the ablest Jews.

Bauman does not mention any prewar Christian friends of the family, except to say that some of them visited just before the ghetto was closed.... Instead, their main point of contact with the outside world was through their servants. Domestic labor was cheap in prewar Poland, and any respectable middle-class family, even one that was not very wealthy, would have a maid or a nanny or a cook. A number of family servants figure in Bauman's story: besides Aunt Maria and Zena Ziegler, there is also Ziegler's husband, a *Volksdeutsche* [a person of German descent living outside the Reich]; a nurse named Sister Franciszka, also a *Volksdeutsche*; and Stefania Bergman's Christian maid, who moved into the ghetto with the family (there were not a few such cases).[21]

Summing up Bauman's story, then: the Lewinsons' beachhead on the Aryan side consisted of the old nanny, Aunt Maria, and the chauffeur's ex-wife, Mrs. Ziegler. They in turn recruited various friends and relatives. Aunt Maria enlisted her sister Helena, her brother Tadeusz and her brother-in-law, the electrician with a pass for the ghetto. This beachhead was then expanded through the further families, friends, and neighbors of these servants. These were working class Poles, most of whom were honest but for whom looking after Jews was primarily a way of supplementing their income. Chmielewski, who as a cousin's lover was tenuously related to the Lewinsons, acted as another beachhead. In helping the Lewinsons, Chmielewski used contacts with the Polish underground, Andrzej Szawernowski and the porter Kazik. Through the daughter of the aristocratic Szawernowskis, in turn, the Lewinsons met the *Reichsdeutsch* prostitute Lily; while the contact with Kazik led to the ill-fated under-

ground printing shop of Tom and Wanda. This was the structure of the Lewinsons' network on the Aryan side.

On the Jewish side, Bauman mentions thirteen relatives and eleven friends who were alive and in Warsaw when the ghetto was closed or subsequently. Of these, two relatives stayed out of the ghetto; seven relatives, five friends and three parents of friends escaped from it, and three relatives died or were deported. We are not told the fate of the remaining six friends. Thus, at least fifteen out of twenty-four—nearly two-thirds—either escaped from the ghetto or never entered it. Of those of whose final fate we are told (excluding Bauman herself), six survived, two died in the 1944 Warsaw Uprising and four died on the Aryan side before that uprising. Thus, at least a quarter of this very well-connected group of Jews survived the war, and more than half of those on the Aryan side survived at least until the uprising in 1944.

... Certain things can be said on the basis of this case history. First of all, relying mainly on the testimony of one Polish and one Jewish witness, we have found our way to more than a hundred Jews, sixty-odd Poles, four Germans (Chmielewski's helper Erich Horst, one of Bauman's blackmailers, the prostitute, Lily, and her brother) and two *Volksdeutsche* (Zena Ziegler's husband and the nurse, Sister Franciszka). Through Kenigswein and his connection with Zabinski, we have also arrived at the Polish and Jewish aid organizations, which ultimately reached thousands of the Jews in hiding. Each of these Jews in turn had, like Bauman, additional contacts with Poles and other Jews, and the Poles also had further contacts of their own. Here, then, is how the secret city arose, spontaneously, through personal networks.

Nechama Tec has suggested that Polish helpers of Jews largely thought of themselves as "outsiders," a proposition that Michael Marrus finds so self-evident that he describes it as "a circular argument."[22] Some of the people described by Chmielewski and Bauman and the others were indeed outsiders: Lily the prostitute, Zena Ziegler the morphine addict, Chmielewski the homosexual. And there is more than a hint that much of Chmielewski's circle was a homosexual underground, helping its fellow victims of Nazi persecution. But the larger network that these accounts reveal reached into the most extraordinary variety of milieus. It included the aristocratic Szawernowskis and the working-class Zielinskis, the extreme right-wing ONR and OWP circles with which Chmielewski was in contact, and also the Communists to whom his friend Dr Plocker belonged. It included Poles, Germans, *Volksdeutsche*, and old Jewish converts, members of the Polish underground and of the Nazi party, sportsmen and boulevardiers, priests and atheists, servants and masters. It included people of great kindness and nobility, others whose interest was purely mercenary, and (counting the *szmalcowniks*) the vilest of criminals. In short, it reached into every corner of Polish society and involved people of every type.

On the Jewish side, the network may in principle have reached most of the Jews in the ghetto—though Bauman's milieu is assimilated, many other memoirists had relatives who remained traditional—but the principle of "charity begins at home" ensured that those with the closest contacts had the best chances. There were also many psychological barriers that held back the less assimilated Jews. For many reasons, the community of Jews on the Aryan side consisted almost entirely of assimilated Jews, except for the relatively small group of political and social activists who escaped through the efforts of their organizations. . . .

Summary and Conclusions

I have estimated that the secret city consisted of some 28,000 Jews in hiding, in addition to 70,000–90,000 Poles who helped them and a few thousand criminals and policemen who preyed on them. Criminal element and all, the secret city thus numbered at least 100,000 people, 10 per cent of the population of Aryan Warsaw. It was linked, as all cities are, by a complex network of personal relationships, of which the individuals who comprised it were only dimly aware.

I have also estimated that about 11,500 of these Jews survived. If these figures are correct, then despite the distress that the city of Warsaw suffered during the war, despite the dangers that all its citizens faced, despite the special dangers that confronted the Jews, and despite the dangers unique to Warsaw, such as the 1944 Warsaw Uprising and the Hotel Polski trap, the survival rate among the Jewish fugitives of Warsaw (about 40 per cent) was not much less than that observed in a Western European country such as the Netherlands, where it has been estimated that 40–60 per cent survived. In Warsaw, some 61 per cent of those in hiding (17,000 out of 28,000) survived until the 1944 uprising. . . .

The fugitives may have amounted to only a small proportion of the nearly 490,000 Jews who passed through the Warsaw ghetto, but as we have seen, the bulk of escapes occurred only after the Great Deportation of 1942, when the ghetto population had been reduced to 55,000–60,000: no fewer than 13,000 escapes took place after that point, nearly a quarter of the remaining population. No less remarkable is that a city so overcrowded, impoverished and terrorized managed to find room for 28,000 Jewish refugees, more than most of the neutral countries of Europe took in over the entire war. . . .

Depending on one's point of view, therefore, the number of Jewish fugitives and ultimate survivors in Warsaw was either very small (5 per cent and 2 per cent of the Jewish population, respectively) or very large (more than anywhere else, remarkable under the circumstances). Both are legitimate points of view. Therefore, two complementary questions can be asked: why so few, and why so many?

Why so few? The most obvious reason is that escape on a large scale took place only at a late date, when the great majority of the Jews of Warsaw were already dead. How we evaluate the importance of this factor depends on our assessment of how many more fugitives the city could have accommodated, a question that can only be a matter for speculation. Certainly the wave of escapes was showing no signs of abating when the Ghetto Uprising broke out: if escape had continued at the same rate for another six months, half the remaining Jews would have got away; by August 1944 they would all have gone. But it is unlikely that this rate of escapes could have been sustained. . . . Indeed, the difficulties that the activists had in placing the surviving ghetto fighters in the summer of 1943 suggests that their possibilities were well-nigh exhausted at that point, though the same may not have been true of the wider network. With an organized effort, it would in principle have been possible to transfer Jews to other centers, or to rural estates like those of the Bersons. But . . . no one at the time seems to have thought of such a scheme. On the contrary, Jews hiding elsewhere were advised to come to Warsaw, as the main center of Polish resistance and of the aid effort. . . .

The lateness of escape, rather than a shortage of hiding-places, explains why 95 per cent of the ghetto population did not flee . . . A variety of factors in turn account for the lateness of escape.

When the ghetto was sealed off in 1940, no one knew what the future held, and it is not surprising that few people wanted to chance disobeying German orders. Nevertheless, more Jews might have stayed out of the ghetto but for the fact that those who did, and even those who escaped in 1940–41, were regarded virtually as traitors, and certainly as cowards. The ghetto famine of 1941–42 might have induced more people to escape, but paradoxically the success of the smuggling effort meant that escape was never perceived as the best prospect for survival. Even Poles who extended aid to their Jewish friends in the ghetto helped by bringing them food, medicine, and money, and rarely by proposing escape. The introduction in October 1941 of the death penalty for leaving the ghetto acted as a further disincentive, making Poles think twice about helping Jews and Jews think twice about exposing their Polish friends. Ominous news reaching the ghetto in the first half of 1942 did induce slightly more people to escape, but the news was contradictory, unreliable and hard to interpret. By the eve of the first *Aktion*, in July 1942, only about 5,000 Jews were to be found on the Aryan side, a little more than 1 per cent of the Jewish population of Warsaw.

Once the first *Aktion* started, escape immediately became more difficult, as the established smuggling routes were sealed off. It took some time before the ghetto became persuaded that those "deported to the east" were in fact being killed, and before new means of escape were worked out. At the same time, the ghetto remained unaware of the scope of German plans, and many people believed that the deportation was to be limited to 'unproductive elements,' sparing those with essential jobs. The Germans took care to promote such illusions by announcing various classes of exemption, which were cancelled one by one.

Even for those who were convinced that the ghetto was doomed, escape was by no means an easy or obvious choice. The chaotic conditions of the *Aktion* left people with little time and energy to organize escape, and adults were reluctant to leave their families and community behind. Many of those who left the ghetto during the *Aktion* were therefore children sent out of the ghetto by their parents, who hoped to be able to follow eventually. . . .

Those who did manage to make their way to the Aryan side, by one route or another, found themselves hunted by German gendarmes, Polish Blue policemen, and an army of *szmalcowniks*. In addition, they had to deal with the complications of underground life in a dictatorship, which aimed to enmesh every citizen in a web of documentary controls, and were also faced with a critical shortage of housing, especially of a kind that offered the privacy that Jews living underground needed. Jews seem to have been easily detectable by the Poles, less because of their Semitic appearance, as was supposed, than by more subtle traits: a characteristic accent or manner of speech, unfamiliarity with Polish cultural and religious traditions, and various other signs—above all, a furtive manner and sad eyes—so that practically every Jew in hiding was successfully tracked down by *szmalcowniks* at least once, and often many times. In addition, Jews could be recognized by prior acquaintances, who were not necessarily friendly, or by other residents in the same building, who might denounce them or put pressure on the porter to have them removed; or rumors might reach them that the police or blackmailers were on their trail. Any of these situations, which Jews in hiding encountered on average seven or eight times in the course of their ordeal on the Aryan side would force a change in hiding place. Each such move confronted Jews with new dangers and uncertainties, and forced them to deal afresh with the problems of housing and documentation.

Money posed a major problem for Jews in hiding, for whom working meant additional public exposure as well as the need to obtain more documents. Some worked nevertheless, preferably at home or as domestics; others operated on the black market, exposing themselves to additional dangers. About a third eventually received financial support from *Zegota*, the ZKN, the Bund or other welfare agencies, but the amounts were small and came late in the day. Most lived either by selling their possessions, or on the charity of their Polish hosts. Those who carried all their possessions with them were soon stripped of them by *szmalcowniks* or unscrupulous landlords, in some cases being left literally penniless and naked. Many Jews therefore left goods for safekeeping with Polish friends, most of whom discharged their obligations honestly; but some, including highly respectable members of Polish society, had no scruples about robbing them. This could leave them in a disastrous situation. . . .

Adding to the terror to which the Jews were subjected, finally, was the unrelenting barrage of antisemitic propaganda, emitting not only from street loudspeakers and the Nazi-sponsored "reptile" press, but also from the underground organs of the Polish right, which for example told Poles to be wary about hiding Jews, since Jews who were captured were supposedly known to denounce their benefactors. Together with the widespread preexisting antisemitism in Polish society, which found its expression in malevolent remarks and, in extreme cases, in denunciation or murder, these expressions of hostility made Jews more apprehensive and hence easier for *szmalcowniks* to recognize, dissuaded many Jews from escaping from the ghetto, and persuaded others to return to the ghetto or take advantage of the various German schemes and "amnesties." . . .

The harrowing underground existence of the Jews of the secret city ended with the outbreak of the Warsaw Uprising on August 1, 1944, but old dangers were now replaced by new ones. By coincidence, the majority of hiding places were located in areas controlled by the insurgents, so that Jews formed a disproportionate number of those killed by military action. Jews were also at risk in various ways from the Polish population. A renegade unit of the AK murdered at least twenty-three Jews in and near the area that they controlled, and there were many other individual murders and summary executions as well. Jews were suspected of being German agents (on the logic that "since they survived, they must have collaborated"), and were arrested and sometimes killed out of hand on the basis of absurd "evidence." Jews descending into bomb shelters often encountered hostility from the Polish occupants, and in at least one case a Jew was forced to leave his shelter during a bombardment and was killed by shrapnel. In total, some 4,500 Jews died during the uprising, several dozen at the hands of Poles. . . .

Jews in hiding faced extraordinary difficulties and dangers, and every Jew in hiding ran a gauntlet in which a single misstep could be fatal. It is no wonder that authors who consider only the negative aspects of this story conclude that the Jews' chances of survival on the Aryan side were "negligible." I have estimated . . . that 16,450 Jews died on the Aryan side in the Warsaw area: 5,400 during and after the Warsaw Uprising, 3,500 as a result of the Hotel Polski trap, a few hundred of what one might call accelerated natural causes, another few hundred for various other reasons, and 6,000 as a result of being caught, betrayed or murdered. Nevertheless, I have also estimated that there were 11,500 survivors. . . .

We therefore need also to ask the complementary question 'Why so many?' How was it possible for nearly a quarter of the remaining ghetto population to escape, once the necessity of escape became evident? And how was it possible for such a relatively large proportion of them to survive the seemingly insuperable challenges that faced them? The following reasons can be adduced:

1. The Jews of Warsaw had many preexisting links with the Gentile community, despite the apparent mutual isolation of and frequent friction between the two societies. A bridging community existed, consisting mainly of converts and people in mixed marriages, who had friends and relatives on both sides of the wall. Jewish assimilants also often had Polish friends and colleagues to whom they could turn, especially those who were politically engaged in the three political parties (the SD, PPS, and PPR) that had both Jewish and non-Jewish members. The small number of Jews—about 2,400—who stayed out of the ghetto in 1940 frequently maintained contacts with their friends and relatives inside the ghetto, as did some Poles. From this nucleus of primary contacts, a network spread out that reached into all milieus on both sides of the wall, so that most Jews had some direct or indirect contacts on the Aryan side.

2. Various factors made the ghetto wall porous. The Warsaw ghetto was in the heart of the city, not in the outskirts as was originally planned. This in turn was a result of the very large number of Jews in Warsaw, which made it impracticable to relocate them all, and also of their economic importance, which persuaded the authorities that isolating or hermetically sealing the ghetto would be disadvantageous. German policies that predated the creation of the ghetto had already given rise to an extensive

black market in Warsaw, and this market continued to operate, on both sides of the ghetto wall and across it. The links that were formed and the methods that were worked out at that time served well later on, when the trade was in guns and people. Physical channels of contact across the ghetto wall included telephones and the postal service, both of which continued to operate until a surprisingly late date, evidently an oversight on the part of the authorities. In addition, some Poles had passes that allowed them to enter the ghetto legally, or else they entered the ghetto with work parties, while others crossed the wall illegally. Through these channels, Jews contemplating escape from the ghetto could get in touch with friends on the "other side," who could make the necessary arrangements. Once on the Aryan side, Jews typically had to keep finding new quarters to avoid blackmailers and police; in the process, they were forced to rely on help from people with whom their connections were increasingly tenuous. That is to say, the group of people involved in helping Jews spread from the original bridging community to encompass a much wider circle, which, I have estimated, ultimately numbered 70,000–90,000 people.

3. In this and other ways the networks that individual Jews relied upon became interconnected to form a single "secret city." Many strands of evidence show that this was so. The rapidity with which news of the Hotel Polski spread, and the fact that organized aid eventually reached about a third of the fugitives (despite their reluctance to expose themselves even by asking for help), testify to the existence of an effective communications system. So does the fact that an argot developed, which included such words as *melina, szmalcownik* and so on (which have become a permanent addition to the Polish language). Most Jewish memoirists report encountering other Jews in hiding, previously unknown to them: each such encounter demonstrates a point of contact between individual networks. The same is true of contacts with previously unknown Poles, and conversely of the involvement of Poles in hiding Jews previously unknown to them. The secret city also had its institutions, its meeting places, its intellectual life, even its publications and nascent culture. If we take into account Jews and their helpers, the secret city numbered about 100,000 people, or one-tenth of the population of supposedly *judenrein* Warsaw.

4. The Germans were almost certainly unaware of the size and extent of this secret city, estimating the number of Jews who had fled the ghetto at only 5,000–6,000. After they had caught 3,500 Jews through the Hotel Polski scheme, they must have thought they had nearly all of them. Subsequent Jew-hunting from the German side was fairly desultory and took second place to action against the Polish underground.

5. Warsaw was the center of this underground, and also accommodated a large number of people who were hiding for various reasons. This meant that there was a parallel Polish "secret city," offering Jews further contacts and opportunities. For example, an extensive document-forging operation came into existence, which also became available to the Jews. Clerks in the municipal administration succeeded in delaying the introduction of the German identity document, the *Kennkarte*, with the fortuitous result that the period of the greatest number of escapes from the ghetto coincided with the registration of the entire population of Warsaw. Thus, thousands of Jews could obtain authentic *Kennkarten* without attracting attention. The large number of non-Jews in hiding also pro-

vided a certain amount of camouflage for the Jews, although they also drew the unwelcome attention of the police.

6. The Blue police [the indigenous collaborationist police force of the *General Gouvernement*] were somewhat cautious about turning suspected Jews over to the Germans, since there were known cases of Poles who had been mistaken for Jews. Therefore, Jews who were arrested were not killed on the spot, as the German authorities had ordered, but held for investigation. This provided opportunities for even those who had been caught to free themselves through bribes or for Polish friends to come and vouch for them. The other main group of Jew-hunters, the *szmalcowniks*, were for the most part interested in money, not blood. Those who accosted Jews on the street were generally satisfied with relatively small sums, while those who found out their victims' hiding places would take whatever they could find. Although in the latter case Jews could be left destitute and desperate, and often died as a consequence, it was relatively uncommon for *szmalcowniks* to turn them over to the police, contrary to the general belief. Actual denunciation was done for personal or ideological reasons, was usually anonymous, brought little material benefit to the denouncer and was relatively rare.

7. Although some Poles to whom Jews had entrusted their belongings for safe-keeping betrayed this trust, the majority did not; and although some Poles who hid Jews for money failed to honor their promises or otherwise cheated or exploited the Jews, the majority did not. Most Poles [in Warsaw] who were hiding Jews did not make money a condition of rescue, and some even refused to accept money when it was offered.[23] Many Jews were thus

able to support themselves on the Aryan side through selling their belongings, or by relying on the help of faithful friends. Work opportunities were very limited, and exposed Jews to additional dangers; nevertheless, some Jews were able to support themselves at least partially by working, most commonly as domestics or doing work that could be performed at home. Some, finally, received help from *Zegota*, the Jewish National Committee, the Bund or other aid agencies, or if politically engaged were supported by their parties.

8. German policy was in many respects self-defeating. Irrational economic policies created the underground economy that sustained the ghetto; they necessitated the use of Jewish labor outside the ghetto, which provided the most frequent means of escape; and they ensured that nearly everyone was engaged in some kind of illegal activity, creating a generally anarchic atmosphere. Indiscriminate and excessively draconian measures, instead of taming the population, forced it into bravado and lawlessness; as a result, hiding Jews became merely one of the many illegal activities for which people routinely risked their lives. The principle of collective responsibility backfired as well: denouncing Jews also meant exposing their Polish helpers to danger, a severe violation of the wartime code of solidarity. (Some Jews, on the other hand, were denounced precisely in order to strike at their helpers, as a result of private vendettas.)

9. The secret city was a self-selecting conspiracy of mainly decent and honest people, which remained secret not only from the Germans but also from the bulk of the Polish population. In this the Jews benefited from, among other things, the unspoken rules of behavior in occupied Poland—at the minimum, to mind your

own business. This is, of course, more generally a principle of big-city life, and was one of the things that attracted Jews to Warsaw as a place to hide. When Jews were exposed in front of Poles who were not involved in the conspiracy, the latter, though not especially sympathetic to the Jews and sometimes openly hostile, rarely went so far as to denounce them. . . . We have noted numerous situations in which Jews were publicly exposed as Jews and yet no one in a large crowd denounced them. Keeping in mind that it required only one person to denounce a Jew but the unanimous silence of the whole crowd to allow him or her to escape, that a significant number of Jews did survive such situations is testimony that most Poles [in Warsaw] were passively protective towards the Jews, even when their attitudes were antisemitic, while only a small minority were actively hostile.

The Polish Blue police can . . . be divided into three types: those who hunted Jews with enthusiasm or cooperated with blackmailers; those who were willing to turn a blind eye in return for a bribe; and those, like Mieczyslaw Tarwid or Eliasz Pietruszko, who used their positions actively to help Jews. The great majority of escapes were accomplished by leaving the ghetto with a work party; this required the guards at the ghetto gate . . . to miscount the members of the party and the party's overseer to allow people to slip away once outside. This could not have been accomplished without the cooperation of a sufficient number of German and Polish policemen, who usually had to be bribed but sometimes acted voluntarily.

Neither the Polish nor the Jewish underground acquitted itself particularly well in helping Jews to escape, both becoming involved in helping Jewish fugitives only on a comparatively small scale

and relatively late in the day. The Jewish underground had its sights fixed on armed resistance and generally persuaded itself that escape was impossible, although each organization managed to smuggle some of its activists out. The organizational structure—the Jewish Coordinating Committee, the Jewish National Committee and the Bund—that later carried out relief work among the Jews in hiding came into existence not for that purpose but as the political arm of the Jewish Combat Organization (ZOB), to organize arms for the ghetto and maintain contacts with the Polish underground. It did not organize escapes from the ghetto (although there is evidence that some ZOB members operated an "underground railroad" from the Poniatowa labor camp), and its relief operations reached a significant scale only toward the end of 1943.

The Polish underground likewise was not involved in arranging escapes from the ghetto. The Jewish Bureau under Henryk Wolinski—with a Jewish wife, he was a member of the "bridging community" described above—had only the functions of observing and reporting, and later served as liaison between Polish and Jewish leaders. *Zegota*, the initiative for which came again from the "bridging community," in this case a group of . . . members of the Democratic Party, came into existence only in October 1942 and operated at first on a very small scale. Like the Jewish organizations, whose representatives joined the *Zegota* council in January 1943, it reached a larger group of fugitives only in the second half of 1943. Eventually the Polish and Jewish underground, between them, provided financial assistance to about 8,900 Jews in hiding.

The roles played by the Polish culture of the time, especially its rampant antisemitism, and by the Catholic church need to be assessed. Here we might reflect on two instances, recounted by

Michael Zylberberg and Stefan Chaskielewicz respectively. In each case, a woman who was risking her life to hide Jews—in Zylberberg's case, refusing to accept money for it—felt obliged to go to her parish priest and confess to this "sin." In each case, the priest reassured her that she was doing a fine and noble thing, and Chaskielewicz writes of his landlady that she subsequently lost her fear and stopped asking him to find another hiding place. These examples show the Catholic church at its best. But it is notable that in both cases an essentially good person had become so confused by Catholic teachings concerning Jews that she was no longer sure where her duty lay. It is no wonder, then, that people who were less good persuaded themselves that hiding Jews was disreputable or even disgraceful. Churchmen on the whole acquitted themselves well: for example, the prelate of All Saints' Church in the ghetto, Msgr. Marceli Godlewski, though notorious before the war as an antisemite, became actively involved in smuggling Jewish converts out of the ghetto. Other priests provided forged parish documents to Jews, and it appears to be true that virtually every convent in the Warsaw area was hiding a few Jewish children. The Father Boduen orphanage also distinguished itself in this regard. Nevertheless, it is also true that the traditional prayer "for the perfidious Jews" continued to be said on Good Friday; that priests were on occasion heard to express crude antisemitic sentiments . . . and on occasion even denounced Jews personally. The record and influence of the Catholic church, which by its own standards should have been unambiguously on the side of the oppressed and persecuted, was in fact mixed: the church was a force for evil as well as good. . . .

Zylberberg, on one occasion, having read the book of medieval lamentations *Gorzkie Zale* (Bitter Sorrows), marveled that despite such influ-

ences many ordinary Poles had managed to retain a humane and compassionate attitude toward the Jews. This can be attributed, first, to the more positive aspects of Polish culture: traditions of hospitality (*Gosc w dom, Bog w dom*—"When a guest is in the house, God is in the house"); Catholic teachings such as the Parable of the Good Samaritan or the Old Testament principle, "Love thy neighbor as thyself" (not to mention "Thou shalt not kill"); the Catholic veneration of altruism and martyrdom and related nationalist traditions of heroic self-sacrifice in adversity; a Polish literary tradition that has generally been sympathetic to the Jews (Mickiewicz, Prus, Orzeszkowa, Boy-Zeleriski, Konopnicka); historic traditions of toleration and liberality stretching back to the old Commonwealth of Both Nations [Poland and Lithuania]. Less positively, Catholics were moved by the hope of gaining converts. Second, the sheer familiarity of the Jews led to curiously inconsistent attitudes, which I have described as antisemitism "present company excepted." We may recall the paradox of the woman who expressed satisfaction that "the Jewish bedbugs are burning" while serving a meal to a Jewish couple for whom she was risking her life. The strength of family ties in Poland also made a contribution: if some members of a family had made a commitment to helping Jews, other members would know that by betraying the Jews they would also be betraying their own family. Third, despite the strength of right-wing politics and antisemitic attitudes, there was also a considerable left in Poland, particularly in the capital, which rejected antisemitism in principle and had been known to defend Jews against antisemitic attacks before the war.

Native antisemitism seems to have played only a marginal role in determining the fate of the Jews of Warsaw, and one that was offset by other factors, such the positive aspects of Christian faith, anti-German solidarity, and the strength and efficiency of the Polish underground. The secret city also effectively isolated the Jews under the protection of what I have called a spontaneous, self-selecting conspiracy of honest and decent people, so that what mattered was not how many enemies the Jews had, but how many friends. . . .

The conditions in Warsaw were inauspicious: a vicious dictatorship intent on destruction, a history of troubled ethnic relations, a nasty criminal element, no possibility of getting to a safe sanctuary abroad, economically difficult conditions all around. As a case study it represents a stiff test. In the end, however, the phenomenon of the Jews on the Aryan side in Warsaw must be assessed positively rather than negatively. To reiterate, the number of Jews who escaped from the ghetto was small in proportion to the whole ghetto population, but large—even extraordinarily large—as a proportion of those who might realistically have been expected to realize the need to escape. It was also extraordinarily large considering the traditional social isolation of the Polish Jews, a situation that had existed for centuries by mutual consent, and considering the conditions of life in occupied Warsaw, particularly the shortage of housing and the prevailing poverty and terror. It was, finally, extraordinarily large in comparison with other cities and even whole countries, which had more space, more resources, fewer barriers, and more freedom. I have estimated that 7–9 percent of the city's population was involved in helping Jews, including 6 per cent who knowingly provided hiding places; and it is possible that even more people would have risen to the occasion if they had been asked: the invisible walls that protected the secret city could at times exclude potential friends as well as enemies. The overcrowding in Aryan Warsaw, amounting to almost two people per habitable room, also meant that many people of goodwill lacked the physical circumstances to provide significant help, while others were restrained by fear. Finally, the proportion of Jews who survived, after hiding for between twenty months and four years, is surprisingly high in view of the dangers that beset them. The "gauntlet effect" multiplied even a small degree of risk through repeated exposure: that so many Jews ran the gauntlet successfully is evidence that the great majority of the population, even people who were hostile, were not prepared to go so far as to hand Jews over to be killed. The secret city protected the Jews; its criminal element hounded them; the rest of Warsaw, whatever it may have thought and felt about the Jews, provided camouflage and above all kept the secret. Thus—under the noses of one of the harshest occupation regimes in history–28,000 Jews managed to hide, and a good number of them lived to see the end of the war.

The secret city of the Jews of Warsaw, 1940–1945, was in short a remarkable achievement, made possible by the initiative, courage, and perseverance of the Jews, the heroic altruism of some Poles and the common decency of many others, and of some of the Germans as well. It casts a welcome and entirely unfamiliar light on the Holocaust as a whole and . . . is a phenomenon well worth further reflection and study.

NOTES

1. The Mongols are said to have massacred 800,000 people in Baghdad in 1258, but like most medieval estimates of this sort, this is probably a considerable exaggeration.
2. AZIH 301/4235; AZIH 301/4659; AZIH 301/5815; Michal Grynberg, ed., *Ksiega sprawiedliwych* (Warszawa: Wydawnicto Naukowe PWN, 1993), 77, 326, 327; AZIH 301/5008; Bartoszewski and Lewin, *Righteous*, 182–85, and Grynberg, *Ksiega*, 91, 410, 643.

3. Grynberg, *Ksiega*, 90; also AZIH 301/5711 YV-RG 0221 1966, and Bartoszewski and Lewin, *Righteous*, 181–85 (from the recollections of Henryk Joffe). Bartoszewski and Lewin, *Righteous*, 4–5 (extract from the memoirs of Adolf Berman), 492–93 (extract from the memoirs of Rachel Auerbach), 496–97 (extract from the memoirs of Basia Temkin-Berman), 500–503 (extract from the memoirs of Janina Buchholtz-Bukowska).

4. Shmuel Krakowski, *The War of the Doomed* (New York: Holmes & Meier, 1984), 278.

5. AZIH 301/5175 (deposition of Stefan Koper), and Bartoszewski and Lewin, *Righteous*, 450–52 (memoirs of Marek Stok).

6. Supporting letter to Chmielewski's deposition, AZIH 301/5815. Janina Bauman, *Winter in the Morning* (New York: Free Press, 1986), 104–5 *et passim*: Bauman refers to him as Karol; he was her mother's cousin.

7. AZIH 301/5815, 4

8. Ibid., 6. "Beat the Jew!" (*Bij Zyda!*) was a common incitement, particularly among right-wing student gangs that attacked Jews in the street before the war.

9. Mosdorf was the prewar editor of *Prosto z mostu*, the main organ of the ONR. As a prisoner in Auschwitz, he became involved in the camp underground and devoted particular attention to helping Jewish prisoners. He perished in the camp. See Philip Friedman, 'Za nasza i wasza wolnosc,' in Bartoszewski and Lewin, eds, *Ten jest z ojczyzny mojej* (Krakow: Znak, 1969), 90–91, and relation of Mieczyslaw Maslanko, in ibid., 668–70.

10. Ringelblum, *Kronika getta warszawskiego*, ed. Artur Eisenbach (Warszawa: Czytelnik, 1988), 204.

11. AZIH 301/4659.

12. AZIH 301/5815, 12.

13. Ibid., 13.

14. Ibid., 18–19.

15. Computer printout of the Yad Vashem database on Righteous Gentiles (Polish cases only) in author's possession, as of April 1994; kindly provided by Dr Mordechai Paldiel.

16. Bauman, *Winter*, 52.

17. Ibid., 121.

18. Bauman uses various pseudonyms in her memoir. For Stefania Bergman: Aunt Maryla; for Bielinska: Zielinska; for Stanislaw: Edward; for Kulesza: Koterba; for Dr Plocker: Uncle Leo; for Simonis: Serbin; for Szawernowski: Sokolnicki; for Tom's partner Wanda: Krystyna; for Zina Ziegler: Zena Richter. She could not remember the real names of the Majewski family or of the prostitute Lily.

19. Ibid., 141.

20. Ibid., 145.

21. Ibid., 33.

22. Nechama Tec, *When Light Pierced the Darkness* (Oxford: Oxford Univeristy Press, 1986), 150–83; Michael Marrus, *The Holocaust in History* (Toronto: Lester & Orpen Dennys, 1982), 106.

23. [These generalizations apply to Warsaw; in the Polish countryside, the picture was quite different. See Jan Grabowski, *The Hunt for the Jews* (Bloomington: Indiana University Press, 2013).]

Saving Jewish Children in Belgium

BOB MOORE

From *Survivors*

The situation in Belgium has some parallels with France, the most obvious being the degree of integration, both personally and institutionally, between Jews and non-Jews in saving children, most notably with the formation of the CDJ [*Comité de Défense des Juifs*] and its children's section, and the greater involvement of churchmen and church institutions in helping to hide the children. As elsewhere in Europe, children were widely seen as a special case and innocent of any "crimes." Those directly involved often cited the heavy-handed and brutal nature of the first round-ups by the Gestapo and *Feldgendarmerie* alongside ideological, patriotic, or religious motives for their actions.[1] However, the first steps to hide children were taken by elements within the Brussels Jewish community itself, even before the deportations began. When the Germans ordered all Jewish children out of the city schools, the community created new schools called *Nos Petits*. The leading light in this movement was Fela Perelman, who used the children to contact their parents, with a view to sending their offspring into hiding with non-Jewish families. Thus if the adults were arrested, the children could be kept safe. At this stage, there was no real question of knowing that "labor service in the East" was just a euphemism, but the motivation was that, even if this was the fate in store for the Jews, the children should be spared it if possible. In this way, some 325 Jewish children were placed with non-Jewish families.[2]

As with the rescue of adults in Belgium, the children benefited from the existence of the CDJ and its separate children's department led by Maurice Heiber. He already had experience with orphans, having been previously involved in the reform of the Jewish orphanage in Brussels. In that role he was then asked to join the AJB [*Association des Juifs de Belgique*], but realizing that it was working for the Germans rather than for the good of the Jewish community, he transferred his allegiance to the CDJ, but remained inside the AJB to cover his illegal activities and to act as a source of information. The main day-to-day work was carried out by four professional social workers, Hava Jospa (Yvonne) and Ida Sterno (Jeanne) who were Jewish, and Andrée Geulen and Suzanne Moons-Lepetit (Brigitte) who were not. It was their task to find addresses and provide money, false papers, and ration cards.[3] These four women travelled the length and breadth of the country searching out addresses and permanent homes for the children. They looked to religious institutions, children's homes, and boarding schools, as well as to individuals for help. Contacts were made with "practical" Catholicism that created, little by little, what was termed, a "chain of solidarity."[4] They also had to provide new identities, papers, money and ration cards, as well as food and clothing for some of the children. Meetings between parents and their children in hiding were organized in a neutral venue so that the adults could not know where the children were sheltered, but this had many dangers, not least the possibility that the parents were being followed by the Gestapo.[5] While face-to-face meetings were a problem, the organization also facilitated other forms of communication, especially the transmission of letters.[6] It also held the view that separating parents from children not only represented the best possible chance for escape for the children, but also gave the parents more chance of survival through increased mobility.[7]

The problem for the CDJ was that it had to go looking for children to hide. Initially it was able to place children from the *Solidarity Juive* and the *Secours Mutuel*.[8] Later, it turned to the *Oeuvre National de l'Enfance* (ONE). Contacting individual Jewish families was far more difficult. There were no central registers, and families who had already gone underground were, by definition, difficult to trace. Those without hiding places only had the AJB to rely on, but CDJ workers took steps to contact those who came to the AJB offices and to offer them help.[9] Other CDJ "agents" were placed in organizations such as the Red Cross, Winterhelp, and ONE to intercept Jews looking for help.[10] The approach here was a subtle one. The "agents" would talk to the parents about placements for children, but claim to know nothing except that another institution might be able to help. The net result was that the parents were sent from pillar to post so that when they were finally contacted by the CDJ, they could have no idea from whom the referral actually came.[11] However, persuading even those in the greatest danger to give up their children remained difficult. After the liberation, Estera Heiber recounted how in July 1942, the Jewish orphanage had been sent seven Jewish mothers with their young children who had been captured trying to escape to Switzerland. Although in imminent danger of deportation, only one of the mothers agreed to give up her child to be placed in a children's home,

where he survived the war. All the others were deported.[12]

This was almost always the most painful element for the parents and the CDJ workers: visiting the home and taking away the children. Yvonne Jospa never made more than one or two "visits" each day, as she described it, invading a Jewish family who knew nothing of her and had never seen her before and taking away the child. She recalled the first time this happened. Visiting a house in the Brussels suburb of Anderlecht, she met the parents of a single, five-year-old child. She told them that they could not know the child's false name, nor where he was being hidden. Then there was a long silence while the child, sitting at their feet, played unconcernedly. Then the mother began to cry and Jospa took the child out into the street. It was important for her that the child did not cry, as this would invariably attract attention. In this case, he held her hand tightly and went with her to the station without protest. Her only problem arose in trying to convince him of the need for a new name that would conceal his Jewish identity, but even this proved a success with the aid of stories and a few sweets. The child was subsequently successfully placed with a foster family in the south-east of the country.[13]

In spite of the fact that contact between parents and children was deliberately broken when they were fostered through the CDJ, some problems remained. One girl in a group of fifteen who were hidden in a convent in Ghent sent word to her mother of her location—in direct contravention of the instructions she had been given. As a result, the mother attempted to sell some leather goods to pay for a journey to visit her daughter, but made the mistake of telling the buyer why she needed the money. The purchaser proved to be a collaborator whose daughter was being educated at the same convent, and he lost no time in passing on his "indignation" to the Mother Superior. This meant that the CDJ had to expedite the immediate removal of all the girls hidden in that convent back to Brussels, where they were collected by ONE staff and hidden, at least temporarily, at the organization's headquarters.[14]

Apart from a "recruitment" section, the CDJ also had a "placement" section that matched children to potential homes and hosts, and a "research" section geared to finding suitable hiding places. As a contemporary report put it, this latter section "moved heaven and earth" to find suitable locations in religious institutions, charitable homes, boarding schools, and with private citizens.[15] CDJ workers were often confronted with potential foster parents who wanted to adopt children and were very clear what sort of child they wanted, not only in terms of gender and age, but also in terms of appearance. Yet even when they had specific details (insofar as they were prepared to deal in this way), their perception of a "pretty and intelligent young girl" could still be very different from [that of] the potential hosts.[16] It is clear that the CDJ was prepared to countenance the adoption of children who had been orphaned or, as Maurice Heiber put it, "had the greatest probability of being alone after the war." To that end, he claimed that the organization developed a special intuition about which children would be best suited to particular environments.[17]

One of the key associates of the CDJ was Yvonne Nevéjean, director of ONE. She made sure that all the orphanages under her supervision were primed to hide Jewish children and her wide range of friends and acquaintances among the directors of Catholic, Protestant, and non-religious institutions ensured the widest network of contacts imaginable. Apart from finding placements, Nevéjean provided nursing, food, and other forms of care to children and also ensured that they were monitored and well looked after—all through the good offices of ONE. Her organization was also officially responsible for the AJB orphanages that had been established to deal with the problems created by the German deportation program. By inflating the figures for the actual number of children in these orphanages, she was able to siphon some ONE money into funds to help children underground.[18] The children's section of the CDJ is credited with having helped to hide around 3,000 Jewish children and provided for 2,443 of them.[19] They were hidden in at least 138 institutions and with at least 700 individual families, the vast majority (c. 95 per cent) in either Brussels or Wallonia [the French-speaking part of Belgium]. The placement process and security systems operated by the CDJ appear to have been highly successful, with betrayals being the exception rather than the rule. However, there were some disasters. Maurice Heiber recalled the case of a Jewish mother who had betrayed members of the organization in Antwerp. Arrested after placing two of her children with the CDJ, she was taken with her newborn infant to Mechelen and questioned about the whereabouts of her two remaining children. She was tortured but refused to give up any names, and it was only when the torturers began burning her baby with cigarette ends that she finally cracked.[20]

CDJ links with the armed resistance of the Independence Front [a multiparty resistance movement founded in 1941] also proved to have some advantages. Thus, in May 1943, some fifteen Jewish children placed by the children's section at the Convent of the Sisters of Très St. Saveur in Anderlecht were discovered by the Jew-hunter Icek Glogowski, otherwise known as "Gros Jacques," and the Gestapo. The Mother Superior, Marie-Aurelie, was ordered, "on pain of death" to prepare them for evacuation to an unknown destination the following day when the authorities would supply a truck. Straightaway she informed Maurice Heiber who arranged for an immediate partisan night raid on the convent to "liberate" the children.[21] This served to remove the children successfully and also provided the Mother Superior and the nuns with an alibi. However, it also cost Heiber his liberty, as he was arrested the following day.

Nevéjean was undoubtedly a remarkable individual. She had been involved with the placement of children in Belgium after the *Anschluss* and was thus no stranger to the specific needs of Jewish children.[22] Forty years old when the German occupation began, she is reputed to have worked for Belgian National Security and also possibly for the British. In 1938, she had been to a *Bund Deutscher Mädel* [League of German Girls] congress in Berlin and made the acquaintance of Erich Hilgenfeld, who later became an ss-General and head of the German *Winterhilfe* [a Nazi charitable program]. These contacts in high places may have given her a degree of protection, for example when the Gestapo in Brussels suspected her of hiding Jewish children. Certainly, she did not limit her activities to the rescue of children as she was also an active member of the *Services et Reseignements* resistance group.[23]

The CDJ also investigated the possibilities of trying to evacuate children to neutral countries. Indirectly, it sounded out the German authorities if this could be done officially, but although they received a positive answer, it was to be at the expense of major monetary payments (taxes)— something that the organization was unwilling to countenance. Contacts were made with an organization specializing in getting people to Portugal, but the journey was considered too onerous to be considered for most children to attempt, but some professional smugglers were employed who had

managed to get children across the frontier into Switzerland. However, their first journey with CDJ-sponsored children saw them caught and taken to Drancy [the principal departure point for deportations from France]. This major dent in morale caused the abandonment of any further organized attempts to move children to safety abroad.[24]

The CDJ was probably responsible for the majority of rescues of Jewish children in Belgium, but there were also many private arrangements. For example, one girl and boy were taken by their father to the home of two women in Ottignes, initially for a summer holiday in 1942 that was turned into a permanent arrangement. Thus the parent had a direct contact with the foster mothers, something that may help to explain the rapid conversion of the children to Catholicism to match their cover as an evacuated niece and nephew. In this case, the introduction to the Catholic faith was a matter of convenience, both for the parents and for the foster mothers, who were described as "wary of too much religion."[25] Even though the children were baptized and went to the local Catholic Church, they were educated separately in a makeshift school for the Jewish children hidden locally. Nonetheless, their presence was well known to the local community but there was no question of betrayal. Ottignes was also the site of a school for disturbed children run by Renée Jacquemotte that, during 1942, slowly filled up with Jewish children as others were sent home. Again, this seems to have been a piece of private enterprise although the venture did receive support from the resistance.[26]

The active role played by the Catholic Church as an institution was a feature of the rescue of Jewish children in Belgium. Thus Monsignor Kerkhofs in Liège was instrumental in mobilizing Catholic institutions around Banneux to help, and also in using three homes (*colonies*) originally established to house the mentally ill children of the middle classes.[27] These homes also sheltered a number of adult Jews as "domestic servants," but they were primarily refuges for children. Their surnames were altered slightly to disguise their Jewish origins, thus Rappoport became Rapport and first names were Christianized where necessary, with Myryam becoming Maria. They would also sometimes be baptized as a further protection, but only in consultation with the parents.[28] The lawyer Albert van den Berg and his brother-in-law, Georges Fonsny, were both on the administrative council of the charity set up to run these homes, and once the war began, it was van den Berg who organized the work and collected the necessary funds. He was helped by the Capuchin Fathers from Venders and by German Franciscans who had fled from Aachen and established themselves in Herstal. This latter group was particularly active in helping the welfare of Jewish boys at *l'Hospitalité*. The other home, *La Vierge des Pauvres*, was based at the Chateau des Fawes and run by the Sisters of St. Vincent de Paul. Here, van den Berg was able to hide dozens of Jewish children, although precise numbers are impossible to determine.[29] Children were also placed in boarding schools, sanatoria, and other convents and abbeys.[30] Their education was something of a problem as the obvious schools for these children would be Catholic ones, designed specifically to provide a Catholic upbringing. The governors of the schools raised the matter and it was decided that the Jewish children hidden in the diocese of Liège would be incorporated into the religious instruction offered. This had two important advantages; namely, that it would not seem odd to the other children in the school, and also that there would be no awkward questions if the schools were subject to state inspection. For the children who had been handed over directly by their parents, it was made a condition that they signed a form indicating their willingness for the child to attend classes and also nominated a guardian. The children were only excused communion and confession.[31] For their part, the parents agreed to pay for their child's upkeep.[32] The fact that educational institutions were subject to state inspection did occasionally cause problems, although not always for the obvious reasons. Thus when the network placed some children in a home near Belleghem, the local schools' inspector deemed it illegal for francophone children to be registered at a Flemish school. The children were therefore moved on to a convent in Wallonia, but the Mother Superior, frightened when she discovered the children were Jewish, took steps to move them on again to another home in Linkebeek, unaware that this was controlled by the Gestapo. The network therefore intervened to save the children and move them elsewhere.[33] In total, it was estimated that the van den Berg-Fonsny network helped at least four hundred children.[34] It is also worthy of note that van den Berg was far more than a distant organizer and took a personal interest in the children placed in his care. Thus one young girl later recalled, "Mr. van den Berg came to visit them regularly. He was for them like a father, talking to them and taking an interest in their joys and their sadnesses, in everything that made up their lives."[35]

The question of state supervision of education seems to have been a major problem for the rescuers insofar as it restricted the places where francophone children could be placed. In one example, a linguistic commission visited an institution near Namur, in the French-speaking part of the country. The commission was reportedly made up of individuals from the *Vlaams Nationaal Verbond* (VNV) "and other blacks" (collaborators), and proceeded to interrogate the children.

One was asked, "Do you speak French?" "Yes" came the reply. "Do you speak Flemish?" Again the reply was in the affirmative. Floored by this, the commissioners then tried to elicit a definitive response. "What language do you speak at home?" To this there was no reply. Frustrated, they tried another avenue, "What language do you speak to your mother?" "Yiddish," replied the child to a stunned audience.[36] The linguistic commission and the VNV were primarily interested in preventing Flemish children being brought up as francophones, and were therefore not directly concerned with unearthing Jewish children in hiding. However, given the collaborationist nature of the VNV, the CDJ could not be certain that this episode would not be reported to the Gestapo, and all the children had to be moved from the home immediately.

Apart from the van den Berg-Fonsny network, there were many other organizations and individuals within Catholic milieux that later came together under the umbrella of *L'Aide Chrétienne aux Israelites* (ACI).[37] Among the most famous of these was Bruno Reynders who in 1942 had become almoner for a small home for the blind in Hodbomont-Thieux.[38] He soon realized that the director, as well as some of the residents were Jews in hiding.[39] After a Gestapo raid removed all the adult Jews but left the children, van den Berg, as the home's supervisor, met Reynders for the first time.[40] In January 1943, they began the process of hiding these and other children, with Reynders doing most of the work of finding hiding places himself from among friends and acquaintances.[41] These included his mother and brother as well as many Catholic institutions, including his own former school. He undertook most of this on a bicycle and at the end of the war, it was estimated he had travelled the equivalent of 40–50 times the distance of the cyclists' Tour of Bel-

gium.[42] He also adopted a peripatetic lifestyle to stay out of the hands of the Gestapo and, with hindsight, can be seen as extremely fortunate not to have betrayed his entire network. Unlike most other illegal workers who understood the importance of secrecy, Reynders actually kept details of all his fellow workers and the people he had hidden in three notebooks.[43] The amount of detail recorded in them would have made it very easy for the Gestapo to have rounded up the entire network in a matter of hours. In the end, he also had to go underground after his base at the Mont César monastery was threatened by the Gestapo.[44] In spite of his apparent lack of personal security, Bruno Reynders refused to work closely with the CDJ because this would have meant sharing information about the location of children in his care.[45]

Reynders and van den Berg were involved in both finding and housing Jewish children. Thus sometimes Reynders would send children, or *colis* (parcels) as they became known, for van den Berg to hide, but on other occasions the "trade" might be reversed.[46] Children had to be moved on for all sorts of reasons, although it was less likely for those in institutions compared to those in private homes.[47] For example, two boys and a girl placed in a chateau that was subsequently requisitioned by the *Feldgendarmerie* had to be moved after the Germans let it be known that they knew the children were Jewish. The lack of effective cooperation (and even active dislike) between the military and the Gestapo undoubtedly saved these particular children, but the fact that they did need to be moved helps to explain contemporary reminiscences of Banneux as a place of permanent comings and goings.[48]

There is no doubt that the network created by van den Berg and Reynders was overwhelmingly successful, not only in finding places for Jewish children to hide, but also in keeping them safe throughout the occupation. Inevitably, the work of the organizers became more onerous as the number of their charges increased and the Gestapo devoted more energy to tracking down resistance networks of all types. Reynders was forced underground when his cloister came under suspicion, and van den Berg was arrested by the Gestapo. As a precaution, the children at the homes in Banneux were moved, but there is no indication that they were under threat or that the existence of the network supporting the children was betrayed in any way.

The network built by Joseph André in his parish of St-Jean-Baptiste in Namur owed much to the priest's friendship with Arthur Burak, a German Jewish refugee who had come to live in his parish.[49] His rectory, known as Notre-Dame-de-Sion, or *Hôme de l'Ange*, became a transit point for several hundred Jewish children smuggled out of Antwerp and Brussels en route for hiding places in Wallonia in the two years between July 1942 and the summer of 1944. The building was close to the German *Kommandantur* but this did not prevent André from hiding both children and adults in the building—up to thirty-five were known to have been there at one time, although only a few were permanently resident and most moved on to other hiding places after a short stay.[50] These were either cloisters or families, although older children were sometimes placed with artisans or shopkeepers as apprentices.[51] Many of his helpers were also engaged in other forms of illegality, thus increasing the risks of accidental betrayal, and André instituted some elements of security, not least in insisting that the children never reveal their real names and that others did not speak about anything they were doing. The rectory was raided on a number of occasions but children were able to escape through an outhouse. Jews were sometimes taken by controls [checks of papers by police or soldiers] on the street and some were arrested in André's own house, leading to his abandonment of the rectory as a hiding place and his decision to go underground in May 1944.[52]

André kept much of the running of his network in his own hands, facilitating meetings of children and parents in hiding, and negotiating treatment for sick individuals in hospital under assumed identities. He also personally monitored the suitability of placements and moved any children he did not think were being properly cared for. His helpers came from many sections of society, including a neurologist who hid Jews in the contagious diseases ward of the St. Camille Hospital in Namur. What was surprising about him was that his prewar career had been as a "mystic and a dreamer," rather than one schooled in the practicalities of day-to-day life under occupation. Yet his dynamism in the cause of helping Jewish children was second to none and surprised even his superiors.[53] At the beginning of 1943, he came into contact with Max Katz of the CDJ in Charleroi and this marked the start of a cooperation between André's network and the CDJ that was to last until the end of the occupation. Records show that he sheltered sixty-six people on CDJ books but refused any financial help, as the CDJ would then insist on knowing all the details of the child and of the foster parents, and this, like Bruno Reynders, André refused to divulge.[54] His reasoning was partly to do with security, but also the fact that in some cases, parents had entrusted their children to him with the stipulation that they should not be placed in the hands of the CDJ . . . . This isolation meant that André had to find money from other sources. He was able to obtain help with ration cards and false papers from sympathizers within the city administration, and appears to have raised money primarily from his own resources, from his family, and from friends and acquaintances, as well as from the Socrates resistance group that catered primarily to *réfractaires* [dodgers of the Nazi labor drafts].[55] His helpers included schoolteachers, youth leaders, and members of the medical profession, as well as the local town clerk and some of his subordinates. Each contributed some essential element to the work but they were increasingly hampered by Gestapo raids that saw the arrests of local civil servants, ration office workers, and policemen. André reputedly made no attempt to convert any of his charges to Catholicism while they were under his care.

Beyond these two networks run by Reynders and André there were many other priests involved specifically in rescuing Jewish children. For example, there was Father Maurice Robinet who was reputed to have helped around 400 children, including twenty-nine whom he sheltered in the cellars of the Gesu Church in Brussels during the last months of the occupation.[56] Likewise, Abbot Bruylants lived in a quarter of the city that had a substantial Jewish population and, when the persecutions began, converted the parochial residence into a hiding place. He also brokered hiding places elsewhere in the city, including a Catholic school and around Mechelen, saving around eighty people. He had contacts with the *Jeunesses Ouvrière Chrétiennes* (JOC) through Cardinal Jozef Cardijn, Queen Elisabeth, and Cardinal van Roey, but he was perpetually short of money for his activities and had no dealings with the resistance. Also in Brussels, Antoon de Breuker established an organization called *l'Ami des Pauvres* to help not only the poor, but also *réfractaires* and Jews on the run from the Germans, including an estimated 265 Jewish children.[57] Again, he used his parishioners and convents to help hide children and cooperated with the JOC, but as with both Robinet and Bruylants, his initial motivation had come from specific conditions in his par-

ticular locality rather than any promptings from his superiors.

Other help came from secular Catholic organizations such as the JOC. It had established the *Entr'aide* service in 1940 run by Father Capart, the self-confessed right-hand man of Cardinal Cardijn, who himself had established the *Kristelijke Arbeidersjeugd* (KAJ) in 1924 to help children in danger and also founded homes at Braine-l'Alleud, Schaltin, Banneux, Lauwe, Dworp, and Leffe-lez-Dinant.[58] Capart was subsequently approached by his father, the Egyptologist Jean Capart, who had in turn been asked by Queen Elisabeth to help provide assistance to the Jews. As a result, the first Jewish child was brought to a JOC home at the end of 1942. After March 1943, contact was established with the CDJ, but it was never the only source of children as others came from individual parishes and other institutions. Essentially, the JOC took full charge of the upbringing of the children held in its homes. It is impossible to say if there were any deliberate attempts to convert Jews hiding in this way, but at least three boys in its care whose mother had died were adopted by a priest responsible for education at Banneux and Leffe. One of them later entered holy orders and became a parish priest.[59]

Like the CDJ, the JOC was able to obtain documentation for those in hiding from sympathetic civil servants. Its headquarters in the Boulevard Poincaré was used as a temporary shelter and distribution point for children, a fact made all the more remarkable in that three-quarters of the building was occupied by the German army and police. One JOC home at Schaltin was raided by the Gestapo, resulting in three leaders, four Jewish children, and three other Jews being arrested and ultimately deported.[60] Unlike the networks created by the priests specifically to help Jewish children, the work of the JOC was far more wide ranging and had been more concerned with providing help to escaping prisoners of war and *réfractaires*. Thus, while the Jews, and Jewish children in particular, were not discriminated against, they were viewed by the JOC as just one of many categories of Belgian citizens in danger from German measures.[61] In total, it was estimated that the JOC had saved fifty-nine Jewish children during the occupation.[62]

Children whose parents or guardians still had access to funds could afford to send their children to boarding schools in the countryside where they were considered safer and could live using false papers and assumed identities. The directors and head teachers of these institutions almost invariably knew the origins of their new charges and sometimes even acted as couriers. However, such institutions would often shelter numbers of fugitives, both children and adults, with each one unaware of others in a similar predicament, or at least warned not to ask any questions. Realizing a possible compromising situation, one headmaster warned an older girl arriving at his school in late 1942 about another pupil who had been at her school in Brussels and that if she was recognized, another hiding place would have to be found for her.[63]

Hosts could and did ask for subsidies to support foster children. In February and March 1943, three farming families in South Hainaut asked for and received 10 francs a day (or 300 francs per month) for each child they sheltered. Other records from the van den Berg network show that Jewish parents were often responsible for the upkeep of their children. Thus a brother and sister were supported with 25 francs per day and a fund of 12,000 francs, and the foster parents of another boy received 300 francs per month.[64] These figures bear some relationship to what is known about other children in hiding where their upkeep was met from other sources. The surviving records show that children were fostered with sums ranging from 400 to 1,000 francs per month.[65] How these amounts were calculated seems impossible to reconstruct. There is no correlation according to age, and no indication of any special needs that individual children might have had. The differences may have just been a result of demands from the foster parents: a conclusion reinforced by one or two examples where children were apparently fostered without charge, or where it was made clear that they were taken in on an *au pair* basis.[66] However, the standard rate seems to have been 600 francs per month during the crucial period from the end of 1942 until the liberation, and the fact that there were accepted "rates" probably reduced the possibilities for profiteering, except where arrangements were made privately and without reference to an aid organization. Charges did change over time and there were increases noted long after the liberation for children still being fostered. Thus for example, the foster parents of a fifteen-month-old child were paid 600 francs per month in December 1942, but this increased to 750 francs per month by October 1944.[67] These increases may simply have been to compensate for inflation, but there were also cases where additional payments were made because the child had or developed a critical illness.[68] It is also clear that not all charges were borne by the organizations involved, as some cards record the fact that part-payments were made by the parents or that the individual case was "free to us," indicating that all the charges were being paid or subsidized by third parties.[69] Food was also an issue, especially later in the occupation. Even with subsistence payments, children still needed ration cards, food stamps, and clothing. This was not so much of a problem if the local civil servants and merchants were sympathetic, but poor relations between hosts and these crucial members of the community could lead to difficulties. This was overcome in some measure by the system set up by van den Berg in Liège where network members presented their own papers to the communal authorities but with false addresses. This allowed them to receive duplicate ration stamps that could then be handed on to those in hiding.[70]

Beyond the Catholic institutions, there were also other networks and organizations that helped save substantial numbers of children. Pastors from the very small Protestant community in Belgium helped by providing baptismal and confirmation certificates and by sheltering Jewish children in orphanages run by their churches. In numerical terms, the most important was the *Foyer Protestant pour Enfants* in Brussels that helped between eighty and ninety Jewish children for longer or shorter periods, usually referred to it by the CDJ. However, other pastors and parishes were also involved.[71] Beyond the confessional organizations there were other secular institutions involved, some at the prompting of the CDJ—others because it represented an extension of their existing resistance work. For example, the *École Nouvelle des Ardennes* had been used by its director to hide arms and a radio, labor service evaders, and resistance workers, as well as Jews. Soon the last-named formed two-thirds of the residents. Ultimately, the whole operation was betrayed to the Germans by a local farmer and they were all arrested and deported.[72] Another haven was the children's homes run by the *Oeuvre Nationale de Service Social aux Families de Militaires*. Its director, Georges Rhodius, established contacts with the CDJ and created a clandestine organization, the *Aide aux Abandonnés*, that ultimately helped around 350 Jews, including 300 children.[73]

The total number of children saved by these major networks will probably never be accurately known, not least because children were sometimes transferred between networks or double-counted in some other way. By the same token there were others who survived as a result of private arrangements that were never formally recorded.[74] For the children hidden in non-confessional environments, there were no problems of religious conformity, but in the many confessional hiding places, this was a major issue, both during and after the occupation. Both André and Reynders were adamant that there should be no pressure placed on Jewish children, either by force or persuasion, to be baptized in the Catholic faith, and that this should only take place with the express permission of the parents.[75] This was mirrored in the attitude of Kerkhofs who reserved all decisions on the baptism of Jewish children in his diocese and only very rarely gave permission if the parents were absent.[76] Nonetheless, the very nature of the hiding places for many children—in Catholic religious or educational institutions—meant that exposure to Christian education and belief were almost inevitable—as any exclusions or exceptions would have immediately drawn attention to the children's presence.[77] Thus even before the occupation was over, claims and counter-claims were being traded and the postwar period saw increasing animosity between the CDJ on the one hand, and the various Catholic-based rescue organizations on the other.[78] While refusing to use the children as a source of converts during the occupation, Reynders nonetheless took the view after the war that orphan children who had been baptized in hiding should not then be returned to the Jewish organizations who claimed them.[79] Nevertheless, even before hostilities were over, he had accused the CDJ of trying to establish a monopoly over all the Jewish orphans created by the Holocaust, and used this as an explanation for the distance between the two groups.[80] For its part, the CDJ had a rather less charitable view of "certain Catholic institutions" that obliged hidden children to say prayers, attend confession, and attempted to convert them. Some complained about this when the CDJ workers visited them, and they in turn raised it with the institutions' leaders. However, such charges were often met with incomprehension, and it was better to change the location of the children involved.[81] Other complications could arise where only some of an institution's staff knew that Jewish children were being sheltered there. Thus one small Jewish boy was removed from a kindergarten when it became clear that one of the nuns—presumably suspecting he was Jewish—had excluded him from the presents given on the feast of St. Nicholas.[82]

It would be impossible to discuss the rescue of children in Belgium without reference to perhaps the strangest case of mass survival, namely the children who were transferred into homes controlled by the collaborationist AJB and with the full knowledge of the Gestapo, but who nonetheless survived the occupation. The AJB had been charged with finding placements for children and the elderly whose nearest relations had been or were about to be deported. For their own reasons, and perhaps because they wanted to maintain the fiction of deportation being for "labor in the East" the young and the very old were excluded from the holding centre at Mechelen but needed to be found shelter elsewhere. Children became de facto orphans through any number of routes. Sometimes they were placed in the care of a Jewish orphanage by their parents before they themselves reported to Mechelen. Others arrived there because their parents were arrested in raids or the people sheltering them took fright at the risks they were taking or the money they received for the upkeep of their charges dried up.[83] Unlike their fellow Jews in hiding, these children retained their own identities and were able to talk openly about their families. Initially, their numbers were small and they were housed at the Jewish orphanages in Antwerp and Brussels. Ultimately, the numbers grew to around 500, although it was estimated that over 700 children had spent some time there.[84] All were under the control of the Gestapo, administered by the children's department of the AJB, and funded by the state organization for child welfare. In the postwar era, the directors of these homes and the members of the AJB were castigated for having collaborated with the Germans, but the fact remains that, although the homes' existence helped to bolster the image of the deportations that the Germans wanted to portray, until the last days of the occupation, they also provided an unlikely sanctuary for a large number of children. Although the CDJ did take over the care of some of the children in the AJB homes, there were never any plans to remove all of them. While the CDJ may have harbored genuine and well-founded fears for the safety of the children, the scale of the task in finding placements for all the other children at risk served to prevent any preemptive action.[85] . . .

As the Allied armies advanced across France in the late summer of 1944, the Germans finally took action against the 4,000 or so "legal" Jews remaining in Belgium. An SS officer arrived at the orphanage in Brussels on August 24 and demanded full details of all the children there. The directors were warned that the Germans intended to clear all the orphanages, hospitals, and old people's homes within forty-eight hours. . . . All the children in the AJB homes were spirited away at very short notice with the help of the CDJ and the resistance, and were doubtless saved from further pursuit by the arrival of Allied forces only a few days later.[86] Many of them ended up in the care of Sister Marie Beirens of the convent at Heverlee, but hiding places varied enormously. Some children were kept in groups while others were placed with local farmers.[87] Thus the children from the home at Aiche-en-Refail were taken to a school where local farmers came to choose those they would take—always preferring the strongest and best nourished of the candidates. Some proved unwilling to hand over their charges after the liberation and pressure had to be exerted so that all the children were returned to the care of the authorities.[88]

The rescue of Jewish children in Belgium was, therefore, a story of relative success, with coordination and cooperation between a range of Jewish and non-Jewish organizations, albeit not without some frictions. As with the rescue of adults, the creation of the CDJ as a counterweight to the later AJB gave Jews in Belgium some measure of choice over whom to trust, and the infiltration of the latter by CDJ activists had major advantages for the clandestine workers in knowing what the Germans had planned. The involvement of both Catholic clergy and laity is also worthy of note. The fact that some leading churchmen were proactive in encouraging help for Jews was undoubtedly important, as was their mobilization of secular organizations such as the van den Berg network. This greater integration was beneficial, although the case studies show that there was still some distrust and reluctance to share information and risks between different networks. That said, Belgium also provided a number of structural advantages for those involved. The most important one was probably the sheer number of religious institutions that could be used as hiding places, in addition to the houses of individual rescuers. The cause was also helped by the nature of the German occupation. The military governance of the country limited the scope of the SS and Gestapo, both in terms of influence and manpower. Thus the officials sent to Brussels from Berlin were never able to call on much help from the Belgian civil service or its police force to track down Jews in hiding, and they had to rely primarily on indigenous national socialists and informers to fulfill their tasks.

NOTES

1. CEGES-SOMA AA1915 Heiber, Dossier 17, "Les Enfants," 1. Brachfeld, *Ze hebben het overleefd*, 63.
2. Brachfeld, *Ze hebben het overleefd*, 64.
3. Saerens, "Die Hilfe fur Juden," 252; Brachfeld, *Ze hebben het overleefd*, 65–66; YV M31/7474 Comité de Défense Juifs. Attestation by Andrée Geulen and letter Sylvain Brachfeld to Mordechai Paldiel, November 19, 1995. Vromen, *Hidden Children*, 98–99.
4. Testimony of Yvonne Jospa, Delpard, *Les enfants cachés*, 172. For example see, Michman, *Encyclopedia of the Righteous: Belgium*, 119–20, Constant and Simone Fooz, who were asked to take Jewish children into their boarding school.
5. Brachfeld, *Ze hebben het overleefd*, 68.
6. USHMM RG 65.001 Roll 1901 File 26386, "Les Enfants," written by Maurice Fleiber in Tombeek Sanatorium, November 1944, 4.
7. USHMM RG 65.001 Roll 1901 File 26386, "Les Enfants," 2.
8. Shlomo Kless, "The Rescue of Jewish Children in Belgium during the Holocaust," *Holocaust and Genocide Studies*, III/3, 275–87, here 281–82, suggest that there was friction between the Zionists and Communists within the organization.
9. Betty Garfinkels, *Les Belges face à la persecution raciale 1940–1944* (Bruxelles: Editions de l'Institut de Sociologie de l'Université Libre de Bruxelles, n.d.), 91.
10. USHMM RG 65.001 Roll 1901 File 26386, "Les Enfants," 2.
11. USHMM RG 65.001 Roll 1901/26386, "Les Enfants," 2–3. Brachfeld, *Ze hebben het overleefd*, 67.
12. CEGES-SOMA AA1915 Heiber Dossier 13 CDJ, Letter from Capt. L. J. Eschelbacher to Messrs. Eschelbacher and Wachenheim, September 26, 1945.
13. Delpard, *Les enfants cachés*, 173–75. For similar stories recounted by Andree Geulen, see Vromen, *Hidden Children*, 93–5.
14. Garfinkels, *Les Belges face a la persecution raciale*, 91–2. USHMM RG 65.001 Roll 1901 File 26386, "Les Enfants," 5.

15. USHMM RG 65.001 Roll 1901 File 26386, "Les Enfants," 3; Kless, "The Rescue of Jewish Children," 279–80.

16. USHMM RG 65.001 Roll 1901 File 26386, "Les Enfants," 8.

17. GEGES-SOMA AA1915 Heiber, Dossier 17, "Les Enfants," 9.

18. Brachfeld, *Ze hebben het overleefd*, 71. She was also involved in funding the work of the CDJ itself and used her contacts to approach the Société Général for money. It provided a monthly sum, and funds later also came via the Belgian government-in-exile.

19. CEGES-SOMA AA1915 Heiber, Roger van Praag to M. Denis, Premier commissaire d'Etat, August 12, 1952.

20. USHMM RG 65.001 Roll 1901 File 26386, 'Les Enfants' II.

21. CEGES-SOMA AA1915 Heiber, Dossier 11, Attestation of Yvonne Vemant (Sister Claire d'Assise), January 10, 1948. See also *La Libre Belgique*, August 3, 1947, which gives her name as Sister Marie-Amelie AA1915 Heiber, Dossiers 31–34. CEGES-SOMA AA1915 Heiber, Roger van Praag to M. Denis, Premier commissaire d'Etat, August 12, 1952.

22. Saerens, "Die Hilfe für juden," 252–53.

23. Brachfeld, *Ze hebben het overleefd*, 71–72. See also CEGES-SOMA BD KD 765, *Le Soir*, August 28, 1987.

24. USHMM RG 65.001 Roll 1901 File 26386, "Les Enfants," 9.

25. Meschman, *Never to be forgotten*, 69, 78.

26. Michman, *Encyclopedia of the Righteous: Belgium*, 146. Renee Jacquemotte.

27. Papeleux, "Un Liégeois," 283. These were *l'Hospitalité* and the *Hôme de la Vierge des Pauvres*.

28. YV M31/6678 Undated note on the conduct of Curé Louis Jamin at Banneaux. Papeleux, "Un Liégeois," 283.

29. Papeleux, "Un Liégeois," 284.

30. Leon Papeleux, "Le Reseau Van Den Berg," *La Vie Wallonie* (1981). *Resistance: Père Bruno Reynders*, 142.

31. Papeleux, "Un Liégeois," 284.

32. Leon Papeleux, "Le Reseau Van Den Berg," *La Vie Wallonie* (1981). *Resistance: Père Bruno Reynders*, 144. Papeleux, "Un Liégeois," 287.

33. Papeleux, "Un Liégeois," 287.

34. Saerens, "Die Hilfe für juden," 272–73.

35. YV M31 /6678 Albert van den Berg. Letter Hanna Kleinberger to Department of the Righteous, May 21, 1995.

36. USHMM RG 65.001 Roll 1901 File 26386, "Les Enfants," 6.

37. Geneviève Thyange, "L'Abbé Joseph André et 1'Aide aux Juifs à Namur," in Maerten *et al.*, eds., *Entre la peste et le cholera*, 272–73.

38. Resistance: *Père Bruno Reynders. Juste des Nations* (Brussels: Les Carrefours de la Cite, 1993), 16.

39. Cf. Teitelbaum-Hirsch, *Enfants caches*, 73–74. See also, Reynders, *Père Bruno Reynders*, 6, and his testimony in English YV M31/84 "Father Bruno (Henry) Reynders," 3.

40. Leon Papeleux, "Le Réseau Van Den Berg," *La Vie Wallonie* (1981). *Resistance: Père Bruno Reynders*, 156.

41. *Resistance: Père Bruno Reynders*, 17. Brachfeld, *Ze hebben het overleefd*, 78. Van den Berg provided funds for the work carried out by Reynders. Van den Wijngaert, "Les Catholiques Belges et les Juifs," 125. Teitelbaum-Hirsch, *Enfants caches*, 73–74.

42. *Resistance: Père Bruno Reynders*, 17.

43. Brachfeld, *Ze hebben het overleefd*, 79. Saerens, "Die Hilfe für Juden," 265–66 gives details of where the children were hidden.

44. Paldiel, *Sheltering the Jews*, 108.

45. Teitelbaum-Hirsch, *Enfants caches*, 73.

46. Papeleux, "Un Liégeois," 286.

47. Vromen, *Hidden Children*, 11.

48. Leon Papeleux, "Le Réseau Van Den Berg," *La Vie Wallonie* (1981). *Resistance: Père Bruno Reynders*, 157. Papeleux, "Un Liégeois," 284.

49. The city had a Jewish community of only 31 souls prior to the summer of 1942.

50. YV M31/186 Joseph André, *Vers L'Avenir*, February 5–6, 1983, Thyange, "L'Abbé Joseph André," 263.

51. Brachfeld, *Ze hebben het overleefd*, 75.

52. Ibid. 77. Thyange, "L'Abbé Joseph André," 270–71.

53. Delpard, *Les enfants cachés*, 177. Paldiel, *The Path of the Righteous*, 70–71.

54. Thyange, "L'Abbé Joseph André," 265–66. See also CEGES R497.235.825. Bruno Reynders "Notes sur le situation légale des enfants israélites," January 9, 1944, 3–4.

55. Brachfeld, *Ze hebben het overleefd*, 75. Thyange, "L'Abbé Joseph André," 266–67.

56. CEGES-SOMA Doc. Enquête Kerk-Eglise AA1448–9/no Rommens. Rommens to Navorsings en Studiecentrum, October 8, 1980.

57. CEGES R497.235.348. Report by M. Dumonceau de Bergendal, "Aide aux Israelites pendant la guerre, 1940–1945," April 6, 1970; Thyange, "L'Abbé Joseph André," 269; Brachfeld, *Ze hebben het overleefd*, 87; YV M31/7474 Letter Sylvain Brachfeld to Mordechai Paldiel, November 19, 1995.

58. Brachfeld, *Ze hebben het overleefd*, 82.

59. CEGES R497.234.655. Report by M. Dumonceau de Bergendai, L'Aide de la JOC: Declaration du R. P. Pierre Capart, February 4, 1970.

60. CEGES R497.238.395. Ofipresse No.21, September 28, 1945, 1–2. Jean Brück, "L'Aide aux Refractaires, aux Juifs, aux Prisonniers de Guerre," in Emilie Arnoud *et al.*, eds., *La Résistance dans la Mouvement Jociste (JOC, JOCF, KAJ, VKAJ) pendant la guerre 1940–1945*, 28. CEGES R497.234.449. Report by M. Dumonceau de Bergendai, L'Aide de la JOC. Declaration de M. Bouton, January 27, 1970.

61. Brück, "L'Aide aux Refractaires, aux Juifs, aux Prisonniers de Guerre," 29.

62. CEGES R497.234.449. Report by M. Dumonceau de Bergendai, L'Aide de la JOC. Declaration de M. Bouton, January 27, 1970.

63. Brodsky, *A Fragile Identity*, 85.

64. Leon Papeleux, "Le Réseau Van Den Berg," *La Vie Wallonie* (1981). *Resistance: Père Bruno Reynders*, 157–58.

65. USHMM CEGES-SOMA Roll 1850, File 25843 Service Social Juif to Inspecteur General, Ministere de la Sante Publique, December 6, 1962. Roll 2028, File 27481 Card Index.

66. USHMM CEGES-SOMA Roll 2028/27481. Index card for Mathilde Stevens.

67. Ibid. Index card for Annie Legros.

68. See, for example, USHMM CEGES-SOMA Roll 2028/27481. Index card for Pierre de Bonnaires where he was described as bronchial and nervous.

69. USHMM CEGES-SOMA Roll 2028/27481. Index card for Suzanne Demoulin.

70. Papeleux, "Un Liégeois," 286.

71. Brachfeld, *Ze hebben het overleefd*, 88–9. Kless, "The Rescue of Jewish Children," 284–85.

72. Brachfeld, *Ze hebben het overleefd*, 86–87, 89.

73. Ibid., 88–89.

74. CEGES R497.235.825. Bruno Reynders "Notes sur le situation légale des enfants Israelites," January 9, 1944, 4.

75. Brachfeld, *Ze hebben het overleefd*, 82.

76. Papeleux, "Un Liégeois," 285.

77. CEGES R497.235.825. Bruno Reynders "Notes sur le situation légale des enfants israélites," January 9, 1944, 5. For a wider discussion, see Vromen, *Hidden Children*, 14–15 and Luc Dequecker, "Baptism and Conversion of Jews in Belgium," in Michman, *Belgium and the Holocaust*, 235–71.

78. Kless, "The Rescue of Jewish Children," 285, notes that the Protestant Ecumenical Council insisted that all Jewish children sheltered by its churches be returned to the Jewish community.

79. Brachfeld, *Ze hebben het overleefd*, 82.

80. CEGES R497.235.825. Bruno Reynders, "Notes sur le situation légale des enfants israélites," January 9, 1944, 3–4.

81. Delpard, *Les enfants cachés*, 177.

82. *Encyclopedia of the Righteous: Belgium*, 70–71, Ferdinand Collin.

83. Brachfeld, *Ze hebben het overleefd*, 108.

84. Ibid. 154.

85. Ibid. 156.

86. Brachfeld, *Ze hebben het overleefd*, 200–201, 224–25.

87. YV M31/7474 Comité de Defense Juifs, Letter Andrée Geulen to Sylvain Brachfeld, March 31, 1999. CEGES-SOMA BD KD 765 *Le Soir*, August 28, 1987. Vromen, Hidden Children, 62–66.

88. Brachfeld, *Ze hebben het overleefd*, 231–32.

American Inhibitions

RICHARD BREITMAN AND ALAN M. KRAUT

From *American Refugee Policy and European Jewry, 1933–1945*

To write about Franklin Roosevelt's reaction to the Nazi murder of approximately six million Jews is to engage in speculation. As far as is known, he said very little about it and wrote virtually nothing. It does not follow, however, that FDR was unconcerned or indifferent to Nazi mass murders of Jews.[1] Some of his comments and his actions during the late 1930s seem to indicate the contrary; he wanted to get Jews out of Germany before the murderers gained full sway.

This complex master of the art of politics was at the same time loquacious and terse. He was outwardly gregarious but kept much to himself and often left associates and subordinates with sharply different impressions about his attitudes. Who else could keep both Breckinridge Long [Assistant Secretary of State, 1939–44] and Stephen Wise [President of the World Jewish Congress, 1936–49] pacified at the same time? His calculated ambiguity may be proof of necessary political skills, but it makes life very difficult for historians of the Roosevelt presidency, whose problems are compounded by the absence of cabinet minutes (expressly prohibited by the president).

To judge Franklin Roosevelt's reaction to the Final Solution, we must first review his prior views on refugee policy, then calculate when he received information about the overall Nazi plan, and finally gauge any immediate or subsequent changes in his behavior. We must keep in mind that outside forces may have limited his ability to react in certain ways. Even a powerful president was not a free agent. But in the end we can assess FDR's attitudes only through his behavior.

In 1940, FDR reversed his previous view that the full German-Austrian quota (27,370) should be available for the many victims of Nazi persecution. Roosevelt did not simply turn visa policy over to the bureaucrats in the State Department. The evidence indicates that he gave the signal to tighten immigration regulations partly out of real concern for national security, partly out of recognition of political realities.

As early as September 6, 1939, he had requested that the attorney general instruct the FBI to take charge of all investigative work regarding espionage, sabotage, and violation of neutrality laws. Representatives of the FBI later held a series of conferences with local law enforcement agents throughout the country, stressing the seriousness of the danger and formulating detailed plans to cope with it. At one conference held in Washington on August 5–6, 1940, Attorney General Robert Jackson read a presidential statement about the danger of espionage, sabotage, and fifth column activity to representatives of forty-two state governments. The president condemned efforts during World War I in this field as inadequate and called for FBI direction of activity this time. Attorney General Jackson added that the Axis powers were now trying to weaken the U.S. as they had already weakened France before war had broken out in Europe.[2]

FDR's worries had been magnified in the spring of 1940. Already embarked upon an anti-Axis course in foreign policy, FDR had learned that an American code clerk named Tyler Kent, serving in the American embassy in London, had turned over to fascist sympathizers in London secret American-British diplomatic correspondence from 1938 on, including the Roosevelt-Churchill exchanges. The material quickly found its way to Rome and Berlin. Another by-product of the leak was that the Germans were able to crack the American codes, which then had to be changed. This was a psychological blow that struck the president hard. From this point on, FDR could hardly overemphasize the fifth column danger.[3]

Another high-ranking official who shared this view of an endangered national security was former Assistant-Secretary of State George Messersmith, who had become ambassador to Cuba. Messersmith told Undersecretary Welles that the German conquest of France had gone so smoothly because French morale had already been undermined, not only by aliens but also by French citizens opposed to the government. Messersmith urged the president to take preventive measures against similar happenings in the U.S. . . . He advocated immediate controls over aliens and over certain native-born and naturalized Americans, whom he considered potentially even more dangerous. With the administration's backing, Congress passed the Smith Act in June 1940, requiring all aliens to be registered and fingerprinted. Those who were presently or previously members of communist or fascist organizations could be deported. The Smith Act also made it a crime to advocate the violent overthrow of the government.[4]

Concern for security meant that the president was no longer willing to take many chances with foreign refugees. When a reporter asked the president how the American public's suspicions about aliens, particularly refugees, could be allayed, FDR in effect referred that task to private immigration organizations. But he defended the need to check refugees, because there were spies—voluntary and involuntary—among them. He specifically cited the German government's alleged threat to shoot the relatives of German Jewish refugees unless the latter agreed to work as spies for Germany.[5]

Precisely where the president obtained this information is uncertain. One possibility was Colonel William Donovan, who was receiving briefings and information from the British during the summer of 1940. British officials made no secret of their fears of a fifth column.[6] But FDR's source was more likely to have been Ambassador William Bullitt in France. In August 1940, having returned to the U.S., Bullitt gave a major foreign policy address backing the sale or lease of U.S. destroyers to Great Britain. In the course of this speech given to the American Philosophical Society in Philadelphia, Bullitt stated that war was coming to the U.S. and that the agents of the dictators were already preparing the way. He went on to describe how hundreds of communist and Nazi agents in France had transmitted the movements of the French army by short-wave radio to Germany. Bullitt then blamed the French for being even more hospitable to refugees from Germany than the United States was; allegedly, more than one-half of the spies captured in France were refugees from Germany. What is of particular interest about this diatribe is that both Undersecretary Welles and the president read Bullitt's speech beforehand. Welles went so far as to say that he approved every word of it. Two days after the speech the New York Times editorialized: "Our own history in the next few years will be happier if our people act now, in the spirit of Mr. Bullitt's warning."[7] Bullitt was an antisemite whose testimony on the issue of "refugee" agents might be doubted. But Roosevelt, Messersmith, Welles, and the New York Times were all reacting to the same fears. In fact, some of those most committed to an anti-Axis foreign policy, including the president, seemed most concerned about the danger of spies among the refugees.

The State Department could hardly show leniency to visa applicants in this atmosphere, nor did Breckinridge Long wish to. Circular telegrams went out in June, July, and September 1940 urging consuls to reject or at least suspend any visa application about which there was any doubt. One consul in Stockholm replied: "Very difficult, sometimes impossible [for] refugees here [to] satisfy us completely [regarding] past and potential future activities, criminal record, etc. . . . Result has naturally been delay and drastic reduction [in the] issuance [of visas]. . . .[8]

Even the privileged lists of intellectuals and labor leaders compiled by the President's Advisory Committee [on Political Refugees, PACPR] and other American organizations came under close scrutiny, which set off a prolonged political battle in Washington. Breckinridge Long told FDR that the emergency visa arrangements were being abused. Some of the applicants were not in entire accord with U.S. policy (i.e., too far to the left, in Long's view), and consular officers considered others not to be "of the desirable element." Moreover, the PACPR was submitting too many names. Long wanted to change the procedure by adding an additional check to weed out German agents and other undesirables and to cut down the number of names added in the future.

Roosevelt heard both sides, and, faced with conflicting testimony, he brought in Sumner Welles and Justice Department officials to help resolve the dispute. But Long eventually got what he really wanted—an interdepartmental visa review board in Washington that would scrutinize visa applications and weed out security problems. The restrictionists were bolstered further in June 1941 when the Congress passed a law enabling consuls to deny any kind of visa to anyone who would endanger public safety. After jurisdictional disputes broke out again in July between State and Justice, Hull consulted FDR, who decided that the basic responsibility on visas should remain with the State Department.[9]

Long's victory over [James] McDonald [Chairman of the PACPR] was not accidental. The president also believed that security came before all else. When McDonald complained again to Eleanor Roosevelt, she spoke to her husband and brought back a message. FDR wanted the PACPR and the Intergovernmental Committee to continue because of the future (not the present). The presidential committee should not be discouraged even if its nominees were not given visas, because sometimes investigations turned up information that made it necessary to refuse admission, and investigations had to be made.[10] This was, in effect, an endorsement of much of Long's position and a renunciation of the short-term changes in the immigration program that the president had advocated as late as October 1939.

Not all bureaucrats took the same view as Long. Taking advantage of a loophole in the immigration law for the Virgin Islands, Henry Hart of the Justice Department and Nathan Margold of Interior devised a plan in late 1940 to have the governor and legislature of the Virgin Islands admit refugees without visitors' visas. But Long and the State Department raised objections. Although Secretary of the Interior Harold Ickes backed the proposal, FDR came down on the other side.

I yield to no person in any department in my deep-seated desire to help the hundreds of thousands of foreign refugees in the present world situation. The Virgin Islands, however, present to this Government a very serious social and economic problem not yet solved. If the Interior Department could find some unoccupied place . . . where we could set up a refugee camp . . . , that would be treated with sympathy by the State Department and by me.[11]

When Margold persisted, the attorney general ultimately ruled the Virgin Islands plan illegal.[12]

Although Long was the administration's point man on the refugee issue, one must really speak of a State Department stance. Undersecretary Welles was free of Long's prejudices. But Welles, too, harbored deep suspicions about German government motives. In December 1940, he wrote to FDR that recent deportations of German Jews to unoccupied France indicated that the Germans were trying to "force our hand on the refugee problem."

> Were we to yield to this pressure all the evidence indicates that in the wake of the ten thousand Jews recently forced into France the Germans would drive on the French the remaining Jews from Germany and the occupied territories, hundreds of thousands of persons, in the expectation that the French in turn would persuade this country and the other American republics to receive them. Information reaching us is conclusive that if we or the other American Republics yield to these blackmailing totalitarian tactics the Germans will inaugurate something approaching a "reign of terror" against the Jewish people. . . .[13]

The undersecretary believed that German persecution and deportation of Jews were primarily instruments to weaken the opponents of Nazi Germany. This indeed had been one aspect of German policy during 1938–39, but Welles and others now failed to perceive that Nazi policy had entered a new and more deadly phase. Assistant Secretary of State Adolf Berle, who had favored a formal American protest against German deportations of Jews to Poland in early 1940, found it "unhappy" but "necessary" in early 1941 to tighten the visa machinery, because the Russians and Germans were forcing some refugees to act as spies.[14] Lower-level State Department officials as well as Foreign Service officers abroad were hardly less diligent in protecting national security and eschewing risky humanitarian undertakings.

After December 1941 the idea of protecting national security remained a prime concern for FDR. The president approved the War Department's plan to intern the Japanese-Americans on the West Coast, and he urged Attorney General Francis Biddle to press criminal charges against his antiwar critics. He even wanted to get rid of alien waiters from Washington restaurants, where customers exchanged all too much confidential information about the war. As other scholars have noted, the war eroded the president's respect for due process and civil liberties.[15] In this context, it is easier to understand why FDR approved of the State Department's tighter visa regulations. Fairness to visa applicants was not even a remote presidential concern then.

Some in Congress were much more extreme. Senator Richard Reynolds of North Carolina announced in June 1941 that, if he had his way, he would, without the slightest hesitation, "build a wall about the United States so high and so secure that no single alien or foreign refugee from any country upon the face of the earth could possibly scale or ascend it."[16] Reynolds was more outspoken than most congressmen, but he was hardly alone on this issue. FDR certainly harbored no fondness for the isolationist Reynolds, but he had to work with an often refractory Congress.

A bill to extend the length of military service to eighteen months passed the House by only one vote in August 1941. The president did not want immigration to add to his foreign policy disputes with the Hill.

Obstructed for years by a strong isolationist faction in Congress, pilloried by right-wing extremists as "President Rosenfeld," depicted as being surrounded by Jews, well aware of a significant antisemitic current among the American public, and seeing the war as the greatest crisis in western history, FDR reacted as most realistic politicians would. He limited his visibility on Jewish issues partly in self-defense, partly in the hope that the public and Congress would be less likely to object to his defense and foreign policies.

As Roosevelt scholar Robert Dallek has observed, FDR wanted more than the support of a bare majority in Congress and among the public. If the United States entered the European war, it would need a broad, stable consensus, which was why the president waited for the other side to strike the first blow.[17] Conveniently, after the Japanese attack at Pearl Harbor, the German government came to the aid of its ally and declared war against the United States first. Hitler's foolhardy action eliminated the need for FDR to go to Congress and explain why the U.S. should work for the defeat of Germany, too. That did not stop former ambassador William Bullitt from telling people that the Roosevelt administration's emphasis on the European war as opposed to the Asian one was the result of Jewish influence.[18]

In actuality, considerations of strategy and propaganda during the war led Roosevelt to temper inclinations to do anything publicly on "Jewish" causes. In October 1942, knowing that political conditions in the Middle East and North Africa were sensitive and that the area was crucial to Allied military success, FDR thought it would be a good idea to have someone do a firsthand analysis on resettlement of refugees, which resulted in a tour of three and one half months for an American lieutenant colonel, Harold Hoskins, and an accompanying British officer. Among Hoskins's findings, reported back to the president in May 1943, were growing tensions between Arabs and Jews in Palestine and in the Middle East and North Africa generally: "There is an ever-present Arab fear of American support for political Zionism with its proposed Jewish State and Jewish Army in Palestine. . . . *The experiences of British troops during their retreat in Burma are a grave and recent warning of the serious effects that a hostile, rather than friendly, native population can have on our military operations* [Hoskins's italics]." The primacy of the war effort dictated FDR's reaction. The president hastened to reassure King Saud of Saudi Arabia that no decision would be reached altering the basic situation in Palestine without full consultation of both Arabs and Jews.[19] He sent this message in spite of the fact that privately, to Morgenthau, FDR had talked about moving Arabs from Palestine to some other part of the Middle East to make room for additional Jews and an independent Jewish state.[20] This pro-Zionist solution was hardly an idea one could even raise publicly in the midst of an all-out war.

FDR also seemed quite sensitive to antisemitic currents in Spain and Latin America. When Gerardo Murillo, alias Dr. Atl, came out with the first booklet of a planned three-volume series entitled *Judios Sobre America* (*Jews over America*), J. Edgar Hoover sent a translated copy to the White House. The author claimed to demonstrate that FDR himself was of Jewish ancestry and that he had surrounded himself with Jewish advisors and cabinet members. Pictures even allegedly showed a physical resemblance between FDR, his family members, and various Jews. The president expressed the hope that the State Department and the Mexican government would be able to prevent publication abroad. The White House asked the attorney general to prevent publication and distribution in the U.S.[21]

When the president addressed the issue of war crimes, he avoided emphasizing the Nazi crimes against Jews. American Jewish organizations arranging a Madison Square Garden rally in July 1942 asked for a presidential statement to be read to the audience. FDR's response was "the American people not only sympathize with all victims of Nazi crime but will hold the perpetrators of these crimes to strict accountability in a day of reckoning which will surely come." Another presidential statement issued in August 1942 simply denounced barbaric crimes against civilian populations in Axis-occupied countries, particularly on the continent of Europe. FDR mentioned crimes carried out in many of the European countries, as well as in Japanese-controlled China and southeast Asia. Those involved in such behavior would eventually be brought to justice, he promised. According to presidential confidant Adolf Berle, Dutch government pressure as well as Berle's own feeling that the statement might deter crimes led to the presidential statement. Another presidential declaration was issued in October. Noting that the Axis crimes continued unabated, the president warned that the U.S. and other nations would bring the perpetrators before courts of law and that all war criminals would have to be surrendered at the end of the war.[22]

There is little question that the president was aware of the Final Solution by November 1942, if not earlier. Given Roosevelt's unwillingness to stir up additional trouble with Congress, certain lobbies, and Middle Eastern nations over European Jewry, he likely resisted believing the early reports of Jews being killed en masse in death factories. If Felix Frankfurter, a Jew, could not force himself to believe them,[23] why should FDR have been different? But the reports kept coming in. It strains credulity to think that Undersecretary Welles would have confirmed the information in [Gerhart] Riegner's telegram of August 1942 [a message from the secretary of the World Jewish Congress in Geneva reporting that a highly placed German informant had stated that the Reich was planning to kill all Jews under German control, possibly with prussic acid, the generic name for Zyklon] and given Rabbi Wise leeway to make the information public without notifying the president of the situation. And there were signs of minor shifts in policy, quite possibly as the result of the accumulated information. In the fall of 1942, the president did not hesitate to approve the admission, as a special case, of 5,000 Jewish children from France—no chance of spies there. But Sumner Welles, who had taken charge of the matter, took pains to avoid adverse publicity.

A second indicator was Roosevelt's request to Congress in the Third War Powers Act for the power to suspend immigration laws in the interest of the war effort. The bill was introduced in November 1942, and Roosevelt lobbied personally with House Speaker Sam Rayburn for the immigration provision only two days after Stephen Wise's press conferences on the Final Solution. To be sure, the president's emissaries expressly denied, under hostile congressional questioning, that he intended to bring civilian refugees into the U.S., but one cannot rule out this possibility. What is clearer is that hostile congressional reaction and suspicion about the entrance of refugees, and the deletion of the provision from the bill, could only have strengthened FDR's inclination not to do battle publicly on behalf of European Jews.

Stephen Wise then asked the president to receive a delegation of Jewish leaders at the White

House in early December as part of an international day of mourning (December 2) for European Jews. The Jewish leaders wished to give FDR specific information about the Final Solution. FDR did not wish to see the group and tried to avoid the meeting. He suggested that the delegation go to the State Department instead. Wise persisted, and, with the assistance of presidential advisor David Niles, he obtained an appointment for a small group of Jewish leaders with the president on Tuesday, December 8, at noon.[24]

The president announced to the group that he had just appointed Herbert Lehman to head the new Office of Foreign Relief and Rehabilitation Operations. It gave him "sadistic satisfaction" to appoint a Jew to this post; "Junkers" would eventually have to go to Lehman on their knees and ask for bread. After Wise read the delegation's declaration and presented a detailed memorandum about the Final Solution, he appealed to FDR to bring the extermination program to the world's attention and "to make an effort to stop it." The president said that the government was familiar with most of the facts, but it was hard to find a suitable course of action. The Allies could not make it appear that the entire German people were murderers or agreed with Hitler's actions. He agreed to release another statement denouncing Nazi mass killings. When the delegation wanted some statement that it could release immediately, FDR authorized the re-release of his statement to July's Madison Square Garden rally, which, he said, had to be quoted exactly. That meant no specific emphasis of Nazi crimes against Jews. The delegation press release exceeded the president's instructions and quoted FDR as saying that he was shocked to learn that two million Jews had, in one way or another, already perished as a result of Nazi rule and crimes.[25]

In his thank-you note to Niles afterward, Wise wrote that the "Chief" could not have been more "friendly and helpful," that he was "cordiality itself." Wise continued:

"The word he gave us will carry through the country and perhaps serve in some degree as warning to the beasts. . . . Thank God for Roosevelt. We ought to distribute cards throughout the country bearing just four letters, TGFR, and as the Psalmist would have said, thank Him every day and every hour."[26] It is hard to escape the conclusion that Wise was more impressed by FDR's cordiality, his anti-Nazism, and his strong war leadership than any specific service to European Jewry. The president had not promised retribution against Germany or changes in refugee policy. And the United Nations Declaration of December 17, 1942, condemning the Nazis' "bestial policy of cold-blooded extermination," resulted more from pressure from the Polish government in exile and Winston Churchill's interest than anything the United States government did.

In early 1943, partly because of growing public pressure, the United States and Great Britain agreed to hold the Bermuda Conference to consider refugee assistance. But the early indications were that both governments would hold to their strict line that nothing could be done that might detract from the war effort. Moreover, the layers of visa committees in Washington had slowed visa approvals to a trickle. When a delegation of seven Jewish congressmen sought an appointment with the president to press their complaints on visas and related issues, again FDR tried to divert them to the State Department. [Congressman Emanuel] Celler refused to accept that and promised an "off the record" session. They got their meeting at the White House on April 1.

White House secretary Edwin Watson subsequently informed Breckinridge Long that the delegation had criticized the voting of the military officials on the visa committees and had urged a simplification of the visa process. They also apparently pointed out the sharp decrease in the number of visas approved, and the president responded that perhaps visitors' visas would again be issued. In a follow-up meeting with Sumner Welles, Judge Joseph Proskauer of the American Jewish Committee, now also representing the Joint Emergency Committee on European Jewish Affairs, pressed for a Jewish delegation to attend the Bermuda Conference. That request was denied, and the Joint Emergency Committee itself was unable to obtain an audience with FDR before the conference, despite an urgent request.[27]

When Secretary of State Cordell Hull reported the results of the Bermuda Conference to the president, he posed a number of questions of "high policy," which needed presidential decisions. FDR agreed to the idea of moving a specific number of refugees from vulnerable locations to designated temporary havens, the costs to be shared by the U.S. and Great Britain. He rejected the idea of trying to bring refugees into the United States without compliance with the immigration laws or in excess of quota limitations. He advised against sending large numbers of Jews to North Africa and agreed that anything that would set off prolonged congressional debate should be avoided. FDR shared Hull's view that refugees should not be admitted to the U.S. as temporary visitors, which would be seen as an evasion of the quota laws.[28] That did not leave a great deal of room for action.

From 1940 until the middle of 1943, Franklin Roosevelt's behavior with regard to European Jewry showed general consistency. He undoubtedly regretted reported Nazi killings of Jews in Europe, but they did not affect him deeply enough to override his basic instinct: for domestic and foreign policy reasons, he could not allow the United States to be seen as giving Jews special leniency or assistance. Many millions of Europeans were suffering under Nazi rule, and Allied troops had their hands full with the Germans. It was not advisable—it was strongly inadvisable politically—to make a public issue of the Holocaust. It is significant that the two moves to relax tight immigration restrictions in the fall of 1942 were both supposed to go through quietly and that, when the immigration provision of Third War Powers Act became controversial, the president backed down.

If there was a deeper, more personal reason for presidential inaction, it may well lie in Roosevelt's upbringing and milieu. The president's mother was antisemitic, his half-brother even more so. The young Franklin Roosevelt absorbed some of this sentiment and only gradually grew out of it. By the time he reached the governorship of New York, he appreciated men and women of talent, whatever their background and descent. Steven Early, his friend and presidential press secretary, apparently did not. Some of FDR's best friends were antisemites.[29] If there was anyone aware of the influence of antisemitism in the United States, it was Franklin Roosevelt. He may have been overly sensitive to the danger of antisemitic reaction to American policies.

By the summer of 1943, three factors began to alter the president's attitude. The first was the improvement of the war situation. The invasion of Italy gave the Americans and British a toehold on the continent; the war on the eastern front was going better for the Allies. The war was far from over, but one could now confidently predict the outcome. The president began to take an interest in matters such as shipping food to suffering populations, but he ran into British resistance. He told Francis Pickett of the American Friends Service Committee that the worst conditions were in Poland and that he felt frustrated by the problem.[30] This was not yet a specific concern for the fate of European Jewry, but it was evidence of humanitarian concern.

The second influence, whose weight is difficult to measure, was a personal presentation of the horrors of the Final Solution. On July 28, 1943, at 10:30 a.m., the Polish ambassador, Jan Ciechanowski, and Jan Karski, a lieutenant in the Polish underground army, went upstairs in the White House to the president's study. Serving as a courier from the Polish underground, Karski had arrived in London with messages for the Polish government in exile, the Allied governments, and Polish Jewish leaders. One of his most important messages concerned the Final Solution: "The unprecedented destruction of the entire Jewish population is not motivated by Germany's military requirements. Hitler and his subordinates aim at the total destruction of the Jews before the war ends and regardless of its outcome. . . . The Jews in Poland are helpless. . . . Only the powerful Allied governments can help effectively."[31]

Roosevelt began to question Karski about German methods of political terrorism. Karski described mass arrests and concentration camps in Poland, some where mass murders were carried out daily. He went on to talk of his own clandestine visit to the Izbica transit camp in 1942, where he entered disguised in the uniform of an Estonian guard. He saw hundreds of dead Jews packed into railway cars, which then were closed and moved outside the camp. When the doors were opened, the corpses were removed and the bodies taken out and burned. He did not actually get to see gas chambers themselves. Karski emphasized that there was no exaggeration in the accounts of how the Nazis were handling the Jewish question. Polish underground sources estimated the number of Polish Jews killed by November 1942 (when Karski left Poland) at 1.8 million, and the

underground was convinced that the Nazis were out to exterminate the entire Jewish population. The president asked many other questions about various underground activities and, after an hour, said goodbye to Karski with a noncommittal comment. "Tell your nation we shall win the war."[32]

Five days before the Roosevelt-Karski meeting, Roosevelt had told Stephen Wise to "go ahead" with his plan for the relief and evacuation of Jewish refugees in Romania and France. That was not quite evidence of presidential backing, although Wise certainly got the impression that FDR approved. Wise followed up his meeting with a letter to the president, who then took the initiative of inquiring with the Treasury Department (not the State Department) on the status of the proposal.[33] That inquiry led to the battle between Treasury and State that resulted ultimately in the formation of the War Refugee Board. The sequence of events suggests that Karski's presentation may have had an impact on the president's action and on initial approval of the rescue plan.

By far the most important factor inducing the president to take action was a changing public and congressional climate. One day after Congressman Will Rogers, Jr., Joseph Baldwin, and Senator Guy Gillette of Iowa introduced House and Senate resolutions calling upon the president to create a rescue commission to save the surviving European Jews from extinction, Undersecretary of State Edward Stettinius, Jr., who had replaced Sumner Welles, reported to high State Department officials that the president was convinced that not enough was being done on the Jewish refugee problem. FDR suggested establishing small offices in Algiers, Naples, Portugal, Madrid, and Ankara to assist Jews. There might also be another refugee camp and a small amount of money available for the purpose. But European Division chief Ray Atherton told Stettinius that the U.S. should avoid unilateral sponsorship of this type of activity, or it would be paying all the bills. Stettinius decided to refer the matter to Breckinridge Long, who was to consult Secretary Hull.[34] Whatever impetus FDR generated was quickly dissipated.

Growing criticism of Long and the State Department in Congress and in the media made FDR aware of a political problem, in addition to a humanitarian one. Even then, it took the decisive intervention of Josiah DuBois relayed by Secretary Morgenthau to make FDR aware, in January 1944, that he had to take the refugee problem away from Long and the State Department or he would face a nasty political scandal. He took what action the Treasury Department contingent wanted but installed Secretary of War Henry Stimson on the War Refugee Board to curb possible impetuousness by Morgenthau and his subordinates.

It is extremely difficult to calculate whether a more active American refugee policy gained significant public support beyond the American Jewish community and liberal circles. There were still plenty of diehard opponents of immigration as well as of any diversion of effort on behalf of non-Americans. The most that one can say is that by 1944 there was less public and congressional resistance to the idea of a special government agency to look after the interests of victims of Nazi persecution.

FDR's willingness to support most of the proposals put forward by the War Refugee Board during 1944, including stern public warnings to the Hungarian government not to turn over its Jews to Germany, represented a significant reversal of earlier wartime policy. The most likely explanation for the turnabout is not that the president saw a chance to score political points during a presidential election year (since the political risks at least

equaled the benefits) but that he was now confident about the outcome of the war and was willing to take some risks on behalf of a cause that he had neglected for some time. Still, there were limits to what the president would approve. The idea of bringing Jewish refugees into the United States outside the quota system and the usual immigration regulations obviously raised political as well as legal concerns that troubled him. . . .

It is true that President Roosevelt might have ordered the bombing of the gas chambers at Auschwitz-Birkenau. Even if he had wished to do so (for which there is no evidence), he must have been aware of the political risks. To send American pilots on a long and dangerous mission for the benefit of European Jews threatened with extinction might be justified morally. But would the American people understand it and approve of it? To override the stance of the War Department and to substitute his own moral impulse for official policy would carry grave risks for the president. If the requests for the bombing of Auschwitz reached him through [Assistant Secretary of War John] McCloy, which is likely, FDR shunned the potentially damaging political repercussions of a risky humanitarian strike. Only in retrospect does the efficacy of bombing Auschwitz and the moral imperative outweigh all else. It is instructive, however, to note that Winston Churchill, against the views of the Foreign Office and military, favored bombing Auschwitz but was unable to prevail.[35] When dealing with large bureaucracies, even chief executives are not all-powerful.

A comparison of Roosevelt's and Churchill's behavior makes it clear that the prime minister was far more concerned and motivated to make public statements on behalf of European Jewry. The same comparison, however, should make one beware of making the president the archvillain of American refugee policy. For despite Churchill and despite less unfavorable public opinion in Great Britain, British refugee policy toward European Jewry during the war was even less humanitarian than American refugee policy.

Although FDR was adept at manipulating government agencies and bureaucrats, he was to some degree the prisoner of bureaucratic government. A president could set general lines of policy in many areas and try to resolve conflicts and priorities. He could not continually supervise implementation of policy in more than one or two spheres, no matter how great his interest. Refugee policy during the depression, the era of Nazi expansion, and the world war could not command much of the president's time. Roosevelt had to depend upon the State Department and the War Department to carry out his foreign policy and military action against the Axis powers. He could force some officials to compete with each other. He could insert some of his own appointees into these agencies, New Dealers who understood his own goals and methods better than traditional civil servants and military officers. He could use Harry Hopkins [confidant of FDR and administrator of the Lend Lease program of aid to Britain and the Soviet Union] and others as troubleshooters. But he could not carry out a radical purge of the bureaucracy, particularly not in time of war, without serious impairment of administrative efficiency and adverse political repercussions in Congress as well. All of this meant that the president had to operate in the bureaucratic world around him, however much he disliked it.

That world was stamped by certain traditions and nationalist values. Before 1933 the United States was far more the aloof isolationist seeking to insulate itself from the world's troubles than it was the defender of universal "human rights." Most American civil servants and military officers had received their training and experience in

this pre-1933 world; they were not about to revolutionize their attitudes overnight. The institutional climate in the State and War departments, as well as in newer agencies such as the Office of War Information, was strongly opposed to active American assistance to European Jews. Proposed measures on behalf of European Jews frequently seemed to interfere with the normal functions of these agencies, and thereby with the success of the war effort. The fact that relatively few American officials could comprehend the extent and horror of the Final Solution only made it easier for them to pass on to other matters. Europe would always have its problems; the important thing now was to win the war.

The fluctuations in American refugee policy during the Roosevelt administration were determined in part by presidential initiatives but in part also by bureaucratic politics. The Labor Department's initiatives to loosen immigration regulations in 1933–34 contributed to the State Department's increased willingness to recognize affidavits from American citizens and residents pledging financial support for their European relatives. The transfer of the Immigration and Naturalization Service from Labor to Justice in 1940 weakened Labor's influence over refugee policy and facilitated the State Department's tightening of immigration regulations. The creation of the War Refugee Board in 1944 gave advocates of humanitarian measures a new foothold within the government and thus made possible a variety of life-saving measures in Europe.

The evidence . . . indicates that the president was quietly more liberal on the admission of Jewish refugees to the United States than the bureaucracy during the 1930s and approximately as restrictionist as the bureaucratic consensus during the 1940s. But, even when FDR chose to intervene personally in refugee policy as he did in

1938–39, he needed help to carry out his ideas. The history of American refugee policy between 1939 and 1945 indicates that most government agencies and officials were more efficient restrictionists than humanitarians.

The United States government did not match Adolf Hitler's single-minded frenzy to wipe out the Jewish "race" with corresponding determination to save those Jews who could be saved during the Holocaust. FDR's reluctance to engage himself directly in the cause of European Jewish refugees resulted first from his almost exclusive focus on the war itself, second from his perception of adverse political realities in the U.S. and in the west generally, and third from his dependence upon a bureaucracy largely unaccustomed to humanitarian initiatives.

There are always questions about how far a politician can be ahead of his own time and his own society and remain a successful politician. American refugee policy was one area where Franklin Roosevelt, so venturesome in other spheres, did not feel free to take on much additional risk.

NOTES

1. Wyman, *Abandonment of the Jews*, 312–13, admits the problem posed by lack of clear evidence of Roosevelt's views. This does not prevent him from labeling FDR as insensitive and indifferent. See also ibid., xi, 103.

2. Copy in Attorney General Jackson to Secretary of War, August 1, 1940, NA RG 107, Fifth Column Correspondence. See also Department of State, Division of Current Information, Radio Bulletin no. 185, August 5, 1940, copy in NA RG 107, Records of the Office of the Secretary of War.

3. Breckinridge Long Diary, May 22, June 22, 1940, LC, cited and discussed in Joseph Lash, *Roosevelt and Churchill, 1939–1941: The Partnership That Saved the West* (New York, 1976), 137.

4. Messersmith to Welles, May 22, 1940, Messersmith Papers, Folder 1360, University of Delaware; and Messersmith to Frankfurter, May 31, 1940, Frankfurter Papers, Box 83, Messersmith Folder LC.

5. Presidential Press Conference, June 5, 1940, in *Presidential Press Conferences*, vol. 13–14.

6. Dunlop, *Donovan*, 210–11; and Wasserstein, *Britain*, 84–102.

7. Bullitt's speech is reprinted in *New York Times*, August 19, 1940. Information about Welles and Roosevelt is in Bullitt's memorandum, August 12, 1940, reprinted in Orville H. Bullitt, ed., *For the President, Personal and Secret: Correspondence between Franklin D. Roosevelt and William C. Bullitt* (Boston, 1972), 499. Bullitt had earlier, well before the fall of France, written FDR much the same thing—that large numbers of Jewish refugees in France were spying for Germany. See Ted Morgan, *FDR* (New York, 1986), 498–99.

8. Circular telegram of September 19, 1940, NA RG 59, 811.111 Refugees/260; Johnson to Secretary of State, September 28, 1940, NA RG 59, 811.111 Refugees/376.

9. Secretary of State Memo, July 26, 1941, NA RG 59, 811.111 War Regulations/366A.

10. Eleanor Roosevelt to McDonald, March 2, 1941, Eleanor Roosevelt Papers, Box 1612, FDRL.

11. FDR Memorandum for the Secretary of the Interior, December 18, 1940, OF 3186, FDRL.

12. Feingold, *Politics of Rescue*, 155–56.

13. Welles to Mr. President, December 21, 1940, NA RG 59, CDF 840.48 Refugees/2352.

14. Berle Diary, March 5, 1941, Berle Papers, FDRL.

15. Dallek, *Franklin D. Roosevelt*, 334–35.

16. *Congressional Record*, June 5, 1941.

17. Dallek, *Franklin D. Roosevelt*, 277, 285, 267.

18. Frankfurter Telephone Conversation with Secretary of War Stimson, June 16, 1943, transcript in Stimson Papers, Roll 127 LC.

19. Hull to FDR, May 7, 1943; Undated Summary of Colonel Hoskins's Report on the Near East; Welles to the President, June 14, 1943; Roosevelt to King Saud, June 15, 1943, President's

Secretary's File: Confidential File, Box 13, State Department 1943, FDRL.

20. Morgenthau Presidential Diaries, December 3, 1942, Box 5, FDRL.

21. Memo to Watson and President, December 2, 1942; Early to Welles, December 4, 1942; Welles to Early, December 12, 1942, President's Secretary's File: Confidential File, State Department, FDRL.

22. The comment of July 1942 is quoted in Jewish Delegation Press Release, December 8, 1942, American Jewish Committee Archives RG-i, EXO-29, Waldman Papers, Germany/Nazism/American Jewish Congress. For the other statements, see OF 5152; White House Press Release, October 7, 1942; and Berle Diary, August 18, 1942, and attached Statement of the President of the United States, Box 214, FDRL.

23. Laqueur, *Terrible Secret*, 3, 237.

24. Watson Memorandum, November 30, 1942; Watson comment about FDR's reaction, December 1, 1942; Wise to Dear Boss, December 2, 1942, OF 76–C, FDRL; Wise to Niles, December 2, 1942, Wise Papers, Box 181, AJHS; and Welles to Watson, December 4, 1942, OF 76–C, FDRL.

25. Held's account of meeting, pt. 3, sec. 1, no. 15, Jewish Labor Committee Archives, quoted by Penkower, *The Jews Were Expendable*, 85–86; and Jewish Delegation Press Release, December 8, 1942, copy in American Jewish Committee Archives RG-i, EXO-29, Waldman Papers, Germany/Nazism/ American Jewish Congress.

26. Wise to Niles, December 9, 1942, Wise Papers, Box 181, AJHS.

27. Watson to Long, April 1, 1943, and attached documents OF 3186, FDRL, copy also in NA RG 59, 811.111 Refugees/4—143. See also Celler's report in Meeting of the Joint Emergency Committee on European Jewish Affairs, April 10, 1943, American Jewish Committee Archives.

28. *FRUS*, 1943, vol. 1, 177–79.

29. Morgan, *FDR*, esp. 23, 37, 47, 275, 445.

30. Pickett Journal, April 12, June 15, 1943, AFSC.

31. Jan Ciechanowski, *Defeat in Victory* (Garden City, 1947), 179–80. Nowak's message is reprinted in Laqueur, *The Terrible Secret*, 232.

32. Ciechanowski, *Defeat*, 182; and Laqueur, *Terrible Secret*, 231, 236.

33. Wise to the President, July 23, 1943, and handwritten comment on Meltzer memorandum, Proposed Arrangement for Relief and Evacuation of Refugees in Rumania and France, July 30, 1943, NA RG 59, CDF 862.4016/2286 and 840.48 Refugees/42 11. On August 10, 1943, Wise reported confidentially and off the record about the evacuation plan to the Joint Emergency Committee for Jewish Affairs, stating that the government had approved the plan. American Jewish Committee Archive, RG-1, EXO-29, Waldman File, Joint Emergency Committee.

34. Meeting of the Undersecretary with the Assistant Secretaries, Political Advisors, and Geographic Division Heads, November 11, 1943; Stettinius to Long, November 1943, Stettinius Papers, Boxes 732, 215, Meeting with Asst. Secretaries, October 1943, and Long Folders, respectively, University of Virginia.

35. Gilbert, *Auschwitz and the Allies*, esp. 267–76.

Sweden Expands Asylum

PAUL A. LEVINE

From *From Indifference to Activism*

At the Wannsee conference in January 1942, *Unterstaatssekretär* Martin Luther argued that the tiny size of Norway's (and Denmark's) Jewish population would make the imposition of the Final Solution difficult, and that great effort would be required with only a small numerical result to be anticipated. Nonetheless, the decision was made to deport Norway's Jews. Unlike other areas of Europe where the SS was the primary agency in charge of arranging and carrying out the deportations, in Norway officials of Germany's Foreign Ministry were in charge of organizing the destruction process. In "the semicircular arc of destruction," *Auswärtiges Amt* [Foreign Office] personnel considered the genocide theirs to conduct.[1]

Thus at least in Berlin any negotiations UD [*Utrikesdepartementet*, the Swedish Foreign Ministry] might undertake to aid Jews in Norway would be conducted with German officials already known to Swedish diplomats. No evidence has been located indicating that diplomats at UD knew in advance when the blow would fall in Norway, but there is no question that for many months they were aware of the by now familiar pattern of persecution to which Norway's Jews were being subjected. Soon after occupation in 1940, anti-Jewish measures began, generally in conjunction with [Vidkun] Quisling's puppet government, and they increased in the intervening months.[2]

In Trondheim in early October 1942, the arrest was ordered of all Jewish males over 14 years.[3] ...

Only in late October was the action in Trondheim brought to the attention of officials in Stockholm, in a report written to UD on the 27th by Swedish Consul-General Claes Westring.[4] ... As of the day before, Westring wrote, raids in the entire country were carried out against all male Jews, with several hundred caught and taken to a camp at Berg. Though the state controlled Norwegian press said that the round up of Jews was in reprisal for the murder of a policeman by two Jews, Westring rejected that explanation, saying a large-scale effort against the Jews had been expected after the arrests in Trondheim.

One of the Jews arrested was a Swedish citizen, motivating Westring to immediately visit *Standartenführer* (Colonel) Heinrich Fehlis, head of German security in Norway, in an attempt to get the Swede released. Fehlis told Westring that Swedish Jews were not the intended targets of the raid, and that he hoped that all such Jews would return to Sweden. Westring also reported the announcement of the recently published law that the wealth of all Jews, Norwegian or stateless, would be confiscated by the Norwegian state.[5]

Information about these events immediately reached the Swedish press, which throughout November published stories on the increasing tide of anti-Jewish measures. On November 1, *Stockholms-Tidningen* reported that "According to the information from Oslo, there appears to be an action against the Norwegian Jews that has reached an extent never before seen."[6] In mid-November, all Jews were ordered to register with the authorities, an action reported in Swedish newspapers on the 19th and directly to UD on the 20th.[7] Though many Jews went into hiding to save themselves, some succumbed to fear and a wave of suicides resulted. This disturbing phenomenon was reported in one newspaper on November 22. The suicides were described as a direct result of the measures taken against the Jews.[8]

Historian Samuel Abrahamsen writes that the Germans were so unconcerned with the Jews of Norway that no transport was arranged in advance of the action, and that Berlin was in fact surprised at the arrests of large numbers of Jews.[9] Though Hilberg agrees that in this case "preparatory measures were started slowly, ". . . on November 26 the transport ship *Donau* left Oslo with 532 men, women, and children bound for Stettin and then Auschwitz. They reached the extermination facility on December 1 and upon arrival were divided into two groups. The women and children were immediately gassed to death and the men sent to slave labor. Twenty-one men of this original group of 532 survived the war.[10]

News of the deportation reached Sweden immediately and the departure of the vessel was front-page news in most of Stockholm's dailies.[11] The numbers given were exaggerated but the description of events was accurate. *Svenska Dagbladet* wrote that "1,000 male and female Jews of all ages are being sent to Germany for further transport to Poland." Noteworthy here is that for the first time since the war began *Dagens Nyheter* not only reported actions against Jews but also commented on the now close-to-home persecution of Europe's Jews. The editorial that day said:

A Horrible Message Comes from Norway . . . a thousand Jews, among them many elderly, women and children . . . have been assembled and shipped to Germany for further transport

to Poland. . . . Merely and only for their origins have these humans been summarily dispatched to an existence of suffering and deprivation which for many of them must mean death . . . these measures are so completely incomprehensible for people with a Nordic and Western conception of justice. . . . Now for the first time we see this happen close by . . . this complete disregard for human dignity.[12]

Of course, diplomats in UD read their newspapers. They and others in government were well [aware] of public opinion. News stories negative to Germany and expressions of anti-German opinion were very common in Swedish newspapers and were a source of tension in German-Swedish relations throughout the war's first three years. Swedish officials, not least within UD, were often anxious to suppress what they considered to be an overly free press that could and sometimes did harm bilateral relations.[13]

Interestingly, not everyone in UD agreed that the anti-German tone of the Swedish press was harmful. In a reflection that would both become more frequent later in the war . . . , Sven Grafstrom expressed this feeling in the wake of a conversation in Berlin with Werner von Grundherr, head of *Auswärtiges Amt*'s Scandinavian Division, about the problems Sweden's press caused: "We should not forget that the vigilance and reaction of the Swedish press towards events in the occupied countries constitutes possibly the only good will in England and America we have, a good will which will most likely become more and more important the longer the war goes on. The government itself surely creates no good will in the Anglo-Saxon countries.[14] Now with German atrocities hitting so close to home efforts to restrain the press were bound to fail. Indeed, the moral problem of being uninvolved and/or uninterested in German atrocities was addressed. On November 28, *Dagens Nyheter* reprinted an editorial from *Östgöten*, a small regional newspaper in central Sweden. "We must react both with our thoughts and feelings against that which has happened in Norway and other occupied counties.... Our neutrality must not become an unfeeling indifference.... Such neutrality can in the long-term work against itself; those who remain quiet can easily give the impression of agreement."[15]

Throughout December Swedish newspapers continued to report on actions against the Jews remaining in Norway, thus maintaining their readers' and the government's attention on the issue. What they didn't report were the various yet still quiet measures being taken by Swedish diplomats in Berlin, Stockholm and Oslo to aid Jews.

The Shift in UD's Response Begins

Those affected by the wave of arrests and the deportation of November 26 were not, as before, Jews from Poland, France or even Germany. These Jews were mostly Norwegian citizens (the remainder were either German or stateless) and thus had a cultural and political claim to Swedish attention—and thus potential aid—that Jews from elsewhere in Europe did not. This is at least partly the explanation for the immediate manner in which UD officials responded.... Efforts on behalf of Jews "with at least ... a connection to Sweden" began as soon as information about the deportations reached Stockholm. On November 27, Gosta Engzell [head of the Legal Division of the UD] sent to Oslo for investigation a list of names received from relatives of Jews in Sweden anxious about family or friends in Norway. Late on the evening of the 30th, a telegram was sent to the Legation in Berlin instructing them to inquire about the "Swedish born or those with close relatives (in) Sweden on the Jewish transport from

Norway, and if this has happened, to request their release for travel to Sweden."[16]

The same day Engzell wrote a letter to [Swedish Ambassador in Berlin Arvid] Richert saying that [Foreign Minister Christian] Günther was greatly disturbed by the deportations and by the furor they aroused within the Swedish public. Thus Günther "considers it necessary to at least try to do something to help those who have a connection to Sweden." Engzell expressed Stockholm's hope that a demarche from the Legation would be of some use.... This important letter concludes by saying that "If these Jews, of whom at most two are Swedish citizens, are transported into Poland's interior, we fear that nothing more can be done." The message intended with such information is clear, and the wording leaves no doubt that Engzell understood, even if the ultimate fate of deported Jews is not directly stated, what was at stake.[17]

Richert responded immediately and in a report which arrived in Stockholm on December 4, told Staffan Soderblom that on the first of the month Chargé Eric von Post went to see Ambassador Erich Albrecht, head of the Legal Division of *Auswärtiges Amt* (and thus Engzell's direct counterpart). Von Post told Albrecht that his government requested "a rapid investigation" whether Jews with a connection to Sweden had been deported, and if so, that they be freed and allowed to return to Sweden. Richert wrote that von Post stressed not only the urgency of the matter for the Swedish government, but more importantly for German-Swedish relations in general. "... von Post added, that if it is determined that any Swedish subject or native-born Swede was included in the Jewish transport, no power in the world will be able to restrain Swedish newspapers; the German measure will be subject to sharp criticism and damage will be done to Swedish-German relations." Richert also noted Albrecht's reply. Its pattern of delay and obfuscation would become familiar for Swedish diplomats negotiating for the lives of Jews. The German told von Post that the issue was actually the responsibility of another division within the Foreign Ministry, but he would look into it and quickly respond.[18]

On December 3, Richert received another telegram from Stockholm [that] encapsulates what Steven Koblik accurately labels "a pivotal point for Swedish policy" toward Germany's campaign of extermination.[19] In a telegram ordered sent by Prime Minister Hansson, Richert was told to discreetly and "in an appropriate manner, indicate that Sweden is prepared to accept all remaining Jews in Norway should they be subject to removal."[20]

The shift in Swedish attitudes from previous episodes when Jews required assistance is striking. First the offer came from the same government that up to that point strove to exclude Jews *because* they were Jews. Now these same officials sought to help some individuals because it was understood that they were under assault *only* because they were Jews. For the first time since Nazi Germany began persecuting its Jewish population in 1933, a sovereign state announced to the Germans, albeit informally and not yet for public knowledge, that it was willing to accept any Jew from a third country who could make it to the Swedish border.

Importantly, no differentiation was made between Jews with a connection with Sweden (although this qualification was not in general revoked), Norwegian citizens or stateless Jews. Though some reluctance remains evident in the fact that the government neither wanted a formal demarche made to the German government or knowledge of the effort becoming public, there is no question that a watershed was reached in Sweden's reaction to the Holocaust.

Why this sudden change when to that point in time the policies formulated in the 1930s remained essentially intact? Material conditions in Sweden had worsened somewhat since the war began, yet now, when there was no sign of the war ending anytime soon, the government was opening its doors to more mouths to feed—and they would be Jewish mouths. . . . Sweden's willingness to act now on behalf of some Jews was aided immeasurably by the fact that these events were occurring not far away in Europe to peoples of a different culture, but in neighboring Norway. Though it is highly probable that Swedes in general retained long-held prejudices against Jews, Norwegian Jews were different. They belonged to a *broderfolk* (a fellow people); they were (or at least most were) fellow Scandinavians. As such, they had claims to the emotions of Swedish citizens, and thus government activity, which other Europeans, Jewish or not, could never have. As Sven Grafstrom told a German diplomat early in November, if similar methods were used, "above all in Norway," the Germans could virtually count on a powerful, unified reaction by Sweden's press and people.[21]

From this point forward Sweden's willingness to help Jews would expand and deepen, while some hesitance continued. This holds true not only in response to anti-Jewish actions in Scandinavia but for the rest of the war, a sometime ambivalence generally losing out to energetic activism. . . . By the end of 1942 a clear pattern had emerged. Swedish diplomats were engaged in regular and normative discussions with their German counterparts regarding direct (and sometimes life-saving) assistance to Jews. The discussions involved both large groups, as with the offer to accept all Jews remaining in Norway, and specific individuals. Structurally these efforts were supported by a method of approach founded on two basic platforms. The first was the authority of their office—a German official speaking to a Swedish diplomat could not doubt that the latter represented a sovereign nation with which the Germans desired calm and normal relations, above all in trade. The second was the non-emotional, almost non-partisan manner and language Swedish diplomats used to try to save lives. For the most part UD diplomats did not employ accusatory language that would not have in any case been effective, and they were too sophisticated to argue, at least as indicated in the written accounts, with the "goals" of Nazi racial policy. That was being left to the Swedish press, which UD could count on to stake out such a position. Indeed, had Swedish officials engaged in such rhetorical exercises they surely would have hurt their chances of intervening with success. Rather, their appeals were interventions almost always couched in the language of citizenship or political interests. This method indicated to their murderous interlocutors that, in effect, the making of an exception in such or such a case would not hinder the "achievement" of the larger "goal." The manner in which UD officials were going about their delicate task shows in fact some sophistication and hard calculations about what might succeed, and what would not....

Shocked by the onset of the Final Solution so close to home, Swedish diplomats—backed by their government—swiftly, wholeheartedly and energetically did what they felt was possible. Rather than engage in public relations exercises designed to relieve public pressure—an option presumably available to the Swedish government as well—the decision was made to assist with genuine and significant diplomatic activity.

Moreover, it was directed not only to Jews of demonstrated Scandinavian citizenship or background, but also encompassed other nationalities and even stateless Jews. The diplomats of UD were trying to help as many people as they could. The

spirit and methods that informed these interventions would continue to expand....

UD's Role in the Salvation of Danish Jewry, September—October 1943

> Several days ago information became available in Sweden that measures were being prepared against Jews in Denmark similar to earlier unlawful actions in Norway and other occupied countries. In accordance with [his] instructions, on October 1 Sweden's Minister in Berlin told German officials of the serious consequences such measures will cause in Sweden. Furthermore, the Minister has put forward an invitation from the Swedish government that it is prepared to accept all Danish Jews in Sweden.
>
> —Official government statement, read on Swedish radio at 18:00, October 2, 1943.[22]

... Immediately after Germany occupied Denmark on April 9, 1940, it was clear that this small Scandinavian nation would be treated differently by its conquerors. Denmark was "the model protectorate" and its Nordic character gave it, in Hitler's eyes, a special status. Crucial to this was the maintenance of its existing form of government and civil administration. According to Danish historian Henrik Nissen, political conditions were "marked above all by the existence of two sides that negotiated with each other concerning practical arrangements for practical problems." One element of these arrangements was that the political situation would remain stable—the German's real goal—as long as three fundamental points were maintained; otherwise the collaborative arrangement would end. The third of these points was, writes Nissen, that no special anti-Jewish legislation be introduced.[23]

On November 17, 1941, Sweden's Minister in Copenhagen Gustaf von Dardel cabled Staffan

Söderblom in UD . . . that Germany's resident envoy [had] told Denmark's King Christian X that the time had come for measures to be taken against the Jews in Denmark. "The King answered," wrote von Dardel, "that he saw no reason for this," and then told his German interlocutor that, "We Danes don't need to do anything in this matter because we don't feel inferior to Jews."[24] In January 1942, von Dardel again informed Stockholm that German pressures to initiate anti-Jewish laws in Denmark (always the first step in the Nazi pattern of destruction) were bound to fail because the Danes simply would not accept them.[25] And late in December, von Dardel wrote that even though all Jews were fired from the civil service, "the Danes hope this will be the only demand."[26] By the summer of 1943, the "practical" relationship between the Germans and Danes finally collapsed. In August an uprising began in the town of Esbjerg, and for the next three weeks riots and confrontations spread throughout Denmark. By the end of the month, it was clear that the previous bilateral relationship was beyond repair. Even though Danish civil servants sought to keep the policy of collaboration alive, it finally collapsed, and on Sunday, August 29, the German military commander declared martial law.[27]

Dr. Werner Best, German Plenipotentiary in Denmark, quickly understood that . . . the time had come to strike against the country's small Jewish population. As noted, historians have made much of the role played by German shipping attaché Georg Ferdinand Duckwitz, [who] is routinely given credit for "warning" both the Danish Jewish community and the Swedish government late in September that action against the Jews was imminent. And though it seems certain that Duckwitz did meet with Prime Minister [Per Albin] Hansson . . . , from the Swedish documentation it seems clear that his role, at least with regard to

"warning" Sweden, has been considerably exaggerated.[28] . . .

This is seen most clearly in a letter written on August 31 by Gosta Engzell to Minister von Dardel in Copenhagen. From this we see that only days after the imposition of martial law, and almost a full month before Duckwitz appears in the picture, Sweden knew that it was only a matter of time before the Jews would come under assault and that the government would be called upon to respond: "We are rather clear on what you can do under current circumstances to rescue Danish Jews by bringing them here. I'm thinking mainly about the Swedish-born and nearest relatives, husbands, and children. If there is anything to be gained by issuing provisional passports you may do that, still with some caution concerning the non-Swedish born. . . ."[29]

The next day Engzell again wrote von Dardel . . . that Swedish-born Jews should first receive assistance.[30] In this report and other documents dated September 1 is evidence that others in Stockholm understood the imminent danger for Danish Jews and were already asking for assistance. Engzell recommended that all possible help be given.[31] Engzell's deep engagement in the entire issue "of doing what was possible" is described in considerable detail in a long letter written only the next day to von Dardel. "As expected we have received a stream of requests and applications concerning Jewish relatives in Denmark . . . we are prepared to do what is possible to allow them to come over to Sweden." . . . Below Engzell's typed signature is the following; "p.s. entry visas may be given to all Jews in question without prior clearance from the Department."[32]

Dozens of letters and reports, requests for assistance and communications with Swedes and others outside of UD leave no doubt that Engzell was well informed of the situation throughout

September and that he was fully prepared to do what he and his colleagues could to assist as many Jews as possible. There was no attempt to diminish the danger Denmark's Jews were in, nor any inclination to distance UD from the already many requests for assistance received throughout September.[33] Engzell knew what was coming, and he prepared himself and his division.

Several interesting matters appear in von Dardel's long response to Engzell's request for his evaluation of the situation. As of September 6, he wrote that no special measures had been taken against Jews "although the Jewish question in some fashion 'is hanging in the air.'" One indication was that the Germans had confiscated the membership rolls of the Jewish community. However, von Dardel advised against anything special being done as long as the situation remained that way. He reported on his visit to Danish Minister of Justice Tunne Jacobsen, who told him that the Germans were unlikely to respect any Swedish documents and that if the Germans treated Danish Jews as they had others, he found it difficult to understand what Sweden might be able to do to help.[34] Engzell also read that some Jews had already visited the Legation looking for assistance and ... that ... it was common knowledge that the Legation received instructions to help Jews. This report was sent, as were several of Engzell's with his instructions and evaluations, to Prime Minister Hansson, Foreign Minister Günther, other Cabinet members, all the important legations abroad, and Jewish leader Gunnar Josephson.[35]

Knowledge of Sweden's willingness to help was evident to people in the United States. On September 9, Swedish Minister in Washington Wollmar Boström cabled Stockholm saying that the American Jewish Congress (a leading establishment Jewish organization) had inquired asking how many Jews had already fled to Sweden, and if others required a visa to enter the country.[36] Five days later a telegram was sent saying that Jewish refugees were being accepted without visas and that to date about 20 had arrived.[37] ...

UD received official confirmation that arrests of Jews had begun the night before when von Dardel telegraphed Stockholm on Saturday, October 2 at 12:11 p.m. ... "Last night at 21:00 1,000 Gestapo and [Danish] Free Corpsmen, since the Danish police refused, turned out and arrested a large but still unknown number of Jews ... Telephone out in whole country. Himmler said to be in Copenhagen." As planned the Germans simultaneously announced in the controlled press that interned Danish soldiers were being released because, as von Dardel repeated," ... the Jews were now segregated from public life and can no longer continue to poison the atmosphere."[38] Less than an hour later another telegram arrived from Copenhagen saying that the Legation secretly received word from Danish police that preliminary information told of 1,600 Jews and half-Jews arrested.[39] It was also reported to Stockholm that ... in the last week or so some 100 provisional passports had been issued and that "masses of people coming to the Legation."[40]

The decision to make the unprecedented offer of unconditional sanctuary was accepted by all leading members of the government, but the manner in which it was done, without consulting most Cabinet members, caused Conservative Leader Gösta Bagge to complain to Günther ... "that such an important thing had not been previously announced to Cabinet members before instructions went to Berlin."[41] ... Foreign Minister Günther called Thomsen, the German envoy in Stockholm, to a meeting where ... "He asked Thomsen to suggest to authorities in Berlin that the vessel which is clearly meant for transporting Jews be redirected to a Swedish port."[42]

Richert was informed of this offer, which was not accepted.

As Engzell expected UD was literally swamped with desperate requests for help, but the news from Sweden's southern coast soon caused a decline in them. Of course all Swedish newspapers reported their government's offer, and editorial comment was for the most part positive. *Göteborgs Handels- och Sjöfarts Tidning* (GHT) said, "The government can be assured that every measure in such a direction will be supported by unified public opinion."[43] By Sunday the 3rd, *Stockholms-Tidningen* was reporting "A wave of Jewish refugees over the entire Scania coast." From the city of Landskrona came the report that "... many policemen have had to sacrifice their day off to function as porters ... the greatest numbers are confessors of Judaism and the streets in Lands-krona are swarming with dark haired Danes of different ages."[44] Indeed by the 3rd UD officials were aware of some two to three thousand Jews having already landed in Sweden.[45] That weekend and for the remainder of October, thousands more would make the journey across the water; all would be accepted and treated well.

Engzell was at the center of efforts in Stockholm to coordinate UD's response. He directed his colleagues, sent off instructions, composed memoranda reviewing the situation, authorized the issuance of provisional passports, and was ceaseless in urging his colleagues, as we see in one report which, after reviewing what had been done in Norway and elsewhere, stated "That which is possible should be done also in Denmark using the ways and means which can be found. The Legation [in Copenhagen] is authorized to cover reasonable costs."[46] In scores of documents from the remainder of October is unequivocal evidence of Engzell's deep personal and professional commitment to save lives.[47]

Not unnoticed in all of the excitement was the praise that many around the world, particularly in the United States, showered on the government and people of Sweden. One telegram received on October 7 from New York to Prime Minister Hansson is typical:

> To you as Chairman of Socialist Party Sweden and Premier of that country we deem it our duty to express our admiration for brave and humanitarian steps taken by Swedish government to rescue Jews of Denmark now in the clutches of Nazis. During the years of untold suffering of Jews under the Nazis this is the first time that a government officially issued a statement announcing readiness to grant asylum to tortured Jews of a neighboring country.[48]

On October 6, the *Washington Post* editorialized that Sweden's action was "the only bright spot" in the years of war and occupation. Finally and not unimportantly, the American government made very clear to Sweden's government how much it "warmly appreciated the spontaneous action for Denmark's Jews."[49]

On the other hand, German officials in Berlin were less pleased with Sweden's actions. On October 5 von Otter went to *Auswärtiges Amt* and there met with Councillor Eberhard von Thadden, [who] complained ... that in no less than forty-five cases it was discovered that non-Swedish Jews possessed provisional passports. Von Otter, in what must have been a good moment for someone who had experienced great frustration dealing with Nazi officials determined to harm Jews, said that no one in the Legation had any knowledge of such matters. "Then, von Otter ... said that there was nothing remarkable about the Swedish side trying to help Jews with special connections to Sweden and possibly also previous Swedish citizens. . . ."[50]

In numbers previously unthinkable the Swedish government and people offered Jews refuge and safety. Of course geography has much to do with this as did the fact that, as with Norway, a Scandinavian people endangered by Nazi policies were involved. All were fortunate that the Germans did not press their assault on Danish Jews as was their custom, and that for whatever reason—lack of manpower or political will—little or no attempt was made to stop the transit of refugees across the Oresund. Yet again there is the issue of choice that explains just as much if not more. Engzell and others chose to do what they did when other options existed. Although there is no evidence to indicate that Engzell and others in the government were motivated in this episode by the prospect of gaining good will with the Allies, they knew that offering shelter to Denmark's Jews would be appreciated in the West at a time when political and economic pressures from the Allies were still increasing. Indeed, an editorial in GHT commented on this connection, arguing that because Sweden had escaped destruction it had a moral duty to help the Danish Jews.[51]

Intriguingly, not all in Sweden were sure that letting in so many Jews was good. An editorial published in the pro-Nazi newspaper *Dagsposten* on October 6 strongly criticized the government's action and predicted that the country would regret any act which,

> . . . doubles the Jewish population in our country at the same time as a weak interest is shown for our own kinsmen, such as Estonian Swedes. They have partly suffered and are threatened by a much harder fate than that threatening Danish Jews. Furthermore from the point of view of the war, the Estonian Swedes are completely innocent. . . . There is however a certain comfort in knowing that the enthusiasm for Jews fanned

in the press is not genuine. Jewish interests that control the Swedish press are responsible for that. . . . All of this actually concerns something completely different than real humanism.[52] . . .

When looking at Sweden and UD reaction to the Final Solution in Denmark one indeed sees a small "bright spot" in a dismal landscape. This conclusion holds whether or not the Germans allowed the Danish Jews to leave or whether they in fact narrowly escaped sure death. There was certainly no equivocation in the appreciation felt by many at the time. . . . Dr. Stephen Wise, a leader of the American Jewish community during the war. . . . cabled UD with words which remain pertinent today. ". . . rescue danish jewry not only constitutes victory for humanity but marks turning point in struggle for reestablishing immemorial spiritual values for common humanity . . . moral grandeur your country's act will hold forever honored place among most cherished memories of eternal people."[53]

The public offer to accept Denmark's Jews was indeed an act of "moral grandeur" that contributed to a significant shift in public opinion in the West toward Sweden. Although this shift did not immediately affect the pressures Allied governments were putting on Sweden, it eventually contributed to this. Perhaps more importantly, Sweden's substantive gesture was an act of humanitarianism that told those Jews still remaining alive in Europe that at least one sovereign government could be turned to in times of dire need. Less than six months later, the Jews of Budapest, knowing of Denmark, knew that they had at least one ally in their struggle to survive the war. . . .

Swedish Diplomacy in Budapest

Assistance activities in Budapest constitute Sweden's most important and most complicated efforts during the Holocaust. They also constitute the most successful. Although the number of those assisted and/or saved (and even those terms are open to discussion) varies greatly, it seems certain that at a minimum between 20,000 and 30,000 Jews received Swedish protection in one form or another. . . . The Holocaust in Hungary may be divided into three fairly specific periods. The first is from occupation on March 19, 1944, until the halting of the deportations in early July. Coincidental to this was Raoul Wallenberg's arrival to Budapest. The second phase, during which few Jews were deported and pressures eased slightly, lasted from early July until October 15. The third phase commenced with the Hungarian Nazi Party, the Arrow Cross (or *Nyilas*) overthrowing the government headed by Regent Miklos Horthy and lasted until the city's liberation by the Red Army in January—February 1945. For the Jews of Budapest the third phase was a nightmare of random but often mass killings, forced marches in winter weather, and desperate living conditions as they clung to life. . . .

In popular imagination and memory Raoul Wallenberg is personally responsible for the success of Swedish diplomacy in Budapest. Yet an analysis of the essential Swedish documents . . . demonstrates that his role and importance in Swedish activities in Budapest have been greatly exaggerated. This exaggeration and concentration on one figure, a circumstance at least partly the result of Wallenberg's disappearance into the Soviet Union, has led to a general and problematic simplification of a very complicated series of events. His individual heroism (and ultimate tragedy) is profound and indisputable, and a careful revision will not lessen this. But sober analysis must be done even when dealing with popular heros, and in this case such a revision is necessary. . . . Without his authority as a Swedish diplo-

mat he simply would not have been in Budapest, let alone able to do what he ultimately did. . . .

Several days after Germany occupied its Hungarian ally on March 19, 1944, Sweden's Minister in Budapest sent a telegram to UD explaining the reasons behind the long expected German move. The primary reason, according to Sweden's Minister Carl Ivan Danielsson, was Hungary's "inability or will to solve the Jewish problem according to the German pattern."[54] Danielsson was told this during a visit to the office of Deputy Foreign Minister Andor Szentmiklosy the day after the occupation. This first analysis of the new situation reached Stockholm on April 6, an indication of the excellent communications between Budapest and Sweden. . . . Szentmiklosy complained that the Germans simply did not understand how difficult it was for Hungary to act against its Jewish population in the German manner. "The Jews' place in the country's economic life and structure was such," Danielsson was told, "that radical measures according to German patterns for the Jews' extermination would have brought catastrophic consequences for the country; only through progressive measures could a satisfactory solution be obtained."[55] Notice was given that the incumbent German minister had already been summarily sent out of Budapest and replaced by a plenipotentiary appointed directly by Hitler and Himmler, Dr. Edmund Veesenmayer.[56] Danielsson then described the first day's attacks on the city's Jewish population:

The city itself is not occupied by German troops; they are encamped around the city. On the other hand, Budapest is flooded with ss formations and Gestapo agents and a merciless hunt is underway for leading Jews. . . . Diplomatic extraterritoriality has not been respected. . . . The Legation is besieged by people, mostly Jews and Poles, who are requesting asylum or seek a paper declaring that they stand under the protection of the Legation.[57]

From March 19 until liberation in early 1945, Danielsson, Attaché Per Anger and others at the Legation would find themselves literally besieged by desperate people, primarily Jews, begging for protection by the Swedes. Most people knew from events in Denmark and elsewhere that the government of Sweden was sometimes willing to offer assistance and protect Jews threatened by the Nazis. In Budapest Swedish diplomats would be challenged on a scale previously unimaginable. Yet aided by their colleagues in Berlin and Stockholm and supported by their political superiors, they responded energetically and often with creativity to the challenge. . . .

The thrust of the Legation's efforts to assist and protect Jews was by issuing "official" documents that, it was hoped, conveyed some measure of protection. Ever since the First World War, when passports again became widely used, physical possession of an official looking piece of paper, generally with an authoritative looking stamp, signature or photo became an obligatory item for all travelers and even for domestic use.[58] Then, from the 1930s on, the possession of an entry visa to a desired destination could mean the difference between life and death. In Budapest the value of documents was particularly high, especially after the German occupation. The operative concept here is another of the vital elements of bureaucratic resistance. Everyone understood that the mere possession of an official looking paper might have some positive effect. Physical possession of a "foreign" document gave the bearer the opportunity to present a persecuting authority—either Hungarian or German—physical evidence of the concern of a foreign power. Such evidence some-

times did stymie arrest; sometimes it had no effect whatsoever.

In Budapest any sort of official looking document that could be easily identified as connecting the bearer with the Swedish government granted some form of protection. Swedish documents were particularly desirable due to . . . Sweden's "unique" position in Hungary. This position was based on favorable attitudes created by previous humanitarian services done by Sweden for Hungarians and because Sweden represented Hungarian interests in belligerent countries.[59]

Sweden was of course not alone in issuing documents, as several neutral legations and organizations provided Jews with various types of documents. The various neutral papers had relative values of perceived protection with Swiss and Swedish documents widely considered most effective.[60] In similar fashion, the various types of documents issued by the Swedes had relative value.

This hierarchy of protective value was discussed and analyzed on several occasions by Danielsson and Anger. All were agreed that the best document was the provisional passport, and not surprisingly that was the one most sought after. The diplomats quickly realized that a document with a signature was worth more than one without it, and that possession of any document with a Swedish letterhead or stamp was better than having nothing at all. On May 4, Danielsson wrote that those Jews who sought a provisional passport but were denied, nonetheless, ". . . still requested a stamped certificate of any type . . . and because the Legation does not want to completely deny those seeking help, a certificate has been issued saying, for example, 'It is hereby certified that the bearer has submitted an application to the Legation for Swedish citizenship' . . . stamped without a signature."[61] It was a terribly confusing and arbitrary time. That which protected on one occasion might be useless and ineffective the next. Presenting a lesser "certificate" could lead to release, and other times even a provisional passport appeared insufficient as a means of protection.[62] ... But there is no question that the documents were much sought after. Otherwise there would not have been thousands of people every day beseeching Legation personnel for help.

Yet even the relative value of Swedish documents shifted. Although by the middle of May Danielsson and Anger had established a hierarchy of value for the documents they were issuing, they remained uncertain about what the authorities were thinking. In one memo there are descriptions of the various values of provisional passports, an entry visa (to Sweden), protective letter A (*skyddsbrev*), and protective letter B. The system was being worked out by trial and error.[63] The frustrating uncertainty was partly caused by not knowing exactly whether Germans or Hungarians were in charge on anti-Jewish policy.[64] ... In addition it was unclear which Hungarian ministry or bureau was responsible for the enforcement of anti-Jewish measures. This confusion was amplified because, Danielsson wrote, within the Hungarian bureaucracy "the left hand commonly does not know what the right is doing."[65]

The Extermination of Hungarian Jewry and UD's Response

Throughout May, information about the conditions of the Jews in the countryside and the onset of deportations came to the Legation. Much of this information was assembled on May 26 into a very lengthy report that arrived only five days later in Stockholm. Titled "persecution of Jews in Hungary," the report is timely, detailed, and for the most part accurate, apart from its failure to fully understand the implication of "transport northward." ... The report was distributed to all the important Legations abroad, such as London, Washington DC, Berlin, and Moscow.[66] A copy was also given on June 13 to the American Legation in Stockholm.[67] [The report] said that since the occupation most Jews in the countryside had been deprived of all employment and housing and that since April they had been subjected to brutal concentration into temporary ghettos where conditions were appalling.... Of special significance was the recent regulation stating that all Jews with "foreign citizenship" were exempt from all the regulations (including wearing the Yellow Star of David) as long as certificates confirming the granting of citizenship had been given to the Hungarian authorities. Confirming the life-threatening situation, Danielsson wrote that plans were known to transfer to German territory "up towards 900,000 people . . . these transports have begun and are taking place daily in sealed freight cars with 70 people in each without any access to facilities for natural needs and without any food apart from that each could bring." Many more details of the plight of Hungarian Jewry are described, as is word received that [Hungarian] State Secretary [Lazslo] Baky "has declared himself very satisfied with arrangements."[68] ...

On June 2, Danielsson again telegraphed Stockholm. . . . He reported that "the Jewish question becomes more acute daily" and that word was received that the deportation of Jews from Budapest to Germany and Poland would soon begin, "except for the 50,000 who will be closed into a ghetto." Two other items are of significant interest in this short telegram. The first is the initial proposal calling for Swedish participation in a coordinated action with other neutrals "to save children, women and elderly. According to available information, unlimited financial support is available for this." The second is a request from the Hungarian Red Cross asking that representatives of the Swedish Red Cross and *Rädda Barnen* (Save the Children) be sent to Hungary to organize relief. This request . . . is the genesis from Sweden's side for the task which eventually fell to Raoul Wallenberg.[69]

The continuing confusion over who could be and who should be helped is demonstrated in dozens of documents from these difficult weeks. Again, some requests for assistance were refused [and] similar others granted.[70] Regarding Danielsson's proposals to help women and children in the telegram of June 2, there was no confusion. Four days after receiving the telegram, Sven Grafström (then temporary head of the Political Division) telegraphed Budapest, "you should explain to Hungarian authorities the gloom which characterizes the reaction of the Swedish people concerning the persecution of Jews now underway. Ascertain whether a Swedish initiative to rescue, for example, women, children, and elderly would lead to anything. . . . If so, the proposal will be given quick examination."[71]

The end of May and the first weeks of June were witness to probably the bloodiest weeks of the entire Holocaust. . . . Danielsson was fully aware of the increased tempo of deportations, and on June 14 he sent the following telegram to Stockholm:

> According to reliable intelligence from various sources, deportation and extermination of the Jews accelerating. In eastern and southern Hungary, the largest portion of Jews already deported primarily to extermination camp Kattovitz (sic). Here in Budapest the order for Jews to concentrate in special houses expected this week. The Legation requests confirmation, in accordance with passport regulation 24, if following our own careful determination, provisional passports can be issued for people with connection to Sweden.[72]

Thus . . . , Danielsson and Anger not only identified in unmistakable language the final fate of the deportees but also urgently insisted that assistance policy be completely liberalized. They now sought to employ the most effective measure at their disposal—the issuance of provisional passports—unhindered by the necessity of waiting for instructions or applications coming from Stockholm. Early the next day the Cabinet gave the Legation freedom to act as requested.[73]

On June 20, Danielsson wrote a brief cover letter as an introduction to an appeal received from the Budapest Jewish Council. Written in French on cheap notebook paper, this was a request for an "intervention" by Sweden's King Gustav V "to save the Hungarian Jewish population from complete destruction."[74] That correspondence arrived in Stockholm on June 28, one day before another appeal to the King arrived from Itzchak Gruenbaum, head of the Jewish Agency's Rescue Committee in Palestine. Using Rabbi Marcus Ehrenpreis as a conduit, Gruenbaum had sent a desperate appeal asking Ehrenpreis to tell the Swedish king that "ten thousands Jews already sent [to] death camps [in] Poland for annihilation. If possible, ask His Majesty to use his personal influence on the Hungarian government to stop deportation. We hope King's personal intervention might be helpful. Wire!"[75] That day, both appeals were sent by Grafström to *kabinettskammarherre* [Privy Counselor] General Major T. af Klercker, [who] minuted on Grafström's letter that "His Majesty desires a suitable intervention which can and should be done. . . ."[76]

. . . the much edited Swedish version of Gustav's famous telegram to Miklos Horthy reads:

> After receiving knowledge of the extraordinarily severe methods that your government is resorting to against Hungary's Jewish popula-

tion, allow me to personally turn to Your Highness and in the name of humanity appeal that You take measures to save those who remain of that unfortunate people. This appeal is motivated by my old feelings of friendship for Your country and by my genuine concern for Hungary's good name and reputation in the community of nations.[77]

The message was telegraphed on June 30 to the Legation and delivered by Danielsson and Anger on July 3 in an audience with the Regent. Writing after returning from the audience, Per Anger said that Horthy understood and appreciated Gustav's message, which was similar, he said, to one recently received from the Vatican. Horthy told the Swedes that "he regretted not having greater possibilities to hinder what was happening to Hungary's Jews . . . the Germans," he said, "stand behind all the measures against the Jews" and that although he did not like the deportations, he understood that local authorities ". . . in Eastern Hungary were anxious to transport Eastern Hungary's Jews away because of the communist elements that in recent decades moved to the area and that had little in common with the Hungarian people." The report ends by saying that Horthy had greeted them in an "extremely personable manner, but he was very tired and deeply distressed over the recent events. . . ."[78]

Gustav's appeal to Horthy was immediately publicized in Sweden and the West. On July 5, the Swedish Legation in Washington DC received a sincere but somewhat hyperbolic telegram from an American Jewish group thanking the Swedish King for his ". . . unceasing efforts on behalf of the doomed Jewish people of Europe . . . Sweden's action again leads the way for all nations."[79]

On June 23, Danielsson sent a short telegram to Stockholm telling not only of a protest by the Hungarian Protestant community, but also that "the rumor that the official aim is to, before July 15, remove all of Hungary's Jews."[80] The next day another long and accurate report was compiled for dispatch to Stockholm. Among the detailed information is notification that, as of the week before, up to 420,000 Jews had been deported and that Budapest's Jews were to be so within three weeks. Danielsson wrote,

> . . . all the captured Jews, men and women, children and elderly are loaded into cattle cars and transported partly to German and partly to the Polish *Generalgouvernement* . . . . In Budapest the Jews are stripped of all the property. They now live 8–10 people in a single room. Those lucky enough for necessary labor are said to be transported to German industrial locations where they have a chance to be treated relatively well. The rest, on the other hand, children, weak women, and the elderly are deported to the extermination camp at Auschwitz-Birkenau near Kattowitz in Poland.[81]

The report also describes the complications and difficulties encountered with the various papers issued by the Legation [and] understandable complaints about Legation personnel being overwhelmed by the situation. Although they wished to do more, "the Legation was in the first place trying to help those with connection to Sweden," an indication of how many others were also pleading for assistance. The difficulties of dealing with Hungarian and German officials who constantly blamed the others for the on-going deportations and persecutions are detailed, as are some specific instances of the different treatment according different people when using the various papers as protective devices—sometimes they worked and sometimes they didn't. . . .

In the next days, several more pessimistic, almost pleading reports were written by Danielsson and Anger describing the increasingly ineffective efforts to intervene in individual cases. In one report Danielsson renewed his appeal for immediate Red Cross intervention and wrote that ". . . stubborn rumors say that large numbers of the transports directed to Poland, where the human cargos are exterminated by means of gas."[82]

Not surprisingly, the despair felt in Budapest was shared by officials in Stockholm. All concerned, even the determined Gösta Engzell, began to seriously doubt the value of the documents issued by the Legation.[83] And though Per Anger was able to report one incident when a Jew in Budapest was released from custody after displaying a "*skyddsbrev B*" to the police, there seemed little room for any optimism that any Jew in Hungary would survive the war. By the 5th of July, Anger felt there was little cause for any hope, "A change in the apparently irrevocable decision on the almost total deportation of Hungary's Jews appears . . . to be unthinkable."[84]

It may have been unthinkable to the Germans and Hungarians organizing the deportations to Auschwitz, but it wasn't to Horthy and others in the Hungarian government. Just three days after that pessimistic conclusion, Anger wired Stockholm to report on the coup attempt by Baky and his supporters. Unconvinced that Horthy was prepared to allow the deportation of Budapest's Jews, Baky and other Hungarian Nazis tried to overthrow Horthy. They failed, and were jailed. On July 7, Horthy ordered the announcement that the deportations were to be halted. He was, at least partly, affected by the appeals of Sweden and the other neutral governments.[85] Horthy's decision gave at least a temporary reprieve to the approximately 450 Jews then under Swedish protection.[86]

In the months to come, thousands more would be, in some way or another, assisted by Swedish diplomats in Budapest, Stockholm, and Berlin.[87] The overworked staff in Budapest received an enormous boost when Raoul Wallenberg arrived on July 9, bringing his tremendous energy, creativity, and sense of humanity to the on-going and determined efforts of Danielsson, Anger, Engzell, and others. With Wallenberg's arrival a new phase of Swedish assistance efforts began, and with it new problems, motives and determining factors. . . .

Unfortunately, everything changed again on October 15 with the successful coup against Horthy that put in power the Arrow Cross, Hungary's Nazi Party. The [group] immediately resumed persecuting and murdering Jews, and between that date and the final liberation of Budapest and Hungary in winter 1945, some tens of thousands more Jews would be brutalized and murdered by Germans and Hungarians. Many thousands, however, survived at least partly due to the heroic efforts of Wallenberg, Anger, Swiss diplomat Charles Lutz, and others.

NOTES

1. R. Hilberg, *The Destruction of the European Jews,* v. 2, 546–47.
2. On the Holocaust in Norway in general, see S. Abrahamsen, *Norway's Response to the Holocaust: A Historical Perspective,* (New York, 1991), and R. Hilberg, *op.cit.,* 555–58. Remarkably, Abrahamsen all but ignores Sweden's diplomatic efforts. . . .
3. R. Hilberg, *op.cit.,* 555.
4. C. Westring to S. Söderblom, #662, October 27, 1942, RA UD Hp 21 An 1070/Ti.
5. Ibid.
6. *Stockholms-Tidningen,* November 1, 1942.
7. *Dagens Nyheter,* November 19, 1942; and Westring to Günther, #1309, November 20, 1942, RA UD Hp 21 An 1070/11.

8. *Stockholms-Tidningen*, November 22, 1942.

9. S. Abrahamsen, *op.cit.*, 102 and n. 29.

10. See R. Hilberg, *op.cit.*, 556–57; and S. Abrahamsen, *op.cit.*, Document #6, 190.

11. *Svenska Dagbladet, Stockholms-Tidningen, Dagens Nyheter*, all November 27, 1942.

12. *Dagens Nyheter*, November 27, 1942.

13. The government's attempt to silence the traditionally free press has been analyzed by Swedish historians. See, e.g., Louise Drangel's, *Den kampande demokratin; En studie i antinazistisk opinionsrörelse 1935–1945*, (Uddevalla, 1976) [and] K. Wahlbäck, ed., *Regeringen och kriget; Ur statsrädens dagböcker 1939–1941*, 126–30. Grafström's diary is replete with efforts by UD officials, particularly Arvid Richert, to quash anti-German criticism.

14. S. Grafström, *op.cit.*, November 5, 1942, 441.

15. *Ostgöten*, November 27, 1942, reprinted in *Dagens Nyheter*, November 28, 1942.

16. Cabinet to Swedish Legation Berlin, #83, November 30, 1942, RA UD Hp 21 An 1070/11.

17. Engzell to Richert, #146, November 30, 1942, RA UD Hp 21 An 1070/11.

18. Richert to Soderblom, #105, December 1, 1942, RA UD Hp 21 An 1070/11.

19. S. Koblik, *op.cit.*, 59.

20. Cabinet to Swedish Legation Berlin, #84, December 3, 1942, RA UD Hp 21 An 1070/11.

21. S. Grafström, *op.cit.*, November 5, 1942, 439.

22. Text of statement given to TT, October 2, 1943, RA UD Hp 21 Ad 1056/11.

23. H. Nissen, "Adjusting to German Domination," in H. Nissen, ed., *Scandinavia during the Second World War* (Minnesota, 1983), 114.

24. G. von Dardel to S. Söderblom, November 17, 1941, RA UD Hp 21 Ad 1056/1.

25. Von Dardel to Günther, #45, January 14, 1942, RA UD Hp 21 Ad 1056/1.

26. Von Dardel to Soderblom, December 28, 1942, RA UD Hp 21 Ad 1056/1.

27. A. Trommer, "Scandinavia and the Turn of the Tide," in Nissen, *op.cit.*, 229–38.

28. On Duckwitz, see Kirschhoff, "Gruppenführer Best," *op.cit.*, 209–11.

29. Engzell to von Dardel, #37, August 31, 1943, RA UD Hp 21 Ad 1056/1.

30. Engzell to von Dardel, #44, September 1, 1944, RA UD Hp 21 Ad 1056/1.

31. See S. Nisell to UD Legal Division, September 1, 1943, RA UD Hp 21 Ad 1056/1.

32. Engzell to von Dardel, #46, September 2, 1943, RA UD Hp 21 Ad 1056/1. Engzell advised von Dardel already to start a card file listing the people seeking assistance!

33. These documents are all located in RA UD Hp 21 Ad 1056/1.

34. Von Dardel to Engzell, #103, September 6, 1943, RA UD Hp 21 Ad 1056/1.

35. Engzell sent Josephson a detailed summary of von Dardel's report on September 10, 1943. RA UD Hp 21 Ad 1056/1.

36. W. Bostrom to UD, #726, September 9, 1943, RA UD Hp 21 Ad 1056/1.

37. Cabinet to UD, #618, September 13, 1943, RA UD Hp 21 Ad 1065/1.

38. Von Dardel to UD, #21, October 2, 1943, RA UD Hp 21 Ad 1056/11. The next day Engzell forwarded this wording to the Legation in Berlin, acidly adding that "it is impossible for children to do this." Cabinet to Legation Berlin, #71, October 3, 1943, Hp 21 Ad 1056/11.

39. Von Dardel to UD, #22, October 2, 1943, RA UD Hp 21 Ad 1056/11.

40. Von Dardel to Engzell, #161, October 1, 1943; and PM by M. Hallenborg, October 2, 1943, both RA UD Hp 21 Ad 1056/11.

41. Gösta Bagge's *Minnesanteckningar*, October 2, 1943, 950 RA.

42. Söderblom to Richert, #1496, October 2, 1943, RA UD Hp 21 Ad 1056/11.

43. *Göteborgs Handels- och Sjöfarts Tidning*, October 2, 1943.

44. *Stockholms-Tidningen*, October 3, 1943.

45. Söderblom to von Dardel, #502, October 4, 1943, RA UD Hp 21 Ad 1056/11.

46. PM "concerning assistance to Danish Jews," October 4, 1943, RA UD Hp 21 Ad 1056/11.

47. See RA UD Hp 21 Ad 1056/III, *passim*, and Hp 21 Ad 1057/IV, V, & VI.

48. American Representation of General Jewish Workers Union of Poland to Per Albin Hansson, October 5, 1943, RA UD Hp 21 Ad 1056/HI.

49. Legation Washington to UD, #795, October 4, 1943, RA UD Hp 21 Ad 1056/11.

50. Richert to Engzell, #70, October 6, 1943, RA UD Hp 21 Ad 1056/111.

51. *Göteborgs Handels- och Sjöfarts Tidning*, October 4, 1943.

52. *Dagsposten* editorial, October 6, 1943, located in RA UD Hp 21 Ad 1056/111.

53. Telegram from Wise sent to M. Ehrenpreis for delivery to UD. RA UD Hp 21 Ad 1057/V.

54. Danielsson to UD, #28, March 23, 1944, RA UD Hp 1 Eu 582/XXI.

55. Danielsson to Gunther, #58, March 21, 1944, RA UD Hp 1 Eu 582/XXI.

56. Dr. Edmund Veesenmayer played a critical role in conducting the Final Solution in Hungary, and represented both the SS and *Auswärtiges Amt* while there. He visited the Hungarian capital late in 1943 and reported to Hitler that Hungary had fallen behind treating its Jews as the Germans had done and that the situation must be rectified. On Veesenmayer in Hungary, see RLB [Randolph L. Braham], both volumes, *passim*, and R. Hilberg, *op. cit.*, vol. 2, 820–60.

57. Danielsson to Günther, # 58, March 21, 1944, *op.cit.*

58. On the use of passports and their significance, see M. Marrus, *The Unwanted; European Refugees in the Twentieth Century* (New York, 1985), 92–94.

59. *RLB*, vol. 2, 1083–84.

60. See ibid., 1054–95.

61. *PM* #6, May 4, 1944, RA UD Hp 21 Eu 1095/V.

62. Danielsson to UD, #118, May 8, 1944, RA UD Hp 21 Eu 1094/III.

63. *PM*, #8, May 17, 1944, RA UD Hp 21 Eu 1095/IV.

64. Per Anger recalled that discussions with German officials often ended with suggestions to take up the mailer with Hungarian officials. Both were trying to maintain a facade of sovereignty for the Hungarians. Author's interview with Per Anger, *op.cit.*

65. *PM* #8, May 17, 1944, RA UD Hp 21 Eu 1095/IV.

66. Danielsson to Günther, #115, May 26, 1944, RA UD Hp 21 Eu 1095/IV.

67. Grafström to American Embassy, June 13, 1944, RA UD Hp 21 Eu 1095/IV.

68. Danielsson to UD, May 16, 1944, RA UD Hp 21 Eu 1095/IV.

69. Danielsson to UD, #157, June 2, 1944, RA UD Hp 21 Eu 1095/V.

70. See, for instance, Engzell to Danielsson, #352, June 2, 1944; De Geer to André Leicht, June 6, 1944; De Geer to unknown, June 16, 1944; Engzell to Dr. Lajos Székely, #1415, June 8, 1944. All located in RA UD Hp 21 Eu 1095/V.

71. Cabinet to Legation Budapest, #150, June 6, 1944, RA UD Hp 21 Eu 1095/V. Of course everyone in Europe had awoken that day to news of the Normandy invasion.

72. Danielsson to UD, #170, June 14, 1944, RA UD Hp 21 Eu 1095/V.

73. Cabinet to Legation Budapest, #165, June 15, 1944, RA UD Hp 21 Eu 1095/V.

74. Danielsson to Günther, #121, June 20, 1944, RA UD Hp 21 Eu 1095/V.

75. Ehrenpreis to UD, June 29, 1944, RA UD Hp 21 Eu 1095/V.

76. Grafström to T. af Klercker, #181/3072, June 29, 1944, RA UD Hp 21 Eu 1095/V.

77. RA UD Hp 21 Eu 1095/VI.

78. Anger to Günther, #143, July 3, 1944, RA UD Hp 1/21 Eu 1095/VI. Jeno Levai's 1948 book about Raoul Wallenberg mistakenly says that Gustav's message was delivered on July 1; see Raoul Wallenberg; *Hjalten i Budapest* (Stockholm, 1948), 41. This mistake has been since repeated by many historians. See RLB, vol. 2, 714, and 730, n. 91.

79. Telegram of July 5, 1944, from G. A. Wechsler, National Secretary, Emergency Committee to Save Jewish People of Europe, to W. F. Bostrom, Swedish Minister in Washington. RA UD Hp 21 Eu 1095/VI. Randolph Braham is incorrect to write that the King's plea "was forwarded as secret diplomatic message without any public-

ity." See *RLB*, vol. 2, 715. At the bottom of the original telegram to Budapest we see the following "Telegraph when message delivered, publicizing here will take place." Moreover, on July 3 UD officials sent a copy to Rabbi Ehrenpreis asking him to publicize its contents as soon as Budapest reported the message delivered. Grafström to Ehrenpreis, July 1944. Finally, on July 4 Grafström sent the telegram to all important Swedish news outlets, including the Swedish-American News Bureau. RA UD Hp 21 Eu 1095/VI.

80. Danielsson to UD, #192, June 23, 1944, RA UD Hp 21 Eu 1095/V.

81. Danielsson to Günther, #127, June 24, 1944, RA UD Hp 1/21 Eu 1095/V.

82. Danielsson to Günther, #131, June 30, 1944, RA UD Hp 1 Eu 583/XXII. This report arrived in Stockholm on July 19.

83. Engzell to Danielsson, #6, July 5, 1944, RA UD Hp 21 Eu 1095/VI.

84. Anger to Engzell, #15, July 5, 1944; and Anger to Günther, #149, July 5, 1944. Both RA UD Hp 21 Eu 1095/VI.

85. *RLB*, vol. 2, 762–63.

86. Anger to UD, #211, July 3, 1944, RA UD Hp 21 Eu 1095/VI. Anger categorized the approximately 450 as having sufficiently strong connection to Sweden to be on a list given to Hungarian authorities. 186 had provisional passports and about 260 had Swedish entry visas stamped on some document.

87. Any accurate estimation of the actual numbers rescued and or assisted directly or indirectly by Swedish diplomats in Budapest requires considerable study from a wide variety of sources. . . . What is clear, however, is that the number of 100,000 people saved by Roul Wallenberg, is a considerable exaggeration. As with other questions regarding this important figure, a considered revision—which will be downward—of the number of humans actually saved by him will do nothing to diminish his heroism.

9 Aftermath

18. Young mothers take their babies for a stroll in the Landsberg DP (Displaced Persons) camp, ca. 1948. Dorit Mandelbaum, in the baby carriage on the left, is being pushed by her mother, Anka. Anka and her family were forced into the Warsaw ghetto in 1940. Jakub Mandelbaum went to the ghetto to persuade his future wife, Anka, to flee. In 1941 Anka escaped, only to be arrested and imprisoned. She managed to jump out of a bathroom window and flee. On the last leg of the long walk to Jakub's hometown of Kozienice, Anka met an elderly Pole who pretended to be her father and helped her to board a boat crossing the Vistula River to Kozienice. Soon after her arrival, Anka and Jakub married. From 1942 until the end of 1944 Jakub was transferred from one forced labor camp to another. Finally, in January 1945 he was transferred to the Mauthausen concentration camp where he was in a *Strafkommando* (punishment commando). On May 5, 1945, the American army liberated the camp, and Jakub Mandelbaum rushed back to Kozienice to search for his family. Anka Mandelbaum had been deported from the Kozienice ghetto to Auschwitz-Birkenau. She was liberated in January 1945. After the war, Jakub and Anka Mandelbaum left Poland for Germany. They spent five years in the Landsberg-am-Lech DP camp, where their only daughter, Dorit, was born on June 2, 1946. (U.S. Holocaust Memorial Museum, courtesy of Dorit Mandelbaum.)

19. Varian Fry, Marseilles, France, August 1940. In June 1940 Varian Fry, an American journalist, volunteered to travel from New York to Marseilles as a representative of the Emergency Rescue Committee, a newly formed relief organization. The U.S. government agreed to provide entry visas to two hundred refugees in France—prominent political leaders, scientists, artists, and writers. Fry's task was to help them get out. He arrived in Marseilles in August 1940 with a list of names and $3,000. Fry was shocked to learn that thousands of refugees were unable to leave due to bureaucratic hurdles that stood in the way. He felt a responsibility to help as many people as possible. He and his accomplices used black-market funds to forge passports and to smuggle refugees out of France. His three-week mission turned into a thirteen-month stay. Both the French authorities and the American consulate in Vichy condemned Fry's efforts. He was detained and questioned on more than one occasion. Among those he saved were artists Marc Chagall and Jacques Lipshitz, writers Lion Feuchtwanger, Heinrich Mann, and Franz Werfel, and philosopher Hannah Arendt. Varian Fry was the first American recognized by Yad Vashem as a Righteous Among the Nations. (U.S. Holocaust Memorial Museum, courtesy of Annette Fry.)

Introduction

PETER HAYES

The Holocaust did not end along with World War II in Europe when the Germans surrendered at Reims and Berlin on May 7–8, 1945. Debilitated camp inmates continued to die for months, some 14,000 at Belsen alone in the weeks following its liberation. The aftereffects on the living were often severe as well. Diverse in their experiences of Nazism—the survivors consisted of camp veterans, people who had gone underground or been hidden across Nazi controlled Europe, others who had fled before the German armies in the East and now returned to their former homes in Poland and Lithuania, and, above all, Jews who the Germans had been prevented from seizing, most of them in the arc of countries that extended south and east from Belgium through France, Italy, Hungary, Bulgaria, and Romania— nearly all of these remnant Jews soon had a common bond. Everywhere, with the partial exception of Western Europe (including Italy), they swiftly found that their continued presence was unwelcome to the surrounding populations. Often subjected to verbal and physical abuse, thousands of now twice-persecuted Jews streamed in 1945–46 into Germany, of all places, primarily into the displaced persons camps established in the American occupation zone, where their hosts learned only gradually how best to cope with the influx and what to do with it.

The first three selections in this chapter detail the frequently difficult postwar experiences of survivors, many of which stemmed from the inability or reluctance of their contemporaries to comprehend the distinctness of what the Nazis had done to Jews. Thus, Mark Wyman's portrait of *survivors* in 1945–49 exposes how unprepared Allied military personnel were for the condition and situation of Jews in postwar Europe, how gradually Allied policy improved, and how in the meantime increasingly large proportions of those survivors set their sights on Palestine as a new home. One should add to Wyman's account the comment that even the architects of the Allies' postwar war crimes trials generally treated Nazi antisemitism as a secondary consequence of the regime's greatest crime (aggression) and homogenized Nazism's victims, blending Jewish suffering at Nazi hands into everyone else's. Such a mindset facilitated, along with the freezing of the cold war, the integration of West Germany into the NATO alliance and the non-prosecution or pardoning of numerous former killers during the postwar decades (though the record was not as bad as is sometimes said; worth remembering in this connection are two statistical facts: every one of the 16 men who ever commanded a death camp was either dead by 1945 or caught and punished afterward; the same is true of every one of the 14 men who ever commanded an *Einsatzgruppe*).

Something similar to the Allied prosecutors' mixture of evasion and embarrassment in the face of the Holocaust is apparent in the next two reading selections, Tom Segev's recounting of *Zion's ambivalence* toward the refugees who reached Palestine, and Beth Cohen's portrait of *America's incomprehension* of the emotional states of many survivors who came to the United States. In both instances, though for different reasons, the receiving communities demanded, often in insensitive fashion, rapid adjustment to new conditions and behavioral expectations and generally turned a deaf ear to survivors' need to talk about their losses. If the results of relocation included many successfully rebuilt and productive existences, these were not the only outcomes, nor were even they achieved easily.

Whereas the first two postwar decades were times of blurring, in which the Holocaust did not stand out in popular or for the most part academic memory from the carnage of World War II, *the great reversal* in this optic, as Tony Judt shows in his examination of European perceptions, began in the 1970s and has continued steadily ever since. As in the United States, the transition "from repression to obsession" (Jeremy Adler) occurred because of the accumulation of cultural productions devoted to the subject, e.g., films, documentaries, and popular dramas; the increasing identification with Israel and its perceived vulnerability on the part of Jews worldwide in the aftermath of the Six Day War; and the rising valuation of toleration and "diversity" brought on by the movements for civil, gay, and women's rights and the progress of European integration. Indeed, Judt makes a strong case for the proposition that the prerequisite for participation in that integration has become a nation's "recognition" of the Holocaust, i.e., confrontation with its citizens' role in it.

With success came the resurgence of old enemies in new guises. Richard Evans provides a devastating case study of not only the deceitful methods, but also the antisemitic motives that characterize the *pathology of denial* that the Holocaust occurred. As an expert witness against David Irving's claim that Deborah Lipstadt had committed libel by calling him a Holocaust denier, Evans meticulously exposed the calculated dishonesty behind Irving's assertions that Jews were not murdered en masse during World War II and certainly not by gas. In the end, the presiding judge concluded that Irving had been shown to be "anti-semitic [and] a right-wing pro-Nazi polemicist." Demonstrated in Irving's case, hostility to Jews is the only conceivable driving motive for the tortured reasoning and sheer mendacity in which he and other deniers of one of the most thoroughly documented events in history engage.

Success also came during the 1990s at the price of some collateral damage, and in this respect courts played a less salutary role. The excerpt by Michael Marrus on *restitution and its discontents* maps both the achievements and the downsides of the most recent and materially rewarding phase of the quest for justice for survivors. The subject is the quest in American courts to obtain payments to Holocaust survivors and/or their heirs from Swiss commercial banks that allegedly had pocketed the unclaimed accounts of victims of the Holocaust; from Swiss, German, and Italian life insurance companies thought to have done the like with victims' policies; and from German enterprises that had employed forced (i.e., generally compulsory foreign) and slave (i.e., camp inmate) laborers. Marrus shows that the resulting multibillion-dollar settlements, while not unwarranted, amounted to very rough and imperfect justice and left behind a trail of legal briefs that significantly distorted the historical record regarding such matters as the autonomy of business in the Third Reich and the profitability of corporate involvement in Holocaust-related crimes.

Finally, Eva Hoffman explores what humanity has learned *after such knowledge* of the Holocaust as this book presents. She contrasts the simple with the subtle lessons taught by the atrocities and suggests in elegiac fashion that in the twenty-first century the time for emotional responses to the subject is giving way to an era of informed reflection upon it, the stage of mourning to an age of moral inspiration.

Survivors

MARK WYMAN

From DPs: Europe's Displaced Persons, 1945–51

Trains were passing in the night across Eastern Europe in the spring and summer of 1946, carrying human cargoes with vastly different expectations. Rolling eastward from the zones of Germany were thousands of repatriated Poles, their trains decorated with leafy branches and Polish flags, their patriotic songs rising above the rumble of the cars as they moved toward repatriation.

But other trains were going toward the West. These carried Polish Jews, traveling across the continent to Germany and Austria in both legal and illegal journeys. These passengers sang, too, but instead of the Polish national hymn and Polish marching airs they chorused a joyful "Pioneers Prepare Themselves for Palestine." Their train cars were not decorated with Polish flags. An American journalist, I. F. Stone, rode with one Jewish group across Czechoslovakia and noted that sometimes an eastbound and a westbound train were stopped at the same time in a station, and Polish Jews and Polish Catholics got out on opposite sides of the platform to stretch their legs. There was no mixing, Stone reported, "no one shouted across the platform from one train to the other. Their mutual misery created no common bond between peoples who regarded each other as oppressors and oppressed. The hate and fear that flowed between us was almost tangible, like a thick current in the hot summer night."[1]

There was a momentous story in this. Groups were choosing their futures: thousands thought, pondered, discussed, and made decisions that would direct the flow of their people for generations.

For many Jews, that decision came easily. Europe had become the graveyard of their people, its major monuments not the Eiffel Tower and Saint Peter's but the Nazi death camps where humans were turned into objects and plundered for their labor, gold fillings, hair. A newly arrived American serving with the UNRRA landed in Munich in July 1945 and made his way to nearby Dachau, one of the most infamous of the concentration camps. It had not yet been made presentable for tourists, and he could still see human ashes before the crematorium, fingernail scratches running down the gas chamber walls. The very silence shrieked.[2] . . . But some European Jews managed to elude the Nazis, hiding with gentile friends or in forests or melting unnoticed into the population; the earliest postwar surveys found 20,000 Jews left in Germany and 7,000 in Austria, with 80,000 surviving inside Poland (over 130,000 others had fled into Russia), 90,000 in Hungary, 100,000 in Romania.[3] . . .

The impact of this Holocaust, as it eventually came to be known, was felt and continues to be felt in many areas of the world, on many activities and institutions. But in 1945 its impact was felt most severely by the *She'erit Ha-pletah*—the spared or surviving remnant of European Jews.

Like the tattoos that large numbers of Jews carried on their arms, . . . many of the psychological scars could also be observed readily. The *katzetler* or *katzetnik* (concentration camp veterans) broke into tears easily, fell apart at a knock at the door, froze when a black limousine stopped nearby. Some refused to enter ambulances being used to transfer ailing Belsen inmates to the ship for Sweden, because they remembered that the Nazis had used such vehicles, complete with Red Cross emblems, to carry Jews away to the gas chambers. And some would cry out in nightmares, shrieking "*Deutschen!*" They dwelt on the past, reliving it in their conversations again and again. Having seen small incidents of hatred in the 1930s lead to catastrophe in the Third Reich, they now became extremely sensitive to any hint of antisemitism, generalizing from and exaggerating any such report.[4]

Many Jewish DPs lacked the capacity for anything sustained, as evidenced in their early responses in the DP camps. "They become fatigued after a few hours work," one American worker reported. A newspaper correspondent in Austria encountered Jews resisting efforts by the American Jewish Joint Distribution Committee (the "Joint") to begin work projects. Some of the camp's DP tailors said they could make more money on their own, while "the rest of the people are too tired and indifferent to bother," the correspondent observed.[5]

One of the continuing effects of the war on Jewish DPs centered on their loss of close relatives. Receiving a tiny bit of evidence that a family member was still alive, they would travel hundreds of miles to track it down, usually returning only with additional details on the final hours of their loved one. Some fantasized against all evidence that one of the family had somehow survived, was still alive, waiting perhaps in another country overseas; they would meet someday. Continually frustrated in their search, they developed a fear of loving anyone, afraid they would lose that person and suffer again. Many developed guilt over having survived. An American traveling with a mixed group of Jewish and Christian DP children found that the Jews put "great importance on kinship; they valued a family tie, however distant."[6]

Outsiders had problems dealing with such people, for cynicism and suspicion were everywhere. Jewish DPs were often hostile, forcing some psychiatrists to give up their efforts in the camps because of a lack of rapport. A British DP official was flabbergasted at the refusal of a group of Jews to move into more commodious huts, but a Jewish writer later saw in the incident the problem of the "concentration camp psychology, which was ridden with inferiority complexes and resulting aggressiveness." Many Jewish DPs simply rejected the right of non-Jews to tell them what to do any longer.[7]

Placing the Jews of the *She'erit Ha-pletah* in the decrepit conditions of the first improvised DP camps created a volatile mixture. One problem lay with the victorious armies. Having just fought a war against an enemy who persecuted individuals according to their religion, the Allies were not willing to resort to such classifications in dealing with the refugees. A British official cautioned in 1944 that just because Jews could be "identified by certain characteristics," and because Nazi policies had inserted the Jewish question into world politics, there were still "not sufficient reasons for treating 'Jews' as a separate national category." As a result, Jews who struggled out of the concentration camps initially found themselves classified as "enemy nationals" if they originated in Germany, Austria, or other Axis nations; in some DP camps they were placed among their former Nazi guards and tormentors. General Eisenhower asserted in early August 1945 that his headquarters "makes no differentiation in treatment of displaced persons."[8]

Differentiation, however, became the goal of Jewish agency workers and DP spokesmen. The basis of their claim was that Jews had been singled out as Jews by the Nazis. "The fact was that we had not faced the Auschwitz crematoriums as Poles, Lithuanians, or Germans," one Auschwitz survivor stressed. "It was as Jews that we had become victims of the greatest catastrophe of our people." . . .

The refugee president of the Landsberg DP camp, Samuel Gringauz, noted that the Nazis' targeting of Jews had produced a sort of Jewish universalism not present before, under which Jews who formerly felt distinct from other Jews now felt one with them. He drew on his own concentration camp experiences:

A Jewish tailor from Rhodes who could find no one in the camp to understand him, and a Hungarian druggist baptized thirty years before, lay in the same wooden bunk with me, shared their experience as Jews with me, and died only because they were Jewish. That is why the *She'erit Ha-pletah* feels itself to be the embodiment of the unity of Jewish experience.[9]

Conditions of Jews in the camps soon caught the eyes of journalists, Western officials, and Jewish spokesmen. As early as July 21, 1945, the World Jewish Congress appealed to the Allied leaders meeting at Potsdam to release the former concentration camp inmates from "conditions of the most abject misery." The WJC charged that Jews at the Lingen DP camp were housed in "indescribably filthy" structures, with inadequate medical and other supplies and personnel. Worse, the Congress found that in some cases ex-Nazis had been placed in charge of their former victims and were "treating them with neglect and contempt."

The *Jewish Chronicle*, a London newspaper, compared American troops with Hitler's SS in reporting an incident in which Jewish DPs were driven from their huts by General Patton's Third Army. DP protests against this rough handling drew the response from the soldiers that "this was the only way to deal with Jews."[10]

These stories reached Washington. President Harry S. Truman, only recently installed in office, soon wrote to the dean of the University of Pennsylvania Law School and asked him to investigate conditions in Europe, especially the situation of the Jewish displaced persons. The dean was Earl G. Harrison, who had been serving as American representative on the Inter-Governmental Committee on Refugees. After making contact with Jewish representatives in Europe, Harrison left the itinerary laid out by the army and probed into situations that, it seems likely, the military would have avoided. An inhabitant at the Belsen DP camp remembered Harrison visiting them, chain-smoking as tears streamed down his face. "He was so shaken he could not speak," the Belsen man recalled. "Finally, he whispered weakly: 'But how did you survive, and where do you take your strength from now?'"[11]

Harrison's report to Truman in early August 1945 was devastating. "As matters now stand, we appear to be treating the Jews as the Nazis treated them except that we do not exterminate them," he wrote. Harrison referred to the DP camps holding Jews as "concentration camps," where they wore the "rather hideous striped pajama" they had worn earlier when controlled by the Nazis (some were forced to wear leftover German SS uniforms) and existed on rations composed principally of bread and coffee, all the while guarded closely by American soldiers. Meanwhile, they could look not far off and see German civilians, "to all appearances living normal lives in their own homes."

Harrison's report, as might be expected, called for a vast improvement in food, clothing, and housing for the Jewish DPs. But he went beyond this to urge two sharp shifts in policy:

> The first and plainest need of these people is a recognition of their actual status and by this I mean their status of Jews. . . . While admittedly it is not normally desirable to set aside particular racial or religious groups from their nationality categories, the plain truth is that this was done for so long by the Nazis that a group has been created which has special needs. Jews as Jews (not as members of their nationality groups) have been more severely victimized than the non-Jewish members of the same or other nationalities.

This meant segregated DP camps for Jews, he stressed, with their own representatives to deal with the military authorities.

Harrison's second major proposal was for immediate help for Jews to leave Germany and Austria—through emigration to the United States and other countries if possible, but mainly through opening the doors into British-controlled Palestine. The Palestine issue "must be faced," he wrote. "For some of the European Jews, there is no acceptable or even decent solution for their future other than Palestine." The main solution lay, he stressed, "in the quick evacuation of all nonrepatriable Jews in Germany and Austria, who wish it, to Palestine."[12]

President Truman responded quickly to Harrison's report. He pressured General Eisenhower to improve conditions in the DP camps and sent a copy of the Harrison document to British Prime Minister Clement Attlee with the recommendation that British-controlled Palestine be opened for Jewish settlement. Truman commented later that year that the issue had stimulated the greatest volume of mail in the history of the White House.[13]

Eisenhower was stung by Harrison's findings. The general made his own inspection, then responded somewhat defensively and emphasized the army's enormous problems in Europe in the aftermath of the war. But he went on to authorize the creation of special Jewish DP centers, the selection of camp guards from among the DPs themselves, and an increase in the daily minimum caloric level to twenty-five hundred for "racial, religious and political persecutees." He also appointed a Jewish adviser and a Jewish liaison officer. In mid-November the British Zone finally permitted segregation of Jews within DP camps, although the new policy stated that "special camps exclusively for Jews will not be established."[14]

As a result of these changes, by early January 1946 the British Zone of Germany had one major heavily Jewish camp at Höhne (near the site of Belsen concentration camp) with 9,000 Jews, while the American Zone had twelve camps that were entirely Jewish, led by Landsberg and Wolfratshausen with more than 5,000 each, and Feldafing with 3,700. In the French Zone more than three-fourths of the Jews lived in households taken from the Germans; no segregation was authorized. The Jewish camps soon were electing their own spokesmen, aided by the formation in July 1945 of the Central Committee of Liberated Jews, an umbrella leadership group for Jews in the western zones.[15]

These new Jewish spokesmen found the occupation authorities in Germany and Austria generally cooperative from late 1945 on. Gen. Mark Clark, head of the U.S. occupation forces in Austria, instructed his assistants in October 1945 that Truman's orders were to be carried out "not only because they were orders" but because Clark believed the Jews' treatment during the war made them "entitled to first consideration." Jewish writers later referred to the months from late

1945 to mid-1947 as the "humanitarian period" of Occupation-Jewish relations. And in the meantime the Jewish DP camps emerged as the new centers of European Jewry, speaking for Jews, settling disputes, offering practical help and spiritual guidance. Remnants of the traditional Jewish centers in Hamburg, Lübeck, Bremen, and Düsseldorf now turned to the camps for leadership.[16]

The environment of the Jewish DPs began to change in other ways as well. The new political environment—perhaps philosophical environment is more accurate—flowed from two major developments, only slightly evident in the summer of 1945 but more apparent with each passing day: (1) a sharp upsurge in support for Zionism, the movement to reestablish Judaism's base in its ancient home of Palestine (Israel), and (2) the continuance and even the increase of virulent antisemitism in Poland and other areas of Eastern Europe.

These two changes in turn affected each other, and were essential ingredients in the growing international debate over the Palestine question. The DP issue, already frustrating to occupying powers and host nations, now took on new complexity.

Zionism's growth came from several factors. It was paradoxical that rising support for a Jewish homeland was accompanied by little or no increase in religiosity among the Jewish remnant—in fact, some argued that religious practice had declined from the thirties, because Orthodox Jews had been more noticeable and for that reason were more readily eliminated by the Nazis. But this new Zionism was not a religious movement: it drew strength from traditional Jewish beliefs, but only because they were given new relevance by events of the Hitler era. Koppel Pinson of "Joint," after working for a year among Jewish DPs, argued that Zionists "were the only ones that had a pro-

gram that seemed to make sense after this catastrophe." The Palestine return became so identified with salvation for Europe's Jews, he emphasized, that "emotionally and psychologically as well as in a real physical sense it became dangerous to think outside this complex."[17]

This was because each week after V-E Day seemed to bring forth new evidence of the degradation and extermination of Europe's Jews during the war. And already whispers were heard of the probability of another war, between Americans and Russians, or even between Americans and the rumored underground Nazi movement. What would be the fate of the Jews then?

The head of the Landsberg DP camp's Jews, Dr. Samuel Gringauz, presented the argument for Jewish pessimism in the camp newspaper:

> We do not believe in progress, we do not believe in the 2,000-year-old Christian culture of the West, the culture that, *for them*, created the Statue of Liberty in New York and Westminster Abbey on the Thames, the wonder gardens of Versailles and the Uffizi and Pitti palaces in Florence, the Strasbourg *Münster* and the Cologne cathedral; but *for us*, the slaughters of the Crusades, the Spanish Inquisition, the blood bath of Khmielnicki, the pogroms of Russia, the gas chambers of Auschwitz, and the massacres of entire Europe.

I. F. Stone encountered older Jews who put it more simply, as they told of their desire to go to Palestine despite not considering themselves Zionists: "I'm a Jew. That's enough. We have wandered enough. We have worked and struggled too long on the lands of other peoples. We must build a land of our own."[18]

In the recorded comments and letters of such people, and in reminiscences of Jews moving through the postwar period, the idea appears repeatedly that Palestine represented *home*. Virtually none had ever been there, but a return—*Aliyah*—to the land of Israel was a foundation block of their faith, repeated each year during Passover Seder prayers: "Next year in Jerusalem." Perhaps this image meant little in earlier years; it is not unusual for ritual to lose significance. But now, with all that had once meant home mixed with the dust, eliminated, destroyed, the thought came forward again. They still had a home. Children traveling on a cold train en route to a French port, to board a Haifa-bound ship, explained to concerned UNRRA workers, "Hardships? It is worth them all. We are going home."[19]

The symbol of Palestine the home also became a positive affirmation of Jewish existence. It was a way to finally show the world the Nazis had failed. Everything—even personal comfort—had to be sacrificed for Palestine. Plans to remove Jewish orphans to better conditions in Jewish homes in England were blocked by the Jewish Central Committee of the British Zone, which resolved that the children "who were with us in the Ghettos and concentration camps . . . must stay where they are until their Aliyah." The committee demanded that the first allocations for Palestine go to the children. At the same time in late 1945, delegates broke into tears as a Rome conference of Polish Jews voted for a ringing declaration to proceed "by all ways and means" to Palestine, despite British opposition. It was their last hope for survival, the delegates asserted, and they would go "because they owed such action to the 5,000,000 or more Jews of Europe exterminated by Nazism." UNRRA staff workers, trying to compile statistics on this phenomenon, distributed a questionnaire among 19,000 Jewish DPs and found that 18,700 listed "Palestine" as their first choice for emigration, but then 98 percent also wrote "Palestine" as their second choice. At the Fürth DP camp near Nürnberg,

however, alert staff members told the DPs not to repeat "Palestine" for second choice, but to write another preference for emigration. One-fourth then wrote in "crematorium."[20]

An important difference in this new Zionism was that it temporarily overwhelmed divisions that had been rife among European Jews, divisions that earlier had left them almost incompetent to meet the challenges of the Hitler era. Earlier generations of Jews had debated extensively over Zionism—whether Jews should dream of resettlement at all, and even where their Land of Zion should be. At various times, Texas, Uganda, and the Argentine had been proposed, as well as Palestine. Britain's Balfour Declaration in 1917, supporting a Jewish national home in Palestine, stimulated the Zionists, although some sought only a federal arrangement with Arabs. Even in wartime, in the face of Nazi attacks, the different groups within Judaism had trouble working together; the antagonists included socialist bundists versus Zionists, Zionists versus assimilationists, the Orthodox versus the nonobservant, radicals versus capitalists, and socialists versus Communists. These and other divisions made a farce of the Third Reich's assertion that Jews represented a powerful conspiratorial group controlling vast areas of European life. In fact, no overall organization existed among the Jews of Europe, not even an information chain that might have kept them abreast of dangers.

That long-sought unity would appear only in 1945, and even then some outsiders might have missed it because of the multiplicity of political parties and organizations visible in the camps. The Belsen DP camp soon had elections fought out by General Zionists and Revisionists, as well as members of *Hashomer Hatzair, Mapai, Mizrachi, Aguda,* and *Poale Zion.* Several groups within the camp ran their own schools; most had their own newspapers. One participant called the Belsen DP camp not only a Jewish community but "an intense Zionist community. . . . I felt there as if I was back in my Lithuanian home town." But despite their differences these groups cooperated, he stressed. "It was based on a genuine compromise and an appreciation that, in the first place, they were all Zionists."[21]

The second major change in the Jewish DPs' environment arose out of events in the newly liberated areas of Eastern Europe. Release from concentration camps or forced labor was usually followed by a frantic search for family members, but for those Jews who returned to their homes in Eastern Europe the search was usually doubly numbing: not only were they unable to locate their kin, but former neighbors often turned upon them with a bitter antisemitism that recalled the recent days of Hitler's reign.

David Lubetkin's story will perhaps speak for thousands.[22] David Lubetkin (not his real name) was liberated in Buchenwald near the end of the war, and a few weeks later, while scanning the names posted on a military bulletin board, he saw his two sisters listed as survivors in the concentration camp at Bergen-Belsen. Soon David and a friend headed off on bicycles to link up with their kin. The next step was to return to Poland, to learn whether others of the family had survived. If three Lubetkins had made it through the war, why not more? David had high hopes for reuniting the entire family—parents and six children—who had been seized and sent away on September 13, 1939, after Germans overran their village. The Russians also wanted David to go home. After taking over the Buchenwald area in midsummer of 1945, when zonal boundaries were redrawn, Soviet officials encouraged all Poles to go back to rebuild their homeland. "Trains are prepared," they announced in the Buchenwald area. "Those

who will not go on train, will have to go on foot." There was no other option.

And so David and his sisters boarded an eastward-bound train, heavily loaded with Buchenwald veterans who traveled with both expectation and apprehension. "It was not a joyful, singing trip," he said. Soon he joined with others, forming a group of eleven Jews from the same Polish town. At the German-Polish border they had to leave the train and wait a day for another to carry them into Poland. While the eleven prepared their night's shelter, however, a Polish border guard— Jewish, it turned out—talked privately with them. He showed some surprise at their return: "Why did you come back to hell? I'm looking to get away from hell." That set them thinking. But they continued on, and two days later David and his friends received another jolt as they disembarked onto the railway platform in their hometown in central Poland. A local policeman, whom they had known before the war as the son of the village ice cream vendor, greeted them: "So many of you lived through the war? Why didn't they get you all?"

It was an ominous welcome. In one respect it should not have been surprising, however, for their village had been torn in the 1930s with antisemitic agitation. Warnings had been stenciled repeatedly on Jewish-owned shops: "*Swoj do Swego*" (Stay with your own) and "*Zyd twoj wrog*" (Jews are your enemies), among other slogans. Despite this history of anti-Jewish activity the returning Jews were taken aback. "I expected they would have learned something from the war," David said. "I expected them to have changed in their thinking and ideas by then, due to the suffering they themselves had experienced." But such was not the case. And so the few Jews making their way back to the village clustered together, sharing food and shelter and fears, welcoming the

Jews starting to trickle in from the Soviet Union as well as the continuing arrivals from liberated Germany. Meanwhile, local antisemitism worsened as Polish nationalism flowered.

By November 1945, David, at his sisters' urging, decided it was time to get out. He and a cousin—the only surviving kinsman they had found—realized they had an advantage in their escape: they looked Polish. On the first leg of their train trip they sat next to a pretty gentile girl and listened respectfully to her diatribes against Jews. It was a fortunate deception. On that day-long ride to Poznan they saw four Jewish passengers thrown out of windows while the train lumbered on, victims of roving bands of ultranationalistic *Armia Krajowa*.

The two cousins had chosen Poznan as their first destination because they knew trains left from there for Berlin. As luck would have it, a Soviet train carrying goods from Moscow to Berlin was then in the station, and by pooling their cash they bought two bottles of whiskey and several sausages, adequate to bribe a Russian soldier to allow them on board. Better than merely boarding, they were hidden in a baggage car filled with office furniture, which was not opened until the train entered Berlin. [There] they made their way to the Zehlendorf transit camp in the United States sector, producing concentration camp release documents to prove they were Jewish. Later they were taken into western Germany, ending up at the Feldafing DP camp in early December 1945. Their next task was to plot the escape of David's sisters.

The experiences of David Lubetkin were repeated over and over across Eastern Europe in the first months after the war. Thousands of Jews returned home, including some 130,000 who had spent the war years in the Soviet Union. But they discovered that the defeat of the Third Reich was not the defeat of anti-Jewish feeling. Reborn anti-

semitism became so widespread that the new Polish regime finally ordered that attacks on Jews were to be punishable by death or life imprisonment.[23] . . .

Only two factors in 1945 were new amid this antisemitism. Many Poles had acquired property (buildings, jewelry, clothing) that Nazis had seized from Jews in 1939–40; now they feared it would be taken away and returned to the prewar Jewish owners. In fact, such returns were being authorized by the new Communist regime. Also, stories were circulating that Jews had helped the Soviet Union in its ultimately successful efforts to take over eastern Poland and were now helping the Soviet-imposed regime.[24]

The latter argument appears to have been widely believed. General Wladyslaw Anders stated in his memoir of the war that when the Russians invaded in 1939, "a number of Polish Jews, especially the young ones, who had made no secret of their joy at the entry of Soviet troops, began to cooperate" with Soviet officials. A book on Poland published in London after the war, *The Dark Side of the Moon*, noted the Soviets' inability to enlist Polish minorities in their cause. This was especially surprising in the case of the Jews, the anonymous author stated, for "nobody in Poland, they say, welcomed the Red Army in the same way as the Jews." (Thirty-five years and thousands of miles away, a Polish ex-DP thought back on those years and remembered that he had been told in the DP camps that when the Russians invaded in 1939, the Jews sided with them. "People resented that," he said.) In addition, several Jews were leading officials in the postwar Communist regime in Warsaw.[25]

There was no time to investigate and refute such charges amid the heated nationalism of 1945 and 1946. Attacks on Jews began even before the Germans were defeated. In the spring of 1945 a right-wing Polish group proclaimed it a sign of patriotism to kill Jews. A Polish government report stated that 351 Jews were murdered in Poland between November 1944 and October 1945, with anti-Jewish riots occurring during 1945 at Cracow on August 20, in Sosnowiec on October 25, and in Lublin on November 19. But none held the terror of the incident at Kielce.[26]

It occurred in July 1946, when a Christian boy in the city some 120 miles south of Warsaw returned after a three-day absence with tales of a blood ritual. Jews had kidnapped him, he said, and took him into a cellar where he watched as fifteen other Christian children were murdered. As the story spread some five thousand protestors gathered around the Jewish community building. Men in Polish army uniforms brought the Jews out, then released them to the mob. Local militia, a Socialist factory director, even some members of the clergy took part in what rapidly turned into a melee. Forty-one Jews were killed at Kielce, and soon Jews were building stockade-like structures in various areas of Poland. The Catholic Church's reaction surprised many: Poland's August Cardinal Hlond criticized Jews for increasing antisemitism by taking leading appointments in a government "that the majority of Poles do not want." When a Cracow priest denounced the riot, he was forbidden to continue ecclesiastical duties. The Kielce boy's story was eventually revealed as a fabrication.[27]

In nearby countries antisemitism also became violent, as nationalism flared up in the aftermath of the German retreat and surrender. Anti-Hungarian demonstrations in Kosice, Czechoslovakia, were soon combined with anti-Jewish demonstrations, while in Presov five Jews were killed in what appeared to be a pogrom. German Jews in Prague, meanwhile, were attacked as Germans. Bucharest crowds screaming their support of king and coun-try "fell to beating up all the Jews they could lay hands on," often with the thick staffs used to carry their Romanian flags.[28]

The piling of murder upon murder, the shouts in the street and the rumors in the marketplace, all helped drive thousands of returned Jews out of Poland and neighboring countries from late 1945 on. The impact of the Kielce killings in 1946 was immediate: some 16,000 Polish Jews fled the country that month; 23,000 more left in August (including almost 4,000 who crossed into Czechoslovakia one night), and another 23,000 left in September. A UNRRA official was on hand as fleeing Polish Jews arrived at the Zeilsheim DP camp near Frankfurt; he gazed out on

> what appeared to be an endless queue of refugees, packs and bundles on their backs, plodding up the path toward the camp. Never had I seen such a bedraggled lot of people. Mothers held infants to their breasts, clutching the hands of tiny youngsters who stumbled alongside them. As I watched, a group halted and, throwing their bundles to the ground, literally fell in their tracks from exhaustion, unable to make the last few yards to the camp. . . . They had arrived in the last few days from Cracow and Polish Silesia, more than seven hundred miles distant. Fathers, mothers and children alike, hitchhiked, rode trucks, jumped freight trains, slept in the forests at night and somehow managed to reach here.[29]

Was this organized or unorganized? Lt. Gen. Sir Frederick E. Morgan, briefly UNRRA's chief of operations in Germany, believed it was organized. This outflow from Poland, he charged, was "nothing short of a skillful campaign of anti-British aggression on the part of Zion aided and abetted by Russia." Although it was presented to the world by "Zionist propaganda" as being the "spontaneous surge of a tortured and persecuted people," Morgan held that it was really a well-organized drive by the American Joint Distribution Committee and related Jewish groups to pack the Jewish DPs into Germany. Their ultimate aim was to force the opening of Palestine for emigration—meaning "death to the British," Morgan charged. The UNRRA officer was called on the carpet for such charges, restored to his post, then fired later by a new UNRRA chief for similar remarks.[30]

Other accounts challenged Morgan's claim that the movement was organized, for journalists found "infiltrees," as they were called, who had fled on their own and linked up with others as they headed west. In fact, soon after Morgan made his comments at a press conference in early 1946, a UNRRA investigator stated that "all the infiltrees with whom we spoke said that there was no organized program." Others noted that many people, not just Jews, wanted to leave their homes in Europe; a Netherlands survey estimated that even 20 percent of the Dutch population wished to emigrate.[31]

But organization was present; that became increasingly obvious. A probe by the U.S. Third Army in January 1946 discovered that a group of 250 Jewish refugees heading for Munich had been detoured at one point, then sent in another direction where better facilities would be available. Within two weeks of the opening of a new camp for Jews, the report stated, a new group of 200 infiltrees arrived there, without having passed through any other camp en route. The report said that Zionist committees along the way gave advice and assistance, and many trying to reach Italy were found in possession of forged passes. When the UNRRA ran an investigation in June and July 1946, interrogation of infiltrees at three major collection points confirmed that "the movements are fairly well organized, but . . . the fear of persecu-

tion is still the predominant motive." And that was before Kielce.[32]

Some evidence was also found for Morgan's charge that the movement aimed at pressuring the British. The western zones were obvious goals for anyone on the loose in Europe then, for few other spots were prepared to care for large numbers of refugees. But it is also on record that David Ben Gurion told the Jewish Agency in October 1945, "If we succeed in concentrating a quarter million Jews in the American zone, it will increase the American pressure [on the British]." This pressure would arise not through financial burdens, Ben Gurion added, "but because they see no future for these people outside *Eretz-Yisrael*." A January 1946 probe by the UNRRA found a "strong impression" that one motive behind the organized flow of Jews was to "bring the questions of the future of the Jews and of Zionism to a head."[33]

The escape of one Polish Jew illustrates the mixed pattern of organized and unorganized flight that became common in late 1945 and much of 1946. Returning to her Polish hometown in April 1945, Chana Wilewska (not her real name) was met by the same apartment building janitor who had thrown out her family in 1939. Then, he had worn a large swastika badge; now he pleaded, "I didn't know what I was doing!" Gaining entry, she struggled in the ensuing weeks to regain family furniture and heirlooms, all the while overhearing anti-Jewish comments in the streets and rumors of attacks on Jews in nearby towns.[34] Then came a letter from her uncle, who was serving with General Anders's Polish army in Italy. He told her to join him and sent forged papers with a fellow soldier who was returning to Poland for a visit. The papers were inadequate, however; two attempts to cross the border using them resulted only in rebuffs.

Chana decided to work out her own plan. Since her mother had been born in Czechoslovakia, she went to the city hall and obtained a permit to visit her relatives in that country. The permit got her across the border in April 1946. Upon arrival at her mother's native city, she went immediately to the Jewish community center, where she met a visiting member of the Jewish Brigade who took her to Prague. [There] she was delivered to the headquarters of the *Bricha*, the organized exodus. (*Bricha* means "flight" in Hebrew.) After several days' wait, persons running the Bricha center in Prague took her with a group of fifty fleeing Jews by train to the German border. All were given forged papers attesting to the legality of their trip in case they were caught. They were taken at night to a house, where they waited until 2:00 a.m. Three guides came for them, leading them in a two-hour trek over the mountains into Germany. (Chana believes that the border guards had been bribed, for the group of fifty traveled with no fear of capture.)

Early the next morning the group walked into a German train station, waited while their Bricha guides purchased their tickets, then boarded a train that eventually crossed into the American Zone. Most entered DP camps, as suggested by their Bricha guides. Chana, meanwhile, elected not to enter a camp and instead registered as a German, which was easy to do since she had grown up in Polish Silesia.

Organized. Unorganized. At times disorganized. All three describe the massive exodus of Jews out of Eastern Europe beginning in late 1945. Undoubtedly many would have fled even without help, for a tenuous string of escape routes had existed sporadically in wartime. It is just as certain, however, that many were encouraged to leave by the knowledge that they would receive assistance along the way. Yehuda Bauer, an Israeli scholar and expert on the *Bricha*, argues that despite what some Israelis would later claim, the postwar exo-

dus from Poland received its early organizational drive from resident Polish and Lithuanian Jews—not from the special agents sent from Palestine, known as *shlichim* (emissaries). Ex-partisans first helped Polish Jews find the best border crossings, then forged Red Cross documents for them. Large numbers were assisted in traveling by train into Berlin, or down through Romania into Yugoslavia or toward Italy.[35] . . .

Finally, in October 1945, the first emissaries arrived from Palestine, ten months after the initial groups of Polish Jews had escaped south into Romania and others had fled through Czechoslovakia and Germany. Now the *Bricha* became an established organization across much of the Continent, although local Jews continued to run most of the day-to-day operations in Poland. Members of the Jewish Brigade, a British military unit from Palestine that saw action near the end of the war in Italy, began to show up anywhere the *Bricha* needed them, helping Jews steal across frontiers, transporting them in disguised military trucks, carrying supplies, foiling occupation forces repeatedly. The Joint Distribution Committee provided food and clothing for many of the travelers.[36]

But six months after Lieutenant General Morgan charged that a well-organized, fully financed operation was moving thousands of Jews out of Eastern Europe, the reality was that the escape routes were being blocked, largely through British pressure and Soviet reluctance to go along with the exodus. And the truth was that the organizers were unable to cope with the mounting flow of refugee traffic.[37]

At that point a major shift occurred: the Czechoslovaks changed their minds. On July 25, 1946, the Czechoslovak cabinet officially recognized the *Bricha*, granting it permission to transport Jews across Czechoslovakia. The only proviso was that travelers were not to remain on Czechoslovak soil. (When I. F. Stone traveled with such a group, he found that a Czechoslovak policeman accompanied it to ensure that no one fled the train; in fact, his presence seems to have assured that none of the Jews would be harmed.) Poland then opened its borders also, so by late 1946 there was no legal barrier between any Polish Jew and the DP camps of Austria and Germany. . . .[38]

As the influx started to crowd western zone reception centers, Allied policymakers began to understand that they faced a new situation. The realization frequently came in a sudden confrontation, as experienced by Alexander Squadrilli, at that time displaced persons executive with the U.S. Army in Frankfurt. Squadrilli began to receive desperate pleas from officials in Austria, calling for trains to transport the infiltrees out of the vastly overcrowded centers there. Squadrilli dispatched empty train cars to Austria and later went to the camp sidings when they were due to return. "I was out there when the first train arrived," he said. "Some Jews were getting off with bundles and children on their backs. I would look into these people's eyes: it was as if they were seeing right through me—they had a hard glitter in their eyes that told me they had reached the end of their tolerance—they would cut my throat if I did anything against them."[39]

Some authorities tried to block entry into their zones. But higher-ups intervened, ordering the infiltrees placed in Jewish camps and provided with regular DP food, shelter, and care; these officials also reversed an order that forbade organized groups from entering the U.S. Zone. In Austria the occupation forces quickly gave up efforts to block these "infiltrees"; they did an about-face and assisted them in moving through. "I could put a division up there on the line but it wouldn't stop the Jews," a high-ranking American officer told one correspondent. And the chief of British DP

operations for Austria added, "I find it good policy to play along with the chaps who can turn the tap on and off. They buzz me and announce they have a thousand for my zone and I usually manage to settle for about 500." This became known as the "Green Plan," and it would be tolerated as long as the Jews were just passing through.[40] In April 1947, however, the United States finally clamped down on the continuing influx. Nothing would be done to stop the infiltrees from coming into the American zones, the new order stated, but they could no longer enter DP camps. Private groups, such as the American Joint Distribution Committee and other Jewish agencies, would have to care for them.[41]

This loosening of occupation policy from 1945 to 1947 opened the doors to the West for thousands of east European Jews. Entering the American zones at rates of 2,000 or more a week, the Jewish population under UNRRA care in Germany and Austria jumped from 18,361 in December 1945 to 97,333 in December 1946; 167,529 were receiving IRO care on September 30, 1947. Thousands of others were not under UNRRA or IRO care. The influx into the U.S. Zone of Germany was so great that the expected decline in camp population from repatriation did not take place. More than 107,000 DPs were repatriated in the last half of 1946, and 16,000 other DPs were removed from the camps as ineligible—but total camp population rose by 8,000.[42]

The 1947 statistics on Jews receiving UNRRA care were dominated by the 122,313 Jews from Poland; there were also 18,593 from Romania, 8,445 from Hungary, 6,602 from Czechoslovakia, and 6,167 from Germany. By then, Jews accounted for 25 percent of displaced persons in Germany and Austria, a sharp rise from the 3.7 percent reported at the end of September 1945 (when many Jews were still classified by nationality).[43]

New camps for infiltrees were opened, a few of them luxurious—as at Bad Gastein in Austria—but most at the other end of the comfort spectrum. A visitor to the Zeilsheim DP camp near Frankfurt found four families crammed into a room measuring twelve by eighteen feet; he learned that a baby had been born that morning on the stoop outside the main office, and that there was no fresh milk for the camp's sixty new-born babies—while nearby German farmers pastured herds of milk cows. Visitors were appalled at the impermanence and squalor of these overcrowded infiltree centers. Various reasons for these conditions were advanced. One observer concluded that the refugees had a "burning desire to get out, and to shut out any implication that they may have to remain where they are for any serious length of time."[44]

As had happened with other DPs, it was this contrast of wretched overcrowding in the camps with well-housed Germans nearby that put bitterness into the hearts of many, and led some in the UNRRA and IRO to urge major shifts in priorities. This was behind the publicized resignation of the Landsberg camp's welfare director in December 1945 and the resulting army investigation. Dr. Leo Srole, a sociologist, protested the overcrowding, underfeeding, and lack of adequate housing (some of which had been declared "unfit for German prisoners of war"), while expressing fear of impending epidemics, since outbreaks of cholera had been reported in Eastern Europe, source of most of the infiltrees. . . . The military made a quick investigation, and additional camp installations for the incoming Jews were ordered. In February 1946 the army ordered that infiltrees were to be housed and cared for according to the same standards applied to earlier arrivals.[45]

In some camps, much of the power was gathered by sophisticated DPs who organized quickly to protect themselves, to block unwanted actions by authorities, or simply to seek more supplies from the UNRRA or voluntary agencies. . . . The situation at the Neustadt camp in March 1946 angered a UNRRA welfare officer in the British Zone:

> There is no control of supplies distributed by the Jewish agencies. . . . They distribute it to whom they will and how they like, taking double ration for themselves. Occasionally food is given to Polish hospital patients, but only those who are friendly with the committee. There is no satisfactory control of the DP population in the camp, consequently the food from Belsen is drawn on the strength of about 650, although the actual number of Jews in Neustadt is only around 400. There is constant movement of displaced persons in and out of the camp without any permit, which makes it possible for the same displaced person to be registered and collect food at Belsen and Neustadt at the same time. . . . The present staff cannot cope with the situation.[46]

Less than four months later another UNRRA official complained of political infighting between Jewish groups—at Schwebda they were "fighting for the souls" of 150 unaccompanied children—and admitted that competent UNRRA personnel refused to leave jobs in stable Polish and Baltic camps "for the immense difficulties which confront personnel in infiltree centers."[47]

But this intense feeling, this anger at the outside world, also led to a burning desire to celebrate everything that was Jewish. The Joint Distribution Committee's supply network strained to provide enough kosher food for the Orthodox, although a donation of ten million pounds of kosher beef from the Irish Republic helped through a difficult period in early 1947. A major need for special foods came during Jewish festivals, the succession of events that mark the seasons of the Jewish year. These were days when Jewish feeling was most concentrated, and they took on special meaning, special poignance, after liberation. For years Jews had met only secretly on those days, had passed messages, exchanged looks. Now they celebrated publicly and, as one escaped Polish Jew explained, "Jewish life began to exist again!"[48]

Several of the holidays were contemplative, sad events, bringing happiness after the war only in that they could now be commemorated openly again. But one holiday was sheer joy—Purim, the annual festival of the deliverance of Jews from a massacre planned by Haman as related in the Book of Esther. Traditionally at that springtime event an effigy of Haman is ridiculed and attacked in a joking manner, to the accompaniment of noisemakers, hooting, and singing. Purim 1946 became very special—perhaps the most special Purim for generations. It was the occasion when Europe's Jews finally threw off the worry and fear under which they had lived since the early 1930s and danced and laughed in the warm sunlight of freedom again. The DPs at Landsberg, one of the largest Jewish camps, turned the event into an exhilarating rebuke to Nazism—in the very city where Hitler wrote *Mein Kampf*.[49] . . . Camp leaders saw an opportunity to turn Purim week at Landsberg into rehabilitative activity that would spruce up the camp, help its Jewish residents shake off their despair and celebrate their joy at having survived. Streets were cleaned and buildings scrubbed all week long, while the DPs secretly planned costumes and floats, all to focus on a carnival on March 24. Haman's defeat was marked as Hitler's defeat: on the day of the carnival the grounds were filled with tombstones for Hitler, walls were decorated and ornamented, slogans and caricatures appeared everywhere. The camp newspaper reported: "Hitler hangs in many variants and in many poses: A big Hitler, a fat Hitler, a small 'Hitler,' with medals, and without medals. Jews hung him by his head, by his feet, or by his belly. Or: a painter's ladder with a pail and brush, near a tombstone with the inscription: 'P.N.' (*po nikbar*) here lies Hitler, may his name be blotted out." Groups from the camp paraded—the orchestra, sports clubs, unions, and *kibbutzim*—along with members of the trade schools, police, and hospital staff.

But the day meant more than merriment. It also included the reading of a chapter from the Megillah, part of the traditional Purim service. And the speeches to the crowd also stressed the broader significance of Purim, 1946, in the DP camps across Europe:

> Hitler Germany was the embodiment of the bestial jungle. The Beast is conquered, not only for us, but for all of humanity. This is the meaning of the festival that we celebrate today. A year ago today, in the concentration camps, we did not imagine that the prophecy of the Prophet Ezekiel would be fulfilled: "dry bones" again become a living people. We must rebuild our lives from the ground up and build our own home.

That night at the Landsberg camp they burned a copy of *Mein Kampf*—the chief testament of Adolf Hitler, who had warned in 1944 that unless Germany was victorious, "Jewry could then celebrate the destruction of Europe by a second triumphant Purim festival." Europe had been nearly destroyed, because of Hitler, but some Jews he had tried to destroy lived on—and now commemorated their escape from both Haman's and Hitler's massacres. Europe was saved. And for the Jews of *the She'erit Ha-pletah*, Purim 1946 was a time of redeeming significance.

Thoughts of Palestine were quickened by these celebrations. The *Mossad le Aliyah Bet*, the underground group aiding emigration, sought to oblige, sending twelve ships illegally to Palestine with forty-four hundred European Jews between May and December 1945. Larger ships left in 1946, with elaborate strategies devised to outwit the British in European ports. The British were increasingly able to catch these ships en route, however. As in the famous case of the *Exodus* in 1947, many ships were forced to return to Europe or deposit their passengers in detention camps on Cyprus.[50]

But some Jews made it into Palestine despite British capture. One was Carl Friedman, who journeyed from a Nazi labor camp to liberated Bucharest and traveled from there into Austria using forged papers provided by the *Bricha*. He then gave up his wristwatch to purchase passage for his group of six Czechoslovak Jews over the Alps into Italy. Their next stop was a Jewish Brigade camp at Padua, from which they went to a new Kibbutz at Nonontola, where five hundred east European Jews gathered to undergo training for Palestine. Friedman recalled that the training even included methods to travel from the ship to the nearby shore. It was almost to no avail. Leaving with 950 others on the *Enzo Sereni* in December 1945, Friedman ultimately saw the ship intercepted by the British off Haifa; the passengers were forced into the British camp at Atlit but then released, apparently included in the shifting British legal admission totals. For Carl Friedman, Palestine—home—had been reached.[51]

World events soon changed the Palestine situation. In April 1946, the Anglo-American Committee of Inquiry called for admission of 100,000 Jews into Palestine immediately, and under mounting pressure the British turned the issue over to the United Nations. On September 1, 1947, the United Nations Special Committee on Palestine unanimously recommended that Britain give up its mandate on Palestine and partition it into separate Arab and Jewish states. This was approved by the UN General Assembly on November 29, 1947, and when word of the UN vote was flashed to Europe around midnight, the lights came on in the Jewish camps, DPs rushed out and the dancing and singing went on for hours. The British mandate would end on May 15, 1948. The state of Israel was born.[52]

By that time some 69,000 European Jews had made it into Palestine since the end of the war or into detention on Cyprus. They were part of the estimated 250,000 east European Jews who had escaped into Western Europe through the *Bricha*. After the state of Israel was established, 331,594 European Jews emigrated there through 1951. Others, however, began looking elsewhere as doors began to open; 165,000 European Jews ultimately emigrated to other countries from 1946 to 1950.[53]

Why did they turn away from Israel? Many had relatives in America or other countries, but it should also be stated that opportunities for emigration began to appear by late 1947 that had not been present in 1945. At war's end only Palestine had seemed possible—that was the only "home." Malcolm Proudfoot, an early student of postwar refugee movements, speculated that the state of Israel might not have come into being if other countries had welcomed Europe's Jews earlier.[54]

The *Bricha* and the Jewish DPs' suffering in overcrowded camps must be counted as major factors in the rise of modern Israel. Armed struggle by the *Haganah* in Palestine was important, but, as Yehuda Bauer argued, the presence of Jewish DPs in Europe kept pressure on American opinion makers, while winning the world's sympathy, and ultimately helped swing the United Nations behind the partition of Palestine.

1. I. F. Stone, *Underground to Palestine* (New York: Boni and Gaer, 1946), 43, 60–62.

2. Leo Srole, autobiographical article in *Harvard Class of 1933: Fiftieth Anniversary Report* (Cambridge MA: Harvard Class of 1933, 1983), 523.

3. Levin, *Holocaust*, 20, 254–55. Malcolm J. Proudfoot, *European Refugees: 1939–1952—A Study in Forced Population Movement* (Evanston IL: Northwestern University Press, 1956), 334–42. Henry L. Feingold, "Who Shall Bear Guilt for the Holocaust: The Human Dilemma," *American Jewish History* 68, no. 3 (March 1979): 278.

4. Stone, *Underground*, 46. Josef Rosensaft, "Our Belsen," in *Belsen* (Israel: Irgun Sheerit Hapleita Me'haezor Habriti, 1957), 29. Helen Epstein, *Children of the Holocaust: Conversations with Sons and Daughters of Survivors* (New York: Putnam's, 1979), 105–7, 115. Samuel Gringauz, "Jewish Destiny as the DPs See It," *Commentary* 4, no. 6 (December 1947): 504.

5. Koppel S. Pinson, "Jewish Life in Liberated Germany—A Study of the Jewish DPs," *Jewish Social Studies* 9 (April 1947): 110. Hal Lehrman, "Austria: Way-Station of Exodus—Pages from a Correspondent's Notebook," *Commentary* 2, no. 6 (December 1946): 571.

6. Pinson, "Jewish Life," 110. Epstein, *Children*, 105–7, 213. Tadeusz Grygier, *Oppression: A Study in Social and Criminal Psychology* (Westport CT: Greenwood Press, 1954, 1973), 200–201. Cornelia Goodhue, "We Gain New Candidates for Citizenship," *The Child*, July 1946, 6–7.

7. Grygier, *Oppression*, 41–44. Yehuda Bauer, *Flight and Rescue: Brichah* (New York: Random House, 1970), 266, 272.

8. British official quoted in Bauer, *Flight and Rescue*, 51–52. Leonard Dinnerstein, "The U.S. Army and the Jews: Policies toward the Displaced Persons After World War II," *American Jewish History* 68, no. 3 (March 1979): 355–56; Dinnerstein, *America and the Survivors of the Holocaust* (New York: Columbia University Press, 1982), 13, 28.

9. Norbert Wollheim, "Belsen's Place in the Process of 'Death-and-Rebirth' of the Jewish People," in *Belsen*, 55. Bauer, *Flight and Rescue*, 35–36. Gringauz, "Jewish Destiny," 503.

10. *Times* (London), July 21, 1945, 4. *Jewish Chronicle*, quoted in Dinnerstein, *America*, 17.

11. Bauer, *Flight and Rescue*, 76. Paul Trepman, "On Being Reborn," *Belsen*, 134.

12. "Report of Earl G. Harrison," *Department of State Bulletin*, September 30, 1945, no. 13, 456–63 (reprinted in Dinnerstein, *America*, a B, 291–305). Earl G. Harrison, "The Last Hundred Thousand," *Survey Graphic*, December 1945, 469–73.

13. Joseph B. Schechtman, *The United States and the Jewish State Movement—The Crucial Decade: 1939–1949* (New York: Herzl, 1966), 137–38, 142.

14. Gen. Dwight D. Eisenhower to President Harry S Truman, October 8, 1945, in *The Papers of Dwight David Eisenhower* (Baltimore: Johns Hopkins University Press, 1978), 6: 414–17. Dinnerstein, *America*, chap. 2, *passim*. Order from R. B. Longe, lt. col., for brigadier, chief PW & DP Div. Hq. PW & DP Div. Main Hq., Control Commission for G (BE), Bunde, BAOR, November 19, 1945, UNRRA Archives, Germany Mission, British Zone (Lemgo) Central Registry, Repatriation.

15. Proudfoot, *European Refugees*, 342n. Bauer, *Flight and Rescue*, 69, 73. Levin, *Holocaust*, 710–11.

16. Bauer, *Flight and Rescue*, 84–87. Samuel Gringauz, "Our New German Policy and the DPs," *Commentary* 5, no. 6 (June 1948): 510–11. Ephraim Londner, "Religious Life in Belsen," in *Belsen*, 184.

17. Pinson, "Jewish Life," 117.

18. Yehuda Bauer, *The Jewish Emergence From Powerlessness* (Toronto: University of Toronto Press, 1979), 63. Gringauz quote from *Landsberger Lager Cajtung*, reprinted in Pinson, "Jewish Life," 114n. Stone, *Underground*, 52.

19. Marion E. Hutton, "UNRRA Shelters Unattended Children," *The Child*, July 1946, 29.

20. S. Adler-Rudel, "The Surviving Children," in *Belsen*, 125. Pinson, "Jewish Life," 116–17. *New*

York Times, November 27, 1945, 5. Gringauz, "Jewish Destiny," 501–9. Bauer, *Flight and Rescue*, 59–60. Gerold Frank, "The Tragedy of the DPs," *New Republic* 114, no. 13 (April 1, 1946): 437–38.

21. Bauer, *Jewish Emergence*, 47, 52–53. M. Lubliner, "Jewish Education in Belsen," 160–61; Josef Fraenkel, "The Cultural Liberation of Belsen," 166; and Z. Zamarion (Halpern), "A Shaliach in Belsen," 179, in *Belsen*. Levin, *Holocaust*, 19–20, 61–62, chap. 17. Bauer, *Flight and Rescue*, 29–30, 36. Jon Kimche and David Kimche, *The Secret Roads: The "Illegal" Migration of a People—1938–1948* (New York: Farrar, Straus and Cudahy, 1955), 171–72.

22. Polish Jew (anonymous), interview with author.

23. Levin, Holocaust, 279. "The Infiltrees," *Commentary* 1, no. 2 (February 1946): 43.

24. Inter-Governmental Committee on Refugees, *Memorandum: From the American Resident Representative*, no. 4, April 30, 1946, 3–4. Bauer, *Jewish Emergence*, 64. Yitzhak Arad, *The Partisan: From the Valley of Death to Mount Zion* (New York: Holocaust Library, 1979), 176–77.

25. Wladyslaw Anders, *An Army in Exile: The Story of the Second Polish Corps* (London: Macmillan, 1949), 19. *The Dark Side of the Moon* (London: Faber and Faber, 1946), 210. Arad, *Partisan*, 27, 160–61, 186. Pole (anonymous), interview with author.

26. Bauer, *Flight and Rescue*, 115. Bauer, *Jewish Emergence*, 65. *Commentary* 1, November 1945, 33–34. Arad, *Partisan*, 186.

27. Dinnerstein, *America*, 107–9. *New York Times*, July 13, 1946, 1, 5. *Commentary* 2, no. 2 (August 1946): 140. Bauer, *Jewish Emergence*, 65.

28. *Commentary* 1, no. 1 (November 1945): 33; 2, no. 4 (October 1946): 327–35.

29. Proudfoot, *European Refugees*, 340–42. Dinnerstein, *America*, 112. Bauer, *Flight and Rescue*, chap. 7 *passim*. Ira A. Hirschmann, *The Embers Still Burn* (New York: Simon and Schuster, 1949), 75–76.

30. Lt.-Gen. Sir Frederick Morgan, *Peace and War—A Soldier's Life* (London: Hodder and Stoughton, 1961), 236–37, 246–51, 256. *Commentary* 1, no. 4 (February 1946): 44–46; March 1946, 66.

31. Frank, "The Tragedy," 437. Genfit, "Letter From Wurzburg," *New Yorker*, November 6, 1948, 116–17. Jay B. Krane, "Observations on the Problem of Jewish Infiltrees" (confidential), January 18, 1946, UNRRA Archives, Germany Mission, Infiltrees. David Bernstein, "Europe's Jews: Summer, 1947," Commentary 4, no. 2 (August 1947): 104.

32. *New York Times*, January 27, 1946, 1, 27. Jay B. Krane, "Report on Infiltrees in the U.S. Zone" (confidential), July 10, 1946; "Observations," January 18, 1946, UNRRA Archives, Germany Mission, Infiltrees.

33. Bauer, *Jewish Emergence*, 66–67. Krane, "Observations," January 18, 1946.

34. Polish Jew (anonymous), interview with author.

35. Bauer, *Flight and Rescue*, VII—VIII, 118–19. Bauer, *Jewish Emergence*, 62–63, 65–67. Kimche and Kimche, *Secret Roads*, 83–84.

36. Bauer, *Flight and Rescue*, 45, 66–67, 118–19, 121. Bauer, *Jewish Emergence*, 63, 67.

37. Kimche and Kimche, *Secret Roads*, 87–89.

38. Ibid., 87–92. Stone, *Underground*, 43.

39. Alexander E. Squadrilli, interview with author.

40. Bauer, *Flight and Rescue*, 81–82, 87–89, 190–91, 248–49. Dinnerstein, *America*, 105. Krane, "Observations," January 18, 1946, 4. Lehrman, "Austria: Way-Station," 565–72.

41. *New York Times*, April 17, 1947, 6. Lucius D. Clay, *Decision in Germany* (Garden City NJ: Doubleday, 1950), 232.

42. U.S. Office of Military Government for Germany, *Weekly Information Bulletin*, no. 78, February 3, 1947, 24.

43. Proudfoot, *European Refugees*, 238–39. Preparatory Commission for the IRO, *pciro News Bulletin*, no. 6, December 8, 1947, 1–3; no. 11, March 24, 1948, 1–2. *New York Times*, October 26, 1946, 7.

44. Stone, *Underground*, 112–13. Hirschmann, *Embers Still Burn*, 74ff. Bernstein, "Europe's Jews," 107.

45. See accounts of Srole's acts in *New York Times*, December 6, 1945, 7; December 7, 1945, 5. U.S.

Army, *Displaced Persons*, Occupation Forces
in Europe Series, 1945–46, Training Packet 53
(Frankfurt am Main, Germany: U.S. Army, n.d.),
105.

46. H. Hrachovska, dist. welfare officer, Hq. 8 Corps
District, to Col. C. J. Wood, UNRRA dist. dir.
Hq. 8 Corps Dist. British Zone, March 29, 1946,
UNRRA Archives, Germany Mission, British
Zone (Lemgo) Central Registry, Repatriation.

47. Krane, "Report on Infiltrees," July 10, 1946, 2.

48. *New York Times*, February 6, 1947, 3. Polish Jew
and former Jewish agency worker (anonymous),
interviews with author.

49. Information on the Landsberg carnival is from
Toby Blum-Dobkin, "The Landsberg Carnival:
Purim in a Displaced Persons Center," Yeshiva
University Museum, 1979 Catalogue, Purim: The
Face and the Mask (New York: Yeshiva Univer-
sity, 1979), 52–58. For information on the Lands-
berg DP camp, see Leo Srole, "Why the DPs
Can't Wait," *Commentary* 3, no. 1 (January 1947):
13–21.

50. Kimche and Kimche, *Secret Roads*, 84, 98, 100–
106. *New York Times*, September 8, 1947, 6.

51. Carl Friedman oral history interview, William
E. Wiener Oral History Library of the American
Jewish Committee, December 1, 1974, 20–23.

52. Schechtman, United States, 153. Bauer, *Jewish
Emergence*, 74–75. Bauer, *Flight and Rescue*, 320–
21. Arad, *Partisan*, 207. *New York Times*, December 1, 1947, 5.

53. Proudfoot, *European Refugees*, 358–61. Bauer,
Flight and Rescue, 319–21. Bauer, *Jewish Emergence*,
73.

54. Proudfoot, *European Refugees*, 361.

Zion's Ambivalence

TOM SEGEV

From *The Seventh Million*

The *yishuv* [the Jewish population of Palestine prior to Israeli independence] felt morally and ideologically responsible for the survivors. Everyone knew that, without them, there was no chance of achieving statehood. During [David] Ben-Gurion's visit to a former Nazi prison camp near Frankfurt, a blonde girl with long braids had approached him. Her name was Malkele; she asked him in Yiddish, "Are you the king of Israel?" Ben-Gurion patted her on the head and said he was not the king. But the girl insisted: "Yes! They told me that you are the king! Take me to the Land of Israel right now!"[1] Everywhere Ben-Gurion went he heard that people wanted to come to Palestine. He estimated their numbers at between 60 and 70 percent of the residents of the camps. Everywhere, he asked them if they were ready to accept the difficulties involved in waiting for immigration certificates, and everywhere they said yes. On his return home, then, he reported to the Jewish Agency executive that most of the residents of the DP camps were "loyal Zionists."[2] . . .

At the same time, the *yishuv* made it clear that the survivors were not ideal "human material." One of the envoys warned that 5,000 Jews of the type he had met in Europe would turn Palestine into "one big madhouse."[3] There were those who said that the survivors were liable to "poison" Zionism, democracy, and progress and to obliterate the country's socialist agricultural foundation, until it became, as Meir Yaari said while

the Holocaust was still in progress, "one big Tel Aviv."[4] There were those who feared for *Mapai*'s [the Workers' Party] future. As long as selection for immigration reflected relative party strength, *Mapai* could ensure its majority. Uncontrolled immigration was liable to bring a "terrible holocaust" on the party, one of its leaders said.[5] One envoy to the displaced persons told Ben-Gurion that, if a hundred thousand of them indeed came to Israel, they would cause a disaster; he called them "scum." Ben-Gurion responded that it was best for "scum" to live in Palestine. "We will have troubles," he granted, "but at least the troubles will come from Jews."[6]

After the war, the envoys still tried to encourage the immigration of helpful and desirable "human material" and to delay the immigration of undesirables, especially right before Israel's War of Independence. During those months they sent the *yishuv* almost exclusively young people fit for combat. In the 1950s, they again debated this point, and for a while even reinstituted what was then still called *selektsia*—that is, choosing candidates for immigration according to their country of origin, age, professional training, family status, and even, as in the past, party affiliation. Yet the dream that guided the Zionist movement before the Holocaust, of an ideal society that would in time create a new man out of the very best of European Jewry, was dead. The slaughter of the Jews forced the Zionists to recognize that it was necessary to bring all those who remained alive to Palestine immediately. One of the organizers of the immigration said that, in practice, they would have to take "everything that comes along," excepting only "absolutely antisocial types and unreformable criminals."[7]

Once the Holocaust had forced the leaders of the Zionist movement to give up the principle of selection, they began to discover, for the first time, the Jews of the Islamic world. Until word of the extermination in Europe had begun to arrive, the Zionist movement had taken little interest in the Jews of North Africa and the Arab countries. "We were used to thinking of the Oriental Jews mostly as subjects for historical and anthropological research," one leader said.[8] The movement's roots were in Europe, and its activists, as Ben-Gurion said, "did not notice" the Jews of the Arab world.[9] The Holocaust dictated a new outlook. When one member of the Jewish Agency executive reported to *Mapai* on the Nazi exterminations, he immediately noted that some three-quarters of a million Jews lived in the Middle East and North Africa and that these henceforth would be Zionism's reservoir of immigration.[10]

The efforts to reach the Jews of the Moslem world and organize them for immigration were intensified as the dimensions of the European Holocaust became known. While there was also concern about the physical safety of these communities, as after the 1941 pogrom in Baghdad, the Jews of Islam were seen mainly as a replacement for the manpower lost in Europe. This, then, was the most dramatic effect of the Holocaust on the composition of Israeli society, culture, and politics. Hitler's rise to power had brought German Jews to Palestine; the extermination of European Jewry in the Holocaust brought Israel the Jews of the Arab world. . . . in large numbers and at a rapid rate, with no selection and before anyone had any idea what to do with them. The main reason they were brought in so hastily was not only because

it was feared that they were in immediate danger, but also because Israeli politicians knew that someday they themselves might be held accountable for the loss of another Jewish population. The same was true for the remaining Jews in Europe. The government of Israel paid some eastern European countries hundreds of dollars for each Jew allowed to come to Israel. When these payments came up for discussion, one member of the Jewish Agency executive said: "We have to live with our consciences. For that reason, we must know that we did everything that could be done!"[11] . . .

In the second half of 1945, some 90,000 Jewish refugees came to Palestine from Europe.[12] All had lived under Nazi occupation; some had been in concentration camps. In the next three years, another 60,000 survivors came, and in the first year of statehood, nearly 200,000 more.[13] At the end of 1949 there were, then, close to 350,000 Holocaust survivors living in Israel—almost one out of every three Israelis. On arrival, they faced a difficult struggle.

It was very hot in the banana groves of the Jordan Valley kibbutz, and life was hard for Miriam Weinfeld and Hanan Yakobowitz. In the first weeks they slept outside, under mosquito nets. At night the wails of the jackals brought back memories of Bergen-Belsen. Weinfeld's memories and her longing for home were stronger than her ability to adjust to the kibbutz. And the kibbutz did not encourage individual soul-searching; members were told to put aside the past and become part of the group. Weinfeld felt shunned by the young people. Although she did not speak Hebrew, their cliquishness hurt; she sensed arrogance, sometimes even mockery and hostility. The older members were more welcoming; they tried to adopt the new couple, but did not know how to make life easier for them. She sensed in their kindness guilt, even shame. She wanted to be asked about herself; her story was the only thing she had to contribute to her relationship with the new country. But no one asked.

For many of the survivors, telling their story seemed a patriotic duty: Many said that in the postwar months, they felt as though they were the last living Jews, who alone knew what had happened to their communities. Each had a moral and historical obligation to preserve the memory of all the others. Yet trying to tell the story also expressed the intense need to share with others the crushing emotional burden. It was a very personal, individual need. But the survivors discovered that people did not always want to listen to them, or could not.

Often, the stories were simply not believed. In 1943, at the forced-labor camp that the Nazis set up near the town of Przemysl, Poland, a seventeen-year-old prisoner named Michael Goldman was brought before the camp commandant, Franz Schwammberger. The commandant whipped and beat him. Goldman fainted. When he woke, the commandant kept on beating him—eighty lashes, until Goldman broke. His back was torn and bloody but he was alive. He survived and came to Israel. When he told his relatives what had happened to him, they refused to believe it. They were sure he was imagining things or exaggerating. "That disbelief was the eighty-first blow," Goldman later said. The story became a symbol.[14] "They didn't believe me!" wrote Yaakov Kurtz, who arrived at the end of 1942. "They asked me questions and interrogated me as if I were a criminal who wanted to mislead people."[15] This was the survivors' first difficulty in their new country.

Weinfeld's new direction in life, at the kibbutz, turned out to be a blind alley. She felt trapped. Then she married her Hanan. They had a modest wedding on a flatbed trailer by the Sea of Galilee. Someone lent them a ring. They received three presents: a tablecloth, a vase, and a Bible. It was not how she had imagined her wedding as a child, a nice, middle-class girl from Poland. What would her mother have said? After the ceremony Miriam and Hanan Yakobowitz crossed the banana grove and went to the neighboring kibbutz, *Beit Zera*, where relatives gave them a room for a night. Years later, she would say that she began her family too early, before she was ready, perhaps before she really wanted to. But back then, she had no one to ask for advice. The first baby died soon after it was born: another reminder of the trauma of the concentration camps.

After the wedding, they moved to another kibbutz, *Ginegar*. She did not feel at home there either, but she worked, took part in the community's social life, learned how to shoot a rifle, and did guard duty during the War of Independence. She felt that she was contributing something to life at the kibbutz but that the kibbutz was giving her less than she gave. Other members of the group that she and her husband had been part of in Sweden arrived in the country, having set out on a *maapilim* [illegal immigrants] ship and spent two years in Cyprus. The experience had given them a group identity. Miriam and Hanan Yakobowitz joined them in founding Kibbutz *Nahsholim* on the coast, near Mount Carmel, where an Arab village, Tantura, had previously been. The two years that had passed since they had last seen the group set them apart, but their seniority in the country gave them a certain advantage. Hanan Yakobowitz became the treasurer of the new kibbutz.

After a time, they left Kibbutz *Nahsholim* as well. They bought a tiny apartment in Neve Amal, near Herzlia—without doors, door frames, or shutters. They were no longer newlyweds, so they did not qualify for the gifts the state gave to young couples—a pressure cooker, a broom, and the like. Living alongside them were immigrants from Yemen and Persia, as well as other Holocaust survivors, struggling young couples. They helped each other. They showered at the neighbors' houses, where there was hot water. Someone brought them a few orange crates for furniture. They had no connection with the old-timers in the country and knew only a few. After a series of medical and psychological complications, Ronit was born. Miriam Yakobowitz's first response was, "She looks like Mama." Suddenly the thought came to her that she was older than her mother had been when she died. A while later, they had another daughter. They earned salaries as employees of public and government organizations; she was a nurse in the *Histadrut* [Jewish labor union] health collective, while he somehow found a job with the internal security service. Once or twice, the government sent them overseas, so in accordance with official regulations they Hebraized their family name. Forty years after Bergen-Belsen, Miriam Akavia writes books, mostly for young people, which have also been published in several European countries, including Germany and Poland. She writes in Hebrew but has never lost her Polish accent: always something of an outsider, always a Holocaust survivor.[16]

Like Miriam Akavia, thousands of Holocaust survivors settled in the country's cities, villages, and kibbutzim, served in the army, learned trades, worked, married, bought apartments, had children, and spoke with them in Hebrew, a testament to the life wish that had helped get them through the war. Many of them very much wanted to be Israelis and so adopted the mores and way of life of their new country. Thousands Hebraized their names, taking on, as it were, a new identity.

From one perspective, their encounter with Israel was an amazing triumph. People who had been dead to the world, at Auschwitz and Bergen-Belsen and Dachau and the rest of the camps, ghet-

tos, and hiding places, returned to life in Israel. This is the significance of a story that appeared in *Maariv* one day early in 1949. On that day Rivka Waxman went out shopping on Herzl Street in Haifa. It was also one of her first days in Israel, she had just come from Poland. Near the Ora cinema she suddenly noticed a young soldier get out of a jeep and go to the ticket booth. She froze in place. "Haim?" she called. The soldier turned to her, and for the next few seconds they stared at each other in disbelief. Then the woman held out her arms, close to fainting, and fell on the youth's shoulder. She was his mother. They had last seen each other eight years before, when he was fourteen. Until she met him in the street, Rivka Waxman believed that her Haim had been killed in the Holocaust.[17] Thousands of people had, like the Waxmans, been torn from their loved ones—in the ghettos, during the deportations, at the death camps, and in the forests—and here in Israel they found one another by chance or through notices published in newspapers and on a heartrending radio program called *Who Knows*. They were new immigrants, on the verge of a new life.

Yet if they found it difficult to start a new life, or if they wanted to preserve their previous identity, they were often in conflict with their new country. Israel was apprehensive about them and wanted to change them. The task the country's leaders set for themselves was to give the survivors a new personality, to imbue them with new values. "They must learn love of the homeland, a work ethic, and human morals," said a *Mapai* leader, and another added that they should be given "the first concepts of humanity." One said, as if they were a huge ball of dough, that it was necessary to "knead their countenances." At one meeting of the *Mapai* secretariat it was said that they should be "reeducated."[18] Such statements did not only give voice to the negative political and social stereotype of the survivor. People sincerely feared meeting the survivors face to face, with their physical and psychological handicaps, their suffering and terror. How will we live with them, they asked themselves over and over again—and their fears were justified. The Holocaust survivors came from another world and to the end of their days they were its prisoners.

... Indeed, liberation came too late for many of the Holocaust survivors, and they did not succeed in rehabilitating themselves. Thousands left Israel, especially in the 1950s.[19] Many needed psychological care, and some continued to need it for years. They did not escape the nightmare of their pasts. Over the years they wrote thousands of books about that "other planet" they had left yet not left, but all they could do was enumerate the atrocities. Those were part of their story that could be told. The rest remained inside. "Even if you studied all the documentation," Elie Wiesel has said, "even if you listened to all the testimonies, visited all the camps and museums and read all the diaries, you would not be able to even approach the portal of that eternal night. That is the tragedy of the survivor's mission. He must tell a story that cannot be told. He must deliver a message that cannot be delivered. . . ."[20]

Miriam Weinfeld was sometimes asked about the blue number tattooed on her arm. She felt that the question reflected only casual interest, not a real desire to hear the true story. So she evaded it. She knew people who had undergone plastic surgery to have the number removed. She did not; but she generally kept it hidden from strangers and never looked at it herself, never learned it by heart. Michael Gilad used to tell his son that it was his telephone number at work.

During the stay in the DP camps before the journey to Palestine, the survivors recuperated; by the time they arrived, they were no longer the walk-ing skeletons the Allied forces discovered in the concentration camps. While still in Europe, they had time to gather themselves and give thought to their futures. There was nothing they wanted more than to return to normalcy: "It is hard to describe their longing for a normal life," commented one of the envoys from Palestine.[21] But they suffered from anxieties, nightmares, and attacks of depression, fury, and apathy; from difficulties in concentrating and in establishing relations with others; from suspicion of strangers, introversion, overwhelming worries about their personal, economic, and professional security, great fear and great aspirations for their children.

Many raised their children with the feeling that their own lives were barely worth living, that their only purpose in living was to ensure the good, the welfare, and the future of their children. Many forced the children to bear the burden of memory by giving them the names of relatives who had died in the Holocaust. Many, perhaps most, could not, and did not want to, tell their children what they had experienced, and the children did not dare ask, as if the answer were a terrible, threatening family secret. Holocaust anxieties could suddenly break into daily life, triggered by routine events at home or at work or on the news. An illness, losing a job, a border incident—everything took them back to "there." For many, the past continued to intrude years after the end of the war.

There were those who became ambitious and tough, able to endure suffering and adjust to crises. Others had trouble dealing with even minor setbacks. Many feared dependence, failure, separation. They were often sick, or thought they were. Many experienced inchoate feelings of grief and violence that had never found release. They were ashamed that they had not been able to resist what had been done to them. They blamed their parents for abandoning them and suffered guilt at having survived their loved ones. "My conscience torments me," one survivor said. "I left children on the way, and they fell into the hands of the Germans."[22] This was a common feeling; and though most survivors owed their lives to chance, not to another's sacrifice, they still felt guilt for having survived. The feeling often served a psychological and moral purpose: It acted as a cover for the powerlessness of the victims. It allowed them to think they had had a choice, and had chosen to live. The sense of guilt had a contrary purpose, too. It was for the survivors a kind of pledge of allegiance to humanistic ethical values, another bid, after the fact, to counter the attempt to rob them of their humanity.[23] The few who had resisted had it easier; many of them tended to set themselves off from the other survivors, even displaying a measure of arrogance. But they too tortured themselves; perhaps they could have done more. "When the Germans entered Poland, had we immediately recognized the danger and started to act," Tzivia Lubetkin said, "perhaps the whole thing would have looked different."[24] In August 1949, the state prosecutor brought the minister of justice's attention to the disturbing rise in the number of new immigrants, among them Holocaust survivors, who were taking their own lives.[25]

Like the survivors, the entire country was in the throes of an emotional crisis. Thousands of those who had come to Palestine before the war had also lost relatives; they too were in mourning. Many tortured themselves with the same guilt feelings that plagued the survivors. Shouldn't they have died in place of a loved one? There were, of course, many who felt an obligation to help the survivors, as if the survivors were their lost parents and siblings. But many others blamed the survivors, as if these had survived at the expense of their relatives and so shared part of the guilt for their deaths. One survivor, Simha Rotem, wrote,

"In almost every contact with the inhabitants of the country, the question would come up of how we had remained alive. It was asked again and again and not always in the most delicate way. I had a feeling that I was being blamed for having stayed alive."[26] The conflict pitted the victims of one trauma against the victims of another.

The earliest immigrants spent their first days in the country in transit camps; later immigrants spent their first weeks and months there. Each received a "primary needs" package from the Jewish Agency. First came cash, 7 to 10 liras (up to $40), which had to suffice for immediate needs in the transit camp or in a Jewish Agency residence while the immigrant looked for work and a permanent place to live. The immigrants were also given iron beds and mattresses. These "agency beds" became an Israeli symbol.

Until they found apartments, immigrants might stay with relatives. But such arrangements could be difficult. Those responsible for absorption complained that few Israelis were willing to accept their immigrant relatives into their houses. There were Israelis who instructed newly arrived relatives not to let the Jewish Agency know that they had family in the country, lest the agency make the local family responsible and not assist the immigrants further. Someone proposed declaring a national voluntary campaign—every family would take an immigrant into its house. Ben-Gurion dismissed the idea. He believed that few people would respond to the call. Later, there was talk of a special law that would allow the confiscation of rooms for immigrants, but it was obvious that it could not be enforced—people would find ways of cheating the government.[27] Many did in fact live in crowded conditions that did not allow them to take in immigrant relatives.

The Jewish Agency and other public bodies built rental apartments for the immigrants—one room and a kitchen. Some apartments were even sparsely furnished. But construction could not keep pace with demand, and the shortage grew month to month, year to year. Neither were jobs created for everyone, nor schools for the children, nor clinics for the ill. The failure was principally due to the lack of funds. But the *yishuv* also tended to scorn organized planning. The Jews, having lived under foreign rule for centuries, had learned to act outside the law, to improvise, and this ability became a valued part of the *yishuv*'s self-image. As one leader said: "We just need to throw the immigrants here and there and they will be absorbed somehow."[28] Furthermore, the *yishuv* was unsure many survivors would come; after all, they had not come in droves before the war and there were indications that most of them would not come now either. Why build them houses before they arrived?

Then the War of Independence broke out, and tens of thousands of homes were suddenly available. This was what Shaul Avigur called "the Arab miracle": Hundreds of thousands of Arabs fled and were expelled from their homes. Entire cities and hundreds of villages left empty were repopulated in short order with new immigrants. In April 1949 they numbered 100,000, most of them Holocaust survivors.[29] The moment was a dramatic one in the war for Israel and a frightfully banal one, too, focused as it was on the struggle over houses and furniture. Free people—Arabs—had gone into exile and become destitute refugees; destitute refugees—Jews—took the exiles' places as a first step in their new lives as free people. One group lost all they had, while the other found everything they needed—tables, chairs, closets, pots, pans, plates, sometimes clothes, family albums, books, radios, and pets. Most of the immigrants broke into the abandoned Arab houses without direction, without order, without permission. For sev-

eral months the country was caught up in a frenzy of take-what-you-can, first-come, first-served.[30] Afterward, the authorities tried to halt the looting and take control of the allocation of houses, but in general they came too late. Immigrants also took possession of Arab stores and workshops, and some Arab neighborhoods soon looked like Jewish towns in prewar Europe, with tailors, shoemakers, dry-goods merchants—all the traditional Jewish occupations.

Soon, though, unemployment, want, and hunger spread among the new settlers. Arab neighborhoods had been damaged during the war, and municipal and community services had not yet been restored. There wasn't enough electricity and water; sewage flowed in the streets. There were no telephones, clinics, or schools. In villages, matters were more organized. To hand outlying villages over to Jewish settlers was, in part, to meet a strategic political need; settlement of the countryside. Most of the abandoned houses in the villages needed renovation, having been damaged or despoiled during the war. Many were far from other Jewish settlements, cut off from the water, electricity, and sewage networks.

The Arab houses were all occupied within a few months after the War of Independence. At the same time, the state of the immigrant camps grew worse from day to day. "If we compare the objective situation—housing, food, family life—in the DP camps with the situation in our camps in Pardes Hannah, Benyamina, or any other place," said Giora Yoseftal, chief of the Jewish Agency's absorption department, "the [current] conditions in Bergen-Belsen are better, because there, 3,000 people live in a camp built for 13,000, while in our camp built for 8,000 there are 10,000 people."[31] When he wrote, 22,000 immigrants lived in transit camps. A few months later, their number had risen to 100,000, about half of them survivors. In later years, the tribulations of the transit camps would be associated with the absorption of immigrants from the Islamic world. In fact, the beginning was also very difficult for the Holocaust survivors. Here and there, they received preferential treatment, but they went through the same stages of absorption, the same humiliating mass disinfecting with DDT, the same intolerably crowded conditions, meager food, fetid blankets, doorless, sometimes dividerless latrines. Not surprisingly, they felt despondent and unsure of the future.

Members of the Jewish Agency, the *Histadrut*, and *Mapai* frequently blamed themselves for the continuing immigrant housing problem. As the months went on, they were seized by a sense of failure, of despair. They described the situation in the camps as "a crime," "a catastrophe," and "God's own horror," and complained, justifiably, that the leaders of the party, with Ben-Gurion at their head, had not put the welfare of the immigrants higher on their list of priorities. Ben-Gurion responded that he unfortunately could not find the time to see to immigrant absorption. He reprimanded his colleagues, telling them not to spoil the immigrants: "People can live in tents for years," he said. "Anyone who does not want to live in a tent shouldn't come here."[32]

The files of the immigration departments of the Jewish Agency, the *Histadrut*, the municipalities, *Mapai*, and the other parties are full of reports that document the misery of the immigrants. Officials generally took note of the applicant's past in the forms they filled out and the letters they wrote trying to help individual survivors. They often recorded, after the names of the applicants, the names of the concentration camps the applicants had been in, as if these were their country of origin. The Holocaust was reason enough to assist them, the letters indicated. But, as is the way of bureaucrats, the officials were loyal to procedure,

and they tended to think the immigrants were demanding too much. "They want the *yishuv* to set them up in the same situation and same position they had before the Nazis came," one writer for Haaretz complained. He thought this an unreasonable demand.[33]

Regina Hitter, "an immigrant from Bergen-Belsen," was thirty-one when she arrived in Palestine in September 1945, widowed, the mother of a baby girl. She was sent to *Beit Hahalutzot*, a hostel for immigrant women in Haifa. Genia Shvadron, director of the hostel, wrote on Hitter's behalf to the Jewish Agency's Haifa immigration department, which forwarded a copy of her letter to the main office in Jerusalem. "The above-mentioned woman wants very much to learn a trade," Shvadron wrote: girdle making. She had begun to learn this skill in Belgium after her release from Bergen-Belsen. The Tel Aviv office of WIZO (the Women's International Zionist Organization) had given her a 40-lira grant (about $160) for that purpose. Now she needed 50 liras to support herself while taking the four-month course. The *Histadrut* had given her 20 liras. *Beit Hahalutzot* was applying on her behalf for a grant of 30 liras that would enable her to complete her training and make an honorable living. The Haifa immigration department's first application to the main office on Hitter's request was made on November 11, 1945, and is marked with a large, official-looking stamp with the number 6253, file number E-914. In Jerusalem the letter was given the number 218/28098. Three weeks passed. Jerusalem sent a questionnaire to Haifa. Haifa filled it out and returned it to Jerusalem. Jerusalem asked for details about the woman's file to the present date: Who was caring for her daughter? Who was paying for her? Haifa responded. Regina Hitter had received 22.5 liras. Her daughter was in a day-care program. Jerusalem checked this information and discovered in its files that Mrs.

Regina Fertig-Hitter was supposed to receive 10 liras, with another 10 for her daughter. Four more weeks went by. Now there was the question of whether Comrade Regina had received something in advance. In any case, Jerusalem directed that she be paid an additional 10 liras and assumed that this would help her "a great deal" and that therefore "the matter is no longer current." The serial number given to the young woman's affairs had in the meantime grown to 7142/5/405/914. Here the matter ended: Regina Fertig-Hitter of Bergen-Belsen was one of tens of thousands of immigrants who managed to find a place for themselves in one of the country's cities. Golda Meir said of them that they had "disappeared"—no one noticed them, no one knew what they were doing.[34] Whether or not Regina Fertig-Hitter managed to get the rest of the money she needed and found happiness as a girdle maker in Israel we shall never know; perhaps she did.[35]

Some of the aid to immigrants, such as education, medical care, and housing, was given on the basis of political party affiliation. The parties set up special divisions for immigrants. *Mapai*, which controlled most of the absorption machinery, had the greatest potential to benefit—but also the most to lose. The discussions in party councils reflected great anxiety about the party's future, but also a sense of national responsibility. Characteristically, no distinction was made between the two. "In my opinion," wrote the director of the *Bnei Brak* immigrant camp to the head of the *Mapai* immigration division, "every camp director interested in the good of the country and the party must ease the hardships of the immigrants and improve, to the extent possible, their housing conditions; this will necessarily increase sympathy with the party and with the government, both of which are responsible for everything done in the country." The director of the *Bnei Brak* camp had

doubts, apparently, about whether to favor party members, "since that is our job and that is what we were sent here for," or whether to avoid favoritism, because it might harm the party.[36]

The task was impossible. In a time of shortages, putting the care of immigrants in the hands of people who saw it as a party mission necessarily led to preferential treatment and discrimination, or as it was called then, *protektsia*. The Labor party archives contain a file with dozens of brief letters from one *Mapai* official to another, each a request for help for "our people." This was called the "note system."[37] Sometimes the Holocaust past of the "protectionee" was cited in the notes: "The bearer of this letter, Comrade Aharon Kutzik (Kamelnitzki), one of the surviving Warsaw ghetto fighters and one of their leaders, is applying with regard to his housing and is deserving of support."[38] Most of these notes were directed to a special committee of the Jewish Agency, the Functionaries Committee. "Please approve an apartment for Comrade Baruch Vinograd from Poland. The above-noted is an activist in our party. Recently he has been a member of our party's central committee in Poland." Activists of the Zionist parties outside the country received special privileges. Sometimes it was enough for a man to be among the senior members of the party, in which case he was directed to the Jewish Agency's Senior Members Committee: "Please approve an apartment in the Tel Aviv area for Comrade Shmuel Brenner, a senior member of our party in Poland." This note was the 1,715th of its type in the file.[39] . . .

On top of all this, there was the ideological dispute. The *yishuv* was permeated with a deep, almost mystic faith in its superiority, as symbolized by a hardy cactus whose fruit was spiked on the outside and sweet inside—the prickly pear, the *sabra*. Author Yehudit Hendel once said on Israeli television:

To put it bluntly, there were almost two races in this country. There was one race of people who thought they were gods. These were the ones who had had the honor and privilege of being born in Degania, or in the Borochov neighborhood of Givataim, and I belong, as it were, to those gods. I grew up in a workers' neighborhood near Haifa. And there was, we can certainly say, an inferior race. People we saw as inferior who had some kind of flaw, some kind of hunchback, and these were the people who came after the war. I was taught in school that the ugliest, basest thing is not the Exile but the Jew who came from there.[40]

"This people is ugly, impoverished, morally suspect, and hard to love," Leah Goldberg said in a meeting Ben-Gurion held with a group of writers. Like Dostoevsky and Gorky, who were unafraid of ugliness, stench, and lowness, the poet added, the Israeli writer had to see in the Holocaust survivor the human image, and not only the man hiding dollars in his belt. Of course, she said, this was a task that required "a tremendous effort."

Itzhak Sadeh, commander of the *Palmach* elite militia, wrote an often-quoted essay called "My Little Sister." He describes meeting a young woman who has just arrived from Europe. Her body bears a tattoo "For Officers Only." It later emerges that the Germans not only forced her into prostitution but also sterilized her. "Why am I here? Do I deserve to be rescued by these strong, healthy young men, who risk their lives to save mine?" she asks. Sadeh responds: "Be our sister, be our bride, be our mother," and he sums up: "For the sake of my sisters I'll be brave. For the sake of my sisters I'll also be cruel: everything, everything!" It was no coincidence that the Holocaust was symbolized by a prostitute; the metaphor was a continuation of a common stereotype that depicted the Exile as weak, feminine, and passive, and the *yishuv* as strong, masculine, and active.[41]

The *sabra* represented a national ideal, and the Holocaust survivor its reverse. Moreover, the survivors threatened that ideal at a time when sabras were still fighting their parents' generation for preeminence in Israeli society. The country fostered the *sabra* image, seeing in it the fulfillment of the Zionist and labor movement dreams of national renewal and return to a "healthy" social structure. Yet most people could not live up to this ideal. They had not lived long in the country, and many had not yet rid themselves of their "Diaspora mentality." Holocaust survivors imposed on earlier immigrants a past that many had not yet succeeded in putting aside, and their disdain of the survivors often reflected a desire to distance themselves, to deny what they themselves were. The survivors forced the Israelis to realize that the vision of the "new man" was not to be. Most came as refugees, not as visionary Zionists. "Many of them are nothing but migrants who have come because they have nowhere else to go," wrote a *Haaretz* reporter scornfully.[42] The same was true, of course, of many who had come before.

The dissonance between ideal and reality made the Israelis harsher with the new immigrants. The newcomers were expected to identify with the sabra stereotype and transform themselves in its image; the effort to do so was seen as a pledge of loyalty and a rite of entry into the tribe. Aharon Appelfeld wrote of a boy newly arrived from Poland whose fellows beat him because he could not get a suntan like theirs. He assured them that he was trying as hard as he could to make his skin darker, but they told him that, if he really wanted it, it would have happened long before. His pallor forced them to confront the Diaspora and the Holocaust, so they hit him.[43]

Even Rozka Korczak, who had fought the Nazis in the Vilna ghetto and who was received as a heroine, found herself under attack. She arrived in Palestine in December 1944 and soon thereafter appeared at a *Histadrut* convention. She spoke in Yiddish. David Ben-Gurion complained that "Comrade Refugee" was speaking "a foreign language" (or, according to another source, "a foreign, discordant language") instead of speaking Hebrew.[44]

Each new arrival was a reminder that the Zionist movement had been defeated in the Holocaust. The leadership could reiterate that the extermination of the Jews occurred before the Zionist movement had enough power to save them. It could repeat that the Holocaust was proof of the need to establish a Jewish state. It could recall that the British were to blame for having blocked entry to the country and that the Arabs were to blame for making them do so and that the entire world was at fault for standing aside and not coming to the aid of the Jews. It could glorify and extol the few rescue attempts that were made. But none of this could change the fact that the Zionist movement had been helpless. Not only did the *yishuv* not come to the rescue, but it now found itself in a position where its existence and future depended on the willingness of the Holocaust survivors to settle in the country and fortify its army against the Arab threat.

There were those who were inclined to blame European Jewry itself for its extermination. If they had only recognized the truth of Zionism. "Did we not warn them?" wrote author Moshe Smilansky. "Build yourself a home in your country, your homeland, soon, so you will not be lost." But the warning did not help: "The people heard but did not act."[45] Avraham Shlonsky wrote:

The storm jolted them with a shower of
    sparks,
With a fiery rune,

Omens, omens, omens,
And the inferno had already engulfed the
    forest
And they fell deaf, they shielded their eyes.[46]

Haim Yahil took this idea one step further: "After all, we cannot forget that the war against the Jews served the Nazis as a major springboard for capturing and maintaining control," he wrote; the implication was that if the Jews had come to Zion, the Nazis would not have gained power in Germany.[47] An article that appeared in *Haaretz* less than four weeks after the German surrender asked: "Did the Jews also have a hand in the horrible bloodshed committed against our nation?"[48] Such sentiments too were a way for native Israelis to defend themselves against the survivors' accusations and to salve their consciences, tormented by impotence, complacency, and above all, psychological detachment from the Jews of Europe while the Holocaust raged.

Many survivors, for their part, resented, even blamed the *yishuv*: "You danced the hora while we were being burned in the crematoriums," said Yosef Rosensaft, a DP leader at Bergen-Belsen, who settled in America.[49] Usually such things were said only in private. But even unsaid, the accusations poisoned relations between the survivors and the *yishuv*. "The question lurks in our hearts," said Dov Shilansky, who would later serve as speaker of the Knesset. "What did our brothers outside of hell do?"[50] . . .

Within a short time after the survivors began to come, a kind of ideological-emotional compact was settled between the Israelis and the "remnants," built on four basic assumptions that united them during the war effort of 1948, the depression of the 1950s, and the mass immigration from the Islamic countries. The first assumption, enshrined in the Declaration of Independence, stated that the Holocaust had proven once again that the only solution to the Jewish problem was an independent state in Israel. The second assumption was that the rest of the world—literally every nation—was hostile and had done nothing to save the Jews during the Holocaust. "This is the most terrible lesson, perhaps, that we have learned in the present generation," wrote a columnist for *Haaretz*.[51] The third assumption was summed up in the phrase "Holocaust and heroism" and held that the two were of equal moment, "two flames burning in one heart." This assumption was also the ideological basis for the memorial culture that developed over the years.[52] The fourth assumption said that the less everybody talked about the Holocaust, the better. Thus the great silence was born; it continued for years and was broken only at the time of the Kastner trial [in 1954 involving a former leader of Hungarian Jewry]. The assumptions were not the product of conscious deliberation; rather, they arose spontaneously from a recognition that without a consensus of this sort, it would be very hard to live together.

In 1949 the composition of the incoming immigrants began to change. Instead of Holocaust survivors, Jews from Asia and North Africa arrived. The result was that the Holocaust survivors experienced what past immigrants had: they suddenly became "old-timers." Like the German Jews and the Holocaust survivors before them, the immigrants from the Islamic world had to deal not only with practical difficulties but also with a hostile atmosphere. "We need to teach them the most elementary things—how to eat, how to sleep, how to wash," a member of the Jewish Agency executive remarked.[53] Many of them were abandoned upon their arrival in miserable conditions, without proper housing, without education for their children, without medical care, without work. Many lived for a while in front yards, public parks, even on the streets; many went hungry. Their situation was so difficult that one *Mapai* leader who dealt with them said the worst thing any real Zionist could say: "Had I known what awaited them here, I would have voted in favor of leaving them in Syria."[54] Their distress lasted for years, passing on to their children and even grandchildren, and has become a central, painful issue in Israeli history. Yet at base their experience was very similar to that of the Holocaust survivors.

With the arrival of the immigrants from the Arab countries, a new kind of social struggle came into existence. It was no longer old-timers versus Holocaust survivors, sabras versus "debris," but European Jews versus Oriental Jews, *Ashkenazim* versus *Sephardim*. Soon the survivors were part of the European establishment that ruled the country. Anticipating the arrival of more immigrants from Poland, the Jewish Agency executive in 1949 considered a proposal to house them in hotels, reserving the transit camps for immigrants from Arab countries. After all, explained one participant in the discussion, the Europeans belong to our tribe.[55] Soon, the Holocaust survivors would begin receiving payments from Germany, compensation for their suffering and the property they had lost. This, too, widened the gap between them and the newcomers from the Islamic countries and helped bring them, finally, into the tribe.

NOTES

1. Aliav testimony, 55.
2. BGD, October 20, 1945; October 26, 1945; David Ben-Gurion at the JAE, November 21, 1945, CZA.
3. Aharon Hoter-Yishai in Bauer, *Briha*, 102.
4. Yehiam Weitz, "Positions and Approaches in Mapai Regarding the Holocaust of European Jewry, 1939–1945," diss., Hebrew University of Jerusalem, 1988, 58.

5. Eliahu Golomb at the *Mapai*. PC, January 26, 1944, LPA, 24/44; Pinhas Lubianiker at the Histadrut EC, September 5, 1945, LA; on a "great holocaust," see also Yonah Kosoi at the *Mapai* CC, August 14, 1945, LPA, 23/45.

6. David Ben-Gurion at the JAE, February 24, 1946, CZA.

7. Shaul Meirov Avigur at the *Mapai* secretariat, May 3, 1943, LPA, 24/43; also Weitz, "Positions and Approaches," 56 ff.

8. Dobkin, *Immigration and Rescue*, 61 ff.

9. David Ben-Gurion at the JAE, February 11, 1945, CZA; Weitz, "Positions and Approaches," 139 ff.

10. Eliahu Dobkin at the *Mapai* secretariat, November 24, 1942, LPA, 24/42.

11. Yitzhak Refael at the JAE, August 19, 1949, CZA.

12. Moshe Sikron, Immigration to Israel from 1948 to 1953 (Jerusalem: Falk Center, 1957), 16.

13. Hannah Turuk Yablonka, "The Absorption and Integration Problems of the Remnants in Israeli Society in Formation: November 29, 1947, to the end of 1949," diss., Hebrew University, 1990, 13.

14. Smadar Golan, "The Story of Michael Gilad," *Koteret Rashit* 204 (October 29, 1986), 24 ff.; Tom Segev, "The 82nd Blow," *Haaretz*, November 20, 1987, B5. *The Eighty-first Blow* became the name of a well-known film, made by Haim Guri and Zako Erlich. Fifteen years after being rescued, Michael Gilad (Goldman), a police officer, was one of Adolf Eichmann's interrogators, and he was present at the execution.

15. Yaakov Kurtz, *Book of Testimony* (Tel Aviv: Am Oved, 1943), 6.

16. Testimony of Miriam Akavia, videotaped (raw footage for the film *Return to Life*), preserved in the Diaspora Museum and quoted with the kind permission of the museum and the subject. See also Tzvika Dror, ed., *Pages of Testimony: Ninety-six Members of Kibbutz Lohamei Hagetaot Tell Their Stories* (Kibbutz Lohamei Hagetaot: Katznelson Ghetto Fighters' Museum, Hakibbutz Hameuhad, 1984).

17. "Dramatic Meeting between a Mother and Her Soldier Son," *Maariv*, February 9, 1949, 4.

18. Yablonka, "Absorption and Integration," 29.

19. Ada Fishman at the *Mapai* immigration and absorption committee, April 1948, 26 ff., LPA, 7/24/48; Haim Yahil, "The Actions of the Mission to the Survivors, 1945–1949," *Yalkut Moreshet* 30 and 31 (November 1980 and April 1981), 31; Yehiel Duvdevani at the *Mapai* secretariat, January 15, 1946, LPA, 24/46.

20. Elie Wiesel, "Questions That Remain Unanswered," papers for research on the Holocaust, collection 7, 4, Haifa University, 1989.

21. Eliahu Dobkin at the *Mapai* CC, April 29, 1946, LAP, 23/46.

22. Testimony of Hanche Sheich, Moreshet Archive, A 964.

23. S. Davidson, "Holocaust Survivors and Their Families: A Psychotherapeutic Clinical Experiment," *Rofeh Hamishpaha* 10 (August 1981), 313 ff.; Yael Danieli, "The Heterogeneity of Postwar Adaptation in Families of Holocaust Survivors," in Randolph L. Braham, ed., *The Psychological Perspectives of the Holocaust and of Its Aftermath* (Boulder: East European Quarterly, 1988), 109 ff.

24. Tzivia Lubetkin, *The Last on the Walls* (Tel Aviv: Ha-kibbutz Hameuhad, 1947), 5.

25. State prosecutor to minister of justice, August 28, 1949, NA, PMO, 5437/9; undated memo NA, PMO, 5437/19.

26. Yablonka, "Absorption and Integration," 284.

27. The Division for Immigrant Care (Histadrut) to the Immigration Department (*Mapai*), January 25, 1945, LA IV 2351–2061; Ada Fishman at the *Mapai* bureau, April 8, 1947, LPA, 25/47; David Remez, Shaul Avigur, and David Ben-Gurion at the *Mapai* bureau, February 12, 1945, LPA, 25/45; Giora Yoseftal at the *Mapai* CC, December 14, 1948, LPA, 23/48.

28. Heshel Frumkin at the *Mapai* CC, August 9, 1948, LPA, 23/48.

29. Shaul Avigur at the *Mapai* secretariat, April 22, 1949, LPA, 24/49; Giora Yoseftal at the *Mapai* secretariat, April 22, 1949, LPA, 24/49; Yablonka, "Absorption and Integration," 36.

30. Tom Segev, *1949: The First Israelis* (New York: Free Press, 1986), 68 ff.

31. Giora Yoseftal at the *Mapai* CC, December 14, 1948, LPA, 23/48.

32. Eliahu Dobkin and Zalman Aharonowitz at the *Mapai* CC, April 22, 1949, LPA, 24/49; Shaul Avigur and David Ben-Gurion at the *Mapai* bureau, February 12, 1945, LPA, 23/45; Ben-Gurion at the *Mapai* secretariat, April 22, 1949, LPA, 24/49; Ben-Gurion to Dr. Sofer, February 5, 1948, BGA, correspondence; see also Ben-Gurion at the Zionist EC, August 22, 1948, CZA, S/5 323.

33. Arieh Gelblum, "Fundamental Problems of Immigrant Absorption," *Haaretz*, September 28, 1945, 3.

34. Golda Meir at the Histadrut EC, April 29, 1946, LA.

35. Regina Fertig Hitter file, CZA, S/6 242 I/4.

36. Yitzhak Salant to Haim Rokah (undated), LPA, 10−1−5.

37. *Mapai* Haifa to Rokah, September 26, 1948; Absorption Department to Avra-mowitz, December 21, 1948, LPA, 10−1−2.

38. B.A. to Karmi, May 21, 1946, LA, 208 IV 4298.

39. Absorption Department to activists committee, January 5, 1950; Absorption Department to senior members committee, March 8, 1950, LPA, 10−1−3.

40. According to the film *Cloudburst*, produced by Orna Ben-Dor-Niv and Dafna Kaplanski, first broadcast on Israeli television in June 1989.

41. *Writers at a Meeting Summoned by the Prime Minister*, March 27, 1949 (Jerusalem: GPO, 1949); see Anita Shapira, *Land for Power* (Tel Aviv: Am Oved, 1992).

42. Gelblum, "Fundamental Problems."

43. Aharon Appelfeld, *Struck by Light* (Tel Aviv: Hakibbutz Hameuhad, 1980), 61; *Tsror Mihtavim* 7, no. 6 (169) 131, January 22, 1943, 143.

44. *The Sixth Histadrut Convention* (Tel Aviv: Histadrut, 1945), 302; see also Yehuda Tubin et al., eds., *Rozka* (Tel Aviv: Sifriat Poalim, 1988).

45. Moshe Smilansky, "Lesson," *Haaretz*, May 10, 1945, 2.

46. Avraham Shlonsky, "Omens," *Poems* (Tel Aviv: Sifriat Poalim 1971), IV 72.

47. Yahil, "Actions of the Mission," 174.

48. Haim Baltzan, "The Jews Among the War Criminals," *Haaretz*, June 3, 1945, 2.

49. Aliav testimony, BGA, 57.

50. Testimony of Dov Shilansky, Jabotinsky Institute, 6/29/18.

51. Haim Baltzan, "Like Foam on the Water," *Haaretz*, January 31, 1947, 2.

52. David Remez at the Histadrut EC, May 26, 1943, LA.

53. Eliezer Kaplan at the JAE, June 20, 1944, CZA.

54. Ada Fishman at the Histadrut EC, January 23, 1946, LA.

55. S. Eisenberg at the JAE, October 9, 1949, CZA.

America's Incomprehension

BETH B. COHEN

From *Case Closed*

In a front-page article in the *New York Times* of January 19, 1950, the writer's conclusions were summed up in the headline: "DPs Quick to Catch Tempo of America, Survey Shows: New Immigrants Become Self-Sustaining in Short Time and Offer Few Problems—Language Barriers Most Serious."[1] The reporter emphasized the rapidity with which refugees adjusted to life in the United States and cited a survey that demonstrated that their acculturation "is proceeding so fast that they are different from older residents only in their stumbling English."[2] Indeed, this assessment of a quick and successful adaptation of the newcomers, in great measure a result of the host communities' help, was the impression commonly reported and accepted at the time. Today's scholars, among them William Helmreich, in *Against All Odds* (1996), arrive at the same conclusion and emphasize the triumph of the survivors in rebuilding their lives after the war.[3]

. . . Employment, more than anything else, defined success in the DPs' adjustment. This was what agencies communicated and what was depicted in the media. Time after time, in publications ranging from USNA's [United Service for New Americans] *New Neighbors* to the *New York Times*, stories boasted of the speed with which the immigrants had entered America's workforce. That the main objective of NYANA [New York Association for New Americans], for one, was to remove the DPs from the agency relief load within a year

was not mentioned. Nor were the many examples of those individuals for whom one year was simply not sufficient time to find a place to live, become self-supporting, begin to learn a new language, and adapt to a new culture.

These were survivors of the Holocaust, and they were still reeling from their experiences. Even as they endeavored to meet agency agendas, the Holocaust intervened. A close examination of the agency files reflects this. Not that refugees did not make great strides in their new lives. Many did. But others did not. For both groups, the early years in America were fraught with difficulties, which have been not only ignored or minimized, but also transformed into a heroic and victorious story.

Important as employment was, it would be myopic to infer adjustment according to that criterion alone. And comforting as it might be to look only at those who appear to have been successful, it is historically inaccurate. The survivors' path was long and bumpy. Some never regained wholeness. Others pieced together a life as best they could. All were scarred. To suggest a unanimous victory belittles the grave challenges with which they struggled, the depths to which they were misunderstood, and the pain of those who were irrevocably damaged.

Lawrence Langer, the scholar of Holocaust testimonies, art, and literature, has identified the phenomenon of the "disintegrated self among Holocaust survivors.[4] Survivors coexist, Langer has asserted, with the presence of those who did not survive. Their deaths are an essential part of the survivors' beings and hover over them throughout their lives. In a similar vein, Langer also has described how survivors experience two separate notions of time: chronological and durational.[5] In the former, survivors mark their lives within a conventional calendar noted by the usual milestones that typify our days: work, holidays, birthdays. At the same time, they live according to the latter—the narrative of their Holocaust experiences.

Langer formulated his ideas from his analysis of hundreds of videotaped interviews with Holocaust survivors. They are equally applicable to the case files that are assessed in this study. So much of what the survivors confronted when they arrived in the United States was experienced through a veil of irrevocable loss: of mothers, fathers, husbands, wives, children, siblings, friends, youth, status, place, home. The refugees moved through two parallel universes. One consisted of their new life and the demands of finding a place in America. The other was a universe of death from which there was no escape. How the survivors experienced this tension between past and present in the context of their postwar experience is at the heart of this chapter.

The survivors' records dramatically illustrate the impact of the refugees' recently endured trauma on their life in America and how it affected their perceptions, their family, and their health. These records also shatter the myth that survivors chose to be silent about their wartime experiences in the early years because they were too painful, too raw to acknowledge. Telling, scholars hold, came later, beginning with the Eichmann trial. It gained momentum after the survivors had led fruitful lives. In the later years, during the quietude of retirement, after the business of work and raising children had diminished in focus, survivors

would be better able to confront their past. Their readiness, so goes popular theory, was part of the reason behind the proliferation of oral history projects and Holocaust memorials that began in the 1980s.

Case files and survivors' oral histories reveal an entirely different sentiment. They are filled, loud and clear, with the refugees' desire and need to address the past. This need at times seems uncontrollable and at other times ambivalently expressed: bringing these feelings to light also awakens the accompanying anguished memories. What the case files show, too, is how little anyone listened. The conspiracy of silence started not with the survivors, but with the agencies and the greater society, which just did not want to hear.

The DPs arrived in a country that needed to be convinced of their value. In light of this, the media endeavored to promote positive impressions of the refugees to combat both antisemitic and nativist sentiments. The intent was to reinforce the notion that the refugees were the kind of people who belonged in the United States. To that end, the United Jewish Appeal and USNA sponsored a series of radio programs titled *I Am an American Day*, which marked the anniversary of the arrival of the first DPs in the United States in May 1946. Three New York stations, WQXR, WNYC, and WMCA, aired programs on May 18, 1947, dedicated to "the new Americans who have recently reached these shores from war-torn countries, and are now making important contributions to life in America."[6]

The choice of personalities determined by the United Jewish Appeal and USNA for this program reflects the images that the organizations wanted to portray. It also reflects the contemporary Jewish establishment, which was of German, not East European, descent. One *I Am an American Day* radio show featured guest Newbold Morris, a leading New York citizen "whose ancestors came to America 300 years ago as refugees from religious persecution and helped formulate democratic foundations in this country—Lewis Morris signed the Declaration of Independence, Governor [*sic*] Morris drafted the Bill of Rights."[7] This reminded the listening public that even some of America's founding fathers were once refugees too. Another guest was Dr. Maurice Davie, chair of Yale University's sociology department, whose book *Refugees in America*, about the settlement and contribution of German Jews, had recently appeared. The two refugee participants had escaped Nazi Germany by 1939. One was both a baritone with the Metropolitan Opera and a cantor. The other had been an insurance broker in Germany and became a successful farmer in New Jersey. Both men had been in the United States for nearly ten years and were hardly representative of the DPs who began to arrive after the war. Moreover, their Jewish identity was minimized. USNA's programming served several goals: universalizing the refugee, negating any *Ostjuden* (unflattering term for Eastern European Jews) image, and assuring its audience that the DPs not only were not troublesome but were adjusting well and making significant contributions to American life.

One year later, in May 1948, other cities joined New York in observing I Am an American Day. A ceremony in Central Park marked the occasion and Governor Thomas Dewey issued a proclamation from Albany urging wide observance of the day. One newspaper highlighted the stories of a few of these "hopeless refugees who have received a new lease on hope, the homeless wanderers who have put down fresh roots in the fruitful soil of American tradition, to whom the 'I am an American' Day ceremonies, inspired and staged on a coast-to-coast scale by the Hearst newspapers, are a symbol and a beacon."[8]

The cast had changed since 1947, but the press was still careful to universalize the victims. Morris Cohen, an Italian refugee who was interviewed for this article, described himself as a man who hated the Fascists. "Because of this hate," the authors wrote, "he was sent to various concentration camps, Italian and German, including Auschwitz and Belsen."[9] Again, the virtues of American democracy were championed and each DP's desire to become a U.S. citizen was duly noted. While brief mention was made of terrible, degrading experiences, and even of the shattered nerves of the newcomers, the writer emphasized the DPs' eagerness to become full-fledged citizens and their joy at being on American soil.

Certainly many New Americans expressed these positive sentiments. They also described a great deal else about their state of being and the reality of their lives in the postliberation world. Often it was not happy. In direct contradiction to the media reports, DPs in both case files and postwar oral histories almost universally anguished over how very, very difficult it was to start life in America. The shiny veneer of the PR images belied the newcomers' torment.

The process of settling in a new land is multilayered—it is complicated and fraught with difficulty for any immigrant. The DPs faced the expected challenges and more. The process of moving forward in America was invaded by the tensions suggested earlier: the presence of the Holocaust and the unfamiliar demands of daily living. Added to this were the agency requirements. What were the manifestations of these conflicting pressures and how did the agencies' staffs respond?

The social workers articulated their expectations for the refugees but they were mute about their clients' wartime history, and there is little—if any—evidence of their recognition or acknowledgment of the significance of that history. This reflects the attitude they communicated to their clients: do not spend too much time thinking about the past. Despite the lack of encouragement they received, the refugees often referred to their past when discussing employment and other issues of resettlement with the agency staff.

One recurring theme that newcomers expressed was a lack of purpose or meaning to their lives after what they had lived through. Mr. B., who was having trouble beginning his search for employment, illustrates this bleakness perfectly. He confided to his social worker that he felt guilty that he had survived, while his first wife and three children had not. "People live on," he told her, "but after such experiences somehow lose their meaning for living or their desire for living. They more or less exist." And he felt "that he [was] in such a state at this time."[10] The social worker responded in a way that no doubt was meant to be sympathetic but that minimized the depth of her client's grief. She encouraged Mr. B. to find satisfaction in his role as breadwinner for his new wife and their three children. Mr. B. responded that her suggestion might help, but he was pessimistic. At the same time, he did want to learn a trade so that he could take care of his family. Mr. B. saw the necessity of working, but he was also struggling to live with his pain over the murder of his first family at the hands of the Germans and their allies.

Facing a new life in America sometimes elicited emotions that were the antithesis of those the media depicted. Like those of Mr. B., Mr. G.'s wife and children had been killed. Mr. G. talked about how "'dark' he [was] finding life here in America."[11] He was nearly paralyzed by the prospect of beginning anew in a strange place. "All of this was extremely frightening to Mr. G.," wrote his caseworker. She noted that "he would need a great deal of help in moving out of this total fear into some sort of ability to begin picking up one piece at a time." He was having trouble locating work in the first several months in New York and "spoke of the pains he has had and his nervousness now."[12]

One woman, after her arrival in 1949, described the past ten years of her life to the social worker so that the latter might better understand why beginning in America was a nightmare for her client. "While she was hiding from Hitler, her main preoccupation was that she may survive. Then when she went to a DP Camp, her thoughts were preoccupied for herself and her family about coming to this wonderful land, America," her social worker recorded. The narrative abruptly changed course, and this survivor then articulated something quite different. Now that she was here, she confided, "she [wished] that she were not alive."[13] The murder of two of her children tormented her. Although she was sixty-five years old, she begged the agency to help her find work so that she would be occupied.

The idea that being occupied would help block out the past was reiterated by others and dovetailed fortuitously with the agencies' aims. Both client and professional sought the same goal—but for very different reasons. Mr. L., a thirty-nine-year-old Polish man who arrived in Denver in 1951, wanted to find work because he "was very much alone." Expressing his loneliness unleashed his longing for his murdered family, and the social worker listened to his story at length. "Living was very hard," reported the social worker. "Many times in thinking over his experiences he cries quietly. His first night in America he had gone to bed and couldn't sleep, thinking over what had happened and had finally cried himself to sleep. He said that he cannot forget his experiences and he will carry the memory as long as he lives." Mr. L. told the worker, "You can understand why life is not worth very much after all I have seen."[14]

The social worker was not uncaring. She responded that "while he could no doubt never forget his experiences he could adjust and be able to live with those experiences and be a better man because of them." The woman was trying to be helpful, but was she listening? One wonders how the murder of his entire family and two years in a concentration camp made him a better person. At Mr. L.'s next meeting, one week later, his social worker "spoke to him of his being strong and that he survived." She also recognized that although "he would not forget what had happened to him and others in the past, it was something he had to try to put aside and work on his readjustment here in America."[15] The agency's sympathy only went so far. Focusing on the future was the order of the day.

Sometimes the professionals were much less kind about their clients' need to talk about their past. One couple was referred to a psychiatrist who stated that "neither of them revealed any psychotic manifestations but were neurotic individuals, self absorbed [sic] and preoccupied with their past."[16] Another refugee, a young woman plagued by memories of her murdered mother, father, three brothers, and sister, said that she tried "not to think about it" and that she had "the future to start over again in." Her social worker agreed and advised her that "it was hard to forget, but we must all descipline [sic] ourselves to that direction." That the client and her husband were so young "was a big thing in their favor." She was sure that the couple would make a good adjustment.[17] The psychiatric diagnosis and the happy future were two sides of the same coin: finding a way to package the newcomers' past in a way that the agencies could more easily handle.

There were many refugees who did not see work as an immediate panacea and requested a recovery period in America so that they could garner the strength to begin looking for work. Chana L.'s social worker wrote in her NYANA file that the young woman did want to work eventually, but did not believe that she was employable at present, since she felt "weak and tired." Chana's uncle, who accompanied her to the interview, "interjected that she had spent a year and a half in a dark, dank cellar with little food and water."[18] The social worker referred Chana to a clinic for a medical evaluation in order to determine her client's condition, employability, and eligibility for financial aid. The agency was willing to support her if she was deemed medically unfit. For the following nine months NYANA did just that. All the while she was tested, without conclusion, to determine the source of numerous symptoms, including headaches, dizziness, and nausea. Eventually, her uncle found her a job that was not physically taxing, and she entered the workforce.... NYANA would, within certain limitations, support those whom a physician confirmed to be ill. Support is not to be confused with sympathy, however. It was an economic equation. Chana did not need relief beyond her one-year allotment. There was little long-term sympathy or financial support for those whose ailments were not easy to diagnose.

Comments about returning to Europe in the face of what seemed insurmountable obstacles were not uncommon. Mr. K., a nineteen-year-old, said, weeping, to the USNA worker that "he had hoped that things would be better in this country. Life had not been so bad for him in Germany where the Joint Distribution Committee had arranged for him to attend University. Disappointment in America," he told the social worker, "hardly described how he felt."[19] He was lonesome, confused, and "miserable." Another newcomer said that "had he known what difficulties he would meet here and what adventures, he would have stayed over there."[20]

Part of this despair was attributable to the refugees' unhappiness and part to the differing messages that the overseas and American agencies conveyed. Many refugees said that the overseas agencies had promised that the U.S. agencies would take care of them in America. Upon arrival, however, the DPs quickly learned the nature and extent of the agencies' help. Morris L., a Czech Jew, had been sent to England on a children's program after the war. For three years, he was cared for under the auspices of the Central British Fund, a Jewish organization located in London, which serviced refugees.[21] He received full support while he learned a trade. He came to New York in 1950 after he learned of the existence of an uncle, his only living relative. He had also been told by the European agency that USNA would support him until he was self-sufficient. When he learned that the agency could not "go along with this plan," he expressed extreme disappointment. His uncle was too poor to help him and his sponsor had provided an affidavit with the understanding that he "would not be bothered about anything."[22] Morris felt as though he had nowhere to turn. Through his own efforts he found work after several months, feeling very much abandoned by the agency. . . .

There were times when families were torn apart with the help of the agencies, not because the agencies sought the dissolution of the families but because the former perceived that there was no other choice or way of helping the family. Mr. and Mrs. D. turned to JFCS when Chaim, their twelve-year-old son, ran away from Denver.[23] He managed to get as far as New York, where he was found staying at a public welfare shelter. Chaim's father told the social worker about "the difficulty which he [had] had in Europe and in adjusting in this country and was able to say that he was impatient with the boy because of his own nervousness and unhappiness." Surviving the war in hiding was brutal and the murder of their daughter was devastating, but after one and a half years in the United States, the family's struggles were hardly over.

For a short time after his return, Chaim was a model of good behavior, assiduously attending both school and his appointments with his social worker. Once again, however, the story did not end there. When the youth began to withdraw from his parents and stayed away from home, sometimes overnight, the couple returned to the agency for guidance. This time there was a psychological evaluation. Chaim "is neither psychotic or neurotic," the psychiatrist wrote, "but . . . this is a simple behavior and [sic] disorder." The parents were at their wit's end. Simple, orthodox people, who spoke little English, they seemed adrift in their new home and puzzled over the agency's explanation of their son's hostile behavior. The agency suggested a solution: give JFCS custody of the boy and he would be sent to Bellefaire, a residential treatment center in Cleveland. . . . The parents agreed, but the decision was taken with heartache. "Having survived, which in itself to them constitutes a miracle," the social worker reported, "it seems particularly tragic to them now that they have to be separated when an opportunity finally presents itself for them to live together normally as a family."[24] Chaim spent nearly three years at Bellefaire. The reports about his progress there and his visits home were mixed. He finally returned to live with his parents in 1953, planning to finish high school. Whether or not he did is an open question; the parents refused to continue working with JFCS. The case was closed.

That the D. family's wartime experiences had a profound impact on their lives in America seems obvious, yet the agency approached their treatment as they would that of any dysfunctional family. The family's wartime experiences seemed to have had little bearing on how the agency handled the family. One woman, a children's worker, did appear to recognize the aftereffects of the trauma that the newcomers had endured and responded with sensitivity. Unfortunately, her contact with Chaim was brief. The agency, however, looked at this family as though its difficulties had begun the day that Chaim first ran away. There is another possibility, too. The social workers' references to the mother's dull mental status, the father's rigidity, and their orthodoxy, raises a question about the agency's attitude toward this family. Did the agency seek what was best for the family or did the social worker see little hope that these Eastern European Jews were capable of coping with their son in the way that the agency deemed effective? The possible tension between the agency, whose executive director was an Austrian Jew, and the worldview of the immigrants brings another level of complexity to JFCS's response to this family crisis.

Occasionally, parents requested that their children be placed in foster care or an institution because they did not feel able to raise them. This was more common with widowed parents who were caring for their children on their own. Mr. B. placed his daughter, Jan, and her older sister in the Jewish National Home for Asthmatic Children in Denver. He was ill, needed to find work, and could not "establish a home for the children." But Jan's file reveals another wrinkle: Mr. B. was not entirely convinced that the child was, in fact, his daughter. He and his wife had placed their daughter, a toddler at the time, in a convent. His wife was killed and he survived. Two years had elapsed by the time he claimed the girl. The child he took away from the convent school did not completely match his memory's image, but he felt fairly confident that he had made the right choice. Still, doubt lingered. That uncertainty combined

with Jan's "serious personality difficulties" had provoked "definite signs of rejection on the part of Mr. B."[25] Then, too, Mr. B. felt himself to be "emotionally and physically broken" and not up to the challenge of caring for an extremely rebellious adolescent. Jan lived at the home for nearly five years, at the end of which time it was determined that there was no longer a place for the girl; she was getting older and more difficult to handle. Her father talked about buying a house and having Jan and her college-age sister come to live with him. He was involved in a relationship with a woman, however, and the plan for the girls did not materialize. At the age of sixteen Jan was discharged from the institution and went to live with a foster family. For most of her early life and in the eleven years after the war's end, she never lived as part of her nuclear family. Jan was not an orphan, but the Holocaust had nonetheless devastated her family life. This was as clear in 1956 as it had been in 1951 when the family came to the United States to start a new life.

The issue of illness looms astonishingly large in these files, and when the file includes both husband and wife, it is not unusual for each to describe somatic complaints. While the agencies tended to view "real" symptoms more seriously than those they considered "merely" psychosomatic, even the former were minimized. Agencies, after all, evaluated illness in the context of the immigrant's employability. And they saw employment as a form of rehabilitation.

Dr. Gary Zucker was a volunteer physician for NYANA whose first encounter with the agency was as a consultant on some recent arrivals who had inactive TB. His wife, a social worker at NYANA, was working with these refugees, who had spent time in sanitariums in Europe and had recovered to the point where they were acceptable to U.S. Immigration Service.... Dr. Zucker educated the social workers "so that they would know how to shorten [the refugees'] period of dependency." . . . [He] emphasized to the staff that TB was not a disease that was permanently disabling and that the refugees' former dependency on sanitarium care was incompatible with the American philosophy of rehabilitation. Said Dr. Zucker, "You know, it was more humanitarian to get people independent and self-employed or working for other people than just to coddle them." The doctor's statement was emblematic of the fundamental attitude of NYANA and perhaps even also of the times. . . . This attitude is a striking example of how lopsided the ideology was. Little attempt was made to address anything besides the DPs' ability to work. Dr. Zucker proudly estimated that the NYANA budget for prolonged care dropped from 1.3 million dollars to less than three hundred thousand dollars after his recommendations were put into action, as though this reflected the success of the DPs' rehabilitation.[26] . . . [I]t is no surprise that Dr. Zucker was asked to remain as the agency's medical consultant. . . .

One discovery gleaned from analysis of hundreds of case files and oral histories is . . . that the newcomers were clearly suffering from a wide array of psychosomatic ailments. Today, we recognize posttraumatic stress disorder as an illness. It is no surprise that survivors fell victim to this syndrome. What is surprising is that the social workers and physicians, including psychiatrists, made little connection between the numerous somatic complaints and their clients' recent history. Clearly, workers seemed quite averse to delving too deeply into the source of their clients' pain. Not surprisingly, when newcomers were referred for psychological help, it was often because their problems interfered with employment. This was the case with a fifty-year-old woman, Mrs. F., who arrived in Denver alone; her husband and daughter had been killed in Europe. She was determined to reclaim some semblance of her former life as a successful cosmetologist by studying for a Colorado license in this field. Her dreams of opening a small shop of her own remained distant as she struggled with preparing for the exam in English, as well as with JFCS's attitude that her time would be better spent by taking a job. During this period Mrs. F. lived alone in a rundown hotel in the city, anxious for companionship but unsure about how to expand her social circle. She began to manifest a number of ailments for which there appeared to be no organic basis. Finally, the agency recommended psychiatric treatment. The psychiatrist's assessment after their initial meeting was that Mrs. F. suffered from depression resulting from menopause. He treated her accordingly. Mrs. F. accepted the doctor's diagnosis.[27]

Even in extreme cases of psychological disorder, the professionals recommended work as the best medicine. Mr. K.'s history illustrates this dramatically. In conversation with his social worker, he said, "Then I must tell you' and poured our [sic] rapidly his story presenting himself as mentally ill." Thus, his file has a brief but fairly detailed description of his wartime and immediate postliberation experiences. His family was from a shtetl near Kraków. They lived in the ghetto from 1940 to 1942 and then were deported. He managed to escape and survived by hiding in a hole in the ground. He had several breakdowns in the DP camp. "He had headaches, lost his hearing, lost all knowledge of reading and writing," the social worker recorded.[28] When the American Joint Distribution Committee located a relative in the United States, there was a question of whether the consulate would grant him a visa. Despite the official's reservations, he arrived in New York in 1949; even though his relatives found him work in a bakery he could not hold down a job. Although he wanted to work, he continually complained of headaches. He had trouble operating within the agency guidelines for seeking employment. His social worker, at a loss about how to approach the problem, asked the consulting psychiatrist to meet with Mr. K. and make a recommendation. The psychiatrist wrote:

> On the basis of this single interview and the appearance he presented I am wondering whether he isn't showing some sort of depressive residuals from his original psychosis. It seems to me that the approach in this case would be to try to have him taken on by some mental hygiene clinic such as Beth Israel or Lebanon. There he could be observed by the psychiatrists and given psychotherapy and a more definite diagnostic impression of his present behavior pattern can be arrived at. If it should be felt by them that we are indeed dealing with a depressive condition, then they might consider giving him a short series of electric shock treatments. On the other hand, it is possible that with time and encouragement his depression might be alleviated and he might find himself. In any event, I think that you or your Vocational Department should make every effort to continue to find employment for him.[29]

Mr. K.'s file ends there. How his emotional state was reconciled with the agency demands remains unanswered. It seems highly likely that this conflict would continue. What is crystal clear is that putting the refugee to work was the aim, even if his condition dictated electric shock treatments.

Infrequently, the refugee himself realized the connection between his physical symptoms and emotional state and attempted to convey that to the professionals. Mr. H., a widower who arrived in New York City in August 1949, exemplifies how futile this could be. Mr. H.'s wife was murdered in 1942 and he still struggled with this loss in 1950.[30] One social worker, with stunning insensitivity, suggested that he find a new girl to overcome his grief. When he continued to have a number of undiagnosed physical symptoms that interfered with finding work, Mr. H. was referred to a psychiatrist, who wrote:

> Mr. H., 43 years old, was examined by me on June 1, 1950. . . . This patient suffers from a psychoneurosis with depressive and hysterical symptoms. I told him that the best way to get over his complaints would be to start a new life here by getting a regular occupation, and that his chances for recovery would not be good if he would have to spend the whole day without useful work. To this he reacted rather violently, saying that this meant an accusation that he was not willing to work. Nothing of this kind has been expressed by the examiner. It is my opinion that this patient should be put to work as soon as feasible and should continue in any case the training course which he is taking now. It might be well to refer him to some psychiatric clinic where he can talk over his problems as well as find further encouragement.[31]

In the cases of both Mr. H. and Mrs. F., work was seen as a remedy for the client's ills, which underscores the agencies' primary goal for their clients. In both files, too, the newcomers themselves articulate that they want nothing more than to find productive work. Despite that, their depression interferes with the objectives that they and the agencies share. Mr. H.'s history raises another point. He emphasized that he had never been ill before, even in the concentration camp. He fell sick only after liberation. Many others shared Mr. H.'s experience. Sometimes the newcomer observed this in puzzling frustration: why should I be sick now when I am living in freedom and need to work? The Holocaust continued to shadow the refugees even when they were most intent on making a new life in America. Despite survivors' willingness and determination to get settled, their past quickly came back to haunt them and undermine their great efforts.

Mr. F. and his wife came to Denver in 1950 and he began to study immediately for his barber's license. A month after their arrival, he passed the required exam and received the license. A few days later, he called the agency to report enthusiastically that he would be starting a job imminently. Shortly thereafter, his wife came into the office for her appointment with the caseworker. She said that both she and her husband were very happy about his new position, but she was concerned about his health; he could not sleep at night and had chest pains and terrible headaches. . . . For several months, Mr. F.'s symptoms persisted. He said, "he was dragging himself to work and hardly [knew] how he [could] go on." This was said despite his new glasses, treatment for a possible infection, and numerous doctor visits. A tonsillectomy was performed, with no visible improvement in his overall well-being. His marriage began to show the strains of his constant health issues.

Nearly five months later, Mr. F. called his caseworker to say that he was not at all well. He had seen five specialists and all reports were negative. He wanted to discuss the possibility of moving to California because he thought that the climate there might benefit his health. At present, he said, "from his right eye down the back of his head and into his back he had constant pains." After that conversation, his social worker conferred with his physician, who recommended a psychiatric evaluation. The patient agreed, although he could not think of any particular problems, "since he was very happy with his wife and work, and was already very nicely settled here." Mr. F. made no

connection between his physical symptoms and his Holocaust experiences. Initially, neither did Dr. Shere, the agency psychiatrist, as recorded by the caseworker, who first explored other possibilities. He concluded, however, according to the caseworker, ". . . Mr. F is suffering from a persecution complex." The psychiatrist explained that his patient had a deep sense of guilt because "his whole family had perished by the hands of the Nazis, yet he, himself, was in a concentration camp working for them as a barber, and lived rather well, considering the times and how other people were getting along." The psychiatrist noted, "Mr. F. feels he cannot afford to be well, and his many symptoms relate to his guilt complex."[32]

Dr. Shere's analysis of Mr. F.'s problems reflected conventional psychiatry of the early 1950s. He did attempt to link the patient's chronic illness to his concentration camp experiences. But the psychiatrist's ability to help was limited. After Dr. Shere presented his diagnosis to the caseworker and to Dr. Neumann, the former recorded, "We thanked Dr. S for his cooperation and services in the case." There is no mention of treatment. Perhaps the agency was at a loss about how to help. Mr. F.'s case was closed when the agency refused to pay for his request for chiropractic visits. Still ill, the patient searched for a way to ease his suffering.

Unfortunately, both Mr. F.'s story and the way that JFCS responded are typical. It illustrates the newcomer's genuine desire and initial success in rapidly getting on his feet, which the agency supported and applauded. The triumph quickly soured, however, when Mr. F., who had "never been sick not even in the concentration camp" began to suffer from a host of symptoms.[33] The agency responded in what appears to be a sympathetic fashion. It accepted that Mr. F. was sick and facilitated doctors' appointments. But, as noted earlier, this was also an economic equation. In barely more than a month after his arrival in Denver, the newcomer was working and supporting himself. The agency offered advice, direction, and an agency discount for medical referrals, but Mr. F. footed the bill. However, Mr. F.'s caseworker did finally suggest psychological intervention when her client seemed to exhaust all other possibilities. Again, it was an ambivalent show of sympathy. The psychiatrist labeled his patient with a host of complexes and sent him on his way. The agency would not finance any other treatment. The case was closed, but it is hard to imagine that Mr. F.'s troubles were over.

An analysis such as this that challenges the idea of the survivors' triumphant return to life must look, too, at the darkest end of the spectrum: those who were irrevocably shattered. The most extreme were the instances of suicide. These were rare, but they did happen.[34] There were those who made an attempt to end their lives but did not succeed.[35] The files reveal that some survivors became transients, traveling from one Jewish community to another, depending on charity for food and a bed.[36] Others struggled to live within normal society but their spirits were broken beyond repair. Pueblo State Hospital in Colorado was host to several; even electroshock treatment, popular at the time, could not cure their ailments. Children, too, found themselves in institutions, helped along by the agencies, when their parents were too devastated to cope with both their own and their youngsters' sufferings. Where do these stories fit in the accepted narrative about the survivors' experiences in America? To confront them is shattering, but a critical analysis of this period must include their history too.

Holocaust survivors' postwar narrative has been constructed as a triumph: lives once destroyed rebuilt in freedom. This myth has its roots in the immediate postwar years when the refugees first

arrived. Politics, antisemitism, and the national mood shaped their stories and cast them in a victorious glow. Underneath this public patina of hope and success that the media promulgated, the DPs struggled to begin life in America with the constant companionship of their recent Holocaust experiences. Moreover, it is generally accepted that survivors would not or could not speak then about their painful memories and instead endeavored to put the past behind them as they moved forward. Contemporary documents voice exactly the opposite. The survivors had much to say, but their listeners were deaf to what the survivors had to tell them.

NOTES

1. H. Faber, *New York Times*, January 19, 1950, 1.
2. Ibid.
3. William Helmreich, *Against All Odds: Holocaust Survivors and the Successful Lives They Made in America* (New Brunswick NJ: Transaction Press, 1996).
4. Lawrence Langer, "Holocaust and Jewish Memory in the Paintings of Samuel Bak," public lecture, Strassler Family Center for Holocaust and Genocide Studies, Clark University, Worcester MA, September 25, 2002.
5. Lawrence Langer, *Admitting the Holocaust* (Oxford: Oxford University Press, 1995), 14, 18, 20.
6. UJA Press Release, Community Relations Department, May 14, 1947, YIVO Institute for Jewish Research Archives RG 246, Box 66, File 2598.
7. Ibid.
8. Jerome Edelberg and Harry Coren, "Pride, Hope Inspire 'I am an American' Day," *New York Daily Mirror*, May 14, 1948.
9. Ibid.
10. NYANA Case File 425–53, NYANA Archive.
11. NYANA Case File 316–49, 2, NYANA Archive.

12. Ibid, 3.

13. NYANA Case File 329–49, 7, NYANA Archive.

14. Report by D. G., JFCS Caseworker, May 15, 1951, Box 35, File 1004, Record Group 1-065, JFCS, Denver, American Jewish Historical Society.

15. Ibid.

16. Report by A. S., JFCS Caseworker, September 23, 1949, 3, Record Group 1-065, JFCS, Denver, Box 16, File, 980; 1, American Jewish Historical Society.

17. Reports by E. M., JFCS Caseworker, July 14–20, 1952, Box 16, File 2106, Record Group 1-065, JFCS, Denver, American Jewish Historical Society.

18. NYANA Case File 331–49, 1, NYANA Archive.

19. NYANA Case File 303–48, 5, NYANA Archive.

20. NYANA Case File 374–50, 1, NYANA Archive.

21. See Gilbert, The Boys. Morris referred to this as "Bloomsbury House," as did many child survivors, as recorded by Gilbert. Bloomsbury House was the building where the Central British Fund was located.

22. NYANA Case File 374–50, 2, NYANA Archive.

23. Case File Report, Box 13, File 424, 1, Record Group 1-065, JFCS, Denver, American Jewish Historial Society.

24. Ibid, 3.

25. Case File Report, Box 3, File 1766B, 4, Record Group 1-065, JFCS, Denver, American Jewish Historical Society, 4–5.

26. Gary Zucker, M.D., interviewed in New York by Liz Jaffee for the NYANA Oral History Project, New York, May 4, 1993. Reproduced with permission of Dr. Zucker, 2–5.

27. Case File Report, Box 16, Mrs. F. (no file number), Record Group 1-065, JFCS, Denver, American Jewish Historical Society.

28. NYANA Case File 325–49, NYANA Archive.

29. Letter from Psychiatrist to NYANA Social Worker, January 31, 1950, NYANA Case File 325–49, NYANA Archive.

30. NYANA Case File 325–49, NYANA Archive.

31. Letter to USNA from Dr. S., June 2, 1950, NYANA Case File 324–49, NYANA Archive.

32. Reports by A. N., R. K., and S. J., JFCS Caseworkers, January 3, 1950–March 10, 1951, Box 17, F. family (no file number), 10, Record Group 1-065, JFCS, Denver, American Jewish Historical Society, 12, 20.

33. Ibid., 21.

34. Examples cited in interviews with Rabbi Trainin and Robert Berger, M.D.

35. Bluma G., "Interview by Survivors of the Shoah Visual History Foundation," Columbia, South Carolina, June 18, 1998, University of Southern California Shoah Foundation Institute for Visual History and Education, 43565, 3:18:05.

36. Case File Reports, Box 36, File 1806, Record Group 1-065, JFCS, Denver, American Jewish Historical Society.

The Great Reversal

TONY JUDT

From *Postwar*

For Jews, concluded Heinrich Heine, baptism is their "European entry ticket." But that was in 1825, when the price for admission to the modern world was the relinquishing of an oppressive heritage of Jewish difference and isolation. Today, the price of admission to Europe has changed. In an ironic twist . . . , those who would become full Europeans in the dawn of the twenty-first century must first assume a new and far more oppressive heritage. Today the pertinent European reference is not baptism. It is extermination.

Holocaust recognition is our contemporary European entry ticket. In 2004 President Kwasniewski of Poland—seeking to close a painful chapter in his nation's past and bring Poland into line with its EU partners—officially acknowledged the wartime sufferings of Polish Jews, including their victimization at the hands of Poles themselves. Even Romania's outgoing President Iliescu, in a concession to his country's ambition to join the European Union, was constrained the following year to concede what he and his colleagues had long and strenuously denied: that Romania, too, played its part in the destruction of the Jews of Europe.

To be sure, there are other criteria for full participation in the family of Europe. Turkey's continuing refusal to acknowledge the "genocide" of its Armenian population in 1915 will be an impediment to its application for EU membership, just as Serbia will continue to languish on the European doorstep until its political class takes responsibility for the mass murders and other crimes of the Yugoslav wars. But the reason crimes like these now carry such a political charge—and the reason "Europe" has invested itself with the responsibility to make sure that attention is paid to them and to define "Europeans" as people who *do* pay attention to them—is because they are partial instances (in this case before and after the fact respectively) of *the* crime: the attempt by one group of Europeans to exterminate every member of another group of Europeans, here on European soil, within still living memory.

Hitler's "final solution to the Jewish problem" in Europe is not only the source of crucial areas of postwar international jurisprudence—"genocide" or "crimes against humanity." It also adjudicates the moral (and in certain European countries the legal) standing of those who pronounce upon it. To deny or belittle the *Shoah*—the Holocaust—is to place yourself beyond the pale of civilized public discourse. That is why mainstream politicians shun, so far as they can, the company of demagogues like Jean-Marie Le Pen. The Holocaust today is much more than just another undeniable fact about a past that Europeans can no longer choose to ignore. As Europe prepares to leave World War Two behind—as the last memorials are inaugurated, the last surviving combatants and victims honored—the recovered memory of Europe's dead Jews has become the very definition and guarantee of the continent's restored humanity. It wasn't always so.

There was never any mystery about what had happened to Europe's Jews. That an estimated 6 million of them were put to death during the Second World War was widely accepted within a few months of the war's end. The handful of survivors, whether in the displaced persons' camps or their countries of origin, paid implicit witness to the number of dead. . . . The returning remnant was not much welcomed. After years of antisemitic propaganda, local populations everywhere were not only disposed to blame "Jews" in the abstract for their own suffering but were distinctly sorry to see the return of men and women whose jobs, possessions, and apartments they had purloined . . . Little wonder that the future French government minister Simone Veil could write of her return from Bergen Belsen, "We had the feeling that our lives did not count; and yet there were so very few of us." In France (as in Belgium) deported resisters who had survived and now returned were treated as heroes: the saviors of their nation's honor. But Jews, deported not for their politics but on account of their race, could serve no such useful purpose. In any case De Gaulle (like Churchill) was curiously blind to the racial specificity of Hitler's victims, understanding Nazism in the context of Prussian militarism instead. At Nürnberg, the French prosecutor François de Menthon was uncomfortable with the very concept of "crimes against humanity"—he preferred "crimes against peace"—and throughout the trial he made no reference to the deportation or murder of Jews.[1]

Nearly three years later an editorial in *Le Monde* on January 11, 1948, headed "The survivors of the death camps," managed to speak movingly of "280,000 deportees, 25,000 survivors" without once mentioning the word "Jew." Under legislation passed in 1948, the term *'déportés'* could be applied only to French citizens or residents deported for political reasons or for resisting the occupier. No distinction was made regarding the camp to which someone was sent or their fate upon arrival. Thus Jewish children who were locked into trains and shipped to Auschwitz for gassing were described in official documents as "political deportees." With mordant if unintended irony these children, most of whom were the sons and daughters of foreign-born Jews and who had been forcibly separated from their parents by French gendarmes, were then commemorated in documents and upon plaques as having "died for France."[2]

In Belgium, Catholic parties in the first postwar parliament protested at the idea of any compensation being paid to "Jews arrested simply for a racial motive"—most of whom, it was hinted, were probably black marketers. Indeed, in Belgium the exclusion of Jews from any postwar benefits was taken a step further. Since 95 percent of the Jews deported from Belgium had been foreign nationals or stateless, it was determined by a postwar law that—unless they had also fought in the organized resistance movements—surviving Jews who ended up in Belgium after the war would not be eligible for any public aid. In October 1944, the Belgian authorities automatically ascribed the nationality "German" to any Jewish survivor in Belgium who could not prove his or her Belgian citizenship. Theoretically this abolished all wartime "racial" distinctions—but it also turned surviving Jews into de facto enemy aliens who could be interned and whose property was seized (and not returned until January 1947). Such rulings had the attendant benefit of marking these Jews for eventual return to Germany, now that they were no longer threatened by Nazi persecution.

In the Netherlands, where, according to the Dutch resistance paper *Vrij Nederland*, the Nazis themselves had been taken aback at the alacrity with which local citizens and civic leaders cooperated in their own humiliation, the handful of returning Jews was decidedly unwelcome. One of them, Rita Koopman, recalled being greeted thus upon her return: "Quite a lot of you came back. Just be happy you weren't here—how we suffered from hunger!" Indeed, the Dutch did suffer greatly through the "Hunger Winter" of 1944–45 and the many houses vacated by deported Jews, in Amsterdam especially, were a valuable source of wood and other supplies. But for all the enthusiastic cooperation of Dutch wartime officialdom in identifying and rounding up the country's Jews, the postwar authorities—their own conscience clear—felt no obligation to make any particular amends to Jews. Instead, they made a rather self-congratulatory point of refusing to distinguish among Dutch citizens on racial or any other grounds and thus froze the country's lost Jews into retrospective anonymity and invisibility. In the Fifties, the Catholic prime ministers of the Netherlands even declined to contribute to a proposed international monument at Auschwitz, dismissing it as "Communist propaganda."

In eastern Europe there was of course never much question of recognizing Jewish suffering, much less compensating it. . . . After Germany's defeat, many Jews in eastern Europe pursued their wartime survival strategy: hiding their Jewish identity from their colleagues, their neighbors, and even their children, blending as best they could into the postwar world and resuming at least the appearance of normal life. And not only in eastern Europe. In France, although new laws forbade the overt antisemitic rhetoric of prewar public life, the legacy of Vichy remained. The taboos of a later generation had not yet taken hold, and behavior that would in time be frowned upon was still acceptable. As in the Thirties, the Left was not immune. In 1948, the Communist parliamentarian Arthur Ramette drew attention to certain prominent Jewish politicians—Leon Blum, Jules Moch, René Mayer—in order to contrast them with the parliamentarians of his own party: "We Communists have only French names" (a claim as unseemly as it was untrue).

In these circumstances, the choice for most of Europe's Jews seemed stark: depart (for Israel once it came into existence or America after its doors were opened in 1950) or else be silent and, so far as possible, invisible. To be sure, many of them felt an overwhelming urge to speak and bear witness. In Primo Levi's words, he was driven by an "absolute, pathological narrative charge" to write down what he had just experienced. But then Levi's own fate is instructive. When he took *Se questo è un uomo*, the story of his incarceration in Auschwitz, to the leading left-wing Italian publisher Einaudi in 1946, it was rejected out of hand: Levi's narrative of persecution and survival, beginning with his deportation as a Jew rather than as a resister, did not conform to uplifting Italian accounts of nationwide anti-Fascist resistance.

Se questo è un uomo was published instead by a small press in just 2,500 copies—most of which were remaindered in a warehouse in Florence and destroyed in the great flood there twenty years later. Levi's memoir was not published in Britain until 1959, when *If This Is a Man* sold only a few hundred copies (nor did the U.S. edition, under the title *Survival in Auschwitz*, begin to sell well until twenty years later). Gallimard, the most prestigious of the French publishing houses, for a long time resisted buying anything by Levi; only after his death in 1987 did his work and his significance begin to gain recognition in France. Like his subject, then, Primo Levi remained largely inaudible for many years: no one was listening. In 1955, he noted that it had become "indelicate" to speak of the camps: "One risks being accused of setting up as a victim or of indecent exposure." Giuliana Tedeschi, another Italian survivor of Auschwitz, made the same point: "I encountered people who didn't want to know anything, because the Italians, too, had suffered, after all, even those who didn't go to the camps. . . . They used to say, 'For heaven's sake, it's all over,' and so I remained quiet for a long time."[3]

Even in Great Britain the Holocaust was not discussed in public. Just as the representative concentration camp for the French was Buchenwald, with its well-organized committees of Communist political prisoners, so in postwar Britain the iconic image of a Nazi camp was Bergen-Belsen (liberated by British troops); and the skeletal survivors recorded on film and shown in cinema newsreels at the end of the war were not typically identified as Jews.[4] In postwar Britain, too, Jews often preferred to maintain a low profile and keep their memories to themselves. Writing in 1996 of his English childhood as the son of camp survivors, Jeremy Adler recalled that whereas there were no taboos at home about discussing the Holocaust, the topic remained off limits everywhere else: "My friends could boast of how dad had fought with Monty in the desert. My own father's experiences were unmentionable. They had no place until recently. The public cycle from repression to obsession in Britain took about fifty years."[5]

In retrospect it is the universal character of the neglect that is most striking. The Holocaust of the Jews was put out of mind not only in places where there were indeed good reasons not to think about it—like Austria, say (which had just one-tenth the population of prewar Germany but supplied one in two of all concentration camp guards), or Poland; but also in Italy—where most of the nation had no cause for shame on this score—or in Britain, where the war years were otherwise looked upon with pride and even some nostalgia. The rapid onset of the Cold War contributed, of course.[6] But there were other reasons

too. For most Europeans, World War Two had not been about the Jews (except in so far as they were blamed for it), and any suggestion that Jewish suffering might claim pride of place was deeply resented.

The Holocaust was only one of many things that people wanted to forget: "In the fat years after the war . . . Europeans took shelter behind a collective amnesia" (Hans-Magnus Enzensberger). Between their compromises with Fascist administrators and occupying forces, their collaboration with wartime agencies and rulers and their private humiliations, material hardships and personal tragedies, millions of Europeans had good reasons of their own to turn away from the recent past, or else misremember it to better effect. What the French historian Henry Rousso would later dub the "Vichy syndrome"—the decades-long difficulty of acknowledging what had really happened during the war and the overwhelming desire to block the memory or else recast it in a usable way that would not corrode the fragile bonds of postwar society—was by no means unique to France.

Every occupied country in Europe developed its own "Vichy syndrome." The wartime privations of Italians, for example, both at home and in prison camps, diverted public attention from the suffering Italians had caused to others—in the Balkans, for example, or in Italy's African colonies. The stories that the Dutch or the Poles told themselves about the war would sustain the national self-image for decades—the Dutch in particular setting great store by their image as a nation that had resisted, while forgetting as best they could that 23,000 Dutchmen volunteered for the Waffen ss: the largest contingent from Western Europe. Even Norway had somehow to digest the memory that more than one in five of its military officers had voluntarily joined Vidkun Quisling's neo-Nazi *Nasjonal Samling* (National Rally) before or after April 1940. But whereas liberation, resistance and deportees—even heroic defeats like Dunkirk or the Warsaw Rising of 1944—could all be put to some service in compensatory national myth-making, there was nothing "usable" about the Holocaust.

In certain respects it was actually easier for *Germans* to engage and acknowledge the scale of their crime. Not, of course, at first . . . History teaching in the early Federal Republic stopped with the Wilhelminian Empire. With the rare exception of a statesman like Kurt Schumacher—who warned his fellow countrymen as early as June 1947 that they had better learn to "talk for once about the Jews in Germany and the world"—German public figures in the Forties and Fifties managed to avoid any reference to the Final Solution. The American writer Alfred Kazin remarked upon the fact that for his students in Cologne in 1952 "the war was over. The war was not to be mentioned. Not a word was said by my students about the war." When West Germans looked back it was to memories of their own sufferings: in polls taken at the end of the Fifties an overwhelming majority identified the Allied postwar occupation as "the worst time of their lives."

As some observers had already predicted in 1946, the Germans successfully distanced themselves from Hitler: evading both punishment and moral responsibility by offering the Führer to the world as a scapegoat. Indeed there *was* considerable resentment at what Hitler had wrought—but at the harm he had brought down upon the heads of Germans rather than because of what he and Germans had done to others. Targeting the Jews, as it seemed to many Germans in these years, was not so much Hitler's greatest crime as his greatest *error*: in a 1952 survey, nearly two out of five adults in West Germany did not hesitate to inform pollsters that they thought it

was "better" for Germany to have no Jews on its territory.

Attitudes like these were facilitated by the relative absence of nearby reminders of Nazi atrocities; the Nazis had carefully located their main death camps far from the "Old Reich." Not that proximity in itself was any guarantee of sensibility. The fact that Dachau was a suburb of Munich, a tram-ride from the city center, did not in itself advance local understanding of what had taken place there: in January 1948 the Bavarian parliament unanimously voted to convert the site of the Nazi camp there into an *Arbeitslager*, a forced labor camp for "work-shy, asocial elements." As Hannah Arendt observed on visiting Germany in 1950: "Everywhere one notices that there is no reaction to what has happened, but it is hard to say whether this is due to an intentional refusal to mourn or whether it is the expression of a genuine emotional incapacity." In 1955, a Frankfurt court acquitted one Dr. Peters, the general manager of a company that provided the SS with *Zyklon* B gas, on the grounds that there was "insufficient proof" that it had been used to kill deportees.

At the same time, however, Germans—uniquely in Europe—could not deny what they had done to the Jews. They might avoid mention of it; they might insist upon their own sufferings; they might pass the blame up to a "handful" of Nazis. But they could not sidestep responsibility for the subject by attributing the crime of genocide to someone else. Even Adenauer, though he confined himself in public to expressions of sympathy for Jewish "victims" without ever naming those who victimized them, had been constrained to sign a reparations treaty with Israel. And whereas neither the British, nor the French, nor even his fellow Italians showed any interest in the memoirs of Primo Levi, *The Diary of Anne Frank* (admittedly a more accessible document) was to become the best-selling paperback in German history, with over 700,000 copies sold by 1960.

The trigger for German self-interrogation . . . was a series of trials prompted by belated investigations into German crimes on the eastern front. Beginning in Ulm in 1958 with proceedings against members of wartime Operations Groups [*Einsatzgruppen*] followed by the arrest and prosecution of Adolf Eichmann, and culminating in the Frankfurt trials of Auschwitz guards between December 1963 and August 1965, these proceedings were also the first opportunity since the end of the war for camp survivors to speak publicly about their experiences. At the same time the Federal Republic's twenty-year Statute of Limitations for murder was extended (though not yet abolished).

This change in mood was driven in large measure by a wave of antisemitic vandalism at the end of the Fifties and by growing evidence that young Germans were utterly ignorant about the Third Reich: their parents had told them nothing and their teachers avoided the subject. Beginning in 1962, ten West German *Länder* [federal states] announced that henceforth the history of the years 1933–1945—including the extermination of the Jews—would be a required subject in all schools. Konrad Adenauer's initial postwar assumption was thus reversed: the health of German democracy now required that Nazism be remembered rather than forgotten. And attention was increasingly directed to genocide and "crimes against humanity," rather than the "war crimes" with which National Socialism had hitherto been primarily associated. A new generation was to be made aware of the nature—and the scale—of Nazi atrocities. No longer would popular magazines like *Stern* and *Quick* be able to downplay the significance of the camps, as they had done in the

Fifties, or sing the praises of "good" Nazis. A certain public awareness of the unacceptability, the indecency of the recent German past began to take hold.

The change should not be exaggerated. During the Sixties both a West German Chancellor (Kiesinger) and the Federal President (Hans Lübke) were former Nazis—a glaring contradiction in the Bonn Republic's self-image that younger commentators duly noted . . . And it was one thing to tell the truth about the Nazis, quite another to acknowledge the collective responsibility of the German people, a subject on which most of the political class was still silent. Moreover, while the number of West Germans who believed that Hitler would have been one of Germany's greatest statesmen "but for the war" fell from 48 percent in 1955 to 32 percent in 1967, the latter figure (albeit composed overwhelmingly of older respondents) was hardly reassuring.

The real transformation came in the following decade. A series of events—the Six-Day Arab-Israeli War of 1967, Chancellor [Willy] Brandt dropping to his knees at the Warsaw Ghetto memorial, the murder of Israeli athletes at the 1972 Munich Olympics and, finally, the German telecast of the "Holocaust" miniseries in January 1979—combined to place Jews and their sufferings at the head of the German public agenda. Of these the television series was by far the most important. The purest product of American commercial television—its story simple, its characters mostly two-dimensional, its narrative structured for maximum emotional impact—'Holocaust' . . . was execrated and abominated by European *cinéastes* from Edgar Reitz to Claude Lanzmann, who accused it of turning German history into American soap opera and rendering accessible and comprehensible that which should always remain unspeakable and impenetrable.

But these very limitations account for the show's impact. It ran for four consecutive nights on West German national television and was watched by an estimated twenty million viewers—well over half the adult population. It also happened to coincide with another trial, of former guards from the Majdanek death camp: a reminder to viewers that this was unfinished business. The public impact was enormous. Five months later the *Bundestag* [lower house of parliament] voted to abolish the Statute of Limitations for murder (though it should be recorded that among those who voted against was the future Chancellor Helmut Kohl). Henceforward Germans would be among the best informed Europeans on the subject of the *Shoah* and at the forefront of all efforts to maintain public awareness of their country's singular crime. Whereas in 1968 there had been just 471 school groups visiting Dachau, by the end of the Seventies the annual number was well in excess of five thousand.

Knowing—and publicly acknowledging—what Germans had done to Jews four decades earlier was a considerable advance; but situating it in German and European history remained a difficult and unresolved dilemma . . . The new salience of the Holocaust in German public discussion—culminating in the Nineties in copious displays of official remorse for past shortcomings, with Germans indulging in what the writer Peter Schneider called "a kind of self-righteous self-hate"—could not last indefinitely. To ask each new generation of Germans to live forever in Hitler's shadow, to require that they take on responsibility for the memory of Germany's unique guilt and make it the very measure of their national identity, was the least that could be demanded—but far too much to expect.

Elsewhere in Western Europe the process of remembering and acknowledging had to first over-come self-serving local illusions—a process that typically took two generations and many decades. In Austria—where the television "Holocaust" was broadcast just two months after its German showing but with no remotely comparable impact—it was not until the country's President, Kurt Waldheim, was revealed in the mid-Eighties to have played a role in the *Wehrmacht*'s brutal occupation of wartime Yugoslavia that (some) Austrians began a serious, and still incomplete, interrogation of their country's Nazi past. Indeed, the fact that Waldheim had previously served as UN Secretary General without anyone in the international community troubling themselves over his war record fuelled the suspicions of many Austrians that they were being held to uniquely high standards. Austria, after all, had had a postwar Jewish Chancellor (the Socialist Bruno Kreisky), which was more than could be said for the Germans. But no one expected very much of the Austrians. Their largely untroubled relationship to recent history—as late as 1990, nearly two Austrians in five still thought of their country as Hitler's victim rather than his accomplice and 43 percent of Austrians thought Nazism "had good and bad sides"—merely confirmed their own and others' prejudices.[7]

Austria's Alpine neighbor Switzerland was another matter. For forty years after 1945, Switzerland secured a free pass for its wartime record. Not only was it forgotten that the Swiss had made strenuous efforts to keep Jews out; on the contrary, in popular fiction and films everywhere the country was represented as a safe, welcoming haven for any persecuted person who could reach its borders. The Swiss basked in their clear conscience and the envious admiration of the world.

In fact, by 1945 the Swiss had taken in just 28,000 Jews—seven thousand of them before the war began. Wartime refugees were refused work permits—they were supported from payments levied upon wealthy Jewish residents. Not until June 1994 did the authorities in Bern officially acknowledge that the Swiss request (made to Berlin in October 1938) for the Letter "J" to be stamped on the passports of all German Jews—the better to keep them out—was an act of "intolerable racial discrimination." If this were the extent of Swiss misbehavior there would hardly have been much fuss—London and Washington never actually requested an identification tag on Jewish passports, but when it came to saving Jewish refugees the British and American records are hardly a source of pride. But the Swiss went considerably further. . . . A September 13, 1996, editorial in Germany's *Die Zeit*, noting that Switzerland had at last been caught by "the long shadow of the Holocaust"—smacked more than a little of *Schadenfreude*. But it was the simple truth.

The burnished image of wartime Holland—where almost everyone was believed to have "resisted" and done their best to impede German plans—was engaged and discredited somewhat earlier, and by local initiative. By the mid-Sixties multivolume official histories of the Second World War provided copious information about the *what* of the Netherlands's wartime experience, including the deportations, but studiously avoided addressing in detail the *who*, the *how*, and the *why* of the Jewish catastrophe in particular. In any case, few people read them. But in April 1965 a Dutch historian—Jacob Presser—published *Ondergang*, the first full history of the extermination of Dutch Jewry; it sold 100,000 copies in 1965 alone and precipitated a torrent of public interest in its subject.[8] It was followed in short order by an avalanche of television documentaries and other programs about the wartime occupation—one of which, *De bezetting* (The Occupation), was to run for over two decades—and by a shift in official mood. It was in 1965 that a Dutch govern-

ment, for the first time, offered to contribute to the memorial at Auschwitz—though it took another seven years before the Netherlands at last agreed to pay to surviving Jewish deportees the pension that had been accorded resisters and other Nazi victims since 1947.

As in Germany, the trigger for Dutch interest in their occluded past was the Israeli and German trials of the early Sixties. And in the Netherlands as elsewhere, the postwar baby-boomers were curious about recent history and more than a little skeptical of the story they had been told—or, rather, not told—by the "silent generation" of their parents. The social changes of the Sixties helped breach the wall of official silence about the occupation: the breaking of social and sexual taboos—which in parts of the Netherlands, notably Amsterdam, had deeply disruptive implications for a hitherto conservative society—drew in its train a suspicion of other received practices and cultural truisms. For a new cohort of readers the core text of the Dutch Holocaust—Anne Frank's diary—was now read in a very different light: Anne and her family, after all, were betrayed to the Germans by their Dutch neighbors.

By the end of the century, the years 1940–45 had become the most thoroughly studied period in Dutch history. But although the truth about the contribution of the Dutch to the identification, arrest, deportation and death of their Jewish fellow citizens first became public knowledge in the Sixties, it took a long time for the full implications to sink in: not until 1995 did a reigning head of state—Queen Beatrice—publicly acknowledge the tragedy of the Dutch Jews, in the course of a visit to Israel. Perhaps only in the mid-Nineties, with the image of armed Dutch UN peacekeepers standing placidly aside to let Serbian militia round-up and murder seven thousand Muslims at Srebrenica, did the lesson finally strike home. A long-postponed national debate about the price the Dutch have paid for their heritage of order, cooperation, and obedience could at last begin....

It is the tortured, long-denied and serially incomplete memory of France's war—of the Vichy regime and its complicitous, pro-active role in Nazi projects, above all the Final Solution—that has back-shadowed all of Europe's postwar efforts to come to terms with World War Two and the Holocaust. It is not that France behaved the worst. It is that France mattered most. Until 1989, Paris ... was still the intellectual and cultural capital of Europe: perhaps more so than at any time since the Second Empire. France was also by far the most influential state in continental western Europe, thanks to Charles De Gaulle's remarkable achievement in reestablishing his country in the corridors of international power. And it was France—French statesmen, French institutions and French interests—that drove forward, on French terms, the project for a united continent. Until France could look its past in the face, a shadow would hang over the new Europe—the shadow of a lie.

The Vichy problem can be simply stated. Marshall Pétain's regime had been voted into office in July 1940 by the last parliament of France's Third Republic; it was thus the only wartime regime that could claim some continuity, however spurious, with prewar democratic institutions. At least until the end of 1942, an overwhelming majority of French men and women regarded Vichy and its institutions as the legitimate authority in France. And for the Germans, Vichy was an immense convenience—it saved them the trouble of installing a costly occupation regime of their own in so large a country as France, while furnishing them with everything they needed from such a regime: acquiescence in defeat, "war reparations," raw materials, cheap labor, and much

else besides.... As a consequence of this successful assertion of French administrative autonomy, most of the Jewish deportees from France never even saw a foreign uniform until they were handed over to the Germans for final trans-shipment to Auschwitz from the train years at Drancy ... Until then the whole affair was in French hands.

Following the Liberation, for all the obloquy poured upon Pétain and his collaborators, his regime's contribution to the Holocaust was hardly ever invoked, and certainly not by the postwar French authorities themselves. It was not just that the French successfully corralled "Vichy" into a corner of national memory and then mothballed it. They simply didn't make the link between Vichy and Auschwitz. Vichy had betrayed France. Collaborators had committed treason and war crimes. But "crimes against humanity" were ... the affair of Germans. This situation still obtained twenty years later. When the present author studied French history in the UK in the late Sixties the scholarly literature on Vichy France—such as it was—paid almost no attention to the "Jewish" dimension.... There was still a respected school of French historians who argued that the Pétainist "shield" had protected France from "Polonization"—as though Hitler ever intended to treat his western conquests with the barbarous ferocity visited upon the East. And any questioning of the myth of a heroic, nationwide resistance was still off limits—in historiography as in national life.

The only concession French authorities in those years would make to the changing mood abroad came in December 1964 when the National Assembly belatedly incorporated the category of "crimes against humanity" (first defined in the London accords of August 8, 1945) into French law and declared them imprescriptible [i.e., inalienable, irrevocable]. But this too had nothing to do with Vichy. It was a response to the Auschwitz Trial then under way in Frankfurt and intended to facilitate any future prosecution on French soil of individuals (whether German or French) for their direct participation in the Nazis' exterminatory schemes. Just how very far it was from official thinking to reopen the question of France's *collective* responsibility became clear in 1969, when the government forbade French television to show *Le Chagrin et la Pitié* (The Sorrow and the Pity) by Marcel Ophuls.

Ophuls's film, a documentary about the wartime occupation of Clermont Ferrand in central France, was based on interviews with French, British and German subjects. There was almost nothing in it about the Holocaust and not much about Vichy: its theme was the widespread venality and daily collaboration of the war years: Ophuls was peering behind the self-serving postwar story of resistance. But even this was too much for the authorities in the last year of De Gaulle's presidency. And not just the authorities: when the film was finally released two years later, not on national television but in a small cinema in Paris's Quartier Latin, one middle-aged woman was heard to comment, upon exiting the cinema: "Shameful—but what do you expect? Ophuls is Jewish, isn't he?"

It is a point of some note that in France, uniquely, the breakthrough into a more honest engagement with wartime history was the work of foreign historians, two of whom—Eberhard Jäckel in Germany and Robert Paxton in the US, both of whose major books were published between the end of the Sixties and the mid-Seventies—were the first to use German sources to demonstrate how much of Vichy's crimes were undertaken at French initiative. This was not a subject that any native-born scholar had felt comfortable addressing: thirty years after the Liberation of France, national feelings were still acutely sensitive. As

late as 1976, on learning the details of an exhibition planned to memorialize French victims at Auschwitz, the *Ministère des Anciens Combattants* (Ministry of Veterans' Affairs) requested certain changes—the names on the list "lacked a properly French resonance."[9]

As so often in France in those years, such sentiments probably had more to do with wounded pride than with unadorned racism. As recently as 1939, France had been a major international power. But in three short decades it suffered a shattering military defeat, a demeaning occupation, two bloody and embarrassing colonial withdrawals, and (in 1958) a regime change in the form of a near-coup. *La Grande Nation* had accumulated so many losses and humiliations since 1914 that the compensatory propensity to assert national honor on every possible occasion had become deeply ingrained. Inglorious episodes—or worse—were best consigned to a memory-hole. Vichy, after all, was not the only thing that the French were in a hurry to put behind them—no one wanted to talk about the "dirty wars" in Indo-China and Algeria, much less the torture practiced there by the army.

De Gaulle's departure changed little in this respect, even though a younger generation of French men and women showed scant interest in national glory and had no personal investment in the myths surrounding France's recent history. In coming years the French undoubtedly became more aware of the Holocaust and sensitive to Jewish suffering in general—in part thanks to the outrage that followed De Gaulle's notorious press conference of November 27, 1967, in the aftermath of Israel's victory in the Six-Day War, when the French President referred to Jews as "a people sure of themselves and domineering." And the 1985 documentary film *Shoah*, by the French director Claude Lanzmann, had a dramatic impact upon French audiences, despite (or perhaps because of) being concerned almost exclusively with the extermination of Jews in the East.

But even though French historians—following in the wake of their foreign colleagues—were now establishing beyond question the overwhelming responsibility of France's wartime rulers for the fate of Jews deported from French soil, the official French stance never varied. From Georges Pompidou (president from 1969 to 1974) through Valéry Giscard d'Estaing (1974–1981) and on to François Mitterrand (1981–1995), the line remained the same: whatever was done under or by the Vichy regime was the affair of Vichy. Vichy may have taken place in France and been the work of certain Frenchmen. But Vichy was an authoritarian parenthesis in the history of the French Republic. Vichy, in other words, was not "France," and thus France's public conscience was clear.

President Mitterrand, the last French head of state to experience World War Two as an adult (he was born in 1916), had special reason to maintain this Jesuitical distinction. A former Vichyite civil servant, Mitterrand built his subsequent political career in large measure by obscuring the compromises and ambiguities of his own biography and by projecting those ambiguities onto the country at large. He studiously avoided any reference to Vichy on public occasions; and while he was never reluctant to speak out about the Holocaust in general—whether in Jerusalem in 1982 or at home on the fiftieth anniversary of the July 1942 roundup of 12,884 Parisian Jews—he never let slip any suggestion that this was an affair in which France had debts to pay.

The taboo that Mitterrand enforced, embodied and would surely have taken to his grave was finally broken (as so often in this matter) by a series of trials. In 1994, after nearly fifty years in hiding, Paul Touvier—an activist in Vichy's wartime *Milice* [paramilitary force]—was caught and brought to trials for the murder of seven French Jews in June 1944 near Lyon. In himself Touvier was unimportant: a cog in the Vichy machinery and a collaborator of Klaus Barbie, the Gestapo head in Lyon who had been captured and tried in 1987. But Touvier's trial—and the evidence that came out concerning the Vichy authorities' collaboration with the Gestapo and their role in the deportation and murder of Jew—served as a kind of *ersatz* for other trials that never happened: notably that of René Bousquet, the senior police administrator at Vichy. The prosecution of Bousquet, who in 1942 personally negotiated with the German authorities for the delivery of Jews, might have provided France with an occasion to confront the truth about Vichy. And not just Vichy, for Bousquet had lived unscathed for many decades in postwar France, protected by friends in very high places—including Mitterrand himself. But before he could be brought to trial Bousquet was conveniently assassinated (by a "lunatic") in June 1993.

In the wake of Touvier's condemnation, and in the absence of Bousquet, the French judiciary at last found the courage (after Mitterrand's death) to inculpate, arrest and prosecute another major figure, Maurice Papon. A sometime government minister and police chief of Paris under De Gaulle, Papon had been employed as secretary-general of the Bordeaux administrative region during the war. This was a purely bureaucratic post, and his stint in Bordeaux in the service of Pétain had proven no impediment to Papon's successful postwar career as a public servant. While in Bordeaux, however, Papon had been directly responsible for authorizing the arrest and dispatch of the region's Jews to Paris and thence into deportation. It was for this—now defined under French law as a crime against humanity—that he was placed on trial in 1997.

The Papon trial, which lasted six months, revealed no new evidence—except perhaps about the man himself, who displayed an astonishing absence of pity or remorse. And of course the trial came fifty years too late: too late to punish the octogenarian Papon for his crimes, too late to avenge his victims, and too late to save the honor of his country. A number of French historians, called to testify as expert witnesses, declined to appear. Their task, they insisted, was to recount and explain what had happened in France fifty years before, not deploy that knowledge in a criminal prosecution.[10] But the trial was exemplary nonetheless. It demonstrated conclusively that the fine distinction between "Vichy" and "France" so carefully drawn by everyone from De Gaulle to Mitterrand had never existed. Papon was a Frenchman who served the Vichy regime and the subsequent French Republic, both of which were fully aware of his activities in the Bordeaux prefecture and neither of which was troubled by them.

Moreover, Papon was not alone—indeed both the man and his record were decidedly commonplace. Like so many others, all he had done was sign the death warrants of people he never met and to whose fate he was indifferent. The most interesting thing about Papon's case (and that of Bousquet, too) was why it had taken official France nearly fifty years to locate them in its midst—and why, at the very end of the century, the crust of silence finally broke open. There are many explanations, not all of them flattering to the French political class or national media. But the passage of time, together with the psychological significance of the ending of an era, is perhaps the most pertinent.

So long as François Mitterrand remained in office, he incarnated in his very person the national inability to speak openly about the shame of the occupation. With Mitterrand's departure, every-thing changed. His successor, Jacques Chirac, had been just eleven years old when France was liberated in 1944. Within weeks of taking office, on the fifty-third anniversary of the same round up of Parisian Jews about which Mitterrand had always been so circumspect, President Chirac broke a fifty-year taboo and pointedly acknowledged for the first time his country's role in the extermination of the Jews of Europe. Ten years later, on March 15, 2005, at the newly inaugurated Holocaust Museum in Jerusalem, Chirac's Prime Minister, Jean-Pierre Raffarin, solemnly declared: "France was at times an accomplice in this shame. She is bound forever by the debt she has incurred."

By the end of the twentieth century the centrality of the Holocaust in Western European identity and memory seemed secure. To be sure, there remained those occasional individuals and organizations—"revisionists"—who persisted in trying to show that the mass extermination of the Jews could not have taken place (though they were more active in North America than in Europe itself). But such people were confined to the extreme political margins—and their insistence upon the technical impossibility of the genocide paid unintended homage to the very enormity of the Nazi crime. However, the compensatory ubiquity with which Europeans now acknowledged, taught and memorialized the loss of their Jews did carry other risks.

In the first place, there was always the danger of a backlash. Occasionally even mainstream German politicians had been heard to vent frustration at the burden of national guilt—as early as 1969 the Bavarian Christian Social leader Franz-Josef Strauss relieved himself in public of the thought that "a people that has achieved such remarkable economic success has the right not to have to hear anymore about 'Auschwitz.' Politicians of course have their reasons."[11] What was perhaps more indicative of a coming cultural shift was a widespread urge, at the beginning of the twenty-first century, to reopen the question of German suffering after years of public attention to Jewish victims. Artists and critics . . . were now starting to discuss another "unmanaged past": not the extermination of the Jews but the under-acknowledged other side of recent German history. Why, they asked, after all these years should we not speak of the burning of Germany's cities, or even of the uncomfortable truth that life in Hitler's Germany (for Germans) was far from unpleasant, at least until the last years of World War II? Because we should speak instead of what Germany did to the Jews? But we've spoken of this for decades; it has become a routine, a habit. The Federal Republic is one of the most avowedly philosemitic nations in the world; for how much longer must we (Germans) look over our shoulder? New books about "the crimes of the Allies"—the bombing of Dresden, the burning of Hamburg, and the wartime sinking of German refugee ships (the subject of Im Krebsgang, "Crabwalk," a 2002 novel by Günter Grass)—sold in huge numbers.

In the second place, the new found salience of the Holocaust in official accounts of Europe's past carried the danger of a different sort of distortion. For the really uncomfortable truth about World War Two was that what happened to the Jews between 1939 and 1945 was not nearly as important to most of the protagonists as later sensibilities might wish. If many Europeans had managed to ignore for decades the fate of their Jewish neighbors, this was not because they were consumed with guilt and repressing unbearable memories. It was because—except in the minds of a handful of senior Nazis—World War Two was not about the Jews. Even for Nazis the extermination of Jews was part of a more ambitious project of racial cleansing and resettlement.

The understandable temptation to read into the 1940s the knowledge and emotions of half a century later thus invites a rewriting of the historical record: putting antisemitism at the center of European history. How else, after all, are we to account for what happened in Europe in those years? But that is too easy—and in a way too comforting. The reason Vichy was acceptable to most French people after the defeat of 1940, for example, was not that it pleased them to live under a regime that persecuted Jews, but because Pétainist rule allowed the French to continue leading their lives in an illusion of security and normality and with minimum disruption. How the regime treated Jews was a matter of indifference: the Jews just hadn't mattered that much. And much the same was true in most other occupied lands.

Today we may find such indifference shocking—a symptom of something gravely amiss in the moral condition of Europe in the first half of the twentieth century. And we are right to recall that there were also those in every European country who did see what was happening to Jews and did their best to overcome the indifference of their fellow citizens. But if we ignore that indifference and assume instead that most other Europeans experienced the Second World War the way Jews experienced it—as a Vernichtungskrieg, a war of extermination—then we shall furnish ourselves with a new layer of mismemory. In retrospect, "Auschwitz" is the most important thing to know about World War Two. But that is not how things seemed at the time.

It is also not how things seemed in Eastern Europe. To east Europeans, belatedly released after 1989 from the burden of officially mandated Communist interpretations of World War Two, the fin-de-siècle Western preoccupation with the Holocaust of the Jews carries disruptive implications. On the one hand, eastern Europe after 1945 had much more than western Europe to remember—and to forget. There were more Jews in the eastern half of Europe and more of them were killed; most of the killing took place in this region and many more locals took an active part in it. But on the other hand, far greater care was taken by the postwar authorities in eastern Europe to erase all public memory of the Holocaust. It is not that the horrors and crimes of the war in the east were played down—on the contrary, they were repeatedly rehearsed in official rhetoric and enshrined in memorials and textbooks everywhere. It is just that Jews were not part of the story.

In East Germany, where the burden of responsibility for Nazism was imputed uniquely to Hitler's West German heirs, the new regime paid restitution not to Jews but to the Soviet Union. In school texts, Hitler was presented as a tool of monopoly capitalists who seized territory and started wars in pursuit of the interests of big business. The "Day of Remembrance" inaugurated by Walter Ulbricht in 1950 commemorated, not Germany's victims, but eleven million dead "fighters against Hitler fascism." Former concentration camps on East German soil—notably Buchenwald and Sachsenhausen—were converted for a while into "special isolation camps" for political prisoners. Many years later, after Buchenwald had been transformed into a memorial site, its guidebook described the stated aims of "German fascism" as "Destruction of Marxism, revenge for the lost war, and brutal terror against all resisters." In the same booklet, photos of the selection ramp at Auschwitz were captioned with a quote from the German Communist Ernst Thälmann: "The bourgeoisie is serious about its aim to annihilate the party and the entire avant-garde of the working class."[12] This text was not removed until after the fall of Communism.

The same version of events could be found throughout Communist Europe. In Poland it was not possible to deny or minimize what had taken place in extermination camps at Treblinka or Majdanek or Sobibór. But some of these places no longer existed—the Germans had taken extraordinary pains to obliterate them from the landscape before fleeing the advancing Red Army. And where the evidence did survive—as at Auschwitz, a few kilometres from Crakow, Poland's second city—it was retrospectively assigned a different meaning. Although 93 percent of the estimated 1.5 million people murdered at Auschwitz were Jews, the museum established there under the postwar Communist regime listed the victims only by nationality: Polish, Hungarian, German, etc. Polish schoolchildren were indeed paraded past the shocking photos; they were shown the heaps of shoes, hair, and eyeglasses. But they were not told that most of it belonged to Jews.

To be sure, there was the Warsaw Ghetto, whose life and death were indeed memorialized on the site where the ghetto had stood. But the Jewish revolt of 1943 was occluded in Polish memory by the Poles' own Warsaw uprising a year later. In Communist Poland, while no one denied what Germans had done to Jews, the subject was not much discussed. Poland's "re-imprisonment" under the Soviets, together with the widespread belief that Jews had welcomed and even facilitated the Communist takeover, muddied popular recall of the German occupation. In any case, Poles' own wartime suffering diluted local attention to the Jewish Holocaust and was in some measure competitive with it: this issue of "comparative victimhood" would poison Polish-Jewish relations for many decades. The juxtaposition was always inappropriate. . . . There was a difference. For Poles, it was difficult to survive under German occupation, but in principle you could. For Jews it was possible to survive under German occupation, but in principle you could not.

Where a local puppet regime had collaborated with its Nazi overlords, its victims were duly memorialized. But scant attention was paid to the fact that they were disproportionately Jews. There were national categories (Hungarians) and above all social categories (workers), but ethnic and religious tags were studiously avoided. The Second World War . . . was labeled and taught as an anti-Fascist war; its racist dimension was ignored. After 1968, the government of Czechoslovakia even took the trouble to close Prague's Pinkus Synagogue and paint over the inscriptions on its walls that gave the names of Czech Jews killed in the *Shoah*.

When recasting recent history in this region, the postwar Communist authorities could certainly count on an enduring reservoir of anti-Jewish feeling—one reason they went to some trouble to suppress evidence of it even in retrospect (during the Seventies, Polish censors consistently banned allusions to the country's interwar antisemitism). But if east Europeans paid less attention in retrospect to the plight of the Jews, it was not just because they were indifferent at the time or preoccupied with their own survival. It is because the Communists imposed enough suffering and injustice of their own to forge a whole new layer of resentments and memories.

Between 1945 and 1989 the accumulation of deportations, imprisonments, show trials, and "normalizations" made almost everyone in the Soviet bloc either a loser or else complicit in someone else's loss. Apartments, shops, and other property that had been appropriated from dead Jews or expelled Germans were all too often re-expropriated a few years later in the name of Socialism—with the result that after 1989 the question of compensation for past losses became hopelessly tangled in dates. Should people be rec-ompensed for what they lost when the Communists seized power? And if such restitution were made, to whom should it go? To those who had come into possession of it after the war in 1945, only to lose it a few years later? Or should restitution be made to the heirs of those from whom businesses and apartments had been seized or stolen at some point between 1938 and 1945? Which point? 1938? 1939? 1941? On each date there hung politically sensitive definitions of national or ethnic legitimacy as well as moral precedence.[13] . . .

The fall of Communism [in the revolutions of 1989] thus brought in its wake a torrent of bitter memories. Heated debates over what to do with secret police files were only one dimension of the affair. The real problem was the temptation to overcome the memory of Communism by inverting it. What had once been official truth was now discredited root and branch—becoming, as it were, officially false. But this sort of taboo breaking carries its own risks. Before 1989 every anti-Communist had been tarred with the "Fascist" brush. But if "anti-Fascism" had been just another Communist lie, it was very tempting now to look with retrospective sympathy and even favor upon *all* hitherto discredited anti-Communists, Fascists included. Nationalist writers of the nineteen thirties returned to fashion. Post-Communist parliaments in a number of countries passed motions praising Marshal Antonescu of Romania or his counterparts elsewhere in the Balkans and central Europe. Execrated until very recently as nationalists, Fascists, and Nazi collaborators, they would now have statues raised in honor of their wartime heroism (the Romanian parliament even accorded Antonescu one-minute's silence).

With this post-Communist reordering of memory in eastern Europe, the taboo on comparing Communism with Nazism began to crumble. Indeed politicians and scholars started to insist upon such comparisons. In the West this juxta-position remained controversial. Direct comparison between Hitler and Stalin was not the issue: few now disputed the monstrous quality of both dictators. But the suggestion that Communism itself—-before and after Stalin—should be placed in the same category as Fascism or Nazism carried uncomfortable implications for the West's own past, and not only in Germany. To many Western European intellectuals, Communism was a failed variant of a common progressive heritage. But to their central and east European counterparts it was an all too successful local application of the criminal pathologies of twentieth-century authoritarianism and should be remembered thus. Europe might be united, but European memory remained deeply asymmetrical.

The Western solution to the problem of Europe's troublesome memories has been to fix them, quite literally, in stone. By the opening years of the twenty-first century, plaques, memorials, and museums to the victims of Nazism had surface all across western Europe, from Stockholm to Brussels. In some cases, they were amended or "corrected" versions of existing sites; but many were new. Some aspired to an overtly pedagogical function: the Holocaust Memorial which opened in Paris in 2005 combined two existing sites, the Memorial to the Unknown Jewish Martyr and a Center for Contemporary Jewish Documentation. Complete with a stone wall engraved with the names of 76,000 Jews deported from France to Nazi death camps, it echoed both the U.S. Vietnam Memorial and—on a much reduced scale—the ambitions of the Holocaust Memorial Museum in Washington DC or Yad Vashem in Jerusalem. The overwhelming majority of such installations were indeed devoted—in part or whole—to the memory of the Holocaust: the most impressive of them all was opened in Berlin on May 10, 2005.

The explicit message of the latest round of memorials contrasts sharply with the ambiguity and prevarication of an earlier generation of lapidary commemorations. The Berlin memorial, occupying a conspicuous 19,000 square meter site adjacent to the Brandenburg Gate, is the most explicit of them all: far from commemorating ecumenically the "victims of Nazism" it is, quite avowedly, a Memorial to the Murdered Jews of Europe.[14] In Austria, young conscientious objectors could now choose to replace military service with a period in the state-financed *Gedenkdienst* (Commemorative Service, established in 1991), working at major Holocaust institutions as interns and guides. There can be little doubt that Western Europeans—Germans above all—now have ample opportunity to confront the full horror of their recent past. As the German Chancellor Gerhard Schroeder reminded his audience on the sixtieth anniversary of the liberation of Auschwitz, "the memory of the war and the genocide are part of our life. Nothing will change that: these memories are part of our identity."

Elsewhere, however, shadows remain. In Poland, where a newly established Institute of National Memory has striven hard to encourage serious scholarly investigation into controversial historical subjects, official contrition for Poland's own treatment of its Jewish minority has aroused vociferous objections. These are depressingly exemplified in the reaction of Nobel Peace Prize winner and Solidarity hero Lech Walesa to the publication in 2000 of Jan Tomasz Gross's book *Neighbors*, an influential study by an American historian of a wartime massacre of Jews by their Polish neighbors: "Gross," Walesa complained in a radio interview, was out to sow discord between Poles and Jews. He was a "mediocre writer . . . a Jew who tries to make money."

The difficulty of incorporating the destruction of the Jews into contemporary memory in post-Communist Europe is tellingly illustrated by the experience of Hungary. In 2001 the government of Viktor Orbán inaugurated a Holocaust Memorial Day, to be commemorated annually on April 16 (the anniversary of the establishment in 1944 of a ghetto in wartime Budapest). Three years later Orban's successor as prime minister, Péter Medgyessy, opened a Holocaust Memorial Centre in a Budapest house once used to intern Jews. But much of the time this Holocaust Centre stands nearly empty, its exhibits and fact sheets seen by a thin trickle of visitors, many of them foreign. Meanwhile, on the other side of town, Hungarians have flocked to the *Terrorhaza*.

The *Terrorhaza* (House of Terror), as its name suggests, is a museum of horrors. It tells the story of state violence, torture, repression, and dictatorship in Hungary from 1944 to 1989. The dates are significant. As presented to the thousands of schoolchildren and others who pass through its gloomy, Tussaud-like reproduction of the police cells, torture equipment, and interrogation chambers that were once housed there (the House of Terror is in the headquarters of the former Security Police), the *Terrorhaza*'s version of Hungarian history draws no distinction between the thugs of Ferenc Szalasi's Arrow Cross party, who held power there from October 1944 to April 1945, and the Communist regime that was installed after the war. However, the Arrow Cross men—and the extermination of 600,000 Hungarian Jews to which they actively contributed—are represented by just three rooms. The rest of the very large building is devoted to a copiously illustrated and decidedly partisan catalogue of the crimes of Communism.

The not particularly subliminal message here is that Communism and Fascism are equivalent.

Except that they are not: the presentation and content of the Budapest *Terrorhaza* makes it quite clear that, in the eyes of the museum's curators, Communism not only lasted longer but did far more harm than its Nazi predecessor. For many Hungarians of an older generation, this is all the more plausible for conforming to their own experience. And the message has been confirmed by post-Communist Hungarian legislation banning public display of all representations of the country's undemocratic past: not just the swastika or the Arrow Cross symbol but also the hitherto ubiquitous red star and its accompanying hammer and sickle. Rather than evaluate the distinctions between the regimes represented by these symbols, Hungary—in the words of Prime Minister Orbán at the opening of the Budapest House of Terror on February 24, 2002—has simply "slammed the door on the sick twentieth century."

But that door, is not so easy to close. Hungary, like the rest of central and eastern Europe, is still caught in the backdraft.[15] The same Baltic states which have urged upon Moscow the duty to acknowledge its mistreatment of them have been decidedly slow to interrogate their own responsibilities: since winning their independence neither Estonia nor Latvia nor Lithuania has prosecuted a single case against the surviving war criminals in their midst. In Romania—despite former President Iliescu's acknowledgement of his country's participation in the Holocaust—the Memorial to the Victims of Communism and to the Anticommunist Resistance inaugurated at Sighet in 1997 (and supported by the Council of Europe) commemorates assorted interwar and wartime Iron Guard activists and other Romanian fascists and antisemites now recycled as martyrs to Communist persecution.

In support of their insistence upon "equivalence," commentators in Eastern Europe can point to the cult of the victim in contemporary Western political culture. We are moving from winners' history to victims' history, they observe. Very well, then let us be consistent. Even if Nazism and Communism were utterly different in intent—even if, in Raymond Aron's formulation, "there is a difference between a philosophy whose logic is monstrous, and one which can be given a monstrous interpretation"—that was scant consolation to their victims. Human suffering should not be calibrated according to the goals of the perpetrators. In this way of reasoning, for those being punished or killed there, a Communist camp is no better or worse than a Nazi camp.

Similarly, the emphasis upon "rights" (and restitution for their abuse) in modern international jurisprudence and political rhetoric has furnished an argument for those who feel that *their* sufferings and losses have passed unrecognized—and uncompensated. Some conservatives in Germany, taking their cue from international condemnation of "ethnic cleansing," have reopened the claims of German communities expelled from their lands at the end of the Second World War. Why, they ask, was theirs a lesser form of victimhood? Surely what Stalin did to the Poles—or, more recently, what Milosevic did to the Albanians—was no different in kind from what Czechoslovakia's President Benes did to the Sudeten Germans after World War Two? By the early years of the new century there was talk in respectable circles of establishing in Berlin yet another memorial: a Center Against Expulsions, a museum devoted to all victims of ethnic cleansing. . . .

There are risks, though, of indulging in the cult of commemoration to excess. On the one hand there is no limit in principle to the memories and experiences worthy of recall. On the other hand, to memorialize the past in edifices and museums is

also a way to contain and even neglect it—leaving the responsibility of memory to others. So long as there were men and women around who really did remember, from personal experience, this did not perhaps matter. But now, as the 81-year-old Jorge Semprun reminded his fellow survivors at the sixtieth anniversary of the liberation of Buchenwald on April 10, 2005, "the cycle of active memory is closing."

Even if Europe *could* somehow cling indefinitely to a living memory of past crimes—which is what the memorials and museums are designed, however inadequately, to achieve—there would be little point. Memory is inherently contentious and partisan: one man's acknowledgement is another's omission. And it is a poor guide to the past. The first postwar Europe was built upon deliberate mismemory—upon forgetting as a way of life. Since 1989, Europe has been constructed instead upon a compensatory surplus of memory: institutionalized public remembering as the very foundation of collective identity. The first could not endure—but nor will the second. Some measure of neglect and even forgetting is the necessary condition for civic health.

To say this is not to advocate amnesia. A nation has first to have remembered something before it can begin to forget it. Until the French understood Vichy as it was—and not as they had chosen to misremember it—they could not put it aside and move on. The same is true of Poles in their convoluted recollection of the Jews who once lived in their midst. The same will be true of Spain, too, which for twenty years following its transition to democracy drew a tacit veil across the painful memory of the civil war. Public discussion of that war and its outcome is only now getting under way.[16] Only after Germans had appreciated and digested the enormity of their Nazi past—a sixty-year cycle of denial, education, debate and consensus—could they begin to live with it, i.e., put it behind them.

The instrument of recall in all such cases was not memory itself. It was *history*, in both its meanings: as the passage of time and as the professional study of the past—the latter above all. Evil, above all evil on the scale practiced by Nazi Germany, can never be satisfactorily remembered. The very enormity of the crime renders all memorialization incomplete.[17] Its inherent implausibility—the sheer difficulty of conceiving of it in calm retrospect—opens the door to diminution and even denial. Impossible, to remember as it truly was, it is inherently vulnerable to being remembered as it wasn't. Against *this* challenge memory itself is helpless: "Only the historian, with the austere passion for fact, proof, evidence, which are central to his vocation, can effectively stand guard."[18]

Unlike memory, which confirms and reinforces itself, history contributes to the disenchantment of the world. Most of what it has to offer is discomforting, even disruptive, which is why it is not always politically prudent to wield the past as a moral cudgel with which to beat and berate a people for its past sins. But history does need to be learned, and periodically relearned. In a popular Soviet era joke, a listener calls up "Armenian Radio" with a question: "Is it possible," he asks, "to foretell the future?" Answer: "Yes, no problem. We know exactly what the future will be. Our problem is with the past: that keeps changing."

The rigorous investigation and interrogation of Europe's competing pasts—and the place occupied by those pasts in Europeans' collective sense of themselves—has been one of the unsung achievements and sources of European unity in recent decades. It is, however, an achievement that will surely lapse unless ceaselessly renewed. Europe's barbarous recent history, the dark "other" against which postwar Europe was laboriously constructed, is already beyond recall for young Europeans. Within a generation the memorials and museums will be gathering dust—visited, like the battlefields of the Western Front today, only by aficionados and relatives.

If in years to come we are to remember why it seemed so important to build a certain sort of Europe out of the crematoria of Auschwitz, only history can help us. It will have to be taught afresh with each passing generation. Memory may be a response to history, but it can never be a substitute.

NOTES

1. The American prosecutor Telford Taylor was struck by this in retrospect but acknowledges that he did not even notice it at the time—a revealing admission. See Telford Taylor, *The Anatomy of the Nuremberg Trials* (New York, 1992), 296.

2. In the town of Pithiviers, near Orléans, where Jewish children rounded up in Paris were kept until their shipment east, a monument was actually erected in 1957 bearing the inscription *"A nos déportés morts pour la France."* Only in 1992 did the local municipality erect a new plaque, more accurate if less reassuring. It reads: "To the memory of the 2300 Jewish children interned at the Pithiviers camp from July 19 to September 6, 1942, before being deported and murdered in Auschwitz."

3. Giuliana Tedeschi is quoted by Nicola Caracciolo in *Uncertain Refuge: Italy and the Jews During the Holocaust* (University of Illinois Press, 1995), 121.

4. In postwar Britain, an unusually thin or sickly person might be described as looking "like something out of Belsen." In France, fairground chambers of horror were labeled "Buchenwalds" as an inducement to voyeuristic trade.

5. See *The Times Literary Supplement* for October 4, 1996.

6. Especially in America. In 1950 the Displaced Persons' Commission of the U.S. Congress stated that "The Baltic Waffen ss units are to be considered as separate and distinct in purpose, ideology, activities and qualifications from the German ss. Therefore the Commission holds them not to be a movement hostile to the government of the United States." The Baltic *Waffen ss* had been among the most brutal and enthusiastic when it came to torturing and killing Jews on the Eastern Front; but in the novel circumstances of the Cold War they were of course "our" Nazis.

7. In October 1991, following the desecration of tombs in Vienna's Jewish cemetery, Gallup polled Austrians on their attitude to Jews: 20 percent thought positions of authority should be closed to Jews; 31 percent declared that they would not want a Jew as a neighbor; fully 50 percent were ready to agree with the proposition that "Jews are responsible for their past persecution."

8. *Ondergang* was published in English in 1968 as *The Destruction of the Dutch Jews*.

9. See Sonia Combe, *Archives interdites: Les peurs françaises face à l'histoire contemporaine* (Paris: Albin Michel, 1994), 14.

10. Professor Paxton of Columbia University, who had initiated historical investigation into Vichy's crimes nearly a quarter of a century earlier (when most of his French colleagues were otherwise engaged), took a less monastic view of his professional calling and gave important testimony.

11. When U.S. President Ronald Reagan, on a visit to West Germany in 1985, was advised to avoid the military cemetery at Bitburg (site of a number of ss graves) and pay his respects at a concentration camp instead, Chancellor Kohl wrote to warn him that this "would have a serious psychological effect on the friendly sentiments of the German people for the United States of America." The Americans duly capitulated; Reagan visited Belsen *and* Bitburg.

12. Quoted by Ian Buruma in "Buchenwald," *Granta* 42 (1992).

13. When the Czechoslovak parliament voted in 1991 to restitute property seized after the war it explicitly limited the benefits to those expropriated after *1948*—so as to exclude Sudeten Germans expelled in 1945–46 before the Communists seized power.

14. The memorial was not uncontroversial: in addition to many who disliked its abstract conception there were those, including a Christian Democrat Mayor of the city, Eberhard Diepgen, who criticized it for helping turn Berlin into "the capital of repentance."

15. In March 2004, eighty-four Hungarian writers, including Péter Esterházy and György Konrád, left the country's Writers' Union in protest at its tolerance of antisemitism. The occasion for the walk out were comments by the poet Kornel Döbrentei following the award of the Nobel Prize for Literature to the Holocaust survivor Imre Kertész. The prize, according to Döbrentei, was "conscience money" for a writer who was just indulging the "taste for terror" of "his minority."

16. The last statue of Franco in Madrid was quietly removed at dawn in front of an audience of one hundred onlookers on March 17, 2005.

17. "We, the survivors, are not the true witnesses. . . . We are . . . an anomalous minority: we are those who by their prevarications or their attributes or their good luck did not touch bottom. Those who did so, those who saw the Gorgon, have not returned to tell about it, or they returned mute." Primo Levi, *The Drowned and the Saved* (New York, 1988), 83–84.

18. Yosef Hayim Yerushalmi, *Zakhor: Jewish History and Jewish Memory* (Seattle, 1982), 116.

The Pathology of Denial

RICHARD J. EVANS

From *Lying about Hitler*

At issue in the [libel] case brought by [David] Irving against [Deborah] Lipstadt was not only her contention that he falsified history, but also her allegation that he was a Holocaust denier (*Denying the Holocaust*, 111). What exactly did this mean? . . . There was wide agreement among historians that there was a systematic attempt undertaken by the Nazi regime in Germany between 1941 and 1945 to kill all the Jews of Europe, and that it succeeded to the extent of murdering between 5 and 6 million of them in a variety of ways, including mass gassings in camps specially constructed for the purpose. . . . Standing apart from this scholarly literature was an attempt by a small number of writers to deny that there was any systematic or organized extermination of Europe's Jews by the Nazis; to suggest that the number of Jews killed was far smaller than 5 or 6 million; and to claim that there were no gas chambers or other specially built extermination facilities. Who were these people? I knew something about them from my reading of Lipstadt's book, but reading them in the original was an altogether different experience from encountering them through the filter of Lipstadt's cool, academic prose. They inhabited an intellectual world that was far removed from the cautious rationality of academic historical scholarship. What moved them seemed to be a strange mixture of prejudice and bitter personal experience.

After the war, perhaps the earliest proponent of these views was the Frenchman Paul Rassinier (1908–67). Rassinier had apparently been beaten by a communist fellow prisoner in the Buchenwald concentration camp for failing to recognize or pay his respects to the imprisoned German communist leader Ernst Thälmann (subsequently murdered by the ss in 1944). His fellow prisoners seemed more dangerous than the ss guards to him. Rassinier eventually got a relatively easy job in the infirmary on his transfer to camp Dora in the Harz mountains, where he was evidently well treated by his boss, a senior ss officer. These experiences seem to have prejudiced him in favor of the Nazis. He initially published a defense of the ss against its critics and denied reports by survivors of atrocities in the camps, then went on to dispute the existence of the gas chambers and to assert that it was the Jews who had started the Second World War.[1]

Another relatively early denier was Austin J. App, author of *The Six Million Swindle: Blackmailing the German People for Hard Marks with Fabricated Corpses*. App estimated the total number of Jewish casualties of the Third Reich at around three hundred thousand, and declared the "six million" to be "an impudent lie." Born in 1902, App was for a time president of the Federation of American Citizens of German Descent, and in 1942 he campaigned in the United States in support of Nazi war aims. In the early years after the war, he defended the Nazi mass murder of the Jews and similar atrocities as legitimate acts of war, minimized the numbers of victims, and denied the existence of gas chambers. In his book, he argued that the "fraudulent six million casualty" figure for Jewish deaths at the hands of the Nazis was used "vindictively as an external club for pressuring indemnities out of West Germany and for wringing financial contributions out of American Jews." He alleged that at least five hundred thousand of the Jews supposedly gassed in the camps had gone to Israel. The perpetuation of the "swindle" was due to Jewish domination of the media. The Americans and the British and above all the Soviet Union colluded in the deception in order to distract attention from their own war crimes.[2]

Perhaps the most influential proponent of such views was Arthur R. Butz, an [electrical] engineering professor at Chicago's Northwestern University, whose book *The Hoax of the Twentieth Century*, published in 1976, constituted the first attempt to present Holocaust denial in a pseudo-academic form. Its eight chapters were adorned with 450 footnotes, 5 appendices, and 32 plates and diagrams and it looked at first glance like an academic treatise. The book argued, *inter alia*, that the Allied bombing of Dresden produced more corpses than had ever been found from the camps, that Zyklon B gas was used strictly as an insecticide, that Auschwitz was an industrial plant, that deaths there were mainly caused by typhus, and that no gassings took place there. In Butz' view, when the Nazis talked or wrote about *Judentum* (Jewry), they meant the destruction of Jewish power, not of Jewish human beings, and when they used the word *annihilation* (*Vernichtung*) or *extirpation* (*Ausrottung*) in this context, they did not mean actual killing. He alleged that the failure of the Yad Vashem memorial to the Holocaust in Jerusalem to collect 6 million names of those who had died proved that the number of dead was far fewer than 6 million. The Nuremberg tri-

als were a frame-up in Butz' view, and the myth of the Holocaust was propagated after the war by the Jews for their own advantage.[3]

Perhaps the most active and vocal of the deniers in the 1980s and 1990s was the Frenchman Robert Faurisson, a former university teacher of French literature who had argued over many years that "the alleged massacres in the 'gas chambers' and the alleged 'genocide' were part of the same lie," which "is essentially Zionist in origin" and "has allowed a huge political and financial swindle of which the state of Israel is the principal beneficiary." Faurisson concentrated in particular on attempting to prove that the gas chambers at Auschwitz and in other camps never existed. He was tried in his native France for slander, violation of Article 382 of the Civil Code by willfully distorting history, and incitement to racial hatred, which had been outlawed under a law of 1972, and was found guilty on all three counts.[4]

As well as these three figures, a role was also played in the denial phenomenon by Wilhelm Staeglich, an academically qualified German lawyer whose book *Der Auschwitz-Mythos: Legende oder Wirklichkeit* (The Auschwitz Myth: Legend or Reality), published in 1979 by the far-right Grabert-Verlag in Germany, followed Butz in presenting Holocaust denial in a pseudo-academic form. The book argued that there had been no mass extermination of Jews in Nazi extermination camps and that guilty verdicts in postwar trials of the perpetrators were wrong. Staeglich used minor discrepancies in postwar documents and reports of the extermination to dismiss all such documents as forgeries and falsifications. As a result of this book, Staeglich was dismissed from state employment, and his doctoral title was withdrawn by his university.[5]

Figures such as these operated on the fringes of public life. Their books were mostly distributed by mail order and could seldom be found on the shelves of respectable bookshops or libraries. They seemed to belong in the world of sensational newspapers such as you could buy in American supermarkets, recounting the experiences of people who had been abducted by little green aliens or who had seen Elvis Presley still alive. . . .

The writings of people like Rassinier, Butz, Faurisson, and Staeglich were different, however. For a start, it was surely deeply offensive to the many thousands of Hitler's victims who had been through the camps and the persecution and were now confronted by people telling them that virtually nothing of what they had suffered had ever happened. Those who had lost relatives and loved ones in the Nazi extermination program were now being told that they had not lost them at all or if they had, it was through disease or secret emigration to Palestine. Moreover, . . . the denial of such a large and complex chunk of history as the systematic extermination of millions of Jews by the Nazis . . . called in question a huge mass of historical evidence carefully gathered and interpreted by professional historians over the decades. [Finally,] the writings of the Holocaust deniers seemed neither morally nor politically harmless. On the contrary, a good many of them seemed to be linked to racial hatred and antisemitic animosity in the most direct possible way. And, . . . the Holocaust deniers were not maverick individualists but fed off each other's work and organized journals, conferences, and institutes to exchange views and disseminate publications.

It was for these reasons that they had attracted a good deal of attention from serious scholars in recent years. Deborah Lipstadt's book, published in the United States in 1993, was the most thorough study of the deniers, but it was by no means the first. Others who sought to describe and explain the phenomenon included the British political scientist Roger Eatwell,[6] the distinguished French historian Pierre Vidal-Naquet . . . ,[7] the Israeli scholar Yisrael Gutman . . . ,[8] the German political scientist Armin Pfahl-Traughber,[9] and Limor Yagil, a researcher . . . at the Faculty of Humanities, Tel Aviv University.[10] An important early book on this phenomenon was Gill Seidel's *The Holocaust Denial: Antisemitism, Racism and the New Right*, published in 1986.[11]

Clearly there were some differences among these various authors' depictions of Holocaust denial, and equally clearly, not all Holocaust deniers subscribed to all the views which they mentioned, or held them to the same degree. However, reducing them all to a lowest common denominator, it seemed clear that Holocaust denial involved the minimum following beliefs:

(a) The number of Jews killed by the Nazis was far less than 6 million; it amounted to only a few hundred thousand, and was thus similar to, or less than, the number of German civilians killed in Allied bombing raids.

(b) Gas chambers were not used to kill large numbers of Jews at any time.

(c) Neither Hitler nor the Nazi leadership in general had a program of exterminating Europe's Jews; all they wished to do was to deport them to Eastern Europe.

(d) "The Holocaust" was a myth invented by Allied propaganda during the war and sustained since then by Jews who wished to use it to gain political and financial support for the state of Israel or for themselves. The supposed evidence for the Nazis' wartime mass murder of millions of Jews by gassing and other means was fabricated after the war.[12]

Lipstadt had alleged in her book that Irving belonged to the weird and irrational world of

Holocaust denial. Whether or not he could reasonably be called a "Holocaust denier" could be determined by examining his public statements to see if these four basic principles of Holocaust denial were present. Did what he had said and written about the Nazi extermination of the Jews conform to what Rassinier, Butz, Faurisson, Staeglich, and others had said and written? And did he have any contacts with such individuals or with organizations devoted to Holocaust denial? I determined to find out.

In his written submission to the court, Irving wrote: "It is a particularly mischievous and damaging libel to call the Plaintiff 'a Holocaust denier,' a lie worthy of the Nazi propaganda minister Dr. Goebbels himself."[13] Irving asserted "that the whole of World War Two can be defined as a Holocaust." He considered it "invidious to single out one single act of mass murder of innocents and to label it 'The Holocaust,' as though there was none other." He went on:

If however the Defendants seek to define the Holocaust as the mass murder of Jews by the Nazis and their cohorts during World War II, then the Plaintiff maintains that he has at no time denied it; on the contrary, he has rendered it more plausible by investigating documents, questioning witnesses, and uncovering fresh sources and making no secret of for example the alleged liquidation of 152,000 Jews at Chelmno . . . , about which he wrote in Hitler's War, 1991 edition, at page 426. At page 7 of his book on aerial warfare against civilians Von Guernica bis Vietnam (From Guernica to Vietnam), the very first page of text, the Plaintiff emphasized: "The massacre of minorities by the National Socialists in Germany . . . probably cost more lives than all the air raids carried out to the present date."[14]

Similarly, Irving maintained that he had "at no time denied that the Nazis established concentration camps throughout their territories." He had "at no time denied that the murder of the Jews began in about June 1941 when the Germans invaded the Soviet Union, or that hundreds of thousands of Jews were shot to death." In this context he referred to pages 270–71 of the 1977 edition of Hitler's War, pages 380–81 of the revised 1991 edition of the same book, and unnumbered pages of his 1996 biography of Goebbels.[15]

When I looked at them more closely, however, it became clear that these points did not really relate to the Holocaust as defined by most historians. Irving wrote only of an alleged liquidation at Chelmno; he did not accept, therefore, that 152,000 Jews were actually killed there. He referred to concentration camps, but the existence of such camps was not at issue, for nobody denied that concentration camps were built to imprison those whom the Nazis regarded as their enemies, above all within the borders of the Reich, at Dachau, Buchenwald, Bergen-Belsen, Flossenbürg, and elsewhere. What was at issue was a different category of camp, namely those constructed in occupied Eastern Europe, such as Belzec, Sobibór, Treblinka, and Chelmno, and built specifically and exclusively to exterminate Jews or, in the case of Auschwitz-Birkenau, with extermination as one of its principal aims: in other words, the extermination camps. Finally, the murder by shooting of hundreds of thousands of Jews was not the same as the extermination by shooting, gassing, starvation, and deliberate neglect of millions of Jews which formed an essential part of the Holocaust as conventionally understood.

Moreover, the book on aerial warfare to which Irving referred was published in 1982. On reading through his many books and speeches, I soon realized that Irving's views on these issues had not stood still over time. In his introduction to the first edition of *Hitler's War*, Irving referred to "the methodical liquidation of Russian Jews during the 'Barbarossa' invasion of 1941," and also to the fact that the Nazis "kept the extermination machinery going until the end of the war."[16] Leaving aside for the moment Irving's view of Hitler's role in all this, it was clear that in 1977 Irving accepted that the Nazis had systematically killed the Jews of Europe in very large numbers. In the index to the 1977 edition of *Hitler's War*, for example, there were seventeen entries under the heading "Jews, extermination of, documenting responsibility for and knowledge of," referring to thirty-one pages of text. Another entry in the index was for "Auschwitz, extermination camp at." These pages made no attempt to deny the fact of the extermination. When the Jews were deported to the East on Hitler's orders, Irving wrote on page 391, their fate was determined by lower level officials. "Arriving at Auschwitz and Treblinka, four in every ten were pronounced fit for work; the rest were exterminated with a maximum of concealment." Similarly, on page 332 of the 1977 edition of *Hitler's War*, Irving referred to "the extermination program," which, he wrote, "had gained a momentum of its own."

All this had made it plain to most commentators that Irving was not a hard-core Holocaust denier in the 1970s or early 1980s.[17] By the end of the 1980s, however, all this had changed, and Irving had clearly moved from "soft-core" to "hard-core" Holocaust denial.[18] When I looked at the 1991 edition of *Hitler's War*, it became clear that the picture painted by Irving here was very different from what it had looked like in the first edition. The references made in 1977 to "the extermination of the Jews," "the methodical liquidation of Russian Jews," and "the extermination machinery" had all been deleted from the introduction by 1991. Indeed, the word *extermination* no longer

appeared at all. Instead, Irving referred vaguely to "the Jewish tragedy," "the Nazi maltreatment of the Jews," or "the entire tragedy." The index entry was still there in 1991, as in 1977, for "Auschwitz, extermination camp at," as it was for "Treblinka, extermination camp at." But on the pages in question (463–67 in 1991, 390–93 in 1977) the account had undergone some significant alterations. In 1991, the 1977 references to the "murder machinery" and "the extermination center at Treblinka," had gone. In their place was new material describing Himmler's visit to Auschwitz on July 18, 1942, and citing the postwar interrogation of Albert Hoffmann, an SS man who accompanied Himmler on the visit, noting that "maltreatment did occur" but adding that he "totally disbelieves the accounts of atrocities as published in the press" after the war. Irving explicitly denied that there was any documentary sanction for the story that Himmler witnessed the "liquidation" of a trainload of Jews on this occasion, and added: "By late 1945 the world's newspapers were full of unsubstantiated, lurid rumors about 'factories of death' complete with lethal 'gas chambers.'"

Perhaps most noteworthy of all was the difference between the two versions of Irving's account of Hitler's address to a group of generals about Hungary's Jews on May 26, 1944:

> 1977: In Auschwitz, the defunct paraphernalia of death—idle since 1943—began to clank again as the first trainloads from Hungary arrived.

> 1991: Four hundred thousand Jews were being rounded up in Hungary; the first trainloads arrived in Auschwitz as slave labor for the now completed [*sic*] I. G. Farben plant.

In 1977, Irving made it clear that the Hungarian Jews were killed. In 1991, he made no mention of this fact but claimed instead that they were being used merely as workers in a chemical factory.

Thus Irving's views had altered substantially between the two editions. The turning point seemed to have been the 1988 trial of Ernst Zündel, a German-Canadian antisemite, Holocaust denier, and self-confessed admirer of Hitler. Zündel's books included *The Hitler We Loved and Why*, published by a firm called White Power Publications, and *ufos: Nazi Secret Weapons?*, which argued that unidentified flying objects, which used to be known as flying saucers, were still being deployed by survivors of the Nazi regime from bases underneath the Antarctic.[19] . . . Zündel's defense lawyers called a number of Holocaust deniers as expert witnesses in an attempt to demonstrate that the information Zündel had been spreading about the Holocaust was not false. Irving also appeared as an expert witness in this trial. Irving repeatedly admitted under questioning in the court that he had changed his mind since 1977 on the issues of the numbers of Jews killed and the use of the gas chambers. "My mind has now changed," he said, "because I understand that the whole of the Holocaust mythology is, after all, open to doubt."[20]

In examining the question of whether or not Irving was a Holocaust denier, I had therefore to concentrate on his publications and statements at and after the Zündel trial in 1988, not before. For Irving himself said quite openly in 1991 that he had removed all references to extermination camps and death factories from the second edition of the book.[21] I could thus disregard work published by Irving before 1988 since it was plainly irrelevant to the issue of whether Lipstadt was correct in 1994 to call him a Holocaust denier.

[**Numbers**]

The first basic element of Holocaust denial was a minimization of the numbers of Jews killed. I looked through Irving's various books, articles, and speeches to see what his estimation of the numbers was. They revealed that until the late 1980s, Irving had paid little attention to this question. In 1986, for example, while confessing that he thought "the six million figure is probably marginally exaggerated," Irving described the minimal figure of one hundred thousand as being put forward by a "school of thought" that was "right out at the fringe," and added that "I have to admit that I haven't examined the Holocaust in any detail."[22]

In his evidence to the Zündel trial in Canada in 1988, however, which he had put in full on his own website for all to consult, Irving was asked to comment on the following statement (put to him by the defense lawyer): "If the 'Holocaust' is represented as the allegation of the extermination of 6 million Jews during the Second World War as a direct result of official German policy of extermination (sic), what would you say to that thesis?" Irving replied:

> I am not familiar with any documentary evidence of any such figure as 6 million . . . it must have been of the order of 100,000 or more, but to my mind it was certainly less than the figure which is quoted nowadays of 6 million. Because on the evidence of comparison with other similar tragedies which happened in the Second World War, it is unlikely that the Jewish community would have suffered any worse than these communities.[23]

As he himself said in 1996, "cutting the Holocaust down to its true size makes it comparable with the other crimes of World War II."[24]

This applied not just to gassing and extermination camps, but also to the mass shootings carried out by the Security Service and Security Police task forces, the *Einsatzgruppen*. In his evidence to the Zündel trial in 1988, Irving cast doubt, for example, on the reports filed by task force leaders giving numbers of Jews shot by their forces. "I don't trust the statistics they contain," he said. "Soldiers who are out in the field doing a job or murderers who are out in the field doing a job, they don't have time to count." Each leader, he suggested, submitted reports whose aim was to "show he's doing a jolly good job," and by inference, therefore, seriously exaggerated or even invented the numbers killed. "Statistics like this are meaningless," Irving said. "I'm suggesting," he continued, "it is possible that at the time some overzealous ss officer decided to put in a fictitious figure in order to do Heinrich Himmler a favor." This of course was pure speculation, unsupported by any documentary evidence. This was characteristic of Irving's methods in disposing of inconvenient documents. If a document did appear that Irving was unable to suggest was not genuine or in some way unreliable, such as a memorandum from Himmler to Hitler in which three hundred thousand Jews were referred to in 1942 as having been exterminated. Irving said he was "unhappy about it because it is such an unusual, isolated document."[25] But of course, it was only "isolated" because Irving had dismissed or ignored other documentary evidence that pointed in the same direction: there was no genuine documentary warrant at all for this remark.

By the middle of the 1990s, Irving was deploying a range of arguments to buttress his minimal estimates for the numbers of Jews killed by the Nazis. In *Nuremberg: The Last Battle*, he claimed that the Auschwitz death books gave 46,000 names of people who had perished in the camp, mainly from disease.[26] Citing British decrypts of German code messages from Auschwitz to Berlin, Irving suggested on a number of occasions that some 25,000 Jews possibly died in Auschwitz by killing, the rest from disease, the cause given

in most of the reports.[27] On occasion, he went so far as to suggest that all the Jews who died in Auschwitz died from disease: "Probably 100,000 Jews died in Auschwitz," he said in 1993, "but not from gas chambers, they died from epidemics."[28]

Irving actually claimed that the official history of British Intelligence during the Second World War, by the late Professor Sir Harry Hinsley, "states . . . that upon analysis of the daily returns of the Auschwitz concentration camp, it becomes completely plain that nearly all of the deaths, nearly all of the deaths, were due to disease. The others were by execution, by hanging, and by firing squad. There is no reference, and I'm quoting this page, there is no reference whatever to any gassings."[29] In fact, when I looked up the passage, Hinsley did not claim that nearly all the deaths were due to disease; all he wrote was that the British decrypts of encoded radio messages sent from Auschwitz did not mention gassings, which was hardly surprising, given the Nazis' policy of not mentioning the gas chambers explicitly in any of their communications with one another. Moreover, although Irving claimed that the radio reports from Auschwitz to the central administration of the camps in Berlin were decrypted by British intelligence at Bletchley Park "from 1942 to the end of 1943,"[30] in fact the decrypts ended on September 1, 1942. . . . Crucially, too, the decrypts were decipherments of radio reports of the additions and subtractions to the *regular, registered* camp population: these reports omitted all *unregistered* Jews (as well as gypsies) selected for gassing immediately on arrival. Thus they proved nothing, except that there were numerous deaths from executions and disease among the long-term camp inmates.[31] . . .

This was far from being the only attempt Irving made to twist the evidence in order to minimize the numbers of Jews deliberately murdered by the

Nazis. "Despite the most strenuous efforts," he also claimed, "the Yad Vashem Museum, Jerusalem, has compiled a list of no more than three million possible Holocaust victims. The same names appear in this list many times over."[32] This did not mean, of course, that the same names referred to the same people; nor did the fact that the number of names compiled totaled less than 6 million mean that 6 million were not killed. The figure of 6 million, Irving said, originated in a guesstimate based on a comparison of European Jewish population figures in 1929 and 1946. It had no basis, he declared, in documented historical fact.[33] Yet the discrepancy in population was a documented historical fact.

When it came to suggesting ways in which the missing Jews might in fact have survived the war, Irving suddenly and conveniently forgot his demand for documented historical fact. Nobody, he alleged, had "explained what became of the one million cadavers" which it was claimed "were produced by killing operations at Auschwitz," nor for that matter what happened to the alleged corpses produced by supposed gassings in other camps.[34] There was no trace in Allied aerial photographs of mass graves at Auschwitz, so where had the bodies gone? he asked.[35] Irving himself supplied more than one answer. He claimed that the Jews who disappeared did not die but were secretly transported to Palestine by the *Haganah*, the Zionist underground, and given new identities. He suggested some of the missing Jews were killed in the February 1945 bombing raid on Dresden: "Many other raids were like that. Nobody knows how many Jews died in them. Nobody knows how many Jews died on the road of hunger or cold, after the evacuation of concentration camps in late 1944 and early 1945. Nobody knows how many Jews survived in displaced persons' camps. None of the Holocaust historians have researched this."[36] . . .

Did this amount to "Holocaust denial"? I thought it did. Irving admitted in 1992 without qualification that "Eichmann's memoirs are an important element of the refutation of the Holocaust story."[37] If engaging in a refutation of the Holocaust story was not Holocaust denial, then what was? "For me as a historian," Irving said in 1992, "the Holocaust is a mere footnote to history. I write about world history; I write about Real History, and I am not going to talk at any great length about something which is of far more obsessive interest to other historians, revisionists, or whatever."[38] Speaking in Toronto on November 1, 1992, Irving declared:

The legend was that Adolf Hitler ordered the killing of six million Jews in gas chambers in Auschwitz. This is roughly how history has had its way for the last forty or fifty years. . . . Well, I am not a Holocaust denier, and that word really offends me, but I am a Holocaust analyst, I think we are entitled to analyse the basic elements of the statement: Adolf Hitler ordered the killing of six million Jews in gas chambers at Auschwitz, and to ask, is any part of this statement open to doubt?[39]

Once again Irving, as in another speech made during his Canadian lecture tour in 1992, was using the term analysis as a euphemism for denial; the difference between analysis and denial here was nonexistent: "I don't like this word 'deny,'" he said in 1993 with reference to the figure of 6 million Jewish victims of Nazism: "the word 'deny' is only one step away from lying, really. I challenge it, I contest it."[40] There was nothing about the word *denial* that implied telling a lie, however, any more than there was anything about the words *challenge*, *contestation*, or *analysis* that implied telling the truth.

At the beginning of his videotape *The Search for Truth in History*, Irving said once more: "The

Holocaust with a capital 'H' is what's gone down in history in this one sentence form, so to speak: 'Adolf Hitler ordered the killing of six million Jews in Auschwitz.'[41] But nobody had ever argued that 6 million Jews were killed by gassing in Auschwitz. Irving's claim that this was what the term Holocaust meant was a figment of his own imagination. The standard works on the Holocaust made it clear both that a substantial proportion of those killed were shot or starved to death or deliberately weakened and made susceptible to fatal disease as a matter of policy, that gassings took place at other centers besides Auschwitz, including notably Belzec, Chelmno, Sobibór, and Treblinka, and that the number killed in Auschwitz was around 1.1 million.[42]

Only on one recorded occasion, during an interview with the Australian journalist Ron Casey on July 27, 1995 (after the publication of Deborah Lipstadt's book) did Irving depart at all significantly from his minimization of the numbers killed:

Casey: What is your estimate of the number of Jews who died at the hands of Hitler's regime in the war years? What number—and I don't like using this word—what number would you concede was killed in concentration camps?

Irving: . . . if putting people into a concentration camp where they die of barbarity and typhus and epidemics is killing, then I would say the four million figure, because, undoubtedly, huge numbers did die in the camps in the conditions that were very evident at the end of the war.[43]

Even in giving, exceptionally, a figure of . . . 4 million however, it was noticeable that Irving strongly qualified his remarks by claiming that "barbarity and typhus and epidemics" were the main causes of death. Irving had a long record of

blaming the high mortality rate in the camps—insofar as he conceded it at all—on epidemics rather than on deliberate, systematic killing. Thus, for example, in 1986 he told an audience, again in Australia, that the piles of dead filmed in Buchenwald and Bergen-Belsen at the end of the war had been the result of epidemics that "had only broken out in the last two or three weeks of the war." And who, in Irving's view, was responsible for these epidemics?

We have to admit probably that we, the British and the Americans, were partially responsible, at least partially responsible for their misfortune. Because we vowed deliberate bombing of the transportation networks, deliberate bombardation, bombarding the German communications, by deliberate destruction of the German pharmaceutical industry, medicine factories. We had deliberately created the conditions of chaos inside Germany. We had deliberately created the epidemics, and the outbreaks of typhus and other diseases, which led to those appalling scenes that were found at their most dramatic in the enclosed areas, the concentration camps, where of course epidemics can ravage and run wild.[44]

In fact, of course, conditions for epidemics were deliberately created by the Nazis, who ran the camps in a way that deprived the inmates of hygiene and medical attention as a matter of policy.[45] . . .

[Gas Chambers]

Closely linked to these views was the denial of the existence of gas chambers at Auschwitz and elsewhere. Irving declared in his written submission to the court: "It is denied that the Plaintiff has denied the Holocaust; it is denied that the Plaintiff has denied that gas chambers were used by the Nazis as the principal means of carrying out that extermination; they may have used them on occasion on an experimental scale, which fact he does not deny."[46] This sentence was remarkably self-contradictory. Was he saying that he accepted that the gas chambers were the principal means of killing, or that their use was only possible ("may have used") and if it did occur, was he merely saying that it was only experimental in scale?

It was also contradicted by another line of defense he took against the accusation of being a Holocaust denier, namely, to deny that there was any authentic wartime archival evidence for the existence of gassing facilities at Auschwitz-Birkenau, Chelmno, Belzec, Sobibór, and Treblinka—a cautious statement stopping short of an outright denial but clearly designed to imply that those gassing facilities therefore did not exist.[47] If Irving was implying here that he would not accept any evidence about the Second World War unless it was written at the time, then how did he justify his own extensive use of the postwar testimony of members of Hitler's entourage given in interviews with them conducted by himself? Here again, he was applying double standards in his approach to different types of evidence. The fact was that historians had to take all kinds of evidence into account, and apply the same standards of criticism to all of them. Irving was wrong to imply that there was no authentic wartime evidence of gassing facilities in the camps he mentioned. But even if he had been right, this would not have meant that there was no authentic evidence of any kind for their existence.

Nevertheless, Irving clearly meant to imply that there was not. In his testimony to the Zündel trial in 1988, he explicitly rejected the use of the term *extermination camps* apart from Chelmno, which "was operating on a very small scale."...[48] In 1992, he put forward the same kind of argu-ment in describing the memoirs of Adolf Eichmann. Irving said:

He also describes—and I have to say this being an honest historian—going to another location a few weeks later and being driven around in a bus; then being told by the bus driver to look through a peephole into the back of the bus where he saw a number of prisoners being gassed by the exhaust fumes. So I accept that this kind of experiment was made on a very limited scale, but that it was rapidly abandoned as being a totally inefficient way of killing people. But, I don't accept that the gas chambers existed, and this is well known. I've seen no evidence at all that gas chambers existed.[49]

This minor concession was characteristic of his technique in admitting small-scale, limited instances of what he devoted much of his attention to denying on the large scale, as a kind of alibi that enabled him to deny that he was really doing the latter at all. He alleged that "equal tonnages of Zyklon B pesticide granules were delivered to Auschwitz and Oranienburg camps, at which latter camp nobody had ever suggested that "gas chambers existed, and to camps in Norway." Recently discovered documents in former Soviet archives showed that Auschwitz prisoners, he said, were released to the outside world on completion of their sentence. This was "incompatible with the character of a top-secret mass extermination center." This again applied only to registered prisoners, and only to a minuscule number of them.[50]

Irving also denied "that diesel engines could be used for killing operations. These engines," he said, "exhaust non-lethal carbon dioxide (CO_2) and only minute quantities of toxic carbon monoxide (CO). These howlers," he says, "typify the flawed historical research into 'the Holocaust' even now, fifty years after the tragedy."[51] In his videoteped speech *The Search for Truth in History*, made in 1993, Irving also asked: "How can you gas millions of people with hydrogen cyanide gas and leave not the slightest significant trace of chemical residue in the walls of the gas chambers?" This was a reference to the so-called Leuchter Report, a document commissioned by the French Holocaust denier Robert Faurisson for use in Zündel's defense in the 1988 trial. In this report, the American Fred Leuchter (pronounced Looshter), designer of gas chambers and lethal injection devices used in the administration of the death penalty in some states in the United States, declared that his examination of the cyanide residues in the inner walls of the gas chambers in Auschwitz proved that they had not been used for gassing at all. Irving accepted the report's findings and published them in Britain. Indeed a reading of the report had proved decisive in bringing Irving round to full-scale Holocaust denial in 1988.[52] Irving went on to claim that Dr. Franciszek Piper of the Auschwitz State Museum had had the tests secretly replicated and when the State Forensic Laboratory in Cracow had confirmed Leuchter's findings the museum suppressed the fact and filed the report away.[53]

It was not difficult to check up on Irving's arguments. They turned out to be specious and derivative, and corresponded closely to a number of the same points put forward by well-known Holocaust deniers such as Robert Faurisson.[54] I was able to establish that the Polish authorities did not suppress findings of their own investigations of the former gas chambers, and these findings did not confirm Leuchter's claims. And of course the literature made it abundantly clear that prisoners sent to Auschwitz for extermination were not enrolled on the camp's list of inmates, but were sent straight away to the gas chamber; so naturally there was no record of their release.[55] . . .

The Leuchter Report had long since been exposed as an incompetent and thoroughly unscientific document compiled by an unqualified person; it was completely discredited, along with its author, at the second Zündel trial in 1988. Leuchter had removed samples from the inner walls of Crematorium II at Auschwitz-Birkenau and had them analyzed, with the result that the concentration of cyanide residues was found to be slight, compared with the concentrations found in the delousing facilities, thus showing, he had triumphantly declared, that the crematorium was not used for gassing people. But he had taken great chunks out of the wall instead of scrapings off the surface, thus greatly diluting whatever residues were to be found there. Even more crass, he had ignored the fact that the concentration of cyanide gas needed to kill humans was far lower than that needed to kill lice in clothing, and so failed to understand that, far from disproving the existence of the gas chamber, his findings actually tended to confirm it. Yet Irving, in his continued championing of the report, had completely ignored—or suppressed—these fatal objections to its credibility.[56] . . .

"There were no gas chambers in Auschwitz," he said on March 5, 1990. In his view, only "30,000 people at the most were murdered in Auschwitz . . . that's about as many as we Englishmen killed in a single night in Hamburg."[57] In 1995 he repeated this view: "We revisionists," he declared, "say that gas chambers didn't exist, and that the 'factories of death' didn't exist."[58] "I'm a gas chamber denier," he told a television interviewer in 1998. "I'm a denier that they killed hundreds of thousands of people in gas chambers, yes."[59] Irving repeatedly denied that there were any functioning gas chambers and that any Jews or other victims of Nazism were killed in them, with the sole exception of a small number who, he conceded, were gassed during experiments. I found plenty of instances of such comprehensive denial in his speeches. In 1989, for instance, he confessed himself "quite happy to nail my colors to the mast on that, and say that to the best of my knowledge, there is not one shower bath in any of the concentration or slave labor camps that turns out to have been some kind of gas chamber."[60] On March 5, 1990, he declared roundly to an audience in Germany once more that there were no gas chambers at all in Auschwitz during the war: "There were no gas chambers in Auschwitz, there were only dummies which were built by the Poles in the postwar years, just as the Americans built the dummies in Dachau . . . these things in Auschwitz, and probably also in Majdanek, Treblinka, and in other so-called extermination camps in the East are all just dummies." Repeating this claim later in the same speech, Irving added that "I and, increasingly, other historians, . . . are saying, the Holocaust, the gas chamber establishments in Auschwitz did not exist."[61] On November 8, 1990, he repeated the same claim to an audience in Toronto: "The gas chambers that are shown to the tourists in Auschwitz are fakes."[62] These statements were clear and unambiguous. Irving's statement to the court of his position on this issue—"it is denied that the Plaintiff has denied that gas chambers were used by the Nazis as the principal means of carrying out that extermination"—was a falsehood.[63]

[Policy]

A third element in Holocaust denial was a refusal to accept that the extermination of the Jews was systematic, organized, or centrally directed. Where did Irving stand on this issue? Even before he changed his mind on the numbers killed and the use of gassing as a murder technique, Irving was denying that the Nazi extermination of the Jews had been carried out in a systematic man-

ner, because he had always denied that it had been ordered by Hitler. . . . The extermination of Jews in Eastern Europe during the war, he repeated, in places like Minsk and Kiev and Riga, was "conducted for the most ordinary and repugnant motives of greed and thievery" by "individual gangsters and criminals," for whom the German state and people could not be held responsible.[64] In fact, of course, those responsible on the ground for directing and carrying out the actual killing operations were . . . officials acting on behalf of the Nazi state and Nazi agencies such as the SS and the police.

As so often when he dealt with these questions, Irving abandoned the pretense of original research and resorted to speculation and innuendo. Testifying at the 1988 Zündel trial, for example, Irving said he was

> puzzled at the apparent lack of logic: that the Nazis are supposed to have had a government policy for the deliberate, ruthless, systematic extermination of the Jews in Auschwitz and other places of murder and yet tens if not hundreds of thousands of Jews passed through these camps and are, I am glad to say, alive and well amongst us now to testify to their survival. So either the Nazis had no such program or they were an exceedingly sloppy race, which isn't the image we have of them today. . . .

"I don't think there was any overall Reich policy to kill the Jews," he repeated later on the same occasion.[65] Of course, his argument here was fallacious. Auschwitz was both a labor camp and an extermination camp, so it is not surprising that many Jews interned there survived the experience. On the other hand, Treblinka, Chelmno, Belzec, and Sobibór, which was presumably what Irving meant by "other places of murder," were designed purely for extermination; Irving presented no evidence to show that any Jews at all survived from these camps, which is not surprising, for hardly any did. . . .

"I don't now believe," Irving said in 1988, "there was anything you could describe as 'extermination machinery' other than the very disorganized *ad hoc* efforts of the criminals and murderers among the ss who were carrying out the liquidations that we described earlier."[66] This was a familiar part of the litany of Holocaust denial. . . . Another Holocaust denier, Austin J. App, had similarly asserted that there was no "single document, order, blueprint" demonstrating the Nazis' intention of murdering the Jews, and went on to argue, as Irving later did, that the Nazis were so efficient that the fact that some Jews undoubtedly survived proves that they never had any intention of murdering them all: had they wanted to, "they would have done so."[67] Speculation such as this struck me as wild, indeed almost desperate in its attempt to distract attention from the hard evidence of various kinds that pointed to the extermination program having been large-scale, systematic, and comprehensive in intent.

[Origins]

Reading through the work of Holocaust deniers like Arthur Butz, it was clear that they wanted their readers to believe that the evidence for the Holocaust was fabricated. In a number of speeches and writings, Irving claimed that the "Holocaust legend" was invented by the Political Warfare Executive of the British Government. "British intelligence," he said in Toronto on August 13, 1988, "deliberately masterminded the gas chamber lie." "Who invented the myth of the gas chambers?" he asked rhetorically in Moers on March 9, 1990. His answer? "We did it. The English. We invented the lie about the gas chambers, just as we invented the lie about the Belgian children

with their hands hacked off in the First World War."[68] . . . So where did Irving believe that the gas chamber "story" originated? In extracts from the forthcoming second volume of his Churchill biography, Irving wrote that it was supplied to the British in 1942 by Gerhard Riegner, director of the Geneva Office of the World Jewish Congress from 1939 until 1945.[69] The Foreign Office disbelieved Riegner; the whole story might have been invented. So when the British used the story as propaganda, they knew it to be untrue. This was already some distance from Irving's claim that they had invented it themselves.

What was the real documentary evidence for this account? I checked it out in the British Public Record Office in Kew, just to the west of London. The documents were well known and a number of other historians such as Sir Martin Gilbert, author of *Auschwitz and the Allies*, published as long ago as 1981, had cited them before. They revealed that on August 8, 1942, Riegner informed the Foreign Office that he had been told by a well-connected German that the Nazis were intending to exterminate 3 to 4 million Jews.[70] The methods under consideration included Prussic acid (hydrogen cyanide).[71] Foreign Office mandarins were reluctant to make use of "this story" in British propaganda against Germany "without further confirmation."[72] In a minute of August 27, Roger Allen of the Foreign Office wrote:

> This [Polish] aide-memoire [on which the declaration was based] is in line with a good deal of information which we have received from time to time. There can, I think, be little doubt that the general picture painted is pretty true to life. On the other hand it is of course extremely difficult, if not impossible, for us to check up on the specific instances or matters of detail. For this reason I feel a little unhappy

about the statement to be issued on the authority of His Majesty's Government, that Poles "are now being systematically put to death in gas chambers."

Allen considered that reports of gassings "may or may not be true, but any event I submit we are putting out a statement on evidence which far from conclusive, and which we have no means of assessing."[73] ... There was no evidence here or anywhere else, indeed, that the British Political Warfare Executive had invented the story of the gas chambers: [it] had on the contrary received a report from people with contacts in Central Europe about them. Nor was there any evidence that [people in] the Foreign Office considered reports of gassings to be a lie; they were simply unsure about them. ...

But Irving's speeches went much further than this in their allegations. Irving also asserted that following on this supposed propaganda lie, further evidence for the Holocaust was fabricated after the end of the Second World War.[74] This included the eyewitness testimony of the thousands of former camp inmates and survivors of the Nazi extermination program. ... In an interview with the right-wing magazine *code* in 1990, Irving, answering a question about how he would judge the credibility of Holocaust survivors, responded: "I say that the psychiatrists should concern themselves with this matter some time. There are many cases of mass hysteria."[75] "I'm afraid I have to say I wouldn't consider what a survivor of Treblinka could tell me in 1988 to be credible evidence," he told the court at the second Zündel trial; one could not rely on "the very human and fallible human memories after a tragic wartime experience forty years after the event."[76] (Irving would have been lucky to have found such a survivor. Only *fifty-four* people are known to have survived

of the million or so who entered the camp in 1942 and 1943; most of them escaped during an uprising of Jewish prisoners on August 2, 1943).[77] ... "The eyewitnesses in Auschwitz ... who claim to have seen the gas chambers," he said in another lecture in 1991, "are liars." They were "an interesting case for the psychiatrist. People over a period of years begin kidding themselves that they have seen something." This was because they had been through a traumatic experience (Irving did not say what this was), and "being in the center of a traumatic experience is liable to induce strange thoughts in eyewitnesses."[78] ...

Irving never used eyewitness testimony from victims of Nazism in any of his voluminous writings; he hardly ever discussed it or even mentioned its existence. When confronted with actual survivors, he picked on technical aspects of their testimony that he tried to use to discredit their memories. A discussion with a survivor in a program broadcast on Australian television in 1997, for example, included the following exchange:

Irving: You said you saw the smoke coming from the crematoria.

Survivor: Absolutely. ...

Irving: But crematoria don't smoke, Mrs. Altman. Go and visit your local crematorium in Sydney.[79]

The thought that the crematoria of Auschwitz might have been designed differently, and with less regard to the susceptibilities of onlookers and neighbors, than the crematoria in Sydney, did not, apparently, enter his mind.

Why, then, did Irving think that such evidence had been concocted? Who could possibly have gone to all the immense trouble necessary to fabricate such a vast quantity of documentary material? Describing various versions of Holocaust denial in 1986, Gill Seidel remarked in her pioneering survey of the subject:

> They all purport to show that Jews are liars and tricksters holding the world to ransom and continuing to extract war reparations. This is a continuation and an extension of the anti-Jewish prejudices and practices. The implication is that after all this time Jews are still liars, parasites, extraordinar[il]y powerful, and fundamentally dishonest—and that maybe Hitler was right.[80]

[Irving's Antisemitism]

As I read Irving's writings and transcripts of his speeches dating from the 1990s, it became clear that after his conversion in 1988 he moved rapidly into line with these views. Fundamentally, he seemed to believe—against all the evidence of the massive amount of scholarly research carried out by non-Jewish historians in many countries—that the history of the Nazi extermination of the Jews had been written by Jewish historians. Thus he could refer, as he did in 1993, to "we independent historians, shall we say, the non-Jewish historians, the ones with an entirely open mind," as if all non-Jewish historians agreed with him.[81] Such agreement existed only in Irving's fantasy.

The political thrust behind such strange views became apparent when I read the following passage in Irving's preface to the English edition of the Leuchter Report, published by his Focal Point publishing house:

> Nobody likes to be swindled, still less where considerable sums of money are involved (Since 1949 the State of Israel has received over 90 billion Deutschmarks in voluntary reparations from West Germany, essentially in atonement for the "gas chambers of Auschwitz"). And this myth will not die easily: Too many hundreds of millions of honest, intelligent people have been duped by the well-financed and brilliantly successful postwar publicity campaign which followed on from the original ingenious plan of the British Psychological (sic) Warfare Executive (PWE) in 1942 to spread to the world the propaganda story that the Germans were using "gas chambers" to kill millions of Jews and other "undesirables."

"The 'big lie,'" he declared in 1991, referring to the Holocaust, "allows Jewish fraudsters to escape unpunished and Israel to torture Arabs and ignore UN resolutions." And who were these Jewish fraudsters? "The big lie is designed to justify both in arrears and in advance the bigger crimes in the financial world elsewhere that are being committed by the survivors of the Holocaust."[82] The idea that survivors were engaged in large-scale financial fraud was new to me. I could not find any evidence in Irving's writings and speeches to support this sweeping claim.

On July 7, 1992, *The Guardian* printed an interview with Irving in which, consistently with views he expressed elsewhere, Irving predicted that

> one year from now the Holocaust will have been discredited. That prediction is lethal because of the vested interests involved in the Holocaust industry. As I said to the Jewish Chronicle, if a year from now the gas chamber legend collapses, what will that mean for Israel? Israel is drawing millions of dollars each year from the German taxpayer, provided by the German government as reparation for the gas chambers. It is also drawing millions from American taxpayers, who put up with it because of the way the Israelis or the Jews suffered. No one's going to like it when they find out that for 50 years they have been believing a legend based on baloney.[83]

Irving's confidence was misplaced. Moreover, many of his points were already familiar to me from a reading of the older Holocaust denial literature. The allegation that the Jews had used the Holocaust story to win reparations from the Germans could also be found in the texts of Paul Rassinier.[84] Austin J. App similarly argued that the Jews had "used the six million swindle to blackmail West Germany into 'atoning' with the twenty billion dollars of indemnities to Israel."[85] In fact, the true figure was $735 million; and the money was paid for resettlement of survivors, not as compensation for the dead; had the state of Israel actually wanted to maximize the amount of reparations, then, as Deborah Lipstadt pointed out, the state of Israel would have tried to argue that—as Irving himself tried to argue—millions of Jews were not killed by the Nazis, but fled to Israel instead.[86]

Irving of course denied being "anti-Jewish" or "anti-Israel," just as he denied being a Holocaust denier. Speaking in Canada in November 1992, he told his audience: "I am not an antisemite."[87] But he realized that his ideas opened him up to the obvious accusation that he was:

> Interviewer: When one reads your speeches, one has the impression that Churchill was paid by the Jews, that the Jews dragged Britain into the war, that many of the Communist regimes have been dominated by Jews subsequently, and that a great deal of control over the world is exercised by Jews.

> Irving: Right, these are four separate facts, to each of which I would be willing to put my signature. They are four separate and unrelated facts. When you string them together like that, you might be entitled then to say: "Question five, David Irving, are you therefore an anti-semite?" This may well have been—

> Interviewer: No, this wasn't my question.

> Irving: But the answer is this, these are in fact four separate facts which happen to be true, in my considered opinion as a historian. And I think we can find the historical evidence for it.[88]

From the end of the 1980s, Irving began referring to Jews as "our traditional enemies."[89] Who these precisely were, he made clear in a speech given in 1992: "our old traditional enemies . . . (are) the great international merchant banks (who) are controlled by people who are no friends of yours and mine," people who were "annoyed" by sixty-foot posters advertising the *Sunday Times* serialization of the Goebbels diaries "in all the Jewish ghettos of Great Britain."

Later in the speech he attacked the "odd and ugly and perverse and greasy and slimy community of 'anti-Fascists' that run the very real risk of making the word fascist respectable by their own appearance!"[90] His particular venom seemed to be reserved for the Board of Deputies of British Jews, to whom he referred in 1991 as "cockroaches."[91] "I never used to believe in the existence of an international Jewish conspiracy," he said. "I'm not even sure now if there's an international Jewish conspiracy. All I know is that people are conspiring internationally against me, and they do mostly turn out to be . . . (drowned out by laughter and applause)."[92] In April 1998, he spoke of American Jews

> moving into the same positions of predominance and influence (media, banking, business, entertainment, and the more lucrative professions like law, medical and dentistry) that they held in Weimar Germany which gave rise to the hatreds and the resulting pogroms; and that this being so, twenty or thirty more years might see in the USA the same dire consequences as happened in Nazi Germany.[93]

This was the classic language of antisemitism that I had encountered in reading texts from German antisemites from the late nineteenth century on: "ghettos," "greasy and slimy," "lucrative professions," "cockroaches," "international Jewish conspiracy." The use of the term ghettos, for example, suggested in standard racist manner that there were districts in Great Britain where Jews were in a majority and, by implication, not integrated into the wider society in which they lived. In fact, such ghettos existed nowhere in the United Kingdom. Irving's language expressed the classic ideology of antisemitism too, with its attempt to whip up jealousies and hatreds of Jews by portraying them—without a shred of evidence—as exerting predominance over key professions and institutions (although why this should have been a cause for pogroms, or indeed objections from anybody, Irving did not say). This alleged "predominance," in the view of Holocaust deniers, was behind the continuing widespread public acceptance of what they called the "Holocaust myth."[94]

Indeed, some of Irving's own speeches contained a veiled threat of violence against Jews in the future as a result of his own "exposure" of the Holocaust "myth":

And gradually the word is getting around in Germany (Irving said in 1991). Two years there from now too the German historians will accept that we're right. They will accept that for fifty years they have believed a lie. And then there will come about a result not only in Germany, but around the world, which I deeply regret and abhor. There will be an immense tidal wave of antisemitism. It's an inevitable result. And when people point an accusing finger at me and say, "David Irving, you are creating antisemitism," I have to say, "It is not the man who speaks the truth who creates the antisemitism, it's the man

who invented the lie of the legend in the first place." (Applause).[95]

Irving's crocodile tears were not to be taken too seriously. . . . For Irving told an audience in Tampa, Florida, on October 6, 1995, referring to the Jews:

What these people don't understand . . . is that they are generating antisemitism by their behavior, and they can't understand it. They wonder where the antisemitism comes from and it comes from themselves, from their behavior. . . . I said to this man from Colindale, this leader of the Jewish community in Freeport, Louisiana, I said . . . "You are disliked, you people. You have been disliked for three thousand years. You have been disliked so much that you have been hounded from country to country, from pogrom to purge, from purge back to pogrom, and yet you never asked yourselves why you're disliked. That's the difference between you and me. It never occurs to you to look into the mirror and say, why am I disliked? What is it that the rest of humanity doesn't like about the Jewish people, to such an extent that they repeatedly put us through the grinder?" And he went berserk. He said: "Are you trying to say that we are responsible for Auschwitz? Ourselves?" And I said, "Well the short answer is yes. The short answer I have to say is yes. . . . If you had behaved differently over the intervening three thousand years, the Germans would have gone about their business and not have found it necessary to go around doing whatever they did to you."[96]

Thus whatever atrocities Irving admitted had been suffered by the Jews over the centuries had been mainly their own fault.

After all, he said in 1991, "they (meaning the Jews) dragged us into two world wars and now, for equally mysterious reasons, they're trying to drag us into the Balkans."[97] Here too, in the 1990s, the machinations of a Jewish conspiracy seemed to be at work. Irving was confronted with his various statements along these lines in 1996:

> Interviewer: At times in your speech to these groups you speak at, you ask if the Jews have ever looked at themselves to find a reason for the pogroms and the persecutions and the extermination. In other words, you're asking, "did they bring it on themselves?"
>
> Irving: Yes.
>
> Interviewer: Thereby excusing the Germans, the Nazis.
>
> Irving: Let us ask that simple question: why does it always happen to the Jews?
>
> Interviewer: But isn't that an ugly, racist sentiment?
>
> Irving: It is an ugly, of course it's an ugly, racist sentiment. Of course it is. You're absolutely right. But you can't just say, therefore let's not discuss it, therefore let's not open that can of worms in case we find something inside there that we don't like looking at.

After all this, it was not surprising that he considered that "the Madagascar solution would probably have been the most peaceful for the present world," because the Jews "would have had no neighbors, nobody who they could feel intimidated by, and of course, nobody whom they in turn could intimidate." In fact, as recent research had made clear, Irving was glossing over the fact that the Nazi regime, in drawing up its never realized plans to deport the Jews there in the early part of the war, would have made no provision to supply them with food and clothing and the basic necessities of life, and that the climate and economy of the island were entirely unsuited to sustaining millions of mostly highly urbanized European settlers.[98]

Irving thus shared the common position of Holocaust deniers that evidence for the Holocaust has been fabricated. He augmented these arguments with a wider range of assertions about the Jews' alleged influence in the postwar world, and their supposed responsibility for provoking attacks on themselves, assertions which in style and content could fairly be called antisemitic.

NOTES

1. Lipstadt, *Denying the Holocaust,* chapter 2.
2. Austin J. App, *A Straight Look at the "Third Reich": Hitler and National Socialism, How Right? How Wrong?* (Tacoma Park, Md., 1974), 5, 18–20; and idem, *The Six Million Swindle: Blackmailing the German People for Hard Marks with Fabricated Corpses* (Tacoma Park, Md., 1973), 2, 29.
3. Arthur Butz, *The Hoax of the Twentieth Century* (Brighton, 1977 ed.), 30, 36–37, 49, 58–59, 69–73, 100–105, 131, 173, 198, 203–5, 246–50.
4. Robert Faurisson, *Mémoire en Défense, contre ceux qui m'accusent de falsifier l'histoire: La question des chambres a gaz* (Paris, 1980); *Le Matin,* November 16, 1978, interview with Faurisson; report of the trial in *Patterns of Prejudice,* vol. 15, no. 4 (October 1981), 51–55. Faurisson was influenced by Rassinier: Paul Rassinier, *Debunking the Genocide Myth* (Torrance, Calif., 1978).
5. Wilhelm Staeglich, *Der Auschwitz-Mythos. Legende oder Wirklichkeit* (Tübingen, 1979); Armin Pfahl-Traghber, "Die Apologeten der "Auschwitz-Lüge"—Bedeutung und Entwicklung der Holocaust-Leugnung im Rechtsextremismus," *Jahrbuch Extremismus und Demokratie,* vol. 8 (1996), 75–101, esp. 86–87. Hermann Graml, "Alte und neue Apologeten Hitlers," in Wolfgang Benz, ed., *Rechtsextremismus in*

Deutschland: Voraussetzungen, Zusammenhänge, Wirkungen (Frankfurt am Main. 1994), 63–92. here 81–83.

6. Roger Eatwell, "How to Revise History (and Influence People?), Neo-Fascist Style," in Luciano Cheles, Ronnie Ferguson, and Michalina Vaughan, eds., *The Far Right in Western and Eastern Europe* (London, 1995), 309–26, here 311. The element of diversity in Holocaust denial was also noted by Kenneth S. Stern, *Holocaust Denial* (New York, 1993), 8–9.

7. Pierre Vidal-Naquet, *Assassins of Memory: Essays on the Denial of the Holocaust* (New York. 1992), 18–23 (originally published in 1980).

8. (Yisrael Gutman), "Die Auschwitz-Lüge," in Jäckel et al., eds., *Enzyklopädie*, vol. I, 121–27, here 121–24.

9. Pfahl-Traghber, "Die Apologeten," 75–77, esp. 75–77.

10. Pierre Vidal-Naquet and Limor Yagil, *Holocaust Denial in France: Analysis of a Unique Phenomenon* (Tel Aviv, 1995).

11. Gill Seidel, *The Holocaust Denial: Antisemitism, Racism and the New Right* (Leeds, 1986).

12. Dokumentationsarchiv des österreichischen Widerstandes/Bundesministerium für Unterricht und Kunst, *Amoklauf gegen die Wirklichkeit. NS-Verbrechen und "revisionistische" Geschichtsschreibung* (Vienna, 1991); similarly (a-c only), the recent study by Michael Shermer and Alex Grobman, *Denying History: Who Says the Holocaust Never Happened and Why Do They Say It?* (Berkeley, 2000).

13. Reply to Defense of Second Defendant, 11.

14. Ibid., 10–11.

15. Ibid., 4.

16. Irving. *Hitler's War*, 1977 ed., xiv–xv.

17. Vidal-Naquet, *Assassins*, 89, 124; Seidel, *The Holocaust Denial*, 121.

18. Stern, *Holocaust Denial*, 31.

19. Lipstadt, *Denying*, 157–58: Shermer and Groban, *Denying*, 65–67.

20. "David Irving's 1988 Testimony at the Trial of Ernst Zündel," on Irving's website, http:www .fpp.co.uk: "Documents on the Auschwitz controversy," 30, 82–83, 138.

21. Videotape 207: NDR (North German Radio) 3, documentary, "Juden wurden nicht vergast," German version of a Danish program by Jens Olaf Jersild, screened on May 9, 1993, at 38 min. 25 secs.; also videotape 189: speech presented in Calgary, September 29, 1991.

22. Audiocassette 89: Terry Lane, ABC 3LO Radio, interview with Irving, March 18, 1986.

23. "David Irving's 1988 Testimony," 12.

24. Videotape 223: Irving interviewed on Australian Channel 7, October 1, 1996, 3 mins. 25 secs.

25. "David Irving's 1988 Testimony," 16, 151, 93.

26. Irving, *Nuremberg: The Last Battle* (London, 1996), 352 n. 13.

27. Videotape 200: "The Search for Truth in History," cited in Nigel Jackson, *The Case for David Irving* (Sidgwick, Australia, 1992), 88. . . . videotape 190: Latvian Hall, Toronto, November 8, 1990—"50,000 people were killed in Auschwitz . . . the number is too high . . . nearly all of the deaths were due to disease" (from 55 mins. 30 secs.); audiocassette 108: speech presented to the Free Speech League, Victoria, British Columbia, October 27, 1990, no. 507)—40,000 killed at Auschwitz in three years; videotape 200: "The Search for Truth in History" (1993)— 100,000 deaths from all causes, "25,000 people murdered in Auschwitz in three years" (from 1 hr. 13 mins. 15 secs.). The variation in the figures was typical of Irving's indifference to statistical accuracy.

28. Videotape 200: "The Search for Truth in History," 1993, at 1 hr. 12 mins.

29. Videotape 190: Irving at Latvian Hall, Toronto, November 8, 1992, from 1 hr. 7 mins. 15 secs.

30. Irving, "Battleship Auschwitz," *jhr*, vol. 10, no. 4.

31. Richard Breitman, *Official Secrets: What the Nazis Planned, What the British and Americans Knew* (London. 1998), 115.

32. Irving, *Nuremberg*, 341 n. 12.

33. Ibid., 62.

34. Reply to Defense of Second Defendant, 5–6.

35. Irving, *Nuremberg*, 24–25, 353.

36. Videotape 200: 1 hr. 15 mins. 40 secs.; also Videotape 184: Leuchter Report Press Conference, June 23, 1989, at 19 mins. 40 secs.

37. "David Irving on the Eichmann and Goebbels Papers" (opening sentence of section: "Eichmann on Höss").

38. "David Irving on Freedom of Speech," October 28, 1992.

39. "Speech by David Irving to a Packed Hall in the Primrose Hotel. Toronto, November 1, 1992." Transcript from Irving's Focal Point website.

40. Videotape 206: "Holmes Show," New Zealand television, June 4, 1993, at 6 mins. 25 secs.

41. Jackson, *The Case for David Irving*, 89.

42. See, for example, Gilbert. *The Holocaust*; Marrus, *The Holocaust in History*; Hilberg, *The Destruction of the European Jews*, etc.

43. Ron Casey interview with David Irving, July 27, 1995, Station 2GB, *Media Monitors* (Sydney etc.), Broadcast transcript S36962003.

44. Audiocassette 86, Irving, "Censorship of History," lecture in Runnymede, Australia, March 18, 1986, 270–91.

45. Wolfgang Sofsky, *Die Ordnung des Terrors. Das Konzentrationslager*, 2nd ed. (Frankfurt am Main, 1997), 237–45; also videotape 180: Toronto 1989.

46. Reply to Defense of Second Defendant, 3.

47. Ibid., 5–6.

48. David Irving's 1988 testimony at the trial of Ernst Zündel, 99–100.

49. Audiocassette 114, Irving, "The Worldwide Anti-Irving Lobby and the Eichmann 'Memoir,'" speech at the 11th International Revisionist Conference, October 1992, 420–30.

50. Reply to Defense of Second Defendant, 5–6.

51. Ibid.

52. Gabriel Weimann and Conrad Winn, *Hate on Trial: The Zündel Affair, the Media, and Public Opinion in Canada* (New York, 1986); Shelly Shapiro, ed., *Truth Prevails: Demolishing Holocaust Denial: The End of "The Leuchter Report"* (New York, 1990); David Irving, foreword to *Auschwitz: The End of the Line: The Leuchter Report* (London, 1989); Shermer and Grobman, *Denying History*, 64–67, 123–67.

53. Jackson, *The Case for David Irving*, 75–79.

54. Robert Faurisson, "The Problem of the Gas Chambers," *jhr*, Summer 1980; Robert Faurisson, foreword to *The Leuchter Report: The End of a Myth: An Engineering Report on the Alleged Execution Gas Chambers at Auschwitz, Birkenau, and Majdanek, Poland* (American edition, 1988).

55. Expert witness reports by Professor Robert Jan Van Pelt, Professor Christopher Browning, and Professor Peter Longerich; see also Shelly Shapiro, ed., *Truth Prevails: Demolishing Holocaust Denial: The End of "The Leuchter Report"* (New York, 1990).

56. TS 24/1, 74–75.

57. Videotape 186: Irving in Moers, March 5, 1990, at 4 mins. 45 secs.

58. David Irving, "Revelations from Goebbels's Diary," *jhr*, vol. 15, no. 1 (1995), 2–17, here 15.

59. BBC2: "Journey to the Far Right" (March 20, 1999).

60. Videotape 184: Leuchter Report Press Conference, June 23, 1989, at 57 mins. 30 secs.

61. Videotape 186: Irving in Moers, March 5, 1990, from 31 mins. 30 sees, and again at 1 hr. 17 mins. 45 secs.

62. Videotape 190, "German reunification and other topics," Latvian Hall. Toronto, November 8, 1990, at 1 hr. 1 min. 50 secs.

63. Reply to Defence of Second Defendant, 3.

64. Audiocassette 99: Irving speech in Toronto, August 1988 (private house), side 1, 727–54.

65. For these statements, see "David Irving's 1988 testimony," 45–46, 88.

66. Ibid., 95–98.

67. App, *The Six Million Swindle*, 7–8, repeating arguments first advanced in App, *Morgenthau Era Letters*, 2nd ed. (Tacoma Park, Md., 1975), 101 (first ed., 1965).

68. Irving, *The Search for Truth in History*, as summarized by Jackson. *The Case for David Irving*, 79; Discovery document, doc. 1, 211: "Auschwitz—the end of the line"; Irving, "Deutsche Historiker—Lügner und Feiglinge, Rede vor der

deutschen Presse in Berlin am 3. Oktober 1989," *Historische Tatsachen*, vol. 42 (1990), 37–40; Irving, "Battleship Auschwitz," *jhr*, vol. 10, no. 4, 1990; Discovery document, doc. 1,697: Irving to Slater, November 15, 1993.

69. David Irving, "Auschwitz, and the Typhus Plague in Poland. More Preview Pages from David Irving's New Biography, Churchill's War, vol. 2. A Sneak Preview," posted on Irving's Internet site, checked February 12, 1999.

70. PRO FO 371/30917, C 7853, telegram no. 2831, Berne to Foreign Office, quoted in Martin Gilbert, *Auschwitz and the Allies*, (London, 1981), 57.

71. Ibid., 58.

72. PRO FO 371/30917, D. Allen, minute, September 10, 1942, quoted in Gilbert, *Auschwitz and the Allies*, 60.

73. PRO FO 371/3455, Roger Allen, minute. August 27, 1943.

74. Reply to Defense of Second Defendant, 5, 6, and 7.

75. *code*, no. 5 1990, 55. CODE (*Confederation organisch denkender Europäer*; "Confederation of organically-thinking Europeans').

76. "David Irving's 1988 testimony." 136–37.

77. Noakes and Pridham, *Nazism*, vol. 3, 1,155–1,156, gave a maximum figure of 70.

78. Videotape 189: Irving speech at Travelport Airport Inn, Calgary, Alberta, September 29, 1991.

79. Videotape 225: "Cover Story" on Australian television program "Sunday," March 4, 1997, at 2 mins. 15 secs.

80. Seidel. *The Holocaust Denial*, 39.

81. Videotape 200: "The Search for Truth in History—Banned!" 1993, at 20 mins.

82. Videotape 190: Irving Speech at the Bayerischer Hof, Milton, Ontario. October 5, 1991, from 2 hrs. 28 mins. 30 secs.

83. "History's Cache and Carry," *The Guardian*, July 7, 1992.

84. Rassinier, *Debunking*, 309.

85. App, *The Six Million Swindle*, 2.

86. Lipstadt, *Denying the Holocaust*, 57; Y. Gutman et al., eds., *Encyclopedia of the Holocaust* (New York, 1990), 1,255–1,259.

87. "Speech by David Irving to a packed hall in die Primrose Hotel. Toronto, November 1, 1992." Transcript on Irving's Focal Point website.

88. Videotape 226: unedited material from *This Week*, November 28, 1991, 1 hr. 30 mins. 15 secs. To 1 hr. 31 mins. 15 secs.

89. Jackson, *The Case for David Irving*, 85.

90. Transcript of first half of David Irving's talk to the Clarendon Club in London, September 19, 1992 (Focal Point website); also audio-cassette 159 (same speech), "self-appointed, ugly, greasy, nasty, perverted representatives of that community (i.e., Jews) in Britain."

91. Videotape 190: Irving Speech at the Bayerischer Hof, Milton, Ontario, October 5, 1991, at 2 hrs. 44 mins.

92. Speech at the Clarendon Club, Town Hall, Bromley, May 29, 1992, at 43 mins. 20 secs.

93. Extract from Irving's "A Radical's Diary," April 13–14, 1998, on Irving's Focal Point website.

94. See App, *A Straight Look*, 18, for alleged Jewish control of the media; Butz, *Hoax*, 87, for an alleged Jewish world conspiracy to persuade the world of the reality of the Holocaust.

95. Videotape 190: Irving Speech at die Bayerischer Hof, Milton. Ontario, October 5, 1991, from 2 hrs. 10 mins. 30 secs.

96. Videotape 220: "David Irving, Historian, in Tampa, Florida," October 6, 1995, from c. 23 mins.

97. Videotape 190: "German reunificaiton and other topics," Latvian Hall, Toronto, November 8, 1990, at 19 mins. 19 secs.

98. Videotape 225: "Cover Story" on Australian television program "Sunday," March 4, 1997, Irving interviewed in Key West. Florida (33 mins. 10 secs.). Audiocassette 90: Irving in Christchurch, New Zealand, March 26, 1986; Magnus Brechtken. *Madagascar für die Juden": Antisemitische Idee und politische Praxis* (Munich, 1997); Peter Longerich, *Politik der Vernichtung: Eine Gesamtdarstellung der nationalsozialistischen Judenverfolgung* (Munich, 1998), 273–89.

Restitution and Its Discontents

MICHAEL R. MARRUS

From *Some Measure of Justice*

Historians are storytellers, among other things, and they like to think of themselves as getting to the bottom of issues, even if they know that the ultimate truth will in the end elude them. Lawyers too tell stories. As the Israeli jurist Leora Bilsky observes, "The courtroom [is] maybe the last public space in our modern society where stories in general and oral stories in particular are still considered to be the privileged way of arriving at the truth."[1] However, along with storytelling, the law has an overriding objective, which is to use legal processes to achieve just outcomes. To do so, storytelling in the legal context is heavily regulated by rules and procedures that have evolved to secure those ends. Hence the point of the comment by the distinguished anthropologist Clifford Geertz: "Whatever it is that the law is after, it is not the whole story."[2]

The Holocaust restitution movement of the 1990s highlights these different approaches, casting into relief law and history and highlighting the degree to which the campaign's contentions about wrongdoing were not necessarily what historians would write about the persecution and murder of European Jewry. What happens to storytelling about the Holocaust in a legal context? Practitioners of both law and history would probably agree that they are both seeking the truth about the matter. "The focus must remain on discovering the truth, on revealing and owning up to the past," wrote Abraham Foxman [National Direc-

tor of the Anti-Defamation League], in a widely circulated article in 1998.[3] But Foxman was worried. He mentioned lawsuits against two American companies, Ford and General Motors, for deeds committed by their German subsidiaries during the war. Was there a problem with the choice of these defendants? Was he uncomfortable with the decision to go after American companies for the doings of their wartime European branches decades ago? There was no indication of this, for Foxman pressed on. He lamented that the Swiss bankers did not pay voluntarily, and that they had to be sued. There was no absolute justice, he said. He was concerned lest Holocaust survivors "be used as political footballs or tickets for financial gain." All fair enough. But what was really his problem?

The nub of the matter seemed to be that, with litigation, the story told about wartime murder of European Jews would be trivialized or distorted: "I fear that all the talk about Holocaust era assets is skewing the Holocaust, making the century's last word on the Holocaust that the Jews died not because they were Jews, but because they had bank accounts, gold, art and property," Foxman wrote. Elie Wiesel has expressed a similar view, explaining why he had not taken up the subject before. "I felt reluctant to define the greatest tragedy in Jewish history in terms of money."[4] For many, as suggested in these views, there was a sense that disputes over restitution would render the Holocaust banal. So what was to be done? It was not quite clear. "We owe it to history and to the six million who died to teach the lessons of the Holocaust to new generations," Foxman commented. Did this mean that he opposed the campaign for restitution? He did not say so, and the reader was left with his unease, his sense that things were somehow on the wrong track. The story was not being told properly, the Holocaust was being "skewed," and the fault seemed to be with the restitution campaign. Was there a real problem here? Or was this just a nervous response to a new chapter of justice seeking for the Holocaust? These questions are the subject of this [excerpt].

Robbery

At the core of the restitution campaign of the 1990s is a view of the Holocaust: "probably the gravest crime against humanity in recorded history," noted Stuart Eizenstat, but also "history's greatest robbery—robbery of personal effects, art, property, insurance, the right to compensation for labor, and ultimately, dignity."[5] Might the attention to robbery cast murder into the shade? Given the salience of property issues in the movement I am discussing, there are grounds to appreciate concerns about how the restitution campaign has framed the spoliation of Jews in the history of the Holocaust. In the slave labor case against the Siemens industrial concern, one of the plaintiffs maintained that the Holocaust should be viewed as if it were "one gigantic robbery." As a contention, this is often bracketed with the assertion that the Holocaust was the largest theft in history, with losses of Jewish assets estimated at between $143 billion and $215 billion in today's dollars.[6] Elaborating on the theme of theft, a commentator on the Siemens case maintained: "The Nazi SS stole their lives, Swiss banks stole their money, European insurance companies stole their insurance claims, some companies stole their gold fillings,

and the Pollack plaintiffs claim the defendants stole their labor."[7] Mass murder, in this view, was simply part of a continuum, with the unifying theme being theft.[8]

Abraham Foxman's worry that the Holocaust would appear out of shape when seen through the optic of restitution has its counterpart in at least one distinguished authority's recent evaluation. At the beginning of his important study of the plunder of Jews in Nazi Germany, historian Götz Aly states that one of his aspirations was to correct impressions created by Eizenstat's negotiations on restitution matters.[9] Aly's concern was not that attention to the robbery of Jews would crowd out mass murder, however. His unhappiness was with what he felt was Eizenstat's mistaken implication that the plunder of German Jews was mainly the work of the leading elements of German industry—"world famous companies like Daimler Benz, Volkswagen, Allianz Insurance, Krupp, the Bertelsmann publishing group, and BMW." Aly sought to redirect attention to ordinary Germans and to the spoliation of Jews that was an inescapable part of everyday life in the Third Reich. The villains in his piece, those ordinary Germans, were far indeed from bourgeois elites who masterminded the victimization of Jews and sought to cover up their greed after the war. "Readers of these pages will encounter not Nazi monsters," writes Aly, "but rather people who are not as different from us as we might like them to be. The culprits here are people striving for prosperity and material security for themselves and their children. They are people dreaming of owning a house with a garden, of buying a car of their own, or of taking a vacation. And they are people not tremendously interested in the potential costs of their short-term welfare to their neighbors or to future generations."[10] As Aly suggests, there is a mistaken view that German businessmen and bank directors were the main beneficiaries of the plundering of Jews. Not so, he argues. Most of the loot went to the state, the German war chest as he puts it, as did the dispossession of entire populations of occupied territories. In turn, the state passed along the benefits to the German population—the welfare or "socialist" side of the National Socialist state. Spectacular profiteering by Nazi satraps doubtless existed, but the real story was in a way much more problematic—the passing on of the stolen property to an entire society, boosting its "domestic consumption and public morale with policies of mass murder and state-organized plunder and terror."[11] . . .

With war, robbery became European-wide. The Wehrmacht confiscated millions of tons of food and shipped whatever the troops could not eat back to the Reich. Those who produced the food often starved. The regime's bureaucrats routinely destroyed currencies to the advantage of the Reich, bled away countries' industrial and agricultural production, stripped them of their businesses, their buildings, their transportation networks, their citizens' personal belongings, bank accounts, furniture, jewelry, art, and libraries. Larceny, one might say, was written into the DNA of the Nazi regime. In addition, one should add the obvious if sometimes forgotten point, that although the victimization of Jews was greater than that of any other group, given the scale and intensity of the Nazis' theft, the amounts stolen from non-Jews dwarfed the amounts taken from Jews.[12] And finally, speaking of Jews, one should not forget the wholesale robbery they suffered at the hands of other occupied and allied societies— the "Aryanization" of businesses, institutions, homes, and apartments, but also, mainly in Eastern Europe, valuables, household goods, clothing, and even things that could be stripped from the dead.[13] . . . Nazis stole from Jews before they

even contemplated a Holocaust; and they stole from non-Jews for whom there was no Holocaust. The regime rested on theft, among other things, and it is complicated enough to work out restitution for it without constant linkages from one crime to another.

From whom, under these circumstances, should restitution come? From the German state, clearly enough, as the agency, or the successor to the agency, that promoted and in many instances directed the process. But beyond that, where does one stop? As Hannah Arendt observed years ago, "There existed not a single organization or public institution in Germany, at least during the war years, that did not become involved in criminal actions and transactions."[14] How is the law to contend with this? When complicity is near universal and when wrongdoing is more often than not a question of degree, to be examined everywhere in a society, how are those to be found liable to be identified and how is the degree of their responsibility to be established?

To questions such as these, plaintiffs' lawyers have a ready answer: In the imperfect world of justice seeking, lawyers choose defendants against whom, for any number of reasons, a case can be mounted and who offer reasonable prospects for recovery. Some maintain that, notwithstanding these apparently arbitrary bases for holding some responsible, justice is served through the process, albeit imperfectly. Gerald Feldman once related that his first exposure to this approach occurred "when a prominent Jewish leader suggested to me at a conference in Vienna that Allianz and the other insurance companies were rich enough to afford to redo the postwar restitutions under the German compensation legislation in a fairer manner."[15] Feldman was flabbergasted. Quite apart from the politics of the matter, historians seek to put matters of responsibility into perspective, telling as much of the story as they can, irrespective of whether specific aspects of wrongdoing lend themselves to successful litigation. In his massive study of the Allianz Feldman found that a preoccupation with restitution could actually limit his inquiry of the company's involvement in the crimes of Nazism. As he discovered, "the central issues involve the political behavior and role of its leaders, their treatment of their Jewish employees, the actions of its leaders during the November 1938 Pogrom, the role of Allianz in Germany's expansion, and its involvement in insuring the facilities and production of places like the Lodz Ghetto and the ss factories in the concentration camps."[16] Much of this, Feldman points out, bore no relationship to restitution at all.

My concern about the litigation process, therefore, involves its implications for the history of the destruction of the European Jews. This is best examined, I think, in the context of the most important legal theory of wrongdoing used in the restitution campaign—"the theme that links the Swiss bank cases, the German slave labor cases, the German bank cases, and the German insurance cases," according to Burt Neuborne—namely, unjust enrichment.[17]

Unjust Enrichment and Related Issues

Unfamiliar to many common law lawyers, the doctrine of unjust enrichment is, in my view, ill suited to the characterization of Holocaust-era wrongdoing and those responsible for those crimes. Conceived for purposes far indeed from genocide and mass murder, this complicated area of law usually deals with far more humdrum matters—the circumstances under which there can be recovery of property to which the defendant is not properly entitled. In the classic statement of the linkage between unjust enrichment and restitution, articulated by the American Law Institute in 1937,

"A person who has been unjustly enriched at the expense of another is required to make restitution to the other."[18] But as the experts agree, such restitution need not involve wrongful conduct. As Emily Sherwin, a close student of the subject observes, a claim of unjust enrichment does not require that the defendant be a wrongdoer: "It is enough that the plaintiff lost an expected benefit, or in some cases that the plaintiff simply has a superior moral claim to whatever enrichment the defendant obtained."[19] Moreover, thinking about Holocaust-era restitution as unjust enrichment conflates two kinds of claims, for which the doctrine applies quite differently: with banks, insurance companies, and art restitution the heart of the issue was the claimants' efforts to have their property returned to them, whereas in the case of forced and slave labor—the largest part of the demands for Holocaust-era restitution and even part, as we have seen, of the Swiss banks settlement—the object of the claim was the value of the labor itself, what is classified technically as claims in *quantum meruit*.[20] In the latter situations, as I shall argue, unjust enrichment is a particularly distorted lens through which to view the Holocaust.

... The key element in Holocaust-related restitution cases is the highly seductive motif of perpetrators becoming fabulously wealthy as a result of theft from persecuted and murdered Jews. And further, this enrichment is widely understood to persist until the present day. In one succinct view, "financial giants worldwide are sitting on billions of dollars in funds made on the backs of World War II victims, which they invested and reinvested many times over during the last century."[21] Gerald Feldman noted "the fantasy about the amount of insurance held by Jews and the value of their policies."[22] Ronald Zweig has written similarly about myths of dizzying levels of wealth on the Hungarian Gold Train, linking these to hoary tales about secret stashes of Jewish valuables.[23] These characterizations have quickened demands for pursuing restitution against particular targets and the emphasis upon greed as the sole explanation for why it is not forthcoming. "Why Won't Those SOBS Give Me My Money?" was the title of one survivor's article on restitution, referring to "the criminals who run European insurance companies that stole hundreds of millions of dollars from those who died prematurely in the gas chambers and who used the money to hire stooges to make sure the money is not given back." Why would they not do so? "It is because they would rather keep it."[24]

A caricature? Of course, even if understandable given the circumstances. But the interrelated issue of unjust enrichment is worth examining closely as an accompaniment of the legal presentation of wartime theft from the Jews, for it is an excellent example, it seems to me, of how history can be misshapen to fit the idiom of the law.

The starting point is the enrichment, understood as the logical consequence of the devastation of European Jews. According to the claimants, what happened during the Holocaust was the wrongful transfer of massive amounts of wealth from the victims, resulting in unjust profits to the defendants. No one disputes the first part of this claim. In one of the earliest estimations of Jewish property losses, published in 1944, the Jewish researcher Nehemiah Robinson calculated that more than $8 billion (in 1944 values) had been lost.[25] In the case of the Swiss banks and the European insurance companies, and speaking more generally about the theft of Jewish-owned property of all kinds, including art, one can trace specific instances of confiscation, instances that occurred in different ways tens and hundreds of thousands of times. Recently, looking closely at

the nearly five million Jews of Germany, Austria, the Netherlands, France, Poland, and Hungary, the economist Helen Junz, the leading authority on the matter . . . , estimated that Jewish wealth in prewar Europe amounted to over $12 billion in value of the time, of which property losses, due to both theft and destruction involve as much as $10 billion—although every assessment recognizes that these numbers can only be approximate.[26] . . . There is no doubt that there was robbery, on an astronomic scale. Enrichment, however, is another matter.

Unfortunately, identifying those who were unjustly enriched and by how much—no small requirements in law—turns out to be a more complicated and historically problematic exercise than might appear at first glance. Proceeding against such parties required a deft legal hand, picking through patterns of ownership and state control, and working around questions of treaty rights, prior history, and involvement in restitution. Some obvious targets were off limits. Volkswagen, for example, owned during the war by the Nazi Party's Labor Front, might well have been protected because of the doctrine of sovereign immunity, which under some circumstances protects state agencies from American courts.[27] For these reasons, there was no possibility of establishing legal liability for forced laborers who worked for railway companies, the post office, or even companies owned by the SS. Some enterprises had long since ceased to exist. Some had divided into successor companies or had been consolidated through one or more mergers. Others had been nationalized by the East German regime. Some companies got off scot free because they did no business in the United States. Because the various contests, in the end, were settled around negotiating tables rather than in the courts, issues raised by this kind of selectivity were never judicially tested. Nor did the lawyers bother overly much with how their choices affected history. "It is understandable that lawyers concentrate on what is actionable rather than on what is simply awful," Gerald Feldman observed. And then he added, ruefully: "The latter seems to be the province of the historian."[28]

For reasons to which I have already alluded, lawyers for the plaintiffs in the various restitution cases chose unhesitatingly to launch their campaign against the "commanding heights" of the corporate world. No litigation lawyer would have dreamed of doing otherwise. This was the only reasonable way to identify defendants clearly and possibly . . . to reach a lucrative settlement. From the historians' point of view this inevitably involved distortions. The most flagrant among these is the implication that the theft was mainly the work of big industry and the major banks—leaving aside what I have seen to be the far more widespread involvement of "ordinary Germans," indeed virtually an entire society. . . . [In addition,] most of the victimized still living today had either worked in agriculture or for a company no longer in existence.[29] As [Lutz] Niethammer elaborates, "The majority of concentration camp prisoners and almost a third of those forced workers deployed outside farming had not been employed by private enterprises but by *public* agencies and organizations." But these facts were irrelevant to the thrust of restitution as negotiated with the industrial giants in the 1990s. Moreover, present-day German farmers . . . did not see themselves as even remotely liable for restitution, nor could the German companies that were no more, nor did the German state, which believed that it had discharged its responsibilities years ago.[30] . . . Of course, this is not to deny that German corporations during the Hitler era were responsible in some sense for slave and forced labor. They most

certainly were. It is rather to point out that the companies that were the subject of litigation and the negotiations for settlement in the 1990s bore only a distant relationship to perpetrators in the Third Reich more than half a century before.[31] The high-profile cases against American parent companies of German subsidiaries provide a particularly vivid example of this problem.

Consider three examples of American companies, Ford, General Motors, and IBM, sued as part of the restitution campaign. Of these, Ford was particularly vulnerable to lawsuit by virtue of its prominence in the United States and because of the high-profile antisemitism of its founder, Henry Ford, a determined Jew hater and a promoter, among other sins, of the anti-Jewish mythology of the *Protocols of the Elders of Zion*. A longtime supporter of Adolf Hitler, Ford had the dubious distinction of being appreciated in *Mein Kampf* in connection with the Führer's fulminations against the Jews.[32] Ford had pride of place in the restitution story when, in March 1998, it was the object of the first in a series of class actions in the United States having to do with forced labor. Begun in New Jersey, this lawsuit was launched on behalf of a single named plaintiff, Elsa Iwanowa, a non-Jewish woman living in Belgium after the war who had been taken from her home in Russia by German soldiers when she was seventeen years old to do heavy labor in the Cologne plant of the company's *Ford-Werke AG*. Iwanowa and her compatriots, altogether some ten thousand workers at the Cologne factory alone, suffered from excruciating conditions at the site. But there was also the enrichment. The complaint against Ford referred to the "enormous profits from the aggressive use of forced labor under inhuman conditions."[33] Without probing too deeply into the details of the case against Ford, the history was at the least problematic.

Ford responded to the allegations by appointing a large investigating team to look into the matter, which eventually produced more than ninety-eight thousand pages of documentation.[34] At the heart of the issue was the relationship between the present-day Ford Motor Company, headquartered in Dearborn, Michigan, and the German branch that had used forced labor during the war. . . . "By the time that slave labor was introduced," according to one of the Ford investigation's team members, Simon Reich, "*Ford-Werke* was clearly under the direct control of the Nazi government, though administered through the company headquarters in Cologne. . . . The meetings of the board of directors had already been suspended and didn't resume until after the war. Although the American parent company desperately sought to retain control of their German assets, [it] failed to do so. *Ford-Werke* became an instrument of the Nazi state."[35]

Similar questions about the links between American companies and their German subsidiaries arose with General Motors and IBM, with results that certainly did not sustain the allegations of culpable collaboration between American industrial firms and Nazi Germany. In the case of General Motors the issue was the use of slave labor by its German subsidiary Opel AG. Asked by GM to look into the question, Yale University Professor Henry Ashby Turner warned about anachronism—the "application of attitudes that became widely held among Americans only later." In Turner's view at least, the wartime links between the forced-labor-employing Opel and GM in the United States were practically nonexistent. "Allegations that GM continued to exercise control over Opel even after Hitler declared war on the United States in December 1941 are unfounded. Well before then, all direct contact with the Rüsselsheim headquarters of Opel had been lost. The last American had departed many months earlier, leaving the subsidiary's German lawyer in Berlin as the sole remaining channel of communications. Trans-Atlantic telephone contact with him ceased during the summer of 1941." Opel certainly had no excuses for the exploitation of forced labor during the war. However, in Turner's view at least, "General Motors cannot . . . be held responsible for the fate of those victims at that time. When the use of forced labor began in 1942, the American corporation had lost all control over its subsidiary and was cut off from information about what was happening there."[36]

In the case of IBM, a much-publicized book appearing in February 2001 by the energetic, strident American journalist Edwin Black, *IBM and the Holocaust: The Strategic Alliance between Nazi Germany and America's Most Powerful Corporation*, claimed that the company significantly facilitated the enslavement of workers and slaughter of European Jews through its German subsidiary *Dehomag* (*Deutsche Hollerith Maschinen Gesellschaft*). IBM did so, claimed Black, and did so knowingly, through the Nazis' supposedly widespread use of the company's precomputer punch card Hollerith machines to prepare lists of prospective victims. Published with considerable fanfare, Black's investigation also implicated the company's eccentric chief executive officer from 1915 to 1956, Thomas J. Watson, portrayed as a war profiteer in alliance with Hitler to facilitate the murder of European Jews.[37]

Almost simultaneously with that book's appearance, attorney Michael Hausfeld filed a class action lawsuit in Brooklyn alleging IBM's facilitation of Nazi persecution, genocide, and postwar cover-up and demanding that the company disgorge profits from the sale of Hollerith machines half a century before. "Book, Lawsuit Claim IBM Abetted the Holocaust" headlined a Jewish newspaper in California, reflecting a general view.[38] As with the other allegations against German and American corporations, these contentions were never tested in court: deferring to the wider settlement with German industry and the agreement to secure "legal peace," Hausfeld soon dropped the case against IBM so as to permit the resolution with German industry to go forward. Only the book remained, stoutly defended by Black himself against critical comments and supported by many popular reviewers.[39]

Once again, however, it turns out that the contentions about an American company's involvement in the Holocaust were highly contestable. IBM's crime, according to the allegations, amounted to the leasing by Dehomag of IBM tabulating machines to the German government, thereby assisting the murder of European Jews. The *New York Times* reviewer of Black's book observed about this supposed link to the Holocaust that it "threatens to obliterate the moral distinction between the sellers of rope and those who use the rope to hang people."[40] Moreover, Black's claim that the machines greatly facilitated the slaughter of European Jewry did not fare well with Holocaust historians.[41] Most seem to have agreed with Michael Allen, a specialist in the field, who wrote that "traditional means of record-keeping more than sufficed for the destruction of the European Jews."[42] Moreover, it has never been proven that Hollerith machines were used to make deportation lists; in many cases at least the lists were drawn up by hand, and sometimes not even by the Germans. As well, Black's estimation of IBM's chief executive officer at the time as a "corporate scoundrel" was sharply challenged. Thomas Watson's biographer, Kevin Maney, portrayed his subject even-handedly as an appeaser, an ambitious peacenik, and a maverick champion of his company's interests, but hardly someone

complicit with genocide. It is true that the Germans honored him with a decoration in 1937. But they probably did so because he was assuming the presidency of the International Chamber of Commerce and they hoped to get something from him. Watson did pander to Hitler in the 1930s, as did many at the time, but in Maney's view at least, he was a decent if naive man who warned about the fate of German Jews and even wrote directly to Hitler urging him to apply "the Golden Rule in dealing with these minorities." And he returned the decoration in 1940.[43]

Commenting on the IBM proceedings, a *New York Times* reporter saw a common thread with other Holocaust restitution cases: "Like other lawsuits based on human rights violations, Holocaust litigation often stands on shaky legal ground because evidence is missing or because it focuses on matters that the courts have traditionally left to politicians and diplomats to negotiate on behalf of citizens. But the sensitivity of multinationals to negative publicity and, in some cases, shame about past activity can sometimes give class-action lawyers a strong hand in negotiating settlements."[44] To be clear, my point is not to resolve the issues of wartime control over the German subsidiaries of these American companies or still less to absolve the latter for their associations with Nazi Germany before or during the war. It is rather to contest the historical representation that emerges from "litigating" the Holocaust in each of these cases, attended as they understandably are by negative publicity and shame. In each of the cases referred to here—that of Ford, General Motors, and IBM—there was plenty of each to go around, justified or not. In each, the one-sided picture presented by the plaintiffs misrepresents the past, at least to some degree. In each, the defendants seem to have been chosen because they appeared easy targets rather than exemplary wrongdoers. In each, the lawsuits seem to have raised more questions than they resolved—good news for historians but not so good for companies that value their good name and resist being stigmatized in this way. And finally in each, the pictures presented in the initial, usually highly publicized complaints, are misleading if taken as a fully rounded explanation of the wartime past.

For me, legal commentator Anthony Sebok sums up the situation well: "One of the consequences of 'litigating' the Holocaust is that actions are painted in very stark terms: a company's acts are either illegal or legal, which often translates into their being either intentionally evil or innocent. This area of law is like that: it needs clearly defined states of mind in order to make sense of the past. But the truth is, some of the guilty parties involved in the Holocaust are not so easy to pigeonhole."[45] Historians would wholeheartedly agree. Most find themselves ill at ease in the litigators' environment of intense, high-pressured rush to judgment against particular defendants. Few would accept the characterization of German corporations in the 1990s as "Hitler's willing business partners"—a designation taken from Daniel Goldhagen's controversial book on German complicity in the Holocaust that made similarly sweeping generalizations.[46] Discomfort with such commentary prompted a fine historian like Gerald Feldman, well accustomed to shades of gray even when dealing with the Nazi era, to cringe when he read what sometimes emerged from the plaintiffs' lawyers. "The briefs in some class actions sometimes make me feel that our worst history students have decided to take up law," he complained.[47]

When choosing defendants, establishing a link between Holocaust-era perpetrators and present-day companies and institutions . . . posed . . . no problems of principle or worries about putting matters into historical perspective. Through the well-worn legal fiction of "corporate personality" and through established legal processes that define it, corporate defendants in the 1990s could, to a court's satisfaction in any event, be understood to retain their identities over time and thereby to have participated in the crimes of the Nazi era.[48] Legal fictions, utilized warily by laymen, are of almost second nature to the lawyers and negotiators.[49] Plaintiffs' lawyers pointedly referred to the German corporations and the banks as "tortfeasors," "wrongdoers," or "malefactors." Survivors unhesitatingly demanded that companies give back what "they had stolen" fifty or sixty years before.

To non-lawyers, however, to those of us who are spectators in legal contests to determine responsibility, this identification of past and present could be problematic. Specifically, it is not always obvious that liability can be passed from a group of perpetrators to their organizational successors so many decades later.[50] . . . Banks or companies in the 1990s were often, in a widely held view, scarcely recognizable as the moral successors to their counterparts of the 1930s and 1940s. Company leaders from that era, of course, had long passed from the scene. As we have seen, the companies themselves had sometimes disappeared. Sometimes they had split into fragments, explicitly terminating the liability for past wrongs Sometimes they had been transformed through their experience under Communism. Sometimes they had cast their lot with others. With Swiss banks, for example, the Volcker Committee noted that since the end of the war there had been more than one hundred mergers among implicated banks that existed in 1945.[51] The structures of public companies also militated against findings of moral responsibility or blameworthiness after a half century—although there may, in some instances, be a case for reparations or the return of assets to claimants.[52] . . .

Even more problematic, one of the least credible historical arguments made by the plaintiffs was that the present-day companies had enriched themselves, or were "sitting on" great wealth that was generated by the Holocaust. Northwestern University's Peter Hayes, one of the few scholars who have inquired deeply into the issues of unjust enrichment with regard to one importantly implicated industrial concern, reached conclusions quite at odds with those proposed by counsel for the plaintiffs. Looking at Degussa, a chemical corporation that not only used slave labor but was responsible, among other things, for the production and sale of the deadly Zyklon gas used to murder Jews in Auschwitz and for processing gold taken from the victims, he found much that was unjust about the company but very little that entailed enrichment as a result of its exploitation of Jewish and East European workers.[53] Degussa used slave laborers at four known branch locations, and in none of these did the company show any profits. Moreover, [these installations] . . . fell largely into the Soviet occupation zone. Mass murder and mass enslavement, it seems, was far less profitable than the Nazis hoped or intended it to be. Summing up, Hayes notes: "The more I explored Degussa's history under the Nazis, the more I thought the firm had engaged in acts that extinguished or gravely damaged the lives of many and for which it clearly 'owed' at least the survivors something, but that it had not made much money directly from any of these deeds—indeed, it probably, in the aggregate, lost some."[54]

Extrapolating from the case against German industry in which unjust enrichment was at the core, Hayes points out how different were the rhetoric of the law and the findings of his history. The former carried "the implication that the evil of the system lay in its profitability"; the latter told a story that was horrible enough even with-

out the profit-making necessary for a finding of liability in American courts.[55] Going over similar ground focusing on Soviet prisoner of war labor, the German researcher Rolf Keller believes that the use of these workers made no economic sense. Although the German war economy had a voracious appetite for labor, the terrible treatment of these victims and their lack of skills or motivation rendered these workers worse than useless to the German economy.[56] Needless to say, none of these points found a place in the plaintiffs' arguments. As Hayes concluded, the restitution settlements "produced financial obligations for the participating corporations that bear no discernable relationship to what each actually did in Nazi Germany or earned by virtue of doing so, as well as payouts to survivors that seldom approximate adequate compensation for what they lost. In other words, the argument from profits served as a club, not a measuring stick, and it was, at best, partially successful."[57]

To be fair, we do not as yet have conclusive research that would bear out Hayes's generalization that "few enterprises, German or otherwise, grew rich from the Holocaust."[58] Furthermore, a legal case can be made that unjust enrichment does not necessarily require profit making. But at the very least the plaintiffs' empirical arguments seem shaky and their history misleading. There are solid grounds for making this point, for example, with regard to the wartime Daimler Benz—an important firm to examine because Manfred Gentz, the chief financial officer of that company's successor, Daimler Chrysler AG, formed in 1998 from a merger with the Chrysler Corporation, was a vigorous spokesman for German industry during the 1990s settlement negotiations and became chairman of the German industry fund that was instrumental in financing the settlement. The British scholar Neil Gregor studied Daimler's wartime use of forced labor and was unsparing in his description of the cruel conditions that took such a toll upon such workers. However, as he pointed out, what really enhanced production at Daimler Benz was its skilled labor force and not its forced workers. This is what made money for the company. Decision makers at this and other corporations did not turn to involuntary labor because it would raise their profits. As Gregor suggests, this recourse was part of the barbarization of the "Third Reich" and a way of keeping afloat in the latter part of the war.[59]

Moreover, even without conclusive findings across German industry, there are ample grounds to fear, as in one recent discussion, that "framing the claim in the language of unjust enrichment will trivialize the defendant's wrongdoing."[60] After all these years, we are still contending with the Holocaust not because of lost value or unfair labor practices but because of lost lives, limitless cruelty, and the targeting of entire categories of individuals. To historians, of course, inapt theories are deplorable, even if they contribute to just resolutions. And not just to historians. I give the last word on this matter to Anthony Sebok, who in my opinion gets it right: "The problem is that [the language of unjust enrichment] buys into a rhetoric and a vocabulary which fundamentally commodifies the wrong. . . . The claims are not about violations of human rights. The claims are not about the destruction of a culture. And the claims are not about the oppression of a people. They are about returning property that has been wrongfully taken."[61] The law, thereby, gets the history wrong.

Defendants as Bystanders

To historians, it should not be surprising that the restitution contests of the 1990s are part of that decade's intellectual climate. Indeed, many of the historical issues disputed in the clashes between plaintiffs and defendants are precisely those that historians of the subject have turned to during recent years. These turn, I argue, on questions about bystanders to the Holocaust, loosely defined as individuals, companies, institutions, or governments who were neither perpetrators nor collaborators nor victims but who, being present in some sense at the destruction of European Jews and aware of what was happening, did not intervene in any meaningful way in the process of mass murder or, even worse, became part of a vast apparatus of exploitation and persecution. Bystanders, or at least some of them, were, to use a word one hears increasingly, "enablers" of the Holocaust.[62] The defendants of the 1990s, it seems to me, fall generally into this category. Particularly in light of the historical interest in bystanders during the 1990s, it makes sense to examine the restitution campaign in relationship to what historians have thought about their role.

From the margins of interest in the murder of European Jews, the subject of the bystanders has come to wider public attention and, some might even say, to the center of the puzzle of how the catastrophe could have happened. "Slowly but surely," observes Regula Ludi, "the behavior of the bystanders . . . has come to be regarded as a decisive factor in the ability of the Nazis to accomplish their murderous goals. Such insights raise new questions about political and moral responsibility during World War II and suggest the need for many nations to rethink their understanding of the Nazi past."[63] . . . This is as good a sketch as any of the historical fallout of the litigation and settlement contests in the period I am discussing.

"Once filed, the lawsuits were used as a public relations platform to mobilize political and public opinion against the defendant companies," writes Owen Pell, a veteran litigator and defense counsel in both Holocaust-related and other human rights issues.[64] Facilitating this process, U.S. rules of procedure permit the presentation of unproven allegations in order to exert maximum pressure on the parties to settle. Repeatedly in the commentary on the restitution campaign, one reads of the frustrated or even angry contentions of the defendants that they had been caricatured through the litigation process and an attendant misshaping of the history of the Holocaust. However judged in the end, one senses among the European defendants a constantly frustrated effort to relay their version of history to their largely American accusers. "Our neutrality was not opportunistic or of recent vintage, formed as a response to the Nazi takeover of Germany," declared Hans Halbheer, honorary secretary of the American Swiss Foundation Advisory Council. "Instead, neutrality has been a condition of our domestic peace and our foreign policy since time immemorial—dating back to 1515."[65] Comforting for those who care about historical representation is the acknowledgment that history is important. "A crucial lesson of the Holocaust asset cases is that companies must invest heavily in historical research so that they will have control and an intimate understanding of the facts," adds Pell.[66] The problem for him, and even more for European executives who contended with what was for them an unfamiliar and unsettling legal environment, was how history seemed to fare when caught up in the litigation process.

At the starting point for all these cases, no one doubts, were massive, unprecedented violations of human rights. Defendants never disputed this element in the restitution cases, and all accepted accounts of the persecution of European Jews, the brutalization of Slavic and other occupied peoples, and the violation of every civilized norm in the conduct of war. But for the defendants in prac-

tically every one of the lawsuits, the real culprits were the German and collaborationist regimes and not those who, in their characterization, were sucked into the perpetration of the crimes of the Third Reich.

Research on German industrialists under the Nazis seems now to bear this out. As Hayes notes, "the prevailing view now traces executives' liability not to their supposed congruence of purpose with Hitler's government, but to their reflexive adaptability."[67] Generally speaking, historians do not believe that the profit motive, and certainly not the profit motive alone, drove corporate complicity with Nazism. At least as important were status, ideology, and the corporate culture of leading-businessmen. "Making money was not the reason the Reich's increasingly counterproductive, cruel, cumbersome, and chaotic program of labor exploitation came into being, and it is neither morally nor historically sound to measure its evil by its lucrativeness," Hayes observes. And he goes on: "Precisely because the 'slave' labor system emerged out of a vortex of macropolitical, not microeconomic forces, international law consistently has defined the German state—and thus its citizens collectively—as the primary party responsible for answering to the financial claims of people exploited under Nazism."[68]

That is why German executives . . . , like most others in that country, believed that the government should assume responsibility for restitution, as indeed it had done over many years. "We are determined that justice is done," insisted Herbert Hansmeyer, a member of the board of the Allianz insurance company at a speech in 1998. Nevertheless, he told his listeners, "the lawsuit came as a surprise to us." As he explained, "the majority of cases were included in postwar compensation programs and treaties among the nations involved in the war. It was our understanding that these programs—initiated after World War II by the Allied governments and continued to this day by the Federal Republic of Germany had, in fact, settled all claims."[69] Count Otto Lambsdorff, the distinguished lawyer, longtime member of the Bundestag, and representative of the German chancellor who worked closely with [Stuart] Eizenstat to secure agreement with German industry, . . . made it clear that whatever the legal liability, moral responsibility lay heavily on the German government: "I have always defended the decision to finance three-quarters of the Foundation by the public sector. It was not only the direct employment of forced labor in the public sector that brought us to that conclusion, but also the fact that a large part of the labor force was recruited—or, to be more accurate, in many cases apprehended—by the German police and army and subject to draconian and racist laws in order to replace German workers employed in Hitler's armies. This put the bulk of the moral responsibility on the German government that represented Germany in succession to the Third Reich."[70]

"We know that there can never be moral closure," Lambsdorff conceded.[71] Still, participants suffered from the continuing climate of recrimination that was never entirely absent from the negotiations and the legal proceedings. "I'm the last person not to want justice for Holocaust victims," protested Amihud Ben-Porat, the Israeli lawyer for the Generali insurance company. "But there were many groundless, vicious accusations made against Generali] in Israel by persons who didn't always verify facts."[72] Reacting to what he felt was a gross injustice, defense attorney Kenneth Bialkin commented on how he and his fellow lawyers defending insurance companies were treated by the plaintiffs. "I went to some of those early meetings with some of these executives from Generali and other companies, many of whom weren't even born when the war ended, and some of my colleagues were addressing them as though it was 1943."[73] A former head of the Conference of Presidents of Major American Jewish Organizations, Bialkin was bitterly attacked for taking on the defense of Generali, part of an intense debate over whether Jewish lawyers ought to have done so.[74] Bialkin stood his ground. "The more I got into it, the more I felt that Generali and others were being pressed and tarred with the anathema of the Holocaust and asked to pay money which they didn't owe in amounts which bore no relationship to what was fair," he said.[75] . . .

A good illustration of . . . problems in the legal assessment of bystanders appeared in the legal responses to accusations about slave labor. Attorneys for the German companies argued that the latter had no choice during the war and had been dragooned into wrongdoing by the Nazi regime. Critically, and in a crucial argument familiar to the story of bystanders, the industries' lawyers insisted that the claims against them "arise out of a *war*, not a run-of-the-mill private dispute." They sought to have the case thrown out of court on grounds of non-justiciability—in layman's terms, because it had to do with war making, that is, interstate relations, held to be out of bounds in civil courts in the United States. Lawyer Stephen Whinston identifies the crucial point: "Since wars are fought between nations, claims arising out of wars can only be resolved by such nations."[76] In rebuttal, lawyers for the plaintiffs made a complicated case that the wrongdoing did not arise out of the war, but instead was part and parcel of a quite separate undertaking, the Nazis' genocidal design for the Jews. The destruction of the Jews, as Whinston notes, "was unrelated to the armed hostilities of World War II and stemmed from a genocidal motivation."[77] Unintentionally, the lawyers found themselves in detailed disputation on one of the most difficult questions of Holocaust historiography—the relationship between the Nazis' genocidal antisemitism and Hitler's imperial war of conquest.[78] Happily, final resolution of these issues was eventually supplanted by settlement negotiations around the bargaining table and the lawyers no longer had to worry about whether the Holocaust "arose" out of the war or not. For history, it was probably just as well.[79]

Claimants and History

As we have seen, in peace settlements following the cessation of hostilities, states were traditionally in charge. Challenging this system in the 1990s litigation, claimants typically pursued settlements outside governmental authority and without institutional support for their efforts except, in some circumstances, in the case of the Claims Conference [the umbrella group formed in 1951 to represent Jewish victims' claims for restitution and compensation for persecution during the Nazi era]. In one exception to this practice, at the very beginning of the Holocaust-era restitution campaign, the United States government took action with respect to Hugo Princz, a Holocaust survivor whose forty-year quest for reparation involved unusual circumstances. A young American citizen living in Slovakia at the beginning of the war, Princz was turned over to the Nazis by local townspeople in 1942, following the United States declaration of war against Germany. Deported to Auschwitz with his family, he managed, miraculously, to survive. After the war, Princz found himself ineligible for reparations because he was not stateless but rather an American citizen for whom there had been no provision for restitution. To rectify this, Princz took the German government to court, but was blocked because of sovereign immunity, the rule that foreign governments cannot be sued in American courts. He later tried,

unsuccessfully, to sue the German companies for whom he had been forced to work. At that point the United States took on Princz's claim, acting on his behalf with the Germans. Following President Bill Clinton's raising the matter with German Chancellor Helmut Kohl in 1995, the issue was resolved through a special American agreement with Germany. Princz and eleven other deportees in related circumstances shared an award of $2.1 million, after a settlement signed with Germany on Capitol Hill. Princz also received undisclosed amounts from Bayer, Messerschmidt-Boelkow-Blohm, BASF, and Hoechst, for his unpaid service as a slave laborer during the war.[80] An individual (in this case, thanks to the eventual assistance of the United States government) achieved some reparation in circumstances that had not been contemplated by the diplomats or international lawyers in the postwar period.

The radical departure of the restitution campaign against the Swiss banks, the German corporations, and insurance was that the United States did not espouse the claims of the plaintiffs as in the Princz case, and the quest for restitution proceeded outside the interstate framework, with the role of the United States government being limited to the encouragement of negotiations and mediation. With respect to the German companies, the American government facilitated talks among representatives of the plaintiffs as well as company representatives, the Claims Conference, several foreign governments, plus Germany and the United States. In all these efforts, there were masses of claimants, represented by private attorneys who had to be satisfied. Moreover, the claimants came from all over the world and were citizens of many different countries.[81] Managing them credibly and in conformity with the strict requirements of the Federal Rules of Procedure on class actions was no mean challenge.

In this new environment, the claimants as a collectivity were far more at the center of attention than ever before. Depending on the stage of the restitution process, whether the lawsuits or the settlements, contacting and informing them about the process was the task of the lawyers, the courts, or in the case of insurance, the ICHEIC [International Commission on Holocaust Era Insurance Claims] machinery agreed to by the insurers. In all, more than two million claimants from around the world appeared on the scene—Jews and non-Jews, victims and their heirs, those who had been in camps, forced laborers, or those who claimed accounts or policies.[82] Reaching out to survivors and communicating with them became a fundamental part of the restitution culture—an overlooked and under researched part of the process that deserves serious inquiry in materials generated by the various participants in the litigation and negotiation process. Of course, no one knew how many survivors there were at the time and there was no template for engaging with them. In the Swiss banks settlement, the notices prescribed in the rules went out around the globe, and an astounding 584,000 questionnaires were returned.[83] ICHEIC developed perhaps the most sophisticated process to communicate with claimants. Its staff produced packets of information and claim forms available in twenty languages. It established a Web site and a twenty-four-hour call center with toll-free numbers in New York and extensive language capabilities. It launched a global press campaign to inform survivors wherever they lived. Anticipating approximately 20,000 claims, in the end ICHEIC received more than 100,000, coming from more than thirty countries, in more than twenty different languages.[84] Similar outreach efforts had to be made on behalf of each of the various class action lawsuits, and these often required

follow-up communications and interaction with survivors.

. . . Roman Kent, chairman of the American Gathering of Holocaust Survivors and treasurer of the Claims Conference, had no illusions about the process. "With time, I . . . realized that the basis for these negotiations on the part of the Germans, as well as the great majority of class action lawyers, was not founded on moral and humanitarian purposes. It was strictly business. For the Germans it was legal closure; for the lawyers who had filed the class action lawsuits against the German companies, it was millions of dollars in fees." Still, Kent believed restitution was worth pursuing:

In spite of this I saw the prospect of utilizing the opportunity at hand to bring some relief to needy survivors in Eastern European countries as well as Jewish Holocaust survivors throughout the world. In addition, from a historical point of view, there was something more important to be gained. The negotiations would bring official exposure and acknowledgment of the evil acts perpetrated by Germans against mankind. They would prove the direct, large-scale involvement of German industry at large. Thus the negotiations would show beyond a shadow of a doubt that not only Hitler and the Nazis were responsible for the atrocities, but the totality of the German nation was also responsible.[85]

. . . . Claimants were rarely satisfied with settlements, although they disagreed with them for many different reasons. Intending to address the rights and the needs of Holocaust survivors, distribution involved tremendous difficulties and disputes, some of which remain unresolved to this day. Stuart Eizenstat refers to a "three month torment" of deciding how to divide the money provided by German industry on the slave and forced labor issues. "The process brought out the worst in everyone," he observed, as the claimants' representatives sought to divide the pie.[86] Debate persists, centering notably on accountability and institutional matters, challenges to the role of the Claims Conference and the administration of settlement claims, the desperate circumstances of some aged Holocaust survivors, and the right balance between material support for survivors and programs for the Jewish world.[87] There were also disputes about process matters, application deadlines, and standards of proof. What I would like to do here is not to review these disagreements but rather to comment briefly on how some settlement distribution decisions shaped and reflected the historical understanding of the Holocaust that lay behind the restitution campaign and the way in which this played itself out in a particularly American context. . . .

Generalizations about claimants are difficult. It is often not appreciated that, for the greatest part of the restitution campaign, having to do with forced and slave laborers, the numbers of non-Jewish victims predominated, receiving more than three-quarters of the funds.[88] Similarly, the Swiss bank settlement included not only Jews but also Jehovah's Witnesses, Sinti and Roma, as well as homosexuals and the disabled.[89] In the settlement with German industry, there were bitter debates between representatives of the Jewish survivors of the Holocaust and East European forced workers, behind which were layers of animosity and utterly different ways of understanding the history of the Second World War. To be divided was some 10 billion deutsche marks, to be paid to claimants for unremunerated labor, in working conditions ranging from a few who were relatively comfortable to some, mostly Jews, who were intended to be worked to death. Of perhaps 12 million people who worked in that capacity, there were estimated

to be between 1.2 million and 1.5 million survivors, including those who had worked in agriculture and who were generally acknowledged to have suffered the least. "Everybody agreed that the other side deserved something, but nobody could agree on how much," observe John Authers and Richard Wolffe.[90] The East Europeans rested their case on the devastation in the conquered territories; the Jews stressed the racially motivated persecution and the fact that so many of them were worked to death. Melvyn Weiss, representing Jewish survivors, denounced the East European claimants as "a bunch of antisemites." "Go file your own suit." he is supposed to have told them in an effort to beat back their case for greater restitution.[91] On the other side, there were accusations based on need: the Jews had received various forms of reparation to that point, but the East Europeans, with their postwar past under Communism, had not.

Eizenstat describes the exceedingly complex, highly contentious bargaining process by which he and Count Lambsdorff worked out a settlement and eventually secured agreement. The upshot was to distinguish between two classes of workers: slave and forced laborers. The former, survivors of camps and ghettos and destined to be worked to death, would each receive $7,500, and the latter, who had worked in somewhat better although extremely variable conditions, would receive approximately $2,500 apiece. Of the former, Jews were the majority, and of the latter most were East European Slavs, although there were many of the other group on each side.[92]

The disputes were hardly limited to the quarrels between plaintiffs and defendants or between Holocaust victims and others. Among Jews, there were sharp divisions between those who claimed survivor status by virtue of having escaped persecution and murder through emigration, flight, and hiding and those who suffered in camps, ghettos, or forests. While all were victimized, some claimed to have suffered more than others, and this unhappy issue played out in complicated ways when the survivor designation translated into restitution. Notably, the United States-based Holocaust Survivors Foundation–USA (HSF-USA) contested the survivor standing of Jews in the former Soviet Union, arguing that they had managed to flee eastward out of the hands of the Germans and had, therefore, not been directly persecuted by the Nazis as had so many others. Similarly, there were passionate arguments over whether restitution should be based on verifiable claims or whether it should be driven by need—or put otherwise, on suffering at the time of the crime or present-day poverty.[93]

Decisions on such matters in the Swiss banks affair fell to Special Master Judah Gribetz, a respected, high-ranking former New York civil servant and attorney charged ... with developing a comprehensive plan of allocation and distribution of the settlement proceeds—including humanitarian funds, specially designated for elderly survivors in need. In a Solomonic resolution, Gribetz recommended that 75 percent of what eventually would be $205 million in humanitarian funds would go to survivors in the former Soviet Union, 13 percent to Israel, and the balance to the rest of the world. HSF-USA received 4 percent. Gribetz accepted the survivor status of the former-Soviet-Union claimants and made the further case that they were most in need, not only due to their circumstances in countries of the former Soviet Union but also due to their not having received reparations in previous years. Representing the HSF, Florida attorney Samuel Dubbin protested bitterly, making the point that many Holocaust survivors in the United States were desperately poor and that they were five times more likely than nonsurvivors to be living below the poverty

line in that country. Dubbin unsuccessfully made the case for a population-based formula, under which humanitarian distributions would be allocated according to the percentage of survivors in each country—under which the American survivors would have received 25 percent of the total.[94] Needless to say, it was impossible to please everyone. Michael Bazyler is certainly correct when he observes that "the distribution of money will always produce discord, especially when the payouts are the consequence of a tragedy, man-made or natural. . . . The real questions of how to serve justice and concurrently balance the claims of memory, responsibility, and group survival will inevitably produce competing visions."[95]

Were these distribution decisions faithful to the historical experience of Nazi-era criminality? Did the outcomes of these momentous disputes confirm or validate Holocaust memory as so many had hoped? An obvious but underappreciated point was the great diversity of the historical events associated with these instances of historic wrongs. Take just one example, the case of "forced and slave labor." As Peter Hayes observes, these categories cover an extraordinarily wide spectrum of circumstances, for both Jews and non-Jews: "Considerable differences arise concerning everything from daily treatment and nourishment to ultimate chances for survival depending on whether the laborer was a Jew; male or female; a civilian, prisoner of war, or a ghetto or camp inmate; could or could not speak German; came from Western or Eastern Europe; and whether he or she had to toil in Germany or the occupied East, in agriculture or industry, directly for the SS or the *Wehrmacht*, in a state-owned or private enterprise, a large or small one, and in construction or mining or on an assembly line."[96] To the extent that this process highlighted the vast scope and diversity of forced and slave labor, it was therefore helpful to history. And, while a blunt instrument indeed, the broad distinction between "forced" and "slave" laborers did make historical sense, and was a point worth making.

It is therefore appropriate that when the claimants finally spoke, they spoke with many different voices, and that their terrible experiences were not easy to categorize or to enlist in one or another distribution scheme. While undoubtedly painful for those who sought a resolution that would achieve universal support, this outcome is nevertheless in keeping with our understanding of the Holocaust. By now, the destruction of European Jews is slipping from justice seeking into history, a realm that lives with complexity and ambiguity, and is becoming more and more the province of the historians rather than the advocates of individuals seeking restitution for themselves and their fellows according to some common formula. Justice seeking is inevitably drawing to an end, and with it will come a diminishing of disagreements that may have been, as some feel, inescapable. Meanwhile, the effort to understand the Holocaust in all its complexity continues.

NOTES

1. Leora Bilsky, *Transformative Justice: Israeli Identity on Trial* (Ann Arbor: University of Michigan Press, 2004), 141.

2. Clifford Geertz, *Local Knowledge: Further Essays in Interpretive Anthropology* (New York: Basic Books, 1983), 173.

3. Abraham Foxman, "The Dangers of Holocaust Restitution," *Wall Street Journal*, December 4, 1998.

4. Elie Wiesel, preface to Stuart E. Eizenstat, *Imperfect Justice: Looted Assets, Slave Labor, and the Unfinished Business of World War ii* (New York: Public Affairs, 2003), ix. But Wiesel goes on to say that Eizenstat's book "is not really about

money. . . . It is about the ethical value and weight of memory." Ibid., xi.

5. Stuart E. Eizenstat, Remarks at the 12th and Concluding Plenary on the German Foundation, July 17, 2000, Deputy Secretary of the Treasury Stuart E. Eizenstat, U.S. Diplomatic Mission to Germany, available at http://usa.usembassy.de /etexts/ga7–000717e.htm, last accessed October 8, 2008, 1. cf. Richard Z. Chesnoff. *Pack of Thieves: How Hitler and Europe Plundered the Jews and Committed the Greatest Theft in History* (New York: Doubleday, 1999).

6. Sidney Zabludoff, "Restitution of Holocaust-Era Assets: Promises and Reality," *Jewish Political Studies Review* 19 (Spring 2007): available at http://www.jcpa.org/jcpa/templates/showpage .asp?drit=3&dbid=1&lngid=1&tmid=111& fid=253&pid=0&iid=i678&ttl=Restitution _of_Holocaust-Era_Assets:_Promises_and _Reality, last accessed October 1, 2008. Michael J. Bazyler, *Holocaust Justice: The Battle for Restitution in America's Courts* (New York: New York University Press, 2003), xi, estimates the losses at between $230 billion and $320 billion.

7. Justin H. Roy, "Strengthening Human Rights Protection: Why the Holocaust Slave Labor Claims Should Be Litigated," *The Scholar* 1 (1999): 162.

8. See Jonathan Petropoulos, "The Nazi Kleptocracy: Reflections on Avarice and the Holocaust," in Dagmar Herzog, ed., *Lessons and Legacies VII* (Evanston IL: Northwestern University Press, 2006), 29–38.

9. Götz Aly, *Hitler's Beneficiaries: Plunder, Racial War, and the Nazi Welfare State*, trans. Jefferson Chase (New York: Metropolitan Books, 2006), 1.

10. Ibid., 4.

11. Ibid., 331–32.

12. This is especially evident in the plundering of precious metals, even of gold taken from private individuals. For a detailed examination of this looting, see Peter Hayes, *From Cooperation to Complicity: Degussa in the Third Reich* (New York: Cambridge University Press, 2004), chap. 5, and for some

calculations, see 175. For a magisterial overview, see Mark Mazower, *Hitler's Empire: How the Nazis Ruled Europe* (New York: Penguin, 2008).

13. Ibid., 453.

14. Hannah Arendt, *Eichmann in Jerusalem: A Report on the Banality of Evil* (New York: Viking, 1965), 159, emphasis mine. Similarly, as she wrote in 1945: "The totalitarian policy has achieved the result of making the existence of each individual in Germany depend either upon committing crimes or upon complicity in crimes." Ron H. Feldman, ed., *Hannah Arendt: The Jew as Pariah: Jewish Identity and Politics in the Modern Age* (New York: Grove Press., 1978), 228.

15. Gerald D. Feldman, "The Historian and Holocaust Restitution: Personal Experiences and Reflections," *Berkeley Journal of International Law* 23 (2005): 352.

16. Ibid., 354.

17. Burt Neuborne, "Preliminary Reflections on Aspects of Holocaust-Era Litigation in American Courts," *Washington University Law Quarterly* 80 (2002): 829. In Neuborne's summary: "The Swiss and German cases were based on classic principles of restitution and unjust enrichment. In each case, a private entity was unjustly enriched by the transfer of identifiable property from a victim of a crime against humanity. The remedy sought by plaintiffs in the Holocaust cases consisted of a simple reversal of the unjust wealth transfer." Neuborne, "A Tale of Two Cities: Administering the Holocaust Settlements in Brooklyn and Berlin," in Michael J. Bazyler and Roger P. Alford, eds., *Holocaust Restitution: Perspectives on the Litigation and Its Legacy* (New York: New York University Press, 2006), 74. See also Black's Law Dictionary's most recent definition of "Restitution": "A body of substantive law in which liability is based not on tort or contract but on the defendant's unjust enrichment." *Black's Law Dictionary* 8th ed. (St. Paul MN: Thomson, 2004), 1339.

18. American Law Institute, *Restatement of the Law of Restitution: Quasi-Contracts and Constructive Trusts* (St. Paul MN: American Law Institute Publishers, 1937), 5.

19. Emily Sherwin, "Reparations and Unjust Enrichment," Cornell Law School Legal Studies Research Paper Series, Paper 6 (2004), 9, available at http://papers.ssrn.com/so13/papers.cfm?abstract_id=580802, last accessed June 5, 2008; Peter D. Maddaugh and John D. McCamus, *The Law of Restitution* (Aurora, Ont.: Canada Law Book Inc., 1990), 33; Peter Birks, *Unjust Enrichment* (Oxford: Oxford University Press, 2003), 3–18; Daniel Friedman, "Restitution for Wrongs: The Basis of Liability," in W. R. Cornish, Richard Nolan, Janet O'Sullivan, and Graham Virgo, eds., *Restitution: Past, Present and Future* (Oxford: Hart Publishing, 1998), 133, 152–54.

20. *Quantum meruit* (Latin: as much as is deserved). See Anthony J. Sebok, "A Brief History of Mass Restitution Litigation in the United States," in David Dyzenhaus and Mayo Moran, eds., *Calling Power to Account: Law, Reparations, and the Chinese Canadian Head Tax* (Toronto: University of Toronto Press, 2005), 359. Sebok argues that the basic claims with respect to dormant accounts— and he might have added unpaid insurance policies—were based on replevin, "where the proceeds of the wrongfully taken property had been held . . . in a constructive trust on behalf of their true owners." Ibid.

21. Michael J. Bazyler, "The Holocaust Restitution Movement in Comparative Perspective," *Berkeley Journal of International Law* 20 (2002): 41. Cf. Chesnoff, *Pack of Thieves.*

22. Gerald Feldman, "The Historian and Holocaust Restitution: Personal Experiences and Reflections," address to the 31st Annual Symposium of the Alexander von Humboldt Foundation Prize Fellows, Bamberg, Germany (March 20–22, 2003), 10, available at http://www\.bepress.com/cgi/viewcontent.cgi?articlc=1080&context=ils, last accessed May 29, 2008.

23. See his aptly titled "The Hungarian Gold Train: Fantasies of Wealth and the Madness of Geno-

cide," in Dean, Goschler, and Ther, *Robbery and Restitution*, 211–22.

24. Si Frumkin, "Why Won't Those SOBs Give Me My Money? A Survivor's Perspective," in Bazyler and Alford, *Holocaust Restitution*, 92.

25. Nehemia Robinson, *Indemnification and Reparations: Jewish Aspects* (New York: Institute of Jewish Affairs), 83.

26. Helen B. Junz, "Report on the Prewar Wealth Position of the Jewish Population in Nazi-Occupied Countries, Germany, and Austria," in Independent Committee of Eminent Persons, *Report on Dormant Accounts of Victims of Nazi Persecution in Swiss Banks* (Bern: Independent Association of Eminent Persons, 1999), Appendix S, 127–206. Cf. Sidney Zabludoff, "Restitution of Holocaust-Era Assets: Promises and Reality," Jerusalem Center for Public Affairs, March 2007, available at http://www.jcpa.org /jcpa/templates/showpage.asp?drit=3&dbid =i&lngid=i&tmid=in&fid=625&pid=i666& iid=i678&111=Restitution_of_Holocaust-Era _Assets:_Promises_and_Reality, last accessed October 1, 2008. See also Dean, Goschler, and Ther, *Robbery and Restitution*, 7–8, and passim.

27. Hans Mommsen with Manfred Grieger, *Das Volkswagenwerk und seine Arbeiter im Dritten Reich* (Düsseldorf: Econ Verlag, 1996); Detlev Vagts and Peter Murray, "Litigating the Nazi Labor Claims: The Path Not Taken," *Harvard International Law* Journal 43 (2002): 510–12.

28. Gerald Feldman, *Allianz and the German Insurance Business, 1933–1945* (New York: Cambridge University Press, 2001), 536.

29. Vagts and Murray, "Litigating the Nazi Labor Claims," 527.

30. Lutz Niethammer, "Converting Wrongs to Rights? Compensating Nazi Forced Labor as a Paradigm," in Dan Diner and Gotthart Wunberg, eds., *Restitution and Memory: Material Restoration in Europe* (New York: Berghahn, 2007), 88.

31. Ibid., 99.

32. Adolf Hitler, *Mein Kampf* (Boston: Houghton Mifflin, 1943), 639. See Keith Sward, *The Legend of Henry Ford* (New York: Rinehart & Co, 1948), 139; Ken Silverstein, "Ford and the Führer," *The Nation*, January 24, 2000.

33. *Iwanowa v. Ford Motor Co.*, 67 F.Su2d, 424 (D.N.J., 1999); Keith Bradsher, "International Business: Suit Charges Ford Profited by Nazi-Era Forced Labor," *New York Times*, March 5, 1998; Bazyler, *Holocaust Restitution*, 63.

34. See *Research Findings about Ford-Werke under the Nazi Regime* (Dearborn mi: Ford Motor Company, 2001), available at http://media.ford.com /events/pdf/0_Research_Finding_Complete .pdf, last accessed September 10, 2008. See also Simon Reich, "Ford's Research Efforts in Assessing the Activities of Its Subsidiary in Nazi Germany," in ibid., 6. For a critical view of the use of historians in this context, see Michael Pinto-Duschinsky, "Selling the Past," *Times Literary Supplement*, October 23, 1998, 16–17. But cf. Gerald D. Feldman, "The Business History of the 'Third Reich' and the Responsibilities of the Historian: Gold, Insurance, 'Aryanization' and Forced Labor," University of California, Berkeley, Center for German and European Studies, *Working Papers*, January 1999, available at http:// www.ciaonet.org/wps/feg01/, last accessed May 28, 2008.

35. Simon Reich, "The Ford Motor Company and the Third Reich," *Dimensions* 13 (December 1999), 15–17; idem, "Corporate Social Responsibility and the Issue of Compensation: The Case of Ford and Nazi Germany," in Francis R. Nicosia and Jonathan Huener, eds., *Business and Industry in Nazi Germany* (New York: Berghahn, 2004), 104–28.

36. Henry Ashby Turner, Jr., *General Motors and the Nazis: The Struggle for Control of Opel, Europe's Biggest Carmaker* (New Haven CT: Yale University Press, 2005), 155, 158. Turner does, however, have some harsh words for GM on its postwar conduct: "General Motors bears full responsibility . . . for laying claim in 1951 to the Opel dividends put aside for it during the war, another aspect of the corporation's relationship to its

German subsidiary that has hitherto escaped notice. That decision appears not to have been made by the top ranks of GM, possibly because the money involved . . . amounted to only a twentieth of one percent of GM's net income for that year. . . ." Ibid. Cf. Reinhold Billstein, Karola Fings, and Anita Kugler, eds., *Working for the Enemy: Ford, General Motors, and Forced Labor in Germany during the Second World War*, (New York: Berghahn, 2000).

37. Edwin Black, *IBM and the Holocaust: The Strategic Alliance between Nazi Germany and America's Most Powerful Corporation* (New York: Crown, 2001).

38. *Jewish News Weekly*, February 16, 2001.

39. Michael Berenbaum, "An Enabler of Genocide," *The Jewish Journal*, March 8, 2001; Drew Cullen, "IBM Escapes Holocaust Suit," *The Register*, March 30, 2001. For a discussion of the relations between this case and the ongoing quest for "legal peace" in the negotiations for the settlement of the lawsuits against the German corporations, see John Authers and Richard Wolffe, *The Victim's Fortune: Inside the Epic Battle over the Debts of the Holocaust* (New York: Perennial, 2003), 336–39. See also Edwin Black's website, available at http://www.edwinblack.com, last accessed October 20, 2008.

40. Richard Bernstein, "IBM's Sales to Nazis: Assessing the Culpability," *New York Times*, March 7, 2001.

41. See, for example, the devastating critiques in Peter Hayes, "Did IBM Really Cozy Up to Hitler?" *Business Week*, March 19, 2001; Omer Bartov, "Did Punch Cards Fuel the Holocaust?" *Newsday*, March 25, 2004; and Henry Ashby Turner in *Business History Review* 75 (2001): 636–39. See also Gabriel Schoenfeld, "The Punch-Card Conspiracy," *New York Times*, March 18, 2001.

42. Michael Allen, "Stranger than Science Fiction: Edwin Black, IBM, and the Holocaust," *Technology and Culture* 43 (2002): 153.

43. Black, *IBM and the Holocaust*, 32; Kevin Maney, *The Maverick and His Machine: Thomas Watson,*

Sr. and the Making of IBM (Hoboken NJ: Wiley, 2003), 218–20 and *passim*, [and] "IBM Founder Wasn't Bad Guy Book Portrays," *USA Today*, February 14, 2001. . . . For Black's view of this matter, see *IBM and the Holocaust*, 217.

44. Barnaby J. Feder, "Lawsuit Says I.B.M. Aided the Nazis in Technology," *New York Times*, February 11, 2001.

45. Anthony J. Sebok, "IBM and the Holocaust: The Book, the Suit, and Where We Go From Here," FindLaw. March 12, 2001, available at http://writ.news.findlaw.com/sebok/20010312.html, last accessed May 29, 2008.

46. Michael J. Bazyler, "Suing Hitler's Willing Business Partners: American Justice and Holocaust Morality," *Jewish Political Studies Review* 16 (2004), available at http://www.jcpa.org/phas/phas-bazyler-f04.htm, last accessed July 2, 2008.

47. Feldman, "Business History of the 'Third Reich' and the Responsibilities of the Historian," 7.

48. Arthur W. Machen, Jr., "Corporate Personality," *Harvard Law Review* 24 (1911): 347: "A corporation, or indeed any group or succession of men . . . is regarded as a person only by way of metaphor or by a fiction of law." See the excellent discussion in Katrina Wyman, "Is There a Moral Justification for Redressing Historical Injustices?" *Vanderbilt Law Review* 61 (2008): 125–96.

49. "Mass restitution suits are remarkable because they are such extraordinary performances of a legal fiction," notes Antony Sebok, "Brief History of Mass Restitution Litigation in the United States," in Dyzenhaus and Moran, *Calling Power to Account*, 366.

50. Janna Thompson, for example, refers to "a robust tradition in American thought, and indeed in liberal thought in general, that holds that a democratic nation of free individuals ought not to tolerate" "the imposition of moral debts on citizens who were unborn when the wrongs occurred." Janna Thompson, "Repairing the Past: Confronting the Legacies of Slavery, Genocide, & Caste," Proceedings of the Seventh Annual Gilder Lehrman International Center at

Yale University, October 27–29, 2005, available at http://www.yale.edu/glc/justice/mccarthy .pdf, last accessed May 30, 2008. Cf. *idem*, *Taking Responsibility for the Past: Reparation and Historical Justice* (Cambridge: Polity, 2002).

51. Independent Committee of Eminent Persons, *Report on Dormant Accounts*, 6.

52. For a discussion of this issue and related questions see Sherwin, "Reparations and Unjust Enrichment." "Moral indignation against a corporate entity, when all the individuals who owned or controlled the corporation at the time of the wrong are long dead, is much like moral indignation against a deodand. It may provide some satisfaction, but it is irrational and should not be encouraged by law." Ibid., 30–31. Cf. Larry May, *Sharing Responsibility* (Chicago: University of Chicago Press, 1992); Eric A. Posner and Adrian Vermeule, "Reparations for Slavery and Other Historical Injustices," *Columbia Law Review* 103 (2003): 704; and Adrian Vermeule, "Reparations as Rough Justice," University of Chicago John M. Olin Program in Law & Economics, Working Paper No. 260, September 2005, available at http://ssrn.com/abstract= 813086, last accessed June 5, 2008.

53. Hayes, *From Cooperation to Complicity*, chap. 7.

54. *Idem*, "Corporate Profits and the Holocaust: A Dissent from the Monetary Argument," in Bazyler and Alford, *Holocaust Restitution*, 201–2.

55. *Idem*, "The Ambiguities of Evil and Justice: Degussa, Robert Pross, and the Jewish Slave Laborers at Gleiwitz," in Jonathan Petropoulos and John K. Roth, eds., *Gray Zones: Ambiguity and Compromise in the Holocaust and Its Aftermath* (New York: Berghahn, 2005), 19. According to Hayes, "this is a distortion imposed by a form of 'path dependency' in the American judicial system, where the language of civil suits emphasizes the 'disgorgement' of unjust proceeds from unlawful conspiracies as the principal means of making them good." Ibid.

56. Rolf Keller, "Racism versus Pragmatism: Forced Labor of Soviet Prisoners of War in Germany (1941–1942)," Center for Advanced Holocaust Studies, *Forced and Slave Labor in Nazi-Dominated Europe: Symposium Presentations* (Washington DC: United States Holocaust Memorial Museum, 2004), 109–23.

57. Hayes, "Corporate Profits and the Holocaust," 203.

58. Ibid. See the similar assessment by Harold James, concluding that while the bank incurred a significant "moral liability" from its involvement in "Aryanization," it did not make a large profit. James illustrates how complicated it is to calculate such a profit or loss and concludes that "there is fundamentally no financial way of correcting an injustice perpetrated over fifty years ago." Harold James, *The Deutsche Bank and the Nazi Economic War against the Jews* (New York: Cambridge University Press, 2001), 209.

59. Neil Gregor, *Daimler-Benz and the Third Reich* (New Haven CT: Yale University Press, 1998), 216–17, 250. Cf. Stephan Linder, *Inside I.G. Farben: Hoechst in the Third Reich* (New York: Cambridge University Press, 2005); Hans Mommsen and Manfred Grieger, *Das Volkswagenwerk und seine Arbeiter im Dritten Reich* (Düsseldorf: Econ Verlag, 1996).

60. Monica Chowdry and Charles Mitchell, "Responding to Historic Wrongs: Practical and Theoretical Problems," *Oxford Journal of Legal Studies* 27 (2007): 345.

61. Anthony J. Sebok, "Reparations, Unjust Enrichment, and the Importance of Knowing the Difference between the Two," *New York University Annual Survey of American Law* 58 (2003): 656. But cf. a critique of this view by Dennis Klimchuk, "Unjust Enrichment and Reparations for Slavery," *Boston University Law Review* 84 (2004): 1257–75.

62. On "enablers," see Bernie M. Farber, "The Nazi Enablers among Us," *National Post*, February 9, 2007; Yossi Klein Halevi, "Iran's German Enablers," *Wall Street Journal*, September 24, 2007.

63. Regula Ludij "Waging War on Wartime Memory: Recent Swiss Debates on the Legacies of the

Holocaust and the Nazi Era," *Jewish Social Studies* 10 (2004): 116–52. More generally on bystanders, see Victoria J. Barnett, *Bystanders: Conscience and Complicity during the Holocaust* (Westport CT: Praeger, 1999); and David Cesarani and Paul A. Levine, eds., *Bystanders to the Holocaust: A Reevaluation* (London: Frank Cass, 2002).

64. Owen C. Pell, "Historical Reparation Claims: The Defense Perspective," in Bazyler and Alford, *Holocaust Restitution*, 333.

65. Hans Halbheer, "To Our American Friends: Switzerland in the Second World War," American Swiss Foundation, available at http://www.americanswiss.org/content/, last accessed June 9, 2008.

66. Pell, "Historical Reparation Claims," 331–32.

67. Peter Hayes, "The Ambiguities of Evil and Justice," 7. Sec also *idem*, "Industry under the Swastika," in Harold James and Jakob Tanner, eds., *Enterprise in the Period of Fascism in Europe* (Aldershot, England: Ashgate, 2002), 14–37.

68. Hayes, *From Cooperation to Complicity*, 271.

69. "Herbert Hansmeyer at the Washington Conference on Holocaust-Era Assets 1998," Allianz Group Portal, available at http://www.allianz.com/dc/allianz_gruppe/ueber_uns/geschichte/firmenhistorisches_archiv_der_allianz/menu_data/ page5.html, last accessed June 5, 2008.

70. Otto Graf Lambsdorff, "The Negotiations on Compensation for Nazi Forced Laborers," in Bazyler and Alford, *Holocaust Restitution*, 173.

71. Ibid., 179.

72. Chesnoff, *Pack of Thieves*, 277.

73. Authers and Wolffe, *Victim's Fortune*, 268.

74. Michael J. Bazyler, "The Gray Zones of Holocaust Restitution: American Justice and Holocaust Morality," in Petropoulos and Roth, eds., *Gray Zones*, 353–54.

75. Authers and Wolffe, *Victim's Fortune*, 267.

76. Memorandum in Support of Defendant's Motion to Dismiss at 33, *Lichtman v. Siemens AG*, No. 98–4252 (D.NJ. filed September 9, 1998), quoted in Stephen Whinston, "Can Lawyers and Judges Be Good Historians? A Critical Examina-tion of the Siemens Slave-Labor Cases," *Berkeley Journal of International Law* 20 (2002): 164, emphasis in original.

77. Ibid., 167.

78. See Hannah Arendt's comments in *Eichmann in Jerusalem*, 257, referring to the Nazis' crimes against the Jews as "not only crimes that 'no conception of military necessity could sustain' but crimes that were in fact independent of the war and that announced a policy of systematic murder to be continued in time of peace." For recent, authoritative evaluations, see Christopher R. Browning, with contributions by Jürgen Matthäus, *The Origins of the Final Solution: The Evolution of Nazi Jewish Policy, September 1939–March 1942* (Lincoln: University of Nebraska Press, 2004), 425–33; and Mazower, *Hitler's Empire*, chap. 12.

79. See the discussion in Libby Adler and Peer Zumbassen, "The Forgetfulness of Noblesse: A Critique of the German Foundation Law Compensating Slave and Forced Laborers of the Third Reich," *Harvard Journal on legislation* 39 (2002): 41–51.

80. Matthew Dorf, "American Holocaust Survivor Wins Fight for Payment," *Jewish News Weekly*, September 22, 1995; Douglas Martin, "Hugo Princz, 78, U.S. Winner of Holocaust Settlement, Dies," *New York Times*, July 31, 2001; Mitchell G. Bard, *Forgotten Victims: The Abandonment of Americans in Hitler's Camps* (Boulder co: Westview Press, 1994).

81. Ronald J. Bettauer, "The Role of the United States Government in Recent Holocaust Claims Resolution," *Berkeley Journal of International IMW* 20 (2002): 1–10.

82. Peter Van Der Auweraert, "Holocaust Reparation Claims Fifty Years After: The Swiss Banks Litigation," *Nordic Journal of International Law* 71 (2002): 560–61, based on his calculations that include Swiss bank claimants and those received as part of the German Foundation settlement. As for the numbers of Holocaust survivors, demographic studies produced different conclu-

sions, ranging from just under 700,000 to just over a million, depending in part on definitions of "survivors." See Bazyler, "Suing Hitler's Willing Business Partners."

83. Burl Neuborne, "A Tale of Two Cities: Administering the Holocaust Settlements in Brooklyn and Berlin," in Bazyler and Alford, *Holocaust Restitution*, 62.

84. Lawrence Eagleburger and M. Diane Koken, with Catherine Lillie, *Finding Claimants and Paying Them: The Creation and Workings of the International Commission on Holocaust Era Insurance Claims* (N.P.: National Association of Insurance Commissioners, 2007), 21–22; International Commission on Holocaust Era Insurance Claims, *Lessons Learned: A Report on Best Practices*, June 2007, 7.

85. Roman Kent, "It's Not about the Money: A Survivor's Perspective on the German Foundation Initiative," in Bazyler and Alford, *Holocaust Restitution*, 206.

86. Eizenstat, *Imperfect Justice*, 261.

87. Daniel Kadden, "Holocaust Restitution and the Claims Conference: Controversies and Organizational Accountability," *Jewish Currents*, July 2006, available at http://www.jewishcurrents .org/2006-july-kadden.htm, last accessed June 10, 2008.

88. Eizenstat, Remarks at the 12th and Concluding Plenary on the German Foundation; Burt Neuborne, letter, *The Nation*, October 23, 2000; Peter Hayes, "Forced and Slave Labor: The State of the Field," in *Forced and Slave Labor*, 1; Bazyler, *Holocaust Justice*, 10.

89. See Holocaust Victim Assets Litigation (Swiss Banks), the official Web site of the *Swiss Banks Settlement: In re Holocaust Victim Assets Litigation*, United States District Court for the Eastern District of New York, available at http:// www.swissbankclaims.com/Overview.aspx, last accessed June 9, 2008.

90. Eizenstat, *Imperfect Justice*, 239, according to Professor Lutz Niethammer's calculation. Niethammer also estimated that of these, 200,000 had

been slave laborers, slightly more than half of whom were Jews. But cf. Authers and Wolffe, *Victim's Fortune*, 217, 231.

91. Authers and Wolffe, *Victim's Fortune*, 226, 233.

92. Eizenstat, *Imperfect Justice*, 239, 263–66; Bazyler, *Holocaust Justice*, 81.

93. David A. Lash and Mitchell A. Kamin, "Poor Justice: Holocaust Restitution and Forgotten, Indigent Survivors," in Bazyler and Alford, *Holocaust Restitution*, 315–21.

94. Stewart Ain, "One-Fourth of Holocaust Survivors in U.S. Living below Poverty Line," *United Jewish Communities*, November 20, 2003, available at http://www.ujc.org/page.aspx?id=5i886, last accessed November 7, 2008; Adam Liptak, "Ideas & Trends: For Holocaust Survivors, It's Law versus Morality," *New York Times*, March 14, 2004; Michael J. Bazyler, "The Gray Zones of Holocaust Restitution," 345.

95. Bazyler, *Holocaust Justice*, 284–85. See also Bazyler, "Suing Hitler's Willing Business Partners." For a good summary of the distribution controversies see Bazyler, *Holocaust Justice*, chap. 6. For Gribetz's perspective and a detailed summary, see Judah Gribetz and Shari C. Reig, "The Swiss Banks Holocaust Settlement," a larger version of a paper presented by Shari C. Reig at the conference on Reparations for Victims of Genocide, Crimes against Humanity and War Crimes: Systems in Place and Systems in the Making, the Peace Palace, The Hague, the Netherlands, March 1–2, 2007.

96. Hayes, "Forced and Slave Labor," in *Forced and Slave Labor*, 1.

After Such Knowledge

EVA HOFFMAN

From *After Such Knowledge*

The statute of limitations on the Holocaust is running out, as it must. Living memory fades, the fierceness of feeling subsides. Even with events of the Shoah's magnitude, this is inevitable. We must reflect on the past, but we cannot dwell in it forever. But how we turn away from the Holocaust matters. For those who lived in its proximity through personal history, it matters for our own sake. But it matters also for the sake of historical fidelity. Once again, the dangers of distortion—of sheer forgetfulness or mythologizing, of partial denial and willful misinterpretation—are considerable. It matters enormously that we do not use the Holocaust for our own self-serving purposes, or pervert its facts for newly hateful ends.

On one level, extreme events teach us simple lessons: Virulent prejudice breeds virulent results. Deadly ideologies permit deadly deeds. The dehumanization of the other leads to mass murder. On the other hand, the claims made for the uses of historical memory have to be modest. The Irish poet Seamus Heaney, in a clearly pessimistic moment, observed that it sometimes seems we can learn as much from history as from a visit to an abattoir. And, in relation to our collective histories, pessimism sometimes seems the only form of realism. Certainly, as we have watched the genocides in Cambodia and Rwanda, and as new methods of atrocity and terror have started presenting themselves at the beginning of the twenty-first century, it is all too clear that to learn from history is not the same as to cure or prevent it.

Nevertheless, we must keep trying to learn; we must keep trying.

Moreover, sometimes, by small increments and not always in dramatically visible ways, we do seem to learn something. It seems to me that in some areas, the concentrated thinking about atrocity we have been forced to do, perhaps especially about the Holocaust and its aftermath, has led to greater collective awareness. One of those areas in which we have tried, at least, to deal with large-scale problems with greater sensitivity has been, precisely, the aftermath of enormity and collective violence.

For one thing, we have come to understand that great crimes and wrongs cannot be left unaddressed; that unless some acknowledgment and recognition of what happened takes place, the suppressed past will rankle and return. Among the ravages of atrocity are the ravages of the moral sense—the moral world—of those so gratuitously injured; and the first need of the victim after such violence is for a restoration of that moral world and moral order through an acknowledgment that wrongs have been committed, and the punishment of those responsible. The need for societies as a whole is also to invert the perverse order of atrocity—its principled injustice, one might say—by establishing the very principles and norms of justice. Whatever the specific criteria of judgment or punishment, the first task after great wrongs have been committed is to name those wrongs *as* wrongs.

At the same time, it has been increasingly recognized—from so many instances of dealing with the aftermath of great wrongs—that large-scale justice in such situations is difficult, in fact impossible, to attain. In recent years, there have been interesting experiments, the most notable among them South Africa's Truth and Reconciliation Commission, in administering symbolic justice instead. The commission, for all its shortcomings and compromises, was a stirring attempt to achieve justice through the symbolic processes of recognition—through bringing the executioners of apartheid face to face with the people they had injured and giving them the opportunity to gain amnesty by telling the full truth of their deeds. Although this was hardly a perfect instrument of redress, it was nevertheless as effective as could perhaps be hoped for in the wake of the great and longstanding evils of apartheid. For some of the victims, at least, the opportunity to face their tormentors and executioners and force them to recognize the victims' pain—in some cases, the expression from the perpetrators of awareness and even remorse for what they have done, seemed to be reparative and cathartic. The balm of recognition seemed to do its work: The South African experiment has become a model for other efforts to cope with the aftereffects of enormous crimes. . . .

Perhaps, after all the causes and mechanisms of the Holocaust—and other atrocities, for that matter—have been examined, the urgent question we are left with is how to establish normative principles and structures that can form a mainstay against eruptions of hatred. For this, neither victimology nor demonology will suffice; neither the idealization nor the denigration of the Other will in the long range assure harmony. Moreover, on such issues, we need to think not only on behalf of our own tribe, or from particular sites of identification, but from the imagination of norms that apply to all. We need justice for others—and for ourselves. We need the kind of tolerance that does not dissolve either others' or our own integrity or legitimacy.

But beyond keeping compact with the past and contemplating its stern lessons, there is one thing that we, as members of the second generation [Eve Hoffman is the daughter of Holocaust survivors] need to do for ourselves—and that is to disentangle the spectral memories that have inhabited us from the realities we inhabit. It was in the United States Holocaust Memorial Museum that I had my strange epiphany. As I walked through this most daunting of museum exhibitions, and as I entered into its hellish world as into a familiar element, I suddenly thought: But there must also be something outside of this. There must be a reality that is not horror, but that is equally foundational. The Holocaust cannot be the norm that defines the world. It is, of course, symptomatic of my second-generation condition that it would have taken so long—half a lifetime—for such an idea to occur. For me, in the beginning was the war, and the Holocaust was the ontological basis of my universe. And indeed, the Holocaust continues to stand as a kind of limiting condition of experience, and therefore, a necessary part of our knowledge about human nature. It is because the Holocaust exposes the negative extremes of human possibility that it has been taken as philosophically central not only by childhood minds but by so many thinkers of our time. Hell, especially if it is of human making, is surely one clue about the human condition—and the Holocaust extends our knowledge of the human hell.

And yet, unless we want to fall into permanent melancholia or nihilistic despair, we cannot take the Holocaust as the norm that governs human lives. We cannot start from it as a basis, or move toward it as a form of transcendence, even of the darkest kind. That is why it is necessary to separate the past from the present and to judge the present in its own light. For me, as for many direct inheritors of that wounding trauma, this has been the difficult and necessary task. After the dark logic of the Shoah, acceptance of a benign world does not come easily. The "normal" may seem suspect, or it may seem thin. How to find richness, authenticity, depth in the temperate zones of ordinary life? How to find sources of significance that do not derive from extremity and to endow with value not only great losses but modest gains? In a sense—as with all aspects of second-generation experience—this is a question that arises in every transition to maturity but that, for children of survivors, is sharpened to a fine acuity. For the inheritors of traumatic historical experience, the ability to separate the past from the present—to see the past as the past is a difficult but necessary achievement.

The moment of that separation, of letting go, is a poignant one, for it is akin to the giving up of mourning. There is pain in the very diminution of pain, the danger that time will dilute morality as it dilutes passion. We do not, generally, forget the facts; anyway, these are always available as information, in books or on the Internet. What we do forget, imperceptibly but inevitably, are the sensations accompanying the facts: the rightful rage, gratitude where it is due, the anguish of loss for the loved one's death. This has to be accepted as part of time's work and its passage. But if we do not want to betray the past—if we want to remain ethical beings and honor our covenant with those who suffered—then moral passion needs to be supplanted by moral thought, by an incorporation of memory into our consciousness of the world.

There is a Jewish tradition that says we must grieve for the dead fully and deeply; but that mourning must also come to its end. Perhaps that moment has come, even as we must continue to ponder and confront the knowledge that the Shoah has brought us in perpetuity.

LIST OF ABBREVIATIONS

AA: Auswärtiges Amt (German Foreign Office)

AEG: Allgemeine Elektrizitäts Gesellschaft (German General Electric corporation)

AO: Auslandsorganisation (Foreign Organization of the Nazi Party)

BASF: Badische Anilin- und Soda-Fabrik (a division of the IG Farben corporation)

BMW: Bayerische Motoren-Werke

CV: Centralverein Staatsbürger jüdischen Glaubens (German Central League of Citizens of the Jewish Faith)

DAF: Deutsche Arbeitsfront (German Labor Front)

DAW: Deutsche Aufrüstungswerke (German Armaments Works, an SS-owned enterprise)

DNVP: Deutschnationale Volkspartei (German National People's Party)

GG: General Government, the German-occupied but not formally annexed part of Poland

GM: General Motors

HSSPF: Höhere SS und Polizeiführer

HTO: Haupttreuhandstelle Ost (Main Trusteeship Office East)

IBM: International Business Machines Corporation

IG: Interessengemeinschaft (Interest Community), the abbreviation for the IG Farben corporation

IMT: International Military Tribunal

KG: Kommanditgesellschaft, a German corporate structure

KGB: Soviet secret police after World War II

KZ: Konzenstrationslager (concentration camp)

MAN: Maschinenfabrik Augsburg-Nürnberg

NKVD: Soviet secret police during World War II

NSBO: Nationalsozialistische Betriebszellenorganisation (the Nazi labor union)

NSDAP: Nationalsozialistische Deutsche Arbeiterpartei (National Socialist German Workers' Party)

OKH: Oberkommando des Heeres (Supreme Command of the German Army)

OKW: Oberkommando der Wehrmacht (Supreme Command of the German Armed Forces)

POW: prisoner of war

RFM: Reichsfinanzministerium (German Ministry of Finance)

RFSS: Reichsführer-SS

RKFDV: Reichskuratorium für die Festigung deutschen Volkstums (Commission for the Strengthening of German Nationhood)

RSHA: Reichssicherheitshauptamt (Reich Security Main Office of the SS)

RWM: Reichswirtschaftsministerium (German Economics Ministry)

SD: Sicherheitsdienst (Security Service of the SS)

SPD: Sozialdemokratische Partei
         Deutschlands (Social Democratic Party
         of Germany)
SS: Schutzstaffel
UNESCO: United Nations Educational, Scientific,
         and Cultural Organization
UNRRA: United Nations Relief and
         Rehabilitation Administration
USHMM: United States Holocaust Memorial
         Museum
WVHA: Wirtschafts- und Verwaltungshauptamt
         (Economics and Administration Main
         Office of the SS)

SOURCE ACKNOWLEDGMENTS

Aly, Götz, and Susanne Heim. "Rearranging Populations." *Architects of Annihilation: Auschwitz and the Logic of Destruction.* Princeton NJ: Princeton University Press, 2002. 73–93. Print.

Aly, Götz. "Plunder, Individual and Governmental." *Hitler's Beneficiaries: Plunder, Racial War, and the Nazi Welfare State.* New York: Metropolitan, 2007. 94–152. Print.

Ancel, Jean. "Romania: Annihilation Aborted." *The History of the Holocaust in Romania.* Lincoln: University of Nebraska, 2011. 217–559. Print.

Barkai, Avraham. "Aryanization." *From Boycott to Annihilation: The Economic Struggle of German Jews, 1933–1943.* Hanover NH: Published for Brandeis University Press by the University Press of New England, 1989. 13–138. Print.

Bauer, Yehuda. "The Fates of Gypsies." *Anatomy of the Auschwitz Death Camp.* Ed. Israel Gutman and Michael Berenbaum. Bloomington: Published by Indiana University Press in Association with the United States Holocaust Memorial Museum, Washington DC, 1994. 441–55. Print.

Blatman, Daniel. "The Final Frenzy." *The Death Marches: The Final Phase of Nazi Genocide.* Cambridge MA: Belknap of Harvard University Press, 2011. 81–136. Print.

Boehling, Rebecca L., and Uta Larkey. "Palestine." *Life and Loss in the Shadow of the Holocaust: A Jewish Family's Untold Story.* Cambridge: Cambridge University Press, 2011. 141–66. Print.

Braham, Randolph L. "The Hungarian Paroxysm." *Studies on the Holocaust.* Boulder CO: The Rosenthal Institute for Holocaust Studies, Graduate Center , City University of New York and Social Science Monographs, 2000. 69–97. Print.

Breitman, Richard, and Alan M. Kraut. "American Inhibitions." *American Refugee Policy and European Jewry: 1933–1945.* Bloomington: Indiana University Press, 1987. 236–49. Print.

Breitman, Richard, and Alan M. Kraut. "The United States and Refugees, 1933–1940." *American Refugee Policy and European Jewry, 1933–1945.* Bloomington: Indiana University Press, 1987. 7–10, 223–35. Print.

Burleigh, Michael, and Wolfgang Wippermann. "Racism." *The Racial State: Germany, 1933–1945.* Cambridge: Cambridge University Press, 1991. 23–37. Print.

Cohen, Beth B. "America's Incomprehension." *Case Closed: Holocaust Survivors in Postwar America.* New Brunswick NJ: Rutgers University Press, 2007. 115–32. Print.

Conze, Eckart, Norbert Frei, Peter Hayes, and Mosche Zimmermann. "Elite Cooperation." *Das Amt und Die Vergangenheit: Deutsche Diplomaten im Dritten Reich und in der Bundesrepublik.* Trans. Peter Hayes. München: Karl Blessing Verlag, 2010. 29–51. Print.

Dean, Martin. "Robbery in the Netherlands." *Robbing the Jews: The Confiscation of Jewish Property in the Holocaust, 1933–1945.* Cambridge: Cambridge University Press, 2008. 264–87. Print.

Elon, Amos. "Contradictions in Central Europe." *The Pity of It All: A Portrait of the German-Jewish Epoch, 1743–1933.* New York: Holt, 2003. 222–340. Print.

Evans, Richard J. "The Pathology of Denial." *Lying about Hitler: History, Holocaust, and the David Irving Trial.* New York NY: Basic, 2001. 104–40. Print.

Fischer, Klaus P. "Germany's Turmoil, 1918–33." *Nazi Germany: A New History*. New York: Continuum, 1995. 42–73, 218–62. Print.

Friedländer, Saul. "Vichy France: 'Our' Jews and the Rest." *The Years of Extermination: Nazi Germany and the Jews, 1939–1945*. New York NY: Harper Collins, 2007. 108–78, 376–421, 550–55. Print.

Goldstein, Jonathan. "The Kovno Connection." *Lessons and Legacies VI: New Currents in Holocaust Research*. Ed. Jeffry M. Diefendorf. Evanston IL: Northwestern University Press, 2004. 71–87. Print. Lessons and Legacies.

Good, Michael. "The Good German of Vilna." *The Search for Major Plagge: The Nazi Who Saved Jews*. New York: Fordham University Press, 2005. 68–167. Print.

Grabowski, Jan. "Poland: The Blue Police." *Hunt for the Jews: Betrayal and Murder in German-Occupied Poland*. Bloomington: Indiana University Press, 2013. 101–20. Print.

Gutman, Yisrael. "Nothing to Lose." *The Jews of Warsaw, 1939–1943: Ghetto, Underground, Revolt*. Bloomington: Indiana University Press, 1982. 367–400. Print.

Haffner, Sebastian. "Street-Level Coercion." *Defying Hitler: A Memoir*. Trans. Oliver Pretzel. New York: Farrar, Straus and Giroux, 2002. 105–98. Print.

Henry, Patrick. "Collective Action in Vivarais-Lignon." *We Only Know Men: The Rescue of Jews in France during the Holocaust*. Washington DC: Catholic University of America, 2007. 9–40. Print.

Herbert, Ulrich. "Forced Labor." *Hitler's Foreign Workers: Enforced Foreign Labor in Germany under the Third Reich*. Cambridge: Cambridge University Press, 1997. 167–299. Print.

Hilberg, Raul. "Bringing Jews to Death." *The Destruction of the European Jews*. New Haven: Yale University Press, 2003. 3rd ed. 921–52. Print.

Hoffman, Eva. "After Such Knowledge." *After Such Knowledge: Memory, History, and the Legacy of the Holocaust*. New York: Public Affairs, 2004. 266–79. Print.

Horwitz, Gordon J. "Choiceless Choices." *Ghettostadt: Lodz and the Making of a Nazi City*. Cambridge MA: Belknap of Harvard University Press, 2008. 203–19. Print.

Independent Commission of Experts Switzerland. "Self-Serving Switzerland." *Switzerland, National Socialism, and the Second World War*. Zürich: Pendo, 2002. 238–77. Print.

Independent Commission of Experts Switzerland. "Switzerland." *Switzerland, National Socialism, and the Second World War*. Zürich: Pendo, 2002. 106–10. Print.

Judt, Tony. "The Great Reversal." *Postwar: A History of Europe since 1945*. New York: Penguin, 2005. 803–31. Print.

Kaplan, Chaim Aron, Abraham Isaac Katsh, and Israel Gutman. "Isolation and Impoverishment." *Scroll of Agony: The Warsaw Diary of Chaim A. Kaplan*. New York: Macmillan, 1965. 52–56, 205–90. Print.

Kaplan, Marion A. "Going and Staying." *Between Dignity and Despair: Jewish Life in Nazi Germany*. New York: Oxford University Press, 1998. 62–144. Print.

Karay, Felicja. "Women Slave Laborers." *Women in the Holocaust*. Ed. Dalia Ofer and Lenore J. Weitzman. New Haven CT: Yale University Press, 1998. 285–304. Print.

Kassow, Samuel D. "Leaving a Record." *Who Will Write Our History? Emanuel Ringelblum, the Warsaw Ghetto, and the Oyneg Shabes Archive*. Bloomington: Indiana University Press, 2007. 145–49, 209–23. Print.

Kühne, Thomas. "The Claims of Community." *Belonging and Genocide: Hitler's Community, 1918–1945*. New Haven: Yale University Press, 2010. 32–50. Print.

Levi, Primo. "Camp Labor." *If This Is a Man (Survival in Auschwitz)*. Trans. Stuart Woolf. London: Orion, 1959. 22–37. Print. Used by permission of Viking Penguin.

Levine, Paul A. "Sweden Expands Asylum." *From Indifference to Activism: Swedish Diplomacy and the Holocaust, 1938–1944*. Uppsala: *Studia Historica*

Upsaliensis 178, Uppsala University, 1998. 2nd ed. 134–55, 229–77. Print.

London, Louise. "The Unreceptive British Empire." *Whitehall and the Jews, 1933–1948: British Immigration Policy, Jewish Refugees, and the Holocaust*. New York NY: Cambridge University Press, 2000. 16–133. Print.

Marrus, Michael Robert. "Restitution and Its Discontents." *Some Measure of Justice: The Holocaust Era Restitution Campaign of the 1990s*. Madison WI: University of Wisconsin Press, 2009. 85–114. Print.

Mendelsohn, Ezra. "The Interwar Jewish Heartland." *The Jews of East Central Europe between the World Wars*. Bloomington: Indiana University Press, 1983. 1–83. Print.

Moore, Bob. "Saving Jewish Children in Belgium." *Survivors: Jewish Self-Help and Rescue in Nazi-Occupied Western Europe*. Oxford: Oxford University Press, 2010. 276–95. Print.

Paulsson, Gunnar S. "The Hidden Jews of Warsaw." *Secret City: The Hidden Jews of Warsaw, 1940–1945*. New Haven: Yale University Press, 2002. 1–5, 42–54, 231–45. Print.

Phayer, Michael. "Papal Priorities." *The Catholic Church and the Holocaust: 1930–1965*. Bloomington: Indiana University Press, 2000. 43–66. Print.

Proctor, Robert. "Culling the German Volk." *Racial Hygiene: Medicine Under the Nazis*. Cambridge MA: Harvard University Press, 1988. 177–94. Print.

Rhodes, Richard. "Bringing Death to Jews." *Masters of Death: The ss-Einsatzgruppen and the Invention of the Holocaust*. New York: A. A. Knopf, 2002. 3–17, 38–47, 170–79, 257. Print.

Roseman, Mark. "Deciding to Kill." *The Wannsee Conference and the Final Solution: A Reconsideration*. New York: Metropolitan, 2002. 39–77. Print.

Segev, Tom. "Zion's Ambivalence." *The Seventh Million: The Israelis and the Holocaust*. New York: Hill and Wang, 1993. 119–86. Print.

Snyder, Timothy. "Racial War in the East." *Bloodlands: Europe Between Hitler and Stalin*. New York: Basic, 2010. 158–86. Print.

"Talk of Annihilation." *Documents Diplomatiques Suisses 1848–1945*, vol. 12 (1937–1938). Trans. Peter Hayes. Wabern-Bern: Benteli-Werd, 1994. 1031. Print. *Das Schwarze Korps*, quoted in Richard Breitman, *The Architect of Genocide: Himmler and the Final Solution*. New York: Alfred A. Knopf, 1991. 58. Print. Hitler's Reichstag speech, quoted in *Nazism, 1919–1945*. Ed. Jeremy Noakes and Geoffrey Pridham, vol. 3. Exeter UK: University of Exeter, 2001. 441. Print.

Trunk, Isaiah. "Indirect Rule." *Judenrat: The Jewish Councils in Eastern Europe under Nazi Occupation*. New York: Macmillan, 1972. 43–50, 317–25, 451–55. Print.

Weber, Eugen. "France: From Hospitality to Hostility." *The Hollow Years: France in the 1930s*. New York: Norton, 1994. 87–109. Print.

Westermann, Edward B. "Political Soldiers." *Hitler's Police Battalions: Enforcing Racial War in the East*. Lawrence: University Press of Kansas, 2005. 4–15, 234–39. Print.

Wistrich, Robert S. "Antisemitism." *Antisemitism: The Longest Hatred*. New York: Pantheon, 1991. 54–65. Print.

Wyman, Mark. "Survivors." *DP: Europe's Displaced Persons, 1945–1951*. Philadelphia: Balch Institute, 1988. 131–55. Print.

Zuccotti, Susan. "The Italian Paradox." *The Italians and the Holocaust: Persecution, Rescue, and Survival*. New York: Basic, 1987. 74–100. Print.

INDEX

Page numbers in italic indicate illustrations.

Comte, Louis, 681

concentration camps: accounts of arrival at, 506–7; accounts of daily life in, 508–12; conversions into extermination camps, 523–24; demoralizing nature of, 506–7, 512; development and growth of, 463–65; evacuations of, 518, 519–24; influence of POW camps on, 297; release from due to emigration, 213, 249; relief organizations in, 681–82; role of Gestapo in, 242, 463–64, 513; statistics on, 475n5; types of inmates, 510. *See also* death camps; labor camps; *specific camps*

Consistoire (Jewish organization), 574–76, 582

conspiracy theories: development of, 4, 14, 26, 27, 132; in Hitler's worldview, 66; of Jewish wealth, 536–37

consulates: of Denmark, 648–53; of Great Britain, 207, 213, 228; of Italy, 591, 596; of Japan, 649, 653–54; of the Netherlands, 648–51; role in emigration difficulties, 178, 242–43; of Switzerland, 220, 647; of United States, 724

Conti, Leonardo, 261, 265, 266

Convent of the Sisters of Très St. Saveur, 710–11

conversions, 26, 34–35, 717–18

Conway, John, 618

Cooper, Ernest Napier, 209, 212, 213

Coordinating Committee (British), 207, 209, 211

corporate personality, 850, 862n48

Coty, François, 191

Council for German Jewry, 158–59

Cracow (Poland): forced labor workers from, 322–24

Craig, Gordon A., 30

Credit Suisse (Swiss bank), 633, 639–40

Criminal Police (Nazi), 484

Croatia: death rates in, xii, 529; Italian protection of Jews in, 588–91; treatment of Gypsies in, 498; *Ustasha* genocide in, 615

Cuba, 179

cultural and intellectual life: in Hitler's worldview, 66; Jewish success in and antisemitism, 13, 14–16; of Jews, 87–88, 96–98, 151–52, 157

Cuno, Wilhelm, 63

Curaçao visa, 649–51, 656n7

currency: exchange rate between franc and mark, 310; exchange rate of reichsmark, 169n45, 232n8; German manipulation of exchange rates, 304; German soldiers' exchange of, 301; Nazi restrictions on exchange of, 223; post-WWI devaluation of mark, 63–64; Swiss role in currency exchange, 632–35

Currie, Laughlin, 633

Currie Agreement (1945), 633–34

Cywiriski, Feliks, 691

Czarnecki, Antoni, 618

Czech, Danuta, 500

Czechoslovakia: death rates in, xii; deportations of Jews, 442, 443; forced labor of citizens, 318; during the interwar period, 85; postwar perceptions of the Holocaust, 815; on postwar refugees, 767–68; in the Versailles Treaty, 61

Czerniakow, Adam, 340, 362, 364–65, 376

Czerniewski, Marian, 539

Dachau concentration camp: creation of, 464; evacuations to, 516–17; gas chamber at, 521; Gypsies in, 496; influence of POW camps on, 297; postwar, 757, 805

Daimler Benz Corporation, 851–52

Dallek, Robert, 726

Daluege, Kurt, 481, 484, 491

Danielsson, Carl Ivan, 744–49

Dannecker, Theodor, 573, 576, 578

Danzig, 61

Darbyites, 675, 680

Darcissac, Roger, 679

Dardel, Gustaf von, 739–41, 750n32Darlan, Francois, 571, 573, 576

Darwin, Charles, 21–22

Darwinism in Hitler's worldview, 65–66

Daszkiewicz, Leszek, 653–54

Davidescu, Gheorge, 559

Davie, Maurice, 791

Day of National Rising celebrations, 122

Day of Potsdam, 122

death camps: design and layout of, 467–68, 479n71; development of, 463–67; postwar denial of, 824, 829–32; temporary nature of, 428. *See also* concentration camps; gas chambers; *specific camps*

death marches, 429, 513–16, 518–19, 554–55

Deckert, Joseph, 14, 15

Les Décombres (Rebatet), 579, 580

de Decker, L. P. J., 648

De Gaulle, Charles, 802, 809, 810

Degussa (chemical corporation), 851

Dehomag (IBM subsidiary), 848–49

de Jong, A. M., 653

de Jong, Johannes, 621

stitution, 58–60; during WWI, 45–50, 53

Germany (Nazi): collaboration with Switzerland, 632–38; compulsory deportation policy of, 333–34; comradeship in, 129–32; conquering Europe, 257–59; counterproductive nature of, 258, 703; creating a new order, 272–73, 275–78; death rates in, xii, 529; development of annihilation policy, 427–29; economic visions of, 285; euthanasia programs of, 260–69; Fighter Aircraft Staff project, 605; foreign policy, 68–69, 116–17; foreign workers in, 315–27; *Ha'avarah Agreement*, 223–24, 227; Hunger Plan, 287–88; indoctrinating German youth, 135–38; initial talk of annihilation, 172; invasion of Austria, 185; invasion of the Soviet Union, 288–92, 296–97, 298; Jewish government employees, 157; justifications for antisemitism in, 178; national boycott of April 1933, 123–26; Nazi Party coming to power, 109, 118–23; obstacles to emigration from, 241–44, 244–45; plundering occupied France, 309–11; and the plunder of Jews, 843–44; policy regarding Gypsies, 499, 502; racial ideology of, xiii–xiv, 485–87; Reichstag fire (1933), 119–20; resettlement policies, 271–74; role of ideology in, 482; seizure of Jewish assets, 167–68, 416, 638–41; special status given to Denmark, 739–40; status of foreign Jews in, 157–58; sterilization legislation, 25. *See also* National Socialist Party (Nazi Party)

Gerstein, Gary, 658
Gerstein, Kurt, 614, 616
Gerstein, Mula, 658
Gerstein, Nina, 658
Gerstel, Else, 238, 240, 241, 242, 245–46
Gertler, Dawid, 359
Gestapo: controlling German citizens, 134–35; in the ghettos, 339, 340, 341–42, 383; and Jewish emigration, 242, 243; murder of Jews in Hungary, 744–45; in the November 1938 pogrom, 165, 166; organizational structure of, 484, 486; relations with German military, 713; role in the concentration camps, 242, 463–64, 513; tracking resistance networks, 714; in Vilna, Lithuania, 666–69; work with AJB children's' homes, 718
Geulen, Andrée, 708
ghettos: aid organizations in, 355–56; firefighters' role in deportations, 367–68; fluctuation of Council members in, 338–44; food supply in, 336–38, 355; Gestapo in, 339, 340, 341–42, 383; group morale in, 356–57; and Nazi annihilation policy, 427; organizational structure of, 336–38; police, 354, 367–68; resistance movements in, 345–47, 392; in Romania, 551, 553; tax system, 356; variations among, 334; welfare services in, 336–38. *See also specific ghettos*
Gilad, Michael, 779, 787n14
Gilmour, Sir John, 201
Giraudoux, Jean, 193
Giterman, Yitzhak, 383
GkFW (Dutch Ministry for Financial and Economic Affairs), 413
Glagau, Otto, 12

Glaser, Ruth, 249
Glatten, Wilfried, 140
Glaue, Walter, 405
Globocnik, Odilo, 430, 440–41, 468
Glogowski, Icek, 710
Glücks, Richard, 523
Gobineau, Count Joseph Arthur de, 21
Goebbels, Joseph: 1932 election campaign, 75, 76; on the annihilation of Jews, 434; and the April 1933 boycott, 147; on the deportations of Jews, 435–36; and the German Section, 115; July 1934 lecture at University of Warsaw, 99; November 1938 pogrom, 165; propaganda of, 73; on removing Jews from cultural life, 151; role in annihilation policies, 442
Goette, Wolf, 302–3
Goffman, Erving, 136
Gohier, Urbain, 191
gold bars, 635–36
Goldberg, Leah, 784
Goldberg, Linka, 410
Goldfeier, Józef, 534
Goldfinger, Józef, 534
Goldhagen, Daniel, 482, 850
Goldin, Leyb, 373
Goldman, Michael, 777
Goldschmidt, Albert, 36–37
Goldstein, Moritz, 43
gold trade, 632–38
Golleschau camp, 513
Goodfriend, Betty, 650
Göring, Hermann: establishment of concentration camps, 463–64; and forced labor, 298, 315; Four-Year-Plan of, 288, 290; and French occupation costs, 309; and Hitler's chancellorship appointment, 79, 80; November

Rathenau, Emil, 41–42
Rathenau, Walther, 40, 41–42, 49
Ravasz, Laszlo, 607
Ravensbrück camp, 519–20
Reagan, Ronald, 820n11
Rebater, Lucien, 579
Reform Judaism, 33–34
refugee and immigration policies: in Canada, 203, 204–5; of
France, 178, 191–92; of Great
Britain, 178, 200–215; impact
of November 1938 pogrom on,
186–87, 204; of Palestine, 177–
78, 222–24; of Sweden, 738–39,
740; of Switzerland, 178–79,
218–21; of the United States, 178,
180–89, 722, 723–25, 732–33
refugees: in Australia, 204, 205,
207; in Britain, 208; in Canada,
182, 204–5; challenges in adapt-
ing to new environment, 237–
38; colonization as option for,
187, 188–89; deciding to flee,
236–41; in France, 175, 176, 179,
191–97; in Great Britain, 182,
201–15; in Hungary, 610n1; in
New Zealand, 203–4; obstacles
encountered by, 177–79, 241–
44; painful farewells of, 236,
246–48; in Palestine, 203, 778–
79, 780–86; Roosevelt's push for
international support for, 186,
187, 188–89; in Shanghai, 650;
in South Africa, 204; on the *St.
Louis, 175, 179, 187–88*; in Switzerland, 218–21; in the United
States, 182, 189n6. *See also* children; emigration; rescue work;
survivors
rehabilitation camps, 522
Reich, Simon, 848
Reich Chamber of Culture Law
(1933), 152
Reich Citizenship Law, 156, 163, 164

Reichsbank, 632–38, 640
Reichsmark: exchange rate, 169n45,
232n8, 310; manipulation of
exchange rate, 304; Nazi restrictions on exchange of, 223; post-
WWI devaluation of, 63–64
Reichstag: fire of 1933, 119–20;
under the Weimar Constitution,
59–60
Reinecke, Hermann, 308
Reinhardt, Fritz, 307, 308
Reinhardt, Max, 45–46
Reitemeier, Johann Georg Friedrich, 20
Reiter, Wladyslaw, 534
relief organizations: in Belgium,
715–16; in concentration camps,
681–82; and emigration, 250,
253n48; in France, 574–76, 582,
678, 681–82; in ghettos, 355–56;
in Great Britain, 158–59, 201–
9, 212–14; Jewish agencies, 159,
160–62, 236, 769; role in the successful escapes, 703; in Switzerland, 220; in Warsaw, 350,
355–56, 689; Winter Aid program, 131. *See also* rescue work
Remarque, Erich Maria, 197n5
repressive terror, 121
rescue work, 645–47; commonal-
ity as motivation for, 645, 738,
743; dangers of hiding, 700–701;
human solidarity as motivation for, 2, 645, 652–53, 684–85;
idealism as motivation for, 645,
691; lack of assistance from the
Catholic Church, 619–20; in Le
Chambon-sur-Ligon village,
643, 675–79, 681–85; lessons
learned from, xi; motivations of
governments participating in,
647, 654–55; obtaining food in,
716–17; payments to host families, 716; penalties for, 645; and

personal networks in Warsaw's
secret city, 690–98; reasons for
successes, 701–6; religious motivations in, 651, 680, 681–82; role
of money in, 693, 700, 714–15; of
Sweden in Denmark, 739–43; of
Sweden in Hungary, 743–49; of
Sweden in Norway, 737–43; in
Warsaw, 644, 688–89, 698–99;
work of AJB in Belgium, 718–19;
work of CDJ in Belgium, 708–11,
714, 717–19; work of ONE in Belgium, 710; work of the Catholic
Church in Belgium, 711–16
resettlement programs: in annexed
Western Poland, 278–82; clas-
sification of people in, 275–78;
development of in Poland, 273–
74
resistance movements: in Belgium,
717; Catholic, 613, 619–20; in
France, 2; in ghettos, 345–47,
392; Gypsies at Auschwitz, 501;
Independence Front, 710–11;
Zegota, 620, 644, 689, 704. *See
also* underground movements
restitution and reparations, 756;
confusion in, 417, 815; definition of, 860n17; denial of, 802,
803; effect on German economy
(WWI), 63–64, 77; German
government's responsibility in,
853–54; Germany's war debts
(WWI), 61–62; Holocaust
deniers and, 835–36; limiting
benefits, 820n13; moral responsibility of, 862n50; typical
means of, 855
restitution campaign (1990s):
bystanders as defendants, 852–
55; claimants in, 855–59; contrasting law and history, 842–43,
849–52, 858–59; robbery at the
core of, 843–45; settlement

Sammern, Ferdinand von, 388–90, 392–93

Sandberger, Martin, 280

Sauckel, Fritz, 317–18, 320, 323, 324

Saur, Karl, 605

Sauvage, Pierre, 680, 683

Schallmeyer, Wilhelm, 23

Scheidemann, Phillip, 54, 56–57, 60

Schein, Edgar H., 483

Schiff, Otto, 205–6, 209, 212

Schiper, Isaac, 374–75, 380

Schirach, Baldur von, 135

Schleicher, Kurt von, 71, 75, 77–78, 79–80

Schlep Decree, 306–7, 308

Schlome (Polish Jew at Auschwitz), 508–9

Schlüsselburg (Soviet Union), 327n1

Schmidt, Helmuth, 490

Schmitt, Carl, 132

Schmitz, Hermann, 404, 405

Schneider, Carl, 265

Schneider, Hans, 405–6

Schnitzler, Arthur, 31

Schobertm, Eugen Ritter von, 550

Schoenerer, Georg von, 16

Scholem, Arthur, 34

Schrader, Otto, 131

Schroeder, Gerhard, 816

Schuker, Stephen, 195

Schulweis, Harold M., xi

Schulz, Erwin, 449

Schumacher, Kurt, 805

Schumburg, Emil, 115, 117

Schüppe, Wilhelm Gustav, 461

Schuster, Heinrich, 521

Schutzpass, 647

Schwarzbard, Shalom, 377

Das Schwarze Korps (ss journal), 172

Schwarzhuber, Johann, 519, 520–21

Schwerin von Krosigk, Graf Lutz, 420

Schwinger, Fritz, 405

sciences, Jewish role in, 43–45

SD (Security Service), 134; organizational structure of, 484–85; resettlement programs and, 274; role in Germanization process, 275; on treatment of foreign workers, 323; in Vilna, Lithuania, 666–70

The Search for Truth in History (Irving), 831, 839n27

Sebastian, Mihail, 560

Sebok, Anthony J., 850, 852, 860n20

Second LiRo Decree (1942), 416–17

Security Police: ideology of, 482; organizational structure of, 484–85; resettlement programs and, 274. See also *Einsatzgruppen* (Order Police); Gestapo; SD (Security Service)

Segal, Lore, 237

Seidel, Gill, 835

Seldte, Franz, 150

selection, theory of, 21

selektsia (immigration selection), 775

Semi-Gotha Almanach (social register), 34

"Semitic," defined, 6

Semprun, Jorge, 818

Sendler, Irena, *644*

Sendung und Gewissen (Unger), 261

Senpo (Chiune), Sugihara. See Sugihara, Senpo (Chiune)

Serbia: death rates in, xii, 529; mass murders of Jews in, 438; treatment of Gypsies in, 498

Setoff, Otto, 202

Seventh Fort massacre (Kovno, Lithuania), 453–54

sexual assault in labor camps, 404–6

sexual relationships: between "Aryans" and "non-Aryans," 404–6

Seydoux, Roger, 573

Seyss-Inquart, Arthur, 412–14, 415, 420, 650

Shanghai, refugees in, 650

Shenker, Rivka, 535

Sherwin, Emily, 845

Shilansky, Dov, 785

Shippers, Franz, 405

Shlonsky, Avraham, 785

Siauliai ghetto, 346–47

Sieff, Rebecca, 212

Siegman, Frania, 408

Siemens reparation case, 843

Simenon, Georges, 193

Simon, Ernst, 50

Simon, James, 35, 41, 44, 50

Simplicissimus (magazine), 34

Simpson, John Hope, 209–10

Sin Against the Blood (Dinter), 27

Singer, Oskar, 368

Sinti (Gypsies), 495, 497, 500

Siret (Romania), 548

The Six Million Swindle (App), 821–22

Skarzysko labor camp: evacuation of, 409–10; organization of, 402–4; relationships within, 407–9; sexual harassment and assault at, 404–6; trade and commerce in, 406–7

skilled workers, 316, 320, 326

Skrzyniarz, Piotr, 541

slave labor: restitution campaign and, 845, 857, 858–59; and unjust enrichment, 845, 846–48, 851–52. See also forced labor

Slovakia: death rates in, 529; deportations of Jews from, 611n8; treatment of Gypsies in, 497

Smallbones, R. T., 213

Smilansky, Moshe, 785

Smith Act of 1940 (U.S.), 723